INTEGRATED EARTH
AND
ENVIRONMENTAL EVOLUTION
OF THE
SOUTHWESTERN UNITED STATES

INTEGRATED EARTH
AND
ENVIRONMENTAL EVOLUTION
OF THE
SOUTHWESTERN UNITED STATES

The Clarence A. Hall, Jr. Volume

W. G. Ernst and C. A. Nelson, editors

Bellwether Publishing, Ltd. **for the**
Geological Society of America

Published by

Bellwether Publishing, Ltd.
8640 Guilford Road, Suite 200
Columbia, MD 21046-2612
for the Geological Society of America

Library of Congress Catalog Card Number 98-86763
ISBN 0-9665869-0-5

Composed by The TypeStudio, Santa Barbara, California
Printed by The Sheridan Press, Hanover, Pennsylvania

INTEGRATED EARTH AND ENVIRONMENTAL EVOLUTION OF THE SOUTHWESTERN UNITED STATES: THE CLARENCE A. HALL, JR. VOLUME

W. G. Ernst and C. A. Nelson, editors

Contents

Sierra Nevada

Western and Baja California

Introduction

CLARENCE HALL, Professor of Geology at the University of California at Los Angeles, served as the Director of the White Mountain Research Station (WMRS) for 15 years (1980–1995), during which time the facility was vastly upgraded and the emphasis broadened from high-altitude physiology, and, later, observational astronomy, to Earth and environmental sciences, anthropology, and field biology (zoology + botany). Hall oversaw and directed the renovation and enhancement of the WMRS facilities from a series of dilapidated, ramshackle buildings at four sites—the Owens Valley Laboratories/Bishop (1,234 m elevation), the Crooked Creek camp (3,093 m elevation), the Barcroft Station (3,801 m elevation), and the White Mountain summit hut (4,342 m elevation)—to national prominence as a modern, well-equipped environmental research complex, sited in rugged alpine desert—truly a unique natural reserve. The current WMRS director, Frank Powell, along with long-time colleague Clem Nelson and myself, agreed that, with his formal retirement, it was high time to call attention to Clarence's administrative and scientific contributions as well as to his dynamic, visionary leadership. We therefore held a symposium during September 13–15, 1997 at the Crooked Creek Conference Center. That remarkable facility, located high in the southern White-Inyo Range of easternmost California, has now been officially designated by the University of California as the Clarence A. Hall, Jr., Lodge. The present volume is the product of that scientific symposium. Its contents reflect the range of subjects that encompass Hall's breadth of research interests, but is not restricted to them. Technical co-editors of the compendium are W. G. Ernst and C. A. Nelson.

In another dimension, Hall's double-barreled research thrusts involve careful paleobiological studies as well as detailed geologic field mapping and innovative plate-tectonic reconstructions. He has documented the paleogeography and water depths of Cenozoic strata that constitute superjacent portions of the California Coast Ranges on the basis of ecological environments and paleotemperatures, conducted meticulous taxonomic studies of gastropods, pelecypods, and echinoids, and related the deceleration of the Earth's rotation to measured variations in molluscan growth stages. In addition, Hall has been the sole, main, or contributory author on more than 35 geologic maps, ranging in scale from 1:20,000 to 1:250,000 and covering regions from the central California Coast Ranges and San Joaquin Valley to the White-Inyo Range and the French Pyrenees. Most contributions are color maps, and the investigated bedrock terranes include Mesozoic and Cenozoic fossiliferous strata as well as pre-Mesozoic metasedimentary, ultramafic, plutonic, and volcanic rocks. Hall is a careful, insightful field observer and a meticulous cartographer. His productivity will leave a lasting legacy to the Earth sciences—especially with regard to a better understanding of the geologic architecture of central California. Seminal research contributions include: (1) recognition and documentation of ~115 km of dextral slip on the San Simeon–Hosgrei fault; (2) demonstration of the offset of Neogene molluscan provinces and paleo-isotherms along the San Andreas system; and (3) synthesis of the geology and invertebrate paleontology of the central California Coast Ranges and hypothesis of the existence of the southern California allochthon. And he is still producing imaginative and insightful tectonic syntheses.

Remarkably, Hall has simultaneously pursued studies in paleobiology and regional geology and served the University of California, Los Angeles as departmental chair (four years) and dean (12 years), in addition to his directorship of the WMRS. This GSA volume is meant to call attention to these lifelong contributions.

—W. G. ERNST AND C. A. NELSON
TECHNICAL EDITORS

1

CRUSTAL EVOLUTION

Archean Tectonics and Magmatism

WARREN B. HAMILTON

Department of Geophysics, Colorado School of Mines, Golden, Colorado 80401

Abstract

The Earth began to form ~4.56 Ga, and probably was entirely molten about 4.45 Ga and likely also before. Felsic igneous rocks of unknown provenance were in the crust by 4.3 Ga (clastic zircons to 4.3 Ga in <3.0 Ga quartzites, and relict zircons to 4.0 Ga in migmatites stabilized <3.6 Ga). Lunar analogy requires that the entire surface of the Earth was recycled by impact melting and brecciation before 3.9 Ga, and greatly modified until 3.8 Ga, but no certain relics of this history have been identified.

When the fog clears and Archean time proper begins, at ~3.6 Ga, the oldest granite-and-greenstone terrains are beginning to form. The granite-and-greenstone terrains that dominate the upper crust, formed from ~3.6 to 2.6 Ga, record magmatic and tectonic processes that have no close younger analogues. They indicate heat loss by the Archean Earth primarily by voluminous magmatism. The upper mantle was 200 °C, perhaps 300 °C, hotter than at present.

Magmatism in the granite-and-greenstone terrains began with regional volcanic plains, erupted over and around discontinuous basements of recently stabilized migmatitic tonalites of unknown provenance. Although the oldest stratified rocks are quartzites or felsic volcanic rocks in a number of regions, the oldest voluminous rocks typically are basalts and ultramafic lavas that were erupted at liquidus temperatures. These typically are succeeded by felsic volcanic rocks and often by repeated intercalations of mafic and felsic rocks. The stratiform rocks are preserved in "greenstone belts"—anastomosing networks of upright synforms formed by crowding aside by, and sinking between, large rising diapiric, elliptical composite batholiths. The belts are defined by late deformation of regionally semiconcordant volcanic and sedimentary successions, not by relics of linear volcanic features. Little deformation generally preceded the diapirism, and metamorphism was primarily of contact type. The regionally uniform spatial density and accordant crustal level of the diapiric batholiths, their contacts primarily against the oldest strata of the synforms, their general age at 10 to 20 m.y. younger than most of the flanking stratiform rocks except the younger felsic volcanic rocks, and considerations of high Archean radiogenic heat productivity all fit the explanation that the batholiths were mobilized by partial melting of hydrous lower crust by radiogenic heating. Diapirism was accompanied by modest regional orthogonal shortening and extension of the hot upper crust, producing the orientations of the batholiths. The rise of the batholiths greatly increased the petrologic fractionation of the crust and the concentration of radionuclides high within it. Cooling of deeper crust and subjacent mantle, and thus cratonization, followed. The upper crust, containing the granite-and-greenstone aggregates, was decoupled from the gneissic middle crust, which underwent flattening and extension subparallel to the elongation of the shallow batholiths. This deep deformation may have been driven by flow of dense restites toward delamination loci.

Plate-tectonic processes were not then operating. The distinctive array of petrologic, structural, and stratigraphic features that characterize Phanerozoic subduction and collision systems—ophiolites, magmatic arcs, accretionary wedges, forearc basins, etc.—have no viable analogues in Archean terrains. Purported Archean plate-tectonic indicators consist merely of rock types that superficially resemble actual Phanerozoic indicators only when considered in isolation from their association and structure. Archean ultramafic and mafic volcanic rocks neither resemble ophiolitic rocks in petrology nor occur in ophiolite-type successions, and they often depositionally overlie felsic basement rocks and commonly are intercalated with sedimentary and felsic-volcanic rocks. Archean graywackes are coherent strata derived from nearby volcanic rocks during the diapiric-granite histories of their regions, and they lack the setting and disruption that characterize modern accretionary wedges. The lithologic, structural, and stratigraphic assemblages that characterize Proterozoic and Phanerozoic rifted and reassembled margins similarly have no Archean analogues, and no evidence has been found for Archean rifting, rotation, and reassembly of continental plates.

Plate-tectonic rifting and convergence were operating by ~2.0 Ga, perhaps earlier, and were in an essentially modern mode by ~0.8 Ga. The nature of the transition from the granite-and-

5

greenstone mode at 2.6 Ga to plate mode by 2.0 Ga is poorly defined, but the change may have been facilitated by the increasing content of water and carbon dioxide in the mantle as dense, but hydrated, delaminated Archean crust sank into it.

Introduction

ARCHEAN CRATONS ARE CHARACTERIZED by igneous and meta-igneous rocks in associations, and in part with compositions that lack modern analogues. Conversely, none of the structural and magmatic associations indicative of plate-tectonic interactions in Phanerozoic assemblages have Archean analogues. Plate tectonics apparently did not operate during Archean time, widespread contrary assumptions notwithstanding. Macgregor (1951) early emphasized, correctly, that the characteristic Archean granite-and-greenstone terrains are strikingly different from modern batholithic provinces, but the differences have been ignored in the rush to force plate models on the Archean because they work well for the Phanerozoic.

Plate-tectonic interpretations work well only for geologic terrains younger than ~2.0 Ga but nevertheless now dominate the literature on Archean terrains also. The basic geometric concepts of plate tectonics were developed in the late 1960s, primarily from marine geophysical data, and comprehension has increased steadily since. Basic understanding of the systematic relationships in active convergent-margin systems between distinctive accretionary wedges, forearc assemblages, magmatic arcs, and back-arc complexes, and of the features of rifted margins, was developed and applied to characterize the Phanerozoic tectonic and magmatic evolution of continental crust during the late 1960s and the 1970s. (I was a contributor during this stage—e.g., Hamilton, 1969a, 1969b, 1970, 1978, 1979—and subsequently.) Many Phanerozoic geologists, and a few Proterozoic specialists (e.g., Hoffman, 1973), quickly picked up the new concepts, and the literature in their fields soon was dominated by plate-tectonic explanations. Archean geologists were, rightly, slower to adopt plate explanations, but influential theorists (e.g., Dewey and Windley, 1981; Sleep and Windley, 1982; Talbot, 1973) rationalized that uniformitarianism required that plate tectonics operated during Archean time; resistance dwindled, and a flood

of papers by Archean specialists has advocated plate-tectonic rationales during the late 1980s and the 1990s. Many of those papers are commented upon here.

Archean rocks are exposed primarily in "cratons," remnants of larger thick-crust constructs that were stabilized in Archean time and then were dismembered, and variably reassembled, in later geologic time. The dominant ages of formation of rocks of these cratons were centered at ~2.7 Ga for some (e.g., Slave and Superior of North America, Yilgarn of Australia) and 3.3 Ga for others (e.g., Pilbara of Australia, Kaapvaal of South Africa). Pilbara and Kaapvaal share late Archean histories and likely once were contiguous, but other initial continuities are less apparent. Some other Archean crust is preserved in reworked form in younger orogenic terrains. What the remainder of the Earth's crust consisted of in Archean time, and how it was recycled into the mantle, are matters for conjecture and contention.

The literature on Archean geology is cluttered with dubious age determinations—particularly whole-rock Rb-Sr pseudochrons—of minimal validity, and I do not generally here cite such ages nor discuss the confusion produced by them. I rely primarily on U-Pb age determinations on zircon by the ion-probe and single-crystal methods as generally dating the crystallization or high-temperature recrystallization of the bits sampled. In some cases, I cite determinations by other methods.

Models and consensus

I argue in this essay that Archean rock associations are so unlike modern ones as to provide no uniformitarian basis for assuming Archean plate tectonics, and that, conversely, none of the indicators of modern plate interactions can be recognized in Archean assemblages. This updates a theme stated earlier (Hamilton, 1993). I regard the general pro-plate consensus, indicated by recent published literature, among Archean specialists as a product of an unwarranted assumption of uniformitarianism, of a general unawareness of the character of plate-tectonic post–2.0 Ga rifts and sutures, and of herd suggestibility. A number of these specialists have argued with me that their consensus itself demonstrates that plate tectonics operated in Archean time—although the history of science should tell them otherwise.

Particularly outspoken among those who claim that groupthinkers define truth is Kusky (1997), who, in a review of Goodwin's (1996) book, berated Goodwin for not accepting the consensus assumption of Archean plate tectonics because that consensus has been presented in "modern peer-reviewed journal literature" and therefore must be correct. If, however, many of the facts are as reported by Goodwin in his excellent book, then those facts cannot be reconciled with plate-tectonic models no matter what assumptions are favored by those Kusky follows.

In my geologic youth, conventional wisdom favored permanent and stable continents and oceans, whereas nowadays collective hunches stretch plate-tectonic models (and, increasingly, plume conjectures) to cover all occasions. Then as now, peer review can represent the tyrrany of the majority. I have run the peer-review gauntlet perhaps a hundred times. My papers describing and interpreting geology in more or less conventional terms have progressed smoothly, whereas publication of my manuscripts challenging accepted concepts has often been impeded, and occasionally blocked.

Scientific progress is made by testing and, where necessary, revising prior assumptions and concepts. Neither I nor any other scientist can rightly claim total objectivity divorced from his own experience and preferred models, but I feel strongly that the minimum statement permitted by the data is that plate tectonics—involving rifting, spreading, and subduction and their products more or less as we now see them—did not operate in Archean time. This can be correct only if many published interpretations are incorrect.

Tonalite

Tonalite and its kin are voluminous in Archean cratons, and arguably were present as early as 4.3 Ga, long before preserved cratons formed. Tonalite crystallizes from hydrous melt generated either by fractionation of hydrous mafic magma or by partial melting of hydrated mafic rock, and it cannot be generated by either partial melting or fractionation of either ultramafic or anhydrous materials. These constraints bear importantly on discussions of both early-Earth and Archean processes, so it is appropriate to examine the conditions under which tonalite can form before going on to such discussions. To the extent that Archean rocks are similar to those of young magmatic arcs (and there are conspicuous contrasts between them), they are evidence for similar pressure-temperature-composition conditions of formation, not necessarily of similar tectonic settings of heat sources.

Gneissic and migmatitic tonalite, trondhjemite, and granodiorite—"grey gneisses," or "TTG suite"—in many regions form basement complexes upon which were erupted mafic and ultramafic volcanic rocks, or intrude or formed beneath such volcanic rocks, or are the oldest rocks known in the region; such occurrences are incompatible with the concept that the mafic volcanic rocks formed directly upon unseen ultramafic mantle newly exposed by spreading. Tonalite and its kin dominate much Archean middle crust and are widespread in variably remobilized or new-melt form in many late diapiric upper-crust batholiths. The gneisses commonly are complexly migmatitic and enclose abundant amphibolite, garnet amphibolite, or garnet-clinopyroxene granulite, noted in order of increasing depth of equilibration. Dacite and rhyodacite, equivalent to tonalite and granodiorite (but not to the generally high-water-pressure, hence mostly midcrustal, trondhjemite) are abundant in supracrustal greenstone-belt assemblages.

Much of the advocacy of plate-tectonic processes during Archean time is based on the recognition that the closest Phanerozoic equivalents of the TTG suite occur typically, but not exclusively, in magmatic arcs, and on the false assumption that tonalitic melts rise directly from ultramafic mantle to crust. I now address that assumption.

Fractionation. Direct derivation of tonalite from peridotitic mantle is precluded, for common mantle peridotite cannot yield tonalitic melt under any mantle conditions (Wyllie et al., 1997); nor can fractionation of basaltic melt controlled by olivine and pyroxene produce tonalite. Crustal-pressure fractionation of hydrous basaltic melt can, however, yield tonalitic melt (Carroll and Wyllie, 1990). The huge crustal volume of Archean tonalite, the relative scarcity of diorite and andesite, and the lack of evidence for hydrous mafic magmatism in such forms as hornblende gabbro are difficult to explain by such fractionation on an intracrustal scale. Fractionation of hydrous basaltic melt on a vast, magma-ocean scale, as proposed by Ridley and Kramers (1990), the tonalite in such a case representing most of the crust, would not meet those objections. Perhaps early-Earth tonalites can be explained in such terms, the necessary water perhaps having been added to the parental basaltic melt from a very dense, pre–water-ocean hydrous atmosphere. Deep-crustal fractionation of mantle-derived basaltic melt heavily contaminated by assimilation of hydrous crustal rocks might also be a viable mechanism (Stern et al., 1994), although this avoids the problem of the origin of the initial rocks.

Intracrustal melting. Most Archean tonalites span the same age range as do the low-magmatic-water-content basalts and komatiites and the other rocks of the granite-and-greenstone assemblage. The origin of these tonalites that accords with experimental data is in intracrustal melting as the second part of a two-stage process (as Condie, 1992, Wyllie et al., 1997, and many others have emphasized). Basaltic melts of mantle origin rose into the crust and there were hydrated and metamorphosed to amphibolite (perhaps via greenstone and greenschist), and the amphibolite was subsequently heated in the stability fields of high-temperature garnetiferous rocks. Many experimenters have shown that when amphibolite is heated, over a broad range of pressure and temperature, the hornblende dissociates and releases water, which combines with other components to produce tonalitic melt, leaving a residue of clinopyroxene plus other minerals at $P < 8$ to 10 kbar, and of garnet, clinopyroxene, and other minerals at greater pressure (Wyllie et al., 1997). This dissociation can occur at either deep-crustal or uppermost-mantle conditions. Partial melting of amphibolite in the uppermost-mantle stability field of high-T eclogite can yield voluminous tonalitic melt at high temperature with a residue of such eclogite (Rapp et al., 1991), although tonalitic melt would lose its character if it reacted with olivine-bearing mantle rocks during subsequent rise. When the two stages follow within a

relatively short period, such as 200 m.y., the second-stage silicic melts will bear a "mantle" signature in isotopes of Nd, Pb, and Sr. Many felsic Archean plutonic and volcanic rocks indeed have mantle-like proportions of isotopes of those elements, but the citation of such proportions as evidence for direct mantle derivation of the magmas (e.g., by Barrie and Shirey, 1991, and Vervoort et al., 1994) is not in fact an argument against two-stage, short-crustal-residence time, explanations which, unlike direct derivation, are compatible with experimental data. Longer crustal-residence times for sources of many other Archean felsic-rock suites are shown by appropriate divergences of the isotope systematics from "mantle" signatures. Champion and Sheraton (1997) and Hill et al. (1992) explained, in these terms, the contrasted systematics and compositions (and the inherited zircons) of young granitic rocks of the Yilgarn craton as resulting from partial melting of mafic rocks of mantle origin to produce calcic, low-silica granodiorites, and partial melting of old, deep tonalitic and granodioritic gneisses to produce low-calcium, high-silica granodiorite and quartz monzonite. Heat needed for Archean second-stage partial melting presumably represented in part the high ambient and radiogenic temperatures of Archean crust and mantle, and in part crustal underplating by mafic and ultramafic melts rising from the mantle.

The voluminous tonalites and allied rocks of Archean crust require, in these terms, the formation of even greater volumes of dense, restitic products of partial melting of amphibolite. An appropriate volume of dense restites cannot be accounted for in exposed or seismically defined Archean crust, so it follows that most of the missing restite is in the mantle, either as the upper part of the preserved lithosphere or as dense material delaminated and sunk into the mantle. Wolf and Wyllie (1993) calculated high densities for the garnet-rich restites, and they, like Rudnick and Taylor (1986) and others, advocated such delamination.

The restites (and cumulates?) complementary to Archean tonalites probably typically were more garnetiferous, and hence denser, than have been those of younger ages. Archean tonalites are characterized by severe depletion in heavy rare-earth elements, and the restite minerals that selectively retained most of the heavy rare earths in the required proportions must have included substantial garnet (Hanson, 1978; Martin, 1986; Rudnick and Taylor, 1986; Rapp et al., 1991; Condie, 1992). This in turn requires a depth of partial melting greater than ~20 km if the restite was garnet amphibolite, 30 km if garnet-clinopyroxene granulite, and 40 km if eclogite. Post-Archean tonalites generally show much less depletion of heavy rare earths, and less garnet was needed for their equilibration. The conclusion that Archean restites were more garnetiferous follows also from the negligible to positive Eu anomalies in Archean tonalites as contrasted to the negligible to negative anomalies in young ones (cf. Gromet and Silver, 1987).

Early Earth, Moon, and impact melts

The oldest preserved coherent rock assemblages are ~3.6 Ga (or ~3.8 Ga, if ambiguous dating of the Isua supracrustals of southwest Greenland is correct), although zircon grains, of unproved provenance, have been dated back to almost 4.3 Ga. Preserved Archean assemblages, ~3.6 to 2.6 Ga, formed closer in time to the beginning of accretion of the Earth than to the present. The early Earth likely was wholly molten, and lunar history requires that the Earth's surface was extremely modified by impacts until 3.8 Ga.

The Earth probably accreted mostly within ~100 m.y. from the time of beginning of condensation of the solar nebula at ~4.56 Ga, and at least the outer part of the accreting Earth was melted, likely above liquidus temperatures, by impacts, core formation, contained heat of impactors, and the mega-impact that formed the Moon (e.g., Taylor, 1992, 1993; Lee and Halliday, 1995; Galer and Goldstein, 1996; Jacobsen and Harper, 1996; papers by many authors in Agee and Longhi, 1992). Crystallization, fractionation, and dynamics of resulting magma oceans have been discussed by Abe (1993), Jacobsen and Harper (1996), Warren (1992), and others, and must have varied complexly with depth and time.

Composition and geochemical evolution of Earth. Most geochemical modeling of terrestrial evolution incorporates the assumption that the Earth has a chondritic bulk composition, whereas in fact the bulk Earth probably is markedly more refractory than chondrite because of its aggregation mostly from materials condensed much closer to the sun than were chondrites (most of which come from the inner part, and the others from the medial part, of the heliocentrically zoned asteroid belt between Mars and Jupiter) and of its high-temperature early history (Hamilton, 1993, and references therein; Taylor, 1993). Most geochemical modeling incorporates the additional dubious assumption, a relic from cold-accretion conjectures of the 1940s, that the Earth's mantle never had a large melt component and that it has fractionated unidirectionally throughout geologic time. Armstrong's (1991) finding that chemical and isotopic relationships cited in support of slow-fractionation models accord equally with the cosmologically, petrologically, and tectonically plausible explanation that mantle heterogeneity has increased during geologic time as crust has been recycled into the mantle is seldom considered. Much speculation specifically regarding Archean tectonics and magmatism is based on the conventional rationale of progressive fractionation of a chondritic Earth (as advocated and summarized, for example, by Hofmann, 1988). For one recent example among, probably, hundreds, Hollings et al. (1997) cantilevered these and other assumptions with measurements of Nd, Zr, and Hf to deduce that Archean mafic and ultramafic lavas in one greenstone section required melting, at a depth of 450 km, of both depleted and subducted-slab parts of the mantle and, thus, that plumes and plate tectonics both then operated. (I discuss Archean ultramafic liquidus lavas and hypothetical plumes in subsequent sections.)

Something like half of the present mass of continental crust was produced from the mantle during Archean time (Rudnick, 1995). As the degree of recycling of continental crust, and of its sedimentary derivatives, into the mantle by subduction and by crustal delamination cannot yet be quantified through time, it is uncertain whether the amount of continental crust has increased, decreased, or been approximately constant through geologic time, and whether mantle heterogeneity has decreased or (more likely) increased (Armstrong, 1991; Bowring and Housh, 1995; Rudnick, 1995).

Origin of the Moon. The only quantitatively viable origin of the Moon known to explain the angular momentum of the Earth-Moon system and the composition, low density, and anhydrous character of the Moon is in the oblique collision with the Earth of a planet at least as large as Mars (Cameron and Benz, 1991; Cameron, 1994; Taylor and Esat, 1996). The impact melted much or all of the Earth; the impactor's core joined the Earth's core; a dense hot-rock-vapor atmosphere formed around the Earth; and the Moon formed mostly from splashed-out impactor mantle. The impact pre-dated the oldest well-dated Moon rocks—a nor-ite crystallized at ~4.46 Ga (Shih et al., 1990 [Sm-Nd]) and a ferroan anorthosite at ~4.43 Ga (Carlson and Lugmair, 1988 [Sm-Nd]; Premo and Tatsumoto, 1993 [Pb-Pb]). Major bolide accretion continued on both Earth and Moon after this event.

Impact history of the Moon. The impact record of the Moon must transfer to Earth, so the Earth also was heavily bombarded by large bolides until ~3.8 Ga. The lunar maria, giant impact basins to ~1000 km in diameter, were formed by large bolides from ~3.90 to 3.83 Ga (Dalrymple and Ryder, 1996) and are well pre-served because large subsequent impacts were sparse. Lunar surfaces older than 3.9 Ga are saturated with impact basins and craters, many of them older than the maria and of diverse relative ages, but not otherwise dated (Wilhelms, 1987). Many of these older basins are as large as the well-preserved maria but have been greatly modified by subsequent impacts. The largest and oldest identified lunar impact basin—itself saturated with younger craters but recognizable by its rim, 2500 km in diameter and 12 km in height (Spudis et al., 1994)—is older than all maria and older than all pre-maria impact structures in its region, and its ejecta probably buried pre-existing features every-where on the Moon (Wilhelms, 1987). Some investigators (Dalrymple and Ryder, 1996, and references therein) advocate a late cataclysmic bombardment from ~3.9 to 3.8 Ga, but alterna-tive correlation of the late maria with the tailing out of main accretion accords better with the extensive pre-maria cratering, with dating noted below, and with orbital-mechanics considerations.

Igneous rocks from the impact-saturated lunar highlands have been retrieved only as clasts in impact breccias, and the rocks are of all ages from 4.4 to 3.8 Ga, with abundances decreasing for the younger rocks. Most lunar geologists define as impact melts primarily those rocks that display obvious partial or com-plete shock-melting (none such have been dated as older than about 3.94 Ga) (Dalrymple and Ryder, 1996), with or without inclusion of some types of basalts but specifically excluding all plutonic rocks. They assume that many plu-tonic rocks are proto-crust products of crystalli-zation of a magma ocean, whereas the other plutonic rocks, including granophyres and most holocrystalline basalts and diabases, are products of endogenic melts unrelated to impacts. No mantle rocks have been recognized. Thus, most investigators explain the "ferroan anorthosite suite" as representing the crystal-flotation protocrust of the initially molten Moon, and the highlands "magnesian suite" and "alkali suite," which largely overlap the anorthositic suite in age, as recording endo-genic magmatism (e.g., Simon, 1990), although these assumptions lead to major problems regarding retention of heat in so small a body.

Alternatively, fractionation of some, even all, of these suites, and formation of all or most basalts, in impact-melt lakes and impact-related secondary magmatic masses accords with their petrology (e.g., Grieve, 1980; Grieve et al., 1991; Norman, 1994; Warren, 1993; cf. Ryder, 1994; Snyder et al., 1995). It is possible that no proto-crust has been sampled even in impact-excavated-breccia form.

Probably the best-defined lunar ages are ion-probe U-Pb determinations of 33 zircon crystals, and these provide support for the declining-bombardment option, not for the cat-aclysmic late-bombardment one. About a quar-ter of the analyzed zircons were found *in situ* in granophyres (such as on Earth are common lava-lake fractionates), a quarter are *in situ* in norites and other rock types, and half are iso-lated crystals, from unknown protoliths, in impact breccias. The 33 zircon ages show an exponential decrease in abundance with time: 4.37 to 4.3 Ga, 14 determinations; 4.3 to 4.2 Ga, 10; 4.2 to 4.1 Ga, 4; 4.1 to 4.0 Ga, 3; 4.0 to 3.9, 2 (Meyer et al., 1989). This progression of ages fits the concept of a declining flux of large melt-lake-producing impacts. Bombardment inten-sity decreased to a flux broadly comparable to that of the Phanerozoic by late Archean time.

Impact history of the Earth. The transfer to the Earth of the impact history of the Moon requires far more impact churning and melting of the Earth's crust and upper mantle than most

Archean geologists incorporate in their theories. The Earth was hit by more bolides per unit area because of its larger capture cross section. Because of Earth's six times greater gravity, the transient crater produced by a bolide would have only half the diameter of one produced on the Moon by a bolide of the same mass; but impact melting increases exponentially with velocity, and the terrestrial event, with its velocity ~5 km/s greater, would produce about two-thirds more melt and vaporized rock, and much deeper melting and excavation (Cintala and Grieve, 1994). Vertical and lateral geothermal-gradient perturbations by impacts would necessarily have produced extensive consequent endogenic melting. Whatever the dynamics of magma oceans and the solid shell of the early Earth, its surface was churned by impacts from 3.9 to 3.8 Ga, and probably throughout its earlier history. Terrestrial crustal materials older than ~3.8 Ga thus also must include abundant impact breccia and products of primary and secondary impact melts, and crustal materials older than ~3.9 Ga likely are dominated by them. The Archean Earth contained much more crustal and mantle melt than the modern one (as discussed subsequently), and the early Earth must have been markedly hotter yet; thus modeling the physical and petrologic effects of early-Earth impacts will be challenging.

The oldest well-documented large terrestrial impact structures and melts are the early Proterozoic Vredefort and Sudbury complexes, but the Archean record must contain unrecognized impact complexes. Obvious Archean subjects in need of evaluation are such fractionated magma lakes as the Stillwater sheet of Montana, Bell River of Ontario, Gaborone of southern Africa, and Windimurra of southwestern Australia. The derivation of the Stillwater complex, for example, from both mantle and crustal melts (e.g., Lambert et al., 1994) accords with an origin by impact melting. Also in need of evaluation for possible impact origin are the dismembered complexes of calcic anorthosite, norite, peridotite, and dunite (mostly low-pressure[?] igneous fractionates whose initial felsic complements have not been recognized) now enclosed within many Archean gneissic and migmatitic domains.

Earth's early crust. Some investigators have deduced that the Earth had a tonalitic, thus hydrous, crust before 4 Ga, but only zircons, not rocks, of that age have been dated: the oldest proved hydrous-melt rocks are only ~3.6 Ga. Zircons as old as 4.3 Ga have been found as clastic grains in much-younger Archean quartzite in Australia. Complexly polycyclic and extremely heterolithic tonalitic and granodioritic migmatites are known to contain relict zircons as old as 4.0 Ga in northwestern Canada (Bowring et al., 1989; W. Bleeker and R. Stern, pers. commun., 1997; Williams et al., 1997), and 3.9 Ga in Greenland (Nutman et al., 1996), Labrador, and Antarctica. These migmatites contain igneous zircons whose U-Pb analyses, from different or zoned grains in the same samples, scatter or cluster from the high values at least as far down concordia as 3.6 Ga, and often as far as 2.8 or even 2.6 Ga, with variable lead loss along the way. The rocks now contain abundant hydrous minerals, typically hornblende and biotite, which, like their distinct plagioclase and potassic feldspars, were formed from, or equilibrated with, relatively cool, hydrous partial and injected melts.

Although the ancient zircons have been cited by Bowring, Nutman, their colleagues, and many others as requiring the presence of hydrous tonalitic crust throughout the time span of their ages, the assumption that because the zircons are now enclosed in hydrated rocks they must have formed initially from hydrous melts has yet to be substantiated. The final hydrous mineralogy of the rocks was the end product of a series of re-equilibrations, partial meltings, and melt additions over hundreds of millions of years, and the initial mineralogy is unknown. Many of the felsic protoliths might have been impact-melt fractionates containing initially nearly anhydrous mafic minerals and, where significantly potassic, containing high-temperature broad-composition feldspars such as sanidine and anorthoclase (which would have exsolved to mesoperthite upon cooling); the mafic and ultramafic components of the migmatites would have originated in part as other fractionates of impact lakes. Alternatively, if the ancient zircons did indeed form from hydrous melts, then the source of those melts might lie in the fractionation of basaltic melts, of either magma-ocean or impact origins, which had been hydrated in at least their upper parts by a dense, hydrous atmosphere to permit the generation of tonalite (Ridley and Kramers, 1990).

The character of the ancient zircons themselves may be found to constrain conditions of initial crystallization and thus to help discriminate between origins in hot, dry impact(?) melts and cooler, hydrous non-impact(?) melts. Zircon morphology tends to vary with temperature of crystallization of igneous rocks and with ratio of Al to alkalis, and between felsic and mafic rocks and between igneous and granulitic-metamorphic rocks (Pupin, 1980; van Breeman et al., 1987). Perhaps magmatic histories of the zircons also can be constrained by studying compositional features such as uranium-thorium ratios, heavy-rare-earth enrichment, and the signs of Ce and Eu anomalies. A start in this direction was made by Maas et al. (1992), who found ten 4.2 to 3.9 Ga clastic zircons in 3.0 Ga quartzite to have steeply fractionated rare earths and low contents of Sc, indicating unusual felsic source rocks uncommonly low in Sc. (The felsites that cap the voluminous silicic differentiates atop the early Proterozoic Bushveld magma lake, which I regard as likely of impact origin and which is larger and more completely fractionated than the proved impact-melt lake of Sudbury, are uncommonly low in Sc; see Twist and French [1983].) Like many Archean quartzites, this one is rich in fuchsite (chromian muscovite), so chromitic ultramafic rocks, such as are to be expected in fractionated magma lakes, apparently were in its source region.

The ancient zircons require that silicic rocks existed at or near parts of the Earth's surface from ~4.3 Ga onward, but no empirical evidence yet defines the specific character of the crust and of whatever tectonic processes might have been operating before 3.6 (or possibly 3.8) Ga and of how those processes were complicated by bolide bombardment. When the fog clears at ~3.6 Ga, we see the granite-and-greenstone tectonomagmatic style that characterizes Archean time from 3.6 to 2.6 Ga.

Archean Granite and Greenstone Terrains

The characteristic Archean assemblages of the upper crust are granite-and-greenstone terrains, the rocks of which vary globally from about 3.6 to 2.6 Ga in age but within any one

craton are mostly contained within an age range of 100 m.y. or so. These assemblages are typified by domiform diapiric batholiths, elliptical or oval in plan, 20 to 100 km long and about two-thirds as wide and regionally subparallel, outlined by anastomosing networks ("greenstone belts") of upright synforms of volcanic and subordinate sedimentary rocks (e.g., Macgregor, 1951; Rhodesia Geological Survey, 1977; Blackburn, 1981; Hickman, 1983; Ayres and Thurston, 1985). The synforms can be tightly appressed and complex where sited between closely spaced plutons, but open, simple, and little strained where more distant from plutons (Hickman, 1983; Hickman and Lipple, 1978). These regular patterns of synformal wall rocks and domiform plutons of uniform areal density contrast strikingly with the complexly irregular patterns of Phanerozoic plutons and wall rocks of magmatic arcs of both island-arc and Andean types. Macgregor (1951) was perhaps the first to recognize that "gregarious batholiths" and intervening synclines characterize Archean shields and distinguish them from younger orogens. He also recognized that the batholiths were diapiric and that they formed because "a relatively thin crust rests upon a mobile substratum with lower specific gravity." Many authors since, with widely varying models in mind, which I will not discuss separately (in part because most of the models pre-dated precise dating of components), also have emphasized the diapiric nature of the batholiths. However, many Archean specialists have lost sight of the confinement of the unique granite-and-greenstone association to Archean cratons.

Prebatholithic continuity of greenstone stratigraphy

Greenstone belts have been shown in various areas to be remnants of subregional stratigraphic assemblages, with much continuity to mafic and ultramafic volcanic sections and some sedimentary rocks, although with more local variations in felsic volcanic rocks. Nowhere have they been shown to have been derived from initially linear volcanic features. Well-studied and well-dated low-strain greenstone belts display thick, coherent sections with repeated stratigraphic intercalations of felsic, mafic, and ultramafic volcanic rocks, as well as subordinate sedimentary rocks, which generally underwent little deformation before late diapiric plutonism. These sections have no modern analogues, for such diverse volcanic rocks now form in widely disparate tectonic settings and do not occur in continuous stratigraphic sections of repeating contrasted types, and the ultramafic lavas lack modern analogues.

The late Archean Swayze greenstone belt of the Superior craton in Ontario presents sequences of felsic, mafic, and ultramafic rocks, and sedimentary rocks, in a coherent and continuously upward-facing section (Heather et al., 1995). The succession, in order upwards, is felsic and intermediate volcanic rocks; iron formation; subaqueous basalts; felsic to intermediate volcanic rocks; komatiite, komatiitic basalt, and pillow basalt; and felsic to intermediate volcanic rocks. Zircon U-Pb dating of the three felsic-volcanic sequences shows the section to be in stratigraphic order and to have been deposited over a total time span of ~40 m.y. Continuity of the iron formation, and its constant position atop the early felsic sequence, is proved over a local area of ~80 × 80 km. The main iron formation of the Abitibi greenstone belt, which extends far eastward from the Swayze area across Ontario into Quebec, closely resembles that of Swayze and similarly overlies felsic volcanic rocks, suggesting regional sheet stratigraphy of this lower part of the section (K.B. Heather, pers. commun., 1997).

In a 60 × 60 km region of mostly supracrustal rocks in the Lake of the Woods greenstone belt of the Superior Province, a lower unit, with an original thickness to ~10 km, is regionally continuous and is dominated by submarine tholeiitic basalt flows but includes intercalated komatiite and intermediate felsic calc-alkaline rocks; a tholeiite and a gabbro are zircon dated as 2.738 and 2.732 Ga, respectively (Ayer and Davis, 1997). A thick overlying subaerial and marine section has considerable vertical and lateral stratigraphic variability and is dominated by calc-alkaline mafic to felsic volcanic rocks, but includes intercalated tholeiite, komatiite, and clastic and chemical sedimentary rocks; zircon dates range from 2.723 to 2.712 Ga. The capping section, preserved only in two synclines, consists mostly of clastic sedimentary rocks but includes mafic to felsic volcanic rocks. Ayer and Davis recognized that the repeated intercalations of tholeiitic,

komatiitic, and calc-alkaline rocks lack modern analogues, emphasized that contacts between the contrasted types are seen to be depositional and concordant, not tectonic, and rightly dismissed the possibility of structural interleaving.

A very thick, late Archean homoclinal, low-strain greenstone-belt section in the Slave craton has been well studied by many geologists (Helmstaedt and Padgham, 1986, and references therein) and constrained by zircon U-Pb dates (Isachsen et al., 1991). The 2.72 to 2.65 Ga section consists of, in order upward: basalt flows with gabbro sills; calc-alkalic dacite and rhyodacite; basalt breccias and pillow flows; intercalated mafic and felsic volcanic rocks and conglomerates; and turbidites. Despite the tholeiitic character of the older basalts, they overlie a >2.9 Ga continental basement of tonalitic gneiss, as well as quartzite that contains 3.7 to 2.9 Ga zircons (Isachsen and Bowring, 1997).

A unit of komatiite and allied ultramafic lavas is widely preserved throughout a well-studied region ~200 km wide across the strike of a number of greenstone belts and domiform batholiths, and 150 km long parallel to the strike, in the eastern Yilgarn craton of Western Australia. For example, the steeply dipping ultramafic unit is 1 to 3 km thick and continuous within the greenstone belts, over the 90 × 110 km area mapped by Walker and Blight (1983). The unit is dated in three places, and closely bracketed in several others, by ion-probe U-Pb zircon determinations as ~2.705 Ga, and records voluminous eruption across the region during a short period (Nelson, 1997). Thick basalts and felsic volcanic rocks below and above the ultramafic unit, and the minor sedimentary rocks above it, lack such obvious regional continuity, but insofar as zircon-dated are mostly within the narrow span of 2.71 to 2.66 Ga; late granites are mostly ~2.67 to 2.66 Ga (Nelson, 1997).

Regional stratigraphic continuity of greenstone-belt rocks has been inferred across the northwest Yilgarn also, although I have not seen support in the form of U-Pb ages. Watkins and Hickman (1990) reported this general section, in order upward: mafic and ultramafic volcanic rocks + banded iron formation; felsic volcanic rocks + volcaniclastic and pelitic sedimentary rocks; basalt + high-Mg basalt ± banded iron formation; calc-alkaline volcanic rocks and volcaniclastic sediments + clastic strata, no iron formation. About 70% of the total section is mafic, basalt > high-Mg basalt > ultramafic lavas.

The most continuously exposed Archean granite-and-greenstone terrain is that of the Pilbara craton, for the greenstone belts of which Hickman (1983) inferred broad regional stratigraphic coherence. His reconnaissance mapping and air-photo interpretation of the craton accords with the color Thematic Mapper imagery now available for the craton. There are large low-strain sectors of the greenstone belts, for example where triangular synforms formed between three domiform batholiths, and in these stratigraphic continuity is strikingly obvious on the imagery. Although some local-area Pilbara geologists emphasize irregularities inherent in volcanic units and dispute regional continuity (references in Trendall, 1995), they have not really addressed the issue of broad continuity. Precise zircon U-Pb dating is still too sparse to rigorously test stratigraphic synthesis in the Pilbara (and much literature discussion hangs on very unreliable ages such as those by whole-rock Rb-Sr determinations), but hopefully will soon be expanded. In the meantime, Hickman's (1983, p. 273) opinions are by far the best we have. "The stratigraphic succession of the Warrawoona Group [the lower part of the supracrustal section, consisting of 8 km or so of basalt, high-Mg basalt, and komatiite, and subordinate chert and banded iron formation] is tabular and extends over an area of at least 60,000 km² [the total area of Pilbara granite-and-greenstone exposures]. Individual formations [within the group] can be traced continuously between some of the greenstone belts, establishing that the major synclines are entirely tectonic in origin and bear no direct relationship to depositional basins" (Hickman, 1983, p. 172–173). This regional character "rules out deposition in geosynclines located in the present positions of the greenstone belts . . . which reveal no evidence of facies changes or primary stratigraphic thinning towards syncline margins. Where attenuation is present, it is accompanied by such features as deformed pillows and development of schistosity, indicating its tectonic origin" (ibid.). The regional character "also precludes any model involving migrating depositories," such as have been pro-

posed in the Yilgarn block and the Canadian Shield.

The oldest well-dated greenstone belt is the Barberton belt of South Africa, where thick sections of komatiitic and basaltic-komatiitic lavas are present, but the oldest preserved supracrustal rocks are felsic metatuffs, with a zircon U-Pb age of ~3.54 Ga, depositionally beneath and interbedded with the oldest of those ultramafic and mafic rocks (Lowe, 1994). The overlying thick mafic and ultramafic lavas contain chert units and rare felsic tuffs, and are conformably overlain in turn by felsic volcanic rocks with an age of ~3.25 Ga, as well as clastic sedimentary rocks (Lowe, 1994). The mafic and ultramafic rocks are in contact with older, to 3.64 Ga, zircon-dated tonalitic gneisses (Kröner and Todt, 1988; de Ronde and de Wit, 1994). The ultramafic and mafic rocks were intruded by tonalites little younger than themselves, so by the time of this tonalitic magmatism substantial hydrated crust underlay the exposed ultramafic rocks. Eruption of the mafic and ultramafic rocks at least partly through older, evolved crust is indicated.

I presume that subregional stratigraphic continuity will be demonstrated across broad tracts of most granite-and-greenstone terrains; certainly, the lack of such continuity has nowhere been demonstrated in well-studied regions of low strain. Whatever their correlations, the lower parts of many greenstone-belt supracrustal sequences are dominated by low-alkali olivine basalts, up to 10 km in present structural thickness, with or without ultramafic rocks, and the upper parts often have thinner sedimentary and felsic or intermediate or bimodal volcanic rocks (Goodwin, 1977, 1982, 1991, 1996; Naldrett and Smith, 1981; Condie, 1984; Ayres and Thurston, 1985; Ayres and Corfu, 1991; Ayer and Davis, 1997). It is highly significant for tectonic and petrogenetic analysis that many mafic sequences, with or without ultramafic rocks, lie depositionally above broadly continuous sedimentary rocks or felsic volcanic rocks, and that many continuous sections contain several mafic-and-felsic sequences (Hickman and Lipple, 1978; Hickman, 1983; Helmstaedt and Padgham, 1986; Card and Sanford, 1989; Thorpe et al., 1990; Williams and Collins, 1990; Heather et al., 1995; Wilson et al., 1995). Inherited zircons in many felsic rocks require that their melts reacted with, or were derived from, petrologically evolved rocks at depth even where only mafic and ultramafic rocks are now exposed beneath them (e.g., Kröner et al., 1991). In many places, mafic and ultramafic lavas lie upon older felsic basement gneisses (e.g., Kröner and Todt, 1988) or even successions of cratonic basement and sediments, as in the upward successions of basement granites, quartz sandstones + conglomerates ± stromatolitic (very shallow water) carbonates, banded iron formations, and tholeiites + ultramafic rocks described by Thurston and Chivers (1990). In one such occurrence in the Pilbara craton of Western Australia, ~3.46 Ga shallow-water basalt, magnesian basalt, and chert lie upon a probable paleosol atop deformed ~3.62 Ga basalt, komatiitic basalt, and shallow-water dacite and rhyolite; the old complex was above sea level before the younger was erupted (Buick et al., 1995).

The mafic sequences of greenstone belts formed both as broad coalescing volcanoes that comprised submarine lava plains, and as large shield volcanoes that reached above sea level (Ayres and Thurston, 1985; Watkins and Hickman, 1990). Ultramafic lavas (komatiites), cumulates, and sills are intercalated in many of the basaltic sections. The voluminous intermediate or felsic volcanic rocks that conformably or semiconformably overlie the basalts, or are intercalated with them, in many regions represent more local volcanic edifices, which commonly reached above sea level, and their clastic debris (Goodwin, 1982, 1996; Lowe, 1982; Ayres and Thurston, 1985; Watkins and Hickman, 1990; Ayer and Davis, 1997). Synvolcanic plutons lie within many sequences.

For most of their histories, the regions that became "greenstone belts" typically evolved as vast terrains of subaerial and submarine volcanoes and lava plains and subjacent plutons and gneisses, which built to crustal thicknesses of perhaps 30, or even 40, km within periods typically shorter than 100 m.y. within any one terrain. Magmatic heat sources were regional, not linear; neither spreading centers nor magmatic arcs existed within the assemblages preserved in surviving cratons. Many successions are seen to be ensialic, built on still older continental plutonic or volcanic assemblages. Others can be inferred on isotopic grounds to have formed directly upon mantle rocks,

although no such contacts have been recognized in the field. All lithologies are explicable in terms of the rise of basaltic and ultramafic magmas from the mantle followed by variable eruption, fractionation, and contamination of such magmas, and by secondary melting of them or produced by them. Deformation generally was only moderate before the climactic episodes of granite diapirism, discussed subsequently.

Ultramafic lavas

Most Archean granite-and-greenstone terrains contain voluminous komatiite, and other ultramafic lavas and sills, crystallized from extremely low-viscosity melts with MgO contents as high as 29 wt%, and hence at eruption temperatures as high as ~1600°C, about 200°C higher than the rare most-magnesian Phanerozoic lavas (Nisbet et al., 1993; Abbott et al., 1994). Closely following eruptions of Archean ultramafic complexes were of enormous volume, as in the Yilgarn example noted previously. Olivine commonly was the only liquidus phase over a broad cooling interval, so that the distinctive komatiitic spinifex textures of bladed olivine could develop in the upper zones of many ponded flows, although many other ultramafic lavas are merely densely olivine-phyric throughout. (In less-magnesian komatiites, the spinifex texture may be developed by clinopyroxene.) Komatiite lavas and associated dunites, peridotites, and other fractionates form composite flows recording individual eruptions with volumes that may have reached several thousand km[3], and wherein the komatiites proper may mostly represent quietly crystallized overbank flows from major channels (Hill et al., 1990, 1995). Much debate centers on the depths and degrees of melting and on the mode of rise to the surface of the ultramafic melts (e.g., Cattell and Taylor, 1990; Herzberg, 1992; Nisbet et al., 1993; Xie and Kerrich, 1994). Most investigators argue for high degrees of partial melting in a late Archean upper mantle 200° or even 300°C hotter than that of the present. Although such temperatures often are attributed to mantle plumes, such a setting is not required, as discussed subsequently.

Thermal erosion by extremely hot ultramafic lavas of their substrates is shown both by contact features and by contamination of the lavas

(Perring et al., 1996). The proportion of ultra-mafic rocks in the final assemblages is probably much smaller than the initial magmatic propor-tion that left the mantle because of widespread and severe contamination. Komatiitic basalts may have formed mostly by assimilation of continental crust in rising ultramafic melts (Cattell and Taylor, 1990; Morris, 1993).

Many of the ultramafic rocks overlie conti-nental crustal rocks and other evolved sedimen-tary and igneous rocks. Komatiites and related intrusive and extrusive ultramafic rocks are voluminous in the Archean, are present also in the very early Proterozoic, and have almost no younger analogues.

Late domiform batholiths

The late diapiric batholiths of Archean upper-crust granite-and-greenstone terrains have subuniform spatial densities over broad tracts. Low-density melts and variably remobil-ized older plutonic rocks rose as aggregating batholiths, and denser volcanic rocks were pushed aside and sank between them. The rising material included new magmas, crystal mushes, and variably remobilized older plutonic rocks, in widely varying proportions. Rise of the domiform batholiths in any one region typically was concentrated within a time span of only ~10 m.y., very late in the magmatic history of that region (Ridley, 1992).

Some batholiths consist of broadly uniform tonalite, granodiorite, or quartz monzonite, and others are complex composites of these plus pre-diapiric gneisses. One well-studied com-posite batholith in the Superior craton is a 30 × 50 km dome of leucotonalite, trondhjemite, and granodiorite, wherein remobilized phases are old and migmatitic and preserve pre-diapiric deep-crustal fabrics, whereas young igneous phases are relatively uniform and carry only the doming fabric (Ayres et al., 1991). A Pilbara-craton domiform upper-crustal batholith simi-larly contains much midcrustal gneiss and mig-matite, ~3.42 to 3.44 Ga, much older than the syn-doming granite (~3.00 to 3.10 Ga) with which it was carried upward (Williams and Collins, 1990). In this Pilbara example, the old gneisses are about the same age as the oldest felsic volcanic rocks in the now-synformal greenstone succession, and the young granites are about the same age as the youngest volcanic rocks (Williams and Collins, 1990) (zircon

U-Pb ages). Similar correlations have been doc-umented for some batholiths and flanking vol-canic rocks in the Superior craton. These relationships are powerful evidence that such greenstone-belt volcanic rocks formed as regional plains that underwent no major defor-mation before late diapiric doming, and that the deeper crust beneath these plains was the site of intrusion, partial melting, and migmatization concurrent with the stratiform volcanism.

The typically upright-synformal character, although often complex in detail, of the vol-canic and sedimentary rocks (e.g., Macgregor, 1951; Hickman and Lipple, 1978; Ayres and Thurston, 1985; Chown et al., 1992) between domiform batholiths in contact with the strati-graphically lowest units preserved provides fur-ther powerful evidence that the batholiths rose into stratiform successions of generally simple prior structural history (although many geolo-gists nevertheless make contrary interpreta-tions). Contacts are irregular and crosscutting in detail but in many sectors have little strati-graphic relief for lengths of many kilometers. Simple triangular synforms are present in three-batholith corners. In the Superior craton, most greenstone-belt metamorphism was contact metamorphism by the batholiths, and aureoles typically are zoned outward from discontinuous hornblende hornfels through narrow amphibolite facies to broad greenschist and, where plutons are most distant, sub-greenschist facies, low-pressure prehnite-pum-pellyite, and sub-prehnite pumpellyite (Ayres, 1978; Jolly, 1978). Most of the deformation in the stratiform rocks was synchronous with con-tact metamorphism and commonly decreases away from the batholiths, and little-strained rocks are widespread. That the synmetamorphic deformation resulted primarily from the rising diapirs is indicated by the characteristic down-dip stretching and crossdip flattening, shown by the common triaxial deformation of pillow lavas and by the common parallelism of downdip pillow elongations, stretching lineations, and mineral lineations (e.g., Chown et al., 1992; Percival et al., 1996). In the Pilbara craton also, metamorphism of the stratiform rocks is mostly of greenschist and subgreenschist facies, but contact metamorphism is less conspicuous, and granite/greenstone contacts commonly are sheared; steep dips, tight folds, and strong folia-tion occur where greenstone belts are narrow, but gentler dips and low strains where belts are wide (Hickman, 1983; Trendall, 1995). Structural patterns in mid- and lower-crustal rocks are strikingly different and require decoupling between upper and middle crust.

"Belts"

Plutons and wall-rock networks are elongated in subparallel fashion across any large remnant of an Archean craton. Geologic study has emphasized the "belts" of volcanic rocks, which contain most Archean ore deposits, between late domiform granites. These belts are late features, defined not by stratigraphic or volcanologic features but instead by the anastomosing trends of the complex synforms into which the volcanic and sedimentary rocks were deformed as late diapiric batholiths shouldered them aside. Regional stratigraphy was emphasized previously. No one has demonstrated that pre-batholithic rocks record in their primary volcanic and sedimentary geology any control of the future trends of the "belts."

The several hundred precise zircon U-Pb age determinations from the many poorly defined zones of the Superior craton show no systematic age progression in either plutonic or volcanic rocks across the 1300 km cross-strike width of the province (Card, 1990, Fig. 3; Corfu and Ayres, 1991; Corfu et al., 1989). Ages of plutonic and felsic-volcanic rocks are generally concentrated within less than 100 m.y. in each belt, overlap broadly between belts, and commonly are centered between ~2.72 and 2.70 Ga in all of them. In a number of belts, sparse ages scatter back to 3.00 or 3.05 Ga, and a few ages are as young as 2.6 Ga. Plutonic and volcanic rocks largely overlap in age, although the large, late, diapiric batholiths commonly postdate most nearby volcanic rocks by 10 to 20 m.y.

Late granites and cratonization

The subuniform spatial density of the upper-crustal Archean batholiths over broad regions accords with the inference that their melts and partial melts were generated by regional sheet-like heating of the lower crust and coalesced and rose as diapirs. The pattern is incompatible with local or linear sources of magmas rising from the mantle, and the geochronology is incompatible with sources sequential across strike. Where stratigraphic, structural, and geochronologic studies are most complete, it is

seen that the granites rose into what previously had been sheetlike stratigraphy in the upper crust.

Deep Archean crust was much hotter than modern crust both because the mantle was hotter and because the crust was more radioactive. Continental crust is heated by conductive and advective (magmatic) transfer of heat upward from the mantle, and by radioactive disintegration of ^{238}U, ^{235}U, ^{232}Th, and ^{40}K within the crust. Decay over time has reduced the amount of heat generated by these isotopes by a factor of two or three since 3 Ga (Fowler, 1990, Table 7.2; Thompson et al., 1995). Ambient temperature in basal Archean crust may have approached 1000°C, deep-crustal melt then being widespread (Ridley, 1992) and the dry peridotite solidus having been crossed high in the upper mantle beneath such crust (Thompson et al., 1995). This great contrast between Archean and Phanerozoic crust and upper mantle is reflected in major differences in tectonic and magmatic processes.

The likely cause of the regional partial melting required to mobilize the regional arrays of huge, subsynchronous diapiric batholiths is radiogenic heat that accumulated after magmatism and sedimentation had suitably thickened the crust (Ridley, 1992). Petrology of the granites requires hydrous deep-crustal partial melting. The felsic melts scavenged the radioactive elements responsible for the melting.

The late diapirism effected an enormous transfer of radioactive isotopes, and of contained heat, from the lower to the upper crust within a short period of time in each region, and greatly increased the petrologic stratification of the crust. This transfer allowed the lower crust and subjacent mantle to cool markedly below prior temperatures and resulted in stabilizion of cratons and stiffening of lithosphere (Ridley, 1992).

Structural trends

The regional fabric of Archean granite-and-greenstone terrains is defined by the rough orientation of elliptical diapiric batholiths and by the anastomosing strikes of the synformal volcanic and sedimentary rocks deformed between them. These trends generally record the final cratonization of a region and require a combination of density-driven diapiric rise of batholiths and of more or less synchronous regional horizontal shortening across strike as well as extension along strike. The shortening was transmitted through the upper crust as a series of diapir-controlled waveforms of semi-constant dimensions. The deformation represented bulk-pure-shear cross-strike shortening and along-strike extension, for the resulting structures are dominantly upright, without the systematic vergences that would be produced by simple shear. Structures commonly are broadly subparallel across any one remnant craton, but in the Superior craton regional structures swing from the eastward trend dominant elsewhere to northward in the northeast part of the craton (for example, see Percival et al., 1994).

The synchroneity of vertical batholithic diapirism and of horizontal orthogonal shortening and extension, and the semiconstant structural level and wavelength of diapirism and upright deformation across broad tracts, indicate the upper crust to have been effectively floating on deeper crust, and both to have been very weak and presumably partly molten. Archean upper crust was in this phase too weak to support high topographic loads or to transmit simple shear. The apparent lack of great Archean crustal thrust faults also precludes an explanation of severe shortening of rigid crust. As discussed subsequently, the middle and lower crust were decoupled from the upper crust and deformed quite differently. The external cause of the shortening, and its relationship to mantle processes and kinematics, is unknown—but it did not represent rigid-plate tectonics.

Turbidites

The youngest stratiform rocks of granite-and-greenstone terrains commonly are dominated by coarse clastic sediments, both subaerial and subaqueous, derived primarily from volcanic and late-granitic complexes of about the same ages. I take this broad synchroneity of late diapiric granites, younger volcanic rocks, and turbidite-dominated sediments to indicate that erosion and sedimentation were responses to the moderate topographic and bathymetric relief created by the rise of the diapiric granites and the concurrent regional shortening and extension of the decoupled upper crust, and by the building of late felsic-volcanic edifices. Conversely, the scarcity of such sediments in

older sections is evidence against the general existence of major basins flanked by uplands before diapir time.

Late Archean graywacke, mudstone, volcani-clastic sediments, quartzose sandstone, and subordinate conglomerate, quartzite, and iron formation, derived mostly from granitic and felsic volcanic rocks, occur discontinuously across the entire Slave craton (400 × 800 km). These strata are intercalated with and overlie the youngest volcanic rocks of the province, locally lie upon older gneiss, and comprise about three-quarters of the preserved area of Archean supracrustal rocks (Henderson, 1981; Padgham and Fyson, 1992; Hoffman, 1993; Padgham, 1995). The late diapiric granites in part were synchronous with turbidite deposition and in part formed within a few million years after it (van Breeman et al., 1992; Davis et al., 1994). Henderson (1981) inferred deposition in many small extensional basins, but no structural evidence for this is apparent. No disruption of accretionary-wedge type has been recognized, and the regional extent and stratigraphic successions preclude an origin in such a wedge. At least a substantial proportion of the sedimentary rocks were deposited in shallow water, and none are proven to be of deep-water origin.

A similar late-basin origin accords with the description by Fralick et al. (1992) of shallow-water turbidites of the Superior craton, which fan away from volcanic edifices and were not deposited longitudinally as would typify trench or forearc basins. The Superior turbidites were deposited in short periods of time following cessation of greenstone-belt magmatism (Davis et al., 1990).

Incomplete granite-and-greenstone cycle?

The Kaapvaal craton of South Africa and Pilbara craton of Western Australia were cratonized by ~3.0 Ga, and sequences >10 km thick of mafic and felsic volcanic rocks and clastic and chemical sedimentary rocks were deposited, with regional stratigraphic continuity, across them in late Archean time. The African succession is preserved in the Witwatersrand basin and outliers, the Australian in the Hamersley basin and outliers—the basins being those of preservation, not necessarily of deposition. The two cratons and these overlying successions may have been contiguous in

Archean time. No Archean granites cut the young successions, but some Australian outliers show slight deformation into gentle synforms formed between the terminal uplifts of the older diapiric granites (Hickman, 1983).

Rock types in these regionally continuous successions are reminiscent of the deformed successions seen in Archean greenstone belts, although ultramafic lavas are lacking. If these late Archean post-cratonization sequences indeed are similar to those that formed the greenstone belts, then perhaps they represent all but the late-stage granitic history of another granite-and-greenstone cycle. Perhaps because the basement beneath the late sequences had already been inverted and stabilized by the regional rise of diapiric granites, such granites could not again form in the lower crust and rise through the sequences.

Archean Middle and Deep Crust and Upper Mantle

Gneiss terrains

Some Archean gneiss complexes are the basements beneath supracrustal sections, and others are the deeper-crustal equivalents of nearby upper-crustal assemblages. Some upper-crustal granite-and-greenstone terrains give way along or across strike, where erosion has cut obliquely deeper into the crust, to gneissic domains, and these often contain rocks older than, as well as equivalent to, the upper-crustal assemblages (e.g., Davis et al., 1995). The older gneisses of such associations generally have not been mapped or characterized against adjacent younger gneisses, having been recognized primarily by spot determinations of ancient zircons. The gneiss complexes typically are in amphibolite facies, but broad tracts are in orthopyroxene-granulite facies recording less hydrous crystallization and higher temperatures than those typical of post-Archean middle crust (e.g., Pan et al., 1994; Percival et al., 1994).

Where broad belts of metasedimentary rocks intervene between granite-and-greenstone terrains, they tend to have medial tracts of gneisses and anatectic micaceous granites, typically more potassic and aluminous than the characteristically tonalitic gneisses of the other assemblages of gneisses (Percival, 1989). Both

types of granitic rocks are of crustal-melt origin, as discussed previously for tonalite.

The best-studied tract of Archean gneisses of widely varying ages, recorded by near-concordia ion-probe U-Pb zircon ages scattering from 3.9 to 2.5 Ga, is in the 100 × 200 km Nuuk region of southwestern Greenland (McGregor et al., 1991; Friend et al., 1996; Nutman et al., 1996). The dominant rocks are tonalitic gneisses and migmatites of amphibolite and orthopyroxene-granulite facies, most of them complexly polycyclic (McGregor, 1993). Gneisses and granites of ~2.8 to 2.7 Ga are widespread. In a well-sampled medial tract ~30 km wide, gneisses with zircons yielding maximum ages of 3.9 to 3.6 Ga also are abundant. Different spots on the same zircon grains, or on different grains from the same samples, can scatter more or less down concordia as far as 2.5 Ga, showing a protracted, or complexly multi-episodic, high-temperature history. The sparse determinations made northwest of the medial tract scatter back to ~3.2 Ga, whereas the few determinations southeast of the medial tract are within the range of 2.9 to 2.7 Ga. The authors cited suggested that the old ages in the well-sampled medial tract require that northwest, medial, and southeast tracts formed far apart and collided, and were complexly interfolded together, when intervening oceanic crust was subducted, shortly before late regional granite formation and migmatitization at ~2.7 Ga. Their work indeed establishes the presence of a coherent belt of polycyclic gneisses that included ancient protoliths of yet-undefined character (see the discussion of ancient gneisses in the early-Earth section), but this in no way requires a plate-tectonic explanation. A similar study of an old migmatite in the Yilgarn craton found igneous zircons scattered widely in U-Pb age, from 3.7 to 3.3 Ga, even within hand specimens or cm-scale layers (Kinny and Nutman, 1996).

Decoupling of upper crust from middle and lower crust

Archean upper-crustal deformation was accomplished by gravitational body forces as low-density domiform batholiths rose through denser stratiform successions and shouldered them aside into complex sinking synforms. The diapirism was accompanied by orthogonal horizontal bulk-pure-shear shortening and extension, the character of which indicates the upper crust to have been effectively floating on deeper material.

Late deformation of middle- and lower-crust Archean assemblages as seen in outcrop is so strikingly different from that of upper-crust assemblages exposed along and across strike from them that decoupling is required. The simple dome-and-syncline pattern, and the steep stretching lineations, that characterize the upper crust are lacking in the lower. A number of studies (e.g., in the Superior craton—Percival, 1989; Moser, 1994; Sawyer and Benn, 1995) have demonstrated that, instead, gently plunging stretching lineations trending subparallel to the long axes of upper-crustal domiform batholiths are typical.

The structural and geochronologic study by Moser (1994) and Moser et al. (1996) in the mid-crustal rocks of the Kapuskasing uplift of Ontario documented subhorizontal late Archean extension parallel to the long dimension of the granite-and-greenstone terrain above. They emphasized that this requires decoupling of the middle from the upper crust. The extension was accomplished by bottom-to-the-west simple shear combined with pure-shear flattening and boudinage. Moser et al. inferred that the initially underlying basal crust in this sector had flowed westward, coalesced into larger masses, and sunk into the mantle, and that the exposed structure thus developed in response to deeper delamination. They suggested that water released by dehydration of the sinking masses had risen into the remaining lower crust and enabled the late partial melting displayed there. The model is appealing.

The middle and deep crust beneath Archean upper-crustal assemblages commonly is displayed on long-sweep seismic-reflection profiles as having a pervasive subhorizontal or gently undulating fabric. Thus, seismic-reflection profiles in the broad Abitibi granite-and-greenstone terrain typically show few apparent reflections in the top 6 to 12 km of the crust: the granites are acoustically transparent, and the volcanic rocks are too steep, or too lacking in impedance contrasts, to produce good reflectors (Bellefleur et al., 1995; Jackson et al., 1995; Lacroix and Sawyer, 1995). Often present at 6 to 12 km is a gently undulating reflector, which is continuous in one sector for 90 km (Lacroix and Sawyer, 1995) and perhaps images the zone of decoupling discussed in both pre-

vious and subsequent sections. Elsewhere, a single distinct reflector is not present, but instead the middle and deep crust are displayed as many variably continuous to highly discontinuous reflectors with gentle apparent inclinations.

This apparent deep fabric may well be real, but strong caveats should be kept in mind when interpreting such records. The common-depth-point methodology of processing reflection data strongly enhances any subhorizontal reflectivity actually present; comparison with super-deep drilling results shows that the strongest reflectors tend to be fractures and minor shear zones rather than lithologic contrasts or foliation-induced anisotropy, and that actual moderate to steep dips are completely masked (Harjes et al., 1997). Subhorizontal pseudoreflectivity can be generated from random noise as an artifact of processing, the effect increasing with moveout (Levander and Gibson, 1991) and hence being greatest in deep profiles. Out-of-section reflectors, even from distant vertical dikes (Zaleski et al., 1997), or scattering artifacts from out-of-section point sources, can be recorded and mistaken for inclined in-section events. Crooked traverses provide still another family of problems for interpretation. Sum these and other complexities, and the two directions of superimposed deep-crustal shortening and thrusting deduced by Bellefleur et al. (1997), by "assuming a connection between reflectivity and strain produced by tectonic processes" in a Superior reflection profile, can only be viewed as tenuous.

Archean lower crust

Obliquely eroded sections through much of the crust in Archean terrains show a general downward progression from low-grade rocks (of greenschist or lower amphibolite facies) and high-level granites in the upper crust through gneisses and migmatites of upper amphibolite facies, and in some regions orthopyroxene granulites (in the middle crust) to mixed mafic to felsic rocks in garnet-amphibolite and granulite facies in the upper part of the lower crust (e.g., Percival et al., 1992). The Proterozoic ramp uplift of Wawa gneisses and Kapuskasing granulites in Ontario displays a well-documented example through this progression (Moser, 1994; Percival and West, 1994). Upper-crustal steep-dipping greenstones and steep-sided granites are seen in this oblique crustal section to give way downward to undulating to steeply domiformal amphibolite-facies mafic gneiss, migmatite, and concordant sheets of tonalite, granodiorite, and quartz monzonite. This assemblage in turn gives way downward to layered mafic and tonalitic rocks in granulite, garnet-amphibolite, and upper amphibolite facies, and subordinate ultramafic and anorthositic rocks, which before thrust ramping mostly were subhorizontal. Each of these three descending assemblages characterizes a depth section 10 km or so thick. Krogh (1993) found that U-Pb zircon ages of granulites in the upper part of the lower crust in the uplift are tens of millions of years younger than the youngest upper-crustal magmatism nearby, noted that similar age discrepancies characterize other Canadian Archean granulites, and suggested that the granulites were produced by late magmatic underplating of the crust; but slow cooling of residual heat in the deep crust might provide an alternative explanation.

Basal Archean crust has nowhere been recognized in outcrop, whereas basal crust and uppermost mantle of Phanerozoic age are exposed in obliquely eroded upramped sections in collision zones in several parts of the world. In such Phanerozoic sections, the basal crust consists of great layered igneous and meta-igneous complexes of mafic rocks, which generally become increasingly rich downward in garnet, both igneous and metamorphic, and the geophysical Mohorovičić discontinuity is seen to be present within the layered complexes well above residual mantle rocks (Hamilton, 1989, 1995; Percival et al., 1992). Underplating of continental crust by voluminous mafic magmas is indicated. Seismic-velocity structure and the study of xenoliths yield the same conclusion (Christensen and Mooney, 1995; Rudnick and Fountain, 1995).

The few studies of xenoliths from the deep crust beneath Archean cratons, found in kimberlites and alkaline mafic igneous rocks, show that Archean basal crust is quite mafic, although comparison of the aggregate thickness of mafic rocks with that in younger crust is not possible with available data, and available petrothermobarometry does not adequately define deep-crustal and upper-mantle depth successions for the xenoliths. Deep-crustal (and uppermost mantle?) xenoliths in kimberlites in the Kaapvaal craton are mafic plagioclase-bearing and plagioclase-free garnet-pyroxene granulites (Pearson et al., 1995). Archean lower-crustal xenoliths studied from Eocene lamprophyres in Montana and Alberta are dominantly mafic granulitic cumulates (Collerson et al., 1989). Xenoliths of upper-crustal tonalite in those lamprophyres yield Archean U-Pb zircon ages (Davis and Berman, 1995). Ages of cores of zircons in a felsic granulite xenolith from the upper part of the lower crust scatter from ~2500 to 3000 Ma, whereas overgrowth ages are ~1760 to 2375 Ma (Collerson et al., 1993). In two high-pressure granulites from the still deeper crust, ages of zircon cores, or of uniform grains of zircon, range from ~1715 to 1815 Ma, with one discordant age of ~2945 Ma. Overgrowth ages range from ~1695 to 1780 Ma (Davis and Berman, 1995). The authors cited attributed this downward-younging trend to Proterozoic reheating of Archean crust, but an alternative explanation is that the deep crust did not cool sufficiently to prevent lead loss from zircon until early Proterozoic time.

Crustal delamination

Much Archean fractionation of crust, and much mixing into the mantle of mafic crustal materials, may have been achieved by the sinking of dense mafic rocks delaminated from the deep crust. Such a process would have been facilitated by the relatively low viscosity of hot Archean mantle. Only basalt and komatiite magmas likely reached the Archean crust as primary melts from the mantle; as the preserved crust is intermediate in bulk composition, much of the complementary mafic and ultramafic deep-crustal material must have been returned to the mantle. Much ultramafic magma was erupted through Archean continental crust, but density considerations make it likely that much more was underplated at the base of the crust. Delaminated and sunken underplated crust and cogenetic uppermost mantle probably included much ultramafic material as well as mafic igneous rocks and dense restites complementary to crustally generated melts. Mid-crustal structural evidence compatible with flow toward delamination sites was noted previously.

Seismic-velocity studies could constrain options, but current results are disputed. Velocity structure can be interpreted to show the present lower part of the lower crust of Archean terrains to be less dense on average than that of Proterozoic and Phanerozoic terrains; if this is correct, then either the uppermost mantle includes much high-density petrologic crust, or much Archean basal crust was delaminated or dripped from higher crust and sank into the mantle during Archean time, or both (Christensen and Mooney, 1995; Rudnick and Fountain, 1995). Others see a more normal velocity structure in Archean crust; thus, Grandjean et al. (1995) deduced a standard-thickness high-velocity lower crust, from 30 to 40 km in depth, with Vp of ~6.9 to 7.3 km/s. The apparent sub-Moho inclined reflector imaged by Calvert et al. (1995) and Bellefleur et al. (1995, 1997) (they inferred it to be an arrested subducting slab) perhaps is a sheet of delaminated lower crust arrested in its sinking into the mantle.

Lack of crustal roots

Archean cratons typically are eroded much less deeply than are Proterozoic and Paleozoic orogenic belts. Rocks of subgreenschist and low-pressure prehnite-pumpellyite facies are widespread in Archean greenstone belts where relatively distant from the nearest large granite; associated relatively impervious, nonhydrated rocks are almost unmetamorphosed. In lower and middle amphibolite-facies rocks, andalusite, not sillimanite, is the dominant Al_2SiO_5 polymorph (although sillimanite is dominant in upper amphibolite-facies gneisses and migmatites); kyanite is rare and is virtually limited to relatively low-temperature rocks. These and other petrologic features indicate that common depths of erosion of granite-and-greenstone terrains are within the range from 3 to 10 km and erosion depths of belts of gneiss and migmatite are commonly less than 15 km (although often more). Archean rocks have been eroded much more deeply than these cratonic depths in Proterozoic uplifts (e.g., Kapuskasing in Canada, Limpopo in Africa), in Proterozoic collision complexes, and in post-Archean rift-shoulder uplifts. As many observers have commented, the general shallow crustal level of exposure of Archean cratons is remarkable. Furthermore, it provides another indication that Archean tectonomagmatic processes were quite different from modern ones.

Apparently Archean granite-and-greenstone terrains did not form with deep crustal roots, or

else they lost incipient roots by delamination and sinking into the mantle concurrent with magmatic growth, for roots would have produced uplift high above sea level and deep erosion. The somewhat deeper erosion of Archean gneiss belts may be a product of retention of roots beneath them.

Archean mantle

Seismic tomography. Some, but not all, of those parts of Precambrian shields that are of Archean and pre–2 Ga Proterozoic age are underlain by mantle of relatively high velocity to depths of 250 to 450 km (Polet and Anderson, 1995; van der Lee and Nolet, 1997). A compositional contrast with mantle elsewhere, not merely a cooler temperature, is required for at least the deeper parts of these mantle roots (Anderson and Polet, 1995). Apparently Archean mantle processes differed from later ones, and the primary(?) deep roots remain attached to their cratons in some regions but elsewhere have been recycled into the rest of the mantle.

Temperature and xenoliths. An Archean mantle on the order of 200°C hotter than the modern one is required by the greater radiogenic and retained heat of the earlier Earth (Schubert et al., 1980) and by the abundance of Archean ultramafic lavas. The upper mantle beneath Archean cratons may have formed primarily from igneous, not residual, ultramafic rocks. Nevertheless, data from mantle xenoliths in Proterozoic and Phanerozoic kimberlites erupted through Archean cratons have been cited widely as indicative of an Archean mantle as cool as that of the present, and that inference in turn has been cited in support of the assumption that Archean crustal and upper-mantle processes were like modern ones.

The dominant mantle xenoliths erupted through the Archean crust of southern Africa (from which comes the best information) are garnet lherzolites that now consist of magnesian olivine, enstatite, and much-subordinate diopside and garnet. This non-igneous mineralogy is broadly compatible with geothermal gradients like modern ones, with allowance for perturbation by rising kimberlite magmas (Boyd, 1987). Some investigators have assumed from this that Archean continental upper mantle was little if any hotter than modern mantle (e.g., Boyd, 1987; Ballard and Pollack, 1988; Richardson,

1990). The problem at issue, however, regards the thermal gradient in Archean time, and hence the mineralogy as it then existed, and not the mineralogy as sampled much later by kimberlites. Various dating methods demonstrate that the xenoliths contain Archean isotopic components but do not date the final mineral assemblages as older than the enclosing kimberlites.

The sampled low-temperature mineralogy apparently was inverted upon cooling from initial igneous assemblages. Textures and compositions, and experimental data, indicate that the studied southern African lherzolites were inverted from harzburgites crystallized at temperatures near the dry peridotite solidus, the final low-temperature garnet and pyroxene having exsolved from initial high-temperature, high-pressure orthopyroxene rich in Ca and Al (Cox et al., 1987; Herzberg, 1993).

Varied eclogitic rocks are a common component of mantle sampled by kimberlites in Archean cratons, and at least many of these also record early temperatures much higher than those of equilibration of the kimberlite-sampled xenoliths. The eclogites have compositions that are, broadly, basaltic to melabasaltic. The protoliths of their mantle sources have been variously interpreted as subducted oceanic crust (MacGregor and Manton, 1986; Helmstaedt and Schulze, 1989; Gurney, 1991; Helmstaedt and Gurney, 1995), as delaminated and sunken crustal cumulates or restites (e.g., Ireland et al., 1994), and as primary mantle igneous rocks. Strong evidence for the origin of at least some of the eclogites as igneous rocks crystallized within the mantle at temperatures much above modern ones comes, again, from study of exsolved mineral phases. Many of the eclogites contain kyanite and garnet exsolved from clinopyroxene, the reconstructed initial composition of which apparently requires crystallization from a melt deeper than 100 km (Smyth et al., 1989).

Origin. Both Archean crust and (assuming the southern African sample to be representative) upper mantle apparently are dominated by igneous rocks and are not merely mobilizate and residue, respectively. Some preserved Archean crust remains attached to upper mantle that escaped the pervasive tectonic and magmatic recycling that affected the rest of the mantle. The African mantle sample is in bulk markedly higher in Mg—and lower in Al, Fe, and Ca (but not Si)—than komatiite, the most mafic melt that penetrated Archean crust (Herzberg, 1993). The preserved Archean mantle may include material that both correlates with and pre-dates the overlying cratons.

Obvious options for the preserved mantle are formation as cumulates, or as direct crystallizates from a magma ocean or from impact-melted mixes of mantle and meteorites (Herzberg, 1993), with, perhaps, admixed material delaminated from the continents above. All of these may be represented as products of superimposed processes. Thermal considerations discussed previously accord with voluminous mantle magmatism after the overlying granite-and-greenstone terrain began to form (between 3.6 and 2.8 Ga, depending on the craton), whereas lunar analogy accords with vast impact melts only older than 3.8 Ga. Magma oceans with hydrous, tonalitic upper layers, as proposed by Ridley and Kramers (1990), could have been present before the granite-and-greenstone assemblages (but not after, for the 10 km thick mafic-volcanic sections would have sunk in them), and might be invoked to explain the puzzling tonalitic basement seen in outcrop and recognized as a contaminant to greenstone sequences.

Minimally disturbed ancient mantle thus may be preserved in the roots of some Archean cratons, where it was much modified during the formation of those cratons but was modified relatively little thereafter. The concepts of crust, mantle, and Mohorovičić discontinuity tend to convey images of processes that change profoundly, as from residuum to construct, at a boundary, and this may be completely wrong with regard to the Archean. Instead, there may have been a magmatic construct, several hundred kilometers thick, high within which the Moho was a leaky self-perpetuating density filter, beneath which most ultramafic melts crystallized, and through which sank many dense rocks that crystallized, or formed as intracrustal restites, above it.

A distinctive feature of Archean cratons is the volume of mafic and ultramafic lavas they display. Probably only mafic and ultramafic magmas left the mantle, and the proportion of initial ultramafic magmas must have been higher than the final proportion of rocks because of contamination by assimilation into the extremely hot ultramafic liquids; yet the bulk crust is of intermediate, not mafic, composition. Something like half of whatever melts originally reached the crust may now be in the mantle. Alternatively, much of the felsic component of Archean cratons may have been recycled during granite-and-greenstone time from older magma-ocean fractionates (cf. Ridley and Kramers, 1990).

Plumes?

Archean tectonics and magmatism are products of a mantle much hotter than the modern one. The effects of greater heat were felt at different times in different craton remnants in the small preserved sample of Archean crust. Although the tectonomagmatic successions were similar, several craton remnants experienced their major evolution hundreds of millions of years before others. Obviously the Archean Earth did not evolve with radial uniformity.

The concept of mantle plumes has become widely accepted in recent years and a voluminous literature elaborates their hypothetical properties and effects. Hot mantle is pictured as piped upward from the core-mantle boundary and spreading or channeling beneath the crust. The notion was devised to explain the "hot spot" time-distance relationships of, particularly, the Hawaiian-Emperor seamount chain, and has since been broadened by proponents to account for practically any magmatism, uplift, or rifting, on any scale or shape or progression in either space or time, not obviously related to two-dimensional subduction and seafloor spreading. The voluminous literature on hypothetical plumes is notable for ingenuity on the one hand and absence of constraints on the other.

Plumes nevertheless probably do not exist in the modern Earth. Upper-mantle temperatures are shown by high-resolution seismic tomography to vary much around the Earth (Anderson et al., 1992). "Hotspots" occur mostly above broad, not local, areas of low-velocity upper mantle, and are not associated with the hottest or central parts of those areas, nor do those low-velocity anomalies extend deep into the mantle. "Hotspots may not be narrow pipelike features but rather the focused effect of upwelling triggered from above by extensional strains or discontinuities in the lithosphere" (Anderson

et al., 1992, p. 1647). Thermal anomalies associated with spreading ridges also are largely limited to the upper mantle: ridges form where plates pull apart, not where great convective upwellings occur, and necessarily migrate independent of the deep mantle. Lateral temperature gradients, particularly near boundaries between thick and thin lithosphere, control major magmatic effects both on the continents and in the oceans (Anderson et al., 1992; King and Anderson, 1995). Deeper mantle heat also is widely variable laterally and indicates locations where plates have been in the past more than where they are now. Tomography does not support the popular concept of "plumes" rising from the base of the mantle, and geochemical, noble-gas, and petrogenetic arguments presented for the existence of plumes are invalid (Anderson, in press).

Wolfe et al. (1997) presented a teleseismic-tomographic model in support of a downward-widening conical plume (not the downward-narrowing mushroom plume of popular conjecture) under Iceland, but their data are equally satisfied by a shallow, non-plume magma chamber of limited vertical extent (Keller et al., 1997; I am indebted to Eugene D. Humphreys and Sean C. Solomon for correspondence clarifying further points in this analysis). The hypothetical plume of Wolfe et al. is the envelope of steeply rising teleseismic rays recorded in small Iceland. Actual tomographic resolution is limited to the small upper-mantle volume, below 100 km, wherein recorded teleseismic rays cross, and in the rest of the raypath envelope there is no resolution of the depth of the retarding mass and the method used "smears" the delay down to the 400 km limit of the analysis. The trend to zero retardation at the margins and top of the Wolfe model is an artifact of an inversion algorithm that forces values to zero where ray density is low, as it necessarily is around the perimeter of Iceland.

Nor are mantle-fixed plumes required by island chains. The archetypical chain, widely cited as requiring a mantle-fixed plume, is the Hawaiian-Emperor volcanic ridge, almost 6000 km long, whereon age of volcanism increases with distance from the active southeastern end at a general rate of ~8 or 9 cm/yr (Clague and Dalrymple, 1989). The abrupt 120° bend, from west-northwestward to northward, at 42 or 43

Ma in the middle of the chain, is incompatible with plume theory, which can explain this bend only by an abrupt 60° change in the direction of motion of the huge Pacific plate, an extreme plate reorganization compatible with no other type of evidence. Uninterrupted spreading of the vast Pacific plate is shown by the smooth progression of its magnetic-anomaly stripes, from the North Pacific to the Southern Ocean, throughout the early Tertiary (e.g., Atwater and Severinghaus, 1989). (Atwater emphasized to the author the importance of this relationship.) Spreading, subduction, and tectonism, of course, were occurring elsewhere at this time, but no great, abrupt global changes occurred near 42 Ma.

Megaplumes of Proterozoic age are widely rationalized to have produced the large circular structures—"coronae" and related features—that saturate most uplands of Venus, and vast basalt outpourings are widely considered to have produced the intervening plains. There certainly are large volcanic edifices on Venus, but the magmatic interpretations of plains and circle-saturated uplands have not in my view been proven. My own analysis (Hamilton, 1993) of Magellan radar imagery, including stereoscopic images in some areas, and of the data from landers on Venutian plains, led me to infer that the old circular structures may be the roots of impact structures (hence presumably mostly older than 3.8 Ga), deeply eroded by wind in the extremely dense atmosphere, and that the plains may be primarily products of eolian deposition.

Archean plumes often have been postulated to explain the high mantle temperatures needed to generate ultramafic lavas, in terms of transient perturbations requiring massive transfer of heat upward in material from a deep source. Such hypothetical plumes would have needed heads the size of the cratons-to-be, which were larger by unknown amounts than the preserved remnants, and to have had two or more abrupt, coextensive upwellings beneath most cratons. Proponents have not attempted more specific plume-tectonomagmatic explanations for Archean terrains, but given the purported ability of modern plumes to account for whatever is observed, such explanations are to be expected in the future. My own preference is for explanations (like those favored by Anderson and his colleagues in many papers, including those just cited) in terms of lateral, lithosphere-controlled variations in temperature, such as are required in the Archean Earth by the lack of synchronous development of cratons.

Lack of Archean Indicators of Plate-Tectonic Processes

No diagnostic indicators of plate tectonics have been found in Archean terrains. The concepts of plate tectonics and the analogy with currently active tectonic systems have permitted much comprehension of the tectonic and magmatic evolution of continental crust during Phanerozoic time. The lithologies, structures, and relationships of the components of active and late Phanerozoic plate-tectonic systems vary much in detail but are broadly similar. In active convergent-plate margins, we see systematic relationships between distinctive accretionary wedges, forearc assemblages, magmatic arcs, and backarc complexes. Where continents have been sundered, we see rifts both along and across the grain of pre-rift terrains, and we see stratal wedges of shelf, slope, and abyssal sedimentary rocks developed along those rifts. In collisional complexes, we find such stratal wedges shoved back onto their flanking cratons in thrust belts, and complex interactions between the opposed tectonic systems. Often we see the development of new subduction systems initiated outboard of the collided aggregates. Where we find similar assemblages in similar relationships in ancient terrains, we infer similar tectonic settings of formation. Ancient convergent margins are no longer open-sided, with oceanic lithosphere preserved outboard of subduction complexes, but instead occur within sutures—scars left where large or small ocean basins disappeared by subduction beneath one or both now-juxtaposed high-standing crustal masses—that join aggregates of convergent and trailing-edge plate-margin assemblages. The various components of the modern open-sided margins can be recognized in suture zones within many Phanerozoic orogenic belts and thus provide strong support for the general assumption that these belts record plate interactions analogous to modern ones. For example, where ancient complexes with characteristics similar to those of modern accretionary wedges can be paired spatially with coeval magmatic complexes that are similar to modern magmatic arcs, we infer that the ancient assemblages also formed in convergent-plate settings, and that the polarity of subduction can be defined.

Identifying plate-interaction features in Proterozoic and Phanerozoic terrains commonly is straightforward where the features are seen in upper-crustal settings and have not been subjected to severe later deformation, metamorphism, and plutonism. Broad regions of Archean cratons expose low-strain, upper-crustal assemblages wherein plate-interaction processes should be well recorded, had they operated. The lack of Archean plate-tectonic indicators cannot be attributed to masking of features once present by greater subsequent deformation and metamorphism in Archean terrains, for the typical depth of erosion in Archean cratons is markedly less than that in most Proterozoic and Paleozoic orogens, and many broad tracts in Archean cratons have been eroded less than 10 km and only minimally strained and metamorphosed. It should therefore be easy to recognize analogues with modern systems if such exist, but none of the modern plate-tectonic components has been demonstrated to have a credible analogue in Archean assemblages.

My career experience has been mostly in Phanerozoic plate tectonics and crustal evolution, and I have worked extensively with convergent-plate tectonics in active island-arc and collisional settings and also in inactive and variably eroded Phanerozoic orogens. When I began to look seriously at Archean assemblages, about 1990, I assumed that I would find evidence for plate interactions. I did not find it. Others who recently have emphasized that Archean assemblages do not fit plate-tectonic models include Bickle et al. (1995), Davies (1992), Goodwin (1996), Hammond and Nisbet (1992), Padgham (1992, 1995), and Rapp et al. (1991). The lithologies, structures, and relationships of the components of active and late Phanerozoic plate-tectonic systems vary widely in detail but are broadly similar. When direct mechanistic analogy to such systems is postulated for ancient rock suites, the prediction thus is implicit that similar assemblages and relationships should prevail in the ancient terrains. This prediction has not been shown to be fulfilled in any Archean terrain. Although the

view that plate tectonics dominated the Archean Earth is widely held by Archean specialists, they have yet to identify what appear to me to be valid analogues for any of the many diagnostic products of plate rifting and convergence.

No evidence for Archean rifting has been recognized in the sundering of cratons or in the development of continent-margin sedimentary wedges, so proponents of plate tectonics presume rifting from the presence of basalts that are considered to be analogous to ophiolites, ocean-floor basalts, and oceanic plateaus, on the basis of slight compositional similarities to modern basalts from such settings, even where the Archean "oceanic" rocks at issue depositionally overlie older continental basement rocks, platform strata, or felsic volcanic rocks. (Archean ultramafic rocks are utterly different from modern ophiolitic ones.) No stratigraphic, spatial, structural, and temporal relationships have been identified between Archean tectonic and magmatic assemblages that would support analogy with modern convergent-margin systems, so felsic volcanic and granitic rocks are assumed to represent "magmatic arcs." Archean turbidites are widely assumed to be "accretionary wedges," even though no appropriate deformation has been recognized within them. Representative papers that base extremely complex tectonic rationales on such vague lithologic analogies are cited in this essay.

Not only do Archean assemblages display none of the relationships that characterize plate-tectonic rifting and accretion in Proterozoic and Phanerozoic domains, but assemblages widespread in the Archean lack counterparts in younger terrains. Granite-and-greenstone terrains typify Archean upper crust and have no structural and magmatic analogues younger than very early Proterozoic. Komatiites and related intrusive and extrusive ultramafic rocks are voluminous in the Archean, are present also in the very early Proterozoic, and have almost no younger analogues.

Tectonics and magmatism are responses to loss of heat by the Earth. The modern Earth loses heat primarily through the thermal windows created by seafloor spreading, and modern lithosphere plates move primarily in response to the sinking of dense slabs. Archean crust and mantle were much hotter than modern ones, and there is no a priori reason that density-driven subduction beneath internally rigid plates should have been an important Archean process.

Convergent-margin features

Had oceanic lithosphere been subducted beneath high-standing Archean crustal masses, in modern tectonic style, then sutures should have formed between disparate collided arcs and continents and fragments thereof, and magmatic arcs should have developed above subducting plates. The subregional continuity of greenstone stratigraphy where well studied is presumptive evidence that no sutures are present within such subregions.

Sutures. Scars between aggregated crustal masses should be marked by, among other features, polymict mélange and broken formation from accretionary wedges; large or small masses of ophiolite (oceanic crust and mantle); and metamorphic rocks recording high ratios of pressure to temperature. None of these have been found in the Archean (although the lack of high P/T rocks can be attributed to the higher geothermal gradients in Archean time).

I know of no documented examples of Archean disrupted rocks analogous to those abundant as indicators of subduction in Phanerozoic orogens. Many geologists (e.g., Percival and Williams, 1989) have assumed that tracts of Archean turbidites represent accretionary-wedge materials preserved in sutures. I have seen no suggestion of accretionary-wedge structure in the many large and small outcrops I have visited of Archean turbidites (although minor soft-sediment deformation is occasionally displayed), in part in the company of proponents of accretionary-wedge interpretations. Kusky (1991) illustrated his speculation that turbidites represent wedges with field photographs (his Figs. 7B, 7C, and 7D) showing well-exposed coherent, unsheared strata. Archean graywackes occur as late, or the latest, components of the continuous stratigraphic sections in their regions; they commonly are volcanigenic, and they probably were deposited in response to accentuation of topographic and bathymetric relief by late diapiric batholiths, as discussed earlier.

There are, of course, many narrow shear zones in Archean rocks that contain tectonic mixtures of local wall rocks, but these are not analogous to subduction-related polymict

mélanges of far-travelled bits. Skulski et al. (1994) described schistose serpentinite, with basal pods of serpentinite-matrix "mélange" of local rock types, a few meters thick, along the base of a section of ultramafic volcanic rocks. Kusky (1991, p. 824) made a specific claim for subduction-related mélange in describing an outcrop of a shear zone of purportedly exotic clasts: "a thin wedge of serpentinite mélange . . . [that] contains small (<1 m), roughly equidimensional blocks of bedded limestone, chert, isotropic gabbro, layered gabbro, basalt, and graywacke." I visited this locality in 1994, and it is not as Kusky stated (except that the clasts indeed are angular blocks, not the sheared lenses or shear-polished ellipsoids that typify accretionary wedges). The matrix and all rocks in the shear zone, which is only a few meters thick, are of local provenance. Kusky's "bedded limestone" is an angular block of talc-tremolite schist with veins of iron-bearing carbonate, and his "chert" is vein quartz.

Most modern subducting plates are dominated by oceanic crust and mantle with a characteristic ophiolitic stratigraphy. This crust and mantle are formed in divergent-plate settings, either by seafloor spreading or by marginal-basin rifting and fast migration of oceanic magmatic arcs, and are preserved as slices and fragments within and along sutures. Old mantle, mostly tectonized harzburgite (orthopyroxene peridotite) residual after extraction of basaltic melts, is overlain by the products of fractionation of those melts. The basal fractionates are ultramafic cumulates (the geophysical Mohorovičić discontinuity is within the petrologic crust), and these give way upward to mafic cumulates, and those to more massive gabbros with or without subordinate plagiogranites. These in turn typically are overlain by complexes of sheeted diabase dikes and sills, those by pillow basalts, the basalts in turn commonly by deepwater pelagic sediments, and those often by trench turbidites. Steady-state magma chambers in dynamic spreading systems are needed to explain such consistent sequences.

Such ophiolites are known in abundance in Phanerozoic suture complexes. They occur as great sheets, commonly forming the leading edges of overriding plates and the basements of forearc-basin strata; such sheets often preserve the entire ophiolite sequence, and are ramped onto accretionary wedges and other subducting-plate materials. Disrupted fragments (from millimeters to kilometers in size) of ophiolite also are widespread in polymict mélange in accretionary wedges. A few possible Proterozoic ophiolites as old as ~2 Ga have been identified (Helmstaedt and Scott, 1992), although these examples lack the tectonized mantle rocks that characterize the bases of modern ophiolites.

Ultramafic lavas and their fractionates are voluminous in Archean terrains, but bear no petrologic similarity either to the residual harzburgites or to the ultramafic cumulates of ophiolites, even as isolated samples; they do not occur in ophiolite-type successions; they often depositionally overlie or are interbedded with continental rocks; and no associated residual harzburgite or other indicators of ophiolite stratigraphy have been found. The Archean ultramafic lavas commonly are intercalated with low-alkali olivine basalts, which differ from modern seafloor basalts in having both generally higher Mg contents and higher Mg/Fe ratios at given Mg contents, and also in having generally lower contents of Al and of incompatible elements (Cattell and Taylor, 1990). The Archean basalts often are pillowed, but these often are coarsely vesicular and amygdaloidal, indicating in such cases water depths of less than several hundred meters and hence precluding deep-ocean analogies.

Kusky (1991, p. 824 and Fig. 5) claimed to have found in the Slave craton an outcrop of an ophiolitic "sheeted dike complex . . . [wherein] Dikes show preferential (70%) one-way chilling with most dikes indicating spreading center to the northwest." These features do not exist. I visited this outcrop in 1994 and my companions and I found it to consist of uniform hornblende schist. Kusky's purported dike contacts, as drawn on his Figure 5, are merely joints following foliation, and there is no change in texture or grain size of the schist at or near these joints.

Many investigators (e.g., de Wit et al., 1987) assume that any occurrence of ultramafic and mafic lavas requires an origin in primitive oceanic crust. Bickle et al. (1995) reviewed the geology of a number of purported Archean ophiolites and rightly concluded, "on the basis of basal unconformities, presence of xenocryst zircons, geochemical and isotopic evidence for crustal contamination, intrusive relationships with older basement and their internal stratigraphy, that none of these examples is derived from Archean oceanic crust" (Bickle et al., 1995, p. 121).

Magmatic arcs. Volcanic rocks in modern magmatic arcs commonly are erupted from centers situated ~100 km above subducting plates of oceanic lithosphere. The composition of volcanic rocks varies with the thickness and petrologic maturity of the crust through which their magmas erupt, and typically is olivine tholeiite in young intra-oceanic island arcs of small crustal volume, and calc-alkalic basalt, andesite, and subordinate dacite in mature oceanic island arcs; however, these compositions are not unique to arc settings. Volcanic-arc melts erupted through continental crust, or through thick terrigenous sedimentary rocks proxying for such crust, commonly contain much crustal material and are much more silicic and potassic in bulk composition, and more evolved isotopically, than are oceanic-arc rocks. Exposed in obliquely eroded crustal sections beneath the volcanic and hypabyssal rocks of magmatic arcs, and broadly paralleling them in composition, are stocks and batholiths; beneath these, in turn, are gneisses and migmatites, and then granulites.

Modern intermediate and felsic volcanic rocks are most common in continental volcanic arcs and highly evolved island arcs, and many investigators assume that Archean intermediate and felsic rocks must have formed above subducting slabs. Such rocks are by no means restricted to arc settings in the modern Earth, however, for they are widespread also in severely extensional settings and in some continental rift-shoulder regions. Similar Archean and modern rocks may reflect similar conditions of melting and equilibration, but such similarity in no way constrains the tectonic settings of their heat sources. Intermediate and felsic calc-alkalic melts require the partial melting of hydrous crustal rocks. Partial melting of amphibolites produces tonalites and dacites, and partial melting of their hydrated equivalents in turn produces trondhjemite; partial melting of micaceous metasedimentary rocks, or pre-existing granites or gneisses, produces granodiorites, quartz monzonites, and granites. Heat commonly is now introduced into the crust by mafic melts rising from the mantle, but it is the tectonothermal setting of those primary melts, and of possible Archean analogues, that is to be determined, not assumed. Furthermore, as emphasized previously, endogenic melting of the much hotter and more radiogenic Archean crust must have been widespread.

In composites of Phanerozoic island arcs accreted to continents and exposed at upper crustal levels—a setting many Archean specialists have mistakenly assumed to be represented by Archean granite-and-greenstone terrains—plutons break irregularly through diverse aggregates of volcanic-arc rocks, ophiolites, and accretionary wedges; many small plutons are domiform but large ones are not (e.g., Davis et al., 1965; Hietanen, 1973; Bateman, 1992, for the southwestern Sierra Nevada). Plutons breaking through pre-existing continental crust and overlying strata severely deform it; early plutons may have intruded concordantly to major lithologic boundaries, but later ones are sharply and irregularly cross cutting (e.g., Bateman, 1992, for the central and northeastern Sierra Nevada). Plutons intruded into thick stratigraphic sections form fat blisters (e.g., Ross, 1967; Sylvester et al., 1978). These pluton-and-wall-rock modes neither geometrically nor structurally resemble the typical Archean association of domiform plutons and synformal wall rocks.

Magmatic arcs form as discrete belts, whereas Archean igneous rocks, where well exposed and well studied, occur in subregional stratigraphic sequences shown by zircon geochronology to have formed more or less synchronously over broad regions. No primary belts have been demonstrated to exist in Archean assemblages on the basis of either field relationships or geochronology. Slight local cross-strike offsets of broadly overlapping ages have been interpreted by a number of investigators (e.g., Card, 1990; Kimura et al., 1993; Jackson and Cruden, 1995) to represent migrating or successively accreted arcs, but no general trends in ages support such inferences, and well-dated rocks in adjacent belts represented by many age determinations have not been shown to differ in age more than do those within belts. As discussed previously, the belts at issue are late features, defined not by stratigraphic or volcanologic features but instead by the anastomosing trends of the complex synforms into which the volcanic and sedimentary rocks were deformed as late diapiric batholiths shouldered them aside. No

one has demonstrated that pre-batholithic rocks record in their primary volcanic and sedimentary geology any control of those future trends.

Rock types in Phanerozoic magmatic-arc complexes, either intrusive or extrusive, are unimodal on large scales (although there is much bimodality on small scales of space and time). Frequency distributions of silica contents are high and narrow for primitive island arcs, and broad and asymmetric, with a peak near the high-silica end, for continental batholithic complexes. Archean volcanic assemblages, by contrast, commonly are bimodal—basalt and ultramafic rocks on the one hand, and dacite, rhyodacite, and in many cases rhyolite, on the other—even where the contrasted rock types are intercalated in continuous sections. Andesites, which are the peak volcanic-rock types in many mature, evolved oceanic island arcs, are uncommon in most Archean assemblages wherein basalt and rhyodacite are voluminous.

The general picture that I, like Goodwin (1996), derive from the mapping and geochronology of greenstone belts is that for most of their histories their regions typically evolved as vast terrains of subaerial and submarine volcanoes and lava plains (and subjacent plutons and gneisses developing simultaneously), which built to crustal thicknesses of perhaps 40 km within periods of less than 100 m.y. within any one terrain. Magmatic heat sources were regional, not linear; neither spreading centers nor magmatic arcs existed within the assemblages preserved in surviving cratons. Many successions are seen to be ensialic, built on still older continental or volcanic assemblages, and recycled ancient crust may be a major component of much Archean crust. Other successions can be inferred on isotopic grounds to have formed directly upon mantle rocks, but no such contacts have been recognized in the field. All lithologies, save perhaps ancient basement gneisses, are explicable in terms of the rise of basaltic and ultramafic magmas from the mantle followed by variable eruption, fractionation, and contamination of such magmas, and by secondary melting of them or produced by them. Deformation generally was only moderate before the climactic episodes of granite diapirism, which record regional, not linear, heating of the lower crust, as discussed previously. None of this accords with magmatic-arc analogies.

Complex-aggregation speculations. Well-studied and well-dated low-strain greenstone belts display thick, coherent sections, often with repeated stratigraphic intercalations of felsic, mafic, and ultramafic volcanic rocks as well as sedimentary rocks, which underwent little deformation before late diapiric plutonism. I see no modern analogues for these sections.

Proponents of Archean plate tectonics working in greenstone belts nevertheless seek modern petrotectonic analogues. Sutures have not been demonstrated by structural and field relationships, so the common methodology of these proponents (e.g., Barrie et al., 1993; Feng et al., 1993; Percival et al., 1994) is to infer from vague or quantitative petrologic discriminants diverse tectonomagmatic settings of igneous rocks in what appears to be a depositional sequence and then to assume that the succession was tectonically assembled, from rocks formed in those diverse inferred settings in widely separated locales, by intricate combinations of rifting, subduction, strike-slip, and collision, all on structures that are effectively invisible. The complexities thus deduced are not supported by observed structures and are incompatible with the common broadly concordant character, both structurally and metamorphically, of continuous thick sections, so the lithologic discriminants used to assign initial tectonic settings apparently have been misapplied. The geochemical relationships commonly used for identification of Archean tectonic settings in fact have only very inconsistent applicability even for rock assemblages in known modern settings, the exceptions within modern assemblages being widespread.

The petrologic discriminants have been derived mostly from fresh volcanic rocks, and from a few among many provinces of each petrotectonic type, and they overlap widely; they have been misapplied not only to all other volcanic assemblages, including highly altered and variably metamorphosed volcanic rocks, but also to plutonic rocks formed at all crustal depths (thus assuming, incorrectly, that pressure, temperature, and volatiles play no role in melt compositions). Many discriminants are expressed as ratios plotted against ratios, or as ratios or values plotted in ternary systems; such expressions obfuscate whatever similarities or differences might in fact exist. The closest lithologic analogues of the classified assemblages are then presumed to have been produced by the same heat sources as those assumed (but in fact poorly constrained) for the classified assemblages, rather than to simply be indicative of similar physical conditions of melting and equilibration. Furthermore, many Archean suites differ markedly in composition (as in the steeper fractionation of rare-earth elements in Archean tonalites and the higher Mg and Mg/Fe contents in typical Archean basalts) from the idealized concepts of those modern assemblages to which they are presumed analogous; the common Archean ultramafic lavas have no modern counterparts.

Exceedingly complex deformation, older than the late granites, has been postulated for many greenstone terrains on the basis almost entirely of speculative petrologic discriminants. Such conjectural deformation has nowhere been well constrained. Where exposures and mapping are good, zircon dating provides tight control, and late deformation of the entire assemblage has not obliterated facing directions and other essential relationships, stratal and depositional continuity, not disruption, is displayed. Particularly where constraints are inadequate because these conditions are not all met, wild structures have in places been inferred on the basis of discriminants. For example, de Wit et al. (1987) invoked complex interthrusting of mafic and felsic rocks, then poorly dated, during several periods of severe deformation to explain concordant juxtapositions of mafic and felsic volcanic rocks in the Barberton greenstone terrain of South Africa. Their speculation was disproved subsequently by many precise zircon U-Pb dates that showed the belt to have a generally nonrepeating stratigraphy and to have been deformed primarily during and after deposition of the youngest part of the section (Kamo and Davis, 1994).

Stratified rocks in the tiny Vizien area in the northeastern Superior craton are dated by a few zircon U-Pb age determinations and were postulated by J. A. Percival and his associates (Percival et al., 1993, 1994; Skulski et al., 1994; Lin et al., 1996; Skulski and Percival, 1996) to be juxtaposed from initially far-distant settings. They looked at the trace-element compositions of volcanic rocks in this 10 × 10 km area and saw a "plume-derived oceanic plateau," a continental volcanic arc, a synmagmatically rifted arc from a different continent, and a back-arc continental rift, the lot having been scrambled by premetamorphic subduction-related thrusting to produce a concordant stack of four thin allochthonous sheets above autochthonous(?) continental basement. (Interpretations became more complex, and more thrust panels were postulated, through time in the series of papers.) The rocks were deformed synmetamorphically at middle-amphibolite facies at a depth of only ~10 km and hence in a contact-metamorphic setting; most rocks are severely flattened and elongated, but thin shear zones of local rock types along several contacts were termed "mélange." The extreme tectonic scrambling, postulated from geochemical conjectures, has no modern analogues and appears to me to be contraindicated by the proponents' own data.

I look at their geologic map and see a simple, nonrepeating stratigraphic stack of diverse volcanic rocks, which accords with their U-Pb zircon dates. In map-order upward: tonalitic basement complex, 3.1 to 2.9 Ga; basal conglomerate (see below) + other clastic sedimentary rocks; mafic and ultramafic lavas and sills, 2.786 Ga (one of the Percival group's hypothetical megathrusts occurs low in this unit); and interbedded mafic and felsic rocks, 2.724 and 2.722 Ga. Late granites in the region, both shallow and mid-crustal, have ages scattered from 2.73 to 2.69 Ga (Stern et al., 1994). Supracrustal assemblages elsewhere in the region also begin with a basal conglomerate upon tonalitic basement (Percival et al., 1996). The basal conglomerate in the Vizien map area is dominated by boulders of the locally underlying tonalitic basement complex (U-Pb zircon dates from one cobble, ~2.955 Ga). The tectonic-aggregation conjecture thus requires that the components have been assembled from their extremely diverse initial settings into an apparently concordant section of upward-younging units.

There is a problem with my simple-section alternative. The basal conglomerate also contains "a large boulder of graphic granite with a heterogeneous population of zircons yielding single-grain Pb/Pb ages from 2708 to >3000 Ma . . . interpreted as a mixture of inherited and igneous zircons" (Percival et al., 1993, p.

321). The youngest determination has been repeatedly cited, later as 2718 Ma, in papers by the Percival group as providing a maximum age for the conglomerate and thus as requiring thrust faulting. This is the only determination among the many in the map area that can be cited in support of such deformation, so I presume that, instead, it has been misinterpreted. The aberrant sample and its immediate setting have not been described in published reports. J. A. Percival gave me in 1997 the unpublished Pb/U concordia plot for this sample, which he assured me is from an obvious, low-strain boulder. The plot shows one almost-concordant single-zircon point, 2718 ± 5 Ma, and three very discordant points, not on a single chord, from which older ages were inferred. The concordance and modest analytical uncertainty assigned the critical 2.718 Ga date show that analytical error is unlikely to account for the problem I perceive. The zircon age could reasonably date the contact metamorphism and perhaps was reset, although the middle-amphibolite grade, near 600°C, is lower than expected to reset a zircon. Perhaps the single grain at issue represents laboratory contamination.

Other inferences of far-traveled components interthrust complexly within concordant, isofacial successions have yet to be tested by dating but will not, I expect, survive such testing. For another Superior craton example, Kimura et al. (1993) speculated that a thick section of ultramafic, mafic, and felsic igneous rocks, turbiditic and shallow-water clastic rocks, and banded iron formation (with many irregular repetitions of types, mapped and described by others as a continuous stratigraphic succession broadly concordant over an area of 140 × 20 km) had been assembled by regionally layer-parallel thrusting by both orthogonal and oblique subduction in a composite "accretionary wedge." They assumed that the diverse rock types formed in widely separated oceanic plateaus, mid-oceanic ridge crests, pull-apart basins, island arcs, and unspecified sedimentary settings had been deformed separately in each of those settings and then had been assembled by subduction into a regionally concordant and metamorphically isofacial stack. Phanerozoic accretionary wedges, of course, lack any such layer continuity of far-transported but non-disrupted materials. Kimura et al. mentioned only one example of shearing observed along a contact, a trivial "several-centimeter-thick mylonite," and recognized no mélange or broken formation.

Ayres and Corfu (1991) interpreted a small Superior area, mapped in reconnaissance with overlapping-wastebasket units, to contain three or four thrust sheets of disparate assemblages. U-Pb zircon age determinations date some rocks, but do not require the inferred structure.

Several geologists have attempted to explain the apparent broad regional stratigraphic continuity of Archean volcanic rocks with numerous hypothetical sutures between amalgamated plates in the Yilgarn craton. (Nothing of the sort is known in the modern Earth.) Myers (1995) speculated that many subduction systems operated simultaneously to produce widely separated, but stratigraphically very similar, build-ups that then were brought together and sutured invisibly to produce the illusion of regional stratigraphy. Swager (1995, 1997) conjectured, quite differently although also appealing to simultaneous development followed by appropriately precise suturing, that Yilgarn "greenstone terranes represent stacked and collapsed basins." His patterns of unexposed duplexed thrust and strike-slip faults make no geometric sense even in his own terms: hypothetical sutures are drawn along layering, bounding lithologic units, or wastebaskets thereof, without offsetting them in any reasonable fashion, and then abruptly end.

Advocates of Archean plate tectonics commonly attribute the granitic rocks of both upper-crustal granite-and-greenstone terrains and mid-crustal gneissic assemblages to arc magmatism (e.g., Stern et al., 1994; Bédard and Ludden, 1997). As the ages of these granites commonly span about the same age range as do the nearby volcanic sections, which are attributed by the same or different plate proponents to tectonic-assembly processes, abundant implicit contradictions falsify the interpretations.

Rifting and aggregation

The splitting of continents and separation of their fragments as ocean basins opened between them—dispersive plate tectonics—is clearly shown by Phanerozoic and Proterozoic geology. Some rifts are irregularly subparallel to pre-existing continental orogenic trends, but many rifts cut directly or irregularly across such trends. Rifted margins consist of tectonically thinned continental crust and thick new gabbroic and basaltic crust. Thinning and rift magmatism open thermal windows into the mantle, steepen vertical geothermal gradients, and produce large horizontal thermal gradients. As the rift crust subsequently cools toward ambient geotherms, its upper surface subsides and is covered by an oceanward-thickening stratal wedge, the distal, deep-water equivalent of which laps far out upon new oceanic crust. When such a rifted margin later collides with an advancing overriding plate—which can be a simple Andean continental plate or an island-arc plate with more ocean behind it, or an already-aggregated composite of island arcs, plateaus, and small continents backed by either ocean or continent—as intervening oceanic lithosphere is subducted, the stratal wedge is driven as a tectonically thickened wedge of imbricated thrust sheets and crumpled rocks onto the continent on which it was deposited. Or the rifted margin can become an active one as subduction is initiated beneath it, and the suite of subduction-system features is then printed across it; this newly active margin can hit either another active margin or another rifted margin.

The possible permutations are many, but the end result of rifting and aggregation is a juxtaposition, across a suture system of complexes diversely recording subduction, of continental masses of contrasting pre-rift histories and geometry. Examples are abundant in orogenic systems younger than ~2.0 Ga around the world. For example, Archean continental crust in North America occurs as disparate fragments truncated by early Proterozoic rifts, in part preserving early Proterozoic rifted-margin stratal wedges, and juxtaposed by younger early Proterozoic suture complexes (Hoffman, 1988; Helmstaedt and Scott, 1992; St-Onge and Lucas, 1996).

Broadly subparallel structures characterize entire Archean cratons, which themselves are remnants separated by post-Archean rifting and rotation. The initial domains must have been larger than these remnants. Nowhere, to my knowledge, has Archean rifting across such trends, accompanied by major extensional structures or appropriate post-cratonization sedimentary packages, been demonstrated. Archean rifts and sutures have been postulated on the basis of superposed volcanic or sedimentary rocks deduced from their chemistry to represent contrasted tectonic settings, but have not been demonstrated by appropriate structures and associations.

The youngest strata preserved in the complex and faulted medial synclines of the Barberton greenstone belt of South Africa comprise a fining-upward sequence of continental and shallow-water conglomerates and quartz arenites that disconformably to unconformably overlie felsic volcanic rocks and turbiditic and other sedimentary rocks, beneath which are mafic and ultramafic lavas. The upper sedimentary sequence was interpreted by Eriksson (1982) to have formed as a rifted-margin coastal plain and continental shelf, and by Heubeck and Lowe (1994) to have formed in local basins bounded by normal faults. Numerous zircon U-Pb dates from volcanic rocks and from surrounding pre-belt tonalitic basement and post-belt granites show the entire volcanic and sedimentary section to span the approximate period 3.48 to 3.15 Ga and, integrated with structural information, show the main synformal deformation of the belt to have occurred in a brief period concurrent with, and ending shortly after, deposition of the young quartzose strata (e.g., Kamo and Davis, 1994). The young clastic strata thus apparently formed in basins produced by early cross-belt shortening, not by extension as required by rifted-margin explanations. Similar inferences were made previously for the late turbidites of the Slave and Superior cratons.

Two broad tracts of upper- and middle-crust granite-and-greenstone assemblages are separated by a belt—200 km in width, in Zimbabwe, Botswana, and South Africa—of mostly granulitic rocks, commonly termed the Limpopo Mobile Belt, which has been widely regarded as a late Archean rift and suture between the older Archean Kaapvaal and Zimbabwe continental plates (Barton, 1983; de Wit et al., 1992; Roering et al., 1992; Treloar et al., 1992; van Reenen et al., 1995). I read the array as, instead, a single Archean craton with a medial Proterozoic uplift of lower-crustal rocks, and as lacking a rift and suture of any age. The dominant strike in all three terrains is east-northeastward (Watkeys, 1983), northern and southern granite-and-greenstone terrains are similar, and no major dislocations have been demonstrated. Both mar-

gins of the granulite belt represent primarily increasing pressure and temperature both of metamorphism and of crystallization of granites, without abrupt changes in protoliths, and hence primarily increasing depth of exposure (Rollinson and Blenkinsop, 1995; van Reenen et al., 1995). Strong to weak retrograde foliation, indicative of minor to moderate strain, dips mostly steeply inward, and has downdip stretching lineations on both sides of the granulite belt (Mkweli et al., 1995; Rollinson and Blenkinsop, 1995; van Reenen et al., 1995), and there is no evidence for megathrusting. There is nothing "oceanic" about the Limpopo belt, and there is no evidence for truncation of northern or southern granite-and-greenstone terrains by rifting, nor for rotation of them prior to hypothetical suturing, nor for juxtapositions of disjunct assemblages, nor for the formation and deformation of trailing-edge stratal wedges. Reliable U-Pb zircon dates show the granulite-facies metamorphism to be of early Proterozoic age (Jaeckel et al., 1997). (Dating in the region was long obfuscated by the dominance of whole-rock Rb-Sr pseudochrons—cf. Beakhouse et al., 1988—and by single-mineral Rb-Sr analyses calculated as ages by assuming initial ratios of $^{87}Rb/^{86}Sr$, which amount to assuming the age.) The Limpopo belt presents a problem in differential uplift rather than in rifting and suturing; that uplift was of early Proterozoic, not Archean, age.

Afterword

A pre-granite-and-greenstone history of the Earth's crust is recorded in ancient zircons recycled in younger Archean quartzites and igneous rocks, and in basement tonalitic gneisses that have prolonged or episodic histories of partial melting, in various cratons. The rest of the granite-and-greenstone crustal assemblages that characterize the later Archean are missing from the pre-Archean basement remnants. Some of these remnants are well-preserved basement to volcanic accumulations, and some have been mostly recycled by partial melting into younger midcrustal complexes. That the remnants are restricted to parts of each craton, and did not belong to a continuous layer of tonalitic crust immediately before granite-and-greenstone magmatism began, appears to be indicated by within-craton variations in geochemical and relict-zircon characteristics of younger volcanic rocks. Final equilibrations were under hydrous-melt conditions, but the roles otherwise are unknown of: (1) hydrous and anhydrous fractionation of magma-ocean and impact-lake melts, of remelting, and of impact brecciation in forming these ancient rocks; (2) the character of whatever materials overlay them when they formed; and (3) the processes that distributed them with apparent irregularity before the development of Archean granite-and-greenstone terrains. Liquid water covered much of the Earth's surface by 3.6 (or 3.8?) Ga, but when before that it condensed from a dense atmosphere is undefined.

The relatively clear geologic record begins with Archean granite-and-greenstone terrains formed after 3.6 (or possibly 3.8) Ga. These typically began with voluminous eruptions of mafic and ultramafic lavas through (and between and around?) old tonalites. Plate tectonics, in the modern sense, played no part in the evolution of the preserved assemblages, which display no apparent analogues for products of the rifting and converging regimes of the modern Earth. Thermal irregularities in the modern Earth are profoundly influenced by plate motions, and if plate tectonics is rejected for the Archean Earth, what might have produced Archean irregularities? Some observers see a major role for plumes from the deep mantle, but I am now dubious of this concept. How otherwise might we explain the broad setting of Archean tectonics and magmatism?

A successful rationale must incorporate the much higher temperatures of Archean mantle and lower continental crust. These temperatures in turn indicate high degrees of uncoupling within and beneath the crust, and permit explanations of differential lateral mobility, albeit not in a modern-plate mode. The temperatures had great lateral variations—some cratons were stabilized before others began to form—and the crust and mantle certainly were not radially symmetrical. Convection of the mantle, profoundly influenced by the discontinuous presence of cratonic mantle roots, must have operated, and there may have been major lateral motions of shallow materials. The cause and broader context of the pervasive shallow syn-diapiric shortening of late-stage-developing cratons has yet to be deduced, let alone documented. The extent to which cratonized continental masses wandered about the Archean Earth is unknown, although perhaps can be constrained by paleomagnetic investigations; the causes of such possible motion are undeduced.

Exposed Archean crust was built primarily by ultramafic and mafic melts rising from the mantle and by the widespread hydrous partial melting of resulting rocks (and of ancient tonalites where present) within the crust. The lavas were variably hydrated both during and after submarine eruption. As the volcanic crust thickened, radiogenic heat accumulating in the deep crust greatly augmented mantle heat, both conducted and introduced in rising melts. The deep crust long was hotter than the water-saturated granite solidus; partial-melt migmatization was active for protracted periods, and partial melts formed granitic sheets within the crust and felsic volcanic rocks at the surface. Deep partial melting increased as the volcanic pile thickened and heat accumulated faster than it was transmitted to the surface until the deep melts and partly molten migmatites rose as great diapiric batholiths, which produced most of the deformation and metamorphism displayed by the stratified rocks. The resulting compositional overturning of the crust moved radioactive isotopes upward and permitted cooling and cratonization of the crust and upper mantle. Major cycles of such behavior affected surface areas >1000 km across, operated for periods of up to 100 m.y., and represented regional transfer of heat to the surface at rates much faster than in the modern Earth.

Much of the restite from the preserved cratons probably was returned to the mantle by density conversion and by delamination. There was a net transfer of continental components from the mantle into the crust within the preserved cratons, but these cratons represent only a small fraction of the Earth's outer shell of the time. We do not know whether similar cratons developed over the entire Earth or represented local aggregations of sialic components concentrated by either vertical or horizontal processes, and whether or not there was a net fractionation of continental components into the crust during Archean time. Perhaps the surviving sample is dominated by the fraction of globe-girdling magmatic piles into which enough water was incorporated to permit generation of voluminous felsic rocks by partial melting; where less water was incorporated, the thick mafic and ultramafic rocks were returned to the mantle. Or perhaps survival of the preserved sample resulted in part from vagaries of distribution of pre-Archean magma-ocean and impact-lake crust. The Archean Earth may have lacked bimodal continents and oceans and had unimodal topography—a continuum between buoyant felsic crust (recording a high degree of recycling and refining by hydrous partial melting), like that selectively preserved in the surviving Archean cratons, and less fractionated crust, quickly returned to the mantle.

That upper continental crust was effectively floating on partially molten lower crust during late-stage evolution of each craton is indicated by the regional uniform-wavelength shortening (and orthogonal elongation?) of the upper crust that accompanied the diapiric rise of regional partial melts from the deeper crust. Similar decoupling of crust from mantle is likely. Quasi-independent motions of layers, or segments thereof, are required for syn-diapiric deformation and can be considered for other and larger effects as well. Cratons may have wandered about the Earth by processes not yet sorted out.

Among major problems is the lack of knowledge regarding the character of the crust-mantle boundary, both as it now exists beneath Archean cratons and as it existed when Archean volcanic piles were forming. There are no exposures of Archean upper mantle and, more particularly, of mantle in contact with crust, such as we have for Phanerozoic oceans and continents. We do not know whether the sub-craton Mohorovičić discontinuity is a break (gradational or otherwise) between old mantle and new crust, or just a change in density within the magmatic pile, and if the latter, whether it represents a change in bulk composition or in present mineral phases. Neither do we know the character of residual mantle complementary to the mafic and ultramafic magmatism that produced the crust. Studies of xenoliths could address these problems.

By 2.0 or 1.9 Ga, plate-tectonic processes—the rifting and aggregation of continental crustal masses that were internally little deformed—were clearly operating. Archean cratons were rifted across as well as along their trends, continental-shelf assemblages were deposited along those truncated margins, and

convergence and collisions juxtaposed disparate Archean and Proterozoic components. The products of the rifting of Archean cratons and the suturing of them into aggregates such as that containing most of the Archean and early Proterozoic terrains of North America are broadly similar to modern rift and suture complexes (Hoffman, 1988), although importantly different in detail. Ophiolites have been recognized in several early Proterozoic sutures (although the term ophiolite has been misapplied to other Proterozoic mafic suites that share no diagnostic features with Phanerozoic ophiolites). Metamorphic rocks recording high ratios of pressure to temperature characterize Phanerozoic sutures and are known locally in late Proterozoic (but not older) sutures. Polymict mélanges with either serpentinite or scaly clay matrixes are known from sutures of all Phanerozoic ages, but the oldest ones described in published reports of which I am aware are those of the late Proterozoic of Arabia (Pallister et al., 1988).

But what was going on during still-earlier Proterozoic time, ~2.5 to 2.0 Ga? Stratified rocks—often as thick sections of bimodal volcanic rocks and of sedimentary rocks, reminiscent of Archean granite-and-greenstone terrains without the climactic crustal melting and rise of late domiform granites—of this age occur atop previously cratonized Archean crust, and may represent a continuation of Archean style without the generation of the granites. Little crust formed during this early Proterozoic span is otherwise preserved (Hoffman, 1988; Goodwin, 1991, 1996). I have attempted no systematic study of that little, but note that others have suggested it to be more like the Archean than like the later Proterozoic. For example, komatiitic basalt and magmatic peridotite, well dated at ~2.4 Ga, occur in the Karelian shield (Puchtel et al., 1997). Condie (1992) showed that the chemical distinctions between Archean and younger igneous rocks change gradationally during the period from ~2.5 to 2.0 Ga.

What was the nature of the transition between the very different tectonic and magmatic regimes of the pre–plate-tectonic, pre-2.5 Ga Archean and the plate-tectonic, post-2.0 Ga Proterozoic, and how did plate-tectonic processes and products evolve toward modern ones during Proterozoic time? I do not treat such important questions here, but do note that the transition may have been facilitated by the increasing content of water and carbon dioxide in the mantle, as dense but hydrated delaminated Archean and early Proterozoic crust sank into it. Also, the great regional swarms of far-traveled very early Proterozoic mafic dikes have no recognized Archean counterparts, and occur on far larger scales than Phanerozoic swarms; this must have significance regarding the evolving rigidity of the crust and mantle heat sources.

Acknowledgments

My career research has emphasized Phanerozoic tectonics, magmatism, and crustal evolution. I have not done detailed field work in Archean assemblages but have field-tripped widely in them in the United States, Canada, Scotland, South Africa, and Western Australia. In part this has been with the guidance of regional experts, most extensively Kenneth Card and Herwart Helmstaedt, and also Stephen Barnes, Robin Hill, William Padgham, and George Snyder, as well as many others. Discussions with many experts in cosmology, mantle problems, and Archean geology have greatly increased my understanding beyond that derived from the literature.

REFERENCES

Abbott, D., Burgess, L., Longhi, J., and Smith, W. H. F., 1994, An empirical thermal history of the Earth's upper mantle: Jour. Geophys. Res., v. 99, p. 13,835–13,850.

Abe, Y., 1993, Physical state of the very early Earth: Lithos, v. 30, p. 223–235.

Agee, C. B., and Longhi, J., eds., 1992, Workshop on the physics and chemistry of magma oceans from 1 bar to 4 mbar: Lunar Planet. Inst. Tech. Rept. 92-03, 79 p.

Anderson, D. L., in press, A theory of the Earth—Hutton and Humpty-Dumpty and Holmes, *in* Geol. Soc. Lond., Hutton Conf. Spec. Publ.

Anderson, D. L., Tanimoto, T., and Zhang, Y.-S., 1992, Plate tectonics and hotspots, the third dimension: Science, v. 256, p. 1645–1651.

Armstrong, R. L., 1991, The persistent myth of crustal growth: Austral. Jour. Earth Sci., v. 38, p. 613–630.

Atwater, T. and Severinghaus, J., 1989, Tectonic maps of the northeast Pacific, *in* Winterer, E. L., Hussong, D. M., and Decker, R. W., eds., The eastern Pacific

Ocean and Hawaii: Boulder, CO: Geol. Soc. Amer., The geology of North America, v. N, p. 188–217.

Ayer, J. A., and Davis, D. W., 1997, Neoarchean evolution of differing convergent margin assemblages in the Wabigoon Subprovince—geochemical and geochronological evidence from the Lake of the Woods greenstone belt, Superior Province, northwestern Ontario: Precamb. Res., v. 81, p. 155–178.

Ayres, L. D., 1978, Metamorphism in the Superior Province of northwestern Ontario and its relationship to crustal development: Geol. Surv. Can. Pap. 78-10, p. 25–36.

Ayres, L. D., and Corfu, F., 1991, Stacking of disparate volcanic and sedimentary units by thrusting in the Archean Favourable Lake greenstone belt, central Canada: Precamb. Res., v. 50, p. 221–238.

Ayres, L. D., Halden, N. M., and Ziehlke, D. V., 1991, The Aulneau Batholith—Archean diapirism preceded by coalescence of granitoid magma at depth: Precamb. Res., v. 51, p. 27–50.

Ayres, L. D., and Thurston, P. C., 1985, Archean supracrustal sequences in the Canadian Shield—an overview: Geol. Assoc. Can. Spec. Pap. 28, p. 343–370.

Ballard, S., and Pollack, H. N., 1988, Modern and ancient geotherms beneath southern Africa: Earth Planet. Sci. Lett., v. 88, p. 132–142.

Barrie, C. T., Ludden, J. N., and Green, T. H., 1993, Geochemistry of volcanic rocks associated with Cu-Zn and Ni-Cu deposits in the Abitibi subprovince: Econ. Geol., v. 88, p. 1341–1358.

Barrie, C. T., and Shirey, S. B., 1991, Nd- and Sr-isotope systematics for the Komiskotla-Montcalm area—implications for the formation of late Archean crust in the western Abitibi Subprovince, Canada: Can. Jour. Earth Sci., v. 28, p. 58–76.

Barton, J. M., Jr., 1983, Our understanding of the Limpopo Belt—a summary with proposals for future research: Geol. Soc. South Afr. Spec. Publ. 8, p. 191–203.

Bateman, P. C., 1992, Pre-Tertiary bedrock geologic map of the Mariposa 1° by 2° quadrangle, Sierra Nevada, California; Nevada: U.S. Geol. Survey Map I-1960, 1:250,000.

Beakhouse, G. P., McNutt, R. H., and Krogh, T. E., 1988, Comparative Rb-Sr and U-Pb zircon geochronology of late- to post-tectonic plutons in the Winnipeg River belt, northwestern Ontario, Canada: Chem. Geol., v. 72, p. 337–351.

Bédard, L. P., and Ludden, J. H., 1997, Nd-isotope evolution of Archaean plutonic rocks in southeastern Superior Province: Can. Jour. Earth Sci., v. 34, p. 286–298.

Bellefleur, G., Barnes, A., Calvert, A., Hubert, C., and Mareschal, M., 1995, Seismic reflection constraints from Lithoprobe line 29 on the upper crustal structure of the northern Abitibi greenstone belt: Can. Jour. Earth Sci., v. 32, p. 128–134.

Bellefleur, G., Calvert, A. J., and Chouteau, M. C., 1997, A link between deformation history and the orientation of reflective structures in the 2.68–2.83 Ga Opatica belt of the Canadian Superior Province: Jour. Geophys. Res., v. 102, p. 15,243–15,267.

Bickle, M. J., Nisbet, E. G., and Martin, A., 1995, Archean greenstone belts are not oceanic crust: Jour. Geol., v. 102, p. 121–138.

Blackburn, C. E., 1981, Kenora-Fort Frances: Ontario Geol. Surv. Map 2443, 1:253,440.

Bowring, S. A., and Housh, T., 1995, The Earth's early evolution: Science, v. 269, p. 1535–1540.

Bowring, S. A., Williams, I. S., and Compston, W., 1989, 3.96 Ga gneisses from the Slave province, Northwest Territories, Canada: Geology, v. 17, p. 971–975.

Boyd, F. R., 1987, High- and low-temperature garnet peridotite xenoliths and their possible relation to the lithosphere-asthenosphere boundary beneath southern Africa, in Nixon, P. H., ed., Mantle xenoliths: Chichester, UK, John Wiley, p. 403–412.

Buick, R., et al., 1995, Record of emergent continental crust ~3.5 billion years ago in the Pilbara craton of Australia: Nature, v. 375, p. 574–577.

Calvert, A. J., Sawyer, E. W., Davis, W. J., and Ludden, J. N., 1995, Archaean subduction inferred from seismic images of a mantle suture in the Superior Province: Nature, v. 375, p. 670–674.

Cameron, A. G. W., 1994, Comparative results from giant impact studies: Lunar Planet. Sci., v. 25, p. 215–216.

Cameron, A. G. W., and Benz, W., 1991, The origin of the Moon and the single impact hypothesis IV: Icarus, v. 92, p. 204–216.

Card, K. D., 1990, A review of the Superior Province of the Canadian Shield, a product of Archean accretion: Precamb. Res., v. 48, p. 99–156.

Card, K. D., and Sanford, B. V., 1989, Bedrock geology, Timmins, Ontario-Quebec: Geol. Surv. Can. Map NM-17G, 1:1,000,000.

Carlson, R. W., and Lugmair, G. W., 1988, The age of ferroan anorthosite 60025—oldest crust on a young Moon?: Earth Planet. Sci. Lett., v. 90, p. 119–130.

Carroll, M. R., and Wyllie, P. J., 1990, The system tonalite-H_2O at 15 kbar and the genesis of calc-alkaline magmas: Amer. Mineral., v. 75, p. 345–357.

Cattell, A. C., and Taylor, R. N., 1990, Archaean basic magmas, in Hall, R. J., and Hughes, D. J., eds., Early Precambrian basic magmatism: Glasgow, Blackie, p. 11–39.

Champion, D. C., and Sheraton, J. W., 1997, Geochemistry and Nd isotope systematics of Archaean granites of the Eastern Goldfields, Yilgarn Craton, Australia—implications for crustal growth processes: Precamb. Res., v. 83, p. 109–132.

Chown, E. H., Daigneault, R., Mueller, W. and Mortensen, J. K., 1992, Tectonic evolution of the Northern Volcanic Zone, Abitibi belt, Quebec: Can. Jour. Earth Sci., v. 29, p. 2211–2225.

Christensen, N. I., and Mooney, W. D., 1995, Seismic velocity structure and composition of the continental crust—A global view: Jour. Geophys. Res., v. 100, p. 9761–9788.

Cintala, M. J., and Grieve, R. A. F., 1994, The effects of differential scaling of impact melt and crater dimensions on lunar and terrestrial craters—some brief examples: Geol. Soc. Amer. Spec. Pap. 293, p. 51–59.

Clague, D. A., and Dalrymple, G. B., 1989, Tectonics, geochronology, and origin of the Hawaiian-Emperor volcanic chain, in Winterer, E. L., Hussong, D. M., and Decker, R. W., eds., The eastern Pacific Ocean and Hawaii: Boulder, CO, Geol. Soc. Amer., The geology of North America, v. N, p. 188–217.

Collerson, K. D., Hearn, B. C., MacDonald, R. A., Upton, B. G. J., and Harmon, R. S., 1989, Composition and evolution of lower continental crust—evidence from xenoliths in Eocene lavas from the Bearpaw Mountains, Montana: New Mex. Bur. Mines Geol. Bull. 131, p. 57.

Collerson, K. D., Scherer, E. E., MacDonald, R., Upton, B. G. J., and Hearn, B. C., 1993, The evolution of Wyoming craton lower crust—U-Pb SHRIMP and Nd-Sr isotopic evidence for middle Archaean and Early Proterozoic events [abs.]: Int. Workshop, The xenolith window into the lower crust, Macquarie Univ., Abs. vol., p. 4.

Condie, K.C., 1984, Archean geotherms and supracrustal assemblages: Tectonophysics, v. 105, p. 29–41.

———, 1992, Evolutionary changes at the Archaean-Proterozoic boundary: Univ. West. Austral. Geol. Dept. Publ. 22, p. 177–189.

Corfu, F., and Ayers, L. D., 1991, Unscrambling the stratigraphy of an Archean greenstone belt—a U-Pb geochronological study of the Favourable Lake belt, northwestern Ontario, Canada: Precamb. Res., v. 50, p. 201–220.

Corfu, F., Krogh, T. E., Kwok, Y. Y., and Jensen, L. S., 1989, U-Pb zircon geochronology in the southwestern Abitibi greenstone belt, Superior Province: Can. Jour. Earth Sci., v. 26, p. 1747–1763.

Cox, K. G., Smith, M. R., and Beswetherick, S., 1987, Textural studies of garnet lherzolites—evidence of exsolution origin from high-temperature harzburgites, in Nixon, P. H., ed., Mantle xenoliths: Chichester, UK, John Wiley, p. 537–550.

Dalrymple, G. B., and Ryder, G., 1996, Argon-40/Argon-39 age spectra of Apollo 17 highlands breccia samples by laser step heating and the age of the Serenitatis Basin: Jour. Geophys. Res., v. 101, p. 26,069–26,084.

Davies, G. F., 1992, On the emergence of plate tectonics: Geology, v. 20, p. 963–966.

Davis, D. W., Pezzutto, F., and Ojakangas, R. W., 1990, The age and provenance of metasedimentary rocks in the Quetico Subprovince, Ontario, from single zircon analysis—implications for Archean sedimentation and tectonics in the Superior Province: Earth Planet. Sci. Lett., v. 99, p. 195–205.

Davis, G. A., Holdaway, M. J., Lipman, P. W., and Romey, W. D., 1965, Structure, metamorphism, and plutonism in the south-central Klamath Mountains, California: Geol. Soc. Amer. Bull., v. 76, p. 933–966.

Davis, W. J., and Berman, R., 1995, U-Pb geochronology and isotopic studies of crustal xenoliths from the Medicine Hat block, northern Montana and southern Alberta: Paleoproterozoic reworking of Archean lower crust [abs.], in Precambrian 95, Montreal, Prog. Abs., p. 287.

Davis, W. J., Fryer, B. J., and King, J. E., 1994, Geochemistry and evolution of Late Archean plutonism and its significance to the tectonic development of the Slave craton: Precamb. Res., v. 67, p. 207–241.

Davis, W. J., Machado, N., Gariepy, C., Sawyer, E.W., and Benn, K., 1995, U-Pb geochronology of the Opatica tonalite-gneiss belt and its relationship to the Abitibi greenstone belt, Superior Province, Quebec: Can. Jour. Earth Sci., v. 32, p. 113–127.

de Ronde, C. E. J., and de Wit, M. J., 1994, Tectonic history of the Barberton greenstone belt, South Africa—490 million years of Archean crustal evolution: Tectonics, v. 13, p. 983–1005.

Dewey, J. F., and Windley, B. F., 1981, Growth and differentiation of the continental crust: Philos. Trans. Roy. Soc. Lond., ser. A., v. 301, p. 189–206.

de Wit, M. J., et al., 1992, Formation of an Archaean continent: Nature, v. 357, p. 553–562.

de Wit, M. J., Armstrong, R., Hart, R. J., and Wilson, A. H., 1987, Felsic igneous rocks within the 3.3- to 3.5-Ga Barberton greenstone belt—high crustal level equivalents of the surrounding tonalite trondhjemite terrain, emplaced during thrusting: Tectonics, v. 6, p. 529–459.

Eriksson, K. A., 1982, Sedimentation patterns in the Barberton Mountain Land, South Africa, and the Pilbara Block, Australia—evidence for Archean rifted continental margins: Tectonophysics, v. 81, p. 179–193.

Feng, R., Fan, J., and Kerrich, R., 1993, Noble metal abundances and characteristics of six magma series, Archean Abitibi belt, Pontiac subprovince: Relationships to metallogeny and overprinting of mesothermal gold deposits: Econ. Geol., v. 88, p. 1376–1401.

Fowler, C. M. R., 1990, The solid Earth: An introduction to global geophysics: New York, Cambridge Univ. Press, 472 p.

Fralick, P., Wu, J., and Williams, H.R., 1992, Trench and slope basin deposits in an Archean metasedimentary belt, Superior Province, Canadian Shield: Can. Jour. Earth Sci., v. 29, p. 2551–2557.

Friend, C. R. L., Nutman, A. P., Baadsgaard, H., Kinny, P. D., and McGregor, V. R., 1996, Timing of late Archaean terrane assembly, crustal thickening and granite emplacement in the Nuuk region, southern West Greenland: Earth Planet. Sci. Lett., v. 142, p. 353–365.

Galer, S. J. G., and Goldstein, S. L., 1996, Influence of accretion on lead in the Earth: Amer. Geophys. Union Geophys. Monog. 95, p. 75–98.

Goodwin, A. M., 1977, Archean volcanism in Superior Province, Canadian Shield: Geol. Assoc. Can. Spec. Pap. 16, p. 205–241.

———, 1982, Archean volcanoes in southwestern Abitibi Belt, Ontario and Quebec—form, composition, and development: Can. Jour. Earth Sci., v. 19, p. 1140–1155.

———, 1991, Precambrian geology: London, Academic Press, 666 p.

———, 1996, Principles of Precambrian geology: London, Academic Press, 327 p.

Grandjean, G., Wu, H., White, D., Mareschal, M., and Hubert, C., 1995, Crustal velocity models for the Archean Abitibi greenstone belt from seismic refraction data: Can. Jour. Earth Sci., v. 32, p. 149–166.

Grieve, R. A. F., 1980, Cratering in the lunar highlands: Some problems with the process, record, and effects: Proc. Conf. Lunar Highlands Crust, p. 173–196.

Grieve, R. A. F., Stoffler, D., and Deutsch, A., 1991, The Sudbury Structure: Controversial or misunderstood?: Jour. Geophys. Res., v. 96, p. 22,753–22,764.

Gromet, L. P., and Silver, L. T., 1987, REE variations across the Peninsular Ranges batholith: Implications for batholithic petrogenesis and crustal growth in magmatic arcs: Jour. Petrol., v. 28, p. 75–125.

Gurney, J. J., 1991, Diamonds deliver the dirt: Nature, v. 353, p. 600–601.

Hamilton, W. B., 1969a, The volcanic central Andes: A model for the Cretaceous batholiths and tectonics of North America: Oregon Dept. Geol. Min. Ind. Bull. 65, p. 175–184.

———, 1969b, Mesozoic California and the underflow of Pacific mantle: Geol. Soc. Amer. Bull., v. 80, p. 2409–2430.

———, 1970, The Uralides and the motion of the Russian and Siberian platforms: Geol. Soc. Amer. Bull., v. 81, p. 2553–2576.

————, 1978, Mesozoic tectonics of the western United States: Pacific Sect. Soc. Econ. Paleontol. Mineral., Pacific Coast Paleogeog. Symp. 2, p. 33–70.

————, 1979, Tectonics of the Indonesian region: U.S. Geol. Surv. Prof. Pap. 1078, 345 p.

————, 1989, Crustal geologic processes of the United States: Geol. Soc. Amer. Mem. 172, p. 743–781.

————, 1993, Evolution of Archean mantle and crust, in Reed, J. C., Jr., et al., eds., Precambrian—Conterminous United States: Boulder, CO, Geol. Soc. Amer., The geology of North America, v. C-2, p. 597–614, 630–636.

————, 1995, Subduction systems and magmatism: Geol. Soc. Lond. Spec. Publ. 31, p. 3–28.

Hammond, R. L., and Nisbet, B. W., 1992, Towards a structural and tectonic framework for the central Norseman-Wiluna greenstone belt, Western Australia: Univ. West. Austral. Geol. Dept. Publ. 22, p. 39–49.

Hanson, G. N., 1978, The application of trace elements to the petrogenesis of igneous rocks of granitic composition: Earth Planet. Sci. Lett., v. 38, p. 26–43.

Harjes, H.-P., et al., 1997, Origin and nature of crustal reflections: Results from integrated seismic measurements at the KTB superdeep drilling site: Jour. Geophys. Res., v. 102, p. 18,267–18,288.

Heather, K. B., Shore, G. T., and van Breeman, O., 1995, The convoluted "layer cake"—an old recipe with new ingredients for the Swayze greenstone belt, southern Superior Province, Ontario: Geol. Surv. Can., Curr. Res. 1995-C, p. 1–10.

Helmstaedt, H., and Gurney, J. J., 1995, Geotectonic controls of primary diamond deposits—implications for area selection: Jour. Geochem. Explor., v. 53, p. 125–144.

Helmstaedt, H., and Padgham, W. A., 1986, A new look at the stratigraphy of the Yellowknife Supergroup at Yellowknife, N.W.T.—implications for the age of gold-bearing shear zones and Archean basin evolution: Can. Jour. Earth Sci., v. 23, p. 454–475.

Helmstaedt, H., and Schulze, D. J., 1989, Southern African kimberlites and their mantle sample—implications for Archaean tectonics and lithosphere evolution: Geol. Soc. Austral. Spec. Publ. 14, p. 358–368.

Helmstaedt, H., and Scott, D. J., 1992, The Proterozoic ophiolite problem, in Condie, K. C., ed., Proterozoic crustal evolution: Amsterdam, Elsevier, p. 55–95.

Henderson, J. B., 1981, Archaean basin evolution in the Slave Province, Canada, in Kröner, A., ed., Precambrian plate tectonics: Amsterdam, Elsevier, p. 213–235.

Herzberg, C., 1992, Depth and degree of melting of komatiites: Jour. Geophys. Res., v. 97, p. 4521–4540.

————, 1993, Lithosphere peridotites of the Kaapvaal craton: Earth Planet. Sci. Lett., v. 120, p. 13–29.

Heubeck, C., and Lowe, D. R., 1994, Depositional and tectonic setting of the Archean Moodies Group, Barberton Greenstone Belt, South Africa: Precamb. Res., v. 68, p. 257–290.

Hickman, A. H., 1983, Geology of the Pilbara Block and its environs: Geol. Surv. West. Austral. Bull. 127, 268 p.

Hickman, A. H., and Lipple, S. L., 1978, Marble Bar, Western Australia: Geol. Surv. West. Austral., 1:250,000 Geol. Series—explan. notes, 24 p. + map.

Hietanen, A., 1973, Geology of the Pulga and Bucks Lake quadrangles, Butte and Plumas counties, California: U.S. Geol. Surv. Prof. Pap. 731, 66 p.

Hill, R. E. T., Barnes, S. J., Gole, M. J., and Dowling, S. E., 1990, Physical volcanology of komatiites: Geol. Soc. Australia, West. Austral. Div., Guide Book 1, 100 p.

————, 1995, The volcanology of komatiites as deduced from field relationships in the Norseman-Wiluna greenstone belt, Western Australia: Lithos, v. 34, p. 159–188.

Hill, R. I., Campbell, I. H., and Chappell, B. W., 1992, Crustal growth, crustal reworking, and granite genesis in the southeastern Yilgarn block, Western Australia, in Glover, J. E., and Ho, S. E., eds., The Archaean—terrains, processes, and metallogeny: Univ. West. Austral. Geol. Dept. Publ. 22, p. 203–212.

Hofmann, A.W., 1988, Chemical differentiation of the Earth—the relationship between mantle, continental crust, and oceanic crust: Earth Planet. Sci. Lett., v. 90, p. 297–314.

Hoffman, P. F., 1973, Evolution of an early Proterozoic continental margin—the Coronation geosyncline and associated aulacogens of the northwestern Canadian Shield: Philos. Trans. Roy. Soc. Lond., ser. A, v. 273, p. 547–581.

————, 1988, United plates of America, the birth of a craton—Early Proterozoic assembly and growth of Laurentia: Ann. Rev. Earth Planet. Sci, v. 16, p. 543–603.

————, 1993, Slave Craton and environs [map]: Geol. Surv. Can. Open File 2559, 1:1,000,000.

Hollings, P., Polat, A., Kerrich, R., and Wyman, D., 1997, Archean komatiites and alkaline basalts with majorite garnet and himu-like signatures in Superior Province ocean plateau volcanic belts [abs.]: Geol. Soc. Amer., Abs. Prog., v. 29, no. 6, p. 247.

Ireland, T. R., Rudnick, R. L., and Spetsius, Z., 1994, Trace elements in diamond inclusions from eclogites reveal link to Archean granites: Earth Planet. Sci. Lett., v. 128, p. 199–213.

Isachsen, C. E., and Bowring, 1997, The Bell Lake group and Anton Complex—a basement-cover sequence beneath the Archean Yellowknife greenstone belt revealed and implicated in greenstone belt formation: Can. Jour. Earth Sci., v. 34, p. 169–189.

Isachsen, C. E., Bowring, S. A., and Padgham, W. A., 1991, U-Pb zircon geochronology of the Yellowstone volcanic belt, NWT, Canada—new constraints on the timing and duration of greenstone belt magmatism: Jour. Geol., v. 99, p. 55–67.

Jackson, S. L., and Cruden, A. R., 1995, Formation of the Abitibi greenstone belt by arc-trench migration: Geology, v. 23, p. 471–474.

Jackson, S. L., Cruden, A. R., White, D., and Milkereit, B., 1995, A seismic-reflection-based regional cross section of the southern Abitibi greenstone belt: Can. Jour. Earth Sci., v. 32, p. 135–148.

Jacobsen, S. B., and Harper, C. L., Jr., 1996, Accretion and early differentiation history of the Earth based on extinct radionuclides: Amer. Geophys. Union Geophys. Monog. 95, p. 47–74.

Jaeckel, P., Kröner, A., Kamo, S. L., Brandl, G., and Wendt, J. I., 1997, Late Archaean to early Proterozoic granitoid magmatism and high-grade metamorphism in the central Limpopo belt, South Africa: Jour. Geol. Soc. Lond., v. 154, p. 25–44.

Jolly, W. T., 1978, Metamorphic history of the Archean Abitibi Belt: Geol. Surv. Can. Pap. 78-10, p. 63–78.

Kamo, S. L., and Davis, D. W., 1994, Reassessment of Archean crustal development in the Barberton Mountain Land, South Africa, based on U-Pb dating: Tectonics, v. 13, p. 167–192.

Keller, W. R., Anderson, D. L., and Clayton, R. W., 1997, Resolution of seismic structure in the mantle beneath Iceland: EOS, v. 78, no. 46 (suppl.), p. 500.

Kimura, G., Ludden, J. N., Desrochers, J.-P., and Hori, R., 1993, A model of ocean-crust accretion for the Superior province, Canada: Lithos, v. 30, p. 337–355.

King, S. D., and Anderson, D. L., 1995, An alternative mechanism of flood basalt formation: Earth Planet. Sci. Lett., v. 136, p. 269–279.

Kinny, P. D., and Nutman, A. P., 1996, Zirconology of the Meeberrie gneiss, Yilgarn Craton, Western Australia—an early Archean migmatite: Precamb. Res., v. 78, p. 165–178.

Krogh, T. E., 1993, High precision U-Pb ages for granulite metamorphism and deformation in the Kapuskasing structural zone, Ontario—implications for structure and development of the lower crust: Earth Planet. Sci. Lett., v. 119, p. 1–18.

Kröner, A., Byerly, G. R., and Lowe, D. R., 1991, Chronology of early Archaean granite-greenstone evolution in the Barberton Mountain Land, South Africa, based on precise dating by single zircon evaporation: Earth Planet. Sci. Lett., v. 103, p. 41–54.

Kröner, A., and Todt, W., 1988, Single zircon dating constraining the maximum age of the Barberton greenstone belt, southern Africa: Jour. Geophys. Res., v. 93, p. 15,329–15,337.

Kusky, T. M., 1991, Structural development of an Archean orogen, western Point Lake, Northwest Territories: Tectonics, v. 10, p. 820–841.

————, 1997, Principles of Precambrian geology [book review]: GSA Today, v. 7, no. 5, p. 29–34.

Lacroix, S., and Sawyer, E.W., 1995, An Archean fold-thrust belt in the northwestern Abitibi Greenstone Belt—structural and seismic evidence: Can. Jour. Earth Sci., v, 32, p. 97–112.

Lambert, D. D., et al., 1994, Re-Os and Sm-Nd isotope geochemistry of the Stillwater Complex, Montana—implications for the petrogenesis of the J-M Reef: Jour. Petrol., v. 35, p. 1717–1753.

Lee, D.-C., and Halliday, A. N., 1995, Hafnium-tungsten chronometry and the timing of terrestrial core formation: Nature, v. 378, p. 771–774.

Levander, A. R., and Gibson, B. S., 1991, Wide-angle seismic reflections from two-dimensional random target zones: Jour. Geophys. Res., v. 96, p. 10,251–10,260.

Lin, S., Percival, J. A., and Skulski, T., 1996, Structural constraints on the tectonic evolution of a late Archean greenstone belt in the northeastern Superior Province, northern Quebec (Canada): Tectonophysics, v. 265, p. 151–167.

Lowe, D. R., 1982, Comparative sedimentology of the principal volcanic sequences of Archean greenstone belts in South Africa, Western Australia, and Canada—implications for crustal evolution: Precamb. Res., v. 17, p. 1–29.

————, 1994, Accretionary history of the Archean Barberton Greenstone Belt (3.55–3.22 Ga), southern Africa: Geology, v. 22, p. 1099–1102.

Maas, R., Kinny, P. D., Williams, I. S., Froude, D. O., and Compston, W., 1992, The Earth's oldest known crust—a geochronological and geochemical study of 3900–4200 Ma old detrital zircons from Mt. Narryer and Jack Hills, Western Australia: Geochim. et Cosmochim. Acta, v. 56, p. 1281–1300.

Macgregor, A. M., 1951, Some milestones in the Precambrian of Southern Rhodesia: Proc. Geol. Soc. South Africa, v. 54, p. 27–71.

MacGregor, I. D., and Manton, W. I., 1986, Roberts Victor eclogites—ancient oceanic crust: Jour. Geophys. Res., v. 91, p. 14,063–14,079.

Martin, H., 1986, Effect of steeper Archean geothermal gradient on geochemistry of subduction-zone magmas: Geology, v. 14, p. 753–756.

McGregor, V. R., 1993, Qôrqut 64 V.1 Syd, Descriptive text: Geol. map of Greenland, 1:100,000: Grønlands Geol. Undersøgelse, 40 p.

McGregor, V. R., Friend, C. R. L., and Nutman, A. P., 1991, The late Archaean mobile belt through Godthabsfjord, southern West Greenland—a continent-continent collision zone?: Bull. Geol. Soc. Denmark, v. 39, p. 179-197.

Meyer, C., Williams, I. S., and Compston, W., 1989, $^{207}Pb/^{206}Pb$ ages of zircon-containing rock fragments indicate continuous magmatism in the lunar crust from 4350 to 3900 million years: Lunar Planet. Sci. Conf., v. 20, p. 691-692.

Mkweli, S., Kamber, B., and Berger, M., 1995, Westward continuation of the craton-Limpopo Belt tectonic break in Zimbabwe and new age constraints on the timing of the thrusting: Jour. Geol. Soc. Lond., v. 152, p. 77-83.

Morris, P. A., 1993, Archaean mafic and ultramafic rocks, Menzies to Norseman, Western Australia: Geol. Surv. West. Austral. Rept. 36, 107 p.

Moser, D. E., 1994, The geology and structure of the mid-crustal Wawa gneiss domain—a key to understanding tectonic variation with depth and time in the late Archean Abitibi-Wawa orogen: Can. Jour. Earth Sci., v. 31, p. 1064-1080.

Moser, D. E., Heaman, L. M., Krogh, T. E. and Hanes, J. A., 1996, Intracrustal extension of an Archean orogen revealed using single-grain U-Pb zircon geochronology: Tectonics, v. 15, p. 1093-1109.

Myers, J. S., 1995, The generation and assembly of an Archaean supercontinent—evidence from the Yilgarn craton, Western Australia: Geol. Soc. London Spec. Publ. 95, p. 143-154.

Naldrett, A. J., and Smith, I. E. M., 1981, Mafic and ultramafic volcanism during the Archean, in Basaltic Volcanism Study Project, Basaltic volcanism on the terrestrial planets: New York, Pergamon Press, p. 5-29.

Nelson, D. R., 1997, Evolution of the Archaean granite-greenstone terranes of the Eastern Goldfields, Western Australia—SHRIMP U-Pb zircon constraints: Precamb. Res., v. 83, p. 57-81.

Nisbet, E. G., Cheadle, M. J., Arndt, N. T., and Bickle, M. J., 1993, Constraining the potential temperature of the Archaean mantle—a review of the evidence from komatiites: Lithos, v. 30, p. 291-307.

Norman, M. D., 1994, Sudbury igneous complex—impact melt or endogenous magma? Implications for lunar crustal evolution: Geol. Soc. Amer. Spec. Paper 293, p. 331-341.

Nutman, A. P., McGregor, V. R., Friend, C. R. L., Bennett, V. C., and Kinny, P. D., 1996, The Itsaq Gneiss Complex of southern West Greenland: The world's most extensive record of early crustal evolution (3900-3600 Ma): Precamb. Res., v. 78, p. 1-39.

Padgham, W. A., 1992, The Slave structural province, North America—a discussion of tectonic models: Univ. West. Austral. Geol. Dept. Publ. 22, p. 381-394.

_____, 1995, Evolution of the Slave craton—comment: Geology, v. 23, p. 863-864.

Padgham, W. A., and Fyson, W. K., 1992, The Slave Province—a distinct Archean craton: Can. Jour. Earth Sci., v. 29, p. 2072-2086.

Pallister, J. S., Stacey, J. S., Fischer, L. B., and Premo, W. R., 1988, Precambrian ophiolites of Arabia—geologic settings, U-Pb geochronology, Pb-isotope characteristics, and implications for continental accretion: Precamb. Res., v. 38, p. 1-54.

Pan, Y., Fleet, M. F., and Williams, H. R., 1994, Granulite-facies metamorphism in the Quetico Subprovince, north of Manitouwadge, Ontario: Can. Jour. Earth Sci., v. 31, p. 1427-1439.

Pearson, N. J., O'Reilly, S. Y., and Griffin, W. L., 1995, The crust-mantle boundary beneath cratons and craton margins—a transect across the south-west margin of the Kaapvaal craton: Lithos, v. 36, p. 257-287.

Percival, J. A., 1989, A regional perspective of the Quetico metasedimentary belt, Superior Province, Canada: Can. Jour. Earth Sci., v. 26, p. 677-693.

Percival, J. A., Card, K. D., and Mortensen, J. K., 1993, Archean unconformity in the Vizien greenstone belt, Ungava Peninsula, Quebec: Geol. Surv. Can. Curr. Res. 1993-C, p. 319-328.

Percival, J. A., et al., 1994, Minto block, Superior province—missing link in deciphering assembly of the craton at 2.7 Ga: Geology, v. 22, p. 839-842.

Percival, J. A., Fountain, D. M., and Salisbury, M. H., 1992, Exposed crustal cross sections as windows on the lower crust, in Fountain, D. M., Arculus, R. J., and Kay, R. W., eds., Continental lower crust: Amsterdam, Elsevier, p. 317-362.

Percival, J. A., Skulski, T., and Nadeau, L., 1996, Granite-greenstone terranes of the northern Minto block, northeastern Superior Province, Quebec: Geol. Surv. Can. Curr. Res. 1996-C, p. 157-167.

Percival, J. A., and Williams, H. R., 1989, Late Archean Quetico accretionary complex, Superior province, Canada: Geology, v. 17, p. 23-25.

Percival, J. A., and West, G. F., 1994, The Kapuskasing uplift—a geological and geophysical synthesis: Can. Jour. Earth Sci., v. 31, p. 1256-1286.

Perring, C. S., Barnes, S. J., and Hill, R. E. T., 1996, Geochemistry of komatiites from Forrestania, Southern Cross Province, Western Australia: Evidence for crustal contamination: Lithos, v. 37, p. 181-197.

Polet, J., and Anderson, D. L., 1995, Depth extent of cratons as inferred from tomographic studies: Geology, v. 23, p. 205-208.

Premo, W. R., and Tatsumoto, M., 1993, U-Pb systematics of ferroan anorthosite 60025: Lunar Planet. Sci., v. 24, p. 1175–1176.

Puchtel, I. S., et al., 1997, Petrology and geochemistry of crustally contaminated komatiitic basalts from the Vetreny Belt, southeastern Baltic Shield: Evidence for an early Proterozoic mantle plume beneath rifted Archean continental lithosphere: Geochim. et Cosmochim. Acta, v. 61, p. 1205–1222.

Pupin, J. P., 1980, Zircon and granite petrology: Contrib. Mineral. Petrol., v. 73, p. 207–220.

Rapp, R. B., Watson, E. B., and Miller, C. F., 1991, Partial melting of amphibolite/eclogite and the origin of Archean trondhjemites and tonalites: Precamb. Res., v. 51, p. 1–25.

Rhodesia Geological Survey, 1977, Provisional geological map of Rhodesia, 1:1,000,000.

Richardson, S. H., 1990, Age and early evolution of the continental mantle, in Menzies, M., ed., Continental mantle: Oxford, Clarendon Press, p. 55–65.

Ridley, J. R., 1992, The thermal causes and effects of voluminous, late Archean monzogranite plutonism: Univ. West. Austral. Geol. Dept. Publ. 22, p. 275–285.

Ridley, J. R., and Kramers, J. D., 1990, The evolution and tectonic consequences of a tonalitic magma layer within Archean continents: Can. Jour. Earth Sci., v. 27, p. 219–228.

Roering, C., et al., 1992, Tectonic model for the evolution of the Limpopo Belt: Precamb. Res., v. 55, p. 539–552.

Rollinson, H., and Blenkinsop, T., 1995, The magmatic, metamorphic, and tectonic evolution of the Northern Marginal Zone of the Limpopo Belt in Zimbabwe: Jour. Geol. Soc. Lond., v. 152, p. 65–75.

Ross, D. C., 1967, Generalized geologic map of the Inyo Mountains region, California: U.S. Geol. Surv. Map I-506, 1:125,000.

Rudnick, R. L., 1995, Making continental crust: Nature, v. 378, p. 571–578.

Rudnick, R. L., and Fountain, D. M., 1995, Nature and composition of the continental crust: a lower crustal perspective: Rev. Geophys., v. 33, p. 267–309.

Rudnick, R. L., and Taylor, S. R., 1986, Geochemical constraints on the origin of Archaean tonalitic-trondhjemitic rocks and implications for lower crustal composition: Geol. Soc. Lond. Spec. Publ. 24, p. 179–191.

Ryder, G., 1994, Coincidence in time of the Imbrium basin impact and Apollo 15 KREEP volcanic flows: The case for impact-induced melting: Geol. Soc. Amer. Spec. Pap. 293, p. 11–18.

St-Onge, M. R., and Lucas, S. B., 1996, Paleoproterozoic orogenic belts: Geol. Surv. Can. Open File 3228, p. 17–24.

Sawyer, E. W., and Benn, K., 1995, Structure of the high-grade Opatica Belt and adjacent low-grade Abitibi Subprovince, Canada—an Archaean mountain front: Jour. Struct. Geol., v. 12, p. 1443–1558.

Schubert, G., Stevenson, D., and Cassen, P., 1980, Whole planet cooling and the radiogenic heat source contents of the Earth and Moon: Jour. Geophys. Res., v. 85, p. 2531–2538.

Shih, C.-Y., Bansal, B. M., and Wiesmann, H., 1990, Sm-Nd age of a pristine norite clast from breccia 15445: Lunar Planet. Sci., v. 21, p. 1146–1147.

Simon, S. B., 1990, Lunar magmatism, in Hall, R. J., and Hughes, D. J., eds., Early Precambrian basic magmatism: Glasgow, Blackie, p. 136–156.

Skulski, T., and Percival, J. A., 1996, Allochthonous 2.78 Ga oceanic plateau slivers in a 2.72 Ga continental arc sequence—Vizien greenstone belt, northeastern Superior Province, Canada: Lithos, v. 37, p. 163–179.

Skulski, T., Percival, J. A. and Stern, R. A., 1994, Oceanic allochthons in an Archean continental margin sequence, Vizien greenstone belt, northern Quebec: Geol. Surv. Can., Curr. Res. 1994-C, p. 311–320.

Sleep, N. H., and Windley, B. F., 1982, Archean plate tectonics—constraints and inferences: Jour. Geol., v. 90, p. 363–379.

Smyth, J. R., Caporuscio, F. A., and McCormick, T. C., 1989, Mantle eclogites—evidence of igneous fractionation in the mantle: Earth Planet. Sci. Lett., v. 93, p. 133–141.

Snyder, G. A., Taylor, L. A., and Halliday, A. N., 1995, Chronology and petrogenesis of the lunar highlands alkali suite—cumulates from KREEP basalt crystallization: Geochim. et Cosmochim. Acta, v. 59, p. 1185–1203.

Spudis, P. D., Reisse, R. A., and Gillis, J. L., 1994, Ancient multiring basins on the Moon revealed by Clementine laser altimetry: Science, v. 266, p. 1848–1851.

Stern, R. A., Percival, J. A., and Mortensen, J. K., 1994, Geochemical evolution of the Minto block—a 2.7 Ga continental magmatic arc built on the Superior proto-craton: Precamb. Res., v. 65, p. 115–153.

Swager, C. P., 1995, Geology of the greenstone terranes in the Kurnalpi-Edjudina region, southeastern Yilgarn Craton: Geol. Surv. West. Austral. Rept. 47, 31 p.

————, 1997, Tectono-stratigraphy of late Archaean greenstone terranes in the southern Eastern Goldfields, Western Australia: Precamb. Res., v. 83, p. 11–42.

Sylvester, A. G., Oertel, G., Nelson, C. A., and Christie, J. M., 1978, Papoose Flat pluton: A granitic blister in the Inyo Mountains, California: Geol. Soc. Amer. Bull., v. 89, p. 1203–1219.

Talbot, C. J., 1973, A plate tectonic model for the Archaean crust: Philos. Trans. Roy. Soc. London, ser. A., v. 273, p. 413–427.

Taylor, S. R., 1992, Solar system evolution: New York, Cambridge Univ. Press, 307 p.

————, 1993, Early accretionary history of the Earth and the Moon-forming event: Lithos, v. 30, p. 207–221.

Taylor, S. R., and Esat, T. M., 1996, Geochemical constraints on the origin of the Moon: Amer. Geophys. Union Geophys. Monog. 95, p. 33–46.

Thompson, P. H., Judge, A. S., and Lewis, T. J., 1995, Thermal parameters in rock units of the Winter Lake–Lac de Gras area, central Slave Province, Northwest Territories—implications for diamond genesis: Geol. Surv. Can. Curr. Res. 1995-E, p. 125–135.

Thorpe, R. I., Hickman, A. H., Davis, D. W., Mortenson, J. K., and Trendall, A. F., 1990, Application of recent zircon U-Pb geochronology in the Marble Bar region, Pilbara Craton, to modelling Archean lead evolution [abs.]: Third Int. Archaean Symp., Perth, ext. abs. vol., p. 11–13.

Thurston, P. C., and Chivers, K. M., 1990, Secular variation in greenstone sequence development emphasizing Superior Province, Canada: Precamb. Res., v. 46, p. 21–58.

Treloar, P. J., Coward, M. P., and Harris, N. B. W., 1992, Himalayan-Tibetan analogies for the evolution of the Zimbabwe Craton and Limpopo Belt: Precamb. Res., v. 55, p. l571–487.

Trendall, A. F., 1995, Paradigms for the Pilbara: Geol. Soc. Lond. Spec. Publ. 95, p. 127–142.

Twist, D., and French, B. M., 1983, Voluminous acid volcanism in the Bushveld Complex—a review of the Rooiberg Felsite: Bull. Volcanol., v. 46, p. 225–242.

van Breeman, O., Davis, W. J., and King, J. E., 1992, Temporal distribution of granitoid plutonic rocks in the Archean Slave Province, northwest Canadian Shield: Can. Jour. Earth Sci., v. 29, p. 2186–2199.

van Breeman, O., Henderson, J. B., Loveridge, W. D., and Thompson, P. H., 1987, U-Pb zircon and monazite geochronology and zircon morphology of granulites and granite from the Thelon Tectonic Zone, Healey Lake and Artillery Lake map areas, N.W.T.: Geol. Surv. Can. Pap. 87-1A, p. 783–801.

van der Lee, S., and Nolet, G., 1997, Upper mantle S velocity structure of North America: Jour. Geophys. Res., v. 102, p. 22,815–22,838.

van Reenen, D. D., McCourt, S., and Smit, C. A., 1995, Are the Southern and Northern Marginal Zones of the Limpopo Belt related to a single continental collisional event?: South Afr. Jour. Geol., v. 98, p. 498–504.

Vervoort, J. D., White, W. M., and Thorpe, R. I., 1994, Nd and Pb isotope ratios of the Abitibi greenstone belt—new evidence for very early differentiation of the Earth: Earth Planet. Sci. Lett., v. 128, p. 215–229.

Walker, I. W., and Blight, D. F., 1983, Barlee, Western Australia: Geol. Surv. West. Austral. 1:250,000 Geol. Ser., Explan. Notes SH/50-8, 22 p. + map.

Warren, P. H., 1992, The three stages of magma ocean cooling: Lunar Planet. Inst. Tech. Rept. 92-03, p. 70–71.

————, 1993, Limits on differentiation of melt "sheets" from basin-scale lunar impacts: Lunar Planet. Sci., v. 24, p. 1481–1482.

Watkeys, M. K., 1983, Provisional geologic map of the Limpopo Belt and environs, 1:1,000,000: Geol. Soc. South Afr. Spec. Publ. 8, colored plate.

Watkins, K. P., and Hickman, A. H., 1990, Geological evolution and mineralization of the Murchison Province, Western Australia: Geol. Surv. West. Austral. Bull. 137, 267 p.

Wilhelms, D. E., 1987, Geologic history of the Moon: U.S. Geol. Survey Prof. Pap. 1348, 302 p.

Williams, I. S., and Collins, W. J., 1990, Granite-greenstone terranes in the Pilbara Block, Australia, as coeval volcano-plutonic complexes; evidence from U-Pb zircon dating of the Mount Edgar Batholith: Earth Planet. Sci. Lett., v. 97, p. 41–53.

Williams, I. S., Bowring, S. A., and Nutman, A., 1997, Earth's earliest crust [abs.]: Geol. Soc. Amer., Abs. Prog., v. 29, no. 6, p. 351.

Wilson, J. F., Nesbitt, R. W., and Fanning, C. M., 1995, Zircon geochronology of Archaean felsic sequences in the Zimbabwe craton—a revision of greenstone stratigraphy and a model for crustal growth: Geol. Soc. Lond. Spec. Publ. 95, p. 109–126.

Wolf, M. B., and Wyllie, P. J., 1993, Garnet growth during amphibolite anatexis—implications of a garnetiferous restite: Jour. Geol., v. 101, p. 357–373.

Wolfe, C. J., Bjarnason, I. T., VanDecar, J. C., and Solomon, S. C., 1997, Seismic structure of the Iceland mantle plume: Nature, v. 385, p. 245–247.

Wyllie, P. J., Wolf, M. B., and van der Laan, S. R., 1997, Conditions for formation of tonalites and trondhjemites: Magmatic sources and products, in de Wit, M. J., and Ashwal, M. D., eds., Tectonic evolution of greenstone belts: New York, Oxford Univ. Press, p. 256–266.

Xie, Q., and Kerrich, R., 1994, Silicate-perovskite and majorite signature komatiites from the Archean Abitibi Greenstone Belt: Implications for early mantle differentiation and stratification: Jour. Geophys. Res., v. 99, p. 15,799–15,812.

Zaleski, E., et al., 1997, Seismic reflections from subvertical diabase dikes in an Archean terrane: Geology, v. 25, p. 707–710.

Ophiolites, the Sierra Nevada, "Cordilleria," and Orogeny along the Pacific and Caribbean Margins of North and South America

E. M. MOORES

Department of Geology, University of California, Davis, California 95616

Abstract

Ophiolites are major expressions of orogeny; they are dominantly oceanic crust and mantle emplaced by collision of a mantle-rooted thrust (subduction zone) with a continental margin or island arc. Ophiolite nappes thus represent remnants of lithospheric plates; their basal thrusts (fossil subduction zones) intrinsically cannot be balanced; their displacements are unknown but very large.

Two major belts of Mesozoic ophiolites and related island-arc complexes extend along the western and Caribbean margins of the Americas from Alaska to Ecuador. An eastern belt (e.g., Stikinia-Intermontane superterranes, Canada, United States; rocks of western Baja California and the Guerrero terrane, Mexico; ophiolitic and related rocks of Guatemala, Cuba, Hispaniola, Puerto Rico, and La Desirade; Cordillera de la Costa, Venezuela; and the Cordillera Central, Colombia) was an active island-arc complex in the Early to Middle Jurassic and was emplaced in Middle Jurassic–Cretaceous time. A western belt (e.g., the Wrangellia/Insular superterrane of Canada and United States; Chocó-Chortis blocks of Central America; Cordillera Occidental (Piñon) of Colombia and Ecuador) experienced activity during the Jurassic–Cretaceous and was emplaced during Late Cretaceous–Tertiary time.

These relations inspire an outrageous hypothesis that in Middle to Late Mesozoic time, a separate intra-oceanic plate similar to the present Philippine plate, herein named "Cordilleria," was separated by active island-arc complexes from the American and Farallon/Kula plates to the east and west, respectively. Basement rocks of the Colombian, Venezuelan, and Yucatan basins may represent remnants of "Cordilleria." Convergence and collision of "Cordilleria" and its island-arc margins with the American continents were major factors in western American and Caribbean orogenic development.

The Mesozoic tectonic history of the North American Cordillera, with its conflicting sinistral and dextal motions at varying locations and times, suggests a model involving a rigid-plastic continuum approximation using slip-line field theory, as successfully applied to the Indian-Eurasian collision. Complex evolution of the northern Sierra Nevada and its surroundings may reflect such tectonics. Direct contact between the Kula/Farallon plates and North America may not have occurred until Late Cretaceous time.

Introduction

. . . subjected to the principle of least astonishment, geologic science has always tended to adopt the most static interpretation allowed by the data, and evidence indicating displacements larger than conceivable . . . has consistently met strong resistance (Seeber, 1983, p. 1528).

A vital lesson of plate tectonics is that there is no validity to any assumption that the simplest and therefore most acceptable interpretation demands a proximal rather than a distant origin (Coombs, 1997, p. 763).

THE PACIFIC AND CARIBBEAN margins of the Americas are regions of complex tectonic evolution that have been the source of considerable interest and controversy. Orogenies in late Mesozoic–early Cenozoic time are well documented from Alaska to Ecuador. These orogenies involve, among other features, deformed continental marginal sequences involved in fold-thrust belts vergent toward continental interiors, major modern and inferred ancient plate margins, entrapped oceanic crust (e.g., Caribbean plate interior), large batholithic belts, subduction-related volcanism and accretionary complexes, and abundant ophiolitic rocks.

For the past quarter century the role of plate processes in the evolution of this region has been generally accepted, but the detailed processes have remained elusive, and the number and polarity of subduction zones and the role of exotic terranes have remained controversial. In this article, I propose a provocative hypothesis that much of the tectonic development of the Pacific and Caribbean margins of North and South America is the result of the interaction of these continents with a Philippine-like plate that existed west of the Americas during Mesozoic–early Cenozoic time. The margins of this plate, which were originally intra-oceanic island arcs or archipelagoes, were key elements in the tectonic development of the American Cordillera. Convergence and collision of these margins with the continents resulted in the orogenic "collage" present in the American Cordillera. The hypothesis violates the "principle of least astonishment" cited above, but it is offered as an addition to the "multiple working hypotheses" (Chamberlin, 1890) that should guide our search for insight into the tectonics of this complex and fascinating region. The hypothesis is a revival and update of an earlier, very general, and somewhat battered model for collisional origin of the Cordilleran orogen (Moores, 1970). In that model, I proposed that the Mesozoic orogenies of North and South America were the result of arc-continent collision, and that the Caribbean and Scotia arcs represented the result of eastward migration of arc segments not involved in the collision (1970, Fig. 6). Hamilton (1963, 1988) and Jones (1991) both expressed similar ideas, but without accompanying illustrations. In a much undercited paper, Wilson et al. (1991) also presented a detailed analysis of the Mesozoic evolution of western North American exotic terranes, including a series of reconstructions for Triassic through Cretaceous time. The hypothesis herein presented is intended also to be "outrageous" in the sense of Davis (1926), in attempting to focus attention on many obscure unsolved problems.

Chamberlin (1890) also cautioned against the pitfalls of having a single dominant theory, which he called the "ruling theory," holding sway over the judgment of a scientific community. Such a theory arises, he argued, from the predilection of scientists to "hastily conjure up an explanation for every new phenomenon that presents itself." A premature explanation becomes a tentative theory, then an adopted theory, and finally, a ruling theory. In such cases, the biases of parenthood skew one's judgment in favor of one's scientific "offspring."

Since the plate tectonics revolution, the "ruling theory" for Cordilleran evolution has been a single subduction zone dipping under the continent. Most, if not all, tectonic phenomena have been explained as variations about such a theme (e.g., "flat-slab" subduction for the Sevier-Laramide deformation). Models that invoke more complex plate interactions, especially with collisions or oceanic subduction zones, have been stoutly resisted. Even with the rise of the terrane concept, few authors have been willing or able to present more complex models, especially in visual form, although several have argued, even passionately, for them (e.g., Hamilton, 1988, 1989; Jones, 1991; Schermer et al., 1984).

Ophiolites and Orogeny

My original hypothesis was based on analysis of the problem of emplacement of ophiolitic rocks in orogenic belts. As originally emphasized by Hess (1939, 1955), ophiolites are a key element in the understanding of any orogenic belt, such as the western American Cordillera. Ophiolites—oceanic crust and mantle preserved on land—are major tectonic elements whose importance often is overlooked. In part, this situation has arisen because ophiolites originally were thought of as igneous rocks, and their emplacement as igneous, rather than tectonic, events. Although no longer commonly held, this pre–plate tectonic misunderstanding has led to widespread ignorance, or at least disregard, for the significance of ophiolites. The following six points emphasize the significance of ophiolites (see Moores, 1982; Hamilton, 1989):

1. Ophiolites represent oceanic crust and mantle formed at oceanic spreading centers and emplaced over island arcs or continental margins

Figure 1 shows diagrammatically the principal settings of origin of ophiolites. Settings include: (1) entrapped older oceanic lithosphere formed at a pre-existing spreading center and preserved in the forearc region of island arcs; (2) pull-apart intra-arc basins; (3) spreading centers in the forearcs of incipient or initially developed island arcs; (4) mid-oceanic

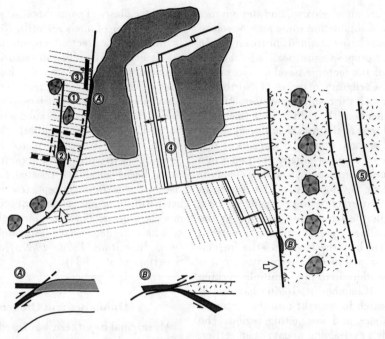

FIG. 1. Generalized sketch of environment of formation and emplacement of ophiolite complexes. Symbols: 1 = entrapped old oceanic crust; 2 = pull-apart basin behind or within island-arc; 3 = spreading within a forearc; 4 = spreading at mid-oceanic ridge; 5 = backarc spreading; A = emplacement of ophiolite by collision of continental margin with subduction zone; B = emplacement of ophiolite by "flake tectonics" or obduction—detachment of antithetic thrust block during subduction of a ridge. Patterns: dotted lines = magnetic lineations; shaded region at A = continental crust; stippled area at B and 5 = island-arc crust.

spreading; and (5) spreading in a small ocean in a backarc setting.

2. Ophiolites preserve spreading structures; they thus provide insight into the tectonics of modern spreading centers and the plumbing of "black-smoker" hot springs

Compositional and stratigraphic differences of ophiolite complexes arise from different processes within such diverse settings. These differences include chemical composition of volcanic and plutonic rocks, presence or absence and thicknesses of extrusive piles, sheeted dike complexes, abundance of such lithologies as serpentinite, ophicalcite, sulfide ore deposits, etc. These will vary with the tectonic environments illustrated in Figure 1.

3. Ophiolites are emplaced by mantle-rooted thrust faults (subduction zones) that form by conversion of normal or strike-slip (transform) faults (originally parallel or perpendicular to the spreading center) to mantle-rooted thrust

faults during changes in plate motion (e.g., Moores, 1982)

In Figure 1, the subduction zone at A developed within previously formed oceanic crust, as at 1.

4. Most ophiolites are emplaced by collision of subduction zones with island arcs or with continental margins

Such a setting is shown at location A in Figure 1. The continent (shaded pattern) has migrated into the subduction zone, and collided with it. Preservation of oceanic crust and mantle thus emplaced (see cross-section A) results in most of the ophiolite complexes preserved. Only a few complexes may have been emplaced by "obduction," as shown in cross-section and location B, where ophiolites are emplaced during subduction of a ridge. These types of complexes seem to be subordinate, however, in the geologic record—e.g., Taitao ophiolite, Southern Chile (Nelson et al., 1993; Lagabrielle et al.,

1994) or, less likely, the Resurrection Bay complex, Alaska (Bradley et al., 1995).

5. Ophiolite-emplacing thrusts represent fossil subduction zones; sedimentary decollement-style fold-thrust belts, often found beneath ophiolite thrusts, are secondary features subsidiary to ophiolite thrusts

Most attention in orogenic studies has been devoted to decollement-style fold-thrust belts because of their ease of analysis and their economic importance. From the point of view of tectonic development, however, they are less significant than are the ophiolite thrusts. An excellent modern example of this situation is the West Taiwan fold and thrust belt, which has resulted from collision of the West Luzon arc with the China continental margin. The West Luzon arc has moved some 1000 km in the past few million years, whereas the West Taiwan fold and thrust belt has a few tens of km of shortening (e.g., Hall, 1996).

6. Ophiolite thrusts, because they represent fossil subduction zones, intrinsically cannot be balanced. Their displacements are unknown, but very large. Consequently ophiolite thrusts are of prime importance in the understanding of the tectonic evolution of any orogenic belt

Again the collision of the West Luzon island arc with the China continental margin in Taiwan is an excellent example of this situation. Another example is the island arc–continental margin collision in New Guinea.

Collisions and Slip-Line Tectonics

If collisions are important in Cordilleran evolution, and many lines of evidence indicate that they are, an important question is the effect of that event on the collided blocks. Both thrusting and strike-slip faulting can be expected, and the latter may well follow the patterns that would be indicated by a slip-line field model.

The application of slip-line field theory to the collision of India with Asia is well known (e.g., Molnar and Tapponnier, 1975; Tapponnier and Molnar, 1976). Less well known in the U.S. is Tapponnier's (1977) attempt to apply a rigid-plastic model to the Alpine-Mediterranean system. In this provocative paper, Tapponnier out-

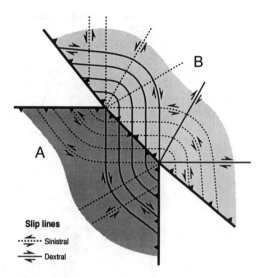

FIG. 2. Hypothetical slip-line tectonic development within two weak plates, outlined in the heavy lines. Plate on left (A) may represent Stikine-Intermontane-Sierra-Guerrero superterrane, plate on right (B) North America, at time of collision. See text for discussion.

lined possible slip-line fields for three cases: (1) where the downgoing plate includes a promontory of crust, which serves as an indentor, as is the case with India colliding with Asia; (2) where the crustal promontory is on the overriding (weak) plate; in this case the promontory is the first part of the weak continent to collide, which essentially is the inverse of the India case; slip lines form in the promontory and it deforms by extrusion to either side; and (3) where two crustal blocks of equal strength are juxtaposed by strike-slip faulting and then compressed; in this case both blocks deform and are extruded to the side as compression proceeds.

Slip-line field theory has not been applied in any comprehensive way to the problem of a collision between an island arc and an active continental margin. In such cases, one might expect that both crusts will be weak, and both will undergo deformation, depending upon the shape of the collided crustal blocks and the direction of convergence. Figure 2 shows a hypothetical slip-line field for a collision between two blocks, which may represent the situation during mid-Mesozoic time off North America, as discussed below. Clearly the details of the deformation will depend upon the shape

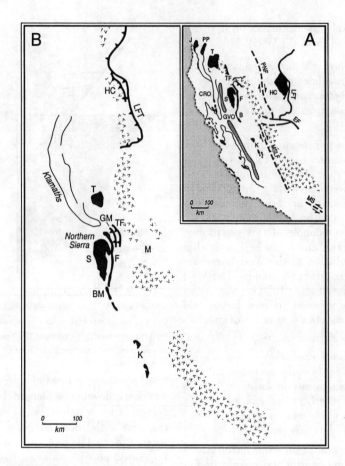

FIG. 3. Generalized map of the western United States, showing several major features discussed in text. A. Present configuration. B. Palinspastic restoration with movement on Pine Nut–Mojave–Snow Lake fault removed. Abbreviations: BM = Bear Mountains ophiolite; CF = Candelaria fault; CRO = Coast Range ophiolite; EF = Excelsior fault; F = Feather River complex; GM = Grizzly Mountain fault; GVO = Great Valley ophiolite; HC = Humboldt complex; J = Josephine ophiolite; K = Kings River ophiolite; LFT = Luning Fencemaker thrust; M = Mojave desert; MSLF = Mojave–Snow Lake Fault; MS = Mojave-Sonora fault; PNF = Pine Nut Fault; P = Preston Peak complex; T = Trinity complex; TF = Taylorsville fault.

of the blocks and the direction of convergence. In any case, both blocks will deform, and both sinistral and dextral faults will form at appropriate orientations and locations within the blocks and along the suture.

U.S. Cordillera

The U.S. Cordillera is a region of complex, diverse tectonics, much disagreement about the significance of various features, and many ophiolite complexes (e.g., references in Schermer et al., 1984; Dilek and Moores, 1993). Of

particular concern for the present discussion are ophiolitic rocks.

Figure 3 is a sketch map of a few principal ophiolitic terranes of the Sierra Nevada and surroundings. The principal elements are as follows.

(1) *The Humboldt complex of NW Nevada (HC)*. This sequence of mafic plutonic, basalt-andesite dikes and extrusives represents a portion of a continental island arc that bordered or fringed North America, which was thrust eastward from Middle to Late Jurassic time (Dilek and Moores, 1995).

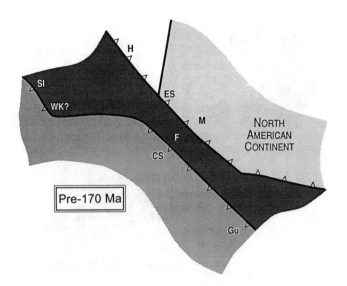

FIG. 4. Generalized tectonic scenario just prior to collision of the Stikine-Sierra-Guerrero terranes with North America. Abbreviations: CS = Central Sierra; ES = Eastern Sierra; F = Feather River complex; Gu = Guerrero terrane; H = Humboldt complex; M = Mojave block; WK = Western Klamaths; SI = Stikine-Intermontane superterrane.

(2) *The Eastern Belt of the northern Sierra Nevada (TF [Taylorsville fault] in Fig. 3; ES in Fig. 4)*. This is a complex stratigraphic sequence of lower Paleozoic quartzose meta-sediments (Shoo Fly complex) overlain unconformably by mid-Paleozoic, Permian and/or Triassic, and Jurassic andesitic complexes, which may represent intraoceanic (mid-Paleozoic) to continental-margin (Jurassic) arcs. These rocks were isoclinally folded and thrust first eastward and then westward, possibly during mid-Jurassic time.[1]

(3) *The Feather River Peridotite belt of the northern Sierra Nevada.* This is a 100-mi-long belt of mantle tectonite, ultramafic cumulate, mafic plutonic rocks, dikes, and pillow lavas, all of which have been deformed and metamorphosed. Radiometric dates of these rocks range from 235 to 315 Ma (Edelman et al., 1989; Saleeby et al., 1989).

(4) *The Smartville–Slate Creek complexes of the northern Sierra Nevada.* These complexes

[1]Harwood (1989) and Jayko (1990) have cast doubt on the previous interpretation of some of the folding in these rocks, as outlined by D'Allura et al. (1977), Hannah and Moores (1986), Moores and Day (1984), and Day et al. (1985). Harwood and Jayko did not take into account much of the indicated evidence for the structures in dispute, particularly within the Shoo Fly complex.

form a ~200-Ma ophiolitic sequence, thrust eastward over the Sierran rocks to the east at ~170 Ma and subsequently intruded by dikes and plutonic bodies at ~160 Ma (Day et al., 1985, 1988; Beard and Day, 1987; Edelman et al., 1989).

(5) *The Great Valley ophiolite.* The Great Valley ophiolite is a major 600-km-long complex buried beneath the Great Valley of California (Godfrey and Mendocino Working Group, 1994; Godfrey et al., 1997).

(6) *The Coast Range ophiolite.* The Coast Range ophiolite is an extensive series of ophiolitic sequences of backarc, forearc, or mid-oceanic-ridge origin (Dickinson et al., 1996).

(7) *The Josephine complex.* This is a complete 160-Ma ophiolite, possibly formed near a fracture zone (e.g., Harper et al., 1985).

Figure 3B is a reconstruction for the Sierra Nevada and surrounding area, with the effects of subsequent Basin and Range extension and strike-slip faulting on the Snow Lake–Pine Nut fault removed. This reconstruction has the effect of placing the northern Sierra Nevada opposite the Mojave Desert (see references in Dilek and Moores, 1995).

Figures 4–7 depict schematic stages in the evolution of the western United States assum-

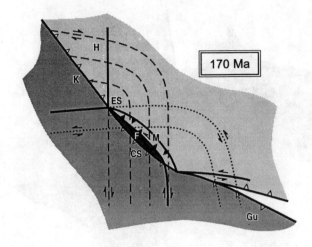

FIG. 5. Tectonic configuration at collision ~170 Ma (Middle Jurassic), and development of slip-line features, as in Figure 2. For abbreviations, see Figure 4.

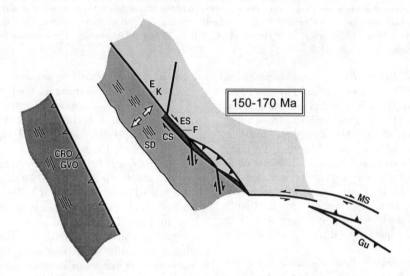

FIG. 6. Development between 150 and 170 Ma (Middle to Late Jurassic): development of both left- and right-lateral faults as a result of collision; formation of Smartville dike complex (SD), Coast Range and Great Valley ophiolites, and the Mojave-Sonora megashear (MS). For abbreviations, see Figure 4.

ing an arc–active continental margin collision. Figure 4 shows the situation just before collision (before 170 Ma, pre-Callovian). An E-facing arc includes the Smartville–Slate Creek complexes in the Central and Western belts of the northern Sierra Nevada (CS) and possible continuations to the Klamaths and the Stikine-Intermontane terranes to the north and the Guerrero terrane of Mexico to the south. The Feather River complex is assumed to be the downgoing plate being consumed by both subduction zones.

In Figure 5 (170 Ma, Middle Jurassic), the two arcs have collided. Deformation of both crustal blocks may have occurred first by the western island arc overriding the eastern one, producing E-vergent structures in the collided blocks (Central belt and Mojave block), which then are overriden by W-vergent structures. Slip-line tectonics may have produced

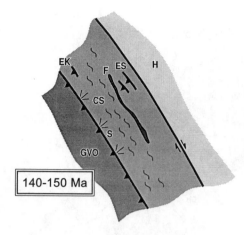

140-150 Ma

FIG. 7. Development between 140 and 150 Ma (Late Jurassic–Early Cretaceous). Emplacement of Great Valley ophiolite (Godfrey et al., 1997) causes deformation of Smartville complex and thrusts in eastern Klamaths and northern Sierra. For abbreviations, see Figure 4.

E-ESE–trending sinistral faults (e.g., Mojave-Sonora megashear) to the south and dextral N-NNE–trending faults to the north (strike-slip faults in the northern Sierra, incipient Snow Lake–Pine Nut fault (?).

In Figure 6 (150 to 170 Ma, Middle to Late Jurassic), dextral strike-slip faulting takes place to the north, juxtaposing the Eastern Sierra and the Central Sierra/Feather River blocks. A new E-facing arc has developed that will emplace the Coast Range and Great Valley ophiolites. Rifting in the collided arc in the Sierra Nevada produces the Smartville plutonic and dike complexes. The Guerrero terrane moves southward along strands of the Mojave-Sonora megashear.

In Figure 7 (140 to 150 Ma, Late Jurassic–Early Cretaceous), emplacement of the Great Valley/Coast Range along the continental margin deforms the Northern Sierra, produces isoclinal folds and the Taylorsville and Grizzly Mountain thrusts in the Eastern belt, isoclinally folds the thrusts that emplaced the Smartville–Slate Creek ophiolite, and produces widespread foliation and deformation in parts of the Smartville dike complex.

American Cordilleran Evolution

Figure 8 shows several principal tectonic elements of western North America, the Caribbean region, and northern South America, from north to south, as follows (abbreviations in parentheses are as shown in Fig. 8).

• The Stikine/Intermontane superterrane (SI), a complex belt of Paleozoic and Mesozoic rocks, which was attached to North America in mid-Jurassic time (e.g., Cowan et al., 1997).

• The Wrangellia/Insular superterrane (WI), a complex belt of Paleozoic and Mesozoic rocks that was attached to North America in Late Cretaceous time (~90 Ma) (Cowan et al., 1997).

• The Sierra Nevada/Klamath and associated rocks (SK), a complex sequence of island-arc, deep-marine clastic, and ophiolitic rocks, which were in place at least by mid-Jurassic time, and which may represent a continuation of the SI superterrane.

• The Great Valley/Coast Range ophiolite (GCO), a Late Jurassic complex of diverse origin, emplaced probably in Early Cretaceous time (Dickinson et al., 1996; Godfrey et al., 1997).

• The Guerrero terrane (G), a Jurassic–Cretaceous island-arc complex deposited on an older metamorphic basement complex (Centeno-Garcia et al., 1993).

• The basement rocks of Cuba (Cu), Hispaniola (H), and Puerto Rico (Pr) of Triassic–Jurassic or older metasediments, ophiolites, subduction-related deposits, and Cretaceous volcanic arc–related rocks and sediments (e.g., Lewis, Draper et al., 1990), which collided with the North American continental margin and/or Bahama platform in Paleogene time.

• The Aves Ridge (A), an E-facing Cretaceous–Paleogene island-arc complex (e.g., Holcombe et al., 1990).

• The Cordillera de la Costa of northern Venezuela (VC), a complex assemblage of nappes involving Paleozoic–Mesozoic metamorphic, ophiolitic, and volcanic-arc rocks, and emplaced chiefly in Late Cretaceous–Paleogene time (Bellizia and Dengo, 1990).

• The Chorotega-Chocó-Chortis blocks of Central America (CH), and correlative rocks of western Colombia and Ecuador (Piñon and related rocks) (P), including Jurassic–Cretaceous deep-sea sediments, ophiolites, and Cretaceous–Paleogene arc-type volcanic rocks (Escalante, 1990).

FIG. 8. Generalized map of the Americas with terranes discussed in text. Symbols: A = Aves Ridge; C = Colombia Basin; CC = Cordillera Central, Colombia; CH = Chorotega-Chocó-Chortis blocks, Central America; Cu = Cuban allochthonous terranes; G = Guerrero terrane, Mexico; GCO = Great Valley–Coast Range ophiolite, California and related rocks; H = Hispaniola allochthonous terranes; SI = Stikine-Intermontane superterrane; SK = Sierra Nevada–Klamath and related terranes, western United States; V = Venezuelan basin; VC = Cordillera de la Costa, Venezuela; WI = Wrangellia-Insular superterrane.

• The Cordillera Central of Colombia (CC), consisting of Paleozoic–Mesozoic metamorphic and batholithic rocks, with extensive ophiolites emplaced in Cretaceous time (Case et al., 1990; Bourgois et al., 1982).

• The basins of the Caribbean—the Yucatan (Y), Colombian (C), and Venezuelan (V)—which possibly represent entrapped Pacific or backarc oceanic crust (e.g., Pindell and Barrett, 1990).

Western Pacific Analogue

The island arc–marginal basin systems of the western Pacific represent a possible analogue for the Mesozoic–Paleogene American margins. To give an idea of the possibility, Figure 9 represents a whimsical tectonic map of the Kurile-Kamchatka, Japan, Philippine, and Indonesian regions, *reversed* and juxtaposed

against the Americas. The western Pacific island arcs themselves contain abundant evidence of active and ancient multiple subduction zones, collisions, backarc-basin development, forearc ophiolites, entrapped oceanic crust, large-scale strike-slip faulting, and numerous other complexities (see Hall, 1996 for a synthesis). If these archipelagoes were to be incorporated into a continental margin, their intraoceanic history would be preserved, and would complicate the interpretation of that margin. Many of the contradictions of timing, vergence, and relative sequence of orogenic events within the American Cordillera may have resulted from such a history.

Model for Evolution of the American Cordillera

Figures 10A to 10E present a provocative hypothesis for evolution of the American Cor-

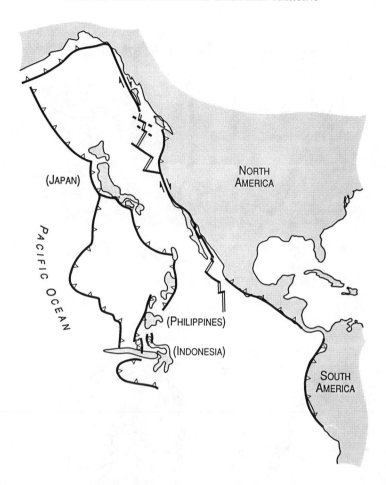

FIG. 9. Whimsical tectonic map of the eastern Pacific, with western Pacific archipelagoes reversed and superimposed at the same latitude. From Simkin et al. (1989).

dillera. The model involves two intraoceanic, intermittently active island arcs or archipelagoes (Hsü, 1994) bordering an intraoceanic plate, labeled "Cordilleria."

Figure 10A shows a possible original configuration in Early Jurassic time (180 Ma, mid-Jurassic). The eastern margin of Cordilleria is a complex island-arc system composed of the Stikine-Intermontane, Sierra-Klamath, and Guerrero terranes; basement terranes of Cuba, Hispaniola, and Puerto Rico; the Cordillera de la Costa of Venezuela; and the Cordillera Central of Colombia. Cordilleria's western margin consists of the Wrangellia/Insular superterrane of Canada and Alaska and the Chorotega-Chocó-Chortis-Piñon terranes of Central America, western Colombia, and Ecuador. The position of WI is that of Debiche et al., 1987).

Figure 10B shows a possible Late Jurassic scenario (160 Ma, Oxfordian). The Stikine-Intermontane and Sierra-Klamath terranes have collided with North America, and a new subduction zone has formed beneath the Great Valley–Coast Range ophiolite, but the Guerrero, Cuba, Hispaniola, Puerto Rico, Cordillera de la Costa, and Cordillera Central terranes are still in an intraoceanic position. The position of the SI terrane is consistent with the paleomagnetic data (see Cowan et al., 1997 for discussion).

Figure 10C shows a possible Jurassic–Cretaceous boundary reconstruction (140 Ma, Jurassic–Cretaceous boundary). The Guerrero and Great Valley–Coast Range ophiolite terranes have collided with southern North America. The Cuba, Hispaniola, and Puerto Rico

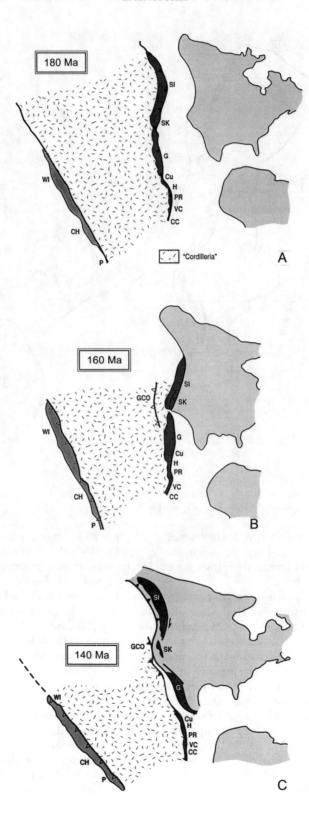

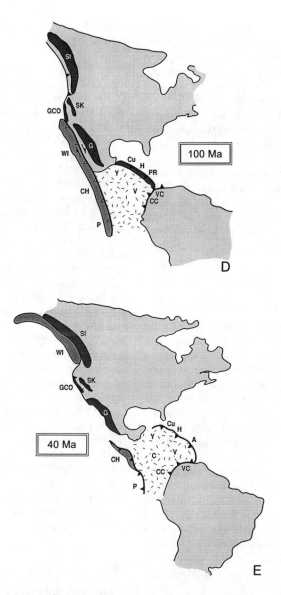

FIG. 10. Hypothetical evolution of Philippine-like eastern Pacific plate—Cordilleria—and its margins (A to C on facing page). Positions of continents after Smith et al. (1980). See text for discussion. A. Configuration at ~180 Ma (mid-Jurassic). Cordilleria and its margins separate American plates from Pacific/Kula/Farallon systems. B. Configuration at ~160 Ma (Late Jurassic). Stikine-Intermontane-Sierra has collided, Guerrero and other terranes are moving southeast along the Mojave-Sonora shear system. C. Configuration at ~140 Ma (Jurassic-Cretaceous boundary). Great Valley–Coast Range ophiolites are emplaced as thrust within Cordilleria; the southern part of the "eastern" archipelago is still west of the Americas. D. Configuration at ~100 Ma (Middle to Late Cretaceous). "Western archipelago" begins collision with Americas in "Baja BC" configuration; interaction of eastern archipelago and South America begins. E. Configuration at ~40 Ma. Western archipelago nears its present location between Guatemala and northwestern South America.

region and the Cordillera de la Costa and Cordillera Central region are still intraoceanic, approaching the edges of the two continents.

Figure 10D shows a possible Late Cretaceous scenario (100 Ma, Albian). The Wrangell-Insular superterrane has collided in its "Baja British

Columbia" position (e.g., Cowan et al., 1997), but the Chorotega-Chocó-Chortis-Piñon terranes are still intraoceanic. The stage has been set for the "hit-and-run" Laramide orogeny (Maxson and Tikoff, 1996). The terranes of Cuba, Hispaniola, Puerto Rico, and the Cordillera de la Costa of Venezuela are beginning to approach their present positions; the ophiolites of the Cordillera Central of Colombia have been emplaced.

Finally, Figure 10E shows a possible Eocene configuration (50 Ma, middle Eocene). Cuba, Hispaniola, and the Aves terranes are nearly in their present positions, whereas the Chorotega-Chocó-Chortis and Piñon terranes are still intraoceanic, but nearing the continental margins.

Discussion and Conclusions

The reconstructions of Figure 10 clearly are quite speculative, and they no doubt have glossed over many important details, some of which may not mesh well with the scenario presented here. They or something like them (e.g., Wilson et al., 1991; see also Jones, 1991) seem, however, to be natural consequences of a western Pacific model for evolution of the eastern Pacific margin. Some general implications can be drawn.

1. Archipelagoes, or island-arc margins of intraoceanic plates, may have been an important part of the tectonic evolution of American continental-margin orogens. Because they tend to be better preserved than the intervening oceanic plates, their histories may be of more importance than those of the intervening oceanic plates (Hsü, 1994; see also Hamilton, 1988, 1989).

2. Many tectonic events—such as ophiolite emplacement, igneous activity, thrusting, or sedimentation—now present in continental-marginal orogenic terranes may have occurred in intraoceanic environments, similar to processes taking place in the modern Philippine and Indonesian regions (see also Hamilton, 1989).

3. Many orogenic events represent collision of continental margins with seaward-dipping subduction zones (Moores, 1970, 1982).

4. Correlative rocks along an archipelago may show very different stratigraphies as a function of the timing of development of island-arcs, their convergence, and collision with continental margins.

5. A full understanding of the tectonic evolution of the orogenic belts along the eastern Pacific may involve correlations of allochthonous terranes from Alaska through the Caribbean to Ecuador.

6. The model depicted in Figure 4 shows the Coast Range–Great Valley ophiolite of California originating as part of "Cordilleria." The analogue for Cordilleria, the Philippine plate, is one of diverse origins—part entrapped oceanic crust, part backarc spreading, and part forearc spreading. As such, it may be a good model for such ophiolite complexes, which exhibit apparently diverse and contradictory origins at various localities (Dickinson et al., 1996).

7. The model provides a plausible origin for the Feather River complex. This complex displays metamorphic assemblages indicating temperatures of 650°C (and presumably 20 km of burial), which differ widely from the surrounding regions (Day et al., 1988). These rocks may have been emplaced by thrusting during suture progradation during the 170 Ma collision. Juxtaposition of these rocks against the Mojave Desert also may give a plausible explanation for the 13-km structural displacement during E-vergent thrusting in that region, as outlined by Howard et al. (1995).

8. The North American and Farallon-Kula plates may not have been in contact with each other until Late Cretaceous time (post-95 Ma), or approximately the time of arrival of the western archipelago.

Acknowledgments

I thank J. S. Davis, K. J. Hsü, R. J. Twiss, and J. R. Unruh for helpful discussions, and Alan Glazner for a thoughtful review of an earlier version of the manuscript. The statements herein are, of course, my sole responsibility.

REFERENCES

Beard, J. S., and Day, H. W., 1987, Smartville intrusive complex, Sierra Nevada, California: The core of a rifted arc: Geol. Soc. Amer. Bull, v. 99, p. 779–791.

Bellizia, A., and Dengo, G., 1990, The Caribbean mountain system, northern South America, a summary, in

Dengo, G., and Case, J. E., eds., The Caribbean region: Boulder, CO, Geol. Soc. Amer., The geology of North America, v. H, p. 167-175.

Bourgois, J., et al., 1982, Ages et structures des complexes basique et ultrabasique de la façade pacifique, Colombie, Panama, et Costa Rica: Bull. Soc. Geol. France, v. 3, p. 545-554.

Bradley, D., Haeussler, P., et al., 1995, Geologic effects of Paleogene ridge subduction, Kenai Peninsula, southern Alaska [abs.]: Geol. Soc. Amer., Abs. Prog., v. 27, no. 5, p. 7.

Case, J. E., Shagam, R., and Giegengack, R. F., 1990, Geology of the northern Andes: An overview, in Dengo, G., and Case, J. E., eds., The Caribbean region: Boulder, CO, Geol. Soc. Amer., The geology of North America, v. H, p. 177-200.

Centeno-Garcia, E., Ruiz, J., Coney, P. J., Patchett, P. J., and Ortega-Gutiérrez, F., 1993, Guerrero terrane of Mexico: Its role in the Southern Cordillera from new geochemical data: Geology, v. 21, p. 419-422.

Chamberlin, T. C., 1890, The method of multiple working hypotheses: Science, v. 15, p. 92-96 (reprinted in Science, v. 148, p. 754-759).

Coombs, D. S., 1997, A note on the terrane concept, based on an introduction to the Terrane '97 conference, Christchurch, New Zealand, February, 1997: Amer. Jour. Sci., v. 297, p. 762-764.

Cowan, D. S., Brandon, M. T., and Garver, J. I., 1997, Geologic tests of hypotheses for large coastwise displacement—A critique illustrated by the Baja British Columbia controversy: Amer. Jour. Sci., v. 297, p. 117-173.

D'Allura, J. A., Moores, E. M., and Robinson, L., 1977, Paleozoic rocks of the northern Sierra Nevada: Their structural and paleogeographic significance, in Stewart, J. H., Stevens, C. H., and Fritsche, A. E., eds., Paleozoic paleogeography of the western United States: Pacific Sect., Soc. Econ. Paleontol. Mineral., Pacific Coast Paleogeog. Symp. 1, p. 394-408.

Davis, W. M., 1926, The value of outrageous geological hypotheses: Science, v. 63, p. 463-468.

Day, H. W., Moores, E. M., and Tuminas, A. C., 1985, Structure and tectonics of the northern Sierra Nevada: Geol. Soc. Amer. Bull., v. 96, p. 436-450.

Day, H. W., Schiffman, P., and Moores, E. M., 1988, Metamorphism and tectonics of the northern Sierra Nevada, in W. G. Ernst, ed., Metamorphism and crustal evolution of the Western United States. Rubey Volume 7: Englewood Cliffs, NJ, Prentice Hall, p. 737-763.

Debiche, M. G., Cox, A., and Engebretson, D., 1987, The motion of allochthonous terranes across the north Pacific Basin: Geol. Soc. Amer. Spec. Pap. 207, 49 p.

Dickinson, W. R., Hopson, C. A., and Saleeby, J. B., 1996, Alternate origins of the Coast Range ophiolite (California): GSA Today, v. 6, no. 2, p. 1-10.

Dilek, Y., and Moores, E. M., 1993, Across-strike anatomy of the Cordilleran orogen at 40°N Latitude: Implications for the Mesozoic paleogeography of the Western United States, in Dunne, G. C., and McDougall, K. A., eds., Mesozoic paleogeography of the Western United States—II, Soc. Econ. Paleontol. Mineral., Pacific Sect., Book 71,p. 333-346.

————, 1995, Geology of the Humboldt igneous complex, Nevada, and tectonic implications for the Jurassic magmatism in the Cordilleran orogen: Geol. Soc. Amer. Spec. Pap. 299, p. 229-248.

Edelman, S. H., Day, H. W., Moores, E. M., Zigan, S. M., Murphy, T. P., and Hacker, B. R., 1989, Structure across a Mesozoic ocean-continent suture zone in the northern Sierra Nevada, California: Geol. Soc. Amer. Spec. Pap. 224, 56 p.

Escalante, G., 1990, The geology of southern Central America and western Colombia, in Dengo, G., and Case, J. E., eds., The Caribbean region: Boulder, CO, Geol. Soc. Amer., The geology of North America, v. H, p. 201-230.

Godfrey, N., Beaudoin, B. C., and Lemperer, S. L., 1997, Ophiolitic basement to the Great Valley forearc basin, California, from seismic and gravity data: Implications for crustal growth at the North American continental margin: Geol. Soc. Amer. Bull., in press.

Godfrey, N., and Mendocino Working Group, 1994, Results from the 1993 Mendocino triple junction experiment: Possible ophiolitic material beneath the western edge of the Great Valley: EOS (Trans. Amer. Geophys. Union), v. 75, p. 483.

Hall, R., 1996, Reconstructing Cenozoic SE Asia, in Hall, R., and Blundell, D., eds., Tectonic evolution of Southeast Asia: Geol. Soc. London Spec. Publ. 106, p. 153-184.

Hamilton, W., 1963, Tectonics of Antarctica: Amer. Assoc. Petrol. Geol. Memoir 2, p. 4-15.

————, 1988, Plate tectonics and island arcs: Geol. Soc. Amer. Bull., v. 100, p. 1503-1527.

————, 1989, Crustal geologic processes of the United States: Geol. Soc. Amer. Memoir 172, p. 743-782.

Hannah, J. L., and Moores, E. M., 1986, Age relationships and depositional environments of Paleozoic strata, northern Sierra Nevada, California: Geol. Soc. Amer. Bull., v. 97, p. 787-797.

Harper, G. D., Saleeby, J. B., and Norman, E. A. S., 1985, Geometry and tectonic setting of seafloor spreading for the Josephine ophiolite, and implications for Jurassic accretionary events along the California margin, in Howell, D. G., ed., Tectonostratigraphic terranes of the Circum-Pacific region: Circum-Pacific Council Energy Min. Resources, Earth Sci. Series, v. 1, p. 239–258.

Harwood, D. S., 1989, Stratigraphy and structure of the northern Sierra Terrane, in Blake, M. C., Jr., and Harwood, P. S., leaders, Sedimentation and tectonics of western North America; Vol. 2, Tectonic evolution of northern California: Washington, DC, Amer. Geophys. Union, 28th Geol. Cong., p. 56–66.

Hess, H. H., 1939, Island arcs, gravity anomalies, and serpentinite intrusions: Int. Geol. Cong., Moscow, 1937, Rept. 17, p. 263–283.

————, 1955, Serpentines, orogeny, and epirogeny: Geol. Soc. Amer. Mem. 62, p. 391–408.

Holcombe, T. L., et al., 1990, Caribbean marine geology; ridges and basins of the plate interior, in Dengo, G., and Case, J. E., eds., The Caribbean region: Boulder, CO, Geol. Soc. Amer., The geology of North America, v. H, p. 231–260.

Howard, K. A., McCaffrey, K. J. W., Wooden, J. L., Foster, D. A., and Shaw, S. E., 1995, Jurassic thrusting of Precambrian basement over Paleozoic cover in the Clipper mountains, southeastern California: Geol. Soc. Amer. Spec. Pap. 299, p. 375–392.

Hsü, K. J., 1994, Tectonic facies in an archipelago model of intra-plate orogenesis: GSA Today, v. 4, no. 12, p. 289–290, 292–293.

Jayko, A., 1990, Stratigraphy and tectonics of Paleozoic arc-related rocks of the northernmost Sierra Nevada, California: The eastern Klamath and northern Sierra terranes: Geol. Soc. Amer. Spec. Pap. 255, p. 307–324.

Jones, D. L., 1991, Synopsis of late Paleozoic and Mesozoic terrane accretion within the Cordillera of western North America, in Dewey, J. F., et al., Allochthonous terranes: New York, Cambridge Univ. Press, p. 23–30.

Lagabrielle, Y., Lemoigne, J., Maury, R. C., Cotten, J., et al., 1994, Volcanic record of the subduction of an active spreading ridge, Taitao Peninsula (southern Chile): Geology, v. 22, p. 515–518.

Lewis, J. F., and Draper, G., et al., 1990, Geology and tectonic evolution of the northern Caribbean margin, in Dengo, G., and Case, J. E., eds, The Caribbean region: Boulder, CO, Geol. Soc. Amer., The geology of North America, v. H, p. 77–140.

Maxson, J., and Tikoff, B., 1996, Hit-and-run collision model for the Laramide orogeny, western United States: Geology, v. 24, p. 968–972.

Molnar, P., and Tapponnier, P., 1975, Cenozoic tectonics of Asia: Effects of a continental collision: Science, v. 189, p. 419–426.

Moores, E. M., 1970, Ultramafics and orogeny, with models for the US Cordillera and the Alps: Nature, v. 228, p. 837–842.

————, 1982, Origin and emplacement of ophiolites: Rev. Geophys. Space Phys., v. 20, p. 735–760.

Moores, E. M., and Day, H. W., 1984, Overthrust model for the Sierra Nevada: Geology, v. 12, p. 416–419.

Nelson, E., Forsythe, R., Diemer, J., Allen, M., et al., 1993, Taitao ophiolite—a ridge collision ophiolite in the forearc of southern Chile (46°S): Rev. Geol. Chile, v. 20, no. 2, p. 137.

Pindell, J., and Barrett, S. F., 1990, Geological evolution of the Caribbean region; a plate tectonic perspective, in Dengo, G., and Case, J. E., eds., The Caribbean region: Boulder, CO, Geol. Soc. Amer., The geology of North America, v. H, p. 405–432.

Saleeby, J. B., Shaw, H. F., Niemeyer, S., Moores, E. M., and Edelman, S. H., 1989, U/PB, Sm/Nd, and Rb/Sr geochronological and isotopic study of northern Sierra Nevada ophiolitic assemblages, California: Contrib. Mineral. Petrol., v. 102, p. 205–220.

Schermer, E. L., Howell, D. G., and Jones, D. L., 1984, The origin of allochthonous terranes: Perspectives on the growth and shaping of continents: Ann. Rev. Earth Planet. Sci., v. 12, p. 107–132.

Seeber, L., 1983, Large-scale thin-skin tectonics: Rev. Geophys. Space Phys., v. 21, p. 1528–1538.

Simkin, T., Tilling, R. I., Taggart, J. N., Jones, W. J., and Spall, H., 1989, This dynamic planet: World map of volcanoes, earthquakes, and plate tectonics: Washington, DC, Smithsonian Institution.

Smith, A. G., Hurley, A. M., and Briden, J. C., 1980, Phanerozoic paleocontinental world maps: Cambridge, UK, Cambridge Univ. Press, 98 p.

Tapponnier, P., 1977, Évolution tectonique du système alpin en Méditerranée: Poinçonnement et écrasement rigide-plastique: Bull. Soc. Geol. France, v. 7, p. 437–460.

Tapponnier, P., and Molnar, P., 1976, Slip-line field theory and large-scale continental tectonics: Nature, v. 264, p. 319–324.

Wilson, K. M., Hay, W. W., and Wold, C. N., 1991, Mesozoic evolution of exotic terranes and marginal seas, western North America: Marine Geol., v. 102, p. 311–361.

A Model for Evolution of Laramide Axial Basins in the Southern Rocky Mountains, U.S.A.

AN YIN AND RAYMOND V. INGERSOLL

Department of Earth and Space Sciences, University of California, Los Angeles, California 90095-1567

Abstract

The structural, stratigraphic, and sedimentologic development of Laramide axial basins of the southern Rocky Mountains is inconsistent with previous models relating them to transpressional tectonics. Axial basins are better explained as broad synclinal troughs in the hanging walls of large pop-up structures, in contrast to perimeter and ponded basins formed in the footwalls of these same structures. Laramide faults in the southern Rocky Mountains can be divided into the E-dipping Park Range thrust system and the W-dipping Sangre de Cristo thrust system. The W-dipping Front Range fault is the backthrust of the Park Range system, and the E-dipping Nacimiento fault is the back-thrust of the Sangre de Cristo system. The broad synclinal troughs formed between these two pairs of oppositely verging thrust systems were the locations for sediment deposition in axial basins, as exemplified by the Galisteo–El Rito basin of northern New Mexico. The Eocene Galisteo and El Rito formations were deposited on a broad syncline of Phanerozoic strata with crystalline basement along the basin margins. Most sediment was derived from the northeast, north, and northwest, except near the NE-trending Tijeras-Cañoncito transfer zone along the southeast margin of the basin. Uplift of the Sangre de Cristo Range occurred first, followed by backthrusting to uplift the Sierra Nacimiento. This model explains Laramide uplifts and basins as the direct response to rapid NE-SW convergence between the North American and Farallon plates, without multiple reorientation of Laramide stress fields, and without major strike-slip along the eastern side of the Colorado Plateau.

Introduction

AN IMPORTANT RECORD of the latest Cretaceous through Eocene Laramide orogeny in the southern Rocky Mountains (United States) is preserved in syntectonic sedimentary basins. Dickinson et al. (1988) classified Laramide basins into perimeter, ponded, and axial types (Fig. 1), based on their architecture and structural settings. The structural origins of the first two types, with their associated basin-vergent thrusts, are well understood; their development has been related to flexural loading of footwalls due to thrusting of hanging walls. On the other hand, the structural setting of axial basins is controversial. Although Dickinson et al. (1988) accepted the suggestion by Chapin and Cather (1981) that axial basins originated by transpressional tectonics, we find this model to be inconsistent with both structural and sedimentological characteristics. In this paper, we review these characteristics and propose a model that relates axial basins to the development of broad synclinal troughs in the hanging walls of large pop-up structures (Yin and Ingersoll, 1993).

Geologic Constraints

Structural geology

The key to understanding the origin of axial basins is the structural history of the Laramide faults that bound them. Documenting this history requires knowledge of the kinematics of the faults, a topic that has been controversial. Two end-member models have been proposed: (1) the N-trending faults along the east side of the Colorado Plateau reflect transpressional tectonics (Chapin and Cather, 1981); and (2) they are thrusts produced by NE-SW compression (i.e., Kelley, 1955; Sales, 1968). The first model is based primarily on the fact that the Uinta Mountains experienced N-S shortening during the Laramide orogeny (e.g., Gries, 1983), apparently requiring northward relative movement of the Colorado Plateau. This argument is potentially flawed, however, because it implicitly assumes that deformation on the northern and eastern sides of the Plateau was produced by the interaction of two rigid blocks: the North American craton and the Colorado Plateau. Considering the presence of complex

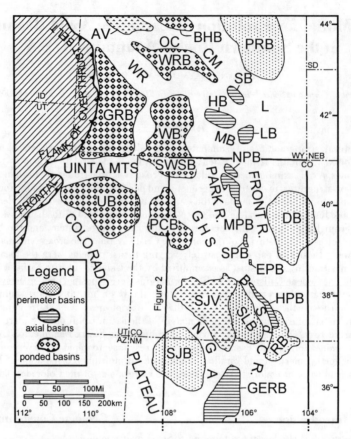

FIG. 1. Laramide basins, uplifts, and related features of southern Wyoming, Colorado, northern New Mexico, and surrounding regions (after Dickinson et al., 1988). Perimeter basins: PRB = Powder River; DB = Denver; RB = Raton; SJB = San Juan. Axial basins: SB = Shirley; HB = Hanna; LB = Laramie; NPB = North Park; MPB = Middle Park; SPB = South Park; EPB = Echo Park; HPB = Huerfano Park (although actually a continuation of the perimeter Raton basin; see text); GERB = Galisteo–El Rito. The axial Monte Vista basin underlies the Neogene San Luis basin (SLB). Ponded basins: BHB = Big Horn; WRB = Wind River; GRB = Green River; WB = Washakie; SWSB = Sand Wash sub-basin; UB = Uinta; PCB = Piceance Creek. Mid-Tertiary volcanic fields: AV = Absaroka; SJV = San Juan. Uplifts: OC = Owl Creek; WR = Wind River; CM = Casper Mountain; L = Laramie; MB = Medicine Bow; GHS = Grand Hogback–Sawatch; NGA = Nacimiento-Gallina-Archuleta; BSdCR = Brazos–Sangre de Cristo Range. Also shown are Park Range, Front Range, Colorado Plateau, and frontal flank of overthrust belt (primarily Cretaceous). Northern part of Figure 2 is outlined by heavy lines.

Laramide faults immediately north of the Plateau, Yin et al. (1992) suggested that E-W compression along the Park Range and Front Range, NE-SW compression along the Laramie and Medicine Bow Mountains, and N-S shortening across the Uinta Mountains could have resulted from the interaction of several blocks, based on the integration of slip vectors across individual Laramide faults. This interpretation is consistent with recent kinematic studies along the Cheyenne belt in the Laramie basin, where NE-striking strike-slip faults are linked with NW-striking thrusts (Stone, 1995), indicating that range-bounding faults are thrusts in the Laramie and Medicine Bow Mountains immediately to the east and south. Also, Paylor and Yin (1993) and Molzer and Erslev (1995) documented oblique convergence during NE-SW Laramide compression along the E-W Owl Creek and Casper Mountain arches in central Wyoming. Furthermore, Erslev et al. (1996) demonstrated that Laramide

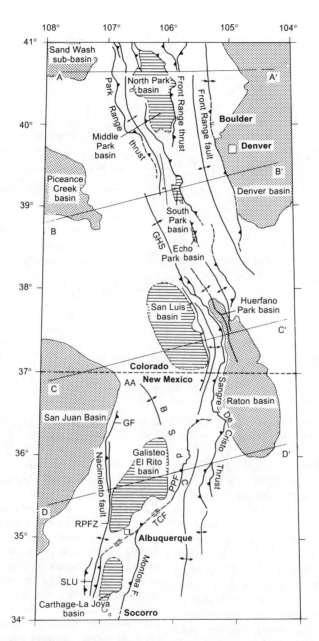

FIG. 2. Tectonic map (modified from Tweto, 1978, and Woodward et al., 1978) of the southern Rocky Mountains in Colorado and northern New Mexico, showing major thrusts and basins and locations of cross-sections (see Fig. 3). Abbreviations: GHS = Grand Hogback–Sawatch uplift; AA = Archuleta arch; GF = Gallina fault; BSdC = Brazos–Sangre de Cristo uplift; PPF = Picuris-Pecos fault; RPFZ = Rio Puerco fault zone; TCF = Tijeras-Cañoncito fault; SLU = Sierra-Ladron uplift. Only a few Neogene normal faults are shown.

faults in the Front Range, Wet Mountains, and Sangre de Cristo Range all experienced a single phase of N75°E-S75°W compression.

Based on this premise, regional compilation of geologic maps, and sedimentologic arguments, we divide the Laramide faults in the

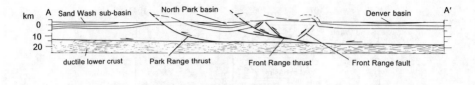

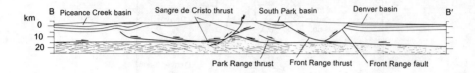

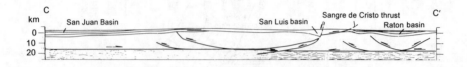

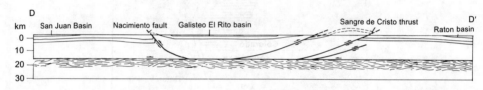

FIG. 3. Structural cross-sections showing positions of Laramide basins, thrusts, uplifts, and a few major Neogene normal faults. See Figure 2 for locations.

southern Rocky Mountains into two large thrust systems: the E-dipping Park Range thrust system to the north and the W-dipping Sangre de Cristo thrust system to the south (Figs. 2 and 3). The two fault systems north of the San Luis basin form an overlapping transfer zone. The Front Range fault (with its minor shortening) is the backthrust of the Park Range thrust. Similarly, the Nacimiento fault is the backthrust of the Sangre de Cristo thrust. Within this structural framework, the tectonic settings of the major Laramide basins are clear. The Sand Wash sub-basin and Piceance Creek basin are the foreland basins of the Park Range thrust, whereas the Raton basin is the foreland basin of the Sangre de Cristo thrust. The broad, shallow Denver and San Juan basins are located at broad asymmetric synclinal troughs in the footwalls of the backthrusts. The axial basins of Dickinson et al. (1988) are all located between the main thrusts and their backthrusts. It is this characteristic structural setting of the axial

basins that produces their unique stratigraphic and sedimentological characteristics, as discussed below.

Although this hypothesis needs to be tested, we assume that the major Laramide thrusts in the southern Rocky Mountains soled into a ductile shear zone in the middle crust. This assumption is based on the following postulates: (1) the inferred rheology for the continental lithosphere consists of a weak and plastic lower crust (e.g., Chen and Molnar, 1983); and (2) intracontinental deformation, both in extension and contraction, may be characterized by detachment zones at mid-crustal levels, as suggested by Burchfiel et al. (1989).

Structural setting of sedimentary basins

Chapin and Cather (1981) used the Echo Park basin (Fig. 1) as the type example for what Dickinson et al. (1988) later named axial basins of the central and southern Rocky Mountains. Utilizing limited (primarily subsurface) data regarding the Echo Park basin, Chapin and

Cather (1981) attempted to demonstrate that the basin primarily resulted from Laramide transpressional deformation. We find their arguments unconvincing in detail for the basin itself, as well as unconvincing by comparison to known transpressional basins (e.g., Ridge basin of southern California; Crowell, 1982). Application of criteria for the recognition of strike-slip-related basins (e.g., Reading, 1980; Christie-Blick and Biddle, 1985; Nilsen and Sylvester, 1995) to Echo Park–type basins results in clear negation of significant strike-slip as a basin-forming process. For example, *none* of the following characteristics has been demonstrated: discordance of paleogeography or stratal thickness, mismatch between source rocks and alluvial fans, significant unconformities of the same age as adjoining thick syntectonic strata, extreme lateral facies variations, simultaneous extensional and compressional tectonics, or major strike-slip offsets of Laramide age (i.e., Reading, 1980).

In addition, we find the characteristics of the Echo Park basin to be distinctly different from those of the Galisteo–El Rito (GER) and other axial basins (discussed below). The structural setting of the Echo Park basin is similar to that of the Huerfano Park basin; both the Echo Park and the Huerfano Park basins are more appropriately described as perimeter basins, northeast of the Sangre de Cristo thrust belt, although late-stage basement deformation renders their relations less clear than for the contiguous Raton perimeter basin. Laramide axial basins developed above hanging-wall blocks, in contrast to perimeter and ponded basins formed on footwall blocks (e.g., Dickinson et al., 1988).

Chapin and Cather (1981), Chapin (1983), Laughlin (1991), and Karlstrom and Daniel (1993) all proposed major (greater than 1 km) N-S right slip along the trend of the modern Rio Grande rift during Laramide time. In contrast, none of the criteria for recognition of major strike-slip deformation (e.g., Reading, 1980; Christie-Blick and Biddle, 1985; Nilsen and Sylvester, 1995) can be applied successfully to any of the Laramide axial basins; Chapin and Cather (1981) did not even apply these criteria to the Echo Park basin, their type "wrench" basin. Right-slip offset of 100 to 170 km along the Rio Grande trend has been proposed, based on offset Precambrian magnetic anomalies (Chapin, 1983) and basement features (Laugh-

lin, 1991; Karlstrom and Daniel, 1993). We do not contest the possible dextral offset of Precambrian features, but we do question whether significant offset occurred during Laramide deformation (also see Woodward et al., 1997). Some dextral offset may have occurred during the late Paleozoic Ancestral Rocky Mountain orogeny (Kluth, 1986), although no significant offsets of this age have been demonstrated; basin and provenance evolution during the late Paleozoic is more consistent with predominantly orthogonal compressional deformation (Miller et al., 1963; Soegaard and Caldwell, 1990; Devaney and Ingersoll, 1993). The only plausible age for significant dextral slip along N-trending faults in northern New Mexico (e.g., Picuris-Pecos fault) is Proterozoic (Miller et al., 1963). Woodward (1994) summarized evidence against significant Laramide dextral offset along the western side of the Nacimiento uplift.

The Laramide compressional direction is identified by the northeast trend of the Tijeras-Cañoncito (TC) fault zone between the Montosa and Sangre de Cristo frontal thrust zones (Fig. 2). Lisenbee et al. (1979) documented the anastomosing nature of this vertical fault zone, which in a complex manner connects the northwest boundary of the Carthage–La Joya basin with the southeast boundary of the GER basin. Of all exposed faults in northern New Mexico, the TC fault best satisfies criteria for recognition of strike-slip faults (e.g., Reading, 1980; Christie-Blick and Biddle, 1985; Nilsen and Sylvester, 1995). On the other hand, magnitude and timing of displacement along the TC fault zone are difficult to constrain; Lisenbee et al. (1979, p. 95) concluded that some motion occurred during the Precambrian and late Paleozoic, but that "post-Cretaceous movement is responsible for most of the structure."

The regional orientation of maximum compression during Laramide deformation in New Mexico was roughly parallel to the TC fault zone (NE or NNE). This interpretation is consistent with geometric characteristics of the Rio Puerco fault zone (Slack and Campbell, 1976), the NNE-striking Gallina fault at the north end of the Nacimiento uplift (Woodward et al., 1992), and the en-echelon NNW-trending folds of the southeastern San Juan Basin (Baltz, 1967). Furthermore, the NNE-striking right-slip faults of the Pecos fault zone (Kelley, 1971) and the NW- and WNW-trending Laramide uplifts of southern New Mexico (Seager and Mack, 1986) are consistent with this compression direction. Locations and orientations of many fault zones may have been determined by reactivation of late Paleozoic and Precambrian structures of diverse orientations, so that strain partitioning among faults was common (e.g., Varga, 1993).

Sedimentology

The best exposed and most studied of the Laramide axial basins is the Galisteo–El Rito (GER) basin of northern New Mexico (Figs. 1 and 2) (Stearns, 1943; Baltz, 1978; Gorham and Ingersoll, 1979; Logsdon, 1981; Ingersoll et al., 1990; Cather, 1992; Abbott et al., 1995). The GER basin is bounded on the northeast by the Brazos–Sangre de Cristo (BSdC) uplift, on the northwest by the Nacimiento-Gallina-Archuleta (NGA) uplift, on the southwest by the Rio Puerco fault zone and the Lucero uplift, and on the southeast by the TC fault zone (Fig. 2).

Key sedimentologic observations regarding the El Rito and Galisteo formations include the following (Gorham and Ingersoll, 1979; Logsdon, 1981):

1. All facies are alluvial or fluvial, with subordinate floodplain and lacustrine(?) deposits.
2. Paleocurrents are strongly southward, with general centripetal patterns along basin borders. Lower Galisteo strata were derived from the northeast (BSdC source), whereas the remainder of the Galisteo had multiple sources, including the NGA uplift.
3. Conglomerate and sandstone provenance consisted of Precambrian crystalline basement and Carboniferous through Cretaceous sedimentary strata; volcanic and volcaniclastic components are absent.
4. Strata rest disconformably on Cretaceous strata near the deepest part of the basin, with angular unconformity on Permian through Cretaceous strata along the northwestern basin margin, and nonconformably on Precambrian basement along the southwestern edge of the BSdC uplift (Baltz, 1978; Kelley, 1978; Gorham and Ingersoll, 1979; Logsdon, 1981). Thus, the GER basin was deposited above a broad syncline of Phanerozoic strata, with crystalline basement along the basin margins.

5. Strata thin to the northwest, north, and northeast; the thickest measured section is 1295 m of primarily fluvial/alluvial strata in the southern Hagan basin, adjacent to the TC fault zone (Gorham and Ingersoll, 1979).

Cather (1992, Fig. 7) summarized surface and subsurface data on stratal thickness of the Galisteo and El Rito formations, and provided paleogeographic and paleotectonic reconstructions. Our structural interpretation and reconstruction contrast markedly (compare his Figs. 9 and 10 to our Figs. 2 and 3). Because our model is based primarily on characteristics of the GER basin, we present a detailed discussion of how our interpretation differs from that of Cather (1992, p. 109), keyed to the four "modifications to the Tertiary history of north-central New Mexico" he proposed.

1. We see no compelling evidence for reverse faulting along the Pajarito fault zone (presently a normal fault along the east side of the Jemez volcanic field, which covers the west-central GER basin). Cather's primary evidence for a "Pajarito uplift" is the presence of basement clasts up to 50 cm in diameter, even though paleocurrents for this unit run southward, parallel to his hypothesized uplift. In contradiction to Cather's hypothesis is the presence of "maximum diameters of 3 feet" (about 90 cm) for clasts in the Hagan basin (Stearns, 1943, p. 307), which Cather's paleogeographic map (and ours) puts ~30 km downstream from Cather's study area. Characteristics of the Galisteo Formation at St. Peter's Dome (near the Pajarito fault) are similar to those of the El Rito Formation formed along the western side of the Brazos–Sangre de Cristo uplift, as described by Logsdon (1981); no "Pajarito uplift" is needed. The nonvolcaniclastic strata at Arroyo Hondo, similarly, can be interpreted as typical El Rito–Galisteo alluvial deposits preserved along the western edge of the BSdC uplift.

2. We know of no evidence that the TC fault zone was a releasing bend. In fact, Cather's Figure 9 shows "late Laramide sigma1" parallel to the TC fault, an interpretation consistent with our model. We interpret the TC fault zone as a transfer zone between the slightly transpressional Montosa fault and the highly compressional frontal thrusts of the Sangre de Cristo uplift (Fig. 2). As such, the TC fault zone may have been either transpressional or trans-

tensional, or possibly both (see Lisenbee et al., 1979).

3. We consider the "development of a flexural hinge" and the presence of the "Santa Ana accommodation zone" (north of Albuquerque and TCF in Fig. 2) as speculation with no supporting data. Southeastward thickening of the El Rito and Galisteo formations is irregular, with no clear break; in fact, Cather (1992) showed thicker Galisteo north of the "Santa Ana accommodation zone" at St. Peter's Dome than south of it, even though his primary criterion for locating it is the abrupt southward thickening of the Galisteo.

4. Because we see no evidence for the Pajarito uplift, we also see no evidence for its subsequent collapse. Normal movement on the Pajarito fault is demonstrably post-Bandelier Tuff (Pleistocene) (Smith et al., 1970). Evidence for Miocene movement is lacking; westward thickening of the Oligo-Miocene Abiquiu Formation within the Española basin probably results from the filling of residual Eocene (Laramide) topography (see Fig. 3 in Ingersoll et al., 1990). Greater normal displacement can be demonstrated along the eastern side of the Nacimiento uplift, which was the western boundary of the Española half-graben during the Miocene (Cavazza, 1989; Ingersoll et al., 1990; Ingersoll and Yin, 1993; Large and Ingersoll, 1997).

Other Laramide basins

In Colorado, the Piceance Creek basin formed in the foreland southwest of the Grand Hogback–Sawatch uplift (Fig. 1); the Denver basin formed in the foreland northeast of the Front Range uplift (see Chapin and Cather, 1981; Dickinson et al., 1988 for regional syntheses and additional references). We suggest that southwestward overthrusting occurred first along the Grand Hogback–Sawatch trend, followed by northeastward compression along the Front Range. If a broad axial basin analogous to the GER basin formed in central Colorado, then little evidence for this remains. We speculate that strata in the North, Middle, and South Park basins once were part of a broad synclinal basin (Hall, 1965), which subsequently experienced latest Laramide deformation and Neogene erosion. In contrast to the uniformly high elevations of northern and central Colorado, the Neogene Rio Grande rift of

southern Colorado to central New Mexico has formed along the trend of the Laramide axial basins, thus downdropping Laramide-age strata and preserving them beneath and along the margins of the rift basins.

In northern New Mexico and southern Colorado, structural events occurred in mirror image to those of northern and central Colorado. Northeastward overthrusting of the Sangre de Cristo Range formed the Raton foreland basin (Baltz, 1965), followed by southwestward compression of the NGA to form the San Juan Basin. Deposition of the Blanco basin and San Jose formations in the San Juan Basin occurred, in part, contemporaneously with deposition of the El Rito and Galisteo formations (Baltz, 1967; Smith et al., 1985; Brister, 1992; Smith, 1992; Brister and Chapin, 1994). San Jose fluvial systems transported detritus southward in the foreland west of the NGA uplift (Smith, 1992).

The Eocene Monte Vista basin underlies the Neogene San Luis basin in southern Colorado (Brister and Chapin, 1994; Brister and Gries, 1994). Little is known about this basin because it underlies Neogene rift strata (Santa Fe Group). Seismic and well studies (Brister and Gries, 1994) suggest that the "Blanco Basin formation" is similar in character to the Blanco Basin Formation along the northeastern side of the San Juan Basin. However, Late Eocene uplift of the Archuleta arch seems to have separated the two areas of deposition. Seismic line 1 of Brister and Gries (1994) clearly shows the "Blanco Basin formation" pinching out eastward against Precambrian basement of the Sangre de Cristo uplift. Thus, the overall setting of the Monte Vista basin is similar to that of the GER basin. Timing of uplift (early in the northeastern BSdC, later in the southwest Archuleta arch) also is similar to timing of development of the GER basin.

The tectonic setting of the Carthage–La Joya basin (south of the GER basin) (Fig. 2) was analogous to that of the GER basin, although the Carthage–La Joya basin was smaller and is less well exposed. The Carthage–La Joya is bordered on the east by the E-vergent Montosa uplift and on the west by the doubly vergent Sierra-Ladron uplift (Cabezas, 1991), from which the basin received sediment (Cather and Johnson, 1984). The TC fault zone separated

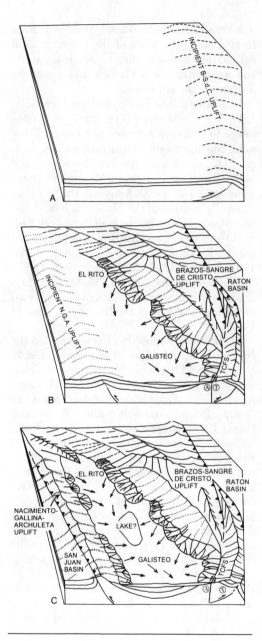

FIG. 4. Block diagrams showing structural and sedimentological evolution of northern New Mexico and southern Colorado during the Laramide orogeny, view to north (after Ingersoll et al., 1990). A. Initiation of movement along Sangre de Cristo thrust system (latest Cretaceous). B. Brazos–Sangre de Cristo uplift forms during thrusting, and provides sediment to the perimeter Raton basin and axial Galisteo–El Rito basin. Nacimiento-Gallina-Archuleta uplift begins to shed sediment into Galisteo–El Rito and San Juan basins as backthrusting begins (Paleocene–early Eocene). C. Galisteo–El Rito basin receives sediment from all directions in intermontane setting as thrusting and backthrusting continue. Raton and San Juan basins subside rapidly as a result of flexural loading as their margins deform (middle to late Eocene).

ment of the GER basin and its bounding uplifts. NE-SW compression was first expressed by basement-involved NE-vergent thrusting of the BSdC block, causing flexural subsidence of the Raton basin. Sediment derived from the BSdC uplift accumulated in the Raton basin most rapidly during the Paleocene (see Figs. 3 and 4 of Dickinson et al., 1988 for summary stratigraphic columns). High-angle, SW-vergent thrusting (possibly with a small transpressional component) began along the western side of the NGA uplift, resulting in subsidence of the San Juan foreland basin, which experienced maximum sedimentation rate in the early Eocene. The TC fault also was active as a dextral transfer zone. Sediment began accumulating as the Galisteo Formation in the deepest part of the synclinal trough as drainages adjusted to the changing topography; lower Eocene sediment came primarily from the BSdC uplift (Gorham and Ingersoll, 1979). Middle to upper Eocene sediment (El Rito and Galisteo formations) was derived from all directions, but primarily from the BSdC and NGA uplifts (Gorham and Ingersoll, 1979; Logsdon, 1981). Laramide compression, erosion, and sedimentation were terminated abruptly at the Eocene–Oligocene boundary as regional calc-alkaline volcanism exploded onto the landscape (Ingersoll et al., 1990).

Laramide axial basins of New Mexico and Colorado formed late during the Laramide orogeny (primarily Eocene) because finite compressional deformation over several million years was required to cause significant uplift in order to trap derived sediment within hanging-wall synclines. Sedimentation ceased soon after compressional deformation ended.

the deep GER basin to the northwest from the shallow Carthage–La Joya basin to the southeast (see Fig. 12 of Russell and Snelson, 1994).

The Model

Figure 4 integrates structural, stratigraphic, and sedimentologic constraints for develop-

Implications and Conclusions

Our model explains Laramide uplifts and basins as the direct response to rapid NE-SW convergence between the North American and Farallon plates (e.g., at 50 Ma of Fig. 8 of Engebretson et al., 1985; also see Coney, 1976; Bird, 1988; Brown, 1988). All observed structures and basins can be explained by this model without the need for multiple stages of Laramide stress orientations (e.g., Chapin and Cather, 1981; Gries, 1983).

The best modern analog for the Laramide orogeny is found in that part of the Andean orogenic system experiencing flat-slab subduction (Dickinson and Snyder, 1978; Jordan et al., 1983). In this setting, the Sierras Pampeanas and surrounding basement-cored uplifts in the Andean retroarc foreland are analogous to the Laramide uplifts. Compressional features are approximately perpendicular to the direction of modern plate convergence (Jordan and Allmendinger, 1986).

A more speculative modern analog for a similar structural setting to the Laramide orogen of the southern Rocky Mountains may be the Tian Shan in central Asia (e.g., Tapponnier and Molnar, 1979; Avouac et al., 1993). In the Tian Shan, two oppositely dipping thrust systems have formed large basement uplifts. Between the two thrust systems are numerous intermontane basins. Although the detailed structural setting is yet to be ascertained and the overall tectonic setting differs, we speculate that the general structural setting of these basins may be similar to that of Laramide axial basins described herein. Other modern and ancient analogs undoubtedly will be found after further research.

Acknowledgments

This work was partially supported by NSF grant EAR-89-04321, awarded to Yin. Ingersoll thanks the Committee on Research of the Academic Senate of the Los Angeles Division of the University of California. We thank G. J. Axen, W. G. Brown, W. R. Dickinson, and T. E. Jordan for reviewing the manuscript, and for many helpful suggestions.

REFERENCES

Abbott, J. C., Cather, S. M., and Goodwin, L. B., 1995, Paleogene synorogenic sedimentation in the Galisteo basin related to the Tijeras-Cañoncito fault system: New Mex. Geol. Soc. Guidebook 46, p. 271–278.

Avouac, J. P., Tapponnier, P., Bai, M., You, H., and Wang, G., 1993, Active thrusting and folding along the northern Tien Shan and late Cenozoic rotation of the Tarim relative to Dzungaria and Kazakhstan: Jour. Geophys. Res., v. 98, p. 6755–6804.

Baltz, E. H., 1965, Stratigraphy and history of Raton basin and notes on San Luis basin, Colorado–New Mexico: Amer. Assoc. Petrol. Geol. Bull., v. 49, p. 2041–2075.

————, 1967, Stratigraphy and regional tectonic implications of part of Upper Cretaceous and Tertiary rocks, east-central San Juan Basin, New Mexico: U.S. Geol. Surv. Prof. Pap. 552, 101 p.

————, 1978, Resume of Rio Grande depression in north-central New Mexico: New Mex. Bur. Mines Min. Resources Circular 163, p. 210–228.

Bird, P., 1988, Formation of the Rocky Mountains, western United States: A continuum computer model: Science, v. 239, p. 1501–1507.

Brister, B. S., 1992, The Blanco Basin Formation (Eocene), San Juan Mountains region, Colorado and New Mexico: New Mex. Geol. Soc. Guidebook 43, p. 321–331.

Brister, B. S., and Chapin, C. E., 1994, Sedimentation and tectonics of the Laramide San Juan sag, southwestern Colorado: The Mountain Geologist, v. 31, p. 2–18.

Brister, B. S., and Gries, R. R., 1994, Tertiary stratigraphy and tectonic development of the Alamosa basin (northern San Luis basin), Rio Grande rift, south-central Colorado: Geol. Soc. Amer. Spec. Pap. 291, p. 39–58.

Brown, W. G., 1988, Deformational style of Laramide uplifts in the Wyoming foreland: Geol. Soc. Amer. Mem. 171, p. 1–25.

Burchfiel, B. C., Deng, Q., Molnar, P., Royden, L., Wang, Y., Zhang, P., and Zhang, W., 1989, Intracrustal detachment within zones of continental deformation: Geology, v. 17, p. 448–452.

Cabezas, P., 1991, The southern Rocky Mountains in west-central New Mexico—Laramide structures and their impact on the Rio Grande rift extension: New Mex. Geol., v. 13, p. 25–37.

Cather, S. M., 1992, Suggested revisions to the Tertiary tectonic history of north-central New Mexico: New Mex. Geol. Soc. Guidebook 43, p. 109–122.

Cather, S. M., and Johnson, B. D., 1984, Eocene tectonics and depositional setting of west-central New

Mexico and eastern Arizona: New Mex. Bur. Mines Min. Resources Circular 192, 33 p.

Cavazza, W., 1989, Sedimentation pattern of a rift-filling unit, Tesuque Formation (Miocene), Española basin, Rio Grande rift, New Mexico: Jour. Sediment. Petrol., v. 59, p. 287–296.

Chapin, C. E., 1983, An overview of Laramide wrench faulting in the southern Rocky Mountains with emphasis on petroleum exploration, in Lowell, J. D., ed., Rocky Mountain foreland basins and uplifts: Denver, Rocky Mountain Assoc. Geol., p. 169–179.

Chapin, C. E., and Cather, S. M., 1981, Eocene tectonics and sedimentation in the Colorado Plateau–Rocky Mountain area: Ariz. Geol. Soc. Digest, v. 14, p. 173–198.

Chen, W.-P., and Molnar, P., 1983, Focal depths of intracontinental and intraplate earthquakes and their implications for the thermal and mechanical properties of the lithosphere: Jour. Geophys. Res., v. 88, p. 1180–1196.

Christie-Blick, N., and Biddle, K. T., 1985, Deformation and basin formation along strike-slip faults: Soc. Econ. Paleontol. Mineral. Spec. Publ. 37, p. 1–34.

Coney, P. J., 1976, Plate tectonics and the Laramide orogeny: New Mex. Geol. Soc. Spec. Publ. 6, p. 5–10.

Crowell, J. C., 1982, The tectonics of Ridge basin, southern California, in Crowell, J. C., and Link, M. H., eds., Geologic history of Ridge basin, southern California: Los Angeles, Pacific Sect., Soc. Econ. Paleontol. Mineral., p. 25–42.

Devaney, K. A., and Ingersoll, R. V., 1993, Provenance evolution of upper Paleozoic sandstones of north-central New Mexico: Geol. Soc. Amer. Spec. Pap. 284, p. 91–108.

Dickinson, W. R., and Snyder, W. S., 1978, Plate tectonics of the Laramide orogeny: Geol. Soc. Amer. Mem. 151, p. 355–366.

Dickinson, W. R., Klute, M. A., Hayes, M. J., Janecke, S. U., Lundin, E. R., McKittrick, M. A., and Olivares, M. D., 1988, Paleogeographic and paleotectonic setting of Laramide sedimentary basins in the central Rocky Mountain region: Geol. Soc. Amer. Bull., v. 100, p. 1023–1039.

Engebretson, D. C., Cox, A., and Gordon, R. G., 1985, Relative motions between oceanic and continental plates in the Pacific basin: Geol. Soc. Amer. Spec. Pap. 206, 59 p.

Erslev, E. A., Jurista, B., and Selvig, B. W., 1996, Thrust kinematics of the Laramide front in Colorado [abs.]: Geol. Soc. Amer. Abs. Prog., v. 28, no. 7, p. A-112.

Gorham, T. W., and Ingersoll, R. V., 1979, Evolution of the Eocene Galisteo basin, north-central New Mexico: New Mex. Geol. Soc. Guidebook 30, p. 219–224.

Gries, R., 1983, North-south compression of Rocky Mountain foreland structures, in Lowell, J. D., and

Gries, R., eds., Rocky Mountain foreland basins and uplifts: Denver, Rocky Mountain Assoc. Geol., p. 9–32.

Hall, W. J., Jr., 1965, Geology of northwestern North Park, Colorado: U.S. Geol. Surv. Bull. 1188, 133 p.

Ingersoll, R. V., and Yin, A., 1993, Two-stage evolution of the Rio Grande rift, northern New Mexico and southern Colorado [abs.]: Geol. Soc. Amer. Abs. Prog., v. 25, no. 6, p. A-409.

Ingersoll, R. V., Cavazza, W., Baldridge, W. S., and Shafiqullah, M., 1990, Cenozoic sedimentation and paleotectonics of north-central New Mexico: Implications for initiation and evolution of the Rio Grande rift: Geol. Soc. Amer. Bull., v. 102, p. 1280–1296.

Jordan, T. E., and Allmendinger, R. W., 1986, The Sierras Pampeanas of Argentina: A modern analogue of Rocky Mountain foreland deformation: Amer. Jour. Sci., v. 286, p. 737–764.

Jordan, T. E., Isacks, B. L., Allmendinger, R. W., Brewer, J. A., Ramos, V. A., and Ando, C. J., 1983, Andean tectonics related to geometry of subducted Nazca plate: Geol. Soc. Amer. Bull., v. 94, p. 341–361.

Karlstrom, K. E., and Daniel, C. G., 1993, Restoration of Laramide right-lateral strike slip in northern New Mexico by using Proterozoic piercing points: Tectonic implications from the Proterozoic to the Cenozoic: Geology, v. 21, p. 1139–1142.

Kelley, V. C., 1955, Regional tectonics of the Colorado Plateau and relationship to the origin and distribution of uranium: Univ. New Mex. Publ. Geol. 5, 120 p.

———, 1971, Geology of the Pecos country, southeastern New Mexico: New Mex. Bur. Mines Min. Resources Memoir 24, 78 p.

———, 1978, Geology of Española basin, New Mexico: New Mex. Bur. Mines Miner. Resources Geol. Map 48, 1:125,000.

Kluth, C. F., 1986, Plate tectonics of the Ancestral Rocky Mountains: Amer. Assoc. Petrol. Geol. Memoir 41, p. 353–369.

Large, E., and Ingersoll, R. V., 1997, Miocene and Pliocene sandstone petrofacies of the northern Albuquerque basin, New Mexico, and implications for evolution of the Rio Grande rift: Jour. Sediment. Res., v. 67, p. 462–468.

Laughlin, A. W., 1991, Fenton Hill granodiorite—an 80 km (50 mi) right-lateral offset of the Sandia pluton?: New Mex. Geol., v. 13, p. 55–59.

Lisenbee, A. L., Woodward, L. A., and Connolly, J. R., 1979, Tijeras-Cañoncito fault system—a major zone of recurrent movement in north-central New Mexico: New Mex. Geol. Soc. Guidebook 30: p. 89–99.

Logsdon, M. J., 1981, A preliminary basin analysis of the El Rito Formation (Eocene), north-central New

Mexico: Geol. Soc. Amer. Bull., v. 92, Part I, p. 968–975, Part II, p. 2308–2317.

Miller, J. P., Montgomery, A., and Sutherland, P. K., 1963, Geology of part of the southern Sangre de Cristo Mountains, New Mexico: New Mex. Bur. Mines Min. Resources Memoir 11, 106 p.

Molzer, P. C., and Erslev, E. A., 1995, Oblique convergence during northeast-southwest Laramide compression along the east-west Owl Creek and Casper Mountain arches, central Wyoming: Amer. Assoc. Petrol. Geol. Bull., v. 79, p. 1377–1394.

Nilsen, T. H., and Sylvester, A. G., 1995, Strike-slip basins, *in* Busby, C. J., and Ingersoll, R. V., eds., Tectonics of sedimentary basins: Cambridge, MA, Blackwell Sci., p. 425–457.

Paylor, E. D., II, and Yin, A., 1993, Left-slip evolution of the North Owl Creek fault system, Wyoming, during Laramide shortening: Geol. Soc. Amer. Spec. Pap. 280, p. 229–242.

Reading, H. G., 1980, Characteristics and recognition of strike-slip fault systems: Int. Assoc. Sedimentol. Spec. Publ. 4, p. 7–26.

Russell, L. R., and Snelson, S., 1994, Structure and tectonics of the Albuquerque basin segment of the Rio Grande rift: Insights from reflection seismic data: Geol. Soc. Amer. Spec. Pap. 291, p. 83–112.

Sales, J. K., 1968, Crustal mechanics of Cordilleran foreland deformation: A regional and scale-model approach: Amer. Assoc. Petrol. Geol. Bull., v. 52, p. 2016–2044.

Seager, W. R., and Mack, G. H., 1986, Laramide paleotectonics of southern New Mexico: Amer. Assoc. Petrol. Geol. Memoir 41, p. 669–685.

Slack, P. B., and Campbell, J. A., 1976, Structural geology of the Rio Puerco fault zone and its relationship to central New Mexico tectonics: New Mex. Geol. Soc. Spec. Publ. 6, p. 46–52.

Smith, L. N., 1992, Stratigraphy, sediment dispersal and paleogeography of the Lower Eocene San Jose Formation, San Juan Basin, New Mexico and Colorado: New Mex. Geol. Soc. Guidebook 43, p. 297–309.

Smith, L. N., Lucas, S. G., and Elston, W. E., 1985, Paleogene stratigraphy, sedimentation and volcanism of New Mexico, *in* Flores, R.M., and Kaplan, S.S., eds., Cenozoic paleogeography of the west-central United States: Denver, Rocky Mountain Section, Soc. Econ. Paleontol. Mineral., Rocky Mountain Paleogeog. Symp. 3, p. 293–315.

Smith, R. L., Bailey, R. A., and Ross, C. S., 1970, Geologic map of the Jemez Mountains, New Mexico: U.S. Geol. Surv. Misc. Invest. Series Map I-571, 1:125,000.

Soegaard, K., and Caldwell, K. R., 1990, Depositional history and tectonic significance of alluvial sedimentation in the Permo-Pennsylvanian Sangre de Cristo Formation, Taos trough, New Mexico: New Mex. Geol. Soc. Guidebook 41, p. 277–289.

Stearns, C. E., 1943, The Galisteo Formation of north-central New Mexico: Jour. Geol., v. 51, p. 301–319.

Stone, D. S., 1995, Structure and kinematic genesis of the Calla wrench duplex: Transpressional reactivation of the Precambrian Cheyenne belt in the Laramie basin, Wyoming: Amer. Assoc. Petrol. Geol. Bull., v. 79, p. 1349–1376.

Tapponnier, P., and Molnar, P., 1979, Active faulting and Cenozoic tectonics of the Tien Shan, Mongolia and Baykal regions: Jour. Geophys. Res., v. 84, p. 3425–3459.

Tweto, O., 1978, Tectonic map of the Rio Grande rift system in Colorado: New Mex. Bur. Mines Min. Resources Circular 163, Sheet 1, 1:1,000,000.

Varga, R. J., 1993, Rocky Mountain foreland uplifts: Products of a rotating stress field or strain partitioning?: Geology, v. 21, p. 1115–1118.

Woodward, L. A., 1994, Restoration of Laramide right-lateral strike slip in northern New Mexico by using Proterozoic piercing points: Tectonic implications from the Proterozoic to the Cenozoic: Comment: Geology, v. 22, p. 862–863.

Woodward, L. A., Anderson, O. J., and Lucas, S. G., 1997, Mesozoic stratigraphic constraints on Laramide right slip on the east side of the Colorado Plateau: Geology, v. 25, p. 843–846.

Woodward, L. A., Callender, J. F., Seager, W. R., Chapin, C. E., Gries, J. C., Shaffer, W. L., and Zilinski, R. E., 1978, Tectonic map of Rio Grande rift region in New Mexico, Chihuahua, and Texas: New Mex. Bur. Mines Min. Resources Circular 163, Sheet 2, 1:1,000,000.

Woodward, L. A., Hultgren, M. C., Crouse, D. L., and Merrick, M. A., 1992, Geometry of Nacimiento-Gallina fault system, northern New Mexico: New Mex. Geol. Soc. Guidebook 43, p. 103–108.

Yin, A., and Ingersoll, R. V., 1993, Tectonic development of Laramide thrusts and basins in southern U.S. Rocky Mountains [abs.]: Geol. Soc. Amer. Abs. Prog., v. 25, no. 5, p. 167.

Yin, A., Paylor, E. D., II, and Norris, A., 1992, Analysis of Laramide crustal strain distribution using relative-slip circuits [abs.]: Geol. Soc. Amer. Abs. Prog., v. 24, no. 6, p. 69.

Paleoelevation Estimated from Tertiary Floras

Daniel I. Axelrod

Section of Ecology and Evolution, University of California, Davis, California 95616

Abstract

One method of estimating the elevation of Tertiary flora involves the difference in elevation indicated by a flora in the uplands that is similar to vegetation in the lowlands, shown by examples from Tibet-Himalayas and the Andes. A second method relies on the difference in estimated paleotemperature between a paleoflora now in the uplands and that of similar vegetation in the lowlands, assuming a normal lapse rate in most cases. The former method provides only a general indication of the amount of uplift. The latter can suggest not only the amount of uplift, but the decrease in length of the growing season (Warmth: days), the frequency of freezing (% hrs/yr), and the degree of temperateness as illustrated by examples from the Sierra Nevada. The latter method also suggests that in the Sierra Nevada, the *condition* for treeline (W 10°C, 0 days warmer) increased 100 m in 10 m.y. between two superposed floras. Following 7 to 5 Ma, the range added 637 m to reach its present level of 2775 m. Regionally, Miocene floras from the central Great Basin represent deciduous hardwood forests that indicate only moderate elevation over the lowlands into the late Tertiary (~5 Ma), following which much of the present relief developed. Eocene floras from the Rocky Mountains, where major volcanism was widespread, show that forests above lowland broadleafed evergreen forests (i.e., Wasatch, Kisinger, etc. floras) were zoned with respect to decreasing Warmth at higher elevation, from W 15°C (227 days) to W 11.3°C (96 days), and from nearly frostless in the Eocene lowlands to fully 15% hrs/yr subfreezing in the uplands at treeline (W 10°C, 0 days), then at 2365 m (6600 ft.).

Comparison with Modern Vegetation

Tibet-Himalayas

Now near 4000 m on the treeless Tibetan Plateau west of Lhasa, the *Miocene Namling flora* is a deciduous hardwood forest with species of *Betula, Carpinus, Populus, Ribes,* and *Ulmus* (Li and Guo, 1976). In the upper beds are small-leafed oaks (three species) as well as some evergreens with moderate-sized leaves, such as *Rhododendron, Thermopsis,* and others. Judging from the principal flora, as well as that in the upper horizon, a position near the upper margin of deciduous forest is indicated. This suggests that elevation probably was near 1500 m, implying that elevation has increased on the order of 2500 m since the Miocene (Li and Guo, 1976).

An *Eocene flora* from the lower Moincer Group in Gar, westernmost Tibet, is dominated by broadleafed evergreen trees (Guo, 1981). Among the taxa are species of *Myrica, Ficus, Eucalyptus, Eugenia, Cassia,* and *Rhamnus,* with species of *Eucalyptus* dominant. The fossil leaves are large, have entire margins, and are similar to plants now in coastal southeast China.

This suggests that the Gar area was a lowland, probably not more than 300 m in elevation. Since the flora now is at 5100 m, the area has been elevated nearly 5000 m.

The *lower Karewa flora* from Kashmir, of early Pleistocene age, occurs at Liddarmarg, on the northern slope of the Pir Pinjal Range at 4000 m. It includes oaks, laurels, figs, maple, mallotus, pittosporum, rhamnus, and a few water plants, such as *Trapa,* as well as conifers, notably pine and spruce. Most of the allied modern species now occur at levels of 2700 to 3000 m. However, the water plant *Trapa* does not live above 2300 m because it is too cold at that level today. This suggests that the Pir Pinjal Range was elevated about 600 m in the late Quaternary.

A *Pliocene flora* now occurs *above* timberline on the northern slope of Mt. Shisha–Pangma in the central Himalayas at 5800 m. The flora includes three small-leafed species of oak as well as pollen of *Quercus, Cedrus, Picea, Pinus,* and *Tsuga.* Plants allied to those in the flora do not occur above 3000 m today. This suggests that the flora has been elevated by roughly 2500 to 3000 m since the late Pliocene (Hsu et al., 1973).

Remains of a *Hipparion fauna* occur in the Bulong Basin, Xizang (e.g., Wu and Yu, 1980; Zeng, 1980). Because *Hipparion* also is in the Siwalik beds at the southern base of the Himalayas, *Hipparion* must have crossed the present site of the range to Tibet before it was elevated to a major degree. At a maximum, it probably was at no more than 2500 to 3000 m elevation, as judged from pollen flora in beds overlying the *Hipparion* fauna. The flora, with species of *Picea, Cedrus, Quercus, Juglans, Ulmus,* a palm, *Castanea, Celtis,* and *Acer,* represents a cool temperate climate. The Bulong region, now at about 4500 m, suggests uplift on the order of 2000 m since the late Miocene.

The Andes

Floristic information provided by Tertiary floras, mostly described by Berry (see refs. in 1930)—and which need recollecting and revision as well as radiometric dating where possible—indicates the nature of topographic change during the Tertiary and later periods.

Loja, Ecuador (Berry, 1929). A large, wet, tropical lowland flora is now at 2100 m in a temperate climate. It is allied to taxa in the Amazonian forests. Miocene in age, it indicates uplift of fully 1500 m.

Potosi, Bolivia (Berry, 1917, 1938). A rich Miocene flora occurs on the high altiplano at 4100 m at Potosi, Bolivia. Its very small leaves and leaflets appear to be similar to those produced by thorn scrub vegetation. Similar vegetation now occurs at elevations of up to 1000 m, suggesting about 3000 m uplift since the late Tertiary. Because arid or drier areas appeared at this general latitude only in the late Miocene–Pliocene (Menendez, 1971), uplift of the Andes of ~3000 m, therefore, is a very recent event.

Zorritos, Peru (Berry, 1919). A rich fossil flora occurs in the semi-desert of coastal Peru at 20° S Lat., within 100 m of the ocean. Associated marine invertebrate megafossils are middle Miocene in age. The fossil flora, with lianas, feather palm, and mesic hardwoods with large leaves, represents a tropical rainforest. This suggests that the Ecuadorian and Peruvian Andes have not yet interposed their mass into the path of moisture-bearing winds from the east that supported the forest. Obviously, the present coastal semi-desert and desert to the north were not then in existence, and the Andes were elevated to a considerable degree only well after the middle Miocene.

Pisillypampa, Bolivia (Berry, 1922b). This Pliocene flora from the Sierra Cochabamba at 3600 m has leaves representing wet tropical forests like those now in the *yungas* of Bolivia below 1000 m in elevation. Uplift of fully 2600 m is indicated.

Concepción-Araco, Chile (Berry, 1922a). This rich, late Oligocene flora of warm temperate aspect is allied to wet forests in the *montana* zone of eastern Peru and northern Bolivia. Living near sea level, it has many species in common with the Rio Pichilefu flora, Argentina (Berry, 1938). This indicates that the intervening Andean range, which now produces an orographic rainshadow, had not yet been elevated.

It seems evident that the present Andes are quite young. They commenced developing during the later Miocene, the Pliocene, and throughout the Pleistocene. Together with the withdrawal of shallow seas in Chile and Argentina, and the development of cold water originating in Antarctica, the change to colder, drier climates resulted in the restriction of older, more mesic vegetation and the rise of modern communities. The late uplift of the Andes probably was contemporaneous with development of the Chilean-Peruvian trench, the rise of massive composite volcanos along the Andean axis, and the accompanying break-up of the upland plateaus, as suggested by Berry (1938). Certainly, there is no evidence to support the notion that the present relief in the Andes, western North America, or southern Asia has considerable antiquity (Taylor, 1991).

Paleotemperature Estimates of Elevation

Because the occurrence of Tertiary floras suggests impressive rates of uplift, it is pertinent to measure the amount of uplift on the basis of paleotemperature. A tested method of determining paleotemperature involves estimating the Warmth (W) of climate in which a fossil flora lived. Warmth measures the length (days) of the growing season, as illustrated by the radiating lines in Figure 1. Warmth is determined from *both* mean annual temperature (T)

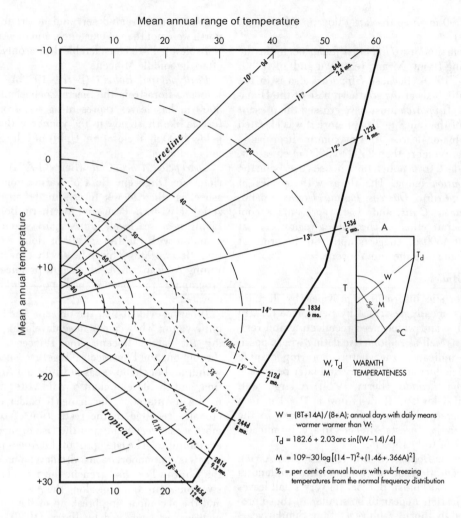

FIG. 1. Nomogram showing Warmth (W) and Temperateness (M) of climate (Bailey, 1960, 1964). Radiating lines represent Warmth (days, d, months, m), arcs are a measure of temperateness (M = moderation), descending lines indicate percentage of hours per year (% hrs/year) with subfreezing temperatures.

and mean annual range of temperature (A = amplitude). A Warmth of W 18°C indicates that all 365 days per year have a mean temperature of at least 18°C. This marks the boundary of a full tropical climate. The vegetation boundary of W 10°C indicates that 0 days have a mean temperature greater than 10°C. This corresponds to the treeline and is the edge of a true polar climate. Other Warmth lines are indicated in Figure 1.

Because Tertiary floras have counterparts in modern vegetation zones, the difference in Warmth (W) between a fossil flora and allied modern vegetation provides an indication of

how much the fossil-bearing rocks have been elevated (Axelrod and Ting, 1960; Axelrod, 1962, 1965, 1981, 1991, 1995; Greller, 1989; Greller and Balasurbamaniam, 1988). Because a well-sampled flora will indicate its position (lower, middle, upper) in a W zone, its elevation can be estimated by the difference in W (°C) between its present upland level and that at which it grew.

The Sierra Nevada

The Mt. Reba flora occurs just below treeline at 2620 m (8600 ft.), 50 km (30 mi.) south of Lake Tahoe in the Sierra Nevada. It is preserved

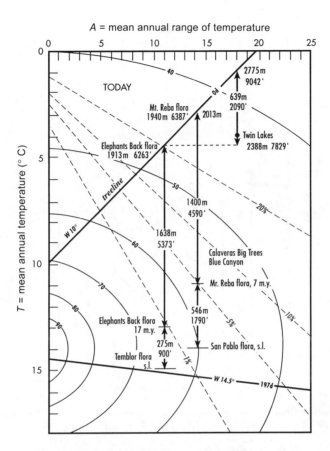

FIG. 2. Estimates of paleotemperature and elevation of the Miocene Mt. Reba and Elephants Back floras, Sierra Nevada, California.

in fine andesitic sandstone associated with mudflows and conglomerates of the Disaster Peak Formation, dated at 7 Ma (Axelrod, 1980). The flora includes species allied to those now on the lower-middle western slope of the range. Among its taxa are evergreen trees allied to gold-cup oak (*Quercus chrysolepis*) and tanbark oak (*Lithocarpus densiflora*) associated with the conifers that include Douglas fir, Sierra redwood, white fir, yellow pine, and cypress. Elm also is part of the flora, indicating that there was effective summer rain. A relatively low range of temperature existed, probably near 14°C, as judged from the San Pablo flora at sea level, with magnolia and avocado, suggesting a Warmth of W 14.4°C (194 days, 6.5 months). The Mt. Reba flora was situated above the San Pablo flora near 545 m (1790 ft.) (3 × 182 m), suggesting that since 7 Ma the fossil flora was uplifted about 1400 m (4590 ft.) above sea level,

based on a decrease in mean temperature of 10.7°C and a normal lapse rate (Fig. 2).

A *Miocene flora* at Elephants Back, situated one mile south of Carson Pass in the Sierra Nevada, is dated at 17 Ma. The flora is in andesitic sediments that form a gentle syncline under Elephants Back, with the plant bed 10 m above the granitic basement. The flora, now at 2750 m (9100 ft.) at timberline, contains broad-leaved evergreens such as *Ilex*, *Magnolia*, *Persea*, *Nectandra*, and *Quercus*, which are adapted to nearly frost-free conditions. Associates include deciduous hardwoods, notably species of *Fagus*, *Liquidambar*, *Platanus*, *Populus*, *Pterocarya*, and *Ulmus*. Conifers (fir, pine, spruce) are not represented. This mixed broad-leafed evergreen–deciduous hardwood forest grew at an elevation of no more than 450 m above sea level. Allied vegetation now occurs in areas with a temperature of T 13.8° and A

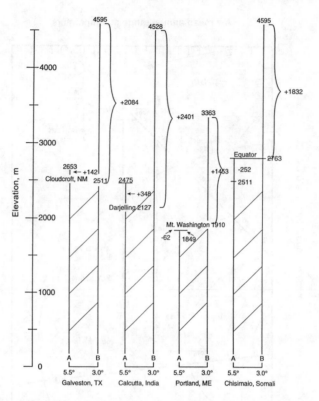

FIG. 3. Difference in estimated elevation using a normal lapse rate and one of 3°C/1000 m, advocated by Wolfe (1992), Gregory (1994), Gregory and McIntosh (1996), and Wolfe and Schorn (1984).

10°C, and a Warmth of W 13.8°C (177 days, ~6 months). Because the flora is now at timberline, uplift has been on the order of 1638 m (5325 ft.) since the flora lived (Fig. 2). This uplift occurred largely since 7 Ma, because a younger flora, collected by Dwight Billings, is in the flat-lying andesitic section at 9400 m, fully 70 m above the Miocene mixed evergreen-deciduous hardwood forest. This upper flora contains white oak, hickory, and oleander, which indicate only moderate elevation (800 m, 2500 ft.). The Elephants Back flora is now at 2775 m (9100 ft.), but during deposition it was near 270 to 300 m (900 to 1000 ft.). This suggests that total uplift of the Sierra in this area was 2500 m (8200 ft.).

These two Miocene floras show that as the range of temperature increased, the *condition* for treeline *(W* 10°C) became progressively higher, although the Sierra Nevada was not then sufficiently high to support treeline vegetation. In these two examples, treeline *condition (W* 10°C) increased from ~1913 m (6263 ft.) to

2013 m (6503 ft.), or by 100 m (328 ft.), between deposition of the two floras (Fig. 2). Since then, elevation of treeline has increased 637 m (2080 ft.) to its present level of 2775 m (Fig. 2). This increase in paleoelevation of vegetation as A increased is paralleled by modern vegetation zones. Examples are provided by the red fir–hemlock–white pine forest. Its lower elevation is at ~1370 m (4500 ft.) in the Siskiyou Mountains some 32 km (20 mi.) inland from Crescent City, in northwestern California. But 160 km (100 mi.) to the southeast, its lower elevation in the interior is near 2290 to 2240 m (7500 to 8000 ft.) because the range of temperature there is much greater (~15 to 25°C). A similar difference in elevation is shown by the fir-spruce forest in coastal British Columbia, as compared with its elevation 500 m higher in the interior. Likewise, the mixed conifer forest rises to higher elevation in interior Oregon as compared with its occurrence in the near-coastal area.

FIG. 4. Geographic occurrence of upland Eocene floras, Rocky Mountain region. Legend: 1 = Jesse Creek; 2 = Haynes Creek; 3 = Cow Creek; 4 = Horse Prairie; 5 = Thunder Mountain; 6 = Coal Creek; 7 = Bullion Gulch; 8 = Copper Basin; 9 = Bull Run; 10 = Florissant.

Lapse rate

Following Wolfe (1992), some investigators (Gregory, 1994; Gregory and McIntosh, 1996) believe that to estimate paleoelevation a lapse rate (LR) of 3°C/1000 m is preferable to the generally accepted rate of 5.5°C/1000 m. That an LR of 3°C/1000 m is not as accurate as a normal rate when used to estimate paleoelevation of a Tertiary flora is apparent from Figure 3. Because estimates with LR 3°C regularly give elevations 1000 to 2000 m *above* modern stations, similar results are to be expected when applied to paleoelevation. The result also would be that numerous subtropicals and evergreen dicots in floras of moderate elevation would be placed at levels where freezing would eliminate many taxa, as in the case of the Florissant (Wolfe, 1992; Gregory, 1994) and other floras (i.e., Wolfe, 1964).

Wolfe and Schorn (1994; Wolfe et al., 1997) have suggested a high elevation (4000 m) for middle Miocene floras (15 Ma) in west-central Nevada. However, the species in these floras do not show adaptations to high elevation and low temperature (i.e., thick leaves, evergreen character, entire margins, small size). Wolfe and

Schorn also found that although many of the same species are in slightly younger floras (14 to 12 Ma) in the area, collapse had by then brought elevation to near its present level. These findings raise several questions: (1) How do "alpine" plants become "normal" in such a brief time? (2) How did some species that now are in a moderate climate, such as *Arbutus*, *Lyonothamnus*, *Populus*, and others, adapt physiologically to near-normal conditions so rapidly? (3) What is the structural evidence for regional collapse of fully 2000 to 2500 m in scarcely 2 to 3 m.y.? Actually, the principal change in vegetation in this area following 15 Ma resulted from the progressive disappearance of summer rain.

Regarding the high Miocene LR favored by Wolfe and Schorn, a climatologist has noted (pers. comm., 1997):

The opinion of high elevation with LR 3°C/1000 m can also be attacked effectively from the standpoint of the static stability of the atmosphere. The present mean global LR of 0.6°C/1000 m represents a global equilibrium of latent heat flux warming up the upper troposphere. If the atmospheric lapse rate were to increase, convection and latent heat would correspondingly increase, further reducing the lapse rate. For this reason, the average global lapse rate probably has been the same ever since the oceans first formed. The estimate of 3°C/1000 m by Wolfe suggests a world where atmospheric convection is minimal, a condition impossible as long as the sun shines and most of the planet is covered with water.

The Great Basin Arch

The old notion that the Great Basin represents a collapsed great arch that extended from the Wasatch Range to the Sierra Nevada, and presumably had a very high elevation over the central region, has been rejected on the basis of geological evidence (i.e., Davis, 1925; King, 1977). The idea certainly has no support from paleobotanical evidence.

The Eocene Elko flora (35 Ma) from Catlin coal mine (abandoned) one mile south of Elko, Nevada, includes species of:

Taxodium	Persea
Metasequoia	Quercus
Alnus	Mahonia
Betula	Ribes
Cercidiphyllum	Diospyros
Sassafras	Acer
Tilia	Rosa.

This deciduous hardwood forest bordered a lake in the Humboldt Formation. Its elevation probably did not exceed 915 m (3000 ft.) compared with fully 1525 m (5200 ft.) today.

A fossil flora (15 Ma) from the northern end of the San Antonio Mountains, 37 km (23 mi) north of Tonopah, is dominated by evergreen oak (*Quercus pollardiana,* cf. *chrysolepis*) and has associates of:

Juniperus	Zelkova
Picea	Sorbus
Mahonia	Acer
Ulmus	Arbutus
Quercus.	

Presently at an elevation of 1830 m (6000 ft.), earlier it was at no more than 915 m (3000 ft.).

The *Miocene Bullhead Ranch flora* (15 Ma), situated at the north end of the Hot Springs Range, 16 km (10 mi) southeast of Paradise in Humboldt County, northern Nevada, has species of:

Juniperus	Amelanchier
Picea	Sorbus
Zelkova	Robinia
Cedrela	Rhus.

They indicate an elevation of no more than 760 to 915 m (2500 to 3000 ft.), as compared with its present level at 1400 m (4600 ft.).

These floras, well distributed over the central Great Basin, suggest a broad region of only moderate elevation, consistent with the widespread distribution of ash-flow tuffs and with little relief apart from local eruptive centers. There certainly is no known plant evidence to indicate an earlier topographic high over the Great Basin area. It is higher now than at any time in the Tertiary. During the later Tertiary, commencing about 7 to 5 Ma, the area was rapidly elevated to its present level and its principal mountains were uplifted and separated by major grabens.

Rocky Mountain upland Eocene floras

During the past two decades I have collected several new Eocene floras from the uplands of Idaho and Nevada (Fig. 4). They are now farther from the ocean than they were earlier, because later Tertiary extension widened the Great Basin by ~300 km, nearly half its present width (Hamilton and Myers, 1966; Hamilton, 1978). This regional extension also brought the uplands of Nevada and Idaho farther apart, as the Snake River Basin opened and widened in later Miocene and Quaternary times. As a result, more equable climate earlier extended farther into the interior, because the ocean then was warmer and closer and the barrier of the Sierra-Cascade axis was not yet elevated.

All these floras from the central Rocky Mountain area (Fig. 4) occur in fine tuffaceous sediments intercalated in thick volcanic piles representing the Challis, Medicine Lodge, Frost Creek, and 39-Mile volcanics and allied rocks in the region. The floras occur *above* the broadleafed evergreen forests of the lowlands, as represented by the Wasatch (Berry, 1930; MacGinitie, 1974) and similar floras. As depicted in Figure 5, these forests represent a sequence of vegetation zones that change in composition with increasing cold and elevation that, in turn,

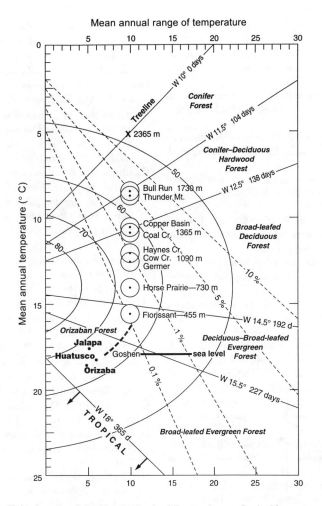

FIG. 5. Elevation, Warmth, and zonal relations of upland Eocene forests, Rocky Mountain region.

reflect shorter growing seasons at higher elevation (Axelrod, 1996). The change (Fig. 5) is from broadleafed evergreen–deciduous hardwood forest (Florissant), to deciduous hardwood forest (Cow Creek, Germer, Haynes Creek), to conifer–deciduous hardwood forest (Copper Basin, Coal Creek, Lower Bull Run), to montane conifer forest (Upper Bull Run, Lower Thunder Mountain). These forests indicate that the growing season (Warmth) decreased gradually from W 15.5°C (227 days, 7.5 months) to W 11.3°C (96 days, 3.2 months) in the uppermost Bull Run florule. Freezing increased from scarcely 1% hrs/yr in the lower zone to ~W 11.3°C (96 days, 3.2 months) in the uppermost Bull Run florule (at $T\,8°$, $A\,10° = 6\%$ hrs/yr),

situated ~546 m (3° C × 182 m) below the treeline condition (W 10°C, 0 days).

REFERENCES

Axelrod, D. I., 1962, Post-Pliocene uplift of the Sierra Nevada, California: Geol. Soc. Amer. Bull., v. 76, p. 183–198.

————, 1965, A method of determining the altitudes of Tertiary floras: The Palaeobotanist, v. 14, p. 144–171.

————, 1980, The Mt. Reba flora from Alpine County, California: Univ. of California Publ. Geol. Sci., v. 121, p. 13–78.

————, 1981, Altitudes of Tertiary forests estimated from paleotemperature, in Geological and ecological studies of the Qinghai-Xizang Plateau: Proc. Symp. Qinghai-Xizang (Tibet) Plateau, Beijing, v. 1: Beijing and New York, Sci. Publ. House and Gordon and Breach, p. 131–138.

————, 1991, The early Miocene Buffalo Canyon flora of western Nevada: Univ. of California Publ. Geol. Sci., v. 135, 76 p.

————, 1992, The middle Miocene Pyramid flora of western Nevada: Univ. of California Publ. Geol. Sci., v. 137, 50 p.

————, 1995, The middle Miocene Purple Mountain flora of western Nevada: Univ. of California Publ. Geol. Sci., v. 139, 62 p.

————, 1996, Diverse upland Eocene forests, western United States: The Palaeobotanist, v. 45, p. 81–97.

Axelrod, D. I., and Ting, W. S., 1960, Late Pliocene floras east of the Sierra Nevada: Univ. of California Publ. Geol. Sci., v. 39, p. 1–118.

Bailey, H. P., 1960, A method of determining the warmth and temperateness of climate: Geografiska Annaler, v. 42, p. 1–16.

————, 1964, Toward a uniform concept of the temperate climate: Geog. Rev., v. 54, p. 516–545.

Berry, E. W., 1917, Fossil plants from Bolivia and their bearing on age of uplift of the eastern Andes: U.S. Nat. Museum Proc., v. 54, p. 103–164.

————, 1919, Miocene fossil plants from northern Peru: U.S. Nat. Museum Proc., v. 55, p. 279–294.

————, 1922a, The flora of the Concepcion-Arauco coal measures of Chili: Johns Hopkins Univ., Stud. Geol., no. 4, p. 73–142.

————, 1922b, Pliocene fossil plants from eastern Eolibia: Johns Hopkins Univ., Stud. Geol., no. 4, p. 145–202.

————, 1929, The fossil flora of the Loja Basin in southern Ecuador: Johns Hopkins Univ., Stud. Geol., no. 10, p. 79–136.

————, 1930, A flora of Green River age in the Wind River Basin of Wyoming: U.S. Geol. Surv. Prof. Paper 165-B, p. 55–81.

————, 1938, Tertiary flora from the Rio Pichileufu, Argentina: Geol. Soc. Amer., Spec. Pap., v. 12, p. 1–140.

Davis, W. M., 1925, The Basin Range problem: Nat. Acad. Sci. Proc., v. 11, p. 387–392.

Gregory, K. M., 1994, Paleoclimate and paleoelevation of the 35 Ma Florissant flora, Front Range, Colorado: Paleoclimates, v. 1, p. 23–57.

Gregory, K. M., and McIntosh, W. C., 1996, Paleoclimate and paleoelevation of the Oligocene Pitch-Pinnacle flora, Sawatch Range, Colorado: Geol. Soc. Amer. Bull., v. 108, p. 545–561.

Greller, A. M., 1989, Correlation of warmth and temperateness with the distributional limits of zonal forests in eastern North America: Bull. Torrey Bot. Club, v. 116, p. 145–163.

Greller, A. M., and Balasurbamaniam, S., 1988, Vegetational composition, leaf size, and climatic warmth in an altitudinal sequence of evergreen forests in Sri Lanka (Ceylon): Trop. Ecol., v. 29, p. 121–145.

Guo, S.-X., 1981, On the elevation and climatic changes on the Qinghai-Xizang Plateau based on fossil angiosperms, *in* Geological and ecological studies of the Qinghai-Xizang Plateau: Proc. Symp. Qinghai-Xizang (Tibet) Plateau, v. 1: Beijing and New York, Sci. Publ. House and Gordon and Breach, 201–206.

Hamilton, W., 1978, Mesozoic tectonics of the Western United States, *in* Howell, D. G., and McDougall, K. A., eds., Mesozoic paleogeography of the Western United States: Pacific Section, Social Econ. Paleontol. Mineral., Pacific Coast Paleogeog. Symp., v. 2, p. 33–70.

Hamilton, W., and Myers, W. B., 1966, Cenozoic tectonics of the western United States: Rev. Geophys., v. 4, p. 509–549.

Hsü, J., 1976, On the paleobotanical evidence for continental drift and the Himalayan uplift: The Palaeobotanist, v. 25, p. 131–145.

Hsü, J., Tao, J.-J., and Sun, H.-J., 1973, On the discovery of a *Quercus semicarpifolia* bed at Mount Shisha Pangma and its significance in botany and geology: Acta Botan. Sinica, v. 15, p. 103–119.

King, P. B., 1977, The evolution of North America: Princeton, NJ, Princeton Univ. Press, 197 p.

Li, H., and Guo, S., 1976, The Miocene flora from Namling of Xizang: Acta Palaeontol. Sinica, v. 15, p. 7–18.

MacGinitie, H. D., 1974, An early Middle Eocene flora from the Yellowstone-Absaroka volcanic province, northwestern Wind River basin, Wyoming: Univ. of California Publ. Geol. Sci., v. 108, 103 p.

Menendez, C. A., 1971, Tertiarias de la Argentina: Ameghiniana, v. 8, p. 209–212.

Taylor, D. W., 1991, Paleobiogeographic relationships of Andean angiosperms of Cretaceous to Pliocene age: Paleogeography, Paleoclimatology, Paleoecology, v. 88, p. 69–84.

Wolfe, J. A., 1964, Miocene floras from Fingerrock Wash, southwestern Nevada: U.S. Geol. Surv. Prof. Paper 454-N.

————, 1992, An analysis of present-day lapse rates in the western conterminous United States and their significance in paleoaltitudinal estimates: U.S. Geol. Surv. Bull. no. 1964, p. 1–15.

Wolfe, J. A., and Schorn, H. E., 1984, Fossil floras indicate high altitude for west-central Nevada at 16 Ma and collapse to about present altitudes by 12 Ma [abs.], *in* Geol. Soc. Amer., Annual Meeting, Seattle, Washington, Abstract A-521.

Wolfe, J. A., et al., 1997, Paleobotanical evidence for high altitudes in Nevada during the Miocene: Amer. Assoc. Adv. Sci., v. 276, p. 1672–1675.

Wu, Y., and Yu, Q., 1980, Pollen spore assemblages from localities of *Hipparion* fauna in Xizang and its sig-

nificance: The fossils of Tibet: Acta Botan. Sinica, v. 22, p. 81–82.

Zheng, S., 1980, The *Hipparion* fauna from Bulong Basin, Biru, Xizang, *in* Paleontology of Xizang, Book 1: Nanking, Academia Sinica, p. 33–47.

Anatomy of an Anomaly: The Devonian Catastrophic Alamo Impact Breccia of Southern Nevada

JOHN E. WARME

Department of Geology and Geological Engineering, Colorado School of Mines, Golden, Colorado 80401

AND HANS-CHRISTIAN KUEHNER

Nederlandse Aardolie Maatschappij B. V., P. O. Box 28000, 9400 HH Assen, Netherlands

Abstract

The Alamo Breccia is a carbonate rock breccia of Late Devonian age in southern Nevada. It is an anomalous sedimentary unit because it has the properties of a massive debris-flow and turbidity-current deposit that would be expected to occur in deep water, but is intercalated over much of its area with typical shallow-water carbonate-platform beds. The Breccia was created by the catastrophic detachment and flow, over a nearly horizontal surface, of previously deposited platform carbonates. It crops out in 14 or more mountain ranges that cover an area of ~10,000 km², conservatively averages ~50 m in thickness, and contains a volume of 500+ km³. Along the base it contains trains of individual detached blocks as much as 500 m long and 90 m high. Clasts generally grade upward to gravel-, sand-, or mud-sized particles at the top.

The Breccia was generated by forces unleashed during the impact of an extraterrestrial object with Earth. The impact produced shocked quartz grains, unique ejecta spherules, and an iridium anomaly—which are present within the Breccia but absent from confining beds. Internally the Breccia is segmented vertically into as many as five sequentially thinner graded units created by successive tsunamis. In one range, peculiar deformed dolostone, shocked quartz sandstone, and sedimentary dikes and sills occur under the Breccia and deep-water limestones rest over it, indicating a near-crater location. Surrounding detached megablocks and tsunamites suggest an annular crater trough.

The Breccia formed within the span of a few hours or days, and falls entirely within a single early Frasnian conodont zone, at ~367 Ma. The well-documented middle Late Devonian (Frasnian/Famennian) extinctions are ~3 Ma later.

An impact scenario explains the known features of the Alamo Breccia: impact occurred on the Late Devonian outer platform or slope; seismic shock delaminated the upper ~50 to 100 m of the platform, loosening carbonate-platform bedrock and creating trains of large blocks that may rest in an annular trough; successive tsunamis reworked the loosened material, which was augmented by unknown proportions of ejecta containing shocked quartz from the crater, carbonate spherules from the vapor cloud, and iridium from the projectile. Mass flows west of the platform likely represent tsunami backwash, shock-induced failure along the platform margin, and slumps from offshore topographic highs.

Introduction

The tsunami effects of oceanic impacts appear to be so energetic as to produce not only widespread erosive disturbances in deep-sea sediments but profound erosional disruptions (with consequent gravity wasting) around margins of basins as large as the modern Pacific basin. Passive margins, in particular, might be expected to retain records of such events in the form of basin-perimeter unconformities, base-of-slope debris slides, instantaneous fans, and broad sedimentary aprons of a typically chaotic character. Actual examples have not yet been identified (Silver, 1982, p. xviii).

THE ALAMO BRECCIA, an Upper Devonian carbonate megabreccia spread over much of southern Nevada (Fig. 1), was created by processes generated from an impact such as Silver (1982) envisioned. The Breccia is a singular and extraordinary sedimentary unit compared to the characteristics of the regional well-known Upper Devonian formations (Fig. 2). It is a

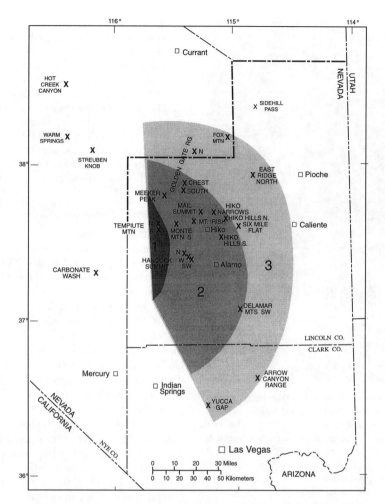

Fig. 1. Index map of southern Nevada, showing the confirmed distribution of the Alamo Breccia (shaded) and projections of Breccia zones based on its thickness: Zone 1 = ~130 m; Zone 2 = ~50 to 100 m; Zone 3 = 1 to 7 m. Studied Upper Devonian sections, both within and beyond the Breccia, are shown by the symbol "X" (from Warme and Sandberg, 1996).

product of mass-flow processes and catastrophic waves and currents. Newly found ejecta and evidence for impact tectonics suggest the close proximity of the impact crater in southern Nevada.

The Alamo Breccia and related phenomena may represent the best-exhibited marine impact deposit now exposed on land (Alvarez, 1997, p. 141). It can be analyzed in three dimensions utilizing outcrops spread across 14 or more mountain ranges in southern Nevada. It is important both for comparison with other impact sites and as a paradigm for marine impact processes. Any reconstruction of the

Breccia, or of the crater, is complicated by pervasive Mesozoic thrusting and Cenozoic extension in Nevada, the cumulative effects of which since the Devonian have not been resolved. However, the concentric distribution of the Breccia in Figure 1 implies that its original relative E-W positions are intact, even if now extended or compressed.

The Alamo event apparently did not produce widespread extinctions (Sandberg and Warme, 1993; Warme and Sandberg, 1995), but did temporarily rearrange Late Devonian geography of parts of southern Nevada and perhaps beyond. The event must have effected, directly

FIG. 2. Exposure of the massive-weathering Alamo Breccia (center), intercalated with typical thinner-bedded, shallow-water carbonate-platform cycles of the Guilmette Formation, West Pahranagat Range. Breccia occupies the central 60 m of the ~100 meters of strata shown. An intrabreccia fold was created during the Alamo event, when a wedge-shaped megaclast (Facies C; see Fig. 5) moved from the right (northeast), underriding and upturning beds in the clast at center and left. Facies D (not visible at this scale; see Fig. 8) extends for several hundred meters along the prominent light-weathering bench at the base of the megaclast interval. Breccia of Facies B (disorganized) and A (graded) occupy the upper half of the Breccia cliff over the folded clast.

or indirectly, the genesis and distribution of Late Devonian regional unconformities and sedimentary formations (Sandberg et al., 1997a, 1997b), as well as the structural fabric, and perhaps influenced the occurrence and timing of mineral deposits and even orogeny.

Because it is distributed in ranges around the desert community of Alamo in the Pahranagat Valley (Fig. 1), it was named the "Alamo breccia" (Warme, 1991), and formalized as the Alamo Breccia Member of the Guilmette Formation by Sandberg et al. (1997a). The convulsive processes that produced it were termed the

Alamo event (Warme et al., 1991). "Alamo" was deemed geographically, and catastrophically, appropriate.

Our understanding of the Alamo Breccia as of 1995 was summarized by Warme and Sandberg (1995, 1996), and new interpretations of the broader Alamo event were presented by Kuehner et al. (1996), Warme and Kuehner (1997), and Sandberg et al. (1997a, 1997b). The descriptions, analyses, and interpretations of the Alamo Breccia and the Alamo event presented here are discussed in more detail by Kuehner (1997).

Discovery and documentation of the Alamo Breccia

During field reconnaissance at Tempiute Mountain (Fig. 1) in January 1990, the thick, well-sorted, upper portion of the Alamo Breccia caught the attention of Colorado School of Mines graduate student Alan Chamberlain and UNOCAL geologist Norman Kent. They showed a sample to the senior author, and the three puzzled over the genesis of this uncharacteristic Guilmette facies. Together, two days later, they discovered a Breccia outcrop near Mount Irish (Fig. 1). It took several days of field work to grasp the character of the Breccia there; it is ~100 m thick and contains clasts tens of meters long, with preserved internal stratigraphy. The clasts were mistaken by past workers as *in situ*. Once the basic characteristics of the Breccia were comprehended, we quickly identified it in several more ranges in southern Nevada.

The Guilmette Formation, including the Breccia, had been measured, described, and interpreted by many academic, government, and mining- and oil-company geologists. Our early reports of the Breccia as a widespread single sedimentary deposit were met with doubt; as a potential impact phenomenon it was regarded with deep skepticism. Therefore, we organized a week-long field workshop in May 1991—attended by authorities on Nevada stratigraphy, paleontology, and tectonics, as well as by specialists on impacts and catastrophic deposits. By the end of the week, all participants agreed that they had surveyed an anomalous deposit, correlative across several different mountain ranges, and that it was a catastrophic sedimentary megabreccia—not one derived from tectonic, karst, solution collapse, or other processes. Charles Sandberg (USGS) joined the project and provided evidence from conodont microfossils that the Breccia was deposited in the lower part of the Frasnian Stage (lower Upper Devonian), within a single conodont (*punctata*) zone (Sandberg and Warme, 1993). Since then we documented the Breccia in its shallow-water framework in 13 different ranges in southeastern Nevada, in a deeper-water setting at Tempiute Mountain, and in deep-water likely equivalents at four other ranges to the west (Sandberg et al., 1997a, 1997b). We also have uncovered evidence for a crater and for the sequence of events that unfolded during the Late Devonian Alamo event, presented below in the section entitled "Synthesis."

Physical characteristics and paleobathymetry from conodont assemblages (Sandberg and Warme, 1993; Warme and Sandberg, 1995, 1996) independently confirmed the shallow-water carbonate-platform environment of the Guilmette. In contrast with the typical thin-bedded Guilmette, the Alamo Breccia is a single depositional unit as much as 130 m thick and possesses sedimentological features more common in deep-water catastrophic mass flows (Fig. 2). It contains transported blocks as much as 90 m high and 500 m long, and rests on a distinctive regional near-horizontal detachment surface within the Guilmette, all uncharacteristic of carbonate platform deposits. The volume of the breccia, 500+ km³, is equal to that of some of the largest deep-water mass flows.

An energy source was sought that could account for the anomalous characteristics of the Alamo Breccia. Earthquakes, volcanic explosions, tsunamis, and impacts all were considered. An impact could yield all of the above—seismic shock, melt rock, and tsunamis. No volcanic debris was noticed in the breccia, or in thin sections or insoluble residues. Brian Ackman (1991) discovered the first quartz grain in thin section that appeared to show shock lamellae, although they were poorly developed, diagenetically altered, and unconvincing to shock-mineral experts that we consulted. Thousands of such grains subsequently were recovered from the insoluble residues of conodont samples. We later found additional independent evidence for an impact—an iridium anomaly, ejecta spherules, tsunami deposits, and a potential crater.

Impact studies

Space exploration programs beginning in the 1960s, together with the Alvarez et al. (1980) impact hypothesis regarding the terminal-Cretaceous extinctions, stimulated interdisciplinary research that created a wealth of knowledge and considerable controversy about Earth-impact processes, products, and possible global effects. The relevant literature is voluminous and scattered, but symposium volumes and monographs provide overviews and reference lists (e. g., Silver and Schultz, 1983; Melosh, 1989; Sharpton and Ward, 1990; Gehrels, 1994; Koeberl and Anderson, 1996; Ryder et al., 1996).

Grieve and Shoemaker (1994) listed ∼140 worldwide impact sites, each confirmed by the presence of meteoroid fragments and/or shock metamorphic minerals. Koeberl and Anderson (1996) summarized the characteristics of 20 of these impact structures in the United States. Evidence for craters includes surface depressions, eroded or exhumed surface remnants, or seismogram records of buried examples. In general, craters larger than 4 km in diameter may exhibit a central uplift surrounded by a concentric depression, peak ring, and annular trough or moat. Clear evidence for rings is rare in Earth examples. Many craters reveal rock deformation such as faulting, injection, melting, and other changes that occurred upon impact.

At least three marine impact craters have been documented in subsurface localities that are partially or wholly offshore—(1) Montagnais, offshore Nova Scotia; (2) Chicxulub, partially offshore Yucatan; and (3) Ust Kara, offshore eastern Russia (Grieve and Shoemaker, 1994). A fourth, Chesapeake Bay, of the eastern United States, was confirmed by Poag (1997a). Inland buried structures may have occurred in epicontinental seas. The characteristics of impacts in various water depths, and in water-saturated rock substrates, are theoretically different from those on dry land (e.g., Oberbeck et al., 1993). The Alamo event may be the best-displayed proven marine impact deposit, including tsunami beds, now exposed on land.

Initial evidence for some of the largest known impacts was discovered indirectly in stratified rocks far from the target area, commonly in the form of thin "boundary clays" that tend to occur at stage or period boundaries. The clays contain widely broadcast impact shock minerals, ejecta tektites or spherules, and anomalous iridium concentrations. Silver's (1982) scenario, cited above, was prompted by the discovery of an iridium anomaly at the Cretaceous/Tertiary boundary in Italy, confined to a bed of submicrometer-sized grains ~1 cm thick. It was interpreted to represent debris from a large impact (Alvarez et al., 1980). The crater site was unknown, but the event was proposed as the cause of the abrupt extinctions at the end of the Cretaceous Period at 65 Ma. Alvarez (1997) recounted the history of the intensive research that eventually yielded the crater location. During the quest, correlative boundary clays were found beyond Italy, and meter-thick beds with tektites, spherules, and shocked quartz were identified around the northern Gulf of Mexico and in Haiti. Beds several meters thick were discovered in Mexico, and results from scientific and commercial drilling in the Gulf of Mexico and at sites on- and offshore in Mexico revealed significant slumps and thick breccias that formed at or near the K/T boundary. The giant Chicxulub Crater was finally identified beneath younger deposits in northern Yucatan. Seismic profiles were interpreted to give an outer ring diameter of ~195 km, with a possible faint ring beyond (Morgan and Warner et al., 1996).

A similar discovery sequence occurred for the 90 km diameter Late Eocene crater documented by drilling and seismic profiling of coastal plain strata under Chesapeake Bay (Poag, 1997a). The event correlates with iridium and shocked quartz found in Italy (Montanari et al., 1993), but much earlier indirect evidence for this impact was known from scattered tektite localities (Koeberl et al., 1996).

Early evidence for the Alamo event as an impact also was indirect. The Alamo Breccia was first recognized to represent some kind of catastrophic event. Conclusive evidence for an impact came with later discovery of the shocked quartz, iridium, and spherules that it contained. Expanded field search yielded a potential crater site.

Stratigraphic Framework of the Alamo Breccia

Regional stratigraphy

During Paleozoic time, the western margin of the North American continent was the seaward edge of a long-lived carbonate platform that trended N-S through central Nevada, with an ocean to the west. The history of this platform was summarized by Cook (1983) and paleogeographic time slices were presented by Poole et al. (1992). The formations of the platform are shown in Figure 3.

Devonian stratigraphy of the Nevada and Utah Great Basin was summarized by Sandberg et al. (1988), Johnson et al. (1991), and Poole et al. (1992). Hurtubise (1989) reviewed the Devonian formations and members of eastern Nevada and western Utah, and provided details on the Devonian in the Seaman Range north of the Alamo Breccia area (Fig. 4A). His stratigraphic units can be extended into our study area. Morrow (1997) provided the most comprehensive synthesis of the Upper Devonian Frasnian and Famennian (F/F) stages in the Great Basin. He presented the latest synthesis of the stratigraphic "events" deciphered from the distribution of formations and unconformities, the course of biotic evolution and extinctions, and mass-extinction issues associated with the F/F boundary. The field trip guidebook of Sandberg et al. (1997a) highlighted these events, including the Alamo event.

The Sevy and Simonson dolostones and the Guilmette Formation (mainly limestones) are platform facies that approximately represent Early, Middle, and Late Devonian time. To the west, equivalent Middle Devonian ramp or slope facies are the Sentinel Mountain and Bay State formations, and equivalent deep-water facies are the Lower and Middle Devonian Denay and Upper Devonian Devils Gate formations. Based on studied outcrops, the platform margin was projected to be ~150 km west of the western edge of the shaded area in Figure 1, indicating that the area was on the shallow platform (Johnson et al., 1991).

The Pilot Shale occupies an intraplatform depression that first developed in east-central Nevada in the early Late Devonian, north of the shaded area in Figure 1. The basin was initiated at about the same time as the Alamo event, so

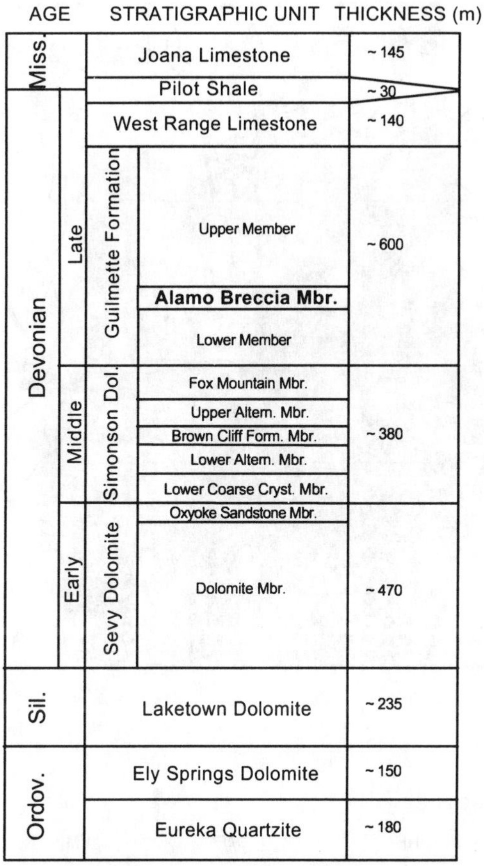

AGE		STRATIGRAPHIC UNIT		THICKNESS (m)
Miss.		Joana Limestone		~145
		Pilot Shale		~30
Devonian — Late	Guilmette Formation	West Range Limestone		~140
		Upper Member		~600
		Alamo Breccia Mbr.		
		Lower Member		
Devonian — Middle	Simonson Dol.	Fox Mountain Mbr.		~380
		Upper Altern. Mbr.		
		Brown Cliff Form. Mbr.		
		Lower Altern. Mbr.		
		Lower Coarse Cryst. Mbr.		
		Oxyoke Sandstone Mbr.		
Devonian — Early	Sevy Dolomite	Dolomite Mbr.		~470
Sil.		Laketown Dolomite		~235
Ordov.		Ely Springs Dolomite		~150
		Eureka Quartzite		~180

FIG. 3. Stratigraphic column showing Paleozoic formations, thicknesses, and ages of shallow-water platform facies in the study area of southern Nevada. Alamo Breccia is the middle member of the Upper Devonian Guilmette Formation.

that lower portions of the Shale correlate with lower portions of the Guilmette and Devils Gate. The Pilot basin enlarged, and the Shale became a regional unit that represents the demise of the shallow platform. The Pilot contains the Devonian/Mississippian boundary (Sandberg et al., 1988, 1997a). The Pilot basin has not been connected to the Alamo event.

Devonian formations and the Alamo Breccia

The Alamo Breccia is currently best known within the zoned semicircle shown in Figures 1 and 4A. Figure 4B is a stratigraphic section that crosses the three zones and shows how the base of the Breccia rests over progressively older rocks from Zones 3 to 1. In Zone 1, it cuts down into the Middle Devonian Sentinal Mountain and Bay State formations, which are discussed below. In the larger Zones 2 and 3, it occurs completely within the Upper Devonian Guilmette Formation.

Carbonate platform facies of the Guilmette Formation

The composition of the Alamo Breccia is the same as that of the carbonate platform from which it was derived. In most localities, the bounding contacts of the Alamo are subtle, and its internal characteristics, within the context of the Guilmette Formation, are not obvious when first encountered in the field. The anticipated normal facies of the Guilmette must be grasped in order to contrast them with those of the Breccia.

Carbonate rocks deposited on shallow platforms, such as represented by the Guilmette Formation, are characteristically cyclic. They reflect deposition driven by repeated changes of relative sea level. Typical cycles, and Devonian ones in particular, were summarized by Wilson (1975) and have been described by many other investigators worldwide. The Guilmette exhibits ~125 typical Devonian meter-scale shallowing-upward carbonate-platform cycles; many of them envelop uncounted thinner subcycles. Guilmette cycles were described and bundled into 11 stratigraphic sequences of regional extent by Chamberlain and Warme (1996). Each sequence contains from 1 to as many as 23 cycles, is bounded by prominent flooding surfaces, facies shifts, exposure surfaces, or karsts, and has a distinctive surface gamma-ray signature. Surface gamma-ray logs, shown in Figure 4B, are similar to subsurface electric logs from boreholes, but are collected by traversing surface outcrops with a hand-held scintillometer. The Alamo Breccia is a single sequence of distinctive lithology and gamma-ray character.

An ideal complete Guilmette shallowing-upward cycle begins with an erosive flooding surface, overlain by a thin trangressive zone of small rip-up lithoclasts and scattered fossil debris. An overlying interval of bioturbated and fossiliferous limestone represents the deepest, subtidal to lower intertidal part of the cycle, and commonly contains abundant stromatoporoids (fossil sponges) and more rarely a diverse marine assemblage including corals, brachio-

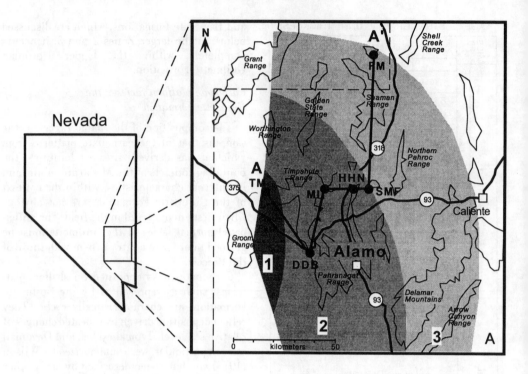

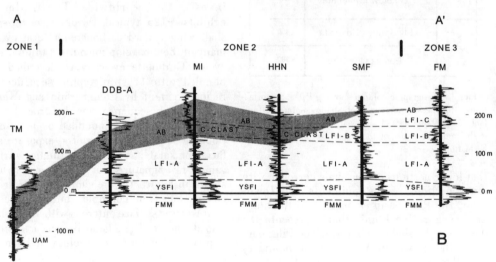

FIG. 4. A. Map showing locations of stratigraphic sections of the Alamo Breccia used for cross section A–A′ (Fig. 4B). Abbreviations: FM = Fox Mountain; SMF = Six Mile Flat; HHN = Hiko Hills North; MI = Mount Irish; DDB = Down Drop Block near Hancock Summit; TM = Tempiute Mountain. Columns in Figure 4B are correlated using the base of the yellow slope-forming interval (YSFI) as a datum and the lithostratigraphic characteristics and surface gamma-ray signatures of ledge-forming intervals (LFI) A to C. Higher gamma values are plotted to the left and lower values to the right, as per standard well logs. Relatively low gamma values of interval LFI-B in the columns at FM and SMF in Zone 3 can be traced into Facies C megaclasts of the Breccia at HHN and MI in Zone 2. The base of the Alamo Breccia is ~200 m above the YSFI datum in Zone 3 and ~100 m above it in Zone 2, and cuts below it in Zone 1 (from Kuehner, 1997).

pods, and gastropods. Upward within the cycle, shallower intertidal sediments are less bioturbated, and the bedding is better preserved, thinner, and contains fewer fossils. The cycle terminates with upper intertidal to supratidal laminated and fenestral dolostones, capped by erosion along the flooding surface of the next cycle. The boundaries of the cycles are not easily identified in deeper portions of the platform, such as in the dolostones under the Alamo Breccia in Zone 1, because they do not culminate with characteristic exposure indicators.

Stromatoporoid facies and members of the Guilmette Formation

The Guilmette Formation was divided into informal lower (~200 m thick) and upper (~400 m thick) members by Reso (1963), who chose the contact between the members to be the top of "a massive biostromal cliff 120–340 feet thick and containing prolific amounts of large spheroidal and encrusting stromatoporoids and other fauna." Some or all of this cliff, depending upon the locality, is the Alamo Breccia, which we designate as an intervening middle member.

Other investigators noticed stromatoporoid-rich intervals, and termed some of them "breccias." Tschantz and Pampeyan (1970) mentioned stromatoporoid-bearing "reef breccias" as much as 30 m thick in the Guilmette throughout western Lincoln County, but did not discuss them. In the Worthington Mountains (Fig. 1), Hurtubise (1989) measured and described a 60 m thick breccia containing abundant stromatroporoids within the Guilmette, which we now know to be the Alamo Breccia.

Past investigators confused three different stromatoporoid occurrences, which caused them to overlook the Alamo Breccia as an anomalous widespread unit within the Guilmette. (1) Under the Breccia, stromatoporoids of Reso's lower member are increasingly common upward as bedded biostromes, within the cycles of the ledge-forming interval (LFI) of Figure 4B. (2) Countless millions of these well-calcified sponges were released from their biostromal matrix in the process of the disintegration of the upper part of the lower member that formed the Alamo Breccia. They comprise 50 percent or more of the Breccia matrix in some localities.

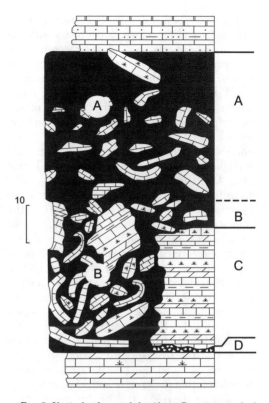

FIG. 5. Vertical column of the Alamo Breccia typical of Zone 2. Facies A and B are polymict carbonate breccias. Sprout-like symbols represent bedded and loose stromatoporoids. Facies A is graded bed(s) near the top. Facies B is disorganized Breccia under Facies A, which extends to the base at the left and to the top of Facies C at the right. Facies C is represented by one of the discontinuous megaclasts that rest at or near the base of the Breccia. Facies D is monomict breccia preserved under Facies C that was generated along the detachment zone at the base of the Breccia (from Warme and Sandberg, 1995, 1996).

They also occur as bedded biostromes in entire intact cycles preserved within the Breccia megaclasts (Fig. 5). (3) Stromatoporoids are present over the Breccia as major components of rare, but large and obvious, bioherms in the upper member.

Stromatoporoids of the lower member occur in the generally muddy matrix of the lower and middle parts of the upward-shallowing cycles. These well-bedded cycles greatly contrast with the massive accumulation of stromatoporoids, abundant large lithoclasts, grainy matrix, and graded units in the Breccia that were generated by disintegration and tsunami reworking of the upper part of Reso's lower member.

Reso's upper member began at the top of the cliff described above, which coincides with the top of the Breccia. He did not recognize the Breccia as a regional stratigraphic unit, but believed that the abundant stromatoporoids of the Breccia were a facies of overlying reefs, whose bases coincided with the base of his upper member. Such a reef is spectacularly exposed at Mount Irish (Fig. 1), and a few similar bioherms exist at the same stratigraphic level directly over the Breccia in the Hiko Range (Fig. 4A). Dunn (1979) puzzled over the relationships between the 50 m thick stromatoporoid bioherm at Mount Irish (Fig. 1) and the underlying breccia. She described as much as 40 m of breccia directly under the reef, and correctly interpreted the breccia as one or more debris-flow deposits, but believed, as did Reso, that the reef and the breccia were related facies. She extended the reef downward into the Breccia, and interpreted large Breccia clasts as reef facies and the Breccia matrix as lateral and vertical facies changes to reef talus. We now know that the reef is a post-breccia structure, that the reef and the breccia are genetically unrelated, that the breccia is thicker (~100 m, Fig. 4) than the reef at this locality, and that the breccia is the regional Alamo Breccia. The large reefs directly over the Breccia perhaps grew in response to increased marine circulation across a platform temporarily deepened by the Alamo event.

In addition to the basal reefs, the thick upper member is more varied than the underlying members. It has significant intervals of interbedded sandstones at some localities and contains ~90 shallowing-upward cycles.

The Alamo Breccia Member

Figure 3 shows the three members of the Guilmette Formation analyzed in this report—the informal lower and upper members, and the now formalized middle Alamo Breccia Member (Sandberg et al., 1997a). The middle member exists only where the upper part of the lower member disintegrated to become the Breccia. The lower member contains ~35 shallowing-upward cycles and numerous subcycles. At or near the base of the lower member is a well-bedded unit of upper intertidal and supratidal dolostones. It weathers to form a distinctive yellow band visible from distances of several kilometers along the ranges of Nevada and

Utah, and provides both a stratigraphic marker during field searches for the Breccia and a reliable datum from which to measure the vertical distribution of the Breccia within the Guilmette. This yellow slope-forming interval (YSFI) also gives a distinctive surface gamma-ray signature that can be followed across Figure 4B. The dolostones give way upward to increasing proportions of dark grey, ledge-forming, stromatoporoid-bearing limestones that indicate an upward trend toward more marine conditions. These are the ledge-forming intervals (LFI) A to C, which also have distinctive gamma-ray signatures.

Figure 4B shows that the base of the middle Alamo Breccia Member cuts through strata in Zone 3, ~200 m above the YSFI datum, and drops down to ~100 m above the datum in Zone 2. Intact platform cycles of the ledge-forming, interval C in Zone 3, and their gross gamma signature, can be traced into the correlative larger Breccia clasts in Zone 2 (Fig. 4B), which may contain 10 or more cycles. The base of the Breccia cuts much deeper in Zone 1, through the yellow slope-forming interval and into underlying Middle Devonian formations (Fig. 4A).

Description of the Alamo Breccia

Age

The Alamo Breccia formed within a day or so in Late Devonian time. It is one of the best constrained of impact deposits, falling within the middle part of the *punctata* conodont zone (Sandberg and Warme, 1993; Warme and Sandberg, 1995, 1996). Analyses of 80+ conodont samples show that strata of *punctata* age lie beneath and above the Breccia in Zones 2 and 3 (Fig. 4), and *punctata*-zone species occur in the Breccia matrix. Thus, the beds that disintegrated during the Alamo event were originally deposited within the *punctata* zone, as were the early post-event beds deposited over it. In Zone 1, the base of the Breccia lies much deeper, cutting out rocks that were deposited over a time span of ~14 Ma (Figs. 9 and 10 in Sandberg et al., 1997a).

Frasnian conodont zones average ~0.5 m.y. each; thus the Breccia is bracketed within this short geologic time span. The *punctata* zone is

FIG. 6. Photo of Facies D interval showing typical progressive disintegration of bedrock under Facies C megaclasts in Zone 2 (Figs. 1 and 5). Hammer shaft is 2 cm wide.

the third oldest of 10 zones within the Frasnian Stage (lower Upper Devonian), so the Breccia formed ~3.5 m.y. before the well-known Frasnian/Famennian events and extinctions. Sandberg et al. (1997a) estimated that the absolute age of the Breccia is ~367.2 Ma, interpolated from radiometric dates tied to underlying and overlying conodont zones. The dates were derived from areas far from our study area and several million years older and younger than *punctata* time. This absolute age will change as radiometric dates increase in number, accuracy, and correlation to faunal zones, and as durations in years of each zone are refined.

Composition

The Alamo Breccia is almost completely composed of carbonate rock. Quartz grains, phosphatic fossils (conodonts), and other insoluble components comprise much less than one percent of the volume. Most identifiable clasts were derived from the Upper Devonian carbonate platform limestone/dolostone cycles. The disintegrating limestone portions of the cycles were better cemented and more brittle than the dolostone portions, which were uncemented and plastically deformed. Because the Breccia incorporated carbonate rock that was deposited within a single conodont zone, probably much less than 0.5 m.y. in duration, it indicates the rate of lithification of the limestones and dolostones in the upper ~100 m of the platform. In

some localities the breccia has been partially (matrix only) or completely (matrix and clasts) dolomitized by later burial diagenesis.

Area and volume

The Breccia has been documented in 14 mountain ranges and encompasses an area of ~10,000 km², based on the rough semicircular pattern shown in Figure 1. If the Breccia has an average thickness of 50 m over this area, its volume would be 500 km³. Localities now under study indicate that the Breccia extended to similar or greater distances westward (bold "x" symbols on Figure 1) as deep-water debris flows (Sandberg et al, 1997a, 1997b) up to 20 m thick, significantly increasing its total area and volume.

Lateral zones

The three concentric zones of Figures 1 and 4B are defined by thickness and other Breccia characteristics discussed by Warme and Sandberg (1995, 1996). Within the Breccia, and even within zones, overall clast/matrix ratios, clast facies compositions, fossil contents, and other characteristics are variable. The breccia as presently documented forms a regional wedge that opens westward from Zone 3 to Zone 1 (Fig. 4). The distribution and thickness of the Breccia west of Zone 1 is still speculative (see below).

Central Zone 1 contains the thickest Breccia—as much as 130 m. In Zone 2, the Breccia

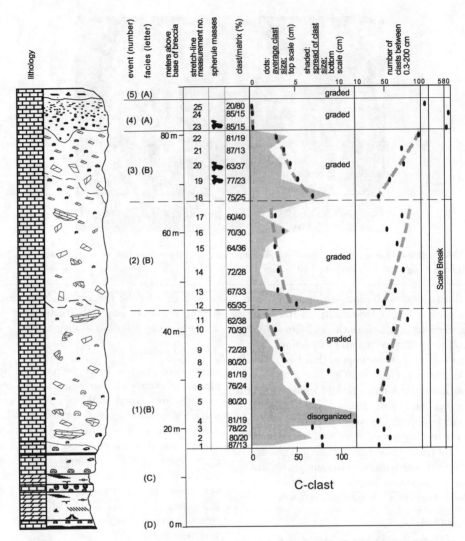

FIG. 7. Stratigraphic column measured through Alamo Breccia at Hiko Hills South locality (Hiko Hills, Fig. 1), representative of Zone 2. Columns indicate vertical distribution of lithology (standard symbols), clasts, erosion/deposition events, distribution of Facies D to A, locations of 2 m stretch-line measurements and of spherule masses, and trends in clast/matrix ratios, average clast sizes, range of clast sizes, and number of clasts per line. Facies D is only 10 to 20 cm thick and very subtle at this locality. The Facies C clast at the base is 18 m thick, overlain by five graded beds that become progressively thinner and finer grained upward. The lowest bed is disorganized debriite at the base, which becomes graded toward the top (from Kuehner, 1997).

ranges from ~50 to 100 m in thickness, averages ~60 m, and rests upon shallow-water platform carbonates ~100 m above the base of the Guilmette Formation. In Zone 3, the Breccia thins from ~7 m to a feather edge, resting on the carbonate platform ~200 above the base of the Guilmette Formation (Fig. 4). There it is commonly dolomitized. The Breccia in these

three zones is interpreted below in the section entitled "Synthesis."

Vertical facies

The diagrammatic column of the Breccia presented in Figure 5 is most representative of the broad Zone 2. The four facies, A to D, are lettered from the top down because A and B are

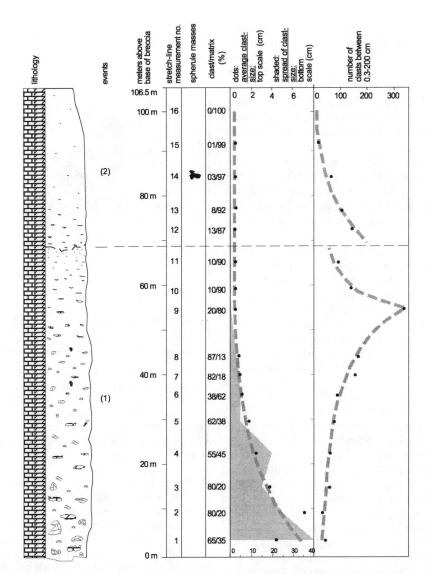

FIG. 8. Stratigraphic column measured through the Alamo Breccia at Tempiute Mountain (Fig. 1) in Zone 1. The Breccia here shows only two internal erosional/depositional events, is thicker and finer grained than in Zone 2, and is partially dolomitized. See Figure 7 for an explanation of the columns and for comparison with Zone 2 (from Kuehner, 1997).

always present and C and D (Fig. 6) are interdependent but discontinuous. Facies A is the graded interval of the upper part of the Breccia; it is commonly 5 to 10 m thick and muddy, sandy, or gravelly at the top, grading downward to polymict fist-, head-, or larger-sized clasts supported by a finer-grained matrix. It exhibits systematic clast imbrications, as discussed below. It originally was interpreted as a single

turbidite (Warme and Sandberg, 1995, 1996), but now is understood to be a compound unit (Figs. 7 and 8).

Facies B is an underlying chaotic polymict breccia of disorganized clasts. They are generally tabular, but some are almost equidimensional, and range in size up to the megaclasts of Facies C. In some localities large clasts are suspended in the upper part of the Breccia, even

protruding from the top, surrounded by graded
matrix (Fig. 5). Facies B exhibits the properties
of a debris-flow deposit (debriite). It extends to
the Breccia base if the megaclasts of Facies C
and detachment breccia of Facies D are not
present. Facies A and B comprise similar heterolithic carbonate breccias derived predominantly from the disintegration of the carbonate
platform.

Facies C represents the giant blocks resting at
or near the base of the Breccia (Figs. 2 and 5)
and overlying the peculiar monomict breccia of
Facies D (Fig. 6). The megaclasts are discontinuous, but common at all localities across
Zone 2.

Facies D represents the detachment interval
of the Breccia across Zone 2, created by some
combination of bedrock fluidization, liquifaction, and mechanical abrasion from the movement of the overlying and confining Facies C
megaclasts. This interval is characteristically a
few decimeters thick, but ranges from zero to
~5 m. It exhibits a sequence of bedrock disintegration that culminates in completely homogenized clasts suspended in a distinctive pale
grey weathering matrix (Fig. 6). In some
localities, the interval of Facies D can be traced
laterally through the following steps: intact
bedrock; bedrock with a mosaic of fractures
that define clasts; fractures progressively
dilated to separate the clasts; and clasts suspended, rotated, and homogenized within a
fine-grained matrix (monomict breccia). This
interval developed independent of various bedrock lithologies within Guilmette carbonate
cycles. It does not obviously follow specific
cycles, finer-grained beds, laminated dolostones, or specific bedding planes. Monomictic
breccias similar to Facies D, resulting from
fluidization, also occur throughout Facies B on
the margins or in cracks of clasts preserved in
the process of disintegration, and along the
margins of the sedimentary dikes and sills at
Tempiute Mountain; these breccias are discussed under the heading of "Shocked Formations" below.

Facies D consists of a low-relief, originally
nearly horizontal interval of detachment over
which the Breccia moved. In some exposures, it
can be traced beneath a single Facies C megaclast for hundreds of meters along the same
stratigraphic level (see caption, Fig. 2) or it

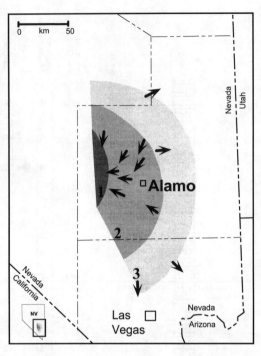

FIG. 9. Map of Alamo Breccia Zones 1–3 that summarizes
667 clast-imbrication measurements from 12 localities.
Results show inward radial flow in Zone 2, interpreted as
clast orientation by tsunami backwash toward Zone 1, and
outward radial flow in Zone 3, interpreted as orientation by
tsunami uprush and particle stranding on the shallower
portion of the platform.

shifts vertically only a few decimeters or
meters. Where the Facies C blocks were parted,
lifted, or transported away, Facies D was
exposed and eroded by flowage along the base of
Facies B. In many places, this detachment interval is thin, subtly expressed, or covered, and is
easily overlooked. Coupled with the Facies C
clasts it revealed that the Breccia has a flat,
nearly horizontal base and similar total thickness across large areas of Zone 2.

Internal stratification

The package of Facies B, C, and D was interpreted by Warme and Sandberg (1995, 1996) as
an interval representing a debriite transi-
tionally overlain by the Facies A turbidite.
Results of a refined analysis of the internal
structure of the Alamo Breccia are shown in
Figures 7 to 9. A cord 2 m long was stretched
across the Breccia and used to objectively
describe the composition and orientation of all
clasts between 3 mm and 2 m long that were

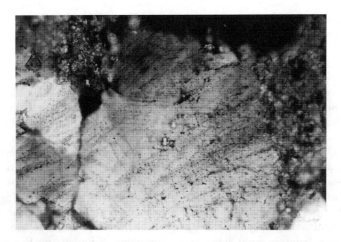

FIG. 10. Quartz grains in the Oxyoke Canyon Sandstone at Tempiute Mountain, showing three or more directions of shock deformation lamellae, decorated by inclusions. Cross polarization also shows mottled extinction. Field of view is ~0.5 mm.

intersected by the line (Kuehner et al., 1996; Kuehner, 1997). The matrix was arbitrarily defined as particles less than 3 mm across. Columns in Figures 7 and 8 illustrate the results from locations in two separate ranges. Shown are positions of the stretch-line measurements, clast/matrix ratios, and distributions of clast sizes and clast numbers through the Breccia. Figure 7 represents the results from the southern end of the Hiko Range, in Zone 2. Analyses in three other ranges within Zone 2 show similar results.

Using this technique, we discovered that the Breccia is internally stratified and contains as many as five separate scours, each overlain by a graded bed. The rapidly deposited Breccia was unstable, and the scour surfaces were pervasively deformed by dewatering and loading that created pockets of breccia-within-breccia—finer within coarser, and coarser within finer. The number of subevents recorded is greater where Facies C clasts are thin or missing at the base of the Breccia, and thus Facies A and B are thicker. They are reduced where more of the Breccia thickness is occupied by megaclasts along the base. Figure 8 shows the results from Tempiute Mountain in Zone 1, where the Breccia is thicker and finer grained, and where only two scour-and-deposit events were detected.

Paleocurrent directions

Figure 9 presents a summary of 12 rose diagrams constructed from 667 imbrication measurements collected along stretch lines in Zones 2 and 3 (Kuehner, 1997). We interpret the radially outward transport and deposition in Zone 3 to result from the uprush of tsunamis that transported Breccia material from deeper water and also reworked shallow-platform material and perhaps ejecta. The tsunamis coming to rest in Zone 3 may have been highly charged rock-and-water slurries that had no backwash component. The graded bed at each locality in Zone 3 has a distinctive Breccia composition derived from the admixture of local platform materials. Radially inward transport in Zone 2 is interpreted to represent slightly deeper water backwash from the tsunamis toward the crater.

Smoking Arsenal

When the Alamo Breccia was confirmed as a large-scale catastrophic unit anomalously resting upon a carbonate platform, we initiated a search for a "smoking gun" that would indicate an impact site. In the absence of an unequivocal crater, proxies for impact include shocked quartz or other shocked grains, iridium anomalies, and impact ejecta, as well as more subtle features such as impact-formed minerals—e. g., coesite, microscopic spinels, and diamond (see review by Koeberl and Anderson, 1996). The Breccia contains an arsenal of such features that unequivocally testify that it is an impact product—shocked quartz grains, an iridium anomaly, and ejecta in the form of distinctive carbonate spherules. Our search for other indicators is not yet completed.

Shocked quartz

Abundant shocked quartz grains from the Alamo event have now been identified in three different frameworks: (1) in the matrix of the Breccia; (2) in ejecta spherules in the Breccia; and (3) in bedrock in Zone 1 (Fig. 10). Several highly dispersed quartz grains were first documented by Ackman (1991) in rock thin sections from the upper few meters of the Breccia at the Worthington Mountains (Fig. 1). When insoluble residues of conodont samples from the Breccia became available, they yielded abundant shocked grains. Samples from above and below the Breccia do not contain these distinctive grains. The grains were incorporated into the Breccia as ejecta, and some may have been borne by tsunamis from sites closer to the impact. They were reworked by the tsunamis, because they tend to be sorted within the Breccia.

The quartz grains from the matrix of the Breccia exhibit an array of shock features. In thin section some are mildly deformed and exhibit only one or a few directions of shock lamellae. Others show as many as six directions. All lamellae are decorated with tiny inclusions, and almost all of the grains within the Breccia are studded with distinctive euhedral crystals of diagenetic displacive hematite. Most grains exhibit a highly irregular mottled extinction pattern under cross-polarized light. Analysis by Transmission Electron Microscopy (TEM) demonstrated unequivocal shock indicators—PDFs (planar deformation features) (Laroux et al., 1995).

Two other shocked quartz occurrences have been discovered since 1995. Silt-sized grains were detected in thin sections of ejecta spherules. The grains occupy much less than one percent of the volume of the spherules and are present in both the spherules and in the matrix of concentrated spherule masses. Elongate quartz grains tend to be arranged tangentially within the concentric grading of the spherules, as are the carbonate grains (Fig. 11).

Thin sections of the bedrock Oxyoke Canyon Sandstone (Fig. 10) under the Breccia at Tempiute Mountain contain rare shocked grains. These grains survived the pervasive post-event silica mobilization and alteration that occurred there.

Iridium

Iridium is proportionally more abundant in space materials than in terrestrial crustal rocks; thus, it is sought as a hallmark of extraterrestrial impacts. Analyses for iridium in the Alamo Breccia were negative except along two closely spaced vertical transects in the Worthington Mountains. Background levels of iridium in Guilmette Formation carbonates are ~2 to 10 ppt. The Worthington Mountains anomalies, concentrated ~1.5 m below the top of the Breccia, were as high as 139 ppt. Because the composition of the Breccia is 99+% pre-existing marine carbonate rock, any space-derived material in the Breccia was heavily diluted, and a detectable anomaly is remarkable.

Spherules

Composition. Spherules recovered from the Alamo Breccia superficially resemble volcanic lapilli (Fig. 11) and closely match the structure of those from the Miocene Ries Crater in Germany (Newsom et al., 1990). However, they are carbonate rather than silicate, implying that the target rocks were carbonates and that the projectile did not penetrate to deep levels of underlying siliceous sedimentary rocks or crystalline basement. The composition of the spherules also indicates that the impactor was an icy comet, rather than an asteroid, because of the absence of meteoritic stony or metallic components. They range from ~2 mm to 3 cm in diameter, have crystalline carbonate or carbonate clast cores, grade outward to very fine silt-sized grains, are rimmed by closely spaced concentric lamellae, and incorporate silt-sized grains of shocked quartz. In cross-section they are circular, deformed, or broken. The broken examples (Fig. 11) indicate that the spherules had relatively brittle rims and ductile interiors. In thin section, their interiors seem to have the same composition as the matrix between spherules.

We believe that the spherules formed by accretion around a nucleus in the dust and vapor cloud created by the impact. Such a cloud may have risen to tens of kilometers above the crater. Many of the spherules have a nucleus of

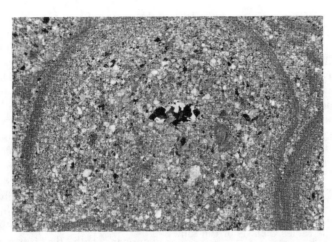

FIG. 11. Photomicrograph of carbonate spherules from the reworked spherule clast in the Alamo Breccia. The central spherule shows a coarsely crystalline nucleus surrounded by a core of grains that fine outward and culminate in very fine grained rims. The spherule is deformed on the right-hand side by an adjoining one, and broken along the base. The matrix consists of the same silt- and clay-sized material as in the spherule interiors. Spherules are commonly deformed or broken by impact or by the loading process that preserved them from tsunami erosion. Spherule rims were more brittle than the soft and unconsolidated cores. Field of view ~0.5 cm.

coarsely crystalline calcite that may represent a water droplet or ice to which pulverized rock particles adhered. To our knowledge, carbonate spherules such as these have not been described from other impact sites or ejecta blankets.

Stratigraphy. The stratigraphic distribution of the spherules helps reveal the depositional sequence within the Breccia. The spherules were formed in the water-charged ejecta cloud, and precipitated in layers, most of which were reworked by tsunamis (Warme and Kuehner, 1997). Figures 7 and 8 show the position of deformed masses of spherules within the Breccia at two localities. The masses are a few decimeters to meters across and are deformed between the Breccia clasts. They occur in the Breccia as deep as 30 m from the top. Zones rich and poor in spherules, and a rough grading, can still be detected in some of these masses. The spherules were preserved in two possible ways: (1) by sinking into the newly deposited underlying breccia, which was unstable and easily loaded, or (2) by incorporation into overlying breccia beds through transportation and deposition by ensuing tsunamis. In either case, the spherule beds must have been cohesive and possessed some strength.

Only one segment of an undistorted spherule bed has been found, apparently in its original position; it is 3 m long and 0.75 m high, and occurs 4 m below the top of the Breccia in Zone 2. The spherules in it tend to be sorted by size in vertical zones and are interbedded with spherule-poor zones of fine-grained matrix, uncoated carbonate fragments, and attenuated carbonate clasts. The spherule bed apparently resisted complete erosion by the tsunami that deposited the next overlying portion of the Breccia.

The spherule beds and the distorted spherule masses accumulated one or more times to a thickness of 0.75 m or more, probably during the short stillstand between uprush and backwash of tsunamis (see the section entitled "Synthesis" below). However, the spherules and related ejecta must have rained down across the platform more or less continuously for several hours. Most of it was eroded, abraded into small components, and incorporated into the matrix of the breccia where it is unidentifiable. We believe that a large volume of spherules was deposited, most of which was disaggregated by the tsunamis that oscillated across the platform.

Attenuated clasts. Attenuated, wispy clasts are incorporated into the spherule masses. They are few centimeters to decimeters in length, are irregularly curved, appear stretched, and have tattered or serrated ends. They resemble the geometry of fragments of melt rock in the siliceous suevite of the Ries Crater (personal observation of the senior author), and may have been hot meltrock when deposited along with the spherules. These fragments rarely form the nuclei of spherules 2 to 3 cm across. If these flame-shaped clasts are a carbonate version of suevite, then the entire spherule bed may have been hot when deposited and partially welded upon cooling, imparting the strength needed to withstand loading in the Breccia or transportation across it by tsunamis.

Reworked conodonts

Conodont assemblages from the matrix of the lower part of the Breccia indicate *punctata*-zone shallow-water environments similar to those recovered from the Facies C clasts of the same interval. Assemblages from the upper part of the Breccia have a high proportion of *punctata*-zone deeper-water forms, as well as rare Ordovician specimens (Warme and Sandberg, 1995, 1996). The deeper-water conodonts were interpreted to be derived from *punctata*-zone strata at the impact site, delivered as ejecta and/or by tsunamis. It is possible that the general upward deepening, documented for the lower member of the Guilmette, produced rare, thin, unrecognized deep-water limestones that liberated the conodonts during the Breccia-forming processes. The Ordovician conodonts were also interpreted as exotics that were transported within impact ejecta and/or by the tsunamis (Figs. 7 and 8). They suggest that the crater may have extended as deep as the Ordovician, or encountered younger rocks with reworked Ordovician fossils. There is no independent evidence of crater penetration as deep as the Ordovician.

"Shocked Formations" and the Crater

The Alamo Breccia is exposed in cross section on numerous uplifted ranges and provides a rare potential to discover and characterize the crater or craters, if preserved, in three dimensions. By following the trail of the deposit across southern Nevada, we have identified characteristics that may signify crater segments.

Zone 1 as a crater

The rocks under, within, and over the Alamo Breccia in Zone 1 are different from those in Zones 2 and 3, and are presumed to be closer to

the center of a crater. The underlying beds are peculiarly deformed, the Breccia itself is thick but comparatively fine grained, and the overlying beds constitute a deep-water facies. The single Breccia locality found to date in Zone 1 is a ridge several kilometers long on Tempiute Mountain (Fig. 1).

Bedrock deformation. The bedrock under the Breccia at Tempiute Mountain has curious characteristics that we first attributed to tectonic and metamorphic processes associated with an adjacent mineralized intrusion, which is the site of 19th-century silver mines and the recently inactivated Tempiute tungsten mine. However, except for stretched clasts near the boundary with the intrusion, the Breccia escaped pervasive fracturing and other distortion that is present in the rocks under it.

About 300 m below the base of the Breccia, the thin Late Lower or Middle Devonian Oxyoke Canyon Sandstone (Fig. 3) is heavily penetrated by a system of sedimentary dikes and sills. These extend upward into the intervening dolostones of the Middle Devonian Sentinel Mountain and Bay State formations (equivalent to the Simonson Formation). The dolostone margins of the dikes and sills are fluidized and preserved in various stages of detachment and incorporation into the sedimentary fill (Kuehner, 1997). The fractures are filled with sand grains, twisted slabs of the Oxyoke preserved in the process of disintegrating, and various kinds of dolostone lithoclasts (Sandberg et al., 1997a) (Fig. 11). These "propants" are interpreted to have been forced upward into fractures formed by the impact, similar to propants within the Roberts Rift near the Upheaval Dome impact crater in Utah (Huntoon and Shoemaker, 1995). The Oxyoke Sandstone was likely to have been less thoroughly cemented, more nearly porous, and more nearly fluid saturated than the overlying dolostones, and thus was more easily overpressured and mobilized by the impact. Shocked quartz grains were identified in the Oxyoke Canyon at this location, as described above (Fig. 10).

Under the Breccia, the entire 300 m thick column of dolostones overlying the Oxyoke Canyon at Tempiute Mountain is internally twisted, sheared, and heavily veined. The dolostones appear to have been partially fluidized. They contain arrays of countless cement-filled

FIG. 12. Three expressions of cavities, showing the variety of sizes and geometries, that permeate dolostones under the Alamo Breccia at Tempiute Mountain. Dark geopetal sediment fills the lower portion, whereas white spar cement fills the remainder. A. Cluster of cavities dispersed in dolostone matrix. B. Stacked, parallel, elongate cavities offset by small faults. C. Tight cluster of cavities ranging from ~1 to 25 mm across. Scale bar equals 5 cm. These pervasive vugs, within the framework of larger-scale dolostone deformation, are interpreted as products of thermal and shock waves under or near the impact crater.

vugs, ~1 mm to 40 cm across (Fig. 12), which represent void formation by some process(es). We propose that some combination of shearing, fluidization, or gas generation by the pressure and heat of impact created the cavities. They occur in various sizes and shapes, but tend to form clusters of similar scale and geometry. The clusters generally follow bedding, which still preserves fossiliferous intervals in the folded and distorted dolostone.

Internally, each vug contains a geopetal deposit, having a lower part filled with sediment and an upper portion filled with carbonate cement (Fig. 12). Vug geometries are highly variable, and some superficially resemble *Stromatactus*, an enigmatic fossil or primary or diagenetic sedimentary structure in carbonate rocks. Many examples appear to represent larger, flatter cavities that were compartmentalized by tiny faults. The vugs of all shapes are commonly connected by thin sinuous seams that appear to have been fluid conduits. Similar vugs and connecting seams are present within the matrix of some of the sedimentary dikes and sills. They appear to represent a dewatering and/or degassing process. To our knowledge, such vugs have not been found or described at other impact sites.

The dikes, sills, and distorted dolostones at Tempiute Mountain are interpreted as entire "shocked" formations at or near the crater. They exhibit properties consistent with processes that occur a few seconds to hours after impact. Field characteristics of the dolostones suggest that seismic shear dilated the bedrock and perhaps released pore pressures and mobilized fluids. A thermal front heated and vaporized formation fluids, and weakened or volatilized the bedrock. Interstitial bubbles coalesced to form vugs that expanded and filled with a mobilized rock, liquid, and/or gas slurry. The shear relaxed, slowly or rapidly, and some of the vugs were faulted into smaller segments (Fig. 12). Compressed fluids migrated between cavities until equilibrium was attained. If the Sentinel Mountain and Bay State dolostones were part of the target rocks, they probably were undolomitized limestone at the time of impact. The spherules derived from the impact, as described above, are limestone and contain little magnesium.

Rock fluidization and liquifaction processes expected to occur during cratering are described in papers in volumes edited by Silver and Schultz (1982), Roddy et al. (1977), and Dressler et al. 1994); in the monograph by Melosh (1989); and in other sources. Several theoretical mechanisms exist to weaken and alter target rock. In a series of experiments, Dey and Brown (1990) showed that saturated limestones are fluidized by much less shear stress than are dry samples, and pervasive microfracturing may occur. Melosh (1989, p. 151) offered a concept whereby rock heated in and around a crater may fluidize, flow briefly as a melt-solid slurry, then cool and solidify.

In a comprehensive field study of the Sierra Madera impact structure in Texas, Wilshire et al. (1971) identified dikes and sills filled with monomictic and polymictic carbonate breccias and sandstones similar to those under the Alamo Breccia in Zone 1. They described penetration and flow of bedrock fragments in the uplifted core of the crater for distances of up to 500 m, both upward and downward from their normal stratigraphic positions. The injected fractures display altered and plucked wall rock. They also documented quartz sandstone dikes that penetrated upward tens of meters from a thin sandstone formation that was interpreted to be relatively unconsolidated and mobilized at the time of impact. The carbonate breccias are similar to those that penetrate the dolostones under the Breccia at Tempiute Mountain, and the sandstone dikes and sills are remarkably like the Oxyoke Canyon examples. These examples suggest that our interpretations of the deformation structures under the Breccia in Zone 1 are realistic.

Zone 1 at Tempiute Mountain is proposed as the closest known Breccia segment to the crater. We envisage that the fluidized and upward-injected Oxyoke Canyon Sandstone represents an interval that focused detachments as outward-directed thrusts or inward-directed listric faults during crater formation. Strong inward and upward movement creates the central uplift of large craters. The overlying dolostones, injected from below by the Oxyoke Canyon and internally deformed, may represent a large-scale detached impact thrust slice or slumped block within or near the crater, similar to those interpreted by Poag (1997a) from seismograms across the Eocene crater under Chesapeake Bay. The small-scale geopetal-filled vugs were formed by shock and thermal pulses during and

shortly after impact. If the 300 m thick dolostone section is detached, it could be regarded as a megablock at the base of the Breccia, and the total Breccia thickness would be 400+ m, rather than 130 m, at Tempiute Mountain.

Alamo Breccia. The Alamo Breccia at Tempiute Mountain may be an early, instantaneous part of the crater fill. The Breccia is the thickest (~130 m) that we have documented (Figs. 4 and 8), but also is the finest grained and contains relatively small megaclasts (maximum ~5 × 15 m). An important observation at Tempiute Mountain is that the Alamo Breccia and the overlying sedimentary formations look fresh compared to the underlying dolostones, even though the Breccia is closer to the Tempiute Mine intrusion. Both dolostones and breccia underwent the same history of burial, nearby intrusion, faulting, and uplift, but only the dolostones are riddled with fractures and carbonate-filled veins, in addition to the geopetals, dikes, and sills described above. These relationships indicate that the dolostones were altered by the impact, and that the Breccia, although it was deposited only a few minutes or hours later, was not.

Devils Gate Formation. It is difficult to delineate the exact top of the Alamo Breccia at Tempiute Mountain. The Breccia grades upward to a thick carbonate mudstone that merges with a deep-water facies interpreted as the Devils Gate Formation, which is 235 m thick and contains the Frasnian/Famennian boundary (Sandberg et al., 1997a). It generally consists of thin-bedded limestones with slumps, shallow channels filled with brecciated slumps and rip-up clasts, and a few quartzose sandy turbidites with limestone rip-ups. The section has been tightly dated and bathymetrically interpreted by Morrow (1997). Benthic fossils are rare, lack diversity, and may have been transported from higher parts of the crater. Trace fossils (burrows) are generally absent, implying a stratified water column that would be expected in a silled crater depression. However, these beds contain pelagic conodonts, styliolinids, and other forms that indicate the water column was connected at the surface to the open sea, and that any crater rim was partially or wholly underwater.

If the Breccia and overlying Devils Gate were deposited within the crater, the finer portions of the Breccia flowed into it freely; no high peak rim acted as a total barrier. This relationship implies that the crater was relatively small (V. Oberbeck, 1997, pers. commun.). It is also possible that a relatively low peak rim formed and blocked the megaclasts from entering the crater, but not the suspended finer-grained debris.

The phenomena displayed at Tempiute Mountain may represent the central crater root or margin, or a location some significant distance from the central impact zone. The site likely portrays a fragment of a larger structure that has not yet been identified. It could also represent a secondary crater, such as that associated with the Chesapeake Bay impact (Poag, 1997a). Tempiute Mountain is surrounded on the north, west, and south by intermontane valleys with no known Devonian outcrops nearby. Moreover, the Paleozoic strata exposed on Tempiute Mountain are bounded by prominent thrusts and other faults, and probably rest within a thrust sheet that may be part of a thick thrust stack (Chamberlain and Gillespie, 1993; Taylor et al., 1993), hiding segments of the crater. No general agreement exists among structural geologists regarding the style, magnitude, and sequence of post–Alamo event crustal shortening and lengthening in our study region of southern Nevada.

Zone 2 as an annular trough

Over all of Zones 2 and 3 (Fig. 1) we see no systematic faults, fractures, shattercones, or other features beneath the Breccia that might imply a crater. There the Breccia was interpreted to have originated by shallow bedrock detachment and disintegration from seismic shock, crustal tilting upon impact, tsunami loading and/or shear, or other impact-related processes. Detachment was followed by transportation of some of the fractured platform into deep water offshore by mass gravity flow, and modification of the remainder by subsequent catastrophic waves and currents (Warme and Sandberg, 1995, 1996). An alternative explanation is that the apparently abrupt change in Breccia thickness between Zones 2 and 3 marks the position of a faulted crater ring that has not been identified in the discontinuous outcrops, and that Zone 2 is an annular crater trough.

Facies D underlying the Breccia in Zone 2 may represent a flat, shallow, crater-detachment floor. The genetic relationships between crater rings, impact-induced faults, and annular moats or troughs are not well understood (Spudis, 1994), but may have been clarified by the recent analysis and summary by Poag (1997a) of the Late Eocene crater (90 km in diameter) under Chesapeake Bay. Results of drilling and seismic profiling show a central depression surrounded concentrically by a zone of peak ring faults, an annular trough, and a zone of rim faults. A widespread ejecta blanket extends beyond the crater. The annular trough is flat floored and contains megablocks defined by listric faults that flatten and merge along the base of the trough. In this example, the detachment surface is the top of the crystalline basement. The thickness of the blocks and impact breccia overlying them varies around the trough, but averages ~500 m, according to Poag's interpreted seismic lines.

Zone 2 of the Alamo Breccia may correspond to such a moat. In this concept the level of Facies D, which floors the breccia and megaclasts in Zone 2, represents the detachment interval and zone where the listric faults merged along the moat floor. A family of more or less evenly spaced listric faults accounts for the approximately equal 400 to 500 m lengths of the largest Facies C megaclasts in Zone 2. Break-up of the platform, movement of the Breccia, and tsunami reworking erase the fault planes. A theoretical impact model offered by Melosh (1989) shows inward rotation and collapse of listric blocks over fluidized bedrock. The blocks flow toward the crater center and the process flattens the rocks across the ring area. A relevant experiment was the Snowball TNT explosion over a saturated substrate that became fluidized. Loosened blocks that rotated and slid radially inward, creating ring fractures and sand fountains, merged to form a central peak (Melosh, 1989).

It is not understood why the D Facies interval was propagated only 50 to 100 m beneath the surface of the contemporary carbonate platform. Possible contributing factors include a small or relatively low-speed impactor, direction and obliquity of impact, specific shock-wave and substrate characteristics, water-saturation and pore-pressure effects, overburden influences, etc. At Chesapeake Bay, the ratio of crater diameter to annular trough depth is ~180:1. By analogy, if the Alamo annular trough fill averages 60 m, then the crater diameter would be 10.8 km.

Western Facies

Figure 1 shows locations of Upper Devonian sections west of Zone 1. At some of these places, there exist thick debriites and turbidites that are strong candidates for deep-water equivalents of the Alamo Breccia, but they have not yet been closely dated. The generally fine-grained frameworks for the candidate beds are diverse western facies of the Devonian whose detailed interrelationships are not well understood.

At Carbonate Wash, a few meters of carbonate breccia is interbedded with other carbonate beds that appear to be deeper facies than the platform facies exposed in our study area to the east (C. A. Sandberg, 1997, pers. commun.). Carbonate Wash is in a restricted military zone and is not readily visited. Streuben Knob is in the Reveille Range, where a poorly exposed section contains a carbonate breccia, ~10+ m thick, with abundant stromatoporoid heads and fragments. This bed contrasts with other, thinner mass flows that contain mainly deeper-water components and probable small coral-bearing olistoliths.

Near Warm Springs in the Hot Creek Range, a well-studied Middle and Upper Devonian section has a significant unconformity, across which there is a gap of 11 conodont zones representing an ~8 m.y. hiatus (Sandberg et al., 1997a; Stop 5). This gap is widespread in central Nevada and brackets the Alamo event. It conceivably could be related to impact-tectonic processes such as crater formation and evolution; to crustal depression, rebound, and erosion; and/or to regional deep-water slumping and tsunami scouring, as speculated by Sandberg et al. (1997a). However, a preserved Alamo Breccia nominee exists at newly discovered localities in the Hot Creek Range north of Warm Springs. It is ~20 m thick and contains abundant stromatoporoid fragments and distinctive attenuated and wispy clasts that may represent possible carbonate melt rocks similar to those associated with the spherule beds described above.

The Reveille Range and Hot Creek Range beds are both rich in platform-derived stromatoporoids, which may be deep-water tracers for the Breccia. The attenuated clasts in

the Hot Creek Range probably were much more fragile than the stromatoporoid heads, and could not survive long transport distances. These distinctive clasts hint that airborne ejecta traveled as far as the Hot Creek Range, 100+ km west of the platform and the proposed crater site.

A distinctive, thin (<1 m) graded bed was discovered ~300 km northwest of Zone 1 in the carbonate-platform facies of the lower Devils Gate Formation (Sandberg et al., 1997a). It occurs within the correct interval to be a candidate for the Alamo Breccia, but has not yet been closely investigated or dated.

Synthesis

Figure 13 summarizes our interpretation of the genesis of the Alamo Breccia. The sequential cross sections show a closely spaced series of impact-related events, and represent a working concept that accounts for the stratigraphic framework and internal properties of the Alamo Breccia as we now know it.

Crater location

As shown in Figure 13A, the impactor probably struck on the shallow-water carbonate platform, near its seaward edge. No deep-water facies have been identified as ejecta in the Breccia, and the spherules that it contains are almost pure limestone where not dolomitized by later diagenesis. Alternatively, the impact could have occurred on a carbonate slope or ramp leading west into deep water; this interpretation is favored by Sandberg (Sandberg and Warme, 1993; Warme and Sandberg, 1995, 1996) because the tsunamites in the upper part of the Breccia contain conodonts that indicate off-platform depths. No clasts of igneous or metamorphic rocks have been found. Quartz grains, although shocked, are quite rare, indicating that the crater did not reach the Eureka Sandstone ~1300 m below the Alamo Breccia at Tempiute Mountain. These observations imply that the impactor was relatively small or struck at a low angle. The recently discovered debris flows in ranges to the west were likely caused by failure along the carbonate margin west of the

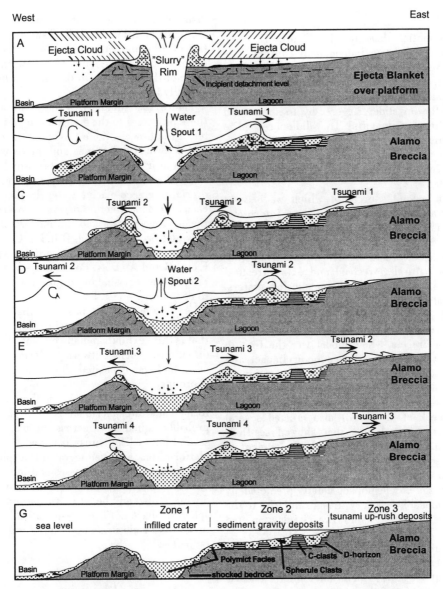

FIG. 13. Scenario for the sequence of processes occurring during the Alamo event, showing the marine impact on the Upper Devonian outer carbonate platform. A–F. Initial impact fractures bedrock and creates transient crater and slurry rim. Rim collapse outward induces initial tsunami. Rim collapse inward creates first waterspout, its collapse, and second tsunami; sequential waterspouts and their collapse create repeated waves that damp with time. High-velocity ejecta curtain and rain of spherules from impact cloud blankets platform, but is mostly eroded by ongoing tsunamis. G. Zone 1 contains crater with sedimentary dikes and sills and shocked dolostones under partial sedimentary fill of polymict Alamo Breccia. Zone 2 exhibits regional monomict Facies D detachment breccia underlying Facies C megaclasts and polymict Breccia Facies B and A. Zone 2 may be an annular crater trough, with rotated Facies C listric fault blocks over Facies D detachment interval. Zone 3 shows thin Breccia stranded above sea level by tsunamis on a shallower part of the platform (from Kuehner, 1997).

crater, triggered by the Alamo event, supplemented by material from Tsunami backwash off the platform. Similar Atlantic basin base-of-

slope slumps, triggered by the impact at Chesapeake Bay, were interpreted by Poag (1997a) from seismograms.

Impact scenario

Sequential diagrams in Figure 13 were adapted from two independent sources. The first was published by Warme and Sandberg (1995, 1996), who explained the Alamo Breccia as an unusual epiplatform detachment and seaward-flowing slide, triggered by an impact and modified by tsunami(s). They did not recognize the internal multiple events shown in Figures 7 and 8, and did not consider the possibility that the Alamo Breccia rested, at least in part, within a crater.

The second source, of which we became aware after publication of the above interpretation, is the comprehensive model of Oberbeck et al. (1993) for a marine impact. Their sequence of events was synthesized from studies of natural terrestrial and extraterrestrial craters, nuclear and other explosion craters, laboratory impact experiments, and crater theory developed by workers at NASA and other organizations. They were not aware of the Alamo Breccia. Their model was the first to predict the outcome of an aqueous impact, and it included a mechanism for propagation of multiple tsunamis and for failure and slumping of a siliciclastic delta across a continental shelf. Oberbeck et al. (1993) also erected several stratigraphic columns that showed sea-floor erosion and deformation, and development of new sedimentary beds and structures that would form at various distances away from the target zone. The impact details predicted by their model bear a very strong similarity to the features of the Alamo Breccia documented across Zones 1 to 3 (Kuehner et al., 1996).

Figure 13A shows the position of the impact, transient crater, fractured bedrock, and development of a slurry rim of water and rock debris near the edge of the carbonate platform. The impact shock wave propagates through the platform, creates the Facies D detachment level, and fractures the platform above it to create Facies C megablock boundaries. The initial high-velocity ejecta curtain is deposited across the platform. Figure 13B shows the slurry rim collapsing outward to generate the first tsunami, and inward to create the first waterspout. The first tsunami erodes and mixes ejecta with nearly *in situ* fragmented carbonate-platform rocks and stirred surficial sediments. In Figure 13C, tsunami 1 breaks across the distal platform, and spout 1 collapses to generate tsunami 2. Figures 13D–F show the formation of subsequent tsunamis and spouts that are damped with time. Tsunami backwash brings some of the Breccia into the crater, where it is partially filled.

Figure 13G summarizes the relationship of these processes to the distribution and character of the Breccia. Zone 1 exhibits the shocked and deformed dolostones and quartzose sandstones near or under the crater, which is partially filled with the thick polymict Breccia and overlain by deep-marine water. In Zone 2, the Facies D detachment horizon is overlain by Facies C megaclasts and the moderately thick polymict Breccia of Facies B and A. Clast orientations indicate mainly seaward transport of Facies B and A clasts. Post-event water depths range from very shallow around the periphery to deep near Zone 1, and a newly formed ramp floored by breccia extends from the shoreline into the crater. Zone 3 contains Alamo Breccia that is thin, exhibits radially outward transport directions, tapers outward to form a feather edge, and was deposited above the post-event shoreline.

Small ejecta fragments, as well as spherules formed at stratospheric levels above the crater, probably rained down across the platform for several hours. The tsunamis mixed ejecta with platform rock and disintegrated the spherules, except for rare loaded masses and intact residual beds that accumulated between tsunamis or during stillstands between turnarounds. The spherules have not been systematically sought in *punctata*-zone strata beyond the reach of the tsunamis.

Discussion

From the evidence presented above, it is certain that the Alamo Breccia is related to the impact of an object from space. Several lines of evidence indicate that the impactor was relatively small, but that it produced wide-ranging effects across the platform and into deep water. We do not yet fully understand, however, important issues such as the size and location of the central crater, the composition of the projectile, the relative proportions of true ejecta versus locally derived platform rocks, the full lateral extent of the Breccia, the distribution of fallout beyond the Breccia, the consequences of the event for regional geological development, and possible global significance.

Crater location and dimensions

We believe that the injected and distorted bedrock under the Breccia at Tempiute Mountain represents impact phenomena at or near the impact site. If so, then ~300 m of stratigraphic section is missing and was blasted or slumped away (Fig. 4) and an additional underlying ~300 m was deformed. Exposures there are limited to a N-S strike ridge a few kilometers in length. It is not known how extensive these features were, only that they do not occur in the numerous Breccia localities to the north, east, and south. No large clasts of Lower Devonian or of the distinctive underlying Paleozoic or Precambrian formations have been identified in the Breccia, indicating that the crater did not penetrate deeply.

If Zone 2 represents an annular trough, it is quite wide and contains a relatively thin (50 to 100 m) layer of megaclasts and breccia. If Zone 2 is not an annular trough, then the Breccia within it is the product of a massive slide, triggered by impact, as proposed by Warme and Sandberg (1995, 1996). In either case, the upper half of the Breccia was reworked by repetitive tsunamis simultaneously with the deposition of spherules and shocked quartz.

Composition of the impactor

No fragments of exotic material that could represent the projectile have been noted in reconnaissance of outcrops, in the course of the stretch-line clast censuses reported above, and, significantly, in the insoluble residues from 40+ conodont samples, each representing acid digestion of several kilograms of Breccia matrix. The results suggest that the impactor was an icy comet, or that it vaporized before reaching the surface of the Earth.

Composition and volume of ejecta

The only unambiguous ejecta identified within the Breccia are spherules, which occur in loaded and deformed masses or in rare beds, together with disseminated shocked quartz grains and unidentified iridium-bearing debris. If any carbonate clasts within the Breccia were transported as ejecta, we have not isolated them from locally derived clasts of the disintegrated

platform. If present, they represent shallow-water Devonian carbonates and indicate only shallow crustal penetration.

Lateral dimensions of the Breccia and fallout

The distribution of the Breccia across the carbonate platform of Zones 1–3, and its probable extension into the deeper Devonian sea to the west, was discussed above. We have not pursued the deposit landward beyond Zone 3, where it may be present as fallout along some horizon within the *punctata* zone. The light grey color of the Breccia in Zone 3 suggests that it may contain a high proportion of fallout spherules that were disaggregated by the tsunamis. Significant volumes of fallout may have been washed into Zone 3 and mixed with the Breccia by torrential post-impact rains. Immediate runoff, or the next post-event platform transgression, may have eroded any record of the Breccia beyond Zone 3.

Regional relationships

Because an impact of some magnitude occurred, it may have caused detectable crustal deformation. The broad unconformity that represents several million years of missing time west of Zone 1, including the *punctata* zone, may be related directly or indirectly to impact or post-impact processes.

When the Alamo event was first documented as a regional phenomenon, we speculated that it had some relationship to the late Paleozoic Antler orogeny. Coincidentally, the Antler foreland and Pilot basins were initiated during *punctata* time. Early publication of this and other speculative notions was declined by journal editors. In a recent overview of the entire problem of the driving forces that created the Antler orogeny and associated foreland, Ketner (in press) found scant evidence, based on field work in several key areas, for classic thrusting. Citing the Alamo event, for example, he suggested that some other cause may account for the field relationships that he documented.

Possible connections between impacts and significant mineral deposits are well known at Sudbury in Canada, Vredefort in South Africa, and elsewhere. We speculate that crustal damage from impact may have influenced the location of the large tungsten mine at the proposed crater site on Tempiute Mountain. The broad central Nevada Carlin gold trend is within the northern part of the study area, and genesis of this trend is enigmatic.

Impacts and extinctions

On a global scale, any substantial Phanerozoic impact may have consequences that affect the rate of extinctions and thus the course of biological evolution. Immense physical damage was caused by the Alamo event, but no regional or global increase in extinction rates is known at this time (Warme and Sandberg, 1995). Raup (1992), Jansa (1993), and others have produced "kill curves" that match the size of craters, and thus of impactors, with given percentages of immediate global extinctions. They proposed threshold magnitudes above which certain levels of extinctions occur. Poag (1997b) questioned the value of the curve, using as examples the large Late Eocene Chesapeake Bay (90 km diameter) and Popigay (100 km diameter) craters that do not narrowly coincide with extinction events.

A related issue is whether some impacts merely destabilize many species, as would any large-scale environmental trauma. Such species never fully recover and then succumb to subsequent changes from repetitive impacts or other causes, such as sea-level shifts or volcanism. The environmental consequences of impacts may last for significant periods of geologic time, and the results of all environmental changes may be cumulative, so that deleterious effects on species longevity are protracted. For example, Late Eocene impacts occurred a few million years before the terminal Eocene extinctions (Poag, 1997b). The Alamo event was one of several Devonian impacts, which—together with orogeny, sea-level change, and possibly other factors—perhaps led to the rapid biotic turnover documented throughout the period (Sandberg et al., 1988, 1997a; Schönlaub, 1996). The most familiar of these mass extinctions occurred around the Frasnian/Famennian boundary, ~3 m.y. after the Alamo event, but others occurred in the Devonian. A series of impacts may have destabilized many species, so that they could not tolerate environmental perturbations from any sources (see the comprehensive review of this topic applied to the Devonian by McGhee, 1996).

Conclusions

The Alamo Breccia was discovered in 1990, interbedded with shallow-water platform carbonates of the Upper Devonian Guilmette Formation in southern Nevada. The Breccia consists of 99+% fragmented and redeposited shallow-water carbonate-platform sediments. It was quickly recognized as a regional catastrophic deposit, and linked to the impact of an extraterrestrial object (the Alamo event) by detection in it of shocked quartz, an iridium anomaly, and ejecta spherules.

The Breccia falls into three concentric, semicircular zones, open to the west, encompassing ~10,000 km². The zones are based on Breccia thicknesses and internal attributes. The Breccia is >100 m thick in Zone 1, ~50 to 100 m in Zone 2, and <1 to ~7 m in Zone 3. The Breccia averages more than 50 meters in thickness over large areas and contains a volume of 500+ km³. From the central Zone 1 outward, the Breccia overlies increasingly younger strata, becomes thinner, and is overlain by progressively shallower facies.

Internally the Breccia is divided into four vertical facies (A–D), which are most characteristic of Zone 2. The basal Facies D represents a regional detachment surface and is overlain by Facies C megaclasts, up to 500 m long, that remain at or near their original positions. Between and over the megaclasts is a Facies B debriite overlain by up to five Facies A turbidites caused by multiple tsunamis.

Bedrock fluidization occurred in three situations—along the detachment interval of Facies D, around the peripheries of clasts in the Breccia, and in bedrock under the Breccia in Zone 1. Shocked quartz grains were recovered within three frameworks—Breccia matrix, ejecta spherules in the Breccia, and bedrock beneath the Breccia in Zone 1. The distinctive carbonate spherules are a new impact phenomenon. They structurally resemble volcanic lapilli, were formed in the ejecta cloud, and blanketed the platform. Most of them were destroyed by tsunamis and/or runoff.

Zone 1 has attributes that suggest that it is located within or near the crater. Beneath the Breccia, dolostone bedrock is penetrated by a network of dikes and sills, emanating from the underlying Oxyoke Canyon Sandstone and injected with sand grains and deformed sandstone slabs. The dolostones are pervasively deformed and crowded with newly described microfaulted cavities. The dikes, sills, and cavities are attributed to impact stress and thermal pulses. Over the Breccia, slumped, thin-bedded limestones were deposited in a stratified water column that may have occupied the crater. West of Zone 1, thick, off-platform, deeper-water mass flows of anomalous composition may correlate with the shallow-water Breccia. Zone 2 was originally interpreted as the area of epiplatform detachment and movement westward into deeper water, triggered by the impact. Alternatively, it may represent an annular trough around the central crater. Zone 3 would lie beyond the trough.

A scenario for shallow-water impacts, adapted from a synthesis of crater-event knowledge, was employed to integrate the diverse attributes of the Breccia. The sequence of impact-induced processes and products in the scenario explains the genesis of the Breccia as we currently understand it.

Rocks that belong to the Alamo Breccia were investigated, measured, described, and variously interpreted in several localities in different mountain ranges of southern Nevada, but no one recognized the character, regional extent, and significance of the deposit prior to the studies reported here. The certain flux of impacts throughout geologic time assures that many more overlooked impact deposits will be discovered in the global stratigraphic record. We must be alert for catastrophic signatures, be aware of new paradigms, and match our imaginations with the scale of these events.

Acknowledgments

We thank UNOCAL and NSF (EAR-9106324) for initial support for work on the Alamo Breccia. The new work reported here was funded by a grant to Kuehner from the German Academic Exchange Foundation, by the Department of Geology and Geological Engineering at the Colorado School of Mines, and by personal funds. Our observations, interpretations, and conclusions were aided by numerous individuals, most of whom accompanied us during field work when the most significant progress was made—Walter Alvarez, Brian Ackman, Alan Chamberlain, Philippe Claeys, Scott Hassler, Fred Hörz, Ken Hsü, Don Lowe, Verne Oberbeck, David Roddy, E. L. Winterer, Yarmanto, and many others who contributed as individuals and as participants in organized field excursions to the Alamo Breccia. Charles Sandberg and Jared Morrow provided data, background, and interpretations that were crucial to our studies. Warren Hamilton's review greatly improved this manuscript; however, the work and the conclusions are our own.

REFERENCES

Ackman, B. W., 1991, Stratigraphy of the Guilmette Formation, Worthington Mountains and Shell Creek Range, southeastern Nevada: Unpubl. M.S. thesis, Colorado School of Mines, 207 p.

Alvarez, L. W., Alvarez, W., Asaro, F., and Michel, H. V., 1980, Extraterrestrial cause for the Cretaceous-Tertiary extinction: Science, v. 208, p. 1095–1108.

Alvarez, W., 1997, T. rex and the crater of doom: Princeton, NJ, Princeton Univ. Press, 185 p.

Chamberlain, A. K., and Gillespie, C. W., 1993, Evidence of late Mesozoic thrusting, Timpahute Range, south-central Nevada: Nevada Petrol. Soc. 1993 Field Conf. Guidebook, p. 139–155.

Chamberlain, A. K., and Warme, J. E., 1996, Devonian sequences and sequence boundaries, Timpahute Range, Nevada, in Longman, M. W., and Sonnenfeld, M. D., eds., Paleozoic systems of the Rocky Mountain Region: Denver, CO, Rocky Mountain Sect. SEPM, p. 63–84.

Cook, H. E., 1983, Introductory perspectives, basic carbonate principles, and stratigraphic and depositional models, in Platform margin and deepwater carbonates: SEPM Short Course No. 12, p. 1:1–1:89.

Dey, T. N., and Brown, J. A., 1990, Liquifaction of fluid saturated rocks due to explosion-induced stress waves: Symposium proceedings, Rock Mechanics, Contributions and Challenges: Rock Mechanics, v. 31, p. 889–896.

Dressler, B. O., Grieve, R. A. F., and Sharpton, V. L., 1994, eds., Large meteorite impacts and planetary evolution: Geol. Soc. Amer. Spec. Pap. 293, 348 p.

Dunn, M. J., 1979, Depositional history and paleoecology of an Upper Devonian (Frasnian) bioherm, Mount Irish, Nevada: Unpubl. M.S. thesis, State University of New York, Binghamton, 133 p.

Gehrels, T., ed., 1994, Hazards due to comets and asteroids: Tucson, AZ, Univ. of Arizona Press, 1300 p.

Grieve, R. A. F., and Shoemaker, E. M., 1994, The record of past impacts on Earth, in Gehrels, T., ed., Hazards due to comets and asteroids: Tucson, AZ, Univ. of Arizona Press, p. 417–462.

Huntoon, P. W., and Shoemaker, E. M., 1995, Roberts Rift, Canyonlands, Utah, a natural hydraulic fracture caused by comet or asteroid impact: Ground Water, v. 33, p. 561–569.

Hurtubise, D. O., 1989, Stratigraphy and structure of the Seaman Range and Fox Mountain area, Lincoln and Nye counties, Nevada, with emphasis on the Devonian System: Unpubl. Ph.D. dissertation, Colorado School of Mines, 443 p.

Jansa, L. F., 1993, Cometary impacts into ocean: Their recognition and the threshold constraint for biological extinctions: Palaeogeography, Palaeoclimatology, Palaeoecology, v. 104, p. 271–286.

Johnson, J. G., Sandberg, C. A., and Poole, F. G., 1991, Devonian lithofacies of western United States, *in* Cooper, J. D., and Stevens, C. H., eds., Paleozoic paleogeography of the Western United States. II: Pacific Sect. SEPM, v. 67, p. 83–105.

Ketner, K. B., in press, The nature and timing of tectonism in the western facies terrain of Nevada and California: An outline of evidence and interpretations derived from geologic maps of key areas: U. S. Geol. Surv. Prof. Pap. 1592.

Koeberl, C., and Anderson, R. R., 1996, Manson and company: Impact structures in the United States, *in* Koeberl, C., and Anderson, R. R., eds., The Manson impact structure, Iowa: Anatomy of an impact crater: Geol. Soc. Amer. Spec. Pap. 302, p. 1–29.

Kuehner, H.-C., 1997, The Late Devonian Alamo Impact Breccia, southeastern Nevada: Unpubl. Ph.D. dissertation, Colorado School of Mines, 321 p.

Kuehner, H.-C., Warme, J. E., and Oberbeck, V. R., 1996, Impact stratigraphy: Comparison of synthetic model with Late Devonian Alamo Breccia [abs.]: Geol. Soc. Amer. Abs. Prog., vol. 28, no. 7, p. A-181.

Laroux, H., Warme, J. E., and Doukhan, J. C., 1995, Shocked quartz in the Alamo breccia, southern Nevada: Evidence for a Devonian impact event: Geology, v. 23, p. 1003–1006.

McGhee, G. R., Jr., 1996, The Late Devonian mass extinction: New York, Columbia Univ. Press, 303 p.

Melosh, H. J., 1989, Impact cratering: New York, Oxford Univ. Press, 245 p.

Montanari, A., Asaro, F., and Kennett, J. P., 1993, Iridium anomalies of Late Eocene age at Massignano (Italy) and ODP Site 689B (Maud Rise, Antarctica): Palaios, v. 8, p. 420–437.

Morgan, J., Warner, M., and the Chicxulub Working Group, 1996, Size and morphology of the Chicxulub impact crater: Nature, v. 390, p. 472–476.

Morrow, J. R., 1997, Shelf-to-basin event stratigraphy, conodont paleoecology, and geologic history across the Frasnian-Famennian (F-F, mid-Late Devonian) boundary mass extinction, central Great Basin, Western U. S.: Unpubl. Ph.D. dissertation, Univ. of Colorado, 355 p.

Newsom, H. E., Graup, G., Iseri, D. A., Geissman, J. W., and Keil, K., 1990, The formation of the Ries Crater, West Germany: Evidence of atmospheric interactions during a larger cratering event, *in* Sharpton, V. L. and Ward, P. D., eds., Global Catastrophes in Earth History: An Interdisciplinary Conference on Impacts, Volcanism, and Mass Mortality: Geol. Soc. Amer. Spec. Pap. 247, p. 195–206.

Oberbeck, V. R., Marshall, J. R., and Aggarwal, H., 1993, Impacts, tillites, and the breakup of Gondwanaland: Jour. Geol., v. 101, p. 1–19.

Poag, C. W., 1997a, The Chesapeake Bay bolide impact: A convulsive event in Atlantic Coastal Plain evolution: Sediment. Geol., v. 108, p. 45–90.

————, 1997b, Roadblocks on the kill curve: Testing the Raup hypothesis: Palaios, v. 12, p. 582–590.

Poole, F. G., Stewart, J. H., Palmer, A. R., Sandberg, C. A., Madrid, R. J., Ross, R. J., Hintze, L. F., Miller, M. M., and Wrucke, C. T., 1992, Latest Precambrian to latest Devonian time: Development of a continental margin, *in* Burchfiel, B. C., Lipman, P. W., and Zoback, M. L., eds., The Cordilleran orogen: Conterminous U. S.: Boulder, CO, Geol. Soc. Amer., The geology of North America, v. G-3, p. 9–56.

Raup, D. M., 1992, Large-body impact and extinction in the Phanerozoic: Paleobiology, v. 18, p. 80–88.

Reso, A., 1963, Composite columnar section of exposed Paleozoic and Cenozoic rocks in the Pahranagat Range, Lincoln County, Nevada: Geol. Soc. Amer. Bull., v. 74, p. 901–918.

Roddy, D. J., Pepin, R. O., and Merrill, R. B., eds., 1977, Impact and explosion cratering: New York, Pergamon.

Ryder, G., Fastovsky, D., and Gartner, S., eds., 1996, The Cretaceous–Tertiary event and other catastrophes in Earth history: Geol. Soc. Amer. Spec. Pap. 307, 580 p.

Sandberg, C. A., Morrow, J. R., and Warme, J. E., 1997a, Late Devonian Kellwasser events and major eustatic events, eastern Great Basin, Nevada and Utah: Brigham Young Univ. Geol. Studies, v. 42, part 1, p. 129–160.

————, 1997b, New light on distribution of Late Devonian Alamo impact phenomena, southern and central Nevada [abs.]: Geol. Soc. Amer. Abs., Ann. Meeting, Salt Lake City, v. 29, no. 6, p. A-80.

Sandberg, C. A., and Warme, J. W., 1993, Conodont dating, biofacies, and catastrophic origin of Late Devonian (early Frasnian) Alamo breccia, southern Nevada [abs.]: Geol. Soc. Amer. Abs. Prog., v. 25, no. 3, p. 77.

Sandberg, C. A., Ziegler, W., Dreesen, R., and Butler, J. L., 1988, Late Frasnian mass extinction: Conodont event stratigraphy, global changes, and possible causes: Courier Forschungs. Senckenberg, v. 102, p. 263–307.

Schönlaub, H. P., 1996, Scenarios of Proterozoic and Paleozoic catastrophes: A review: Abhand. der Geol. Bundesanstalt, v. 53, p. 59–75.

Sharpton, V. L., and Ward, P. D., eds., 1990, Global Catastrophes in Earth History: An Interdiscipinary Conference on Impacts, Volcanism, and Mass Mortality: Geol. Soc. Amer. Spec. Pap. 247, 631 p.

Silver, L. T., 1982, Introduction, *in* Silver, L. T., and Schultz, P. H., eds., Geological implications of impact of large asteroids and comets on the Earth: Geol. Soc. Amer. Spec. Pap. 190, p. xiii–xix.

Silver, L. T., and Schultz, P. H., 1982, Geological implications of impacts of large asteroids and comets on the Earth: Geol. Soc. Amer. Spec. Pap. 190, 528 p.

Spudis, P. D., 1994, The large impact process inferred from the geology of lunar multiring basins: Geol. Soc. Amer. Spec. Pap. 293, p. 1–10.

Taylor, W. J., Bartley, J. M., Fryxell, J. E., Schmitt, J. G., and Vandervoort, D. S., 1993, Tectonic style and regional relations of the central Nevada thrust belt, *in* Lahren, M. M., Trexler, J. H., and Spinosa, C., eds., Crustal evolution of the Great Basin and Sierra Nevada: Cordilleran/Rocky Mountain Sections, Geol. Soc. Amer. Guidebook, p. 57–96.

Tschanz, C. M., and Pampeyan, E. H., 1970, Geology and mineral deposits of Lincoln County, Nevada: Nevada Bur. Mines Geol., Bull. 73, 188 p.

Warme, J. E., 1991, The Alamo breccia: Catastrophic Devonian platform deposit in southeastern Nevada [abs.]: Event markers in Earth history, Int. Union Geol. Sci., Joint Meeting of IGCP Projects 216, 293, 303, August 28–30, 1991, Calgary, Prog. Abs., p. 75.

Warme, J. E., Chamberlain, A. K., and Ackman, B. W., 1991, The Alamo event: Devonian cataclysmic breccia in southeastern Nevada [abs.]: Geol. Soc. Amer. Abs., Cordilleran Sect. Meeting, San Francisco, Abs. Prog., v. 23, no. 2, p. 108.

Warme, J. E., and Kuehner, H.-C., 1997, Accretionary carbonate impact-ejecta spherules in the Upper Devonian Alamo Breccia, south-central Nevada [abs.]: Geol. Soc. Amer. Abs., Ann. Meeting, Salt Lake City, v. 29, no. 6, p. A-80.

Warme, J. E., Kuehner, H.-C., and Oberbeck, V. R., 1997, Carbonate platform landslide and multiple tsunami triggered by asteroid or comet impact, Devonian, Nevada [abs.]: Geol. Soc. Amer., Cordilleran Sect. Meeting, Kona, Hawaii, Abs. Prog., v. 29, no. 5, p. 73.

Warme, J. E., and Sandberg, 1995, The catastrophic Alamo breccia of southern Nevada: Record of a Late Devonian extraterrestrial impact: Courier Forschungs. Senckenberg, v. 188, p. 31–57.

————, 1996, Alamo megabreccia: Record of a Late Devonian impact in southern Nevada: GSA Today, v. 6, p. 1–7.

Wilshire, H. G., Howard, K. A., and Offield, T. W., 1971, Impact breccias in carbonate rocks, Sierra Madera, Texas: Geol. Soc. Amer. Bull., v. 82, p. 1009–1018.

Wilson, J. L., 1975, Carbonate facies in geologic history: New York, Springer-Verlag, 471 p.

GREAT BASIN

Cenozoic Tectonism in the Central Basin and Range: Motion of the Sierran-Great Valley Block

BRIAN WERNICKE AND J. KENT SNOW

Division of Geological and Planetary Sciences, California Institute of Technology, Pasadena, California 91125

Abstract

According to geologic reconstructions, the motion of the Sierran-Great Valley block with respect to the Colorado Plateau was mainly westerly at more than 20 mm/yr from 16 to 10 Ma, changing to northwest or NNW since 8 to 10 Ma, at an average rate of 15 mm/yr. These kinematics are consistent with two other independent methods of determining the position of the block since 20 Ma—reconstructions based on paleomagnetic data from range blocks that bound the Basin and Range on the west, and a revised history of Pacific–North America plate motion based on a global plate circuit (Atwater and Stock, 1998, this issue). The plate-tectonic reconstruction shows a change to more northerly motion between the Pacific and North American plates at ~8 Ma, in concert with the motion of the Sierran-Great Valley block. Moreover, the northeast limit of extant oceanic crust (as indicated by the reconstruction of the continental geology) tracks closely with the southwest limit of extant continental crust (as indicated by the positions of oceanic plates) since 20 Ma. The coordination between plate motions and the intraplate geology suggests that plate-boundary forces strongly influenced deformation within the continent.

Introduction

PLATE MOTION absorbed within continental crust tends to result in wide belts of deformation, as opposed to the narrow belts characteristic of oceanic crust. An instantaneous picture of this deformation may be determined using geodetic and seismic data for comparison with plate motions (e.g., Davies et al., 1997). However, structural geology provides the only means of reconstructing the full kinematic history of large-scale intracontinental deformation (e.g., Burchfiel, 1980; Trümpy, 1980; Price, 1981; Wernicke et al., 1988). These reconstructions provide a strong basis for comparing the kinematics of crustal deformation with plate-tectonic reconstructions, and, in particular, to address: (1) whether intraplate deformation is controlled primarily by boundary forces applied at the edge of plates, or (2) whether body forces resulting from potential energy gradients (e.g., Humphreys and Dueker, 1994; Jones et al., 1996; Sonder et al., 1987) or forces exerted on the plate from beneath (for example by plume activity; Parsons et al., 1994) are important factors.

In another paper (Snow and Wernicke, 1998), we present a detailed kinematic model of finite intraplate deformation across the central Basin and Range province, a 400 × 200 km area between the southern Sierra Nevada and the Colorado Plateau. Global plate reconstructions based on recent geophysical surveys of the heretofore poorly understood ridges surrounding the Antarctica plate provide a revised history of Pacific–North America plate motion (Atwater and Stock, 1998, this issue) that is significantly more precise than previous reconstructions (e.g., Stock and Molnar, 1988). The late Cenozoic structural evolution of the central Basin and Range constrains the motion of the Sierra Nevada–Great Valley block, accommodating a large fraction of the total plate motion since 16 Ma (Wernicke et al., 1988; Dickinson and Wernicke, 1997). The details of this path may be compared directly to the new plate reconstruction, so as to test whether the reconstruction results in kinematically unacceptable overlap between continental and oceanic crust (Atwater, 1970; Atwater and Stock, 1998, this issue) and whether changes in plate-boundary kinematics during growth of the transform margin significantly influenced intraplate deformation patterns.

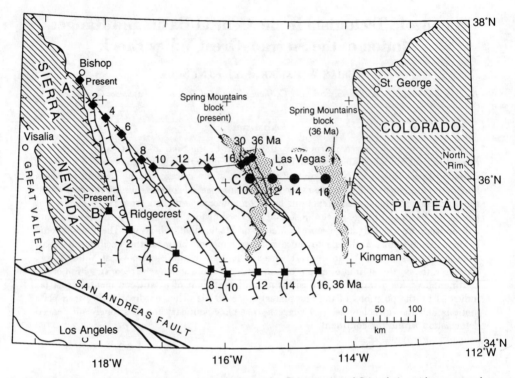

FIG. 1. Map showing positions of three points—A (diamonds), B (squares), and C (circles)—with respect to the Colorado Plateau since 36 Ma. Motion of point C represents the motion of the Spring Mountains block with respect to the Plateau. Paths of points A and B are the sum of point C and the reconstruction of Snow and Wernicke (1998) for the region west of the Spring Mountains block. All times on paths are in Ma.

Cenozoic Kinematic Evolution of the Central Basin and Range

The total finite deformation field in the central Basin and Range derived by reconstructing pre-extensional markers defines two major zones of severe Neogene extension of the upper crust—namely, the Lake Mead extended domain to the east and the Death Valley extended domain to the west (Wernicke, 1992). These realms are separated by a relatively mildly extended medial domain, referred to as the Spring Mountains block (Wernicke et al., 1988; Wernicke, 1992; Snow and Wernicke, 1998) (Fig. 1). In Snow and Wernicke (1998), we presented a kinematic model for the evolution of the Death Valley domain in 6 m.y. increments from 36 to 18 Ma and in 2 m.y. increments from 18 Ma to the present. This reconstruction defined the motion of the Sierra Nevada relative to the Spring Mountains block. The reconstruction showed very minor

amounts of extension in the central Basin and Range prior to 16 Ma, even though significant extension was occurring in late Oligocene and early Miocene time in areas to both the north and south (e.g., Wernicke, 1992).

In order to determine the total displacement of the Sierra with respect to the Colorado Plateau, we must specify a kinematic model for the relative motion of the Spring Mountains. The net displacement is constrained by two independent data sets to be ~100 km, oriented E-W (Wernicke et al., 1988; Rowland et al., 1990), but the kinematics are somewhat uncertain. The easternmost major normal fault block in the system (Gold Butte block) had been unroofed by ~15 Ma (Fitzgerald et al., 1991). In the south-central portion of the system (central Eldorado Mountains), most of the stratal tilting of fault blocks occurred between 15 and 14 Ma (Gans and Bohrson, 1998). In the central portion of the system, a NE-trending strike-slip fault has ~20 km of post–12.7 Ma slip (Hamblin

Bay fault) (Anderson, 1973), but its relationship to regional extension is controversial (Anderson et al., 1994; Duebendorfer and Simpson, 1994). The westernmost steeply tilted fault block in the system, Frenchman Mountain, was tilted between 12 and 9 Ma (Duebendorfer and Wallin, 1991). These observations suggest that the displacement occurred mainly between 16 and 10 Ma, with somewhat more rapid motion early in the deformational history. The local direction of extension ranges from WNW in some areas (Brady et al., 1996) to WSW in others (Anderson et al., 1994), with no clear temporal trend. Therefore, we selected a model with motion of the Spring Mountains block due west throughout the interval 16–10 Ma, with average displacement rates of 22 mm/yr from 16 to 14 Ma and 16.5 mm/yr from 14 to 10 Ma, for a total of 110 km of westerly motion. This estimate is at the upper limit of possible westerly motion in the Lake Mead system, as discussed below, and is somewhat slower than a model discussed in Snow and Wernicke (1998).

Combining the two paths results in ~250 to 300 km of WNW motion of the Sierra Nevada with respect to the Colorado Plateau. The direction and rate of motion is westerly at ~22 mm/yr between 16 and 10 Ma. Beginning no earlier than 10 Ma and no later than 8 Ma, the tracks of two reference points on the Sierra—one just south of Bishop and the other just west of Ridgecrest, California (points A and B, respectively, in Fig. 1)—show contrasting paths. This is the result largely of the Death Valley reconstruction, which indicates a more westerly path for the southern reference point than for the northern point, requiring a net 20° clockwise rotation of a line joining the two reference points since ~10 Ma (Snow and Wernicke, 1998). The average direction and rate of displacement of the northern point since 10 Ma is 16 mm/yr N42°W, whereas that of the southern point is 19 mm/yr N63°W. The apparent low rate from 8 to 10 Ma is probably an artifact of the model for the Lake Mead belt, where a significant part of the deformation may have occurred in the 8 to 10 Ma interval, particularly in the western part of the belt. Rapid northwesterly extension and shear in the Death Valley domain predominate after 8 Ma. Because there is no evidence of strong northwesterly extension within the Lake Mead domain in its latter stages of development, the change in

direction of motion of the Sierra at some time between 8 and 10 Ma (Figs. 1 and 2) appears to be real.

Discussion

The displacement history of the Sierran–Great Valley block suggested by geologic reconstruction of the central Basin and Range may be tested for consistency with two independent data sets—paleomagnetic constraints from the Sierra Nevada and ranges to the north (Magill and Cox, 1980; Frei et al., 1984; Frei, 1986), and plate-tectonic reconstructions (Stock and Molnar, 1988; Atwater and Stock, 1998, this issue).

Paleomagnetic data from two groups of Late Cretaceous plutons in the Sierra—one near Kings Canyon and the other near Yosemite (latitudes 37° N and 38° N, respectively)—yield high-temperature magnetizations oriented close to their Late Cretaceous expected directions (Frei et al., 1984; Frei, 1986). The group means from the two areas, now ~150 km apart, are indistinguishable, suggesting little if any differential rotation (<10°) within the central part of the Sierran block. The mean declination indicates 6 ± 8° of post–90 Ma clockwise rotation at 95% confidence. This does not agree with the 20° of clockwise rotation since 10 Ma indicated by our reconstruction (Fig. 1).

It is possible that either the reconstruction or the paleomagnetic data are in error, but the overall kinematics of Basin and Range extension suggests that they both may be correct. Significant extension, including the development of most Cordilleran metamorphic core complexes, occurred in Oligocene and early Miocene time (35 to 15 Ma) both north and south of the central Basin and Range, which in contrast resisted significant extension during this interval (Wernicke et al., 1987; Wernicke, 1992). Palinspastic reconstructions of the strongly extended Snake Range core complex and environs at latitude 39° N suggest that ~70 to 90 km of extension (Bartley and Wernicke, 1984; Gans, 1987; Wernicke, 1992) developed mainly between 50 and 15 Ma (Lee, 1995), whereas negligible extension occurred at the latitude of the central Basin and Range (36° to

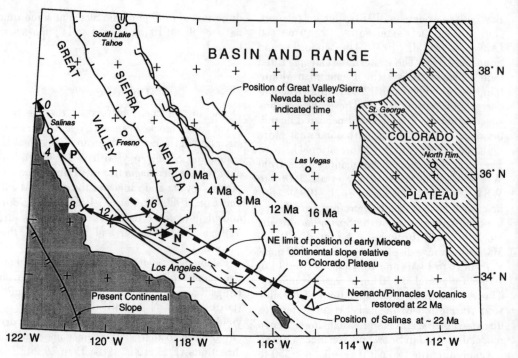

FIG. 2. Map showing the position of the Sierran–Great Valley block with respect to the Colorado Plateau in 4 m.y. increments since 16 Ma. Dashed lines in southern California are present traces of the San Andreas fault system. Arrows show the track of a point on the southwestern side of the Sierran–Great Valley block, presently near the city of Los Gatos, California, corresponding to point Q on Figure 3. Open triangles show restored positions of the Pinnacles and Neenach volcanics, generally considered to constrain the post-22 Ma offset on the central San Andreas fault.

37°N). If differential extension of 50 to 100 km over a N-S distance of 250 km was accommodated by rigid-body rotation of the Sierra between latitudes 37°N and 39°N, then a pre-15 Ma counterclockwise rotation of 11° to 22° is predicted. By adding the 20° post-15 Ma clockwise rotation suggested by the reconstruction to these counterclockwise rotations, a net post-90 Ma rotation of -2 to +9° is obtained (clockwise reckoned positive), which is in good agreement with the 6 ± 8° indicated by the paleomagnetic data.

On a larger scale, paleomagnetic data on Tertiary strata from the Oregon Coast Ranges and Cascades suggest substantial Miocene clockwise rotations of these ranges (Magill and Cox, 1980). Back-rotating them in a counterclockwise fashion restores the southern and central Sierra ~200 to 300 km eastward. When these rotations are integrated with the post-90 Ma rotation history of the central Sierra, and

it is assumed that each of the major blocks is internally rigid, the central and southern Sierra Nevada restore to a position ~100 km west of the Colorado Plateau (Frei, 1986). In the reconstruction preferred by Frei (1986), the Sierran reference point just west of Ridgecrest (point B, Fig. 1) restores back to the current position of Las Vegas, roughly 100 km WNW of its position in our reconstruction (Fig. 1). Given that they are based on entirely independent data and assumptions, the agreement between the two reconstructions is noteworthy.

The motion of the entire Sierran–Great Valley block since 16 Ma may be compared with offshore plate motions. Neglecting minor internal northeast shortening of the western margin of the block since 16 Ma, its southwestern edge represents the northeast limit of extant oceanic lithosphere along the continental margin (Figs. 2 and 3). The edge of the block is defined by the current position of the San Andreas fault. The

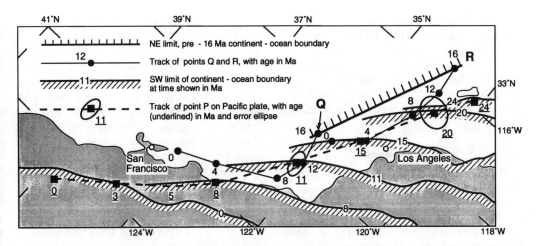

FIG. 3. Map comparing the paths of two points Q and R on the southwestern edge of the Sierran–Great Valley block (this report) with the path of point P on the Pacific plate (Atwater and Stock, 1998, this issue), relative to North America. Limits on the position of the boundary between continental and oceanic crust, indicated by hachured lines, are discussed in the text. Note that the moving oceanward limit coincides closely with the stationary continentward limit from 24 to 16 Ma. From 16 to 8 Ma, motion of the continentward limit, as defined by the track of point Q, tracks closely with the oceanward limit, both of which have a component of margin-normal displacement of >10 mm/yr. After 8 Ma, both limits track more nearly parallel to the margin.

crust directly east of the fault is underlain by a pre-Tertiary "basement" (Great Valley sequence, Coast Range ophiolite, and Franciscan complex), mildly shortened normal to the trace of the San Andreas in late Miocene to Recent time (e.g., Page, 1981). The reconstruction of the central Great Basin positions the edge of the block now bordering the San Joaquin Valley nearly parallel to, and about 25 km northeast of, the present trace of the southern San Andreas fault south of the Big Bend (Fig. 2). The reconstruction of Atwater and Stock (1998, this issue) indicates that oceanic crust at 20 to 15 Ma lay only ~10 km southwest of the restored edge of the block and no more than ~50 km to the southwest, within uncertainties of their reconstruction (Fig. 3).

Retrodeformation of the shortening along the western margin of the block, and the fact that some amount of continental material probably lay southwest of where the Miocene continental margin was truncated by the San Andreas, leaves very little room for reconstructing the block to a more southwesterly position. Therefore, the choice of the upper extreme for extension in the Lake Mead belt discussed above is not only reasonable, but is required in order to avoid significant overlap between the

Pacific ocean floor and continental crust at ~15 Ma. The Rio Grande Rift may account for some post–15 Ma westward motion of the Colorado Plateau relative to North America. However, reconstructions across the rift based on seismic reflection profiles near latitude 35° N suggest that the motion of the eastern margin of the Colorado Plateau relative to the Great Plains is approximately 10 to 20 km (e.g., Russell and Snelson, 1994), and hence Neogene Colorado Plateau–North America motion is not significant with respect to the reconstructed positions of Pacific ocean floor and the Sierran–Great Valley block.

An intriguing aspect of the comparison between geologic and plate-tectonic constraints is that from 20 to 10 Ma the motions of both the Sierran–Great Valley block and the Pacific plate are more westerly than they are between 8 Ma and the present (Atwater and Stock, 1998, this issue). The northeastern limit of where oceanic crust could have existed (defined by the position of the continent) and the southwestern limit of where continent could have existed (defined by the position of oceanic crust) both have a significant component of motion normal to the continental margin from ~20 to 10 Ma, and track more nearly parallel to the margin thereafter (Fig. 3). Comparison of the track of point P along the northeastern margin of the Pacific plate with the track of a point Q on the southwestern margin of the Sierran–Great Valley block (Fig. 3) suggests that southwesterly continental "expansion" and ocean-floor "retreat" from 20 to 8 Ma are well correlated.

Conclusions

The kinematics of Cenozoic tectonism in the central Basin and Range based on reconstruction of geologic markers yields 250 to 300 km of net WNW displacement of the Sierran–Great Valley block with respect to the Colorado Plateau since 16 Ma. The motion was mainly westerly at >20 mm/yr from 16 to 10 Ma, changing to NW to NNW motion since 8 Ma, at an average rate of 15 mm/yr. Given the contemporary rate of 11 mm/yr NNW (e.g., Bennett et al., 1998; Dixon et al., 1995), the rates appear to have significantly slowed since middle and late Miocene time. These kinematics are consistent with reconstructions based on paleomagnetic data from ranges along the western margin of the Basin and Range, and with plate-tectonic reconstructions, which also show a change to more northerly motion between the Pacific and North American plates at 8 to 10 Ma (Atwater and Stock, 1998, this issue). This change is consistent with the change in regional stress directions throughout the Basin and Range province at about this time (Zoback et al., 1981) and appears to reflect coupling of the Sierran–Great Valley block to the Pacific plate.

The slowing of relative motion between the Sierran–Great Valley block and North America, and an increase in dextral shear since 10 Ma east of the block, appear to reflect a growing localization of plate-boundary deformation along the San Andreas fault system (e.g., Dickinson and Wernicke, 1997). According to models based on the thin-sheet approximation of lithospheric deformation (England et al., 1985), one might expect that plate margins with significant boundary-normal motion would be accompanied by diffuse intraplate deformation, at a length scale normal to the margin comparable to the length scale of the plate boundary. In contrast, sheared plate boundaries should develop deformation zones that are narrow in comparison to boundary length. The evolution

of the Pacific–North America boundary—from being relatively diffuse with significant boundary-normal motion before 10 Ma to a boundary dominated by shear after 8 Ma that becomes progressively more localized toward the margin—would appear to be in at least qualitative agreement with the thin-sheet models. If so, the motion of Sierran–Great Valley block, and therefore most or all intraplate deformation since 16 Ma, has been strongly influenced by the Pacific–North America plate boundary and by relatively subtle changes in relative plate motion as the transform grew.

REFERENCES

Anderson, R. E., 1973, Large-magnitude late Tertiary strike-slip faulting, north of Lake Mead, Nevada: U.S. Geol. Surv. Prof. Pap. 794, 18 p.

Anderson, R. E., Barnhard, T. P., and Snee, L. W., 1994, Roles of plutonism, midcrustal flow, tectonic rafting, and horizontal collapse in shaping the Miocene strain field of the Lake Mead area, Nevada and Arizona: Tectonics, v. 13, p. 1381–1410.

Atwater, T., 1970, Implications of plate tectonics for the Cenozoic tectonic evolution of western North America: Geol. Soc. Amer. Bull., v. 81, p. 3513–3535.

Atwater, T., and Stock, J., 1998, Pacific–North America plate tectonics of the Neogene southwestern United States: An update: INT. GEOL. REV., v. 40, p. 375–402.

Bartley, J. M., and Wernicke, B. P., 1984, The Snake Range decollement interpreted as a major extensional shear zone: Tectonics, v. 3, p. 647–657.

Bennett, R. A., Wernicke, B. P., and Davis, J. L., 1998, Continuous GPS measurements of contemporary deformation across the northern Basin and Range province: Geophys. Res. Lett., v. 25, p. 563–566.

Brady, R. J., Wernicke, B. P., Fryxell, J. E., and Lux, D. R., 1996, Large magnitude Miocene extension in the Lake Mead region [abs.]: Geol. Soc. Amer. Abs. Prog., v. 28, p. 449.

Burchfiel, B. C., 1980, Eastern European Alpine system and the Carpathian orocline as an example of collision tectonics: Tectonophysics, v. 63, p. 31–61.

Davies, R., England, P., Parsons, B., Billiris, H., Paradissis, D., and Veis, G., 1997, Geodetic strain of Greece in the interval 1892–1992: Jour. Geophys. Res., v. 102, p. 24571–24588.

Dickinson, W. R., and Wernicke, B. P., 1997, Reconciliation of San Andreas slip discrepancy by a combination of interior Basin and Range extension and transrotation near the coast: Geology, v. 25, p. 663–666.

Dixon, T. H., Robaudo, S., Lee, J., and Reheis, M. C., 1995, Constraints on present-day Basin and Range deformation from space geodesy: Tectonics, v. 14, p. 755–772.

Duebendorfer, E. M., and Simpson, D. A., 1994, Kinematics and timing of tertiary extension in the western Lake Mead region, Nevada: Geol. Soc. Amer. Bull., v. 106, p. 1057–1073.

Duebendorfer, E. M., and Wallin, E. T., 1991, Basin development and syntectonic sedimentation associated with kinematically coupled strike-slip and detachment faulting, southern Nevada: Geology, v. 19, p. 87–90.

England, P. C., Houseman, G., and Sonder, L., 1985, Length scales for continental deformation in convergent, divergent, and strike-slip environments: Analytical and approximate solutions for a thin viscous sheet model: Jour. Geophys. Res., v. 90, p. 3551–3557.

Fitzgerald, P. G., Fryxell, J. E., and Wernicke, B. P., 1991, Miocene crustal extension and uplift in southeastern Nevada—constraints from fission-track analysis: Geology, v. 19, p. 1013–1016.

Frei, L. S., 1986, Additional paleomagnetic results from the Sierra Nevada—further constraints on Basin and Range extension and northward displacement in the western United States: Geol. Soc. Amer. Bull., v. 97, p. 840–849.

Frei, L. S., Magill, J. R., and Cox, A., 1984, Paleomagnetic results from the central Sierra Nevada: Constraints on reconstructions of the western United States: Tectonics, v. 3, p. 157–177.

Gans, P. B., 1987, An open-system, two-layer crustal stretching model for the eastern Great Basin: Tectonics, v. 6, p. 1–12.

Gans, P. B., and Bohrson, W. A., 1998, Suppression of volcanism during rapid extension in the Basin and Range province, United States: Science, v. 279, p. 66–69.

Humphreys, E. D., and Dueker, K. G., 1994, Western U.S. upper mantle structure: Jour. Geophys. Res., v. 99, p. 9615–9634.

Jones, C. H., Unruh, J. R., and Sonder, L. J., 1996, The role of gravitational potential energy in active deformation in the southwestern United States: Nature, v. 381, p. 37–41.

Lee, J., 1995, Rapid uplift and rotation of mylonitic rocks from beneath a detachment fault—insights from potassium-feldspar Ar-40/Ar-39 thermochronology, northern Snake Range, Nevada: Tectonics, v. 14, p. 54–77.

Magill, J., and Cox, A., 1980, Post-Oligocene tectonic rotation of the Oregon western Cascade Range and Klamath Mountains: Geology, v. 9, p. 127–131.

Page, B. M., 1981, The southern Coast Ranges, in Ernst, W. G., ed., The geotectonic development of California. Rubey Vol. I: Englewood Cliffs, NJ, Prentice-Hall, p. 329–417.

Parsons, T., Thompson, G. A., and Sleep, N. H., 1994, Mantle plume influence on the Neogene uplift and extension of the U.S. western Cordillera?: Geology, v. 22, p. 83–86.

Price, R. A., 1981, The Cordilleran foreland thrust and fold belt in the southern Canadian Rocky Mountains, in McClay, K. R., and Price, N. J., eds., Thrust and nappe tectonics: Geol. Soc. Lond. Spec. Publ. 9, p. 427–448.

Rowland, S. M., Parolini, J. R., Eschner, E., McAllister, A. J., and Rice, J. A., 1990, Sedimentologic and stratigraphic constraints on the Neogene translation and rotation of the Frenchman Mountain structural block, Clark County, Nevada, in Wernicke, B. P., ed., Basin and Range extensional tectonics near the latitude of Las Vegas, Nevada: Geol. Soc. Amer. Mem. 176, p. 99–122.

Russell, L. R., and Snelson, S., 1994, Structural style and tectonic evolution of the Albuquerque Basin segment of the Rio Grande Rift, New Mexico, U.S.A., in Landon, S. M., ed., Interior rift basins: Amer. Assoc. Petrol. Geol. Mem. 59, p. 205–258.

Snow, J. K., and Wernicke, B. P., 1998, Cenozoic tectonism in the Central Basin and Range: Magnitude, rate and distribution of upper crustal strain: Amer. Jour. Sci., in review.

Sonder, L. J., England, P. C., Wernicke, B. P., and Christiansen, R. L., 1987, A physical model for Cenozoic extension of western North America, in Coward, M. P., Dewey, J. F., and Hancock, P. L., eds., Continental extensional tectonics: Geol. Soc. Lond. Spec. Publ. 28, p. 187–201.

Stock, J., and Molnar, P., 1988, Uncertainties and implications of the Late Cretaceous and Tertiary position of North America relative to the Farallon, Kula, and Pacific plates: Tectonics, v. 7, p. 1339–1384.

Trümpy, R., 1980, Geology of Switzerland—a guide book. Part A, outline of the geology of Switzerland: Basel, Wepf and Company, 104 p.

Wernicke, B., 1992, Cenozoic extensional tectonics of the U.S. Cordillera, in Burchfiel, B. C., Lipman, P. W., and Zoback, M. L., eds., The geology of North America, v. G-3: The Cordilleran orogen: Conterminous U.S.: Boulder, CO, Geol. Soc. Amer., p. 553–581.

Wernicke, B., Axen, G. J., and Snow, J. K., 1988, Basin and Range extensional tectonics at the latitude of Las Vegas, Nevada: Geol. Soc. Amer. Bull., v. 100, p. 1738–1757.

Wernicke, B. P., Christiansen, R. L., England, P. C., and Sonder, L. J., 1987, Tectonomagmatic evolution of Cenozoic extension in the North American Cordillera, *in* Coward, M. P., Dewey, J. F., and Hancock, P. L., eds., Continental extensional tectonics, Geol. Soc. Lond. Spec. Publ. 28, p. 203–221.

Zoback, M. L., Anderson, R. E., and Thompson, G. A., 1981, Cainozoic evolution of the state of stress and style of tectonism of the Basin and Range Province of the Western United States: Phil. Trans. Roy. Soc. Lond., v. 300, p. 407–434.

Paleozoic and Mesozoic Evolution of East-Central California

CALVIN H. STEVENS,

Department of Geology, San Jose State University, San Jose, California 95192

PAUL STONE,

U.S. Geological Survey, 345 Middlefield Road, MS 975, Menlo Park, California 94025

GEORGE C. DUNNE,

Department of Geological Sciences, California State University, Northridge, Northridge, California 91330

DAVID C. GREENE,

Department of Geology and Geophysics, Dennison University, Granville, Ohio 43023

J. DOUGLAS WALKER,

Department of Geology, University of Kansas, Lawrence, Kansas 66045

AND BRIAN J. SWANSON

Allan E. Seward Engineering Geology Inc., 25570 Rye Canyon Rd., Suite G, Valencia, California 91355

Abstract

East-central California, which encompasses an area located on the westernmost part of sialic North America, contains a well-preserved record of Paleozoic and Mesozoic tectonic events that reflect the evolving nature of the Cordilleran plate margin to the west. After the plate margin was formed by continental rifting in the Neoproterozoic, sediments comprising the Cordilleran miogeocline began to accumulate on the subsiding passive margin. In east-central California, sedimentation did not keep pace with subsidence, resulting in backstepping of a series of successive carbonate platforms throughout the early and middle Paleozoic. This phase of miogeoclinal development was brought to a close by the Late Devonian–Early Mississippian Antler orogeny, during the final phase of which oceanic rocks were emplaced onto the continental margin. Subsequent Late Mississippian–Pennsylvanian faulting and apparent reorientation of the carbonate platform margin are interpreted to have been associated with truncation of the continental plate on a sinistral transform fault zone.

In the Early Permian, contractional deformation in east-central California led to the development of a narrow, uplifted thrust belt flanked by marine basins in which thick sequences of deep-water strata accumulated. A second episode of contractional deformation in late Early Permian to earliest Triassic time widened and further uplifted the thrust belt and produced the recently identified Inyo Crest thrust, which here is correlated with the regionally significant Last Chance thrust. In the Late Permian, about the time of the second contractional episode, extensional faulting created shallow sedimentary basins in the southern Inyo Mountains. In the El Paso Mountains to the south, deformation and plutonism record the onset of subduction and arc magmatism in late Early Permian to earliest Triassic time along this part of the margin.

Tectonism had ceased in most of east-central California by middle to late Early Triassic time, and marine sediment deposited on the subsiding continental shelf overlapped the previously deformed Permian rocks. Renewed contractional deformation, probably in the Middle Triassic, is interpreted to be associated with emplacement of the Golconda allochthon onto the margin of the continent. This event, which is identified with certainty in the Sierra Nevada, also may have significantly affected rocks in the White and Inyo Mountains to the east.

Subduction and arc magmatism that created most of the Sierra Nevada batholith began in the Late Triassic and lasted through the remainder of the Mesozoic. During this time, the East Sierran thrust system (ESTS) developed as a narrow zone of intense, predominantly E-vergent contractional deformation along the eastern margin of the growing batholith. Activity on the ESTS took place over an extended part of Mesozoic time, both before and after intrusion of voluminous Middle Jurassic plutons, and is interpreted to have been mechanically linked to emplacement of the batholith. Deformation on the ESTS and magmatism in the Sierra Nevada both ended prior to the close of the Cretaceous.

Introduction

Geologic and geographic setting

EAST-CENTRAL CALIFORNIA, defined here as the triangular region bounded by the Garlock fault, the crest of the Sierra Nevada, and the Nevada state line (Fig. 1), occupies a unique and critical paleogeographic position for studies of Cordilleran continental-margin evolution from Neoproterozoic through Mesozoic time. In this region, the SW-trending Cordilleran miogeocline, a thick succession of sedimentary rocks formed along a generally passive continental margin during Neoproterozoic and early Paleozoic time, is crosscut and overprinted by the NW-trending Sierra Nevada batholith that formed as part of a magmatic arc along a convergent (subducting) margin during the Mesozoic. Paleozoic and Mesozoic rocks and structures throughout this region provide evidence of many significant tectonic events interpreted to be direct or indirect responses to changes in relative plate motions along the evolving western edge of the North American continent, especially an episode of convergent-margin tectonism in the Late Devonian and Early Mississippian (Antler orogeny), the inferred development of a sinistral, transform margin in Late Mississippian or Pennsylvanian time, and the subsequent transition to a predominantly convergent margin by the Late Triassic. The late Paleozoic change from SW- to NW-trending paleogeographic features in the region is of particular interest; the associated rocks and structures provide a framework for testing the hypothesis that this change was initiated by tectonic truncation of the continental margin, an idea first postulated by Hamilton and Myers (1966).

The region under consideration is divided by the Owens Valley and other valleys to the northwest and southeast that bound the east flank of the Sierra Nevada (Fig. 1). Ranges east of these valleys contain extensive exposures of sedimentary and metasedimentary rocks of Neoproterozoic to Early and Middle(?) Triassic age, which are intruded by locally abundant plutonic

rocks of mostly Jurassic and Cretaceous ages. Middle to late Mesozoic volcanic and associated sedimentary rocks locally overlie Triassic strata in the southern Inyo Mountains and the Argus, Slate, and southern Panamint ranges. Rocks in these eastern ranges are complexly deformed by folds and faults of Permian to Cretaceous age, as well as by diverse Cenozoic structures. By contrast, to the west, in the eastern Sierra Nevada, Paleozoic sedimentary rocks comprise scattered pendants enclosed within Mesozoic intrusive rocks. Until recently, only limited stratigraphic ties had been established between the Paleozoic rocks exposed in these pendants and the more widely exposed sequences to the east (e.g., Moore and Foster, 1980). Recent work (e.g., Stevens and Greene, 1995) has resulted in additional stratigraphic and structural ties between the eastern Sierran pendants and the sequences to the east, thus providing a basis for paleogeographic and tectonic interpretations that integrate data from both areas. Paleozoic rocks closely related to those in the northwesternmost part of the region under consideration here also are exposed in the El Paso Mountains immediately north of the Garlock fault (Fig. 1).

Reconstructions of the pre-Cenozoic paleogeography of east-central California are challenging because of uncertainties in the amounts of contractional, strike-slip, and extensional faulting that have occurred in the region, and no attempt is made here to resolve these problems. East of Owens Valley, large-magnitude late Paleozoic and Mesozoic thrust faulting and Cenozoic extension and associated dextral strike-slip displacements are interpreted to have reoriented apparent Paleozoic trends from an original NNE trend to a present-day, more northeasterly trend (Wernicke et al., 1988; Snow, 1992, 1994). In Owens Valley proper the amount of Cenozoic extension apparently has been modest (Wernicke et al., 1988), but large-scale thrust faulting inferred at some locations (Stevens, 1995) may have telescoped facies significantly. Dextral faulting (Stevens, Pelley et al., 1995; Stevens and Greene, 1997) has fur-

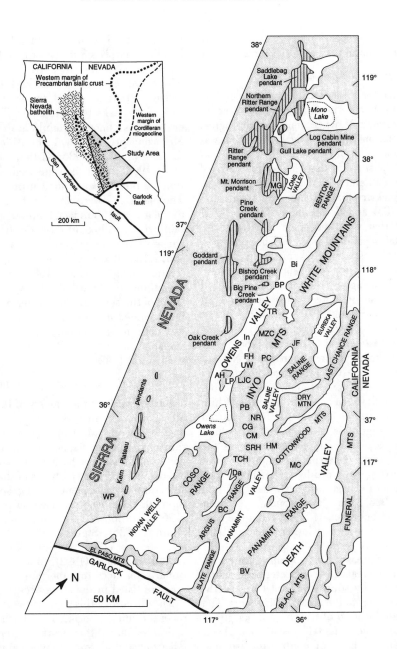

FIG. 1. East-central California, showing localities discussed in this report. Abbreviations: AH = Alabama Hills; BC = Bendire Canyon; BP = Big Pine; Bi = Bishop; BV = Butte Valley; CG = Cerro Gordo; CM = Conglomerate Mesa; Da = Darwin area (includes Darwin Hills and Darwin Canyon); FH = Fossil Hill; HM = Hunter Mountain; In = Independence; JF = Jackass Flats; LP = Lone Pine; LJC = Long John Canyon; MC = Marble Canyon; MG = McGee Mountain; MZC = Mazourka Canyon; NR = Nelson Range; PC = Paiute Canyon; PB = Permian Bluff; SLC = San Lucas Canyon; SRH = Santa Rosa Hills; TCH = Talc City Hills; TR = Tinemaha Reservoir; UW = Union Wash; WP = Walker Pass. Areas with vertical line pattern represent roof pendants of eastern Sierra Nevada discussed in text. Inset shows location of study area in relation to Sierra Nevada batholith, the isotopic boundary marking the western margin of Precambrian sialic crust, and the western margin of the Cordilleran miogeocline.

ther hindered comparison between the White-Inyo Mountains and the eastern Sierra Nevada.

Pre-Phanerozoic background

The stage for Phanerozoic geologic development of the North American margin was set in the Neoproterozoic, when, most workers agree, the western margin of North America was formed as a result of continental rifting. Stewart (1972) postulated that this event occurred between ~850 and 570 Ma; subsequent stratigraphic backstripping studies by Armin and Mayer (1983) and Bond and Komnitz (1984) suggested that the final stage of rifting and continental separation occurred between 555 and 600 Ma. Westward-thickening sequences of mostly clastic strata of Neoproterozoic and Early Cambrian age are interpreted as the initial deposits that accumulated on the rifted margin (Stewart and Suczek, 1977; Stewart, 1991). Strata of this assemblage are extensively exposed in east-central California, where they attain a thickness of more than 6 km (Nelson, 1962; Stewart, 1970). Lithologic changes in Neoproterozoic to Lower Cambrian strata from the Death Valley area westward into the White and Inyo Mountains (Stewart, 1970) produced distinct stratigraphic assemblages that have been used as markers in tectonic models for identifying and reconstructing major faults in the southwestern Cordillera, such as the Mojave-Sonora megashear (Anderson and Schmidt, 1983), the Mojave–Snow Lake fault (Lahren and Schweickert, 1989), and the Last Chance thrust system (Corbett et al., 1988; Corbett, 1989).

In terms of present-day geography, the continental margin created by Neoproterozoic rifting extends generally southwestward from north-central Nevada into the area of this report. The approximate location of the western margin of Precambrian continental crust has been inferred on the basis of contrasting isotopic characteristics of Phanerozoic igneous rocks and distribution of exposures of contrasting shallow-shelf and deep-water marine facies in Paleozoic sedimentary rocks (Kistler and Peterman, 1973; Kistler, 1978, 1990, 1993). In detail, this boundary extends southward across Nevada and then bends sharply westward to pass north of the White Mountains into the Mono Lake basin (Fig. 1). The boundary undergoes several right-lateral offsets in the Sierra

Nevada, totaling more than 200 km, before bending sharply southeastward and continuing down the axis of the range (Kistler, 1990, 1993), where Lahren and Schweickert (1989) have proposed that it follows the western edge of their Snow Lake tectonic block. The right-lateral offsets almost certainly are the result of Mesozoic pre- or synbatholithic strike-slip faulting (Saleeby, 1986; Kistler, 1990; Stevens et al., 1992) rather than the original configuration of the Precambrian continental margin. The major westward and southeastward bends of the inferred boundary, however, are of uncertain origin, and could reflect either the initial shape of the Neoproterozoic margin (Dickinson, 1981; Oldow, 1984) or later tectonic modifications (e.g., Stewart, 1985). Recent interpretations for the origin of the southeastward trend of the boundary in the Sierra Nevada have incorporated a model involving truncation of the continental margin on a late Paleozoic transform fault system (e.g., Walker, 1988; Stevens et al., 1992).

Previous work and purpose of this study

Earlier work on the geology of Paleozoic and Mesozoic rocks in east-central California has been extensive. Most of the 15-minute quadrangles have been mapped by various workers, and topical studies have been conducted by many others. Broad syntheses of the geology or structural development during specific time intervals have been provided by Stewart et al. (1966), Dunne et al. (1978), Nelson (1981), Dunne (1986), Stevens (1986, 1991), Stone and Stevens (1984, 1988b), Wernicke et al. (1988), and Snow (1992), to name a few. Additional references to important studies in this area are listed in the above-mentioned papers.

The purpose of this paper is to synthesize our recent findings, together with those of our colleagues and other workers, regarding the Paleozoic and Mesozoic geological evolution of east-central California. Our primary emphasis is on the middle Paleozoic to Mesozoic structural events and related rock assemblages, especially in ranges immediately east of the Sierra Nevada batholith; these are the areas where we have focused much of the research that forms the core of this paper.

Because of the broad scope of this synthesis and the different (although complementary) geologic interests of the contributing authors,

different parts of this paper have been written
by different authors or combinations of
authors. Thus, in the subsequent sections, representing successive intervals of geologic time,
the authors of each contribution are acknowledged separately. These component sections
were integrated into a single coordinated work
by Stevens, Stone, and Dunne. Geologic ages
used in this paper follow the time scale of
Harland et al. (1982).

Early Paleozoic Subsidence and Sedimentation[1]

The generally SW-trending continental shelf
and adjacent continental slope created by Neoproterozoic rifting of western North America
remained tectonically quiescent and received
marine sediment until Late Devonian time.
During the Early Cambrian, shallow-water
environments extended throughout the region,
at least as far west as the eastern Sierra Nevada,
as recorded by the presence of archaeocyathids
in carbonate-platform deposits in the Benton
Range (Renne and Turrin, 1987) and the Big
Pine Creek pendant in the Sierra Nevada
(Moore and Foster, 1980). No deeper-water
equivalents of these rocks are known in either
east-central California or west-central Nevada.

During Middle and Late Cambrian time,
however, sequences of massive dolomite, representing very shallow-water, restricted environments, were deposited only as far northwest as
the southernmost White Mountains and central Last Chance Range (Fig. 2). Farther west
and north, in the Sierra Nevada (Bishop Creek
and Mount Morrison pendants) and west-central Nevada, thin-bedded carbonates and very
fine grained clastic rocks represent a substantially deeper-water, more offshore facies. This
facies apparently also is represented by rocks
mapped as Emigrant Formation by Nelson
(1966a) in the central White Mountains.
Nelson (1966a) showed thrust faults beneath
these rocks in the White Mountains, but the
section there is essentially coherent and the
rocks are in the correct stratigraphic position;
therefore, the rocks of the Emigrant Formation
probably have not been significantly displaced.
The northwest margin of the platform on which

[1]This section of the paper was written by C. H. Stevens.

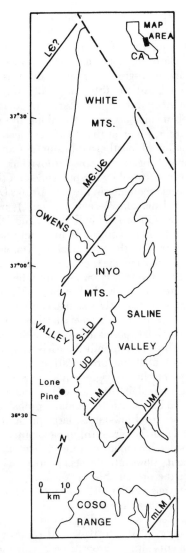

Fig. 2. Positions of lower and middle Paleozoic shelf
margins in White-Inyo Mountains structural block. LC =
Lower Cambrian; MC–UC = Middle and Upper Cambrian;
O = Ordovician; S-LD = Silurian through Lower Devonian;
UD = Upper Devonian; lLM = lowest Mississippian; mLM =
middle Lower Mississippian; UM = Upper Mississippian.
Position of Lower Cambrian shelf margin is uncertain, but
it is at least as far northwest as drawn. Figure is modified
from Stevens (1986).

the shallow-water carbonates were deposited
may have been sharply terminated, as suggested
by the presence of sedimentary breccias and
carbonate grain-flow deposits in the Bonanza
King Dolomite in the northern Last Chance

Range (Kepper, 1981; Montanez and Osleger, 1993).

After the Late Cambrian, SW-trending, rimmed-platform margins were developed repeatedly in progressively more southeasterly (landward) positions (Stevens, 1986) (Fig. 2). For instance, during the Early Ordovician, banks of oncoids accumulated along the platform margin, which at that time was located in the position of northern Mazourka Canyon. This general location of the Ordovician shelf margin is confirmed by the presence of a thick chert-breccia sequence in the Ely Springs Dolomite near Tinemaha Reservoir (Fig. 1), interpreted as a fault breccia by Stevens and Olson (1972), but now recognized as an accumulation of debris within the Ely Springs Dolomite, probably deposited at the base of the slope (C. H. Stevens and P. Stone, unpubl. data, 1997). Later, in the Early Devonian, the platform margin apparently was marked by a prograding coral-rich bank or reef, the debris apron of which is well exposed in southern Mazourka Canyon. Thus, throughout the early Paleozoic, episodes of platform progradation alternated with major marine transgressions. Twice during this time interval, in the Middle Ordovician and in the Middle to Late Devonian, probably at times of sea-level lowstands, large amounts of quartz sand spread across the miogeoclinal shelf and considerable amounts were carried in sediment-gravity flows into the deep-water environments of the present Sierra Nevada (Stevens, 1986; Stevens, Pelley et al., 1995). Overall, however, because the rate of subsidence generally exceeded that of sedimentation, the seaward margin of shallow-water marine environments shifted progressively continentward. By the Late Devonian, when the Antler orogeny began, the shelf margin had receded to a position somewhere between southern Mazourka Canyon and the Long John Canyon area northeast of Lone Pine (Fig. 2).

Antler Orogeny[2]

The Antler orogeny, represented by both structural and stratigraphic features, is the earliest Phanerozoic contractional event to have affected east-central California. In the type

[2]This section of the paper was written by C. H. Stevens and D. C. Greene.

region in central Nevada, where the effects of this orogeny have been extensively studied, contraction is interpreted to have begun in the mid-Frasnian (Late Devonian) and to have culminated in mid-Osagean (Early Mississippian) time with emplacement of the Roberts Mountains allochthon (Johnson and Pendergast, 1981; Goebel, 1991). Most workers have considered these Late Devonian and Early Mississippian events as constituting the Antler orogeny, although some (e.g., Silberling et al., in press) consider later phases of uplift and deformation, lasting throughout the Mississippian and perhaps into the Early Pennsylvanian, as belonging to the same orogenic event. Here, we restrict the concept of the Antler orogeny to those deformational phases leading up to and including emplacement of the allochthon in the Early Mississippian.

Sylvester and Babcock (1975) and Dunne et al. (1978) speculated that NE-trending structures in the White and Inyo Mountains were formed during the Antler event. They noted, however, that meaningful, temporal constraints are lacking, and it now seems probable that these structures formed much later. Demonstrable Antler structures in east-central California were first recognized by Schweickert and Lahren (1987) in the Saddlebag Lake pendant in the Sierra Nevada northwest of Mono Lake (Fig. 3). In this pendant, the rocks have the important characteristics of the Antler orogenic belt in west-central Nevada, including highly disrupted, deep-water sedimentary rocks of presumed early Paleozoic age with some intercalated mafic volcanic rocks, unconformably overlain by less disturbed strata similar to and correlated with the Permian Diablo and Triassic Candelaria formations of the Antler overlap assemblage (Schweickert and Lahren, 1987). Although the only direct paleontologic dating in the Saddlebag Lake pendant is of a clast in the Diablo Formation, which yielded Permian conodonts (Schweickert and Lahren, 1987), the lithology and sequence of units permit confident correlation of the succession in the Saddlebag Lake pendant with that in west-central Nevada. Rocks and structures similar to those in the lower Paleozoic section of the Saddlebag Lake pendant also have been mapped by Greene (1995) farther south in the northern Ritter Range pendant, where a thrust fault at

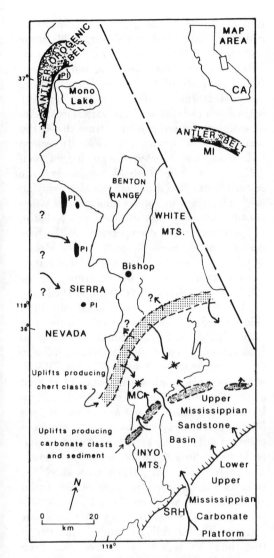

FIG. 3. Upper Mississippian paleogeography in east-central California, showing inferred uplifts. Antler orogenic belt is interpreted to have originiated tens of kilometers to the northwest but is shown here in its present position. Arrows indicate interpreted directions of sediment dispersal; synclinal symbols indicate areas of mixing of clasts from different sources. Abbreviations: Pl = Pennsylvanian–lowest Permian limestone in Sierra Nevada that originated in shallow water; MC = Mazourka Canyon; MI = Miller Mountain; SRH = Santa Rosa Hills.

the base of the allochthon has been correlated with the Early Mississippian Roberts Mountains thrust in Nevada (Greene et al., in press).

Farther south and east, in the Mount Morrison and other pendants containing a correla-tive succession of strata (Stevens and Greene, 1995), here referred to as the Morrison succession, the effects of the Antler orogeny are controversial. In the Mount Morrison pendant, Russell and Nokleberg (1977) interpreted three folding events to have affected the lower Paleozoic rocks, but only two to have affected the upper Paleozoic rocks. The additional event, represented by folds involving primarily lower Paleozoic rocks, was interpreted to be the result of Antler deformation. Wise (1996) did not find evidence of Antler folding in the Mount Morrison pendant, but he interpreted the lower Paleozoic section there as having been tilted to subvertical prior to deposition of the upper Paleozoic rocks. In contrast, we have concluded that the structural effects of the Antler event in these pendants were minor because angular discordance between the Devonian and Mississippian parts of the Morrison succession is lacking where the contact is exposed (Stevens and Greene, 1997). In both the Log Cabin Mine and Bishop Creek pendants, Mississippian rocks of the Bright Dot Formation overlie the Upper Devonian Squares Tunnel Formation paraconformably, and at one locality in the Mount Morrison pendant, the typical brown quartz sandstone and siltstone of the basal Bright Dot Formation is interbedded with light-grey, calcareous, quartz sandstone typical of one facies of the Squares Tunnel Formation, suggesting a continuity of deposition between the Upper Devonian and Mississippian.

Although there is no observed angularity within the Devonian–Mississippian part of the Morrison succession, low-amplitude warping prior to deposition of the Mississippian strata may be indicated by apparent large variations in thickness of Middle and Late Devonian rocks in the pendants (C. H. Stevens and D. C. Greene, unpubl. data, 1977). Alternatively, these differences in thickness could be the result of unresolved structural complexities, especially in the Gull Lake pendant, or to fault juxtaposition of sections that originated far from one another (all sections are in different fault blocks or are isolated from one another by intrusions or cover). The change in the type of sediment deposited at about the Devonian–Mississippian boundary probably reflects a change in depositional environment, perhaps a distal effect of tectonic activity associated with development of the Antler orogenic belt, which we interpret to have originated far (probably many tens of kilometers) to the north and west of the area where the Morrison succession accumulated.

Observations made in the pendants of the Sierra Nevada have important implications for interpreting the position of the southeastern (frontal) trace of the Antler orogenic belt in west-central Nevada. Stewart and Poole (1974) and Stewart (1980) placed this trace in the Miller Mountain area (Fig. 3), whereas others (e.g., Schweickert and Lahren, 1987) have placed it south and east of all exposures of Ordovician black shale, about 50 km southeast of Miller Mountain. We place the frontal trace through Miller Mountain because the Cambrian and Ordovician stratigraphy on the southern side of this mountain and farther southeastward corresponds to that of the Morrison succession; by analogy with the Sierra Nevada, these rocks are interpreted as not belonging to the Antler orogenic belt. By contrast, on the north side of Miller Mountain, the highly deformed lower Paleozoic rocks, including volcanics, are overlain unconformably by the Diablo and Candelaria formations. These rocks definitely represent part of the Antler orogenic belt.

Lower Paleozoic deep-water rocks that may have been affected by the Antler orogeny also are present far to the south in the El Paso Mountains (Carr et al., 1984). Here, two Upper Cambrian-Ordovician facies have been recognized: a western eugeoclinal facies that is lithologically similar to rocks of the Antler orogenic belt, and an eastern "transitional" facies (Carr et al., 1984), which appears to match the Upper Cambrian-Ordovician part of the Morrison succession quite well except for an upper sequence in the El Paso Mountains that contains detrital limestone. These two facies evidently have been juxtaposed tectonically, but the timing is uncertain. Carr et al. (1984) inferred that this juxtaposition occurred during the Antler orogeny, although they pointed out that this has not been proven and that the two facies could have been faulted together later. The eugeoclinal rocks in the El Paso Mountains, as well as similar eugeoclinal rocks of presumed early Paleozoic age in the southeastern Sierra Nevada (Dunne and Suczek, 1991), have been interpreted to be southward-displaced fragments of the westward continua-

tion of the Antler orogenic belt now in the Saddlebag Lake pendant (Walker, 1988; Stone and Stevens, 1988b; Stevens et al., 1992).

In most of eastern California and southern Nevada, effects of the Antler orogeny were subdued. In southwestern Nevada, a foredeep basin developed that was filled with at least 2 km of sediment derived primarily from the Antler belt to the west (Trexler et al., 1996). In eastern California, the foredeep basin is not well defined. The entire Inyo Mountains and the eastern Sierra Nevada, where the Mississippian is characterized by mostly fine-grained siliciclastic strata, may represent the foredeep basin.

The thinning and disappearance of the Kinderhookian to lowest Osagean (Lower Mississippian) Tin Mountain Limestone northwestward under a disconformity in the southern Inyo Mountains (Merriam, 1963) and in the Dry Mountain area (Burchfiel, 1969) (Fig. 1) also may be related to the Antler orogeny. This disconformity could have resulted from erosion of a migrating forebulge similar to that recognized in Nevada (Goebel, 1991), which formed at the beginning of emplacement of the allochthon onto the continental margin farther west. Later, in the early Osagean, the Mississippian carbonate platform throughout eastern California and southern Nevada apparently was depressed rather suddenly, an event interpreted by Stevens, Klingman et al. (1995) to mark the final emplacement of the Antler allochthon. A few sediment-gravity flows were generated in the western part of the carbonate platform (Darwin Hills and Santa Rosa Hills) at this time. No angularity, however, has been reported between lower Paleozoic and Mississippian or younger Paleozoic rocks in the miogeocline of eastern California or southern Nevada.

Late Mississippian-Early Pennsylvanian Faulting[3]

A faulting event interpreted to be primarily Late Mississippian-Early Pennsylvanian in age affected several areas extending from the eastern Sierra Nevada eastward into the Inyo Mountains and southward into the El Paso

[3]This section of the paper was written by C. H. Stevens.

Mountains. Although exposed faults of this age have not been identified, stratigraphic evidence for this event is provided by an unusual sequence of rocks assigned to the Mississippian Kearsarge Formation in southern Mazourka Canyon. There, the base of the formation is marked by a basal boulder conglomerate, which is considered to be Upper Mississippian because it is overlain, apparently conformably, by sandstone identical to that which characterizes the Upper Mississippian Mexican Spring Formation in the eastern Inyo Mountains. These rocks are overlain in turn by limestone turbidites dated as late Meramecian (early Late Mississippian) (Stevens et al., 1996). This limestone detritus is anomalous because the Meramecian carbonate platform margin lay in the Santa Rosa Hills, about 50 km southeast (Fig. 3), and no limestone of this age is known between Cerro Gordo and Mazourka Canyon (Fig. 1). Even more anomalous are Chesterian (late Late Mississippian) carbonate debris-flow deposits and turbidites at the top of the Kearsarge Formation, one of which contains abundant ooids. No other Chesterian carbonates are known in the region, yet somewhere nearby there was a carbonate bank or platform that provided this sediment. Stevens (1986, 1991) postulated a series of Late Mississippian fault-bounded uplifts surrounded by carbonate platforms (Fig. 3), extending through the Inyo Mountains, to explain these anomalous carbonates in Mazourka Canyon.

Mississippian uplifts, the ages of which are poorly constrained but are here considered to be Upper Mississippian, also were formed in several other areas in east-central California. One is located near Tinemaha Reservoir, ~12 km southeast of Big Pine along the eastern edge of Owens Valley (Fig. 1). There, in a thrust plate, Lower Triassic rocks disconformably overlie a Middle Devonian unit of conglomerate, limestone turbidites, and black chert. The unconformity could have formed at any time between the Middle Devonian and Early Triassic, but we suggest that the original uplift was Mississippian because this readily explains the distribution and grain-size trends of Mississippian black-chert-pebble conglomerates in the region. Such conglomerates are thickest and coarsest along a belt extending from northern Mazourka Canyon to the Nevada state line (Fig. 3). Similar conglomerates that are thinner and

much finer grained crop out in the Bishop Creek pendant, and a few fragments have been seen in float in the Log Cabin Mine pendant. These chert-pebble conglomerates thus thicken and coarsen eastward away from the Antler orogenic belt, suggesting a source to the east, most likely the terrain now exposed in the thrust plate near Tinemaha Reservoir, where black chert occurs beneath Triassic rocks. In contrast, rare, coarse Mississippian conglomerates in the Mount Morrison and Pine Creek pendants that lack the predominant black-chert-clast content characteristic of the Inyo Mountains conglomerates may have had an Antler-belt source.

The eastern Sierra Nevada, where the Morrison succession accumulated, could have constituted another uplifted block. In Early Pennsylvanian time, the type of sediment deposited throughout the Inyo Mountains and eastern Sierra Nevada changed from siliciclastic to carbonate. However, whereas deep-water carbonate turbidites were deposited throughout the Inyo Mountains, shallow-water carbonate-platform rocks accumulated in the eastern Sierra Nevada (Fig. 3). Thus, at least compared to the Inyo Mountains, the eastern Sierra Nevada block was elevated in Late Mississippian or Early Pennsylvanian time. Farther south, in the El Paso Mountains, at least one uplift of about the same age has been recognized by Carr et al. (1984). They noted that in one area a shallow-water Pennsylvanian carbonate section unconformably overlies Devonian argillite, and suggested that late Paleozoic deposition occurred in a terrain of marine troughs and submarine ridges that were structurally controlled.

In Nevada, a post-Antler faulting event, possibly associated with extension, resulted in deposition of conglomerate-bearing successions on the older Antler orogenic belt at various locations along its length (Miller et al., 1992). Trexler and Nitchman (1990) and Silberling et al. (in press) pointed out that in north-central Nevada, two widespread Mississippian sequences are separated by a regional and locally angular unconformity, reflecting Late Mississippian tilting and uplift. In southwestern Nevada, Trexler et al. (1996) indicated the presence of both Lower and Upper Mississippian conglomerates, again suggesting renewed uplift after the Early Mississippian Antler event.

Exposures of Mississippian chert-pebble conglomerates deposited along the western margin of the Cordilleran miogeocline continue northward from Nevada to the Yukon (Eisbacher, 1983; Smith et al., 1993). Eisbacher (1983) suggested that these conglomerates were deposited in strike-slip or rift basins formed during a continent-wide, left-lateral shearing event along the western margin of North America that presumably resulted in transtensional and transpressional deformation. Smith et al. (1993), on the other hand, suggested that these conglomerates were generated during contractional orogeny that affected the entire continental margin during the Late Devonian and Mississippian. It is possible that both hypotheses are valid, with a Late Devonian–Early Mississippian contraction, resulting in the Antler orogeny, having been replaced by sinistral shear in the Late Mississippian. Perhaps the sudden relative drop in sea level in the Meramecian (Stevens, Klingman et al., 1995), resulting in the widespread exposure of the Mississippian carbonate platform, and a major episode of subsidence later in the Early Pennsylvanian throughout east-central California and southern Nevada were related to the initiation of continent-wide sinistral shearing, which ultimately led to truncation of the continental margin.

Late Paleozoic Truncation of the Continental Margin[4]

The origin of the southeastward bend in the inferred margin of the Precambrian continental crust in the Sierra Nevada and the termination of SW-trending early and middle Paleozoic isopach lines, facies boundaries, and paleogeographic features against the Sierra Nevada batholith have long been controversial. Some workers, notably Dickinson (1981), have suggested that these patterns reflect the initial shape of an irregular Neoproterozoic rifted margin, and that the overlying Paleozoic facies belts developed more or less parallel to that margin. Others have interpreted the patterns to have

[4]This section of the paper was written by Paul Stone and C. H. Stevens.

resulted from tectonic truncation of an originally SW-trending continental margin, either in latest Paleozoic to Middle Triassic time, following the Sonoma orogeny (e.g., Burchfiel and Davis, 1975; Davis et al., 1978), or during the urassic along the inferred Mojave-Sonora megashear (e.g., Anderson and Schmidt, 1983). More recent studies have supported the concept of continental truncation, but have presented evidence that truncation took place in Pennsylvanian to Permian time (Stone and Stevens, 1988b; Walker, 1988; Saleeby and Busby-Spera, 1992; Stevens et al., 1992). As discussed by Stone and Stevens (1988b), some of the strongest evidence for a late Paleozoic age of continental truncation is provided by rocks exposed in the area of the present report.

Differences between pre–latest Mississippian and Pennsylvanian facies trends in east-central California perhaps best demonstrate relations along the inferred truncational boundary. The Early to early Late Mississippian carbonate shelf-margin and related facies belts extend southwestward without a change in orientation to the point where outcrops are lacking (Fig. 4A). In contrast, the Pennsylvanian shelf margin and related facies belts enter California from Nevada on a southwesterly trend, but bend to a southeasterly orientation between the Panamint and Argus ranges (Fig. 4B). This bend is interpreted to have formed when the area of the Argus Range, which had been part of the Mississippian shelf, subsided and became a relatively deep submarine slope where little sediment accumulated from Pennsylvanian through earliest Permian time (Stone and Stevens, 1988b). Later, but still within the Early Permian (middle and late Wolfcampian), isopachs and paleocurrent indicators in deepwater rocks of the Argus Range and Darwin area show that the basin in which these strata accumulated was elongate and sloped southeastward (Stevens et al., 1989), parallel to the Pennsylvanian shelf margin and oblique to the Mississippian facies trends. The associated Early Permian shelf margin, marked by the occurrence of distinctive colonial corals (Stevens, 1982), formed a belt that clearly demonstrates the change in trend from southwesterly in Nevada to southeasterly in California. These paleogeographic trends suggest that the continental margin of eastern California underwent

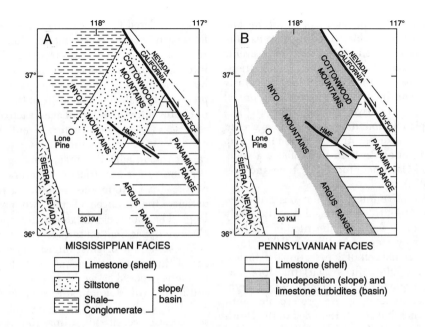

FIG. 4. Lithofacies maps of the Inyo Mountains region showing change in orientation of shelf margin from Mississippian to Pennsylvanian time. A. Mississippian facies, showing SW-trending facies boundaries. B. Pennsylvanian facies, showing southeasterly bend in shelf margin between Panamint and Argus ranges. Note right-lateral offset of facies boundaries on late Cenozoic Hunter Mountain fault (HMF). Abbreviations: DV-FCF = Death Valley–Furnace Creek fault zone of late Cenozoic age.

a major change in orientation between Mississippian and Early Permian time, most likely as the result of continental truncation.

Although the tectonic setting of the truncation event is speculative, several studies have suggested that truncation took place on a SE-trending, sinistral transform fault zone. As discussed by Stevens et al. (1992), ~500 km of displacement along such a fault zone in late Paleozoic time would account for the presence of eugeoclinal Paleozoic strata in the El Paso Mountains, which would represent a sinistrally offset fragment of the eugeoclinal rocks in the east-central Sierra Nevada, and for the presence of miogeoclinal Paleozoic strata in the Caborca-Hermosillo region of Sonora, Mexico, which would represent a sinistrally offset portion of the Cordilleran miogeocline of eastern California. Consistent with this hypothesis, Saleeby (1992) interpreted a SE-trending belt of upper Paleozoic ophiolites in the western foothills of the Sierra Nevada as typical of major oceanic transform fracture zones and to have formed along the inferred truncation boundary.

As noted in the previous section, Late Mississippian faulting and conglomerate deposition

in eastern California and other parts of the Cordilleran margin could have been related to deformation along a major zone of long-lived left-lateral shear, as suggested by Eisbacher (1983). It thus is conceivable that continental truncation began as early as the Late Mississippian after deposition on the extensive Mississippian carbonate platform had ceased, rather than Early or Middle Pennsylvanian as originally proposed by Stone and Stevens (1988b).

Permian to Earliest Triassic Deformations[5]

Complex deformational events and sedimentary patterns characterized Permian to earliest Triassic time in east-central California. Our initial studies of Permian events in the Inyo Mountains region culminated in a series of reports that presented evidence for local thrust faulting and the coeval development of deep-marine sedimentary basins in Wolfcampian (early Early Permian) time followed by Leonardian (late Early Permian) to Guadalupian (Mid-

[5]Written by Paul Stone, C. H. Stevens, and B. J. Swanson.

dle Permian) folding and uplift (Stone and Stevens, 1984, 1988a, 1988b; Stevens and Stone, 1988). We suggested that these events resulted from transpressional and transtensional deformation along the previously truncated continental margin and interpreted deformation to have ended prior to late Guadalupian (Capitanian) time, the age then assigned to the oldest strata observed to overlap deformed Lower Permian rocks above a widespread angular unconformity (Stone and Stevens, 1988a).

An alternative interpretation was presented by Snow (1992), who considered the Early Permian thrust faults documented in the Inyo Mountains by Stevens and Stone (1988) to be part of a regional belt of contractional deformation (Death Valley thrust belt) that foreshortened an originally narrow continental margin unmodified by any post-Neoproterozoic continental truncation event. Included in the Death Valley thrust belt of Snow (1992) were the Last Chance thrust and other major E-vergent thrust faults in the region previously thought to be of Triassic or Jurassic age (e.g., Stewart et al., 1966; Dunne et al., 1978; Dunne, 1986; Corbett et al., 1988). These alternative interpretations were further debated by Stone and Stevens (1993) and Snow and Wernicke (1993).

Recent work by the authors (Swanson, 1996; P. Stone and C. H. Stevens, unpubl. data, 1995–1997) provides a basis for refining the Permian history of the Inyo Mountains region. This work documents a second major episode of probable Late Permian (or earliest Triassic) contractional deformation as well as an extensional faulting event of Late Permian age. Below, we attempt to summarize current knowledge of Permian to earliest Triassic structural events in east-central California, mainly in the Inyo Mountains region, by integrating published work with our more recent work still in progress.

Regional unconformities

On the basis of unconformable relations exposed at several key localities, we previously proposed a widespread angular unconformity separating deformed Lower Permian rocks from an overlapping sequence of Upper Permian and Lower Triassic rocks throughout the Inyo Mountains region (Stone and Stevens, 1987, 1988a; Stone et al., 1991). This unconformity

was considered to reflect a regional episode of late Early Permian deformation followed by relative tectonic quiescence from Late Permian into Early Triassic time. Recent work shows, however, that the unconformity as originally proposed actually is a composite of two separate unconformities of different ages, each of which represents a separate structural event. The recognition of two unconformities has significantly modified our understanding of the Permian to earliest Triassic structural history of the Inyo Mountains region, particularly because the younger of the two post-dates Upper Permian rocks previously interpreted to place an upper limit on the age of deformation.

We based our original interpretation of the age of this composite unconformity largely on relations exposed along the western side of the southern Inyo Mountains between Fossil Hill and Union Wash (Fig. 1). On a ridge 1 km southeast of Fossil Hill, a limestone sequence once considered Late Permian in age (Merriam, 1963) unconformably overlaps the Reward Conglomerate Member and members C and B of the Lone Pine Formation, all of which we regarded previously as Lower Permian (e.g., Stone and Stevens, 1987), with an angular discordance of ~15°. We previously recognized that the upper part of this limestone sequence should be assigned to the Lower Triassic lower member of the Union Wash Formation (e.g., Stone et al., 1991), but we considered the lower part of the sequence to be correlative with the Upper Permian member B of the Conglomerate Mesa Formation (Fig. 5A). Recently, however, conodonts from the presumed Upper Permian limestone above the unconformity 1 km southeast of Fossil Hill have been identified as Early Triassic (B. R. Wardlaw, pers. commun., 1996), negating the previous constraint on the upper age limit of the unconformity and indicating that the entire limestone sequence at this locality is correlative with the lower member of the Union Wash Formation. As a result of this new paleontologic information and new mapping in the area (P. Stone and C. H. Stevens, unpubl. data, 1996), we now interpret the northwestward continuation of the unconformity at Fossil Hill to separate limestone confirmed as the Upper Permian member B of the Conglomerate Mesa Formation from the overlying conglomerate assigned to member C of that

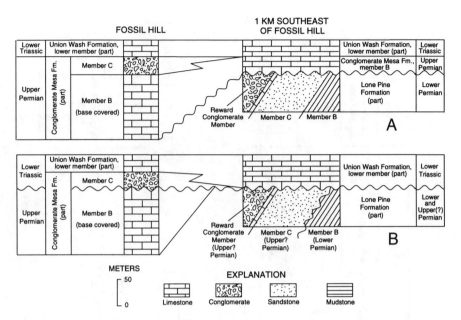

FIG. 5. Interpretations of angular unconformity in Permian–Triassic sequence in Fossil Hill/Union Wash area, southern Inyo Mountains. A. Previous interpretation (Stone and Stevens, 1987, 1988a; Stone et al., 1991) shows unconformity as separating units of Early and Late Permian age. B. Unconformity is reinterpreted in this report as separating units of Late Permian and Early Triassic age. See text for details. Lithology is generalized.

formation, rather than extending beneath member B (Fig. 5B). Member C of the Conglomerate Mesa Formation, which previously was considered Upper Permian, apparently is conformable with the overlying Union Wash Formation and is here reinterpreted as Lower Triassic. Thus, the age of deformation associated with the unconformity originally described in the Fossil Hill/Union Wash area by Stone and Stevens (1988a) now is considered to be Late Permian or earliest Triassic.

Other important relations are exposed in the type area of the Lone Pine and Conglomerate Mesa formations at Permian Bluff, about 20 km southeast of Union Wash. Here, nonmarine or shallow-water marine conglomerate and sandstone of probable Late Permian age (member A of the Conglomerate Mesa Formation) overlie the deep-water marine calcareous mudstone and siltstone of the Lower Permian member B of the Lone Pine Formation (Fig. 6). This disconformable, although concordant, contact previously was considered correlative with the angular unconformity in the Fossil Hill/Union Wash area (Stone and Stevens, 1987, 1988a), an interpretation that no longer is tenable.

Instead, this contact records a separate, late Early to early Late Permian event during which rocks of the Lone Pine Formation apparently were uplifted but not significantly folded or tilted. In the Fossil Hill/Union Wash area, as shown in Figure 6, the same event may be represented by the sharp, concordant contact between members B and C of the Lone Pine Formation (Stone and Stevens, 1987), which similarly marks abrupt shoaling of the depositional environment without significant folding or tilting. Because of the lithostratigraphic similarity to member A of the Conglomerate Mesa Formation, member C and the Reward Conglomerate Member of the Lone Pine Formation are here considered to be of possible Late Permian age (Figs. 5B and 6) rather than Early Permian, as previously interpreted by Stone and Stevens (1987).

Permian to earliest Triassic contractional deformations in the Inyo Mountains region

The primary evidence of Permian to earliest Triassic contractional deformation in the Inyo Mountains region is located in the vicinity of Conglomerate Mesa (Fig. 1), an area largely

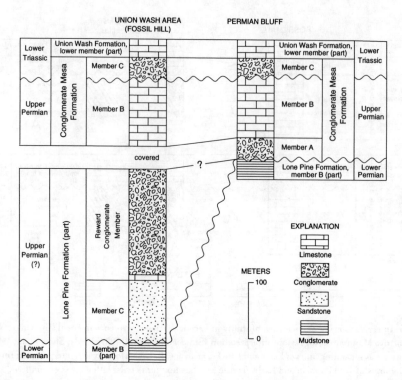

FIG. 6. Diagram showing stratigraphic positions of two unconformities in Permian to Lower Triassic sections at Fossil Hill (Union Wash area) and Permian Bluff, southern Inyo Mountains. At Permian Bluff, lower unconformity separates member B of Lone Pine Formation from member A of Conglomerate Mesa Formation; this unconformity is correlated with contact between members B and C of Lone Pine Formation in Union Wash area. Upper unconformity separates members B and C of Conglomerate Mesa Formation. Lithology is generalized.

underlain by stratigraphically and structurally complex strata of Mississippian to Early Triassic age (Elayer, 1974; Stone, 1984; Magginetti et al., 1988; Stone et al., 1989; Swanson, 1996). Two major episodes of Permian thrust faulting and folding are now recognized in this area. Key geologic units for the recognition of these events are: the Upper Mississippian Rest Spring Shale and the overlying Pennsylvanian to lower middle Wolfcampian (Lower Permian) Keeler Canyon Formation, deep-water units that pre-date contractional deformation; the informally named sedimentary rocks of Santa Rosa Flat, middle Wolfcampian to Leonardian (Lower Permian) in age, which post-date the first major episode of deformation but pre-date the second; and Lower Triassic rocks assigned to the upper part (member C) of the Conglomerate Mesa Formation and the Union Wash Formation, which post-date the second major episode of deformation. Folding and faulting of post-Triassic age has further affected all of these

rocks, hindering recognition of the Permian structures.

Early Permian deformation. Permian thrust faulting in this area was first recognized by Stevens and Stone (1988) in the informally named Fishhook Hills about 3 km east of Conglomerate Mesa (see also Stone et al., 1989). Here, an antiformally folded, E-vergent thrust fault (Fishhook thrust) places lithologically similar sequences of Rest Spring Shale and Keeler Canyon Formation upon one another (Fig. 7). Field relations show that the Keeler Canyon Formation in the upper plate of this thrust is overlapped by the slightly younger, lowermost units of the sedimentary rocks of Santa Rosa Flat, which constrains the age of thrusting as middle Wolfcampian. A structurally lower, more fundamental thrust fault of the same age (Lee Flat thrust) is inferred to lie beneath alluvial cover between the Fishhook Hills and the nearby Santa Rosa Hills. On this thrust, Mississippian through lowermost Per-

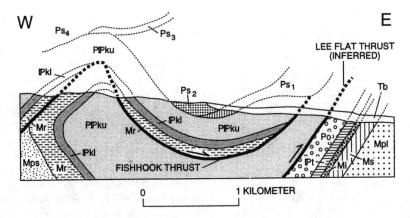

FIG. 7. Cross-section of Fishhook and Lee Flat thrusts in the Fishhook-Santa Rosa Hills area east of Conglomerate Mesa. Modified from Stevens and Stone (1988) and Stone et al. (1989). Cover rocks: Tb = basalt (Tertiary). Units overlapping upper plate of Fishhook thrust: Ps$_4$, Ps$_3$, Ps$_2$, Ps$_1$ = units 4, 3, 2, and 1, respectively, of sedimentary rocks of Santa Rosa Flat (Lower Permian). Basinal units in upper plate of Fishhook thrust: P|Pku, |Pkl = upper and lower members of Keeler Canyon Formation, respectively (Lower Permian and Pennsylvanian); Mr = Rest Spring Shale (Mississippian); Mms = Mexican Spring Formation of Stevens et al. (1996) (Mississippian). Outer shelf units in lower plate of Fishhook thrust: Po = Osborne Canyon Formation (Lower Permian); |Pt = Tihvipah Limestone (Pennsylvanian); Mi = Indian Springs Formation (Mississippian); Ms = Santa Rosa Hills Limestone (Mississippian); Msc = Stone Canyon Limestone of Stevens et al. (1996) (Mississippian). Rocks in lower plate of Lee Flat thrust, covered by Tertiary basalt in the line of the cross-section, are exposed along strike to the south in the Santa Rosa Hills. Stratigraphic overlap of upper plate of Fishhook thrust by units 3 and 4 of sedimentary rocks of the Santa Rosa Flat, inferred in the line of the cross-section, is exposed elsewhere in the Fishhook Hills.

mian basinal strata that include the Rest Spring Shale and Keeler Canyon Formation exposed in the Fishhook Hills are interpreted to have been moved eastward and emplaced above a coeval but lithostratigraphically distinct sequence of outer-shelf strata exposed in the nearby Santa Rosa Hills (Fig. 7). Although the Lee Flat thrust is nowhere exposed, its existence is suggested by the magnitude of the facies contrast between these two areas.

This Early Permian thrust faulting and folding produced a NNE-oriented ridge at least 10 km wide (Stevens and Stone, 1988) that was composed of uplifted and deformed strata of the Keeler Canyon Formation and older units (Fig. 8). This ridge, interpreted as part of the Lee Flat/Fishhook allochthon, separated two later Early Permian sedimentary basins in which distinctly different stratigraphic sequences were deposited. In the basin to the northwest, primarily thin-bedded, calcareous mudstone and siltstone assigned to the Lone Pine Formation of Stone and Stevens (1987) were deposited; to the southeast, the thicker, more heterogeneous, generally coarser-grained sedimentary rocks of Santa Rosa Flat (Magginetti et

al., 1988; Stone et al., 1989) and the laterally equivalent Osborne Canyon and Darwin Canyon formations (Stone et al., 1987) were deposited. These Lower Permian rocks, about 1000 m thick in the northwest basin and perhaps as thick as 3500 m in the southeast basin, gradually buried the intervening ridge from middle Wolfcampian through middle Leonardian time, forming buttress-type unconformities against the underlying Keeler Canyon Formation on the relatively steep, southeast flank of the ridge. These onlapping rocks thin toward the inferred crest of the ridge in the vicinity of Cerro Gordo, where middle Wolfcampian to Leonardian strata are absent and may never have been deposited.

The northeasterly trend of the interbasinal ridge (Fig. 8) that resulted from Early Permian thrust faulting in the study area is oblique to the southwesterly trend of the truncated late Paleozoic continental margin that we infer to have developed previously. Evidently, the trend of the Early Permian Lee Flat/Fishhook thrust zone and the associated interbasinal ridge was controlled by Mississippian and older stratigraphic trends, particularly those associated with the

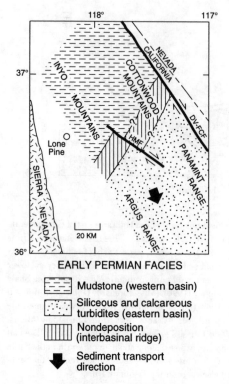

EARLY PERMIAN FACIES

▦ Mudstone (western basin)

▦ Siliceous and calcareous
turbidites (eastern basin)

▥ Nondeposition
(interbasinal ridge)

⬇ Sediment transport
direction

FIG. 8. Early Permian lithofacies map of Inyo Mountains
region showing western and eastern deep-water marine
basins separated by interbasinal ridge interpreted to have
been formed by uplift on the Fishhook/Lee Flat thrust
zone. Northeastward extension of the ridge into the Cottonwood Mountains is inferred.

margin of the Late Mississippian carbonate platform, and was not strongly influenced by the
trend of the truncated margin.

Mapped lithologic units of latest Wolfcampian to Leonardian age in the sedimentary rocks
of Santa Rosa Flat are characterized by complex
facies patterns, depositional pinchouts, and
internal unconformities throughout the Conglomerate Mesa area (Stone et al., 1989; Swanson, 1996). These features, in addition to the
local presence of coarse conglomerate, suggest
that some deformation in the area of the
Lee Flat/Fishhook allochthon continued or
recurred during deposition of the overlapping
upper Wolfcampian to Leonardian strata.

*Late Early Permian to earliest Triassic deforma-
tion.* The second major episode of Permian contractional deformation in the southern Inyo
Mountains was recognized by Swanson (1996)
on the basis of relations exposed 2 to 3 km west

of Conglomerate Mesa. Here, a W-dipping,
E-vergent thrust fault (Inyo Crest thrust) cuts
the Keeler Canyon Formation, which forms
both the footwall and the hanging wall of the
thrust (Fig. 9). In the footwall, the Keeler
Canyon Formation and the unconformably
overlying sedimentary rocks of Santa Rosa Flat
are folded by a large, E-vergent overturned
syncline (Upland Valley syncline), which is
subparallel to the thrust and is interpreted as
kinematically related to it. As demonstrated by
Swanson (1996), this deformation pre-dated
deposition of the Early Triassic member C of the
Conglomerate Mesa Formation and the lower
member of the Union Wash Formation, which
overlie the overturned west limb of the Upland
Valley syncline with a measured angular discordance of 58° at one well-exposed outcrop. The
late Leonardian (Early Permian) age of the
youngest-dated strata in the folded sedimentary
rocks of Santa Rosa Flat (Stone et al., 1989;
C. H. Stevens and P. Stone, unpubl. data, 1997)
places a lower limit on the age of deformation.

At their southern ends, the Inyo Crest thrust
and Upland Valley syncline are cut by W-dipping normal faults of late Cenozoic age that
contain Lower Triassic rocks of the Union Wash
Formation in their hanging walls (Swanson,
1996). Neither the thrust nor the syncline can
be traced through these rocks, reinforcing the
interpretation that these structures are no
younger than middle Early Triassic in age.

The Inyo Crest thrust, Upland Valley syncline, and other related folds comprise a distinct zone of deformation that is younger and
structurally higher than the Early Permian
Fishhook/Lee Flat thrust zone exposed farther
east, with the lower plate of the Inyo Crest
thrust consisting of the upper plate of the
Fishhook/Lee Flat thrust and the overlapping
sedimentary rocks of the Santa Rosa Flat. From
its area of exposure, the Inyo Crest thrust
apparently dips west beneath the main part of
the Inyo Mountains, probably carrying all pre-
Triassic strata of the range in its upper plate.

Cessation of movement on the Inyo Crest
thrust in Late Permian or earliest Triassic time
likely is recorded by the higher of the two
unconformities recognized in the Permian
Bluff and Fossil Hill/Union Wash areas,
beneath member C of the Conglomerate Mesa
Formation. Areas east of the Inyo Crest thrust

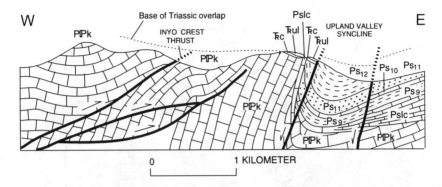

FIG. 9. Cross-section of Inyo Crest thrust and Upland Valley footwall syncline in the southern Inyo Mountains west of Conglomerate Mesa. Generalized from Swanson (1996). Rock units: Qa = alluvium (Quaternary); Jd = diorite (Jurassic?);Ŧul = lower member of Union Wash Formation (Lower Triassic);Ŧc = member C of Conglomerate Mesa Formation (Lower Triassic); Ps₁₂, Ps₁₁, Ps₁₀, Ps₉ = units 12, 11, 10, and 9, respectively, of sedimentary rocks of Santa Rosa Flat (Lower Permian); Pslc = limestone and limestone conglomerate unit of sedimentary rocks of Santa Rosa Flat (Lower Permian); P|Pk = Keeler Canyon Formation (Lower Permian and Pennsylvanian). Note unconformable overlap of Lower Triassic rocks above overturned west limb of Upland Valley syncline.

zone also may have been tilted or folded and uplifted during this episode of deformation, as reflected by an angular unconformity between Lower Permian and Lower Triassic rocks in the Darwin area and Argus Range (Stone and Stevens, 1988a).

Regional correlations. The lateral continuity of the Permian to earliest Triassic contractional structures recognized in the Conglomerate Mesa area is a topic of recent and ongoing investigation. Snow (1992) postulated that the inferred Early Permian Lee Flat thrust of Stevens and Stone (1988) represents the southward continuation of the Last Chance thrust, which is cut by Middle Jurassic plutonic rocks and previously had been presumed to be no older than Triassic (Stewart et al., 1966; Dunne et al., 1978; Dunne, 1986). In addition to the Last Chance thrust, the Death Valley thrust belt was defined by Snow (1992) to include the E-vergent Racetrack, Marble Canyon, and Lemoigne thrusts and a major W-vergent structure called the White Top backfold—all of which are exposed in the Cottonwood Mountains area east of Saline Valley (Fig. 1)—as well as the E-vergent Eureka thrust of Corbett (1989), which previously had been considered part of the Last Chance thrust. Snow (1992) additionally inferred that these structures are Permian in age on the basis of several lines of evidence and reasoning, including the recogni-

tion that the Marble Canyon thrust, its footwall syncline, and the White Top backfold are intruded by plutonic rocks no younger than early Late Triassic and possibly as old as Late Permian (Snow et al., 1991).

Identification of the Inyo Crest thrust by Swanson (1996) supports the existence of a major belt of Permian to earliest Triassic contractional deformation in the Inyo Mountains region and dispels many of our previous concerns regarding Snow's (1992) interpretations of this belt (Stone and Stevens, 1993). For two reasons, however, we still consider a direct connection between the Lee Flat and Last Chance thrusts (Snow, 1992) unlikely. First, the Last Chance thrust apparently does not underlie a northeastward continuation of the Early Permian interbasinal ridge formed by the upper plate of the Fishhook/Lee Flat thrust zone. Instead, Lower Permian rocks in both plates of the Last Chance thrust appear to represent the basin northwest of the Fishhook/Lee Flat interbasinal ridge in which the Lone Pine Formation (Stone and Stevens, 1987) was deposited. Second, based on mapping by Burchfiel (1969) in the Dry Mountain area (Fig. 1), deformation related to the Last Chance thrust apparently post-dates deposition of the Lone Pine Formation and thus is younger than the Fishhook/Lee Flat thrust zone, which is overlapped by strata of the sedimentary rocks of Santa Rosa Flat correlative with the Lone Pine Formation.

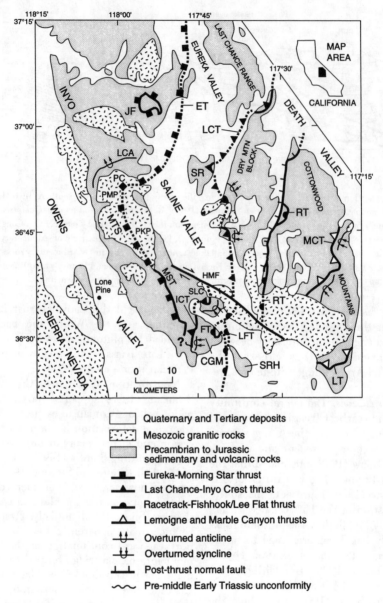

FIG. 10. Map showing major thrust faults of known or possible Permian to earliest Triassic age (Death Valley thrust system) in the Inyo Mountains region and proposed connections of thrusts in the southern Inyo Mountains with thrusts to the north and east. Frontal trace of Last Chance thrust (LCT) is interpreted to connect southward with thrust in San Lucas Canyon (SLC) and Inyo Crest thrust (ICT); Racetrack thrust (RT) is interpreted to connect southward with Fishhook/Lee Flat thrust zone (FT, LFT); and Eureka thrust (ET) is interpreted to connect southward with Morning Star thrust of Elayer (1974) (MST). Note inferred right-lateral offsets of thrusts on late Cenozoic Hunter Mountain fault (HMF). Other symbols: CGM = Conglomerate Mesa; JF = Jackass Flats window of Eureka thrust; LCA = Lead Canyon anticline; LT = Lemoigne thrust; MCT = Marble Canyon thrust; PKP = Pat Keyes pluton; PMP = Paiute Monument pluton; SR = Saline Range; SRH = Santa Rosa Hills.

As an alternative candidate for the southward extension of the Last Chance thrust, we suggest the Inyo Crest thrust, the age and paleogeo-graphic position of which are more compatible with such a correlation. By this interpretation the Inyo Crest thrust is considered continuous with the frontal trace of the Last Chance thrust exposed in the Dry Mountain area (Stewart et al., 1966; Burchfiel, 1969), possibly through connecting structures exposed in the northwestern Nelson Range (Fig. 10). There, the Rest Spring Shale and Keeler Canyon Formation are folded into a large overturned syncline (McAllister, 1956; Werner, 1979) that we interpret to be overridden by a duplicate section of Keeler Canyon Formation on a poorly exposed thrust fault not shown on existing geologic maps (P. Stone, C. H. Stevens, and G. C. Dunne, unpubl. data, 1996). The geometry and style of these structures are similar to those of the Inyo Crest thrust and Upland Valley syncline and thus are consistent with the proposed connection, although additional work is needed to fully document the structural relations in the Nelson Range. Because the upper plate of the Last Chance thrust in the Dry Mountain area contains rocks as old as Ordovician (Burchfiel, 1969), our proposed structural correlation would require this thrust to cut laterally upsection into the Nelson Range, where no rocks older than Pennsylvanian are exposed in the upper plate.

In keeping with its proposed correlation with the Inyo Crest thrust, we consider the Last Chance thrust to be of late Early Permian to earliest Triassic age, younger than the Early Permian age suggested by Snow (1992). Because the age of the Last Chance thrust is nowhere independently constrained to be as old as we suggest, this correlation is somewhat speculative.

Stewart et al. (1966) depicted the Last Chance thrust as a single dislocation surface that underlies a large area extending from the southern Last Chance Range to the northern Inyo Mountains in the vicinity of Jackass Flats (Fig. 1). Corbett et al. (1988), Corbett (1989), and Snow (1992) have proposed, alternatively, that two separate thrusts are present, a structurally lower Last Chance thrust that underlies the Last Chance Range, and a structurally higher Eureka thrust, exposed in southwestern Eureka Valley and at Jackass Flats, that underlies the northern Inyo Mountains. The two-thrust model is supported by the presence of a major structural break in the vicinity of Paiute Canyon, 20 km southwest of Jackass Flats, that likely represents the southwestern continuation of the Eureka thrust. Here, the Jurassic

Paiute Monument pluton intrudes an inferred major thrust fault that apparently placed Cambrian rocks forming the large, recumbent Lead Canyon anticline above rocks as young as Mississippian to the south (Ross, 1967a; Stevens and Olson, 1972; Dunne, 1986). If the Last Chance and Inyo Crest thrusts are connected, as we propose, regional map relations indicate that the thrust at Paiute Canyon is distinct from the Last Chance thrust, occupies a higher structural position, and is best interpreted as a continuation of the Eureka thrust.

No significant structural break that might represent a farther southwestward continuation of the Eureka thrust has been identified beyond the margins of the Paiute Monument and Pat Keyes plutons (Ross, 1967b, 1969). Dunne (1986) hypothesized that a substantial part of the slip inferred for the thrust (then considered to be part of the Last Chance thrust) might be transformed into shortening accommodated by the Lead Canyon anticline, which to the south is represented by smaller folds and faults of less obvious significance. Snow (1992) accepted these interpretations and depicted the Eureka thrust as terminating as a discrete structure in the Lead Canyon anticline.

An alternative possibility, not previously considered in the published literature, is that the Eureka thrust diverges from the Lead Canyon anticline and continues southeastward through the Inyo Mountains. Southeast of the Paiute Monument and Pat Keyes plutons, the Eureka thrust could continue as a fault zone called the Morning Star thrust (Fig. 10), which was first recognized and named by Elayer (1974) in the Cerro Gordo area. This fault zone follows the generally W-dipping contact between the Rest Spring Shale and the overlying Keeler Canyon Formation along the crest and western flank of the Inyo Mountains, a contact others have mapped as stratigraphic (e.g., Merriam, 1963; Ross, 1967b). Recent mapping, in addition to the earlier work of Elayer (1974), shows that rocks along this contact are everywhere sheared or faulted and locally include anomalous slices of Mississippian and Pennsylvanian strata that apparently were dragged into the contact zone by faulting (P. Stone and C. H. Stevens, unpubl. data, 1996). Thus, although this contact zone exhibits little stratigraphic separation, it clearly is a fault zone that could accommodate substantial slip.

A structural correlation between the Eureka and Morning Star thrusts would require that the thrust fault ramp upsection through hanging-wall strata, forming the southern flank of the Lead Canyon anticline, from a level below Lower Cambrian units in areas north of Paiute Canyon to the base of the Keeler Canyon Formation south of the Pat Keyes pluton. In this model, the Morning Star thrust would be a decollement representing a hanging-wall flat located at the base of the Keeler Canyon Formation juxtaposed above a footwall flat located near the top of the Rest Spring Shale.

The trace of the Morning Star thrust has not been conclusively delineated south of Cerro Gordo because of unresolved structural complexities. The thrust could continue to follow the contact between the Rest Spring Shale and Keeler Canyon Formation eastward through a series of folds into the Conglomerate Mesa area, or it could depart from that contact and cut southward and upsection through the Keeler Canyon Formation. Although these options differ in their implications for the geometry, map relations in either case (Swanson, 1996) would imply that the thrust is Permian or earliest Triassic in age. Because neither option is certain, relations at the south end of the Morning Star thrust are shown as questionable in Figure 10.

Other age constraints on both the Eureka and Morning Star thrusts are nondefinitive. The Eureka thrust pre-dates the Paiute Monument and Pat Keyes plutons, which are considered to be ~167 and 182 Ma, respectively (Dunne et al., 1978), and the Morning Star thrust is locally intruded by undated plutonic rocks that may be related to the Jurassic Hunter Mountain batholith (P. Stone, unpubl. data, 1996). These relations permit but do not require a Permian to earliest Triassic age for both thrusts.

An independent line of reasoning, based on relations exposed near Tinemaha Reservoir, leads to a possible alternative interpretation of the age of the Eureka thrust. In that area, Stevens and Olson (1972) identified a low-angle fault, which they named the Inyo thrust, that they suggested extends beneath the northern Inyo Mountains to connect with the Eureka thrust on the eastern side of the range. If this interpretation is correct, the Eureka thrust would have to be post–Early Triassic, because the Inyo thrust is now known to contain Lower Triassic strata of the Union Wash Formation in its upper plate (Stevens, 1995; Stevens and Greene, this report). In addition, this interpretation could preclude a connection between the Eureka and the Morning Star thrust to the southeast, which probably is Permian to earliest Triassic in age, as discussed above. On the other hand, the geology of the Tinemaha Reservoir area also leaves open the possibility that the Inyo thrust originally passed over the Inyo Mountains and later was downdropped to its present position on a prominent rangefront fault first mapped by Nelson (1966b). In this case, the Eureka thrust would root beneath the Inyo Mountains, separate from the Inyo thrust, and could be of Permian to earliest Triassic age. At present, evidence for either structural model in inconclusive.

In concert with the possible interpretations of the Eureka/Morning Star and Last Chance/Inyo Crest thrusts discussed above, we suggest that the Fishhook/Lee Flat thrust zone may represent the southwestern continuation of the Racetrack thrust (Fig. 10), which is structurally below the Last Chance thrust in the Cottonwood Mountains (Stewart et al., 1966). The Racetrack thrust is located between outcrop areas of contrasting Lower Permian sedimentary sequences similar to those separated by the Fishhook/Lee Flat thrust zone (Lone Pine Formation to the west in the Dry Mountain area, Osborne Canyon and Darwin Canyon formations to the east in the Marble Canyon area), and therefore could be associated genetically with a northeastward continuation of the same interbasinal ridge associated with the Fishhook/Lee Flat allochthon (Stone and Stevens, 1988b).

Structurally below the Racetrack thrust is the Marble Canyon thrust, which involves rocks as young as middle Wolfcampian (Stone, 1984) and is intruded by plutonic rocks no younger than ~230 Ma (early Late Triassic according to Harland et al., 1982) (Snow et al., 1991; Snow, 1992). We consider this thrust as being Permian to earliest Triassic in age because of its general proximity to the Last Chance and Racetrack thrusts and because it is structurally similar (although not equivalent) to the Inyo

Crest thrust of known Permian to earliest Triassic age.

Structurally below the Marble Canyon thrust is the Lemoigne thrust, the lowest thrust assigned to the Death Valley thrust belt by Snow (1992). This thrust involves rocks as young as early middle Wolfcampian (Stone, 1984) and pre-dates the Middle Jurassic Hunter Mountain batholith (Snow, 1992), but is not tightly constrained as Permian to earliest Triassic.

Snow (1992) also proposed that the Talc City and Ophir Peak thrusts in the Talc City Hills–Darwin Hills area (Hall and MacKevett, 1962; Stone et al., 1989) represent the southwestern continuation of the Permian Death Valley thrust belt. The Talc City thrust has been interpreted as structurally similar to the Last Chance thrust (Gulliver, 1976) and could be Permian in age, although its exposed relations permit any age younger than Pennsylvanian. The Ophir Peak thrust cuts rocks as young as Early Permian in age and underwent most of its displacement prior to intrusion of the Middle Jurassic Darwin pluton (Stone et al., 1989). Although these relations permit a Permian age of slip on this thrust, Lower Triassic rocks of the Union Wash Formation immediately to the east rest on the Lower Permian Darwin Canyon Formation in the footwall of the thrust with only slight angular discordance, and both units are involved in coaxial E-vergent folds, suggesting that most or all of the deformation associated with thrusting was Middle Triassic or younger.

Snow (1992) noted that the southward continuations of the Lemoigne and Marble Canyon thrusts are poorly constrained, but suggested that one or both of these thrusts could project southward into the Argus Range near Bendire Canyon (Fig. 1). Here, on the basis of stratigraphic relations, Stone (1984) recognized a significant post–middle Wolfcampian, pre–Early Triassic uplift, which Snow (1992) suggested could represent the leading edge of either the Lemoigne or Marble Canyon thrusts. Although this interpretation is possible, Mesozoic plutonism and deformation have so obscured the geology that any specific correlation is problematic.

Summary. We recognize a major, N- to NE-trending belt of Permian to earliest Triassic contractional deformation in the Inyo Mountains region. This belt of deformation includes the Early Permian Fishhook/Lee Flat thrust and the late Early Permian to earliest Triassic Inyo Crest thrust in the southern Inyo Mountains, which we suggest connect northeastward with the Racetrack and Last Chance thrusts, respectively. Other faults that also may be part of this belt of deformation include the Eureka, Marble Canyon, and Lemoigne thrusts, as well as the Morning Star thrust, which may correlate with the Eureka thrust. From the Inyo Mountains, the belt of deformation probably continued southward or southwestward into the Darwin area and Argus Range, where an angular unconformity separates Lower Permian from Lower Triassic rocks. No major thrust faults of Permian to earliest Triassic age have been positively identified in these areas, perhaps owing to later intrusion and overprinting deformations, so the full southward or southwestward extent of this belt of contractional deformation remains unknown.

Late Permian extensional faulting in the southern Inyo Mountains

New information relating to the deposition and structural significance of the Conglomerate Mesa Formation (P. Stone and C. H. Stevens, unpubl. data, 1996) has altered some of our previous interpretations of the Late Permian to earliest Triassic evolution of the Inyo Mountains region (e.g., Stone and Stevens, 1988a). Perhaps the most unexpected discovery was that deposition of the lower (Upper Permian) part of this formation (members A and B of Stone and Stevens, 1987) was controlled by normal faults, which reflect a previously unrecognized episode of extensional deformation.

The clearest evidence of this extensional event is ~3 km northwest of Permian Bluff at a prominent hill we informally call West Peak (Fig. 11), where Upper Permian rocks comprising members A and B of the Conglomerate Mesa Formation undergo dramatic changes in thickness and lithology over very short distances along strike. On this peak, a section of conglomerate ~100 m thick, representing member A of the Conglomerate Mesa Formation, abuts southeastward and pinches out abruptly against the Lower Permian Lone Pine Formation; northwestward, the upper 50 m of this conglomerate interfingers with sandy to pebbly limestone, which represents member B of the Conglomerate Mesa Formation. Mapping has

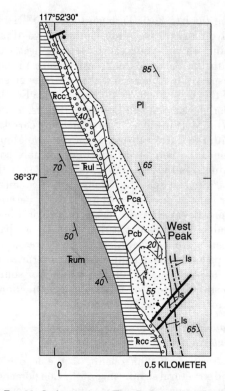

FIG. 11. Geologic map of West Peak area near Permian Bluff in the southern Inyo Mountains, showing pre-Triassic normal faults bounding a small Upper Permian depositional basin. Abbreviations:Ŧum,Ŧul = middle and lower members of Union Wash Formation (Lower Triassic), respectively;Ŧcc = member C of Conglomerate Mesa Formation (Lower Triassic); Pcb, Pca = members B and C of Conglomerate Mesa Formation (Upper Permian); Pl = Lone Pine Formation (Lower Permian); ls = limestone marker beds near top of the Lone Pine Formation.

revealed that the lenticularity of the Conglomerate Mesa Formation here was the result of faulting. Key to this mapping are two conspicuous limestone turbidite beds near the top of the underlying Lone Pine Formation south of West Peak. Traced northwestward, these beds are not erosionally truncated by the thick conglomerate at West Peak, but instead are displaced downward along a series of NE-striking faults to a structural position below the thick conglomerate (Fig. 11). One of the two faults that is large enough to map is aligned with the abutting contact between the Conglomerate Mesa and Lone Pine formations on the south side of West Peak, and both faults are overlapped by conglomerate assigned to the Lower Triassic member C of the Conglomerate Mesa

Formation. Thus, space for the excess thickness of the Conglomerate Mesa Formation was created by displacement on nonrotational normal faults prior to deposition of member C. Members A and B of the Conglomerate Mesa Formation also are truncated against the Lone Pine Formation at the opposite end of the outcrop belt, 1 km northwest of West Peak, by a fault that in this case extends into, but not through, member C.

Because of the moderately steep dip, the map view of the West Peak area (Fig. 11) approximates a vertical section when oriented to look down bedding. This section shows members A and B of the Conglomerate Mesa Formation occupying an asymmetric graben bounded by normal faults, with greater displacement on the southeast than on the northwest. The interfingering of member A conglomerate and member B limestone in the southwestern part of the graben suggests that these faults were syndepositional and mark the original margins of the sedimentary basin. Evidently faulting continued locally during deposition of the lower part of member C, but was terminated prior to deposition of the upper part.

This Late Permian extensional event postdated contractional deformation on the Fishhook/Lee Flat thrust in the Conglomerate Mesa area as well as regional uplift that terminated deep-water sedimentation of the lower part (members A and B) of the Lone Pine Formation. The age relative to that of the youngest-known pre–middle Early Triassic contractional deformation in the region (Inyo Crest thrust), however, is uncertain. If the regional angular unconformity between members B and C of the Conglomerate Mesa Formation developed as a result of deformation and uplift associated with the Inyo Crest thrust, the extensional event predated the youngest contraction.

The full geographic extent of Late Permian extensional faulting that we have documented in the Permian Bluff area is not known, because members A and B of the Conglomerate Mesa Formation, which mark the sedimentary basins formed by this faulting, crop out only in the southern Inyo Mountains (Stone and Stevens, 1987). Elsewhere, as in the Darwin area and Argus Range, Lower Permian strata are unconformably overlain by the Union Wash Formation or, locally, by conglomerate representing member C of the Conglomerate Mesa Formation, with any record of Late Permian extensional faulting and related sedimentation having been destroyed by uplift and erosion prior to the middle Early Triassic. Thus, it is unknown whether the extensional faults and related shallow sedimentary basins observed in the southern Inyo Mountains formed as a response to a discrete, regionally significant episode of extensional deformation or, alternatively, as relatively minor space accommodation structures reflecting local extension within a dominantly contractional deformational system.

Permian to earliest Triassic deformation and plutonism in the El Paso Mountains

Rocks and structures exposed in the El Paso Mountains (Fig. 1) record a major episode of contractional deformation, metamorphism, and associated plutonism during the latter part of Permian and earliest Triassic time. Here, Permian and older eugeoclinal strata of the Garlock assemblage, which includes andesite of Leonardian or younger age at the top of the stratigraphic sequence, are folded into a large, W-vergent synclinorium complicated by E-dipping, W-directed thrust faults (Carr et al., 1984). Deformation was accompanied by greenschist-facies metamorphism and intrusion of a synkinematic quartz monzonite pluton. Recent U-Pb geochronologic studies by Miller et al. (1995) indicate that this pluton has a crystallization age of 260 ± 5 Ma, somewhat older than the U-Pb age of 249 ± 3 Ma originally reported for this pluton by Carr et al. (1984). The pluton and its deformed eugeoclinal host rocks are cut by the undeformed Last Chance Canyon pluton, which has a U-Pb age of 246 ± 3 Ma (Miller et al., 1995). These data document a late Early to early Late Permian age of deformation, metamorphism, and synkinematic plutonism, and a latest Permian to earliest Triassic age of post-deformational plutonism.

Miller et al. (1995) showed that the El Paso Mountains are part of a NW-striking belt of eugeoclinal Paleozoic rocks and Late Permian to Early Triassic plutons ~150 km long, extending from the southeastern Sierra Nevada into the Mojave Desert. The deformation and plutonism that characterize this terrane have been interpreted as an early manifestation of plate convergence and arc magmatism along a NW-trending, tectonically truncated continental margin (Miller and Cameron, 1982; Walker,

1988; Miller et al., 1995).

The deformation and plutonism in the El Paso Mountains were broadly synchronous with the later stages of Permian to earliest Triassic deformation and uplift in the Inyo Mountains region, which included uplift and extensional faulting associated with deposition of the lower part of the Conglomerate Mesa Formation and contractional deformation associated with the Inyo Crest/Last Chance thrust. Snow (1992) proposed a direct connection between Permian deformation in the El Paso Mountains and deformation related to the Death Valley thrust belt. Such a connection, however, appears unlikely because of the opposite vergence of deformation in these two regions and because of the evidence presented by Miller et al. (1995) that the El Paso Mountains terrane was not thrust into its present position until Mesozoic time (240 to 175 Ma). We suggest that Permian to earliest Triassic events in the El Paso and Inyo mountains regions were not directly connected, but probably took place in structurally distinct areas in response to similar convergent or transpressional plate motions that affected a large segment of the continental margin.

Summary and tectonic implications

The Permian to earliest Triassic in east-central California was a time primarily of contractional deformation. In the southern Inyo Mountains, where the timing of events is most tightly constrained, deformation began in the middle Wolfcampian (Early Permian) with development of the Fishhook/Lee Flat thrust zone, was punctuated by a period of relative quiescence and overlapping sedimentation during the remainder of the Early Permian, but resumed in late Early Permian to earliest Triassic time with development of the Inyo Crest thrust. This latter stage of deformation in the Inyo Mountains region was broadly coeval with deformation and plutonism in the El Paso Mountains region to the south.

Permian to earliest Triassic contractional deformation in east-central California apparently reflects convergent plate motion on the previously truncated continental margin, in keeping with some previous tectonic syntheses (e.g., Miller et al., 1992; Saleeby and Busby-Spera, 1992). The western edge of the continental plate may have followed the Kings-Kaweah ophiolite belt in the southwestern foothills of the Sierra Nevada (Saleeby, 1992), which is interpreted to have developed along the late Paleozoic truncational boundary. Subduction along the plate edge, beginning no later than late Early Permian time, led to the development of a diffuse magmatic arc to the east, as discussed by Miller et al. (1995), that included the El Paso Mountains and extended at least as far south as the San Bernardino Mountains (Barth et al., 1997) and as far north as the Walker Pass area (Fig. 1) (Dunne and Saleeby, 1993). Permian to earliest Triassic contractional structures in the Inyo Mountains region (Death Valley thrust belt) developed east of the northward projection of this arc, although no tectonic relationship between the arc and thrust belt has been identified.

Early Triassic Downwarping and Sedimentation[6]

East-central California was tectonically quiescent during the Early Triassic. In the southern Inyo Mountains, the Darwin area, and the Argus Range, dominantly fine-grained sedimentary rocks were deposited unconformably upon Permian rocks that had been involved in the episode of deformation described above (Lewis et al., 1983; Stone et al., 1991). Basal nonmarine conglomeratic rocks of the upper part (member C) of the Conglomerate Mesa Formation, which we now consider to be of Early Triassic age, pass upward into the shallow- to moderately deep-water marine strata of the Union Wash Formation, which is of middle Early Triassic (Smithian) to early Middle(?) Triassic (Anisian?) age (Stone et al., 1991). The Union Wash Formation also is present near Tinemaha Reservoir southeast of Big Pine (Fig. 1), where it unconformably overlies Devonian rocks (Stevens, 1995), as described earlier. Other Lower Triassic strata in the study area include the Butte Valley Formation (Johnson, 1957; Cole, 1986) in the southern Panamint Range, which is similar to the Union Wash Formation, and rocks assigned to the somewhat different Candelaria Formation in the Saddlebag Lake pendant of the Sierra Nevada (Schweickert and Lahren, 1987).

[6]Written by C. H. Stevens and Paul Stone.

The Lower and Middle(?) Triassic sequence of the Inyo Mountains region records initial erosion of the underlying Permian strata, followed by rapid subsidence of the continental margin and deposition of relatively deep-water marine sediment. By latest Early or earliest Middle Triassic time, however, the upper part of the Union Wash Formation aggraded into shallow subtidal to intertidal environments. This shoaling is best exemplified by strata near the top of the section near Cerro Gordo, which contain ooliths, stromatolite-like bedding, and possible birdseye structures (Lewis et al., 1983). After deposition of these beds, marine sedimentation in the Inyo Mountains region ceased.

Facies patterns indicate that the Union Wash Formation accumulated on a gently sloping shelf that deepened to the northwest. The imprecisely defined shelf margin probably was located in the Argus Range, where supratidal and very shallow water shelf deposits are present near the base of the formation. To the NNW in the Darwin area, a base-of-slope environment is indicated by the presence of slump structures, slide blocks, and debris-flow deposits intercalated in a predominantly pelagic and hemipelagic sequence. Sections in the Inyo Mountains farther northwest are composed primarily of very fine grained sediment indicative of a deep shelf or basinal environment.

Lower and Middle(?) Triassic rocks of the Inyo Mountains region contain no evidence of nearby syndepositional tectonism or magmatism. Except for the basal conglomeratic rocks, the sequence lacks coarse detritus, and no part of the sequence contains volcanic or plutonic detritus. In the Mojave Desert region to the south, arc plutonism that had begun in the Late Permian continued intermittently throughout the Early and Middle Triassic (Miller et al., 1995; Barth et al., 1997), thus spanning the time of deposition of the Union Wash Formation in the Inyo Mountains region. There is no evidence, however, that this arc plutonism extended as far north as the latitude of the Inyo Mountains.

The Union Wash Formation represents a change from a structural setting characterized by contractional deformation and uplift to one of subsidence and passive sedimentation. The tectonic significance of this change is unknown, although it could reflect a local, temporary shift from contractional or trans-pressional to transtensional stresses along this part of the continental margin.

Middle Triassic Contraction[7]

A Triassic contractional deformational event, first recognized by Schweickert and Lahren (1987) in the Sierra Nevada and correlated by them with the Sonoma orogeny in central Nevada, brought the quiescent Early to Mid-dle(?) Triassic depositional phase to a close. In the Saddlebag Lake pendant, a thrust correlated by Schweickert and Lahren (1987) with the Golconda thrust in Nevada is constrained to have been emplaced in about Middle Triassic time (Fig. 12). This thrust structurally super-imposes rocks interpreted as part of the Gol-conda allochthon over rocks as young as the Candelaria Formation, which in west-central Nevada was deposited throughout the Early Triassic (Speed, 1984). The Golconda thrust in the Saddlebag Lake pendant is cut by the late Middle or Late Triassic Lundy Canyon thrust, which also cuts a volcanic sequence with an age of ~222 ± 5 Ma and itself is intruded by a 219 ± 2 Ma pluton (Schweickert and Lahren, 1987, 1993), showing that the Golconda allochthon in the Saddlebag Lake pendant probably was emplaced in about Middle Triassic time.

Folds and thrust faults probably belonging to the same contractional episode also occur in the Mount Morrison pendant where they are cut by the Laurel-Convict fault, which is sealed by a granitic dike dated at 225 ± 16 Ma (Greene et al., 1997). Because rocks as young as late Early Permian are involved in structures cut by the Laurel-Convict fault, this major deformational event can be dated as post-late Early Permian and pre-Late Triassic.

Closer direct dating of the deformation in the Mount Morrison pendant is not possible, but a post-Early Triassic age is suggested by correla-tion of rocks and structures between McGee Mountain in the Mount Morrison pendant and outcrops in the Owens Valley near Tinemaha Reservoir, ~65 km to the southeast (Fig. 1). Middle Devonian rocks both near Tinemaha Reservoir and at McGee Mountain, unique among all strata of this age in the Inyo Moun-

[7]Written by C. H. Stevens and D. C. Greene.

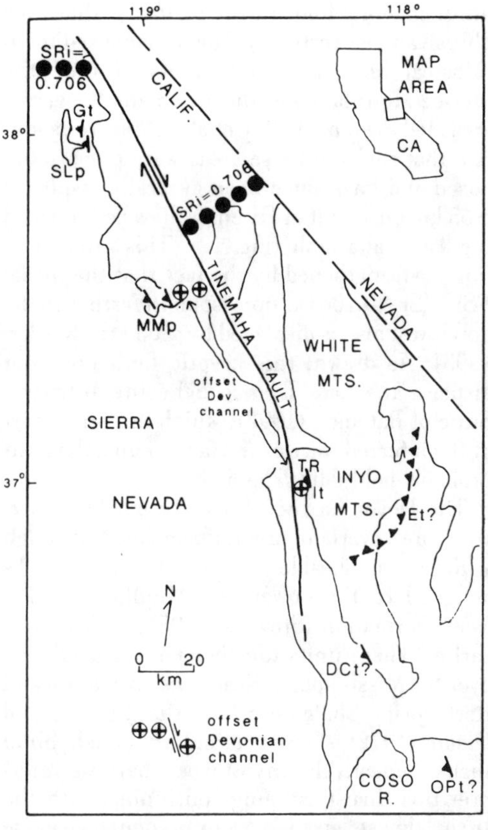

FIG. 12. Possible elements of Golconda thrust system in east-central California. Sri = 0.706 isopleth (Kistler, 1993), and an Upper Devonian channel as well as the Golconda thrust system are shown displaced by a dextral fault, here termed the Tinemaha fault. Abbreviations: DCt = Dolomite Canyon thrust; Et = Eureka thrust; Gt = Golconda thrust; It = Inyo thrust; MMp = Mount Morrison pendant; OPt = Ophir Peak thrust; SLp = Saddlebag Lake pendant; TR = Tinemaha Reservoir. Question marks indicate structures that are questionably assigned to the Golconda thrust system.

tains and Sierra Nevada, contain fragments of tabulate corals in a coarse conglomerate com-posed of limestone and black chert clasts set in a calcareous, fine- to coarse-grained quartz sand-stone matrix. These conglomeratic rocks are interpreted to be the fill of a major submarine channel that carried sediment from the exposed Middle Devonian shelf in the Inyo Mountains to a large submarine fan complex in the eastern Sierra Nevada (Stevens et al., 1995b). In addi-tion, post-Early Triassic folds in the Tinemaha outcrop and in the NE part of the Mount Mor-rison pendant, including McGee Mountain, are unique among folds in the region in that they plunge almost vertically. The unusual sedimentological and structural similarities of the McGee Mountain and the Tinemaha Reservoir areas led Stevens, Pelley et al. (1995) to postulate that rocks in these areas were once juxtaposed and have since been dextrally displaced ~65 km on a fault in Owens Valley, here termed the Tinemaha fault (Fig. 12). This interpretation is strengthened by the fact that the initial $^{87}Sr/^{86}Sr = 0.706$ isotopic isopleth farther to the northwest also is displaced by ~65 km (Kistler, 1993). As drawn, this cryptic fault does not displace the Late Triassic Scheelite Intrusive Suite of Bateman (1992), which underlies part of the inferred trace of the fault. Thus, the fault probably is Middle Triassic in age.

The Devonian rocks near Tinemaha Reservoir are overlain unconformably, although without noticeable angularity, by rocks assigned to the Lower and Middle(?) Union Wash Formation (Stevens, 1995), as described earlier. These units together have been thrust over the Mississippian Kearsarge Formation and Rest Spring Shale on a fault that Stevens and Olson (1972) showed as an unnamed, blind thrust beneath the Inyo thrust; here we interpret this thrust as being continuous with the Inyo thrust itself. A prominent cleavage extends across the thrust fault, and recent observations show that the thrust surface is deformed around tight, steeply plunging folds. These relations support the original interpretation of Stevens and Olson (1972) that the Inyo thrust is a Mesozoic contractional fault, and not a late Cenozoic extensional fault as suggested by Dunne and Gulliver (1978). Here, we interpret the Inyo thrust to represent the same deformation as the post–late Early Permian, pre–Late Triassic event in the Mount Morrison pendant because of the close stratigraphic and structural similarities between these two areas. If this interpretation is correct, the age of thrusting is Middle Triassic, constrained by the age of the dike intruding the Laurel-Convict fault (225 ± 16 Ma) in the Mount Morrison pendant and the age of the Union Wash Formation (embracing the entire Early Triassic) near Tinemaha Reservoir.

One probable effect of the Middle Triassic contractional event was the telescoping of the previously formed Antler belt against the Paleozoic rocks of the Morrison succession. This interpretation is based upon the great difference in the upper Paleozoic stratigraphy in the two sequences. The upper Paleozoic section overlying the deformed Antler belt sequence in the Saddlebag Lake pendant consists of ~30 m of Permian conglomerate (Schweickert and Lahren, 1987), whereas that of the Morrison succession consists of ~2500 m of primarily very fine grained rocks, including at least 1800 m of Permian strata (Willahan, 1991). Outcrops of undoubted Antler belt rocks in the Saddlebag Lake pendant today lie only ~5 km from outcrops of Pennsylvanian rocks of the now somewhat tectonically dismembered Morrison succession. Stevens, Pelley et al. (1995) and Stevens and Greene (1997) have suggested that these different facies were juxtaposed by tens of kilometers of post-Paleozoic thrust faulting after deposition of the Lower Triassic Candelaria Formation (probably during the Middle Triassic), as it seems quite unlikely that these two vastly different sequences could have been deposited anywhere close to one another.

Extension of the Middle Triassic contractional event into the Inyo Mountains south and east of Tinemaha Reservoir, where the Inyo thrust is exposed, is problematic (Fig. 12). As discussed in a previous section of this paper, the Inyo thrust may connect eastward beneath the Inyo Mountains with the Eureka thrust, although it is possible that the Inyo thrust was significantly downdropped to its present location at the western base of the Inyo Mountains and originally passed over the range instead. If the Ordovician rocks near Tinemaha Reservoir are in the upper plate of the Inyo thrust, as proposed by Stevens and Olson (1972) and still accepted by these writers, their similarity to correlative rocks in northern Mazourka Canyon would favor the first option.

Various other folds and thrust faults in the region, including the Dolomite Canyon thrust and Front Ridge anticline in the southwestern Inyo Mountains, the Ophir Peak thrust and related folds in the Darwin Hills, and large folds in the northern and central Argus Range—all of which are intruded by Middle Jurassic plutonic rocks (Dunne et al., 1978; Dunne, 1986; Stone et al., 1989)—also could represent a Middle Triassic contractional event, but their ages are not tightly constrained. The structures in the Darwin Hills and Argus Range are particularly noteworthy because they involve the Union

Wash Formation and thus are post–Early Triassic and pre–Middle Jurassic in age. These structures, however, could instead represent early phases of deformation in the East Sierran contractional belt, as previously interpreted (Dunne et al., 1978; Dunne, 1986).

Late Triassic to Cretaceous Magmatism, Sedimentation, and Deformation[8]

By early Late Triassic time, east-central California came fully under the influence of an east-dipping, continental-margin subduction zone exposed at the surface in the vicinity of what is now the western foothills of the Sierra Nevada (e.g., Burchfiel et al., 1992). The study area encompasses the eastern fringe of the resulting magmatic arc as well as the immediately adjacent back arc. As the arc evolved from Late Triassic to Late Cretaceous time, numerous plutons and a major dike swarm intruded the region, while volcanic complexes accumulated on the surface. During this same time span, these rocks, as well as their Early Triassic and older substrate and host rocks, experienced repeated episodes of predominantly compressional and/or transpressional deformation. The resulting structures compose a long-lived, NW-trending deformation belt located along the eastern margin of the magmatic arc that probably was linked genetically to emplacement of the arc.

Late Triassic to Cretaceous rock assemblages

Intrusive rocks. Radiometrically dated Triassic intrusions in the study area are sparse. Whether this reflects sparse Triassic magmatism or substantial obliteration and/or radiometric resetting of a modestly more voluminous Triassic arc by subsequent Jurassic and Cretaceous episodes of plutonism is unknown. Several small granitoid intrusions in the Cottonwood Mountains (Fig. 1) have yielded Ar-Ar and U-Pb radiometric data permissive of a minimum date for these rocks of ~230 Ma (Snow et al., 1991). These may be the oldest arc-related rocks of post–Early Triassic age in the study area, although an older age for them and a different tectonic setting is possible. The oldest volumetrically significant plutons that most

[8]Written by G. C. Dunne and J. D. Walker.

workers would place in the Sierran arc (e.g., Barth et al., 1997) are those composing the Scheelite Intrusive Suite exposed in the northern Owens Valley and Mono Lake basin areas (Chen and Moore, 1982; Bateman, 1992; Schweickert and Lahren, 1993). These have yielded Late Triassic U-Pb dates ranging from ~220 to ~210 Ma. Major-element compositions of these Late Triassic plutons indicate that they are slightly alkalic (Unruh, 1985), which is consistent with the slightly alkalic nature of Late Triassic plutons in the Mojave Desert and Transverse Ranges to the south (Barth et al., 1997).

Jurassic plutons are much more abundant than those of Triassic age, forming several large composite batholiths along the eastern flank of the arc (e.g., Inyo batholith, Hunter Mountain batholith, Coso/Argus batholith, Sacatar batholith of the eastern Kern Plateau) and scattered plutons elsewhere. The majority of Jurassic intrusions have yielded Middle Jurassic U-Pb radiometric dates ranging from ~186 to ~161 Ma, whereas a smaller group of plutons have yielded Late Jurassic U-Pb dates, mostly in the range from ~152 to ~147 Ma. Major-element compositions and mineralogic characteristics indicate that many Middle Jurassic plutons exposed in ranges east of the Sierra Nevada are slightly alkalic in nature (Dunne et al., 1978; Sylvester et al., 1978; Dunne, 1979).

Also intruded across much of the study area during Late Jurassic time (U-Pb dates of ~148 Ma) was part of the ~500-km-long, NW-trending Independence dike swarm (Chen and Moore, 1979; James, 1989), which has figured prominently in many tectonic models relating the effects of plate motions on evolution of the Sierran arc and its wallrocks (e.g., Wolf and Saleeby, 1995; Carl et al., 1996). The report of Cretaceous dikes within the swarm (Coleman et al., 1994; Ernst, 1997) has highlighted the need for caution in assuming that all NW-trending mafic dikes in the region are ~148 Ma and for development of non-geochronologic methods for distinguishing Late Jurassic from Cretaceous (or other age) dikes within the swarm (J. Bartley, pers. commun., 1997).

Cretaceous plutons form the greatest volume of intrusive rocks in the study area. Radiometric dates ranging from ~110 to ~72 Ma have been determined for these plutons, with a majority yielding ages in the ranges from ~110 to ~98 Ma and ~92 to ~83 Ma (e.g., Bateman, 1992; Saleeby et al., 1990). Plutons of the older interval are widely scattered, whereas a substantial number of the plutons emplaced during the younger interval form three large composite, nested intrusive suites along the crest of the Sierra Nevada (e.g., Tikoff and Saint Blanquat, 1997). Several plutons emplaced in ranges east of the Sierra Nevada during the interval from ~100 to ~72 Ma are highly evolved two-mica granites interpreted to have been derived in part from the melting of continental crust. Examples include the Hall Canyon pluton (Mahood et al., 1996), Skidoo pluton (Hodges et al., 1990), Kern Knob pluton (Griffis, 1986), Papoose Flat pluton (Miller, 1996), and Birch Creek pluton (Barton et al., 1994). Development of these magmas temporally overlapped the development of Late Cretaceous crustal-melt magmas across much of the Great Basin (Barton, 1990; Wright and Wooden, 1991).

Volcanic complexes. Mesozoic volcanic complexes preserved in two NW-trending belts— one in pendants in the eastern Sierra Nevada and one in ranges to the east (Fig. 1)—have yielded radiometric dates ranging from ~222 Ma to ~98 Ma. Lithostratigraphic contrasts suggest that these two belts formed in adjacent yet distinctive Jurassic settings that reflect transverse paleogeographic changes across the arc. Complexes in the eastern Sierra Nevada (Saddlebag Lake, Ritter Range, Mt. Morrison, Goddard, Oak Creek, Alabama Hills) accumulated in what we informally call the arc-core paleogeographic province, whereas those located east of the Sierra Nevada (White Mountains, southern Inyo Mountains, Argus Range, Slate Range, Butte Valley) accumulated in what we call the arc-flank province (Dunne and Walker, 1996; Dunne et al., in press). Schematic stratigraphic columns for the best-documented complexes in each province are presented in Figure 13.

Late Triassic radiometric dates ranging from ~222 to ~213 Ma have been obtained from volcanic strata known or inferred to represent some of the oldest parts of the volcanic complexes in the Saddlebag Lake, Ritter Range, and Goddard pendants in the Sierra Nevada (Fiske and Tobisch, 1978; Saleeby et al., 1990; Schweickert and Lahren, 1993). These dates, together with a similar range of dates determined for most of the oldest documented Trias-

sic plutons in the region, are interpreted to represent the approximate time of initiation of significant magmatism along much of the eastern fringe of the arc in the study area. Most Upper Triassic volcanic units appear to be remnants of widespread sheets, but a Late Triassic caldera has been invoked as the setting for the Dana sequence in the southern part of the Saddlebag Lake pendant and in the northern Ritter Range pendant (Schweickert and Lahren, 1993; Greene, 1995). Evidence indicating specific depositional environments is sparse for most Triassic units, but a fluvial origin has been proposed for the widespread conglomerate of Coony Lake in the Saddlebag Lake and northern Ritter Range pendants (Schweickert and Lahren, 1993).

Jurassic volcanic rocks and epiclastic strata have been identified in most complexes in the study area, and are known or inferred to form the bulk of many. Lower Jurassic rocks have been documented only in the Ritter Range and Saddlebag Lake pendants, but could be present in the undated lower parts of other complexes as well. Substantial thicknesses of volcanogenic rocks accumulated in many complexes during Middle and/or Late Jurassic time. Jurassic sections in the arc-core province, interpreted to have formed in or adjacent to major eruptive centers, are characterized by large-volume, siliceous pyroclastic eruptions in a terrain marked by episodic to continuous shallow-marine conditions and generally modest topographic relief, as judged by the paucity of epiclastic strata (Dunne et al., in press). In contrast, most complexes in the arc-flank province were located in areas somewhat removed from major eruptive centers in predominantly to exclusively fluvial, alluvial-fan, and lacustrine environments; local coarse alluvial-fan deposits suggest substantial topographic relief. Limited paleocurrent data obtained from three arc-flank complexes consistently indicate paleoslopes inclined toward the northeast (Dunne and Walker, 1996).

The paleogeographic picture that emerges for Middle Jurassic time is of a low-relief, episodically to predominantly shallow-marine, high-magma-flux arc-core province grading irregularly eastward to a subaerial, low- to moderate-magma-flux, arc-fringe province bounded on the southwest at times by volcanic terrains elevated sufficiently to generate substantial

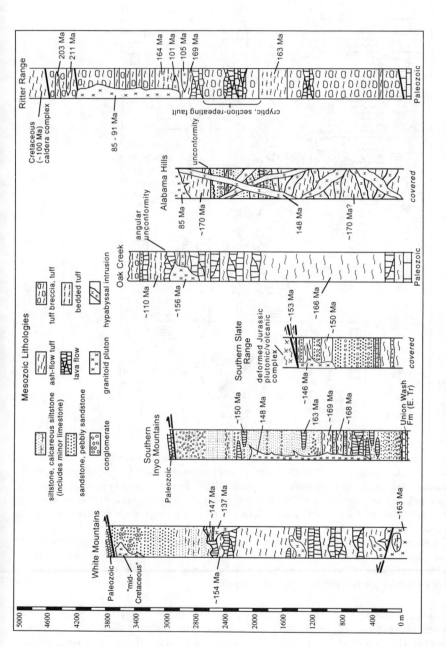

FIG. 13. Schematic stratigraphic columns and U.-Pb dates for selected Mesozoic volcanic complexes in east-central California. White Mountains, southern Inyo Mountains, and southern Slate Range represent the arc-flank paleogeographic province, whereas Oak Creek, Alabama Hills, and Ritter Range represent the arc-core paleogeographic province (see text for discussion). Data for columns are from the following sources: White Mountains (Fates, 1985; Hanson, 1986); southern Inyo Mountains (Dunne and Walker, 1993; Dunne et al., 1994; J. D. Walker, unpubl. data); Southern Slate Range (Dunne et al., in press); Oak Creek (Longiaru, 1987; Saleeby et al., 1990); Alabama Hills (Dunne and Walker, 1993; Dunne et al., in press); Ritter Range (Fiske and Tobisch, 1978; Tobisch et al., 1986; Sorenson et al., in press).

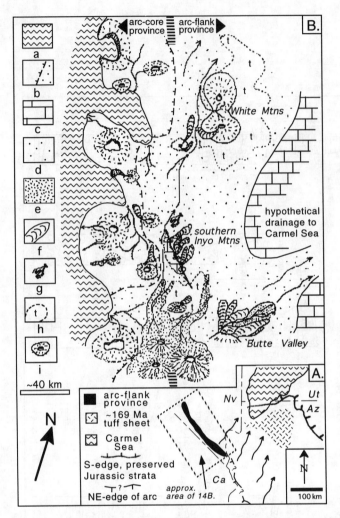

FIG. 14. Schematic paleogeography of Middle to Late Jurassic volcanic provinces discussed in text. A. Middle Jurassic regional setting, showing positions of arc-flank province and northeastern edge of arc as palinspastically restored for Mesozoic contraction and Cenozoic extension by Marzolf (1994). Features in northwestern Arizona and southwestern Utah are from Blakey and Parnell (1995). B. Middle to Late Jurassic paleogeography of arc-core and arc-flank provinces in east-central California. Elements depicted in arc-core province are best documented for Middle Jurassic time; elements of arc-flank province are documented for both Middle and Late Jurassic time. Legend: a = marine environments; b = fluctuating inland edge of periodically inundated coastal plain (unpatterned) covered mostly by slightly reworked ash and minor epiclastic sediment; c = pre-arc strata; d = predominantly epiclastic sediments accumulating in fluvial settings; e = alluvial-fan complexes; f = mafic to intermediate lava flows; g = felsic lava flows; h = ash-flow tuff sheets; i = volcanic edifices.

amounts of epiclastic material (Fig. 14). The relative abundance of volcanic rocks in the Butte Valley complex (Dunne et al., in press) and the lower part of the White Mountains complex is inferred to reflect the local development of high-magma-flux volcanic centers in the arc-flank province; these created volcanic

salients. The volcanic complex in the southern Inyo Mountains received abundant epiclastic sediment and thus is inferred to have accumulated in a low-magma-flux "recess" along the margin of the arc except during times of exceptionally high magma flux in the arc, as during the Middle Jurassic. A pattern of volcanic salients and recesses like that envisioned above is commonly observed along the inland sides of modern continental-margin volcanic arcs (Tatsumi and Eggins, 1995).

The arc-flank province in east-central California provides a view of Middle Jurassic paleogeography along the eastern flank of the arc that is complementary to that inferred for the east side of the magmatic arc in southern Utah and western Arizona. Palinspastic reconstruction of that region by Marzolf (1993) reveals a >200-km-wide gap between volcanic outcrops of the Jurassic arc and closest preserved Jurassic strata on the Colorado Plateau, which contain small amounts of epiclastic sediment derived from the arc. Riggs and Blakey (1993) and Blakey and Parnell (1995) have inferred that during Jurassic time, epiclastic detritus was transported across a N- to NE-inclined, topographically subdued fluvial plain occupying this >200-km-wide gap, and that the ash-flow tuff was deposited on the plain close to the Colorado Plateau at ~169 Ma during especially vigorous magmatic activity in the arc. We infer that the arc-flank province in the study area is to some degree representative of the paleogeography of the intervening region that is missing farther south, a view that is consistent with the inferred NE-inclined drainages of the arc-flank province and with the influx of Middle Jurassic ash-flow sheets into this province at ~168 to 170 Ma—best documented in the southern Inyo Mountains—the same time, Blakey and Parnell (1995) suggested, that silicic ash flows spread farthest northeast from the arc axis.

Volcanic strata yielding Cretaceous U-Pb dates ranging from ~143 to ~100 Ma are known from the Goddard, Oak Creek, and Ritter Range complexes (Saleeby et al., 1990). Some of the youngest strata of the White Mountains complex also could be of Early Cretaceous age. However, conglomerates in that section apparently lack clasts of plutonic rock (Fates, 1985), whereas coarse plutonic clasts are common in Lower Cretaceous strata of the Ritter Range pendant (Fiske and Tobisch, 1994). Mid-Cretaceous strata in the Ritter Range and Oak Creek pendants rest unconformably on previously rotated and deformed Lower Cretaceous and Middle Jurassic strata, respectively (Saleeby et al., 1990; Fiske and Tobisch, 1994), and mid-Cretaceous strata in the Ritter Range are part of a caldera fill (Fiske and Tobisch, 1994). Similar

to Jurassic strata in these same pendants, epiclastic material is sparse, and the pendant strata probably accumulated in settings proximal to major eruptive centers. In contrast to the Jurassic setting, however, mid-Cretaceous topographic relief in the Ritter Range apparently was significant, and granitic plutons had been exposed by this time (Fiske and Tobisch, 1994).

East Sierran thrust system

Rocks along the eastern flank of the Sierran arc were subjected to repeated episodes of contractional and transpressional deformation over a significant span of Mesozoic time. The resulting structures form a coherent, NW-trending belt characterized by NE-vergent thrust and reverse faults, folds, locally well-developed cleavage, and less common shear zones and conjugate strike-slip faults, located along the eastern margin of the continuous granitic terrain forming the Sierra batholith. Dunne et al. (1983) applied the name East Sierran thrust system (ESTS) to this group of structures, and we use that name here.

The East Sierran thrust system is most characteristically developed over a distance of ~150 km from the southern Owens Valley area to the Garlock fault; we consider this reach the type area of the ESTS. Discontinuously exposed contractional structures that we infer to be correlative with the ESTS are present as far north as the Saddlebag Lake pendant (Schweickert and Lahren, 1993) and southward into the Mojave Desert (Walker et al., 1990). Although the northeastern margin of the belt is indistinct, the greatest width of continuously exposed pre-Cenozoic rocks containing abundantly developed structures characteristic of the belt is ~20 km.

NW-striking, SW-dipping thrust and reverse faults are the most apparent structures in the ESTS. Representative dips of individual faults range from ~30°SW to ~90°, with an average value of ~55°SW. These faults commonly are anastomosing, locally producing interleaved arrays of Paleozoic and Mesozoic strata and Mesozoic intrusive rocks. In many areas, the footwall of the structurally lowest thrust is composed of SW-dipping, SW-facing Mesozoic strata, either of the Lower and Middle(?) Triassic Union Wash Formation or of overlying Jurassic volcanic and epiclastic strata. The hanging wall of the structurally highest thrust is com-

posed of Paleozoic strata in areas north of
Darwin and predominantly of Jurassic granitoids of the Sierran batholith in most areas
south of Darwin. Thrusts are ductile in nature
and most are marked by zones of exotic lenses
("horses") of partly to thoroughly transposed
and/or foliated rock a few meters to a few
hundred meters in width. Stretching lineations
of many kinds—pressure shadows, stretched
pebbles, mineral streaks, and rods—oriented
parallel to the known or inferred slip direction
of the fault commonly are well developed in
these fault rocks. Fault slip lines as determined
at 18 locations throughout the full length of the
type area by the Hansen (1971) method indicate
that the upper plates of all major thrust faults
moved ENE.

Although hanging-wall and footwall cutoffs
needed to determine exact slip amounts are
lacking, we infer from limited evidence that slip
amounts generally are less than a few kilometers on any one fault. Such evidence includes
lack of significant contrasts in grade of metamorphism between the footwall and hanging
wall, stratigraphic throws rarely exceeding several hundred meters, and amounts of structural
overlap of less than 2 km. Swanson (1996)
estimated a minimum slip of ~3.9 km for the
Flagstaff fault in the southern Inyo Mountains,
one of the longest individual faults (>29 km) in
the ESTS.

Folds and associated axial-plane cleavage,
locally of two or more approximately coaxial
generations, are widely developed in the ESTS.
Folds predominantly range from upright to
locally E-vergent, and in a few areas, notably the
northern Darwin Hills, are reclined. Small isoclinal folds are present locally, but most folds
have interlimb angles of between 30° and 90°.
Fold axes typically plunge up to 30°NW, but in
some areas, such as the southern Inyo Mountains and central Argus Range, axes alternate
between more common northwest and less common southeast plunges. Typical amplitudes and
half wavelengths are less than ~100 m,
although a few isolated folds such as the Cerro
Gordo and Argus Range anticlines, which we
provisionally include in the ESTS, are several
times larger.

Scattered younger folds of atypical style and
orientation that we provisionally include in the
ESTS locally overprint the common folds and
axial plane cleavage noted above. These younger
folds lack axial-plane cleavage, most commonly
trend west to southwest, and are upright to
inclined. Less common are NW-trending,
W-vergent folds.

NW-trending subvertical shear zones containing evidence of lateral slip crop out in two
areas of the Inyo Mountains. One such shear
zone, located east of Lone Pine, can be traced a
few hundred meters across a pluton and its
Paleozoic wall rock before disappearing beneath
Cenozoic strata. It contains S-C fabrics indicative of left-lateral slip and, as constrained by
dated intrusive rocks with which it interacts,
was active during the interval from ~165 to
~140 Ma. The other shear zone, located east of
Independence, affects a >13-km-long, >3-km-
wide zone at the western exposed edge of the
~164 Ma Santa Rita Flat pluton. It contains
right-slip kinematic indicators that formed
prior to intrusion of the shear zone by NW-
trending dikes of uncertain age (Brudos and
Paterson, 1993). It is unknown whether these
two shear zones are far-field effects of lateral
components of plate-boundary motions or
responses to more locally created stresses.

Numerous near-vertical, conjugate strike-
slip faults that we provisionally include in the
ESTS crop out in the southern Inyo Mountains.
NNE-trending faults accommodate a few to ~30
m of right slip, whereas ENE-trending faults
accommodate similar amounts of left slip,
together indicating modest NE-SW contraction. The faults cut all fold and thrust structures as well as all intrusive rock units in the
vicinity, and are interpreted to represent a last,
locally developed, brittle phase of Creta-
ceous(?) contraction in the ESTS.

We estimate that total contraction across the
ESTS in the southern Inyo Mountains is no
greater than 20 km. Based on cross-sections and
a reconnaissance study of penetrative strain,
Swanson (1996) estimated that contraction
caused by thrust faulting, folding, and penetrative strain across a 5-km-wide transect of the
western half of the belt in the southern Inyo
Mountains is ~100 percent, or about 5 km,
including slip on the Flagstaff thrust. The full
width of the ESTS in this region includes two
additional outcrop belts, one ~5 km wide to the
west of the area studied by Swanson (1996) and
the second ~10 km wide to the east. Both of
these additional areas seem less intensely
deformed than Swanson's study area, and we

think it likely that they accommodated substantially less than 100 percent shortening.

Based principally on relations in the Saddlebag Lake pendant (Schweickert and Lahren, 1993), we consider evolution of the ESTS to be a different, younger deformational event than the Middle Triassic contraction described by Stevens and Greene (this paper). In that pendant, Middle Triassic thrust faults correlated with the Golconda thrust of Nevada are truncated by younger NW-trending, NE-vergent thrusts that cut Sierran arc volcanic strata dated at ~222 Ma (U-Pb), and which in turn are intruded by a ~219 Ma pluton. These relations define a brief, Late Triassic interval of post-Golconda thrusting that we consider to mark the earliest recognized phase of contraction in the ESTS.

Available data (Dunne et al., 1983, 1994; Dunne, 1986; Dunne and Walker, 1993; Dunne et al., 1994; G. C. Dunne and J. D. Walker, unpubl. data) indicate that the ESTS was active over an extended part of Mesozoic time. In addition to the Late Triassic structures noted above, early deformation in the ESTS also may be represented by several thrust faults and major folds in the Inyo Mountains and areas to the southeast that pre-date emplacement of plutons, yielding U-Pb dates of ~174 to ~186 Ma. Examples of such structures include the Dolomite Canyon thrust in the southern Inyo Mountains and the Ophir Peak thrust in the Darwin Hills. We prefer the interpretion that these structures formed during the opening phase of contractional deformation in the ESTS beginning in Late Triassic time, although we acknowledge that most of them lack definitive lower age limits and conceivably could have formed earlier, perhaps as a result of Middle Triassic or even Permian deformation, as pointed out by Stevens and Greene (this paper).

Additional deformation in the ESTS occurred during the latest Jurassic, at which time Mesozoic volcanic complexes in the southern Inyo Mountains and southern Slate Range were tilted to the west and folded and cleaved, and another important phase of thrust faulting took place, burying and preserving these complexes (Dunne et al., 1994). Widespread folding may have affected Paleozoic strata at this time as well. Most folding and cleavage formation were completed prior to emplacement of widespread, steeply dipping, NW-trending mafic and less common felsic dikes that have been correlated with the Independence dike swarm (Chen and Moore, 1979) of Late Jurassic age (~148 Ma), placing an upper age limit on this deformation if the correlation is correct.

Additional contractional deformation, best documented in the southern Inyo Mountains, created structures that overprint those formed during the deformational episodes noted above. Effects of this younger deformation include: (1) reactivation of some thrust faults and tightening of older folds; (2) development of scattered, locally W-vergent folds that, unlike older folds, lack axial-plane cleavage; (3) rotation of SW-dipping cleavage and thrust faults to vertical or steep northeast dips and development of locally significant subvertical stretching of rock units; and (4) development of the conjugate strike-slip faults described earlier. These structures overprint rocks and structures that are known or likely to be Late Jurassic or older. We provisionally infer that they formed in Cretaceous time, perhaps correlating with mid-Cretaceous contractional deformation recognized in the Oak Creek pendant (Saleeby et al., 1990) and the eastern Mojave Desert (Walker et al., 1995).

Contractional structures that we correlate on the basis of alignment, orientation, and age with those in the type region of the ESTS are exposed in the northern Inyo Mountains, White Mountains, Benton Range, and Saddlebag Lake pendant (Fig. 1). In the northern Inyo Mountains, Paterson et al. (1991) argued, deformational fabrics in and adjacent to the mid-Cretaceous Papoose Flat pluton and possibly other mid- to Late Cretaceous plutons in the White and Inyo Mountains resulted from regional contractional deformation during and following intrusion. In the White Mountains, the ~48-km-long, >1-km-wide White Mountains shear zone (Crowder and Sheridan, 1972; Crowder et al., 1972) was correlated with the ESTS by Dunne et al. (1983), an interpretation supported by Hanson's (1986) detailed study of the southern part of the zone. Hanson (1986) interpreted patterns of metasomatism associated with the Pellisier pluton of probable mid-Cretaceous age (McKee and Conrad, 1996) as indicating that the pluton intruded already-sheared rocks and was in turn sheared during continued activity along the zone. The Late

Cretaceous (~73 Ma) Boundary Peak pluton post-dates all significant shearing in the zone.

Hanson (1986) and Fates (1985) recognized an episode of W-vergent thrusting and folding along the west flank of the White Mountains that post-dates the Barcroft Granodiorite (~163 Ma), shearing on the White Mountains shear zone, and deposition of the Late Jurassic(?) metavolcanic and epiclastic strata in the White Mountains volcanic complex. Hanson (1986) suggested that these structures were domed by emplacement of the Pellisier pluton and further noted that they are intruded by granite that Krauskopf (1972) correlated with the mid-Cretaceous Indian Garden Creek pluton. These W-vergent structures may correlate with the minor W-vergent "late" folds in the southern Inyo Mountains noted by Dunne (1986).

Numerous N- to NW-trending folds that developed in lower Paleozoic strata of the southern White Mountains (e.g., Bateman, 1965) also may belong to the ESTS, although their age is poorly constrained. On the west flank and in the middle of the southern White Mountains, these folds overprint NE-trending, SE-vergent folds (Sylvester and Babcock, 1975; Welch, 1979). At the southeast corner of the White Mountains, Morgan and Law (1994) reported the reverse overprinting relations. However, more recent research suggests that the NW-trending folds are younger than the NE-trending folds and that both fold sets pre-date Middle Jurassic plutons (S. Morgan, pers. commun., 1997).

Lower Paleozoic strata in the Benton Range contain numerous NW-trending and plunging, upright to NE-vergent folds that may correlate with the ESTS. These folds are intruded by a dike swarm that cuts the Late Triassic (~212 Ma, U-Pb) intrusions and that is in turn intruded by a Late Jurassic (~161 Ma, U-Pb) pluton (Rinehart and Ross, 1957; Hallee, 1985; Renne and Turrin, 1987). These age constraints, as well as the orientation of these folds, are consistent with their inclusion in the ESTS.

Finally, NW-trending, NE-vergent contractional structures that formed during two episodes of deformation in the Saddlebag Lake pendant are inferred to be part of the ESTS. Late Triassic thrust faults that developed during the first of these episodes were described earlier in this section. A second family of thrust faults with associated folds and cleavage overprints

the older thrusts. This younger family of structures affects Upper Triassic and Lower Jurassic volcanic strata in the pendant and is intruded by mid-Cretaceous plutons (Schweickert and Lahren, 1993).

The observations that the ESTS is located along the immediate eastern margin of the continuous granitic terrain of the Sierra Nevada batholith and that deformation within the ESTS can be interpreted as spanning much of the same time interval as intrusion of the batholith (Chen and Moore, 1982; Bateman, 1992) have led to speculations that development of the ESTS and emplacement of the arc were mechanically linked. In seeking an explanation for Cordilleran-wide back-arc contractional deformation, Burchfiel and Davis (1975) proposed that lithosphere in the vicinity of the arc would have thinned and weakened in response to increased heat flow, thereby establishing a preferred zone of contractional failure at the interface between the arc and cooler, thicker, stronger lithosphere to the east. Dunne and Gulliver (1976) and Moore (1976) applied this hypothesis to the ESTS. An alternative mechanical linkage was proposed by Saleeby and Busby-Spera (1992), who hypothesized that the ESTS reflects downward return flow of eastern wall rocks of the batholith in response to rising, spreading granitic magma. We believe it likely that both phenomena influenced the location, orientation, and predominant sense of vergence of the ESTS, but that the return-flow phenomenon was the less important of the two. In support of this view, we note that while numerous plutons were intruded into the arc during late Middle Jurassic time (~175 to ~160 Ma) in east-central California, deposition of the Inyo Volcanic Complex in the southern Inyo Mountains was mostly on broad, low-gradient floodplains, and no significant angular unconformities of this age span that might reflect uplift or deformation have been recognized within the complex (Dunne et al., in press). Moreover, a major phase of ESTS deformation involving tilting, folding, and overthrusting of Jurassic volcanic complexes that is temporally constrained to the interval from ~150 to ~140 Ma corresponds to a time of greatly reduced plutonic intrusion in the arc (Glazner, 1991).

At present we can only set forth the general interpretation that timing of deformational episodes in the ESTS principally reflected a complex interplay between two partly independent, time-variable phenomena—the strength of the immediate eastern wall rocks of the arc and the stresses developed in those rocks. The former evolved through time as the crust in the region was thickened, as the rocks became increasingly deformed and increasingly intruded by plutons, and as variable amounts of heat and fluid flowed through the rocks. The magnitude and orientation of principal stresses evolved through time as well, responding to changes in the rate and direction of relative convergence and degree of coupling across the plate boundary (e.g., Burchfiel et al., 1992), to relief of components of plate-margin stress within the arc through development of contractional and/or lateral shear zones (e.g., Tobisch et al., 1995; Tikoff and Saint Blanquat, 1997), and to build-up and subsequent relief of gravitational potential energy developed in the arc as a result of changes in surface elevations there (e.g., Hamilton, 1988). More detailed interpretations of the effects of such factors on the timing of deformation in the ESTS await an improved geologic and geochronologic framework for correlating specific events in the ESTS with possible causative events in the arc.

Conclusions

The Paleozoic and Mesozoic rocks of east-central California provide an unusually complete record of continental-margin evolution along part of the western edge of North America. In this paper, we have traced the development of this plate margin from its origin by rifting in the Neoproterozoic through emplacement of the Sierra Nevada batholith in the Mesozoic, focusing principally on major tectonic events that we interpret to have significantly affected east-central California during this period of time. These include: (1) the Late Devonian to Early Mississippian Antler orogeny, which ended the early Paleozoic phase of passive-margin miogeoclinal sedimentation; (2) Late Mississippian–Early Pennsylvanian faulting related to the inferred development of a NW-trending, transform fault zone that truncated the continental margin; (3) Permian to earliest Triassic contractional deformation that marked the initiation of convergence along the previously truncated transform margin; (4) a brief interlude of relative tectonic quiescence in the Early Triassic; (5) Middle Triassic contractional deformation, correlated with emplacement of the Golconda allochthon, followed by dextral strike-slip faulting; and (6) Late Triassic onset of widespread, subduction-driven plutonism, volcanism, and E-vergent contractional deformation, including emplacement of the Sierra Nevada batholith and development of the East Sierran thrust system, that dominated the remainder of the Mesozoic history. These superposed events resulted in development of complex assemblages of structural and stratigraphic features that reflect the tectonic evolution of the Cordilleran plate edge to the west.

In this review, we have made a special effort to highlight recent and ongoing studies by ourselves and others that have provided a basis for updating our own earlier syntheses of the Paleozoic and Mesozoic evolution of east-central California (e.g., Dunne et al., 1978; Dunne, 1986; Stevens, 1986; Stone and Stevens, 1988b). Important recent advances described herein include the identification of post-Antler Mississippian–Early Pennsylvanian uplifts, recognition that Permian contractional deformation in the region was of much larger scale, greater intensity, and longer duration than we originally had thought, and the addition of much new detailed information on the timing of volcanic, intrusive, and structural events along the eastern margin of the Mesozoic arc. Such advances have substantially altered some of our previous perceptions of the Paleozoic and Mesozoic history of this complex region, and underscore the continuing need for additional data and observations that can be used to test and refine existing interpretations.

Acknowledgments

Some of the research reported here was supported by NSF grants EAR-9218174 to C. H. Stevens, EAR-9204703 to G. C. Dunne, and EAR-9205096 to J. D. Walker, and by a grant to Walker from the Petroleum Research Fund administered by the American Chemical Society. In addition, Dunne acknowledges support for research expenses and release time from teaching duties provided by a CSUN Faculty Research Grant and by the CSUN Department of Geological Sciences. We thank R. B. Miller and J. H. Stewart for thoughtful reviews of the manuscript.

REFERENCES

Anderson, T. H., and Schmidt, V. A., 1983, The evolution of Middle America and the Gulf of Mexico–Caribbean Sea region during Mesozoic time: Geol. Soc. Amer. Bull., v. 94, p. 941–966.

Armin, R. A., and Mayer, L., 1983, Subsidence analysis of the Cordilleran miogeocline: Implications for timing of late Proterozoic rifting and amount of extension: Geology, v. 11, p. 702–705.

Barth, A. P., Tosdal, R. M., Wooden, J. L., and Howard, K. A., 1997, Triassic plutonism in southern California: Southward younging of arc initiation along a truncated continental margin: Tectonics, v. 16, p. 290–304.

Barton, M. D., 1990, Cretaceous magmatism, metamorphism, and metallogeny in the east-central Great Basin, in Anderson, J. L., ed., The origin of Cordilleran magmatism: Geol. Soc. Amer. Memoir 174, p. 283–302.

Barton, M. D., Ghidotti, G. A., Holden, P., and Grossman, J. N., 1994, Petrological characterisitcs of the strongly peraluminous end-member of Cretaceous magmatism in the Great Basin: The Birch Creek pluton [abs.]: Geol. Soc. Amer. Abs. Prog., v. 26, no. 7, p. 369.

Bateman, P.C., 1965, Geology and tungsten mineralization of the Bishop district, California: U.S. Geol. Surv. Prof. Pap. 470, 208 p.

————, 1992, Plutonism in the central part of the Sierra Nevada batholith, California: U.S. Geol. Surv. Prof. Pap. 1483, 186 p.

Blakey, R. C., and Parnell, R. A., 1995, Middle Jurassic magmatism: The volcanic record in the eolian Page Sandstone and related Carmel Formation, Colorado Plateau, in Miller, D. M., and Busby, C., eds., Jurassic magmatism and tectonics of the North American Cordillera: Geol. Soc. Amer. Spec. Pap. 299, p. 393–411.

Bond, G. C., and Komnitz, M. A., 1984, Construction of tectonic subsidence curves for the early Paleozoic miogeocline, southern Canadian Rocky Mountains: Implications for subsidence mechanisms, age of breakup, and crustal thinning: Geol. Soc. Amer. Bull., v. 95, p. 155–173.

Brudos, T. C., and Paterson, S. R., 1993, The Santa Rita shear zone: Major Mesozoic deformation along the western flank of the White-Inyo Range, California [abs.]: Geol. Soc. Amer. Abs. Prog., v. 25, no. 5, p. 15.

Burchfiel, B. C., 1969, Geology of the Dry Mountain quadrangle, Inyo County, California: Calif. Div. Mines and Geol. Spec. Report 99, 19 p.

Burchfiel, B. C., and Davis, G. A., 1975, Nature and controls of Cordilleran orogenesis, western United States: Extensions of an earlier synthesis: Amer. Jour. Sci., v. 275-A, p. 363–396.

Burchfiel, B. C., Cowan, D. S., and Davis, G. A., 1992, Tectonic overview of the Cordilleran orogen in the western United States, in Burchfiel, B. C., Lipman, P. W., and Zoback, M. L., eds., The Cordilleran orogen: Conterminous U.S.: Boulder, CO, Geol. Soc. Amer., The geology of North America, v. G-3, p. 407–479.

Carl, B. S., Bartley, J. M., and Glazner, A. F., 1996, Mechanical model for synintrusive Nevadan deformation in the eastern Sierra Nevada [abs.]: EOS (Trans., Amer. Geophys. Union), v. 77, no. 46 suppl., p. F641.

Carr, M. D., Poole, F. G., and Christiansen, R. L., 1984, Pre-Cenozoic geology of the El Paso Mountains, southwestern Great Basin, in Lintz, J., Jr., Western geological excursions: Geol. Soc. Amer. Ann. Meeting, Reno, NV, 1984, Field Trip Guidebook, v. 4, p. 84–93.

Chen, J. H., and Moore, J. G., 1979, The Late Jurassic Independence dike swarm in eastern California: Geology, v. 7, p. 129–133.

————, 1982, Uranium-lead isotopic ages from the Sierra Nevada batholith, California: Jour. Geophys. Res., v. 87, p. 4761–4784.

Cole, R. D., 1986, Geology of the Butte Valley and Warm Springs formations, southern Panamint Range, Inyo County, California: Unpubl. M.S. thesis, California State Univ., Fresno, 126 p.

Coleman, D. S., Bartley, J. M., Glazner, A. F., and Carl, B. S., 1994, Late Cretaceous dikes in the Independence dike swarm, California [abs.]: EOS (Trans. Amer. Geophys. Union), v. 75, no. 44 suppl., p. 686.

Corbett, K. P., 1989, Structural geology of the Last Chance thrust system, east-central California: Unpubl. Ph.D. dissertation, Univ. of California, Los Angeles, 245 p.

Corbett, K. P., Wrucke, C. T., and Nelson, C. A., 1988, Structure and tectonic history of the Last Chance thrust system, Inyo Mountains and Last Chance Range, California, in Weide, D. L., and Faber, M. L., eds., This extended land: Geological journeys in the southern Basin and Range: Geol. Soc. Amer. Annual Meeting, Cordilleran Section, Las Vegas, NV, 1988, Field Trip Guidebook, p. 269–292.

Crowder, D. F., Robinson, P. T., and Harris, D. L., 1972, Geologic map of the Benton quadrangle, Mono County, California and Esmeralda and Mineral Counties, Nevada: U.S. Geol. Surv. Geol. Quad. Map GQ-1013, scale 1:62,500.

Crowder, D. F., and Sheridan, M. F., 1972, Geologic map of the White Mountain Peak quadrangle, Mono

County, California: U.S. Geol. Surv. Geol. Quad. Map GQ-1012, scale 1:62,500.

Davis, G. A., Monger, J. W. H., and Burchfiel, B. C., 1978, Mesozoic construction of the Cordilleran "collage," central British Columbia to central California, in Howell, D. G., and McDougall, K. A., eds., Mesozoic paleogeography of the western United States: Soc. Econ. Paleontol. Mineral., Pacific Sect., Book 8, p. 1–32.

Dickinson, W. R., 1981, Plate tectonics and the continental margin of California, in Ernst, W. G., ed., The geotectonic development of California: Rubey Volume I: Englewood Cliffs, NJ, Prentice-Hall, p. 1–28.

Dunne, G. C., 1979, Hunter Mountain batholith: A large, composite alkalic intrusion of Jurassic age in eastern California [abs.]: Geol. Soc. Amer. Abs. Prog., v. 11, no. 3, p. 76.

————, 1986, Geologic evolution of the southern Inyo Range, Darwin Plateau, and Argus and Slate Ranges, east-central California—An overview, in Dunne, G. C., compiler, Mesozoic and Cenozoic structural evolution of selected areas, east-central California: Geol. Soc. Amer. Annual Meeting, Cordilleran Section, Los Angeles, CA, 1986, Guidebook and Volume, Field Trips 2 and 14, p. 3–21.

Dunne, G. C., and Gulliver, R. M., 1976, Superposed synbatholithic deformations in eastern wallrocks, Sierra Nevada batholith, California [abs.]: Geol. Soc. Amer. Abs. Prog., v. 8, no. 6, p. 846.

————, 1978, Nature and significance of the Inyo thrust fault, eastern California: Discussion: Geol. Soc. Amer. Bull., v. 89, p. 1787–1791.

Dunne, G. C., and Saleeby, J. B., 1993, Kern Plateau shear zone, southern Sierra Nevada—New data concerning age and northward continuation [abs.]: Geol. Soc. Amer. Abs. Prog., v. 25, no. 5, p. 33.

Dunne, G. C., and Suczek, C. A., 1991, Early Paleozoic eugeoclinal strata in the Kern Plateau pendants, southern Sierra Nevada, California, in Cooper, J. D., and Stevens, C. H., eds., Paleozoic paleogeography of the Western United States—II: Soc. Econ. Paleontol. Mineral., Pacific Sect., Book 67, v. 2, p. 677–692.

Dunne, G. C., and Walker, J. D., 1993, Age of Jurassic volcanism and tectonism, southern Owens Valley region, east-central California: Geol. Soc. Amer. Bull., v. 105, p. 1223–1230.

Dunne, G. C., and Walker, J. D., 1996, Paleogeographic implications of Jurassic sedimentation and volcanism along the east fringe of the Sierran arc, east-central California [abs.]: Geol. Soc. Amer. Abs. Prog., v. 20, no. 7, p. 308–309.

Dunne, G. C., Garvey, T. P., Oborne, M., Schneidereit, D., Fritsche, A. E., and Walker, J. D., in press, Geology of the Inyo Mountains Volcanic Complex: Implications for Jurassic paleogeography of the Sier-

ran magmatic arc in eastern California: Geol. Soc. Amer. Bull..

Dunne, G. C., Gulliver, R. M., and Sylvester, A. G., 1978, Mesozoic evolution of rocks of the White, Inyo, Argus and Slate Ranges, eastern California, in Howell, D. G., and McDougall, K. A., eds., Mesozoic paleogeography of the western United States: Soc. Econ. Paleontol. Mineral., Pacific Section, Book 8, p. 189–207.

Dunne, G. C., Moore, S. C., Gulliver, R. M., and Fowler, J., 1983, East Sierran thrust system, eastern California [abs.]: Geol. Soc. Amer. Abs. Prog., v. 15, no. 5, p. 322.

Dunne, G. C., Walker, J. D., Stern, S. M., and Linn, J. K., 1994, New U-Pb age constraints on Late Jurassic magmatism and contractile deformation in east-central California [abs.]: Geol. Soc. Amer. Abs. Prog., v. 26, no. 7, p. 386.

Eisbacher, G. H., 1983, Devonian-Mississippian sinistral transcurrent faulting along the cratonic margin of western North America: A hypothesis: Geology, v. 11, p. 7–10.

Elayer, R. W., 1974, Stratigraphy and structure of the southern Inyo Mountains, Inyo County, California: Unpubl. M.S. thesis, San Jose State Univ., 121 p.

Ernst, W. G., 1997, Metamorphism of mafic dikes from the central White-Inyo Range, eastern California: Contrib. Mineral. Petrol., v. 128, p. 30–44.

Fates, D. G., 1985, Mesozoic(?) metavolcaniclastic rocks, northern White Mountains, California: Structural style, lithology, petrology, depositional setting and paleogeographic significance: Unpubl. M.S. thesis, Univ. of California, Los Angeles, 222 p.

Fiske, R. S., and Tobisch, O. T., 1978, Paleogeographic significance of volcanic rocks of the Ritter Range pendant, Central Sierra Nevada, California, in Howell, D. G., and McDougall, K. A., eds., Mesozoic paleogeography of the western United States: Soc. Econ. Paleontol. Mineral., Pacific Sect., Book 8, p. 209–221.

————, 1994, Middle Cretaceous ash-flow tuff and caldera-collapse deposit in the Minarets caldera, east-central Sierra Nevada, California: Geol. Soc. Amer. Bull., v. 106, p. 582–593.

Glazner, A. F., 1991, Plutonism, oblique subduction, and continental growth: An example from the Mesozoic of California: Geology, v. 19, p. 784–786.

Goebel, K. A., 1991, Paleogeographic setting of Late Devonian to Early Mississippian transition from passive to collisional margin, Antler foreland, eastern Nevada and western Utah, in Cooper, J. D., and Stevens, C. H., Paleozoic paleogeography of the Western United States—II: Soc. Econ. Paleontol. Mineral., Pacific Sec., Book 67, v. 1, p. 401–418.

Greene, D. C., 1995, The stratigraphy, structure, and regional tectonic significance of the Northern Ritter

Range pendant, eastern Sierra Nevada, California: Unpubl. Ph.D. dissertation, Univ. of Nevada, Reno, 270 p.

Greene, D. C., Schweickert, R. A., and Stevens, C. H., in press, The Roberts Mountains allochthon and the western margin of the Cordilleran miogeocline in the Northern Ritter Range pendant, eastern Sierra Nevada, California: Geol. Soc. Amer. Bull.

Greene, D. C., Stevens, C. H., and Wise, J. M., 1997, The Laurel-Convict fault, eastern Sierra Nevada, California: A Permo-Triassic left-lateral fault, not a Cretaceous intrabatholithic break: Geol. Soc. Amer. Bull., v. 109, p. 483–488.

Griffis, R., 1986, Mesozoic intrusions of the Long John Canyon area, southern Inyo Mountains, in Dunne, G. C., compiler, Mesozoic and Cenozoic structural evolution of selected areas, east-central California: Geol. Soc. Amer. Ann. Meeting, Cordilleran Section, Los Angeles, CA, 1986, Guidebook and Volume, Field Trips 2 and 14, p. 57–66.

Gulliver, R. M., 1976, Structural analysis of Paleozoic rocks in the Talc City Hills, Inyo County, California: Unpubl. M.S. thesis, University of California, Santa Barbara, 105 p.

Hall, W. E., and MacKevett, E. M., Jr., 1962, Geology and ore deposits of Darwin quadrangle, Inyo County, California: U.S. Geol. Surv. Prof. Pap. 368, 87 p.

Hallee, M., 1985, The geology of the central Benton Range, California: Unpubl. M.S. thesis, Univ. of Nevada, Reno, 152 p.

Hamilton, W., 1988, Tectonic settings and variations with depth of some Cretaceous and Cenozoic structural and magmatic systems in the western United States, in Ernst, W. G., ed., Metamorphism and crustal evolution of the western United States: Rubey Volume VII: Englewood Cliffs, N.J., Prentice-Hall, p. 1–40.

Hamilton, W., and Myers, W. B., 1966, Cenozoic tectonics of the western United States: Rev. Geophys., v. 4, p. 509–549.

Hansen, E., 1971, Strain facies: New York, Springer-Verlag, 207 p.

Hanson, R. B., 1986, Geology of Mesozoic metavolcanic and metasedimentary rocks, northern White Mountains, California: Unpubl. Ph.D dissertation, Univ. of California, Los Angeles, 231 p.

Harland, W. B., Cox, A. V., Llewellyn, P. G., Pickton, C. A. G., Smith, A. G., and Walters, R., 1982, A geologic time scale: Cambridge, UK, Cambridge Univ. Press, 131 p.

Hodges, K. V., McKenna, L. W., and Harding, M. B., 1990, Structural unroofing of the central Panamint Mountains, Death Valley region, southeastern California, in Wernicke, B. P., ed., Basin and Range extensional tectonics near the latitude of Las Vegas, Nevada: Geol. Soc. Amer. Memoir 176, p. 377–390.

James, E. W., 1989, Southern extension of the Independence dike swarm of eastern California: Geology, v. 17, p. 587–590.

Johnson, B. K., 1957, Geology of a part of the Manly Peak quadrangle, southern Panamint Range, California: Univ. Calif. Publ. Geol. Sci., v. 30, no. 5, p. 353–424.

Johnson, J. G., and Pendergast, A., 1981, Timing and mode of emplacement of the Roberts Mountains allochthon, Antler orogeny: Geol. Soc. Amer. Bull., v. 92, p. 648–658.

Kepper, J. A., 1981, Sedimentology of a Middle Cambrian outer shelf margin with evidence for syndepositional faulting, eastern California and western Nevada: Jour. Sediment. Petrol., v. 51, p. 807–821.

Kistler, R. W., 1978, Mesozoic paleogeography of California: A viewpoint from isotope geology, in Howell, D. G., and McDougall, K. A., eds., Mesozoic paleogeography of the western United States: Soc. Econ. Paleontol. Mineral., Pacific Sect., Book 8, p. 75–84.

————, 1990, Two different lithosphere types in the Sierra Nevada, California, in Anderson, J. L., ed., The origin of Cordilleran magmatism: Geol. Soc. Amer. Memoir 174, p. 271–281.

————, 1993, Mesozoic intrabatholithic faulting, Sierra Nevada, California, in Dunne, G. C., and McDougall, K. A., eds., Mesozoic paleogeography of the western United States–II: Soc. Econ. Paleontol. Mineral., Pacific Sect., Book 71, p. 247–261.

Kistler, R. W., and Peterman, Z. E., 1973, Variations in Sr, Rb, K, Na, and initial $^{87}Sr/^{86}Sr$ in Mesozoic granitic rocks and intruded wall rocks in central California: Geol. Soc. Amer. Bull., v. 84, p. 3489–3512.

Krauskopf, K. B., 1972, Geologic map of the Mt. Barcroft quadrangle, California-Nevada: U.S. Geol. Surv. Geol. Quad. Map GQ-960, scale 1:62,500.

Lahren, M. M., and Schweickert, R. A., 1989, Proterozoic and Lower Cambrian miogeoclinal rocks of Snow Lake pendant, Yosemite-Emigrant Wilderness, Sierra Nevada: Evidence for major Early Cretaceous dextral translation: Geology, v. 17, p. 156–160.

Lewis, M., Wittman, C., and Stevens, C. H., 1983, Lower Triassic marine sedimentary rocks in east-central California, in Gurgel, K. D., ed., Geologic excursions in stratigraphy and tectonics: From southeastern Idaho to the southern Inyo Mountains, California, via Canyonlands and Arches National Parks, Utah: Geol. Soc. Amer. Ann. Meeting, Rocky Mountain and Cordilleran Sect., Salt Lake City, Utah, 1983, Guidebook—Part 2 (Utah Geol. Mineral Surv. Spec. Studies 60), p. 50–54.

Longiaru, S., 1987, Tectonic evolution of the Oak Creek volcanic roof pendant, eastern Sierra Nevada: Unpubl. Ph.D. dissertation, Univ. of California, Santa Cruz, 205 p.

Magginetti, R. T., Stevens, C. H., and Stone, P., 1988, Early Permian fusulinids from the Owens Valley Group, east-central California: Geol. Soc. Amer. Spec. Pap. 217, 61 p.

Mahood, G. A., Nibler, G. E., and Halliday, A. N., 1996, Zoning patterns and petrologic processes in peraluminous magma chambers; Hall Canyon pluton, Panamint Mountains, California: Geol. Soc. Amer. Bull., v. 108, p. 437–453.

Marzolf, J. E., 1993, Palinspastic reconstruction of early Mesozoic sedimentary basins near the latitude of Las Vegas: Implications for the early Mesozoic Cordilleran cratonic margin, in Dunne, G. C., and McDougall, K. A., eds., Mesozoic paleogeography of the western United States—II: Soc. Econ. Paleontol. Mineral., Pacific Sect., Book 71, p. 433–462.

————, 1994, Reconstruction of the early Mesozoic Cordilleran cratonal margin adjacent to the Colorado Plateau, in Caputo, M. V., Peterson, J. A., and Franczyk, K. J., eds., Mesozoic systems of the Rocky Mountains: Denver, CO, Soc. Econ. Paleontol. Mineral., Rocky Mountain Section, p. 181–216.

McAllister, J. F., 1956, Geologic map of the Ubehebe Peak quadrangle, California: U.S. Geol. Surv. Geol. Quad. Map GQ-95, scale 1:62,500.

McKee, E. H., and Conrad, J. E., 1996, A tale of 10 plutons—Revisited: Age of granitic rocks in the White Mountains, California and Nevada: Geol. Soc. Amer. Bull., v. 108, p. 1515–1527.

Merriam, C. W., 1963, Geology of the Cerro Gordo mining district, Inyo County, California: U.S. Geol. Surv. Prof. Pap. 408, 83 p.

Miller, E. L., and Cameron, C. S., 1982, Late Precambrian to Late Cretaceous evolution of the southwestern Mojave Desert, California, in Cooper, J. D., Troxel, B. W., and Wright, L. A., eds., Geology of selected areas in the San Bernardino Mountains, western Mojave Desert, and southern Great Basin, California: Geol. Soc. Amer. Ann. Meeting, Cordilleran Sect., Anaheim, CA, 1982, Volume and Guidebook, Field Trip 9, p. 21–34.

Miller, E. L., Miller, M. M., Stevens, C. H., Wright, J. E., and Madrid, R., 1992, Late Paleozoic paleogeographic and tectonic evolution of the western U.S. Cordillera, in Burchfiel, B. C., Lipman, P. W., and Zoback, M. L., eds., The Cordilleran orogen: Conterminous U.S.: Boulder, CO, Geol. Soc. Amer., The geology of North America, v. G-3, p. 57–106.

Miller, J. S., 1996, Pb-U crystallization age of the Papoose Flat pluton, White-Inyo Mountains, California [abs.]: Geol. Soc. Amer. Abs. Prog., v. 28, no. 5, p. 91.

Miller, J. S., Glazner, A. F., Walker, J. D., and Martin, M. W., 1995, Geochronologic and isotopic evidence for Triassic-Jurassic emplacement of the eugeoclinal allochthon in the Mojave Desert, Californa: Geol. Soc. Amer. Bull., v. 107, p. 1441–1457.

Montanez, I. P., and Osleger, D. A., 1993, Parasequence stacking patterns, third-order accommodation events, and sequence stratigraphy of Middle to Upper Cambrian platform carbonates, Bonanza King Formation, southern Great Basin, in Loucks, R. G., and Sarg, J. F., eds., Carbonate sequence stratigraphy: Recent developments and applications: Amer. Asssoc. Petrol. Geol. Memoir 57, p. 305–326.

Moore, J. N., and Foster, C. T., Jr., 1980, Lower Paleozoic metasedimentary rocks in the east-central Sierra Nevada, California: Correlation with Great Basin formations: Geol. Soc. Amer. Bull., pt. 1, v. 91, p. 37–43.

Moore, S. C., 1976, Geology and thrust fault tectonics of parts of the Argus and Slate Ranges, Inyo County, California: Unpubl. Ph.D. dissertation, Univ. of Washington, 127 p.

Morgan, S., and Law, R., 1994, Forceful intrusion of Jurassic plutons in the White-Inyo Range, eastern California [abs.]: Geol. Soc. Amer. Abs. with Prog., v. 26, p. 134.

Nelson, C. A., 1962, Lower Cambrian–Precambrian succession, White-Inyo Mountains, California: Geol. Soc. Amer. Bull., v. 73, p. 139–144.

————, 1966a, Geologic map of the Blanco Mountain quadrangle, Inyo and Mono Counties, California: U.S. Geol. Surv. Geol. Quad. Map GQ-529, scale 1:62,500.

————, 1966b, Geologic map of the Waucoba Mountain quadrangle, Inyo County, California: U.S. Geol. Surv. Geol. Quad. Map GQ-528, scale 1:62,500.

————, 1981, Basin and Range Province, in Ernst, W. R., ed., The geotectonic development of California: Rubey Volume I: Englewood Cliffs, NJ, Prentice-Hall, p. 203–216.

Oldow, J. S., 1984, Spatial variability in the structure of the Roberts Mountains allochthon, western Nevada: Geol. Soc. Amer. Bull., v. 95, p. 174–185.

Paterson, S. R., Brudos, T., Fowler, K., Carlson, C., Bishop, K., and Verson, R. H., 1991, Papoose Flat pluton: Forceful expansion or postemplacement deformation?: Geology, v. 19, p. 324–327.

Renne, P. R., and Turrin, B. D. 1987, Constraints on timing of deformation in the Benton Range, southeastern California, and implications to Nevadan orogenesis: Geology, v. 15, p. 1031–1034.

Riggs, N. R., and Blakey, R. C., 1993, Early and Middle Jurassic paleogeography and volcanology of Arizona and adjacent areas, in Dunne, G. C., and McDougall, K. A., eds., Mesozoic paleogeography of the western United States—II: Soc. Econ. Paleontol. Mineral., Pacific Sect., Book 71, p. 433–462.

Rinehart, C. D., and Ross, D. C., 1957, Geologic map of the Casa Diablo quadrangle, California: U.S. Geol. Surv. Geol. Quad. Map GQ-99, scale 1:62,500.

Ross, D. C., 1967a, Geologic map of the Waucoba Wash quadrangle, Inyo County, California: U.S. Geol. Surv. Geol. Quad. Map GQ-612, scale 1:62,500.

————, 1967b, Generalized geologic map of the Inyo Mountains region, California: U.S. Geol. Surv. Misc. Geol. Invest. Map I-506, scale 1:125,000.

————, 1969, Descriptive petrography of three large granitic bodies in the Inyo Mountains, California: U.S. Geol. Surv. Prof. Pap. 601, 47 p.

Russell, S., and Nokleberg, W., 1977, Superimposition and timing of deformations in the Mount Morrison roof pendant and in the central Sierra Nevada, California: Geol. Soc. Amer. Bull., v. 88, p. 335–345.

Saleeby, J. B., 1986, Centennial continent-ocean transect #10, C-2 central California offshore to Colorado Plateau: Boulder, CO, Geol. Soc. Amer., 63 p.

————, 1992, Petrotectonic and paleogeographic settings of U.S. Cordilleran ophiolites, in Burchfiel, B. C., Lipman, P. W., and Zoback, M. L., eds., The Cordilleran orogen: Conterminous U.S.: Boulder, CO, Geol. Soc. Amer., The geology of North America, v. G-3, p. 653–682.

Saleeby, J. B., and Busby-Spera, C., 1992, Early Mesozoic tectonic evolution of the western U.S. Cordillera, in Burchfiel, B. C., Lipman, P. W., and Zoback, M. L., eds., The Cordilleran orogen: Conterminous U.S.: Boulder, CO, Geol. Soc. Amer., The geology of North America, v. G-3, p. 107–168.

Saleeby, J. B., Kistler, R. W., Longiaru, S., Moore, J. G., and Nokleberg, W. J., 1990, Middle Cretaceous silicic metavolcanic rocks in the Kings Canyon area, central Sierra Nevada, California, in Anderson, J. L., ed., The nature and origin of Cordilleran magmatism: Geol. Soc. Amer. Memoir 174, p. 251–270.

Schweickert, R. A., and Lahren, M. M., 1987, Continuation of Antler and Sonoma orogenic belts to the eastern Sierra Nevada, California, and Late Triassic thrusting in a compressional arc: Geology, v. 15, p. 270–273.

————, 1993, Tectonics of the east-central Sierra Nevada—Saddlebag Lake and Northern Ritter Range pendants, in Lahren, M. M., Trexler, J. H., Jr., and Spinosa, C., eds., 1993, Crustal evolution of the Great Basin and Sierra Nevada: Geol. Soc. Amer. Ann. Meeting, Cordilleran and Rocky Mountain Sect., Reno, NV, 1993, Field Trip Guidebook, p. 313–351.

Silberling, N. J., Nichols, K. M., Trexler, J. H., Jr., Jewell, P. W., and Crosbie, R. A., in press, Overview of Mississippian depositional and paleotectonic history in the Antler foreland, eastern Nevada and western Utah: Provo, UT, Brigham Young Univ. Press.

Smith, M. T., Dickinson, W. R., and Gehrels, G. E., 1993, Contractional nature of Devonian-Mississippian Antler tectonism along the North American continental margin: Geology, v. 21, p. 21–24.

Snow, J. K., 1992, Large-magnitude Permian shortening and continental-margin tectonics in the southern Cordillera: Geol. Soc. Amer. Bull., v. 104, p. 80–105.

————, 1994, Mass balance of Basin and Range extension as a tool for geothermal exploration: Geotherm. Res. Council Trans., v. 18, p. 23–30.

Snow, J. K., and Wernicke, B., 1993, Large-magnitude Permian shortening and continental-margin tectonism in the southern Cordillera: Reply: Geol. Soc. Amer. Bull., v. 105, p. 281–283.

Snow, J. K., Asmerom, Y., and Lux, D. R., 1991, Permian-Triassic plutonism and tectonics, Death Valley region, California and Nevada: Geology, v. 19, p. 629–632.

Sorenson, S. S., Dunne, G. C., Hanson, R. B., Barton, M. D., Becker, J., Tobisch, O. T., and Fiske, R. S., in press, From Jurassic shores to Cretaceous plutons: Geochemical evidence for paleo-alteration environments of metavolcanic rocks, eastern California: Geol. Soc. Amer. Bull.

Speed, R. C., 1984, Paleozoic and Mesozoic continental margin collision zone features, in Lintz, J., Jr., Western geological excursions: Geol. Soc. Amer. Ann. Meeting, Reno, NV, 1984, Field Trip Guidebook, v. 4, p. 66–80.

Stevens, C. H., 1982, The Early Permian Thysanophyllum coral belt: Another clue to Permian plate-tectonic reconstructions: Geol. Soc. Amer. Bull., v. 93, p. 798–803.

————, 1986, Evolution of the Ordovician through Middle Pennsylvanian carbonate shelf in east-central California: Geol. Soc. Amer. Bull., v. 97, p. 11–25.

————, 1991, Paleozoic shelf-to-basin transition in Owens Valley, California: Soc. Econ. Paleontol. Mineral., Pacific Sect., Book 69, 37 p.

————, 1995, Middle Devonian–Early Triassic unconformity in Owens Valley, eastern California [abs.]: Geol. Soc. Amer. Abs. Prog., v. 27, no. 5, p. 79.

Stevens, C. H., and Greene, D. C., 1995, Stratigraphy of Paleozoic rocks in eastern Sierra Nevada roof pendants, eastern California [abs.]: Geol. Soc. Amer. Abs. Prog., v. 27, no. 5, p. 79.

————, 1997, Manifestation of the mid-Paleozoic Antler orogeny in parautochthonous rocks in the eastern Sierra Nevada, California [abs.]: Geol. Soc. Amer. Abs. Prog., v. 29, no. 5, p. 67.

Stevens, C. H., Klingman, D., and Belasky, P., 1995, Development of the Mississippian carbonate platform in southern Nevada and eastern California on the eastern margin of the Antler foreland basin, in

Dorobek, S. L., and Ross, G. M., eds., Stratigraphic evolution of foreland basins: SEPM (Soc. Sediment. Geol.) Spec. Publ. 52, p. 175–186.

Stevens, C. H., Klingman, D. S., Sandberg, C. A., Stone, P., Belasky, P., Poole, F. G., and Snow, J. K., 1996, Mississippian stratigraphic framework of east-central California and southern Nevada with revision of Upper Devonian and Mississippian stratigraphic units in Inyo County, California: U.S. Geol. Surv. Bull. 1988-J, p. J1–J39.

Stevens, C. H., Lico, M., and Stone, P., 1989, Lower Permian sediment-gravity-flow sequence, eastern California: Sediment. Geol., v. 64, p. 1–12.

Stevens, C. H., and Olson, R.C., 1972, Nature and significance of the Inyo thrust fault, eastern California: Geol. Soc. Amer. Bull., v. 83, p. 3761–3768.

Stevens, C. H., Pelley, T., and Greene, D. C., 1995, Middle Devonian submarine fans in the eastern Sierra Nevada, California [abs.]: 1995 Pacific Sect. Conv.: Amer. Assoc. Petrol. Geol., Pacific Sect., p. 46.

Stevens, C. H., and Stone, P., 1988, Early Permian thrust faults in east-central California: Geol. Soc. Amer. Bull., v. 100, p. 552–562.

Stevens, C. H., Stone, P., and Kistler, R. W., 1992, A speculative reconstruction of the middle Paleozoic continental margin of southwestern North America: Tectonics, v. 11, p. 405–419.

Stewart, J. H., 1970, Upper Precambrian and Lower Cambrian strata in the southern Great Basin, California and Nevada: U.S. Geol. Surv. Prof. Pap. 620, 206 p.

————, 1972, Initial deposits in the Cordilleran geosyncline: Evidence of a Late Precambrian (<850 m.y.) separation: Geol. Soc. Amer. Bull., v. 83, p. 1345–1360.

————, 1980, Geology of Nevada: Nev. Bur. Mines Geol. Spec. Publ. 4, 136 p.

————, 1985, East-trending dextral faults in the western Great Basin: An explanation for anomalous trends of pre-Cenozoic strata and Cenozoic faults: Tectonics, v. 4, p. 547–564.

————, 1991, Latest Precambrian and Cambrian rocks of the western United States—An overview, in Cooper, J. D., and Stevens, C. H., eds., Paleozoic paleogeography of the western United States—II: Soc. Econ. Paleontol. Mineral., Pacific Sect., Book 67, p. 13–37.

Stewart, J. H., and Poole, F. G., 1974, Lower Paleozoic and uppermost Precambrian Cordilleran miogeocline, Great Basin, western United States, in Dickinson, W. R., ed., Tectonics and sedimentation: Soc. Econ. Paleontol. Mineral. Spec. Publ. 22, p. 28–57.

Stewart, J. H., and Suczek, C. A., 1977, Cambrian and latest Precambrian paleogeography and tectonics in the western United States, in Stewart, J. H., Stevens, C. H., and Fritsche, A. E., eds., Paleozoic paleogeography of the western United States: Soc. Econ. Paleontol. Mineral., Pacific Sect., Book 7, p. 1–17.

Stewart, J. H., Ross, D. C., Nelson, C. A., and Burchfiel, B. C., 1966, Last Chance thrust—A major fault in the eastern part of Inyo County, California: U.S. Geol. Surv. Prof. Pap. 550-D, p. D23–D34.

Stone, P., 1984, Stratigraphy, depositional history, and paleogeographic significance of Pennsylvanian and Permian rocks in the Owens Valley–Death Valley region, California: Unpubl. Ph.D. dissertation, Stanford Univ., 399 p.

Stone, P., and Stevens, C. H., 1984, Stratigraphy and depositional history of Pennsylvanian and Permian rocks in the Owens Valley–Death Valley region, eastern California, in Lintz, J., Jr., Western geological excursions: Geol. Soc. Amer. Ann. Meeting, Reno, NV, 1984, Field Trip Guidebook, v. 4, p. 94–119.

————, 1987, Stratigraphy of the Owens Valley Group (Permian), southern Inyo Mountains, California: U.S. Geol. Surv. Bull. 1692, 19 p.

————, 1988a, An angular unconformity in the Permian section of east-central California: Geol. Soc. Amer. Bull., v. 100, p. 547–551.

————, 1988b, Pennsylvanian and Early Permian paleogeography of east-central California: Implications for the shape of the continental margin and timing of continental truncation: Geology, v. 16, p. 330–333.

————, 1993, Large-magnitude Permian shortening and continental-margin tectonics in the southern Cordillera: Discussion: Geol. Soc. Amer. Bull., v. 105, p. 279–280.

Stone, P., Dunne, G. C., Stevens, C. H., and Gulliver, R. M., 1989, Geologic map of Paleozoic and Mesozoic rocks in parts of the Darwin and adjacent quadrangles, Inyo County, California: U.S. Geol. Surv. Misc. Invest. Map I-1932, scale 1:31,250.

Stone, P., Stevens, C. H., and Magginetti, R. T., 1987, Pennsylvanian and Permian stratigraphy of the northern Argus Range and Darwin Canyon area, California: U.S. Geol. Surv. Bull. 1691, 30 p.

Stone, P., Stevens, C. H., and Orchard, M. J., 1991, Stratigraphy of the Lower and Middle(?) Triassic Union Wash Formation, east-central California: U.S. Geol. Surv. Bull., 1928, 26 p.

Swanson, B. J., 1996, Structural geology and deformational history of the southern Inyo Mountains east of Keeler, Inyo County, California: Unpubl. M.S. thesis, California State Univ., Northridge, 125 p.

Sylvester, A. G., and Babcock, J. W., 1975, Regional significance of multiphase folding in the White-Inyo Range, eastern California [abs.]: Geol. Soc. Amer. Abs. Prog., v. 7, no. 7, p. 1289.

Sylvester, A. G., Miller, C. F., and Nelson, C. A., 1978, Monzonites of the White-Inyo Range, and their relation to the calc-alkaline Sierra Nevada batholith: Geol. Soc. Amer. Bull., v. 89, p. 1677–1687.

Tatsumi, Y. and Eggins, S., 1995, Subduction zone magmatism: Cambridge, UK, Blackwells, 211 p.

Tikoff, B., and Saint Blanquat, M., 1997, Transpressional shearing and strike-slip partitioning in the Late Cretaceous Sierra Nevada magmatic arc, California: Tectonics, v. 16, n. 3, p. 442–459.

Tobisch, O. T., Saleeby, J. B., and Fiske, R. S., 1986, Structural history of continental volcanic arc rocks, eastern Sierra Nevada, California: A case for extensional tectonics: Tectonics, v. 5, p. 65–94.

Tobisch, O. T., Saleeby, J. B., Renne, P. R., McNulty, B., and Tong, W., 1995, Variations in deformation fields during development of a large-volume magmatic arc, central Sierra Nevada, California: Geol. Soc. Amer. Bull., v. 107, p. 148–166.

Trexler, J. H., Jr., and Nitchman, S. P., 1990, Sequence stratigraphy and evolution of the Antler foreland basin, east-central Nevada: Geology, v. 18, p. 422–425.

Trexler, J. H., Jr., Cole, J. C., and Cashman, P. H., 1996, Middle Devonian–Mississippian stratigraphy on and near the Nevada Test Site: Implications for hydrocarbon potential: Amer. Assoc. Petrol. Geol. Bull., v. 80, p. 1736–1762.

Unruh, M. E., 1985, Geochemistry and petrology of Triassic granitoids on the Sierra Nevada batholith, California and Nevada: Unpubl. M.S. thesis, California State Univ., Northridge, 94 p.

Walker, J. D., 1988, Permian and Triassic rocks of the Mojave desert and their implications for timing and mechanisms of continental truncation: Tectonics, v. 7, p. 685–709.

Walker, J. D., Burchfiel, B. C., and Davis, G. A., 1995, New age controls on initiation and timing of foreland belt thrusting in the Clark Mountains, southern California: Geol. Soc. Amer. Bull., v. 107, p. 742–750.

Walker, J. D., Martin, M. W., Bartley, J. M., and Coleman, D. S., 1990, Timing and kinematics of deformation in the Cronese Hills, California, and implications for Mesozoic structure of the southwestern Cordillera: Geology, v. 18, p. 554–557.

Welch, T., 1979, Superposed Mesozoic deformations in the southern White Mountains, eastern California [abs.]: Geol. Soc. Amer. Abs. Prog., v. 11, no. 3, p. 134–135.

Werner, M. R., 1979, Superposed Mesozoic deformations, southeastern Inyo Mountains, California: Unpubl. M.S. thesis, California State Univ., Northridge, 69 p.

Wernicke, B. P., Axen, G. J., and Snow, J. K., 1988, Basin and Range extensional tectonics at the latitude of Las Vegas, Nevada: Geol. Soc. Amer. Bull., v. 100, p. 1738–1757.

Willahan, D. E., 1991, Biostratigraphy of Upper Paleozoic rocks in the Mount Morrison roof pendant, Sierra Nevada: Evidence for its original paleogeographic position: Unpubl. M.S. thesis, San Jose State Univ., 92 p.

Wise, J. M., 1996, Structure and stratigraphy of the Convict Lake block, Mount Morrison roof pendant, eastern Sierra Nevada, California: Unpubl. M.S. thesis, Univ. of Nevada, Reno, 321 p.

Wolf, M. B., and Saleeby, J. B., 1995, Late Jurassic dike swarms in the southwestern Sierra Nevada Foothills Terrane, California: Implications for the Nevadan orogeny and North American plate motion, in Miller, D. L., and Busby, C., eds., Jurassic magmatism and tectonics of the North American Cordillera: Geol. Soc. Amer. Spec. Pap. 299, p. 203–228.

Wright, J. E., and Wooden, J. L., 1991, New Sr, Nd, and Pb isotopic data from plutons in the northern Great Basin: Implications for crustal structure and granite petrogenesis in the hinterland of the Sevier thrust belt: Geology, v. 19, p. 457–460.

An Overview of Paleozoic–Mesozoic Structures Developed in the Central White-Inyo Range, Eastern California

Sven S. Morgan and Richard D. Law

Department of Geological Sciences, Virginia Polytechnic Institute and State University, Blacksburg, Virginia 24061

Abstract

The central White-Inyo Range of eastern California is composed of a 7.5 km thick succession of Neoproterozoic to Upper Cambrian sedimentary rocks that have been deformed into a series of NE- and N- to NW-trending folds. The map distribution of the sedimentary rocks is primarily controlled by the younger N- to NW-trending folds that define the White Mountain–Inyo anticlinorium. Smaller-scale folds and associated cleavage, which strongly fans in a divergent pattern about the fold hinge surfaces, are associated with both periods of fold development. Older NE-trending folds and associated cleavage are developed in a NW-trending belt that crosses the range in a structural saddle between the White Mountain and Inyo anticlines. These NE-trending folds are of smaller wavelength than the older N- to NW-trending regional-scale folds, although both fold generations are developed on the cm–km scale. The intensity of both fold and cleavage development generally increases toward the west. Interference between the NE- and the N- to NW-trending folds has led to the development of a series of structural basins. We correlate formation of the NE-trending structures to the Antler orogeny, and formation of the younger N- to NW-trending structures with translation on the Last Chance thrust, which is exposed in the Inyo Range and presumably underlies the entire central White-Inyo Range.

In the eastern and central portions of the range, it is clear that both periods of folding pre-date the emplacement of Jurassic and Cretaceous plutons that are correlatives to the intrusive suites exposed in the Sierra Nevada batholith to the west. On the western margin of the range another set of N- to NW-trending structures, which are coaxial with the earlier N- to NW-trending set, is probably associated with the East Sierran thrust belt; this thrust belt is better recorded in the southern Inyo Mountains, and developed in the Jurassic period.

Introduction

The central White-Inyo Range is located within the transition zone between the Mesozoic magmatic arc (i.e. Sierra Nevada batholith) to the west and the deformed foreland of the Phanerozoic North American craton to the east. Whereas the magmatic arc is dominated by Mesozoic plutons, the central White-Inyo Range is composed of a Neoproterozoic to Upper Cambrian passive-margin shallow shelf sequence that has been intruded by much smaller volumes of Jurassic and Cretaceous plutons; the latter are time correlatives of the much larger intrusive suites to the west. The ages and styles of deformation features preserved within the White-Inyo Range are important for understanding how the passive-margin sequence in eastern California responded to the protracted series of Paleozoic and Mesozoic orogenic events, which are better documented to the north, east, and south, and also how these

rocks were affected by development of the Mesozoic magmatic arc and associated subduction zone located to the west.

Late Mesozoic deformation has been documented in the northern White Mountains (Hanson et al., 1987), and evidence for protracted deformation throughout the Mesozoic era has been recorded in the southern Inyo Mountains (Dunne et al., 1978; Stevens et al., 1997). However, the orientations and ages of structures exposed within the central portion of the White-Inyo Range, and their relationships to the Mesozoic plutons discussed herein, has attracted only brief reviews (Sylvester and Babcock, 1975; Dunne et al., 1978; Nelson et al., 1991; Paterson et al., 1991). Our purpose in this paper is to describe the dominant Paleozoic through Mesozoic structures exposed in the central White-Inyo Range, and to present an overview of the relative sequence of deformational and intrusive events. Detailed descriptions of the sedimentary rocks in the central

White-Inyo Range can be found elsewhere
(Nelson, 1962, 1978; Mount and Signor, 1989);
a more regional account of the geologic evolution of eastern California can be found in Stevens et al. (1997). The central White-Inyo
Range has been mapped at 1:62,500 scale under
the auspices of the U.S. Geological Survey
(Nelson 1966a, 1996b; McKee and Nelson,
1967; Ross, 1967a; Nelson, 1971) and many of
the structural observations and interpretations
reported in this paper are based on these USGS
maps. A regional-scale map of the central
White-Inyo Range and adjacent areas to the
south and east was compiled by Ross (1967b);
more detailed compilation maps subsequently
were published by Nelson et al. (1991) and
Ernst et al. (1993).

Structural Geology

The dominant structures throughout the
range are N- to NW-trending folds of all scales
(cm to km wavelengths) and an associated N- to
NW-striking slaty-spaced cleavage that fans
about the fold hinge planes in a divergent pattern (terminology after Ramsay, 1967). The
range is defined by the N- to NW-trending
White Mountain–Inyo anticlinorium so that,
in general, the western and eastern flanks of the
range are coincident with the western and eastern limbs of the anticlinorium (Fig. 1). Older
NE-trending folds and cleavage are less commonly observed, and are of smaller scale, than
the range-dominating N- to NW-trending structures. The areal distribution of the NE-trending
structures is domainal and they are best developed in a NW-trending belt that crosses the
range. Cleavage formation is believed to be
associated with both periods of folding, because
cleavage consistently strikes subparallel to the
strike of bedding on the limbs of both the N- to
NW- and NE-trending folds and dips more
steeply than bedding on the limbs of both fold
sets (Fig. 2). For both fold sets, cleavage fans in
a divergent manner about the hinge surfaces of
the folds.

In most of the range, sedimentary structures
and fossils are well preserved. Locally, intense
penetrative strains within pelitic horizons have
resulted in the complete transposition of bedding into the overprinting cleavage. Cleavage is

most strongly developed in the pelitic and carbonate units of the Poleta and Harkless formations. In contrast, cleavage is either absent or
only weakly developed in the more competent
quartzites, sandstones, and siltstones that are
abundant throughout the Neoproterozoic
through Upper Cambrian section. In the pelitic
units, cleavage is slaty and is defined by a
preferred alignment of elongate micron-scale
white mica, quartz, and chlorite grains. In the
carbonate units, cleavage is defined by a series
of dark-colored pressure solution seams that are
spaced at the cm scale.

Excluding the western margin of the range
(discussed below), one cleavage is predominantly observed in the rocks. Rarely, two cleavages are preserved, an older NE-trending
cleavage and a younger, cross-cutting, NW-
trending cleavage (Fig. 3). Both are generally
slaty, but the younger fabric is developed in cm-
scale zones. In only a few outcrops are three
generations of cleavage visible. The oldest cleavage is preserved as dark, cm-spaced seams with a
N-trending strike and a variable dip. The significance of this fabric is unknown. Numerous
minor faults and joint sets are observed in the
sedimentary rocks of the White-Inyo Range. A
detailed analysis of these structures remains to
be undertaken.

We correlate folds and cleavage in the central
White-Inyo Range to separate events primarily
on the basis of orientation (Williams, 1985),
but also on scale. NE- and N- to NW-trending
folds are similar in style; both are dominantly
upright and horizontal, except in the western
part of the range, where both sets of folds can be
inclined, and deformation is more intense.

NE-trending structures

NE-trending folds are mostly observed in a
linear belt that trends northwest and crosses the
range crest in the saddle between the White
Mountain and Inyo anticlines (Fig. 1). Beginning on the southeastern limb of the Inyo
anticline, the NE-trending structures can be
traced northwest to the saddle region between
the White Mountain and Inyo anticlines, and
then northward along the western limb of the
White Mountain anticline; the saddle includes
the Poleta folds area (see Fig. 1, basin B3;
Nelson, 1980). The intensity of the NE-trending structures increases to the west. Along the

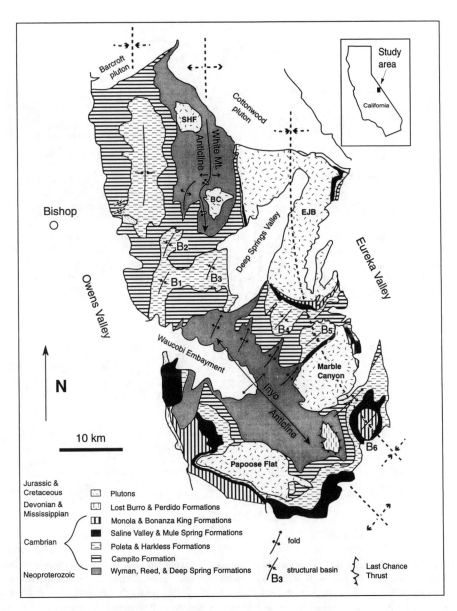

FIG. 1. Simplified geologic map of the central White-Inyo Range. Adapted from Nelson (1966a, 1996b, 1971), Nelson et al. (1991), and McKee and Nelson (1967).

eastern limb of the Inyo anticline, NE-trending folds have km-scale wavelengths and are upright and open, whereas in the Poleta folds area located in the saddle region between the White Mountain and Inyo anticlines (Fig. 1, structural basin B3), folds are of smaller wavelength, slightly inclined and tighter, and are associated with low-angle, small-displacement thrusts. On the western limb of the White Mountain anti-

cline, between Poleta and Silver canyons (Fig. 2, area 2), NE-trending folds are predominantly recumbent and isoclinal, verging toward the southeast (Welch, 1979). The domainal nature of the NE-trending structures is not well understood. Whether folding and cleavage formation associated with the first deformation event was restricted to certain areas, or if they were developed on a regional scale and then largely over-

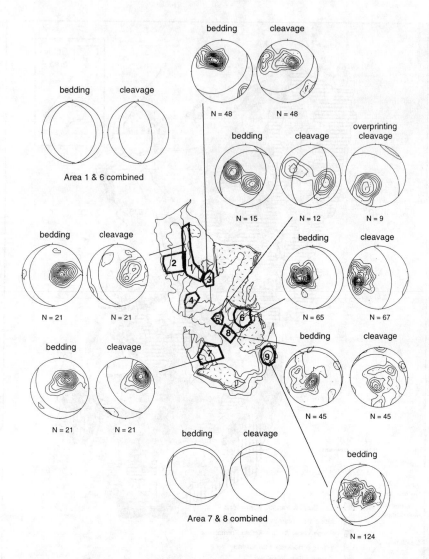

FIG. 2. Location map and bedding-cleavage data from areas selected for structural analysis; see Figure 1 for details of regional geology. Area 2 previously studied by Welch (1979 and unpubl. data); area 4 previously studied by Sylvester and Babcock (1975) and A. G. Sylvester (unpubl. data). Data from all other areas (1, 3, and 5–9) are presented in this paper. Poles to bedding and cleavage were plotted and contoured on lower-hemisphere nets using the program STEREOPLOT; contour intervals: 1, 2, 3, 4 . . . 12 times uniform distribution. With the exception of the cleavage plot for area 3, the great circles defining the average orientation of bedding and cleavage in each area were calculated from the maximum pole concentrations in the contoured diagrams. The great circle defining the average orientation of cleavage in area 3 was calculated by taking an average pole position located at an equal angular distance between the dominant and subordinate point maxima of poles to cleavage. See text for discussion.

printed by the N- to NW-oriented structures, is unknown.

We originally assumed that the NE-trending structures post-dated the N- to NW-trending structures according to map-scale relations (Morgan and Law, 1994). More recently, both cleavages have been observed by the authors in the same outcrop and the NW-striking cleavage clearly overprints the NE-striking cleavage, documenting the older nature of the NE structures (Fig. 3). This is consistent with the observations of Sylvester and Babcock (1975) in the

FIG. 3. Photographs of crosscutting cleavages. A. Older, NE-striking slaty cleavage is parallel to pencil, and slightly oblique to bedding, which is horizontal and can be seen in the upper portion of the photograph. Younger, NW-striking cleavage is slaty in cm-scale zones and crosscuts the NE-striking cleavage. B. Close-up view of the relationship seen in A. Pencil in both photographs is 15 cm long.

saddle region, Welch (1979) in the western part of the White Mountains (Fig. 2, area 2), and Dunne (1986) in the southern Owens Valley region, where NE-trending structures are overprinted by N- to NW-trending structures.

The area of overprinting cleavage is located on the eastern limb of the Inyo anticline, where map-scale NE-trending folds and associated slaty cleavage are observed (Fig. 1). Poles to bedding from one of these folds (Fig. 2, area 5) document an upright, horizontal fold where cleavage dips approximately 20° more steeply than bedding on both limbs of the fold. Also observed on both limbs of this km-scale fold is a NW-striking and NE-dipping cleavage (Fig. 2, area 5) that crosscuts the NE-striking slaty cleavage (Fig. 3) and apparently is related to the development of the larger-scale Inyo anticline.

The NW-striking cleavage is slaty in appearance, but is only found in zones 1 to 2 cm thick, spaced 10 to 15 cm apart, that crosscut the more prevalent NE-striking cleavage.

The change in trend from the White Mountain anticline to the Inyo anticline occurs where the belt of older NE-trending folds and cleavage crosses the composite White Mountain-Inyo anticline. This leads us to believe that the change in fold trend from north to northwest may have been controlled by the location of pre-existing NE-trending structures during the development of the White Mountain–Inyo anticlinorium.

N- to NW-trending structures

The White Mountain anticline trends N-S and can be traced southward through a depression in the fold hinge to the NW-trending Inyo anticline. Cleavage and bedding data for both anticlines (Fig. 2) illustrate that cleavage strikes subparallel to bedding and also consistently dips 5 to 20° more steeply than does bedding. Poles to bedding and cleavage measured along the western limb of the Inyo anticline (Fig. 2, area 7) define clear point maxima. In contrast, poles to bedding and cleavage measured from the eastern limb of the Inyo anticline (Fig. 2, area 8) are more diffuse; we infer this to be caused by the stronger development of the earlier NE-trending folds in this region. The average strike and dip of bedding and cleavage for both limbs of the Inyo anticline have been combined (Fig. 2, area 7 and 8 combined) to illustrate the shallow plunge of the NW-trending fold and the geometric (and inferred genetic) relationship of cleavage to fold formation.

Orientation data from the White Mountain anticline are limited to the western limb of the fold and the southeastern section of the fold's eastern limb (Fig. 2, areas 1 and 3), because on the eastern limb of the White Mountain anticline, much of the cleavage has been overprinted by strain and metamorphism associated with emplacement of the composite Eureka Valley–Joshua Flat–Beer Creek (EJB) pluton. Bedding and cleavage from the western limb of the fold (Fig. 2, area 1) strike north and dip west, whereas bedding and cleavage from the southeastern portion of the White Mountain anticline strike northeast and dip southeast (Fig. 2, area 3). We associated the NE-striking orientation of bedding and cleavage in the southeast portion of the White Mountain anticline with the earlier NE-trending fold event on the basis of orientation and also spatial continuity to the NE-trending structures in the B3 structural basin located to the south (Fig. 1).

We recognize a regionally developed N- to NW-trending syncline, with a fold hinge, located 10 to 15 km east of the White Mountain–Inyo anticline (Fig. 1), on the basis of structures outlined by the USGS geologic quadrangle maps of Soldier Pass (McKee and Nelson, 1967), Waucoba Spring (Nelson, 1971), the simplified geologic map of Nelson et al. (1991), and cleavage-bedding data included in this report (Fig. 2). The syncline forms an anticline-syncline fold pair with the White Mountain–Inyo anticline and is believed to have been modified in shape and dimension as a result of subsequent emplacement of the EJB and Marble Canyon plutons (Fig. 1).

Structural basins

One of the consequences of two periods of folding in the central White-Inyo Range, especially inasmuch as the fold axes from the two events are nearly perpendicular to one another, should be the formation of a series of structural domes and basins as a result of fold interference (Ramsey, 1967). Six structural basins (Fig. 1, B1–6) have been identified, the three most eastern basins (B4–6) being produced by interference between the older NE-trending folds and the regional-scale N- to NW-trending syncline that forms the eastern fold pair to the White Mountain–Inyo anticline (Fig. 1). The other three structural basins (B1–3) are located in the saddle region between the White Mountain and Inyo anticlines. T. C. Welch (unpubl. data) also has identified cm- to m-scale dome and basin structures from the western portion of the southern White Mountains (Fig. 2, area 2).

Map-scale structural domes have not been identified in the range. One possibility is that on the eastern side of the Inyo anticline, they were significantly modified by the intrusion of the Jurassic plutons. In the saddle region, it is possible that the interference patterns produced by orthogonally superimposing large-scale anticlines on smaller anticlines is not as pronounced as that produced by superimposing large-scale anticlines on smaller synclines. In addition, the two generations of fold axes are at a lower angle to each other in the saddle region than on the eastern limb of the Inyo anticline, and the closer the two sets of fold axes are to one another in orientation, the less well developed the resultant dome and basin structures will be.

The most obvious structural basin produces a bull's-eye map pattern defined by inward-dipping Lower and Middle Cambrian formations and is located in the southeast corner of the region (Fig. 1, B6). The orientation of bedding at individual outcrops within this basin has been taken from the Waucoba Spring USGS geologic quadrangle map (Nelson, 1971) and plotted as poles to bedding in Figure 2, area 9. Contouring of these poles reveals a WNW-ESE–striking girdle distribution of poles with two point maxima that define the limbs of a SSW-plunging fold. However, the distribution of poles within this girdle is attenuated in a NE-SW direction, suggesting local reorientation of bedding about a NW-SE–trending fold axis.

Structural saddle between the White Mountain and Inyo anticlines

A structural saddle (or fold depression) defines the transition between the southward-plunging White Mountain anticline and the NW-plunging section of the Inyo anticline. The exposed stratigraphic units range from the Neoproterozoic Wyman Formation, located in the cores of both anticlines, to Middle Cambrian Harkless Formation in the saddle, passing through almost 6000 m of section measured along the hinge of the anticline. Development of the saddle also may be the result of fold interference associated with the two periods of folding. As mentioned previously, the belt of NE-trending structures crosses the N- to NW-trending White Mountain–Inyo anticline in the saddle region. Imposing a larger-wavelength, N- to NW-trending anticline on an already existing, smaller-wavelength, NE-trending syncline could produce the observed structural depression in the White Mountain–Inyo anticline.

Structures associated with pluton emplacement

Emplacement of the Jurassic to Cretaceous plutons in the central White-Inyo Range post-dates the two dominant phases of folding and cleavage development outlined above. This conclusion is based on four lines of evidence.

(1) The composite Middle Jurassic EJB pluton (dated at 161 to 174 Ma by U/Pb methods (Sylvester et al., 1978; Gillespie, 1979) and the Marble Canyon pluton (179 Ma U/Pb) (Sylvester et al., 1978) are the oldest plutons in the study area, and both crosscut structural basins produced by interference between the two fold sets. The structural basins (labeled B4 and B5 in Fig. 1) located between the two plutons are characterized by moderately dipping (20 to 60°) beds. Traced away from the basin troughs toward the pluton margins, however, the beds abruptly change their dip direction at a distance of 1 to 2 km from the pluton margins and rapidly rotate to become subvertical or locally overturned. These rapid changes in the dips of bedding terminate the structural basins and begin at the outer margins of the contact aureoles. The steeply dipping beds within the aureoles strike subparallel to the pluton margin. Glazner and Miller (in press) have recently suggested that these rotations may indicate that the granodioritic-dioritic Jurassic plutons began to sink during crystallization as they became more dense than the surrounding country rocks.

(2) At a distance of 1 to 2 km from the Jurassic plutons, bedding rotates from the regional structural grain into concordancy with the pluton margins, and the cleavage (where measurable) also is rotated by a similar amount, hence preserving the angular relationship between bedding and cleavage observed throughout the range. We interpret cleavage to have rotated passively along with bedding as bedding was deformed into concordancy with the plutons. At a distance of ~1 km from the pluton margins, this cleavage is overprinted by (and transposed into) a new grain-shape fabric parallel to the pluton margins, which is associated with contact metamorphism and emplacement-related strains (Morgan and Law, 1994). For example, near the southwestern margin of the EJB pluton (Fig. 1), bedding can be traced from its regional NNE strike toward the pluton margin, where bedding rapidly steepens and is rotated into a northwest strike to become concordant to the contact. The southeast dip of bedding increases from moderate angles to those that are subvertical, and in several areas is overturned. Cleavage can be traced along with bedding, striking subparallel to bedding and dipping more steeply. Where the overturned

beds strike to the northwest and dip to the southwest, cleavage also strikes to the northwest, but dips less steeply to the southwest, suggesting that cleavage has been rotated passively along with bedding and also has been rotated through the vertical.

(3) On the southwest limb of the Inyo anticline (Fig. 1), bedding and the regionally developed NW-striking cleavage both have been rotated into concordancy with the margin of the Cretaceous Papoose Flat pluton (dated at 83 Ma by U/Pb) (Miller, 1996) within the pluton aureole. Original angular relationships between bedding and cleavage, observed away from the pluton, are preserved as inclusion trails in andalusite porphyroblasts within the contact metamorphic aureole (Morgan et al., in press).

(4) The Cretaceous Birch Creek pluton deflects N-trending folds and faults in the core of the White Mountain anticline (Nelson and Sylvester, 1971) (Fig. 1). Traced southward toward the pluton, N-trending folds become overturned and more appressed as they wrap around the northwestern margin of the pluton, indicating that the folds were deformed by the western expansion of the pluton as it was emplaced (Nelson and Sylvester, 1971).

In addition to the structural evidence above—that fold and cleavage development predate emplacement of the Jurassic and Cretaceous plutons—supporting petrologic evidence has recently been described by Ernst (1996), who conducted a detailed geochemical study of the variably metamorphosed sedimentary rocks of the central White-Inyo Range. This study indicates that metamorphic isograds transect the N- to NW-oriented folds and possibly the NE-oriented folds. Ernst (1996, p. 1528) interpreted the observed higher-grade metamorphic zonation of the region as being "a composite of local recrystallization episodes attending calc-alkaline pluton emplacement over an approximately 100 m.y. interval, overprinting a pervasive, weak, chloritic metamorphism," indicating that the last resetting of isograds could be as young as 80 Ma, at least adjacent to the Cretaceous intrusives.

Discussion

Three orientations of folds and cleavage have been recorded in the central White-Inyo

Range—northeast, north, and northwest. We correlate the NE-trending structures with the first deformation event; we associate the N- and NW-trending structures with a later event, and favor the hypothesis of two dominant periods of deformation resulting in formation of the structures observed in most of the central White-Inyo Range. On the basis of deformation features observed along the western margin of the White Mountains (Welch, 1979) and in the southern Inyo Mountains (Dunne, 1986; Stevens et al., 1997), it is likely that the increase in intensity of the N- to NW-trending structures observed on the western margin of the range is associated with a third period of deformation that post-dates both formation of the NE-trending structures and the earlier N- to NW-trending structures.

We attribute the N-trending White Mountain anticlinorium and the NW-trending Inyo anticlinorium to the same deformation event for several reasons. (1) They are of the same scale and probably are related to the same structure at depth (i.e., the Last Chance thrust system—see justification below). (2) We would expect to see large-scale NW-oriented folds (similar in scale to the Inyo anticline) in the White Mountains, and large-scale N-oriented folds (similar in scale to the White Mountain anticline) in the Inyo Mountains, if the White Mountain–Inyo anticlinorium was produced by two periods of folding. (3) The change in orientation from N- to NW-trending fold hinges occurs where the anticlinorium crosses the NW-oriented belt of NE-trending structures, suggesting a genetic link. In this scenario, the regional-scale bend in structures is related to the architecture of the previously deformed sedimentary sequence. We restate, however, that we do not understand why the NE-trending structures are confined to a NW-trending belt.

The transition between the N- and the NW-trending structures has been investigated by combining bedding and cleavage data from the northeastern limb of the Inyo anticline, where the regional structural grain curves northward from a northwest trend (Fig. 1; Fig. 2, area 6), with data from the western limb of the White Mountain anticline (Fig. 2, area 1). The result is a NNW-trending upright fold pattern with a subhorizontal hinge and equally dipping western and eastern fold limbs (Fig. 2, see the data from areas 1 and 6 combined); cleavage dips

more steeply than does bedding on both limbs. This suggests that the range-scale curvature from the N-S–trending White Mountain anticline to the NW-SE–trending Inyo anticline occurs more to the south in the eastern part of the range, and is consistent with the curvature in our proposed regional-scale syncline to the east of the White Mountain–Inyo anticline (Fig. 1). We believe that this further supports our interpretation that the curvature from the N-S–oriented structures in the White Mountains to NW-oriented structures in the Inyo Mountains is an original feature associated with simultaneous formation of the White Mountain and Inyo anticlinorium.

In contrast, the area of N-striking bedding and cleavage in the eastern Inyo Mountains (Fig. 2, area 6) may be related to an earlier structure that was largely overprinted by NW-oriented structures in the rest of the Inyo Mountains. A. G. Sylvester (pers. commun., 1997) and students at the University of California at Santa Barbara have measured the orientations of hundreds of folds in the saddle region between the White Mountain and Inyo anticlines (Fig. 2, area 4) and concluded that NE-trending folds are refolded by N- to NW-trending folds. Sylvester's data also indicate that there is a third set of structures that trend due north and are of intermediate age between the older NE-trending folds and the younger NW-trending folds (Sylvester and Babcock, 1975). It is possible that the youngest NW-trending folds in area 4 (Fig. 2) are related to the younger NW-oriented structures observed on the western side of the White Mountains (Fig. 2, area 2) (Welch, 1979).

Welch (1979) noted that on the western side of the southern White Mountains, the intensity of the NW-trending deformation increases abruptly toward the west, folds become tighter, and cleavage intensity increases. In addition, early N- to NW-trending structures may be overprinted coaxially by later N- to NW-oriented structures (T. C. Welch, unpubl. data). The increase in intensity of structures, and the possibility of successive events being recorded on the western margin of the range, is consistent with a second period of N- to NW-oriented deformation recognized in the southern Inyo Mountains and associated with the East Sierran thrust system (Dunne, 1986; Stevens et al., 1997).

Relationship of the NE-trending folds to the Antler orogenic belt

NE-trending folds and cleavage are associated with the Late Devonian to Early Mississippian Antler orogenic belt in: (1) the Silver Peak Range, 60 km to the northeast in Nevada (Oldow, 1984); (2) the Candelaria Hills (Oldow, 1984), 100 km to the north in Nevada; and (3) the Northern Ritter Range pendant (Greene et al., 1997), which is located 120 km to the northwest in the eastern Sierra Nevada Mountains. In all three areas, NE-trending folds are upright, and are associated with emplacement of the Roberts Mountain allochthon. NE-trending folds and cleavage in the central White-Inyo Range are similar in orientation and style to early folds and cleavage in Nevada, although northeast folds in the Northern Ritter Range can be tighter and locally isoclinal (Greene et al., 1997).

We tentatively correlate the early NE-trending folds observed in the central White-Inyo Range with the Antler-age NE-trending folds observed to the north and northeast in Nevada and to the northwest in the eastern Sierra Nevada, as previously proposed by Sylvester and Babcock (1975) and Dunne et al. (1978). However, it should be noted that opinions differ as to the deformational event to which the NE-trending folds in the central White-Inyo Range are related (see Stevens et al., 1997). The Antler orogenic belt is defined by fault juxtaposition of allochthonous Lower Paleozoic, dominantly siliceous rocks of deep-water basinal environments with autochthonous Lower Paleozoic carbonate- to clastic-dominated shallow-shelf rocks, such as those found in the White-Inyo Range. The NE-trending folds in the Northern Ritter Range and in both localities in Nevada are observed in the deep-water sedimentary rocks of the allochthon. If the NE-trending folds in the central White-Inyo Range are related to the Antler orogeny, then they are unusual in being recorded in the shallow-shelf sequence. It also should be noted that the central White-Inyo Range probably was located much farther to the west in Antler time. Tens of kilometers of eastward displacement on the Last Chance thrust in the Late Paleozoic is supported by fault juxtaposition and strain analyses (see below).

The only timing constraint on formation of the NE-trending folds in the central White-Inyo Range is that they developed prior to the NW-trending folds (which are associated with Permian[?] Last Chance thrusting; see below). In the Candelaria Hills of Nevada, NE-trending folds are observed only in pre-Permian-age rocks, and are possibly of pre-Mississippian age (Oldow, 1984).

In the three areas discussed above, as well as in the central White-Inyo Range, NE-trending folds are overprinted by NW-trending folds and cleavage. However, correlation of the NW-trending structures in these areas is problematic, because they may be of different ages in each area.

Relationship of N- to NW-oriented structures to the Last Chance thrust

A structural window through the Last Chance thrust (Stewart et al., 1966; Dunne et al., 1978; Corbett et al., 1988), which places the Neoproterozoic to Upper Cambrian sequence of the White-Inyo Range on Devonian and Mississippian strata, is located in the southeastern part of the range in the Jackass Flat area (Fig. 1). The thrust is constrained to have formed between Early Permian and earliest Triassic times (see Snow, 1992 and Stevens et al., 1997 for details); palinspastic restoration incorporating strain analyses indicates a minimum of 75 km of displacement on the thrust (Corbett et al., 1988). Because of the extensive amount of thrusting necessary to place the ~7750 m thick Neoproterozoic to Upper Cambrian section (Stewart and Suczek, 1977; Nelson, 1980) on top of Devonian and Mississippian strata in the Inyo Mountains, it is assumed that all of the central White-Inyo Range section lies above the thrust surface and therefore is allochthonous (Stewart et al. 1966; Nelson et al., 1991).

Extensive strain and kinematic analyses have been conducted by Corbett (1989) on the hanging-wall and footwall rocks. Corbett recorded NNW-trending folds and associated cleavage in the footwall rocks and inferred a N60° E transport direction for the thrust, based on the orientation of the NNW-trending folds. Corbett et al. (1988) have suggested that the regional-scale N- to NW-trending White Mountain and Inyo Mountain anticlines are actually ramp anticlines associated with movement on the underlying Last Chance thrust. This suggestion is supported by the similarity between orientation of structures in the footwall to the thrust and the N- to NW-trending structures we have measured throughout the central White-Inyo Range. Following the suggestions of Corbett et al. (1988) and Corbett (1989), we associate formation of the younger N- to NW-oriented structures exposed in the central White-Inyo Range with motion on the underlying Last Chance thrust. We further speculate that the NW-trending folds observed in the Candelaria Hills and Silver Peak Range of Nevada also may be related to Last Chance thrusting. However, in the Candelaria Hills, NW-trending folds affect rocks as young as Lower Triassic and possibly younger (Oldow, 1984); this would indicate that the NW-trending folds in Nevada may be younger than the Last Chance thrusting recognized in eastern California.

Earlier interpretations by Dunne (1986) that the NE-trending folds represent Last Chance structures are not consistent with the data of Corbett et al. (1988) for the northern Inyo Mountains. However, NE-trending folds in the Nelson Range (located 5 km east of the southern Inyo Mountains), are compatible with motion on thrust faults in the southern Inyo Mountains that are correlated with the Last Chance thrust (G. Dunne, pers. commun., 1997).

We correlate the increase in intensity of N- to NW-oriented structures—and possible coaxial overprinting of structures—on the western margin of the White Mountains (Welch, 1979) with the East Sierran thrust system (Dunne et al., 1978; Stevens et al., 1997), which was active intermittently from latest Triassic to mid-Cretaceous time and is associated with emplacement of the Mesozoic magmatic arc to the west. Renne and Turrin (1987) documented a dominant NW-trending set of folds in the Lower Cambrian section in the Benton Range, 15 km west of the northern White Mountains; these folds are intruded by undeformed dikes with emplacement ages ranging from 209 to 168 Ma, indicating that NW-trending deformation must be older than 168 Ma (i.e., mid-Jurassic) in that area.

Conclusions

The sedimentary rocks of the central White-Inyo Range have been subjected to at least two regionally important phases of deformation, each being characterized by folds and cleavage that are variably developed throughout the range. A third period of deformation seems to have affected rocks on the western margin of the White Mountains, and may have affected rocks throughout the central White-Inyo Range.

In both the NE- and N- to NW-trending fold sets, cleavage fans in a divergent pattern about the hinge planes of the folds and maintains a strike subparallel to the strike of bedding. The N- to NW-trending White Mountain–Inyo anticlinorium defines the large-scale structure of the range, but N- to NW-trending folds of all scales are observed. NE-trending folds are older and of smaller scale than the N- to NW-trending folds, and are observed mainly in a NW-striking belt that crosses the range crest in the saddle between the White Mountain and Inyo anticlines.

Six structural basins have been identified as the products of interference between the two fold sets, although no structural domes have been identified. Superimposed folding also offers an explanation for development of the structural saddle (i.e., fold hinge depression) between the White Mountain and Inyo anticlines. The structural basins are abruptly terminated against the Jurassic plutons, and both bedding and cleavage are rotated (maintaining their angular relationship) into concordancy with the Jurassic plutons, indicating that the two dominant phases of folding and associated cleavage formation pre-date emplacement of the Jurassic plutons.

The NE-trending structures are associated with the deformation observed to the north in the Antler orogenic belt, on the basis of similarity in fold orientation and scale. Formation of the N- to NW-oriented structures is correlated with movement on the underlying Last Chance thrust. This correlation is based on similarity in orientation of structures in the immediate footwall of the thrust, with N- to NW-trending structures found throughout the central White-Inyo Range. The change in trend from NW-oriented structures to N-oriented structures is probably an original feature of the regional-scale folding that produced the White Mountain–Inyo anticline. This interpretation is consistent with development of the structural saddle between the S-plunging White Mountain anticline and the NW-plunging section of the

Inyo anticline by superimposing the N- to NW-trending White Mountain–Inyo anticlinorium on an earlier NE-trending synclinal structure.

The observations that (1) a structural saddle exists at this location, (2) the NW-trending belt of NE-trending structures crosses the range at the saddle, and (3) the White Mountain–Inyo anticlinorium changes trend at the saddle lead us to believe that there is a structural control at depth in this area. It was certainly active during formation of the N- to NW-trending structures, and previously may have influenced the formation and location of the older NE-trending belt of folds.

On the basis of deformation features observed, both along the western margin of the White Mountains (Welch, 1979) and in the southern Inyo Mountains (Dunne, 1986; Stevens et al., 1997), it is likely that the increase in intensity of the N- to NW-trending structures observed on the western margin of the range is associated with a third period of deformation that postdates both formation of the NE-trending structures and the N- to NW-trending White Mountain–Inyo anticlinorium.

Acknowledgments

The authors gratefully acknowledge discussions with George Dunne, Gary Ernst, Alan Glazner, Clem Nelson, Calvin Stevens, and Art Sylvester, which have helped us to understand their research on the structural evolution of the central White-Inyos. Constructive comments by George Dunne on an earlier draft of the manuscript are gratefully acknowledged. The authors also wish to thank Neil Mancktelow for providing the computer program STEREO-PLOT. This project was supported by research grants from the Geological Society of America, Sigma Xi, and University of California White Mountain Research Station to S. S. Morgan, and National Science Foundation grants EAR-9018929 and EAR9506525 to R. D. Law.

REFERENCES

Corbett K. P., 1989, Structural geology of the Last Chance thrust system, east-central California: Unpubl. Ph.D. dissertation, Univ. of California, Los Angeles, 218 p.

Corbett, K. P., Wrucke, C. T., and Nelson, C. A., 1988, Structure and tectonic history of the Last Chance thrust system, *in* Weide, D. L., and Faber, M. L., eds., This extended land, geologic journeys in the southern Basin and Range: Geol. Soc. Amer., Cordilleran Sect. Guidebook, p. 269–292.

Dunne, G. C., 1986, Mesozoic evolution of southern Inyo, Argus, and Slate ranges, *in* Dunne, G. C., ed., Mesozoic-Cenozoic structural evolution of selected areas, east-central California: Geol. Soc. Amer., Cordilleran Sect., Guidebook and volume, fieldtrips 2 and 14, p. 3–22.

Dunne, G. C., Gulliver, R. M., and Sylvester, A. G., 1978, Mesozoic evolution of rocks of the White, Inyo, and Slate ranges, eastern California, *in* Howell, D. G., and McDougal, K., eds., Mesozoic paleogeography of the western United States: Soc. Econ. Paleontol. Mineral., Pacific Sect., Pacific Coast Paleogeography Symp. 2, p. 189–208.

Ernst, W. G., 1996, Petrochemical study of regional/ contact metamorphism in metaclastic strata of the central White-Inyo Range, eastern California: Geol. Soc. Amer. Bull., v. 108, p. 1528–1548.

Ernst, W. G., Nelson, C. A., and Hall, C. A., Jr., 1993, Geology and metamorphic mineral assemblages of Precambrian and Cambrian rocks of the central White-Inyo Range, eastern California: Calif. Div. Mines and Geol. Map Sheet 46, scale 1:62,500.

Gillespie, J. G., 1979, U-Pb and Pb-Pb ages of primary and detrital zircons from the White Mountains, eastern California [abs.]: Geol. Soc. Amer. Abs. Prog., v. 11, no. 30, p. 79.

Glazner, A. F., and Miller, D. M., in press, Late-stage sinking plutons: Geology, v. 26.

Greene, D. C., Schweickert, R. A., and Stevens, C. H., 1997, Roberts Mountains allochthon and the western margin of the Cordilleran miogeocline in the Northern Ritter Range pendant, eastern Sierra Nevada, California: Geol. Soc. Amer. Bull., v. 109, p. 1294–1305.

Hanson, R. B., Saleeby, J. B., and Fates, D. G., 1987, Age and tectonic setting of Mesozoic metavolcanic and metasedimentary rocks, northern White Mountains, California: Geology, v. 15, p. 1074–1078.

McKee, E. H., and Nelson, C. A., 1967, Geologic map of Soldier Pass Quadrangle: U.S. Geol. Surv. Geol. Quadrangle Map GQ-654, scale 1:62,500.

Miller, J., 1996, U/Pb crystallization age of the Papoose Flat pluton, White-Inyo Mountains, California [abs.]: Geol. Soc. Amer., Abs. Prog., v. 28, no. 5, p. A91.

Morgan, S. S., and Law, R. D., 1994, Forceful intrusion of Jurassic plutons in the central White-Inyo Range, eastern California [abs.]: Geol. Soc. Amer., Abs. Prog., v. 26, no. 7, p. A134.

Morgan, S. S., Law, R. D., and Nyman, M. W., 1998, Lacolith-like emplacement model for the Papoose

Flat pluton based on porphyroblast-matrix analysis: Geol. Soc. Amer. Bull., v. 110 (in press).

Mount, J. F., and Signor, P. W., 1989, Paleoenvironmental context of the metazoan radiation event and its impact on the placement of the Precambrian-Cambrian boundary: Examples from the southwestern Great Basin, USA, *in* Christie-Blick, N., and Levy, J., eds., Late Proterozoic and Cambrian tectonics, sedimentation, and record of metazoan radiation in the western United States, Amer. Geophys. Union, Field Trip Guidebook T331, p. 39–46.

Nelson, C. A., 1962, Lower Cambrian–Precambrian succession, White-Inyo Mountains, California: Geol. Soc. Amer. Bull., v. 73, p. 139–144.

————, 1966a, Geologic map of the Waucoba Mountain Quadrangle, Inyo County, California: U.S. Geol. Surv. Geol. Quadrangle Map GQ-528, scale 1:62,500.

————, 1966b, Geologic map of the Blanco Mountain quadrangle, Inyo County, California: U.S. Geol. Surv. Geol. Quadrangle Map GQ-529, scale 1:62,500.

————, 1971, Geologic map of the Waucoba Spring quadrangle, Inyo County, California: U.S. Geol. Surv. Geol. Quadrangle Map GQ-921, scale 1:62,500.

————, 1978, Late Precambrian–early Cambrian stratigraphic and faunal succession of eastern California and the Precambrian-Cambrian boundary: Geol. Mag., v. 115, p. 121–126.

————, 1980, Guidebook to the geology of a portion of the eastern Sierra Nevada, Owens Valley, and White-Inyo Range: Univ. of California, Los Angeles, Dept. of Earth and Space Sciences, ESSSO Guidebook 12, 107 pp.

Nelson, C. A., Hall, C. A., and Ernst, W. G., 1991, Geologic history of the White-Inyo Range, *in* Hall, C. A., ed., Natural history of the White-Inyo Range, eastern California: Berkeley and Los Angeles, CA, Univ. of California Press, p. 42–74.

Nelson, C. A., and Sylvester, A. G., 1971, Wall rock decarbonation and forcible emplacement of Birch Creek pluton, southern White Mountains, California: Geol. Soc. Amer. Bull., v. 82, p. 2891–2904.

Oldow, J. S., 1984, Spatial variability in the structure of the Roberts Mountains allochthon, western Nevada: Geol. Soc. Amer. Bull., v. 95, p. 174–185.

Paterson, S. R., Brudos, T., Fowler, K., Carlson, C., Bishop, K., and Vernon, R. H., 1991, Papoose Flat pluton: Forceful expansion or post-emplacement deformation?: Geology, v. 19, p. 324–327.

Ramsay, J. G., 1967, Folding and fracturing of rocks: New York, McGraw-Hill, 568 p.

Renne, P. R., and Turrin, B. D., 1987, Constraints on the timing of deformation in the Benton Range, southeastern California, and implications for Nevadan orogenesis: Geology, v. 15, p. 1031–1034.

Ross, D. C., 1967a, Geologic map of the Waucoba Wash Quadrangle, Inyo County California: U.S. Geol. Surv. Geol. Quadrangle Map GQ-612, scale 1:62,500.

————, 1967b, Generalized geologic map of the Inyo Mountains region, California: U.S. Geol. Surv. Misc. Geol. Invest. Map I-506, scale 1:125,000.

Snow, J. K., 1992, Large magnitude Permian shortening and continental margin tectonics in the southern Cordillera: Geol. Soc. Amer. Bull., v. 104, p. 80–105.

Stevens, C. H., Stone, P., Dunne, G. C., Greene, D. C., Walker, J. D., and Swanson, B. J., 1997, Paleozoic and Mesozoic evolution of east-central California: Int. Geol. Rev., v. 39, p. 788–829.

Stewart, J. H., Ross, D. C., Nelson, C. A., and Burchfiel, B. C., 1966, Last Chance thrust—a major fault in the western part of Inyo County, California: U.S. Geol. Surv. Prof. Pap. 550-D, p. D23–D34.

Stewart, J. H., and Suczek, C. A., 1977, Cambrian and latest Precambrian paleogeography and tectonics in the western United States, *in* Stewart, J. H., Stevens, C. H., and Fritsche, A. E., eds., Paleozoic paleogeography of the western United States: Soc. Econ. Paleontol. and Mineral., Pacific Sect., Pacific Coast Paleogeography Symp. 1, p. 1–18.

Sylvester, A. G., and Babcock, J. W., 1975, Significance of multiphase folding in the White-Inyo Range, eastern California [abs.]: Geol. Soc. Amer., Abs. Prog., v. 7, p. 1289.

Sylvester, A. G., Miller, C. F., and Nelson, C. A., 1978, Monzonites of the White-Inyo Range, California, and their relation to the calc-alkalic Sierra Nevada batholith: Geol. Soc. Amer. Bull., v. 89, p. 1677–1687.

Welch, T. C., 1979, Superposed Mesozoic deformations in the southern White Mountains, eastern California [abs.]: Geol. Soc. Amer., Abs. Prog., v. 11, p. 134–135.

Williams, P. F., 1985, Multiply deformed terrains—problems of correlation: Jour. Struct. Geol., v. 7, p. 269–280.

Ten Plutons Revisited—A Retrospective View

KONRAD B. KRAUSKOPF

Abstract

The rapid change in ideas about the origin and significance of silicic intrusive rocks over the past 30 years is well illustrated by a succession of studies of plutons in the Mount Barcroft quadrangle and adjacent parts of the White-Inyo Range, California-Nevada.

Introduction

THE ASSORTMENT OF granitic rocks exposed in the Mount Barcroft quadrangle presented an intriguing subject for research 30 years ago (Krauskopf, 1968) and remains equally intriguing today. Our continuing interest does not reflect a lack of progress in understanding the granitic bodies, but rather the fact that the questions we ask about them today are different. The change in questioning reflects much alteration over a few decades in our ideas about how granite bodies originate and find their way into the Earth's crust. This paper surveys briefly this evolution in ideas as it applies to the components of the White-Inyo batholith.

Plutons of the Mount Barcroft Area

Siliceous intrusives in the Mount Barcroft area have a variety of sizes and of structural relations to the assemblage of slightly metamorphosed sedimentary and volcanic rocks that encloses them (Emerson, 1966; Krauskopf, 1971; Ernst et al., 1993). Back in the early 1960s when I first started puzzling over the problems of these rocks, two questions seemed especially pertinent: (1) how many granitic masses should be mapped as separable entities, and (2) what was the mechanism of their emplacement? The question of number was frustrating because most of the bodies were variable in composition and outcrops were far from continuous, so that decisions were needed recurrently as to whether a given exposure should be mapped as part of a nearby mass or as a separate intrusive. Ten bodies, or "plutons," ultimately were distinguished, but the count could as well have been half that number or twice as great. The problem of emplacement was

the familiar one in studies of granitic areas: are structural and textural relations best interpreted as indicating forcible intrusion, sloping, or making over ("granitization") of the country rock?

The state of geologic thinking about granitic rocks in the early 1960s is reflected in the quotation marks I have placed around "plutons" and "granitization" in the previous sentences. Both terms had been known for many years, but only recently had come into common use in geologic discussions. Another innovation that dates from shortly after that time was the extensive use of isotopic measurements in determining the ages of granite bodies (McKee and Nash, 1967; Crowder et al., 1973). Age data, had they been available, would have helped greatly in assigning isolated outcrops to specific granitic bodies, hence in fixing the number of plutons—but the problem would not have been completely resolved, because the many ages determined in subsequent decades are not always uniform over the rocks of any one pluton. Still another change in thinking about granites that came a bit later is the system of classification according to composition and origin, embodied in the now-familiar terms S, I, A, and M types (e.g., Ernst et al., 1993). These changes of ideas during the past 30 years suggest that in the early 1960s, granites still were regarded for the most part in the classical sense as bodies of magma that rise into the crust from some mysterious place below, shouldering aside the existing rocks or engulfing parts of them, and in places accompanied by enough heat and volatile constituents to partially transform some contact material into rock resembling that of the granite itself (e.g., Buddington, 1959).

Plutons and Plate Tectonics

Of all the changes in thinking about granites in the past three decades, the most profound, of course, has come from plate tectonics. The concept of moving plates had appeared in the early 1960s, but by the middle of the decade it still was not widely used in solving geologic problems. In short order thereafter, plate movements and plate collisions became immensely popular, and the origin of granites was nicely explained by the making over of crustal materials above a subducting plate as hot fluids rose from the descending slab. Many details still needed attention: the composition of materials in specific parts of the crust, the nature of the fluids ascending from the slab, movements of the newly formed granitic magma, interaction of the magma with its surroundings, effects of temperature and pressure, and tectonic disturbance. But granitic rocks had lost much of their mystery. No longer strange masses of liquid that somehow had risen hit-or-miss from unknown depths, they now seemed products of well-established geologic processes, formed at specific times and places during the movement and interaction of huge crustal plates. Important questions about granites were not limited to their structures and compositions, but now concerned their relations to the plate collisions from which they were generated.

Specifically, with respect to the plutons of the Mount Barcroft quadrangle, these bodies are merely a small sample out of a great chain of intrusives formed along the border between the North American plate and plates under the Pacific Ocean. Subduction of paleo-Pacific plates under the margin of North America, not once but many times since the Triassic, has led to formation of intrusive rocks that now are the backbone of many ranges, including the Sierra Nevada and the Cascades as well as the White Mountains and the Inyos (Burchfiel and Davis, 1975; Ernst et al., 1993). Therefore, a study of the Mount Barcroft plutons is no longer a matter of working out intricate details of their number, their structure, and their contacts, but now must be on a grander scale that includes the relations over time of the great crustal plates that underlie the continent and the adjacent ocean.

The change in scale does not mean that the old questions have lost their interest. We can still argue at length about the meaning of structures in each pluton, about whether its composition is closer to S type or I type, and about its relation to faults and folds in adjacent rocks. But at least we can wonder if such questions are as important as they used to seem. Should our primary attention now be focused rather on the global problems of moving plates and the relation of plutons to subduction? Should we be asking how each of the White-Inyo plutons is related to a particular encounter of the North American plate with a plate from the ocean? Questions like these, of course, have no easy answer. But at least we can say that our point of view has changed profoundly in the course of 30 years. Perhaps it is useful to ponder also whether a comparable change in thinking about the White-Inyo plutons may lie ahead in the next three decades.

REFERENCES

Buddington, A. F., 1959, Granite emplacement with special reference to North America: Geol. Soc. Amer. Bull., v. 70, p. 671–747.

Burchfiel, B. C., and Davis, G. A., 1975, Nature and controls of Cordilleran orogenesis, western United States; extensions of an earlier synthesis: Amer. Jour. Sci., v. 275-A, p. 353–396.

Crowder, D. F., McKee, E. H., Ross, D. C., and Krauskopf, K. B., 1973, Granitic rocks of the White Mountains area, California-Nevada: Age and regional significance: Geol. Soc. Amer. Bull., v. 84, p. 285–296.

Emerson, D. O., 1966, Granitic rocks of the Mt. Barcroft quadrangle, Inyo batholith, California-Nevada: Geol. Soc. Amer. Bull., v. 77, p. 127–152.

Ernst, W. G., Nelson, C. A., and Hall, C. A., 1993, Geology and metamorphic mineral assemblages of Precambrian and Cambrian rocks of the central White-Inyo range, eastern California: Calif. Div. Mines and Geol., Map Sheet 46, p. 1–25.

Krauskopf, K. B., 1968, A tale of ten plutons: Geol. Soc. Amer. Bull., v. 79, p. 1–18.

————, 1971, Geologic map of the Mt. Barcroft quadrangle, California-Nevada: U.S. Geol. Surv., Quadrangle Map GQ-960.

McKee, E. H., and Nash, D. B., 1967, Potassium-argon ages of granitic rocks in the Inyo batholiths, east-central California: Geol. Soc. Amer. Bull., v. 78, p. 669–680.

The Beer Creek-Cottonwood Igneous Contact, Southern White Mountains, California

C. A. NELSON

University of California, White Mountain Research Station, 3000 East Line Street, Bishop, California 93514

Abstract

New geologic mapping has documented the nearly E-W–trending igneous contact between two large leucocratic plutons in the White-Inyo Range of easternmost California. The megacrystic Cottonwood Granite (~170 Ma) on the north and its apophyses intrude the slightly older, medium-grained, grey Beer Creek Granodiorite on the south. Construction of this portion of the Andean calc-alkaline arc evidently was well under way by mid-Jurassic time.

Introduction

IN 1966, the quartz monzonite of Beer Creek was named for exposures of the leucocratic medium-grained plutonic rocks occupying much of the area of Deep Springs Valley and surrounding ranges (Nelson, 1966; McKee and Nelson, 1967); it is intrusive into the slightly older hornblende-augite monzonite of Joshua Flat (Nelson, 1966). At the time, it was assumed to be continuous to the north with the more porphyritic quartz monzonite named the Cottonwood Porphyritic Adamellite by Emerson (1966).

Krauskopf (1968) applied the informal name Cottonwood pluton to what then was considered to be the northern extension of the Beer Creek body. This leucocratic, uniformly porphyritic rock with large phenocrysts of potassium feldspar occupies the Cottonwood Basin and much of the surrounding area. In the Geologic Map of the Mt. Barcroft pluton, however, Krauskopf (1971) followed Nelson (1966) in naming the rocks of the Cottonwood Basin the Beer Creek, on the assumption that no contact between the two bodies existed.

In 1984, Bateman (pers. comm., February 27, 1984) made reference to a contact, observed by Krauskopf in 1974 while collecting samples for modal and chemical analysis, between leucocratic and megacrystic rock to the north (Cottonwood) and fine to medium-grained, grey, equigranular rock to the south (Beer Creek). This led to the remapping (Fig. 1) of the region of Dead Horse Meadow, in the northern end of the Blanco Mountain quadrangle, and hence

this report. The designations of Granodiorite of Beer Creek and Cottonwood Granite by Bateman (1992, Fig. 88, p. 171) are followed here.

Field Relations

The contact of the Beer Creek Granodiorite and the metasediments is grossly concordant for the entire distance from Deep Springs Valley northward to the contact with the Cottonwood Granite. In Figure 1, the metasedimentary screen is confined to small patches of recrystallized grey limestone of the Poleta Formation, and the entire thickness of the underlying Campito sandstone is overturned steeply to the west. The strongly discordant Cottonwood contact transects the Beer Creek and the metasedimentary screen down to the Deep Springs–Reed–Wyman formations. Thus, the southern edge of the Cottonwood body is marked essentially by an E-W line extending from just east of the eastern edge of Figure 1, where it is in contact with exposures of Beer Creek along a left-lateral fault. The Cottonwood contact continues eastward, where it lies against poorly exposed Beer Creek rocks and a large mass of Joshua Flat Monzonite and the uppermost units of the Lower Cambrian succession. Farther east, beyond another left-lateral fault, the Cottonwood body lies against another metasedimentary screen of Cambrian rocks for a distance of 6.5 km southeastward to its termination against the right-lateral Furnace Creek fault zone. Beyond the Furnace Creek fault zone, the Cottonwood body occurs along the eastern part of the Soldier Pass quadrangle (McKee and

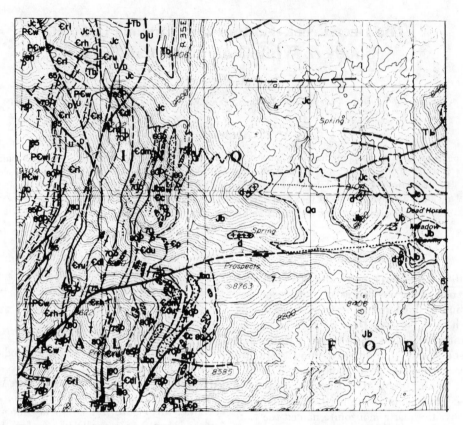

Fɪɢ. 1. Revised geologic map of Dead Horse Meadow region and accompanying legend (facing page).

Tᴀʙʟᴇ 1. Summary of Age Dates[1]

Author	Beer Creek Granodiorite	Cottonwood Granite
McKee and Nash, 1967	151 Ma—biotite 170 Ma—biotite 158 Ma—hornblende	162 Ma—biotite
McKee, 1968	170 Ma—biotite	162 Ma—biotite 155 Ma—biotite
Evernden and Kistler, 1970	174 Ma—biotite	166 Ma—biotite
Crowder et al., 1973		161 Ma—biotite 170 Ma—hornblende 176 Ma—hornblende
Gillespie, 1979	161 Ma—zircon 180 Ma—zircon	
Stern et al., 1981		168 Ma—zircon 172 Ma—zircon
McKee and Conrad, 1996		175 Ma—hornblende

[1]The Gillespie and Stern dates are Pb-U; all others are K-Ar.

Legend, Fig. 1

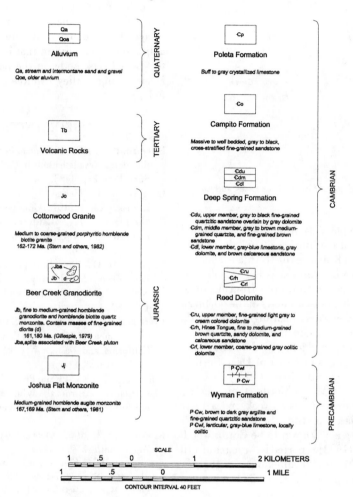

Nelson, 1967) and into the central part of the Magruder Mountain quadrangle (McKee, 1985), where it encompasses the Sylvania Mountain pluton.

In Dead Horse Meadow, the contact of the Cottonwood body diverges northwestward from the left-lateral fault. The intrusive contact is exposed for only a short distance, slightly less than one-half kilometer, where it is expressed by numerous dikes and irregular apophyses of Cottonwood cutting Beer Creek, as well as several xenoliths of Beer Creek engulfed in Cottonwood.

The critical exposures of the western boundary of the Beer Creek and the southern boundary of the Cottonwood form a "T" (Fig. 2).

Farther west the Cottonwood Granite is largely unfaulted against the metasedimentary screen rocks, which consist of overturned Campito–Deep Spring–Reed–Wyman formations, for a distance of nearly 1.5 km; this clearly illustrates the intrusive relations of the two large granitic bodies.

Age Dating

The earliest age dating of granitic rocks in the Inyo batholith was by McKee and Nash (1967), who dated three samples pertinent to this study by the K-Ar method. Their samples 5 and 6, from Beer Creek exposures, yielded biotite ages of 151 and 170 Ma and a hornblende age of 158

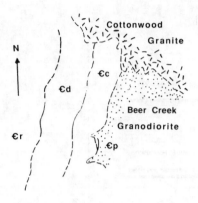

FIG. 2. T-shaped contact of the Beer Creek and Cottonwood bodies.

Ma. Their sample 7 is from the Cottonwood body and yielded a biotite age of 162 Ma. McKee (1968) reported K-Ar ages of 162 Ma (on biotite from rocks then interpreted as Beer Creek, but now known to be Cottonwood) from north of the contact with metasediments in the northern part of the Soldier Pass quadrangle and 155 Ma on biotite from rocks in the Sylvania Mountains. He also reported a biotite date of 170 Ma on Beer Creek rocks just east of Deep Springs College. Evernden and Kistler (1970) reported a K-Ar date of 174 Ma on biotite (their locality 579) on exposures of Beer Creek and a K-Ar date of 166 Ma on biotite (their locality 902) from exposures now known to be Cottonwood. Crowder et al. (1973) reported K-Ar dates of 170 Ma and 176 Ma on hornblende and 161 Ma on biotite from rocks now known to be Cottonwood.

Gillespie (1979) reported discordant Pb-U ages of 161 Ma and 180 Ma on zircon from samples of Beer Creek. Stern et al. (1981) reported a concordant age of 168 Ma and a discordant age of 172 Ma on zircon from exposures now known to be Cottonwood. In 1996, McKee and Conrad (1996) reviewed the ten plutons of Krauskopf (1968). One sample of Cottonwood yielded an age of 175 Ma. This was included under the name Beer Creek, although it is clear that the sample was collected within the Cottonwood body, as defined in this study. A summary of these age dates is presented in Table 1.

The metasedimentary rocks adjacent to the Beer Creek body contain numerous aplite dikes, which are here mapped as part of the Beer Creek

intrusive. They are assumed to be part of the main body at depth although separate at the level of erosion. They may, however, be similar in age (Cretaceous) to the numerous dikes of aplite and microgranite that occur adjacent to the Beer Creek body on the northwest side of Deep Springs Valley (McKee and Nash, 1967, Fig. 3).

REFERENCES

Bateman, P. C., 1992, Plutonism in the central part of the Sierra Nevada batholith, California: U.S. Geol. Surv. Prof. Pap. 1483, 186 p.

Crowder, D. F., McKee, E. H., Ross, D. C., and Krauskopf, K. B., 1973, Granitic rocks of the White Mountains area, California-Nevada—age and regional significance: Geol. Soc. Amer. Bull., v. 84, no. 5, p. 385–396.

Emerson, D. O., 1966, Granitic rocks of the Mount Barcroft quadrangle, Inyo batholith, California-Nevada: Geol. Soc. Amer. Bull., v. 77, no. 2, p. 127–152.

Evernden, J. F., and Kistler, R. W., 1970, Chronology of emplacement of Mesozoic batholithic complexes in California and western Nevada: U.S. Geol. Surv. Prof. Pap. 623, 42 p.

Gillespie, J. G., Jr., U-Pb and Pb-Pb ages of primary and detrital zircons from the White Mountains, eastern California [abs.]: Geol. Soc. Amer. Abs. Prog., v. 11, p. 79.

Krauskopf, K. B., 1968, A tale of ten plutons: Geol. Soc. Amer. Bull., v. 79, p. 1–18.

——, 1971, Geologic map of the Mt. Barcroft pluton, California-Nevada: U.S. Geol. Surv. Geol. Quad. Map GQ-960, scale 1:62,500.

McKee, E. H., 1968 Geology of the Magruder Mountain area, Nevada-California: U.S. Geol. Surv. Bull. 1250-IH, 40 p.

——, 1985, Geologic map of the Magruder Mountain quadrangle, Esmeralda County, Nevada, and Inyo County, California: U.S. Geol. Surv. Geol. Quad. Map 1587, scale 1:62,500.

McKee, E. H., and Conrad, J. E., 1996, A tale of 10 plutons—revisited: Age of granitic rocks in the White Mountains, California and Nevada: Geol. Soc. Amer. Bull., v. 108, no. 12, p. 1515–1527.

McKee, E. H., and Nash, D. B., 1967, Potassium-argon ages of granitic rocks in the Inyo batholith, east-central California: Geol. Soc. Amer. Bull., v. 78, p. 669–680.

McKee, E. H., and Nelson, C. A., 1967, Geologic map of the Soldier Pass quadrangle: U.S. Geol. Surv. Geol. Quad. Map GQ-654, scale 1:62,500.

Nelson, C. A., 1966, Geologic map of the Blanco Mountain quadrangle, Inyo and Mono counties, California: U.S. Geol. Surv. Geol. Quad. Map 529, scale 1:62,500.

Stern, T. W., Bateman, P. C., Morgan, B. A., Newell, M. F., and Peck, D. L., 1981, Isotopic U-96 ages of zircon from the granitoids of the central Sierra Nevada: U.S. Geol. Surv. Prof. Pap. 1185, 17 p.

Depositional Sequence Stratigraphy of Lower Cambrian Grand Cycles, Southern Great Basin, U.S.A.

Jeffrey F. Mount and Katherine J. Bergk

Department of Geology, University of California, Davis, California 95616

Abstract

The Lower Cambrian of the southern Great Basin records third-order cyclical alternation between siliciclastic- and carbonate-dominated sedimentation in a rapidly subsiding passive margin. These alternations, termed Grand Cycles, are a prominent feature of Cambrian stratigraphy on the Laurentian continent and have been the subject of study for more than 30 years. A sequence-stratigraphic analysis of Lower Cambrian Grand Cycles in the southern Great Basin indicates that the alternating siliciclastic- and carbonate-dominated depositional systems record cyclical changes in accommodation volume along the Laurentian passive margin. In outer ramp/platform settings, type-1 sequence boundaries coincide with the top of the carbonate half-cycle; in mid-ramp settings, the sequence boundaries lie within the siliciclastic half-cycle. Thick depositional sequences contain well-developed lowstand wedge, transgressive, and highstand systems tracts. Thinner depositional sequences lack a well-developed lowstand systems tract.

At least five (and as many as seven) third-order cycles of accommodation change, superimposed on a long-term, second-order cycle, are preserved in the Lower Cambrian of the southern Great Basin. This study, like most studies, supports the view that Grand Cycles, and their associated depositional sequences, are a product of cyclical eustatic changes in sea level. However, this does not rule out the possibility that allogenic forcing resulting from changes in climate also played an important role. Periods of wet/cool climate may have promoted siliciclastic half-cycle development, whereas periods of dry/warm climate promoted carbonate half-cycles.

Introduction

During the Cambrian Period, the northern edge of Laurentia (currently the N-S–trending margin of western North America) was a passive margin that accumulated a thick succession of basin, slope, shelf, coastal-plain, and braidplain sediments. One of the more distinctive aspects of this sedimentary pile is the large-scale alternation between siliciclastic- and carbonate-dominated units. First termed "Grand Cycles" by Aitken (1966), these alternations have been widely interpreted to reflect synchronous, regional shifts in depositional conditions on the Laurentian margin in response to eustatic change in sea level.

During the past 15 years, the concepts and principles of sequence stratigraphy, which involves the subdivision of strata into genetic packages bounded by unconformities and their correlative conformities, have come to dominate the manner in which we describe, categorize, and interpret the stratigraphic record

(reviews in Posamentier et al., 1993; Christie-Blick and Driscoll, 1995; Van Wagoner, 1995). Grand Cycles have not escaped re-interpretation using the modern methods of sequence stratigraphy (discussed below), with numerous authors assigning sequence boundaries and systems tracts to various, often conflicting, portions of the cycle.

In this paper, we reexamine the lithostratigraphic and biostratigraphic record of Lower Cambrian Grand Cycles of the southern Great Basin using sequence-stratigraphic concepts. The goal of this paper is to critically evaluate previous attempts to identify sequence boundaries and systems tracts within these Lower Cambrian units. We present a speculative model that links alternation between carbonate and siliciclastic depositional systems to third-order cyclical changes in the creation and destruction of the volume available for accumulation of sediment. We find that the diachronous boundaries of Grand Cycles do not

180

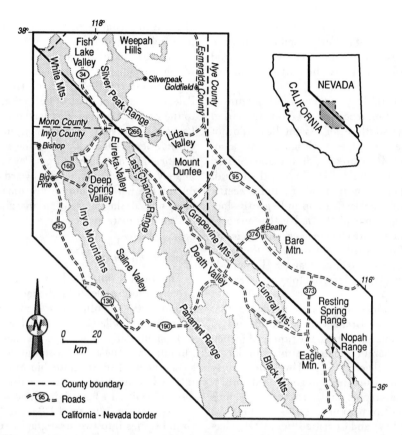

Fig. 1. Index map of the southern Great Basin illustrating the distribution of pertinent upper Precambrian and Lower Cambrian outcrops.

correlate everywhere with sequence boundaries. For this reason, in this paper Grand Cycles are not considered synomymous with depositional sequences. In addition, although we interpret Lower Cambrian accommodation cycles as a function of eustatic sea-level change, the lithologic character of the cycles may record periodic climate change as well.

Lower Cambrian Grand Cycles

Paleotectonic and paleogeographic setting

Lower Cambrian strata crop out extensively in the Cordillera, with particularly thick, heterolithic units occurring in the southern Great Basin (Stewart, 1970). The best-studied and most complete Lower Cambrian section of the Great Basin occurs in a belt stretching from the White-Inyo/Esmeralda County, Nevada region to the Death Valley region (Fig. 1). Mesozoic

and Cenozoic tectonics have dismembered portions of this belt, shifting the relative paleogeographic position of outcrops. However, palinspastic reconstructions by Levy and Christie-Blick (1989) indicate that the general spatial relationships between Death Valley and White-Inyo/Esmeralda County outcrops remain relatively intact.

Lower Cambrian units of the Great Basin form a roughly N-S–striking, W-thickening sedimentary wedge. The asymmetrical geometry of these units reflects rapid thermotectonic subsidence of the passive margin following a late Proterozoic rifting event, with the most rapid subsidence taking place in the most basinward locations (Stewart and Suczeck, 1977; Levy and Christie-Blick, 1991). In the southern Great Basin, depositional strike was oriented NE-SW, with the White-Inyo/Esmeralda County region representing the most basinward deposits and the Death Valley region the most cratonward. A

N-S–oriented tectonic hingeline, which marks the eastward extent of Early Cambrian thermotectonic subsidence, is inferred by Stewart and Suczeck (1977) to lie to the north and east of the Death Valley region.

The sedimentology and facies architecture of uppermost Proterozoic and Lower Cambrian units of the southwestern Great Basin do not reflect a well-developed shelf-margin and associated shelf-slope break (Mount and Signor, 1989; Mount et al., 1991). Rather, the overall basin geometry appears to alternate between a low-gradient siliciclastic ramp and a gently sloping carbonate ramp/platform. For the purposes of this paper, the area located near the hingeline (Death Valley area) is referred to as the inner ramp; the most basinward areas (Esmeralda County, Nevada) are referred to as outer ramp/platform.

Although most workers acknowledge that Lower Cambrian Grand Cycles were deposited in a passive-margin setting, the timing of formation of this margin remains a subject of debate (review in Dalziel, 1997). This uncertainty stems, in part, from the ambiguous and contradictory stratigraphic and structural evidence for a rift-drift transition and associated crustal extension (Levy and Christie-Blick, 1991). Tectonic subsidence curves developed by Bond et al. (1989) and Levy and Christie-Blick (1991) point toward continental separation during the very latest Proterozoic, with dramatic post-rift thermal subsidence occurring during the Early Cambrian.

The paleogeographic and associated paleoclimatologic setting of the Early Cambrian Laurentian passive margin also is a subject of recent controversy. Paleomagnetic-pole data for the Early Cambrian of Laurentia and other continents show a high degree of variability and, presumably, reliability (reviews in Van der Voo, 1994; Torsvik et al., 1996). Recently, Kirschvink et al. (1997) have noted that the highly varied paleomagnetic-pole data for units of latest Proterozoic and Cambrian age represent a global phenomenon and may reflect a short period of extremely fast plate motion. Apparent polar wander paths from Laurentia and Gondwana illustrate dramatic rotations of as much as 90° during the Early Cambrian, implying plate motions at rates higher than 30 cm/year, a rate unmatched in modern settings and, for many,

difficult to reconcile with modern understanding of plate mechanics.

The Kirschvink et al. (1997) hypothesis, which remains to be tested, has important implications for the origin of Grand Cycles. Paleomagnetic-pole data indicate that just prior to the Early Cambrian, the northern margin of Laurentia (current western margin) lay at a latitude of more than 40° S; by the early Middle Cambrian, this same margin lay at approximately 10° N. This 50° northward migration during the Early Cambrian presumably would have moved the Laurentian margin through multiple climate belts over a relatively short period of time.

Stratigraphic setting

The term Grand Cycle was first used by Aitken (1966) to describe the large-scale alternation between siliciclastic- and carbonate-dominated Middle Cambrian to Lower Ordovician shelf deposits of the Canadian Rocky Mountains. These lithostratigraphic cycles span one to two trilobite biozones, and are inferred to be capped by a regionally correlative disconformity. In his original and subsequent papers, Aitken (1966, 1978, 1989) divided Grand Cycles into two stratigraphic units. The basal unit was termed the "shaly half-cycle" for its preponderance of fine terrigenous material (referred to here as the siliciclastic half-cycle). In Middle and Upper Cambrian strata, this half-cycle typically consists of interstratified shallow subtidal to intertidal siltstones and mudstones with lesser amounts of subtidal carbonate. The siliciclastic half-cycle is gradationally overlain by a carbonate-dominated unit, termed the "carbonate half-cycle," which typically contains a range of peritidal lithofacies. Aitken also noted that the shaly half-cycle contained numerous subcycles that broadly mimic the overall Grand Cycles.

On the basis of trilobite biostratigraphy and the regional stratigraphy described by Nelson (1962, 1976), Fritz (1975) defined three Lower Cambrian Grand Cycles in the southern Great Basin (Fig. 2). Termed A, B, and C, these Grand Cycles range in thickness from less than 100 m in the Death Valley region near their stratigraphic pinchout to more than a kilometer in the White-Inyo/Esmeralda County region (Fig. 3). Fritz (1975) limited his observations to what

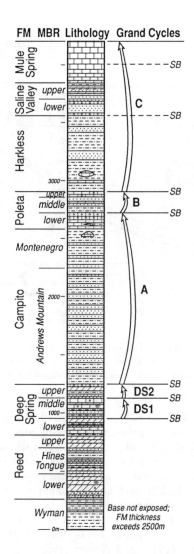

FIG. 2. Uppermost Precambrian and Lower Cambrian stratigraphy of the White-Inyo/Esmeralda County, Nevada region illustrating the location of Grand Cycle boundaries and sequence boundaries (SB). Grand Cycles A, B, and C were originally defined by Fritz (1975). Grand Cycles DS1 and DS2 were defined by Mount et al. (1991). Within the outer-ramp/platform areas, the major sequence boundaries coincide with Grand Cycle boundaries. This is not true for inner-ramp settings.

was then believed to be the Lower Cambrian. In later work, Mount et al. (1991) described at least two pre-trilobite Lower Cambrian Grand Cycles, termed DS1 and DS2 for their expression within the Deep Spring Formation (Fig. 2).

In his original study of Lower Cambrian Grand Cycles, Fritz (1975) concentrated his observations in the more basinward exposures of the southern Great Basin. In a later study, Palmer and Halley (1979) argued that the carbonate half-cycle of Lower Cambrian Grand Cycle C—represented by the Eagle Mountain, Thimble Limestone, Echo Shale, and Gold Ace Limestone members of the Carrara Formation in the Death Valley region—could be subdivided into at least two Grand Cycles (Fig. 3).

In a stratigraphic analysis of the Zabriskie Quartzite in the Death Valley region, Prave (1992) argued for the placement of a Grand Cycle boundary at the facies dislocation that occurs at the contact between the Resting Springs and Emigrant Pass members of the Zabriskie Quartzite (Fig. 3). Prave (1992), like most recent authors (discussion below), assumed that Lower Cambrian Grand Cycle boundaries are sequence boundaries and that all Lower Cambrian sequence boundaries are, in turn, Grand Cycle boundaries. Based on the stratigraphic position of this facies dislocation, he inferred that it was the Grand Cycle B/C contact. As is shown below, the assumption that Grand Cycle boundaries and sequence boundaries are the same, especially for more cratonward exposures, may not be valid. However, this does not rule out Prave's suggestion that a sequence boundary, lying within Grand Cycle C rather than at its boundaries, occurs at this contact.

It is important to note that Lower Cambrian Grand Cycles differ significantly from their Middle and Upper Cambrian counterparts. The most striking differences lie in the "shaly" or siliciclastic half-cycles. The siliciclastic half-cycle of Middle and Upper Cambrian units typically is very fine grained and contains abundant mixed siliciclastic-carbonate subcycles or parasequences (Aitken, 1978). In contrast, most Lower Cambrian Grand Cycles are more siliciclastic rich, with complete absence of carbonate in the lower portions of some half-cycles. Thick, fluvial conglomerates and sandstones occur in at least two Lower Cambrian cycles (A and C). Lower Cambrian carbonate half-cycles contain fewer well-developed Milankovitch-style peritidal cycles (see Adams and Grotzinger, 1996) and a greater overall abundance of dolomite than do younger cycles.

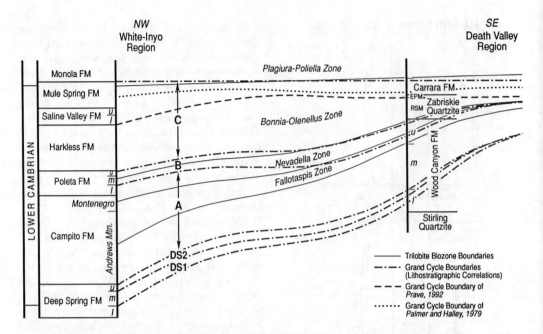

Fig. 3. Lithostratigraphic cross section of the Lower Cambrian, White-Inyo Region to the Death Valley region, southern Great Basin, illustrating lithostratigraphic correlation of Grand Cycles DS1, DS2, A, B, and C, and estimated correlation of trilobite biozones. Note that biozone boundaries cross Grand Cycle boundaries. See text for discussion.

In addition, Lower Cambrian cycles A, B, and C contain wave-resistant, ecological reefs, usually composed of archaeocyathan and calcimicrobe framebuilders (Rowland, 1984). These kinds of reef-builders were absent from Middle and Upper Cambrian Grand Cycles.

Biostratigraphy

An essential element of the evaluation of Grand Cycles as depositional sequences is a biostratigraphic evaluation of the isochroneity of their boundaries. Although there was rapid turnover of most Early Cambrian taxonomic groups, the biostratigraphic resolution of this interval in the southern Great Basin remains relatively weak (Signor and Mount, 1989; Mount and Signor, 1992). Three trilobite zones—the *Fallotaspis*, *Nevadella*, and *Bonnia-Olenellus*—remain the standard for regional biostratigraphic correlation, with support from key archaeocyathan taxa (Nelson, 1962, 1976). The pre-trilobite interval of the Lower Cambrian is sparsely fossiliferous, affording little opportunity for correlation.

In his original description of Lower Cambrian Grand Cycles from the Esmeralda County

and White-Inyo region, Fritz (1975) suggested that Lower Cambrian trilobite biozones do not cross Grand Cycle boundaries. On the basis of this apparent relationship, he argued that Lower Cambrian Grand Cycle boundaries are, like their Middle and Upper Cambrian counterparts, isochronous surfaces.

In their detailed examination of the upper Lower Cambrian in Death Valley, Palmer and Halley (1979) and Palmer (1981) argued that close scrutiny of trilobite data reveals that not all Grand Cycle boundaries are isochronous. This observation was corroborated by Hunt (1990) and Mount et al. (1991), who noted that Lower Cambrian biozones cross both Grand Cycle boundaries and siliciclastic half-cycle/carbonate half-cycle transitions.

We have constructed a regional cross section of the southern Great Basin that compares our lithostratigraphic and biostratigraphic correlations of Lower Cambrian Grand Cycles (Fig. 3). We acknowledge that facies control can influence the pattern of trilobite biozones by controlling the apparent timing of first and last appearances of key taxa (discussions in Mount and Signor, 1986, 1992; Mount et al., 1991).

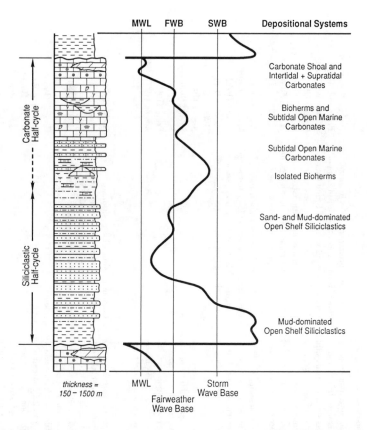

FIG. 4. Generalized facies succession for an idealized Grand Cycle in the outer-ramp/platform region illustrating depositional systems and approximate placement of sequence boundaries and systems tracts (modified from Mount et al., 1991).

However, at present, trilobite biozones offer the highest level of biostratigraphic resolution in the Lower Cambrian.

The crossing of biozone and lithostratigraphic boundaries has important implications for the interpretation of Lower Cambrian Grand Cycles. It appears that carbonate sedimentation characteristic of the carbonate half-cycle began first in mid-ramp settings and shifted progressively seaward until the eventual termination of the cycle. In addition, contacts between Grand Cycles, recognized by the transition from carbonate to siliciclastic strata, are not regional disconformities. Rather, initiation of siliciclastic deposition, typically assumed to be part of the next Grand Cycle, occurred in mid-ramp settings prior to termination of carbonate sedimentation in outer-ramp/platform settings.

Lower Cambrian depositional systems and Grand Cycles

Lower Cambrian Grand Cycles exhibit a broad array of sedimentary environments typical of early Paleozoic ramp/platform settings. Nearly 40 different sedimentary environments have been described from the Lower Cambrian of the southern Great Basin (see summaries in Mount et al., 1991; Prave, 1992; Adams, 1993, 1995). For the purpose of this review, we have grouped genetically linked environments into nine depositional systems. Their sedimentary features and stratigraphic distribution are summarized in Table 1.

Using a synthesis of published descriptions and an application of biostratigraphic constraints outlined above, we have developed a model stratigraphic succession for Grand Cycle deposition in inner- and outer-ramp settings

TABLE 1. Depositional Systems and Systems Tracts of Lower Cambrian Grand Cycles

Depositional system	Paleoenvironments	Lithology	Depositional sequences and systems tracts	Data sources
		Siliciclastic-dominated		
Braidplain/braid delta	Braided river channels and floodplains, tidally influenced braid delta channels, distal alluvial-fan channels	Channelized arkosic conglomerates, medium- to coarse-grained trough and tabular/planar cross-stratified feldspathic arenites, lenticular and flaser-bedded siltstones, mud-chip conglomerates, desiccation features, and low-diversity or absent trace- and body-fossil assemblages.	Form thick, prominent units in inner- and mid-ramp areas. Significant component of lowstand wedge of Grand Cycles A and C. May occur in portions of DS1. Common at base of depositional sequences. Often associated with regional erosion at sequence boundary.	Diehl (1974, 1979); Prave and Wright (1986); Fedo and Cooper (1990); Hunt (1990); Mount et al. (1991); Prave (1992)
Mud-dominated intertidal	Includes mid- to high-intertidal, supratidal, and tidal channel deposits as well as shallow-subtidal to intertidal lagoon and interdistributary bay deposits	Thinning-fining- or coarsening-thickening-upward successions of siltstone/mudstone and lesser amounts of channelized quartz arenite and feldspathic arenite. Flaser, wavy, and lenticular bedding, abundant small-current, wave, and combined flow ripples, climbing ripples, desiccation features, trough and tabular cross-stratification, reactivation surfaces and rare mud chips; relatively low diversity, but abundant trace fossils and rare body fossils.	Abundant in all depositional sequences. Prominent in outer-ramp lowstand wedge systems tracts, inner-ramp transgressive and highstand systems tracts.	Diehl (1974, 1979); Moore (1976); Mount (1982a, 1982b); Dienger (1986); Mount and Signor (1986, 1989, 1992); Hunt (1990); Mount et al. (1991); Prave (1992); Adams (1993, 1995)
Sand-dominated low intertidal/shoreface	Environments of energetic, sand-dominated low intertidal, foreshore, and shoreface settings	Range of medium- to fine-grained quartz and feldspathic arenites. Trough and tabular cross-stratified sands with abundant reactivation surfaces, small-current ripples, climbing ripples and rare mud-chip conglomerates. Swaley and hummocky cross-stratification, parallel lamination in fine-grained deposits. Body fossils nearly absent; abundant trace fossils typical of energetic marine environments. Includes frequently described medium-grained mixed siliciclastic and carbonate sediments. Dienger (1986) demonstrated that these deposits are part of the spectrum of energetic, transgressive, low intertidal deposits.	Common within all depositional sequences. Prominent in outer-ramp transgressive systems tract of DS1, B; across entire ramp in lowstand systems tract and transgressive systems tracts of A and C.	Diehl (1974, 1979); Moore (1976); Mount and Signor (1985, 1989); Dienger (1986); Greene (1986); Prave and Wright (1986); Mount et al. (1991); Prave (1992); Adams (1993, 1995)

Sand-dominated open shelf	Inner-shelf depositional settings at or below fairweather wave base but above storm wave base.	Fine-grained feldspathic/quartz arenites interstratified with dark-colored siltstones and mudstones, allochemic sandstones, and sandy allochemic limestones. Laterally continuous, often amalgamated sand bodies with sharp, erosional bases and gradational tops. Hummocky cross-stratification, combined flow and wave ripples and structures indicative of soft-sediment deformation. Highest trace-fossil diversity and abundance, and for Grand Cycles A and B, moderately diverse body-fossil assemblages.	Occurs in all depositional sequences. Prominent in outer-ramp and mid-ramp lowstand systems tracts and transgressive systems tracts of DS2, A, and C.	Diehl (1974, 1979); Mount (1980, 1982); Mount and Signor, (1985, 1989, 1992); Greene (1986); Hunt (1990); Mount et al. (1991); Prave (1992)
		Carbonate-dominated		
Mud-dominated open shelf	Dominated by accumulation of muds in paleodepths near or below storm wavebase	Dark green to black, bioturbated mudstones and siltstones with thin, laterally continuous sandstone interbeds. Parallel laminae, small-current, and combined-flow ripples with rare flaser and lenticular bedding. Trace fossils abundant and diverse; within Grand Cycle A and B there are highly diverse body-fossil assemblages.	Occurs in all depositional sequences. Prominent in outer-ramp transgressive systems tracts and lower highstand systems tracts of DS2, A, B, and C. Occurs near base of sequence boundary in outer-ramp lowstand systems tract of A.	Moore (1976); Mount and Signor, (1985, 1989, 1992); Greene (1986); Adams (1993, 1995)
Carbonate shoal	Includes all carbonate deposits that accumulated in energetic shoal environments. Dominated by oölite shoals.	Primarily trough and tabular cross-stratified oölitic and peloidal grainstones with lesser quartz sand. Contain discrete horizons reflecting episodic emergence, meteoric cementation, and recrystallization. Additional shoal units consist of trough and tabular cross-stratified bioclastic grainstones, dolomitic grainstones, and sandy allochemic dolostones.	Common in all depositional sequences. Prominent in outer- and mid-ramp/platform highstand systems tracts of DS2, A, B, and C.	Moore (1976); Rowland (1978); Diehl (1979); Mount (1980); Mount and Rowland (1981); Greene (1986); Hunt (1990); Mount et al. (1991); Adams (1993, 1995)

(continued)

TABLE 1. (*continued*)

Depositional system	Paleoenvironments	Lithology	Depositional sequences and systems tracts	Data sources
Intertidal and supratidal	Restricted or evaporitic carbonate lagoons, intertidal flats, evaporitic supratidal environments, and tidal channels	Dominated by dolomicrite and peloidal dolowackestones and dolopackstones. Tepee structures, desiccation structures, evaporite psuedomorphs, and low, laterally linked stromatolites rare; small-current ripples, parallel laminae, cryptalgal lamination, fenestral or birdseye fabric, intraclast horizons, and mud cracks locally abundant. Low-diversity trace and body fossils.	Irregularly distributed within depositional sequences. Common in mid-ramp and outer-ramp/platform of highstand systems tracts of DS2, A, and B. Most common in highstand systems tract of C.	(Diehl, 1974, 1979); Moore (1976); Mount and Rowland (1981); Mount and Signor (1985, 1989, 1992); Greene (1986); Hunt (1990); Mount et al. (1991); Adams (1993, 1995)
Subtidal, open marine	Records normal marine, shallow subtidal environments that lay above and below storm wave base. May have accumulated in open shelf or back-bank settings.	Interstratified peloidal and bioclastic grainstones, packstones, and wackestones with rare lime mudstones and subtidal algal laminites. Admixtures of siliciclastic silt and fine sand common. Contain combined flow and small-current ripples and parallel lamination. Bioturbation locally abundant. In Grand Cycles A and B, body fossils reach peak diversity within subtidal carbonates.	Preserved primarily within outer-ramp/platform settings of highstand systems tracts. Most prominent in early and late highstand systems tract of A and C.	Moore (1976); Rowland (1978); Mount and Rowland (1981); Mount and Signor (1985, 1989, 1992); Greene (1986); Hunt (1990); Mount et al. (1991); Adams (1993, 1995)
Bioherm	Includes all biologically controlled build-ups. Dominated by archaeocyathan and calcimicrobe bioherms.	Co-occurrence of archaeocyathans and calcimicrobes such as *Renalcis* and *Epiphyton*. Bioherms occur as isolated, *Renalcis*-dominated, archaeocyathan framestones and bafflestones built on subtidal siliciclastic or carbonate muds; as framestones and bindstones in shallow, energetic environments; and as ecologically zoned, internally cavernous reefs.	Makes up relatively small portion of depositional sequences. Occurs in transgressive systems tract/highstand systems tract transition in outer- and mid-ramp/platform of A and B; occurs in lowstand wedge/transgressive systems tract transition of C.	Diehl (1974, 1979); Rowland (1978, 1984); Mount (1980); Mount and Rowland (1981); Mount and Signor (1985, 1989); Savarese and Signor (1989); Hunt (1990); Mount et al. (1991)

(Fig. 4). This represents a modification of the model first proposed in Mount et al. (1991) and accommodates several key elements of Lower Cambrian Grand Cycles, including: (1) apparent abrupt termination of the carbonate half-cycle and initiation of the overlying siliciclastic half-cycle in outer-ramp/platform settings; (2) deepening-shoaling-deepening facies successions in outer-ramp settings of siliciclastic half-cycles; (3) sharp, erosional bases overlain by a succession of coarse fluvial to coastal-plain deposits in thick, inner-shelf Grand Cycles (A and C); (4) fine-grained, shallow subtidal to intertidal deposits at the base of thin Grand Cycle sequences (DS1, DS2, B); (5) gradational and diachronous siliciclastic-carbonate half-cycle transitions with apparent seaward progradation of ramp carbonate sedimentation during the latter half of the cycle; (6) karsted surfaces at the Grand Cycle boundary in outer-ramp/platform settings; and (7) siliciclastic tidal channels within and near the top of some carbonate half-cycles, reflecting siliciclastic bypass of carbonate ramp depocenters prior to formation of the Grand Cycle boundary. The following sequence-based analysis of the origin of Grand Cycles is predicated upon these key observations.

Sequence Stratigraphy of Lower Cambrian Grand Cycles

Background

Sequence stratigraphy is based upon the recognition and interpretation of depositional sequences within sedimentary basin fill. Depositional sequences, as originally defined by Mitchum et al. (1977), are "conformable successions of genetically related strata bound at their base and top by unconformities and their correlative conformities." It is beyond the scope of this paper to thoroughly review the concepts of depositional sequence stratigraphy. Excellent summaries, including the necessary definitions that accompany the burgeoning sequence-stratigraphic terminology, are contained in Mitchum and Van Wagoner (1991), Posamentier et al. (1993), Christie-Blick and Driscoll (1995), Christie-Blick et al. (1995), and Van Wagoner (1995). The key features of sequence stratigraphy, as it applies to analysis

of Grand Cycles in outcrop, are summarized below.

The formation of depositional sequences, and their internal facies architecture, is a response to the interplay between basin subsidence (or uplift), eustatic sea-level change, and the abundance and composition of sediment supply. The result of these interactions is spatial and temporal change in *accommodation volume*, or the space available to accumulate sediment. Cyclical change in the rate of generation or destruction of accommodation volume in a sedimentary basin drives the formation of multiple sequence boundaries and dictates the geometry, dynamics, and character of depositional systems. Although depositional sequences can form from infinite combinations of sea level, subsidence, and sediment supply, in the vast majority of published examples, it is assumed (although rarely proven) that accommodation change is driven by eustatic changes in sea level.

The goal of sequence-stratigraphic analysis is to identify the surfaces that bound depositional sequences and to distinguish aspects of the sedimentary units that can be tied to various phases of an accommodation cycle (again, usually assumed to be a eustatic sea-level cycle). The unconformities and their correlative conformities that bound depositional sequences have been grouped into two classes—type 1 and type 2—primarily on the basis of their expression in seismic sections. Type-1 sequence boundaries are associated with extensive subaerial erosion of the shelf, rejuvenation of rivers and streams, and dramatic basinward shifts in facies and coastal onlap. The formation of a type-1 sequence boundary is caused by a significant decline in accommodation volume, leading to relative sea-level decline, coupled with erosion and sediment bypass of the shelf. Type-1 sequence boundaries are the most easily recognized in outcrop studies. They typically exhibit the strongest evidence for development of a regional unconformity or disconformity, including formation of incised valleys and sharp facies dislocations that juxtapose coarse fluvial units on top of shallow-marine sandstones and mudstones. In ramp-like settings similar to those examined in this study, the lack of a shelf-slope break precludes the formation of deep fluvial incision at the sequence boundary, making it difficult to recognize sequence boundaries. This is especially true in interfluve areas where marine shale-on-shale contacts may occur at the sequence boundary. Type-2 sequence boundaries are formed when declines in the rate of generation of accommodation volume lead to basinward shifts in coastal onlap. Because this involves a decline in the *rate* of generation of accommodation volume, and not widespread destruction of accommodation volume, type-2 sequences are not associated with dramatic relative sea-level fall and widespread erosion typical of type-1 sequence boundaries.

The sedimentary deposits that make up a depositional sequence are used to reconstruct discrete episodes of accommodation change. This is accomplished through analysis of *systems tracts*, the fundamental mapping units of depositional sequences. Systems tracts are discrete packets of genetically linked, contemporaneous deposits. Their internal geometry, as well as their boundaries, indicates shifts in onlap and offlap, as well as changes in the relationship between rate of accommodation-volume creation and sediment supply. The internal geometry of systems tracts usually is reflected in stacked facies successions. Termed *parasequences*, or parasequence sets, these successions typically consist of beds or bedsets that are bounded by marine flooding surfaces.

Four different systems tracts are inferred to reflect variations in the accommodation cycle—*lowstand systems tracts, shelf-margin systems tracts, transgressive systems tracts*, and *highstand systems tracts*. In type-1 depositional sequences on ramp margins, the lowstand systems tract is usually referred to as a lowstand wedge (Van Wagoner et al., 1988). Formed during a period of relative decline in sea level followed by a slow relative rise, the lowstand wedge typically consists of incised valley-fill deposits in the up-dip inner ramp, and progradational to aggradational parasequence sets in the down-dip outer ramp. In type-2 depositional sequences, the decline in the rate of creation of accommodation volume across the sequence boundary leads to the formation of shelf-margin systems tracts. Where recognizable, shelf-margin systems tracts are composed of progradational to aggradational parasequence sets. The transgressive systems tract comprises the middle systems tracts of both type-1 and type-2 sequences. It forms in response to rapid increases in the rate of generation of accom-

modation volume, leading to relative sea-level rise and retrogradational parasequence stacking patterns. The contact between the transgressive systems tract and the underlying systems tract or sequence boundary is called the *transgressive surface*. Declines in the rate of generation of new accommodation volume leads to the formation of the uppermost systems tract in both type-1 and type-2 depositional sequences—the highstand systems tract. The contact between the highstand systems tract and the underlying systems tract is the *maximum flooding surface*, representing the maximum landward migration of the shoreline. The parasequence stacking patterns in highstand systems tracts typically are aggradational followed by progradational.

The tectonic, eustatic, and sedimentary processes that drive the formation of depositional sequences operate at a range of superimposed scales and frequencies. This has led workers to develop a hierarchical classification of sequences based on their relative order of duration (summary in Mitchum and Van Wagoner, 1991). First-order stratigraphic cycles have durations of 50 m.y. or more and are associated with long-term cycles of onlap and offlap of the supercontinents. Second-order cycles range from 5 to 50 m.y. or more. These cycles, which typically consist of multiple, stacked depositional sequences that reflect an overall onlap-offlap trend, are referred to as supersequences. Third-order cycles, with a duration of approximately 0.5 to 5 m.y., are the scale of cycle commonly associated with depositional sequences. As Mitchum and Van Wagoner (1991) and others have pointed out, many third-order sequences are actually *composite sequences*, where successions of genetically related higher-order sequences stack into lowstand, transgressive, and highstand sequence sets.

Sequence-stratigraphic model

A synthetic model for an ideal Lower Cambrian depositional sequence is presented in Figures 5 and 6. This model incorporates and reconciles the seven key stratigraphic criteria noted above, including the assumption that Grand Cycle boundaries do not precisely correlate everywhere with depositional sequence boundaries. This model is based primarily on

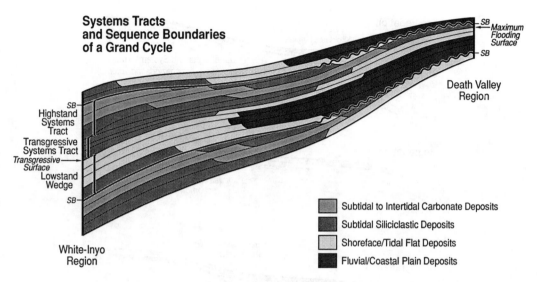

FIG. 5. Sequence-stratigraphic cross section of an idealized, thick depositional sequence. See text for discussion.

the thickest depositional sequence of the section, which includes most of the units of Grand Cycle A. The thinner depositional sequences (approximately correlative with Grand Cycles DS1, DS2, and B) are incomplete and may not contain all of the systems tracts shown in Figure 5. Two additional depositional sequences occur within the thick sequence that correlates approximately with Grand Cycle C (after Palmer and Halley, 1979; Prave, 1992; and Adams, 1995). These are inferred to be higher-order sequences within a composite depositional sequence.

On the basis of trace-fossil and body-fossil data (Signor and Mount, 1986, 1989; Mount and Signor, 1992), the Grand Cycles described here span an interval from the mid-Tommotian, near the base of the Cambrian System, through the end of the Toyonian at the Lower–Middle Cambrian boundary. Recent radiometric dates (Grotzinger et al., 1995) indicate that the duration of this interval is ~15 m.y. This points to an average duration of close to 3 m.y. for the five Grand Cycles, consistent with third-order cyclicity. However, if a relatively constant sedimentation rate is assumed for each of the five Grand Cycles, their duration varies from a minimum of approximately 0.6 m.y. (DS2), a possible fourth-order cycle, to a maximum of 7.3 m.y. (A), a possible second-order cycle.

Grand Cycle and sequence boundaries

The regional biostratigraphic studies cited here indicate that the tops of Grand Cycles A, B, and C are diachronous surfaces. The transition from carbonate-dominated to siliciclastic-dominated sedimentation that defines Grand Cycle tops appears to take place first in mid-ramp settings and later in outer-ramp/platform settings. Therefore, as noted above, by definition Lower Cambrian Grand Cycle boundaries are *not* regionally correlative depositional-sequence boundaries since the Grand Cycle tops do not correspond exactly with the bounding unconformity. However, as discussed in Mount et al. (1991), this does not preclude the possibility that Grand Cycle boundaries coincide locally with sequence boundaries and that most Grand Cycles *approximate* depositional sequences.

Multiple type-1 sequence boundaries can be placed within the Lower Cambrian section on the basis of evidence for widespread erosion coupled with sharp basinward shifts in facies. In outer-ramp/platform settings, Grand Cycle tops and sequence boundaries appear to coincide. The cycle tops typically are eroded and exhibit well-developed karst, indicating emergence of the outer carbonate ramp/platform and a drop in relative sea level prior to initiation of siliciclastic deposition (Mount et al., 1991; Bergk et al., 1996). In more proximal

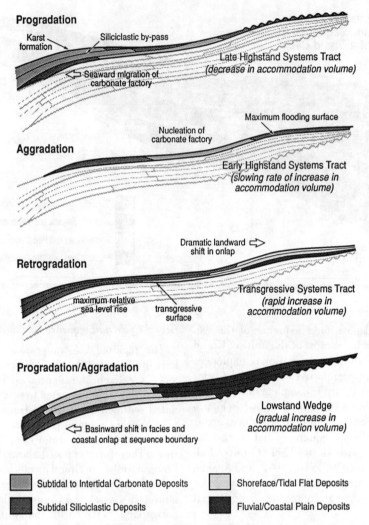

FIG. 6. Evolution of an idealized thick, siliciclastic-rich depositional sequence. Symbols are similar to those shown in Figure 5. See text for discussion.

sections of the Death Valley region, within the lower portions of Grand Cycles A and C, there are two stratigraphic intervals composed of coarse-grained fluvial and coastal-plain units. These units sharply overlie shallow subtidal to intertidal siliciclastic and carbonate deposits along an erosional contact. The juxtaposition of fluvial and subtidal deposits reflects significant, abrupt seaward shifts in facies following erosion, and is inferred to reflect the loss in accommodation volume and associated erosion and sediment bypass typical of a type-1 sequence boundary. In mid-ramp areas, it is difficult to detect the sequence boundary on the

basis of either evidence for erosion or abrupt facies changes. Biostratigraphic correlations suggest that the sequence boundary must lie within, or on top of, intertidal to subtidal mudstone units within the siliciclastic half-cycle. This may indicate that the sequence boundary lies in shale-on-shale contacts within interfluves, and may be difficult to locate.

Most workers who have explored the sequence stratigraphy of Grand Cycles, including the authors of this paper, have suggested that Grand Cycle boundaries are type-2 sequence boundaries. The rationale for this choice usually has been the lack of evidence for incised valleys and, in outer-ramp/platform locations, the lack of evidence for dramatic seaward shift in facies. As Van Wagoner et al. (1988, 1990) and Posamentier and James (1993) have remarked, the gradual change in accommodation volume across a type-2 boundary should make them exceptionally difficult to detect in outcrop. The expression of the boundary may be as subtle as a change in progradational stacking patterns of parasequences, with no sharp dislocation of facies. This is clearly not the case with the depositional sequences that approximate Grand Cycles. In outer-ramp/platform areas, there is a significant drop in relative sea level, leading to widespread karst development. In addition, in at least two instances (Grand Cycles A and C) there is substantial seaward shift in fluvial and coastal-plain facies across the boundary, preceded by broad erosion of the inner ramp. For these reasons, we have reinterpreted the sequence boundaries that occur at or near the base of Grand Cycles as type-1 boundaries.

Lowstand systems tract

In all locations, in outer-ramp/platform settings, the type-1 sequence boundaries that coincide with Grand Cycle contacts are overlain by subtidal to intertidal siliciclastic mudstones and siltstones (Table 1). As noted above, in proximal portions of the ramp, the sequence boundary that occurs in the lower portions of Grand Cycles A and C is overlain by sandstones and coarse conglomerates of braidplain and coastal-plain environments. Within both inner- and outer-ramp settings, facies stacking patterns consist of coarsening- and thickening-upward successions followed by fining- and thinning-upward successions. This indicates that, following formation of the sequence boundary, there was basinward progradation of the fluvial, coastal-plain, nearshore, and tidal-flat enviironments, followed by aggradation and retrogradation.

On the basis of their composition, facies stacking patterns, and occurrence above an erosional unconformity, the units that overlie the sequence boundaries at or near the base of Grand Cycles A and C are inferred to reflect a period of slowly increasing generation of accommodation volume. In most ramp-margin settings, this pattern of change in accommodation volume is associated with the lowstand wedge (after Van Wagoner et al., 1988).

The basal portions of the depositional sequences defined by Grand Cycles DS1, DS2, and B are distinctly different from those of the thicker sequences. The siliciclastic units that overlie the basal sequence boundary are typically finer grained, reflecting shallow subtidal to intertidal, mud-dominated environments. Facies stacking patterns do not appear to show well-developed progradational and aggradational sets. This suggests that the lowstand systems tract that is a prominent feature of thicker depositional sequences is not present in the relatively thinner sequences.

The two lowstand wedges noted here are significantly different from most lowstand wedges described in the literature. First, the lowstand wedge appears to be unusually thick and is laterally persistent across the ramp. However, the thickness of any systems tract is a function of the length of time over which accumulation takes place and the interaction of eustatic change, subsidence, and sediment supply. In settings where there are relatively high sedimentation and subsidence rates, such as postulated for the early Laurentian margin (Levy and Christie-Blick, 1991), the total accommodation volume created and filled during formation of the lowstand wedge would be potentially large. Second, lowstand wedges typically contain incised valleys and associated incised valley fill in up-dip regions. To our knowledge, although there is evidence for widespread erosion at the base of the lowstand wedge, no one has described deeply incised valleys in the Lower Cambrian of the Death Valley region. The geometry of incision of a shelf or ramp during accommodation minima is a function of a range of factors. One of the most important is the relationship between the slope of the ramp and the fluvial gradient (Schuum, 1993; Westcott, 1993; Shanley and McCabe, 1994). Where the gradient of the exhumed ramp is close to the gradient of the lower reaches of rivers that feed into the ramp, channel systems will tend to develop broad alluvial valleys, rather than the narrow, steep-sided valleys typically associated with incised valleys at type-1 sequence boundaries. The low-relief sequence boundaries of the Lower Cambrian ramp therefore may reflect the relatively low-gradient nature of the ramp margin.

Transgressive systems tracts

Within the thick depositional sequences that contain lowstand wedge systems tracts, there appears to be a gradational transition from progradational/aggradational to fining-upward, retrogradational facies stacking patterns. This pattern is most recognizable where thick coastal-plain and nearshore sand units give way upsection to finer-grained, shallow subtidal units (Table 1). This change in stacking patterns is inferred to reflect a significant increase in the rate of creation of accommodation volume, typical of transgressive systems tracts. Because of the gradational nature of this transition in the thicker sequences, it is difficult to identify the transgressive surface.

In the thinner depositional sequences associated with Grand Cycles DS1, DS2, and B, the basal siliciclastic units contain poorly defined retrogradational facies stacking patterns. This implies that the lowermost units of these sequences lie within the transgressive systems tract and that the transgressive surface coincides with, and may have modified, the sequence boundary.

Highstand systems tract

One of the most distinctive stratigraphic features of Early Cambrian Grand Cycles and depositional systems is the gradational, diachronous regional transition from siliciclastic-dominated sedimentation to carbonate-dominated sedimentation (Figs. 2 and 3). The biostratigraphic and stratigraphic data cited here indicate that the initial nucleation of carbonate sedimentation took place in the mid-ramp areas, apparently in shallow subtidal settings. Following nucleation, carbonate depositional systems appear to have shoaled, expanded, and eventually prograded seaward, leading to the formation of a broad, low-gradient ramp/platform (Mount et al., 1991; Table 1). During the later stages of expansion of carbonate sedimentation, subtidal to intertidal carbonate deposition predominated in outer-ramp/platform areas while intertidal siliciclastic and mixed carbonate-siliciclastic sedimentation occurred in mid-ramp areas (Figs. 5 and 6). Siliciclastic mud-filled tidal channels are encased within the subtidal to intertidal limestones that cap Grand Cycles in the outer ramp/platform (Rowland, 1984; Mount and Signor, 1989). These channels indicate that siliciclastic sediments were actively bypassing the outer-ramp carbonate belt during the later stages of Grand Cycle deposition.

The mid-ramp nucleation and shoaling of carbonates, followed by basinward expansion of carbonate sedimentation, is inferred to reflect an episode of decline in the rate of generation of new accommodation volume typical of a highstand systems tract. This episode can be divided into two phases. The initial phase, or early highstand systems tract, involves the establishment of the carbonate sedimentation factory. Because these early carbonates appear to coincide with the beginning of an aggradational phase, their nucleation is linked genetically to the formation of the maximum flooding surface that caps the underlying transgressive systems tract. The second phase, or late highstand systems tract, is associated with the change from aggradation to progradation during which the carbonate factory fills available mid-ramp accommodation volume and migrates toward the outer-ramp/platform margin. The decline in accommodation volume generation in the late highstand systems tract leads to the bypass of siliciclastic material that normally is trapped in the mid- and inner ramp behind shoal carbonates. This episode culminates with a loss of accommodation volume and formation of the sequence boundary that caps outer-ramp/platform carbonates.

The most robust and widespread carbonate sedimentation recorded in Grand Cycles appears to have occurred in the outer-ramp/platform setting during accumulation of the late highstand systems tracts. This is a surprising result, since declining accommodation volume should lead to progradation of fluvial and coastal-plain siliciclastic depositional systems (Van Wagoner et al., 1990). Decline in factors that promote carbonate production, and a tendency to produce mixed carbonate-siliciclastic deposits, should logically be the signature of the late highstand systems tract, rather than relatively clean carbonate sedimentation. Mount and Rowland (1981) and Mount et al. (1991) suggested that the development of a shoaled carbonate platform would lead to trapping of siliciclastic material in the low-energy moat that forms behind the shoal carbonates (similar to that described by Read [1989] elsewhere), reducing their impact on the carbonate depositional systems. If, as suggested above, the slope of the ramp/platform was at or below fluvial gradient, coarse siliciclastics also may have been trapped well inboard of the ramp, reducing their impact on carbonate depositional systems. Alternatively, runoff and associated siliciclastic sediment supply may simply have declined during deposition of the highstand systems tract (discussed below).

Composite depositional sequences

In their study of the Carrara Formation, Palmer and Halley (1979) identified two Grand Cycles within the upper portions of Grand Cycle C. Adams (1995) and Prave (1992) support this and have assigned sequence boundaries to the bases of these cycles. Both of these Grand Cycles have yet to be described from the outer-ramp/platform area (Bergk, in progress).

Based on the descriptions of Palmer and Halley (1979), Prave (1992), and Adams (1993, 1995), the upper Grand Cycle C subcycles strongly resemble the thinner Grand Cycles DS1, DS2, and B. The basal sequence boundaries appear to coincide with flooding surfaces that are overlain by retrogradationally stacked intertidal to subtidal siliciclastic facies. This suggests that the lowstand systems tract is missing and that a transgressive systems tract overlies the inferred sequence boundary. Change from retrogradational to aggradational/progradational stacking patterns appears to coincide with increasing carbonate content, suggesting that the carbonate half-cycle of these subcycles is part of the highstand systems tract (Adams, 1993, 1995).

The occurrence of subcycles within Grand Cycle C that strongly resemble the thinner Grand Cycles suggests that there is a hierarchical succession of sequence-stratigraphic units within the Lower Cambrian section. The subcycles that occur within Grand Cycle C are inferred to be higher-order sequences within a composite sequence (after Mitchum and Van Wagoner, 1991). Because these sequences fall entirely within and define the highstand systems tract of Grand Cycle C, they form a highstand sequence set. Thin Grand Cycles DS1, DS2, and B also may be higher-order sequences, although their relationship to the larger cycles has yet to be determined (Bergk, in progress).

Discussion: Origin of Lower Cambrian Grand Cycles and Depositional Sequences

Lower Cambrian Grand Cycles of the southern Great Basin appear to record cyclical changes in accommodation volume on a nascent Laurentian passive margin (Fig. 7). These changes led to the development of at least five third-order unconformity-bounded depositional sequences that can be traced across the Early Cambrian ramp/platform. In the outer-ramp areas, Grand Cycle boundaries appear to coincide with sequence boundaries, whereas in mid-ramp areas the sequence boundary appears to lie within the siliciclastic half-cycle. At least one cycle, Grand Cycle C, is a composite depositional sequence, which appears to contain two higher-frequency sequences within its highstand systems tract.

Accommodation change (and by association the formation of depositional sequences) is a function of the interaction between eustatic sea level, subsidence, and sediment source/supply. Despite multiple potential allocyclic and autocyclic causes for depositional sequences, the overwhelming majority of studies point to, or imply that, eustatic sea level is the driving external force (see discussions in Miall, 1991, 1992; Mitchum and Van Wagoner, 1991). Grand Cycles have been no exception to this. Most recent workers consider Cambrian Grand Cycles to be expressions of third-order (0.5 to 5 m.y.) variations in eustatic sea level (Mount and Rowland, 1981; Chow and James, 1987; Bond et al., 1988, 1989; Aitken, 1989; Bond and Kominz, 1991; Mount et al., 1991; Adams, 1993, 1995; Cowan and James, 1993; Osleger and Read, 1993; Osleger, 1995; Adams and Grotzinger, 1996; Osleger and Montañez, 1996).

The support for an interpretation of Early Cambrian Grand Cycles as the product of eustatic sea-level changes comes from several independent lines of evidence. Despite the isochroneity of their boundaries, individual stratigraphic elements of Grand Cycles indicating bathymetric change can be correlated interbasinally (see, for example, the high-resolution studies of Osleger, 1995), suggesting an external forcing mechanism that synchronously affected the Laurentian continent. Subsidence analyses of Middle and Upper Cambrian Grand

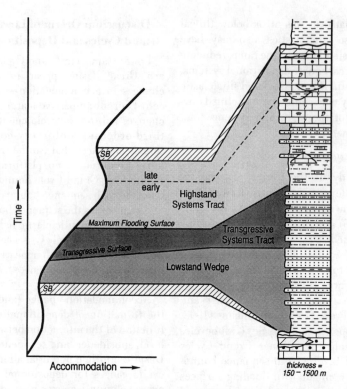

FIG. 7. Conjectural model for cycles of accommodation and the formation of sequence boundaries and systems tracts within Grand Cycles. The overall increase in accommodation volume with time reflects cumulative effects of Early Cambrian second-order rise in sea-level and subsidence of the passive margin.

Cycles, in which the effects of tectonic subsidence and sediment loading are incrementally removed from decompacted total subsidence, indicate systematic, regional changes in accommodation volume. Accommodation maxima, occurring within the siliciclastic half-cycle, and accommodation minima, occurring near the top of the carbonate half-cycle (Bond et al., 1989; Osleger, 1995), provide an additional indication of an external forcing mechanism such as eustacy. Based on these lines of evidence, the alternation of carbonate-dominated and siliciclastic-dominated deposition that constitutes Grand Cycles and their associated depositional sequences is logically inferred to reflect cyclical changes in accommodation volume, driven by eustatic sea level.

Although eustatic sea level controlled the formation of Grand Cycles and depositional sequences, the possibility that other allogenic processes are recorded in Grand Cycles cannot be ruled out. The formation of the cyclical

alternation of siliciclastic- and carbonate-dominated systems tracts depends upon processes that turn the carbonate factory off and on and retard or enhance the delivery of siliciclastic material to and across the ramp. In particular, it is the apparently abrupt termination of carbonate sedimentation in the outer-ramp/platform areas that produces the unique asymmetry of Grand Cycles.

Previous workers, including the senior author, have argued that eustatic sea-level change is sufficient to explain the seemingly abrupt termination of carbonate sedimentation and the initiation of siliciclastic sedimentation that marks Grand Cycle boundaries. Mount and Rowland (1981), Mount et al. (1991), and Adams (1993, 1995) have argued that Lower Cambrian Grand Cycle boundaries are essentially drowning unconformities (after Schlager, 1981), where relative sea-level rise in the outer-ramp/platform area outpaces the capacity of the carbonate factory, leading to elimination of carbonate production. The causes of drowning unconformities are difficult to pinpoint in outcrop (review in Schlager, 1989), but probably involve the coincidence of sea-level rise and changes in environmental conditions, including water chemistry, nutrient supply, temperature, and turbidity.

In a sequence-stratigraphic study of cyclical Upper Cambrian peritidal platform deposits of northwestern Newfoundland, Cowan and James (1993) argued that the influx of terrigenous material, and associated deltaic freshwater dilution, can be tied directly to the suppression of the skeletal and non-skeletal carbonate factory, but not to eustatic sea-level change. According to Cowan and James (1993), the so-called "Grand Cycles" of the Upper Cambrian of western Newfoundland, as originally described by Chow and James (1989), are not characterized by alternation between siliciclastic-dominated and carbonate-dominated half-cycles. Terrigenous muds appear to be irregularly distributed between a "shaly half-cycle," dominated by subtidal to peritidal carbonate-ribbon rock cycles, and a "carbonate half cycle," dominated by subtidal oölite shoal cycles. The appearance of siliciclastic material on the shelf was interpreted to record the independent superimposition of climate-driven runoff cycles on the third-order eustatic cycles that controlled the alternation between ribbonrock and oölite shoal deposits.

The example cited by Cowan and James (1993) illustrates an important concern about the role of climate change in the formation of Lower Cambrian Grand Cycles. Lower Cambrian Grand Cycles are distinguished from their Middle and Upper Cambrian counterparts by an abundance of siliciclastic material. Additionally, the basal portions of most of the Lower Cambrian siliciclastic half-cycles (DS1, DS2, A, and B) are devoid of *any* detrital carbonate. This observation is consistent even in the shallow subtidal and intertidal environments that typically contain some carbonate when they occur in the highstand systems tracts of Grand Cycles. The complete cessation of both organic and inorganic carbonate production in relatively shallow-water facies is enigmatic, especially when compared with the stratigraphic evidence for a relatively vigorous carbonate factory during the later stages of the previous half-cycle.

Explanations for the termination and initiation of carbonate sedimentation solely through eustatic sea-level change both are intellectually unsatisfying and necessitate invoking special circumstances or mechanisms (see previous discussion of highstand systems tract as an example). As Mount et al. (1991) and others have suggested, the rise in relative sea level that follows emergence of the carbonate platform leads to a complete cessation of carbonate production. If, as assumed by most previous workers, the Early Cambrian northern Laurentian margin lay within a tropical, low-latitude setting, it seems unlikely that all carbonate production would cease during initiation of the siliciclastic half-cycle. Even in modern settings, such as the Amazon Delta, where exceptionally high rates of runoff and siliciclastic sedimentation are occurring, there is still generation and preservation of significant organic and inorganic carbonate (see review in Mount, 1984).

In their analysis of the Neoproterozoic–Early Cambrian transition in southern and central Australia, Mount and McDonald (1992) argued that climate change played an important role in the facies composition and architecture of third-order depositional sequences. Onlap of the Australian continent during this interval was associated with a progressive change from deltaic-dominated deposition to carbonate platform-dominated deposition, with significant change occurring following the formation of regionally correlative type-1 sequence boundaries. Based on the distribution of key stratigraphic indicators, Mount and McDonald (1992) argued that this change reflected a shift from wet/cool to warm/dry climatic conditions coincident with long-term eustatic sea-level rise and inundation of the Australian continent.

Lower Cambrian Grand Cycles, with their thick, siliciclastic-dominated half-cycles, also may reflect the superimposition of climate change on eustatic sea-level cycles. However, unlike the examples cited by Cowan and James (1993), these changes would appear to coincide with phases of the accommodation cycle rather than being fully independent. The termination of the carbonate half-cycle in outer-ramp/platform settings, the formation of a sequence boundary, and the initiation of the siliciclastic half-cycle may coincide with a change from a warm/dry climate to cool/wet conditions. This is consistent with the seaward progradation of thick braidplain deposits within the lowstand systems tracts of Grand Cycles A and C. In addition, it would explain the dramatic decline or virtual elimination of carbonate production during the initiation of Lower Cambrian Grand Cycles.

The initiation and expansion of carbonate sedimentation during the latter portions of Grand Cycle deposition may be tied to a change of climate toward more warm/dry conditions. In most Grand Cycle models (including the one proposed here), the nucleation of the carbonate half-cycle typically is assumed to reflect suppression of siliciclastic supply by regional transgression. However, this process does not adequately explain the persistence of carbonate deposition during the late highstand, when declining rate of accommodation generation should promote the delivery of siliciclastic material and associated fresh water to the shelf. If anything, it appears that the carbonate factory should be *most* stressed during the late highstand, and generating mixed siliciclastic/ carbonate sediments.

Although conjectural, the hypothesis that climate change played a role in Early Cambrian Grand Cycles is consistent with a number of recent observations about the Early Cambrian. If, as Kirschvink et al. (1997) suggested, there was exceptionally rapid plate motion during the Early Cambrian, then the Laurentian continent would have traversed multiple climate regimes during accumulation of the Great Basin Grand Cycles. Dramatic changes in continental configuration, which would have accompanied rapid plate motions, also would have produced abrupt changes in oceanographic and climatic circulation. Brasier et al. (1994) and others have shown that the Early Cambrian was characterized by numerous, dramatic oscillations in marine $\delta^{13}C$ values of more than 6 per mil, reflecting large fluctuations in primary productivity. Additionally, the Sr-isotopic record for the Early Cambrian indicates equally unusual fluctuations in values (Derry et al., 1994; Nicholas, 1996). As Kirschvink et al. (1997) noted, the Sr- and C-isotopic variations may record bursts of deep-ocean ventilation, coupled with large sea-level swings and dramatic shifts in rates of continental weathering—all presumably associated with rapid plate motions.

The speculative hypothesis that coeval climate change and eustatic sea-level change drove the formation of Lower Cambrian Grand Cycles and depositional sequences remains to be tested. Moreover, as noted above, Early Cambrian Grand Cycles, and, by analogy, Early Cambrian depositional sequences, are substantially different from their Middle and Upper Cambrian counterparts. These differences may record fundamental change in the processes that formed Grand Cycles, unique global climatic and oceanographic conditions during the Early Cambrian, or simply the unique tectonic and paleogeographic setting during the early stages of development of the Laurentian passive margin.

Acknowledgments

This paper is dedicated to Clarence Hall, whose perseverance and vision made the White Mountain Research Station one of the jewels of the University of California system, and to Clemens Nelson, who graciously shared his 40 years of work on the structure and stratigraphy of the southern Great Basin. D. Sumner and L. Benninger reviewed an earlier version of this manuscript. This research was supported by NSF EAR 85-18018, 88-21192, and 90-04442 and the University of California White Mountain Research Station.

REFERENCES

Adams, R. D., 1993, Sequence-stratigraphic analysis of mixed carbonate-siliciclastic Cambrian sediments, Carrara Formation, southwest Basin and Range, California and Nevada: Unpubl. Ph.D. thesis, Massachusetts Inst. Technol., 750 p.

————, 1995, Sequence stratigraphy of Early–Middle Cambrian Grand Cycles in the Carrara Formation, southwest Basin and Range, California and Nevada, in Haq, B. U., Sequence stratigraphy and depositional response to eustatic, tectonic and climatic forcing: Amsterdam, Kluwer Academic, p. 277–328.

Adams, R. D., and Grotzinger J. P., 1996, Lateral continuity of facies and parasequences in Middle Cambrian platform carbonates, Carrara Formation, southeastern California, USA: Jour. Sedimen. Res., v. 66, p. 1079–1090.

Aitken, J. D., 1966, Middle Cambrian to Middle Ordovician cyclic sedimentation, southern Rocky Mountains of Alberta: Bull. Canad. Petrol. Geol., v. 14, p. 405–411.

————, 1978, Revised models for depositional Grand Cycles, Cambrian of the southern Rocky Mountains, Canada: Bull. Canad. Petrol. Geol., v. 26, p. 515–542.

————, 1989, Birth, growth and death of the Middle Cambrian Cathedral carbonate lithosome, southern Rocky Mountains: Bull. Canad. Petrol. Geol., v. 37, p. 316–333.

Bergk, K., Maggi, J. M., Maxson, D., and Mount, J. F., 1996, Sequence stratigraphy of the basal portion of the Lower Cambrian Harkless Formation, Esmeralda County, Nevada and the White-Inyo Mountains, eastern California [abs.]: Geol. Soc. Amer., Abs. Prog., v. 28, p. 46.

Bond, G. C., Kominz, M. A., and Grotzinger, J. P., 1988, Cambro-Ordovician eustacy: Evidence from geophysical modeling of subsidence in Cordillera and Appalachian passive margins, in Kleinspehn, K. L., and Paola, C., eds., New perspectives in basin analysis: New York, Springer Verlag, p. 129–160.

Bond, G. C., Kominz, M. A., Steckler, M. S., and Grotzinger, J. P., 1989, Role of thermal subsidence, flexure and eustacy in the evolution of Early Paleozoic passive-margin carbonate platforms, in Crevello, P. D., Wilson, J. L., Sarg, J. F., and Read, J. F., eds., Controls on carbonate platform and basin development: Soc. Econ. Paleontol. Mineral. Spec. Publ. 44, p. 39–61.

Bond, G.C., and Kominz, M.A., 1991, Some comments on the problem of using vertical facies changes to infer accommodation and eustatic sea-level histories with examples from Utah and the southern Canadian Rockies, in Franseen, E. K., Watney, W. L., Kendall, C. G. S. C., and Ross, W., eds., Sedimentary modeling: Computer simulations and methods for improved parameter definition: Kansas Geol. Surv. Bull. 233, p. 273–291.

Brasier, M. D., Corfield, R. M., Derry, L. A., Rozanov, A. Y., and Zhravleva, A. Yu., 1994, Multiple $\delta^{13}C$ excursions spanning the Cambrian explosion to the Botomian crisis in Siberia: Geology, v. 22, p. 455–458.

Chow, N., and James, N. P., 1987, Cambrian Grand Cycles: A northern Appalachian perspective: Geol. Soc. Amer. Bull., v. 93, p. 735–750.

Christie-Blick, N., and Driscoll, N. W., 1995, Sequence stratigraphy: Ann. Rev. Earth Planet. Sci., v. 23, p. 451–478.

Christie-Blick, N., Dyson, I. A., and Von der Borch, C. C., 1995, Sequence stratigraphy and the interpretation of Neoproterozoic Earth history: Precamb. Res., v. 73, p. 3–26.

Christie-Blick, N., and Levy, M., 1989, Concepts of sequence stratigraphy, with examples from strata of late Proterozoic and Cambrian age in the western United States, in Christie-Blick, N., and Levy, M., eds., Late Proterozoic and Cambrian tectonics, sedimentation and record of metazoan radiation in the Western United States: Amer. Geophys. Union, 28th Int. Geol. Cong. Field Trip Guidebook T331, p. 23–38.

Cowan, C. A., and James, N. P., 1993, The interactions of sea-level change, terrigenous-sediment influx, and carbonate productivity as controls on Upper Cambrian Grand Cycles of western Newfoundland, Canada: Geol. Soc. Amer. Bull., v. 105, p. 1576–1590.

Dalziel, I. W. D., 1997, Neoproterozoic–Paleozoic geography and tectonics: Review, hypothesis, environmental speculation: Geol. Soc. Amer. Bull., v. 109, p. 16–42.

Derry, L. A., Brasier, M. D., Corfield, R. M., Rozanov, A. Y., et al., 1994, Sr- and C-isotopes in Lower Cambrian carbonates from the Siberian craton—a paleoenvironmental record during the Cambrian explosion: Earth Planet. Sci. Lett., v. 128, p. 671–681.

Diehl, P. E., 1974, Stratigraphy and sedimentology of the Wood Canyon Formation, Death Valley area, California, in Death Valley region, California and Nevada: Geol. Soc. Amer., Cordilleran Sect. Guidebook, p. 38–48.

————, 1979, The stratigraphy, depositional environments, and quantitative petrography of the Precambrian–Cambrian Wood Canyon Formation, Death Valley: Unpubl. Ph.D. dissertation, Pennsylvania State Univ., 322 p.

Dienger, J. L., 1986, Facies modeling of siliciclastic and carbonate sediments in the Lower Cambrian Middle Member Deep Spring Formation, White-Inyo Range, California: Unpubl. M.S. thesis, Univ. of California, Davis, 108 p.

Fedo, C. M., and Cooper, J. D., 1990, Braided fluvial to marine transition: The basal Lower Cambrian Wood Canyon Formation, southern Marble Mountains, Mojave Desert, California: Jour. Sediment. Petrol., v. 60, p. 220–234.

Fritz, W. H., 1975, Broad correlations of some Lower and Middle Cambrian strata in the North American Cordillera: Geol. Surv. Canada Pap. 75-1A, p. 145–159.

Greene, L. R., 1986, Cyclic sedimentation within the Upper Member of the Deep Spring Formation (Lower Cambrian), eastern California and western Nevada: The anatomy of a Grand Cycle: Unpubl. M.S. thesis, Univ. of California, Davis, 198 p.

Grotzinger, J. P., Bowring, S. A., Saylor, B. Z., and Kaufman, A. J., 1995, Biostratigraphic and geochronologic constraints on early animal evolution: Science, v. 270, p. 598–604.

Hunt, D. L., 1990, Trilobite faunas and biostratigraphy of the Lower Cambrian Wood Canyon Formation, Death Valley region, California: Unpubl. M.S. thesis, Univ. of California, Davis, 140 p.

Kirschvink, J. L., Ripperdan, R. L., and Evans, D. A., 1997, Evidence for a large-scale reorganization of Early Cambrian continental masses by inertial interchange true polar wander: Science, v. 277, p. 541–545.

Levy, M., and Christie-Blick, N., 1989, Pre-Mesozoic palinspastic reconstruction of the eastern Great Basin (western United States): Science, v. 245, p. 1454–1462.

————, 1991, Tectonic subsidence of the early Paleozoic passive continental margin in eastern California and southern Nevada: Geol. Soc. Amer. Bull., v. 103, p. 1590–1606.

Miall, A. D., 1991, Stratigraphic sequences and their chronostratigraphic correlation: Jour. Sediment. Petrol., v. 61, p. 497–505.

————, 1992, Alluvial deposits, in Walker, R. G., and James, N. P., eds., Facies models—response to sea-level change: Waterloo, Ont., Geol. Assoc. Can., p. 119–142.

Mitchum, R. M., Jr., Vail, P. R., and Thompson, S., III, 1977, Part Two: The depositional sequence as a basic unit for stratigraphic analysis, in Payton, C. E., ed., Seismic stratigraphy—applications to hydrocarbon exploration: Amer. Assoc. Petrol. Geol., Memoir 26, p. 53–62.

Mitchum, R. M., Jr., and Van Wagoner, J. C., 1991, High-frequency sequences and their stacking patterns: Sequence-stratigraphic evidence of high-frequency eustatic cycles: Sediment. Geol., v. 70, p. 131–160.

Moore, J. N., 1976, Depositional environments of the Lower Cambrian Poleta Formation and its stratigraphic equivalents, California and Nevada: Brigham Young Univ. Geol. Studies, v. 23, p. 23–38.

Mount, J. F., 1980, The environmental stratigraphy and depositional systems of the Precambrian(?)–Cambrian Campito Formation, eastern California and western Nevada: Unpubl. Ph.D. dissertation, Univ. of California, Santa Cruz, 239 p.

————, 1982a, Storm-surge-ebb origin of hummocky cross-stratified units of the Andrews Mountain Member, Campito Formation (Lower Cambrian), White-Inyo Mountains, Eastern California: Jour. Sediment. Petrol., v. 52, p. 941–958.

————, 1982b, Earliest Cambrian paleoenvironments of the southern Great Basin, in Cooper, J. D., Troxel, B. W., and Wright, L. A., eds., Geology of selected areas in the San Bernardino Mountains, western Mojave desert and southern Great Basin, California: Geol. Soc. Amer., Cordilleran Sect. Guidebook, p. 187–193.

————, 1984, Mixing of siliciclastic and carbonate sediments in shallow shelf environments: Geology, v. 12, p. 432–435.

Mount, J. F., Hunt, D. L., Greene, L. R., and Dienger, J., 1991, Depositional systems, biostratigraphy and sequence stratigraphy of Lower Cambrian Grand Cycles, southwestern Great Basin, in Cooper, J. D., and Stevens, C. H., eds., Paleozoic paleogeography of the Western United States—II: Bakersfield, CA, Soc. Econ. Paleontol. Mineral., Pacific Sect., p. 209–226.

Mount, J. F., and McDonald, C., 1992, Influences of changes in climate, sea level and depositional systems on the fossil record of the Neoproterozoic–Early Cambrian metazoan radiation: Geology, v. 20, p. 1031–1034.

Mount, J. F., and Rowland, S. M., 1981, Grand Cycle A (Lower Cambrian) of the southern Great Basin: A product of differential rates of sea level rise, in Taylor, M. E., ed., Short papers for the Second Int. Symp. Cambrian System: U.S. Geol. Surv. Open-File Report 81-743, p. 143–146.

Mount, J. F., and Signor, P. W., 1985, Early Cambrian innovation in low-stress environments: Paleoenvironments of Early Cambrian shelly fossils: Geology, v. 13, p. 730–733.

————, 1986, The record of Cambrian Radiation Event in the White-Inyo region, eastern California and western Nevada: Bishop, CA, Nello Pace Symp. Vol., White Mountain Res. Station, August, 1985, p. 16–26.

————, 1989, Paleoenvironmental context of the metazoan radiation event and its impact on the placement of the Precambrian–Cambrian boundary: Examples from the southwestern Great Basin, U.S.A., in Christie-Blick, N., and Levy, M., eds., Late Proterozoic and Cambrian tectonics, sedimentation, and record of metazoan radiation in the Western United States: Amer. Geophys. Union, 28th Int. Geol. Cong. Field Trip Guidebook T331, p. 39–46.

————, 1992, Faunas and facies, fact and artifact: Paleoenvironmental controls on the distribution of Early Cambrian faunas, in Signor, P. W., and Lipps, J. H., eds., Origins and early evolution of metazoa: New York, Plenum Press, p. 27–52.

Nelson, C. A., 1962, Lower Cambrian–Precambrian succession, White-Inyo Mountains, California: Geol. Soc. Amer. Bull., v. 73, p. 139–144.

————, 1976, Late Precambrian–Early Cambrian stratigraphic and faunal succession of eastern California and the Precambrian–Cambrian boundary, in Moore, J. N., and Fritsche, A. E., eds., Depositional environments of Lower Paleozoic rocks in the White-Inyo Mountains, Inyo County, California: Pacific Sect., Soc. Econ. Paleontol. Mineral., Pacific Coast Paleogeog. Field Guide 1, p. 31–42.

Nicholas, C. J., 1996, The Sr isotope evolution of the oceans during the "Cambrian Explosion": Jour. Geol. Soc. London, v. 153, p. 243–254.

Osleger, D. A., 1995, Depositional sequences on Upper Cambrian carbonate platforms: Variable sedimentologic responses to allogenic forcing, in, Haq, B. U., ed., Sequence stratigraphy and depositional response to eustatic, tectonic and climatic forcing: Amsterdam, Kluwer Academic, p. 247–276.

Osleger, D. A., and Montañez, I. P., 1996, Cross-platform architecture of a sequence boundary in mixed siliciclastic-carbonate lithofacies, Middle Cambrian, southern Great Basin, USA: Sedimentology, v. 43, p. 197–217.

Osleger, D. A., and Read, J. F., 1993, Comparative analysis of methods used to define eustatic variations in outcrop: Late Cambrian interbasinal sequence development: Amer. Jour. Sci., v. 293, p. 157–216.

Palmer, A. R., 1981, On the correlatability of Grand Cycle tops, in Taylor, M. E., ed., Short papers for the Second Int. Symp. on the Cambrian System: U.S. Geol. Surv. Open-File Report 81-743, p. 193–197.

Palmer, A. R., and Halley, R. B., 1979, Physical stratigraphy and trilobite biostratigraphy of the Carrara Formation (Lower and Middle Cambrian) in the southern Great Basin: U. S. Geol. Surv. Prof. Pap. 1047.

Prave, A. R., 1992, Depositional and sequence stratigraphic framework of the Lower Cambrian Zabriskie Quartzite—implications for regional correlations and the Early Cambrian paleogeography of the Death Valley region of California and Nevada: Geol. Soc. Amer. Bull., v. 104, p. 505–515.

Prave, A. R., and Wright, L. A., 1986, Isopach pattern of the Lower Cambrian Zabriskie Quartzite, Death Valley region, California-Nevada: How useful in tectonic reconstructions?: Geology, v. 14, p. 251–254.

Posamentier, H. W., and James, D. P., 1993, An overview of sequence stratigraphic concepts: Uses and abuses, in Posamentier, H. W., Summerhays, C. P., Haq, B. U., and Allen, G. P., eds., Sequence stratigraphy and facies associations: Int. Assoc. Sedimentol. Spec. Publ., no. 18, p. 3–18.

Posamentier, H. W., Summerhays, C. P., Haq, B. U., and Allen, G. P., eds., 1993, Sequence stratigraphy and facies associations: Int. Assoc. Sedimentol. Spec. Publ., no. 18, 644 p.

Read, J. F., 1989, Controls on evolution of Cambrian-Ordovician passive margin, U.S. Appalachians, in Crevello, P. D., Wilson, J. L., Sarg, J. F., and Read, J. F., eds., Controls on carbonate platform and basin development: Soc. Econ. Paleontol. Mineral. Spec. Publ. 44, p. 147–165.

Rowland, S. M., 1978, Environmental stratigraphy of the Lower Member of the Poleta Formation (Lower Cambrian), Esmeralda County, Nevada: Unpubl. Ph.D. dissertation, Univ. of California, Santa Cruz, 116 p.

————, 1984, Were there really framework reefs in the Cambrian?: Geology, v. 12, p. 181–183.

Savarese, M. and Signor, P. W., 1989, New Archaeocyathan occurrences in the Upper Harkless Formation (Lower Cambrian of western Nevada): Jour. Paleontol., v. 63, p. 539–549.

Schlager, W., 1981, The paradox of drowned reefs and carbonate platforms: Geol. Soc. Amer. Bull., v. 92, p,. 197–211.

————, 1989, Drowning unconformities on carbonate platforms, in Crevello, P. D., Wilson, J. L., Sarg, J. F., and Read, J. F., eds., Controls on carbonate platform and basin development: Soc. Econ. Paleontol. Mineral. Spec. Publ. 44, p. 15–25.

Schuum, S. A., 1993, River response to base level change: Implications for sequence stratigraphy: Jour. Geol., v. 101, p. 279–294.

Shanley, K. W., and McCabe, P. J., 1994, Perspectives on the sequence stratigraphy of continental strata: Amer. Assoc. Petrol. Geol. Bull., v. 78, p. 544–568.

Signor, P. W., and Mount, J. F., 1986, Position of the Lower Cambrian boundary in the White-Inyo Mountains of California and in Esmeralda County, Nevada: Newslett. Stratig., v. 16, p. 9–18.

————, 1989, Paleontology of the Lower Cambrian Waucoban Series in eastern California and western Nevada, in Christie-Blick, N., and Levy, M., eds., Late Proterozoic and Cambrian tectonics, sedimentation, and record of metazoan radiation in the Western United States: Amer. Geophys. Union, 28th Int. Geol. Cong. Field Trip Guidebook T331, p. 47–54.

Stewart, J. H., 1970, Upper Precambrian and Lower Cambrian strata in the southern Great Basin, California and Nevada: U.S. Geol. Surv. Spec. Pap. 620, 206 p.

Stewart, J. H., and Suczeck, 1977, Cambrian and latest Precambrian paleogeography and tectonics in the western United States, in Stewart, J. H., Stevens, C. H., and Fritsche, A. E., eds., Paleozoic paleogeography of the western United States, Pacific Coast Paleogeog. Symp. 1: Soc. Econ. Paleontol. Mineral., Pacific Sect., Book 7, p. 1–17.

Torsvik, T. H., Smethurst, M. A., Meert, J. G., Van der Voo, R., et al., 1996, Continental break-up and collision in the Neoproterozoic and Palaeozoic—A tale of Baltica and Laurentia: Earth Sci. Rev., v. 40, p. 229–258.

Van der Voo, R., 1994, True polar wander during the Middle Paleozoic: Earth Planet. Sci. Lett., v. 122, p. 239–243.

Van Wagoner, J. C., 1995, Overview of sequence stratigraphy in foreland basin deposits: Terminology, summary of papers, and glossary of sequence stratigraphy, *in* Van Wagoner, J. C., and Bertram, G. T., eds., Sequence stratigraphy of foreland basin deposits: Outcrop and subsurface examples from the Cretaceous of North America: Amer. Assoc. Petrol. Geol. Memoir 64, p. ix–xxi.

Van Wagoner, J. C., Posamentier, H. W., Mitchum, R. M., Vail, P. R., Sarg, J. F., Loutit, T. S., and Hardenbol, J., 1988, An overview of the fundamentals of sequence stratigraphy and key definitions, *in* Wilgus, C. K., Hastings, B. S., Kendall, C. G. St. C., Posamentier, H. W., Ross, C. A., and Van Wagoner, J. C., eds., Sea-level changes: An integrated approach: Soc. Econ. Paleontol. Mineral. Spec. Publ. 42, p. 39–45.

Van Wagoner, J. C., Mitchum, R. M., Jr., Campion, K. M., and Rahmanian, V. D., 1990, Siliciclastic sequence stratigraphy in well logs, cores and outcrop: Concepts for high resolution correlation of time and facies: Amer. Assoc. Petrol. Geol. Methods in Explorat. Series, no. 7, 55 p.

Westcott, W. A., 1993, Geomorphic thresholds and complex response of fluvial systems—some implications for sequence stratigraphy: Amer. Assoc. Petrol. Geol. Bull., v. 77, p. 208–218.

Geology of the Wilson Cliffs-Potosi Mountain Area, Southern Nevada

B. C. BURCHFIEL,

Department of Earth, Atmospheric, and Planetary Sciences, Massachusetts Institute of Technology, Cambridge, Massachusetts 02139

C. S. CAMERON,

Shell Exploration and Production Company, P.O. Box 2403, Houston, Texas 77252

AND L. H. ROYDEN

Department of Earth, Atmospheric, and Planetary Sciences, Massachusetts Institute of Technology, Cambridge, Massachusetts 02139

Abstract

Detailed mapping of seven lithologic subunits in the Bonanza King Formation in the Wilson Cliffs-Potosi Mountain area, eastern Spring Mountains, Nevada, demonstrates the existence of two thrust plates between the NW-trending Cottonwood and La Madre faults. The structurally lower Wilson Cliffs thrust plate is thrust eastward along a spectacularly exposed contact juxtaposing nearly black Cambrian Bonanza King dolomite above white to pale red Jurassic Aztec Sandstone. This thrust has been called the Keystone thrust by previous workers, but the Keystone thrust can be traced from its type area in the Goodsprings District northward, where it forms the base of the Keystone thrust plate lying structurally above the Wilson Cliffs plate. The Wilson Cliffs plate is a remnant of the Contact thrust plate to the south and the Red Spring thrust plate to the north. Emplacement of the Contact-Wilson Cliffs-Red Spring thrust plate preceded the emplacement of the Keystone thrust and the two events are separated by movement on the La Madre fault and a period of erosion that locally removed the Wilson Cliffs plate. The Cottonwood fault displaces the Wilson Cliffs plate, but ends to the northwest by warping of the Keystone plate. The deformation along the Cottonwood fault can be explained by post-Keystone south-side-down displacement of 3500 to 3800 feet (1060 to 1150 m), and suggests that Cenozoic deformation may be more important within the Spring Mountains than currently recognized.

Presently the Contact-Wilson Cliffs-Red Spring thrust plate lies below and east of the Keystone thrust plate, a relationship that has been used to demonstrate that this part of the Cordilleran thrust belt did not become progressively younger eastward. However, at a low structural level, the ramp for the Keystone thrust fault lies east of the ramp for the Contact-Wilson Cliffs-Red Spring thrust fault and thus is in sequence. At a higher structural level, the Keystone thrust fault propagated across the Contact-Wilson Cliffs-Red Spring thrust plate, placing the leading edge of this plate east and below the surface trace of the Keystone thrust. Thus, the present map pattern gives the erroneous impression of an out-of-sequence relationship.

Introduction

THE KEYSTONE THRUST FAULT of southeastern Nevada is one of the best-exposed thrust faults in the world (Figs. 1 and 2). For more than half a century, geologic relations along the thrust fault and its lateral correlatives have been used: (1) as an example of typical geometric relations along the hanging wall and footwall of a ramp thrust (Serra, 1977); (2) to support various hypotheses for the mechanics of thrust faulting

(Raleigh and Griggs, 1963; Johnson, 1981; Burchfiel et al., 1982; Price and Johnson, 1982; Axen, 1984); and (3) to establish timing relations between deformation in the hanging wall and footwall to show that in this part of the Cordilleran orogenic belt, thrust faults did not become progressively younger eastward (Longwell, 1926; Davis, 1973; Axen, 1984). Surprisingly, the best-exposed part of the thrust plate, where black and grey Cambrian dolomites over-

203

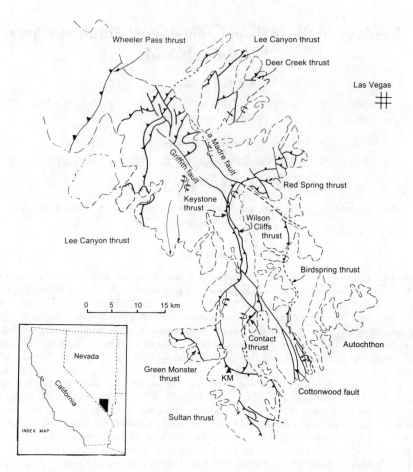

FIG. 1. Generalized tectonic map showing the major structural features of the eastern Spring Mountains, Nevada. KM locates the Keystone Mine, the type locality of the Keystone thrust fault. Inset map gives the location of the eastern Spring Mountains relative to Nevada and California.

lie white or tan Jurassic sandstone (Fig. 2), had not been mapped in detail. This paper presents results of mapping at a scale of 1:15,000 from the Red Rock Canyon area in the north to the Goodsprings mining district in the south.

Hewett (1931, 1956) first mapped and described the Keystone and structurally lower Contact thrust plates in the Goodsprings area immediately south of the area covered by this report (Fig. 1). The area at the Keystone Mine was designated as the type area of the Keystone thrust fault. Carr's (1983) restudy of the Goodsprings area has shown the complexity of structural events in that area, and he presented evidence that the Contact thrust is older than the Keystone thrust. Recent work by Fleck and Carr (1990) demonstrated that the Key-

stone thrust is younger than 100 ± 2 Ma, but the age of the Contact plate remains poorly constrained.

Longwell (1926) and Glock (1929) first mapped the Keystone and structurally lower Red Spring thrust plates in the northeastern Spring Mountains, north of the area covered in this report (Fig. 1). Longwell (1926) first concluded that the Red Spring thrust was older than the Keystone thrust, but later (1960) interpreted the two thrusts to be correlative and the complex relations between them to be related to thrusting contemporaneous with rotation and strike-slip displacement on the nearby Las Vegas Valley shear zone.

Davis (1973) restudied parts of the Red Spring thrust and concluded that Longwell's

FIG. 2. Aerial photographs of the thrust fault at the top of the Wilson Cliffs. Light-colored rocks are the Jurassic Aztec Sandstone overlain along a planar thrust fault contact by dark Paleozoic rocks composed mostly of the Cambrian Bonanza King Formation. This thrust fault, commonly referred to as the Keystone thrust fault, is in fact the Wilson Cliffs thrust fault, which is structurally lower and older than the Keystone thrust fault. A. View looking north along the Wilson Cliffs thrust fault to the Red Rock Canyon area in the upper right. B. View looking west at the Wilson Cliffs thrust fault showing the distinctly planar character of the fault.

(1926) original interpretation that the Red Spring thrust pre-dated the Keystone thrust was correct. Davis also correlated the Red Spring and Contact thrusts and suggested they were remnants of a once continuous thrust. He further suggested that following the emplacement of the Red Spring–Contact thrust plate, it was cut by high-angle faults, uplifted on a horst block bounded by the Cottonwood and La Madre faults, and removed by erosion from the horst prior to emplacement of the structurally higher Keystone thrust plate (Fig. 1). Axen (1984, 1985) remapped in detail the area studied by Longwell, Glock, and Davis and concluded that the structural relationships support an older emplacement age for the Red Spring

thrust plate relative to the Keystone plate, a
concept challenged by Matthews (1988, 1989),
but adequately defended by Axen (1989).

The area between the Goodsprings district
and the northeastern part of the Spring Mountains was mapped by Secor (1962), and his
mapping was incorporated into maps by Longwell et al. (1965) and Burchfiel et al. (1974) as
part of more regional studies in the Spring
Mountains. Their work was completed before
the structural complexities of the adjacent two
areas had been realized. Our mapping of the
Wilson Cliffs–Potosi Mountain area was done
at scales of 1:15,000 and 1:24,000 as part of
detailed studies of thrust faults in this region to
better understand their geometry and timing, as
well as the character of the thrust surfaces
in relation to hanging-wall and footwall rocks,
and to set realistic boundary conditions for
mechanical studies of the thrust faults in this
area and thrust faults in general. The Potosi
Mountain area was mapped by Cameron (1977)
and the Wilson Cliffs area was mapped later by
Burchfiel and Royden. One of the results of this
study is that the well-exposed thrust fault at the
top of the Wilson Cliffs—and described by all
previous works as the Keystone thrust fault—
is, in fact, not the Keystone thrust. This conclusion will be documented and some of its ramifi-
cations presented below.

Stratigraphy

The oldest rocks exposed in the Wilson
Cliffs–Potosi Mountain area are limestone and
dolomite of the Middle and Upper Cambrian
Bonanza King Formation. Seven informal subdivisions of this formation were made for mapping purposes to show the geometry of the
thrust faults in the area relative to hanging-wall
and footwall rocks. Detailed mapping of these
units has revealed that there are two major
thrust faults present throughout the mapped
area, and that the structurally lowest thrust
fault, which places Cambrian rocks above the
Jurassic Aztec Sandstone, is not the Keystone
thrust. To document the stratigraphic level at
which the two thrust faults in the map area
detached, it is necessary to discuss the stratigraphy of the Bonanza King and older formations
from the Las Vegas–Spring Mountains region

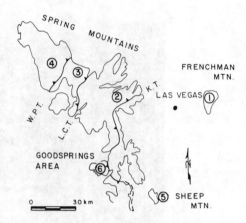

FIG. 3. Location of sections (Figs. 4A and 4B) within the
craton, Keystone thrust plate (KT), Lee Canyon thrust
plate (LCT), and Wheeler Pass thrust plate (WPT).

beyond the limits of the mapped area. Younger
parts of the stratigraphic sequences ranging
from Ordovician to Jurassic are adequately
described in the studies by Cameron (1977),
Gans (1974), Axen (1984, 1985), and Carr
(1983) and will not be presented here.

Tapeats Sandstone–Zabriskie Quartzite

East of the Spring Mountains at Frenchman
Mountain and at Sheep Mountain (Figs. 3 and
4) the Lower Cambrian Tapeats Sandstone rests
unconformably on Precambrian metamorphic
rocks (Hewett, 1956; Longwell et al., 1965).
The Tapeats Sandstone is ~50 meters thick and
consists of red, tan, and white quartzite; quartz-
rich sandstone; and conglomerate. The rocks at
Frenchman and Sheep mountains lie east of the
Cordilleran thrust belt and are part of the North
American cratonal succession.

Rocks correlative to the Tapeats do not crop
out in the easternmost thrust faults of the
Cordilleran thrust belt because detachment of
these faults occurred at a higher stratigraphic
level. Farther west, rocks correlative to the
Tapeats crop out in the Wheeler Pass thrust
plate (Figs. 3 and 4). Work by Stewart (1970)
demonstrated that within these thrust plates, a
conformable succession of Upper Precambrian
and Cambrian sedimentary rocks is present,
and that the Zabriskie Quartzite and the uppermost part of the Wood Canyon Formation, both
of Early Cambrian age, correlate with the
Tapeats. The thickness of the Lower Cambrian

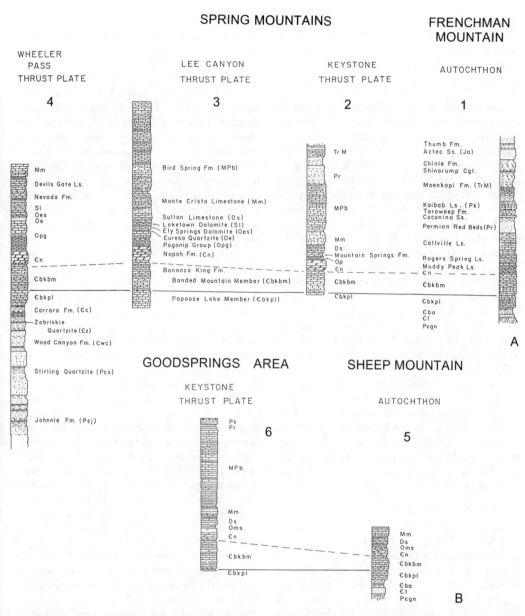

FIG. 4. Stratigraphic sections from cratonal areas east of the Spring Mountains (Frenchman Mountain and Sheep Mountain) to miogeoclinal sections in different thrust plates in the Spring Mountains. A. Spring Mountains and Frenchman Mountain. B. Goodsprings area and Sheep Mountain. Units discussed in the text are the Tapeats Sandstone (Єt), Bright Angel Shale (Єba), and the Bonanza King Formation and its two members—the lower, Papoose Lake Member (Єbkpl) and the upper, Banded Mountain Member (Єbkbm). Even though the Papoose Lake Member is not fully present, and older units are not exposed within the eastern Spring Mountains, their presence can be confidently inferred because of the correlation of units in detail from the craton to the miogeocline in the western part of the Spring Mountains.

rock sequence and the conformable addition of the Upper Precambrian sedimentary rocks beneath the Lower Cambrian rocks toward the west indicate the presence of a depositional hinge zone between cratonal and miogeoclinal rock sequences. This hinge zone has been telescoped by E-directed Mesozoic thrust faulting and it cannot be accurately reconstructed because transitional rock sequences are not exposed in the Las Vegas region.

Bright Angel Shale–Carrara Formation

Conformably above the Tapeats Sandstone in the cratonal section, and above the Zabriskie Quartzite in the miogeoclinal section, is a sequence of green calcareous shale and fine-grained quartz-rich siltstone, with beds of grey, mottled limestone that commonly contain round to elliptical algae pisolites ranging up to 5 cm in diameter. Maroon shale and orange-weathering silty limestone also are present. In the cratonal areas of Frenchman and Sheep mountains, these rocks are ~100 to 150 m thick, and they are assigned to the Lower and Lower Middle Cambrian Bright Angel Shale (Figs. 3 and 4); (Hewett, 1956; Longwell, 1965). Within the Wheeler Pass thrust plate, correlative rocks are 300 to 400 m thick and are assigned to the Carrara Formation (Figs. 3 and 4) (Burchfiel and Davis, 1971; Burchfiel et al., 1974). At the tops of both formations, mottled, silty limestone becomes progressively less silty through about 5 to 15 m and grades into dark grey, mottled limestone and dolomite at the base of the Bonanza King Formation. Like the Tapeats Sandstone, transitional rocks of the Bright Angel Shale (cratonal section) and Carrara Formation (miogeoclinal section) are not exposed in the Las Vegas region.

Bonanza King Formation

Conformably above the Carrara Formation and Bright Angel Shale, both in the miogeoclinal and cratonal sequences, is a thick succession of limestone, dolomite, and silty dolomite of Middle and early Late Cambrian age that was assigned to the Bonanza King Formation of Hazzard and Mason (1936) by Gans (1974). The Bonanza King Formation is the oldest formation that crops out at the base of the easternmost thrust faults in the Cordilleran thrust belt in this region.

Identification and mapping of seven units in the upper part of the Bonanza King Formation has been the key to unraveling the complex structure of the Wilson Cliffs–Potosi Mountain area. In addition, regional correlations show that both major thrust faults recognized in the mapped area detached along basal decollements

that were within the lower part of the Bonanza King Formation and not within the shales of the underlying Bright Angel–Carrara interval (Burchfiel et al., 1982).

The Bonanza King Formation of Hazzard and Mason (1936) was subdivided into two members—the lower, Papoose Lake and upper, Banded Mountain members—by Barnes and Palmer (1961). Since their subdivision, these two members have been recognized and mapped regionally throughout the Las Vegas–Death Valley area (Figs. 3 and 4). In the eastern Spring Mountains and adjacent areas, subdivisions of the members have been identified and widely correlated (Fig. 5) (Gans, 1974), but not mapped areally.

Papoose Lake Member. The Papoose Lake Member of the Bonanza King Formation consists of medium to dark grey limestone and dolomite. Characteristically the limestone and dolomite form irregularly bedded to mottled interbeds 1 to 5 cm thick. Also present is thin-bedded to laminated, medium to dark grey limestone and rare beds of pisolitic or oolitic limestone. Very rare beds of grey to light grey laminated or wavy bedded limestone are present as well. The main rock types occur in units 2 to 20 m thick that crop out as subdued ledges and benches, with the thin-bedded and laminated limestone forming the more recessive units.

In cratonal sections, the Papoose Lake Member is about 100 to 150 m thick at Frenchman Mountain and about 150 to 200 m thick at Sheep Mountain (Figs. 3 and 4). In both places, its top is poorly defined because the basal rocks of the overlying Banded Mountain Member are not as typically developed as they are where the two members were first defined. Within the Wheeler Pass thrust plate, in the miogeoclinal section, the Papoose Lake Member is 200 to 250 m thick and contains rare thin units of white-weathering, laminated dolomite and silty dolomite. The upper part of the Papoose Lake Member also is present in the Lee Canyon and Green Monster thrust plates that structurally overlie the Keystone plate (Figs. 1, 3, and 4). Thus, in regional correlations it is clear that rocks equivalent to the Papoose Lake Member were present in the eastern Spring Mountains, but only the upper few tens of meters of the Papoose Lake Member crop out locally at the base of the two thrust plates in the Wilson Cliffs–Potosi Mountain area.

KEYSTONE THRUST PLATE

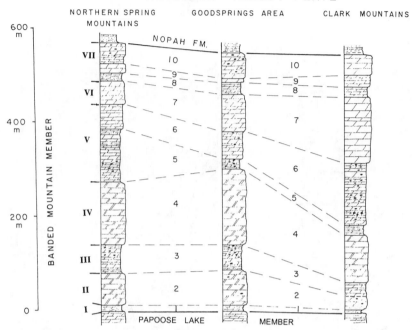

FIG. 5. Subdivisions of the Banded Mountain Member of the Bonanza King Formation from the northern Spring Mountains through the Goodsprings area (covered in this report) to the Clark Mountains, California, 60 km farther south. Detailed stratigraphy by Gans (1974) demonstrated that the Banded Mountain Member could be subdivided into the 10 units shown in this figure. These 10 units can be correlated for more than 100 km along the eastern part of the Spring Mountains to the Clark Mountains. For mapping purposes, we found that seven subdivisions (shown in roman numerals) were more useful, because some of the units described by Gans were difficult to follow in structurally complex areas.

Banded Mountain Member. The Banded Mountain Member of the Bonanza King Formation consists of alternating units (50 to 100 m thick) of dark and light grey dolomite that give the member its distinctive banded outcrop appearance. These bands have been subdivided into seven informal units that were mapped during this study to decipher the internal structure within the Bonanza King Formation (Fig. 5). By mapping these units, we were able to determine the existence of two major thrust faults in the Wilson Cliffs area, to demonstrate that the detachment of both thrust plates occurred within the Bonanza King Formation and not within the underlying Bright Angel Shale, and to show that the internal structures of the two thrust plates are quite different.

The thickness of the Banded Mountain Member is uncertain, varying between 400 and 500 m. Most of the variation in thickness is related to numerous faults that cut bedding at a low angle. From a distance, the light and dark units of the Banded Mountain Member appear to be continuous and in many places structurally simple, but in detail there are numerous small repetitions of beds or groups of beds within each unit along faults that cut bedding at angles from 5 to 15°. Most of these faults could not be mapped at a scale of 1:15,000 because in some cases their displacement is small and they could not be traced along strike. However, their presence is clear and makes the detailed stratigraphy (at a scale of tens of meters) in each unit uncertain. Some variations in thickness may be the result of deposition, particularly where low-angle faults could not be observed, but many of these faults are so subtle that they could be detected only where the outcrop is excellent. Seven units were mapped in the Banded Mountain Member, which correlate generally with the

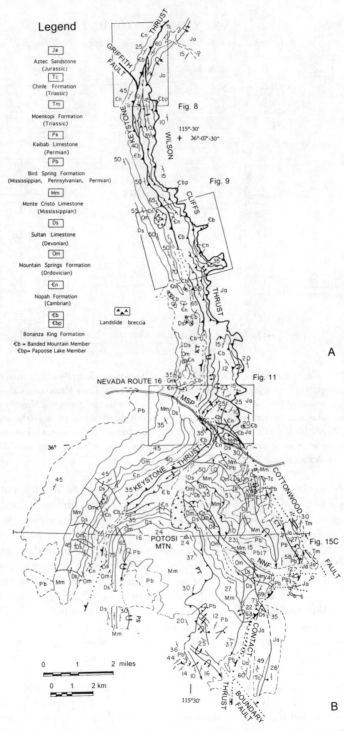

FIG. 6. Generalized geologic map of the Wilson Cliffs–Potosi Mountain area, Nevada. Location of detailed Figures 8, 9, and 11 are shown, as is the location of the geological cross section in the Potosi Mountain area (see Fig. 15C). Abbreviations: CT = Contact thrust; KT = Keystone thrust; MSP = Mountain Springs Pass; NNF = Ninety-Nine fault zone; PS = Potosi syncline; PT = Potosi thrust.

10 units identified by Gans (1974). It will be noted in the descriptions below where our units differ from his. On the generalized geological map (Fig. 6), these units are not distinguished, but they are shown on Figures 8, 9, and 11, which are parts of a detailed map of the Wilson Cliffs–Potosi Mountain area at 1:15,000.[1]

The basal unit, Unit I, consists of 10 to 15 m of yellow- to orange-weathering, thin-bedded to laminated, fine-grained silty dolomite. This unit is known to most local geologists as the "silty unit." It is easily recognized by the formation of orange-weathering slopes within the otherwise light and dark grey dolomite succession. The base of this unit is the contact between the two members of the Bonanza King Formation.

Unit II consists of ~30 to 50 m of grey dolomite and dark grey limestone in irregular or mottled beds 2 to 5 cm thick. This unit and the higher two dark grey, mottled units (Units IV and VI) form rugged cliffs between more slope-forming, lighter grey banded units with mixed rock types. Unit II, unlike units IV and VI above, locally contains beds of light grey mottled and laminated dolomite. In some places it can be demonstrated that these beds are faulted into the sequence, but in other places they appear to be stratigraphically part of Unit II.

Unit III is formed predominantly by a light and medium grey, generally slope-forming, sequence that consists of several different interbedded rock types. Light grey to nearly white laminated dolomite forms beds 10 cm to 1 m thick and alternates with medium to dark grey dolomite that is thin to medium bedded, locally laminated, or mottled. Some beds contain large (10 to 50 cm) irregular grey chert nodules that weather with concentric grey, tan, and orange rings. The contrasting rock types in Unit III appear to facilitate the development of small faults that cut bedding at low angles and duplicate or eliminate section. Thus, the thickness of these units varies considerably along strike. The interbedding of different rock types makes it easy to recognize the faults. Unit III varies in thickness between 50 and 150 m, and its true thickness may be ~50 m.

[1]This detailed map can be obtained by contacting Doug Walker at the University of Kansas (email address: jdwalker@kuhub.cc.ukans.edu).

Unit IV is a cliff-forming, uniform dark grey, mottled limestone and dolomite. Of the dark mottled units within the Bonanza King Formation, it is the darkest and most uniform in composition. Minor rock types present all are dark grey and include thin beds of flat-pebble conglomerate, laminated dolomite, and dolomite with rare wispy stringers of white dolomite 1 to 2 cm long. Unit IV varies from 75 to 200 m in thickness, and its original thickness probably is ~100 to 150 m.

Unit V is similar to Unit III and consists of dominantly slope-forming light and medium grey sequences of different rock types. The dominant rock types are the same as those of Unit III, but also include laminated dolomites with algal heads of 5 to 30 cm in diameter, pisolitic and rare oolitic dolomite, and beds with vertical worm tubes up to 10 cm long. Unit V also contains large chert nodules at several horizons. Some beds of dark grey, mottled dolomite similar to Units II, IV, and VI are present, but they never reach the thickness of these three units. Unit V varies from 50 m to more than 300 m in thickness; its true thickness is difficult to determine because it is the locus of numerous faults and folds. We estimate a thickness of 200 to 250 meters for Unit V, which in our scheme correlates approximately with Units 5 and 6 of Gans (1974).

Unit VI is the highest cliff-forming, dark grey, mottled limestone and dolomite in the Banded Mountain Member. Like Unit IV, it is quite uniform in lithology and can be distinguished from Unit IV by its slightly lighter grey color. In the southern part of the area, the color is a dark grey with a distinctive brown tint. Unit VI varies from 30 to 200 m in thickness and its original thickness is ~75 to 100 m. However, it may have been 150 m thick in the southern part of the mapped area. Our Unit VI corresponds approximately to Unit 7 of Gans (1974).

Unit VII is the most variable unit in the Banded Mountain Member. Within the lower thrust plate of the Wilson Cliffs area, it consists of a basal section of well-bedded, light grey, mottled dolomite; light grey to white laminated dolomite; and rare beds of grey to dark grey dolomite that contain 1- to 5-cm-long wispy stringers of white dolomite. The upper part of Unit VII is a massive to well-bedded sugary dolomite with some rare stringers of silty dolomite. Within the upper thrust plate, Unit VII consists of only poorly bedded to massive, medium- to coarse-grained, white to very light grey dolomite. In the upper thrust plate, Unit VII is ~30 to 70 m thick, whereas in the lower thrust plate it is 100 to 150 m thick. Our Unit VII corresponds approximately to Units 8, 9, and 10 of Gans (1974).

Nopah Formation

The Nopah Formation of Hazzard (1937) was recognized by Gans (1974) in his revision of the Goodsprings Dolomite in the eastern Spring Mountains. Two members—a lower Dunderberg Shale Member and an upper unnamed member—were mapped during this study.[2] The Dunderberg Shale Member consists of 20 to 40 m of orange-weathering silty dolomite and rare green and tan shale with distinctive beds of grey limestone and brown dolomite 1 to 50 cm thick. The limestone beds characteristically contain abundant flat-pebble conglomerate. Lying gradationally above the slope-forming Dunderberg Shale, the upper member consists of cliff-forming, white, massive coarse-grained dolomite. The upper member is 100 to 150 m thick. Both members are present in the upper and lower thrust plates in the Wilson Cliffs–Potosi Mountain area.

Significance of the stratigraphic sequence

The Cambrian stratigraphy is important for two reasons. It shows (1) that initial detachment of both thrust faults in the map area took place within the lower part of the Bonanza King Formation; and (2) that subdivisions of the Banded Mountain Member can be mapped to determine the details of the local structure.

Considering the first point, Cambrian stratigraphic units can be recognized and show continuity from cratonal rocks east of the thrust belt at Frenchman and Sheep mountains to miogeoclinal rocks in the central and western Spring Mountains (Fig. 3). Because of this continuity and the gradual change in thickness and facies of these units, we infer that they originally had continuity throughout the eastern Spring Mountains. Units below the upper part of the Papoose Lake Member of the Bonanza King Formation are not exposed within the two thrust plates of the Wilson

[2]The two members are not shown in Figure 6, but are shown on the detailed maps in Figures 8, 9, and 11.

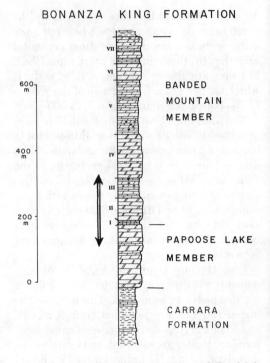

FIG. 7. Throughout the map area and beyond (Burchfiel et al., 1982), thrust faults along the eastern margin of the miogeocline detach within the Bonanza King Formation, from the upper part of the Papoose Lake Member to about Unit IV of the Banded Mountain Member (interval shown by the arrow to the left of the stratigraphic column).

Cliffs–Potosi Mountain area because of thrust faulting. If the Cambrian units did have lateral continuity throughout this region before thrusting, the stratigraphic level at which the two thrust plates detached ranges from a few tens of meters below to about 100 m above the contact between the two members of the Bonanza King Formation (i.e., at the base of Unit I—the "silty unit"), and 200 to 300 m above the Bright Angel Shale (Fig. 7). There is no preferred detachment horizon within that part of the section. Perhaps even more surprising is the fact that both thrust plates detached within that interval even though they were emplaced at two different times: the lower plate was emplaced, cut by high-angle faults, and eroded before the upper plate was emplaced (see below). This level of detachment is present on a regional scale for correlative thrust plates that can be followed for ~100 to 150 km both north and south of the Wilson Cliffs–Potosi Mountain area (Burchfiel et al., 1982).

Considering the second point above, we have shown that seven units can be mapped within the Banded Mountain Member. Gans (1974) demonstrated that stratigraphic subdivisions within the Banded Mountain Member could be correlated within the eastern Spring Mountains, but he did not attempt to map them. We have found a sevenfold subdivision to be most useful for mapping purposes (Fig. 5). This has allowed us to recognize the existence of two different thrust plates and to demonstrate that they contain two different structural styles.

Structure

Detailed mapping in the area between the Cottonwood and La Madre faults demonstrates the presence of two major thrust plates lying above the Jurassic Aztec Sandstone of the Wilson Cliffs (Figs. 1 and 6). The structurally lower thrust plate places the Cambrian Bonanza King Formation above the Jurassic Aztec Sandstone (Fig. 6). This thrust plate, called the Keystone plate by earlier workers, is spectacularly exposed (Fig. 2) and has figured prominently in several models on the mechanics of thrust faulting (e.g., Longwell, 1926; Serra, 1977; Johnson, 1981; Burchfiel et al., 1982; Price and Johnson, 1982). Mapping by two of us (Burchfiel and Royden) demonstrates that this plate is not the Keystone thrust plate, and we refer to it here as the Wilson Cliffs plate. The higher thrust plate places the Bonanza King Formation above Cambrian dolomites of the Bonanza King and Nopah formations throughout much of the map area, but locally it rests on Mesozoic rocks in the northern part of the area (Fig. 6). The higher thrust plate is the Keystone plate, because it is continuous with the Keystone from its type area in the Goodsprings district to the south (Figs. 1 and 6). We also will show that the two thrust plates are of different ages. We correlate the Wilson Cliffs plate to the Contact-Red Springs plates (see below) and document, as Davis (1973) first suggested, that this plate once was continuous below the younger Keystone thrust plate and was emplaced before the higher Keystone plate. Products of the erosion that occurred in the interval separating emplacement of the two plates still are present in the northern part of the area. Sedimentary rocks also are present

below the Wilson Cliffs plate, indicating that both thrust plates moved across erosion surfaces in the area where they are presently exposed.

Footwall of the Wilson Cliffs–Contact thrust plate

Rocks below the Wilson Cliffs–Contact thrust plate belong to the upper part of the structurally lower and more easterly Bird Spring thrust plate (Fig. 1). Throughout the map area they consist of the Jurassic Aztec Sandstone that dips 10 to 15° to the west. Because the Aztec contains abundant large-scale cross beds, attitudes on the map (Fig. 6) do not reflect the overall dip of the formation. Rarely, conglomerate is present—filling channels or as thin beds immediately below the Wilson Cliffs thrust. The channels, up to 3 m deep, consist of rounded pebbles and cobbles of quartzite set in a matrix of reworked Aztec quartz sand. The bedded conglomerates consist of pebbles of angular to rounded Cambrian and younger carbonate rocks, also set in a matrix of reworked Aztec quartz sand. The beds usually are no more than 20 to 30 cm thick and are poorly exposed. In the northern and central part of the area, the Aztec quartz-rich sandstone lies 3 to 5 meters below the thrust; it is white, dense, and composed of shattered and silicified material.

Excluding the high-angle faults discussed below, the only major structure in the footwall rocks within the map area is a NE-trending, E-vergent syncline in the northern part of the map area (Fig. 6). The west limb of the fold is overturned and rocks of the Triassic Chinle Formation are exposed. Toward the south, the axial trace of the fold trends obliquely to, and passes beneath, the Wilson Cliffs plate, but before it does, the western overturned limb of the fold is overlain by three thin thrust slices. The thrust slices consist of, in ascending order, redbeds of the Triassic Chinle and/or Moenkopi formations, limestone of the Moenkopi and Permian Kaibab formations, and Cambrian dolomite of the Wilson Cliffs plate (Fig. 8). This relationship, as well as the relationship of the fold to conglomerates discussed below, indicates that the fold is related to the emplacement of the Wilson Cliffs plate, not the higher Keystone plate, which overlies the fold in the northernmost part of the area. Throughout the

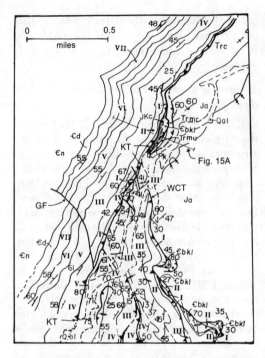

FIG. 8. Detailed geologic map of the northern part of the map area (for location, see Fig. 6). In this area, the Keystone (KT) and Wilson Cliffs (WCT) thrust faults merge. Units in the Banded Mountain Member (I through VII) are mapped separately and the uppermost part of the Papoose Lake Member (€bkp) is present locally at the base of the Wilson Cliffs thrust plate. Above the overturned footwall syncline in the Jurassic Aztec Sandstone (Ja) are thrust slices of Kaibab Limestone (Pk), Moenkopi Formation lower limestone (Trmn), and upper redbeds (Trmr). They are overlain by a thin brecciated sheet of dolomite of the Papoose Lake Member, which we assign to the Wilson Cliffs plate. Lying west of these thrust slices and below the Keystone thrust is a narrow zone of bedded, reworked Aztec Sandstone interbedded with conglomerate composed of clasts of Bonanza King Formation and derived from the east (Jkc, shaded area). The eastern contact with the Wilson Cliffs plate is not exposed, but relations suggest that it was deposited on rocks of the Wilson Cliffs plate (see text). Other units mapped in the Keystone plate are €d = Dunderberg Shale; €n = upper Nopah Formation. The location of the cross section in Figure 15A is shown.

remainder of the area, the Aztec Sandstone is unfolded except by local small-scale folds below the Contact thrust in the very southern part of the mapped area.

Wilson Cliffs–Contact thrust plate

The thrust plate that lies above the Jurassic Aztec Sandstone and below the Keystone thrust

plate, as mapped during this study, can be divided conveniently into a northern and a southern segment divided by the Cottonwood fault (Fig. 6). The segment south of the fault is the Contact thrust plate mapped by Hewett (1931, 1956), Cameron (1977), Carr (1983), and Carr and Pinkston (1987). The segment north of the Cottonwood fault here is referred to as the Wilson Cliffs plate. Our mapping will demonstrate that the Contact and Wilson Cliffs plates are the same, but it is convenient to refer to them separately until all the evidence is presented.

Wilson Cliffs plate. The Wilson Cliffs plate can be traced from the Cottonwood fault 9 km north to where it is truncated by the Keystone thrust (Fig. 6). Before it ends, the Wilson Cliffs plate consists of a thin sequence of white dolomite (probably part of the uppermost Papoose Lake Member of the Bonanza King Formation) overlying thin slices of footwall rocks, and overlain by a conglomerate of post–Wilson Cliffs and pre-Keystone age (Figs. 6 and 8; see below). Southward, the plate contains a complex imbricate structure formed within rocks of the Banded Mountain Member and, more rarely, by rocks of the uppermost Papoose Lake Member of the Bonanza King Formation to the Nopah Formation (Fig. 6).

The Wilson Cliffs plate consists of numerous imbricate slices, and the fault at the base of the plate is a compound fault because it consists of fault segments that bound the base of different thrust imbricates. Figure 6 clearly shows the anastomosing faults that bound and imbricate the base of the plate. Where units are truncated or repeated by thrust faults they are easy to map; however, along strike, some of these faults enter a single map unit, often parallel to bedding, and cannot be traced further (if in fact they exist at all beyond that point). The thrust surfaces usually are sharp planar breaks with little or no breccia. However, the fault at the base of the plate commonly has breccia up to 5 m thick in its hanging wall. The thrust fault at the base of the plate dips from 8° to 20° west, steepening to 30° locally in western re-entrants (Fig. 6). Thrust faults within the plate commonly dip more steeply, and locally may dip from 60° to 75°; some thrust faults are folded (Fig. 9).

Eastward-overturned folds with subhorizontal axes are common within the imbricates of

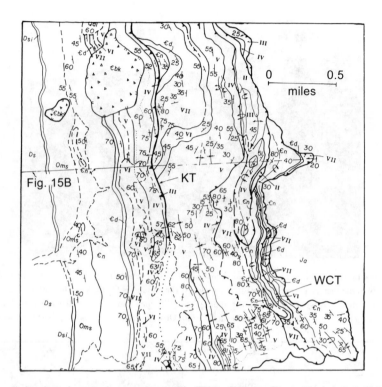

FIG. 9. Detailed geological map in the central part of the Wilson Cliffs (see Figure 6 for location). This area shows the contrast in style between the Wilson Cliffs and Keystone plates. The Keystone plate generally is a homoclinal slab, whereas the Wilson Cliffs plate consists of imbricate thrust slices, folded thrust faults, and upright and E-vergent folds. The nested folded thrust slices in the eastern part of the Wilson Cliffs plate are shown in Figure 10. The dotted line is the key unit traced in Unit V. Banded Mountain units are shown by roman numerals. Other units: Єd = Dunderberg Shale; Єn = upper Nopah Formation; Oms = Mountain Springs Formation; Dsi = Ironside Member of the Sultan Limestone; Ds = Sultan Limestone; Ja = Aztec Sandstone. Brecciated landslide masses are depicted by open triangles. Thrusts: KT = Keystone thrust; WCT = Wilson Cliffs thrust. The location of the cross section in Figure 15B is shown.

the Wilson Cliffs plate. Some synclines lie below thrust faults as footwall synclines, but corresponding hanging wall anticlines are rare (Fig. 10). In some places, E-vergent anticlines lie below thrust faults. More open folds with subvertical axial surfaces also are present. All fold axes trend generally NNW in the northern half of the plate, and north or NNE in the southern half. Some fold axes are curvilinear. Locally, E-trending folds are present. Most thrust surfaces are planar and fold axial surfaces parallel them or are truncated by them, except in one area. In the east-central part of the plate, two thrust faults are folded by E-vergent overturned folds (Figs. 9 and 10).

In the southern 3 to 4 km of the Wilson Cliffs plate, the structure is somewhat simpler. Its eastern part consists of a broad open anticline

in the south and generally gentle W- or S-dipping strata farther north within Units V, VI, and VII of the Banded Mountain Member (Figs. 6 and 11). Imbricates are present, but generally are discontinuous. Its western part consists of tight folds, some overturned eastward, with W-dipping axial surfaces and segments of imbricate faults.

Contact thrust plate. The Contact plate is juxtaposed against the Wilson Cliffs plate and its footwall rocks across the Cottonwood fault (Figs. 6 and 11). The Contact plate carries rocks from the Bonanza King Formation to the Pennsylvanian–Permian Bird Spring Formation thrust eastward over the Aztec Sandstone (Fig. 6). Because the Contact thrust fault lies 3 km east of the Wilson Cliffs thrust fault south of the Cottonwood fault, and because the thrust

FIG. 10. View looking north at folded nested thrust faults in the eastern part of the Wilson Cliffs plate (folded Units IV and V in the eastern part of Figure 9). Wilson Cliffs thrust fault is the dark-white contact at the right of the photo. The prominent E-vergent syncline in the upper part of the ridge folds a thrust slice of Units IV (dark) and V (white) into Cambrian Nopah Formation (white on skyline). Other overturned folds are present on the ridge below.

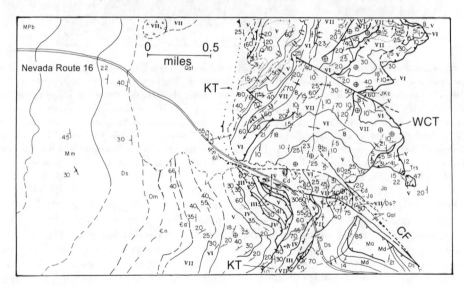

FIG. 11. Detailed geological map of the Mountain Springs Pass area (see Fig. 6 for location). This area contains the critical relations between the Wilson Cliffs (WCT) and Keystone (KT) thrust plates across the Cottonwood fault (CF). Units in the Banded Mountain Member are shown by roman numerals. Other units: €d = Dunderberg Shale; €n= upper Nopah Formation; Oms = Mountain Springs Formation; Ds = Sultan Limestone; Mm = Monte Cristo Limestone (locally subdivided into Ma = Anchor Limestone, Md = Dawn Limestone); Mpb = Bird Spring Formation; Trs = Shinarump Conglomerate; Jkc = channel conglomerate beneath the Wilson Cliffs thrust; Ja = Aztec Sandstone. Brecciated landslide masses are shown with open triangles. Silicified breccia along the Cottonwood fault is shown with solid triangles. Some of the key beds mapped are shown by dotted lines.

plate contains younger Paleozoic rocks than does the Wilson Cliffs plate, separation on the Cottonwood fault is south-side-down.

The structure of the Contact plate is somewhat different from that of the Wilson Cliffs plate. A frontal overturned anticline that has a

FIG. 12. View looking northwestward along the E-vergent frontal anticline of the Contact thrust plate. The S-plunging anticline is outlined in the center of the photo by the prominent light-colored beds of the Monte Cristo Limestone.

FIG. 13. View looking northward along the E-vergent Potosi syncline. Here the syncline is entirely within banded limestones of the Bird Spring Formation.

40° W-dipping axial surface is present in the eastern part of the plate (Figs. 6, 12, and 15C). The plunge of the fold axis varies from 8°S4–16°E in its northern part to 24°S 22–43°W in its southern part. A N-trending eastward overturned syncline, the Potosi Mine syncline, is present in the western part of the plate (Fig. 13). The syncline dies out to the north and downsection. The Potosi thrust fault, in the central part of the plate, dips 20° to 22° west. It cuts upsection to the east in both its

hanging wall and footwall, and small folds associated with the thrust suggest an eastward direction of movement.

The frontal anticline, and the Potosi and Contact thrust faults, are displaced by the NNW-trending Ninety-Nine fault zone (Fig. 6). The fault zone, however, does not offset the Keystone thrust; the fault zone consists of several strands, and separation across the fault zone is north-side-down. Piercing points on both sides of the Ninety-Nine fault zone can be established by using the axis of the frontal anticline within beds of the basal Mississippian rock units. Because the piercing points must be projected onto the fault plane, they have a range of possible positions. Offsets of the extreme positions of the piercing points yield oblique-slip, a north-side-down component of 739 to 968 m, and a right-slip component of 1490 to 1823 m.

Along the northwestern part of the plate, there are several imbricates of Cambrian rocks that rest above younger Paleozoic rocks (Fig. 6). These are interpreted to be derived from the Contact plate, but it is not clear whether some of these might be derived from the higher Keystone plate. The imbricates in the southwestern part of the map area clearly are part of the Contact plate because their boundary faults die out within Cambrian rocks of the Contact plate. Even though the structure of the Contact plate appears to be somewhat different from that of the Wilson Cliffs plate, relations across the Cottonwood fault indicate that they are the same plate.

Cottonwood fault

Previous workers have interpreted the fault here mapped as the Wilson Cliffs thrust to be continuous across, or displaced only a few tens of meters by, the Cottonwood fault (see: Secor, 1962; Longwell et al., 1965; Davis, 1973; Burchfiel et al., 1974). They regarded the Wilson Cliffs thrust fault to be the continuation of the Keystone thrust fault and correlated it to the faults that place Cambrian rocks above younger Paleozoic rocks to the south of the Cottonwood fault. Mapping of units within the Bonanza King Formation shows that the Cottonwood fault has several branches that cut all units and structures within the Contact and Wilson Cliffs plates, but generally warp only the higher Keystone thrust plate (Fig. 11).

At least three WNW- to NW-striking faults comprise the Cottonwood fault in the poorly exposed Paleozoic rocks near Nevada Route 16, east of Mountain Springs Pass. These faults dip from 60° to 75° south and are marked by several meters of breccia. Locally the breccia is silicified and forms prominent red- and white-weathering boulders. Rocks as young as the Nopah Formation are contained within faulted blocks; the very characteristic shale and edge-wise-limestone conglomerate of the Dunder-

berg Shale Member are present at two locations. Unlike the parallel Ninety-Nine fault zone to the south, the Cottonwood fault has a north-side-up separation and has affected the Keystone thrust plate.

Structures are not continuous across the Cottonwood fault. The imbricate thrust slices that contain rocks of the Banded Mountain Member, and include locally the Nopah Formation, south of the fault are juxtaposed against a broad open anticline within Units V, VI, and VII of the Banded Mountain Member to the north of the fault (Fig. 11). The two eastern imbricate thrust slices and their basal thrust faults are folded into a N-plunging syncline adjacent to the Cottonwood fault on its southern side. The rocks and thrust faults are overturned and dip eastward adjacent to the fault. Southeastward, Devonian and Mississippian rocks of the Contact plate are juxtaposed against slivers of Banded Mountain Member and Nopah Formation (including the Dunderberg Shale Member) within the Cottonwood fault zone and Jurassic Aztec Sandstone in the footwall of the Wilson Cliffs plate on the northern side of the fault. Thus, the relations indicate a large displacement on the Cottonwood fault.

The relations across the Cottonwood fault support the interpretation that the Wilson Cliffs and Contact plates are the same plate. Devonian and Mississippian formations of the higher Keystone plate are continuous, and unbroken, across the projected western continuation of the Cottonwood fault (Figs. 6 and 11; see below), and both the Wilson Cliffs and Contact plates rest on the Jurassic Aztec Sandstone; thus the two plates have the same structural position. The overturning of structures along the southern side of the Cottonwood fault and the fault slivers of Cambrian rocks within the fault zone are best explained by a south-side-down (or left-slip) displacement or by an oblique-slip combination of the two displacements, again supporting the correlation of the two plates. Correlation of structures offset across the Cottonwood fault can be made as follows. Western imbricates and overturned folds are present in both plates. They lie west of the open anticline north of the fault, a location that corresponds to the gently folded, upright western limb of the recumbent fold in the Contact plate to the south (Fig. 6). The recumbent fold within the eastern part of the Contact plate would have been removed by erosion from the eastern part of the Wilson Cliffs plate. If these correlations are correct, the slip on the Cottonwood fault post-dated emplacement of the Contact–Wilson Cliffs plate.

Earlier interpretations suggested two periods of displacement on the Cottonwood fault, one following emplacement of the Contact thrust and preceding the emplacement of the Keystone thrust, and the second following emplacement of the Keystone plate (see Davis, 1973; Burchfiel et al., 1974). The magnitude and sense of slip were not treated in detail by earlier workers, who suggested only a south-side-down sense of displacement on the Cottonwood fault. Detailed mapping shows warping of the Keystone plate, and folding of the imbricates of the Contact plate might suggest that the Cottonwood fault also had a left-slip component.

Even with detailed mapping, the timing and magnitude of displacement across the Cottonwood fault are difficult to reconstruct. There is considerable difficulty in supporting left-slip movement on the Cottonwood fault. Piercing lines can be constructed from the intersection of Units V–VII with the Contact and Wilson Cliffs thrust faults. Units V–VII are exposed north of (and within) the Cottonwood fault zone (Fig. 11); however, the Contact thrust exposes only rocks as old as the Ordovician Mountain Springs Formation in the core of its frontal anticline ~0.5 mile (800 m) farther southeast on the southern side of the fault. Detailed cross sections indicate that Units V–VII would be present above the Contact thrust about one-quarter to one-half mile (400–800 m) west of the surface expression of the axial trace of the frontal anticline (see cross section in Figure 15C). This would place them almost directly south of the same units in the Cottonwood fault zone. Thus, the amount of left-slip on the fault would be only a few hundred meters at most and could be zero; this is insufficient to explain the 2.0- to 2.25-mile (3.2- to 3.6-km) left-separation of the Contact and Wilson Cliffs thrusts.

A single period of post-Keystone south-side-down displacement can explain all the mapped geological relations. Cross sections drawn across the Cottonwood fault indicate that the Contact thrust is ~3100 feet (940 m) lower on the southern side of the fault than is the Wilson Cliffs thrust on the northern side. The Wilson Cliffs thrust dips ~10 to 15° to the west. Assuming a 15° dip, a south-side-down displacement of ~3500 feet (1060 m) is necessary to cause a 2.0- to 2.25-mile (3.2- to 3.6-km) left-separation on the thrust. Warping of the Keystone thrust is more difficult to quantify, because exposures are poor in the area where it intersects the Cottonwood fault. The thrust front is shifted sinistrally about 3800 feet (1150 m) across the projected trend of the Cottonwood fault. The Keystone thrust dips more steeply than the Contact–Wilson Cliffs thrust. Assuming a dip of ~45° to the west, a south-side-down displacement on the Cottonwood fault of 3800 feet (1150 m) would accomplish the measured shift. Thus, on the basis of the crude measurements that can be made, it is possible that the present map patterns of the thrust faults could be accomplished by a single, post-Keystone, south-side-down displacement of ~3500 to 3800 feet (1060 to 1150 m). The displacement on the Cottonwood fault still must fade out into warping at, or just west of, its intersection with the Keystone thrust. Other, more complex, multistage displacements are possible, but the present data do not require them.

The Keystone plate

The structurally higher thrust plate, and its basal thrust fault, can be traced from the type area of the Keystone plate at the Keystone Mine (Fig. 1) (Hewett, 1931; Carr, 1983) northward into the higher thrust plate in the map area (Fig. 6); thus, the higher thrust plate is the Keystone plate. In contrast to the Wilson Cliffs–Contact thrust plate, the Keystone plate is structurally simple. Throughout most of the map area, and south to the Keystone Mine, it consists of a W-dipping panel of rocks ranging from the Banded Mountain Member of the Bonanza King Formation at the base to the Mississippian Monte Cristo Formation; westward beyond the map area, the sequence continues into the Triassic Moenkopi Formation. The Keystone thrust fault, and its hanging-wall stratigraphic units, can be traced continuously over the length of the map area. Only locally are they covered by older alluvial deposits and landslide masses of brecciated Bonanza King rocks in the south-central part of the area.

Where exposed, the thrust surface is a sharp break and is marked by little or no evidence of

Fig. 14. Unit I of the Banded Mountain Member of the Bonanza King Formation, lying less than 50 cm above the Keystone thrust. Very thin laminae and burrow mottling are preserved with no evidence of brecciation or proximity to a major thrust fault. This characteristic is common along the Keystone thrust and along many of the subsidiary thrust faults in the map area.

either brittle or ductile deformation (Fig. 14). The trace of the Keystone thrust fault trends generally N-S and is gently arcuate, except where it interacts with the Cottonwood fault at Mountain Springs Pass. The thrust fault is mostly parallel to bedding, dipping 30° to 40° in the northern and southern part of the area and 55° or 65° in the central part of the area. No rocks of the lower member of the Bonanza King Formation are present in its hanging wall over the entire map area. Cross sections indicate that the Keystone thrust truncates the Wilson Cliffs–Contact thrust fault at depth (Fig. 15). Only in the southern part of the map area does the Keystone plate contain a few E-vergent to upright folds and possible imbricates. Some of the imbricates below the Keystone thrust near the Cottonwood fault could be interpreted as derived from the Keystone plate. Otherwise, internal structure of the Keystone plate is a homoclinal slab shallowing in dip west of the map area.

Near the Cottonwood fault, the Keystone plate is folded in the same sense as the displacement of the Wilson Cliffs–Contact plate across the Cottonwood fault (Figs. 6 and 11). At Mountain Springs Pass, the intersection of the Keystone thrust and the Cottonwood fault is covered by alluvium, but Devonian and younger formations are continuous across the

western projection of the Cottonwood fault, indicating that the Keystone plate is warped but not offset by movement on the Cottonwood fault. Warping of the Keystone plate must be at least partly post-Keystone in age. Earlier workers considered movement on the Cottonwood fault to be entirely pre-Keystone in age, whereas the evidence presented here suggests that it may be entirely post-Keystone in age.

No rocks older than the Banded Mountain Member of the Bonanza King Formation are present in the hanging wall of the Keystone thrust fault. Although there appears to be a stratigraphic control of the thrust fault, in detail the fault follows different units of the Banded Mountain Member along strike. The thrust fault lies within Units I to IV, transgressing them locally at a low angle except where the high-angle Griffith fault is truncated by the Keystone in the northern part of the area.

Age Relations of Structures within the Map Area

The oldest structure in the area is the Boundary fault in the southeasternmost part of the area. It is never exposed, but its presence is indicated by displaced Mesozoic rocks in the footwall of the Contact plate; Jurassic Aztec Sandstone to the north strikes into Triassic

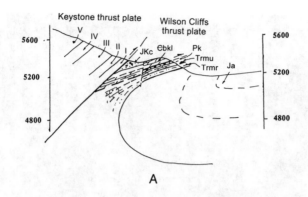

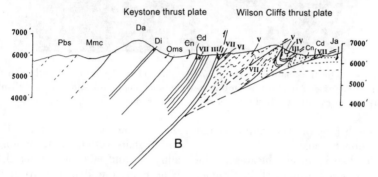

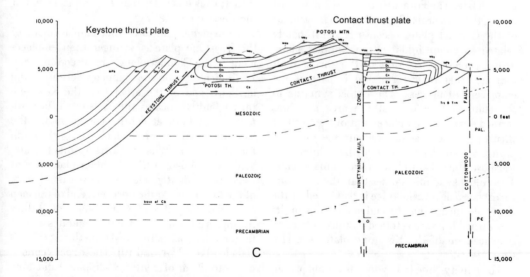

FIG. 15. Cross sections through the Wilson Cliffs area (no vertical exaggeration). Locations are shown in Figures 6, 8, and 9. Note that each cross section has a different scale. A. Section through the northern part of the area, showing that the Keystone thrust truncates the Wilson Cliffs thrust at depth. It also shows the relations between the JKc conglomerate and sandstone unit and the two thrust plates. The basal and eastern contacts of the JKc unit are not exposed in the field. B. Cross section through the middle part of the Wilson Cliffs area; location is shown on Figures 6 and 9. This cross section depicts the difference in structural style between the strongly folded and imbricated Wilson Cliffs plate and the slab-like character of the Keystone plate. Figure 10 shows the folded thrust in the eastern part of the section. C. Cross section through the Potosi Mountain area in the southern part of the map area, showing the truncation of the Contact thrust by the younger Keystone thrust.

Fig. 16. Close-up of the JKc sandstone and conglomerate unit that lies below the Keystone thrust in the northern part of the area (see also Figs. 8 and 15A). White beds are quartz sandstone reworked from the Aztec Sandstone; dark beds are conglomerate consisting only of clasts of Bonanza King Formation with quartz sand matrix.

rocks to the south (Fig. 6). The fault does not displace the Contact thrust.

The next oldest structures in the area are the result of eastward emplacement of the Contact thrust plate. The Potosi thrust in the southern part of the area probably is related to movement of the Contact plate, because it is intimately related to major folds in the Contact plate, whose geometric relation to the thrust fault indicates that their formation is part of the emplacement process. The Potosi syncline in the southwestern part of the area also was formed during the emplacement of the Contact thrust plate, because its axial surface and axial plunge are similar to those of the frontal eastward overturned anticline in the Contact plate. The Potosi syncline is older than the Keystone thrust because its axial trace is truncated by the Keystone thrust (Fig. 6) and small folds on its overturned limb are refolded by folds related to emplacement of the Keystone plate (see also Carr, 1983).

The Ninety-Nine fault zone also is older than the Keystone thrust, but probably is younger than the emplacement of the Contact plate. It displaces the Potosi thrust by normal-right oblique slip (see above), but cannot be considered a tear fault in the contact plate because right-lateral displacement on this NW-trending fault is the wrong sense for a tear fault in the E-vergent Contact plate. Thus, it is younger

than the emplacement of the Contact plate. Although its western continuation is covered by alluvium and landslide material, the Ninety-Nine fault zone does not offset the Keystone thrust; thus it is older than the emplacement of the Keystone plate (Fig. 6).

All evidence indicates that emplacement of the Keystone plate is younger than emplacement of the Contact plate. Cross sections (Fig. 15) indicate (as do the mapped relations at the northern end of the area) that the Keystone thrust fault truncates the Wilson Cliffs–Contact thrust fault at depth. The ramp for the Keystone thrust, therefore, lay east of the ramp for the lower Wilson Cliffs–Contact plate. Thus, the Wilson Cliffs–Contact plate cannot be simply a slightly older and more easterly part of the Keystone. At the northern end of the map area, about 2 miles (3.2 km) south of Willow Spring, sandstones and conglomerates are in fault contact below the Keystone thrust (Figs. 8 [labeled Jkc], 15A, and 16). These rocks consist of 15 to 20 m of gently W-dipping sandstone composed of reworked Aztec Sandstone interbedded with boulder and cobble conglomerate (Fig. 16). The cobbles consist of Bonanza King dolomite and limestone set in a matrix of reworked Aztec Sandstone. Cross-bedding indicates that the sand was derived from the east, suggesting that the rocks are not a synorogenic deposit derived from an advancing Keystone plate, but are erosional products from the Wilson Cliffs plate.

We interpret these rocks to have been deposited unconformably on the Wilson Cliffs plate following a period of erosion between the emplacement of the Wilson Cliffs–Contact plate and the Keystone plate. Unfortunately, the basal and eastern contacts of the conglomerate and sandstone unit are not exposed along its 100- to 200-m outcrop length. Except for being cut by the Keystone thrust at the top, the conglomerate and sandstone unit is undeformed and right-side-up, in contrast to the overturned and highly brecciated rocks beneath it. This suggests that the unit was deposited after emplacement and considerable erosion of the Wilson Cliffs plate. In fact, we suggest that the northern termination of the Wilson Cliffs plate occurred principally through erosion before the Keystone plate was emplaced. This interpretation suggests that a considerable period of time separated the emplacement of the Wilson Cliffs–Contact and Keystone thrust plates, and it is consistent with regional tectonic relations discussed below.

Very small deposits of conglomerate are present in two other locations resting unconformably on the Wilson Cliffs plate, but are too small to appear in Figure 6.[3] Both deposits are fault bounded on at least one side, but nowhere are they in contact with the Keystone plate. Thus, their correlation with structural events is unknown, except that they were deposited after emplacement of the Wilson Cliffs plate. They represent remnants of the deposits discussed above, because the more northerly of the two deposits contains reworked Aztec Sandstone. Dating of the emplacement of the two plates, however, cannot be determined in the map area and must be ascertained from regional relations.

Without additional constraints, a single, south-side-down displacement on the Cottonwood fault is all that is required to explain the mapped geological relations across the fault. This displacement would be younger than emplacement of the Keystone thrust. Mapping in progress in the Bird Spring Range to the southeast is focused partly on the unresolved

[3]These are shown on the detailed geologic map of the area available elsewhere; see note 1.

question of the history of, and displacement on, the Cottonwood fault.

The nearly vertical Griffith fault in the northern part of the map area offsets map units in the hanging wall of the Keystone plate, but does not offset the Keystone thrust (Figs. 6 and 8). Where the two faults intersect there is a broad area of brecciated rocks, and the Griffith fault curves south to merge with the Keystone thrust. The Griffith fault could be interpreted as a tear fault in the Keystone plate, or as a younger fault that merged with the Keystone thrust, reactivating it. Not enough of the Griffith fault was mapped during this study to resolve the interpretation.

Regional Tectonic Relations

The major difference between this study and earlier studies is the interpretation that the spectacularly exposed thrust fault at the top of the Wilson Cliffs, referred to by previous workers as the Keystone thrust, is not the Keystone thrust, but is the basal fault of an older thrust plate (Fig. 17A). In addition, previous workers interpreted the Cottonwood fault to be one of several demonstrable pre-Keystone NW-trending faults (Fig. 17B). Davis (1973), as well as Burchfiel et al. (1974), suggested that the oldest structural event in the area was the emplacement of the Contact thrust plate and its northern correlative, the Red Spring plate. Younger, high-angle faults, such as the La Madre and Cottonwood faults, displaced and locally rotated the Contact–Red Spring thrust plate. At least one of these high-angle faults, the Ninety-Nine fault zone, has a component of strike-slip. Extensive erosion ensued and removed the once-continuous Contact–Red Spring plate from the horst between the Cottonwood and La Madre faults. The Keystone thrust plate was emplaced across an erosion surface in its eastern part that is now exposed in the mapped area (Fig. 17B).

The sequence of events determined from this study modifies two parts of the events described above: (1) the Contact–Red Spring thrust plate was not entirely removed by erosion from the horst between the Cottonwood and La Madre faults, as a remnant of that plate remains as the Wilson Cliffs plate; and (2) the displacement

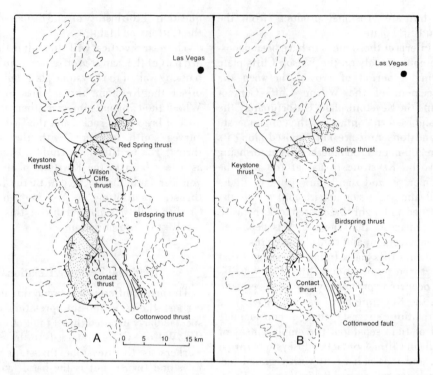

FIG. 17. Previous (B) and present (A) interpretations of the tectonic relations between the Keystone and structurally lower thrust plates in the eastern Spring Mountains.

on the Cottonwood Fault is mostly, if not entirely, post-Keystone in age (Fig. 17A). Mapped relations indicate that the Wilson Cliffs plate is the lateral continuation of the Contact plate and probably also of the Red Spring plate. The conglomerate deposits at the northern end of the map area are interpreted to represent one of the few places where rocks deposited during the post–Wilson Cliffs and pre-Keystone erosion interval are preserved.

Dating of these events remains uncertain, and there is no evidence within the map area to bound these deformations other than to assign them a post–Aztec Sandstone, pre-Quaternary age. Recent work by Fleck et al. (1994) has indicated that the Keystone plate was emplaced probably between 100 and 83 Ma. Emplacement of the Contact–Wilson Cliffs–Red Spring plate and movement on the high-angle faults that displace it were earlier, but how much earlier remains unknown.

Some or all of the movement on both the Cottonwood and Griffith faults could have occurred after emplacement of the Keystone

thrust plate. It is possibile that some or all of the movement on these two faults is Cenozoic in age. The NW-striking Las Vegas shear zone is a Late Cenozoic transfer fault that accommodates Basin and Range extension (Liggett and Childs, 1974; Wernicke et al., 1982); these two faults have the same strike and could have formed at the same time. Recent mapping in the Bird Spring Range along the southeastern continuation of the Cottonwood fault shows that this fault displaces boulder conglomerate of undated, but probable Cenozoic, age (K. V. Hodges, pers. commun., 1996). If these faults do have a Cenozoic history, there may be a greater imprint of Cenozoic deformation on this area than previously thought.

Conclusions

Results of this study are relevant to local and regional structural interpretations and to considerations of the mechanics of thrust faulting. Locally, detailed mapping demonstrates the presence of two thrust plates in the Wilson

Cliffs–Potosi Mountain area—the lower Wilson Cliffs plate, a remnant of a once more extensive Contact–Red Spring thrust plate, and the higher Keystone thrust plate. The thrust fault so magnificently exposed atop the Wilson Cliffs is not the Keystone thrust, but a part of the structurally lower and older Contact–Wilson Cliffs–Red Spring thrust fault.

The emplacement of the Keystone and Contact–Wilson Cliffs–Red Spring thrust plates belongs to two different thrusting events that are separated by a period of high-angle faulting and erosion. The Cottonwood fault, previously interpreted to be one of these high-angle faults, probably experienced most or all of its displacement after emplacement of the Keystone plate. The Contact–Wilson Cliffs–Red Spring thrust plate lies east of and structurally below the younger Keystone plate. However, because the ramp for the Keystone thrust lies east of the Contact–Wilson Cliffs–Red Spring thrust, there was eastward progression of the younger thrust at a low structural level. But the Keystone thrust cut across the Contact–Wilson Cliffs plate at a high structural level so that its present erosional trace lies west of the trace of the Contact–Wilson Cliffs thrust, and the present map pattern gives an erroneous impression. Work in progress in the Bird Spring Range suggests that the Bird Spring thrust (Fig. 1) is older than the Keystone thrust, thus supporting: (1) the concept that a more easterly thrust is older than the Keystone thrust (i.e., the Keystone thrust is "out of sequence" with respect to the Bird Spring thrust, but not with respect to the Contact–Wilson Cliffs thrust); and (2) similar conclusions of other studies of the thrust faults farther south by Burchfiel and Davis (1971, 1981, 1988) and Carr (1983).

Geometric relations suggest that the ramp for the Keystone plate lay east of the ramp for the Contact–Wilson Cliffs–Red Spring plate (Fig. 15A); thus the Keystone plate must have carried parts of both the hanging wall and footwall of the Contact–Wilson Cliffs–Red Spring plate in its eastern part as well as the high-angle faults that cut them. These parts of the Keystone plate must have been removed by erosion, as they are not exposed. Furthermore, the Keystone plate of the map area detached within a narrow stratigraphic interval that was not affected by older high-angle faults. These relations suggest that the Keystone plate was displaced eastward relative to its footwall by a considerable (but unknown) distance, a suggestion supported by differences in Cambrian stratigraphic units (particularly Unit VII and the Nopah Formation) in its hanging wall and footwall.

After ramping up-section, both thrust plates moved across erosion surfaces. Below the Contact–Wilson Cliffs–Red Spring plate, this erosion surface was developed on the Jurassic Aztec Sandstone; below the Keystone plate, however, the erosion surface was developed across highly varied and complex geology.

Even though the two thrust plates are of different ages, they both detached at about the same stratigraphic interval within the Bonanza King Formation. Detachment occurred within an interval of ~100 m between the uppermost part of the Papoose Lake Member and Unit IV of the Banded Mountain Member. Reasons for a detachment in this interval are not obvious, particularly when the Bright Angel Shales almost certainly lay only 100 to 200 m lower stratigraphically. The boundary between the two members of the Bonanza King Formation marks a change from rocks that are predominantly limestone below to predominantly dolomite above. However, the detachment does not follow this lithological change precisely, but for the most part stays within that part of the sequence dominated by dolomite. New interpretations for the Cottonwood and Griffith faults suggest that Cenozoic deformation was more important in the eastern Spring Mountains than previously recognized.

Acknowledgments

This work was supported by National Science Foundation grants EAR 7913637 and EAR 8306863, and the Schlumberger Chair of Geology awarded to B. C. Burchfiel. Part of Cameron's work was supported by a Fannie and John Hertz Foundation fellowship and Geological Society of America research grants.

REFERENCES

Axen, G. J., 1984, Thrusts in the eastern Spring Mountains, Nevada: Geometry and mechanical implications: Geol. Soc. Amer. Bull., v. 95, p. 1202–1207.

————, 1985, Geologic map and description of structure and stratigraphy, La Madre Mountain,

Spring Mountains, Nevada: Geol. Soc. Amer. Map
and Chart Series MC-51.

————, 1989, Reinterpretations of the relations
between the Keystone, Red Spring, Contact, and
Cottonwood faults, eastern Spring Mountains, Clark
County, Nevada: Discussion: Mountain Geol., v. 26,
no. 3, p. 69–70.

Barnes, H., and Palmer, A. R., 1961, Revision of the
stratigraphic nomenclature of Cambrian rocks,
Nevada Test Site and vicinity, Nevada: U. S. Geol.
Survey Prof. Paper 424-C, p. C100–C103.

Burchfiel, B. C., and Davis, G. A., 1971, Clark Mountain
thrust complex, in The cordillera of southeastern
California: Geologic summary and field trip guide:
Riverside Museum Contrib. 1, Univ. of California at
Riverside, p. 1–28.

Burchfiel, B. C., and Davis, G. A., 1981, Structural
evolution of the Mojave Desert and environs, in
Ernst, W. G., ed., Geotectonic development of California. Rubey Volume 1: Englewood Cliffs, NJ, Prentice Hall, Inc., New Jersey, p. 217–282.

————, 1988, Mesozoic thrust faults and Cenozoic
low-angle normal faults, eastern Spring Mountains,
Nevada and Clark Mountains Thrust Complex, California, in Weide, D. L., and Faber, M. L., eds., This
extended land: Geol. Soc. Amer., Cordill. Sect. Meeting, Field Trip Guide Book, Univ. of Nevada, Dept. of
Geoscience, Spec. Publ. No. 2, p. 87–106.

Burchfiel, B. C., Fleck, R. H., Secor, D. T., Vincellete,
R. R., and Davis, G. A., 1974, Geology of the Spring
Mountains, Nevada: Geol. Soc. Amer. Bull., v. 85, p.
1013–1023.

Burchfiel, B. C., Wernicke, B., Willemin, J. H., Axen,
G. J., and Cameron, C. S., 1982, A new type of
decollement thrusting: Nature, v. 300, p. 513–515.

Cameron, C. S., 1977, Structure and stratigraphy of the
Potosi Mountain area, southern Spring Mountains,
Nevada: Unpubl. M. S. Thesis, Rice Univ., 83 p.

Carr, M. D., 1983, Geometry and structural history of
the Mesozoic thrust belt in the Goodsprings District,
southern Spring Mountains, Nevada: Geol. Soc.
Amer. Bull., v. 94, p. 1185–1198.

Carr, M. D., and Pinkston, J. C. 1987, Geologic map of
the Goodsprings district, southern Spring Mountains, Nevada: U.S. Geol. Surv., Misc. Field Studies
Map 1514, 1:24,000.

Davis, G. A., 1973, Relations between the Keystone and
Red Spring thrust faults, eastern Spring Mountains,
Nevada: Geol. Soc. Amer. Bull., v. 84, p. 3709–3716.

Fleck, R. J., and Carr, M. D., 1990, The age of the
Keystone thrust: Laser-fusion ^{40}Ar/^{39}Ar dating of
foreland basin deposits, southern Spring Mountains,
Nevada: Tectonics, v. 9, p. 467–476.

Fleck, R. J., Carr, M. D., Davis, G. A., and Burchfiel,
B. C., 1994, Isotopic complexities and the age of the

Delfonte volcanic rocks, eastern Mescal Range,
southeastern California: Stratigraphic and tectonic
implications: Geol. Soc. Amer. Bull., v. 106, p.
1242–1253.

Gans, W. T., 1974, Correlation and redefinition of the
Goodsprings Dolomite, southern Nevada and eastern
California: Geol. Soc. Amer. Bull., v. 85, p. 189–200.

Glock, W. S., 1929, Geology of the east-central part of
the Spring Mountain Range, Nevada: Amer. Jour.
Sci., 5th ser., v. 17, p. 326–341.

Hazzard, J. C., 1937, Paleozoic section in the Nopah and
Resting Springs Mountains, Inyo County, California: Calif. Jour. Mines and Geol., v. 33, p. 273–339.

Hazzard, J. C., and Mason, F. J., 1936, Middle Cambrian
formations of the Providence and Marble Mountains, California: Geol. Soc. Amer. Bull., v. 47, p.
229–240.

Hewett, D. F., 1931, Geology and ore deposits of the
Goodsprings quadrangle, Nevada: U.S. Geol. Surv.
Prof. Pap. 162, 172 p.

————, 1956, Geology and mineral resources of the
Ivanpah quadrangle, California and Nevada: U. S.
Geol. Surv. Prof. Pap. 275, 172 p.

Johnson, M. R. W., 1981, The erosion factor in the
emplacement of the Keystone thrust sheet (southeast Nevada) across a land surface: Geol. Mag., v.
188, p. 501–507.

Liggett, M. A., and Childs, J. F., 1974, Crustal extension
and transform faulting in the southern Basin and
Range Province: Argus Exploration Company
(Report of Investigation, NASA 5-21809), 28 p.

Longwell, C. R., 1926, Structural studies in southern
Nevada and western Arizona: Geol. Soc. Amer. Bull.,
v. 37, p. 551–584.

————, 1960, Possible explanation of diverse structural patterns in southern Nevada: Amer. Jour. Sci.,
v. 258-A, p. 192–203.

Longwell, C. R., Pampeyan, E. H., Bowyer, B., and
Roberts, R. J., 1965, Geology and mineral deposits of
Clark County, Nevada: Nev. Bur. Mines Geol., Bull.
62, 218 p.

Matthews, V., III, 1988, Reinterpretations of the relations between the Keystone, Red Spring, Contact,
and Cottonwood faults, eastern Spring Mountains,
Clark County, Nevada: Mountain Geol., v. 25, no. 4,
p. 181–191.

————, 1989, Reinterpretations of the relations
between the Keystone, Red Spring, Contact, and
Cottonwood faults, eastern Spring Mountains, Clark
County, Nevada: Reply: Mountain Geol., v. 26, no. 3,
p. 71–74.

Price, N. J., and Johnson, M. R. W., 1982, A mechanical
analysis of the Keystone–Muddy Mountain thrust
sheet in southeastern Nevada: Tectonophysics, v. 84,
p. 131–150.

Raleigh, C. B., and Griggs, D. T., 1963, Effect of the Toe in the mechanics of overthrust faulting: Geol. Soc. Amer. Bull., v. 74, p. 819–830.

Secor, D. T., Jr., 1962, Geology of the central Spring Mountains, Nevada: Unpubl. Ph.D. thesis, Stanford Univ., 152 p.

Serra, S., 1977, Styles of deformation in the ramp regions of overthrust faults: Wyoming Geol. Assoc. Guidebook, 29th Ann. Field Conf., Jackson, Wyoming.

Stewart, J. H., 1970, Upper Precambrian and Lower Cambrian strata in the southern Great Basin, California and Nevada: U.S. Geol. Surv. Prof. Pap. 620, 206 p.

Wernicke, B., Spencer, J. E., Burchfiel, B. C., and Guth, P. L., 1982, Magnitude of crustal extension in the southern Great Basin: Geology, v. 10, p. 499–502.

Climatic-Ecological Aspects of the Arid American Southwest, with Special Emphasis on the White Mountains, California

S. Hetzner, M. Richter, M. Rien, T. Spengler, and K. Verleger

Department of Geography, Friedrich-Alexander University of Erlangen-Nürnberg,
Kochstrasse 4, D-91054 Erlangen, Germany

Abstract

The main purpose of the present study is the development of concepts and methods suitable for deriving climatological information on the basis of phytoindication in semiarid-semihumid regions where no climatological data are available. The macroclimate of the southwestern United States can be clearly defined using regression analysis. The humid oceanic and temperate climate in the western part of this region is distinguished from the dry continental climate of the Great Basin east of the Sierra Nevada. The very important role of summer precipitation for the distribution of vegetation is explained from a climatic-ecological point of view. Although microclimatic conditions point to unfavorable conditions for plant growth—extreme amounts of radiation lead to increasing thermal stress with altitude—the gradients of soil moisture during the warm season explain high vegetation densities.

Phytogeographical aspects show a clear separation between the Sierra Nevada and the White Mountains and between the White Mountains and Wheeler Peak. Lowest vegetation density is found in the Owens Valley and not, as might be expected, in the eastern part of the Great Basin. Thus, although the White Mountains are situated adjacent to the Sierra, their vegetation shows weak relations to the Sierran and Californian floristic province. In fact, Great Basin plants constitute the majority. An overall floristic comparison establishes a continuous change from the White Mountains to Wheeler Peak and an abrupt transition between the vegetation of the Sierra Nevada and the White Mountains.

Introduction

THIS PAPER BEGINS by presenting an overall view of the climatic patterns of the southwestern United States,[1] followed by investigations of altitudinal microclimatic change in the arid region from Death Valley to the high elevations of the White Mountains.[2] Following this, these climatological facts are assessed[3] with consideration of vegetational data of the Sierra Nevada and three ranges of the Basin and Range Province—the White Mountains, the Toiyabe Range, and Wheeler Peak of the Snake Range. By compiling data at both macro- and microscales, the climatic-ecological position of the White Mountains can be defined.

[1]Elaborated by K. Verleger.
[2]Conducted by T. Spengler.
[3]By S. Hetzner and M. Rien.

Coverage initially focuses on a climatic characterization of the general environs of the White Mountains, providing a climatological survey encompassing the region from 35° to 42° N Lat. and from 109° to 122° W Long. The White Mountains are located in the southwestern quadrant (Fig. 1) of this sector, which extends from the Sierra Nevada to the Colorado Plateau.

Special attention will be devoted to the eastern part of the region, as climatic and floristic relations between the White Mountains and the Basin and Range Province are much closer than those between the White Mountains and the Sierra Nevada (Morefield, 1988). This results from the barrier (rain-shadow) effect exerted by the Sierra Nevada relative to humid westerly airflow in all seasons (Barry, 1992). This barrier effect plays an important role in delineating floristic provinces. Although the Californian floristic province extends marginally over the

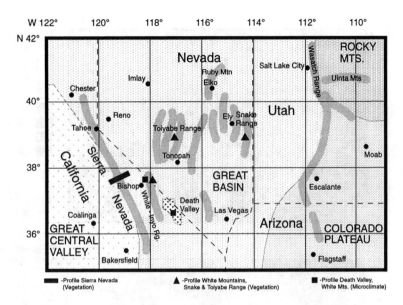

FIG. 1. General map of the study area. Studies on macroclimate cover the entire area.

watershed, the Owens Valley actually belongs to the Basin and Range Province (Barbour and Major, 1988).

Macroscale Climatic Patterns and Gradients

Temperature

Thermal conditions usually are portrayed on maps (Fig. 2A) using isotherms to represent mean annual temperatures. Although such maps show normal mean conditions, they do not provide information on relative regional temperature conditions in relation to the mean. It is hardly possible on such maps to identify areas with a high or low range of values around the mean. This is especially true for high mountain areas, which may be subject to marine influence in the west and continentality in the east. Additionally, net radiation varies with latitude and results in warming from the north toward the south.

Latitudinal and longitudinal effects can be eliminated by calculation of regressions and residuals. Maps of residuals provide an ideal method for interpreting vegetational differentiation. In the present case, residuals of January minimum temperature and July maximum temperature were used, as the presence or absence of species strongly depends on

extremes. To analyze January minimum temperatures (Fig. 2B), relatively cold/warm regions are sorted out by determining their distance left/right of the regression line in Figure 2C. The Sierra Nevada turns out to be relatively mild in winter, whereas the Great Basin between Wheeler Peak and the Wasatch Mountains, and especially the Colorado Plateau north of Moab, is especially cold in winter. Interpolation based on 401 widely scattered weather stations (NCDC, 1900–1995) allocates intermediate temperature values to the White Mountains. Interpretation of the isotherms (IDRISI interpolation program) reveals that the Owens Valley (open to the south) is warmer than Fish Lake Valley to the east. July maximum temperatures (Fig. 2D) reveal Death Valley to be a pronounced "hot spot" not only in absolute but also in relative terms, as a result of the build-up of heat above the deep valley floor. In July, the White Mountains and the Owens and Fish Lake valleys exhibit medium heating conditions. The Sierra Nevada and also western California turn out to be cold poles in what overall is a quite hot region.

Mild conditions in winter and summer cause only a small annual range in temperature for the Sierra Nevada and the extreme west. The map of absolute annual temperature ranges (Fig. 2E) shows light colors for these areas and

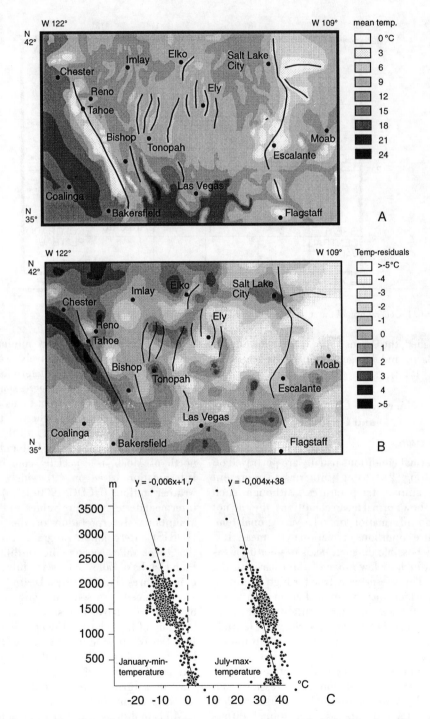

FIG. 2. Patterns and gradients of temperature. A. Mean annual temperature on the basis of data from 401 weather stations, 1948–1995. B. Residuals from regression, January minimum temperature ($y = -0.006x + 1.7$). C. Regression analysis of temperature and elevation. D. Residuals from regression, July maximum temperature and elevation ($y = -0.004x + 38$). E. Amplitude between July maximum temperature and January minimum temperature on the basis of data of 401 weather stations, 1948–1995.

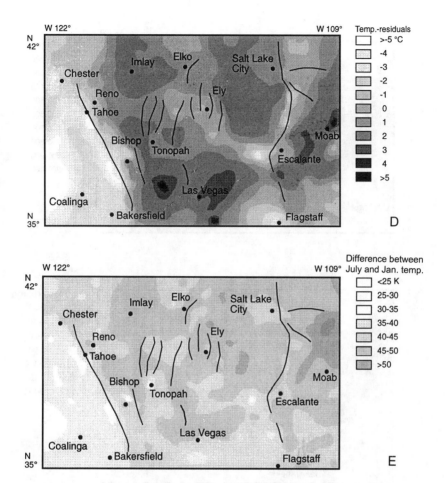

FIG. 2. (continued).

dark colors for the more continental region farther east, with great annual ranges. North of Moab, for instance, the mean difference between the January minimum and July maximum is 54 K. On the oceanic western slope of the Sierra Nevada, the analogous value is 25 K. For the White Mountains, a thermal range of 35 K marks a transition to the continental desert climate. To put it differently, the White Mountain escarpment is the western edge of a climate zone where plants have to adapt to enormous seasonal temperature ranges in order to survive.

Precipitation and evaporation

The region east of the Sierra Nevada is characterized by pronounced aridity in the basins in addition to thermal continentality (Fig. 3A).

The reason for this extreme dryness of the basins can be found in the lowest and driest place in the United States, Death Valley. During the day and during the warm season, most of the precipitation falling out of cumulonimbus clouds evaporates before reaching the earth. Humid mountain "islands" extend from the northern Wasatch Range south to the San Francisco Peaks north of Flagstaff, Arizona. More of these "humid spots" probably exist in other parts of the ranges; unfortunately they could not be determined because of a lack of comparable data sets.

However, the Sierra Nevada represents something of an exception to this rule. The altitudinal increase in annual precipitation (Fig. 3D) is applicable, but here, unlike locations farther east, mountain precipitation falls mainly in winter (Fig. 3B). Eastward-moving cyclones

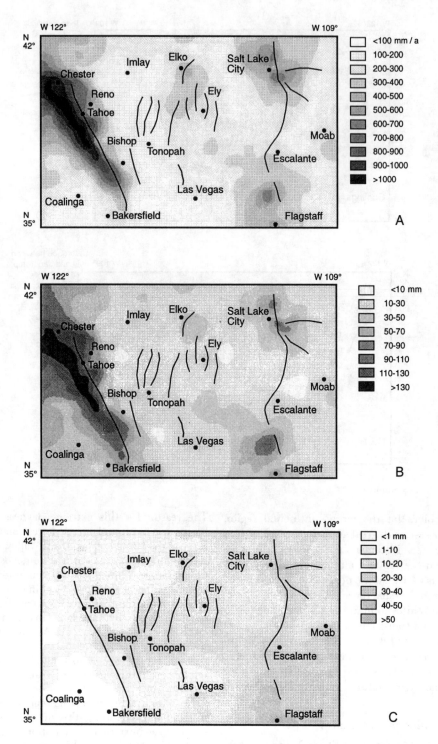

Fig. 3. Patterns and gradients of precipitation on the basis of data from 189 weather stations, 1948–1995. A. Mean annual precipitation. B. Mean January precipitation. C. Mean July precipitation. D. Regression analysis of precipitation and elevation (on facing page).

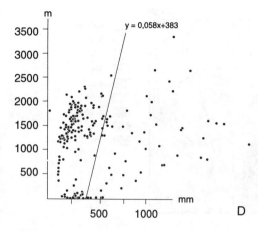

$$pV = (7.5*(E_{tmax} - E_{tmin-2}))*0.7,$$

FIG. 3. (continued).

in which pV is potential evaporation in mm/month, E_{tmax} is the saturation deficit (mm Hg) for the mean daily maximum temperature, and E_{tmin-2} is the saturation deficit (mm Hg) for the mean daily minimum temperature - 2 K. In continental areas such as the arid Southwest, this varied method exhibits a quite close correlation with Penman results.

Naturally, the driest sections should have an increased saturation deficit and therefore a high potential for evaporation. Additionally, this effect varies with the influence of wind as a cooling vis-à-vis an evaporation factor. Consequently, with altitude, decreasing temperature and increasing precipitation work to reduce evaporation rates, whereas increased wind velocity and direct solar radiation intensify them. However, evaporation usually does not decrease with altitude in tropical and subtropical mountains (Henning and Henning, 1981). Nevertheless, evaporation might decrease in areas with a long period of snow cover. The processes of sublimation and melting, which alter soil moisture and albedo, modify microclimates and ultimately influence the energy budget as evaporation rates decrease.

This situation applies to mountains of the subtropical southwestern United States with relatively high amounts of snow. Figures 4A–4D clearly show decreasing evaporation values with elevation. Thus, the Sierra Nevada, the greater Salt Lake City area, and the San Francisco Peaks show positive water balances. For the White Mountains, this is true only in subalpine and alpine locations above 3000 m. Using a Death Valley–Barcroft transect, Richter and Schröder (1991) found that arid conditions prevailed year-round below the lower timberline of the montane woodland at ~2000 m (Fig. 4D). Elevations of 3000 m experienced six humid months, whereas Barcroft (3800 m), with ~500 mm precipitation versus 200 mm evaporation, had nine humid months. The existence of dense alpine meadows between Mount Barcroft and White Mountain Peak provide evidence of this positive moisture balance.

bring mean annual precipitation amounting to more than 1000 mm and "tons of snow" to the western slopes and high elevations, whereas the Owens Valley on the leeward side receives less than 200 mm of precipitation. Föhn effects intensify the aridity and seem to be responsible for the asymmetrical distribution of the vegetation on the eastern and western slopes of the range (Powell et al., 1991). Higher elevations of the White Mountains receive an increasing share of convective summer precipitation that has been transported north from the Gulf of Mexico. The region around Flagstaff especially benefits from those convective rains (Fig. 3C), which are essential for desert and mountain vegetation (e.g., the Sonoran ocotillo could not survive without this summer rainfall). Finally, the Wasatch Range in the northeastern part of the study area benefits equally from both winter frontal precipitation and summer convective rain.

Evaporation, the negative part of the ecological water balance, is much more difficult to determine than precipitation. A network of Class A pans exists in the study area, but according to Jauregui et al. (1978), in arid zones these measurements are subject to a microclimatic "oasis effect" that results in exaggerated values. Similarly, the more accurate calculation method of potential evaporation following Penman (1948) is not practical in this case, as several of the required climatic parameters are measured in only a few locations. It is because of this that the simpler Papadakis method (1966) as modified by Schmiedecken (1978) is applied:

Significance of summer rain on the macroclimate of the Basin and Range Province

A further important variable for the ecology of the Basin and Range Province, the percent-

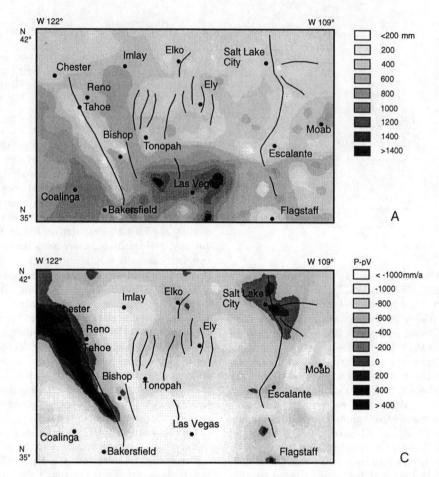

FIG. 4. Patterns and gradients of evaporation. A. Mean annual potential evaporation (pV): pV = (7.5 (E_{tmax} – E_{tmin-2})) × 0.7. B (facing page). Regression analysis: evaporation and elevation. C. Annual moisture balance (precipitation – potential evaporation): N – pV > 0 = moisture surplus; N – pV < 0 = moisture deficit. D (facing page). Gradients of annual precipitation, potential evaporation, and number of humid months in the Death Valley region (after Richter and Schröder, 1991).

age of total precipitation falling as rain in summer, is shown in Figure 4D. A transect from Death Valley to the White Mountains indicates an increase of summer rainfall of up to 40% in open forests between 2000 m and 3500 m, versus 20% in the dry and low basin floors. The importance of this increase follows from Figure 3C. It is evident that the Basin and Range Province in July receives higher amounts of precipitation than the western slopes of the Sierra Nevada, where annual mean values point to much more humid conditions.

Given that the high elevations of the arid complex east of the Sierra Nevada profit

especially from this ecologically favorable situation, a short explanation is in order. The E-W profile in Figure 5 elucidates the importance of the Sierra Nevada as a climatic divide between moist temperate Pacific and dry continental air masses. The location of the White Mountains and the Panamint Range in the rain shadow of the Sierra Nevada in the winter half of the year can be seen in the upper profile sketch. During that time, advective-cyclonic air flow patterns often cause föhn effects on the eastern side, above all in Owens Valley. Occasionally, humid air masses surmount the Sierran barrier and bring snowfall to the White Mountains.

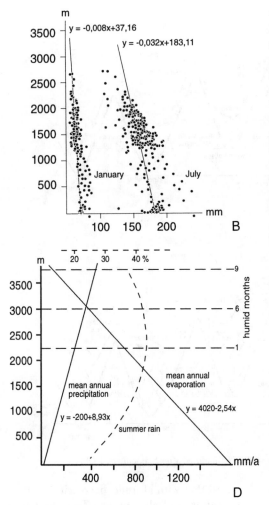

FIG. 4. (CONTINUED).

that Wildrose Canyon, located in the Panamint Range ~150 km east of Bishop (Fig. 6), shows a slight increase in summer maximum precipitation (arrow), a feature that does not occur at the Bishop weather station, located at about the same elevation. The following analysis of the microclimatic measurements also explains why this phenomenon gives rise to generally higher temperatures and lower humidity in Bishop relative to Wildrose Canyon. Again, it is important to note that the high-altitude stations of Crooked Creek and Barcroft show a distinct secondary maximum of precipitation in July/August vis-à-vis Bishop (Fig. 6). The Owens Valley is obviously located in a leeward position relative to tropical air masses invading from the southeast during this period. From a synoptic point of view, because of its double leeward position,[4] the Owens Valley is the driest region of the southwestern United States. That Death Valley is even drier (in absolute numbers) reflects the very low elevation of its valley floor, below sea level. The extremely dry and hot air evaporates rain before it can reach the ground. It must be stressed that although the high elevations of the White Mountains are humid in winter (P-pV > 0), they have a moisture deficit (P-pV < 0) during the warm vegetation period. Consequently, even high altitudes should present challenging conditions for vegetation development.

Detailed Microclimatic Studies

Radiation and temperature

Given the importance of summer rain and winter snow cover for vegetation, the microclimatic status of those factors should be investigated. Up to now, the greater regional climatic structures were explained on the basis of weather-station data. However, plants are actually much more responsive to microclimate—the climate of their immediate surroundings (surfaces of soils or parts of plants), with condi-

During the summer half of the year, schematically illustrated in the lower profile of Figure 5, the Sierra Nevada stays particularly dry. This is the period of intense fire events, which, for instance, sequoia tree populations need for reproduction. Symbolically exaggerated (because it is infrequent but important), a mass of thunderclouds is marked above the White Mountains; obviously, it also could be drawn above the Panamint Range or farther east (e.g., above the San Francisco Peaks) where it plays an important role as well (compare Fig. 3C). Especially the east-facing flanks of the ranges profit from the thunderstorms caused by northerly invasions of moist tropical air from the Gulf of Mexico. It is because of these conditions

[4]The double leeward position follows from the winter and summer circulation pattern of the atmosphere. In winter frontal precipitation comes from the west, and the Owens Valley is in the rain shadow of the Sierra Nevada. In summer most precipitation is brought in with air masses of moist tropical air from the southeast, so during this time of year the Owens Valley is leeward of the White Mountains.

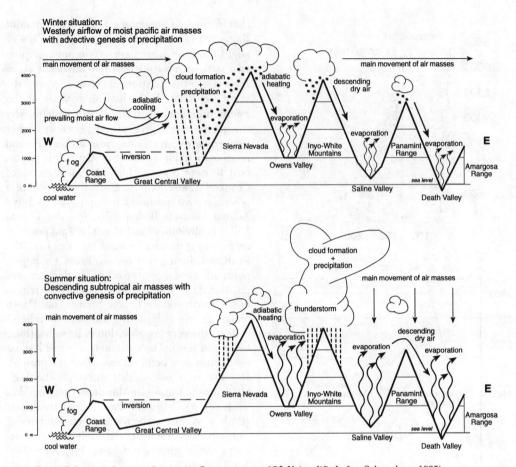

FIG. 5. Schematic diagram of major air-flow patterns at 37° N (modified after Schoenherr, 1995).

tions being more extreme than indicated by macroclimatic values. Unlike the macroclimatic observations, where long-term data are easily available, microclimatic studies are based on sampling and selected short-term measurements. The following results were obtained during field work from May to September 1996. Monthly measurements were made at the locations marked in Figure 6. A composite profile from Furnace Creek to Barcroft was selected so as to include a large altitudinal gradient, between 0 m and 3800 m. In order to link the data sets of Death Valley and the White Mountains, the 1550 m niveau was measured twice. Wildrose Canyon served as measuring point in Death Valley and Redding Canyon as the connection in the White Mountains.

The measurements of global radiation show that this method is necessary. It has to be assumed that with altitude, decreasing air density, scatter, and absorption effects lead to a lower percentage of diffuse radiation in favor of direct solar radiation. Especially in thermodynamic low-pressure cells of arid mountain ranges below the peplopause (inversion layer of the lower troposhere at ~1000 m to 2000 m altitude), high dust densities lead to a gradual increase in radiation. Above these dust bodies, radiation increases exponentially (Fig. 7A). For Death Valley and Owens Valley, the peplopause has different altitudes—~1300 m in the former and up to 3000 m in the latter (Fig. 7B). Under partly cloudy conditions that often occur in the study area, radiation—in addition to the effects of altitude—can increase further as a result of cloud reflection (Barry, 1992). In June, at an elevation of 3000 m, radiation increased by more than 124 W/m² as single altocumulus

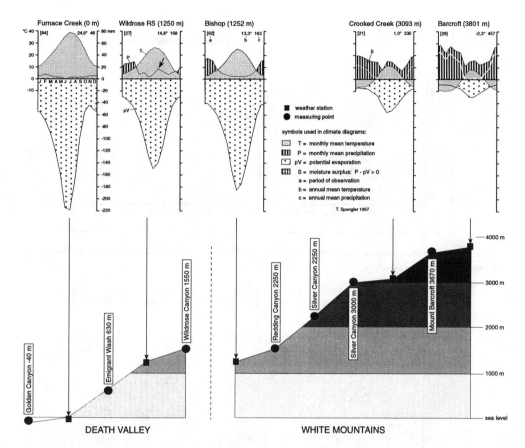

FIG. 6. Schematic profile from Death Valley to the White Mountains showing locations of weather stations and microclimate measuring points.

clouds approached. This represents an increase of nearly 10% above the normal value of 1278 W/m^2, which already is a remarkable 93% of the solar constant (1370 W/m^2). Under optimal conditions, nearly maximum possible radiation amounts were measured in the White Mountains, and maximum surface temperatures higher than 70°C occurred on dark soils. In addition, these special reflection and radiation conditions in high altitudes under partly cloudy skies cause variations of the surface temperatures of up to 15 K within a few minutes. To put it differently, the vegetation of high-mountain areas, particularly in the White Mountains, must adapt to extreme microclimatic stress.

This microclimatic thermal stress also is reflected in the daily amplitude of surface tem-perature. Figure 8A shows a mean temperature amplitude of 50 K for the elevation of Barcroft from May to September, whereas the analogous value at the elevation of Death Valley only reaches 33 K. This regularity is formed by both extremes—early-morning minimum temperatures caused by increased outgoing radiation and afternoon maxima caused by increased incoming radiation at high altitudes. The slightly anomalous zone between 1500 m and 3000 m is explained below.

In sum, it can be seen that under such radiation and microclimatic conditions, the basic ecological requirements for plant growth, especially in dry mountain ranges, clearly are disadvantageous. This raises the question of why the vegetation in the White Mountains turns out to be quite dense and of high floristic diversity.

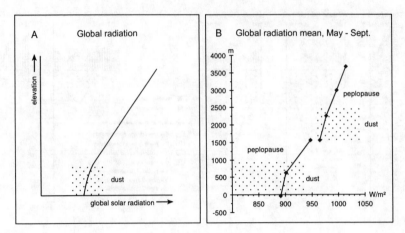

FIG. 7. Altitudinal variation of global radiation on the Death Valley–White Mountains transect. A. Theoretical variation. B. Measured variation.

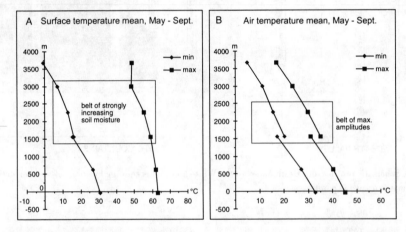

FIG. 8. Altitudinal variation of surface (A) and air (B) temperature along the Death Valley–White Mountains transect.

Soil moisture

Extreme thermal conditions need not inevitably influence the ecological water balance. With regard to the study area, winter snow and convective summer rain were described as two positive moisture sources. Theoretically, this situation influences microclimate, as a considerable part of the soil moisture will be transformed into latent energy. However, this shift of the Bowen ratio (i.e., ratio of sensible versus latent energy) is not significant in the study area, as soil surfaces heat up considerably in midsummer. This does not, however, mean that the soils dry out rapidly and intensively. Here an important factor is soil texture. Loamy sands

and sandy loams that were found all along the Death Valley–White Mountains transect provide favorable infiltration and water storage conditions for plants.

Mean soil moisture values from May to September clearly show the influence of increasing precipitation at altitudes above 2000 m (Fig. 9A). In May, moisture from melting snow is evident above 1500 m, as moisture values positively deviate from the mean (Fig. 9B). This moisture, however, disappears by June, except for the highest measuring point (Fig. 9C). July has similar deficit conditions (Fig. 9D). The fact that most drainage is toward the eastern slopes and the presence of extremely high sublimation rates of up to 95% (Beaty, 1975) lower

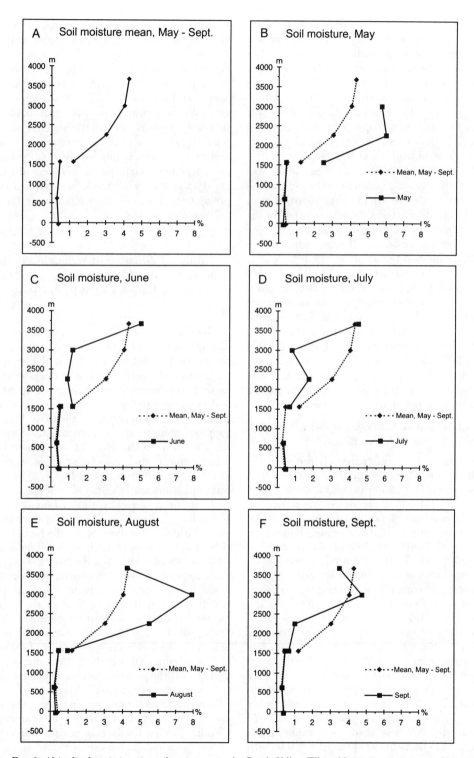

FIG. 9. Altitudinal variations in soil moisture on the Death Valley–White Mountains transect. A. Mean of measurement period. B–F. Monthly variation.

the input of ablation moisture. During this time of the year, no snowfields were found on the western slopes in the study area, but instead on the eastern flank, where wind-drift accumulates high amounts of snow in winter. With increasing activity of thunderstorms in August, which are especially effective above 2250 m, a renewed moisture maximum appears at that elevation (Fig. 9E). Only above 3000 m does soil moisture decrease until September (Fig. 9F).

The woodlands between 2000 m and 3000 m therefore only suffer from drought in June and July, before the conditions improve in August. The latter appears to be the main reason for the development of such dense vegetation. It can be seen from Figure 8A that this is the belt where strongly increasing soil moisture temporarily moderates the increase in amplitude of surface temperature. It must be taken into account, however, that convective rains in summer are characterized by very high spatial and temporal variability. For instance, while a thunderstorm with heavy rain flooded Silver Canyon on July 28, 1996, Black Canyon only 12 km away remained almost dry. Vegetation must consequently adapt to high inter- and intra-annual variations of the moisture balance.

Global comparison with other high-mountain areas in dry subtropical latitudes

The findings of this paper characterize the high-mountain areas of the Basin and Range as a type in which summer rain is of major importance for the relatively dense vegetation in middle and high elevations. In comparison to the extremely dry high Atacama of northern Chile and the more humid Karakorum of Kashmir, the White Mountains occupy an intermediate position. In the Karakorum, precipitation increases from 100 mm on the valley floors to 800 mm at the 4000 m level. At low elevations in this region, as at the Owens Valley, xerophytic vegetation types such as *Artemisia* dominate. Summer rain plays an important role in the Karakorum as well, but here the northern slopes, with dense, dark spruce forests, indicate a much higher humidity than in eastern California. The High Atacama is incomparably drier. Here precipitation increases from ~25 mm at the 2000 m level to a maximum of 150 mm at elevations of 4000 m. In regions with summer rain, this leads to a maximum vegetation density of 40% with scrubs and tussocks,

whereas in regions with winter rain, the same amount of precipitation is sufficient only for 2% vegetation coverage. This comparison clearly indicates two basic climatic-ecological characteristics of the Basin and Range Province (and therefore also the White Mountains): (1) generally arid conditions yield to a moderate increase of precipitation in the high mountains, resulting in the altitudinal extension of semi-deserts up to open montane forest; (2) summer rain, despite its high spatial and temporal variability and its overall moderate share of total precipitation, is of decisive importance for the existence of forests.

Altitudinal Zonation of Vegetation in the Sierra Nevada, the White Mountains, the Toiyabe Range, and Wheeler Peak

Method

The climatological facts outlined above indicate that a clear separation exists between the Sierra Nevada and the Basin and Range Province, which should be obvious in the vegetation as well. Furthermore, increasing precipitation and summer rainfall as one moves from the western to the eastern part of the Great Basin is supposed to affect the vegetation assemblage in the same way. In this context, we have to take into account that vegetation also can be affected by different petrologic situations. Such situations are considered to be less important for the geologically almost homogeneous Sierra Nevada (Mooney, 1962), but might be a major influence for the geologically highly variable ranges of eastern California, Nevada, and Utah/ Colorado. Thus far, the Sierra Nevada is characterized as diverse in climate and homogenous in a geologic or petrologic sense. This situation is exactly the reverse in the White Mountains and the adjacent ranges of the Great Basin, which are geologically diverse and more homogeneous climatically. A matter of interest is the question of which factor—climate or geology—is the principal ecological factor controlling the vegetation assemblage.

Valuable tools for answering these questions are resemblance or similarity computations (Wildi, 1986). These numerical, computer-assisted methods are used to derive floristic, climatic, and ecological groups (Wildi and Orlocki, 1990). According to Müller-Dombois and Ellenberg (1974), the fact that similar species combinations recur under similar habitat conditions enables us to derive ecological relationships. In the present case, the data that can be utilized are floristic, phytomorphologic, and structural in character. More than 250 vegetation samples were taken in the Sierra Nevada, the White Mountains, the Toiyabe Range, and Wheeler Peak to elaborate altitudinal and west–east changes in vegetation. The size of the sampling areas was constant at 100 m² and the sampling method was standardized to make the data sets comparable. All samples were taken along transects at the western and eastern slopes of the ranges so that the maximum vertical distance between adjacent sample plots was 150 m. Sample stands were chosen preferentially—that is, typical units of vegetation were examined. Non-natural or azonal vegetation patterns (e.g., riparian cottonwood stands) were discounted. The elaborated phytogeographic aspects of the Toiyabe Range are not further discussed in this paper, as there are no striking differences with the White Mountains. Different features of vegetation composition, assemblage, and structure primarily occur between the Sierra Nevada and the White Mountains, and between the White Mountains and Wheeler Peak.

Comparison of the ranges

Floristic similarity and altitudinal zonation. Figure 10A illustrates that the petrologically homogeneous Sierra Nevada as the westernmost part of the study area shows a clear separation in vegetation between the windward (western) and leeward (eastern) slopes. Rainshadow effects generally are more pronounced at lower elevations.

The drier eastern side of the Sierra Nevada is characterized by a uniform vertical sequence from desert scrub to montane woodland. The western slope exhibits a more heterogeneous vertical zonation, indicated by a higher rate of species alteration, especially between the lower montane mixed forest and the upper montane coniferous forest. Only the subalpine and alpine zones exhibit reduced exposure (east versus west) differences with increasing altitude and climatic homogenization. This can be seen as an effect of humid Pacific air masses sweeping over the ridges and bringing rain to the higher elevations on the east side. The distinction between the west and east slope of the Sierra Nevada is outlined in Figure 10B. Established by similarity computations, the dendrogram of floristic similarity shows the sample groups clustering according to their exposure. If there would be no climate-induced separation in exposure and altitudinal zonation, the groups would not arranged according to this clearly divided structure. The derived exposure differences also are illustrated in Figure 10C. It is clear from the figure that floristic and climatic similarity between groups on the two sides of the range is low in the foothills, but increases toward higher elevations.

The White Mountains show a different situation. Although highly diverse in a geological sense, the vegetation zonation shows no striking exposure (east versus west slope) differences (see Fig. 11C). This can be seen from the vertical sequence apparent from the dendrogram, in which the groups of the western and eastern slopes are close together (Fig. 11B). It appears that these vegetation patterns reflect a more uniform climate for both exposures, with no extreme weather and rainshadow effect as in the Sierra Nevada. Striking similarities are apparent for the eastern slope of the Sierra Nevada and for both exposures in the White Mountains up to an elevation of 2800 m. The high similarity in the desert scrub and montane pinion/juniper woodland is a result of overwhelming aridity. Relationships between the Sierra Nevada and the White Mountains disappear toward higher elevations at the transition to the subalpine zone. These differences are caused by convectional summer precipitation which is absent from the Sierra Nevada. The latter is seen to be responsible for the presence of bristlecone pines and high-elevation sagebrush in the White Mountains and other Great Basin Ranges (e.g., Toiyabe Range) but not in the Sierra Nevada. Furthermore, a subalpine treeless "bald" zone, which separates a lower from an upper woodland, is a phenomenon absent from the Sierra Nevada and Wheeler Peak, but is found in the White Mountains and in most of the higher ranges of Nevada. "Balds" always occur at a more-or-less constant elevation, and are thus not explained by climatic or geologic patterns, i.e., lack of moisture or substrate differences; they may be explained by the concept of the "unoccupied niche" advanced

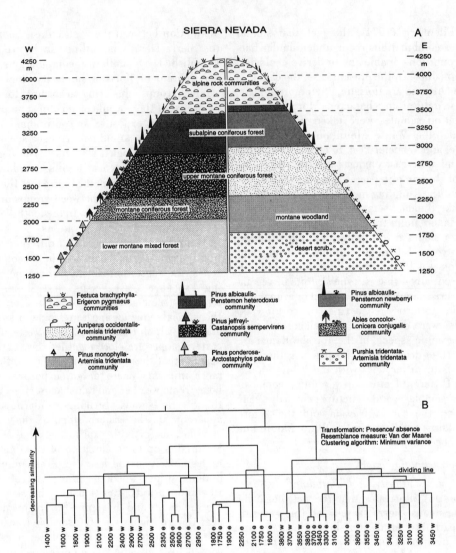

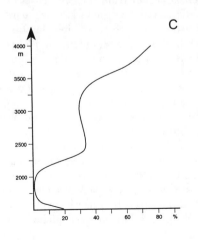

FIG. 10. Floristic similarity and altitudinal zonation for the Sierra Nevada. A. Vegetation profile. B. Dendrogram of floristic similarity. The number of groups formed is indicated by the position of the dividing line. C. Similarity at various exposure levels.

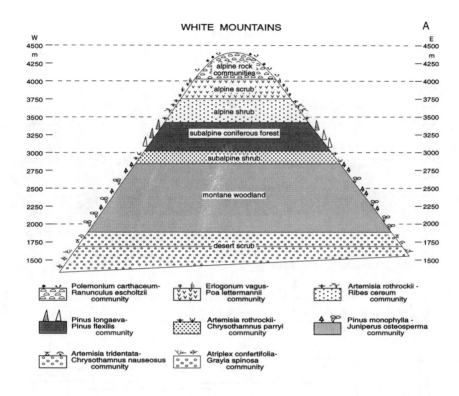

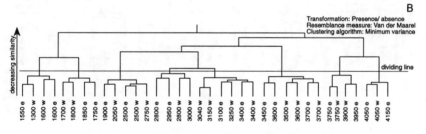

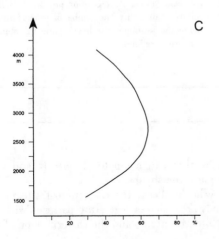

Fig. 11. Floristic similarity and altitudinal zonation for the White Mountains. A. Vegetation profile. B. Dendrogram of floristic similarity. The number of groups formed is indicated by the position of the dividing line. C. Similarity at various exposure levels.

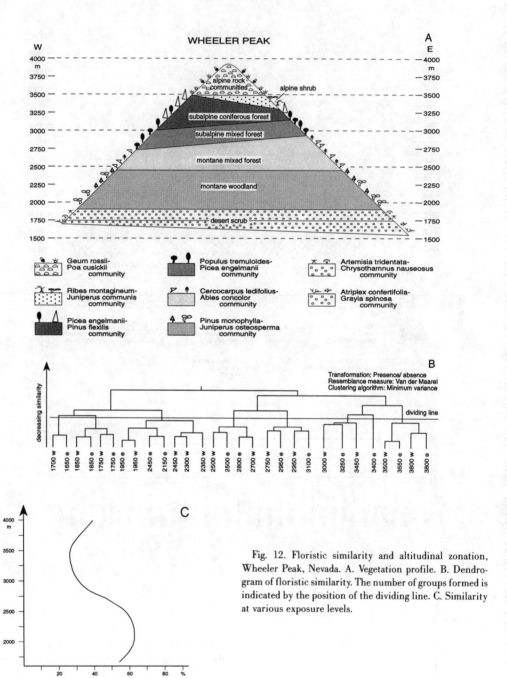

Fig. 12. Floristic similarity and altitudinal zonation, Wheeler Peak, Nevada. A. Vegetation profile. B. Dendrogram of floristic similarity. The number of groups formed is indicated by the position of the dividing line. C. Similarity at various exposure levels.

by M. Richter for such areas in the Tien Shan of Central Asia. Under this theory, the lack of trees is an effect of floristic history. Climate-ecological conditions would favor tree growth, but there are actually no trees that fit into this niche that can compete effectively and thus displace the shrubs.

Wheeler Peak, the easternmost site in the study area, shares vegetation patterns with the White Mountains and the eastern slope of the

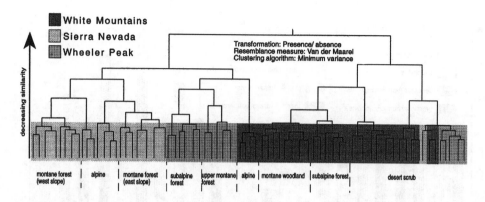

Fig. 13. Dendrogram of floristic similarity of all samples.

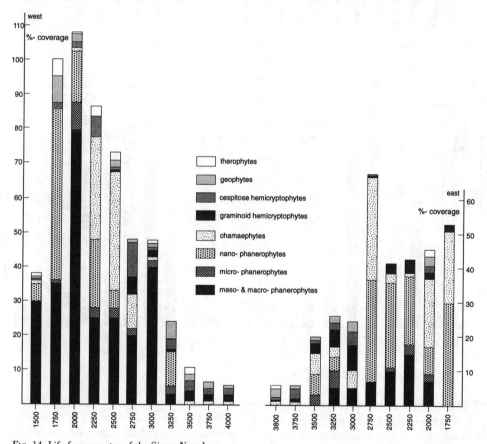

Fig. 14. Life-form spectra of the Sierra Nevada.

Sierra Nevada in the semi-arid foothill zone and in the adjacent pinion/juniper woodland (see Fig. 12A). These similarities disappear at elevations of over 2500 m, when the pinion/juniper community is replaced by a mixed forest community including white fir, which also is present on the humid western slope of the Sierra Nevada. The increasing moisture availability finally becomes obvious with the occurrence of Engelmann spruce between 3050 m and 3100

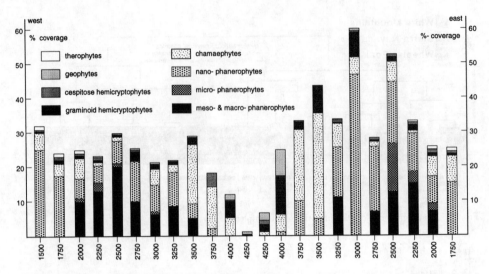

FIG. 15. Life-form spectra of the White Mountains.

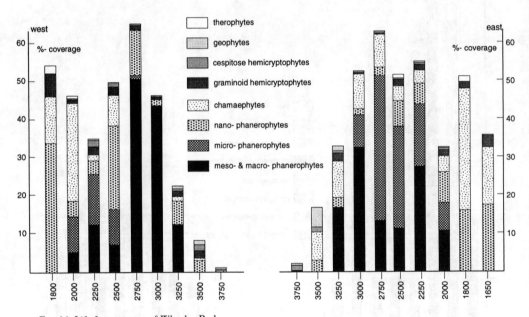

FIG. 16. Life-form spectra of Wheeler Peak.

m. The altitudinal zonation is almost the same for both exposures. Deviations occur at the transition to the upper timberline on the eastern side. Here, a community including common juniper, which is missing along the western slope, causes an asymmetry in the profile. This appears to be an effect of extremely strong westerly winds, which are restricted to higher elevations. Wind effects are further emphasized by the fact that the upper boundaries of the

lower forest communities extend to higher elevations on the eastern side. The climatic influence and the resulting differences in vegetation for both exposures are emphasized in Figure 12C. Evidently similarities at various exposures decrease towards higher elevations.

An overall floristic comparison of the three ranges establishes the obvious separation between the Sierra Nevada and the Wheeler Peak units. The Sierra Nevada and Wheeler

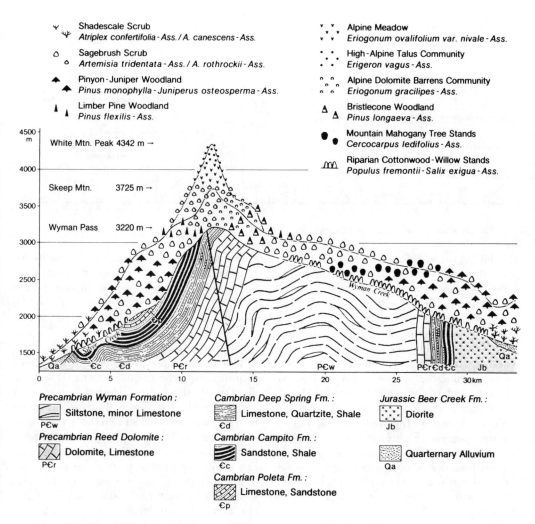

Shadescale Scrub
Atriplex confertifolia - Ass. / A. canescens - Ass.

Sagebrush Scrub
Artemisia tridentata - Ass. / A. rothrockii - Ass.

Pinyon - Juniper Woodland
Pinus monophylla - Juniperus osteosperma - Ass.

Limber Pine Woodland
Pinus flexilis - Ass.

Alpine Meadow
Eriogonum ovalifolium var. nivale - Ass.

High - Alpine Talus Community
Erigeron vagus - Ass.

Alpine Dolomite Barrens Community
Eriogonum gracilipes - Ass.

Bristlecone Woodland
Pinus longaeva - Ass.

Mountain Mahogany Tree Stands
Cercocarpus ledifolius - Ass.

Riparian Cottonwood - Willow Stands
Populus fremontii - Salix exigua - Ass.

White Mtn. Peak 4342 m →

Skeep Mtn.   3725 m →

Wyman Pass   3220 m →

Precambrian Wyman Formation :
Siltstone, minor Limestone
PЄw

Precambrian Reed Dolomite :
Dolomite, Limestone
PЄr

Cambrian Deep Spring Fm. :
Limestone, Quartzite, Shale
Єd

Cambrian Campito Fm. :
Sandstone, Shale
Єc

Cambrian Poleta Fm. :
Limestone, Sandstone
Єp

Jurassic Beer Creek Fm. :
Diorite
Jb

Quarternary Alluvium
Qa

FIG. 17. Profile for Silver Canyon–Wyman Creek.

Peak are more similar to one another than each is to the White Mountains, which appear to be a more-or-less isolated block. This is visible on the dendrogram of all samples outlined in Figure 13. Here, the White Mountains are compared to the Sierra Nevada and Wheeler Peak and exhibit a high level of dissimilarity. The White Mountain samples, dark grey in color, are isolated on the right side. Only some desert scrub samples show Wheeler Peak being more similar to the White Mountains than to the Sierra Nevada. However, this is likely an effect of grazing. Therefore, we can postulate that: (1) floristic similarities between the White Mountains and Wheeler Peak are limited to the basins, and are caused by extreme drought; and (2) similarities in the higher elevations of Wheeler Peak and the Sierra Nevada are a response to more favorable humidity.

Morphological and structural aspects. Another method of determining relationships between climate and vegetation in the dry southwestern part of the United States is afforded via analysis of life-form compositions (physiognomy). Here annual therophytes, bulbous geophytes, branched and graminoid hemicryptophytes (herbs), and chamaephytes (shrubs) are distinguished. Woody plants are further differentiated according to their size in nano-, micro-, and macro-phanerophytes. The diagrams (Figs. 14,

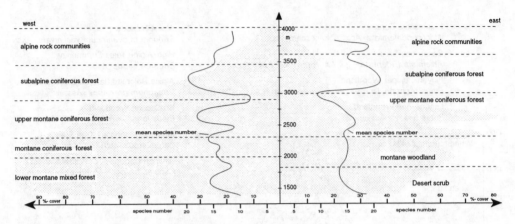

FIG. 18. Mean species number and coverage for the Sierra Nevada.

15, and 16) show lifeform spectra—that is, the percentage share of each life form in the total sample—arranged in columns. Analysis of physiognomic diversity should establish structural similarities and regularities among the three ranges. In the present case, diversity analysis is limited to species richness (alpha or within-habitat diversity), which in its most simple form—number of species per unit—is an adequate and easily derived measure that is useful for comparison of floristic samples.

Certain aspects of the life-form diagrams are readily apparent. Figure 14 shows that the humid western side of the Sierra Nevada has the highest total degree of coverage and predominance of meso- and macro-phanerophytes—in other words, the highest percentage share of trees.

The western side of Wheeler Peak shows similar or even more favorable climatic conditions for tree growth at elevations between 2500 m and 3250 m (see Fig. 16). This clearly indicates the higher moisture availability for the Sierra Nevada and Wheeler Peak, which distinguishes both ranges from the White Mountains. The White Mountains are characterized by a lower total degree of coverage and generally more open vegetation with fewer tree species (Fig. 15). Furthermore, the western side appears to be climatically "disadvantaged" in comparison with the eastern side. The eastern side has a higher total coverage, although the share of trees (phanerophytes) is lower. The treeless "bald" zone shows coverage values of striking height. These differences in coverage—which are less obvious at Wheeler Peak—likely

are a response to different moisture conditions. It appears that summer convectional rain from the Gulf of Mexico is more intense on the eastern than on the western slopes of the White Mountains. A geological profile illustrates another aspect. The Silver Canyon–Wyman Creek profile (Fig. 17) shows strong asymmetry in substrate and topography. The western slope is quite steep, whereas the eastern slope has a more gentle slope. After precipitation, a water loss entailed by interflow (subsurface drainage) is thus more likely to occur on the western side. Furthermore, tilted strata may cause an additional water loss. That the geologic situation can modify vegetation patterns in the White Mountains in at least certain ways is documented by the fact that bristlecone pine stands are found only on dolomite or on similar calcareous substrates (Wright and Mooney, 1965).

Finally, other aspects of diversity analysis should be noted briefly. Figures 18, 19, and 20 show that in many cases the species number is negatively correlated with the total degree of coverage. In other words, open vegetation stands with low tree coverage are not considered to have fewer plant species than do closed forests. In fact, the inverse is the case. This becomes obvious in the curve for number of species in the White Mountains (Fig. 19). Although the White Mountains are the driest of the three ranges, they have the same or even higher species diversity than does either the Sierra Nevada or Wheeler Peak. Locally, more than 15 different species were found per sample unit (100 m²). This is almost the same number of species observed in the humid, dense forests

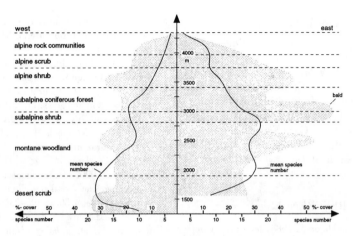

FIG. 19. Mean species number and coverage for the White Mountains.

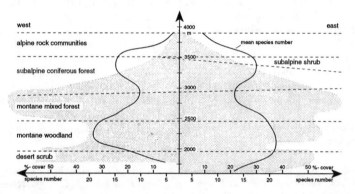

FIG. 20. Mean species number and coverage for Wheeler Peak.

on the western flank of the Sierra Nevada. The reason for this might be a greater range of resource conditions or niches available as a result of microclimatic variability. This relationship is not found in the lowest portions of the range, where alkali soils, excessive temperatures, and grazing seem to reduce the species number. Positive deviations are expected in late winter or spring, when heavy episodic rains make the desert bloom and encourage a large number of short-lived annuals to dominate the scenery.

Conclusions

The derivation of climatic features based on computer-assisted phyto-indication can be an important tool. However, exact evaluations are almost impossible, because no or little data are available. For this reason phyto-indication is seen to afford an opportunity to organize climatological facts without the expensive purchase, installation, and maintenance of several weather stations. It is evident that in some parts of the world, where no climatological data are present, numerical analysis of vegetation data is being used to develop strategies for agro-ecological evaluations and for planning the effective use of water resources. In this context, we call attention to the importance of high-mountain areas as water storage areas, which has been emphasized in the United Nations Mountain Agenda 1992 (UNCED, 1992). It is clear that more work is needed, in developed areas where logistical and infrastructural possibilities are better, to develop better methods, strategies, and concepts of phyto-indication, in order that these may be applied to research in other areas such as the semiarid and semihumid mountains of Central Asia, where much basic information is lacking.

Acknowledgments

This paper presents the climatological and phytogeographical aspects of four master's theses supervised by M. Richter. The authors thank the University of California for generous research support and for the invitation to participate in the Clarence Hall Symposium. Our special thanks go to W. Gary Ernst, Clarence A. Hall, Frank Powell, and the staff of the White Mountain Research Station, who made us feel at home.

REFERENCES

Barbour, M. G., and Major, J., 1988, Terrestrial vegetation of California: New York, Wiley-Interscience.

Barry, R. G., 1992, Mountain weather and climate, second ed.: London/New York, Routledge.

Beaty, C. B., 1975, Sublimation or melting: Observations from the White Mountains, California and Nevada, USA: Journal Glaciol., v. 14, p. 275-286.

Henning, I., and Henning, D., 1981, Potential evaporation in mountain geoecosystems of different altitudes and latitudes: Mount. Res. Devel., v. 1, p. 267-274.

Hill, H. A., 1973, Diversity and evenness: A unifying notion and its consequences: Ecology, v. 54, p. 427-432.

Jauregui, E., Klaus, D., and Lauer, W., 1978, On the estimation of potential evaporation and evapotranspiration in Central Mexico: Colloq. Geographicum, v. 13.

Mooney, H. A., 1962, Alpine and subalpine vegetation patterns in the White Mountains of California: Amer. Midl. Nat., v. 68, p. 257-273.

Morefield, J. D., 1988, Vascular flora of the White Mountains of California and Nevada: An updated working checklist, in Hall, C. A., ed., Plant biology of eastern California: Berkeley, CA, Univ. of California Press, p. 310-364.

Müller-Dombois, D., and Ellenberg, H., 1974, Aims and methods of vegetation ecology: New York, John Wiley and Sons.

NCDC (National Climatic Data Center), Climate data summaries on CD-Rom: Reno, NV, Desert Research Institute, 1900-1995.

Papadakis, J., 1966, Climates of the world and their agricultural potentialities: Buenos Aires.

Penman, H. L., 1948, Natural evaporation from open water, bare soil and grass: Proc. Roy. Soc. Lond., ser. A., Math. and Phys. Sci., v. 193A, p. 120-145.

Powell, D. R., and Klieforth, H. E., in Hall, C. A.. Jr., ed., 1991, Natural history of the White-Inyo Range: Berkeley, CA, Univ. of California Press, p. 3-26.

Richter, M., 1996, Klimatologische und pflanzenmorphologische Vertikalgradienten in Hochgebirgen: Erdkunde, v. 50, p. 205-237.

Richter, M., and Schröder, R., 1991, Klima und Vegetation im Death Valley National Monument: Erdkunde, v. 45, p. 38-51.

Schmiedecken, W., 1978, Die Bestimmung der Humidität und ihrer Abstufungen mit Hilfe von Wasserhaushaltsberechnungen, in Lauer, W., ed., Klimatologische studien in Mexiko und Nigeria: Colloq. Geographicim, v. 13, p. 135-159.

Schoenherr, A. A., 1995, A natural history of California: Berkeley, CA, University of California Press.

Whittaker, R. H., 1975, Communities and ecosystems: New York, Macmillan.

————, 1978, Classification of plant communities: The Hague, Junk.

Wildi, O., 1986, Analyse vegetationskundlicher daten: Zürich, Geobotanischen Instituts ETH Zürich.

Wildi, O., and Orloci, L., 1990, Numerical exploration of community patterns: The Hague, SPB Acad. Publ.

Wright, R. D., and Mooney, H. A., 1965, Substrate-oriented distribution of Bristlecone pine in the White Mountains of California: Amer. Midl. Nat., v. 73, p. 257-284.

UNCED (United Nations Commission for Economic Development), 1992, Mountain agenda 1992: An appeal for the mountains: Berne, Institute of Geography.

SIERRA NEVADA

The Sierra Crest Magmatic Event: Rapid Formation of Juvenile Crust during the Late Cretaceous in California

Drew S. Coleman

Department of Earth Sciences, Boston University, 675 Commonwealth Avenue, Boston, Massachusetts 02215

and Allen F. Glazner

Department of Geology, CB 3315, University of North Carolina, Chapel Hill, North Carolina 27599

Abstract

The Late Cretaceous was a period of extremely voluminous magmatism and rapid crustal growth in the western United States. From approximately 98 to 86 Ma, greater than 4000 km² of exposed granodioritic to granitic crust, including the largest composite intrusive suites in the Sierra Nevada batholith, were emplaced in eastern California. Plutons intruded during this period include the highest peaks in the Sierra; we informally refer to this as the Sierra Crest magmatic event. Field, petrologic, geochemical, and geochronologic data indicate that, although they comprise an insignificant volume of exposed rocks (less than 100 km²), mafic magmas were intruded contemporaneously with each episode of intermediate and high-silica magmatism in the event. This observation attests to the fundamental importance of high-alumina basaltic magmas during crustal-growth episodes in continental arcs. Geochemical data for suites of coeval plutonic rocks of the Sierra Crest magmatic event, ranging in composition from basalt to high-silica rhyolite, demonstrate that recycling of pre-existing crust locally played a minor role in the growth of new crust. Thus, major chemical and isotopic characteristics of Sierra Crest plutons, such as variable isotopic compositions, were inherited from the mantle source of the high-alumina basalts and are not necessarily the result of interaction with the overlying crust. Consequently, we interpret isotopic boundaries in the western United States, such as the $^{87}Sr/^{86}Sr = 0.706$ isopleth, to be largely features of the continental lithospheric mantle. Furthermore, isotopic data demonstrate that enrichment of the lithospheric mantle in the western United States probably occurred in the Precambrian during assembly of the North American craton. Geophysical and xenolith investigations by other workers support the hypothesis presented here that Cretaceous magmatism in the Sierra Nevada may have locally restructured most, if not all, of the crustal column. The timing of Sierra Crest magmatism correlates with voluminous magmatism elsewhere in the Cordilleran arc. We speculate that this intense episode of magmatism may have played a role in the global marine geochemical excursions and extinctions at the Cenomanian–Turonian boundary.

Introduction

Although the exposed continental crust is largely granodioritic in average composition (Rudnick and Fountain, 1994; Weaver and Tarney, 1984), the important role that mafic magmatism plays in its genesis has been recognized since the dawn of modern igneous petrology (Bowen, 1928). A record of mafic magmatism associated with construction of intermediate-composition crust is preserved in rocks ranging from the ancient Acasta gneisses (Bowring and Housh, 1995) to active continental arcs (Hamilton, 1995). Although it is widely accepted that melting of the mantle leads to basaltic (*sensu lato*) magmas, the processes by which these magmas are refined to granodiorites and granites are not fully understood. Understanding the origin and chemical evolution of entire suites of arc plutonic rocks, ranging in composition from basalt to high-silica rhyolite, is critical to understanding the growth and development of continental crust.

The Sierra Nevada batholith of California (Fig. 1) provides an outstanding natural laboratory for the study of these processes. In this paper we discuss recent work on the field relations, age, and geochemistry of voluminous Late Cretaceous plutons that crop out along a 200-km length of the Sierra Nevada Crest. About half of the exposed rocks along the crest were intruded at 92 ± 6 Ma. A principal focus of

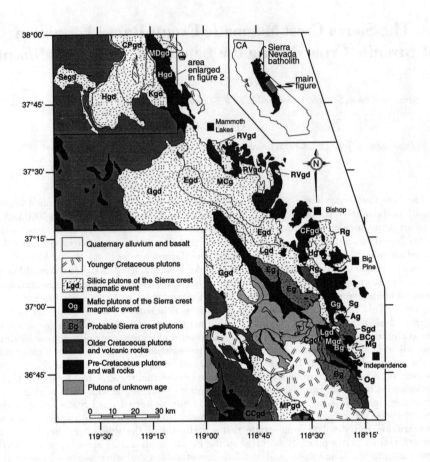

FIG. 1. Simplified geologic map of the east-central Sierra Nevada batholith. Rocks are divided on the basis of age, and all plutons of the Sierra Crest magmatic event (see text) are labeled. Map is simplified from Bateman (1992) and Moore and Sisson (1987). Ages are derived from Stern et al. (1981), Chen and Moore (1982), Coleman et al. (1995), Evernden and Kistler (1970), and this study. Some ages are inferred from field relations with dated plutons. The total area of exposed plutons of the Sierra Crest magmatic event depicted on the map is ~4600 km². Mafic plutons intruded as a part of the Sierra Crest magmatic event comprise the largest area of mafic plutons in the eastern Sierra, yet they crop out over an area of only ~60 km². Nearly all of the Cretaceous plutons on the eastern Sierra front were intruded as part of the Sierra Crest magmatic event. Abbreviations: Ag = Aberdeen mafic sill complex; Bg = granite of Bullfrog Lake; BCg = gabbro of Black Canyon; Cgd = granodiorite of Mount Cotter; CCgd = granodiorite of Castle Creek; CFgd = granodiorite of Coyote Flat; CPgd = Cathedral Peak Granodiorite; Eg = Evolution Basin Alaskite; Egd = Lake Edison Granodiorite; Gg = granite of Goodale Mountain; Ggd = Mount Givens Granodiorite; Hgd = Half Dome Granodiorite; Kgd = granodiorite of Kuna Crest; Lgd = Lamarck Granodiorite; Hg = gabbro of the Hunchback; Mg = granite of McGann Springs; Mgd = granodiorite of Mount McDoogle; MCg = Mono Creek Granite; MDgd = granodiorite of Mono Dome; MPgd = Mitchell Peak Granodiorite; Og = mafic sill complex of Onion Valley; Rg = leucogranite of Rawson Creek; RVgd = Round Valley Peak Granodiorite; Sg = granite of Siberian Lake; Sgd = granodiorite of Spook Canyon; Segd = Sentinel Granodiorite.

our research has been to determine the variation in isotopic compositions across the entire compositional range of individual intrusive suites, with emphasis on the isotopic compositions of the most mafic units present. The goal of this research is to determine the nature and role of the mantle involved in batholith construction, and the processes involved in the evolution of voluminous intrusive suites emplaced rapidly within continental arcs.

Cretaceous Magmatism in the Sierra Nevada

The Sierra Nevada batholith was built along the continental margin of western North America during Mesozoic subduction. Excellent summaries of the geologic history of the batholith and its wall rocks are presented in Hamilton (1978), Schweickert (1981), and Bateman (1992). Geochronologic data suggest that there were distinct peaks of magmatic activity in the Triassic, Jurassic, and Cretaceous (Evernden and Kistler, 1970; Stern et al., 1981; Chen and Moore, 1982). Most geochemical and geochronological investigations of the batholith have concentrated on the voluminous intermediate and silicic plutons (e.g., Bateman et al., 1963; Kistler and Peterman, 1978; DePaolo, 1981; Chen and Tilton, 1991). Only recently has the ubiquity and importance of mafic plutons in the batholith been recognized (Frost and Mahood, 1987; Coleman et al., 1992, 1995; Sisson et al., 1996).

Investigations of mafic plutons in the Sierra Nevada batholith mark a change in thought regarding the origin of the batholith and the evolution of silicic plutons. Prior to such work, geochemical investigations of the batholith focused on E-W variations in geochemical parameters (e.g., K_2O and $^{87}Sr/^{86}Sr$) and attributed these to an eastward increase in the proportion of ancient crustal rocks in the batholith (Kistler and Peterman, 1973, 1978; DePaolo, 1981; Ague and Brimhall, 1988a, 1988b; Chen and Tilton, 1991). In particular, E-W variations in isotope ratios were attributed to mixing of asthenospheric mafic magmas with old crustal rocks (e.g., DePaolo, 1981). However, several recent studies show that mafic plutons in the east-central Sierra Nevada probably were derived from a lithospheric mantle source with low ϵNd and high $^{87}Sr/^{86}Sr$ (Coleman et al., 1992; Sisson et al., 1996). Data from Cenozoic mafic volcanic rocks and entrained mantle xenoliths also indicate that enriched mantle is present beneath the area (Domenick et al., 1983; Beard and Glazner, 1995; Ducea and Saleeby, 1996a). If an enriched mantle component is truly present, then the amount of new crust generated during the Cretaceous in the east-central Sierra Nevada is approximately double that of earlier estimates (Coleman et al., 1992).

The Sierra Crest Magmatic Event

A growing database of high-precision, U-Pb zircon geochronology suggests that from ~98 to 86 Ma, the east-central Sierra Nevada was the site of the most extensive plutonism in its history. Relevant plutons are shown in Figure 1. We refer to this magmatic pulse as the Sierra Crest magmatic event. Other plutons of the event, including parts of the Whitney Intrusive Suite (Hirt, 1989; Hirt and Glazner, 1995), occur both north and south of the area shown in Figure 1, where mapping and dating are less complete. Plutons that were intruded during this event comprise most of the John Muir and Tuolumne intrusive suites of Bateman (1992), and include the huge Mount Givens, Half Dome, Cathedral Peak, Lake Edison, Mono Recesses, and Lamarck plutons. Most of these plutons are exposed along the range crest and along the John Muir Trail.

The Sierra Crest magmatic event overlaps in large part the Cathedral Range intrusive epoch (81 to 92 Ma) of Evernden and Kistler (1970), which was defined on the basis of K-Ar cooling ages, but includes a number of plutons older than 92 Ma. Zircon U-Pb ages from several Cretaceous plutons in the Pacific Northwest also fall within this interval (Walker and Brown, 1991; Brown and Walker, 1993), indicating that it might encompass an area larger than just California.

Geochronology of the Sierra Crest Rocks

Early isotopic dating of Sierran plutons (Curtis et al., 1958; Bateman, 1965; Kistler et al., 1965; Evernden and Kistler, 1970) established that most of the plutonic rocks in the range are Mesozoic in age, chiefly Jurassic and Cretaceous. Evernden and Kistler (1970) argued on the basis of a large number of K-Ar ages that, although magmatism was continuous from ~210 to 80 Ma, dates for Sierran plutons tended to cluster into five intrusive epochs. More recent U-Pb dates have refined and shortened these intrusive episodes. These new data include both large regional studies (Stern et al., 1981; Chen and Moore, 1982) and more detailed, multi-fraction, high-precision studies (e.g., Saleeby et al., 1990; Coleman et al., 1995; Tobisch et al., 1995; Fleck et al., 1996). A large number of recently determined U-Pb ages of rocks in the central Sierra fall within the narrow window of 92 ± 6 Ma (Fig. 1). These include all but a few Cretaceous plutons along the Sierra Crest from the Whitney Intrusive Suite to the Tuolumne Intrusive Suite, as well as newly recognized Cretaceous dikes in the Independence swarm (Coleman et al., in review). Rocks intruded during the Sierra Crest magmatic event are roughly equivalent to the Cathedral Range intrusive epoch of Evernden and Kistler (1970); however, because the K-Ar cooling ages reported by these authors are inconsistent with U-Pb ages for the same units (Stern et al., 1981), we have abandoned the older nomenclature.

Exposed rocks emplaced during the Sierra Crest magmatic event crop out over an area greater than 4600 km². Between 36° and 38° N. Lat., they comprise ~50% of exposed Sierra Nevada plutons, making this the most significant magmatic episode in the central Sierra. The overwhelming majority of the Sierra Crest rocks are granodioritic in composition; however, rocks of intermediate composition nearly always occur in association with high-silica granite, diorite, and gabbro. Mafic plutons comprise less than 100 km² of exposure within the Sierra Crest magmatic event plutons, but include the most voluminous mafic plutons exposed anywhere in the eastern Sierra.

Below we present new data on the age of the Tuolumne Intrusive Suite. These data fall within the Sierra Crest magmatic event, but exhibit noticeable inheritance in their zircon systematics. This is in distinct contrast to the more concordant intrusive suite of Mount Lamarck and other plutons of the central Sierra Nevada.

Age of the Tuolumne Intrusive Suite

Previous work

The Tuolumne Intrusive Suite is the best-known and most-studied zoned intrusive suite in the Sierra Nevada (Frey et al., 1978; Bateman and Chappell, 1979; Kistler et al., 1986; Kistler and Fleck, 1994). Field data suggest that the suite was emplaced in a series of pulses, with each successive pulse displacing older units outward, resulting in a concentrically zoned suite with the most mafic phases in the outer zones. Contacts between phases are variably

gradational and sharp. Units dated here, from outermost to innermost, include the Sentinel Granodiorite, the Half Dome Granodiorite, the Cathedral Peak Granodiorite, and the Johnson Granite Porphyry. The Half Dome Granodiorite is subdivided into an outer equigranular and an inner megacrystic phase. The Cathedral Peak Granodiorite is subdivided into outer and inner phases on the basis of geochemical and isotopic differences (Kistler and Fleck, 1994). Following Kistler and Fleck (1994), we include the megacrystic Half Dome Granodiorite with the outer Cathedral Peak Granodiorite. Zonation of the Tuolumne also is evident in geochemical and isotopic profiles across the suite (Kistler et al., 1986; Kistler and Fleck, 1994), but geochemical and isotopic boundaries are not always coincident with petrologic boundaries (Fleck et al., 1996).

Existing geochronologic data for the Tuolumne Intrusive Suite are complicated, but appear to indicate progressively younger ages toward the center of the suite (Kistler and Fleck, 1994). Fleck et al. (1996) suggested that complications in the ages reflect problems resulting from inheritance and partial resetting by successive magma pulses. For these reasons, we are cautious about interpreting Rb-Sr, K-Ar, and ^{40}Ar/^{39}Ar dates as anything but cooling dates. The most reliable crystallization ages can be obtained from U-Pb zircon and sphene dates, because these minerals have the highest closure temperatures and therefore are the least susceptible to resetting. However, as noted by Fleck et al. (1996) and shown below, even these ages may be susceptible to resetting. Problems with inheritance in zircon can be identified using ion microprobe (SHRIMP) dating techniques and can be addressed through dating extremely small (and even single-zircon) fractions using conventional U-Pb dating techniques.

Existing conventional U-Pb zircon and sphene dates are published for the granodiorite of Kuna Crest (≈90 Ma, one-fraction U-Pb zircon) (Stern et al., 1981), the Sentinel Granodiorite (94 Ma, U-Pb sphene) (Fleck et al., 1996), the outer equigranular phase of the Half Dome Granodiorite (88 Ma, U-Pb zircon) (Kistler and Fleck, 1994), and the inner Cathedral Peak Granodiorite (84 to 86 Ma, U-Pb zircon and sphene) (Stern et al., 1981; Kistler and Fleck, 1994). SHRIMP dating of the Sentinel Granodiorite yielded concordant dates ranging from 95 to 143 Ma; however, these are all interpreted as inheritance ages (Fleck et al., 1996). Similarly, SHRIMP dating of the Johnson Granite Porphyry revealed significant inheritance and an interpreted minimum age of 82 Ma (Fleck et al., 1996). These data suggest an episodic intrusive history that spanned a 12-m.y. period for the Tuolumne intrusive suite.

New U-Pb data

We present new conventional U-Pb zircon and sphene ages for four of the principal phases in the Tuolumne Intrusive Suite. Samples of the Sentinel Granodiorite (YO94-23), the equigranular Half Dome Granodiorite (YO94-21), and the megacrystic Cathedral Peak Granodiorite (YO94-20) were collected along Route 120 in Yosemite National Park with the assistance of Dr. Ronald Kistler (Fig. 2). A sample of the Johnson Granite Porphyry (YO94-28) was collected at Elizabeth Lake, south of Tuolumne Meadows. All samples were crushed, and zircon and sphene were separated and analyzed using conventional techniques (Table 1). As with previous data sets, the U-Pb data for the samples show the effects of Pb loss and inheritance; however, the small size of the samples and concordance of zircon and sphene dates permit fairly robust interpretation of crystallization ages.

Sentinel Granodiorite. Despite significant evidence for zircon inheritance in SHRIMP data for the Sentinel Granodiorite (Fleck et al., 1996), our conventional data for this unit show little evidence of inheritance (Table 1; Fig. 3). Two of the sphene fractions (s3 and s6) and one zircon fraction (d-2 #1 1/2) yield a weighted mean $^{206}Pb/^{238}U$ age of 94.6 ± 1.1 Ma (M.S.W.D. = 2.8). The second zircon fraction (d-2 #2) is slightly older, but reversely discordant. The third sphene fraction (s5) yields a significantly younger date ($^{206}Pb/^{238}U$ = 92.7 Ma) than all of the other fractions analyzed. We interpret this date to reflect either Pb loss or a cooling date, because this fraction included small grains and grain fragments that are most susceptible to these complications. Therefore, we accept 94.5 ± 1 Ma as an estimate of the crystallization age of the Sentinel Granodiorite. This age overlaps the age estimate of 94 Ma for the Sentinel Granodiorite made by Fleck et al. (1996). Finally, our age estimate agrees well

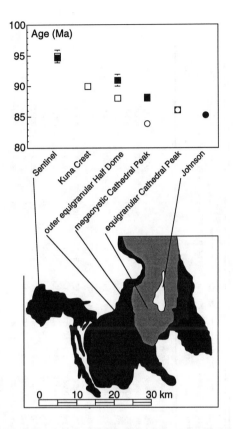

FIG. 2. Summary of U-Pb geochronologic data for the Tuolumne Intrusive Suite. Data are from Kistler and Fleck (1994), Fleck et al. (1996), and this study. Error bars are shown only for points for which errors are larger than the plot symbol. Solid symbols represent data from this study, square symbols are zircon dates, and round symbols are sphene dates. Samples are arranged spatially: units to the right side of the plot crop out in the center of the intrusive suite and units to the left lie progressively farther from the center. The inset below is a simplified geologic map of dated units from Bateman (1992). There is a distinct progression toward the younger ages in the center of the suite in all data sets.

with the minimum SHRIMP dates of 95 Ma obtained by Fleck et al. (1996). Although these authors interpreted the 95-Ma dates to result from inheritance, we interpret these as crystallization dates because of the concordance of the oldest sphene dates and the youngest zircon date.

Half Dome Granodiorite. Unlike the Sentinel Granodiorite, the equigranular Half Dome Granodiorite is characterized by significant inheritance that complicates age interpretation

TABLE 1. U-Pb Isotopic Data for Zircon and Sphene from the Tuolumne Intrusive Suite[1]

Fractions and properties	Concentrations			206Pb[3]/204Pb	208Pb[2]/206Pb	Atomic ratios						Ages (Ma)			Corr. coeff.	Total common Pb, pg
	Weight, mg	U, ppm	Pb[2], ppm			206Pb[4]/238U	Pct. error	207Pb[4]/235U	Pct. error	207Pb[4]/206Pb	Pct. error	206Pb/238U	207Pb/235U	207Pb/206Pb		
Sentinel Granodiorite (YO94-23, UTM[5] 266900, 4192650)																
d-2 #2	0.015	379.3	6.13	941.90	0.171	0.01499	(.61)	0.09886	(.66)	0.04782	(.23)	95.9	95.7	90.3	0.937	6.0
d-2 #1 1/2	0.0089	480.9	7.61	812.59	0.157	0.01489	(.81)	0.09853	(.86)	0.04800	(.26)	95.3	95.4	99.1	0.954	5.2
s3	0.23	253.6	7.35	160.61	0.710	0.01474	(.15)	0.09742	(1.2)	0.04793	(1.1)	94.3	94.4	95.6	0.446	390
s5	0.21	178.8	5.90	130.64	0.932	0.01449	(.24)	0.09464	(1.5)	0.04736	(1.4)	92.7	91.8	67.6	0.451	310
s6	0.24	211.8	6.54	150.64	0.818	0.01475	(.20)	0.09682	(1.3)	0.04761	(1.1)	94.4	93.8	79.8	0.490	360
Equigranular Half Dome Granodiorite (YO94-21, UTM 281200, 4187700)																
nm	0.15	591.2	9.30	4886.7	0.139	0.01517	(.15)	0.1122	(.16)	0.05362	(.07)	97.1	108	355	0.900	17
m0.5	0.041	1964	29.1	2610.2	0.139	0.01421	(.16)	0.09381	(.19)	0.04789	(.11)	90.9	91.0	93.9	0.828	28
m0.75	0.046	831.9	12.8	1330.2	0.154	0.01425	(.12)	0.09415	(.16)	0.04793	(.10)	91.2	91.4	95.6	0.787	27
m1	0.035	1922	28.0	8510.4	0.146	0.01413	(.13)	0.09337	(.15)	0.04791	(.05)	90.5	90.6	94.7	0.926	7.2
s1	0.0010	43400	1600	143.05	1.39	0.01416	(.17)	0.09338	(.42)	0.04781	(.37)	90.7	90.6	89.9	0.492	320
s2	0.012	5764	207	145.76	1.31	0.01414	(.13)	0.09310	(.48)	0.04774	(.44)	90.5	90.4	86.4	0.430	410
s4+5	0.022	1814	46.7	145.72	0.511	0.01400	(.19)	0.09221	(.40)	0.04777	(.33)	89.6	89.6	88.1	0.541	260
Megacrystic Cathedral Peak Granodiorite (YO94-20, UTM 285700, 4192750)																
d-3 #1 1/2	0.0094	1811	25.9	3443.0	0.159	0.01373	(.23)	0.09055	(.26)	0.04784	(.12)	87.9	88.0	91.3	0.897	4.4
d-3 #1 2/2	0.017	1704	24.3	5930.0	0.152	0.01376	(.15)	0.09081	(.18)	0.04785	(.11)	88.1	88.3	91.9	0.822	4.3
d-3 #2	0.0093	533.9	7.98	1077.8	0.142	0.01444	(.73)	0.09565	(.85)	0.04805	(.41)	92.4	92.8	102	0.873	4.4
d-3 #3 1/3	0.0036	900.6	15.1	251.78	0.133	0.01382	(1.1)	0.09104	(1.3)	0.04778	(.56)	88.5	88.5	88.4	0.895	12
d-3 #3 2/3	0.0033	1105	16.4	560.79	0.151	0.01374	(1.0)	0.09062	(1.1)	0.04784	(.37)	88.0	88.1	91.2	0.942	5.9
d-3 #3 3/3	0.0067	1053	16.0	847.62	0.145	0.01424	(.61)	0.09433	(1.0)	0.04805	(.75)	91.1	91.5	102	0.662	7.8
Johnson Granite Porphyry (YO94-28, UTM 291530, 4190810)																
nml #1	0.0011	51790	701	5270.3	0.109	0.01350	(.10)	0.08896	(.14)	0.04778	(.10)	86.5	86.5	88.3	0.737	8.6
nml #2	0.0013	11760	201	2627.7	0.144	0.01647	(.27)	0.1253	(.28)	0.05518	(.07)	105	120	420	0.967	4.8
s1	0.012	13660	411	97.74	0.624	0.01333	(.10)	0.08759	(.45)	0.04764	(.42)	85.4	85.3	81.5	0.389	1500
s2	0.011	11200	464	61.77	0.814	0.01334	(.12)	0.08762	(1.3)	0.04765	(1.2)	85.4	85.3	81.8	0.633	2200

[1]All samples analyzed at Massachusetts Institute of Technology in 1994 using mixed 205Pb/233U/235U spike. Zircon grains are designated as diamagnetic (d), non-magnetic (nm), and magnetic (m) in terms of degrees of tilt on a Frantz LB-1 magnetic separator. Sphene fractions are indicated with an "s." Sample weights are estimated using a video monitor with a gridded screen and are known to within 10%. All zircon fractions were air abraded prior to dissolution. Zircon dissolution followed methods of Krogh (1973) and Parrish (1987). Separation of Pb and U was accomplished using HCl chemistry. Decay constants used are $^{238}U = 0.15513 \times 10^{-9}$ yr^{-1}, and $^{235}U = 0.98485 \times 10^{-9}$ yr^{-1} (Steiger and Jäger, 1977). Common Pb corrections were made using feldspar common Pb data provided by Joe Wooden (unpubl. data) for each intrusive unit. Values used are: Sentinel Granodiorite—206Pb/204Pb = 19.27, 207Pb/204Pb = 15.70, 208Pb/204Pb = 38.94; equigranular Half Dome Granodiorite—206Pb/204Pb = 19.00, 207Pb/204Pb = 15.67, 208Pb/204Pb = 38.80; megacrystic Cathedral Peak Granodiorite—206Pb/204Pb = 19.01, 207Pb/204Pb = 15.66, 208Pb/204Pb = 38.78. Common Pb values in each of the intrusive units are variable about these values (J.L. Wooden, pers. commun., 1996); however, small variations in these values do little to affect the results. U blank = 1 pg ± 50%; Pb blank = 3.5 pg ± 50% for zircon analyses and 7.0 pg ± 50% for sphene analyses. Data reduction and error analysis was performed using the algorithms of Ludwig (1989, 1990) within Pb MacDat-2 by D.S. Coleman (unpubl.). All errors are reported in percent at the 2-σ confidence interval.

[2]Radiogenic Pb.

[3]Measured ratio corrected for fractionation only. Mass fractionation correction of 0.15 ± 0.08%/amu was applied to all Pb analyses.

[4]Corrected for fractionation, spike, blank, and initial common Pb.

[5]UTM (Universal Transverse Mercator) coordinates, referenced to Zone 11.

(Table 1; Fig. 3). Two sphene fractions (s1 and s2) and one zircon fraction (m1) yield a weighted mean $^{206}Pb/^{238}U$ age of 90.6 ± 0.3 Ma (M.S.W.D. = 4) and an identical $^{207}Pb/^{235}U$ age of 90.6 ± 0.1 Ma (M.S.W.D. = 0.4). The third sphene fraction (s4 + 5) is somewhat younger ($\approx$90 Ma); however, as with the young sphene fraction from the Sentinel Granodiorite, this sample includes small grains that may have experienced Pb loss. Two of the remaining zircon fractions (m0.5 and m0.75) yield dates slightly older than 90.6 Ma, whereas the final zircon fraction (nm) is characterized by significant inheritance and plots far away from concordia. None of the zircon fractions are concordant, and given problems with sphene fractions from this (s4 + 5) and other samples from the Tuolumne Intrusive Suite yielding anomalously young cooling and Pb-loss dates, we are hesitant to interpret the age of the equigranular Half Dome Granodiorite precisely with these data. However, we believe that an estimate of 91 ± 1 Ma for this sample is reasonable. This age is significantly older than the published U-Pb zircon age of 88 Ma for the same unit (Kistler and Fleck, 1994). The discrepancy in ages might reflect heterogeneities within the Half Dome Granodiorite that are apparent in chemical data and cooling dates (Kistler and Fleck, 1994). Alternatively, all of our zircon fractions may be characterized by inheritance and yield anomalously old ages. Because the youngest zircon dates and oldest sphene dates for this sample agree so well, we believe that this latter interpretation is unlikely.

Cathedral Peak Granodiorite. The megacrystic phase of the Cathedral Peak Granodiorite exhibits fairly simple zircon systematics (Table 1; Fig. 3). The four most concordant fractions (d-3 #1 1/2, d-3 #1 2/2, d-3 #3 1/3, and d-3 #3 2/3) yield a weighted mean $^{206}Pb/^{238}U$ age of 88.1 ± 0.2 Ma (M.S.W.D. = 1.4). Two additional fractions (d-3 #2 and d-3 #3 3/3) are slightly less concordant and show evidence for inheritance. Therefore, we accept 88.1 Ma as the age of the megacrystic phase of the Cathedral Peak Granodiorite. Both the Stern et al. (1981) and Kistler and Fleck (1994) samples of the Cathedral Peak Granodiorite were collected from the inner phase of the unit, and therefore may be slightly younger (84 to 86 Ma) than our sample, as the data suggest.

Johnson Granite Porphyry. Zircon from the Johnson Granite Porphyry is characterized by excessive inheritance (Table 1; Fig. 3). Two sphene fractions from this unit yield identical concordant U-Pb dates of 85.4 Ma that we accept as the crystallization age. As with sphene dates for other Tuolumne intrusive rocks, this age may be younger than the crystallization age. However, because the Johnson Granite porphyry was the last intrusive phase in the suite, sphene dates could not have been reset by later exposed intrusions (Fleck et al., 1996). Furthermore, the excellent agreement of the two sphene dates makes it unlikely that they suffered identical Pb loss. SHRIMP dating of zircon from the Johnson Granite Porphyry confirms the problems with inheritance in this unit, but yields zircon ages as young as 82 Ma (Fleck et al., 1996). We tentatively interpret these young ages to reflect Pb loss; however, it is possible that part or all of the Johnson Granite Porphyry is 82 Ma or younger.

Summary

The geochronologic data presented here confirm that the Tuolumne Intrusive Suite was emplaced as progressive pulses of magma between 95 and 85 Ma (a somewhat narrower interval than determined by Fleck et al., 1996). Furthermore, the data confirm that the intrusive suite becomes younger toward the center (Fig. 2), although the single-fraction age for the granodiorite of Kuna Crest reported by Stern et al. (1981) suggests that it may have intruded out of sequence. The new dates for the Tuolumne Intrusive Suite also place all but the Johnson Granite Porphyry within our defined limits of the Sierra Crest magmatic event. The Sentinel Granodiorite is 4 to 5 m.y. older than the next younger intrusive unit and therefore may represent an independent intrusive event. This contrasts sharply with other plutons of the suite that intruded within 1 to 2 m.y. of each other. If the Sentinel is indeed an early part of the Tuolumne Intrusive Suite (Kistler and Fleck, 1994), then the entire set of plutons, excluding the Johnson Granite Porphyry, took approximately 7 m.y. for emplacement. This is significantly longer than the interval of a few m.y. inferred by Chen and Moore (1982) for crystallization of the Giant Forest sequence in Sequoia National Park.

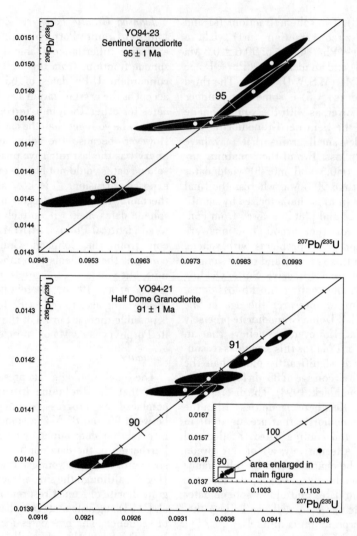

FIG. 3. U-Pb concordia diagrams for rocks of the Tuolumne Intrusive Suite. On all plots, black ellipses represent zircon data and shaded (grey) ellipses represent sphene data. Most samples are characterized by zircon inheritance and by sphene dates that are statistically younger than the youngest zircon dates. Such complicated systematics are difficult to interpret; however, for all but the Johnson Granite Porphyry (facing page), young sphene dates may be interpreted as cooling dates or dates partially reset by later intrusions (Fleck et al., 1996). For samples in which the oldest sphene dates overlap the youngest zircon dates, we interpret this overlap as a crystallization age (Sentinel Granodiorite and equigranular Half Dome Granodiorite). The cluster of concordant zircon dates at 88 Ma for the megacrystic Cathedral Peak Granodiorite (facing page) is interpreted as the crystallization date of that unit. The date of two sphene fractions for the Johnson Granite Porphyry is taken as the crystallization age because of the concordance and agreement of the data.

Mafic-Felsic Interaction

Mafic plutons (diorite and gabbro) make up only a few percent of the Sierra Crest magmatic event, but their significance far outweighs their limited exposure. Mafic plutons are little stud-

ied relative to their more felsic counterparts. Early reports (e.g., Mayo, 1941; Bateman, 1965) considered them to be among the oldest igneous rocks in the batholith and generally unrelated to the granitoids. However, more

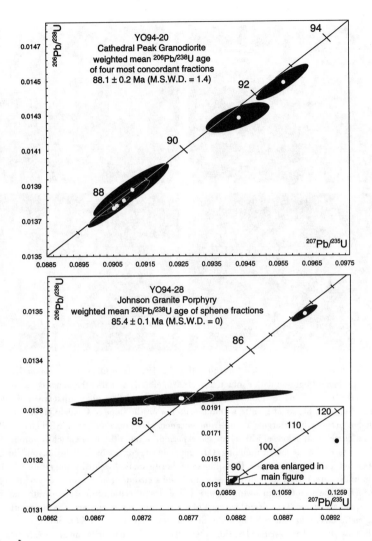

Fig. 3. (*continued*).

recent studies (Frost and Mahood, 1987; Coleman et al., 1995; Sisson et al., 1996) provide compelling evidence that the mafic rocks are commonly mingled and mixed with enclosing Cretaceous granitoids. They were thus an integral part of the Cretaceous plutonic system.

The largest mafic bodies in the batholith have an age of ~92 Ma. These include the Onion Valley, Goodale Canyon, and Black Canyon plutons (Fig. 1)—all of which are exposed in deep canyons east of the range crest—and numerous diorite and gabbro plutons associated with the Lamarck granodiorite along the range crest.

Mafic plutons mingled with granites in and around Yosemite Valley (Fig. 1) have an age of ~102 Ma (Ratajeski and Glazner, 1997).

The style of mafic-felsic interaction expressed in outcrop includes synplutonic dikes, piles of diorite sills with leucocratic inter-sill septa, chilled mafic enclaves, granitoid diapirs in diorites and gabbros, composite dikes, and small mafic plutons whose borders are mingled with adjacent granitoids (Fig. 4). Precise U-Pb dating of these mafic rocks and their commingled granitoids confirms the field interpretation that both magma types were mol-

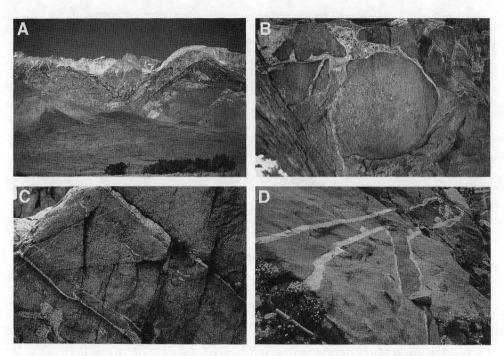

FIG. 4. A. View looking west up Goodale Canyon at the Aberdeen mafic sill complex. Total relief in the photo is
~2700 m. The prominent light-on-dark contact, at ~3000 m elevation, marks the upper contact of the complex.
Both granite on the crest of Goodale Mountain (right side of photo) and diorite beneath it are 92 Ma old (Coleman et
al., 1995). Building-sized blocks of granite within diorite low on the slope of Goodale Mountain are extensively
mingled with diorite along their margins. Range-front volcanoes of the Big Pine volcanic field have spilled lava down
the alluvial fan. These basalts, some of which bear spinel peridotite xenoliths, have enriched isotopic signatures like
those of the diorites. B. Granite-diorite mingling at the upper diorite contact in Goodale Canyon. The diorite-granite
contact at 3000 m is extensively mingled. Here pillows of diorite are back-veined with granite. The large pillow in
center (~1 m in diameter) has a strongly chilled margin and a medium-grained core. After chilling, it was back-
veined on the left by the granite against which it was chilled. These relationships demonstrate that the diorite and
granite were liquids at the same time. Note load casts of diorite into granite septum in the upper left of the photo. C.
West-dipping mafic sills in the Onion Valley mafic sill complex (Sisson et al., 1996). Sills (here ~1 m thick) have
strongly chilled margins and are separated by thin inter-sill septa of granodiorite and granite. Note load casts of sill
into underlying thin granodiorite septum on left side of photo. These sills probably were originally horizontal and
later tilted, perhaps by sagging of the dense diorite body (T. W. Sisson, pers. commun., 1996; Glazner and Miller, in
press). D. Composite dike cutting the Lamarck Granodiorite near Blue Lake. This spectacular dike, which is typical
of many cutting the Lamarck (Frost and Mahood, 1987), consists of an aplite border and a gabbro core. Laboratory
experiments show that when fluids of different viscosity enter a conduit together, the more viscous fluid may plate
onto the walls of the conduit, leaving a channel for the lower-viscosity, faster fluid (Koyaguchi, 1985). The opposite
case also may occur (Carrigan, 1994). The lower (right) aplite appears to have sent several small diapirs upward into
the diorite core. The hammer in the left foreground is 40 cm long (caption continues, next page).

ten at the same time (Coleman et al., 1995).
These relationships establish that mafic
magmas were present during emplacement of a
large proportion of the Cretaceous batholith.
The style of mafic-felsic interaction is remarkably similar to that described by Chapman and
Rhodes (1992) and Wiebe (1993) for analogous
occurrences in Maine.

Sr- and Nd-Isotope Data
for Intrusive Suites

Two fundamentally different patterns of isotopic variation occur within individual suites of
the Sierra Crest magmatic event. Some show a
"normal" isotopic evolution, with mafic rocks
having less radiogenic Sr and more radiogenic

FIG. 4. (*continued*). E. Swarm of mafic pillows in El Capitan Granite at Elephant Rock landslide near the mouth of Yosemite Valley (these rocks are somewhat older than the Sierra Crest event) (Ratajeski and Glazner, 1997). Pillows in this fallen block typically have chilled margins and locally indent one another. They probably settled onto the interface at the right of the photo. Larger pillows are ~1.5 m in diameter. F. Tabular mafic pillow swarm near Independence. Diorite and gabbro in Black Canyon are mingled with the McGann pluton; here a thick SE-striking dike of diorite has entered the McGann pluton and broken into a large swarm of 1- to 3-m diorite pillows, flattened in the dike plane, that disperse as enclave swarms into the quartz monzonite. The diorite has a preliminary age of 94 Ma (U-Pb on sphene) (B. S. Carl, pers. commun., 1997). Photograph by T. W. Sisson. G. View looking down on a horizontal surface cut through granitic to granodioritic pipes that cut diorite near First Lake, Big Pine Creek. Pipes commonly are pegmatitic. Identical pipes in coastal Maine (Chapman and Rhodes, 1992; Wiebe, 1993) emanate from fractionated diorite and evidently rose as diapirs into overlying gabbro. Pipes typically are 20 to 40 cm in diameter. H. Vertical section through a pegmatite pipe cutting diorite near First Lake. Hammer is 40 cm long.

Nd than associated felsic rocks, whereas other suites show almost no isotopic variation across a broad range of bulk compositions.

Isotopic variation in the granodiorites and granite of the Tuolumne Intrusive Suite is well documented (Kistler et al., 1986). The range of variability reported in that paper increases significantly when diorites mingled with the Yosemite Creek Granodiorite and Sentinel Granodiorite (new data reported here) are included (Table 2; Fig. 5). Isotopic composition correlates well with bulk composition across the entire compositional range for this data set. Data for the Mount Whitney Intrusive Suite and the intrusive suite of Rock Creek show variation similar to the Tuolumne series (Fig. 5). Note, however, that isotopic compositions of

the most mafic rocks are highly variable between these intrusive suites, ranging from $\epsilon Nd(t) = -1.6$ to -6.2 and $^{87}Sr/^{86}Sr_i = 0.7051$ to 0.7074.

In contrast to intrusive suites with significant isotopic variation, the intrusive suite of Goodale Canyon shows almost no variability in isotopic composition for rocks with SiO_2 concentrations ranging from 48 to 68 wt% ($\epsilon Nd(t)$ $= -5.7$ to -7.6 and $^{87}Sr/^{86}Sr_i = 0.7070$ to 0.7078) (Table 2; Fig. 5). Furthermore, the limited isotopic variation that is present is not correlated with bulk composition. Similar isotope systematics are reported for the intrusive suites of Mount Lamarck (Coleman et al., 1992), Onion Valley (Sisson et al., 1996), and Yosemite Valley (Ratajeski and Glazner, 1997). The mafic end

TABLE 2. New Isotopic Data for East Sierra Nevada Batholith Intrusive Suites[1]

| Sample | SiO2 | wt% | | ppm | | 87Rb/86Sr | 87Sr/86Sr | 87Sr/86Sr_i | ppm | | 147Sm/144Nd | 143Nd/144Nd | eNd(t) |
		MgO	K2O	Rb	Sr				Sm	Nd			
							Tuolumne Intrusive Suite						
YO94-24	55.3	7.27	2.14	90	538	0.4844	0.705950	0.70532	1.89	19.8	0.05075	0.512445	-2.05
YO94-25	54.7	3.35	2.99	150	737	0.5886	0.705870	0.70510	4.92	23.5	0.1115	0.512502	-1.65
							Mount Whitney Intrusive Suite						
LP-6	66.7	1.68	3.25	110	512	0.6212	0.707713	0.70694	21.4	4.11	2.773	0.513816	-5.95
LP-8	66.5	1.80	3.42	120	565	0.6147	0.707601	0.70683	24.9	4.20	3.151	0.514050	-5.64
P-6	68.2	1.40	3.42	120	495	0.7013	0.708363	0.70749	18.9	3.15	3.185	0.513974	-7.49
P-11	68.5	1.27	3.62	110	590	0.5392	0.708235	0.70756	19.9	3.21	3.293	0.514020	-7.82
S-5	65.6	1.93	3.12	110	545	0.5844	0.707756	0.70703	26.1	4.80	2.888	0.513823	-7.10
W-19	72.3	0.69	3.98	140	465	0.8717	0.708546	0.70746	16.7	2.55	3.482	0.514163	-7.14
MW94-15	59.5	3.86	1.89	100	728	0.3977	0.707337	0.70684	4.00	19.4	0.1279	0.512275	-6.31
MW94-16	55.9	5.24	2.58	120	630	0.5511	0.707602	0.70691	4.00	18.5	0.1150	0.512271	-6.24
							Intrusive suite of Goodale Canyon						
AD1a-93	48.6	4.31	1.82	46	949	0.1394	0.707430	0.70725	6.55	31.6	0.1254	0.512293	-5.90
AD15-93	52.2	4.89	2.47	94	827	0.3282	0.707520	0.70709	6.96	46.8	0.0899	0.512247	-6.38
AD18-93	47.0	3.90	2.07	59	1170	0.1469	0.707750	0.70756	8.24	41.6	0.1197	0.512175	-8.12
AD21-93	47.9	5.86	1.86	47	674	0.2005	0.707220	0.70696	5.37	24.3	0.1337	0.512308	-5.69
AD22-93	50.9	4.08	2.22	71	820	0.2506	0.707470	0.70714	5.68	26.2	0.1312	0.512290	-6.03
LS4-93	56.7	2.29	1.60	52	1060	0.1409	0.707530	0.70735	3.54	18.9	0.1134	0.512199	-7.59
AC2-93	67.2	1.41	3.87	150	425	1.021	0.708580	0.70724	3.62	21.6	0.1016	0.512230	-6.85
AQM1-93	67.7	1.46	4.22	160	419	1.105	0.708800	0.70736	3.29	16.3	0.1221	0.512253	-6.64
							Intrusive suite of Rock Creek						
L1	53.9	4.30	1.46	38.4	711	0.1562	0.705844	0.70565	3.99	18.9	0.1278	0.512484	-2.22
L25	51.1	4.03	0.89	10.9	802	0.03932	0.705752	0.70570	4.18	19.7	0.1286	0.512480	-2.30
cc2b	66.0	1.96	2.62	89.6	574	0.4513	0.706971	0.70639	3.12	15.4	0.1227	0.512277	-6.20

[1]Major-element oxide concentrations determined by direct-current plasma spectrometry (DCP) at the University of North Carolina (UNC), except samples from Mount Whitney (from Hirt, 1989) and Rock Creek (from Link, 1991). Rb analyzed by DCP at the University of North Carolina except for samples from Mount Whitney (from Hirt, 1989). Samples were spiked with mixed ^{150}Nd-^{149}Sm and ^{84}Sr and dissolved in a mixture of HF and HNO_3 in a sealed teflon bomb at 220°C for 5 days. After conversion to chlorides, separation of Sm and Nd was accomplished using standard cation-exchange techniques and alpha-hydroxyisobuturic acid chemistry on cation-exchange resin (Eugster et al., 1970). Sr was separated using Sr-specific resin and HNO_3. Nd was loaded on triple filaments (side Ta, center Re) with H_3PO_4, and Sm was loaded on single-Ta filaments with H_3PO_4. Sr was loaded with H_3PO_4 on a Ta filament. All analyses were performed on the VG sector-54 mass spectrometer at UNC. Nd was analyzed in dynamic multicollector mode with $^{144}Nd = 1.5$ V, and Sm was analyzed in static multicollector mode with $^{147}Sm = 200$ mV. Sr was analyzed in dynamic multicollector mode with $^{88}Sr = 3$V. Nd data are normalized to $^{146}Nd/^{144}Nd = 0.7219$. Sr data are normalized to $^{86}Sr/^{88}Sr = 0.1194$. Replicate analyses of Ames Nd metal standard give $^{143}Nd/^{144}Nd = 0.512139 \pm 0.000005$ (2 standard errors; $n = 33$). Replicate analyses of SRM-987 yielded $^{87}Sr/^{86}Sr = 0.710246 \pm 0.000010$ (2 standard errors; $n = 25$). eNd and T(DM) were calculated using $^{143}Nd/^{144}Nd_{CHUR} = 0.512638$, $^{147}Sm/^{144}Nd_{CHUR} = 0.1967$, and $\lambda^{147}Sm = 6.54 \times 10^{-12}yr^{-1}$, as well as the depleted mantle model of DePaolo (1981). Initial Sr ratios were calculated using $\lambda^{87}Rb = 1.42 \times 10^{-11}yr^{-1}$.

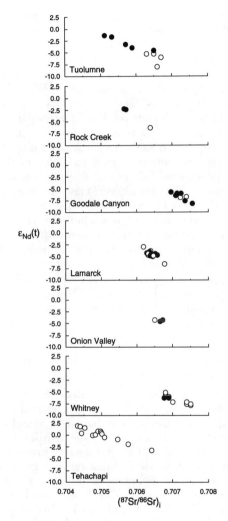

$\varepsilon_{Nd}(t)$

FIG. 5. Sr and Nd data for rocks in the east-central Sierra Nevada batholith. Data are from Kistler et al. (1986), Coleman et al. (1992), Pickett and Saleeby (1994), Bradford (1995), Sisson et al. (1996), and this study. Data are shown for suites containing a wide variety of compositions (i.e., from gabbro or diorite to granite). Sample suites are arranged geographically with the northernmost rocks (Tuolumne Intrusive Suite) in the top plot and the southernmost rocks (Tehachapi Mountains) in the bottom plot. In each plot, samples are divided on the basis of silica concentration: solid (black) symbols = <55 wt% SiO_2; grey symbols = 55 wt% < SiO_2 < 65 wt%; open symbols = >65 wt% SiO_2. No silica concentrations are available for the rocks from the Tehachapis. It should be noted that toward the central part of the batholith, the isotopic composition of the mafic rocks shifts toward more radiogenic Sr and less radiogenic Nd. These suites (Lamarck, Goodale Canyon, and Onion Valley) also are characterized by a lack of

members of each of these suites are very similar, with $\epsilon Nd(t)$ = –4.5 to –6.0 and $^{87}Sr/^{86}Sr_i$ = 0.706 to 0.707.

Discussion

Crust and mantle involvement in the Sierra Crest magmatic event

Through investigation of mafic rocks in the Sierra Nevada batholith, several research groups (Coleman et al., 1992; Bradford, 1995; Sisson et al., 1996) have suggested that the mantle involved in Sierran magmatism was not depleted, MORB-type mantle, as originally proposed by DePaolo (1981), but was instead an enriched lithospheric mantle like that recognized elsewhere in the western United States. Studies of mantle xenoliths entrained in Cenozoic basalts demonstrate the existence of this mantle throughout the central Sierra (Beard and Glazner, 1995; Ducea and Saleeby, 1996a, 1996b). This is an important realization because it dramatically changes estimates of crustal growth rates made on the basis of isotopic data for intrusive suites of the Sierra Crest magmatic event (Coleman et al., 1992).

The lack of variation in isotopic composition for rocks ranging from gabbro to granite in the intrusive suite of Mount Lamarck led Coleman et al. (1992) to suggest that the entire suite was derived from a lithospheric mantle source and perhaps related by fractional melting or crystallization. New work on the intrusive suites of Goodale Canyon (Bradford, 1995) and Onion Valley (Sisson et al., 1996) support this hypothesis. Sisson et al. (1996) went further to demonstrate that the major- and trace-element chemistry of the intermediate-composition rocks could be reproduced through mixing the high- and low-silica end members of the intrusive suites. Given the assumption that the high-silica end member can be derived from the low-silica end member, no pre-existing crust need be involved in the generation of these intrusive suites. Thus, they represent entirely new additions to the crust.

isotopic variation over a wide range of composition. North and south of these suites, the mafic end member shifts to more depleted Sr and enriched Nd isotopic compositions and there is a larger variation in isotopic composition.

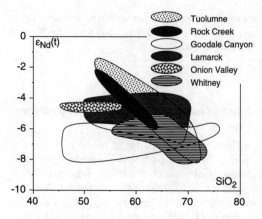

FIG. 6. ϵNd(t) vs. SiO_2 for plutons in the Sierra Crest magmatic episode. Data fields are shown to emphasize trends in individual intrusive suites. Data are from the sources cited in Figure 5. It should be noted that the Tuolumne, Rock Creek, and Whitney suites show a "normal" isotopic variation, with more evolved rocks exhibiting more evolved isotopic compositions, whereas the Goodale Canyon, Lamarck, and Onion Valley suites show almost no isotopic variation across a wide range of silica concentrations. Differences in isotopic variations among the suites also are reflected in zircon systematics: suites with no isotopic variation have no inheritance, whereas suites with substantial isotopic variation have substantial inheritance.

In contrast to these monotonous isotopic compositions, the Tuolumne and Whitney intrusive suites and the intrusive suite of Rock Creek show wide variation in isotopic composition that requires involvement of older crust in their formation. The distinction between the isotopically heterogeneous and homogeneous suites is apparent on plots of SiO_2 vs. isotopic composition (Fig. 6). A further contrast between the two types of intrusive suites is that the zircon systematics of the isotopically variable intrusive suites are characterized by inheritance (Fleck et al., 1996; Wooden et al., 1996; this study), whereas the isotopically homogeneous suites show essentially no inheritance in their systematics (Coleman et al., 1995). The zircon systematics thus are consistent with the hypothesis that pre-existing crust was involved in the development of the intrusive suites at Whitney, Tuolumne, and Rock Creek, but that pre-existing crust played little or no role in the evolution of intrusive suites at Mount Lamarck, Goodale Canyon, and Onion Valley.

It is interesting to speculate regarding the true magnitude of the Sierra Crest magmatic event, assuming that there was little or no involvement of ancient crust. Kay and Kay (1991) estimated that every unit of mass of exposed intermediate-composition crust derived indirectly from the mantle leaves a residue with a mass 1.3 times greater. Our estimates for the mass of residue left after generating average Sierran granodiorite is on the order of 10 parts residue for every part of granodiorite (Coleman et al., 1996). For intrusive suites such as the Lamarck Granodiorite, the true magnitude of material added to the crust during the Sierra Crest magmatic event is at least 10 times the exposed mass of granodiorite. Evidence for the existence of such residue is apparent in xenolith studies (Ducea and Saleeby, 1996a, 1996b) combined with seismic experiments across the batholith (Fliedner et al., 1996; Wernicke et al., 1996), which suggest that parts of the batholith are underlain by a thick, Mesozoic eclogite root. Thus, the entire crustal column may have been reconstructed locally during the event (Ducea and Saleeby, 1997).

The origin of isotopic boundaries in the western United States

Since its definition, the initial $^{87}Sr/^{86}Sr = 0.706$ line (the "706 line") was recognized as a fundamental lithospheric boundary that has existed since Precambrian time (Kistler and Peterman, 1973, 1978). Subsequent investigations have demonstrated that regional geology and Nd isotopes define similar boundaries (e.g., Farmer and DePaolo, 1983). Kistler and Peterman (1973, 1978) argued that the Sr-isotopic signature of rocks in the western United States was derived from a deep source (upper mantle/ lower crust), but later studies suggested that the isotopic boundaries may originate through crustal processes (e.g., DePaolo, 1981).

Our data demonstrate that the isotopic compositions of the granites and granodiorites in a given intrusive suite reflect that of the mafic end member of each suite. For example, the isotopic compositions of the diorites and gabbros in the suites shown in Figures 5 and 6 change regularly from north to south across the batholith. Mafic rocks in the suites from the central part of the Sierra Nevada (Goodale Canyon, Lamarck, Onion Valley, and Whitney) are distinctly more enriched in Rb, Sr, and Nd than mafic rocks from the north (Rock Creek and Tuolumne) and south (Tehachapi Mountains).

This change corresponds with the position of the "706 line" defined by intermediate and felsic rocks. Similarly, studies of Cenozoic basalts and mantle xenoliths throughout the western United States show that the upper mantle east of the "706 line" has an initial Sr-isotopic composition of 0.706 or greater (consistent with the definition of the "706 line") where the lithospheric mantle was not removed by extension (e.g., Kistler and Peterman, 1973; Farmer and DePaolo, 1983; Fitton et al., 1988). A growing database for mantle xenoliths demonstrates that the isotopic character of the mafic rocks in the Sierra Nevada is inherited from the lithospheric mantle and does not reflect extensive crustal interaction (Beard and Glazner, 1995; Ducea and Saleeby, 1996a). Thus, the "706 line" seems to reflect a lithospheric mantle, not a crustal, feature. It appears that the upper mantle can exert first-order control on granite-isotope geochemistry.

Timing of enrichment of the lithospheric mantle

Recognition that the "706 line" is a feature of the upper mantle has important implications for the age of isotopic enrichment of that mantle. Many authors have speculated on the age of mantle enrichment, usually on the basis of "isochrons" for xenoliths or mafic magmas interpreted to have been derived from the lithospheric mantle. A Precambrian age for the lithospheric mantle in the western United States was inferred on the basis of Sr- and Nd-isotopic data for Cenozoic basalts (Menzies et al., 1983). Similarly, both Farmer et al. (1989) and Coleman and Walker (1992) interpreted a Precambrian age for the lithospheric mantle in Nevada and Utah on the basis of Pb-isotope data for mafic rocks. Most recently, Beard and Johnson (1997) interpreted Hf-isotopic data for Cenozoic basalts in the Basin and Range province to be consistent with Proterozoic enrichment. Using Sm-Nd systematics, Beard and Glazner (1995) inferred a latest Precambrian age for the enrichment. Finally, in contrast to the previous studies, Lange et al. (1993) suggested that significant enrichment may be associated with Mesozoic subduction.

The fact that similar isotopic boundaries can be mapped in rocks ranging in age from Mesozoic to Recent suggests that the boundaries are old (Kistler and Peterman, 1973, 1978). The antiquity of the boundaries (and by implica-

tion, the time of enrichment) is also supported by the apparent lack of appreciable isotopic evolution of the lithospheric mantle since Mesozoic time (Fig. 7). For example, the isotopic composition of mafic rocks from the Big Pine area has changed insignificantly since Jurassic time; Jurassic and Cretaceous mafic rocks (Coleman et al., 1992) are isotopically similar to enriched mantle xenoliths erupted in Recent basalts (Beard and Glazner, 1995). Using Sr-isotope evolution as an example, the assumption of a simple, one-stage evolution of the isotopic composition of the mantle from primitive values to measured enriched values in Mesozoic rocks requires either: (1) extreme enrichment in the mantle in the early Mesozoic, or (2) moderate enrichment in the mantle in the Precambrian (Fig. 7). However, whereas extreme Mesozoic enrichment predicts that the mantle should have evolved significantly since Jurassic time, Proterozoic enrichment allows for little additional evolution in the composition of the mantle source from the Mesozoic to the present. Thus, ancient enrichment appears to fit the data, and better explains the lack of significant Sr evolution of the lithospheric mantle throughout the Mesozoic and Cenozoic.

Alternatively, the isotopic evolution of the lithospheric mantle may not reflect a simple, one-stage model. The lack of change in the Sr-isotopic composition of Jurassic to Recent mafic rocks could, for example, be explained by Rb enrichment of any age followed by Rb depletion in the Mesozoic. However, the consistency of Proterozoic enrichment ages estimated for the lithospheric mantle from a variety of different isotopic systems (Rb-Sr, Pb-Pb, Sm-Nd, Lu-Hf) suggests that some memory of a Proterozoic event is preserved. Thus, we suggest that the formation of lithospheric mantle beneath the western United States and establishment of fundamental isotopic boundaries occurred during Proterozoic assembly of the stable North American craton (e.g., Jordan, 1975, 1981).

An interesting coincidence? Sierra Crest magmatism and the Cenomanian–Turonian boundary event

The middle of the Sierra Crest magmatic event approximately coincides with significant oceanographic events at the Cenomanian–Turonian boundary (~93 Ma). The Cenomanian–

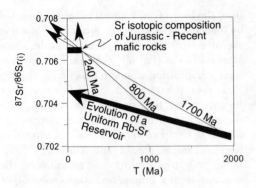

FIG. 7. Simple, one-stage Sr-isotope evolution of a uniform reservoir over the last 2 g.y. Box at $^{87}Sr/^{86}Sr_{(i)} = 0.7065$ shows Sr-isotopic composition of Jurassic to Recent mafic rocks and mantle xenoliths from the Big Pine area (see text for discussion). Thin arrows show Sr evolution of enriched sources initiating at different times and evolving to the composition of the inferred Jurassic enriched mantle. Note that the older the enrichment event, the lower the trajectory of evolution and the less significant the evolution over the past 180 m.y. If a one-stage model is assumed (see text for discussion), enrichment must have occurred in the Precambrian in order to account for the minimal evolution of the lithospheric mantle since Jurassic time.

Turonian event involved a major marine $\delta^{13}C$ excursion, a $^{87}Sr/^{86}Sr$ excursion, widespread deposition of organic carbon, and a marine mass extinction (Schlanger et al., 1987; Jarvis et al., 1988; Eaton et al., 1997; Bralower et al., 1997). Additionally, four bentonite beds found through much of the western interior basin of the United States are stratigraphically quite close to the Cenomanian–Turonian time boundary and have been shown to have sources within the Late Cretaceous Cordilleran arc (Elder, 1988). The causes and consequences of the Cenomanian–Turonian boundary event are controversial and may involve changes in eustatic sea level, oceanic temperature fluctuations, and oceanic anoxia (Arthur et al., 1987; Bralower, 1988; Jarvis et al., 1988; Paul et al., 1994; Eaton et al., 1997). It is interesting to speculate that Cretaceous arc magmatism in the North American Cordillera might have contributed to the Cenomanian–Turonian event, given the effect that magmatism can have on global climate and seawater isotope values (Rampino et al., 1988).

Conclusions

Major conclusions of this study are as follows:

1. The Late Cretaceous interval of 98 to 86 Ma was a period of extremely voluminous plutonism in the eastern Sierra Nevada. Approximately 50% of the plutons along the range crest were intruded during this interval.

2. Zircon and sphene U-Pb systematics of the Tuolumne Intrusive Suite are complicated, but indicate a prolonged intrusive interval ranging from 94.5 to 85.5 Ma.

3. Mafic rocks are sparse but ubiquitous throughout the Sierra Nevada. Virtually all granodiorite plutons are mingled with coeval diorites and gabbros.

4. Plutons in the central High Sierra, between the latitudes of Bishop and Independence, generally show little correlation of isotope ratios with bulk composition and little zircon inheritance. Plutons north and south of this area generally show correlations between isotope ratios and bulk compositions, as well as zircon inheritance. This suggests that pre-existing crust played a minor role in the genesis of the central Sierran plutons.

5. The isotopic compositions of mafic rocks in the Sierra are generally enriched (low $\epsilon Nd(t)$ and high $^{87}Sr/^{86}Sr_i$) relative to a depleted-mantle end member, indicating that enriched mantle played an important role in Sierran magmatism. The enrichment event probably occurred in the Proterozoic.

Acknowledgments

This research was supported by National Science Foundation grants EAR-9219521 and EAR-9526803 to AFG. We are indebted to a great many coworkers who assisted us with the field work, sample collection, and analysis in this project. In particular, we thank Tom Frost and Tom Sisson for their work with us on mafic rocks. John Bartley collaborated on much of the field work and hauled the heaviest zircon samples out of the high country. Ron Kistler, Joe Wooden, and Bob Fleck provided assistance and lively discussions regarding the rocks from the Tuolumne Intrusive Suite. Special thanks go to Joe Wooden for freely sharing data and ideas regarding geochronologic data for the Tuolumne. Many UNC students have been a part of this project, including Carolyn Bachl, Kevin Bradford, Brian Carl, Jennifer Joye, and Kent Ratajeski. Kathy Davidek prepared all samples for zircon analysis. Jonathan Miller, C. J. Northrup, Kent Ratajeski, and Jennifer Wenner are thanked for formal reviews of the manuscript and many enlightening conversations regarding the data and ideas presented here.

REFERENCES

Ague, J. J., and Brimhall, G. H., 1988a, Magmatic arc asymmetry and distribution of anomalous plutonic belts in the batholiths of California: Effects of assimilation, crustal thickness, and depth of crystallization: Geol. Soc. Amer. Bull., v. 100, p. 912–927.

————, 1988b, Regional variations in bulk chemistry, mineralogy, and the compositions of mafic and accessory minerals in the batholiths of California: Geol. Soc. Amer. Bull., v. 100, p. 891–911.

Arthur, M. A., Schlanger, S. O., and Jenkyns, H. C., 1987, The Cenomanian–Turonian oceanic anoxic event. II. Paleoceanographic controls on organic matter production and preservation, *in* Brooks, J., and Fleet, A. J., eds., Marine petroleum source rocks: Geol. Soc. Spec. Publ., v. 26, p. 401–420.

Bateman, P. C., 1965, Geology and tungsten mineralization of the Bishop district, California: U.S. Geol. Surv. Prof. Pap., v. 470, p. 208.

————, 1992, Plutonism in the central part of the Sierra Nevada batholith, California: U.S. Geol. Surv. Prof. Pap., v. 1483, p. 186.

Bateman, P. C., and Chappell, B. W., 1979, Crystallization, fractionation, and solidification of the Tuolumne intrusive series, Yosemite National Park, California: Geol. Soc. Amer. Bull., v. 90, p. 465–482.

Bateman, P. C., Clark, L. D., Huber, N. K., Moore, J. G., and Rinehart, C. D., 1963, The Sierra Nevada batholith—a synthesis of recent work across the central part: U.S. Geol. Surv. Prof. Pap., v. 414-D, p. 46.

Beard, B. L., and Glazner, A. F., 1995, Trace element and Sr and Nd isotopic composition of mantle xenoliths from the Big Pine volcanic field, California: Jour. Geophys. Res., v. 100, p. 4169–4179.

Beard, B. L., and Johnson, C. M., 1997, Hafnium isotope evidence for the origin of Cenozoic basaltic lavas from the southwestern United States: Jour. Geophys. Res., v. 102, p. 20149–20178.

Bowen, N. L., 1928, The evolution of the igneous rocks: Princeton, NJ, Princeton Univ. Press, 333 p.

Bowring, S. A., and Housh, T., 1995, The Earth's early evolution: Science, v. 269, p. 1535–1540.

Bradford, K. J., 1995, Petrology of a mafic intrusive suite in the central Sierra Nevada batholith, California: Unpubl. M.Sc. thesis, Univ. North Carolina, 63 p.

Bralower, T. J., 1988, Calcareous nannofossil biostratigraphy and assemblages of the Cenomanian–Turonian boundary interval: Implications for the origin and timing of oceanic anoxia: Paleoceanography, v. 3, p. 275–316.

Bralower, T. J., Fullagar, P. D., Paull, C. K., Dwyer, G. S., and Leckie, R. M., 1997, Mid-Cretaceous strontium-isotope stratigraphy of deep-sea sections: Geol. Soc. Amer. Bull., v. 109 (in press).

Brown, E. H., and Walker, N. W., 1993, A magma-loading model for barrovian metamorphism in the southeast Coast Plutonic Complex, British Columbia and Washington: Geol. Soc. Amer. Bull., v. 105, p. 479–500.

Carrigan, C. R., 1994, Two-component magma transport and the origin of composite intrusions and lava flows, *in* Ryan, M. P., ed., Magmatic systems: International geophysics series: San Diego, Academic Press, p. 319–354.

Chapman, M., and Rhodes, J. M., 1992, Composite layering in the Isle-Au-Haut igneous complex, Maine—evidence for periodic invasion of a mafic magma into an evolving magma reservoir: Jour. Volcanol. Geotherm. Res., v. 51, p. 41–60.

Chen, J. H., and Moore, J. G., 1982, Uranium-lead isotopic ages from the Sierra Nevada batholith, California: Jour. Geophys. Res., v. 87, p. 4761–4784.

Chen, J. H., and Tilton, G. R., 1991, Applications of lead and strontium isotopic relationships to the petrogenesis of granitoid rocks, central Sierra Nevada batholith, California: Geol. Soc. Amer. Bull., v. 103, p. 439–447.

Coleman, D. S., Frost, T. P., and Glazner, A. F., 1992, Evidence from the Lamarck Granodiorite for rapid Late Cretaceous crust formation in California: Science, v. 258, p. 1924–1926.

Coleman, D. S., Glazner, A. F., Bartley, J. M., and Carl, B. S., in review, Late Cretaceous, and Jurassic, Independence dike swarm in eastern California: Geol. Soc. Amer. Bull..

Coleman, D. S., Glazner, A. F., and Hirschmann, M. M., 1996, Growth of continental lithosphere during continental arc magmatism, an example from the Sierra Nevada batholith, CA [abs.]: Geol. Soc. Amer. Abs. Prog., v. 28, p. 56.

Coleman, D. S., Glazner, A. F., Miller, J. S., Bradford, K. J., Frost, T. P., Joye, J. L., and Bachl, C. A., 1995, Exposure of a Late Cretaceous layered mafic-felsic magma system in the central Sierra Nevada batholith, California: Contrib. Mineral. Petrol., v. 120, p. 129–136.

Coleman, D. S., and Walker, J. D., 1992, Generation of juvenile granitic crust during continental extension: Jour. Geophys. Res., v. 92, p. 11011–11024.

Curtis, G. H., Evernden, J. F., and Lipson, J., 1958, Age determinations of some granitic rocks in California by the potassium-argon method: Calif. Div. Mines Spec. Report 54, p. 16.

DePaolo, D. J., 1981, A neodymium and strontium isotopic study of the Mesozoic calc-alkaline granitic batholiths of the Sierra Nevada and Peninsular ranges, California: Jour. Geophys. Res., v. 86, p. 10470–10488.

Domenick, M. A., Kistler, R. W., Dodge, F. C. W., and Tatsumoto, M., 1983, Nd and Sr isotopic study of crustal and mantle inclusions from the Sierra Nevada and implications for batholith petrogenesis: Geol. Soc. Amer. Bull., v. 94, p. 713–719.

Ducea, M., and Saleeby, J., 1996a, Lithospheric mantle origin for the isotopic gradients within the Sierra Nevada batholith [abs.]: Geol. Soc. Amer. Abs. Prog., v. 28, p. A381.

_____, 1996b, Buoyancy sources for a large, unrooted mountain range, the Sierra Nevada, California: Evidence from xenolith thermobarometry: Jour. Geophys. Res., v. 101, p. 8229–8244.

_____, 1997, A case for delamination of the deep batholithic crust beneath the Sierra Nevada, California: INT. GEOL. REV., v. 39 (in press).

Eaton, J. G., Kirkland, J. I., Hutchison, J. H., Denton, R., O'Neill, R. C., and Parrish, J. M., 1997, Non-marine extinction across the Cenomanian–Turonian boundary, southwestern Utah, with a comparison to the Cretaceous–Tertiary extinction event: Geol. Soc. Amer. Bull., v. 109, p. 560–567.

Elder, W. P., 1988, Geometry of Upper Cretaceous bentonite beds: Implications about volcanic source areas and paleowind directions, western interior, United States: Geology, v. 16, p. 835–838.

Eugster, O., Tera, F., Burnett, D. S., and Wasserburg, G. J., 1970, The isotopic composition of gadolinium and neutron capture effects in some meteorites: Jour. Geophys. Res., v. 75, p. 2753–2768.

Evernden, J. F., and Kistler, R. W., 1970, Chronology of emplacement of Mesozoic batholithic complexes in California and western Nevada: U.S. Geol. Surv. Prof. Pap., v. 623, p. 42.

Farmer, G. L., and DePaolo, D. J., 1983, Origin of Mesozoic and Tertiary granite in the western United States and implications for pre-Mesozoic crustal structure: 1. Nd and Sr isotopic studies in the Geocline of the northern Great Basin: Jour. Geophys. Res., v. 88, p. 3379–3401.

Farmer, G. L., Perry, F. V., Semken, S., Crowe, B., Curtis, D., and DePaolo, D. J., 1989, Isotopic evidence on the structure and origin of subcontinental lithospheric mantle in southern Nevada: Jour. Geophys. Res., v. 94, p. 7885–7898.

Fitton, J. G., James, D., Kempton, P. D., Ormerod, D. S., and Leeman, W. P., 1988, The role of lithospheric mantle in the generation of late Cenozoic basic magmas in the western United States: Jour. Petrol., v. 29, p. 331–349.

Fleck, R. J., Kistler, R. W., and Wooden, J. L., 1996, Geochronological complexities related to multiple emplacement history of the Tuolumne intrusive suite, Yosemite National Park, California [abs.]: Geol. Soc. Amer. Abs. Prog., v. 28, p. 65–66.

Fliedner, M. M., Ruppert, S., and the Southern Sierra Continental Dynamics Working Group, 1996, Three-dimensional crustal structure of the southern Sierra Nevada from seismic fan profiles and gravity modeling: Geology, v. 24, p. 367–370.

Frey, F. A., Chappell, B. W., and Roy, S. D., 1978, Fractionation of rare-earth elements in the Tuolumne Intrusive Series, Sierra Nevada batholith, California: Geology, v. 6, p. 239–242.

Frost, T. P., and Mahood, G. A., 1987, Field, chemical, and physical constraints on mafic-felsic magma interaction in the Lamarck Granodiorite, Sierra Nevada, California: Geol. Soc. Amer. Bull., v. 99, p. 272–291.

Glazner, A. F., and Miller, D. M., in press, Late-stage sinking of plutons: Geology.

Hamilton, W., 1978, Mesozoic tectonics of the western United States, in Howell, D. G., and McDougall, K. A., eds., Mesozoic paleogeography of the western United States: Los Angeles, Pacific Sect. Soc. Econ. Paleontol. Mineral., Pacific Coast Paleogeog. Symp., p. 33–70.

_____, 1995, Subduction systems and magmatism, in Smellie, J. L., ed., Volcanism associated with extension at consuming plate margins: Geol. Soc. Lond. Spec. Publ. 81, p. 3–28.

Hirt, W. H., 1989, The petrological and mineralogical zonation of the Mount Whitney intrusive suite, eastern Sierra Nevada, California: Unpubl. Ph.D. thesis, Univ. Calif. at Santa Barbara, 278 p.

Hirt, W. H., and Glazner, A. F., 1995, Sr and Nd isotopic compositions of granitoids from the Mount Whitney intrusive suite, southern Sierra Nevada, California: EOS (Trans. Amer. Geophys. Union), v. 76, p. F657.

Jarvis, I., Carson, G. A., Cooper, M. K. E., Hart, M. B., Leary, P. N., Tocher, D. A., Horne, D., and Rosenfeld, A., 1988, Microfossil assemblages and the Cenomanian–Turonian (late Cretaceous) oceanic anoxia event: Cretaceous Res., v. 9, p. 3–103.

Jordan, T. H., 1975, The continental tectosphere: Rev. Geophys. Space Phys., v. 13, p. 1–12.

_____, 1981, Continents as a chemical boundary layer: Philos. Trans. Roy. Soc. Lond., v. 301, p. 359–373.

Kay, R. W., and Kay, S. M., 1991, Creation and destruction of lower continental crust: Geolog. Rundschau, v. 80, p. 259–278.

Kistler, R. W., Bateman, R. W., and Brannock, W. W., 1965, Isotopic ages of minerals from granitic rocks of the central Sierra Nevada and Inyo Mountains, California: Geol. Soc. Amer. Bull., v. 76, p. 155–164.

Kistler, R. W., Chappell, B. W., Peck, D. L., and Bateman, P. C., 1986, Isotopic variation in the Tuolumne intrusive suite, central Sierra Nevada, California: Contrib. Mineral. Petrol., v. 94, p. 205–220.

Kistler, R. W., and Fleck, R. J., 1994, Field guide for a transect of the central Sierra Nevada, California; geochronology and isotope geology: U.S. Geol. Surv. Open File Report, v. 94-0267, 50 p.

Kistler, R. W., and Peterman, Z. E., 1973, Variations in Sr, Rb, K, Na, and initial $^{87}Sr/^{86}Sr$ in Mesozoic granitic rocks and intruded wall rocks in central California: Geol. Soc. Amer. Bull., v. 84, p. 3489–3512.

————, 1978, Reconstruction of crustal blocks of California on the basis of initial strontium isotopic compositions of Mesozoic granitic rocks: U.S. Geol. Surv. Prof. Pap., v. 1071, p. 17.

Koyaguchi, T., 1985, Magma mixing in a conduit: Jour. Volcanol. Geotherm. Res., v. 25, p. 365–369.

Krogh, T. E., 1973, A low-contamination method for hydrothermal decomposition of zircon and extraction of U and Pb for isotopic age determination: Geochim. et Cosmochim. Acta, v. 37, p. 485–494.

Lange, R. A., Carmichael, I. S. E., and Renne, P. R., 1993, Potassic volcanism near Mono basin, California: Evidence for high water and oxygen fugacities inherited from subduction: Geology, v. 21, p. 949–952.

Link, T. E., 1991, Geochemistry, petrology, and contact relationships of the Rock Creek gabbro, Inyo County, California: Clues to the origin of Sierra Nevadan mafic enclaves: Unpubl. B.A. thesis, Hampshire College, Amherst, Massachusetts.

Ludwig, K. R., 1989, PBDAT for MS-DOS, a computer program for IBM-PC compatibles for processing raw Pb-U-Th isotope data, version 1.06: U.S. Geol. Surv. Open-File Report, v. 88-542, 40 p.

————, 1990, ISOPLOT, a plotting and regression program for radiogenic-isotope data, for IBM-PC compatible computers, version 2.02: U.S. Geol. Surv. Open-File Report, v. 88-557, 44 p.

Mayo, E. B., 1941, Deformation in the interval Mt. Lyell–Mt. Whitney, California: Geol. Soc. Amer. Bull., v. 52, p. 1001–1084.

Menzies, M. A., Leeman, W. P., and Hawkesworth, C. J., 1983, Isotope geochemistry of Cenozoic volcanic rocks reveals mantle heterogeneity below western USA: Nature, v. 303, p. 205–209.

Moore, J. G., and Sisson, T. S., 1987, Preliminary geologic map of Sequoia and Kings Canyon National Parks, California: U.S. Geol. Surv. Open-File Report 87-651, scale 1:250,000.

Parrish, R. R., 1987, An improved micro-capsule for zircon dissolution in U-Pb geochronology: Chem. Geol., v. 66, p. 99–102.

Paul, C. R. C., Mitchell, S., Lamolda, M., and Gorostidi, A., 1994, The Cenomanian–Turonian boundary event in northern Spain: Geol. Mag., v. 131, p. 801–817.

Pickett, D. A., and Saleeby, J. B., 1994, Nd, Sr, and Pb isotopic characteristics of Cretaceous intrusive rocks from deep levels of the Sierra Nevada batholith, Tehachapi Mountains, California: Contrib. Mineral. Petrol., v. 118, p. 198–215.

Rampino, M. R., Self, S., and Stothers, R. B., 1988, Volcanic winters: Ann. Rev. Earth Planet. Sci., v. 16, p. 73–99.

Ratajeski, K. R., and Glazner, A. F., 1997, Field and isotopic characteristics of mafic rocks associated with the El Capitan granite in Yosemite Valley, California [abs.]: Geol. Soc. Amer. Abs. Prog., v. 29, p. 58.

Rudnick, R. L., and Fountain, D. M., 1994, Nature and composition of the continental crust: A lower crustal perspective: Rev. Geophys., v. 33, p. 267–309.

Saleeby, J. B., Kistler, R. W., Longiaru, S., Moore, J. G., and Nokleberg, W. J., 1990, Middle Cretaceous silicic metavolcanic rocks in the Kings Canyon area, central Sierra Nevada, California: Geol. Soc. Amer. Memoir 174, p. 251–270.

Schlanger, S. O., Arthur, M. A., Jenkyns, H. C., and Scholle, P. A., 1987, The Cenomanian–Turonian oceanic anoxic event. I. Stratigraphy and distribution of organic carbon-rich beds and the marine $\delta^{13}C$ excursion, *in* Brooks, J., and Fleet, A. J., eds., Marine petroleum source rocks: Geol. Soc. [Lond.] Spec. Publ. 26, p. 371–399.

Schweickert, R. A., 1981, Tectonic evolution of the Sierra Nevada, *in* Ernst, W. G., ed., The geotectonic development of California: Rubey volume 1: Englewood Cliffs, NJ, Prentice-Hall, p. 87–131.

Sisson, T. S., Grove, T. L., and Coleman, D. S., 1996, Hornblende gabbro sill complex at Onion Valley, California, and a mixing origin for the Sierra Nevada batholith: Contrib. Mineral. Petrol., v. 126, p. 81–108.

Steiger, R. H., and Jäger, E., 1977, Subcommission on geochronology: Convention on the use of decay constants in geo- and cosmochronology: Earth Planet. Sci. Lett., v. 36, p. 359–362.

Stern, T. W., Bateman, P. C., Morgan, B. A., Newell, M. F., and Peck, D. L., 1981, Isotopic U-Pb ages of zircons from the granitoids of the central Sierra Nevada: U.S. Geol. Surv. Prof. Pap., v. 1071, p. 17.

Tobisch, O. T., Saleeby, J. B., Renne, P. R., McNulty, B., and Tong, W., 1995, Variations in deformation fields during development of a large-volume magmatic arc, central Sierra Nevada, California: Geol. Soc. Amer. Bull., v. 107, no. 148–166.

Walker, N. L., and Brown, E. H., 1991, Is the Coast Plutonic Complex the result of accretion of the Insular terrane? Evidence from geochronometry in Washington Cascades: Geology, v. 19, p. 714–717.

Weaver, B. L., and Tarney, J., 1984, Chemical composition and fractionation of the continental crust: Nature, v. 310, p. 575–577.

Wernicke, B. P., Clayton, R., Ducea, M., Jones, C. H., Park, S., Ruppert, S., Saleeby, J., Snow, J. K., Squires, L., Fliedner, M., Jiracek, G., Keller, R., Klemperer, S., Luetgert, J., Malin, P., Miller, K.,

Mooney, W., Oliver, H., and Phinney, R., 1996, Origin of high mountains in the continents: The southern Sierra Nevada: Science, v. 271, p. 190–193.

Wiebe, R. A., 1993, The Pleasant Bay layered gabbro-diorite, coastal Maine—ponding and crystallization of basaltic injections into a silicic magma chamber: Jour. Petrol., v. 34, p. 461–489.

Wooden, J. L., Kistler, R. W., and Fleck, R. J., 1996, Problems using the U-Pb zircon technique to determine the time of crystallization—lessons from the western U.S. cordillera [abs.]: Geol. Soc. Amer. Abs. Prog., v. 28, p. 126.

A Case for Delamination of the Deep Batholithic Crust beneath the Sierra Nevada, California

Mihai Ducea and Jason Saleeby

California Institute of Technology, Division of Geological and Planetary Sciences 100-23, Pasadena, California 91125

Abstract

Surface exposures as well as deep-crustal and upper-mantle xenoliths constrain the composition of the lithospheric column beneath the Sierra Nevada mountain range (California) as it resulted from the generation of the Mesozoic Sierra Nevada batholith (SNB). After the cessation of magmatism at ~80 Ma, the SNB consisted of a ~30 to 35 km thick granitic crust underlain by a batholithic "root," a ~70 km thick sequence of mafic-ultramafic, mainly eclogite-facies cumulate and residues. The deeper root assemblages consist largely of garnet and pyroxenes that precipitated as igneous cumulate phases during the SNB magmatism. The root assemblages were present beneath the SNB as recently as ~8 to 12 Ma, when they were sampled as xenoliths in fast-ascending magmas erupted through the batholith.

Several lines of evidence suggest that the eclogitic root may have disapeared from beneath the SNB since Miocene time, leading to a major change in the lithospheric column. There are no garnet-bearing xenoliths in the Pliocene and Quaternary volcanic rocks; instead, all xenolith lithologies found in the younger volcanic outcrops are peridotitic, have equilibrated at depths between 35 and 70 km, possess locked-in temperatures of ~1150 to 1200°C, and display an asthenospheric-like adiabatic P-T trend. Some of the Pliocene uppermost-mantle peridotitic xenoliths contain exotic silica-rich glass inclusions that may have originated by partial melting of the eclogitic root. Geophysical evidence suggests that anomalously high seismic velocity may represent eclogitic bodies present at depths of 100 to 200 km beneath the SNB. All of these observations indicate that the "eclogitic" root may have detached and delaminated (sunk) into the underlying mantle, a process compensated by diapiric rise of asthenospheric peridotitic material to the base of the shallow (~35 km) remnant crust. The delamination hypothesis is consistent with observations documenting the existence of a shallow Moho, a low-velocity, partially molten upper mantle observed today beneath the SNB, a gradual change in Miocene volcanism in the Sierra toward more primitive compositions, and significant late Miocene–Pliocene uplift in the area.

If the magmatic arc has indeed lost its root, delamination is an important mechanism in the differentiation of the continental crust at Cordilleran-type margins. The present-day crustal column in the Sierra (the SNB) is a mass extracted from the Earth's mantle predominantly during the Phanerozoic, although not necessarily only during batholithic magmatism. The ~35 km thick present-day crustal composition of the Sierra Nevada is similar to, or more evolved than, the average continental crust.

Introduction

CONTINENTAL MARGINS riding over subducting oceanic plates often are accompanied by large-scale granitic magmatism that leads to the formation of batholiths. Some of the largest batholiths on Earth are found in the American Cordillera, along the western margins of the American continents. The Sierra Nevada batholith (SNB) of California is the type-Cordilleran batholith (Bateman, 1983).

Deep segments of thick crustal sections in orogenic belts, including continental magmatic arcs, are prone to eclogite-facies metamorphism (e.g., Dewey et al., 1993), which leads to the formation of crustal roots denser than the underlying mantle. Most young and extinct continental arcs display a shallow Moho (30 to 40 km crustal thickness) (Christensen and Mooney, 1995) and are underlain by typical peridotitic mantle material. This observation contradicts the petrological prediction that thick, residual, garnet-rich and olivine-poor mafic-ultramafic masses should reside beneath granitic batholiths (e.g., Kay and Kay, 1991).

Kay and Kay (e.g., 1991, 1993) have proposed that eclogite-facies magmatic arc roots (e.g., in the Andes) become gravitationally unstable and founder into the underlying mantle.

The Sierra Nevada mountain range exemplifies this contradiction. The Sierra Nevada crustal thickness is ~35 to 42 km (e.g., Wernicke et al., 1996; Fliedner and Ruppert, 1996), and the crust is almost entirely "granitic" (6 to 6.3 km/sec). The sub-Moho material appears to be partially molten peridotite (Jones and Phinney, 1997). In contrast, deep-crustal and mantle xenoliths accidentally sampled by Miocene (8 to 12 Ma) volcanic rocks indicate the presence of a thick eclogitic root beneath the Sierra Nevada as late as Miocene time (Ducea and Saleeby, 1996a). In this paper, we present evidence that suggests that the eclogitic arc root has delaminated into the upper mantle since Miocene time. This process can explain the apparent contradiction between the predicted and observed lithospheric sections. If viable, arc-root delamination may be the most efficient process responsible for Phanerozoic granitic crustal addition.

Volcanic Rocks

Late Cenozoic volcanic rocks as well as lower-crustal and mantle xenoliths contain some of the most important information concerning the composition of the Sierra Nevada at depth. Many of the observations used in this study to argue for crustal delamination are based on studies of volcanic rocks and xenoliths from the Sierra Nevada. As background information, we provide below a brief description of the Late Cenozoic volcanism in the southern and central Sierra Nevada.

Late Cenozoic mafic to intermediate rocks erupted through the Mesozoic batholith in the southern and central Sierra Nevada (Moore and Dodge, 1980; van Kooten, 1980; Luedke and Smith, 1981; Ormerod et al., 1988), probably as a result of extensional collapse of the Cordillera at Sierra Nevada latitudes. The Late Cenozoic mafic to intermediate volcanic activity in the Sierra Nevada can be temporally divided into three episodes (Moore and Dodge, 1980)—late Miocene (8 to 12 Ma), Pliocene (3 to 4 Ma) and Quaternary (0 to 1 Ma).

Figure 1 is a map showing the distribution of mafic to intermediate Late Cenozoic volcanic rocks in the Sierra Nevada at latitudes south of 38° N. The hachured fields in Fig. 1A cover the areas in which various mafic-intermediate volcanic exposures have been mapped. The volcanic rocks consist of dikes, plugs, and flows and occupy a small area (~1%) of the hachured areas in Figure 1. The Miocene volcanic rocks (MV) are mainly subvolcanic conduits, whereas most Pliocene volcanics (PV) and Quaternary volcanics (QV) are lava flows.

There are sufficient published radiometric data on these rocks to show that both MV and PV cluster in fields elongated in an ENE-WSW direction, as shown in Figure 1. These fields can be followed across the Owens Valley rift into the White-Inyo Mountains. The MV and PV fields alternate from north to south, except for a gap at the latitude of Mount Whitney. Volcanic rocks younger than 1 Ma (QV) erupted along the eastern margin of the Sierra Nevada, more or less following the NNW-SSE trend of the Owens Valley rift. At least 17 of the volcanic outcrops, representing all three age groups, contain xenoliths from the Sierra Nevada lower crust and upper mantle.

Cretaceous to Miocene Lithospheric Column

The Sierra Nevada mountain range consists primarily of a large composite batholith. We will refer to the exposed fragments of these plutons as the Sierra Nevada batholith. The SNB represents ~90% of the surface exposures in the southern and central Sierra. The magmatic arc formed as a product of prolonged ocean-floor subduction beneath the southwestern edge of the North American continent (Dickinson, 1981). Magmatism occurred in the Sierra Nevada between 220 and 80 Ma (Chen and Moore, 1982), although most of the plutons exposed at the surface yield ages between 125 and 85 Ma (Saleeby, 1990). Below we summarize the geologic information that constrains the composition of the Sierra Nevada lithosphere at the end of the batholithic magmatism. Apparently, the section remained intact in the central Sierra until at least 8 to 12 Ma, but subsequently changed, at least at depths greater than ~35 km.

An idealized lithospheric column based on observations made in the central Sierra Nevada

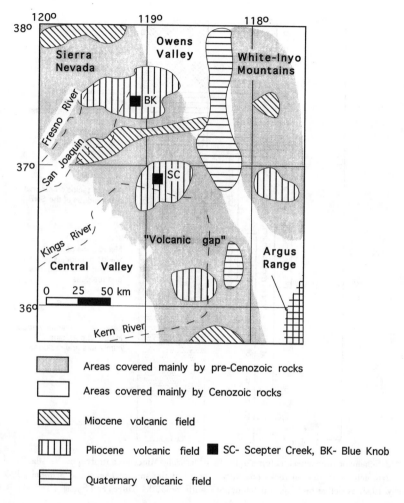

FIG. 1. Schematic map of the distribution of Late Cenozoic volcanic rocks in the southern and central Sierra Nevada region, including the Owens Valley and White-Inyo mountains to the east. The volcanism is divided into three temporal groups—Miocene, Pliocene, and Quaternary—as in the text. Volcanic rocks cover only ~1% of the areas outlined as volcanic fields. Miocene and Pliocene volcanic groups alternate from north to south in the Sierra Nevada, with the exception of a volcanic "gap" between the Kings River and Kern River fields. Locations of the xenolith-bearing areas of Scepter Creek (SC) and Blue Knob (BK), mentioned in text, are indicated by black squares.

is shown in Figure 2. This section was constructed on the basis of the geology of the surface batholith (see reviews in Bateman, 1983 and Saleeby, 1990), geophysical observations in the upper part of the column (Fliedner and Ruppert, 1996; Wernicke et al., 1996), and petrologic, thermobarometric, and geochronometric studies of deep-crustal and mantle xenoliths in the MV that have been reported by the authors elsewhere (Ducea and Saleeby, 1996a, 1996b).

Most SNB plutons are tonalitic to granodioritic in composition. The igneous crystallization depths of the rocks presently exposed vary from 0 to ~30 km (Ague and Brimhall, 1988; Saleeby, 1990). The deepest exposures of the batholith are preserved in the southernmost Sierra Nevada, where igneous and meta-igneous rocks have crystallized at 20 to 30 km depth in the crust during the late stages of magmatism of the Cretaceous batholith (Pickett and Saleeby, 1993). The average chemistry of these deep

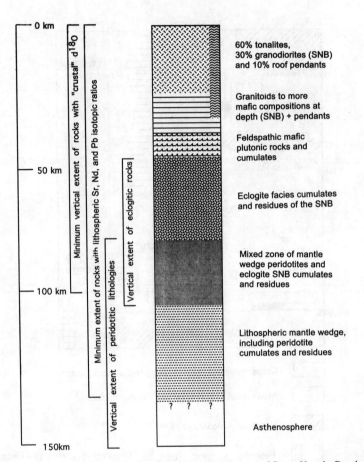

FIG. 2. Schematic lithospheric column of the Late Mesozoic–Miocene central Sierra Nevada. Depths are based on barometric determinations on rocks presently exposed at the surface (Ague and Brimhall, 1988; Pickett and Saleeby, 1993) as well as on lower-crustal/upper-mantle xenoliths (Ducea and Saleeby, 1996a).

exposures corresponds to that of a low-silica tonalite (Saleeby, 1990). Therefore, geological results indicate that throughout the upper 30 km of the Mesozoic Sierra Nevada lithosphere, the rocks are mainly "granitoids," suggesting that the SNB was at least 30 km thick. This conclusion is supported by recent geophysical results (Fliedner and Ruppert, 1996) that documented low compressional velocities (6 to 6.3 km/sec) throughout the seismologically defined crust, in a seismic refraction experiment undertaken across the southern part of the mountain range.

The composition of the Sierra Nevada lithosphere at depths greater than 30 to 35 km is constrained by xenoliths accidentally sampled by some of the Miocene volcanic plugs and dikes (Domenick et al., 1983; Dodge et al.,

1986, 1988; Mukhopadhyay and Manton, 1994; Beard and Glazner, 1995; Ducea and Saleeby, 1996a). Only the MV carry deep samples proven to be related to the Mesozoic lithosphere beneath the SNB (Ducea and Saleeby, 1996a, 1996b). A thermobarometric study conducted by Ducea and Saleeby (1996a) suggested that mafic rocks (diorites, gabbros) become progressively more abundant in the 30- to 40-km depth interval, although quantitative barometric determinations are not available for garnet-free diorites and gabbros. Many of the deep xenoliths in the MV contain garnet, and representative lithologies have been analyzed for thermobarometry and dated by Sm-Nd techniques (Ducea and Saleeby, 1996b). The results provide a link between the pressures of equilibration (and inferred depths) and the time at which pressures were locked in the mineral-chemistry equilibrium. All analyzed rocks yield Cretaceous (81 to 121 Ma) Sm-Nd ages as well as initial Sr-, Nd-, Pb-, and O-isotopic ratios similar to the SNB, suggesting batholith consanguinity. Most of the xenoliths have igneous cumulate textures. Textural, whole-rock isotopic, geochronologic, and trace-element arguments all point to a cumulate/residua origin for most of the garnet-rich xenoliths from the MV.

Garnet-bearing feldspathic xenoliths with intermediate to mafic compositions generally display equilibration pressures lower than 1.2 GPa ($\sim$40 km), while feldspar-free, mainly garnet pyroxenite and hornblende garnet pyroxenite xenoliths equilibrated at pressures exceeding 1.0 GPa ($\sim$35 km), reaching as high as 3.3 GPa ($\sim$100 km). A few xenoliths whose pressures of equilibration were calculated to be in the 1 to 1.4 GPa ($\sim$35 to 45 km) interval are cumulates with alternating feldspar-rich and garnet pyroxene–rich layers.

We interpret these observations as indicating a downward transition to gradually more mafic lithologies, and from feldspathic to feldspar-free ("eclogitic") assemblages. Our data suggest that such a transition may have occurred 35 to 45 km beneath the surface of the SNB.

Rocks that equilibrated at pressures higher than 1.5 GPa are mainly garnet pyroxenites and eclogites. The relatively elevated $\delta^{18}O$ ratios (6.5 to 9) in these xenoliths (Ducea et al., 1997) require the presence of a supracrustal component $\sim$45 to 100 km beneath the batholith, and argues for a crustal rather than a mantle origin for the pyroxenites. We interpret the garnet pyroxenitic xenoliths as being the predominant lithologies of a deep-crustal, eclogite-facies batholithic root (MASH zone of Hildreth and Moorbath, 1988), which extended to at least 100 km. We also have recovered peridotitic xenoliths (spinel-garnet and garnet) that equilibrated at pressures of 2.5 to 4.2 GPa ($\sim$75 to 130 km), indicating that a transition from eclogitic to peridotitic material may have existed at depths somewhere between 75 and 100 km. All analyzed xenoliths, including the deepest garnet peridotite, possess isotopic characteristics consistent with a lithospheric origin. The relatively low temperatures measured in all deep xenoliths—e.g., 975°C at 4.2 GPa (130 km) in the deepest sample—also suggest a litho-

spheric origin. The Mesozoic to middle Miocene lithosphere therefore was at least 130 km thick.

In conclusion, the Sierra Nevada Late Mesozoic to Miocene lithosphere appears to have been composed of granitoids $\sim$30 km in thickness, about twice as much residues and cumulates (mainly ultramafic rocks in eclogite facies), and deeper peridotites; in aggregate, these units constrain the minimum thickness of the post-batholith lithosphere to be at least 130 km.

Observations Supporting Root Delamination

Three geological and geophysical observations suggest that the eclogitic lower crust has delaminated, possibly together with its underlying mantle lithosphere, since the Miocene. They are: (1) contrasting xenolith populations in the MV and PV-QV; (2) the presence of crustal-derived silicic glass inclusions in peridotitic xenoliths from PV and QV; and (3) the existence of anomalously fast (high-compressional-velocity) bodies at great depth beneath the Sierra Nevada today.

Temporal change in xenolith lithology. Seventeen volcanic sequences of the three groups previously defined (MV, PV, and QV) contain lower-crustal and/or mantle xenoliths. Xenoliths of the MV differ from the xenoliths in the PV and QV (Table 1). Although the MV contains mainly garnet pyroxenites corresponding to equilibration depths of 40 to 100 km, the PV and QV contain only spinel peridotites and olivine-clinopyroxenites that equilibrated between $\sim$35 and 65 km. In fact, no garnet-bearing xenolith has been recorded from any PV or QV rock. The MV xenoliths display a negative P-T slope, indicative of cooling from near-igneous temperatures to the low Cenozoic thermal gradients of the Sierra Nevada (Ducea and Saleeby, 1996a). More specifically, we interpreted this trend to be a "false" geotherm: deeper rocks cooled more slowly and locked in younger, lower temperatures (Ducea and Saleeby, 1996a). The PV peridotites from the same depth interval, in contrast, are high-temperature assemblages that define an adiabatic P-T slope and have tectonitic textures.

Based on these thermobarometric arguments, we believe that the aforementioned dif-

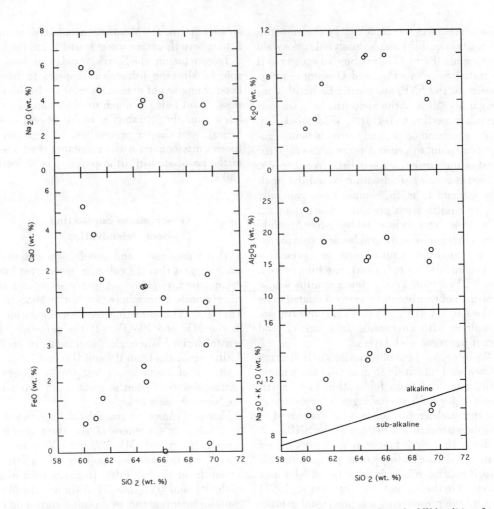

FIG. 3. Major-element compositions of representative glass inclusions in peridotites from the MV localities of Blue Knob and Scepter Creek (simplified after Ducea and Saleeby, 1997). The shaded areas represent data from similar glasses previously reported in the literature.

TABLE 1. Summary of Relevant Differences between the MV and PV–QV
Xenolith Suites in the Sierra Nevada

MV (8 to 12 Ma) xenoliths	PV–QV (0 to 4 Ma) xenoliths
Mainly cumulate-textured, olivine-free lower crust (granulite and eclogite facies) at depths >35 km	Olivine-rich (peridotitic) ultramafic assemblages at depths >35 km
Rocks in the 35 to 100 km depth interval have Cretaceous (synbatholithic) Sm-Nd ages	Rocks that equilibrated deeper than 35 km yield Late Cenozoic ages
Garnet very common in lower-crustal and upper-mantle xenoliths	Garnet absent in all xenoliths
Rocks with crustal $\delta^{18}O$ are found as deep as 100 km	Rocks with crustal $\delta^{18}O$ are not found below ~35 km
Lithospheric P-T slopes, and temperatures <1000°C as deep as 130 km	Adiabatic, asthenospheric P-T slopes and temperatures of 1200 to 1250°C below 35 km

TABLE 2. Average Rb, Sr, Sm, and Nd Elemental Concentrations and $^{87}Sr/^{86}Sr$ and $^{143}Nd/^{144}Nd$ Ratios of the Scepter Creek and Blue Knob Glasses[1]

	SC9	H8-1	Mafic oceanic crust[2]	Oceanic sediments[3]	Sierra lower crust[4]
Rb	33.14	3.42			
Sr	427.86	232.2			
Sm	1.61	1.12			
Nd	9.24	6.68			
Rb/Sr	0.077	0.036	0.06–0.1	0.5	0.01–0.1
Sr/Nd	46.63	35.00	10–20	1–10	20–70
$^{87}Sr/^{86}Sr$	0.708509	0.707772	0.702–0.710	>0.7075	0.706–0.712
$^{143}Nd/^{144}Nd$	0.512438	0.512436	0.5129–0.5132	0.5118–0.5126	0.51235–0.5126

[1]Also includes tyical trace-element and isotopic ratios in mafic oceanic crust, oceanic sediments, and Sierra Nevada lower-crustal root (modified from Ducea and Saleeby, 1977).
[2]From Faure, 1985 and McCulloch et al., 1980.
[3]From Taylor and McLennan, 1985.
[4]From Domenick et al., 1983; Dodge et al., 1988; Mukopadhyay and Manton, 1994; Ducea and Saleeby, 1996b.

ferences in xenolith lithology between the MV and PV represent a fundamental change in composition and thermal structure beneath the batholith. This change must have taken place between 8 to 12 and 3 to 4 Ma, at least in the central Sierra areas rich in xenolith-bearing MV and PV units. These observations suggest that the cold, mainly eclogitic root of the SNB was replaced during the late Miocene by hot, peridotitic, asthenospheric-like mantle.

Crustal-derived glass inclusions in mantle xenoliths. Some of the spinel lherzolites and olivine clinopyroxenites included in the PV lavas contain glass inclusions trapped as films along grain boundaries and as pockets, commonly included in olivine. Ducea and Saleeby (1997) analyzed the major- and trace-element compositions as well as Sr- and Nd-isotopic ratios of glasses included in peridotites from two PV localities, Scepter Creek and Blue Knob (Fig. 1), which are 75 km apart. Representative glass major-element concentrations are plotted on Harker diagrams in Figure 3, while the trace elements and isotopic ratios analyzed on two glass-rich xenoliths are presented in Table 2. Glass inclusions in both Scepter Creek and Blue Knob peridotites have unusually high SiO_2 concentrations, commonly between 65 and 69% SiO_2. These silica-rich glasses (SRG) also are characterized by high alkali and alumina concentrations as well as low Mg, Fe, and Ca abundances (Ducea and Saleeby, 1997). The SRG are, on average, trachytic in composition. Similar SRG inclusions in mantle xenoliths described previously (e.g., Ionov et al., 1994; Schiano and Clocchiatti, 1994; Schiano et al., 1995) have been interpreted as exotic melts with respect to the peridotitic host. The large difference between the glass and peridotite chemical compositions, and the preservation of glassy material at mantle depths, indicates near contemporaneity of the SRG melting with the eruption of the xenolith-bearing basalts.

The glass $^{87}Sr/^{86}Sr$ (0.7077 to 0.7085) and $^{143}Nd/^{144}Nd$ (~0.51244) are higher than those of the residual peridotitic xenoliths and quite different from those of the host basalts (Fig. 4). Therefore, the glasses are exotic with respect to the surrounding peridotites and the basalt hosts. Melting of a hydrous phase in the mantle (e.g., phlogopite or amphibole)—which, although not present in the analyzed samples, may exist at deeper levels in the Sierra Nevada mantle—could explain the radiogenic Sr signature as well as the enrichment in K_2O but not the high silica concentrations and the unusually low Rb/Sr ratios. Young subducted oceanic crust and the product of its partial melting may have a wide range of $^{87}Sr/^{86}Sr$ isotopic ratios, as a result of interactions with seawater (McCulloch et al., 1980), but the $^{143}Nd/^{144}Nd$ should remain fairly close to depleted MORB–like ratios (>0.5130). The SRG $^{143}Nd/^{144}Nd$ ratios are much lower, therefore negating a mafic oceanic crustal origin.

Overall, the K_2O/Na_2O > unit value is indicative of a continental origin for the glasses. These glasses could have formed by melting

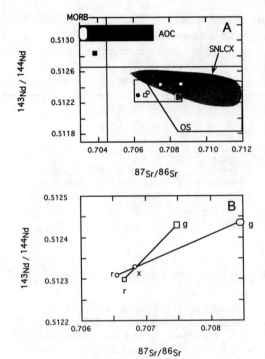

FIG. 4. A. $^{87}Sr/^{86}Sr$ versus $^{143}Nd/^{144}Nd$ diagram (modified from Ducea and Saleeby, 1997) showing the isotopic ratios of Blue Knob (filled squares) and Scepter Creek host volcanics (filled circles), glass inclusions in peridotites (large open symbols), and ultramafic residue after glass extraction (small open symbols). The fields of mid-oceanic ridge basalts (MORB), altered oceanic crust (AOC), oceanic sediments (OS), and Sierra Nevada lower-crustal xenoliths (SNLCX) also are shown (see details in text). B. Detail of Figure 4A. Symbols: g = glass inclusions; r = residue after glass extraction; x = peridotite + glass. Blue Knob analyses are represented by square symbols and Scepter Creek analyses by circles.

subducted sediments, which are similar to (if not fully derived from) a continental source. However, the high Sr/Nd and low Rb/Sr SRG ratios are indicative of a lower-crustal origin, as opposed to an upper-crustal derivation typical for oceanic sediments. The Sierra Nevada eclogitic root has precisely the $^{143}Nd/^{144}Nd$, $^{87}Sr/^{86}Sr$, Sr/Nd, and Rb/Sr ratios required for the SRG source. In particular, the source rocks that upon melting would be likely to produce the trace-element and isotopic ratios measured in the SRG glasses would be amphibolites or hornblende garnet pyroxenites (Fig. 3). Wolf and Wyllie (1993) have demonstrated experimentally that silica-rich glasses similar to the

ones presented here can form by partially melting a basalt + H_2O protolith.

In conclusion, the SRG appear to be the products of late Miocene–Pliocene partial melting of the batholith root. These melts were incorporated into hot peridotitic assemblages where they were trapped and froze. These observations are consistent with the foundering of the batholith root and diapiric ascent of mantle peridotite at the new base of the remnant light crust.

The presence of high-velocity and high-density anomalies at great depth beneath the batholith. Geophysical data grossly characterize the present-day vertical dimension of the Sierra Nevada. A recent seismic refraction experiment performed across the axis of the SNB has revealed that the Sierra Nevada mountain range is underlain by a relatively thin (35–42 km) crust (Fliedner and Ruppert, 1996; Wernicke et al., 1996). At least two independent teleseismic data sets collected from the Sierra Nevada at different latitudes (Jones et al., 1994; Zandt and Ruppert, 1996) contain information on the existence of one or more dense and fast bodies at 100 to 200 km, which may represent fragments of the delaminated eclogitic keel.

Zandt and Ruppert (1996) have combined the crustal model proposed for the Sierra Nevada by Fliedner and Ruppert (1996) with a tomogram of the upper mantle beneath the Sierra Nevada to generate an E-W P-velocity cross section to ~200 km depth. Their results indicate the presence of a high-velocity anomaly in the upper mantle. The anomaly is most clearly defined at depths between 100 and 180 km; it has a nearly vertical cylindrical form and a model density of 3500 g/cm³, typical of eclogites. These results may indicate that the eclogitic lowermost crust from beneath the Sierra Nevada detached and sank into the mantle, leaving behind a relatively thin, felsic remnant crust, according to Zandt and Ruppert (1996).

Jones et al. (1994) used teleseismic data to define a similar high-velocity anomaly in the upper mantle beneath the southern Sierra Nevada, northwest of Lake Isabella. The N-S extent of this anomaly (named the "Isabella anomaly") is ~40 to 60 km. The compressional velocities of the Isabella anomaly are ~4 to 5% higher than its surroundings at depths between 100 and 200 km. The Isabella anomaly could

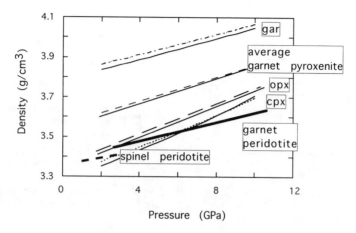

FIG. 5. Density of the Sierra Nevada lower-crustal and upper-mantle xenoliths as a function of pressure, calculated using the program of Niu and Batiza (1991). We used average xenolith mineral chemistry for garnet, orthopyroxene, and clinopyroxene. We calculated the densitites of orthopyroxene, clinopyroxene, and average garnet pyroxenite (average modal composition mixture of the three minerals) at 650°C and 950°C, i.e., the temperature interval measure by thermometry in the "eclogitic" samples analyzed by Ducea and Saleeby (1996a). The garnet pyroxenites are significantly more dense than are peridotites at any upper-mantle depth of interest.

represent a fragment of delaminated mantle lithosphere or eclogitic lowermost crust.

Proposed Sierra Nevada Delamination Model

The xenolith data suggest that the post-Cretaceous lithosphere contained a 40 to 70 km thick eclogite-facies mafic-ultramafic root underlying the granitic batholith. The densities of Sierran eclogites are at least 0.2 g/cm³ higher than those of peridotite, the material in which the eclogite probably was rooted (Appendix 1 and Fig. 5). On the basis of the observations presented above, we hypothesize that gravitational instability of the eclogitic root caused the splitting of the lithosphere at a depth of 35 to 40 km and its eventual delamination into the mantle. The foundered root probably was replaced by hot peridotitic mantle, which rose to the new base of the crust (Fig. 6).

The trigger for this process is not understood. Geochronological data on xenoliths demonstrate that eclogitic assemblages existed as batholith cumulates since at least the Late Cretaceous (Ducea et al., 1997). The presence of garnet pyroxenites in volcanics with an age of 8 to 12 Ma indicates that the eclogitic keel resided under the SNB for at least 70 m.y. before it foundered into the mantle. Density itself is not a sufficient condition for delamination, as dis-

cussed by Kay and Kay (1991). The heat from the Basin and Range–type extension may have been the cause for an increase in the Sierra Nevada heat flow in the Late Cenozoic (Saltus and Lachenbruch, 1990). Heating of the lithospheric column may significantly decrease the strength of the deepest levels rich in silica. Wernicke (1990) predicted lateral flow of a weak middle- to deep-crustal silica-rich layer in response to Basin and Range extension. The postulated mechanically weak layer at midcrustal levels in the Sierra Nevada, perhaps near the transition from granitic to mafic lithologies, could enhance the splitting of the eclogitic root and result in its eventual delamination.

Predictions of the Delamination Hypothesis

Lower-crustal foundering must have a number of geological consequences (Kay and Kay, e.g., 1991, 1993), including (1) the upwelling of asthenospheric material at the base of the crust and an increase of the heat flow in the area; (2) a change in the regional style of volcanism toward more primitive, mantle-like magmas; and (3) regional uplift. Of course, none of the three processes mentioned above need to be generated by delamination, and therefore cannot be used as a priori evidence for delamination. However, one would expect to see some evi-

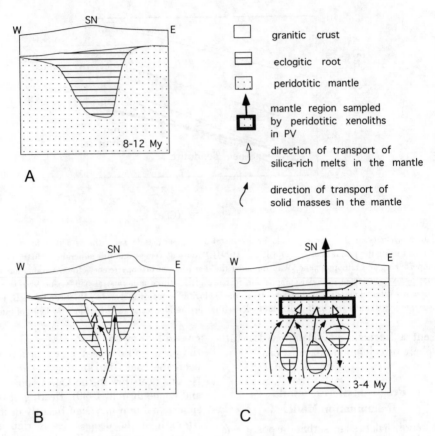

Fig. 6. Schematic diagram of the delamination process. The diagrams are E-W cross sections perpendicular to the Sierra Nevada (SN) axis. The vertical scale for each cross section is ~150 km. A. During the Miocene (8 to 12 Ma), the SNB was underlain by a thick mafic-ultramafic crustal root, consisting mainly of eclogite-facies rocks, at depths greater than 35 to 40 km. B. During the late Miocene, the root started foundering and has been intruded by hot asthenospheric peridotite. C. By Pliocene time (3 to 4 Ma), silica-rich melts derived from the delaminated keel were trapped within spinel peridotites at the new base of the Sierra Nevada crust and were accidentally brought to the surface by fast-ascending Pliocene volcanic lavas.

dence for all three in order to support the delamination hypothesis. In the Sierra Nevada, data exist that support the presence of shallow, partially molten asthenospheric mantle as well as the occurrence of a change in volcanism toward more primitive compositions. Evidence for late Miocene uplift also exists (e.g., Huber, 1981), although it has been questioned recently (Small and Anderson, 1996; Wernicke et al., 1996). Below we present the data that support delamination-model predictions for the Sierra Nevada.

Anomalously hot and slow sub-Moho mantle. The Jones et al. (1994) data set shows that the uppermost mantle (30 to 70 km) has relatively slow compressional velocities (≤ 7.6 km/s),

indicating the presence of hot (asthenospheric?) material at the base of the crust. Upwelling of asthenosphere would be expected in response to the detachment of a dense crustal root. The presence of hot, buoyant asthenospheric mantle at the base of the thin Sierra Nevada crust also has been suggested by the P-wave image of the upper mantle structure of the southern Sierra Nevada (Biasi and Humphreys, 1992), the teleseismic study of Benz et al. (1992) beneath the eastern part of the mountain range in northern California, and the larger-scale teleseismic study of Humphreys and Dueker (1994). At a regional scale, the uppermost (35 to 100 km) mantle beneath the western United States at the latitude of the

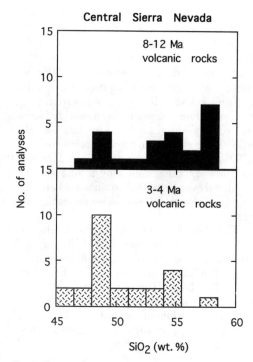

FIG. 7. Histogram comparing the silica concentrations in MV (8 to 12 Ma) and PV (3 to 4 Ma) rocks from the central Sierra Nevada. Both data sets cover a wide range of SiO_2, but the younger volcanic rocks on average are more mafic. Data from Ducea and Saleeby (unpubl.) and Huber (1977).

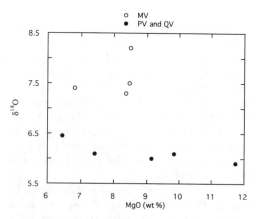

FIG. 8. $\delta^{18}O$ vs. MgO for xenolith-bearing volcanic rocks of the MV and PV groups. PV have more primitive (mantle-like) oxygen-isotope ratios.

Sierra Nevada alternates zones of high and low seismic velocities (Humphreys and Dueker, 1994), suggesting instability of a thick, pre-existing mantle lithosphere that in certain regions has been replaced by asthenosphere, possibly by diapiric ascent.

Humphreys and Dueker (1994) concluded that the low seismic velocities of the uppermost mantle beneath the Sierra Nevada are indicative of the presence of partial melt, expected from mantle volumes decompressing adiabatically as they rise to shallower levels in the mantle. Magnetotelluric data collected along a profile perpendicular to the Sierra Nevada axis show that the regions of slow, shallow-mantle seismic velocity also are characterized by extremely high electrical conductivity, most likely reflecting the presence of partial melt (Park et al., 1996). The presence of very young basaltic volcanic fields in the Sierra Nevada proper and along its eastern edge (e.g., Luedke and Smith, 1981) is consistent with these data.

Compositional change in regional volcanism.
The MV appear to be distinct from the PV. The MV from the central Sierra Nevada on average are more silicic than the PV (Fig. 7). The MV and PV (trachyandesites, potassic and ultra-potassic basalts) are clearly distinct from the QV alkali basalts.

In order to avoid volcanic samples that may have been crustally contaminated, we have further analyzed only volcanic occurrences that carry lower-crustal and/or mantle xenoliths. Xenolith-bearing volcanic rocks are fast-ascending rocks that experienced a minimum of crustal interaction.

The equilibration pressures and stability fields of xenoliths present in the volcanic groups suggest that the MV originated at depths similar to or greater than those of the PV and QV. The presence of diamond and graphite pseudomorphs after diamond in pipes of the MV (Hausel, 1995; Ducea and Saleeby, 1977), as well as equilibration pressures as high as 4.2 GPa, indicate that the source of these trachyandesites is at least 120 to 140 km deep. In contrast, the equilibration pressures of mantle xenoliths of the PV and QV (Ducea and Saleeby, 1996a), as well as the absence of garnet in the peridotites, suggest that the xenolith-bearing PV and QV may have originated at shallower depths. Depths of as much as 120 km were established by van Kooten (1980) for the source of some PV from the Fresno River area. Therefore, the source depths for the PV were shallower than or similar to those of the MV;

there is no indication that the PV and QV originated at greater depths than did the MV.

The oxygen-isotope ratios of fresh, xenolith-bearing PV and MV are shown in Figure 8 against MgO concentrations. Interestingly, the deeper MV magmas have crustal $\delta^{18}O$ ratios (7.1 to 8.2), whereas the PV and QV have mantle-like $\delta^{18}O$ (5.9 to 6.5) values. These results indicate that a crustal oxygen signature during Miocene time at ~120 km was replaced by a mantle signature at similar and/or shallower depths by the Pliocene.

In conclusion, Late Cenozoic volcanic rocks erupted through the Sierra Nevada record a progressive change at depth, from crustal-like (8 to 12 Ma) to mantle sources (0 to 4 Ma), as predicted by the delamination hypothesis.

Young uplift of the mountain range. Sierra Nevada geologists have long presented data suggesting that the mountain range experienced significant Late Cenozoic uplift accompanied by westward tilting, mainly because of tectonic forces (Lindgren, 1911; Christensen, 1966; Huber, 1981; Unruh, 1991). There is abundant evidence that most of the unroofing of the Mesozoic batholith to its present-day exposed levels took place shortly after batholith generation (Unruh, 1991; Renne et al., 1993). The region experienced little erosion during the first half of the Cenozoic, which led most researchers to believe that the Sierran topography was reduced from the presumed Mesozoic Andean-like relief to an unimpressive lowland during the Early Cenozoic (Huber, 1981). Christensen (1966) and Huber (1981) used paleofloral and geomorphological arguments to postulate that uplift was under way in the central Sierra Nevada during 50 to 25 Ma and continued subsequently, but has accelerated mainly over the past 10 m.y. and was demonstrably significant between 10 and 3 Ma.

However, this young uplift event in many ways is enigmatic, as it is not explained by tectonic thickening in an arc environment. The Sierra Nevada ceased to be an active magmatic arc at ~80 Ma (Chen and Moore, 1982). Furthermore, the region stopped being a convergent margin before the time of the fastest postulated uplift. A different cause for uplift must be found. Crough and Thompson (1977) were the first to propose that the late Miocene uplift of the Sierra Nevada must be related to the thinning of the mantle lithosphere beneath the Sierra Nevada, a hypothesis further developed by Eaton et al. (1978) and Jones (1987). Recently, some researchers have challenged all lines of evidence used to document Late Cenozoic uplift (Small and Anderson, 1996; Wernicke et al., 1996), claiming that although there is strong evidence for young westward tilting of the mountain range, it need not be accompanied by an increase in mean elevation. However, the large incision rates measured by Huber (1981) in the Sierran major drainages for the 10 to 3 Ma age range following a long period of erosional quiescence call upon some Late Cenozoic tectonic process to provide buoyancy in the area.

We believe that the cooling and development of the eclogitic root beneath the SNB during the late stages of magmatism and following its cessation inhibited erosion during the Early Cenozoic. The Late Cenozoic detachment of the eclogitic root (possibly a multi-step process) and its replacement by hot peridotite could have provided buoyancy and triggered renewed uplift of the mountain range.

Alternative Interpretations

Crustal foundering into the mantle is a mechanism capable of explaining the present-day relatively shallow crustal thickness and recent uplift of the Sierra Nevada mountain range. We presented above several geological and geophysical lines of evidence that are consistent with the delamination model. There are, however, alternative explanations for some of the observations presented above that support the concept of delamination.

Change in xenolith lithology

One could argue that the xenolith data are not representative of the composition of the deep lithosphere beneath the SNB. The Miocene pipes may have sampled preferentially garnet-rich lithologies, whereas the PV could have selectively sampled peridotitic material from similar depths. Therefore, the depth interval between 35 and 100 km may have been represented by a mixture of peridotites and eclogites at all times during the Late Cenozoic. However, the significant change in peridotite equilibration temperatures, from low values in MV units to near-solidus values in PV and QV units, argues against a sampling bias.

Crustal-derived glass inclusions in
mantle peridotites

While crustal-derived glasses in mantle peri-
odites clearly document interactions between
deep-crustal and mantle materials, they may not
necessarily require crustal delamination. It also
is possible that hot diapirs of peridotitic material locally intruded the lowermost Sierra
Nevada crust, resulting in the partial melting of
the eclogitic assemblages and the incorporation
of trapped SRG inclusions in peridotites (stage
"B" in Fig. 6). Pliocene and Quaternary volcanism in the Sierra Nevada, however, is not a
local feature, shallow-level (35 to 70 km) spinel
peridotite–bearing PV and QV being scattered
throughout the region. Since the Sierra Nevada
did not experience lateral extension comparable to the Basin and Range region to the east,
we believe that regional peridotitic diapirism
must have been accompanied by vertical
removal of the lower crust.

High-velocity anomaly beneath the
Sierra Nevada

The presence of partially molten material
with low seismic compressional velocities measured below the base of the present-day seismologically defined crust could lead to the
erroneous interpretation that dense eclogitic
material is present at depth. The measured
anomaly may instead simply represent a transition from partially molten to solid peridotite,
rather than reflecting a chemical change.

Tectonic Implications

The data outlined above support the hypothesis that a thick, eclogite-facies mafic-ultramafic
root that developed under the Sierra Nevada
during and possibly after the formation of the
composite Mesozoic batholith delaminated and
foundered into the mantle. With the present
data resolution, this interpretation is not
unique, although it does satisfy all the important pertinent geologic and geophysical observations. If our favored interpretation is correct,
it may have important tectonic implications for
the post-arc evolution of the Sierran lithosphere and crustal growth at Cordilleran margins. These implications are discussed below.

Missing root

The Sierra Nevada arc resulted in the formation of an upper crustal structure characteristic
of most Cordilleran-type magmatic arcs. The
Andes, for example, represent a good equivalent in which magmatism is still active today.
Despite the complex nature of the crust-mantle
interface beneath batholiths (Hildreth and
Moorbath, 1988; Pitcher, 1993), it is expected
that a magmatic arc at a Cordilleran margin
would contain large volumes of garnet-rich,
non-peridotitic residues/cumulates beneath
the granitic sections of the crust. Observations
and mass balance calculations demonstrate that
the ratio of arc cumulates to granitoids exceeds
unity (Kay and Kay, 1991) and could be as
much as 10 to 20 if a large fraction of the
magmatic input is mantle derived. Since Cordilleran granitoids can be as thick as ~30 km
(e.g., Saleeby, 1990), one would expect to find
cumulate/residue roots at least 30 km in thickness, but more likely 60 km or more.

The presence of eclogitic roots has not been
recorded sesimically beneath extinct arcs, or
even beneath the larger of the Cordilleran
batholiths (e.g., Zandt and Ammon, 1995). The
Sierra Nevada is one example of an extinct
Mesozoic Cordilleran batholith whose crustal
thickness today is ~35 km, and which is underlain by peridotitic mantle (Wernicke et al.,
1996). Root delamination of defunct arcs is an
appealing mechanism with the capacity for
resolving this apparent contradiction between
geophysical and petrological lines of evidence.

Crustal growth at Cordilleran margins

Although Andean margins have been considered to be prime sites for Phanerozoic crustal
growth (e.g., Taylor and McLennan, 1985), geochemical studies show that the generation of
typical Cordilleran granitoids requires a minimum two-step distillation from the mantle (e.g.,
Hildreth and Moorbath, 1988). Young accreted
crustal masses, which commonly originated
within island-arc settings, are found at Cordilleran margins in front of the magmatic arcs.
These arc-related rocks are composed of water-
rich volcanics intermixed with a variety of
sediments that are melt-fertile in mid- to lower-
crustal environments. Tectonic thickening can
emplace young accreted arc sections and
various other "non-subductable" units at considerable depths and lead to granitic magmatism

via extensive melting in the lower parts of the crust (e.g., Pitcher, 1993). If the residue left after granitoid extraction remains in the crust, batholithic magmatism will lead primarily to the internal differentiation of the crust, whereas if the residue returns to the mantle, the addition of silica-rich material to the crust will be significant.

In the Sierra Nevada, there is evidence for widespread Jurassic submarine arc rocks along the western edge of the batholith and as wall-rock screens within the Cretaceous batholith (e.g., Saleeby, 1990, and references therein). Saleeby (1990) presented strong evidence for downward flow of volcanic-arc rocks during the Cretaceous. Deep-crustal remelting of the Jurassic arc (blended with new mantle additions and possibly some other lower-crustal components) may represent the second event required for generating the silica-rich Cretaceous batholith in the Sierra Nevada (Ducea et al., 1997).

The post-Cretaceous upper 30 km of the Sierra Nevada crust, almost entirely occupied by SNB granitoids, therefore has a composition slightly more silicic than the average continental crust. Precambrian material no older than 1.8 Ga also may have been involved in the source of the SNB, but the ratio of Precambrian to Phanerozoic SNB source rocks based on Nd model ages is <1/4. If delamination has recycled the ultramafic residues back into the mantle, the Sierra Nevada represents today a Mesozoic silica-rich crustal addition to the North American continent.

Acknowledgments

This research was funded by NSF grant EAR-9526859. M. Ducea also acknowledges grant #5810-96 from the Geological Society of America and a 1996 research fellowship from the University of California White Mountain Research Station. Earlier versions of this paper were reviewed by Gary Ernst and Doug Yule. We thank George Zandt and Craig Jones for discussions on the geophysics of the Sierra Nevada. This is California Institute of Technology Division of Geological and Planetary Sciences contribution 8482.

REFERENCES

Ague, J. J., and Brimhall G. H., 1988, Magmatic arc asymmetry and distribution of anomalous plutonic belts in the batholiths of California: Effects of assimilation, crustal thickness, and depth of crystallization: Geol. Soc. Amer. Bull., v. 100, p. 912–927.

Bateman, P. C., 1983, A summary of critical relationships in the central part of the Sierra Nevada batholith, California, U.S.A., in Roddick J. A., ed., Circum-Pacific plutonic terranes: Geol. Soc. Amer. Memoir 159, p. 241–254.

Beard, B. L., and Glazner, A. F., 1995, Trace elements and Sr and Nd isotopic composition of mantle xenoliths from Big Pine Volcanic Field, California: Jour. Geophys. Res., v. 100, p. 4169–4179.

Benz, H. M., Zandt, G., and Oppenheimer, D. H., 1992, Lithospheric structure of northern California from teleseismic images of the upper mantle: Jour. Geophys. Res., v. 97, p. 4791–4807.

Biasi, G. P., and Humphreys, E. D., 1992, P-wave image of the upper mantle structure of central California and southern Nevada: Geophys. Res. Lett., v. 19, p. 1161–1164.

Chen, J. H., and Moore, J. G., 1982, Uranium-lead isotopic ages from the Sierra Nevada batholith, California: Jour. Geophys. Res., v. 87, p. 4761–4784.

Christensen, M. N., 1966, Late Cenozoic crustal movements in the Sierra Nevada of California: Geol. Soc. Amer. Bull., v. 77, p. 163–182.

Cristensen, N., and Mooney, W. D., 1995, Seismic structure and composition of the continental crust: A global view: Jour. Geophys. Res., v. 100, p. 9761–9788.

Crough, S. T., and Thompson, G. A., 1977, Upper mantle origin of the Sierra Nevada uplift: Geology, v. 5, p. 396–399.

Dewey, J. F., Ryan, P. D., and Anderson, T. B., 1993, Orogenic uplift and collapse, crustal thickness, fabrics, and metamorphic phase changes: The role of eclogites, in Prochard, H. M., et al., eds., Magmatic processes and plate tectonics: Geol. Soc. Amer. Spec. Publ. 76, p. 325–343.

Dickinson, W., 1981, Plate tectonics and the continental margin of California, in Ernst, W. G., ed., The geotectonic development of California: Englewood Cliffs, NJ, Prentice-Hall, p. 1–28.

Dodge, F. C. W., Calk, L. C., and Kistler, R. W., 1986, Lower crustal xenoliths, Chinese Peak lava flow, Central Sierra Nevada: Jour. Petrol., v. 27, p. 1277–1304.

Dodge, F. C. W., Lockwood, J. P., and Calk, L. C., 1988, Fragments of the mantle and crust beneath the Sierra Nevada batholith: Xenoliths in a volcanic pipe near Big Creek, California: Geol. Soc. Amer. Bull., v. 100, p. 938–947.

Domenick, M. A., Kistler, R. W., Dodge, F. C. W., and Tatsumoto, M., 1983, Nd and Sr study of crustal and mantle inclusions from the Sierra Nevada and implications for batholith petrogenesis: Geol. Soc. Amer. Bull., v. 94, p. 713–719.

Ducea, M. N., and Saleeby, J. B., 1996a, Buoyancy sources for a large unrooted mountain range, the Sierra Nevada, California: Evidence from xenolith thermobarometry: Jour. Geophys. Res., v. 101, p. 8229–8241.

———, 1996b, Rb-Sr and Sm-Nd mineral ages of some Sierra Nevada xenoliths: Implications for crustal growth and thermal evolution: EOS (Trans. Amer. Geophys. Union), v. 77, p. 780.

Ducea, M. N., and Saleeby, J. B., 1997, Silica-rich glass inclusions in ultramafic xenoliths from the Sierra Nevada, California: Evidence for crustal delamination?: Earth Planet. Sci. Lett., in press.

Ducea, M. N., Taylor, H. P., and Saleeby, J. B., 1997, The age and origin of a thick mafic-ultramafic keel from beneath the Sierra Nevada batholith; Part II, Petrogenesis [abs.]: Abs. submitted to GSA Annual Meeting, 1997.

Eaton, G. P., Wahl, R. R., Prostka, H. J., Mabey, D. R., and Kleinkopf, M. D., 1978, Regional gravity and tectonic patterns: Their relations to the late Cenozoic epeirogeny and lateral spreading in the western Cordillera, in Smith, R. B., and Eaton, G. P., eds., Cenozoic tectonics and regional geophysics of the western Cordillera: Geol. Soc. Amer. Memoir 152, p. 51–91.

Faure, G., 1985, Principles of isotope geology: New York, John Wiley and Sons, 590 p.

Fliedner, M., and Ruppert, S., 1996, Three-dimensional crustal structure of the southern Sierra Nevada from seismic fan profiles and gravity modelling: Geology, v. 24, p. 367–370.

Hausel, W. D., 1995, Diamonds and their host rocks in the United States: Mining Engineering, v. 47, p. 723–732.

Hildreth, W., and Moorbath, S., 1988, Crustal contributions to arc magmatism in the Andes of central Chile: Contrib. Mineral. Petrol., v. 98, p. 455–489.

Huber, N. K., 1977, Silica content of some Late Cenozoic volcanic rocks from the southern Sierra Nevada, California—applications as a correlation tool: U.S. Geol. Surv. Open File Report 77-755, 40 p.

———, 1981, Amount and timing of Late Cenozoic uplift and tilt of the central Sierra Nevada, California—evidence from the upper San Joaquin River basin: U.S. Geol. Surv. Prof. Pap. 1197, 28 p.

Humphreys, E. D., and Dueker, K. G., 1994, Western United States upper mantle structure: Jour. Geophys. Res., v. 99, p. 9615–9634.

Ionov, D. A., Hofmann, A. W., and Shimizu, N., 1994, Metasomatism-induced melting in mantle xenoliths from Mongolia: Jour. Petrol., v. 35, p. 753–785.

Jones, C. H., 1987, Is extension in Death Valley accommodated by thinning of the mantle lithosphere beneath the Sierra Nevada, California?: Tectonics, v. 6, p. 449–473.

Jones, C. H., Kanamori, H., and Roecker, S. W., 1994, Missing roots and mantle drips: Regional P_n and teleseismic arrival times in the southern Sierra Nevada and vicinity, California: Jour. Geophys. Res., v. 99, p. 4567–4601.

Jones, C. H., and Phinney, R., 1997, Seismic structure of the lithosphere from teleseismic converted arrivals observed at small arrays in the southern Sierra Nevada and vicinity, California: Jour. Geophys. Res., submitted.

Kay, R. W., and Kay, S. M., 1991, Creation and destruction of the lower continental crust: Geol. Rundsch., v. 80, p. 259–270.

———, 1993, Delamination and delamination magmatism: Tectonophys., v. 219, p. 177–189.

Lindgren, W., 1911, The Tertiary gravels of the Sierra Nevada, California: U.S. Geol. Surv. Prof. Pap. 73, 226 p.

Luedke, R. G., and Smith, R. L., 1981, Map showing the distribution, composition, and age of Late Cenozoic volcanic centers in California and Nevada: U.S. Geol. Surv. Misc. Invest. Ser. Map., 1091-C.

McCulloch, M. T., Gregory, R. T., Wasserburg, G. J., and Taylor, H. P., 1980, A neodymium, strontium, and oxygen isotopic study of the Cretaceous Samail ophiolite and implications for the petrogenesis and seawater-hydrothermal alteration of the oceanic crust: Earth. Planet. Sci. Lett., v. 46, p. 201–211.

Moore, J. G., and Dodge, F. C. W., 1980, Late Cenozoic volcanic rocks of the southern Sierra Nevada, California; I. Geology and petrology: Geol. Soc. Amer. Bull., v. 91, p. 515–518.

Mukhopadyay, B., and Manton, W. I., 1994, Upper mantle fragments from beneath the Sierra Nevada batholith: Partial fusion, fractional crystallization and metasomatism in a subduction-enriched ancient lithosphere: Jour. Petrol., v. 35, p. 1418–1450.

Niu, Y., and Batiza, R., 1991, DENSCAL: A program for calculating densities of silicate melts and mantle minerals as a function of pressure, temperature, and composition in melting range: Comp. Geosci., v. 17, p. 679–687.

Ormerod, D. S., Hawkesworth, C. H., Rogers, N. K., Leeman, W. P., and Menzies, M., 1988, Tectonic and magmatic transitions in the western Great Basin, U.S.A.: Nature, v. 333, p. 349–353.

Park, S., Hirasuna, B., Jiracek, G., and Kinn, C., 1996, Magnetotelluric evidence for lithospheric mantle thinning beneath the southern Sierra Nevada: Jour. Geophys. Res., v. 101, p. 16, 241-16, 255.

Pickett, D. A., and Saleeby, J. B., 1993, Thermobarometric constraints on the depth of exposure and conditions of plutonism and metamorphism at deep levels of the Sierra Nevada batholith, Tehachapi Mountains, California: Jour. Geophys. Res., v. 98, p. 609-629.

Pitcher, W. S., 1993, The nature and origin of granite: London, Blackie, 321 p.

Renne, P. R., Tobish, O. T., and Saleeby, J. B., 1993, Thermochronologic record of pluton emplacement, deformation, and exhumation at Courtright shear zone, central Sierra Nevada, California: Geology, v. 21, p. 331-334.

Saleeby, J. B., 1990, Progress in tectonic and petrogenetic studies in an exposed cross-section of young (c. 100 Ma) continental crust, southern Sierra Nevada, California, in Salisbury, M. H., and Fountain, D. M., eds., Exposed crustal sections of the continental crust: Norwell, MA, Kluwer Acad., p. 137-158.

Saltus, R. W., and Lachenbruch, A. H., 1990, Thermal evolution of the Sierra Nevada: Tectonic implications of new heat flow data: Tectonics, v. 10, p. 325-344.

Schiano, P., and Clocchiatti, R., 1994, Worldwide occurrence of silica-rich melts in sub-continental and sub-oceanic mantle minerals: Nature, v. 368, p. 621-624.

Schiano, P., Clocchiatti, R., Shimizu, N., Maury, R. C., Jochum, K. P., and Hofmann, A. W., 1995, Hydrous, silica-rich melts in the sub-arc mantle and their relationships with erupted arc lavas: Nature, v. 377, p. 595-600.

Small, E. E., and Anderson, R. S., 1996, Geomorphologically driven Late Cenozoic rock uplift in the Sierra Nevada, California: Science, v. 270, p. 277-280.

Taylor, S. R., and McLennan, S. M., 1985, The continental crust: Its compositional evolution: Cambridge, MA, Blackwell Sci., 312 p.

Unruh, J. R., 1991, The uplift of the Sierra Nevada and implications for the Late Cenozoic epeirogeny in the western Cordillera: Geol. Soc. Amer. Bull., v. 103, p. 1395-1404.

van Kooten, G. K., 1980, Mineralogy, geochemistry, and petrology of an ultrapotassic basaltic suite, central Sierra Nevada, California, U.S.A.: Jour. Petrol., v. 21, p. 631-684.

Wernicke, B., 1990, The fluid crustal layer and its implications for continental dynamics, in Salisbury, M. H., and Fountain, D. M., eds., Exposed crustal sections of the continental crust: Norwell, MA, Kluwer Acad., NATO Adv. Study Ser C., Math. Phys. Sci., v. 317, p. 509-544.

Wernicke, B., et al., 1996, Origin of high mountains on continents: The southern Sierra Nevada: Science, v. 271, p. 190-193.

Wolf, M. B., and Wyllie, P. J., 1993, Garnet growth during amphibolite anatexis: Implications for a garnetiferous restite: Jour. Geol., v. 101, p. 357-373.

Zandt, G., and Ammon, C. J., 1995, Continental crust composition constrained by measurements of crustal Poisson's ratio: Nature, v. 374, p. 152-154.

Zandt, G., and Ruppert, S., 1996, Lower crustal detachment and the evolution of the continental crust: Evidence from the Sierra Nevada [abs.]: EOS (Trans. Amer. Geophys. Union), v. 77, p. 831.

APPENDIX: THE DENSITY OF SIERRA NEVADA XENOLITHS

The density of the garnet pyroxenites as well as peridotite lithologies can be estimated from xenolith data. The densities of average compositions of minerals from garnet pyroxenites recovered in MV units are shown in Figure 5. More than 100 analyses were taken into account in the averaging of mineral densities. The mineral densities were calculated using the program provided by Niu and Batiza (1991) at two different temperatures—650°C and 950°C—as end values of a reasonable spectrum of temperatures in the lower crust. The average modal proportions of garnet, orthopyroxene, and clinopyroxene in our collection were used to calculate an average garnet pyroxenite density as a function of pressure (depth), which is shown in Figure 4. The average densities for garnet peridotites from MV (using a mean temperature of 1000°C recorded in xenoliths) and spinel peridotites from PV and QV units (using a mean temperature of 1200°C) also are shown in Figure 5 as a function of pressure. The peridotite densities are at least 0.2 g/cm^3 lower than those of pyroxenites at all pressures.

Late Cretaceous-Paleocene Extensional Collapse and Disaggregation of the Southernmost Sierra Nevada Batholith

David J. Wood and Jason B. Saleeby

Division of Geological and Planetary Sciences, 170-25, California Institute of Technology, Pasadena, California 91125

Abstract

Geobarometric studies have documented that most of the metasedimentary wall rocks and plutons presently exposed in the southernmost Sierra Nevada batholith south of the Lake Isabella area were metamorphosed and emplaced at crustal levels significantly deeper (~15 to 30 km) than the batholithic rocks exposed to the north (depths of ~3 to 15 km). Field and geophysical studies have suggested that much of the southernmost part of the batholith is underlain along low-angle faults by the Rand Schist. The schist is composed mostly of metagraywacke that has been metamorphosed at relatively high pressures and moderate temperatures. NNW-trending compositional, age, and isotopic boundaries in the plutonic rocks of the central Sierra Nevada appear to be deflected westward in the southernmost part of the batholith. Based on these observations, in conjunction with the implicit assumption that the Sierra Nevada batholith formerly continued unbroken south of the Garlock fault, previous studies have inferred that the batholith was tectonically disrupted following its emplacement during the Cretaceous. Hypotheses to account for this disruption include intraplate oroclinal bending, W-vergent overthrusting, and gravitational collapse of overthickened crust. In this paper, new geologic data from the eastern Tehachapi Mountains, located adjacent to and north of the Garlock fault in the southernmost Sierra Nevada, are integrated with data from previous geologic studies in the region into a new view of the Late Cretaceous–Paleocene tectonic evolution of the region. The thesis of this paper is that part of the southernmost Sierra Nevada batholith was unroofed by extensional faulting in Late Cretaceous–Paleocene time. Unroofing occurred along a regional system of low-angle detachment faults. Remnants of the upper-plate rocks today are scattered across the southern Sierra Nevada region, from the Rand Mountains west to the San Emigdio Mountains, and across the San Andreas fault to the northern Salinian block.

Batholithic rocks in the upper plates of the Blackburn Canyon fault of the eastern Tehachapi Mountains, low-angle faults in the Rand Mountains and southeastern Sierra Nevada, and the Pastoria fault of the western Tehachapi Mountains are inferred to have been removed from a position structurally above rocks exposed in the southeastern Sierra Nevada and transported to their present locations along low-angle detachment faults. Some of the granitic and metamorphic rocks in the northern part of the Salinian block are suggested to have originated from a position structurally above deep-level rocks of the southwestern Sierra Nevada. The Paleocene–lower Eocene Goler Formation of the El Paso Mountains and the post–Late Cretaceous to pre–lower Miocene Witnet Formation in the southernmost Sierra Nevada are hypothesized to have been deposited in supradetachment basins that formed adjacent to some of the detachment faults.

Regional age constraints for this inferred tectonic unroofing and disaggregation of the southern Sierra Nevada batholith suggest that it occurred between ~90 to 85 Ma and ~55 to 50 Ma. Upper-plate rocks of the detachment system appear to have been rotated clockwise by as much as 90° based on differences in the orientation of foliation and contacts between inferred correlative hanging-wall and footwall rocks. Transport of the upper-plate rocks is proposed to have occurred in two stages. First, the upper crust in the southern Sierra Nevada extended in a south to southeast direction, and second, the allochthonous rocks were carried westward at the latitude of the Mojave Desert by a mechanism that may include W-vergent faulting and/or oroclinal bending. The Late Cretaceous NNW extension of the upper crust in the southernmost Sierra Nevada postulated in this study is similar to Late Cretaceous, generally NW-directed, crustal extension that has been recognized to the northeast in the Funeral, Panamint, and Inyo mountains by others. Extensional collapse of the upper crust in the southern Sierra Nevada batholith may be closely linked to the emplacement of Rand Schist beneath the batholith during Late Cretaceous time, as has been suggested in previous studies.

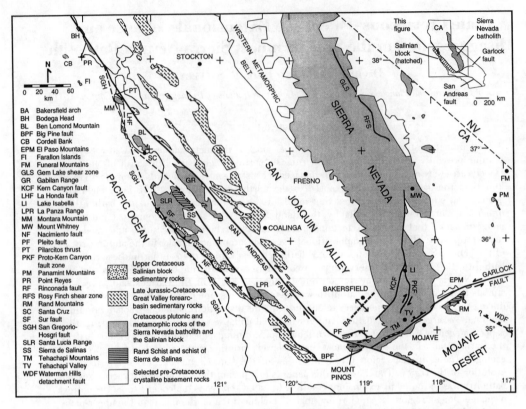

FIG. 1. Geologic and index map of central California and the Sierra Nevada batholith, showing selected geologic features and localities discussed in the text. The Salinian block is bounded on the northeast by the San Andreas fault, on the south by the Big Pine fault, and on the southwest by the Sur fault, the Nacimiento fault, and the Rinconada fault south of its intersection with the Nacimiento fault. The faults with triangular teeth are thrust faults and the faults with square teeth are detachment faults. Geology modified from Jennings (1977) and Powell (1993). Nomenclature of faults west of the San Andreas fault from Hall (1991) and Powell (1993).

Introduction

THE CRETACEOUS SIERRA NEVADA batholith in central California represents one of the best exposures in the world of the root zone of an Andean-type magmatic arc (Fig. 1). Most of the plutonic rocks currently exposed in the batholith appear to have been emplaced at depths of 3 to 15 km in the crust (Ague and Brimhall, 1988). Exhumation of the batholith commonly has been assumed to have occurred by erosion, with much of the removed material deposited immediately to the west of the batholith as forearc basin sediments that today are exposed along the western side of the San Joaquin and Sacramento valleys (Mansfield, 1979; Bateman, 1992). The southernmost part of the batholith south of Lake Isabella, in contrast,

has been exhumed to much deeper crustal levels of ~15 to 30 km (Sharry, 1981; Ague and Brimhall, 1988; Pickett and Saleeby, 1993), which means that more of the batholithic crust in the south has been removed and transported elsewhere. Malin et al. (1995) suggested that crustal thickening related to emplacement of Rand Schist beneath the southernmost Sierra Nevada batholith in Late Cretaceous time may have led to the subsequent collapse of the crust and exhumation of the deep-level rocks in the region along normal faults. The geologic complexity of the southernmost Sierra Nevada–Mojave Desert region, however, has made it difficult to recognize structures involved in this postulated collapse. In this report, recent geologic mapping in the eastern Tehachapi Mountains (Wood et al., 1993; Wood, 1997), which are located immediately south of Tehachapi Valley in the southernmost Sierra Nevada (Fig. 1), is integrated with a synthesis of previous geologic studies in the region into a new model that generally supports the hypothesis of crustal collapse.

The thesis of this paper is that part of the southernmost Sierra Nevada batholith was unroofed by extensional faulting in Late Cretaceous–Paleocene time along a regional system of low-angle faults, and that remnants of the upper-plate rocks today are scattered across the southern Sierra Nevada region from the Rand Mountains west to the San Emigdio Mountains, and possibly across the San Andreas fault to the northern Salinian block (Fig. 1). Formulation of this model for the collapse and disaggregation of the southern Sierra Nevada would not have been possible without the extensive regional geologic studies of Ross (1989b, 1990) and Dibblee (1967), and the identification by Crowell (1952, 1964) and Silver (1982, 1983, 1986) of important low-angle faults in the region.

This paper covers the following main topics. First, the geologic and tectonic setting of the area is summarized, and the geobarometric evidence that suggests that the southernmost part of the Sierra Nevada batholith has been exhumed to a greater depth than the batholith to the north is reviewed. Second, low-angle faults that may have been involved in the inferred extensional unroofing of the southernmost part of the batholith are discussed. Third, a number of possible correlations between distinctive geologic features in the footwall and hanging-wall rocks of this regional fault system are suggested. Fourth, a possible genetic relationship between Late Cretaceous (?)–Paleogene sedimentary deposits in the area and the detachment fault system is proposed. In the last section of this paper, the inferred Late Cretaceous–Paleocene age, extension direction, and upper-plate rotations of this hypothesized extensional faulting event are discussed. In addition, an attempt is made to differentiate and reconcile the evidence for this deformation event with the results of other studies that have documented younger—i.e., early Miocene— extension in the region. Finally, the possible causes of this postulated Late Cretaceous– Paleocene extensional deformation are dis-

cussed, and the important results of this study are summarized.

Geologic and Tectonic Overview of the Region

The Cretaceous Sierra Nevada batholith, the Great Valley forearc-basin sequence, and the Franciscan subduction complex in central California form a classic convergent margin triad. Plutons of the Cretaceous batholith intruded into a complex assemblage of wall rocks along the continental margin of California, including Jurassic and Triassic plutonic rocks and Mesozoic, Paleozoic, and Precambrian metamorphic rocks (Saleeby and Busby, 1993). Coeval sedimentary rocks of the uppermost Jurassic to Cretaceous Great Valley sequence were deposited in the forearc basin located immediately west of the magmatic arc (Ingersoll, 1983; Cowan and Bruhn, 1992) (Fig. 1). Today Upper Jurassic–Cretaceous Great Valley rocks are exposed in uplifts along the western margin of the San Joaquin Valley in central California, and they are present in the subsurface throughout most of the valley beneath a thick sequence of Cenozoic sedimentary deposits (Moxon, 1988) (Fig. 1). The Great Valley sequence appears to be absent, however, southeast of the Bakersfield arch, where early Cenozoic sedimentary rocks are deposited directly on the Sierra Nevada batholith and its wall rocks (Goodman and Malin, 1992).

The NNW-trending Sierra Nevada batholith is transversely zoned in composition, age, and isotopic properties. Moore (1959) defined a "quartz diorite line" that divided the batholith, approximately along strike, into a western, more mafic-rich, gabbroic to quartz-dioritic part and an eastern, granitic part. Following the work of Moore (1959), more detailed studies of the central and southern parts of the batholith (Bateman and Dodge, 1970; Ross, 1989b, 1990; Bateman, 1992) confirmed that Sierra Nevada plutons become less mafic and richer in quartz and potassium feldspar from west to east. This compositional zonation is obvious in the southernmost Sierra Nevada (Fig. 2). The emplacement ages of Cretaceous plutons in the batholith, as indicated by U-Pb ages on zircon,

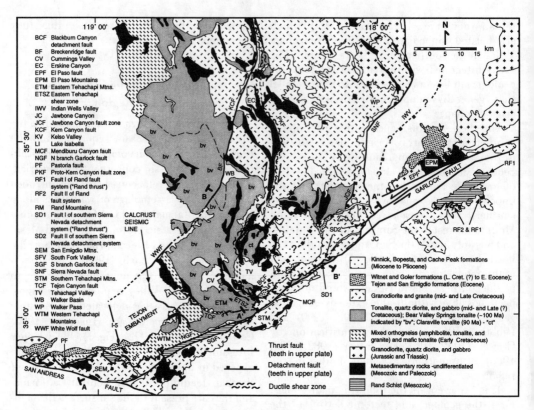

Fig. 2. Geologic and index map of the southernmost Sierra Nevada region. The eastern Tehachapi Mountains are bounded by Tehachapi Valley, the Tejon Canyon fault, and the Cummings Valley; the southern Tehachapi Mountains are located between the southern branch of the Garlock fault and the Mojave Desert; the western Tehachapi Mountains are bounded by the Tejon Canyon fault, the San Joaquin Valley, Interstate Highway 5, and the southern branch of the Garlock fault; the San Emigdio Mountains are bounded by the San Joaquin Valley and the San Andreas fault and are located west of Interstate 5. Faults RF2 and RF1 in the Rand Mountains are too close together to differentiate at the scale of this figure. Geology is modified from Ross (1989b, 1990) and Dibblee (1959, 1967). Modifications of the geology from G. I. Smith (1951), Michael (1960), Samsel (1962), A. R. Smith (1964), Dibblee and Louke (1970), Dibblee and Warne (1970), Peters (1972), Sharry (1981), Silver (1986), Silver and Nourse (1986), Sams (1986), Cox (1987), Sams and Saleeby (1988), Nourse (1989), Busby-Spera and Saleeby (1990), Gazis and Saleeby (1991), Pickett and Saleeby (1993), and Wood (1997).

decrease from west to east (Chen and Moore, 1982). In the southern part of the batholith, the westernmost gneissic and mafic plutons have Early Cretaceous (~130 to 105 Ma) U-Pb zircon ages (Saleeby and Sharp, 1980; Saleeby et al., 1987). East of those plutons, the voluminous tonalitic and gabbroic intrusive suite of Bear Valley has a medial Cretaceous age of ~100 Ma (Saleeby et al., 1987), and in the central to eastern part of the southernmost Sierra Nevada, the plutons have Late Cretaceous U-Pb zircon ages (Saleeby and Busby-Spera, 1986; Saleeby et al., 1987). The easternmost part of the southern Sierra Nevada and most of the El Paso

Mountains are underlain by Jurassic and Triassic plutonic rocks (Ross, 1990; Dunne et al., 1991; Miller et al., 1995) (Fig. 2). The initial $^{87}Sr/^{86}Sr$ ratio of plutonic rocks in the southern part of the batholith also varies systematically, with values generally increasing from ~0.704 in the west to ~0.709 in the central and eastern parts (Saleeby et al., 1987; Kistler and Ross, 1990; Pickett and Saleeby, 1994).

It has long been recognized that the NNW-trending Sierra Nevada Mountains and the generally NNW-trending compositional and isotopic zones of the central Sierra Nevada batholith exhibit an apparent westward deflection at the latitude of the Tehachapi Mountains (Locke et al., 1940; Moore, 1959; Kistler, 1978). After Neogene displacement along the San Andreas fault system is restored, it appears that a number of Sierra Nevadan geologic features are deflected and/or offset westward across the trace of the San Andreas fault into the Salinian block (Burchfiel and Davis, 1981; Silver, 1982, 1983; Ross, 1984). The Salinian block consists of metasedimentary rocks of presumed Mesozoic and/or Paleozoic ages that have been intruded by variably deformed plutons that have compositions, ages, and isotopic properties similar to plutons present in the southern Sierra Nevada batholith (Ross, 1984; Silver and Mattinson, 1986; James, 1992). Upper Cretaceous to Cenozoic sedimentary rocks lie unconformably on the crystalline basement of the Salinian block (Grove, 1993). Among the different mechanisms hypothesized to have produced the apparent offset of the Salinian block from similar rocks in the southern Sierra Nevada batholith are early Cenozoic, dextral, intraplate, oroclinal bending (Burchfiel and Davis, 1981) and transport along a complicated system of Paleogene, W-vergent, low-angle faults (Silver, 1982, 1983; Hall, 1991). In the latter interpretation, the Great Valley forearc-basin sequence and the Franciscan subduction complex are inferred to be partially overridden by the Salinian block along the low-angle faults. Hall (1991) suggested that the Sur fault or Sur-Nacimiento fault exposed along the western side of the Santa Lucia Range is one of these faults (Fig. 1).

The plutonic and metamorphic basement rocks of the southernmost Sierra Nevada region are structurally complex. The Rand Schist is exposed beneath the low-angle Rand fault in the Rand Mountains (Ehlig, 1968; Silver et al., 1984; Postlethwaite and Jacobson, 1987; Nourse, 1989) and the southeastern Sierra Nevada (Silver, 1986), and between the northern and southern branches of the Garlock fault in the western Tehachapi Mountains (Sharry, 1981). In the western Tehachapi Mountains, recent geophysical and geological studies along the Calcrust seismic line (Fig. 2) suggest that Rand Schist underlies the range along a shallowly NW-dipping fault (Malin et al., 1995). The Rand Schist is composed predominantly of metagraywacke with subordinate mafic schist and pelite, and it was metamorphosed at rela-

tively high pressures and moderate temperatures (Sharry, 1981; Jacobson et al., 1988). The schist is thought to have been tectonically emplaced beneath the southern Sierra Nevada batholith by underthrusting from the west in Late Cretaceous time (Malin et al., 1995). In addition to the Rand fault, there are a number of other low-angle faults in the southern Sierra Nevada area that are discussed in detail below. Bisecting the southern Sierra Nevada longitudinally is the proto–Kern Canyon fault, which is a subvertical, dextral-strike-slip, ductile shear zone that was active at ~85 Ma during emplacement of the batholith (Busby-Spera and Saleeby, 1990; Gazis and Saleeby, 1991; Saleeby, 1992) (Figs. 1 and 2). The proto–Kern Canyon fault zone is inferred to be continuous and coeval with the eastern Tehachapi shear zone south of Tehachapi Valley, which is a shallowly NE-dipping, greenschist-facies, ductile shear zone with a top-to-the-SSW shear sense (Wood et al., 1993; Wood, 1997) (Fig. 2).

Thrust-sense shearing along the eastern Tehachapi shear zone appears to be the culmination of a complex and protracted Late Cretaceous contractional and dextral transpressional deformation event in the middle to lower structural levels of the batholith in the southernmost Sierra Nevada. Following intrusion of the ~100 Ma intrusive suite of Bear Valley, the batholith and its wall rocks south and west of Tehachapi Valley locally were deformed by SW-vergent folds with subhorizontal, NW-trending axes, and then the batholith south of roughly the latitude of Walker Basin is inferred to have been folded in a map-scale, dextral, oroclinal fold (Wood, 1997). This oroclinal fold is a different and smaller structure than the regional-scale, dextral, oroclinal fold inferred to be present in the Salinian–Mojave–southern Sierra area by Burchfiel and Davis (1981), and it also is not the simple, concave-northwest, "hook-shaped" structure envisioned by Kanter and McWilliams (1982) and McWilliams and Li (1985) that is suggested by the outcrop pattern of crystalline basement rocks in the region. The oroclinal fold referred to here is evident in the curving metasedimentary screens and pendants between Lake Isabella and the eastern Tehachapi Mountains, which define a rounded "z" (Fig. 2). The metasedimentary screens and pendants all are inferred to have had ~NNW trends prior to the folding event. Dextral oroclinal folding in the vicinity of Tehachapi Valley is interpreted to have occurred before and during development of the eastern Tehachapi shear zone (Wood, 1997).

Late Cretaceous dextral transpressional shear zones have been documented in the central Sierra Nevada and include the Gem Lake shear zone (Greene and Schweickert, 1995) and the Rosy Finch shear zone (Tikoff and de Saint Blanquat, 1997) (Fig. 1). Dextral shearing along the proto–Kern Canyon fault zone, accompanied by dextral oroclinal folding in the southernmost Sierra Nevada, may be a different manifestation of a regional Late Cretaceous dextral transpressional deformation of the magmatic arc. Emplacement of Rand Schist beneath the southernmost part of the batholith in the Late Cretaceous (Malin et al., 1995) may have caused the different deformation styles in the southern and central Sierra Nevada. Thrust-sense shearing along the eastern Tehachapi shear zone may reflect relative NNE-directed underthrusting of Rand Schist at a lower structural level beneath the batholith (Wood, 1997).

The oldest sedimentary rocks deposited on the crystalline basement rocks of the southernmost Sierra Nevada batholith include the Goler Formation in the El Paso Mountains, the Witnet Formation in the southeastern Sierra Nevada, and the Tejon and San Emigdio formations in the San Emigdio and western Tehachapi Mountains (Fig. 2). The Goler Formation consists mostly of Paleocene and lower Eocene nonmarine clastic sedimentary rocks that are exposed on the north flank of the El Paso Mountains in a N-dipping homoclinal sequence that is at least 4 km thick (Dibblee, 1952; Cox, 1987). The lower part of the Goler Formation consists of a basal conglomerate that interfingers upward with alluvial-fan deposits derived from sources to the north, and the upper part of the Goler Formation consists of sediments deposited by westward-flowing streams (Cox, 1987). The lowermost part of the Goler Formation may be as old as latest Cretaceous, but it probably is not older than ~91 Ma, which is the biotite K-Ar apparent age of a clast of silicic metavolcanic rock collected from near the base of the formation (Cox, 1987). Intercalated near the top of the Goler Formation is a thin interval of lower Eocene marine sediments (Cox and Diggles, 1986; McDougall, 1987). Following deposition, the Goler Formation was tilted to the north and eroded, and then lower Miocene volcanic rocks of the Ricardo Formation were deposited unconformably on it (Cox, 1987).

The Witnet Formation, composed of nonmarine arkosic sandstone interbedded with conglomerate and locally with shaley layers, is exposed in three separate areas in the southern Sierra Nevada (Fig. 2). The type locality of the Witnet Formation is located at the western end of the Tehachapi Valley (TV in Fig. 2). The sedimentary rocks in the Tehachapi Valley area were first described by Lawson (1906), and the Witnet Formation was subsequently defined and named by Buwalda (1934). The Witnet Formation at the western end of Tehachapi Valley has been mapped and described in a number of studies (Smith, 1951; Buwalda, 1954; Michael, 1960; Dibblee, 1967; Dibblee and Louke, 1970; Quinn, 1987). Arkosic and conglomeratic sedimentary rocks in upper Jawbone Canyon and south of Tehachapi Valley are lithologically similar to, and have been correlated with, the Witnet Formation (Dibblee, 1959, 1967; Dibblee and Louke, 1970). The age of the Witnet Formation is not definitely known, but it may correlate with the Goler Formation in the El Paso Mountains (Dibblee and Louke, 1970), which is Paleocene to early Eocene (and possibly as old as latest Cretaceous) in age, as noted above.

The Witnet Formation, exposed both south and north of Tehachapi Valley, is folded into a NE-trending NW-vergent syncline, and locally the strata of the southeastern limb are overturned. The contact between the Witnet Formation of the southeast limb of the syncline and the adjacent granitic rocks west of Tehachapi Valley has been interpreted as a SE-dipping thrust fault called the Oil Canyon thrust (Smith, 1951; Buwalda, 1954; Michael, 1960) and as a folded depositional contact (Dibblee and Louke, 1970). South of Tehachapi Valley, the Witnet Formation appears to have been overthrust from the southeast and locally overturned along the Mendiburu Canyon fault (Wood et al., 1993; Wood, 1997). The deformation of the Witnet Formation in the Tehachapi Valley area is no younger than 17.6 Ma, which is the radiometric age of volcanic rocks in the middle part of the Kinnick Formation, which unconformably overlies the Witnet Formation (Evernden et al., 1964; Cox, 1987; Quinn, 1987).

The Tejon and San Emigdio formations unconformably overlie the crystalline rocks of the western end of the southern Sierra Nevada batholith along the southern margin of the San Joaquin Valley (Fig. 2). The Tejon and San Emigdio formations are composed largely of marine sandstone and shale beds that have an Eocene age (Nilsen et al., 1973; Nilsen, 1987a).

Exposure Depth of Rocks in the Southern Sierra Nevada

Regional geobarometric and geologic studies in the Sierra Nevada (Ague and Brimhall, 1988; Saleeby, 1990) indicate that most of the batholithic and framework rocks currently exposed south of about the latitude of Lake Isabella were intruded and/or metamorphosed at a deeper level in the crust than were the rocks exposed north of Lake Isabella (LI in Fig. 2). Estimates of the crustal depth represented by the current level of exposure in the central Sierra Nevada batholith north of the Lake Isabella area range from ~5 to 15 km (Ross, 1985; Bateman, 1992). North of Lake Isabella, the crystallization pressures of plutons determined from Al-in-hornblende barometry are mostly 3 to 4 kbar along the western margin of the batholith, and generally decrease eastward to values of 1 to 2 kbar along the eastern side of the batholith (Ague and Brimhall, 1988). The low pressures indicated for the eastern side of the batholith are consistent with the presence in that area of upper-crustal-level calderas and vent phases of the batholith (Saleeby, 1990).

In contrast, much of the batholith and its metasedimentary wall rocks south of the Lake Isabella area and north of the Garlock fault appears to have been emplaced and metamorphosed at pressures greater than ~3 to 4 kbar (Ague and Brimhall, 1988; Saleeby, 1990; Pickett and Saleeby, 1993; Dixon et al., 1994; Dixon, 1995; Ague, 1997) (Fig. 3). The deepest exposures of rocks in the Sierra Nevada are in the southernmost part of batholith in the western Tehachapi Mountains where the rocks were intruded and metamorphosed at pressures of 7 to 9 kbar, based on geobarometric studies (Sharry, 1981, 1982; Pickett and Saleeby, 1993;

Ague, 1997). On the basis of a synthesis of the available geobarometric and geologic data, Saleeby (1990) suggested that the exposure depth of the Sierra Nevada batholith increases progressively in a southward direction from shallow crustal levels north of Lake Isabella to deep crustal levels in the western Tehachapi Mountains, thus defining an apparent northwardtilted section of the batholithic crust. In contrast, the results of recent geobarometric studies in the southern Sierra Nevada suggest that the rocks from the Lake Isabella area southward to the Tehachapi Valley area were uplifted from crustal depths corresponding to pressures of ~5 to 8 kbar to crustal depths corresponding to pressures of ~1 to 4 kbar without appreciable tilting (Dixon et al., 1994; Dixon, 1995).

Examination of the available geobarometric data for the southern Sierra Nevada region, which are compiled in Figure 3, suggests that both of the above interpretations may be correct. There appears to be a longitudinal discontinuity or step in the observed pressures that approximately coincides with the N-trending proto–Kern Canyon fault zone, which is a Late Cretaceous, subvertical, reverse-dextral-sense ductile shear zone (Busby-Spera and Saleeby, 1990). West of the proto–Kern Canyon fault zone, pressures appear to increase southward more or less progressively from ~1 to 3 kbar near Lake Isabella to ~5 to 8 kbar in the vicinity of Tehachapi. East of the proto–Kern Canyon fault zone, peak pressures in the batholith appear to be moderately high, ~5 to 7 kbar throughout most of the region from Lake Isabella southward to the Tehachapi area. This pattern in the regional geobarometric data is consistent with the observation of Saleeby and Busby-Spera (1986) and Busby-Spera and Saleeby (1990) that there is an abrupt eastward increase in depth of exposure across the proto–Kern Canyon fault zone in the Lake Isabella area. They noted that peperitic textures in ~100 Ma hypabyssal volcanic rocks in Erskine Canyon west of the fault zone indicated nearsurface emplacement, whereas contact metamorphism in the aureole of a ~100 Ma pluton on the eastern side of the fault zone occurred at pressures of ~3 kbar, according to work by Elan (1985). The geobarometric data of Dixon et al. (1994) and Dixon (1995) suggest a more pronounced step in depth of exposure across the proto–Kern Canyon fault zone.

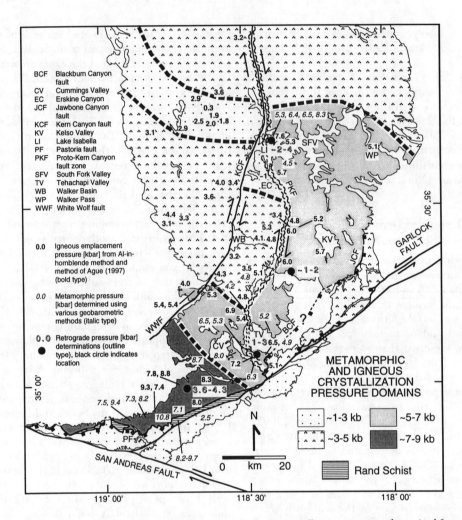

BCF   Blackburn Canyon
      fault
CV   Cummings Valley
EC   Erskine Canyon
JCF   Jawbone Canyon
      fault
KCF   Kern Canyon fault
KV   Kelso Valley
LI   Lake Isabella
PF   Pastoria fault
PKF   Proto-Kern Canyon
      fault zone
SFV   South Fork Valley
TV   Tehachapi Valley
WB   Walker Basin
WP   Walker Pass
WWF   White Wolf fault

0.0 Igneous emplacement
         pressure [kbar] from Al-in-
         hornblende method and
         method of Ague (1997)
         (bold type)

0.0   Metamorphic pressure
         [kbar] determined using
         various geobarometric
         methods (italic type)

●*0.0*   Retrograde pressure [kbar]
         determinations (outline
         type), black circle indicates
         location

METAMORPHIC
AND IGNEOUS
CRYSTALLIZATION
PRESSURE DOMAINS

~1-3 kb   ~5-7 kb
~3-5 kb   ~7-9 kb

Rand Schist

N

0   km   20

Fig. 3. Compilation of peak metamorphic pressures and igneous crystallization pressures determined for wall rocks and plutons in the southernmost part of the Sierra Nevada batholith. The ~1 kbar pressure estimate at Erskine Canyon is based on evidence for shallow-level emplacement of 105 Ma volcanic rocks (Busby-Spera and Saleeby, 1990). Over part of its length, the proto–Kern Canyon fault zone appears to mark an abrupt discontinuity between higher-pressure rocks to the east and lower-pressure rocks to the west. Pressures that are interpreted to be retrograde have been determined in four different areas. Sources of geobarometric data include Kim (1972), Haase and Rutherford (1975), Sharry (1981), Elan (1985), Ague and Brimhall (1988), Pickett and Saleeby (1993), Dixon et al. (1994), Dixon (1995), and Ague (1997).

The distribution of aluminosilicate minerals in the wall rocks of the southern Sierra Nevada batholith is generally consistent with the regional geobarometric data, in the sense that andalusite appears to be restricted primarily to the areas of lowest pressure. If the upper stability limit of andalusite is taken to be ~4 kbar (Holdaway, 1971) then the presence of andalusite in the wall rocks implies metamorphic pressures of ~4 kbar or less. East of the proto–Kern Canyon fault zone, andalusite is present only in the Lake Isabella region, where it coexists with sillimanite (Ross, 1990); west of that fault zone, andalusite is present only as far south as the latitude of Walker Basin, where it mostly occurs in the Pampa Schist exposed directly west of Walker Basin (Dibblee and Chesterman, 1953; Ross, 1989b). These occurrences of andalusite are significant in that they are generally consistent with geobarometric data from the same areas that indicate metamorphic and igneous emplacement pressures of mostly 4 to 5 kbar or less (Fig. 3). Everywhere else in the wall rocks of the southern Sierra Nevada batholith north of the Garlock fault, sillimanite is the only aluminosilicate found, except for one locality in the western Tehachapi Mountains, where white mica appears to have pseudomorphed kyanite (Pickett and Saleeby, 1993). Andalusite is largely absent in the areas of the batholith where geobarometric data indicate metamorphic and emplacement pressures greater than 4 to 5 kbar (Fig. 3). South of the Garlock fault in the southern Tehachapi Mountains, andalusite is abundant in pelitic rocks of the Bean Canyon Formation (Ross, 1989b), which is consistent with the metamorphic pressure estimate of 2 to 3 kbar for those rocks (Haase and Rutherford, 1975; Sharry, 1981, 1982).

Age of Decompression in the Southern Sierran Region

From the above review of geobarometric data, it is apparent that the Sierra Nevada batholith south of the Lake Isabella region and east of much of the proto–Kern Canyon fault zone has been exhumed to a greater degree than has the batholith to the north and west, and there is evidence that suggests that much of this unroofing took place in Late Cretaceous time (Fig. 3). Pickett and Saleeby (1993) inferred that ~15 km of unroofing, corresponding to a decrease from peak metamorphic pressures of ~8 kbar to retrograde (?) pressures of ~4 kbar, took place in the western Tehachapi Mountains after the rocks were intruded at ~100 Ma and before ~87 Ma, which is the K-Ar biotite age of nearby rocks in the gneiss complex. Their inference is based on the observation that the 4 kbar gneisses record a temperature of ~590°C, which is well above the closure temperature of Ar in biotite. Fission-track ages of ~70 Ma on apatite and ~80 Ma on zircon from gneissic basement in the western Tehachapi Mountains (Naeser et al., 1990) suggest that the rocks at the surface today were within several kilometers of the surface by the end of the Cretaceous, assuming a geothermal gradient of ~30°C/km and a closure temperature of ~100°C for fission tracks in apatite. In addition, Dixon (1995)

suggested that the entire region of the Cretaceous batholith between Lake Isabella and Tehachapi may have been uplifted from depths with pressures of ~5 to 8 kbar to depths with pressures of ~1 to 4 kbar before the rocks cooled below ~500°C. $^{40}Ar/^{39}Ar$ apparent ages of hornblende from plutons and amphibolites in the southern Sierra Nevada range from 92 to 85 Ma (Dixon, 1995). If the 92 to 85 Ma $^{40}Ar/^{39}Ar$ apparent ages of hornblende in the rocks of the Lake Isabella and Tehachapi areas represent the time the rocks cooled through ~500°C, which is the approximate closure temperature for Ar in hornblende (Harrison, 1981), then that would suggest that the region had begun to decompress between 92 and 85 Ma (Dixon, 1995). Unroofing of the southernmost part of the batholith was completed by Eocene time, when the Tejon Formation was deposited unconformably on the high-pressure gneisses in the western Tehachapi Mountains at ~52 Ma (Nilsen, 1987b; Pickett and Saleeby, 1993).

Erosional or Extensional Unroofing?

The apparent rapid Late Cretaceous–Paleocene unroofing in the southern Sierra Nevada could have been accomplished by erosional and/or tectonic removal of the upper crust. One major problem with the notion of erosional removal of 15 to 30 km of crust from the southernmost part of the batholith between ~100 Ma and ~50 Ma is that nearby sedimentary deposits of that age are not nearly sufficiently voluminous to account for the missing material. The most likely resting place for much of the material eroded from the batholith is the Great Valley sequence of forearc-basin deposits (Mansfield, 1979; Ingersoll, 1983). The Cretaceous Great Valley sequence in the San Joaquin Valley region, however, is no thicker than ~10 to 12 km (Moxon, 1988), and it is thought to be absent south of the Bakersfield arch (Goodman and Malin, 1992) (BA in Fig. 1). Paleocene-Eocene rock units in the San Joaquin Valley do not appear to be thicker than ~2 km south of the latitude of Fresno (Bartow, 1987) (Fig. 1). The point of this discussion is not to attempt a detailed mass balance, which would be difficult because of the many uncertainties involved, but merely to point out that there appear to be first-

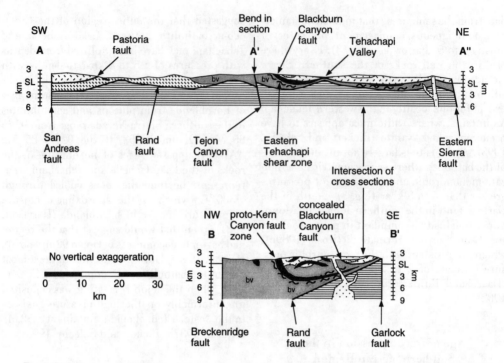

FIG. 4. Geologic cross sections through the southernmost Sierra Nevada, illustrating the low-angle orientation of most of the faults. Locations of the cross sections are shown in Figure 2. Section A-A″ trends approximately parallel to the Garlock fault and Section B-B′ trends at a high angle to the Garlock fault. Lithologic patterns are the same as those in Figure 2.

order problems with a model in which the southern Sierra Nevada batholith is unroofed solely by erosion in the Late Cretaceous. The alternative to erosional exhumation of the southern Sierra Nevada batholith is tectonic unroofing along a detachment fault system. A number of low-angle faults in the southern Sierra Nevada region are suggested to be part of a regional system of upper-crustal extensional faults along which a large part of the southern Sierra Nevada batholith was unroofed. These faults include the Blackburn Canyon fault, a fault in the Rand Mountains region, the Jawbone Canyon fault zone, and the Pastoria fault.

Extensional Faults in the Southern Sierra Nevada

Blackburn Canyon fault

The Blackburn Canyon fault is located in the eastern Tehachapi Mountains, south of Tehachapi Valley (Fig. 2), and it represents a

significant structural, petrologic, metamorphic, and isotopic break in the southern Sierra Nevada batholith (Wood, 1997). The fault is a N- to NE-trending, shallowly to moderately SE-dipping detachment fault with a gently undulating surface. It is truncated to the south by the Garlock fault, and to the north the fault is concealed by the alluvium of Tehachapi Valley. Two regional cross sections across the Blackburn Canyon fault are shown in Figure 4. Rocks in the footwall are upper-amphibolite-grade, ductilely deformed paragneiss and mostly gabbroic to tonalitic orthogneiss, whereas the hanging wall is composed of greenschist and lower-grade, dominantly cataclastically deformed rocks of mostly granodioritic composition (Wood et al., 1993; Wood, 1997). Present locally in the hanging-wall granodiorite are several NE-trending pendants (too small to show at the scale of Fig. 2) of silicic metavolcanic rocks with local hornfelsic textures. The Blackburn Canyon fault contact is sharp, and the base of the hanging wall usually consists of several meters of brownish green, hackly fracturing, mostly fine-grained granodiorite chloritic breccia that lies directly on the footwall. Slip lineations present in shear surfaces in the Blackburn Canyon fault zone are defined by smears of chlorite, elongate quartzofeldspathic aggregates, and striations. The lineations trend mostly to the southeast and south and have shallow southeast plunges. Kinematic indicators in the fault zone indicate that the latest direction of shearing along the fault was top to the south or southeast (Wood, 1997). The Blackburn Canyon fault also corresponds locally to the 0.706 initial Sr isopleth of Kistler and Ross (1990).

The age of the Blackburn Canyon fault is loosely constrained. The fault crosscuts tonalite gneiss in the footwall that appears to be continuous with the less deformed tonalite of Bear Valley Springs, which has a U-Pb zircon age of ~100 Ma (Saleeby et al., 1987). The Blackburn Canyon fault also is inferred to be younger than a locally cataclastically deformed granodiorite present in the hanging wall. The granodiorite has a preliminary U-Pb zircon age of ~90 Ma (J. B. Saleeby and D. J. Wood, unpubl. data). Much if not all of the activity along the fault most likely is older than dacite and felsite dikes in the area, which are inferred to be Miocene in age (Dibblee and Louke, 1970). Although none of the volcanic dikes that were mapped in detail clearly could be traced completely across the fault, several of the dikes intrude the brecciated granodiorite within a few meters of the fault and those dikes appear to be undeformed. A pre–early Miocene minimum age of activity along the Blackburn Canyon fault also is suggested by indirect structural evidence related to deformation of the Witnet Formation. The early Tertiary (?) Witnet Formation (Dibblee and Louke, 1970), composed mostly of conglomerate and arkosic sandstone, is unconformable on the hanging-wall rocks of the Blackburn Canyon fault, but it is not in visible contact with the fault (Fig. 2). The Witnet Formation appears to have been overthrust from the southeast and folded along the Mendiburu Canyon fault (MCF in Fig. 2), which projects to an intersection with the Blackburn Canyon fault zone. In the area where the two faults appear to intersect, Blackburn Canyon fault deformation fabrics are crosscut by top-to-the-NW shear surfaces inferred to be related to the deformation of the Witnet Formation. The

Witnet Formation exposed northeast of Tehachapi Valley is similarly deformed, and there the folded Witnet Formation is overlain by the lower Miocene Kinnick Formation along an angular unconformity (Dibblee and Louke, 1970; Quinn, 1987). A tuff bed in the middle part of the Kinnick Formation has been radiometrically dated at 17.6 Ma (Evernden et al., 1964; Cox, 1987; Quinn, 1987). Thus, activity along the Blackburn Canyon fault is inferred to have occurred between ~90 Ma and the start of Kinnick Formation deposition, which began prior to ~18 Ma.

The Blackburn Canyon fault exhibits a number of characteristics that suggest it is an extensional fault. First, it intersects the surface of the Earth when its trace is followed in a direction opposite to the direction of hanging-wall transport, which is a characteristic of true extensional faults according to the criteria of Wheeler and Butler (1994). Second, the fault places dominantly cataclastically deformed granitic rocks that locally have been deformed at greenschist-facies and lower temperatures structurally above severely and ductilely deformed gneisses that have been metamorphosed at upper-amphibolite facies and subsequently retrograded to greenschist facies. It is reasonable to interpret a fault that juxtaposes low-grade rocks above high-grade rocks as an extensional fault, although this should be considered as evidence and not as proof, as noted by Hodges and Walker (1992).

Third, there is some suggestion that the granitic and metavolcanic rocks in the hanging wall may have been emplaced and deformed at a higher level in the crust than were the footwall gneisses. Some of the silicic metavolcanic rocks in the upper plate of the Blackburn Canyon fault have a black-colored, aphanitic groundmass with a glassy appearance, which appears to be composed mostly of microcrystalline quartz grains less than 0.01 mm in diameter. The extremely fine grain size of the matrix in these rocks suggests that they cooled relatively rapidly after emplacement and have not been subjected to extensive metamorphic recrystallization since then. Rapid cooling of these metavolcanic rocks most likely would occur at a relatively shallow level in the batholithic crust. Elsewhere in the Sierra Nevada batholith, pendants of fine-grained, silicic, metavolcanic rocks commonly are present in regions where geobarometric data indicate that levels of the batholith corresponding to 1 to 3 kbar are exposed (Saleeby and Busby-Spera, 1986; Saleeby, 1990). A somewhat higher crystallization pressure of 5.1 kbar is indicated for a sample of granodiorite in the hanging wall (Fig. 3) on the basis of Al-in-hornblende barometry (Dixon, 1995). In contrast, geobarometric data on nearby footwall gneisses (Fig. 3) indicate that they crystallized and/or were metamorphosed in the mid- to lower crust at pressures of 5 to 8 kbar (Dixon, 1995). In summary, the orientation and transport direction of the Blackburn Canyon fault, the juxtaposition of low- to moderate-grade, cataclastically deformed rocks above high-grade, ductilely deformed rocks by the fault, and the evidence indicating that the hanging-wall rocks were deformed at a generally shallower crustal level than the footwall rocks all suggest that the Blackburn Canyon fault is an extensional fault.

Faults in the Rand Mountains area

Geologic studies of the Rand Mountains region south of the Garlock fault have documented a series of low-angle faults separating several thin plates of crystalline rock (Silver et al., 1984; Nourse and Silver, 1986; Silver and Nourse, 1986; Nourse, 1989). The structurally lowest fault of this Rand fault complex ("thrust" I of Silver and Nourse, 1986, and fault I of Nourse, 1989) is the Rand thrust (RF1 in Fig. 2), which separates mafic schist and metagraywacke in the footwall from multiply deformed, amphibolite-grade ortho- and paragneiss of the Johannesburg Gneiss in the hanging wall (Ehlig, 1968; Silver et al., 1984; Postlethwaite and Jacobson, 1987). Structurally above the Rand thrust fault on the southern side of the Rand Mountains is fault II of the Rand fault complex (RF2, Fig. 2); this is a low-angle, cataclastic, and locally mylonitic fault that juxtaposes high-grade Johannesburg Gneiss in its footwall against hanging-wall rocks composed of cataclastic hornblende-biotite-granodiorite deformed under greenschist facies (Nourse, 1989; Nourse and Silver, 1986; Silver and Nourse, 1986).

Kinematic analyses of structures and fabrics associated with fault II in the Rand Mountains indicate that the granodiorite in the upper plate was transported in a south to southeastward direction (Nourse, 1989; Nourse and Silver,

1986). Postlethwaite and Jacobson (1987) found that kinematic indicators in the thin sheet of mylonitic Johannesburg Gneiss between faults I and II in the southern Rand Mountains indicated a similar shear sense of top to the SSW, and they considered the shearing to be related to exhumation of the Rand Schist along fault I. Nourse (1989) inferred that the granodiorite, the Johannesburg Gneiss, and the Rand Schist were juxtaposed along faults II and I during the same S-vergent deformation event. According to this interpretation, the age of fault II in the Rand fault complex is constrained between the ~87 Ma age of the granodiorite in the upper plate and the ~79 Ma age of an undeformed, post-tectonic granodiorite stock that intrudes the Rand Schist and contains xenoliths of Johannesburg Gneiss (Nourse, 1989; Silver and Nourse, 1991). Fault II of the Rand fault complex is similar to the Blackburn Canyon fault in a number of respects. First, both faults place largely brittlely deformed greenschist-facies granodioritic rocks above high-grade paragneiss and orthogneiss. Second, the lower-plate rocks in the eastern Tehachapi Mountains and in the Rand Mountains both appear to have orthogneiss components with ages of ~100 Ma (Saleeby et al., 1987; Silver and Nourse, 1991). Third, the south to southeast direction of hanging-wall transport of the Blackburn Canyon fault is similar to the S- to SE-directed, upper-plate transport along fault II in the Rand Mountains.

Silver (1986) correlated the system of low-angle faults in the Rand Mountains with a similar sequence of low-angle faults exposed north of and along the Garlock fault in the southeastern Sierra Nevada. As in the Rand Mountains, fault II of the southern Sierra Nevada detachment fault system (SD2 in Fig. 2) juxtaposes cataclastic granodiorite structurally above high-grade mixed orthogneiss and paragneiss that is lithologically similar to the Johannesburg Gneiss (Silver, 1986; Nourse, 1989). The Blackburn Canyon fault is inferred to correlate with fault II of the detachment fault system in the southeastern Sierra Nevada based on lithologic similarities between the rocks in the upper and lower plates in both areas.

Jawbone Canyon fault zone

Another zone of faulting in the southernmost Sierra Nevada that has characteristics similar to the Blackburn Canyon fault is exposed in Jawbone Canyon in the southeastern Sierra Nevada and is referred to as the Jawbone Canyon fault zone (Fig. 2). In lower Jawbone Canyon, Samsel (1962) originally mapped the fault zone as a series of N- to NNE-trending, E-dipping, high-angle normal faults that locally juxtapose granodiorite on the west against downdropped Tertiary sedimentary and volcanic rocks to the east. He interpreted these normal faults to be segments of the Sierran fault system, which bounds the eastern side of the Sierra Nevada. Dibblee (1967) depicted the fault zone in lower Jawbone Canyon as an interval of crushed granodiorite, over 1 km wide in places, hosting numerous E-dipping faults, one of which has a dip of 30° to the east. Silver (1986) suggested that this zone of faulting in the Jawbone Canyon area may be part of the system of low-angle faults exposed adjacent to the Garlock fault discussed above. In contrast, Tennyson (1989) suggested that the normal faulting in the lower Jawbone Canyon area might be part of a regional episode of early Miocene extensional faulting. As shall be discussed in greater detail below, we believe that any Neogene activity along the Jawbone Canyon fault zone most likely represents relatively minor local reactivation of a regional detachment fault that was active principally during Late Cretaceous–Paleogene time.

The trace of the easternmost part of the Jawbone Canyon fault zone shown in Figure 2 is the E-dipping fault contact mapped by Dibblee (1967) north of Jawbone Canyon between crushed granodiorite to the east and quartz diorite and migmatitic gneiss to the west. The eastern Jawbone Canyon fault zone north of lower Jawbone Canyon juxtaposes hanging-wall granitic and granodioritic rocks that are locally overlain by Miocene(?)-age sedimentary and volcanic rocks above footwall rocks composed of mafic hornblende diorite (locally garnet bearing) and tonalite (Dibblee, 1967; Ross, 1989b). Reconnaissance examination of the fault zone in this area indicates that it is similar in some respects to the Blackburn Canyon fault. The hanging-wall granitic rocks north of lower Jawbone Canyon are extensively cataclasized and hydrothermally altered, and the footwall is composed of gneissic gabbro and tonalite, some of which has a subhorizontal foliation.

The location of the Jawbone Canyon fault zone immediately to the west of its intersection with lower Jawbone Canyon is uncertain, but exposed several kilometers to the west in upper Jawbone Canyon is a NE-trending, shallowly SE-dipping, detachment fault that may be the westward continuation of the Jawbone Canyon fault zone (D. J. Wood, unpubl. mapping). This fault in upper Jawbone Canyon (Fig. 2) juxtaposes amphibolitic and granitic gneiss in the footwall against sheared and fractured granodioritic rocks and the Witnet Formation in the hanging wall. The upper part of the footwall is extensively sheared and fractured, and adjacent to the fault, it commonly consists of up to several meters of light greenish, quartz-rich breccia. The fault zone itself is composed of up to 20 to 30 cm of brown to dark-gray microbreccia of unrecognizable protolith. The hanging wall adjacent to the fault consists of either granodioritic rocks stained a rusty red color or arkosic sandstone and conglomerate of the Witnet Formation. The Witnet Formation in the vicinity of the fault commonly is deformed by discrete shear surfaces, but it generally does not appear to be pervasively sheared or shattered. At one location, coarse-grained sandstone of the Witnet Formation, which in outcrop appears to be only moderately fractured, seems to unconformably rest directly on the microbreccia of the fault zone. Striations in the microbreccia and lineations defined by mineral smears in footwall shear surfaces have mostly NNW trends and they plunge shallowly (20 to 30°) to moderately (40 to 50°) to the SSE. Preliminary kinematic analysis of the fault zone, on the basis of the deflection of foliation into shear surfaces, indicates top-to-the-SSE shear sense.

The above-described detachment fault in upper Jawbone Canyon is inferred to be the westward continuation of the Jawbone Canyon fault zone that is exposed in lower Jawbone Canyon, on the basis of similarities in the character and orientation of the two faults. The connection between the inferred eastern and western segments of the Jawbone Canyon fault zone may correspond to the ENE-trending contact between quartz diorite gneiss and granodiorite that is partly concealed beneath alluvial deposits of Jawbone Canyon as shown by Dibblee (1967) and Ross (1989b). The break in the trace of the Jawbone Canyon fault shown in Figure 2 marks the location where the fault has not been mapped.

The northwest contact of the Witnet Formation and the trace of the detachment fault coincide for a distance of several kilometers along eastern exposures of the Witnet Formation in upper Jawbone Canyon (Fig. 2), but the location of the fault west of this area is not known. Similarities between the geology of the upper Jawbone Canyon area near the western Jawbone Canyon fault and the geology in the vicinity of the Blackburn Canyon fault south of Tehachapi Valley suggest that the two faults may be continuous and buried beneath the Kinnick, Bopesta, and Cache Peak formations (Figs. 2 and 4). In both areas, the Witnet Formation is deposited on the hanging wall of a NE-trending, SE-dipping, detachment fault. One difference between the two areas is that the Witnet Formation is not in visible contact with the Blackburn Canyon fault. South of Tehachapi Valley, this unit originally may have been in contact with the Blackburn Canyon fault, however, and subsequent deformation and erosion may have obliterated that relationship (Wood, 1997). As will be discussed later, deposition of the Witnet Formation may have been in a structural basin formed by the Blackburn Canyon and Jawbone Canyon faults.

Pastoria fault

The Pastoria fault in the western Tehachapi and San Emigdio Mountains (Fig. 2) is similar to the Blackburn Canyon fault in that it is a low-angle fault that juxtaposes cataclastically deformed granitic and granodioritic rocks structurally above high-grade, predominantly dioritic to tonalitic orthogneiss (Crowell, 1952; Ross, 1989b; Davis and Lagoe, 1988). Also like the Blackburn Canyon fault, the Pastoria fault represents an isotopic discontinuity, and it corresponds to the initial Sr 0.706 isopleth (Kistler and Ross, 1990). Sharry (1981, 1982) noted that the Pastoria fault appears to be a break between rocks from very different levels of the crust. Sharry correlated the rocks in the upper plate of the Pastoria fault with similar rocks in the southern Tehachapi Mountains south of the southern branch of the Garlock fault (Fig. 2) where the metasedimentary pendants were metamorphosed at a pressure of 2.5 kbar (Haase and Rutherford, 1975; Sharry, 1981). In contrast, north of the southern branch of the Garlock fault, the Rand Schist and mafic orthogneiss both were metamorphosed at pressures

of ~8 kbar (Pickett and Saleeby, 1993; Sharry, 1982). Silver (1983, 1986) correlated the Pastoria fault with the low-angle faults in the Rand Mountains and the southeastern Sierra Nevada that were described above. The Pastoria fault exhibits characteristics similar to the other low-angle detachment faults in the region and we agree with the suggested correlation of the Pastoria fault with these other structures.

The Pastoria fault dips to the south at ~20° toward the Garlock fault (Crowell, 1952), which suggests that it might be truncated and sinistrally offset at depth along the Neogene Garlock fault. The total slip on the western end of the Garlock fault is not well constrained, but similarities between the granodiorite of Lebec north of the fault and the granodiorite of Gato-Montes south of the fault led Ross (1989b) to suggest that the two units may be correlative. This would imply that the granodiorites have been sinistrally offset from one another along the Garlock fault by ~45 km. If the Pastoria fault also has been sinistrally offset ~45 km along the Garlock fault, then that would suggest that the granitic and metamorphic rocks south of the Garlock fault at the western end of the Mojave Desert in the southern Tehachapi Mountains might be underlain at depth by a low-angle fault. There is some indirect evidence that suggests such a low-angle fault does exist beneath the southern Tehachapi Mountains.

Low-angle faults have not been identified at the surface in the southern Tehachapi Mountains, but in a study of the geology in and around two tunnels of the California Aqueduct in the western and southern Tehachapi Mountains, Peters (1972) suggested that a low-angle fault underlies the Tehachapi Mountains south of the Garlock fault. The location of the aqueduct tunnels lies along section C-C' in Figure 2. Figure 5 is a cross section of the geology along the tunnel lines, modified from Peters (1972). Peters documented a moderately to shallowly SE-dipping fault zone in granite that is exposed in two test adits near the north portal of the C. V. Porter aqueduct tunnel, and he interpreted this fault zone as a thrust that flattens with depth to the south because the upper contact of the zone dips more shallowly to the south in the structurally lower of the two adits. In addition, based on study of drill logs from along the C. V. Porter tunnel line, Peters (1972) noted that

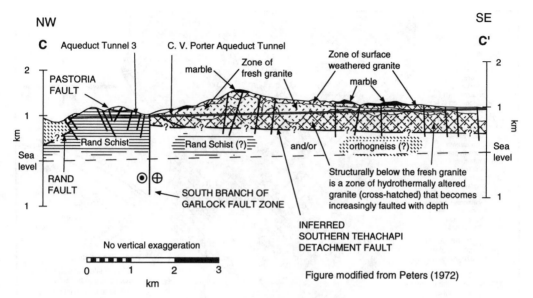

FIG. 5. Geologic cross section through the southern and western Tehachapi Mountains along the line of the California aqueduct tunnels (modified from Peters, 1972). Location of the cross section and lithologic patterns is shown in Figure 2. The cross-hatched pattern indicates granitic rock that is weathered or hydrothermally altered. The short, nearly vertical, heavy black lines in the cross section are steeply dipping fault zones. The existence and location of the southern Tehachapi detachment fault is inferred based on the observations of Peters (1972) and regional geologic relations as described in the text.

fresh granite encountered along the tunnel appears to be underlain by hydrothermally altered granite that becomes increasingly altered and faulted with depth (Fig. 5). Peters suggested that the alteration could be the result of hot fluids ascending along faults and shear surfaces developed after intrusion of the granite.

The increasing degree of fracturing and alteration with depth suggests that a post-batholith, low-angle detachment fault may underlie the southern Tehachapi Mountains south of the southern branch of the Garlock fault (Fig. 5). As noted above, this inferred low-angle fault may be the sinistrally offset continuation of the Pastoria fault. Although the Pastoria fault may have been a thrust during part of its history, the contrast in level of crustal exposure across the Pastoria fault, with probable low-pressure rocks structurally above high-pressure rocks (Sharry, 1981, 1982), is consistent with an interpretation of the Pastoria fault as an extensional fault similar to the Blackburn Canyon fault.

Source Region for Sierran Upper-Plate Rocks

The crystalline rocks in the southern Sierra Nevada region underlain by the low-angle faults discussed above are inferred to be out of place, as has been suggested previously (Silver, 1982, 1983). The current distribution of these allochthonous rocks is shown in Figure 6. On the basis of the apparent offset of petrologic, age, isotopic, and chemical zonation patterns in the batholithic rocks, Silver (1982, 1983) inferred that the out-of-place rocks were emplaced by W-vergent overthrusting, which suggests that the source region for the allochthonous rocks may lie to the east. In contrast, the kinematic and structural data from Wood (1993, 1997) indicate an episode of S- to SE-directed transport for rocks in the upper plate of the Blackburn Canyon detachment fault, which suggests that the source region for the hanging-wall rocks may be in the Sierra Nevada batholith to the north. The transport direction of upper-plate rocks along fault II in the Rand Mountains

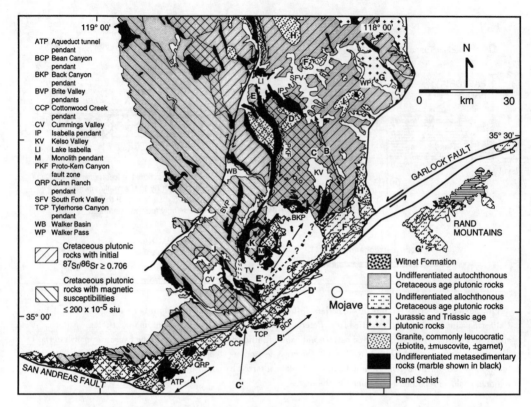

FIG. 6. Geologic map of the southern Sierra Nevada region showing plutonic rocks that are inferred to be in the hanging wall of a regional detachment fault system and out of place relative to regional geologic trends. Low-angle faults underlying the allochthonous rocks are shown by heavy lines with square teeth in the hanging wall. Discontinuous wavy lines indicate the location of ductile shear zones. As discussed in the text, certain geologic features of the hanging wall, labeled with bold, primed letters in the figure, are inferred to correlate with similar features exposed in the footwall that are labeled with the same bold letters. Cretaceous plutonic rocks, with Sr_i $\geq$0.706 (Kistler and Ross, 1990; Pickett and Saleeby, 1994) are shown by NE-trending hatching. The allochthonous rocks in the Rand Mountains are assumed to have Sr_i $\geq$0.706 on the basis of their correlation with similar rocks in the southeastern Sierra Nevada (Silver, 1986). Cretaceous plutonic rocks with magnetic susceptibilities $\leq$200 × 10⁻⁵ siu (standard international units) are from Ross (1989a) and are indicated by NW-trending hatching. Sources for the geology in this figure are the same as those for Figure 2.

also is to the south or southeast (Nourse, 1989; Nourse and Silver, 1986), and the direction of hanging-wall transport along the western Jawbone Canyon fault in upper Jawbone Canyon appears to be to the SSE as well. Although a source to the east for the allochthonous rocks cannot be ruled out at this time, additional geologic evidence discussed below supports a source location to the north.

The source area for the rocks in the upper plate of the Pastoria fault and the inferred allochthonous rocks in the southern Tehachapi Mountains south of the Garlock fault is suggested to be the region in the southern Sierra Nevada east of the proto–Kern Canyon fault zone, west of Kelso Valley, south of the Isabella pendant, and north of Tehachapi Valley (Fig. 6). Most of the Cretaceous plutonic rocks in those areas are characterized by Sr_i $\geq$0.706 (Kistler and Ross, 1990) and magnetic susceptibilities $\leq$200 × 10⁻⁵ siu (standard international units) (Ross, 1989a), as indicated by the cross-hatched pattern in Figure 6. The inferred allochthonous rocks in the southeastern Sierra Nevada and Rand Mountains are suggested to have originated from the area in the southern Sierra Nevada northeast of Kelso Valley, southwest of Walker Pass, and mostly southeast of

South Fork Valley. Both the footwall and hanging-wall Cretaceous plutonic rocks in those areas have $Sr_i \geq 0.706$ (Kistler and Ross, 1990) and most of the plutonic rocks in those areas also have magnetic susceptibilities $>200 \times 10^{-5}$ siu (Ross, 1989a).

There also are a number of specific geologic features in the allochthonous upper-plate rocks, labeled with bold primed letters in Figure 6, that may correlate with similar features exposed in the autochthonous rocks of the southern Sierra Nevada batholith, which are labeled with the same bold letters without the prime mark. The metasedimentary rocks in the Aqueduct Tunnel and Quinn Ranch pendants (A' in Fig. 6) may correlate with the metasedimentary rocks of the Monolith and Back Canyon pendants (A in Fig. 6). All four of these pendants are characterized by thick layers of marble, and they also are distinctive compared to other pendants in the southern Sierra Nevada batholith because most of their contacts are subhorizontal to shallowly dipping, as is much of the compositional layering of the rocks in the pendants (Wiese, 1950; Crowell, 1952; Troxel and Morton, 1962; Kim, 1972; Ross, 1989b). In addition, these four pendants are intruded by relatively large bodies of leucocratic (color index ≤ 5) biotite ($\pm$ garnet, $\pm$ muscovite) granite (Kim, 1972; Ross, 1989b), and the granite of Tejon Lookout (near A' in Fig. 6) may correlate with part of the granite of Tehachapi Airport (near A in Fig. 6). The REE abundances of the Tejon Lookout and Tehachapi Airport granites are similar (see Figure 75 in Ross, 1989b).

The steeply dipping Cottonwood Creek, Tylerhorse Canyon, and Bean Canyon metasedimentary pendants along the southern edge of the southern Tehachapi Mountains (near B' in Fig. 6) may have formerly occupied the gap between the Isabella pendant and the pendant south of Kelso Valley in the southern Sierra Nevada (near B in Fig. 6). The metasedimentary rocks in the Bean Canyon and Tylerhorse Canyon pendants lithologically resemble Upper Triassic rocks in the Mineral King pendant (Dunne et al., 1975; Rindosh, 1977). More recent work indicates that the metasedimentary rocks in both the Mineral King and Isabella pendants are part of the Triassic–Jurassic Kings Sequence (Saleeby and Busby, 1993). Ross (1989b) considered all of the rocks in the differ-

ent pendants of the southern Tehachapi Mountains to be part of the Bean Canyon Formation. Metasedimentary rocks of the Bean Canyon Formation were first described and named the Bean Canyon series by Simpson (1934); Dibblee (1963) renamed the rocks the Bean Canyon Formation.

The Bean Canyon Formation in the Tylerhorse Canyon and Bean Canyon pendants includes a prominent marble layer that is ~300 meters in thickness locally, thick intervals of psammitic and pelitic schist, calc-silicate hornfels, and various metamorphosed volcanic rocks including basalt, andesite, and dacite (Simpson, 1934; Dibblee, 1963; Dunne et al., 1975; Rindosh, 1977; Ross, 1989b). The age of this unit is poorly constrained. The metasedimentary rocks are intruded by plutons of presumed Cretaceous (?) age (Dunne et al., 1975), and Rb-Sr ages on dacitic metavolcanic rocks in the Bean Canyon pendant average ~150 Ma (R. A. Fleck, pers. commun. in Ross, 1989b). Poorly preserved macrofossils in the Bean Canyon Formation are not age diagnostic (Dunne et al., 1975). Map-scale fold axes or fold closures have not been observed in the Tylerhorse Canyon and Bean Canyon pendants, and fault repetition of section cannot be ruled out (Rindosh, 1977); lack of a clear stratigraphic or structural-up direction in the Bean Canyon Formation makes correlation difficult. There do, however, appear to be a number of lithologic similarities between the Bean Canyon Formation and the Triassic–Jurassic Kings Sequence in the Isabella pendant.

The Bean Canyon Formation and the rocks of the Kings Sequence in the Isabella pendant both are characterized by abundant marble with some layers ranging up to ~300 m in thickness (Rindosh, 1977; Saleeby and Busby, 1993). Metamorphosed basalt layers, up to ~100 m thick, are present in the Bean Canyon pendant (Dibblee, 1963), and a layer of amphibolitic mafic volcanic rocks several hundred meters thick is present in the Kings Sequence north of Lake Isabella (Saleeby and Busby, 1993). Both the Bean Canyon Formation and the Kings Sequence in the Kern Canyon pendant also host a distinctive marble horizon containing lenses and boudins of amphibolite that is adjacent to a section of white and grey quartz-rich gneiss (Rindosh, 1977; Saleeby and Busby-Spera, 1986). Finally, Late Triassic to Early Jurassic

Weyla bivalves that have been found in the Isabella pendant are from a calcareous quartzite unit immediately adjacent to a thick Late Triassic (?) marble, and the localities of the poorly preserved fossils in the Tylerhorse Canyon pendant are in a calc-silicate hornfels, quartzite, and marble-bearing unit that is adjacent to a 300-m-thick marble layer (Rindosh, 1977; Saleeby and Busby, 1993).

Between the Cottonwood Creek and Tylerhorse Canyon pendants at C′ (Fig. 6), small bodies of mafic granodiorite and hornblende diorite are engulfed in the granodiorite of Gato-Montes (Dibblee, 1963; Ross, 1989b). A localized exposure of dark granodiorite, gabbro, and mafic-inclusion-rich granodiorite within the Claraville granodiorite at C (Fig. 6) (Ross, 1989b) in the autochthonous rocks of the Sierra Nevada is suggested to correlate with the mafic rocks in the upper plate at C′ (Fig. 6).

One or more of the small bodies of felsic, coarse-grained, biotite granite of Tejon Lookout located near the eastern end of the basement rock exposures south of the Garlock fault and which locally intrude metasedimentary rocks of the Bean Canyon Formation (Ross, 1989b) near D′ (Fig. 6) may correlate with part of the felsic, coarse-grained, biotite granite of Bob Rabbit Canyon (Ross, 1990), which is located adjacent to the Isabella pendant southeast of Lake Isabella at D (Fig. 6).

The small pendants of silicic metavolcanic rocks found near E′ (Fig. 6) in the upper plate of the Blackburn Canyon fault may be related to the ~100 Ma Erskine Canyon and related rhyolitic volcanic rocks exposed west of the proto–Kern Canyon fault in the Lake Isabella area near E (Fig. 6) (Busby-Spera and Saleeby, 1990; Saleeby and Busby-Spera, 1986). The lack of exposures of the mid-Cretaceous Erskine Canyon silicic volcanic rocks east of the proto–Kern Canyon fault zone in the Lake Isabella area may be because they were removed by upper-crustal detachment faulting. Samples of the ~100 Ma metavolcanic rocks from the Piute Lookout area south of Lake Isabella resemble the metavolcanic rocks from the eastern Tehachapi Mountains, although the age of the Tehachapi area metavolcanic rocks is not known.

The small granite plug of Lone Tree Canyon that intrudes the granodiorite of Claraville (Ross, 1989b) in the allochthonous upper-plate rocks at F′ (Fig. 6) may be the offset equivalent

of the granite of Onyx (Ross, 1990) located at F (Fig. 6). Ross (1989b) described the granite of Lone Tree Canyon near the Garlock fault as a fine-grained, aplitic-textured, biotite granite and noted that it is very similar in appearance and composition to the small body of Onyx granite that is located ~50 km north, east of Lake Isabella in South Fork Valley.

Within the granitic rocks in the southern Rand Mountains at G′ (Fig. 6), there is a small exposure of gneissic rocks as well as several larger exposures of hornblende diorite (Dibblee, 1967). The hornblende diorite and the gneiss in the Rand Mountains may correlate with the Summit gabbro and the locally strongly foliated quartz diorite of Walker Pass, respectively, in the vicinity of Walker Pass at location G (Fig. 6) (Miller and Webb, 1940; Ross, 1990). The Summit gabbro and Walker Pass quartz diorite are probable Jurassic to Triassic plutonic rocks in the dominantly Cretaceous southern Sierra Nevada batholith (Ross, 1990). The Jurassic and Triassic rocks also may be present along strike from the exposures in the Sierra Nevada beneath the alluvial deposits southeast of the Sierran frontal fault, so the potential source area for the possibly correlative rocks in the Rand Mountains is relatively large.

The large exposure of leucocratic (<5% biotite) granite of Bishop Ranch (Ross, 1989b) in the upper plate at H′ (Fig. 6) may be offset from the biotite-bearing felsic granite of Long Meadow that is located north of South Fork Valley at H (Fig. 6) (Ross, 1990). The mass of Bishop Ranch leucogranite at I′ (Fig. 6) in the upper plate may match the body of Onyx granite found southwest of Walker Pass at I (Fig. 6).

The possible correlations above support the hypothesis that the allochthonous rocks in the southern Sierra Nevada region originated from a position structurally above the current southeastern Sierra Nevada batholith. Removal of the upper crust in this area by extensional faulting also is consistent with the geobarometric evidence reviewed earlier, which indicates that the southern Sierra Nevada batholith east of the proto–Kern Canyon fault zone has been exhumed from a deeper level than has the batholith to the north and west. We speculate that formation of the relatively broad, ENE-trending South Fork Valley, which is restricted to the area east of Lake Isabella (Fig. 6), may be indirectly related to extensional removal of the upper crust above it and to the southeast. The valley may be located in the area where a mid-crustal subhorizontal detachment in the south-eastern Sierra Nevada ramped up to the north to a breakaway zone at the surface located north of the valley. Isostatic rebound of the footwall in the vicinity of the breakaway zone, as described by Wernicke and Axen (1988), may have caused fragmentation of the rocks along steeply dipping faults and cataclastic cleavages, thus making the rocks more susceptible to later erosion. Late E- to NE-trending, steeply-dipping non-penetrative cleavage and fractures locally present in basement rocks north of Lake Isabella (D. J. Wood, unpubl. mapping) may be structures that formed in response to footwall uplift.

Location of Southwestern Sierra Nevada Upper Crust

The rocks east of the proto–Kern Canyon fault that are inferred to have been unroofed along the detachment fault system were metamorphosed and/or emplaced at pressures of ~5 to 7 kbar (Fig. 3). If the ~5 to 9 kbar rocks exposed in the southwestern Sierra Nevada batholith also were unroofed along extensional faults, then the upper-plate rocks might be found nearby. Silver (1982) suggested that the granitic rocks of the northern 150 to 200 km of the Salinian block were removed from the upper levels of the eastern side of the southern Sierra Nevada batholith by W-directed overthrusting prior to displacement along the San Andreas fault system. Based on similarities between their metamorphic and plutonic histories, James (1992) suggested that Cretaceous basement rocks in the Santa Cruz Mountains of the northern Salinian block may have evolved along strike to the south from rocks exposed north of Tehachapi Valley in the southern Sierra Nevada prior to being displaced westward to the Salinian block. In view of these earlier studies, it is worthwhile to consider whether or not the rocks of the northern Salinian block might have originated from a position structurally above the southwestern part of the Sierra Nevada batholith.

Figure 7A is a palinspastic reconstruction of the northern Salinian block and the southwesternmost Sierra Nevada region for early Miocene time, showing the relative positions of exposures of crystalline basement rocks prior to disruption by the San Andreas fault system and the Garlock fault. Strike-slip displacements on the faults of the San Andreas system and the Garlock fault have been removed while holding the Mojave Desert area fixed. In the figure, dextral displacement of 315 km has been restored along the main strand of the San Andreas fault, on the basis of the offset of the Pinnacles and Neenach volcanic formations (Matthews, 1976).

About 45 km of sinistral displacement has been restored on the western Garlock fault in order to align similar granodiorites on opposite sides of the fault (Ross, 1989b). To close the triangular gap between the San Emigdio Mountains and the southern Tehachapi Mountains that results from restoration of the Garlock fault, the San Emigdio Mountains were rotated ~40° counterclockwise to bring the ranges adjacent to one other. Restoring this amount of rotation is compatible with paleomagnetic data that indicate that early Miocene (23 Ma) basalts in the San Emigdio Mountains have been rotated 44° clockwise since they were erupted (Graham et al., 1990; Goodman and Malin, 1992). Clockwise rotation of the basalt in the San Emigdio Mountains has been assumed to have occurred prior to 16 Ma, based on comparisons with paleomagnetic studies in the Mojave and Tehachapi Valley areas (Graham et al., 1990; Goodman and Malin, 1992). Goodman and Malin, however, suggested that clockwise rotation of the San Emigdio Mountains may have occurred after 16 Ma, so the rotation might have been coeval with motion along the Garlock fault, which may have started ~10 Ma (Burbank and Whistler, 1987; Loomis and Burbank, 1988).

Another difficulty with unslipping ~45 km of displacement along the Garlock fault is that a "hole" is created adjacent to the San Andreas fault. Restoring ~19 km of Pliocene and Quaternary shortening along the Pleito thrust (Fig. 1) and related faults in the southern San Joaquin Valley (Namson and Davis, 1988) while back-rotating the San Emigdio Mountains would fill some of that gap, and there may be unrecognized structures that could be retro-deformed to fill the gap. Straightening the trace of the San Andreas fault in the vicinity of its

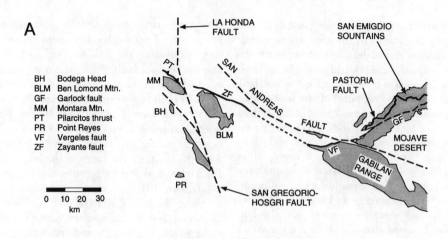

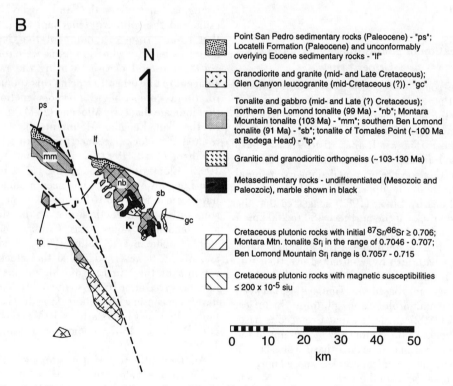

Fig. 7. A. Basement rocks of the northern Salinian block and southwestern Sierra Nevada palinspastically restored to pre–San Andreas fault system (earliest Miocene) configuration. The Mojave Desert region is held fixed in the restoration. The prerestoration disposition of the basement rocks is shown in Figure 1. See text for a description of the reconstruction. B. Earliest Miocene palinspastic restoration of basement rocks of the northern Salinian block showing the geology (Leo, 1967; Ross and Brabb, 1973; Nilsen, 1981; Ross, 1984; Wakabayashi and Moores, 1988), the U-Pb zircon ages of plutonic rocks (in parentheses after unit name in legend) (James and Mattinson, 1985; James, 1992), the initial strontium ratios of plutons (Mattinson, 1990; Kistler and Champion, 1991), and the magnetic susceptibility of the plutons (Ross, 1989a). The lithologic patterns are the same as those in Figure 2 for the southernmost Sierra Nevada. The crystalline basement rocks of the Salinian block are inferred to be underlain by low-angle faults at depth (Silver, 1982, 1983; Hall, 1991). Compare this figure with the region in Figures 2 and 5 that is in the vicinity of Walker Basin, Cummings Valley, and Tehachapi Valley.

juncture with the Garlock fault in a palinspastic restoration also might alleviate some of the misfit problem.

Displacement along two faults of the San Andreas system that are present within the northern Salinian block has been restored in Figure 7A. The granitic rocks from Bodega Head to Point Reyes have been brought southward by restoring 150 km of slip along the San Gregorio–Hosgri fault zone (Ross, 1984). During activity along the San Gregorio–Hosgri fault, 40 km of its slip is inferred to have passed inboard of Montara Mountain along the now-buried La Honda fault (Champion, 1989; Champion and Kistler, 1991; Powell, 1993). Forty kilometers of dextral displacement along the La Honda fault has been restored in Figure 7A in order to align plutonic basement rocks that have similar compositions and ages (Ross, 1984; James and Mattinson, 1985), and to align distinctive isotopic patterns in the plutonic rocks (Champion, 1989; Champion and Kistler, 1991).

The geology of the early Miocene palinspastically restored crystalline basement rocks of the northern Salinian block (Fig. 7B) is remarkably similar to the geology of the southern Sierra Nevada in the vicinity of Tehachapi and Cummings valleys (Fig. 2). The plutonic rocks at Montara Mountain, northern Ben Lomond Mountain, and Bodega Head (indicated by J' in Fig. 7B) are all hornblende biotite tonalites (Leo, 1967; Ross, 1984) that have similar U-Pb zircon ages of 99 to 103 Ma (James and Mattinson, 1985; James, 1992). In the southern Sierra Nevada, the tonalite of Bear Valley Springs (in the vicinity of J in Fig. 6) is compositionally similar to the northern Salinian block tonalites, and it also has a similar range in U-Pb zircon ages of 97 to 101 Ma (Saleeby et al., 1987). The northern Ben Lomond tonalite in the Salinian block and the tonalite of Bear Valley Springs in the southern Sierra Nevada also are similar in that they both are characterized by abundant decimeter-scale, elongate, flattened mafic inclusions, and both are associated with ~100-Ma comagmatic gabbro intrusives (Leo, 1967; James, 1992; Sams and Saleeby, 1988).

The sequence and ages (where known) of the rocks exposed at Ben Lomond Mountain appear to be a good match to the rocks exposed immediately north of Tehachapi Valley as noted by James (1992). At Ben Lomond Mountain (see locality K' in Fig. 7A) a screen of metasedimen-tary rocks that hosts bodies of granitic orthogneiss of 103 to 130 Ma is located between 103 Ma northern Ben Lomond tonalite to the west and 91 Ma southern Ben Lomond tonalite to the east; east of the 91 Ma tonalite are more metasedimentary rocks followed by exposures of the Glen Canyon leucocratic granite (James, 1992). North of Tehachapi Valley, at locality K in Figure 6, a screen of metasedimentary rocks that contains the 117 Ma granitic augen gneiss of Tweedy Creek separates ~100 Ma Bear Valley Springs tonalite on the west from the 90 Ma "granodiorite" of Claraville on the east (Saleeby et al., 1987). The sample of Claraville granodiorite dated at 90 Ma is from an area shown as granodiorite on most maps, but more recent mapping indicates that much of the rock in that area is tonalite (Fig. 2) (D. J. Wood, unpubl. data). East of the Claraville granodiorite/tonalite are more screens of metasedimentary rocks that are intruded on the east by the Tehachapi Airport leucogranite (Ross, 1989b).

The plutonic rocks of the northern Salinian block have similar patterns in initial $^{87}Sr/^{86}Sr$ values as do the rocks of the southern Sierra Nevada batholith in the Tehachapi Valley area (compare Fig. 6 with Fig. 7B). Initial $^{87}Sr/^{86}Sr$ values (Fig. 6) for most of the large Bear Valley Springs tonalite pluton (Fig. 2) range from 0.7043 to less than 0.706, except in the vicinity of Cummings Valley, where there is a local increase in values to at least as high as 0.7064 (Kistler and Ross, 1990; Pickett and Saleeby, 1994). Similarly, measurements of initial $^{87}Sr/^{86}Sr$ of the tonalite plutons in the northern Salinian block range from 0.7046 to at least 0.707 (James and Mattinson, 1985; Kistler and Champion, 1991). The low magnetic susceptibility of the plutonic rocks in the northern Salinian block (Fig. 7B) also is similar to the magnetic susceptibility of the plutons in the Tehachapi Valley area (Ross, 1989a).

In summary, the geology, the initial $^{87}Sr/^{86}Sr$, and the magnetic susceptibility values of the basement rocks in the northern Salinian block all appear to be compatible with the rocks having been derived from a position structurally above the southern Sierra Nevada batholith in the vicinity of Tehachapi and Cummings valleys. Exposed structures along which the northern Salinian block rocks might have been transported from the Sierra Nevada region have not been found, but low-angle faults are inferred to exist in the subsurface (Silver, 1982, 1983; Hall, 1991). The Lower and Middle Cretaceous orthogneisses of the western Tehachapi Mountains gneiss complex (Fig. 2) were metamorphosed at 7 to 9 kbar (Fig. 3), and uppercrustal rocks formerly overlying them also may have been removed along detachment faults. There do not appear to be any presently exposed rocks in the southern Sierra Nevada and northern Salinian regions that may be upper-plate correlatives of those gneisses, however. The locations where these inferred missing upperplate rocks might be found are discussed in a later section of this paper.

Tectonic Significance of Paleogene Sedimentary Deposits

Two hypotheses have been proposed prior to this study regarding the origin and tectonic significance of the Witnet and Goler formations. Based on the alignment of the exposures of the Goler and Witnet close to and parallel to the Garlock fault and the coarseness, composition, and thickness of these formations, Nilsen and Clarke (1975) suggested that the sediments may have been deposited in fault-bounded, strike-slip basins that formed during activity along a proto-Garlock fault in the Early Tertiary. Hewett (1954, 1955) suggested that the Mojave Desert region underwent major uplift in the early Tertiary, and Cox (1987) proposed that the Witnet and Goler formations may have been deposited in a NE-trending tectonic basin that was located along the northern margin of this uplifted region. Cox (1987) noted that subsidence of the basin may have resulted from northward overthrusting of the Mojave Desert block.

Another model for the deposition of the Witnet Formation (and the Goler Formation as well) is suggested here based on the recent recognition of the Blackburn Canyon detachment fault in the eastern Tehachapi Mountains (Wood, 1997). The proximity of the Witnet Formation deposits to the Blackburn Canyon and Jawbone Canyon faults leads to speculation that the faults might have created the basin into which the sediments were deposited. The Witnet Formation is deposited on the hanging wall of the Blackburn Canyon and western Jawbone Canyon faults, and locally the Witnet

Formation appears to be unconformable on the Jawbone Canyon fault. Sedimentary basins formed in the hanging wall adjacent to detachment faults, sometimes referred to as supradetachment basins, commonly are characterized by a half-graben geometry, basin elongation normal to the hanging-wall transport direction, and the presence of coarse-grained, high-gradient alluvial fan deposits and rockavalanche or gravity slide–block deposits (Fedo and Miller, 1992; Fillmore et al., 1994; Friedmann et al., 1994).

The Witnet basin exhibits some of the characteristics of a supradetachment basin. Although the Witnet Formation is not now in visible contact with the Blackburn Canyon fault, and thus cannot unequivocally be demonstrated to have been deposited in a half-graben basin, it may have been in contact with the fault in the past and subsequently has been removed by erosion, for which there is ample evidence in the unconformity between the Witnet and Kinnick formations (Dibblee and Louke, 1970). The Witnet Formation in upper Jawbone Canyon, however, does exhibit some evidence of being deposited in a half-graben basin. The Witnet Formation in that area is deposited on the hanging wall of the western Jawbone Canyon fault, and locally it appears to be unconformable on the fault zone, as discussed earlier (Fig. 2). The northeast trend of the Witnet Basin appears to be oriented normal to the approximate SSE direction of transport for the upper plate of the Blackburn Canyon detachment fault, which is one of the characteristics of a supradetachment basin (Fillmore et al., 1994). The upper-plate transport direction for the detachment fault in upper Jawbone Canyon also appears to be to the SSE as noted earlier. Finally, the local coarse-grained, conglomeratic character of the Witnet Formation (Michael, 1960; Dibblee and Louke, 1970) is consistent with interpretation of the formation as a supradetachment basin deposit.

The timing of deposition of the Witnet Formation, relative to activity on the Blackburn Canyon fault, is not directly constrained because the formation is not in visible contact with the fault. Deposition of the Witnet Formation in the eastern Tehachapi Mountains at least locally appears to postdate cataclastic deformation and chloritic alteration of the underlying granodiorite, which may have occurred during activity along the Blackburn Canyon fault. At one locality near the contact between the grano-diorite and the overlying basal conglomerate of the Witnet Formation, the granodiorite clearly is altered and cataclastically deformed, whereas the nearby Witnet Formation appears to be undeformed and unaltered (Wood, 1997). The relationship of this unit to the detachment fault in upper Jawbone Canyon suggests that some of it was deposited after much of the activity on the fault. At one locality, Witnet Formation that appears to be only moderately deformed rests directly on a layer of microbreccia over 20 cm thick that is present along the fault. Local shear surfaces and fractures in the Witnet Formation near the Jawbone Canyon fault suggest that some activity along the fault zone occurred after—or perhaps during—its deposition.

The Goler Formation also may have been deposited in a supradetachment basin, but the northern margin of the Goler Basin and any detachment fault that might bound it are not exposed. Cox (1987) inferred that the Goler Basin was bounded on the north by a fault. He noted that the generally N-trending Sierra Nevada fault changes to an anomalous north-east trend northwest of the Goler Formation exposures (Fig. 2), and suggested that an ancient fault that bounded the north side of the Goler Basin may have controlled the location of the NE-trending segment of the modern Sierra Nevada fault. There is some evidence that suggests indirectly that the El Paso Mountains may be underlain by an ancient, low-angle detach-ment. Nitchman (1989) proposed that the El Paso fault along the southeastern margin of the range (Fig. 2) is a NW-dipping thrust fault that shallows in dip with depth and was active in the Neogene. The El Paso fault may be a latest Cretaceous to early Eocene, low-angle detach-ment fault that was reactivated as a thrust fault during regional late Cenozoic contractional deformation. Assuming that the basement rocks of the El Paso Mountains and the Goler Forma-tion are in the upper plate of a shallowly SE-dipping detachment, the location of this hypo-thetical fault, concealed beneath the alluvial deposits of Indian Wells Valley, is shown in Figure 2. It appears unlikely that displacement along this inferred fault is great. Restoring ~14 to 15 km of displacement on such a fault by moving the El Paso Mountains due north would result in slightly better alignment of the

screens of metasedimentary rocks and exposures of Triassic and Jurassic plutons exposed in the El Paso Mountains with their possible along-strike counterparts in the east-ern Sierra Nevada. By analogy with the other hanging-wall and footwall geologic correlations in the southern Sierra Nevada, it may also be the case that the rocks in the El Paso Mountains originated structurally above the eastern Sierra Nevada rocks and were transported in a south-eastward direction to their current location.

Synthesis and Discussion

Timing of detachment faulting and disaggrega-tion of the southern Sierra Nevada

A review of direct and indirect evidence for the age of detachment faulting and tectonic disruption of the southern Sierra Nevada batho-lith reveals that it may have been ongoing for a period of 30 to 40 million years, from the Late Cretaceous to the early Eocene. As discussed earlier, the Blackburn Canyon fault was active between ~90 Ma and the early Miocene deposi-tion of the Kinnick Formation in the area. If the Witnet Formation is comparable in age to the nearby and lithologically similar Paleocene-lower Eocene Goler Formation, as has been suggested in other studies, then the relation-ship of the Witnet Formation to the western Jawbone Canyon fault in upper Jawbone Can-yon described earlier suggests that much of the activity along that fault may have occurred prior to and during the Paleocene. Fault II of the Rand fault complex in the Rand Mountains, located between the ~100 Ma Johannesburg Gneiss and the structurally overlying, cata-clastically deformed 87 Ma Atolia granodiorite, is inferred to have been active between 87 Ma and 79 Ma (Nourse, 1989; Silver and Nourse, 1991). The Pastoria fault in the San Emigdio Mountains is younger than the 98 Ma U-Pb zircon age of the Brush Mountain granite in the upper plate of the fault (James, 1986), and the fault is older than the middle to upper Eocene Tejon and San Emigdio formations, which unconformably overlap the fault (Davis and Lagoe, 1988).

Transport of the crystalline basement rocks of the northern Salinian block (Figs. 1 and 7) to a position west of the southern Sierra Nevada is inferred to have occurred after intrusion of the

91 Ma southern Ben Lomond tonalite pluton (James, 1992), the youngest dated pluton in the area. Final emplacement of the northern Salinian block basement in a position west of the Sierra Nevada batholith most likely occurred prior to deposition of the Eocene Butano Sandstone in the area, as has been suggested by Hall (1991). In the northern Salinian block (Fig. 7B), the Paleocene Locatelli Formation is unconformable on the inferred upper-plate northern Ben Lomond tonalite, and the Paleocene rocks in turn are unconformably overlain by the Eocene Butano Sandstone (Nilsen, 1981). The Butano Sandstone has been inferred to correlate across the San Andreas fault with the Point of Rocks Sandstone in the southern San Joaquin Valley (Clarke and Nilsen, 1973). The paleolatitude of the Butano Sandstone determined from paleomagnetic study in conjunction with the above correlation ties the sandstone and the underlying northern Salinian block to the position that is shown in Figure 8A by the early Eocene or ~54 Ma (Kanter, 1988). Thus, transport of the northern Salinian block along detachment faults from an original position inferred to have been structurally above the southwestern Sierra Nevada batholith most likely was complete by the beginning of Eocene time.

As discussed earlier, there also is indirect control on the age of the exhumation in the southern Sierra Nevada. Dixon et al. (1994) and Dixon (1995) documented a decompression event from 5 to 8 kbar to 1 to 4 kbar in the Lake Isabella and Tehachapi regions of the southern Sierra Nevada batholith that occurred at temperatures $\geq$~500°C. Assuming that the Blackburn Canyon and related extensional faults are responsible for this exhumation of the southeastern Sierra Nevada, and if the hornblende $^{40}Ar/^{39}Ar$ apparent ages of 83 to 91 Ma on amphibolites and plutons east of the proto–Kern Canyon fault zone (Dixon, 1995) are interpreted as the time the rocks cooled through ~500°C, then the extensional unroofing of the batholith most likely began between 91 and 83 Ma. This age range overlaps the firm, maximum age of 87 Ma for fault II in the Rand Mountains. As summarized earlier, there is a ~3 kbar difference in the level of exposure of rocks metamorphosed at ~100 Ma across the proto–Kern Canyon fault in the Lake Isabella area, with the deeper rocks exposed to the east.

Since there is little evidence along the proto–Kern Canyon fault zone for major vertical uplift since ~85 Ma, the time when it clearly was active as a dextral strike-slip fault, that would suggest that the differential uplift across the fault occurred between 85 and 100 Ma (Busby-Spera and Saleeby, 1990). If the apparent uplift of the rocks east of the proto–Kern Canyon fault zone occurred during extensional unroofing, then the extension may have begun prior to ~85 Ma. In summary, the inferred unroofing of the southernmost Sierra Nevada along extensional faults and the subsequent dispersion of the upper-plate rocks appears to have occurred between ~90 to 85 Ma and ~55 to 50 Ma. The ranges in the maximum and minimum age constraints for the regional deformation, however, suggest that it may have begun and ended at slightly different times in different places.

Regional extension direction

Determination of the regional Late Cretaceous–early Cenozoic extension direction of the upper crust in the southern Sierra Nevada region is difficult because other coeval or younger tectonic events may have contributed to the apparent displacement of some of the allochthonous rocks. The kinematic data from Nourse and Silver (1986), Nourse (1989), and Wood (1997) indicate that the allochthonous rocks in the upper plates of the Blackburn Canyon fault and fault II of the Rand fault complex were transported in a southeastward to southward direction, at least during part of their activity. Upon restoration of ~45 km of sinistral displacement along the western Garlock fault, this generally southward transport direction is more or less consistent with the inferred source location in the Sierra Nevada to the north for these out-of-place rocks. In contrast, the allochthonous rocks of the batholith in the upper plate of both the Pastoria fault and the hypothesized correlative fault beneath the Tehachapi Mountains south of the Garlock fault clearly are displaced westward relative to potentially correlative rocks located on the eastern side of the Cretaceous batholith in southern California, as noted in previous studies (Silver, 1982, 1983), as well as being displaced in a southward direction from

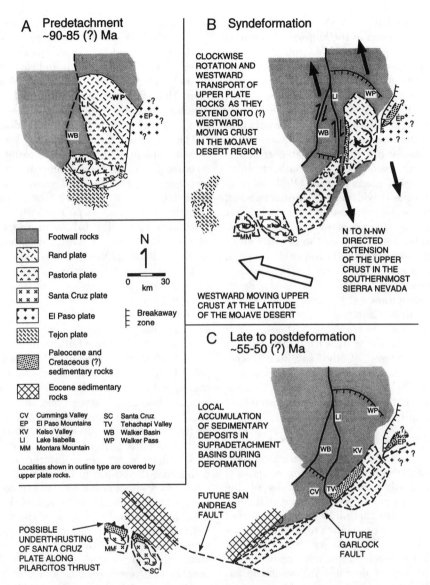

FIG. 8. Diagrams showing hypothesized evolution of detachment faulting in the southernmost Sierra Nevada batholith, and subsequent westward displacement of the upper-plate rocks. A. Early Late Cretaceous palinspastic reconstruction of the southernmost Sierra Nevada. See text for discussion of restoration. The heavy dashed lines in (A) are the future locations of the dextral Kern Canyon and proto–Kern Canyon fault zones. B. Inferred two-stage transport of upper-plate rocks, first to the SSE along extensional faults, and then to the west at the latitude of the Mojave Desert along a complicated series of generally W-vergent faults (Silver, 1982, 1983; May, 1989; Hall, 1991; Malin et al., 1995). C. Configuration of the southernmost Sierra Nevada batholith following Late Cretaceous–Paleocene extensional collapse and disaggregation.

their suggested source region (Fig. 6). The apparent westward component of displacement of these rocks will be discussed below.

The south to southeast direction of extension for the Late Cretaceous and possibly younger activity along the Blackburn Canyon fault, the western Jawbone Canyon fault, and fault II in the Rand Mountains is similar to Late Cretaceous extension directions documented in a number of localities northeast of the southern

Sierra Nevada batholith (Fig. 1). Late Cretaceous age extension in the Funeral Mountains,
which was ongoing at ~72 Ma and over by 70
Ma, was directed to the northwest (Hodges and
Walker, 1990; Applegate et al., 1992; Applegate
and Hodges, 1995). Hodges and Walker (1992)
suggested that some NNW-directed extension
in the Panamint Mountains may have occurred
in Late Cretaceous time, based on a summary of
geologic studies in that area. In an overview of
the geologic history of the southern Inyo,
Argus, and Slate ranges, Dunne (1986) summarized the regional evidence for Late Cretaceous,
Laramide-age deformation and concluded that
it involved a component of NW-SE–directed
crustal extension, based on the orientation of
conjugate, strike-slip faults and subhorizontal,
NW-trending stretching lineations in moderate-
grade gneisses in the Panamint Range. Palinspastic restoration of Miocene and younger
extension in the Basin and Range Province east
of the southern Sierra Nevada (Snow, 1992)
would move the above areas from their current
position northeast of the southern Sierra
Nevada to a relative position NNE of the southern Sierra Nevada, but the distance between
them and the southern Sierra Nevada would not
change significantly.

Apparent rotation of hanging-wall rocks

The location and trend of the metasedimentary pendants and the orientation of igneous
foliation in the hanging-wall rocks of the
regional detachment system suggest that some
of the upper-plate rocks may have been rotated
up to 90° clockwise relative to the autochthonous rocks in the southern Sierra Nevada
batholith. Igneous foliation in the granodioritic
rocks of the upper plate of the Blackburn Canyon fault, which is inferred to be magmatic
based on its parallelism to schlieren and mafic
enclaves, has mostly east to northeast trends,
and the small pendants of metavolcanic rocks
also have northeast trends (Wood, 1997). In the
region east and southeast of Lake Isabella,
where the rocks above the Blackburn Canyon
fault are inferred to have originated, the metasedimentary pendants have northwest trends
and the plutons have a primary foliation that is
generally NW- to NNW-trending (Ross, 1990).
The NE-trending Tylerhorse Canyon and Bean
Canyon pendants south of the Garlock fault
appear to have been rotated about 90° clock-

wise relative to the Isabella pendant in the
Sierra Nevada (Fig. 6). Paleomagnetic data from
the Cretaceous Lebec granodiorite in the upper
plate of the Pastoria fault indicate that the
granodiorite has been rotated clockwise by
more than 90° (McWilliams and Li, 1983),
which is consistent with the estimates of rotation that are based on other geologic data.

The Aqueduct Tunnel pendant, the Quinn
Ranch pendant, and the Tejon Lookout granite
do not appear to be substantially rotated relative
to their inferred footwall correlatives—the
Monolith pendant, the Back Canyon pendant,
and the Tehachapi Airport granite north of
Tehachapi Valley (Fig. 6). We interpret this to
be a result of the pendants and granite body
north of Tehachapi Valley also originally having
had an approximately northwest trend, but they
subsequently were rotated during dextral
oroclinal folding of the footwall rocks described
earlier. Map-scale, oroclinal folding, dextral
shearing along the proto–Kern Canyon fault
zone, and ductile thrust faulting along the eastern Tehachapi shear zone in the middle to lower
part of the batholithic crust may have in part
overlapped in time, with extension and clockwise rotation of the upper crust along the low-
angle detachment faults (Wood, 1997). Paleomagnetic data from sites in the Bear Valley
Springs tonalite pluton immediately northwest
of Tehachapi Valley can be interpreted as indicating that the pluton in that area was rotated
~45° clockwise about a vertical axis sometime
after emplacement (Kanter and McWilliams,
1982). The amount and sense of the paleomag-
netically estimated rotation of the pluton is
consistent with the rotation of the adjacent
metasedimentary screens from a former
roughly northwest trend to a current roughly
northern trend during oroclinal folding.

Miocene extension versus Late Cretaceous–Paleocene extension

The purpose of this section is to review
briefly some of the evidence for Miocene extension and tectonism in the Mojave Desert and
southern San Joaquin Valley regions, and to
differentiate and attempt to reconcile those
data with other evidence that suggests that Late
Cretaceous–Paleocene extensional faulting
occurred in the southernmost Sierra Nevada
area. Recent studies have documented early
Miocene, NE-directed extensional faulting in

the central Mojave Desert along the Waterman Hills detachment fault (Fig. 1) and other faults in the area (Dokka, 1989; Glazner et al., 1989; Walker et al., 1990; Fletcher et al., 1995). Dokka (1989) and Dokka and Ross (1995) suggested that the extension direction originally was N-S and subsequently was rotated clockwise to its current NE-SW orientation, but this contention has been disputed by Glazner et al. (1996). Presently NW-striking normal faults in the southern San Joaquin basin, including the Edison and Tunis faults, were active during a late Oligocene–early Miocene extensional tectonic event (Dibblee and Warne, 1988; Tennyson, 1989; Goodman and Malin, 1992). It is clear that early Miocene extension is an important part of the tectonic evolution of the region surrounding the southernmost Sierra Nevada, and some of the faults that we infer to have been active in the Late Cretaceous most likely were reactivated to some degree during the early Miocene. For example, the Jawbone Canyon fault zone in lower Jawbone Canyon exhibits signs of having been active during the Miocene (Tennyson, 1989). One major difference between the Late Cretaceous–Paleocene detachment faulting event proposed in this paper and early Miocene extension in the region, however, is the direction of extension. The early Miocene regional extension is NE-directed, whereas the inferred Late Cretaceous extension directions range mostly from NW to NNW. Even if the early Miocene extension direction originally was to the north, as proposed by Dokka (1989) and Dokka and Ross (1995), it still would not coincide with the Cretaceous direction regardless of whether the Cretaceous direction was subsequently rotated in the Miocene.

Most thermochronologic data from metamorphic and intrusive rocks exposed in the vicinity of the detachment fault system in the central Mojave Desert appear to be consistent with unroofing and cooling of the rocks in the early Miocene (Dokka et al., 1991; Glazner et al., 1994). Some workers have suggested, however, that partial exhumation of these rocks might have occurred in the Cretaceous (Henry and Dokka, 1991, 1992). Based on local thermobarometric and cooling-age data Henry and Dokka (1991; 1992) proposed a two-stage exhumation history for high-grade gneisses exposed in the footwall of one of the detach-

ment faults in the central Mojave Desert. They suggested that an initial phase of inferred extensional exhumation occurred in the Cretaceous and that a second phase occurred in the early Miocene. This hypothesized two-stage exhumation history is controversial, however, because Glazner et al. (1994) did not see evidence for the early phase of isothermal decompression in thermobarometric data they obtained from metamorphic rocks in the same area. In the southern Sierra Nevada–Tehachapi Mountains area, the Rand Schist was exposed at the surface in the middle Miocene, based on the presence of schist clasts in the middle Miocene unnamed conglomerate that is present in the southern San Joaquin basin (Goodman and Malin, 1992; Malin et al., 1995). Final exhumation of the Rand Schist that formerly resided at depths of ~30 km in the crust (Sharry, 1981; Pickett and Saleeby, 1993) may have occurred in the early Miocene during regional extensional faulting. Based on 74 to 72 Ma ^{40}Ar/^{39}Ar apparent ages on hornblende and muscovite from the Rand Schist in the Rand Mountains, Jacobson (1990) suggested, however, that the Rand Schist was already at moderately shallow crustal levels prior to early Miocene extensional faulting in the region. Late Cretaceous cooling of the schist may have been accomplished in part by extensional unroofing.

Other data and observations on the geology in the southern Sierra Nevada–Salinian–Mojave Desert region can be interpreted indirectly as evidence for Late Cretaceous through early Eocene crustal extension in the region. The regionally averaged topography of extended domains of the crust generally is lower than adjacent unextended areas (Wernicke, 1990). Wernicke et al. (1996) suggested that thick batholithic crust (~60 km) beneath the central Sierra Nevada in the vicinity of Mount Whitney (Fig. 1) maintained the range at a high elevation of 4 to 5 km from the late Mesozoic until Miocene time, when extension in nearby areas caused the elevation to subside to 2 to 3 km. In contrast, the sedimentary record in the southernmost Sierra Nevada–Mojave Desert–Salinian region indicates that parts of the batholith in that area were at sea level during the latest Cretaceous through the early Eocene. Marine sedimentary rocks of early Eocene age in the Goler Formation indicate that the El Paso Mountains region was at sea level at that time

(Cox, 1987). Cretaceous plutonic rocks in the Salinian block that have compositional, age, and isotopic affinities with the southernmost Sierra Nevada batholith (Ross, 1984; Silver and Mattinson, 1986; James, 1992) locally are unconformably overlain by Upper Cretaceous to Eocene marine sedimentary rocks (Compton, 1966; Nilsen, 1987a; Grove, 1993). These observations suggest that the Cretaceous batholith in the southern Sierra Nevada–Mojave–Salinian region was considerably lower in average elevation than the batholith in the central Sierra Nevada during the latest Cretaceous and earliest Cenozoic, which is consistent with Late Cretaceous–Paleocene extensional collapse of the former region.

Deformation model

A generalized kinematic model for the Late Cretaceous–Paleocene regional extensional collapse and disaggregation of the southern Sierra Nevada batholith is illustrated in Figure 8. This model focuses on the large-scale fragmentation and transport patterns of the upper crust. As discussed below, it is based in part on the deep-crustal, tectonic model of Malin et al. (1995) for the Late Cretaceous–Paleogene tectonic evolution of the southernmost Sierra Nevada–Mojave Desert regions. In Figure 8, the rocks of the batholith that comprise the footwall of the regional detachment fault system are shown in grey. Batholithic rocks in the hanging wall of the detachment fault system have been subdivided into five plates, which are indicated by different lithologic patterns. The units that comprise the El Paso, Rand, Pastoria, and Santa Cruz plates have all been discussed earlier in this paper, but none of those rocks appear to be good upper-plate counterparts to the extensive exposures of Early Cretaceous deep-level orthogneiss in the westernmost Tehachapi Mountains (Fig. 2). Thus, a hypothetical upper-crustal plate composed largely of Early Cretaceous orthogneiss, and labeled Tejon plate in Figure 8, is inferred to have formerly overlain some of the deep-level Early Cretaceous orthogneisses now exposed in the westernmost Tehachapi Mountains. Rocks of the inferred Tejon plate do not appear to be exposed today, and the possible locations of this apparently missing plate are discussed below.

In the predeformation configuration of the southern Sierra Nevada batholith (Fig. 8A), the upper-plate rocks have been restored to a position structurally above footwall rocks with which they are inferred to correlate. The El Paso plate has been restored by moving it ~14 km to the north. The hypothetical Tejon plate is shown structurally above the southwesternmost part of the gneiss complex of the western Tehachapi Mountains, but the predeformation orientation and extent of the Tejon plate and the underlying gneiss complex are uncertain, as indicated by question marks. Some deformation of the footwall is inferred to have been coeval with the upper-crustal extensional faulting and has been restored. The map-scale, dextral oroclinal fold in the footwall rocks that was discussed earlier and is apparent in the curving trace of the metasedimentary pendants south of the latitude of Walker Basin in Figure 2 has been straightened in Figure 8A (Wood, 1997). In addition, ~12 km of latest Cretaceous (?) dextral displacement along the Kern Canyon fault (Ross, 1986) has been restored. Displacement on the dextral, strike-slip proto–Kern Canyon fault zone has not been restored. Although a detailed discussion of the proto–Kern Canyon fault zone is beyond the scope of this report, the offset of lithologies in the region where it merges with the Kern Canyon fault (Ross, 1986) and minimum offset estimates for the eastern Tehachapi shear zone at its southern end (Wood, 1997) indicate that offset along the fault zone may be within the range of 4 to 9 km. Neglecting this amount of displacement does not significantly affect this model.

The configuration and relative motion of the upper- and lower-plate rocks in the southern Sierra Nevada region during deformation are shown in Figure 8B. The upper-plate rocks extended along the detachment faults in an overall SSE direction relative to the footwall. Coeval with the upper-crustal extensional faulting, the footwall is inferred to have deformed by map-scale oroclinal folding, thrust faulting along the eastern Tehachapi shear zone, and dextral strike-slip faulting along the proto–Kern Canyon and Kern Canyon faults. Also at the same time, the upper crust at the latitude of the Mojave Desert is inferred to have been moving relatively westward, conceivably by transport along low-angle faults (Silver, 1982, 1983; Hall, 1991; Malin et al., 1995). As the southern Sierra Nevadan upper-plate rocks extended onto (?) the westward-moving crust in the Mojave Desert area, they are inferred to have been progressively deflected to the west and rotated clockwise as they were transported to the west. During and following detachment faulting, the Witnet and Goler formations are inferred to have accumulated in supradetachment basins.

Figure 8C illustrates the final position of the upper-plate rocks following their detachment and westward transport. In the northern Salinian block, a segment of the Pilarcitos fault north of Montara Mountain (Figs. 7B and 8C) has been interpreted as a thrust fault along which Paleocene sedimentary rocks of Point San Pedro and the underlying Montara Mountain tonalite were underthrust to the northeast beneath rocks of the Franciscan Complex prior to ~50 Ma (Wakabayashi and Moores, 1988). The hypothetical Tejon plate, which is inferred to have preceded the Santa Cruz plate in moving to the west (Fig. 8B), may have been involved in a similar deformation. The Tejon plate, if it existed, possibly was thrust beneath the Franciscan Complex and now is no longer exposed. Alternatively, the Tejon plate may have been eroded away, it might be located offshore and has not been recognized, or it may have detached and moved to the northwest relative to the western Tehachapi gneiss complex, to be subsequently buried beneath the thick Cenozoic fill of the southernmost San Joaquin Valley.

Development of low-angle extensional faults in the southernmost Sierra Nevada region may represent collapse of the crust following and/or during a major Late Cretaceous crustal thickening event in southern California. The southern Sierra Nevada is located along the northern margin of a region in southern California that is inferred to have been severely deformed by generally W-vergent, low-angle faulting during Late Cretaceous and early Cenozoic time (Silver, 1982, 1983; May, 1989; Hall, 1991). In the early stages of this regional deformation, the crust may have been thickened to the point where it collapsed under the influence of gravity along low-angle normal faults (Dewey, 1988). Malin et al. (1995) proposed that exhumation of the southern part of the Sierra Nevada batholith is directly related to the Late Cretaceous emplacement of the Rand Schist beneath it. The northern margin of the area, thought to be underlain by Rand Schist at relatively shallow levels (Malin et al., 1995),

corresponds closely to the area in the southern Sierra Nevada batholith that is inferred to have been unroofed along detachment faults. Thrusting of Rand Schist beneath the batholith in the Late Cretaceous may have contributed to its collapse by causing the overlying crust to thicken by folding and thrust faulting. The SW-vergent folds in the igneous suite of Bear Valley and the top-to-the-SSW shearing along the eastern Tehachapi shear zone may record crustal thickening in the batholith prior to and during its collapse. In addition, the NNE trend of slip lineations in the shear zone may record the direction in which the Rand Schist was thrust beneath the batholith at a lower structural level. Removal of the mafic root of the batholith and its replacement with less dense Rand Schist also would tend to buoy up the batholith, making it more susceptible to uplift-driven collapse, and fluids escaping upward from the Rand Schist would weaken the overlying crust, making it more likely to fail (Malin et al., 1995). A large crustal welt centered in the southern California region, forming and gravitationally collapsing, is consistent with the regional differences in the direction of upper crustal transport. The southern Sierra Nevada region may have extended in a north to northwest direction because it was located on the northern flank of the collapsing welt. In contrast, the Mojave Desert region, which was centered over the welt, extended to the west across the adjacent forearc basin, and ultimately across the corresponding subducting trench complex.

Summary and Conclusions

1. The southern part of the Sierra Nevada batholith differs from the batholith to the north in several important respects. Geobarometric data from many different studies indicate that much of the batholith south of Lake Isabella has been exhumed to crustal levels of 15 to 30 km, in contrast to the 5 to 15 km crustal depths exposed in the batholith to the north. The southernmost part of the Sierra Nevada batholith is inferred to be underlain by Rand Schist along low-angle faults. The regular NNW trends of metasedimentary pendants, compositional boundaries, and isotopic zones in the central Sierra Nevada batholith have been modified by oroclinal folding and disrupted by low-angle

faulting in the southern part of the Sierra Nevada.

2. The Blackburn Canyon fault, the Jawbone Canyon fault zone, the Pastoria fault, and other previously mapped, low-angle detachment faults in the Rand Mountains and southeastern Sierra Nevada region are inferred to be extensional faults along which part of the southern Sierra Nevada batholith was exhumed. Most of these faults juxtapose high- to moderate-pressure, ductilely deformed gneissic footwall rocks against low- to moderate-pressure, largely cataclastically deformed granitic hanging-wall rocks.

3. Similarities between the upper- and lower-plate geology of the detachment fault system and SSE-directed upper-plate transport along some of the faults are consistent with derivation of the hanging-wall rocks from a position structurally above the southeastern Sierra Nevada east of the proto–Kern Canyon fault zone and mostly south of South Fork Valley. The presence of higher-pressure rocks east of the northern part of the proto–Kern Canyon fault zone is consistent with greater unroofing of that part of the batholith.

4. After restoring displacement along strike-slip faults of the San Andreas and Garlock fault systems, the Cretaceous and older crystalline basement rocks of the northern Salinian block are palinspastically restored to a relatively compact configuration that is located WNW of the southern Sierra Nevada. Based on previous geologic correlations, the crystalline rocks of the northernmost part of the Salinian block are suggested to have originated from a position structurally above the southwestern Sierra Nevada batholith.

5. Arkosic sandstones and conglomerates of the Upper Cretaceous (?)–Paleogene Witnet Formation and the Paleocene–lower Eocene Goler Formation are inferred to have been deposited in supradetachment basins. The Witnet Formation is suggested to have been deposited in a half-graben basin that formed adjacent to the Blackburn Canyon and Jawbone Canyon fault zones.

6. Regional age constraints indicate that detachment and disaggregation of the southern part of the Sierra Nevada batholith occurred between ~90 to 85 Ma and ~55 to 50 Ma. The age and south to southeast direction of upper-crustal extension in the southern Sierra Nevada correspond to NW-directed Late Cretaceous extension that has been documented nearby in the Funeral, Panamint, and Inyo mountains. The southeast direction of inferred Late Cretaceous–Paleocene age extension in the southern Sierra Nevada region is substantially different than the northeast direction for early Miocene extension that has been documented in the region.

7. Upper-plate rocks of the southern Sierra Nevada detachment system are inferred to have been rotated clockwise by as much as 90° along the low-angle faults, whereas rocks in the footwall of the regional low-angle fault system appear to have been dextrally oroclinally folded. This style of deformation in the southernmost Sierra Nevada batholith may be a different manifestation of a regional Late Cretaceous dextral transpressional deformation of the magmatic arc that is expressed by subvertical, dextral, transpressional shear zones in the central Sierra Nevada to the north.

8. Extensional collapse of the upper crust in the southernmost Sierra Nevada along low-angle detachment faults may have occurred in response to the underthrusting of the Rand Schist beneath the batholith during low-angle Laramide subduction. Transport of the upper-plate rocks is proposed to have occurred in two stages. First, the upper crust in the southern Sierra Nevada extended in a south to southeast direction, and second, the allochthonous rocks were carried westward at the latitude of the Mojave Desert by a mechanism that may include W-vergent faulting and/or oroclinal bending.

Acknowledgments

Partial financial support for this work came from N.S.F. grant EAR-9316105 awarded to J. B. Saleeby and an N.S.F. graduate fellowship, a G.S.A. Penrose grant, and a Caltech Koons Field Fellowship awarded to D. J. Wood. The authors especially would like to acknowledge and thank L. T. Silver for his extensive geologic and geochronologic work in the southern Sierra Nevada–Rand Mountains region. He recognized the importance of low-angle faults in the tectonic evolution of the area, and the authors have benefited from his experience and insights through numerous discussions and field trips.

Formulation of the tectonic model in this paper would not have been possible without the regional geologic studies of D. C. Ross, T. W. Dibblee, Jr., and J. C. Crowell. E. T. Dixon is acknowledged and thanked for sharing unpublished thermobarometric and geochronologic data from her master's thesis research. Thanks also are due to the many private landowners in the area who allowed access to their property. In the course of this work, the authors have benefited from discussions with many other people, including J. A. Nourse, J. Sharry, T. Atwater, J. K. Snow, C. F. Lough, and T. H. Anderson. The authors would like to thank C. A. Hall, Jr. and W. G. Ernst for careful and critical reviews of the manuscript.

REFERENCES

Ague, J. J., 1997, Thermodynamic calculation of emplacement pressures for batholithic rocks, California: Implications for the aluminum-in-hornblende barometer: Geology, v. 25, p. 563–566.

Ague, J. J., and Brimhall, G. H., 1988, Magmatic arc asymmetry and distribution of anomalous plutonic belts in the batholiths of California: Effects of assimilation, crustal thickness, and depth of crystallization: Geol. Soc. Amer. Bull., v. 100, p. 912–927.

Applegate, J. D. R., and Hodges, K. V., 1995, Mesozoic and Cenozoic extension recorded by metamorphic rocks in the Funeral Mountains, California: Geol. Soc. Amer. Bull., v. 107, p. 1063–1076.

Applegate, J. D. R., Walker, J. D., and Hodges, K. V., 1992, Late Cretaceous extensional unroofing in the Funeral Mountains metamorphic core complex, California: Geology, v. 20, p. 519–522.

Bartow, J. A., 1987, Cenozoic nonmarine sedimentation in the San Joaquin Basin, central California, *in* Ingersoll, R. V., and Ernst, W. G., eds., Cenozoic basin development of coastal California. Rubey Volume VI: Englewood Cliffs, NJ, Prentice-Hall, p. 146–171.

Bateman, P. C., 1992, Plutonism in the central part of the Sierra Nevada batholith, California: U. S. Geol. Surv. Prof. Paper 1483, 186 p.

Bateman, P. C., and Dodge, F. C. W., 1970, Variations of major chemical constituents across the central Sierra Nevada batholith: Geol. Soc. Amer. Bull., v. 81, p. 409–420.

Burbank, D. W., and Whistler, D. P., 1987, Temporally constrained tectonic rotations derived from magnetostratigraphic data: Implications for the initiation of the Garlock fault, California: Geology, v. 15, p. 1172–1175.

Burchfiel, B. C., and Davis, G. A., 1981, Mojave Desert and environs, *in* Ernst, W. G., ed., The geotectonic development of California. Rubey Volume I: Englewood Cliffs, NJ, Prentice-Hall, p. 217–252.

Busby-Spera, C. J., and Saleeby, J. B., 1990, Intra-arc strike-slip fault exposed at batholithic levels in the southern Sierra Nevada, California: Geology, v. 18, p. 255–259.

Buwalda, J. P., 1934, Tertic tectonic activity in Tehachapi region: Pan-Amer. Geol., v. 61, p. 309–310.

————, 1954, Geology of the Tehachapi mountains, California, *in* Jahns, R. H., ed., Geology of Southern California: Calif. Div. Mines Bull. 170, p. 131–142.

Champion, D. E., 1989, Identification of the Rinconada fault in western San Mateo County, CA, through the use of strontium isotopic studies [abs.]: Geol. Soc. Amer. Abs. Prog., v. 21, p. 64.

Champion, D. E., and Kistler, R. W., 1991, Paleogeographic reconstruction of the northern Salinian block using Sr isotopic properties [abs.]: Geol. Soc. Amer. Abs. Prog., v. 23, p. 12.

Chen, J. H., and Moore, J. G., 1982, Uranium-lead isotopic ages from the Sierra Nevada batholith, California: Jour. Geophys. Res., v. 87, p. 4761–4784.

Clarke, S. H., Jr., and Nilsen, T. H., 1973, Displacement of Eocene strata and implications for the history of offset along the San Andreas fault, central and northern California, *in* Kovach, R. L., and Nur, A., eds., Proc., Conf. on Tectonic Problems of the San Andreas Fault System: Stanford Univ. Publ. Geol. Sci., p. 358–367.

Compton, R. R., 1966, Granitic and metamorphic rocks of the Salinian block, California Coast Ranges: Calif. Div. Mines Geol. Bull. 190, p. 277–287.

Cowan, D. S., and Bruhn, R. L., 1992, Late Jurassic to early Late Cretaceous geology of the U.S. Cordillera, *in* Burchfiel, B. C., Lipman, P. W., and Zoback, M. L., eds., The Cordilleran Orogen: Conterminous U. S.: Boulder, CO, Geol. Soc. Amer., The geology of North America, p. 169–203.

Cox, B. F., 1987, Stratigraphy, depositional environments, and paleotectonics of the Paleocene and Eocene Goler formation, El Paso mountains, California—geologic summary and roadlog, *in* Cox, B. F., ed., Basin analysis and paleontology of the Paleocene and Eocene Goler Formation, El Paso Mountains, California: Los Angeles, Pacific Sect. Soc. Econ. Paleontol. Mineral., p. 1–29.

Cox, B. F., and Diggles, M. F., 1986, Geologic map of the El Paso Mountains wilderness study area, Kern County, California: U. S. Geol. Surv. Misc. Field Studies Map MF-1827, scale 1:24,000.

Crowell, J. C., 1952, Geology of the Lebec quadrangle, California: Calif. Div. Mines and Geol. Spec. Report 24, 23 p.

————, 1964, The San Andreas fault zone from the Temblor Mountains to Antelope Valley, southern California: Pacific Sect., Amer. Assoc. Petrol. Geol., Soc. Econ. Paleontol. Mineral., and San Joaquin Geol. Soc. Guidebook, p. 1–39.

Davis, T. L., and Lagoe, M. B., 1988, A structural interpretation of major tectonic events affecting the western and southern margins of the San Joaquin valley, California, *in* Graham, S. A., ed., Studies of the geology of the San Joaquin basin: Los Angeles, Pacific Sect., Soc. Econ. Paleontol. Mineral., p. 65–87.

Dewey, J. F., 1988, Extensional collapse of orogens: Tectonics, v. 7, p. 1123–1139.

Dibblee, T. W., Jr., 1952, Geology of the Saltdale quadrangle: Calif. Div. Mines Bull. 160, p. 1–43.

————, 1959, Preliminary geologic map of the Mojave Quadrangle, California: U. S. Geol. Surv. Mineral Invest. Field Studies Map MF-219, scale 1:62,000.

————, 1963, Geology of the Willow Springs and Rosamond quadrangles, California: Geologic investigations of Southern California deserts: U. S. Geol. Surv. Bull. 1089-C, p. 141–253.

————, 1967, Areal geology of the western Mojave Desert, California: U. S. Geol. Surv. Prof. Pap. 522, 153 p.

Dibblee, T. W., Jr., and Chesterman, C. W., 1953, Geology of the Breckenridge Mountain quadrangle: Calif. Div. Mines Geol. Bull. 168, 56 p.

Dibblee, T. W., Jr., and Louke, G. P., 1970, Geologic map of the Tehachapi quadrangle, Kern County, California: U. S. Geol. Surv. Misc. Geol. Investig. Map I-607, scale 1:62,500.

Dibblee, T. W., Jr., and Warne, A. H., 1970, Geologic map of the Cummings Mountain quadrangle, Kern County, California: U. S. Geol. Surv. Misc. Geol. Investig. Map I-611, scale 1:62,500.

Dibblee, T. W., Jr., and Warne, A. H., 1988, Inferred relation of the Oligocene to Miocene Bealville fanglomerate to the Edison fault, Caliente canyon area, Kern County, California, *in* Graham, S. A., ed., Studies of the geology of the San Joaquin basin: Los Angeles, Pacific Sec., Soc. Econ. Paleontol. Mineral., p. 223–231.

Dixon, E. T., 1995, $^{40}Ar/^{39}Ar$ hornblende geochronology and evaluation of garnet and hornblende barometry, Lake Isabella to Tehachapi area, southern Sierra Nevada, California: Unpubl. M.S. thesis, Univ. Michigan, 63 p.

Dixon, E. T., Essene, E. J., and Halliday, A. N., 1994, Critical tests of hornblende barometry, Lake Isabella to Tehachapi area, southern Sierra Nevada, California: EOS (Trans. Amer. Geophys. Union), v. 75, p. 744.

Dokka, R. K., 1989, The Mojave extensional belt of southern California: Tectonics, v. 8, p. 363–390.

Dokka, R. K., Henry, D. J., Ross, T. M., Baksi, A. K., Lambert, J., Travis, C. J., Jones, S. M., Jacobson, C., McCurry, M. M., Woodburne, M. O., and Ford, J. P., 1991, Aspects of the Mesozoic and Cenozoic geologic evolution of the Mojave Desert, *in* Walawender, M. J., and Hanan, B. B., eds., Geological excursions in Southern California and Mexico: Geol. Soc. Amer. Guidebook 1991 Annual Meeting, San Diego, California, p. 1–43.

Dokka, R. K., and Ross, T. M., 1995, Collapse of southwestern North America and the evolution of early Miocene detachment faults, metamorphic core complexes, the Sierra Nevada orocline, and the San Andreas fault system: Geology, v. 23, p. 1075–1078.

Dunne, G. C., 1986, Geologic evolution of the southern Inyo range, Darwin plateau, and Argus and Slate ranges, east-central California—an overview, *in* Dunne, G. C., ed., Mesozoic and Cenozoic structural evolution of selected areas, east-central California: Geol. Soc. Amer., Cordill. Sect. Fieldtrip Guidebook: Calif. State University, p. 3–21.

Dunne, G. C., Moore, J. N., Anderson, D., and Galbraith, G., 1975, The Bean Canyon formation of the Tehachapi mountains, California: An early Mesozoic arc-trench gap deposit? [abs.]: Geol. Soc. Amer. Abs. Prog., v. 7, p. 314.

Dunne, G. C., Saleeby, J. B., and Farber, D., 1991, Early synbatholithic ductile faulting in the southern Sierra Nevada: New U/Pb age and geobarometric constraints for the Kern plateau fault zone [abs.]: Geol. Soc. Amer. Abs. Prog., v. 23, p. 20.

Ehlig, P. L., 1968, Causes of distribution of Pelona, Rand, and Orocopia schists along the San Andreas and Garlock faults, *in* Proc. Conf. Geol. Problems of San Andreas Fault System, p. 294–306.

Elan, R., 1985, High grade contact metamorphism at the Lake Isabella north shore roof pendant, southern Sierra Nevada, California: Unpubl. M.S. thesis, Univ. Southern California, 202 p.

Evernden, J. F., Savage, D. E., Curtis, G. H., and James, G. T., 1964, Potassium-argon dates and the Cenozoic mammalian chronology of North America: Amer. Jour. Sci., v. 262, p. 145–198.

Fedo, C. M., and Miller, J. M. G., 1992, Evolution of a Miocene half-graben basin, Colorado River extensional corridor, southeastern California: Geol. Soc. Amer. Bull., v. 104, p. 481–493.

Fillmore, R. P., Walker, J. D., Bartley, J. M., and Glazner, A. F., 1994, Development of three genetically related basins associated with detachment-style faulting: Predicted characteristics and an example from the central Mojave Desert, California: Geology, v. 22, p. 1087–1090.

Fletcher, J. M., Bartley, J. M., Martin, M. W., Glazner, A. F., and Walker, J. D., 1995, Large-magnitude continental extension: An example from the central Mojave metamorphic core complex: Geol. Soc. Amer. Bull., v. 107, p. 1468-1483.

Friedmann, S. J., Davis, G. A., Fowler, T. K., Brudos, T., Parke, M., Burbank, D. W., and Burchfiel, B. C., 1994, Stratigraphy and gravity-glide elements of a Miocene supradetachment basin, Shadow Valley, east Mojave Desert, in McGill, S. F., and Ross, T. M., eds., Geological investigations of an active margin: Geol. Soc. Amer. Cordill. Sect. Guidebook, 27th Annual Meeting, p. 302-318.

Gazis, C., and Saleeby, J. B., 1991, Southward continuation of the proto-Kern Canyon fault zone (PKF) to the upper Caliente Creek area, southern Sierra Nevada [abs.]: Geol. Soc. Amer. Abs. Prog., v. 23, p. 28.

Glazner, A. F., Bartley, J. M., and Ingersoll, R. V., 1996, Collapse of southwestern North America and the evolution of early Miocene detachment faults, metamorphic core complexes, the Sierra Nevada orocline, and the San Andreas fault system: Comment: Geology, v. 24, p. 858-859.

Glazner, A. F., Bartley, J. M., and Walker, J. D., 1989, Magnitude and significance of Miocene crustal extension in the central Mojave Desert, California: Geology, v. 17, p. 50-53.

Glazner, A. F., Walker, J. D., Bartley, J. M., Fletcher, J. M., Martin, M. W., Schermer, E. R., Boettcher, S. S., Miller, J. S., Fillmore, R. P., and Linn, J. K., 1994, Reconstruction of the Mojave block, in McGill, S. F., and Ross, T. M., eds., Geological investigations of an active margin: Geol. Soc. Amer. Cordill. Sect. Guidebook, 27th Annual Meeting, p. 3-30.

Goodman, E. D., and Malin, P. E., 1992, Evolution of the southern San Joaquin Basin and mid-Tertiary "transitional" tectonics, central California: Tectonics, v. 11, p. 478-498.

Graham, S. A., Decelles, P. G., Carroll, A. R., and Goodman, E. D., 1990, Middle Tertiary contractile deformation, uplift, extension, and rotation in the San Emigdio range, southern California: Amer. Assoc. Petrol. Geol. Bull., v. 74, p. 665.

Greene, D. C., and Schweickert, R. A., 1995, The Gem Lake shear zone: Cretaceous dextral transpression in the northern Ritter Range pendant, eastern Sierra Nevada, California: Tectonics, v. 14, p. 945-961.

Grove, K., 1993, Latest Cretaceous basin formation within the Salinian terrane of west-central California: Geol. Soc. Amer. Bull., v. 105, p. 447-463.

Haase, C. S., and Rutherford, M. J., 1975, The effect of pressure and temperature on the compositions of biotite and cordierite coexisting with sillimanite + quartz + sanidine (muscovite) [abs.]: Geol. Soc. Amer. Abs. Prog., v. 7, p. 1094-1095.

Hall, C. A., Jr., 1991, Geology of the Point Sur-Lopez Point region, Coast Ranges, California: A part of the southern California allochthon: Geol. Soc. Amer. Spec. Pap. 266, 40 p.

Harrison, T. M., 1981, Diffusion of ^{40}Ar in hornblende: Contrib. Mineral. Petrol., v. 78, p. 324-331.

Henry, D. J., and Dokka, R. K., 1991, Multiple extensional events as a mechanism for exposure of granulites: Example from the Mojave Desert [abs.]: Geol. Soc. Amer. Abs. Prog., v. 23, p. A83.

————, 1992, Metamorphic evolution of exhumed middle to lower crustal rocks in the Mojave extensional belt, southern California, USA: Jour. Metamor. Geol., v. 10, p. 347-364.

Hewett, D. F., 1954, General geology of the Mojave Desert region, California, part 1 of chapter 2, in Jahns, R. H., ed., Geology of Southern California: Calif. Div. Mines Bull. 170, p. 5-20.

————, 1955, Structural features of the Mojave Desert region: Geol. Soc. Amer. Spec. Pap. 62, p. 377-390.

Hodges, K. V., and Walker, J. D., 1990, Petrologic constraints on the unroofing history of the Funeral Mountain metamorphic core complex, California: Jour. Geophys. Res., v. 95, p. 8437-8445.

Hodges, K. V., and Walker, J. D., 1992, Extension in the Cretaceous Sevier orogen, North American Cordillera: Geol. Soc. Amer. Bull., v. 104, p. 560-569.

Holdaway, M. J., 1971, Stability of andalusite and the aluminum silicate phase diagram: Amer. Jour. Sci., v. 271, p. 97-131.

Ingersoll, R. V., 1983, Petrofacies and provenance of late Mesozoic forearc basin, northern and central California: Amer. Assoc. Petrol. Geol. Bull., v. 7, p. 1125-1142.

Jacobson, C. E., 1990, The ^{40}Ar/^{39}Ar geochronology of the Pelona schist and related rocks, southern California: Jour. Geophys. Res., v. 95, p. 509-528.

Jacobson, C. E., Dawson, M. R., and Postlethwaite, C. E., 1988, Structure, metamorphism, and tectonic significance of the Pelona, Orocopia, and Rand schists, southern California, in Ernst, W. G., ed., Metamorphism and crustal evolution of the Western United States. Rubey Volume VII: Englewood Cliffs, NJ, Prentice-Hall, p. 976-997.

James, E. W., 1986, U/Pb age of the Antimony Peak tonalite and its relation to Rand Schist in the San Emigdio Mountains [abs.]: Geol. Soc. Amer. Abs. Prog., v. 18, p. 121.

————, 1992, Cretaceous metamorphism and plutonism in the Santa Cruz mountains, Salinian block, California, and correlation with the southernmost Sierra Nevada: Geol. Soc. Amer. Bull., v. 104, p. 1326-1339.

James, E. W., and Mattinson, J. M., 1985, Evidence for 160 km post–mid-Cretaceous slip on the San Gregorio fault, coastal California: EOS (Trans. Amer. Geophys. Union), v. 66, p. 1093.

Jennings, C. W., compiler, 1977, Geologic map of California: Geologic data map 2: Sacramento, CA, Calif. Div. Mines and Geol., scale 1:750,000.

Kanter, L. R., 1988, Paleolatitude of the Butano Sandstone, California, and its implications for the kinematic histories of the Salinian terrane and the San Andreas fault: Jour. Geophys. Res., v. 93, p. 11,699–11,710.

Kanter, L. R., and McWilliams, M. O., 1982, Rotation of the southernmost Sierra Nevada, California: Jour. Geophys. Res., v. 87, p. 3819–3830.

Kim, H. S., 1972, Polymetamorphism of metasedimentary rocks in the southern Sierras, California: Unpubl. Ph.D. thesis, Case Western Reserve Univ., 199 p.

Kistler, R. W., 1978, Mesozoic paleogeography of California: A viewpoint from isotope geology, in Howell, D. G., and McDougall, K. A., eds., Mesozoic paleogeography of the Western United States: Pacific Coast Paleogeog. Symp.: Los Angeles, Pacific Sect., Soc. Econ. Paleontol. Mineral., p. 75–84.

Kistler, R. W., and Champion, D. E., 1991, A strontium and oxygen isotopic study of granitic rocks from Bodega Head to the Santa Lucia Range in the northern Salinian block, California [abs.]: Geol. Soc. Amer. Abs. Prog., v. 23, p. 42.

Kistler, R. W., and Ross, D. C., 1990, A strontium isotopic study of plutons and associated rocks of the southern Sierra Nevada and vicinity, California: U. S. Geol. Surv. Bull. 1920, 20 p.

Lawson, A. C., 1906, The geomorphogeny of the Tehachapi valley system: Univ. Calif. Publ. Bull. Dept. Geol., v. 4, p. 431–462.

Leo, G. W., 1967, The plutonic and metamorphic rocks of the Ben Lomond mountain area, Santa Cruz County, California: Calif. Div. Mines and Geology Spec. Report 91, 27–43 p.

Locke, A., Billingsley, P., and Mayo, E. B., 1940, Sierra Nevada tectonic pattern: Geol. Soc. Amer. Bull., v. 51, p. 513–539.

Loomis, D. P., and Burbank, D. W., 1988, The stratigraphic evolution of the El Paso basin, southern California: Implications for the Miocene development of the Garlock fault and uplift of the Sierra Nevada: Geol. Soc. Amer. Bull., v. 100, p. 12–28.

Malin, P. E., Goodman, E. D., Henyey, T. L., Li, Y. G., Okaya, D. A., and Saleeby, J. B., 1995, Significance of seismic reflections beneath a tilted exposure of deep continental crust, Tehachapi mountains, California: Jour. Geophys. Res., v. 100, p. 2069–2087.

Mansfield, C. F., 1979, Upper Mesozoic subsea fan deposits in the southern Diablo Range, California:

Record of the Sierra Nevada magmatic arc: Geol. Soc. Amer. Bull., Part 1, v. 90, p. 1025–1046.

Matthews, V., III, 1976, Correlation of Pinnacles and Neenach volcanic formations and their bearing on San Andreas fault problem: Amer. Assoc. Petrol. Geol. Bull., v. 60, p. 2128–2141.

Mattinson, J. M., 1990, Petrogenesis and evolution of the Salinian magmatic arc, in Anderson, J. L., ed., The nature and origin of Cordilleran magmatism: Geol. Soc. Amer. Memoir 174, p. 237–250.

May, D. J., 1989, Late Cretaceous intra-arc thrusting in southern California: Tectonics, v. 8, p. 1159–1173.

McDougall, K., 1987, Foraminiferal biostratigraphy and paleoecology of marine deposits, Goler Formation, California, in Cox, B. F., ed., Basin analysis and paleontology of the Paleocene and Eocene Goler Formation, El Paso Mountains, California: Los Angeles, Pacific Sect., Soc. Econ. Paleontol. Mineral., p. 43–67.

McWilliams, M., and Li, Y., 1983, A paleomagnetic test of the Sierran orocline hypothesis: EOS (Trans. Amer. Geophys. Union), v. 64, p. 686.

McWilliams, M., and Li, Y., 1985, Oroclinal bending of the southern Sierra Nevada batholith: Science, v. 230, p. 172–175.

Michael, E. D., 1960, The geology of the Cache Creek area, Kern County, California: Unpubl. M.A. thesis, Univ. Calif., Los Angeles.

Miller, J. S., Glazner, A. F., Walker, J. D., and Martin, M. M., 1995, Geochronologic and isotopic evidence for Triassic–Jurassic emplacement of the eugeoclinal allochthon in the Mojave Desert region, California: Geol. Soc. Amer. Bull., v. 107, p. 1441–1457.

Miller, W. J., and Webb, R. W., 1940, Descriptive geology of the Kernville quadrangle, California: Calif. Jour. Mines and Geol., v. 36, p. 343–378.

Moore, J. G., 1959, The quartz diorite boundary line in the western United States: Jour. Geol., v. 67, p. 198–210.

Moxon, I. W., 1988, Sequence stratigraphy of the Great Valley basin in the context of convergent margin tectonics, in Graham, S. A., ed., Studies of the geology of the San Joaquin basin: Los Angeles, Pacific Sect., Soc. Econ. Paleontol. Mineral., p. 3–28.

Naeser, N. D., Naeser, C. W., and McCulloh, T. H., 1990, Thermal history of rocks in southern San Joaquin valley, California: Evidence from fission-track analysis: Amer. Assoc. Petrol. Geol. Bull., v. 74, p. 13–29.

Namson, J., and Davis, T., 1988, Structural transect of the western Transverse Ranges, California: Implications for lithospheric kinematics and seismic risk evaluation: Geology, v. 16, p. 675–679.

Nilsen, T. H., 1981, Geology of the Santa Cruz Mountains, California, in Frizzell, V., ed., Upper Cretaceous and Paleocene turbidites, central California coast: Los Angeles, Pacific Sect., Soc. Econ. Paleontol. Mineral., p. 5–12.

_____, 1987a, Paleogene tectonics and sedimentation of coastal California, *in* Ingersoll, R. V., and Ernst, W. G., eds., Cenozoic basin development of coastal California. Rubey Volume VI: Englewood Cliffs, NJ, Prentice-Hall, Inc., p. 81–123.

_____, 1987b, Stratigraphy and sedimentology of the Eocene Tejon Formation, western Tehachapi Mountains and San Emigdio Mountains, California: U. S. Geol. Surv. Prof. Pap. 1268, 110 p.

Nilsen, T. H., and Clarke, S. H., 1975, Sedimentation and tectonics in the early Tertiary continental borderland of central California: U. S. Geol. Surv. Prof. Pap. 925, 64 p.

Nilsen, T. H., Dibblee, T. W., Jr., and Addicott, W. O., 1973, Lower and middle Tertiary stratigraphic units of the San Emigdio and western Tehachapi Mountains, California: U. S. Geol. Surv. Bull. 1372-H, H1–H23 p.

Nitchman, S. P., 1989, The El Paso fault, a Neogene thrust fault in the southwestern Basin and Range, Kern County, California [abs.]: Geol. Soc. Amer. Abs. Prog., v. 21, p. 123.

Nourse, J. A., 1989, Geologic evolution of two crustal scale shear zones. Part I: The Rand thrust complex, northwestern Mojave desert, California. Part II: The Magdalena metamorphic core complex, north central Sonora, Mexico: Unpubl. Ph.D. thesis, California Inst. Technol., 394 p.

Nourse, J. A., and Silver, L. T., 1986, Structural and kinematic evolution of sheared rocks in the Rand "Thrust" complex, northwest Mojave Desert, California [abs.]: Geol. Soc. Amer. Abs. Prog., v. 18, p. 165.

Peters, C. M. F., 1972, A structural interpretation of the Garlock fault zone at the Tehachapi crossing, *in* Lane, K. S., and Garfield, L. A., eds., Proc. North Amer. Rapid Excavation and Tunneling Conference, Chicago, Illinois, June 5–7, 1972, Volume 1: New York, Amer. Inst. Mining, Metallurg. Petrol. Eng., Inc., p. 133–155.

Pickett, D. A., and Saleeby, J. B., 1993, Thermobarometric constraints on the depth of exposure and conditions of plutonism and metamorphism at deep levels of the Sierra Nevada batholith, Tehachapi Mountains, California: Jour. Geophys. Res., v. 98, p. 609–629.

_____, 1994, Nd, Sr, and Pb isotopic characteristics of Cretaceous intrusive rocks from deep levels of the Sierra Nevada batholith, Tehachapi Mountains, California: Contrib. Mineral. Petrol., v. 118, p. 198–215.

Postlethwaite, C. E., and Jacobson, C. E., 1987, Early history and reactivation of the Rand thrust, southern California: Jour. Struct. Geol., v. 9, p. 195–205.

Powell, R. E., 1993, Balanced palinspastic reconstruction of pre-late Cenozoic paleogeology, southern California: Geologic and kinematic constraints on the evolution of the San Andreas fault system, *in* Powell, R. E., Weldon, R. J., II, and Matti, J. C., eds., The San Andreas fault system: Displacement, palinspastic reconstruction, and geologic evolution: Geol. Soc. Amer. Memoir 178, p. 1–106.

Quinn, J. P., 1987, Stratigraphy of the middle Miocene Bopesta Formation, southern Sierra Nevada, California: Los Angeles, Natural History Museum of Los Angeles County, Contrib. Sci., No. 393, 31 p.

Rindosh, M. C., 1977, Geology of the Tylerhorse Canyon pendant, southern Tehachapi Mountains, Kern County, California: Unpubl. Masters thesis, Univ. Southern California, 80 p.

Ross, D. C., 1984, Possible correlations of basement rocks across the San Andreas, San Gregorio–Hosgri, and Rinconada–Reliz–King City faults, California: U. S. Geol. Surv. Prof. Pap. 1317, 37 p.

_____, 1985, Mafic gneissic complex (batholithic root?) in the southernmost Sierra Nevada, California: Geology, v. 13, p. 288–291.

_____, 1986, Basement-rock correlations across the White Wolf–Breckenridge–southern Kern Canyon fault zone, southern Sierra Nevada, California: U. S. Geol. Surv. Bull. 1651, 25 p.

_____, 1989a, Magnetic susceptibilities of modally analyzed granitic rocks from the southern Sierra Nevada, California: U. S. Geol. Surv. Open-File Report 89-204, 53 p.

_____, 1989b, The metamorphic and plutonic rocks of the southernmost Sierra Nevada, California, and their tectonic framework: U. S. Geol. Surv. Prof. Pap. 1381, 159 p.

_____, 1990, Reconnaissance geologic map of the southern Sierra Nevada, Kern, Tulare, and Inyo counties, California: U. S. Geol. Surv. Open-File Report 90-337, 163 p.

Ross, D. C., and Brabb, E. E., 1973, Petrography and structural relations of granitic basement rocks in the Monterey Bay area, California: U. S. Geol. Surv. Jour. Res., v. 1, p. 273–282.

Saleeby, J. B., 1990, Progress in tectonic and petrogenetic studies in an exposed cross-section of young (~100 Ma) continental crust, southern Sierra Nevada, California, *in* Salisbury, M. H., and Fountain, D. M., eds., Exposed cross-sections of the continental crust: Dordrecht, Netherlands, D. Reidel Publ. Co., p. 137–158.

_____, 1992, Structure of the northern segment of the proto–Kern canyon fault zone (PKCFZ), southern Sierra Nevada [abs.]: Geol. Soc. Amer. Abs. Prog., v. 24, p. 80.

Saleeby, J. B., and Busby, C., 1993, Paleogeographic and tectonic setting of axial and western metamorphic framework rocks of the southern Sierra Nevada, California, in Dunne, G., and McDougall, K., eds., Mesozoic Paleogeography of the Western United States-II: Los Angeles, Pacific Sect., Soc. Econ. Paleontol. Mineral., p. 197–226.

Saleeby, J. B., and Busby-Spera, C. J., 1986, Fieldtrip guide to the metamorphic framework rocks of the Lake Isabella area, southern Sierra Nevada, California, in Dunne, G. C., ed., Mesozoic and Cenozoic structural evolution of selected areas, east-central California: Geol. Soc. Amer., Cordilleran Section Fieldtrip Guidebook: Los Angeles, California State Univ., p. 81–94.

Saleeby, J. B., Sams, D. B., and Kistler, R. W., 1987, U/Pb zircon, strontium, and oxygen isotopic and geochronological study of the southernmost Sierra Nevada batholith, California: Jour. Geophys. Res., v. 92, p. 10,443–10,466.

Saleeby, J., and Sharp, W., 1980, Chronology of the structural and petrologic development of the southwest Sierra Nevada foothills, California: Geol. Soc. Amer. Bull., Part II, v. 91, p. 1416–1535.

Sams, D. B., 1986, U/Pb zircon geochronology, petrology, and structural geology of the crystalline rocks of the southern Sierra Nevada and Tehachapi mountains, Kern County, California: Unpubl. Ph.D. thesis, California Inst. Technol., 315 p.

Sams, D. B., and Saleeby, J. B., 1988, Geology and petrotectonic significance of crystalline rocks of the southernmost Sierra Nevada, California, in Ernst, W. G., ed., Metamorphism and crustal evolution of the Western United States. Rubey Volume VII: Englewood Cliffs, NJ, Prentice-Hall, p. 865–893.

Samsel, H. S., 1962, Geology of the southeast quarter of the Cross Mountain quadrangle, Kern County, California: Calif. Div. Mines Geol. Map Sheet 2, scale 1:48,000.

Sharry, J., 1981, The geology of the western Tehachapi Mountains, California: Unpubl. Ph.D. thesis, Massachusetts Inst. Technol., 215 p.

————, 1982, Minimum age and westward continuation of the Garlock fault zone, Tehachapi Mountains, California [abs.]: Geol. Soc. Amer. Abs. Prog., v. 14, p. 233.

Silver, L. T., 1982, Evidence and a model for west-directed early to mid-Cenozoic basement overthrusting in southern California [abs.]: Geol. Soc. Amer. Abs. Prog., v. 14, p. 234.

————, 1983, Paleogene overthrusting in the tectonic evolution of the Transverse Ranges, Mojave and Salinian regions, California [abs.]: Geol. Soc. Amer. Abs. Prog., v. 15, p. 438.

————, 1986, Evidence for Paleogene low-angle detachment of the southern Sierra Nevada [abs.]: Geol. Soc. Amer. Abs. Prog., v. 18, p. 750.

Silver, L. T., and Mattinson, J. M., 1986, "Orphan Salinia" has a home: EOS (Trans. Amer. Geophys. Union), v. 67, p. 1215.

Silver, L. T., and Nourse, J. A., 1986, The Rand Mountains thrust complex in comparison with the Vincent thrust–Pelona schist relationship, southern California [abs.]: Geol. Soc. Amer. Abs. Prog., v. 18, p. 185.

————, 1991, Timing of the Rand thrust and its implication for late Cretaceous tectonics in southern California [abs.]: Geol. Soc. Amer. Abs. Prog., v. 23, p. A480.

Silver, L. T., Sams, D. B., Bursik, M. I., Graymer, R. W., Nourse, J. A., Richards, M. A., and Salyards, S. L., 1984, Some observations of the tectonic history of the Rand Mountains, Mojave Desert, California [abs.]: Geol. Soc. Amer. Abs. Prog., v. 16, p. 333.

Simpson, E. C., 1934, Geology and mineral deposits of the Elizabeth Lake quadrangle, California: Calif. Jour. Mines and Geol., v. 30, p. 371–415.

Smith, A. R., compiler, 1964, Bakersfield sheet of the geologic map of California: Sacramento, California, Calif. Div. Mines and Geol., scale 1:250,000.

Smith, G. I., 1951, The geology of the Cache Creek region, Kern County, California: Unpubl. master's thesis, California Inst. Technol., 72 p.

Snow, J. K., 1992, Large-magnitude Permian shortening and continental-margin tectonics in the southern Cordillera: Geol. Soc. Amer. Bull., v. 104, p. 80–105.

Tennyson, M. E., 1989, Pre-transform early Miocene extension in western California: Geology, v. 17, p. 792–796.

Tikoff, B., and de Saint Blanquat, M., 1997, Transpressional shearing and strike-slip partitioning in the Late Cretaceous Sierra Nevada magmatic arc, California: Tectonics, v. 16, p. 442–459.

Troxel, B. W., and Morton, P. K., 1962, Mines and mineral resources of Kern County, California: Calif. Div. Mines Geol. County Report 1, 370 p.

Wakabayashi, J., and Moores, E. M., 1988, Evidence for the collision of the Salinian block with the Franciscan subduction zone, California: Jour. Geol., v. 96, p. 245–253.

Walker, J. D., Bartley, J. M., and Glazner, A., 1990, Large-magnitude Miocene extension in the central Mojave Desert: Implications for Paleozoic to Tertiary paleogeography and tectonics: Jour. Geophys. Res., v. 95, p. 557–569.

Wernicke, B., 1990, The fluid crustal layer and its implications for continental dynamics, in Salisbury, M. H., and Fountain, D. M., eds., Exposed cross-sections of the continental crust: Dordrecht, Netherlands, D. Reidel Publ. Co., p. 509–544.

Wernicke, B., and Axen, G. A., 1988, On the role of isostasy in the evolution of normal fault systems: Geology, v. 16, p. 848–851.

Wernicke, B., Clayton, R., Ducea, M., Jones, C. H., Park, S., Ruppert, S., Saleeby, J., Snow, J. K., Squires, L., Fliedner, M., Jiracek, G., Keller, R., Klemperer, S., Luetgert, J., Malin, P., Miller, K., Mooney, W., Oliver, H., and Phinney, R., 1996, Origin of high mountains in the continents: The southern Sierra Nevada: Science, v. 271, p. 190–193.

Wheeler, J., and Butler, R. W. H., 1994, Criteria for identifying structures related to true crustal extension in orogens: Jour. Struct. Geol., v. 16, p. 1023–1027.

Wiese, J. H., 1950, Geology and mineral resources of the Neenach quadrangle, California: Calif. Div. Mines Bull. 153, 53 p.

Wood, D. J., 1997, Geology of the eastern Tehachapi Mountains and Late Cretaceous–early Cenozoic tectonics of the southern Sierra Nevada region, Kern County, California: Unpubl. Ph.D. thesis, California Inst. Technol., 287 p.

Wood, D. J., Saleeby, J. B., and Silver, L. T., 1993, Structure and tectonic setting of the eastern Tehachapi range, California [abs.]: Geol. Soc. Amer. Abs. Prog., v. 25, p. 165.

The Origin and Evolution of Large-Volume Silicic Magma Systems: Long Valley Caldera

Kurt M. Knesel and Jon P. Davidson

Department of Earth and Space Sciences, University of California, Los Angeles, California 90095

Abstract

Despite extensive study, the origin of large-volume silicic magma systems remains poorly constrained. We review the source regions and processes involved in the generation, differentiation, and eruption of caldera-related silicic magma with particular reference to the Bishop Tuff erupted from Long Valley Caldera, California. Nd-isotopic compositions of the earliest-erupted rhyolites (between 2.1 and 1.2 Ma) at Glass Mountain, which may be associated with the Bishop Tuff magma chamber, are consistent with extensive fractional crystallization of basaltic magmas derived from an enriched lithospheric mantle source. In contrast, Nd-isotopic compositions of late Glass Mountain lavas (1.2 to 0.8 Ma) and the Bishop Tuff (0.76 Ma) suggest significant incorporation of continental crust.

Shallow-crustal residence histories inferred from Sr-isotopic studies at Long Valley suggest that large-volume silicic magmas reflect either: (1) continuous growth with episodic eruption from a single, large, long-lived magma chamber; or (2) rapid generation and eruption of separate, short-lived magma batches. Residence histories that require several rapid differentiation events ($\leq 10^4$ yr) followed by extended periods ($\geq 10^5$ yr) over which magmas are maintained without significant cooling and crystallization are difficult to reconcile with numerical models of the thermal evolution of shallow-crustal magma reservoirs. Sr-isotopic compositions of the Bishop Tuff and precursor Glass Mountain lavas alternatively may reflect assimilation of wall-rock melts undergoing high-$^{87}Sr/^{86}Sr$, low-Sr concentration dehydration during convective sidewall fractional crystallization of parental rhyolites. If so, the reported apparent Sr-isochronal relationships may have little or no age significance.

Sr-isotopic systematics of the Bishop Tuff also provide insights into the influence of eruption dynamics on compositional gradients recorded in pyroclastic deposits. Sr-isotopic compositions of individual fall and flow pumice are consistent with recent field studies that suggest that the Bishop ignimbrite is intraplinian, and that fall and flow deposits previously interpreted to be sequential are largely coeval. Moreover, the distribution of Sr-isotopic compositions of pumice as a function of stratigraphic height suggests that magmas from different depths with different $^{87}Sr/^{86}Sr$ ratios were intimately mixed before exiting the vent and can be qualitatively predicted from numerical models of magma withdrawal from zoned crustal reservoirs.

Introduction

THE ADVENT OF MODERN geochemical and isotopic methods together with the development of physical volcanology as a rigorous quantitative endeavor has led to a vast improvement of our understanding of volcanic systems over the past 20 years. Despite this, large-volume silicic magma systems remain relatively enigmatic from many perspectives. To some extent this is because of the infrequency of such eruptions and their sheer magnitude, which have precluded direct observation and have demanded reconstruction on the basis of interpretive studies of the geometry and characteristics of the resultant tephra. Several problems are still outstanding:

1. What are the relative mass contributions of crust and mantle to the magma system? This is a particularly important question in evaluating the mass flux from mantle to crust, and in the growth and evolution of large vertical tracts of the continental lithosphere.

2. What processes are responsible for the generation of magma in large-volume silicic magma systems? A spectrum of potential petrogenetic processes might be imagined, falling largely between the extremes of fractional crystallization of a purely mantle-derived liquid and whole-scale crustal anatexis. In the former case, the greatest problem to be surmounted is the implication that

an enormous volume of primitive magma is generated, resulting in a similarly large volume of cumulate material relative to the volume of silicic magma erupted. Geophysical data are generally inconsistent with the existence of large volumes of dense cumulate material at depth. Although crustal anatexis alleviates this predicament, it nevertheless requires large quantities of heat, which is itself unrealistic in the absence of a significant advected mass of basaltic magma.

3. How, and over what time scales, do large-volume silicic magma systems evolve? The occurrence of large magma chambers that are compositionally zoned infers some mechanism of stratification and the prevention of thorough stirring through convection. Recent isotopic studies have suggested that such zoned systems develop significantly earlier than the time of eruption (hundreds of thousands of years), which, in turn, would require a mechanism for prevention of solidification simply through cooling over such a long period of time.

4. What are the relative roles of open- versus closed-system processes in the generation of isotopic variations in zoned silicic magmas? Time scales of the silicic magma differentiation and residence in the shallow crust have been estimated from Sr-isotopic variations recorded by Glass Mountain lavas and the Bishop Tuff (e.g., Halliday et al., 1989; Christensen and DePaolo, 1993; Davies et al., 1994; Christensen and Halliday, 1996). The inferred time scales rely on the assumption that the magmas behaved as closed systems such that the observed Sr-isotopic variations result from *in situ* decay of ^{87}Rb to ^{87}Sr in liquids with distinct but variable Rb/Sr ratios over extended periods of time. *In situ* decay might also occur in differentiated solidified bodies that later are remelted to produce rhyolites (Sparks et al., 1990). Other workers have suggested, however, that Sr-isotopic variations may reflect minor yet isotopically significant additions of wall-rock material (e.g., Noble and Hedge, 1969; Johnson, 1989; Duffield et al., 1996). Consequently, establishing the dominance of open- versus closed-system differentiation of silicic magmas is critical to the evaluation of the time scales of magma residence in the shallow continental crust.

5. Finally, how do eruption dynamics influence pre-eruptive compositional gradients now preserved in pyroclastic flow and fall deposits? Compositional zonation recorded in pyroclastic deposits is generally interpreted to represent *in situ* gradients in source magma reservoirs inverted by tapping the magma body from the top down during eruption (Smith, 1979). Accurate reconstruction of pre-eruptive magma gradients therefore is critically dependent upon careful field mapping and interpretation of eruptive chronology and stratigraphy. Complicating this issue is the uncertain extent to which withdrawal mechanics promote mixing of magma from various levels within a chamber during eruption.

We review these issues, along with some preliminary data from the Bishop Tuff, Long Valley Caldera, California. Our approach is to consider mass, thermal, and fluid-mechanical requirements for the generation, differentiation, and eruption of large volumes of silicic magma in light of studies of the Long Valley magma system.

Caldera-Related Silicic Volcanism at Long Valley

The Long Valley Caldera is a 17 × 32 km elliptical depression, situated along the western edge of the Basin and Range Province at the eastern base of the Sierra Nevada batholith in central California (Fig. 1). The reader is directed to Bailey et al. (1976) and Hill et al. (1985) for excellent reviews of the volcanic development and active tectonic and magmatic processes beneath the Long Valley Caldera.

The earliest eruptions that can be related to the Long Valley magma chamber are the high-silica rhyolite lavas and associated pyroclastic rocks of Glass Mountain, situated on the northeast rim of the present caldera (Fig. 1). Early Glass Mountain rhyolites erupted from 2.1 to 1.2 Ma are significantly more evolved than late Glass Mountain rhyolites and the Bishop Tuff, whereas late Glass Mountain rhyolites erupted from 1.2 to 0.8 Ma are slightly less to slightly more evolved in comparison to the Bishop Tuff

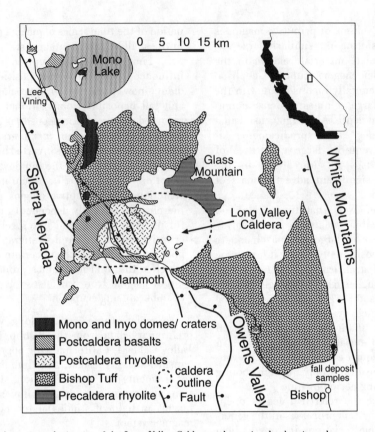

FIG. 1. Schematic geologic map of the Long Valley Caldera and associated volcanic rocks.

(Metz and Mahood, 1991). The chemical, isotopic, and mineralogical heterogeneity, the eruption of magmas with different compositions at the same time in different parts of the field, and the small volume of individual early Glass Mountain lavas are consistent with the concept of eruption from multiple magma bodies, and indicate that an expansive chamber did not exist beneath Long Valley during this early phase of silicic volcanism. However, the relative chemical, isotopic, and mineralogical homogeneity of late Glass Mountain lavas suggest that a large, integrated magma chamber directly related to the Bishop Tuff magma reservoir may have coalesced by or shortly after 1.2 Ma (Metz and Mahood, 1991).

Partial emptying of the magma chamber at 0.76 Ma (van den Bogaard and Schirnick, 1995) resulted in a widespread plinian fall deposit and voluminous partially welded ignimbrite (collectively termed the Bishop Tuff) and collapse of the roof to form the Long Valley Caldera

(Gilbert, 1938). Early field studies by Hildreth (1977) and Hildreth and Mahood (1986) suggested that the eruption began with widespread deposition of fall pumice from a plinian eruption column from an initial vent site near the intersection of the Hilton Creek fault with the ring fracture system along the present-day southern-central caldera wall. Pyroclastic flow followed as a result of column collapse as the vent system migrated counterclockwise toward Glass Mountain and eventually toward the northwestern margin of the caldera. Recent reexamination of the stratigraphy of the Bishop Tuff now suggests that the eruption sequence is more complicated than previously recognized (Wilson and Hildreth, 1997) and forms the framework for interpretation of new Sr-isotopic data related to the development of the Bishop Tuff magma reservoir.

Petrologic studies suggest that the Bishop Tuff reflects the inverted contents of a source reservoir that was zoned with respect to phenocryst content, temperature, trace-element and volatile concentrations, Sr-isotope composition, and oxygen fugacity (Hildreth, 1977, 1979). Over the last 20 years, numerous geochemical, isotopic, and volcanologic studies (Michael, 1983; Cameron, 1984; Halliday et al., 1984; Miller and Mittlefehldt, 1984; Snow and Yund, 1985, 1988; Anderson et al., 1989, Anderson, 1991; Gardner et al., 1991; Dunbar and Hervig, 1992; Hervig and Dunbar, 1992; Lu et al., 1992; Christensen and DePaolo, 1993; Duffield et al., 1996; Christensen and Halliday, 1996) have expanded upon Hildreth's initial studies of the physical and chemical structure of the parental Bishop Tuff magma reservoir.

Origin and Sources of Large-Volume Silicic Magma Systems

Isotopic constraints on crustal versus mantle contributions

Isotope systematics have become the tool of choice in distinguishing the contributions to magma systems of different sources. Continental crust and the asthenospheric mantle, in principle, have distinct radiogenic isotope ratios (such as $^{87}Sr/^{86}Sr$, $^{143}Nd/^{144}Nd$, $^{206, 207, 208}Pb/^{204}Pb$, $^{176}Hf/^{177}Hf$), reflecting long-term partitioning of parent/daughter elements during crust-forming processes. This first-order observation, however, is moderated by a number of factors: (1) the difference in isotopic characteristics is a function of age; therefore, the isotopic contrast between young continental crust and the mantle (or basalts derived therefrom) may be negligible (e.g., Davidson et al., 1987; Johnson, 1989); (2) the contributions determined on the basis of isotope ratios are weighted according to elemental concentrations (of Sr, Nd, Pb, Hf) that may vary over orders of magnitude and may be poorly known; and (3) even though closed-system magmatic processes do not modify isotope ratios, secondary processes may have a significant influence. This problem is particularly acute in the case of Sr, which is both relatively mobile in fluids and of characteristically extremely low abundance in high-silica rhyolites, making such rocks highly vulnerable to secondary modification by hydrothermal alteration or weathering (e.g., Halliday et al., 1984; Bohrson and Reid, 1997).

Notwithstanding these problems, no large-volume silicic magma systems (LVSMS) are characterized by geochemical and isotope systematics consistent with derivation solely from an incompatible-element-depleted asthenosphere. Furthermore, all LVSMS eruptions occur in regions of continental rather than oceanic lithosphere. This likely reflects, in part, the role of thick, low-density lithosphere in impeding magma ascent and promoting accumulation of evolved magmas, although the geochemical and isotopic data also require some mass contribution from the continental lithosphere itself. The lithospheric contribution may be simply continental crust mixed into asthenosphere-derived basalt, or may involve a mantle component from the subcontinental lithosphere.

Neodymium isotopes have proven particularly useful in evaluating crustal versus mantle contributions to silicic magmas (e.g., Farmer and DePaolo, 1983; DePaolo et al., 1992; Perry et al., 1993). The fraction of magma derived from the crust as opposed to that derived from the mantle can be assessed by the neodymium crustal index (NCI) (DePaolo et al., 1992):

$$NCI = \frac{\Delta\varepsilon_{Nd(rock-mantle)}}{\Delta\varepsilon_{Nd(crust-mantle)}},$$

where NCI represents the fraction of Nd derived from the crust. Relative *mass* contributions may be poorly constrained, however, since the Nd-isotope composition and, more significantly, Nd content of the primary basalts and crustal contaminants are largely unknown. To convert NCI to a mass (or volume) fraction, the concentrations of Nd in the crust-derived and mantle-derived (primary basalt) end members must be specified. The relationship between the NCI and mass fraction of crust is shown in Figure 2. Although for simplicity the ratio of Nd in the crustal component to Nd in the mantle-derived component is commonly assumed to be 1, values ranging over two orders of magnitude are possible. This range in estimated Nd contents of crustal and mantle-derived basalt reservoirs may lead to significant uncertainty in the calculated mass fraction of magma derived from the crust (Fig. 2). This exercise serves to illustrate the poor constraints on physically significant (in terms of energy budgets) component

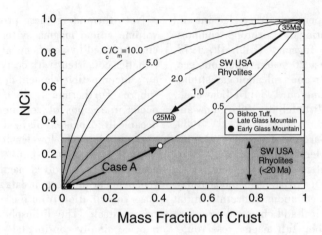

FIG. 2. Relationship between NCI and mass fraction of crust in silicic magma systems. NCI is defined as the fraction of Nd contributed by the crust, after DePaolo et al., 1992 (see text). Curves are for varying crustal (c) and mantle-derived (m) basalt Nd concentrations. Case A represents mixing of Sierran crust (e.g., DePaolo, 1981) with mantle lithosphere–derived basalts (Cousens, 1996) to produce Bishop Tuff and precursor rhyolite magmas.

volumes, even in cases where the relative contributions of specific elements are quite well constrained.

Neodymium-isotopic data for Cenozoic granites and rhyolites of the western United States indicate that crustal contributions of Nd range from less than 10% to greater than 80% (DePaolo et al., 1992; Perry et al., 1993). Perry et al. (1993) showed that rhyolite NCI values correlate with eruption ages; Oligocene systems have NCI values that systematically decrease (from 0.9 to 0.4) with age between 35 and 26 Ma, whereas Miocene to Pleistocene systems have NCI values of <0.3 (Fig. 2). Rhyolite systems younger than 20 Ma appear to be dominated by mantle components. DePaolo and co-workers have suggested that decreasing crustal contributions to rhyolite systems from early Oligocene time to the beginning of the Miocene reflect the thermal evolution of the Cordilleran crust. Regional cooling of the crust corresponding to a decrease in the geothermal gradient from 30°C/km to 20°C/km over this ~15 m.y. period may have progressively limited the amount of lower crustal material assimilated by silicic systems (Perry et al., 1993).

NCI values calculated for the Bishop Tuff and precursor Glass Mountain lavas (Fig. 2) are in general agreement with the results of DePaolo et al. (1992) and Perry et al. (1993). Rhyolite Nd-isotopic compositions used in the calculations represent (1) melt inclusions in quartz phenocrysts (Christensen and Halliday, 1996) and whole-rock and sanidine samples (Halliday et al., 1984) for the Bishop Tuff, and (2) whole-rock, glass, and mineral separates from early and late lavas of Glass Mountain (Halliday et al., 1989; Davies et al., 1994). Estimates of the ϵ_{Nd} values and Nd concentrations of the crustal and mantle components (Fig. 2) reflect the considerable uncertainty of the chemical and isotopic structure of the mantle in the western Great Basin (Ormerod et al., 1988, 1991; Beard and Glazner, 1995; Cousens, 1996; Reid and Ramos, 1996).

Basalts erupted at Long Valley prior to and during Glass Mountain activity (Pliocene series ~3.6 to 2.2 Ma) and just prior to the catastrophic eruption of the Bishop Tuff (older basalts ~1.0 to 0.8 Ma) have ϵ_{Nd} values between –4.8 and –2.8, whereas those erupted after the Bishop Tuff show a systematic shift toward less enriched or depleted sources with time (Moat-Postpile series ~0.42 to 0.02 Ma with ϵ_{Nd} = –4.0 to –0.9; younger basalts < 0.013 Ma with ϵ_{Nd} = +0.6 to +2.6) (Cousens, 1996). We consider the following two hypotheses for the shift with time from enriched to less enriched mafic magmatism at Long Valley. (A) Combined isotopic and trace-element systematics suggest that the temporal shift in composition reflects the increasing contribution of a high-ϵ_{Nd} mafic crustal component similar to deep-level tonalitic to gabbroic roots of the Sierra Nevada batholith

(Cousens, 1996). (B) Alternatively, the temporal isotopic shift in Long Valley basalts may reflect a second, "less enriched" lithospheric mantle source beneath the Long Valley area, which has become a progressively more important contributor to basaltic magmas with time (Cousens, 1996; Reid and Ramos, 1996). Accordingly, crustal contributions to silicic volcanism at Long Valley fall into two categories.

Case A. If the Long Valley Pliocene series and older basalts are parental to Glass Mountain and Bishop Tuff magmas, a positive ϵ_{Nd} crustal source is required to shift the Glass Mountain and Bishop Tuff Nd-isotopic compositions to more radiogenic values. Assuming a mantle component of ϵ_{Nd} = -3.6 (average Pliocene series/older basalt of Cousens, 1996) and a crustal component of ϵ_{Nd} = + 6.3 (average Sierran quartz diorite of DePaolo, 1981), we calculate a NCI value of 0.04 for early Glass Mountain lavas erupted from 2.1 Ma to 1.2 Ma, whereas late Glass Mountain lavas erupted between 1.2 and 0.79 Ma and the Bishop Tuff (0.76 Ma) has NCI values of 0.26 (Fig. 2). These NCI values correspond to an increasing mass fraction of the crustal component from ≤5% for early Glass Mountain lavas to ~40% for late Glass Mountain lavas and the Bishop Tuff (Fig. 2). The increasing crustal contribution with time is consistent with increasing crustal temperature during magmatic growth in a basalt-driven magmatic system (Hildreth, 1981).

Case B. If the compositional variation recorded by Long Valley mafic lavas reflects temporally controlled contributions from distinct lithospheric mantle sources beneath the Long Valley area, the rhyolitic magmas for both Glass Mountain and Bishop Tuff can be derived solely by fractional crystallization of lithospheric mantle–derived basalts with no crustal input (i.e., NCI = 0). The shift in Nd-isotopic compositions from ϵ_{Nd} = -3 to ϵ_{Nd} = -1 is accounted for by variable contributions of enriched and less-enriched lithospheric mantle sources.

Although the above exercise is plagued by the uncertainty of the chemical and isotopic structure of lithosphere in the western Great Basin, particularly near the proposed edge of the Precambrian continental margin as defined by Sr- and Nd-isotopic studies (Kistler and Peterman, 1978; Farmer and DePaolo, 1983), the end-member cases presented here can be used to evaluate the material and thermal roles of basalt in Long Valley silicic magmas.

Reconciling mass and thermal inputs and the role of fractional crystallization in basalt-driven silicic magma systems

Material budgets. In principle, the basaltic input to LVSMS can be derived from petrogenetic modeling of the geochemical and isotopic characteristics of a particular system using expressions that describe the evolution of a magma body undergoing recharge, assimilation, and fractional crystallization (DePaolo, 1985). However, such models require knowledge of the rates of recharge, assimilation, and crystallization in addition to the isotopic and elemental compositions of end members. We propose an alternative approach in which NCI values are converted to actual mass-fraction values based on estimated crustal and mantle Nd concentrations, and then absolute masses or volumes are calculated on the basis of known eruptive volumes.

In Figure 2, we show that, for the open-system model (Case A), the mass fraction of crust in the Bishop Tuff is ~0.4. Given an eruptive volume of ~600 km³ for the Bishop Tuff, this translates to a crustal contribution of ~240 km³. The volume of basalt needed to produce the remainder of the erupted rhyolitic magma then can be calculated on the basis of the degree of fractionation required to produce rhyolitic liquid from a mantle-derived basaltic progenitor, taken here to be ~90% (see discussion below). We estimate that ~3600 km³ of mantle-derived basalt was needed to produce the remaining 360 km³ of Bishop Tuff rhyolite (Fig. 3).

We also consider the basalt budget required to produce the Bishop Tuff through closed-system fractional crystallization (Case B). Least-squares fractionation models, although plagued by the vagaries of phase assemblages and primitive magma composition, suggest that fractionation on the order of 90% or more is required to produce rhyolitic magma from a basaltic parent. Trace-element constraints may be equally useful in constraining the degree of fractionation. Given a wholly incompatible element (D_i = 0), the amount of liquid remaining during fractional crystallization is given by the ratio of concentrations in the primitive (c_0) versus evolved (c_l) magmas:

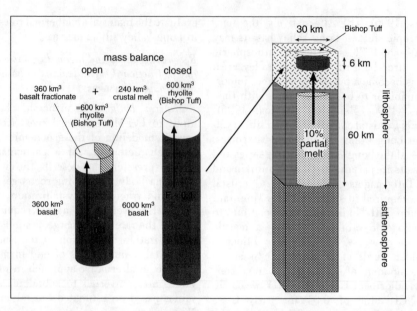

FIG. 3. Schematic illustration of relative volumes involved in open- and closed-system differentiation of the Bishop Tuff from a basaltic parent. The letter F represents the relative volume of liquid produced by fractional crystallization. The right-hand column indicates the volumes relative to the crust and mantle, and the amount of mantle processed by partial melting.

$$F = \frac{c_0}{c_1}.$$

Incompatible trace-element concentrations in high-silica rhyolites are greater by at least a factor of 10 than those in potential primitive basalts from the lithospheric mantle, again suggesting crystallization of 90% or more to produce the extreme trace-element enrichments and depletions typical of LVSM. Given the volume of differentiates erupted at such systems, the equivalent volume of cumulates can be calculated. In the case of the 600 km³ Bishop Tuff, this translates to 6000 km³ of cumulate material, which is approximately twice that required for the open-system model (Case A). The Long Valley Caldera from which the Bishop Tuff was erupted is ~1000 km² in area; thus a column of crustal cumulate of this cross-sectional area would need to be ~6 km thick in order to produce the observed volume of rhyolite (Fig. 3). If the basaltic flux is considered to represent a time period of ~1 m.y. (Christensen and DePaolo, 1993), then the volume inferred for closed-system crystallization (6000 km³) exceeds estimates for the emplace-

ment of the Sierra Nevada batholith (~1000 km³ per m.y.) (Crisp, 1984). Nonetheless, basalt influx rates of 0.006 km³yr⁻¹ and 0.003 km³yr⁻¹ suggested by the closed- and open-system models, respectively, are within the limits of influx rates inferred from studies of magmatism in regions of lithospheric extension, which suggest that caldera-forming volcanic activity results from intrusion of basaltic magmas into the lower crust at rates of ~0.01 km³yr⁻¹ for 10⁵ to 10⁶ years (Shaw, 1985).

Closed-system fractionation seems problematic, however, when it is realized that the large volume of basalt inferred would require an even greater volume of mantle to be partially melted. A conservative estimate of partial melting (e.g., 10%) requires processing of ~60,000 km³ of mantle (nearly twice that required by the open-system model)—equivalent to a cylindrical source region with a cross-sectional area of Long Valley extending over the entire thickness of the mantle lithosphere (Fig 3).

We favor the open-system model for the derivation of the Bishop Tuff, considering: (1) the geochemical arguments discussed in the previous section; (2) the extensive basalt volume and expansive mantle source region required by the closed-system model; and (3) the enormous heat budget provided by both the sensible and latent heat of large volumes of basalt (see discussion below), which undoubtedly would heat and melt an extensive region surrounding a large basalt reservoir in the middle to deep crust. Accordingly, Nd-isotopic studies suggest that the crustal input to the Bishop Tuff is on the order of 40 vol%.

Thermal balance. The basaltic input needed to drive the system thermally can be evaluated by a simple thermodynamic approach, whereby the enthalpy produced during cooling and crystallization of the basaltic magma (right side of equation) is balanced with the enthalpy required to heat (first term on left side of the equation) and melt the crust (terms in parentheses on left side of the equation) to produce rhyolitic crustal component (Reiners et al., 1995):

$$M_c \int C_p^c dT^c + (M_{cm}\Delta H_f^{cm} + M_{cm}\int C_p^{cm} dT^{cm})$$

$$= M_{xtl}\Delta H_f^{xtl} + M_b \int C_p^b dT^b,$$

where M_c, M_{cm}, M_{xtl}, and M_b are the masses of crustal rock, crustal melt, crystals, and basalt; ΔH_f^{cm} and ΔH_f^{xtl} are the latent heats of fusion and crystallization; C_p^c, C_p^{cm}, and C_p^b are the heat capacities of the crust, crustal melt, and basalt; and dT^c, dT^{cm}, and dT^b are the temperature changes of the crustal rock, crustal melt, and basalt. The mass of the basaltic magma needed to heat, melt, and assimilate the crust is then given by:

$$M_b = \frac{1}{C_p^b \Delta T^b}[M_c C_p^c \Delta T^c + M_{cm}C_p^{cm} \Delta T^{cm}$$

$$+ M_{cm}\Delta H_f^{cm} - M_{xtl}\Delta H_f^{xtl}].$$

To facilitate comparison with estimates (Grunder, 1995) of the material and thermal roles of basalt in intermediate to silicic magmas erupted in eastern Nevada, we assume: (1) equal and constant latent heats for all phases of 3×10^5 Jkg^{-1}; (2) equal and constant heat capacities of 1100 Jkg^{-1}°K^{-1}; (3) a basalt density of 2890 kgm^{-3}; and (4) initial temperatures of crust and basalt of 400°C and 1300°C, respectively. Based on isotopic and geochemical

arguments outlined by Cousens (1996), we also assume a contaminant similar to Sierra Nevada mafic residues with a solidus temperature of 900°C for dehydration melting of biotite gneiss at 10 kbar to produce a granitic melt (~73 wt% SiO$_2$) and a final crustal melt fraction of ~0.5 for the biotite-out temperature of 950°C (Patiño-Douce and Beard, 1995). We calculated a crustal density of 2835 kg/m^{-3} based on the modal contents reported by Patiño-Douce and Beard (1995) and mineral densities from Deer et al. (1992). In keeping the Fe-Ti oxide equilibration temperatures for the Bishop Tuff (Hildreth, 1979), we assume a final magma (basalt after ~90 crystallization + crustal melt) temperature of 800°C. With these assumptions and assuming a rhyolite magma density of 2200 kgm^{-3}, we calculate that ~1350 km^3 of basalt is needed to thermally generate the rhyolitic magma erupted to form the Bishop Tuff. Interestingly, this value is only ~40% of the input required by the mass balance.

The lesser basalt budget required thermally in comparison to material requirements for the Bishop Tuff appears incompatible with the results of Grunder (1995), who reported the volume of basalt needed to thermally drive Oligocene magmatism in eastern Nevada was 1.5 to 2 times the amount needed materially. We suggest, however, that the disparate thermal and material role of basalt in these two systems is consistent with the extent of crystal fractionation required to produce the erupted volcanic rocks. The Oligocene volcanic output in eastern Nevada is volumetrically dominated by andesitic to dacitic lavas (Grunder, 1995), and therefore requires considerably less fractional crystallization during differentiation from a basaltic progenitor than that required by high-silica rhyolites such as the Bishop Tuff. Consequently, the energy provided by crystallization (i.e., latent heat) of mafic parental magmas is substantially greater in rhyolitic magma systems than in systems dominated by intermediate compositions. Apparently, andesitic to dacitic systems require a larger proportion of sensible heat in the overall energy balance and thus a larger relative amount of mantle-derived basalt to thermally drive magmatism in comparison to LVSMS.

Shallow Crustal Residence Histories of Large-Volume Silicic Magma Systems

Sr-isotopic constraints on differentiation events and time scales

There is considerable debate regarding whether long-lived silicic volcanic centers record continuous evolution of a single, pluton-sized, upper-crustal magma chamber, or repeated pulses of magma emplaced and erupted from separate, discrete chambers. Recent studies of the Bishop Tuff and precursor rhyolites of Glass Mountain lavas have suggested that compositional variation among magmas (and between phases that constitute the magmas) was established well before the time of eruption. At Glass Mountain, Rb/Sr isochrons are defined among rhyolite glasses and whole-rock samples at 2.1, 1.9, 1.15, and 1.09 Ma, and are interpreted to reflect differentiation "events" pre-dating eruption by up to 360 k.y. (Halliday et al., 1989; Davies et al., 1994; Davies and Halliday, 1997). Time scales for the evolution of the Bishop Tuff based on sanidine Rb/Sr model ages and the time necessary to establish the isotopic differences among homogeneous layers of distinct Sr-isotopic compositions range from 300 to 500 k.y. (Christensen and DePaolo, 1993). However, Rb/Sr model ages for melt inclusion–bearing quartz crystals in the Bishop Tuff now suggest differentiation ages of between 1.3 and 2.5 Ma for air-fall pumice, whereas those for ignimbrite samples suggest differentiation ages between 1.04 and 1.18 Ma (Christensen and Halliday, 1996). Thus, the isotopic data appear to indicate extremely protracted residence times (300 to 1800 Ka) for the Bishop Tuff magma and its precursors.

Sparks et al. (1990) argued that, although the Glass Mountain isotopic data may reflect discrete differentiation events, they do not unequivocally indicate the existence of a single, long-lived magma body. They suggest that the Sr-isotopic systematics of the Glass Mountain lavas are more consistent with separate melting and differentiation events in response to basaltic intrusion into a heterogeneous lower crust, yielding several discrete magma bodies with differing Sr-isotopic signatures. Although these bodies would solidify rapidly to form granitoids, they still would evolve isotopically and, upon later basaltic influx, would rapidly remelt

and erupt as rhyolitic lavas and pyroclastic units.

A third model, proposed by Mahood (1990) to explain the isochronal relationships of Glass Mountain lavas, shifts the site of final magma generation into the upper crust through remelting or "defrosting" of partially to wholly crystallized low-Sr high-silica rhyolite. The model of Mahood (1990) differs from the Halliday et al. (1989), and Sparks et al. (1990) end members in that the isochron ages reflect the residence times for the Sr-poor material either as a liquid, crystal mush, or solid in the roof zone of the Long Valley magma system. The model still allows for, but does not require, long magma residence times (Mahood, 1990).

At present this spirited debate remains unresolved, as consideration of geochemical and isotopic data alone cannot definitively distinguish between the models. Consideration of the thermal evolution of large volumes of magma emplaced within the shallow crust provide independent constraints on the longevity of silicic magma reservoirs and therefore may ultimately provide insights into the interpretation of isochronal relationships in LVSMS.

Thermal constraints on magma-chamber longevity

Evaluation of the viability of maintaining chemically zoned rhyolitic magma bodies for long periods (10^5 to 10^6 yr) without significant cooling or crystallization requires consideration of the thermal evolution of such bodies. A qualitative assessment of the thermal requirements of the various models discussed above can be found in Sparks et al. (1990), Halliday (1990), and Mahood (1990). Here we consider some quantitative constraints imposed by the modeling of the thermal evolution of magma bodies (Spera, 1980) and resulting implications for the chemical and thermal evolution of the Long Valley magma system.

Using a parameterized approach to model the thermal history of plutons, Spera (1980) demonstrated that the dominant factors controlling cooling histories are: (1) depth of magma emplacement, (2) heat-transfer characteristics of the local environment, (3) size of the magma body, and (4) bulk composition of the melt. Solidification times, defined as the time necessary for magma to cool from the initial emplacement temperature to the solidus temperature (i.e., to solidify completely) vary as $R^{1.3}$, where R is the pluton radius (assuming spherical geometry). Solidification times for granitic magma bodies emplaced at a depth of 2 km with radii of 1, 5, and 10 km are $\sim 5 \times 10^4$, $\sim 4 \times 10^5$, and $\sim 1.1 \times 10^6$ years, respectively (see Fig. 1b of Spera, 1980). These chamber sizes are roughly equivalent to inferred dimensions of parental early Glass Mountain, late Glass Mountain, and Bishop Tuff reservoirs, respectively, assuming that: (1) early Glass Mountain lavas were erupted from more than one magma body (Metz and Mahood, 1991); (2) late Glass Mountain lavas reflect a large, integrated magma chamber (Metz and Mahood, 1991); and (3) silicic magma reservoirs are typically an order of magnitude larger than eruptive products, since only a fraction of the magma chamber is evacuated during eruption (Smith, 1979).

In light of the thermal restrictions outlined above, the long residence times inferred for Glass Mountain and Bishop Tuff magmas demand an external heat source (e.g., basaltic underplating) in order to prevent inevitable cooling and crystallization (Halliday et al., 1989; Halliday, 1990; Mahood, 1990; Sparks et al., 1990; Christensen and DePaolo, 1993). A simple thermal balance of the sensible and latent heats of the basaltic input required to generate the Bishop Tuff in 500 k.y. developed by Christensen and DePaolo (1993) suggests that the rate of heat addition to the base of the system (2.8×10^8 Js^{-1}) is in agreement with estimates of the current heat loss for the Long Valley Caldera (2.9×10^8 Js^{-1}) (Sorey et al., 1978). This observation also is compatible with the suggestion that the thermal perturbations of new arrivals of basalt into the base of the system are dampened by the transfer of heat through the system and the buffering effect of the latent heats of silicate minerals in the crystallized rind along the chamber margins (Halliday, 1990; Mahood, 1990). It should be noted, however, that a relatively constant balance between heat lost through the top of the system and basalt addition to the base seems inconsistent with the existence of multiple, discrete differentiation events for Long Valley silicic magmas. The generation of distinct batches of rhyolitic magma at 2.1, 1.9, 1.15, and 1.09 Ma requires episodic rapid cooling and differentiation ($\leq 10^4$ yr) followed by similarly rapid reestablishment of thermal balance so as to pre-

vent further crystallization. Each thermal perturbation then must be followed by extended periods ($\geq 10^5$ yr) during which the thermal balance is maintained. We concur with Sparks et al. (1990) that the thermal requirements of any model that requires both rapid thermal oscillations and long thermal balances seems suspect. Unfortunately, the lack of quantitative constraints on the temporal and spatial thermal evolution of open-magma systems leads to considerable frustration in formulating precise models for the magmatic development of large volumes of silicic magma.

Influence of magma–wall-rock interaction on isotopic systematics

Although variations in ^{87}Sr/^{86}Sr ratios in high-silica rhyolites may be attributed to closed-system *in situ* decay of ^{87}Rb in magmas with steep Rb/Sr gradients (Mahood and Halliday, 1988; Halliday et al., 1989; Christensen and DePaolo, 1993; Davies et al., 1994; Christensen and Halliday, 1996), many ash-flow tuffs record isotopic zonations that appear to require assimilation of country-rock material along the roof and/or sidewalls of magma bodies (Noble and Hedge, 1969; Matty et al., 1987; Johnson, 1989; Tegtmeyer and Farmer, 1990). For example, unlike the Sr-isotopic variations noted for Long Valley silicic magmas, Nd-isotopic zonations recorded in the Double-H Mountains Tuff in the McDermitt volcanic field of north-central Nevada and the Topopah Spring Tuff in the Timber Mountain–Oasis Valley caldera complex of southwestern Nevada (Tegtmeyer and Farmer, 1990) cannot be attributed to closed-system decay of ^{147}Sm to ^{143}Nd because of the low parent/daughter ratios (Sm/Nd < 1.0) of analyzed samples and the long half-life of ^{147}Sm (106 Ga). Neodymium-isotopic variations at the Timber Mountain–Oasis Valley caldera complex (Tegtmeyer and Farmer, 1990; Farmer et al., 1991) support the early suggestion by Noble and Hedge (1969) that Sr-isotopic variations in these tuffs resulted from assimilation of radiogenic country-rock material by the parent magmas prior to eruption. Similarly, Pb-isotopic variations in ash flow tuffs at the San Juan caldera complex (Matty et al., 1987) and the Amalia Tuff erupted from the Questa Caldera in northern New Mexico (Johnson, 1989; Johnson et al., 1989) require open-system evolution for the magma bodies tapped to produce these tuffs.

Direct evidence for the influence of shallow-level magma–wall-rock interaction on Sr-isotope systematics in silicic magmas is preserved in the Taylor Creek Rhyolite, a group of mid-Tertiary lava flows and domes in southwestern New Mexico. Detailed studies of the Taylor Creek Rhyolite reveal abundant geochemical evidence of minor, yet easily measurable assimilation of roof rock material (Reece et al., 1990; Duffield and Ruiz, 1992a, 1992b; Wittke et al., 1996). Strontium-isotopic compositions of Taylor Creek Rhyolite whole-rock samples yield an Rb/Sr isochron "age" of 26.8 ± 0.2 Ma (Fig. 4). However, high-precision $^{40}Ar/^{39}Ar$ analysis of sanidine phenocrysts indicate that the Taylor Creek Rhyolite was emplaced in ≤ 100 k.y. at 27.9 Ma (Duffield and Dalrymple, 1990). The Rb/Sr isochron "age" is 1.1 m.y. younger than the known eruption age and thus has no age significance. The apparent Rb/Sr isochron appears to reflect open-system processes, in accord with: (1) independent geochemical evidence for crustal contamination of the Taylor Creek Rhyolite lavas (Duffield and Ruiz, 1992a, 1992b; Wittke et al., 1996); and (2) the fact that Sr-isotopic zonation in the Taylor Creek Rhyolite could not have been produced by *in situ* decay, as Rb/Sr gradients defined by early and late eruptive units are opposite to the sense of isotopic zoning (Duffield and Ruiz, 1992b). Although integrated chemical and isotopic data suggest that contamination of the Taylor Creek Rhyolite magma body occurred by a complex process involving incongruent melting and assimilation of country rock (Duffield and Ruiz, 1992a, 1992b), for the sake of simplicity, we note that bulk assimilation of ≤ 1 wt% of Precambrian rocks that crop out in southwestern New Mexico by the least contaminated Taylor Creek Rhyolite magma (Sr ~ 3 ppm and $^{87}Sr/^{86}Sr_i \sim 0.7046$) would produce the most contaminated magma (Sr ~ 20 ppm and $^{87}Sr/^{86}Sr_i \sim 0.7131$) (Reece et al., 1990).

The important point is that differences between known eruption ages and apparent Rb/Sr isochron ages for silicic magmas zoned with respect to Sr isotopes do not necessarily reflect magma residence ages. In the Taylor Creek Rhyolite, the linear correlation of $^{87}Sr/^{86}Sr$ with $^{87}Rb/^{86}Sr$ is better explained as a "mixing-

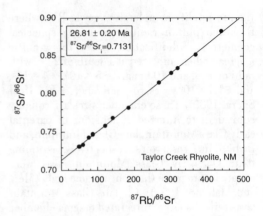

FIG. 4. Rb/Sr isochron formed by whole-rock samples from the Taylor Creek Rhyolite, New Mexico. Rb/Sr isotopic data from Reece et. al. (1990). The pseudo-isochron age of these rocks indicated by the slope is 26.8 ± 0.2 m.y., which is 1.1 m.y. younger than the known eruption age of 27.9 ± 0.1 Ma (Duffield and Dalrymple, 1990).

chron" rather than an age-significant isochron. A similar conclusion was reached by Verplanck et al. (1995) to explain an apparent Rb/Sr isochron age ~ 10 m.y. older than the known age of the Organ Needle pluton in south-central New Mexico. The role of magma–wall-rock interaction in the production of Rb/Sr isochronal relationships is easily recognized in these two silicic systems because of the extreme differences between the Sr-isotopic composition of the magmas and Precambrian wall rocks (Reece et al., 1990; Verplanck et al., 1995). Although significant Sr-isotopic differences exist between parental Bishop Tuff magma and Mesozoic to Paleozoic wall rocks, the younger age and hence lower $^{87}Sr/^{86}Sr$ ratios of the local country rocks fails to provide the dramatic leverage on Sr-isotopic systematics exhibited in the Taylor Creek Rhyolite and Organ Needle pluton systems. Thus the effect of volumetrically minor contamination is not as readily detectable in the isotopic record at Long Valley.

Halliday et al. (1989), Halliday (1990), and Mahood (1990) argued against wall-rock contamination as a viable mechanism for the generation of Sr-isotopic variations among Glass Mountain lavas because incorporation of high-Sr (Sr = 100 to 1000 ppm) Sierran granites and metamorphic rocks appears inconsistent with the generation and preservation of the isochronal relationships and low Sr concentrations of

TABLE 1. Composition of Selected Experimental and Natural Anatectic Melts

Protolith	Melting reaction[1]	SiO$_2$, wt%	Rb, ppm	Sr, ppm	[87]Sr/[86]Sr	Reference[2]
Granite	bt ± pl ± ks ± qtz = mlt ± crd ± ox ± rt	73–77	391–427	20–114	0.7079–0.7082	1
Granite	bt ± pl ± ks ± qtz = mlt ± px ± ox	78	325–427	27–30	0.7082–0.7089	2
Granodiorite	bt ± pl ± ks ± qtz = mlt ± px ± ox	70–74	234–271	61–80	0.7140–0.7128	3
Quartz monzonite	bt + ? = mlt				0.7229	4
Granite	bt ± pl ± ks ± qtz = mlt ± ox	60–77	370–768	46–241	0.8559–2.227	5, 6
Sierra Nevada granitoids			38–205	180–726	0.7041–0.7102	7, 8, 9

[1]Mineral abbreviations: bt = biotite; pl = plagioclase; ks = alkali-feldspar; qtz = quartz; mlt = melt; crd = cordierite; ox = Fe-Ti oxides; rt = rutile.
[2]References: 1 = Kaczor et al., 1988; 2 = Tommasini and Davies, 1997; 3 = Knesel and Davidson, 1997; 4 = Pushkar and Stoeser, 1975; 5 = Knesel and Davidson, 1996; 6 = Knesel, 1997; 7 = Kistler and Peterman, 1973; 8 = DePaolo, 1981; 9 = Kistler et al., 1986.

Glass Mountain lavas. We note, however, that: (1) the Taylor Creek Rhyolite and Organ Needle pluton studies clearly demonstrate that open-system processes can result in the generation of pseudo-isochronal relationships, and (2) experimental and field studies of wall-rock melting at shallow-crustal conditions suggest that preferential breakdown of hydrous phases such as biotite may result in the production of high-[87]Sr/[86]Sr, low-Sr contaminant liquids (Pushkar and Stoesser, 1975; Kaczor et al., 1988; Knesel and Davidson, 1996, 1997; Tommasini and Davies, 1997) (see Table 1 for a compilation of selected high-[87]Sr/[86]Sr, low-Sr anatectic melts). Volumetrically minor assimilation of wall-rock melts similar to those listed in Table 1, when coupled with fractional crystallization, allows for significant increases in [87]Sr/[86]Sr ratios without raising the low Sr concentrations typical of high-silica rhyolites. Evidence for minor assimilation of granitoid wall-rock material may be recorded in scarce biotite xenocrysts found in both Glass Mountain lavas (Metz and Mahood, 1991) and the Bishop Tuff (Christensen and DePaolo, 1993). Although we do not at this time advocate an open-system origin for the Rb/Sr isochronal relationships among Long Valley rhyolites, we do caution that the lessons learned from other silicic systems, such as the Taylor Creek Rhyolite and Organ Needle pluton, in which open-system processes

are more easily recognizable, warrant re-evaluation of the Glass Mountain and Bishop Tuff isotopic data.

Reconstructing Pre-Eruptive Gradients of Large-Volume Silicic Magma Systems

Vertical zonation in compositional and physical parameters in ash flow tuffs are generally interpreted to reflect stratification in the source magma reservoir that was inverted during eruption (Smith, 1979). Monotonic gradients in density, viscosity, temperature, trace elements, isotopes, phenocrysts, and volatiles are common (Hildreth, 1981; Wolff et al, 1990). The origin of these zonations in the Bishop Tuff and other large-volume silicic systems is the subject of considerable debate (e.g., Noble and Hedge, 1969; Hildreth, 1979, 1981; Michael, 1983; Cameron, 1984; Halliday et al., 1984; Miller and Mittlefehldt, 1984; Johnson, 1989; Hervig and Dunbar, 1992; Duffield and Ruiz, 1992a; Christensen and DePaolo, 1993; Christensen and Halliday, 1996; Duffield et al., 1996). Complicating this issue is the uncertain extent to which magma withdrawal and emplacement dynamics influence actual gradients observed in pyroclastic deposits in relation to pre-eruptive compositional gradients in the magma chamber. Accurate reconstruction of *in situ* gradients requires detailed knowledge of: (1) eruptive chronometry and stratigraphy, which can only be established through detailed field study of pyroclastic deposits and (2) fluid dynamics of magma withdrawal, which may promote mixing of magmas as a result of simultaneous withdrawal of magma from different locations within the chamber.

Eruptive systematics

Pyroclastic eruption columns often are categorized as either stable (buoyant) plumes, which produce fall deposits, or unstable collapsing plumes, which generate pyroclastic flows with co-ignimbrite ash-fall deposits (Wilson and Hildreth, 1997). This either/or classification has led to the common assumption that most eruptions, including the Bishop Tuff, begin with plinian fall deposits followed by emplacement of ignimbrite sheets. However, recent detailed re-examination of the stratigraphy of the Bishop Tuff by Wilson and Hildreth (1997) demonstrated that much of the Bishop ignimbrite is intraplinian, and that fall deposits and flow units previously interpreted as sequential are largely coeval.

Although a detailed review of the new eruptive stratigraphy of Wilson and Hildreth (1997) is not feasible here, the following points provide the foundation for the present discussion of the influence of eruption dynamics on the zonation recorded in the Bishop Tuff. (1) The fall deposit, exposed to the east and southeast of the caldera, both beneath and within the ignimbrite, is divided into nine units (F1–F9) based on grain size, grading characteristics, and lithic content. (2) Comparison of maximum clast sizes with other deposits where accumulation rates are known indicates an accumulation time of ~90 hours for F1–F8. No evidence for significant time breaks exists, except possibly between F8 and F9. (3) Glass Mountain lithics occur only after 60 to 80% deposition of F8, suggesting that below this level, much of the magma was vented from the initial Hilton Creek site of Hildreth and Mahood (1981). (4) Fall and flow activity proceeded together from the earliest stages of the eruption at least until the early stages of emplacement of ignimbrite north of the caldera. (5) The ignimbrite is divided into chronological and/or geographically distinct packages of material. Earlier packages (Ig1) were erupted eastward from the initial plinian

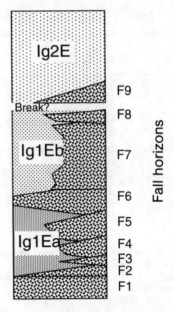

Fig. 5. Schematic illustration of revised Bishop Tuff stratigraphy of Wilson and Hildreth (1997), showing contemporaneity of fall deposits (F) and ash flows (Ig), rather than traditional interpretation of fall deposit overlain by flow(s).

vent location coeval with F1–F8, lack pyroxenes, and contain few or no Glass Mountain lithics. Later packages (Ig2), which contain pyroxenes and are rich in Glass Mountain lithics and other lithologies exposed in the north wall of the caldera, are divided into two groups. Ignimbrite erupted to the east (Ig2E) resulted from eastward and northward vent migration from the Hilton Creek site toward Glass Mountain. Ignimbrite Ig2N erupted from vents that moved from west to east along the northern caldera margin.

These time-stratigraphic relations are summarized schematically in Figure 5. The important point is that the new eruptive stratigraphy belies the commonly invoked linear model of fall-to-flow activity and therefore requires reassessment of the nature and origin of pre-eruptive compositional zonation in the Bishop Tuff magma reservoir (Wilson and Hildreth, 1997).

Zonation of the Bishop Tuff is illustrated in Figure 6, where Rb is plotted against Sr for pumice and fiammé samples representative of fall and flow material. Samples from this study are labeled using the nomenclature of Wilson

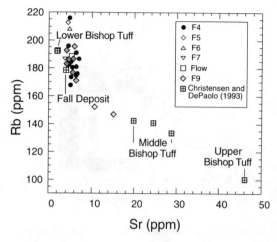

FIG. 6. Rb and Sr concentrations of Bishop Tuff glasses (Knesel, unpubl. data). Pumice analyzed in this study is from site 21 of Wilson and Hildreth (1997), with sample location shown in Figure 1.

and Hildreth (1997) to allow comparison with approximate positions within the time-stratigraphy framework illustrated in Figure 5. In the following discussion, we consider Rb as a moderately incompatible element, whereas Sr is strongly compatible (i.e., Rb increases and Sr decreases during differentiation of rhyolitic magmas).

Preliminary observations drawn from Figure 6 include the following. (1) Much of the fall pumice, which previously was assumed to have been deposited prior to ignimbrite emplacement and therefore representative of the most evolved liquids residing nearer the roof of the magma chamber, appears, in fact, to be less evolved than the lower Bishop Tuff ignimbrite samples of Christensen and DePaolo (1993) (samples BT-29 and BT-39, which represent I1SWa and I1Eb in Wilson and Hildreth's nomenclature) and the I1Eb ignimbrite sample from this study. This observation is consistent with Wilson and Hildreth's conclusion that flow activity accompanied early fall activity. (2) Several individual pumice clasts from fall units F4, F5, and F6 appear to be significantly more evolved (i.e., higher Rb) than the lower Bishop Tuff samples of Christensen and DePaolo (1993) and the single I1Eb sample of this study. Furthermore, pumice from the lowest fall unit reported here (F4) represents the most evolved sample, whereas the highest unit sampled (F9)

represents the least evolved material. (3) Analysis of multiple samples from units F4 and F9 indicates significant heterogeneity on the hand-sample scale. The overall sample distribution confirms that in general F4 is more evolved than F9; however, the significant overlap of the two units in Rb/Sr space indicates mixing of magmas during eruption. Although pumice may be mixed within a turbulent eruption column (Wilson, 1976), the short residence time in the column (typically minutes) and the significant difference in the inferred cumulative times for eruption and deposition of unit F4 (23 hr) to F9 (90 hr) (Wilson and Hildreth, 1997) indicate that most of the mixing must have occurred prior to exiting the vent (Spera, 1984).

In summary, the new Rb/Sr data presented here clearly reflect the revised eruptive stratigraphy of Wilson and Hildreth (1997) in the context of a zoned magma chamber becoming progressively more evolved toward the roof. They also demonstrate that detailed field studies are crucial to geochemical and petrologic study of magmatic systems.

Magma withdrawal dynamics

Despite the large number of detailed petrologic and geochemical studies that document various styles of magma zonation in large-volume silicic volcanic systems (e.g., Smith, 1960, 1979; Lipman et al., 1966; Smith and Bailey, 1966; Hildreth, 1979, 1981; Mahood, 1981; Bacon, 1983; Wörner and Schmincke, 1984; Fridrich and Mahood, 1987; Johnson and Fridrich, 1990; Streck and Grunder, 1997), there are relatively few studies of the dynamics of magma withdrawal from stratified chambers (e.g., Blake, 1981; Spera, 1984; Blake and Ivey, 1986; Spera et al., 1986; Trial et al., 1992) and even fewer applications of fluid dynamic constraints to eruptive sequences (e.g., Wolff, 1985; Sigurdson et al., 1990; Wolff et al., 1990). Simulations of withdrawal dynamics suggest that magma from different depths will arrive at the entrance to the chamber conduit concurrently (as a result of upwelling through a conduit of much narrower width than the underlying reservoir) and therefore will be intimately mixed before exiting the vent (Spera, 1984; Spera et al., 1986; Trial et al., 1992). The relationship between the hydrodynamics of magma withdrawal and preserved composi-

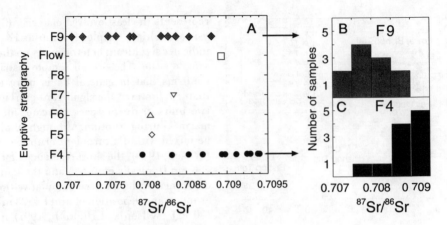

FIG. 7. A. Variation of initial ^{87}Sr/^{86}Sr ratios of Bishop Tuff fall deposit pumice glasses with eruptive stratigraphy (Knesel, unpubl. data). Units are as defined in Figure 6. B and C. ^{87}Sr/^{86}Sr$_i$ distributions for pumice-fall units F9 and F4.

tional gradients remains unclear, however. This deficiency arises in part because of the limited number of eruptions of zoned magma bodies for which sufficient information regarding eruption conditions (e.g., variation in discharge rate and spatial variation of vent locations with time) are known. Below we examine Sr-isotopic data for Bishop Tuff fall and flow pumice to explore the potential relationships between magma withdrawal dynamics and compositional gradients recorded in pyroclastic deposits.

Sr-isotopic compositions of single pumice clasts from the intercalated fall and flow deposit discussed in the previous section indicate a significant but random variation in initial ^{87}Sr/^{86}Sr with stratigraphic height (Fig. 7A), which does not reflect a simple monotonic decrease in ^{87}Sr/^{86}Sr$_i$ with height upsection (inferred to correspond to increasing depth in the magma chamber). Clasts near the base and top of the deposit reveal large ranges in ^{87}Sr/^{86}Sr ratios, with (1) maximum and minimum ^{87}Sr/^{86}Sr$_i$ near the base (F4) and top (F9), respectively (Fig. 7A) and (2) two distinct population distributions (Figs. 7B and 7C). We suggest that the observed Sr-isotopic stratigraphy is qualitatively predictable from numerical simulations of magma withdrawal from zoned crustal reservoirs. Although some of the Sr-isotopic variation among pumice clasts may reflect low-temperature post-eruptive interaction with meteoric water (Halliday et al., 1984), we argue against a dominant role for secondary

alteration in the isotopic variability of pumice clasts by comparison with the Sr-isotopic compositions of melt inclusions in quartz crystals in fall-deposit pumice reported by Christensen and Halliday (1996). When corrected for decay since the time of eruption, melt-inclusion-bearing quartz (MIBQ) yields initial ^{87}Sr/^{86}Sr ratios between 0.7065 and 0.7115. It is highly unlikely that secondary alteration processes could have produced the range in Sr-isotopic compositions of these melt inclusions, as they are enclosed within quartz crystals. The similarity in the Sr-isotopic compositions between the MIBQ data of Christensen and Halliday (1996) and our pumice data argue against a significant role for post-eruptive alteration of the Sr-isotopic compositions of pumice clasts. This conclusion will be tested by acid leaching experiments performed on pumice glass separates.

Spera (1984) and Trial et al. (1992) demonstrated that the stratigraphy of volcanic deposits can be related to pre-eruptive zonation with the aid of evacuation isochron diagrams, which show what part of a magma chamber is feeding an eruption at any instant in time. An evacuation isochron (EI) represents the loci of magma parcels that arrive at the conduit concurrently (Spera, 1984). Hypothetical EIs for the withdrawal of magma through a caldera margin vent to form the Bishop Tuff are illustrated in Figure 8. The EI diagram was constructed assuming: (1) in eruptions driven by

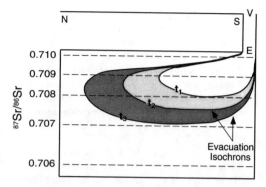

FIG. 8. Schematic portrayal of magma withdrawal from the zoned Bishop Tuff magma chamber. Times after the initiation of eruption (t = 0) are marked for three of an infinite number of evacuation isochrons (EI). EIs modified from Spera (1984). In the time interval t_1 to t_2, magma (with varying $^{87}Sr/^{86}Sr_i$ ratios) lying between the two isochrons (light shaded region) will simultaneously arrive at the vent entrance (E), and will be intimately mixed before exiting the vent at point V, to be deposited as unit F4. Magma lying in the dark-shaded region will erupt later to form unit F9.

caldera collapse, EIs are laterally elongated relative to those driven by magma recharge (Spera, 1984); (2) compared to central vent eruptions, EIs deepen more slowly over time during ring-fracture eruptions (Trial et al., 1992); and (3) $^{87}Sr/^{86}Sr_i$ decreased with increasing depth in the magma chamber of the Bishop Tuff (regardless of the mechanism responsible for the zonation). Whether the gradient is manifested as distinct layers or continuous zonation ultimately will control the efficiency of mixing; however, this distinction does not significantly influence the qualitative model presented here.

Magma vented early in the eruption (t_1 in Fig. 8), now represented by material near the base of the section studied here (approximated by F4 in Fig. 7A), records a zonation in $^{87}Sr/^{86}Sr_i$ ratios of ~0.7080 to 0.7095. The skewed distribution of pumice toward high $^{87}Sr/^{86}Sr_i$ ratios (Fig. 7C) suggests that withdrawal at this early stage of the eruption was dominated by roofward magma with limited mixing with underlying layers (Fig. 8). Progressive tapping of deeper levels (time interval t_2 to t_3 recorded as F9) resulted in eruption of magma with a less radiogenic Sr-isotopic range (~0.7071 to 0.7088). Mixing at this later stage of the eruption appears to have been more extensive (Fig. 7B) and is consistent with a monotonic increase in maximum withdrawal depth as an eruption pro-

ceeds, which results in a greater extent of vertical mixing with time (Spera, 1984).

The preliminary results presented here are consistent with mixed crystal populations in fall pumice reported by Christensen and Halliday (1996) and the concurrent eruption of pumice with different compositions and thus magmatic temperatures noted by Wilson and Hildreth (1997). These features further demonstrate the importance of understanding the dynamics of magma withdrawal in reconstruction of pre-eruptive magma zonation. Accurate reconstruction of *in situ* gradients in the Bishop Tuff magma chamber awaits detailed study of compositional variations at a large number of sites, both to the north and east of the Long Valley Caldera.

Concluding Remarks

Despite a large number of geochemical and petrological studies, the origin of the Bishop Tuff remains poorly understood. Determination of the relative mass contributions from mantle and crustal sources is hindered by the lack of constraints on end-member compositions, although thermal and volume considerations make an entirely mantle-derived origin unlikely. The time scales over which large-volume rhyolite magmas are differentiated and stored are equally poorly known. Detailed isotope studies appear to define differentiation "events" occurring up to 10^5 to 10^6 years prior to eruption, yet the delicate thermal balance required to prevent solidification or mineral dissolution is inconsistent with a history apparently punctuated by discrete magmatic events. Inasmuch as reconstruction of the compositional characteristics of the Bishop Tuff magma chamber relies critically on the interpretation of stratigraphic relations among the erupted products, the newly elucidated chronology for the Bishop Tuff (Wilson and Hildreth, 1997) may provide a framework for better understanding both differentiation and withdrawal mechanisms.

Acknowledgments

We thank Colin Wilson for re-introducing us to the Bishop Tuff and encouraging us to examine the geochemical characteristics of the tephra in detail. Wendell Duffield did likewise for the Taylor Creek Rhyolite system. John Wolff and Shan de Silva have stimulated our interest in ignimbrites and have reviewed the manuscript. Frank Ramos has been instrumental in the isotope laboratory in helping us achieve ultrahigh-quality analyses of very small samples. Thanks also to Gary Ernst for organizing the symposium to honor Clarence Hall, and special thanks to Clarence himself for his enduring support of field geology at UCLA, and for his support as a friend and colleague.

REFERENCES

Anderson, A. T., Jr., 1991, Hourglass inclusions: Theory and application to the Bishop rhyolitic tuff: Amer. Mineral., v. 76, p. 530–547.

Anderson, A. T., Jr., Newmann, S., Williams, S. N., Druitt, T. H., Skirius, C., and Stolper, E., 1989, H_2O, CO_2, Cl, and gas in plinian and ash-flow Bishop rhyolite: Geology, v. 17, p. 221–225.

Bacon, C., R., 1983, Eruptive history of Mount Mazama and Crater Lake Caldera, Cascade Range, U.S.A.: Jour. Volcanol. Geotherm. Res., v. 18, p. 57–115.

Bailey, R. A., Dalrymple, G. B., and Lanphere, M. A., 1976, Volcanism, structure, and geochronology of the Long Valley Caldera, Mono County, California: Jour. Geophys. Res., v. 81, p. 5.

Beard, B. L., and Glazner, A. F., 1995, Trace element and Sr and Nd isotopic composition of mantle xenoliths from the Big Pine volcanic field, California: Jour. Geophys. Res., v. 100, p. 4,169–4,179.

Blake, S., 1981, Eruptions from zoned magma chambers: Geol. Soc. Lond. Jour., v. 138, p. 281–287.

Blake, S., and Ivey, G. N., 1986, Density and viscosity gradients in zoned magma chambers, and their influence on withdrawal dynamics: Jour. Volcanol. Geotherm. Res., v. 30, p. 201–230.

Bohrson, W. A., and Reid, M. R., 1997, Genesis of silicic peralkaline volcanic rocks in an ocean island setting by crustal melting and open-system processes: Socorro Island, Mexico: Jour. Petrol., v. 38, p. 1137–1166.

Cameron, K. L., 1984, Bishop Tuff revisited: New rare-earth-element data consistent with crystal fractionation: Science, v. 224, p. 1338–1340.

Christensen, J. N., and DePaolo, D. J., 1993, Time scales of large-volume silicic magma systems: Sr-isotopic systematics of phenocrysts and glass from the Bishop Tuff, Long Valley, California: Contrib. Mineral. Petrol., v. 113, p. 100–114.

Christensen, J. N., and Halliday, A. N., 1996, Rb/Sr ages and Nd isotopic compositions of melt inclusions from the Bishop Tuff and the generation of silicic magma: Earth Planet. Sci. Lett., v. 144, p. 547–561.

Cousens, B. L., 1996, Magmatic evolution of Quaternary mafic magmas at Long Valley Caldera and the Devils Postpile, California: Effects of crustal contamination on lithospheric mantle-derived magmas: Jour. Geophys. Res., v. 101, p. 27,673–27,689.

Crisp, J. A., 1984, Rates of magma emplacement and volcanic output: Jour. Volcanol. Geotherm. Res., v. 20, p. 177–211.

Davidson, J. P., Dungan, M. A., Ferguson, K. M., and Colucci, M. T., 1987, Crust-magma interactions and the evolution of arc magmas: The San Pedro-Pellado Volcanic Complex, Southern Chilean Andes: Geology, v. 15, p. 443–446.

Davies, G., R., and Halliday, A. N., 1997, Development of the Long Valley Rhyolitic magma system: Sr and Nd isotope evidence from glasses, individual phenocrysts and core-rim relationships: Earth Planet. Sci. Lett., in press.

Davies, G., R., Halliday, A. N., Mahood, G. A., and Hall, C., M., 1994, Isotopic constraints on the production rates, crystallization histories, and residence times of pre-caldera silicic magmas, Long Valley, California: Earth Planet. Sci. Lett., v. 125, p. 17–37.

Deer, W. A., Howie, R. A., and Zussman, J., 1992, An introduction to the rock-forming minerals, 2nd ed.: Harlow, UK, Longmann, 696 p.

DePaolo, D. J., 1981, A neodymium and strontium isotopic study of the Mesozoic calc-alkaline granitic batholiths of the Sierra Nevada and Peninsular Ranges, California: Jour. Geophys. Res., v. 86, p. 10,470–10,488.

————, 1985, Isotopic studies of processes in mafic magma chambers: I. The Kiglapait Intrusion, Labrador: Jour. Petrol., v. 26, p. 925–951.

DePaolo, D. J., Perry, F. V., and Baldridge, W. S., 1992. Crustal versus mantle sources of granitic magmas: A two-parameter model based on Nd isotope studies: Trans. Roy. Soc. Edinb., v. 83, p. 439–446.

Duffield, W. A., and Dalrymple, G. B., 1990, The Taylor Creek Rhyolite of New Mexico: A rapidly emplaced field of lava domes and flows: Bull. Volcanol., v. 52, p. 475–487.

Duffield, W. A., and Ruiz, J., 1992a, Evidence for reversals of gradients in the uppermost parts of silicic magma reservoirs: Geology, v. 20, p. 1115–1118.

————, 1992b, Compositional gradients in large-volume reservoirs of silicic magma as evidenced by ignimbrites versus Taylor Creek Rhyolite lava domes: Contrib. Mineral. Petrol., v. 110, p. 192–210.

Duffield, W. A., Ruiz, J., and Webster, J. D., 1996, Roof-rock contamination of magma along the top of the reservoir for the Bishop Tuff: Jour. Volcanol. Geotherm. Res., v. 69, p. 187–195.

Dunbar, N. W., and Hervig, R. L., 1992, Petrogenesis and volatile stratigraphy of the Bishop Tuff: Evidence from melt inclusion analysis: Jour. Geophys. Res., v. 97, p. 15,129–15,150.

Farmer, G. L., Broxton, D. E., Warren, R. G., and Pickthorn, W., 1991, Nd, Sr, and O isotopic variations in metaluminous ash-flow tuffs and related volcanic rocks at Timber Mountain/Oasis Valley caldera complex, SW Nevada: Implications for the origin and evolution of large-volume silicic magma bodies: Contrib. Mineral. Petrol., v. 109, p. 53–68.

Farmer, G. L., and DePaolo, D. J., 1983, Origin of Mesozoic and Tertiary granite in the Western United States and implications for pre-Mesozoic crustal structure 1. Nd and Sr isotopic studies in the geocline of the northern Great Basin: Jour. Geophys. Res., v. 88, p. 3379–3401.

Fridrich, C. J., and Mahood, G. A., 1987, Compositional layers in the zoned magma chamber of the Grizzly Peak Tuff: Geology, v. 15, p. 299–303.

Gardner, J. E., Sigurdsson, H., and Carey, S. N., 1991, Eruption dynamics and magma withdrawal during the plinian phase of the Bishop Tuff eruption, Long Valley Caldera: Jour. Geophys. Res., v. 96, p. 8097–8111.

Gilbert, C. M., 1938, Welded tuff in eastern California: Geol. Soc. Amer. Bull., v. 49, p. 1829–1862.

Grunder, A. L., 1995, Material and thermal roles of basalt in crustal magmatism: Case study from eastern Nevada: Geology, v. 23, p. 952–956.

Halliday, A. N., 1990, Reply to comment of Sparks, R. S. J., Huppert, H. E., and Wilson C. J. N., 1990, on "Evidence for long residence times of rhyolitic magma in the Long Valley magmatic system: The isotopic record in precaldera lavas of Glass Mountain" by Halliday, A. N., Mahood, G. A., Holden, P., Metz, J. M., Dempster, T. J., and Davidson, J. P.: Earth Planet. Sci. Lett., v. 99, p. 395–399.

Halliday, A. N., Fallick, A. E., Hutchinson, J., and Hildreth, W., 1984, A Nd, Sr, and O isotopic investigation into the causes of chemical and isotopic zonation in the Bishop Tuff, California: Earth Planet. Sci. Lett., v. 68, p. 379–391.

Halliday, A. N., Mahood, G. A., Holden, P., Metz, J. M., Dempster, T. J., and Davidson, J. P., 1989, Evidence for long residence times of rhyolitic magma in the Long Valley magmatic system: The isotopic record in precaldera lavas of Glass Mountain: Earth and Planet. Sci. Lett., v. 94, p. 274–290.

Hervig, R. L., and Dunbar, N. W., 1992, Cause of chemical zoning in the Bishop (California) and Bandelier (New Mexico) magma chambers: Earth Planet. Sci. Lett., v. 111, p. 97–108.

Hildreth, W., 1977, The magma chamber of the Bishop Tuff: Gradients in temperature, pressure, and composition: Unpubl. Ph.D. thesis, Univ. of California, Berkeley, 328 p.

————, 1979, The Bishop Tuff: Evidence for the origin of compositional zonation in silicic magma chambers: Geol. Soc. Amer. Spec. Pap., 180, p. 43–75.

————, 1981, Gradients in silicic magma chambers: Implications for lithospheric magmatism: Jour. Geophys. Res., v. 86, p. 10153–10192.

Hildreth, W., and Mahood, G. A., 1986, Ring-fracture eruption of the Bishop Tuff: Geol. Soc. Amer. Bull., v. 97, p. 396–403.

Hill, D. P., Bailey, R. A., and Ryall, A. S., 1985, Active tectonic and magmatic processes beneath Long Valley Caldera, eastern California: An overview: Jour. Geophys. Res., v. 90, p. 11,111–11,120.

Johnson, C. M., 1989, Isotopic zonations in silicic magma chambers: Geology, v. 17, p. 1136–1139.

Johnson, C. M., and Fridrich, C. J., 1990, Non-monotonic chemical and O, Sr, Nd, and Pb isotope zonations and heterogeneity in the mafic- to silicic-composition magma chamber of the Grizzly Peak Tuff, Colorado: Contrib. Mineral. Petrol., v. 105, p. 677–690.

Johnson, C. M., Lipmann, P. W., and Czamanske, G. K., 1989, H, O, Sr, Nd, and Pb isotope geochemistry of the Latir volcanic field and cogenetic intrusions, New Mexico, and relations between evolution of a continental magmatic center and modifications of the lithosphere: Contrib. Mineral. Petrol., v. 104, p. 99–124.

Kaczor, S. M., Hanson, G. N., and Peterman, Z. E., 1988, Disequilibrium melting of granite at the contact with a basic plug: A geochemical and petrographic study: Jour. Geol., v. 96, p. 61–78.

Kistler, R. W., Chappell, B. W., and Bateman, P. C., 1986, Isotopic variation in the Tuolomne Intrusive Suite, central Sierra Nevada, California: Contrib. Mineral. Petrol., v. 94, p. 205–220.

Kistler, R. W., and Peterman, Z. E., 1973, Variations in Sr, Rb, K, Na and initial in Mesozoic granitic rocks and intruded wall rocks in central California: Geol. Soc. Amer. Bull., v. 84, p. 3489–3512.

————, 1978, Reconstruction of crustal blocks of California on the basis of initial strontium isotopic compositions of Mesozoic granitic rocks: U. S. Geol. Surv. Prof. Pap. 1071.

Knesel, K. M., 1997, Sr-isotopic systematics during crustal anatexis and crust-magma interaction: Ph.D. thesis: Los Angeles, Univ. of California.

Knesel, K. M., and Davidson, J. P., 1996, Isotopic disequilibrium during melting of granite and implications for crustal contamination of magmas: Geology, v. 24, p. 243–246.

————, 1997, Strontium isotope systematics during basalt-crust interaction, in Seventh Ann. V. M. Gold-schmidt Conf., p. 113–114, LPI Cont. No. 921, Lunar and Planetary Inst., Houston.

Lipman, P. W., Christiansen, R. L., and O'Conner, J. T., 1966, A compositionally zoned ash-flow sheet in southern Nevada: U. S. Geol. Surv. Prof. Pap., 524-F, p. F1-F47.

Lu, F., Anderson, A. T., and Davis, A. M., 1992, Melt inclusions and crystal-liquid separation in rhyolitic magma of the Bishop Tuff: Contrib. Mineral. Petrol., v. 110, p. 113–120.

Mahood, G. A., 1981, A summary of the geology and petrology of the Sierra La Primavera, Jalisco, Mexico: Jour. Geophys. Res., v. 86, p. 10,137–10,152.

————, 1990, Second reply to comment of Sparks, R. S. J., Huppert, H. E., and Wilson C. J. N., 1990, on "Evidence for long residence times of rhyolitic magma in the Long Valley magmatic system: The isotopic record in precaldera lavas of Glass Mountain" by Halliday, A. N., Mahood, G. A., Holden, P., Metz, J. M., Dempster, T. J., and Davidson, J. P.: Earth Planet. Sci. Lett., v. 99, p. 395–399.

Mahood, G. A., and Halliday, A. N., 1988, Generation of high-silica rhyolite: A Nd, Sr, and O isotopic study of Sierra La Primavera, Mexican neo-volcanic belt: Contrib. Mineral. Petrol., v. 100, p. 183–191.

Matty, D. J., Lipmann, P. W., and Stormer, J. C., Jr., 1987, Common-Pb isotopic characteristics of central San Juan ash flow tuffs [abs.]: Geol. Soc. Amer. Abs. Prog., v. 19, p. 319–320.

Metz, J. M., and Mahood, G. A., 1991, Development of the Long Valley, California, magma chamber recorded in precaldera rhyolite lavas of Glass Mountain: Contrib. Mineral. Petrol., v. 106, p. 379–397.

Michael, P. J., 1983, Chemical differentiation of the Bishop Tuff and other high-silica magmas through crystallization processes: Geology, v. 11, p. 31–34.

Miller, C. F., and Mittlefehldt, D. W., 1984, Extreme fractionation in felsic magma chambers: A product of liquid-state diffusion or fractional crystallization?: Earth Planet. Sci. Lett., v. 68, p. 151–158.

Noble, D. C., and Hedge, C. E., 1969, $^{87}Sr/^{86}Sr$ variations within individual ash-flow sheets: U. S. Geol. Surv. Prof. Pap., 650-C, p. C133-C139.

Ormerod, D. S., Hawkesworth, C. J., Rogers, N. W., Leeman, W. P., and Menzies, M. A., 1988, Tectonic and magmatic transitions in the Western Great Basin, USA: Nature, v. 333, p. 349–352.

Ormerod, D. S., Hawkesworth, C. J., and Rogers, N. W., 1991, Melting in the lithospheric mantle: Inverse modeling of alkali-olivine basalts from the Big Pine Volcanic Field, California: Contrib. Mineral. Petrol., v. 108, p. 305–317.

Patiño-Douce, A. E., and Beard, J. S., 1995, Dehydration-melting of biotite gneiss and quartz amphibolite from 3 to 15 kbar: Jour. Petrol., v. 36, p. 707–738.

Perry, F. V., DePaolo, D. J., and Baldridge, W. S., 1993, Neodymium isotopic evidence for decreasing crustal contributions to Cenozoic ignimbrites of the Western United States: Implications for the thermal evolution of the Cordilleran crust: Geol. Soc. Amer. Bull., v. 105, p. 872–882.

Pushkar, P., and Stoeser, D. B., 1975, $^{87}Sr/^{86}Sr$ ratios in some volcanic rocks and some semifused inclusions of the San Francisco volcanic field: Geology, v. 3, p. 669–671.

Reece, C., Ruiz, J., Duffield, W. A., and Patchett, P. J., 1990, Origin of the Taylor Creek Rhyolite, Black Range, New Mexico, based on Nd-Sr isotope studies: Geol. Soc. Amer. Spec. Pap. 246, p. 263–273.

Reid, M. R., and Ramos, F. C., 1996, Chemical dynamics of enriched mantle in the southwestern United States: Thorium isotope evidence: Earth Plan. Sci. Let., v. 138, p. 67–81.

Reiners, P. W., Nelson, B. K., and Ghiorso, M. S., 1995, Assimilation of felsic crust by basaltic magma: Thermal limits and extents of crustal contamination of mantle-derived magmas: Geology, v. 23, p. 563–566.

Shaw, H. R., 1985, Links between magma-tectonic rate balances, plutionism, and volcanism: Jour. Geophys. Res., v. 90, p. 11,275–11,288.

Sigurdson, H., Cornell, W., and Carey, S., 1990, Influence of magma withdrawal on compositional gradients during the AD 79 Vesuvius eruption: Nature, v. 345, p. 519–521.

Smith, R. L., 1960, Zonal and azonal variations in welded ash flows: U. S. Geol. Surv. Prof. Pap. 354-F, p. F149–F159.

————, 1979, Ash flow magmatism: Geol. Soc. Amer. Spec. Pap. 180, p. 5–28.

Smith, R. L., and Bailey, R. A., 1966, The Bandelier Tuff: A case study of ash-flow eruption cycles from zoned magma chambers: Bull. Volcanol., v. 29, p. 83–104.

Snow, E., and Yund, R., 1985, Thermal history of a Bishop Tuff section as determined from the width of cryptoperthite lamellae: Geology, v. 13, p. 50–53.

————, 1988, Origin of cryptoperthites in the Bishop Tuff and their bearing in its thermal history: Jour. Geophys. Res., v. 93, p. 8975–8984.

Sorey, M. L., Lewis, R. E., and Olmsted, F. H., 1978, The hydrothermal system of Long Valley Caldera, California: U. S. Geol. Surv. Prof. Pap. 1044-A, p. A1–A60.

Sparks, R. S. J., Huppert, H. E., and Wilson, C. J. N., 1990, Comment on "Evidence for long residence times of rhyolitic magma in the Long Valley magmatic system: The isotopic record in precaldera lavas of Glass Mountain" by Halliday, A. N., Mahood, G. A., Holden, P., Metz, J. M., Dempster, T. J., and Davidson, J. P.: Earth Planet. Sci. Lett., v. 99, p. 387–389.

Spera, F. J., 1980, Thermal evolution of plutons: A parameterized approach: Science, v. 207, p. 299–301.

————, 1984, Some numerical experiments on the withdrawal of magma from crustal reservoirs: Jour. Geophys. Res., v. 89, p. 8222–8236.

Spera, F. J., Yuen, D. A., Greer, J. C., and Sewell, G., Dynamics of magma withdrawal from stratified magma chambers: Geology, v. 14, p. 723–726.

Streck, M. J., and Grunder, A. L., 1997, Compositional gradients and gaps in high-silica rhyolites of the Rattlesnake Tuff, Oregon: Jour. Petrol., v. 38, p. 133–163.

Tegtmeyer, K. J., and Farmer, G. L., 1990, Nd-isotopic gradients in upper crustal magma chambers: Evidence for *in situ* magma–wall-rock interaction: Geology, v. 18, p. 5–9.

Tommasini, S., and Davies, G. R., 1997, Isotopic disequilibrium during anatexis: A case study of contact melting, Sierra Nevada, California: Earth Planet. Sci. Lett., in press.

Trial, A. F., Spera, F. J., Greer, J., and Yuen, D. A., 1992, Simulations of magma withdrawal from compositionally zoned bodies: Jour. Geophys. Res., v. 97, p. 6713–6733.

van den Bogaard, P., and Schirnick, C., 1995, ^{40}Ar/^{39}Ar laser probe ages of Bishop Tuff quartz phenocrysts substantiate long-lived silicic magma chamber at long Valley, United States: Geology, v. 23, p. 759–762.

Verplanck, P. L., Farmer, G. L., McCurry, M., Mertzman, S., and Snee, L. W., 1995, Isotopic evidence on the origin of compositional layering in an epizonal magma body: Earth Planet. Sci. Lett., v. 136, p. 31–41.

Wilson, C. J. N., and Hildreth, W., 1997, The Bishop Tuff: New insights from eruptive stratigraphy: Jour. Geol., v. 105, p. 407–439.

Wilson, L., 1976, Explosive volcanic eruptions, III. Plinian eruption columns: Geophys. Jour. Roy. Astron. Soc., v. 45, p. 543–556.

Wittke, J. H., Duffield, W. A., and Jones, C., 1996, Roof-rock contamination of Taylor Creek Rhyolite, New Mexico, as recorded in hornblende phenocrysts and biotite xenocrysts: Amer. Mineral., v. 81, p. 135–140.

Wolff, J. A., 1985, Zonation, mixing, and eruption of silica-undersaturated alkaline magma: A case study from Tenerife, Canary Islands: Geol. Mag., v. 122, p. 623–640.

Wolff, J. A., Wörner, G., and Blake, S., 1990, Gradients in physical parameters in zoned felsic magma bodies: Implications for evolution and eruptive withdrawal: Jour. Volcanol. Geotherm. Res., v. 43, p. 37–55.

Wörner, G., and Schmincke, H. U., 1984, Petrogenesis of the zoned Laacher See tephra: Jour. Petrol., v. 25, p. 805–851.

WESTERN AND BAJA
CALIFORNIA

Phanerozoic Tectonic Evolution
of Central California and Environs

RAYMOND V. INGERSOLL

Department of Earth and Space Sciences, University of California, Los Angeles, California 90095-1567

Abstract

The use of actualistic analog models for paleotectonic reconstruction produces significant advances in our understanding of evolutionary continental tectonics. The sequential application of such models is possible in a cross section from the central California coast to Utah. This transect represents one of the best-understood Phanerozoic continental margins on Earth. Excellent exposure, detailed local studies, and regional syntheses all contribute to the choice of appropriate plate-tectonic models for successive intervals from the latest Neoproterozoic to the Quaternary. These models include craton, terrestrial rift, nascent ocean, intraplate continental margin, intraoceanic magmatic arc (both extensional and neutral), continental-margin magmatic arc (both neutral and contractional), transform continental margin, remnant ocean, suture, and successor basin. These models are useful for understanding the following stages of development of the Cordilleran margin of central California and its environs—latest Proterozoic rifting, early Paleozoic intraplate margin, Devonian–Mississippian Antler orogeny (arc-continent suturing), Mississippian–Pennsylvanian intraplate margin, Pennsylvanian–Permian Ancestral Rockies orogeny (Ouachita-Marathon continental suturing), Permian–Triassic Sonoma orogeny (arc-continent suturing), Triassic–Jurassic continental-margin magmatic arc, Late Jurassic Nevadan orogeny (arc-arc suturing), latest Jurassic–Late Cretaceous continental-margin magmatic arc, latest Cretaceous–Eocene Laramide orogeny, Oligocene ignimbrite flare-up, and Miocene–Holocene triple-junction migration, transform boundary, and regional extension of the Great Basin. The integrated result of sequential superposition of the actualistic models produces a reasonable representation of the complexity of the study area. The discipline of applying actualistic models to the evolution of this continental margin provides new insights and forces one to consider new implications of the models. The complexity of the tectonic history of this continental margin argues against simplistic general models for the growth of continental crust.

Introduction

TRADITIONAL REGIONAL geologic studies were conducted in the absence of actualistic plate-tectonic models. As a result, virtually all paleotectonic reconstructions prior to adoption of the plate-tectonic paradigm involved inverse modeling based on ad hoc hypotheses (e.g., local observations were interpreted in terms of geosynclinal theory; e.g., Kay, 1951). Following the plate-tectonic revolution, actualistic models based on modern processes were developed, which allowed forward (predictive) modeling (e.g., Dewey and Bird, 1970; Dickinson, 1974; Ingersoll, 1988; Ingersoll and Busby, 1995).

Modern geophysical inverse modeling has the advantage of precision, but does not easily lead to understanding of the temporal component of lithospheric evolution. Quantitative process-oriented forward modeling also is precise, but

can only address a few processes at once, thus limiting its application in reconstructing complex ancient systems. Thus, quantitative digital models have limited applicability to the reconstruction of complex ancient lithosphere that has formed over hundreds of millions of years. Well-constrained actualistic analog models, used in iterative, both forward and inverse applications, produce the most significant advances in our understanding of evolutionary continental tectonics. The iterative application of these models, with subsequent modification and improvement, produces new insights. "Truth emerges more readily from error than from confusion" (Francis Bacon) (Kuhn, 1970, p. 18).

The most successful paleotectonic reconstructions involve iterative forward and inverse modeling, which is self-correcting. "Heidegger

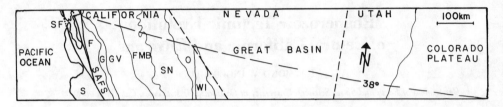

FIG. 1. Location map of study area, showing approximate line of section for Figure 3 (after King, 1969). SF = San Francisco; S = Salinian block; SAFS = San Andreas fault system; F = Franciscan Complex; G = Great Valley Group outcrop belt; GV = Great Valley; FMB = Foothill metamorphic belt; SN = Sierra Nevada; O = Owens Valley; WI = White-Inyo Range.

(1927, 1962) argued that understanding is fundamentally circular; when we strive to comprehend something, the meaning of its parts is understood from its relationship to the whole, while our conception of the whole is constructed from an understanding of its parts" (Frodeman, 1995, p. 963). This is the philosophical underpinning of the present study.

The overall purpose of this study is twofold. The first-order objective is to clarify constraints on interpretations of the tectonic history of the study area. The second-order objective is to illustrate the complexity of Phanerozoic tectonic processes along one of the best-understood continental margins on Earth. It is hoped that similar syntheses of other continental margins will benefit from the present synthesis, and that our knowledge of how continental crust has evolved will be increased through these syntheses.

Central California and Environs

The study area (Fig. 1) is a transect across the southwestern conterminous United States. The paleotectonic history of this margin is relatively well understood from the latest Proterozoic to the present. Unlike many other long-lived continental margins, the transect across the central California Coast Ranges, Great Valley, Sierra Nevada, Owens Valley, White Mountains, Nevada, and Utah exposes all ages of rocks from Proterozoic to Quaternary. Essential to the present study is the fact that the oldest rocks of the latest Proterozoic–early Paleozoic continental margin have experienced all subsequent deformation, and yet are not so thoroughly deformed that events are impossible to decipher. The most recent events have primarily extended the

crust, so that mid-crustal levels are exposed, thus increasing the likelihood that the record of older events is exposed. In addition, the semi-arid climate of much of the area minimizes vegetative and soil cover. In short, this area is uniquely conducive to the type of iterative forward and inverse study outlined above.

The choice of analog model to be applied to each time interval is based on regional relations, rather than local observations. The models are testable using local observations, which may lead to modifications of either the class of model (e.g., convergent continental margin versus intraplate setting) (less likely) or some of the detailed aspects of the model (e.g., contractional arc-trench system versus neutral arc-trench system) (more likely). Choice of appropriate models for each time interval is based on regional syntheses of other workers (e.g., Burchfiel and Davis, 1972, 1975; Dickinson, 1981a, 1981b; Oldow et al., 1989) and specific models that have withstood numerous tests (e.g., Schweickert and Cowan, 1975; Speed and Sleep, 1982).

The models utilized in the present study are two-dimensional (unless one considers time as a third dimension). The choice of model is determined by four-dimensional relations, including sequential paleogeographic and paleotectonic maps. The weakest aspect of the models is their insensitivity to strike-slip movements. During some of the time intervals discussed below, significant strike slip is likely to have occurred, especially within magmatic arcs and along subduction zones. Truncation of the Proterozoic–Paleozoic continental margin during the latest Paleozoic and/or early Mesozoic is problematic. The cross-sectional view of the study area cuts obliquely across NE-SW Proterozoic-Paleozoic trends and only slightly obliquely across NNW-SSE Mesozoic and

Cenozoic trends. Comparable cross sections of continental margins to the north and south of the study area need to be modified accordingly.

Actualistic Models

General

Dickinson (1981a, 1981b) used actualistic analog models to analyze the paleotectonic development of the California continental margin from the latest Proterozoic to the present. Dickinson's (1981a) models are the prototypes for the models shown in Figure 2. His general margin types for the California margin are refined below. The models used below are described by plate-tectonic genetic terms, such as "intraoceanic magmatic arc," rather than by geographic terms, such as "Japan-type margin." Terminology for sedimentary basins related to the models may be found in Ingersoll (1988) and Ingersoll and Busby (1995).

Craton

An intraplate continental interior (Fig. 2A) is described by the simplest model, which includes continental crust of average thickness (~50 km) underlain by mantle lithosphere arbitrarily shown as 130 km thick. The surface is near sea level, with no significant topography. Isostatic balance prevails everywhere.

Terrestrial rift

Rifting of cratonal continental crust (Fig. 2B) can be initiated by asthenospheric (active) or lithospheric (passive) processes (Sengör and Burke, 1978; Sengör, 1995). Whatever the initiating causes, mature rifts are characterized by thinning of crust and mantle lithosphere, upwelling of asthenosphere, high heat flow, predominantly basaltic volcanism, normal faults, downdropped central sedimentary basins containing arkosic sediment and basalt, and regional uplift (Leeder, 1995). Detailed characteristics of basins and structure vary greatly (e.g., Buck, 1991; Ingersoll and Busby, 1995).

Nascent ocean

With continued extension of continental lithosphere, terrestrial rifts evolve into nascent oceans (Fig. 2C), as upwelling asthenosphere interacts with the hydrosphere and seafloor spreading begins. The Red Sea is the best mod-

ern example (e.g., Cochran, 1983), with the Gulf of California providing a transtensional example (e.g., Lonsdale, 1989). Transitional crust is formed during this transitional stage, by thinning of continental crust (forming quasicontinental crust) or the interaction of rising asthenosphere with sediment (forming quasioceanic crust) prior to the onset of seafloor spreading (Dickinson, 1974). As newly formed continental margins move away from a spreading ridge, they cool and subside, and basal transgressive strata are deposited.

Intraplate continental margin

As young continental margins migrate away from a spreading ridge, they evolve into intraplate margins (Fig. 2D). Mantle lithosphere cools and thickens away from the ridge, and continental margins, therefore, also subside thermally (Bond et al., 1995). The continental margins tilt seaward as the lithosphere flexes as a result of sedimentary loading along the margin, especially as thick deep-marine deposits accumulate on adjoining transitional and oceanic crust (Pitman, 1978). Broad shelves form above these seaward-thickening prisms; landward-to-seaward facies belts result, with the classic fining of sediment away from the shore, including thick carbonate strata in low-latitude settings.

Intraoceanic magmatic arc

Extensional. Sinking of oceanic lithospheric slabs generates melts at depths of ~150 km (e.g., Coney and Reynolds, 1977; Keith, 1978, 1982; Lipman, 1992). Rising magmas form magmatic arcs at the surface, as part of either oceanic or continental crust. If the sinking slab is old and, therefore, thick, it sinks faster, and slab rollback is common. This leads to extension in the overriding plate, which is expressed as rifting wherever the lithosphere is weakest. Most commonly, the weakest lithosphere is along the magmatic arc, where mantle lithosphere is thin. Intra-arc rifting (e.g., Smith and Landis, 1995) usually evolves into backarc rifting to form new oceanic crust (Karig, 1971). Extensional intraoceanic arcs (Fig. 2E) may generate several backarc basins with intervening remnant arcs, as in the modern Marianas system (e.g., Karig, 1971; Marsaglia, 1995). All modern extensional intraoceanic systems face east (W-dipping subduction) and result from the subduction of old lithosphere (Dickinson, 1978; Molnar and Atwater, 1978; Dewey, 1980; Jarrard, 1986).

Neutral. Subduction of oceanic lithosphere beneath oceanic lithosphere may occur without backarc spreading (e.g., Aleutian arc and Bering Sea) (e.g., Marsaglia, 1995) (Fig. 2F). Backarc continental margins, such as the Bering Sea coast, are intraplate settings. The rate of slab rollback is balanced by the trenchward motion of the overriding plate in neutral arcs (Dickinson, 1978; Dewey, 1980; Jarrard, 1986).

Continental-margin magmatic arc

Neutral. Subduction of oceanic lithosphere beneath continental lithosphere also may occur in a neutral dynamical setting (Fig. 2G). Most of the Sunda arc of Indonesia is such a setting, with backarc continental crust experiencing neither extension nor contraction (Hamilton, 1979). Backarc areas may be slightly above or below sea level, depending on local isostatic and flexural effects.

Contractional. Subduction of young oceanic lithosphere is resisted by its relative buoyancy. The result is contractional arc-trench systems (e.g., the modern Andes), including retroarc foldthrust belts (Sevier style) and associated foreland basins (Dewey, 1980; Jordan, 1995) (Fig. 2H). In the special case of rapid overriding of young (buoyant) oceanic lithosphere, basement-involved deformation (Laramide style) may propagate far inland of the normal retroarc foldthrust belt (e.g., Sierras Pampeanas of Argentina) (Jordan, 1995) (Fig. 2I). All arc-trench systems include trenches, subduction complexes (accretionary wedges), and forearc basins with diverse characteristics (e.g., Dickinson, 1995; Underwood and Moore, 1995).

Transform continental margin

Continental margins along transform plate boundaries are complex (Fig. 2J) (e.g., Crowell, 1974a, 1974b; Reading, 1980; Christie-Blick and Biddle, 1985; Nilsen and Sylvester, 1995). Continental transform faults are far more complex than oceanic transforms, and it may even be difficult to define where a transform boundary is within a broad zone of continental shear (e.g., modern California margin and Basin and Range Province). Transtensional, transpressional, and transrotational settings result in a

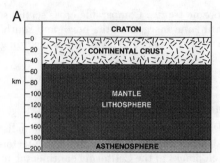

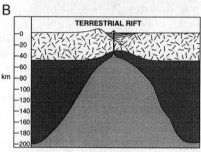

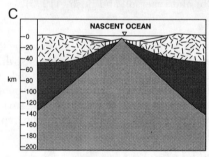

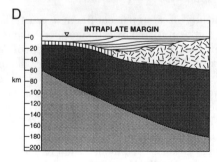

FIG. 2. Actualistic plate-tectonic models utilized in this study (after Dickinson, 1981a) (continues on facing page). Mantle lithosphere is defined geophysically rather than geochemically. A. Craton. B. Terrestrial rift. C. Nascent ocean. D. Intraplate margin. E. Intraoceanic magmatic arc (extensional). F. Intraoceanic magmatic arc (neutral). G. Continental-margin arc (neutral). H. Continental-margin arc (contractional; Sevier type). I. Continental-margin arc (contractional; Laramide type). J. Transform margin. K. Remnant ocean. L. Suture.

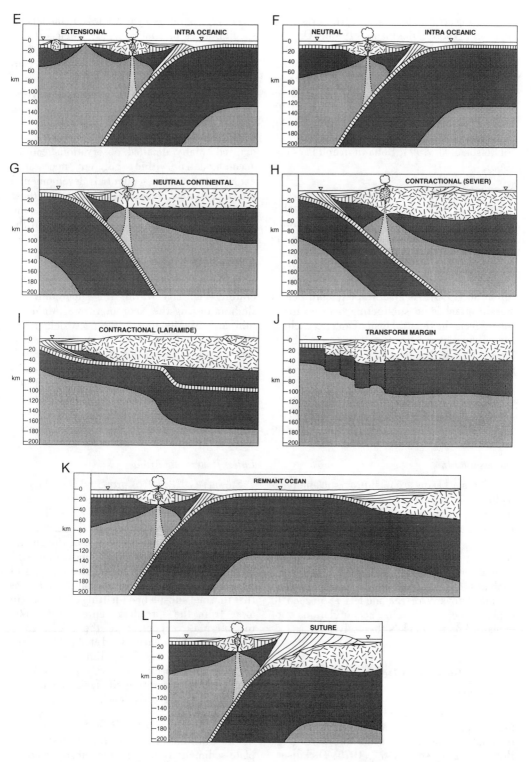

FIG. 2. (continued).

bewildering array of basins and structures (e.g., Ingersoll, 1988; Dickinson, 1996). On the other hand, the preservation of oceanic lithosphere formed at extinct spreading centers near young transform margins (e.g., California) provides unprecedented constraints on paleotectonic reconstructions (e.g., Atwater, 1970, 1989; Dickinson and Snyder, 1979a, 1979b; Ingersoll, 1982a; Stock and Hodges, 1989; Nicholson et al., 1994; Bohannon and Parsons, 1995).

Remnant ocean and suture

Subduction of oceanic lithosphere inevitably leads to the attempted subduction of buoyant continental or arc lithosphere, resulting in the closing of remnant ocean basins (Fig. 2K) to form suture belts (Fig. 2L) (Dewey and Burke, 1974; Graham et al., 1975; Cloos, 1993; Ingersoll et al., 1995). As an intraplate continental margin attached to subducting oceanic lithosphere feels the flexural load of an encroaching overriding plate, it flexes to form a peripheral foreland basin (Dickinson, 1974; Miall, 1995). In extreme cases, usually involving continents of unequal size (e.g., India and Asia), cratonal areas of continents may be deformed far from the suture belt (Molnar and Tapponnier, 1975; Tapponnier and Molnar, 1976; England and McKenzie, 1982; Ingersoll et al., 1995).

Successor basin

Successor basins are post-orogenic and post-taphrogenic basins that cannot be classified according to other criteria (Ingersoll, 1988; Ingersoll and Busby, 1995). As such, they are primarily intermontane basins devoid of evidence for syndepositional faulting or folding. They do not constitute a single analog model, such as those described above; rather, they can be added to any of the models as needed to explain local sediment accumulations not explained by the models themselves.

Sequential Development

Introduction

The following succinct summary of the evolution of the study area depends heavily on regional syntheses of other workers (e.g., Burchfiel and Davis, 1972, 1975; Dickinson, 1981a, 1981b; Oldow et al., 1989; Burchfiel et

al., 1992), as well as local studies and models for specific areas or times (e.g., Schweickert and Cowan, 1975; Stewart, 1976; Ingersoll, 1982b; Speed and Sleep, 1982; Bird, 1984, 1988; Wernicke, 1990). Many readers with knowledge of local details may prefer different models. However, it is hoped that the overall approach will provide tests for evolutionary processes, and predict local characteristics not previously recognized. Many detailed observations can be accommodated within, but not necessarily explained by, the sequential developmental model presented below. The final result of these superposed models is suitably complex in comparison to known or suggested features in the study area.

Proterozoic supercontinent

The western United States was part of a craton (Fig. 2A) within the supercontinent Rodinia during the Neoproterozoic (McMenamin and McMenamin, 1990; Dalziel, 1991; Hoffman, 1991; Moores, 1991). A consensus seems to be building that Australia-Antarctica was adjacent to the Cordilleran margin prior to latest Proterozoic rifting (e.g., Dalziel, 1991; Hoffman, 1991; Moores, 1991), although for the purposes of the present discussion, we are concerned only with the North American remnant of Rodinia.

Latest Proterozoic rifting

Stewart (1972, 1976) proposed that the Cordilleran margin originated after 850 Ma during rifting of the North American craton. The age of initiation of terrestrial rifting (Fig. 2B) is less well constrained than is the age of the rift-to-drift transition (formation of a nascent ocean) (Fig. 2C). Quantitative subsidence analysis of the early Paleozoic intraplate margin indicates that thermal subsidence (drifting of the margin away from the spreading center) began 600 to 550 Ma, very close to the Proterozoic–Phanerozoic boundary (Bond et al., 1985). This transition is expressed as a time-transgressive breakup unconformity (e.g., Falvey, 1974; Bond et al., 1995), separating rift facies from overlying basal transgressive marine strata.

Early Paleozoic intraplate margin

The Cordilleran miogeocline records intraplate sedimentation along the subsiding continental margin, bordered on the west by a growing ocean basin (Fig. 2D). The predominantly shallow-marine strata of the miogeocline thicken westward, culminating in Neoproterozoic–Cambrian strata exceeding 7 km in thickness in the White-Inyo Range (Nelson, 1962), including the Proterozoic–Cambrian boundary (Nelson, 1978). Detailed knowledge of the stratigraphy and paleoenvironments of lower Paleozoic strata (e.g., Poole et al., 1992) constrains palinspastic reconstruction of late Paleozoic through Holocene deformation (Wernicke et al., 1988; Levy and Christie-Blick, 1989). In fact, it is unlikely that most aspects of Cordilleran orogenic and taphrogenic deformation could be understood in the absence of the nearly layer-cake stratigraphy of the lower Paleozoic miogeocline. Knowledge of this stratigraphy is one of the keys to understanding Cordilleran structure.

Devonian–Mississippian Antler orogeny

By Middle Devonian time, an intraoceanic magmatic arc was approaching the Cordilleran intraplate margin (Fig. 3A). Whether this intraoceanic magmatic arc originated far from the Cordilleran margin or resided off the coast of North America is still debated (e.g., Burchfiel and Davis, 1972; Nilsen and Stewart, 1980). Nonetheless, it is clear that by the Late Devonian, subduction of North American oceanic lithosphere under this intraoceanic arc resulted in attempted subduction of the quasicontinental crust of the intraplate margin, resulting in the Antler orogeny (Speed and Sleep, 1982) (Fig. 3B). Lithospheric flexure of the intraplate margin created a peripheral foreland basin (e.g., Dickinson, 1974; Miall, 1995), within which the synorogenic Antler "flysch" accumulated (Poole, 1974; Dickinson et al., 1983). Extension of the Antler orogenic belt into the White-Inyo Range and the Sierra Nevada is problematic, but the presence of deformed, metamorphosed strata of appropriate age in the eastern Sierra Nevada suggests that the orogenic belt continued southwest from its well-documented locales in Nevada (Schweickert and Lahren, 1987).

Mississippian–Pennsylvanian intraplate margin

Following cessation of convergence in Early Mississippian time, uplifted parts of the Antler arc, forearc, and accretionary prism eroded, cooled, subsided, and were buried as the new continental margin regained isostatic equilibrium (Fig. 3C). An intraplate margin likely existed for part of this interval, although transform tectonics may have affected parts of this margin during the Pennsylvanian (Stone and Stevens, 1988b).

Pennsylvanian–Permian Ancestral Rockies orogeny

The Pennsylvanian–Permian suturing of Gondwanaland to Laurasia along the Ouachita-Marathon orogenic belt (Graham et al., 1975; Viele and Thomas, 1989; Ingersoll et al., 1995) caused intracontinental deformation of much of the southwestern United States. This deformation included formation of the Ancestral Rocky Mountains (Kluth, 1986) (Fig. 3D) and may have coincided with transform motion along the Cordilleran margin (Stevens and Stone, 1988; Stone and Stevens, 1988a, 1988b; Walker, 1988). Concurrently with this deformation, an intraoceanic magmatic arc, including the microcontinent Sonomia, approached from the west as North American oceanic lithosphere descended below it (Fig. 3D). The pre-Pennsylvanian position of Sonomia relative to North America is poorly constrained.

Permian–Triassic Sonoma orogeny

By Late Permian time, the intraplate or transform margin of North America had been drawn into the Sonomia subduction zone, and the Sonoma orogeny began with the emplacement of the Golconda allochthon (Speed, 1979; Speed and Sleep, 1982; Snow, 1992) (Fig. 3E). The Sonoma orogeny resembled the Antler orogeny in terms of overall tectonic process. However, the former differed in the following ways: (1) Sonomia was a larger landmass; (2) the North American margin was more complex prior to collision, including a residual Antler orogen; (3) a significant peripheral foreland basin did not form; and (4) subduction polarity reversal occurred following the Sonoma orogeny (Fig. 3F). Following suturing, all components of the Sonoma arc-trench system eroded, subsided, and were buried and intruded by the new continental-margin magmatic arc.

Triassic–Jurassic continental-margin magmatic arc

Following the Sonoma orogeny, subduction initiated along the Cordilleran margin

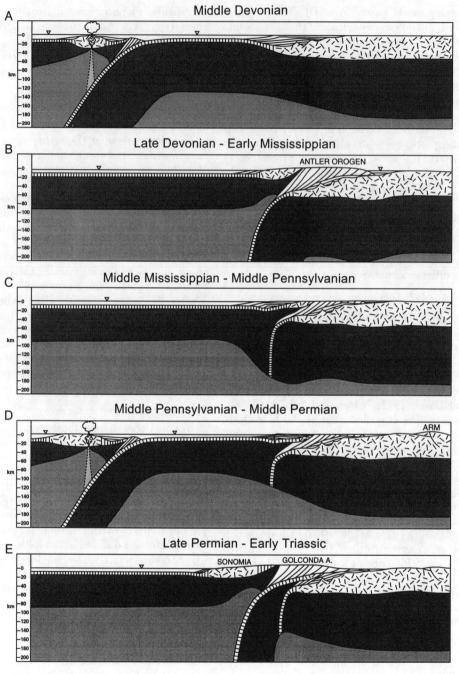

FIG. 3. Sequential cross sections of study area from middle Paleozoic time to the present (see Figs. 2A–2D for Neoproterozoic through early Paleozoic) (see Fig. 1 for approximate location) (continues on pages 965 and 966). Mantle lithosphere is defined geophysically rather than geochemically (see text for discussion). A. Middle Devonian. B. Late Devonian–Early Mississippian. C. Middle Mississippian–Middle Pennsylvanian. D. Middle Pennsylvanian–Middle Permian. E. Late Permian–Early Triassic. F. Middle Triassic–Middle Jurassic. G. Late Jurassic. H. Latest Jurassic. I. Cretaceous. J. Latest Cretaceous–Eocene. K. Oligocene. L. Miocene. M. Pliocene–Quaternary.

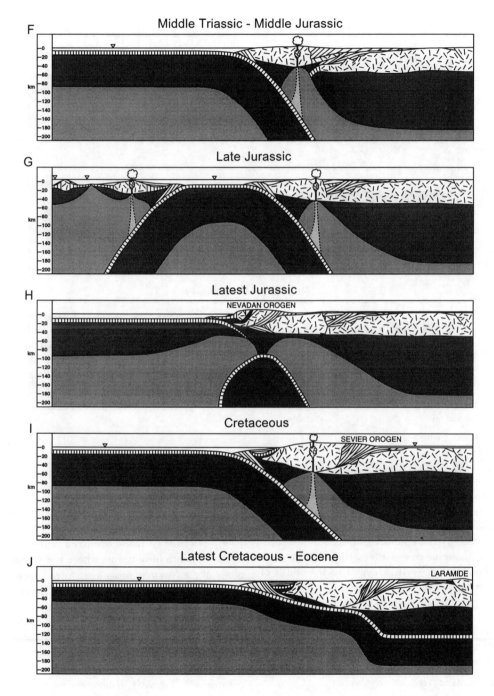

FIG. 3. (continued).

(Hamilton, 1969; Dickinson, 1981a, 1981b) (Fig. 3F). The resulting continental-margin magmatic arc (Schweickert, 1976; Busby-Spera, 1988) obliquely overprinted Proterozoic and Paleozoic belts; transform truncation of the Cordilleran margin may have preceded the

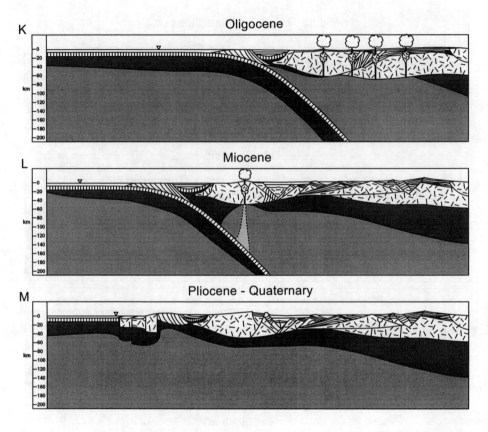

K

FIG. 3. (continued).

initiation of subduction (Stone and Stevens, 1988a, 1988b; Walker, 1988) or it may have been concurrent with subduction or both. In any case, by the end of the Triassic, the continental-margin arc was interacting with the edge of Proterozoic North America to the south of our study area (Figs. 1 and 3F). This early Mesozoic arc was dominantly dynamically neutral, so that shallow-marine and nonmarine conditions prevailed over wide areas of the backarc region (e.g., Bilodeau and Keith, 1986; Stewart et al., 1986; Marzolf, 1988).

Late Jurassic Nevadan orogeny

By the Late Jurassic, an E-facing intraoceanic magmatic arc with backarc basins and a remnant arc approached the W-facing continental-margin arc (Fig. 3G) (Schweickert and Cowan, 1975). As the intervening oceanic lithosphere subducted, the remnant ocean basin closed and a suture formed during the Sierran phase of the Nevadan orogeny (Fig. 3H) (Schweickert and Cowan, 1975; Ingersoll and Schweickert, 1986). No such collision occurred to the north in the Klamath Mountains, where the Klamath phase of the Nevadan orogeny involved opening and closing of a backarc basin behind the continental-margin arc concurrently with collision in the study area (Harper and Wright, 1984; Ingersoll and Schweickert, 1986). As the arc-arc collision progressed, a new subduction zone began in what was the backarc of the intraoceanic arc (Fig. 3H), thus creating a new W-facing forearc underlain by young backarc oceanic crust (now the Great Valley ophiolite) (Schweickert and Cowan, 1975). Most of the colliding arc, remnant arc, and oceanic crust was uplifted and eroded or rapidly buried or intruded by the new continental-margin arc, so that present relations are complex (e.g., Saleeby, 1992).

Latest Jurassic–Late Cretaceous arc-trench system

The Cretaceous continental-margin arc-trench system of the study area is one of the most-studied and best-understood ancient examples on Earth (Fig. 3I). The Franciscan accretionary prism grew westward and upward, forming a barrier behind which the Great Valley forearc basin grew (Ernst, 1970; Dickinson and Seely, 1979; Ingersoll, 1979, 1982b, 1983; Dickinson, 1995). The magmatic front migrated eastward gradually across the present Sierra Nevada, overprinting all pre-existing terranes (Evernden and Kistler, 1970; Schweickert and Cowan, 1975; Ingersoll, 1979, 1982b; Linn et al., 1992). Concurrently, contraction in the retroarc area thickened the crust and created the Sevier foldthrust belt and retroarc foreland basin (Armstrong, 1968; Dickinson, 1976; Jordan, 1995). Cordilleran crust probably reached its maximum thickness during the Late Cretaceous.

Latest Cretaceous–Eocene Laramide orogeny

Rapid relative westward motion of North America over the Farallon plate between approximately 80 and 40 Ma led to flat-slab subduction, with associated continental deformation of the Laramide orogeny (Fig. 3J) (Coney, 1976; Dickinson and Snyder, 1978; Bird, 1984, 1988; Engebretson et al., 1985; Cross, 1986; Spencer, 1996). The magmatic arc migrated eastward rapidly and then dissipated as the Farallon plate no longer interacted with asthenosphere underlying the Cordillera (Coney and Reynolds, 1977; Keith, 1978). Continental lithosphere likely was stripped from beneath the western part of the continental margin and accumulated in the modern Rocky Mountain and Great Plains areas (Bird, 1984, 1988). Laramide thick-skinned deformation and related sedimentation are consistent with NE-SW rapid convergence with the Farallon plate (Dickinson et al., 1988; Yin and Ingersoll, 1997).

Oligocene ignimbrite flare-up

Global plate reorganization resulted in a sudden decrease in the Farallon–North American convergence rate at ~40 Ma (Coney and Reyn-

olds, 1977; Cross and Pilger, 1978; Engebretson et al., 1985). As convergence slowed, the flat Farallon plate delaminated from beneath North America and either sank rapidly or disintegrated (Fig. 3K). In either case, the result was the rapid decompression melting of the inflowing asthenosphere, with resulting outpouring of silicic magma over much of the southwestern United States—the "ignimbrite flare-up" (Coney and Reynolds, 1977; Cross and Pilger, 1978; Keith, 1978; Lipman, 1992). Rapid extension of parts of the Cordilleran region began concurrently with this thermal event, although space-time relations of magmatism and taphrogeny are complex (Axen et al., 1993). Mantle lithosphere grew beneath cooling parts of the North American plate, whereas rapidly extending and hot areas remained weak because of thin lithosphere (Figs. 3K, 3L).

Miocene–Holocene triple-junction migration

As the Farallon slab steepened and a magmatic arc was re-established near the Pacific margin, the East Pacific Rise approached this margin (Atwater, 1970, 1989). Soon after 30 Ma, the Pacific plate began interacting with the North American plate in complex ways (e.g., Dickinson and Snyder, 1979a, 1979b; Severinghaus and Atwater, 1990; Nicholson et al., 1994; Bohannon and Parsons, 1995). Rapid extension of the southwestern United States was coincident with these plate interactions, although cause and effect are debated (e.g., Ingersoll, 1982a; Wernicke, 1992; Axen et al., 1993; Bohannon and Parsons, 1995). The overall effect of regional extension was the thinning of crust, the maintenance of high heat flow, including local volcanism, and widening of the Basin and Range Province (Fig. 3M). The structural style of extension in the Basin and Range also is debated (e.g., Hamilton, 1988; Wernicke, 1992). The Mendocino triple junction migrated northward along the Pacific margin through the study area between 10 and 5 Ma (Atwater, 1970, 1989; Severinghaus and Atwater, 1990; Dickinson, 1996), during which time the Salinian block was juxtaposed with the forearc region of central California (Fig. 3M).

Conclusions

The integrated result of sequential superposition of the actualistic models of Figure 2 is a cross section of the study area that is a reasonable representation of known relations (Fig. 3M). It is important to remember that this cross section was created by analog forward modeling, in contrast with the common inverse method of creating geological cross sections based on surface mapping. In fact, both forward and inverse methods were used iteratively in order to guide the choice of model and to modify each model; in this way, the process is partially self-correcting and circular. The next step might be to create four-dimensional models using supercomputers, but this is beyond the scope of the present study. It is hoped that this exercise provides new insights for the reader, as it has for the author. The discipline of applying actualistic models to the evolution of a continental margin forces one to consider many aspects of an area that one might not normally consider. Suggestions for improvements and tests of the models are welcome.

General models for the evolution of continental crust must account for the complexity of tectonic processes along long-lived continental margins, as illustrated herein. Similar syntheses of other continental margins should be attempted to further refine these models.

Acknowledgments

I thank W. G. Ernst for inviting me to write this paper in honor of C. A. Hall, Jr., former Director of the White Mountain Research Station, where this paper was first conceived. I also thank the Committee on Research of the Academic Senate of the Los Angeles Division of the University of California for support, and G. J. Axen, P. Bird, W. R. Dickinson, and A. Yin for reviewing the manuscript.

REFERENCES

Armstrong, R. L., 1968, Sevier orogenic belt in Nevada and Utah: Geol. Soc. Amer. Bull., v. 79, p. 429–458.

Atwater, T., 1970, Implications of plate tectonics for the Cenozoic tectonic evolution of western North America: Geol. Soc. Amer. Bull., v. 81, p. 3513–3535.

————, 1989, Plate tectonic history of the northeast Pacific and western North America, in Winterer, E. L., Hussong, D. M., and Decker, R. W., eds., The eastern Pacific Ocean and Hawaii: Boulder, CO, Geol. Soc. Amer., The geology of North America, v. N, p. 21–72.

Axen, G. J., Taylor, W. J., and Bartley, J. M., 1993, Space-time patterns and tectonic controls of Tertiary extension and magmatism in the Great Basin of the western United States: Geol. Soc. Amer. Bull., v. 105, p. 56–76.

Bilodeau, W. L., and Keith, S. B., 1986, Lower Jurassic Navajo-Aztec-equivalent sandstones in southern Arizona and their paleogeographic significance: Amer. Assoc. Petrol. Geol. Bull., v. 70, p. 690–701.

Bird, P., 1984, Laramide crustal thickening event in the Rocky Mountain foreland and Great Plains: Tectonics, v. 3, p. 741–758.

————, 1988, Formation of the Rocky Mountains, western United States: A continuum computer model: Science, v. 239, p. 1501–1507.

Bohannon, R. G., and Parsons, T., 1995, Tectonic implications of post-30 Ma Pacific and North American relative plate motions: Geol. Soc. Amer. Bull., v. 107, p. 937–959.

Bond, G. C., Christie-Blick, N., Kominz, M. A., and Devlin, W. J., 1985, An Early Cambrian rift to postrift transition in the Cordillera of western North America: Nature, v. 316, p. 742–745.

Bond, G. C., Kominz, M. A., and Sheridan, R. E., 1995, Continental terraces and rises, in Busby, C. J., and Ingersoll, R. V., eds., Tectonics of sedimentary basins: Cambridge, MA, Blackwell Sci., p. 149–178.

Buck, W. R., 1991, Modes of continental lithospheric extension: Jour. Geophys. Res., v. 96, p. 20,161–20,178.

Burchfiel, B. C., and Davis, G. A., 1972, Structural framework and evolution of the southern part of the Cordilleran orogen, western United States: Amer. Jour. Sci., v. 272, p. 97–118.

————, 1975, Nature and controls of Cordilleran orogenesis, western United States: Extensions of an earlier synthesis: Amer. Jour. Sci., v. 275-A, p. 363–396.

Burchfiel, B. C., Lipman, P. W., and Zoback, M. L., eds., 1992, The Cordilleran orogen: Conterminous U.S.: Boulder, CO, Geol. Soc. Amer., The geology of North America, v. G-3, 734 p.

Busby-Spera, C. J., 1988, Speculative tectonic model for the early Mesozoic arc of the southwest Cordilleran United States: Geology, v. 16, p. 1121–1125.

Christie-Blick, N., and Biddle, K. T., 1985, Deformation and basin formation along strike-slip faults: Soc. Econ. Paleontol. Mineral. Spec. Publ. 37, p. 1–34.

Cloos, M., 1993, Lithospheric buoyancy and collisional orogenesis: Subduction of oceanic plateaus, continental margins, island arcs, spreading ridges, and seamounts: Geol. Soc. Amer. Bull., v. 105, p. 715–737.

Cochran, J. R., 1983, A model for development of Red Sea: Amer. Assoc. Petrol. Geol. Bull., v. 67, p. 41–69.

Coney, P. J., 1976, Plate tectonics and the Laramide orogeny: New Mex. Geol. Soc. Spec. Publ. 6, p. 5–10.

Coney, P. J., and Reynolds, S. J., 1977, Cordilleran Benioff zones: Nature, v. 270, p. 403–406.

Cross, T. A., 1986, Tectonic controls of foreland basin subsidence and Laramide-style deformation, western United States: Inter. Assoc. Sedimentol. Spec. Publ. 8, p. 15–39.

Cross, T. A., and Pilger, R. H., Jr., 1978, Constraints on absolute motion and plate interaction inferred from Cenozoic igneous activity in the western United States: Amer. Jour. Sci., v. 278, p. 865–902.

Crowell, J. C., 1974a, Sedimentation along the San Andreas fault, California: Soc. Econ. Paleontol. Mineral. Spec. Publ. 19, p. 292–303.

————, 1974b, Origin of late Cenozoic basins in southern California: Soc. Econ. Paleontol. Mineral. Spec. Publ. 22, p. 190–204.

Dalziel, I. W. D., 1991, Pacific margins of Laurentia and East Antarctica-Australia as a conjugate rift pair: Evidence and implications for an Eocambrian supercontinent: Geology, v. 19, p. 598–601.

Dewey, J. F., 1980, Episodicity, sequence and style at convergent plate boundaries: Geol. Assoc. Can. Spec. Pap. 20, p. 553–573.

Dewey, J. F., and Bird, J. M., 1970, Plate tectonics and geosynclines: Tectonophysics, v. 10, p. 625–638.

Dewey, J. F., and Burke, K., 1974, Hot spots and continental break-up: Implications for collisional orogeny: Geology, v. 2, p. 57–60.

Dickinson, W. R., 1974, Plate tectonics and sedimentation: Soc. Econ. Paleontol. Mineral. Spec. Publ. 22, p. 1–27.

————, 1976, Sedimentary basins developed during evolution of Mesozoic-Cenozoic arc-trench system in western North America: Can. Jour. Earth Sci., v. 13, p. 1268–1287.

————, 1978, Plate tectonic evolution of north Pacific rim: Jour. Phys. Earth, v. 26, Supplement, p. S1–S19.

————, 1981a, Plate tectonics and the continental margin of California, in Ernst, W. G., ed., The geotectonic development of California: Englewood Cliffs, NJ, Prentice-Hall, p. 1–28.

————, 1981b, Plate tectonic evolution of the southern Cordillera: Ariz. Geol. Soc. Digest, v. 14, p. 113–135.

————, 1995, Forearc basins, in Busby, C. J., and Ingersoll, R. V., eds., Tectonics of sedimentary basins: Cambridge, MA, Blackwell Sci., p. 221–261.

————, 1996, Kinematics of transrotational tectonism in the California Transverse Ranges and its contribution to cumulative slip along the San Andreas transform fault system: Geol. Soc. Amer. Spec. Pap. 305, 46 p.

Dickinson, W. R., Harbaugh, D. W., Saller, A. H., Heller, P. L., and Snyder, W. S., 1983, Detrital modes of upper Paleozoic sandstones derived from Antler orogen in Nevada: Implications for nature of Antler orogeny: Amer. Jour. Sci., v. 283, p. 481–509.

Dickinson, W. R., and Seely, D. R., 1979, Structure and stratigraphy of forearc regions: Amer. Assoc. Petrol. Geol. Bull., v. 63, p. 2–31.

Dickinson, W. R., and Snyder, W. S., 1978, Plate tectonics of the Laramide orogeny: Geol. Soc. Amer. Memoir 151, p. 355–366.

————, 1979a, Geometry of triple junctions related to San Andreas transform: Jour. Geophys. Res., v. 84, p. 561–572.

————, 1979b, Geometry of subducted slabs related to San Andreas transform: Jour. Geol., v. 87, p. 609–627.

Dickinson, W. R., et al., 1988, Paleogeographic and paleotectonic setting of Laramide sedimentary basins in the central Rocky Mountain region: Geol. Soc. Amer. Bull., v. 100, p. 1023–1039.

Engebretson, D. A., Cox, A., and Gordon, R. G., 1985, Relative motions between oceanic and continental plates in the Pacific Basin: Geol. Soc. Amer. Spec. Pap. 206, 59 p.

England, P., and McKenzie, D., 1982, A thin viscous sheet model for continental deformation: Geophys. Jour. Roy. Astron. Soc., v. 70, p. 295–321.

Ernst, W. G., 1970, Tectonic contact between the Franciscan melange and the Great Valley sequence, crustal expression of a late Mesozoic Benioff zone: Jour. Geophys. Res., v. 75, p. 886–902.

Evernden, J. F., and Kistler, R. W., 1970, Chronology of emplacement of Mesozoic batholithic complexes in California and western Nevada: U.S. Geol. Surv. Prof. Pap. 623, 42 p.

Falvey, D. A., 1974, The development of continental margins in plate tectonic theory: Austral. Petrol. Explor. Assoc. Jour., v. 14, p. 95–106.

Frodeman, R., 1995, Geological reasoning: Geology as an interpretive and historical science: Geol. Soc. Amer. Bull., v. 107, p. 960–968.

Graham, S. A., Dickinson, W. R., and Ingersoll, R. V., 1975, Himalayan-Bengal model for flysch dispersal in the Appalachian-Ouachita system: Geol. Soc. Amer. Bull., v. 86, p. 273–286.

Hamilton, W., 1969, Mesozoic California and the underflow of Pacific mantle: Geol. Soc. Amer. Bull., v. 80, p. 2409–2430.

————, 1979, Tectonics of the Indonesian region: U.S. Geol. Surv. Prof. Pap. 1078, 345 p.

————, 1988, Tectonic setting and variations with depth of some Cretaceous and Cenozoic structural and magmatic systems of the western United States, in Ernst, W. G., ed., Metamorphism and crustal evolution of the western United States: Rubey Volume VII: Englewood Cliffs, NJ, Prentice-Hall, p. 1-40.

Harper, G. D., and Wright, J. E., 1984, Middle to Late Jurassic tectonic evolution of the Klamath Mountains, California-Oregon: Tectonics, v. 3, p. 759-772.

Heidegger, M., 1927, Sein und zeit: Tübingen, Germany, Neomarius Verlag, 488 p.

————, 1962, Being and time [Macquarrie, J., and Robinson, E., trans.]: New York, NY, Harper and Row, 589 p.

Hoffman, P. F., 1991, Did the breakout of Laurentia turn Gondwanaland inside-out?: Science, v. 252, p. 1409-1412.

Ingersoll, R. V., 1979, Evolution of the Late Cretaceous forearc basin, northern and central California: Geol. Soc. Amer. Bull., v. 90, Part I, p. 813-826.

————, 1982a, Triple-junction instability as cause for late Cenozoic extension and fragmentation of the western United States: Geology, v. 10, p. 621-624.

————, 1982b, Initiation and evolution of the Great Valley forearc basin of northern and central California, in Leggett, J. K., ed., Trench-forearc geology: Sedimentation and tectonics on modern and ancient active plate margins: Geol. Soc. Lond. Spec. Publ. 10, p. 459-467.

————, 1983, Petrofacies and provenance of late Mesozoic forearc basin, northern and central California: Amer. Assoc. Petrol. Geol. Bull., v. 67, p. 1125-1142.

————, 1988, Tectonics of sedimentary basins: Geol. Soc. Amer. Bull., v. 100, p. 1704-1719.

Ingersoll, R. V., and Busby, C. J., 1995, Tectonics of sedimentary basins, in Busby, C. J., and Ingersoll, R. V., eds., Tectonics of sedimentary basins: Cambridge, MA, Blackwell Sci., p. 1-51.

Ingersoll, R. V., Graham, S. A., and Dickinson, W. R., 1995, Remnant ocean basins, in Busby, C. J., and Ingersoll, R. V., eds., Tectonics of sedimentary basins: Cambridge, MA, Blackwell Sci., p. 363-391.

Ingersoll, R. V., and Schweickert, R. A., 1986, A plate-tectonic model for Late Jurassic ophiolite genesis, Nevadan orogeny and forearc initiation, northern California: Tectonics, v. 5, p. 901-912.

Jarrard, R. D., 1986, Relations among subduction parameters: Rev. Geophys., v. 24, p. 217-284.

Jordan, T. E., 1995, Retroarc foreland and related basins, in Busby, C. J., and Ingersoll, R. V., eds., Tectonics of sedimentary basins: Cambridge, MA, Blackwell Sci., p. 331-362.

Karig, D. E. 1971, Origin and development of marginal basins in the western Pacific: Jour. Geophys. Res., v. 76, p. 2542-2561.

Kay, M., 1951, North American geosynclines: Geol. Soc. Amer. Memoir 48, 143 p.

Keith, S. B., 1978, Paleosubduction geometries inferred from Cretaceous and Tertiary magmatic patterns in southwestern North America: Geology, v. 6, p. 516-521.

————, 1982, Paleoconvergence rates determined from K_2O/SiO_2 ratios in magmatic rocks and their application to Cretaceous and Tertiary tectonic patterns in southwestern North America: Geol. Soc. Amer. Bull., v. 93, p. 524-532.

King, P. B., 1969, Tectonic map of North America: Washington, DC, U.S. Geol. Surv., 1:5,000,000 scale.

Kluth, C. F., 1986, Plate tectonics of the Ancestral Rocky Mountains: Amer. Assoc. Petrol. Geol. Memoir 41, p. 353-369.

Kuhn, T. S., 1970, The structure of scientific revolutions, second ed.: Chicago, IL, Univ. of Chicago Press, 210 p.

Leeder, M. R., 1995, Continental rifts and proto-oceanic rift troughs, in Busby, C. J., and Ingersoll, R. V., eds., Tectonics of sedimentary basins: Cambridge, MA, Blackwell Sci., p. 119-148.

Levy, M., and Christie-Blick, N., 1989, Pre-Mesozoic palinspastic reconstruction of the eastern Great Basin (western United States): Science, v. 245, p. 1454-1462.

Linn, A. M., DePaolo, D. J., and Ingersoll, R. V., 1992, Nd-Sr isotopic, geochemical, and petrographic stratigraphy and paleotectonic analysis: Mesozoic Great Valley forearc sedimentary rocks of California: Geol. Soc. Amer. Bull., v. 104, p. 1264-1279.

Lipman, P. W., 1992, Magmatism in the Cordilleran United States; progress and problems, in Burchfiel, B. C., Lipman, P. W., and Zoback, M. L., eds., The Cordilleran orogen: Conterminous U.S.: Boulder, CO, Geol. Soc. Amer., The geology of North America, v. G-3, p. 481-514.

Lonsdale, P., 1989, Geology and tectonic history of the Gulf of California, in Winterer, E. L., Hussong, D. M., and Decker, R. W., eds., The eastern Pacific Ocean and Hawaii: Boulder, CO, Geol. Soc. Amer., The geology of North America, v. N, p. 499-521.

Marsaglia, K. M., 1995, Interarc and backarc basins, in Busby, C. J., and Ingersoll, R. V., eds., Tectonics of sedimentary basins: Cambridge, MA, Blackwell Sci., p. 299-329.

Marzolf, J. E., 1988, Controls on late Paleozoic and early Mesozoic eolian deposition of the western United States: Sediment. Geol., v. 56, p. 167-191.

McMenamin, M. A. S., and McMenamin, D. L. S., 1990, The emergence of animals: The Cambrian breakthrough: New York, NY, Columbia University Press, 217 p.

Miall, A. D., 1995, Collision-related foreland basins, in Busby, C. J., and Ingersoll, R. V., eds., Tectonics of sedimentary basins: Cambridge, MA, Blackwell Sci., p. 393–424.

Molnar, P., and Atwater, T., 1978, Interarc spreading and Cordilleran tectonics as alternates related to age of subducted oceanic lithosphere: Earth Planet. Sci. Lett., v. 41, p. 330–340.

Molnar, P., and Tapponnier, P., 1975, Cenozoic tectonics of Asia: Effects of a continental collision: Science, v. 189, p. 419–426.

Moores, E. M., 1991, Southwest U.S.–East Antarctic (SWEAT) connection: A hypothesis: Geology, v. 19, p. 425–428.

Nelson, C. A., 1962, Lower Cambrian–Precambrian succession, White-Inyo Mountains, California: Geol. Soc. Amer. Bull., v. 73, p. 139–144.

————, 1978, Late Precambrian–Early Cambrian stratigraphic and faunal succession of eastern California and the Precambrian-Cambrian boundary: Geol. Mag., v. 115, p. 121–126.

Nicholson, C., Sorlien, C. C., Atwater, T., Crowell, J. C., and Luyendyk, B. P., 1994, Microplate capture, rotation of the western Transverse Ranges, and initiation of the San Andreas transform as a low-angle fault system: Geology, v. 22, p. 491–495.

Nilsen, T. H., and Stewart, J. H., 1980, The Antler orogeny—mid-Paleozoic tectonism in western North America: Geology, v. 8, p. 298–302.

Nilsen, T. H., and Sylvester, A. G., 1995, in Busby, C. J., and Ingersoll, R. V., eds., Tectonics of sedimentary basins: Cambridge, MA, Blackwell Sci., p. 425–457.

Oldow, J. S., Bally, A. W., Ave Lallement, H. G., and Leeman, W. P., 1989, Phanerozoic evolution of the North American Cordillera; United States and Canada, in Bally, A. W., and Palmer, A. R., eds., The geology of North America; an overview: Boulder, CO, Geol. Soc. Amer.,The geology of North America, v. A, p. 139–232.

Pitman, W. C., III, 1978, Relationship between eustacy and stratigraphic sequences of passive margins: Geol. Soc. Amer. Bull., v. 89, p. 1389–1403.

Poole, F. G., 1974, Flysch deposits of Antler foreland basin, western United States: Soc. Econ. Paleontol. Mineral. Spec. Publ. 22, p. 58–82.

Poole, F. G., et al., 1992, Latest Precambrian to latest Devonian time; development of a continental margin, in Burchfiel, B. C., Lipman, P. W., and Zoback, M. L., eds., The Cordilleran orogen: Conterminous U.S.: Boulder, CO, Geol. Soc. Amer., The geology of North America, v. G-3, p. 9–56.

Reading, H. G., 1980, Characteristics and recognition of strike-slip fault systems: Int. Assoc. Sedimentol. Spec. Publ. 4, p. 7–26.

Saleeby, J. B., 1992, Petrotectonic and paleogeographic settings of U.S. Cordilleran ophiolites, in Burchfiel, B. C., Lipman, P. W., and Zoback, M. L., eds., The Cordilleran orogen: Conterminous U.S.: Boulder, CO, Geol. Soc. Amer., The geology of North America, v. G-3, p. 653–682.

Schweickert, R. A., 1976, Shallow-level plutonic complexes in the eastern Sierra Nevada, California and their tectonic implications: Geol. Soc. Amer. Spec. Pap. 176, 58 p.

Schweickert, R. A., and Cowan, D. S., 1975, Early Mesozoic tectonic evolution of the western Sierra Nevada, California: Geol. Soc. Amer. Bull., v. 86, p. 1329–1336.

Schweickert, R. A., and Lahren, M. M., 1987, Continuation of Antler and Sonoma orogenic belts to the eastern Sierra Nevada, California, and Late Triassic thrusting in a compressional arc: Geology, v. 15, p. 270–273.

Sengör, A. M. C., 1995, Sedimentation and tectonics of fossil rifts, in Busby, C. J., and Ingersoll, R. V., eds., Tectonics of sedimentary basins: Cambridge, MA, Blackwell Sci., p. 53–117.

Sengör, A. M. C., and Burke, K., 1978, Relative timing of rifting and volcanism on Earth and its tectonic implications: Geophys. Res. Lett., v. 5, p. 419–421.

Severinghaus, J., and Atwater, T., 1990, Cenozoic geometry and thermal state of the subducting slabs beneath western North America, in Wernicke, B. P., ed., Basin and Range extensional tectonics near the latitude of Las Vegas, Nevada: Geol. Soc. Amer. Memoir 176, p. 1–22.

Smith, G. A., and Landis, C. A., 1995, Intra-arc basins, in Busby, C. J., and Ingersoll, R. V., eds., Tectonics of sedimentary basins: Cambridge, MA, Blackwell Sci., p. 263–298.

Snow, J. K., 1992, Large-magnitude Permian shortening and continental-margin tectonics in the southern Cordillera: Geol. Soc. Amer. Bull., v. 104, p. 80–105.

Speed, R. C., 1979, Collided microplate in the western United States: Jour. Geol., v. 87, p. 279–292.

Speed, R. C., and Sleep, N. H., 1982, Antler orogeny and foreland basin: A model: Geol. Soc. Amer. Bull., v. 93, p. 815–828 (also see v. 94, p. 684–686).

Spencer, J. E., 1996, Uplift of the Colorado Plateau due to lithosphere attenuation during Laramide low-angle subduction: Jour. Geophys. Res., v. 101, p. 13,595–13,609.

Stevens, C.H., and Stone, P., 1988, Early Permian thrust faults in east-central California: Geol. Soc. Amer. Bull., v. 100, p. 552–562.

Stewart, J. H., 1972, Initial deposits in the Cordilleran geosyncline: Evidence of a late Precambrian (850 m.y.) continental separation: Geol. Soc. Amer. Bull., v. 83, p. 1345–1360.

————, 1976, Late Precambrian evolution of North America: Plate tectonics implication: Geology, v. 4, p. 11–15.

Stewart, J. H., Anderson, T. H., Haxel, G. B., Silver, L. T., and Wright, J. E., 1986, Late Triassic paleogeography of the southern Cordillera: The problem of a source for voluminous volcanic detritus in the Chinle Formation of the Colorado Plateau region: Geology, v. 14, p. 567–570.

Stock, J. M., and Hodges, K. V., 1989, Pre-Pliocene extension around the Gulf of California and the transfer of Baja California to the Pacific plate: Tectonics, v. 8, p. 99–115.

Stone, P., and Stevens, C. H., 1988a, An angular unconformity in the Permian section of east-central California: Geol. Soc. Amer. Bull., v. 100, p. 547–551.

————, 1988b, Pennsylvanian and Early Permian paleogeography of east-central California: Implications for the shape of the continental margin and the timing of continental truncation: Geology, v. 16, p. 330–333.

Tapponnier, P., and Molnar, P., 1976, Slip-line field theory and large scale continental tectonics: Nature, v. 264, p. 319–324.

Underwood, M. B., and Moore, G. F., 1995, Trenches and trench-slope basins, in Busby, C. J., and Ingersoll, R. V., eds., Tectonics of sedimentary basins: Cambridge, MA, Blackwell Sci., p. 179–219.

Viele, G. W., and Thomas, W. A., 1989, Tectonic synthesis of the Ouachita orogenic belt, in Hatcher, R. D., Jr., Thomas, W. A., and Viele, G. W.. eds., The Appalachian-Ouachita orogen in the United States: Boulder, CO, Geol. Soc. Amer., The geology of North America, v. F-2, p. 695–728.

Walker, J. D., 1988, Permian and Triassic rocks of the Mojave Desert and their implications for timing and mechanisms of continental truncation: Tectonics, v. 7, p. 685–709.

Wernicke, B. P., ed., 1990, Basin and Range extensional tectonics near the latitude of Las Vegas, Nevada: Geol. Soc. Amer. Memoir 176, 511 p.

————, 1992, Cenozoic extensional tectonics of the U.S. Cordillera, in Burchfiel, B. C., Lipman, P. W., and Zoback, M. L., eds., The Cordilleran orogen: Conterminous U.S.: Boulder, CO, Geol. Soc. Amer., The geology of North America, v. G-3, p. 553–582.

Wernicke, B., Axen, G. J., and Snow, J. K., 1988, Basin and Range extensional tectonics at the latitude of Las Vegas, Nevada: Geol. Soc. Amer. Bull., v. 100, p. 1738–1757.

Yin, A., and Ingersoll, R. V., 1997, A model for evolution of Laramide axial basins in the southern Rocky Mountains, USA: INT. GEOL. REV., v. 39, in press.

Late Miocene-Pleistocene Extensional Faulting, Northern Gulf of California, Mexico and Salton Trough, California

GARY J. AXEN

Department of Earth and Space Sciences, University of California, Los Angeles, California 90095-1567

AND JOHN M. FLETCHER

Departamento de Geología, Centro de Investigación Científica y de Educación Superior de Ensenada (CICESE), Baja California, México

Abstract

A belt of low-angle normal (or detachment) faults ~250 km long extends from the northern end of the Salton Trough, California to southern Laguna Salada, Baja California, Mexico. The detachment system is divided into two principal segments. The northern segment, here termed the "west Salton detachment system," comprises top-to-the-east detachment faults along the eastern Peninsular Ranges that root under the Salton Trough. The southern segment, here termed the Laguna Salada detachment system, comprises top-to-the-west detachment faults in northeastern Baja California and the Yuha Desert region of the southwesternmost Salton Trough. Detachments of that system root under Laguna Salada and the Peninsular Ranges of northern Baja California. Both of these systems experienced a major episode of activity in late Miocene to Pleistocene time, synchronous with deposition of the Imperial and Palm Spring formations, and the Laguna Salada detachment system may still be active. Thus, their activity temporally overlapped, partly or completely, with activity on dextral faults of the San Andreas boundary between the Pacific and North American plates, and with accretion of new transitional crust. Some of the detachment faults in the northern segment may have had mid-Miocene normal slip and/or Cretaceous thrust or normal slip as well, although compelling evidence for either is lacking. These detachment faults are distinctly younger than detachments east of the San Andreas fault, which generally ceased activity by middle or late Miocene time and are overlapped by marine or lacustrine rocks (Bouse Formation); these units are equivalent in age to the syntectonic strata of the Salton Trough but are much thinner and essentially undeformed.

Introduction

OBLIQUE RIFTS, in which rift margins are oblique to the direction of continental separation, are reasonably common in the modern record—e.g., the Red Sea and Gulf of Aden (McKenzie et al., 1970; Cochran, 1983; Tamsett, 1984), the Tanganyika-Malawi-Rukwa rifts (Tiercelin et al., 1888; Rosendahl et al., 1992), and the Gulf of California (Atwater, 1970; Stock and Hodges, 1989)—as well as in the ancient record—e.g., Ghana–Ivory Coast (Blarez and Mascle, 1988) and western Tethys (Channell and Kozur, 1997). Such structures may be quite important in the evolution and paleotectonics of many continental margins (e.g., Schermer et al., 1984; Umhoefer and Dorsey, 1997). Significant advances in understanding oblique rifts have been made using analytical and analog models as well (e.g., With-

jack and Jamison, 1986; Tron and Brun, 1991; McClay and White, 1995). Nevertheless, processes of oblique rifting remain poorly understood relative to those of orthogonal rifts, where the rift margins are approximately perpendicular to the extension direction, and to strike-slip systems. Such processes are difficult to study directly in ancient settings because the rifting process leads inexorably to subsidence, causing the products to become submerged and inaccessible to direct observation.

The Gulf of California is one of the premier modern examples of oblique continental rifting, and arguably is the best place in the world in which to study the processes of such rifting as they lead to the interplate transfer of a continental fragment. Opening of the southern Gulf has progressed to the point of creating magnetically lineated ocean crust at the Alarcón Rise (Fig. 1) that records Pacific–North

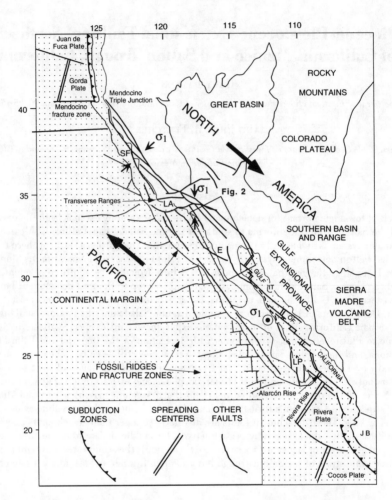

FIG. 1. Tectonic summary map showing Pacific–North America relative motion, major faults of the plate boundaries, and physiographic provinces. The direction of maximum principal stress, inferred from Zoback et al. (1991) is shown by arrows labeled σ_1 (bulls's-eye where vertical). Box shows location of Figure 2. Abbreviations: IT = Isla Tiburón; JB = Jalisco Block; SF = San Francisco; LA = Los Angeles; E = Ensenada; LP = La Paz.

American plate motion since ~3.6 Ma (DeMets, 1995). In contrast, the northern Gulf and Salton Trough region remains in the transitional stage from continental to oceanic rifting, with formation of new crust comprising sedimentary strata intruded and metamorphosed by generally mafic magma (Elders et al., 1972; McKibben et al., 1987; Elders and Sass, 1988; Herzig and Jacobs, 1994). The Gulf depression ends northward where the San Andreas bends westward and transpressional tectonics dominate (Allen, 1957).

We present new data from the Laguna Salada area and review the existing literature from both the Laguna Salada area and the Salton Trough, which show that low-angle normal faults (or detachments) of late Miocene, Pliocene, and Pleistocene(?) age were an integral part of the oblique rift system for ~250 km along strike in the northern Gulf of California–Salton Trough region, and were at least partly synchronous with major dextral slip on plate-boundary faults. This differs from previous interpretations of the detachment faults as late Mesozoic–early Cenozoic thrusts (Sharp, 1979) or normal faults (Erskine and Wenk, 1985; George and Dokka, 1994), or as mid-Miocene normal faults that pre-dated dextral faulting in the region (Frost, Fattahipour et al., 1996; Frost, Suitt et al., 1996). Late Miocene–Pleistocene(?) detachment faults had top-to-the-west slip in the Laguna Salada segment and top-to-the-east slip along the Salton Trough, with the two segments bounded by the Ocotillo accommodation zone (Fig. 2) (Axen, 1995).

Tectonic Setting

The modern Pacific–North American plate boundary is dominated by dextral faulting concentrated along faults of the San Andreas system with other subsidiary, but important, crustal deformation accommodated across a wider zone. The boundary can be divided into three domains from north to south, in which the partitioning of strain differs (Fig. 1). This strain partitioning is also reflected in lateral variations in the stress field (Zoback et al., 1991). Terranes west of the San Andreas may pass from one domain into the next northerly domain as they are translated northwest relative to North America.

The northern domain extends from the Mendocino triple junction to the north side of the Transverse Ranges. It is characterized by transpression in a zone several to tens of kilometers wide that runs along the northern San Andreas and related faults combined with diffuse and spatially separated E-W to SW-NE extension in the Great Basin (Wernicke et al., 1988; Zoback et al., 1991). Thus, a transpressional zone in California is separated from a region of transtension by the relatively rigid Sierra Nevada.

The central domain includes the Transverse Ranges (Fig. 1) and the "big bend" of the San Andreas fault, where the fault changes strike WNW. Strain partitioning in the central domain is characterized by dextral wrench faulting along the San Andreas with N-S compression and clockwise rotation of crustal slivers (see the recent review by Dickinson, 1997). Extension occurs locally and primarily as a result of block rotation.

The southern domain runs from the Transverse Ranges to the Alarcón Rise at the mouth of the Gulf of California (Fig. 1). Strain in the southern domain is dominated by dextral wrench faulting on the southernmost San Andreas and related right-lateral faults south of the big bend (e.g., Crowell, 1981; Goff et al.,

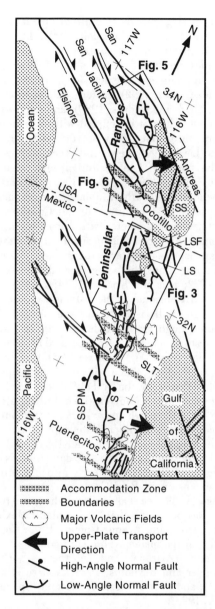

FIG. 2. Fault map of the northern Gulf of California–Salton Trough region, showing three segments of the extensional belt to the west, the accommodation zones that bound them, and the locations of Figures 3, 5, and 6. Stippled areas are below sea level, so the Laguna Salada and the Salton Sea appear to be larger than they actually are. Abbreviations: LS = Laguna Salada; LSF = Laguna Salada fault; SLT = Sierra Las Tinajas; SS = Salton Sea; SSPM = Sierra San Pedro Mártir; VSF = Valle San Felipe.

1987; Lonsdale, 1991) combined with NW-SE extension in the Gulf basins south of Isla

Tiburón (Fig. 1), where seafloor spreading is active or initiating (Lonsdale, 1991; DeMets, 1995). Strain in the southern domain also includes significant approximately E-W extension in mainland Mexico (e.g., Henry and Aranda-Gomez, 1992), eastern Baja California (e.g., Stock and Hodges, 1989), and the northern Gulf, where it is coupled with distributed dextral shear and clockwise vertical-axis rotations (Lewis, 1994; Lewis and Stock, in press).

The northern Gulf–Salton Trough region, discussed here (see Figs. 2–6), lies at the northern end of the southern domain; its northern end passes into the central domain. Continental crust has been completely rifted apart and transitional crust—comprising sedimentary strata, young metasedimentary rocks, and mainly mafic intrusions—is being formed (Elders et al., 1972; Fuis and Kohler, 1984; Fuis et al., 1984). Extensional fault systems exposed in northeastern Baja California and west of the Salton Trough are divisible into top-east and top-west segments that are separated by accommodation zones (Fig. 2) (Axen, 1995).

A subduction-related volcanic arc occupied the area that is now the Gulf of California in late Oligocene to early Miocene time, shutting off at ~16 Ma in the north and ~12 Ma in the south, concomitant with microplate capture events offshore to the west (Lonsdale, 1991, Sawlan, 1991; Stock and Lee, 1994). To date, there is no evidence of Oligocene to early Miocene intra-arc extension in Baja California (Stock and Hodges, 1989; Lee et al., 1996), although extension was occurring then in mainland Mexico (e.g., Henry and Aranda-Gomez, 1992; Gans, 1997), in the metamorphic core complexes of southern Arizona and northern Sonora (Spencer and Reynolds, 1989; Nourse et al., 1994), and in southwestern Arizona (Spencer et al., 1995).

On Isla Tiburón (Fig. 1), rifting apparently had begun by mid-Miocene time, as indicated by marine deposits overlain in angular unconformity by volcanic rocks of ~12 to 13 Ma age (Smith, 1991). Extension north of there was under way between 11 and 6 Ma (Stock and Hodges, 1989; Lee et al., 1996). By ~8 Ma, marine waters had reached the northern Gulf and Salton Trough region (see below). From ~12 to 5 Ma, oblique transtension between the Pacific and North American plates is thought to have been partitioned between ENE-directed

extension in the Gulf region and dextral slip on the Tosco-Abreojos and related faults along the western continental margin (Fig. 1) (Spencer and Normark, 1979; Stock and Hodges, 1989). During or after that time interval, strike-slip motion was transferred into the Gulf, initiating the modern transtensional regime there.

Laguna Salada

Laguna Salada (Figs. 2 and 3) is an actively subsiding, sub–sea-level basin that is bounded on the west by the main Gulf escarpment (Gastil et al., 1975) along the front of the Sierra Juárez, which rises 1500 m over a horizontal distance of 5 km. The sierras El Mayor and Cucapá, east of Laguna Salada, are lower than the Sierra Juárez. The most active subsidence is on the eastern side of the basin, adjacent to the northern Sierra El Mayor and central Sierra Cucapá (Savage et al., 1994).

Laguna Salada has generally been interpreted as a pull-apart basin with up to 5–6 km of fill in its center (e.g., Kelm, 1972; Fenby and Gastil, 1991). More recently, however, it has been interpreted as a shallow half-graben, formed above the Cañada David detachment fault, which subsequently was overprinted by slip on the Laguna Salada and related active faults (Axen, 1995). The depth to basement below Laguna Salada is strongly asymmetric (Kelm, 1972; Miele, 1986; García-Abdeslem et al., in review). The basin fill is inferred to thicken to 4 km on the eastern side, which is reflected in a rapid decrease in the Bouguer gravity anomaly from 0 to –60 mgal over a 10 km distance (García-Abdeslem et al., in review). In contrast, the western margin shows only a 5 to 10 mgal change over the same distance. Recently completed geothermal exploration wells also show this eastward thickening (A. Martín Barajas, pers. commun., 1996).

Rocks along the margins of Laguna Salada are cut by a complex network of low- and high-angle faults. We divide areas along the margin of Laguna Salada into four structural domains based on the patterns of faulting and exhumation of basement blocks. On the eastern side of Laguna Salada, the Sierra El Mayor domain is dominated by a sequence of stacked, top-to-the-west detachment faults. In contrast, no detach-

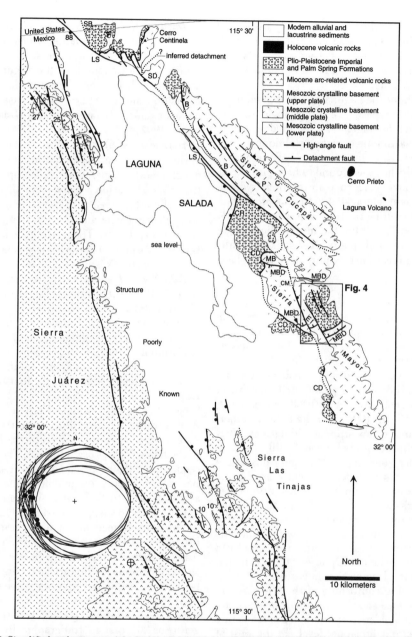

FIG. 3. Simplified geologic map of the Laguna Salada region showing distribution of faults and tectono-lithologic map units. Inset shows a lower-hemisphere, equal-area stereonet plot of detachment-fault planes ($n = 19$) and striae on them (filled circles, $n = 11$); filled square is average striae. Abbreviations: B = Borrego fault; C = Cucapá fault; CD = Cañada David detachment; CM = central Mayor fault; CR = Cañon Rojo fault; LS = Laguna Salada fault; MB = Monte Blanco dome; MBD = Monte Blanco detachment; P = Pescadores fault; SB = Sunrise Buttes fault; SD = Sanchez Diaz fault. Box shows location of Figure 4. Modified from INEGI (1983), Gastil et al. (1975), Siem (1992), Siem and Gastil (1994), Vásquez-Hernández (1996), Romero-Espejel (1997), and unpublished mapping by Axen, Fletcher, and Ramón Mendoza-Borunda.

ment faults have been documented in the Sierra Cucapá domain, where major faults are NW-striking high-angle faults. Detachment faults are found to the north in the Cerro Centinela domain, where they are intimately associated with a series of closely spaced high-angle faults. On the western side of Laguna Salada, the entire Sierra Juárez range front is dominated by high-angle faults.

Throughout the Laguna Salada region, high-angle faults typically cut low-angle detachments. The high-angle faults predominantly show normal dip slip or strongly oblique normal right-lateral slip. However, none of the macroscopic faults has been found to have pure strike slip. Although modern plate motion is dominated by right-lateral strike slip, the proportion of normal faulting to strike slip is only slightly greater than 50:50 for the most oblique high-angle faults, and many NW-striking faults in the area record nearly pure normal displacement.

Rock units

Bedrock in the region consists predominantly of polydeformed metamorphic rocks and granitoids emplaced as part of the Cretaceous continental-margin magmatic arc. These crystalline rocks are intruded by hypabyssal basaltic to andesitic dikes that typically strike northwest and dip steeply (Barnard, 1968; Siem, 1992; Siem and Gastil, 1994). On the basis of mineralogical and compositional similarities, Barnard (1968) interpreted the mafic dikes to have been feeder conduits of Miocene calcalkaline volcanic rocks that depositionally overlie the crystalline basement in the northwestern Sierra Cucapá. Essentially all faults in the Laguna Salada region cut, or can be inferred to cut, the crystalline basement, mafic dikes, and Miocene volcanic strata. Thus, we infer these rocks to have existed prior to the phase of tectonism that produced the Laguna Salada basin.

The basal unconformity of the Miocene volcanic sequence and the erosional surface upon which it and older strata were deposited define the pretectonic erosional level. To the west of the Sierra Juárez escarpment, these form a broad undisrupted surface that dips gently ($\sim$0 to 5°) to the west (Gastil et al., 1975). In contrast, the basal contact dips as much as 30° to the east where it is exposed within the Sierra Juárez escarpment (Gastil et al., 1975; Axen, 1995; Romero-Espejel, 1997). On the eastern side of Laguna Salada, Miocene volcanic rocks are exposed only in a small area at the northern tip of Sierra Cucapá (Fig. 3).

The Imperial Formation. Although we infer that the Imperial Formation overlies lower to middle Miocene volcanic-arc strata, this relationship is not exposed in the Laguna Salada area. Instead, contacts between the Imperial Formation and older crystalline basement are almost exclusively fault contacts (Isaac, 1987; Siem, 1992; Siem and Gastil, 1994; Vásquez-Hernández, 1996). The base of the Imperial Formation consists of a continentally derived conglomeratic facies that grades upward into fine-grained marine siltstone and shale, which is locally interleaved with coarse-grained fault-scarp debris (Siem and Gastil, 1994; Vásquez-Hernández, 1996). The marine facies of the Imperial Formation in the Laguna Salada area is lower Pliocene (Vásquez-Hernández, 1996).

Palm Spring Formation and overlying conglomerate. In the northern Sierra El Mayor, the base of the Palm Spring Formation is generally a fault contact with the Imperial Formation, but elsewhere it is an angular unconformity or is gradational (Stock et al., 1996). There, the Palm Spring Formation grades up into syntectonic conglomerate shed off the footwall of the Laguna Salada fault (Siem and Gastil, 1994; Stock et al., 1996; Vásquez-Hernández, 1996). A correlative, but detachment-related, sequence exists in the central Sierra El Mayor, in the Lopez Mateos basin (Fig. 4). There, a thin sequence of Palm Spring Formation sandstone lies depositionally on middle-plate basement and dips 45° to 80° east. This sandstone is gradationally to abruptly overlain by fault-scarp sedimentary breccia and conglomerate, monolithologic granite megabreccia, and stratigraphically higher polymict conglomerate. Based on sparse data from well-imbricated conglomerate beds, this sequence appears to have been derived from an easterly source. The sequence forms a growth-fault geometry with dips as gentle as 20° east at stratigraphically high levels. A detachment along the southern margin of the basin projects north beneath it and forms its southern outcrop boundary. These relations strongly indicate syndetachment deposition, although the eastern source region subsequently must have subsided below Mexicali Valley. Identical steeply tilted upper-plate conglomerates cut by the range-front detachment are preserved in scattered exposures along the entire Sierra El Mayor range front. Locally,

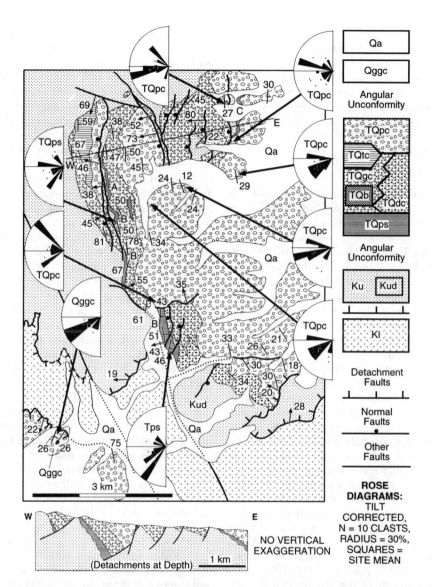

FIG. 4. Simplified geologic map of the Lopez Mateos basin in the east-central Sierra El Mayor, showing sediment transport direction inferred from imbricated clasts in conglomerates (rose diagrams over lower-hemisphere stereonet plots of poles to imbricated clasts). Note that poor exposure over much of the area precludes mapping of fault traces in detail; more faults are probably present within basin sediments than are shown. Units: Qa = Recent and older alluvial deposits; Qggc = older Quaternary(?), locally derived pediment deposits, containing distinctive garnet-bearing granite clasts probably derived from exposures of similar granite immediately to the east in the basement complex; TQpc = well-bedded, polymict, primarily traction-deposited conglomerate and gravel; TQtc = conglomerate transitional between over- and underlying units; TQgc = poorly and massively bedded porphyritic granite-boulder conglomerate probably deposited as debris flows; TQb = landslide megabreccia composed mainly of porphyritic granite plus other subsidiary basement lithologies; TQdc = poorly and massively bedded mafic diorite conglomerate probably deposited as debris flows and derived from a paleotopographic high of mafic diorite (Kud), similar to the one it overlies; TQps = Palm Spring Formation—pebbly quartz sandstone at locality A, arkosic pebble conglomerate at localities B, and marine fossil–bearing pebbly quartz sandstone at locality C; Ku = Cretaceous basement complex of middle plate; Kud = mafic diorite of middle plate; Kl = basement complex of lower plate. From preliminary mapping by Axen in 1996 and 1997.

these are unconformably overlapped by gently dipping "older" Quaternary pediment deposits (Qggc in Fig. 4) that also are faulted by the low-angle range-front fault. The youngest pediment deposits overlap that fault but themselves are semipenetratively normal faulted. Thus, the detachment still may be active in the shallow subsurface west of the bedrock front and under Laguna Salada.

Sierra El Mayor

Cañada David and Monte Blanco detachments. In northern Sierra El Mayor, Siem (1992; Siem and Gastil, 1994) subdivided the detachment system into two major strands that collectively bound the Monte Blanco dome, which comprises the lowest structural level exposed there. The dome is a geomorphic feature that reflects the gently curviplanar nature of the detachment faults and of the Cretaceous foliation that they are subparallel to there. The two detachments merge toward the west in the direction of upper-plate transport, so that only one major fault is present along the western end and northern flank of the dome. These two strands can be mapped and correlated throughout the Sierra El Mayor (Fig. 3) because they juxtapose three slabs from distinct crustal levels (Fig. 3). The upper plate consists entirely of strata of the Imperial and Palm Spring formations and younger conglomerates described above, and is bounded below by the Cañada David detachment (Siem, 1992; Siem and Gastil, 1994).

The lower plate is composed entirely of Cretaceous metamorphic rocks and granitoid intrusions, and is bounded above by the Monte Blanco detachment (Fig. 3), named here for the fault originally mapped by Siem (1992) along the southern side of the Monte Blanco dome. The granitoids range in composition from hornblende gabbro to two-mica garnet-bearing granite, with felsic compositions dominant. The intrusions mainly are found as discordant, subvertical or subhorizontal dikes and sills. Metasedimentary rocks include schist, migmatitic gneiss, para-amphibolites, and marble. Peak metamorphic parageneses in pelitic rocks include garnet + biotite + sillimanite + K feldspar ± white mica ± quartz. Garnets typically are anhedral, strongly embayed, 3 to 15 mm in diameter, and compositionally homogeneous except for relatively thin retrograde zoned margins. A high-grade gneissic foliation forms the

dominant Cretaceous deformational fabric in the lower plate. The foliation generally dips shallowly and only rarely contains a measurable lineation that trends E-W where present. Small-scale folds are present but relatively rare in the lower-plate gneisses, which suggests that the transposing foliation records very high strain magnitudes or that compositional layering was never oriented in the finite or incremental shortening field.

The middle plate consists of moderately intruded metamorphic basement overlain depositionally by Palm Springs Formation and stratigraphically higher conglomerate in the Lopez Mateos basin (Fig. 3). Metasedimentary rocks of the middle and lower plates have similar inferred protoliths, but metamorphic grade was significantly lower in the middle plate. Peak metamorphic parageneses in pelitic rocks include white mica + quartz + biotite ± sillimanite ± andalusite ± garnet. Garnets are only 1 to 3 mm in diameter and euhedral; some preserve prograde compositional zoning that we infer formed during porphyroblast growth. Metamorphic rocks of the middle plate typically record two generations of ductile fabrics. The first is a penetrative schistosity oriented parallel to compositional layering. The second is a spaced crenulation cleavage that defines the axial surfaces of a prominent series of recumbent folds. The intersection lineations and fold hinges plunge shallowly to the north and south, nearly orthogonal to the lineations measured in the gneissic rocks of the lower plate.

Detachment fault anatomy and synkinematic alteration. The low-angle fault zones range from 5 to 300 m in thickness and display variable degrees of cataclasis. Up to three well-developed joint sets are found in the weakly deformed rocks near the external portions of the fault zones. Striated shear fractures and zones of penetrative cataclasis that contain a mosaic of angular clasts, ranging from 0.5 to 10 cm in diameter, become more abundant toward the higher-strain, internal portions of the fault zones. Brecciated fabrics are typically better developed in feldspathic gneisses and granitoid rocks than in adjacent schists and marbles. The most intense fabric development occurs as zones of foliated microbreccia, clay gouge, and striated fault planes. The microbreccia is commonly black and flinty because of the presence of manganese oxide and/or graphite.

Kinematic indicators are abundant in the clay gouge and microbreccia and include SC fabrics, Reidel shear fractures, tensile fractures, and tool marks. In the detachment fault zones, the kinematic indicators consistently show top-to-the-west or WSW transport, and the measurements of detachment planes show general warping of the faults about a similar axis (Fig. 3, inset).

Secondary mineralization is common throughout the fault zones. Quartz, native sulfur, and interlayered illite-smectite clays are dominant secondary minerals, and we infer them to have originated by direct precipitation from high-temperature fluids and by inhomogeneous dissolution of feldspars. These minerals generally occur only in the fault zones, and are themselves overprinted by cataclastic deformation, which suggests that they were deposited synkinematically. Gypsum also commonly occurs in the fault zones, but is typically not overprinted by cataclasis. We infer the gypsum to have formed as a low-temperature alteration of native sulfur by near-surface supergene fluids or to have originated from infiltrating basin brines.

Patterns of exhumation and magnitude of detachment slip. The magnitude of tectonic exhumation is uncertain in many parts of the Sierra El Mayor, but the most pronounced unroofing seems to have occurred in the Monte Blanco dome area. Here, $^{40}Ar/^{39}Ar$ release spectra from potassium feldspar, which record cooling through the range of $\sim400\,°C$ to $150\,°C$, are highly disturbed, and fission-track studies of apatite (closure temperature $\sim110\,°C$) yield cooling ages of 4.8 Ma from the lower plate and 6.5 Ma from the middle (Axen et al., 1997). The fission-track data suggest rapid late Miocene–early Pliocene unroofing, consistent with short-term uplift rates of ~1 to 2 mm/yr calculated from Holocene soils offset across fault scarps along the western side of the Sierra Cucapá (Mueller and Rockwell, 1991). In contrast, $^{40}Ar/^{39}Ar$ release spectra of potassium feldspar from the southernmost Sierra El Mayor define undisturbed Cretaceous plateaus and do not indicate significant Cenozoic cooling (Axen et al., 1997). Therefore, we interpret exhumation magnitudes in the Sierra El Mayor to systematically decrease southward.

The magnitude of slip on the Laguna Salada detachment system may vary in a fashion similar to that inferred above for exhumation, with slip decreasing north and south away from the Monte Blanco area. Minimum estimates are made below. High-grade lower-plate rocks overlap lower-grade middle-plate rocks along the Monte Blanco detachment fault in the transport direction for ~10 km in the central Sierra El Mayor and for ~12 km in the northern part of the range (Fig. 3). Upper-plate strata in the Lopez Mateos basin overlie crystalline basement along a detachment fault for ~4 km in the transport direction, and transport-parallel overlap in the west-central Sierra El Mayor is closer to 7 km (Fig. 3). East-west overlap of sedimentary strata along the Cañada David detachment in the Monte Blanco dome area is ~6 km (Siem, 1992). These numbers suggest a minimum of ~14 km (central Sierra El Mayor) to ~18 km (Monte Blanco dome area) of horizontal extension accommodated by detachment faults in the Sierra El Mayor. East-west overlap of sedimentary strata in detachment-fault contact above basement in the Cerro Centinela area (see discussion below) is ~8 km (Fig. 3).

Central Mayor fault. The high-angle central Mayor fault, named here, strikes north through the range and cross-cuts the detachment system (Fig. 3). Gastil et al. (1975) and Siem (1992) mapped it as a W-down normal fault, but geomorphologically it appears to truncate the eastern end of the Monte Blanco dome with a clear sense of E-down separation, similar to a subparallel fault mapped by Siem (1992) a few kilometers farther west. The fault zone is up to 3 m wide and comprises highly fractured and crushed rock; kinematic indicators are difficult to identify.

Sierra Cucapá

The Sierra Cucapá is a narrow but rugged range that is bounded and internally cut by several high-angle NW-striking faults (Fig. 3). Fault strikes range from N60°W to N20°E, but the major faults typically strike between N30°W and N50°W (Barnard, 1968). Traced northwest, the faults commonly split into several branches and take on a more northerly strike.

The dextral-normal Laguna Salada fault (Fig. 3) bounds the range on its linear southwestern side against Laguna Salada, where the most active basin subsidence occurs (Savage et al., 1994). Both the Laguna Salada fault and the

NNE-striking, normal Cañon Rojo fault apparently ruptured in a widely felt 1892 earthquake (Mueller and Rockwell, 1991, 1995). Traced southeast, the Laguna Salada fault appears to lose displacement rapidly as it approaches the eastern side of the sierras Cucapá and El Mayor. Both of these facts suggest that major displacement on the Laguna Salada fault is transferred to the western Sierra El Mayor range front via the Cañon Rojo fault. The detachment faults in the Sierra El Mayor may have had a similar relationship to the Laguna Salada fault, bounding the Plio-Pleistocene basin preserved in the northern part of the range. Subsequently, slip on both the detachments and the part of the Laguna Salada fault southeast of the Cañon Rojo fault has ceased or slowed as the northern Sierra El Mayor was transferred to the footwall of the northern Laguna Salada–Cañon Rojo fault system.

The Borrego fault can be traced for 25 km north of the point where it splays from the Laguna Salada fault (Fig. 3). The fault dips 50 to 60° toward the northeast where exposed, but much of the fault trace is covered by Holocene alluvium of the narrow basin along its trace. Barnard (1968) interpreted the displacement to have been dominated by normal dip slip of as much as 4300 m in the central portion of the range but only 1300 m in the northern part.

The Cascabel fault (not shown in Fig. 3) lies 500 m east of the Borrego fault and is noteworthy because it shows a component of E-side-up reverse displacement with Mesozoic tonalite thrust over Holocene alluvium. Barnard (1968) suggested that the dip-slip component may be small (tens to hundreds of meters). The Cascabel fault has an irregular orientation, but predominantly dips east. At its northern and southern ends, it is cut by the Borrego fault (Barnard, 1968; Mueller and Rockwell, 1991, 1995).

The Pescadores fault is exposed for 24 km along strike (Fig. 3) and is oriented N40°W, 55°E (Barnard, 1968). The fault displays 3.3 to 3.5 km of right-lateral normal slip with a rake angle of 40 to 70°S, on the basis of the offset of two lithologic contacts with different orientations (Barnard, 1968). At the southern end of the fault, Barnard (1968) reported a 50 m wide fumarole marked by altered alluvium that is too hot to touch at depths greater than 20 cm.

Along the eastern margin of the Sierra Cucapá, the trace of the Cucapá fault is defined by a narrow valley that is generally less than 200 m wide but that extends more than 20 km along strike (Fig. 3). Holocene sediments there show no surface deformation, but the crystalline basement along the valley margins is strongly fractured (Barnard, 1968). Hot springs observed near the southern end of the fault may suggest that the fault is still active (Barnard, 1968). Barnard correlated a tonalite contact that displays 2900 m separation across the Cucapá fault, which is consistent with right-lateral and/or E-down normal displacement.

No low-angle detachment faults have been observed in the Sierra Cucapá. We infer that the crystalline basement in the range is of lower-plate affinity, but probably was located east of and in the footwall of the original detachment breakaway, which may have been located along the present trace of the Laguna Salada fault. Barnard (1968) reported that fold axes in the metamorphic rocks in Sierra Cucapá trend about N60°W, which is similar to the orientation of fold axes in high-grade lower-plate rocks in Sierra El Mayor. However, Miocene Progreso volcanics in the northernmost Sierra Cucapá, which pre-date extension, lie depositionally on crystalline basement (Barnard, 1968). This implies that the northwestern Sierra Cucapá lay nearby and east of the detachment breakaway, and has not been significantly eroded since the onset of detachment faulting. Because the Sierra Cucapá is unlikely to contain a detachment that juxtaposes crystalline basement from significantly different crustal levels, the pre-extensional crustal level apparently grades from shallow in the northwest to deeper in the southeast.

Cerro Centinela

Detachment faults and high-angle faults are intimately associated in the low hills near Cerro Centinela (Fig. 3). Although the detachment faults are strongly dismembered, Isaac (1987) showed that the individual pieces can be reconstructed to form a single laterally continuous detachment fault that juxtaposes Imperial and Palm Spring formations in the hanging wall with Mesozoic crystalline basement in the footwall. The hanging-wall strata define a series of upright open folds that predominantly trend N53–56°E and are interpreted to have formed during detachment faulting, parallel to the extension direction (Isaac, 1987). Although Isaac (1987) did not document the sense of tectonic transport across the detachment, it is likely that displacement was of the same W- to SW-directed polarity as observed in the Sierra El Mayor.

It also is possible that a structurally lower detachment lies just south of Cerro Centinela (Fig. 3). Barnard (1968) documented an abrupt change in orientation of fold hinges and intersection lineations from N60W in the Sierra Cucapá to due north in the Cerro Centinela area. In Sierra El Mayor, W- to NW-trending fold axes are characteristic of the lower-plate crystalline basement, whereas N-trending fold axes are characteristic of the middle-plate basement. This implies that Cerro Centinela may lie in the hanging wall of a N-dipping detachment fault, the footwall of which comprises the Sierra Cucapá. If true, this region would have a stacked detachment sequence similar to the Monte Blanco and Cañada David detachments in the Sierra El Mayor.

Several high-angle faults cut and reorient the detachment fault and NE-trending folds mapped by Isaac (1987). The high-angle faults dip both to the northeast and southwest, and they strike between N60°W and N10°W, with the more northerly strikes occurring in the eastern part of the Cerro Centinela (Isaac, 1987). In the extreme western Cerro Centinela domain, fault strands associated with the Laguna Salada fault rotate extension-related folds in a clockwise sense from their dominant northeast orientation to almost due east (Isaac, 1987). This indicates that those faults record a significant component of right-lateral movement. However, most of the other high-angle faults in the area display down-dip striae indicating nearly pure normal displacement (Isaac, 1987). For example, the Sanchez Diaz fault (Fig. 3) dips steeply west and has striae that rake 90° (Barnard, 1968). These high-angle normal faults accomplish NE-SW extension, which is similar to the extension direction that produced the earlier detachment faults. Isaac (1987) interpreted the transition from detachment faulting to high-angle normal faulting to reflect either a change in style during a single progressive deformation or the superposition of two kinematically similar deformational events. No relative timing relationships were documented

between the Laguna Salada fault system and the high-angle normal faults, and it is possible that they formed coevally.

The magnitude of exhumation in the Cerro Centinela area is poorly known. The area lies very close to the exposed Miocene depositional contact in the extreme northern Sierra Cucapá (Fig. 3). Therefore, although as many as two detachment horizons are found in the Cerro Centinela area, we infer that extensional exhumation was not as great as in the northern Sierra El Mayor.

Eastern Sierra Juárez

The eastern margin of the Sierra Juárez is structurally dominated by NW-striking faults that dip steeply to the east and west. W-dipping faults are abundant but faults with the largest documented vertical separation dip east. For example, two E-down faults in the southernmost Sierra Juárez combine to accommodate about 700 m of vertical separation (CETENAL, 1976b, 1977b) (Fig. 3). Low-angle faults are not common in the Sierra Juárez but two subhorizontal faults, one of which is surrounded by tens of meters of chloritic fault gouge and penetrative breccia, were observed in basement rocks of the northern Sierra Juárez (Romero-Espejel, 1997). The low-angle faults have N-trending striae, with one showing top-north kinematic indicators and the other showing top-south indicators. Relative timing relations between these faults and the high-angle faults in the area are uncertain.

Gently E-dipping, lower or middle Miocene sedimentary and volcanic strata are found in the escarpment of both the northern and southern Sierra Juárez, where they are faulted by both E- and W-dipping faults (CETENAL, 1976a, 1976b, 1976c, 1977a, 1977b; Mendoza-Borunda and Axen, 1995; Romero-Espejel, 1997). Farther west, on top of the range, these sequences are subhorizontal (CETENAL, 1977b, 1977c, 1977d; Romero-Espejel, 1997), so that they define a faulted E-dipping monocline as the escarpment is traversed. This geometry has been attributed to reverse drag above the detachment system exposed in the Sierra El Mayor, which roots west under the Sierra Juárez (Axen, 1995), although a strike-slip component has been documented on many of these faults (Mendoza-Borunda et al., 1995) and may account for their east dip as well.

Summary

Laguna Salada has apparently developed since late Miocene time, principally in response to generally E-W extension accommodated on low-angle detachment faults that root west under Laguna Salada and Sierra Juárez and that have the sierras El Mayor and Cucapá in their footwalls. Detachment faulting overlapped in time with dextral-normal oblique slip on the Laguna Salada fault and may have been intimately tied to slip on that fault throughout most or all of its history. Detachment slip may continue in the subsurface of Laguna Salada.

Salton Trough

A tremendous amount has been written about the Salton Trough, which is one of the best studied rift basins in the world. The geologic setting of the Salton Trough was laid out by Dibblee (1954), who named many of the stratal units and faults in the area. The importance of the San Andreas fault with regard to the opening of the Salton Trough and Gulf of California was initially emphasized by Hamilton (1961). Much of the subsequent literature focuses on the subsurface (e.g., Fuis et al., 1984; Fuis and Kohler, 1984), basin fill (e.g., Winker and Kidwell, 1996), heat flow (e.g., Lachenbruch et al., 1985), geothermal resources (e.g., McKibben et al., 1987; Elders and Sass, 1988), and active faulting, neotectonics, and seismicity (e.g., Weaver and Hill, 1978; Doser and Kanamori, 1986). These studies generally assume or conclude that the Salton Trough opened primarily as a pull-apart basin along NW-striking dextral faults of the San Andreas system (e.g., Hamilton, 1961; Elders et al., 1972; Lonsdale, 1991). However, the western side of the Salton Trough is bounded by a Miocene–Quaternary detachment system that we view as fundamentally important to Salton Trough tectonics. These faults have received much less attention in this regard than the San Andreas system, despite the fact that they are reasonably well mapped and described, because they have been considered to be older than the San Andreas fault system. Below we review this body of literature, emphasizing the geometry of the detachment system and the evidence for significant late Miocene to Pleistocene slip.

Historical background

The brittle detachment faults of the California Peninsular Ranges (Fig. 2) were first recognized by Sharp (1968, 1979), who noted that they are spatially associated with the eastern Peninsular Ranges mylonite zone for most of their length. The mylonite zone consists of moderately E-dipping (30 to 60°), reverse-sense mylonites (Simpson, 1984; O'Brien et al., 1987) of Cretaceous age (George and Dokka, 1994). Sharp used the words "cataclastic" and "mylonitic" differently from their presently accepted usage, which implies grain-size reduction via predominantly brittle deformation during cataclasis, and via significant crystal plastic behavior of at least the weaker constituents (such as quartz) during mylonitization. He described mylonitic gneiss as "cataclastic" and used "mylonite" for rocks that most Cordilleran geologists would assign to the "microbreccia ledge" commonly present for a few to several meters beneath detachment faults developed on quartzofeldspathic footwalls. Sharp interpreted these faults as having formed as thrusts related to, but having outlived, the Cretaceous shortening event that created the mylonitic gneisses. Engel and Schultejann (1984) also interpreted many of the faults this way, but Simpson (1985) pointed out several problems with their structural interpretations. Sharp (1979, p. 264) noted that the "thrusts" locally displace Neogene sediments, a fact that he interpreted to indicate reactivation, noting that "low angle normal faulting . . . played a significant role in the formation and east-west extension of the Salton Trough."

Several other interpretations of the brittle low-angle faults have been made. Erskine and Wenk (1985) considered them to be extensional faults of Cretaceous age, as did George and Dokka (1994). Wallace and English (1982), Engel and Schultejann (1984), Schultejann (1984), Pridmore and Frost (1992), Lough (1993), Frost et al. (1996a, 1996b), and Stinson and Gastil (1996) interpreted the detachments as Miocene structures, based on structural similarities to the well-known Oligocene to mid-Miocene detachment faults in the southwestern United States and on interpretation of poorly dated upper-plate conglomerates as mid-Miocene. Several of these authors (e.g., Frost et al., 1996a, 1996b) suggested that detachment faults in the western Salton Trough pre-dated San Andreas slip and are correlative with detachments in the lower Colorado River extensional belt (e.g., Frost and Martin, 1982), so that their offset along the San Andreas fault can be used to gauge that fault's offset.

We argue below that the dominant phase of slip on the detachments was latest Miocene–Pleistocene, largely was contemporaneous with San Andreas slip, and entirely or almost entirely post-dated detachment slip in the lower Colorado River region. Locally, extension in the western Salton Trough may have begun in mid-Miocene time or earlier, but the case for widespread detachment faulting of that age is weak. Also, we cannot strictly rule out the presence of either brittle Cretaceous thrusts or detachments within the eastern Peninsular Ranges mylonite zone, which is clearly Cretaceous (George and Dokka, 1994). Such structures have been postulated (e.g., Sharp, 1979; Frost and Shafiqullah, 1989; George and Dokka, 1994), but compelling evidence has not been given.

Geologic setting, geometry, and extent of the west Salton detachment system

Crystalline rocks of the eastern Peninsular Ranges consist of granitoid bodies and their pre–middle Cretaceous metasedimentary country rocks, which commonly are amphibolite facies (e.g., Theodore, 1970; Todd et al., 1988). Both have been overprinted locally by the eastern Peninsular Ranges mylonite zone, which affects middle Cretaceous plutonic rocks (see George and Dokka, 1994 for review of ages). Crystalline rocks of the Peninsular Ranges form the footwall of the detachment system everywhere and, like the Laguna Salada detachment system, hanging walls of detachments comprise both crystalline rocks and Neogene–Quaternary sedimentary strata. Footwall quartzofeldspathic rocks typically are overprinted by chloritic alteration, black manganese–rich hydrothermally altered cataclastic shear zones, and/or brecciation for at least a few meters below the detachments, and commonly are capped by a resistant, fine-grained "microbreccia" ledge subjacent to detachment faults (Wallace and English, 1982; Wallace, 1982; Erskine and Wenk, 1985; Stinson and Gastil, 1996). Hanging-wall crystalline rocks typically are brecciated or fractured for tens of meters above

the detachments (Sharp, 1979; Wallace and English, 1982; Wallace, 1982; English, 1985; Lough, 1993; Stinson and Gastil, 1996).

Sedimentary fill of the Salton Trough is complicated, both in terms of depositional systems and architecture as well as in terms of nomenclature. The oldest strata of the Salton Trough crop out in the southwestern part (see Fig. 6) and comprise lower to mid-Miocene volcanic strata and underlying and interbedded fluvial deposits. These are overlain by mid(?)- to late Miocene alluvial-fan and landslide megabreccia deposits and evaporites, which are overlain, in turn, by Pliocene to Pleistocene deposits of the Imperial and Palm Spring formations, their lateral equivalents, and overlying eolian and lacustrine deposits. The Imperial and Palm Spring formations are related largely to construction of the Colorado River delta in the southern Salton Trough and northern Gulf of California (Merriam and Bandy, 1965), but earliest Imperial Formation marine deposits pre-date arrival of the delta and represent an early Gulf incursion. Imperial and Palm Spring strata coarsen westward into the basin-margin Canebrake Conglomerate (Dibblee, 1954), which we view as the main fault-scarp facies of the west Salton detachment system (see below). The apex of the Colorado River delta has remained approximately fixed with respect to North America, while the main body of the delta in the Salton Trough has been translated northwest by San Andreas slip (Winker and Kidwell, 1986; Kerr and Kidwell, 1994). In general, the upper Imperial Formation is composed of marine deposits of this complicated deposystem, whereas the Palm Spring Formation consists of fluvial deposits. The modern Salton Sea and older lacustrine deposits from similar saline lakes accumulated after the delta separated the Salton Trough from Gulf waters. Stratigraphic nomenclature of Salton Trough deposits is problematical because of rapid lateral and vertical facies changes and because of different usage by various authors through the years. Winker and Kidwell (1996) provided a recent review of this problem. Aspects of the Neogene–Quaternary sequence that are key to our interpretation of the detachment system are discussed in more detail below.

The northernmost known exposures of the west Salton detachment system are in Palm Canyon, between the San Jacinto and Santa

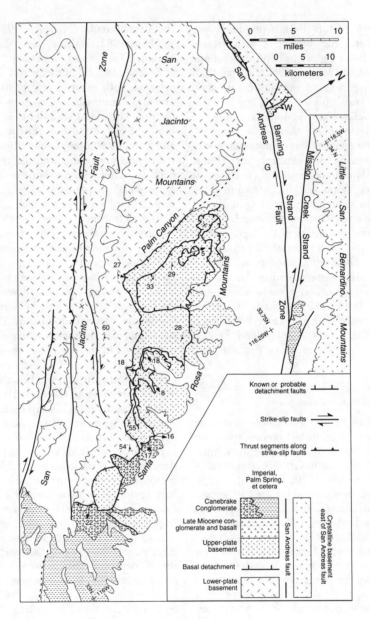

Fig. 5. Simplified geologic map of the northwestern part of the west Salton detachment system. Abbreviations: G = Garnet Hill; W = Whitewater area. Modified from Rogers (1965), Sharp (1979), Wallace (1982), Calzia (1988), Calzia et al. (1988), and Dibblee (1996a).

Rosa Mountains (Fig. 5) (Sharp, 1979; Calzia, 1988). From there, the detachment faults run south through the Santa Rosa Mountains (Sharp, 1979; Wallace, 1982; Wallace and English, 1982; English, 1985; Calzia et al., 1988), where they are apparently cut by the San Jacinto fault system (Sharp, 1967). Detachments also are found striking ESE along the

northeast flank of the Pinyon Ridge–Yaqui Ridge area (Fig. 6) (Sharp, 1979; Schultejann, 1984), but authors disagree about their continuation along the southern side of Pinyon and Yaqui ridges. Sharp (1979) and Lough (1993) showed the detachments doubling back upon themselves and bounding the south side of Yaqui Ridge on its eastern end, but Schultejann

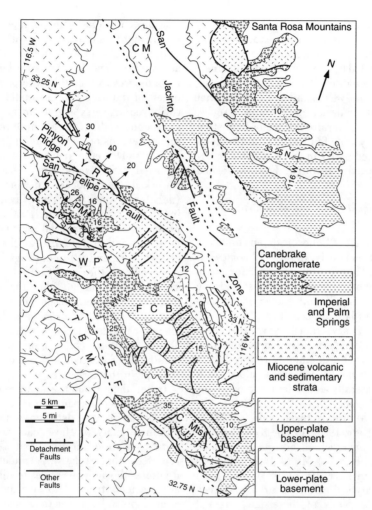

Fig. 6. Simplified geologic map of the southern part of the west Salton detachment system. Abbreviations: CM = Coyote Mountain; C Mts. = Coyote Mountains; FCB = Fish Creek–Vallecito basin; PM = Pinyon Mountains; TBM = Tierra Blanca Mountains; WP = Whale Peak; YR = Yaqui Ridge. Modified from Strand (1962), Rogers (1965), Jennings (1967), Todd (1977), Sharp (1979), Schultejann (1984), Stinson and Gastil (1996), Lough (1993), and Dibblee (1996a, 1996b).

(1984) and Engel and Schultejann (1984) showed the southern sides of those ridges bounded by the dextral San Felipe fault. Detachments also extend from the western to the eastern Pinyon Mountains (Sharp, 1979), with Whale Peak in the western Vallecito Mountains forming their footwall (Fig. 6) (Sharp, 1979; Lough, 1993; Stinson and Gastil, 1996).

Sharp (1979) located the southernmost strands of the detachment system along the northeastern margin of the Tierra Blanca Mountains (Fig. 6), although most authors

showed a strand of the Elsinore fault zone there (e.g., Dibblee, 1954; Todd, 1977; Pinault, 1984). The frontal fault zone of the Tierra Blanca Mountains is abnormally wide relative to other parts of the Elsinore fault zone, with faults that cut alluvium extending for 1 km from the range; intense fracturing and discontinuous faulting characterize the frontal 1.5 km of the range (Todd, 1977; Pinault, 1984). Todd (1977) mapped at least three low-angle fault strands in the Tierra Blanca Mountains and interpreted them as Cretaceous thrusts, although her descriptions (p. 10) of the associated fault rocks ("crush zone . . . up to 9 m thick . . . consists of one or more zones of dark greenish-brown cataclasite and waxy-appearing gouge surrounded by brecciated and hydrothermally altered tonalite with many thin cataclastic planes") are very similar to faults that elsewhere cut Imperial and younger rocks. Based on existing literature, it seems likely that this abnormally wide fault zone could be composite, produced partly in an early detachment phase and partly through Elsinore-related overprinting.

Age of detachment faults and extension in the Salton Trough

The age of onset of Cenozoic extension in the Salton Trough is poorly known and somewhat controversial. There is some evidence for a mid-Miocene onset of extension, but most evidence suggests that significant detachment slip largely began in late Miocene time.

The oldest Tertiary strata in the southwestern Salton Trough comprise lower to middle Miocene volcanic rocks, commonly referred to as Alverson or Jacumba volcanics, along with underlying, laterally equivalent, or overlying continental deposits, typically included in the Anza or Split Mountain formations (e.g., Kerr et al., 1979; Kerr, 1982, 1984). K/Ar ages on the volcanic rocks, which are mainly basalts, range from 24.8 ± 7.4 Ma to 14.9 ± 0.5 Ma (summarized in Kerr, 1982, 1984), with most overlap of analytical errors occurring between 22 and 14 Ma. Many of these dates are not stratigraphically consistent within analytical error (compare table 15 and plates II and IV of Ruisaard, 1979), so their individual accuracy is questionable, although the general age range probably is approximately valid. The intercalated sedimentary strata comprise braided-stream deposits with northward paleoflow indicators. The braided-stream deposits locally interfinger with the basal deposits of otherwise stratigraphically higher, alluvial-fan deposits derived from the west that are overlain, in turn, by a widespread landslide megabreccia deposit (Kerr, 1982, 1984).

Kerr (1984) interpreted the lower to middle Miocene braided-stream and volcanic sequence as recording the onset of extension in the southwestern Salton Trough. In contrast, Winker and Kidwell (1996) inferred that these strata were pre-extensional, because of paleo-flow direction (generally parallel to the axis of the trough) and clast content (presence of "Poway-type" clasts) different from the alluvial-fan deposits that were locally derived from the west, which they interpret to mark the onset of faulting. Unfortunately, this unresolved controversy results in an age discrepancy, conceivably >10 Ma in duration, for the earliest extension in the Salton Trough.

K. McDougall (pers. commun., 1997) reported two important occurrences of reworked mid-Miocene marine nanofossils (nanofossil zones CN5A and CN4, corresponding to ages between 16 and 12 Ma)—(1) in the upper Miocene Imperial Formation of the northern Salton Trough near the Whitewater area (Fig. 5), and (2) in cuttings from geothermal wells southeast of Cerro Prieto (Fig. 3). These fossils indicate that the mid-Miocene marine embayment responsible for strata of that age on Isla Tiburón (Fig. 1; mentioned above) extended as far north as the Salton Trough–northern Gulf region, and suggest the possibility of extensional basin development of that age in the latter area as well.

Other data from the southwestern Salton Trough also support an early or middle Miocene age for the onset of detachment faulting there, although many of those data are subject to reinterpretation. Stinson and Gastil (1996) reported that relatively undeformed and unaltered hornblende-andesite dikes are present in cataclastically deformed and chloritically altered footwall rocks in the Pinyon Mountains. One of these dikes yielded a K/Ar age of 17.2 ± 0.4 Ma (Stinson and Gastil, 1996) that is broadly consistent with other volcanic ages in the region, although the potential for contamination by Cretaceous Ar from the surrounding basement rocks is difficult to evaluate. These dikes were not observed to cut the microbreccia ledge there. Stinson and Gastil (1996) interpreted these facts to indicate that dike injection post-dated earliest detachment-related(?) fracturing, but pre-dated most of the detachment slip. Similarly, Miller and Kato (1990, 1991) reported cataclasis of basement rocks in the Coyote Mountains (Fig. 6) area that pre-dated deposition of the Alverson volcanics. No descriptions of kinematic indicators within the cataclasites were given. We speculate that there may have been an important, if somewhat cryptic, cataclastic event that is represented in these two areas and in the northern Sierra Juárez nearby (see above). In the latter area, fault lineations trend N-S and if similar kinematics characterize the Pinyon Mountains, then it may provide an alternative explanation for the N-trending lineations reported by Stinson and Gastil (1996) that were discussed above. Miller and Kato (1990, 1991) also reported growth-fault relationships in mid-Miocene volcanic and fluvial strata that are preserved in blocks bounded by younger faults. Frost and Shafiqullah (1989) reported a K/Ar age of 10.4 ± 0.3 Ma on feldspar concentrates from the microbreccia matrix at Yaqui Ridge, suggesting that detachment slip may have been ongoing by then, although the significance of this K/Ar age is unclear. Todd (1977) mapped one of three detachment strands in the Tierra Blanca Mountains (Fig. 6) as overlapped by Imperial Formation strata, indicating that slip on that fault ceased before the end of Imperial time, although continued slip on the other detachment strands there cannot be ruled out.

We favor the interpretation that significant, widespread top-to-the-east detachment faulting along the western side of the Salton Trough began in late Miocene time rather than in early or mid-Miocene time, because it is in better agreement with (1) regional constraints favoring a late Miocene onset of extension in the northern Gulf Extensional Province (e.g., Stock and Hodges, 1989; Lee et al., 1996), and (2) widespread constraints provided by Salton Trough deposits (see below). Regardless of the age of earliest extension in any specific area in the Salton Trough, we regard the main phase of slip on the west Salton detachment system to have been concurrent with deposition of the Imperial and Palm Spring formations and their immediate precursors, which were all deposited in late Miocene to Pleistocene time.

Such strata are exposed along much of the western margin of the Salton Trough (Dibblee, 1954) and mainly are represented by marine, marginal marine, and deltaic deposits of the Imperial Formation overlain by fluvial, deltaic, and lacustrine deposits of the Palm Spring Formation (e.g., Winker and Kidwell, 1996). Both the Imperial and Palm Spring formations grade westward into the coarse Canebrake Conglomerate (Dibblee, 1954, 1996a, 1996b; Winker and Kidwell, 1996), which we interpret as the fault-scarp facies of the detachment sys-

tem for the following reasons: (1) the conglomerate is locally derived from the west and has been widely interpreted as a fault-scarp facies, yet the controlling faults had not been clearly identified (Winker and Kidwell, 1996); (2) the conglomerate crops out in a band only a few kilometers wide (Dibblee, 1954; Weber, 1963; Winker and Kidwell, 1996) that is adjacent to the west Salton detachment system for most of its length (Figs. 5 and 6), from the Ocotillo accommodation zone of Axen (1995) to the central Santa Rosa Mountains; and (3) conglomerates assigned to the Canebrake typically are faulted by the detachment system (Figs. 5 and 6) (e.g., Sharp, 1979; Calzia et al., 1988). These observations are easily explained if the west Salton detachment system controlled subsidence of the Imperial–Palm Spring basin and accumulation of the Canebrake Conglomerate. This timing also is identical to that discussed above for the Laguna Salada region.

Undoubtedly, the most well-studied and continuous section of Salton Trough fill is that of the Fish Creek–Vallecito basin (Fig. 6) (e.g., Kerr and Kidwell, 1995; Winker and Kidwell, 1996). Johnson et al. (1983) showed that Imperial and Palm Spring sedimentation and subsidence rates in the Vallecito–Fish Creek area declined exponentially from highs of 5.5 mm/yr and 1.5 mm/yr, respectively, at ~4.3 Ma to rates of 0.5 mm/yr and 0.1 mm/yr at ~0.9 Ma, when the Elsinore fault began to move and induced uplift. Ingle (1974) demonstrated that lowest Imperial Formation beds near the section studied by Johnson et al. (1983) were deposited at upper bathyal depths (>100 m). The landslide megabreccia (mentioned above) is overlain by the Fish Creek Gypsum, which is, in turn, overlain by a second landslide deposit that is overlain by the Imperial Formation (Kerr et al., 1979; Winker and Kidwell, 1996). The Fish Creek Gypsum is the oldest marine deposit in the southwestern Salton Trough, and fossils from the gypsum limit its age to between 6.3 and 4.3 Ma (Dean, 1990, 1996).

These facts agree well with the hypothesis of Winker and Kidwell (1996) that the onset of major extension post-dated deposition of the lower to mid-Miocene braided-stream and volcanic deposits in the southwestern Salton Trough (see above) and suggest that major extension began in latest Miocene time with alluvial-fan deposition, followed by rapid con-

struction of topographic relief that allowed
landslides to be shed into the basin, and led
almost immediately to submergence of the
Salton Trough to upper-bathyal depths. We
obtain a range of reasonable ages for onset of
extension through conservative extrapolation
back in time using sedimentation rates and
thickness of probable syntectonic, postvolcanic
deposits below those studied by Johnson et al.
(1983). The thickness of alluvial-fan deposits,
landslide megabreccias, Fish Creek Gypsum
deposits, and Imperial Formation strata below
those studied by Johnson et al. (1983) is almost
certainly <1 km (see Winker and Kidwell,
1996). Using the range of sedimentation rates
determined for the Imperial Formation and
Palm Spring formations of 0.5 to 5.5 mm/yr, we
conclude that onset of rapid basin subsidence,
and presumably of rapid extension and detachment faulting, could reasonably have been
between 6.3 and 4.5 Ma, respectively, in the Fish
Creek–Vallecito area.

The Fish Creek–Vallecito basin and its crystalline basement all lie in the upper plates of
detachment faults (Sharp, 1979). Dibblee
(1996b) has shown how some of the sedimentary relationships there can be explained if the
basin fill was deposited amidst W-tilting fault
blocks that he considered to be bounded by, and
contemporaneous with, subvertical dextral
faults of the San Jacinto and Elsinore systems.
Such tilted blocks are common in the hanging
walls of detachment faults elsewhere and we
view this interpretation as likely valid in the
Fish Creek–Vallecito area also, with the dextral
faults having developed later.

We are skeptical of assignment of upper-plate
conglomerate and breccia in the Pinyon
Ridge–Yaqui Ridge and Pinyon Mountains
areas (Fig. 6) to units older than Plio-Pleistocene Canebrake Conglomerate. Schultejann
(1984), working in the Pinyon Ridge–Yaqui
Ridge area, suggested that upper-plate megabreccia there belongs to the lower to mid-Miocene Anza Formation, although she emphasized
the uncertainty of this correlation. Similarly,
Stinson and Gastil (1996), working in the
Pinyon Mountains, designated upper-plate conglomerate as "Tertiary." In both cases, Dibblee
(1954) assigned the strata in question to the
Plio-Pleistocene Canebrake Conglomerate. We
follow Dibblee's assignment because: (1) he
paid particular attention to sedimentary

deposits and their structure; (2) he mapped
large areas nearby, so was well qualified to
develop and apply a lithologically consistent
stratigraphic nomenclature; (3) both Schultejann (1984) and Stinson and Gastil (1996)
strongly emphasized characteristics of the crystalline basement with little attention paid to
upper-plate strata; (4) Lough (1993) recognized
Canebrake Conglomerate in fault contact along
the detachment faults at Whale Peak; and (5)
maps of the Pinyon Ridge–Yaqui Ridge area
show the Pleistocene Borrego Formation in
fault contact with the bedrock (Dibblee, 1954;
Schultejann, 1984), indicating that detachment
faulting there continued well past mid-Miocene
time.

Stratigraphic relationships in the northern
Salton Trough also indicate late Miocene onset
of rapid sedimentation and marine incursion,
although it is impossible to tie this directly to
detachment tectonics. Rymer et al. (1994)
reported that the Imperial Formation at Garnet
Hill (Fig. 5) in the northeast Salton Trough is
underlain by a sandstone unit that contains an
ash bed that, on the basis of glass chemistry, has
been correlated with an ash bracketed between
7.6 and 8.0 Ma (according to diatom biostratigraphy). In the Whitewater area (Fig. 5),
Allen (1957) mapped the Coachella Fanglomerate and interfingered intermediate flows,
which are the oldest units there. The fanglomerate laps northward onto bedrock paleohighs
along a buttress unconformity (Allen, 1957)
and paleocurrents were southward into the
trough from a source now displaced dextrally to
the southeast by the San Andreas fault (Peterson, 1975). One of the Coachella flows has been
dated by K/Ar methods as 10.0 ± 1.2 Ma
(Peterson, 1975), suggesting a late Miocene
onset of rapid basin subsidence. The Coachella
Fanglomerate is faulted against crystalline basement along E-striking faults and the entire
assemblage is unconformably overlain by a thin
(<100 m) section of Imperial Formation that
contains fossils indicative of late Miocene or
early Pliocene deposition, probably after 8.3 Ma
(Ingle, 1974; McDougall et al., 1994). The
northwesternmost exposures of Imperial Formation and related sedimentary deposits are
located between San Andreas–related thrusts
(Fig. 5). The Imperial there lies conformably on
the undated Hathaway Formation, which comprises >330 m of arkosic sandstone, siltstone,

conglomerate, and local spring-deposited fresh-water limestone, overlain conformably by >200 m of coarse conglomerate (Allen, 1957). The Imperial Formation in both areas is conformably overlain by the Painted Hill Formation— >1000 m of continental sandstone, conglomerate, and intercalated basalt flows (Allen, 1957), two of which have been dated at 6.04 ± 0.18 and 5.94 ± 0.18 Ma by the K/Ar method (Matti and Morton, 1993). Thus, marine deposition, but not tectonism, in the northernmost Salton Trough ended before Pliocene time.

Direction of slip on the west Salton detachment system

The direction of slip on the west Salton detachment system is somewhat difficult to characterize because: (1) some authors have equated slip direction on brittle faults with lineation directions in the older east Peninsular Ranges mylonite zone (e.g., Sharp, 1979; Erskine and Wenk, 1985); (2) subsequent deformation related to late dextral faults of the San Jacinto and Elsinore fault systems may have rotated detachments and surrounding rocks around subvertical axes (e.g., Johnson et al., 1983) or subhorizontal axes (e.g., Dibblee, 1996a); and (3) some faults interpreted here as part of the detachment system may have developed earlier so, whether reactivated or not, may record unrelated kinematic indicators. Below, we review the evidence for direction of slip on the detachments of the west Salton system, beginning from the north and continuing south.

Sharp (1979, p. 4) described the lower 30 m of "thrust" (detachment) hanging walls as "progressively comminuted country rock that becomes microcrystalline ultramylonite and possibly pseudotachylite, typically 0.5 to 3 m in thickness" and lacking "internal linear structures," and used the plunge of troughs in the faults to infer movement direction on the low-angle faults: E-W in the Pinyon Mountains–Whale Peak area and central Santa Rosa Mountains but NNE-SSW in the northern Santa Rosa Mountains. On the basis of these directions, Sharp (1979) inferred top-to-the-west or SSW transport because he favored a thrust interpretation, but we feel that, if the troughs record detachment slip direction, it was to the east and/or northeast. However, folding subsequent to cessation of detachment slip may

have been important in formation of these troughs.

In the northern Santa Rosa Mountains (northern trough of Sharp, 1979), Erskine and Wenk (1985, p. 274) described a "well-developed chloritic breccia zone . . . commonly present beneath the fault surfaces," consistent with detachment-related, rather than thrust-related, development, with "trend of linear slip-related structures on the fault surfaces" (p. 275) toward the northeast and normal-sense drag-related structures near some of the fault surfaces. They also summarized oxygen-isotope and mineralogical data for upper-plate rocks that suggest a southwesterly source relative to regional trends.

In the southern Santa Rosa Mountains, Wallace (1982) studied a detachment fault that dips southeast and commonly juxtaposes Canebrake Conglomerate over crystalline rocks. Striae on the fault, measured in two places, trend N48°E and N50°E (Wallace, 1982). Upper-plate strata generally dip southwest and are cut by normal faults that mostly strike between northwest and northeast (Wallace, 1982). We interpret these data to suggest top-to-the-northeast transport on the detachment in the southern Santa Rosa Mountains. In contrast, Wallace and English (1982; see also Wallace, 1982) suggested top-to-the-southwest motion on the detachment in the southern Santa Rosa Mountains based on the N50°W average strike of tension veins and a Hansen analysis of asymmetric folds in sheared footwall rocks subjacent to the faults. However, they did not describe the dip of the tension gashes relative to that of the faults, which is critical for inferring shear sense as opposed to extension direction, and the asymmetric folds shown in their Figure 4 (which unfortunately is not oriented) are sigmoidal tails of lithons between shear bands within the footwall shear zone. Hence, we do not feel that the southwest sense of transport inferred by Wallace and English (1982) is robust.

Schultejann (1984) reported NE-plunging striae on the Yaqui Ridge detachment and inferred top-to-the-northeast transport of the upper plate. Stinson and Gastil (1996) showed two sets of striae and mullions on the detachments in the Pinyon Mountains, one set plunging moderately to gently north and the other set plunging gently west. They also show N- to NNW-striking tension gashes in the footwall and two sets of footwall normal faults, dipping moderately east and west. Together, these data suggest an overall E-W extension direction with top-to-the-east displacement on the detachment zone (Stinson and Gastil, 1996). N-trending striae may be explained by late flexural-slip folding, but this interpretation is uncertain.

Magnitude of slip on the west Salton detachment system

Late Miocene–Pleistocene net slip on the detachments of the west Salton system also is difficult to determine precisely. For most of its length, the detachment system is parallel to the eastern Peninsular Ranges mylonite zone, which Sharp (1979) argued is terminated southward, where it is gently cross-cut by low-angle faults that we interpret as detachments. This truncation occurs near the Pinyon Mountains (Fig. 6), but he traced the brittle faults several kilometers farther south, to the northeast side of the Tierra Blanca Mountains, where the Elsinore fault exits from the Peninsular Ranges (Rockwell et al., 1986) in the region of the Ocotillo accommodation zone of Axen (1995). We tentatively interpret this to indicate that displacement on the west Salton detachment system may increase northward, exposing progressively more of the mylonite belt in that direction, and die out southward, as is typical of normal fault systems as they enter accommodation zones (e.g., Bosworth, 1985).

Most displacement estimates for the detachment system are based on the fact that upper- and lower-plate rocks are distinct, which implies that the horizontal overlap in the direction of transport is a minimum displacement. This amount is ~11 km in the Santa Rosa Mountains (Sharp, 1979). However, significantly greater extension is permissible based on the fact that several fault strands are present and that mineralogy and oxygen isotopes of the upper-plate intrusive rocks are consistent with an origin tens of kilometers farther west in the Peninsular ranges (Erskine and Wenk, 1985). At present, it is impossible to say how much, if any, of this extension may have accumulated in Cretaceous time (e.g., Erskine and Wenk, 1985; George and Dokka, 1993). Furthermore, much or all of the overlap between upper- and lower-plate rocks may have occurred during Cretaceous thrust emplacement of Santa Rosa Mountains rocks, so that little extension is required

along the late normal faults between the mismatched rock units. In the Pinyon Mountains–Whale Peak area, Stinson and Gastil (1996) and Lough (1993) suggested ~5 to 7 km of east-west extension on the basis of inferred vertical offset of an Eocene erosion surface on the Peninsular Ranges.

Cretaceous and Paleocene apatite fission-track cooling ages (Dokka, 1984; George and Dokka, 1994) from the Santa Rosa and San Jacinto Mountains suggest that the footwall of the Santa Rosa detachment system was rapidly cooled through the temperature range from 130° to 70°C by ~76 Ma and that the mylonite belt itself was cooled through that range by ~60 Ma. Wolf et al. (1997) present U-Th/He age data for apatites from the San Jacinto Mountains. Such ages record cooling through the range of ~100°–45°C, and were interpreted to indicate that the San Jacinto block did not undergo rapid cooling due to tectonic unroofing until after ~17 Ma, if at all. These data potentially place constraints on the displacement of the fault system. However, the present lack of detailed geometric control on the fault system(s) and mylonite zone along with the fact that upper-plate apatite fission track ages (~60 Ma, Dokka, 1984) are younger than lower-plate ages (~76 Ma, George and Dokka, 1994), which is opposite of most detachment terranes, hinder use of the low-temperature cooling ages for structural purposes.

We find none of the existing estimates of detachment slip compelling, but note that the range of 5 to 7 km is probably a minimum. If the detachments originated at very low dips, or if the Peninsular Ranges geothermal gradient was abnormally low (e.g., due to cooling by the underlying subducted slab; Dumitru et al., 1991), then much larger displacements are possible within the limits of apatite fission-track and U-Th/He data (e.g., Dokka, 1984; George and Dokka, 1994; Wolf et al., 1997). Slip distributed across stacked, anastomosing faults, as is common in the west Salton detachment system, can also allow increased slip without unroofing hot rocks in any particular slice. Also, the present exposure of the detachment terrane is arguably within a few to several kilometers of its breakaway. Because net slip on basal detachments increases downdip as the slip of hanging-wall faults is cumulatively transferred to the detachment, the net slip on the detachment system beneath the Salton Trough is almost certainly greater than the amounts argued for near the breakaway. An estimate of 10 to 20 km is consistent with the available data but poorly constrained.

Discussion and Conclusions

The bulk of the data we present is consistent with an important late Miocene–Pleistocene brittle detachment faulting event in the Laguna Salada–Salton Trough region. The detachment terrane has a strike length of ~250 km and can be divided into two segments of opposite vergence—the top-to-the-west Laguna Salada segment and the top-to-the-east west Salton segment—each of which apparently has less displacement as the Ocotillo accommodation zone is approached. The Laguna Salada system may still be active under the Laguna Salada basin and Sierra Juárez. Each segment is characterized by lower-plate crystalline rocks and an upper plate of internally detachment-faulted crystalline rocks and upper Miocene–Pleistocene strata. The magnitude and direction of net slip on the detachment systems are poorly constrained, but net slip is at least 5 to 7 km, likely on the order of 10 to 20 km, and is generally top-to-the-west or -southwest on the Laguna Salada system and top-to-the-northeast or -east on the west Salton system. These relations and the timing of detachment slip require rethinking of several widely held ideas.

Age data discussed here indicate that the two detachment systems were active synchronously and largely overlapped temporally with slip on the San Andreas fault system and formation of transitional and oceanic crust in Gulf spreading centers and the Salton Trough. The San Andreas system in the Salton Trough is thought to have been active since at least 4 or 5 Ma, may have been active between 12 and 5 Ma, and conceivably may have begun activity as long ago as 17 Ma (e.g., Crowell, 1981; Powell and Weldon, 1992; Matti and Morton, 1993; Powell, 1993; Dickinson, 1997). Although it is beyond the scope of this paper to discuss relationships among the detachment systems, the San Andreas fault, and the formation of new transitional crust, it is clear that such a re-evaluation is needed.

Paleomagnetic declination anomalies from northeastern Baja California and the south-western Salton Trough suggest that clockwise rotations about vertical axes have been important at least locally and may have been regionally important. Clockwise rotations have been reported from: (1) red Pliocene(?) mudstones (Palm Spring Formation?) in the footwall of the Cañon Rojo fault (~30°) (Fig. 3) and (2) along the coast near the Puertecitos accommodation zone (~30°) (Fig. 2) (both in Strangway et al., 1971); (3) mid-Miocene Alverson Volcanics in the Coyote Mountains (45° to 111°) (Fig. 6) (Mace, 1981); (4) Plio-Pleistocene strata in the Fish Creek basin (35°) (Fig. 6) (Johnson et al., 1983); and (5) ignimbrites of 12 to 6 Ma age in the Sierra San Fermín immediately northeast of the eastern end of the Puertecitos accommodation zone (~30°) (Fig. 2) (Lewis and Stock, in press). Lewis and Stock identified NE-striking sinistral-normal faults that have accommodated clockwise rotation in the Sierra San Fermín, and argued that similar faults are present along the entire length of the Valle San Felipe–Sierra San Pedro Mártir segment (Fig. 2) based on mapping by Gastil et al. (1975). They suggested that a regional shear couple is reflected by the rotation and postulated that blocks there rotated above either a deep, vertical, dextral shear zone or above low-angle normal faults at depth. The northern sites (Cañon Rojo, Coyote Mountains, and Fish Creek basin) lie near or within dextral fault zones and so may reflect local wrench-related rotation. All five areas lie above major listric normal faults or detachment faults, and we suspect that rotations may be limited to upper plates of such faults regionally. Paleomagnetic studies to test for rotation of detachment footwalls are needed to verify this hypothesis and determine if detachment-slip directions inferred here should be corrected for vertical-axis rotation.

The only area where low-temperature thermochronometers (e.g., apatite fission-track dates) are known to have been reset is in the northern Sierra El Mayor. We interpret this as probably resulting from the west Salton detachment system rooting east into a region of formation of transitional crust that may have accommodated part of the E-W extension, a component that probably was entirely absorbed on the Laguna Salada detachment system farther south. Alternatively, the west Salton system may have been shut off earlier than the Laguna system as it entered the transpressional/transrotational "big-bend" segment of the San Andreas system.

Gastil and Fenby (1991) suggested that detachment and listric normal faults along the east side of the Peninsular Ranges in California and Baja California may have been driven by gravity, sliding into the Gulf as a mechanism to infill the gap created by its opening. The data discussed here do not support this model in that: (1) the Laguna Salada detachment system roots in the wrong direction; and (2) the detachment faults may have initiated before formation of transitional crust, which would require that they formed before the "hole" that needed filling. Like Frost et al. (1996a, 1996b) we view these detachments as rooted crustal responses to whole-lithosphere extension, not as slides in response to gravity tectonics.

However, Frost et al. (1996a; 1996b) interpreted the west Salton detachment system as mid-Miocene in age, similar to detachments farther east in southern California and western Arizona (see also Wallace and English, 1982; Stinson and Gastil, 1996). We know of no data that prove that any E- or W-directed detachment faults in the region discussed here were active in latest Oligocene–middle Miocene time, the period of peak detachment slip in the lower Colorado River trough (e.g., Davis and Lister, 1988; Spencer and Reynolds, 1989; Spencer et al., 1995). Thus, we cannot support correlations of the west Salton detachment system to the system in the lower Colorado River trough (Wallace and English, 1982; Frost et al., 1996a, 1996b). The fact that the upper Miocene marine or lacustrine Bouse Formation (Buising, 1990; Spencer and Patchett, 1997) in the lower Colorado region is generally <0.5 km thick and little deformed is consistent with the late Miocene deposition there in a topographic low remnant from earlier extensional events (Buising, 1990); Laguna Salada and the Imperial–Palm Spring basin in the Salton Trough continued to actively subside and deform in response to detachment and wrench tectonics into Pleistocene–Recent time, reaching thickness roughly an order of magnitude greater than that of the Bouse Formation. Nevertheless, the thin upper Miocene Imperial Formation exposed in the northern Salton Trough may well have been adjacent to the southern Bouse Formation exposures in late Miocene time and subse-

quently been separated dextrally by San Andreas slip.

Acknowledgments

We would like to thank the many individuals with whom we have discussed the Gulf extensional province, and without whose input this paper would not have been conceived: Arturo Martín-Barajas, Joann Stock, Gordon Gastil, Rick Siem, Juan García-Abdeslam, Sergio Vásquez-Hernández, Hector Romero-Espejel, Ramón Mendoza-Borunda, and Danny Stockli. Ray Ingersoll, Joann Stock, and Paul Umhoefer have provided thoughtful and helpful reviews. This research was supported by grants awarded to G. J. Axen (while at CICESE, subsequently transferred to A. Martín-Barajas) and to J. Fletcher from the Consejo Nacional de Ciéncias y Tecnología (CONACYT), and to G. Axen from the University of California Mexico–United States program (UC-MEXUS) and the UCLA Academic Senate Research Grant program. Field assistance by Deanna Cummings, Lisa Skerl, and Sarah Yoder is greatly appreciated.

REFERENCES

Allen, C. R., 1957, San Andreas fault zone in San Gorgonio Pass, southern California: Geol. Soc. Amer. Bull., v. 68, p. 315–349.

Atwater, T., 1970, Implications of plate tectonics for the Cenozoic tectonic evolution of western North America: Geol. Soc. Amer. Bull., v. 81, p. 3513–3536.

Axen, G. J., 1995, Extensional segmentation of the main Gulf escarpment, Mexico and United States: Geology, v. 23, p. 515–518.

Axen, G. J., Stockli, D., Rothstein, D., Grove, M., and Cadkin, J., 1997, Transition from detachment to strike-slip faulting along the Pacific–North American plate margin, NE Baja California, Mexico [abs.]: Geol. Soc. Amer. Abs. Prog., v. 29, no. 5, p. 2.

Barnard, F. L., 1968, Structural geology of the Sierra de los Cucapas, northeastern Baja California, Mexico, and Imperial County, California: Unpubl. Ph.D. thesis, Univ. of Colorado, Boulder, 157 p.

Blarez, E., and Mascle, J., 1988, Shallow structures and evolution of the Ivory Coast and Ghana transform margin: Marine Petrol. Geol., v. 5, p. 54–64.

Bosworth, W. R., 1985, Geometry of propagating continental rifts: Nature, v. 316, p. 625–627.

Buising, A. V., 1990, The Bouse Formation and bracketing units, southeastern California and western Arizona: Implications for the evolution of the proto-

Gulf of California and the lower Colorado River: Jour. Geophys. Res., v. 95, p. 20,111–20,132.

Calzia, J. P., 1988, Mineral resources and resource potential map of the Pyramid Peak Roadless Area, Riverside County, California: U. S. Geol. Surv. Misc. Field Studies Map MF-1999, scale 1:62,500.

Calzia, J. P., Madden-McGuire, D. J., Oliver, H. W., and Schreiner, R. A., 1988, Mineral resources of the Santa Rosa Mountains Wilderness Study Area, Riverside County, California: U.S. Geol. Surv. Bull., v. 1710, p. D1–D14.

CETENAL (Comisión de Estudios del Territorio Nacional), 1976a, Agua Caliente carta geológica H11B25: Comisión de Estudios del Territorio Nacional: Mexico City, CETENAL, 1:50,000 scale.

————, 1976b, Jose Saldaña carta geológica H11B 15: Comisión de Estudios del Territorio Nacional: Mexico City, CETENAL, 1:50,000 scale.

————, 1976c, La Poderosa carta geológica I11D74: Comisión de Estudios del Territorio Nacional: Mexico City, CETENAL, 1:50,000 scale.

————, 1977a, El Centinela carta geológica I11D64: Comisión de Estudios del Territorio Nacional: Mexico City, CETENAL, 1:50,000 scale.

————, 1977b, El Rayo carta geológica H11B14: Comisión de Estudios del Territorio Nacional: Mexico City, CETENAL, 1:50,000 scale.

————, 1977c, Heroes de la Independencia carta geológica H11B24: Mexico City, CETENAL, 1:50,000 scale.

————, 1977d, La Rumorosa carta geológica I11D63: Comisión de Estudios del Territorio Nacional: Mexico City, CETENAL, 1:50,000 scale.

Channell, J. E. T., and Kozur, H. W., 1997, How many oceans? Meliata Vardar, and Pindos oceans in Mesozoic Alpine paleogeography: Geology, v. 25, p. 183–186.

Cochran, J. R., 1983, A model for development of Red Sea: Amer. Assoc. Petrol. Geol. Bull., v. 67, p. 41–69.

Crowell, J. C., 1981, An outline of the tectonic history of southeastern California, *in* Ernst, W. G., ed., The geotectonic development of California: Rubey Vol. I: Englewood Cliffs, NJ, Prentice-Hall, p. 583–600.

Davis, G. A., and Lister, G. S., 1988, Detachment faulting in continental extension: Perspectives from the southwestern U.S. Cordillera, *in* Clark, S. P., Jr., Burchfiel, B. C., and Suppe, J., eds., Processes in continental lithospheric deformation: Geol. Soc. Amer. Spec. Pap. 218, p. 133–159.

Dean, M. A., 1990, The Neogene Fish Creek Gypsum: Forerunner to the incursion of the Gulf of California into the western Salton Trough [abs.]: Geol. Soc. Amer. Abs. Prog., v. 22, no. 3, p. 18.

————, 1996, Neogene Fish Creek Gypsum and associated stratigraphy and paleontology, south-

western Salton Trough, California, *in* Abbott, P. L., and Seymour, D. C., eds., Sturzstroms and detachment faults, Anza-Borrego Desert State Park, California: Santa Ana, CA, South Coast Geol. Soc., p. 123–148.

DeMets, C., 1995, A reappraisal of seafloor spreading lineations in the Gulf of California: Implications for the transfer of Baja California to the Pacific plate and estimates of Pacific–North America motion: Geophys. Res. Lett., v. 22, p. 3545–3548.

Dibblee, T. W., Jr., 1954, Geology of the Imperial Valley region, California, Geology of Southern California: Calif. Div. Mines Bull. 170, p. 21–28.

————, 1996a, Stratigraphy and tectonics of the San Felipe Hills, Borrego Badlands, Superstition Hills, and vicinity, *in* Abbott, P. L., and Seymour, D. C., eds., Sturzstroms and detachment faults, Anza-Borrego Desert State Park, California: Santa Ana, CA, South Coast Geol. Soc., p. 45–58.

————, 1996b, Stratigraphy and tectonics of the Vallecito–Fish Creek Mountains, Vallecito Badlands, Coyote Mountains, and Yuha Desert, southwestern Imperial basin, *in* Abbott, P. L., and Seymour, D. C., eds., Sturzstroms and detachment faults, Anza-Borrego Desert State Park, California: Santa Ana, CA, South Coast Geol. Soc., p. 59–79.

Dickinson, W. R., 1997, Kinematics of transrotational tectonism in the California Transverse Ranges and its contribution to cumulative slip along the San Andreas transform fault system: Geol. Soc. Amer. Spec. Pap. no. 305, p. 1–46.

Dokka, R. K., 1984, Fission-track geochronological evidence for Late Cretaceous mylonitization and early Paleocene uplift of the northeastern Peninsular Ranges, California: Geophys. Res. Lett., v. 11, p. 46–49.

Doser, D. I., and Kanamori, H., 1986, Spatial and temporal variations in seismicity in the Imperial Valley: Bull. Seismol. Soc. Amer., v. 76, p. 421–438.

Dumitru, T. A., Gans, P. B., Foster, D. A., and Miller, E. L., 1991, Refrigeration of the western Cordilleran lithosphere during Laramide shallow-angle subduction: Geology, v. 19, p. 1145–1148.

Elders, W. A., Rex, R. W., Meidav, T., Robinson, P. T., and Biehler, S., 1972, Crustal spreading in southern California: Science, v. 178, p. 15–24.

Elders, W. A., and Sass, J. H., 1988, The Salton Sea scientific drilling project: Jour. Geophys. Res., v. 93, p. 12,953–12,968.

Engel, A. E. J., and Schultejann, P. A., 1984, Late Mesozoic and Cenozoic tectonic history of south central California: Tectonics, v. 3, p. 659–675.

English, D. J., 1985, Regional structural analysis of the Santa Rosa Mountains, San Diego and Riverside Counties, California: Implications for the geologic history of southern California: Unpubl. M.S. thesis, San Diego State Univ., 170 p.

Erskine, B. G., and Wenk, H.-R., 1985, Evidence for Late Cretaceous crustal thinning in the Santa Rosa mylonite zone, southern California: Geology, v. 13, p. 274-277.

Fenby, S. S., and Gastil, R. G., 1991, Geologic-tectonic map of the Gulf of California and surrounding areas, in Dauphin, J. P., and Simoneit, B. R. T., eds., The Gulf and Peninsular provinces of the Californias: Tulsa, OK, Amer. Assoc. Petrol. Geol., p. 79-83.

Frost, E. G., Fattahipour, M. J., and Robinson, K. L., 1996, Neogene detachment and strike-slip faulting in the Salton Trough region and their geometric and genetic interrelationships, in Abbott, P. L., and Cooper, J. D., eds., Field conference guidebook and volume for the annual convention, San Diego, California, May, 1996: Bakersfield, CA, Pacific Sect. Amer. Assoc. Petrol. Geol., p. 263-294.

Frost, E. G., and Martin, D. L., 1982, Mesozoic–Cenozoic tectonic evolution of the Colorado River region, California, Arizona, and Nevada: San Diego, Cordilleran Publ., 608 p.

Frost, E. G., and Shafiqullah, M., 1989, Pre–San Andreas opening of the Salton Trough as an extensional basin: K-Ar ages on regional detachment faults along the western margin of the Salton Trough [abs.]: Geol. Soc. Amer. Abs. Prog., v. 21, no. 5, p. 81.

Frost, E. G., Suitt, S. C., and Fatahipour, M., 1996, Emerging perspectives of the Salton Trough region with an emphasis on extensional faulting and its implications for later San Andreas deformation, in Abbott, P. L., and Seymour, D. C., eds., Sturzstroms and detachment faults, Anza-Borrego Desert State Park, California: Santa Ana, CA, South Coast Geol. Soc., p. 81-121.

Fuis, G. S., and Kohler, W. M., 1984, Crustal structure and tectonics of the Imperial Valley region, California, in Rigsby, C. A., ed., The Imperial Basin—tectonics, sedimentation, and thermal aspects: Los Angeles, Pacific Sec. Soc. Econ. Paleontol. Mineral., p. 1-13.

Fuis, G. S., Mooney, W. D., Healy, J. H., McMechan, G. A., and Lutter, W. J., 1984, A seismic refraction survey of the Imperial Valley region, California: Jour. Geophys. Res., v. 89, no. B2, p. 1165-1189.

Gans, P. B., 1997, Large-magnitude Oligo-Miocene extension in southern Sonora: Implications for the tectonic evolution of northwest Mexico: Tectonics, v. 16, p. 388-408.

Garcia-Abdeslem, J., Sánchez-Monclú, A., Martin-Barajas, A., Suarez-Vidal, F., Munguía-Orozco, L., and Wong-Ortega, V. M., in review, Residual isostatic gravity, magnetics, seismicity, focal mechanisms, and crustal structure at Laguna Salada, Baja California, Mexico: Geophysics.

Gastil, R. G., and Fenby, S. S., 1991, Detachment faulting as a mechanism for tectonically filling the Gulf of California during dilation, in Dauphin, J. P., and Simoneit, B. R. T., eds., The Gulf and Peninsular provinces of the Californias: Tulsa, OK, Amer. Assoc. Petrol. Geol. Memoir, v. 47, p. 371-376.

Gastil, R. G., Phillips, R. P., and Allison, E. C., 1975, Reconnaissance geology of the state of Baja California: Geol. Soc. Amer. Memoir, v. 140, p. 170.

George, P. G., and Dokka, R. K., 1994, Major late Cretaceous cooling events in the eastern Peninsular Ranges, California, and their implications for Cordilleran tectonics: Geol. Soc. Amer. Bull., v. 106, p. 903-914.

Goff, J. A., Bergman, E. A., and Soloman, S. C., 1987, Earthquake source mechanisms and transform fault tectonics in the Gulf of California: Jour. Geophys. Res., v. 92, no. B10, p. 10,485-10,510.

Hamilton, W., 1961, Origin of the Gulf of California: Geol. Soc. Amer. Bull., v. 72, p. 1307-1318.

Henry, C. D., and Aranda-Gomez, J. J., 1992, The real southern Basin and Range: Mid- to late Cenozoic extension in Mexico: Geology, v. 20, no. 8, p. 701-704.

Herzig, C. T., and Jacobs, D. C., 1994, Cenozoic volcanism and two-stage extension in the Salton Trough, southern California and northern Baja California: Geology, v. 22, p. 991-994.

INEGI (Instituto Nacional de Estadística Geografía e Informática), 1983, Mexicali carta geológica I11-12: Mexico City, INEGI, 1:250,000 scale.

Ingle, J. C., Jr., 1974, Paleobathymetric history of Neogene marine sediments, northern Gulf of California, in Gastil, G., and Lillegraven, J., eds., The geology of Peninsular California: Los Angeles, Pacific Sect. Soc. Econ. Paleontol. Mineral., p. 121-138.

Isaac, S., 1987, Geology and structure of the Yuha Desert between Ocotillo, California, U.S.A., and Laguna Salada, Baja California, Mexico: Unpubl. M.S. thesis, San Diego State Univ., 165 p.

Jennings, C. W., 1967, Geologic map of California, Salton Sea sheet: Calif. Div. Mines Geol., 1:250,000 scale.

Johnson, N. M., Officer, C. B., Opdyke, N. D., Woodard, G. D., Zeitler, P. K., and Lindsay, E. H., 1983, Rates of late Cenozoic tectonism in the Vallecito–Fish Creek basin, western Imperial Valley, California: Geology, v. 11, p. 664-667.

Kelm, D. L., 1972, A gravity and magnetic study of the Laguna Salada area, Baja California, Mexico: Unpubl. M.S. thesis, San Diego State Univ., 103 p.

Kerr, D. R., 1982, Early Neogene continental sedimentation, western Salton Trough, California: Unpubl. M.S. thesis, San Diego State Univ., San Diego, California, 138 p.

————, 1984, Early Neogene continental sedimentation in the Vallecito and Fish Creek Mountains, western Salton Trough, California: Sedim. Geol., v. 38, p. 217–246.

Kerr, D. R., and Kidwell, S. M., 1991, Late Cenozoic sedimentation and tectonics, western Salton Trough, California, in Walawender, M. J., and Hanan, B. B., eds., Geological excursions in Southern California and Mexico: San Diego, CA, Dept. Geol. Sci., San Diego State Univ., p. 397–416.

Kerr, D. R., Pappajohn, S., and Peterson, G. L., 1979, Neogene stratigraphic section at Split Mountain, eastern San Diego County, California, in Crowell, J. C., and Sylvester, A. G., eds., Tectonics of the juncture between the San Andreas fault system and the Salton Trough, southeastern California: Santa Barbara, CA., Dept. Geol. Sci., Univ. of California, Santa Barbara, p. 111–124.

Lachenbruch, A. H., Sass, J. H., and Galanis, S. P., Jr., 1985, Heat flow in southernmost California and the origin of the Salton Trough: Jour. Geophys. Res., v. 90, no. B8, p. 6709–6736.

Lee, J., Miller, M. M., Crippen, R., Hacker, B., and Ledesma-Vasquez, J., 1996, Middle Miocene extension in the Gulf Extensional Province, Baja California: Evidence from the southern Sierra Juarez: Geol. Soc. Amer. Bull., v. 108, p. 505–525.

Lewis, C. J., 1994, Constraints on extension in the Gulf Extensional Province from the Sierra San Fermín, northeastern Baja California, Mexico: Unpubl. Ph.D. thesis, Harvard Univ., Cambridge, MA, 361 p.

Lewis, C. J., and Stock, J. M., in press, Paleomagnetic evidence of localized vertical-axis rotation during Neogene extension in the Sierra San Fermín, northeastern Baja California, Mexico: Jour. Geophys. Res.

Lonsdale, P., 1991, Structural patterns of the Pacific floor offshore of Peninsular California, in Dauphin, J. P., and Simoneit, B. T., eds., The Gulf and peninsular provinces of the Californias: Tulsa, OK, Amer. Assoc. Petrol. Geol. Memoir, v. 47, p. 87–125.

Lough, C. F., 1993, Structural evolution of the Vallecitos Mountains, Colorado Desert and Salton Trough geology: San Diego, CA, San Diego Assoc. Geol., p. 91–109.

Mace, N. W., 1981, A paleomagnetic study of the Miocene Alverson Volcanics of the Coyote Mountains, western Salton Trough: Unpubl. M.S. thesis, San Diego State Univ., 142 p.

Matti, J. C., and Morton, D. M., 1993, Paleogeographic evolution of the San Andreas fault in southern California: A reconstruction based on a new cross-fault correlation, in Powell, R. E., Weldon, R. J., II, and Matti, J. C., eds., The San Andreas fault system: Displacement, palinspastic reconstruction, and geologic evolution: Boulder, CO, Geol. Soc. Amer., p. 107–160.

McClay, K. R., and White, M. J., 1995, Analogue modelling of orthogonal and oblique rifting: Marine Petrol. Geol., v. 12, p. 137–151.

McDougall, K., Powell, C. L., II, Matti, J. C., and Poore, R. Z., 1994, The Imperial Formation and the opening of the ancestral Gulf of California [abs.]: Geol. Soc. Amer. Abs. Prog., v. 26, no. 2, p. 71.

McKenzie, D. P., Davies, D., and Molnar, P., 1970, Plate tectonics of the Red Sea and east Africa: Nature, v. 226, p. 243–248.

McKibben, M. A., Williams, A. E., Elders, W. A., and Eldridge, C. S., 1987, Saline brines and metallogenesis in a modern sediment-filled rift: The Salton Sea geothermal system, California, U.S.A.: Appl. Geochem., v. 2, p. 563–578.

Mendoza-Borunda, R., and Axen, G. J., 1995, Preliminary analysis of the Late Cenozoic structural history of the southern Sierra Juárez fault zone in the vicinity of the main Gulf escarpment [abs.]: Third Int. Meeting on the Geology of Baja California, Abs. Peninsular Geol. Soc., La Paz, Baja California Sur, p. 126–127.

Mendoza-Borunda, R., Axen, G. J., and Frias-Camacho, V., 1995, Fallamiento normal en la parse sur de la zone de falla de Sierra Juarez, en la vecinidad del escarpe principal del Golfo: Evidencias de cambios en la direccion de extension en esa latitud(?): Geos, v. 15, no. 2, p. 69.

Merriam, R., and Bandy, O. L., 1965, Source of upper Cenozoic sediments in the Colorado Delta region: Jour. Sediment. Petrol., v. 35, p. 911–916.

Miele, M. J., 1986, A magnetotelluric profiling and geophysical investigation of the Laguna Salada Basin, Baja California: Unpubl. M.S. thesis, San Diego State Univ., 154 p.

Miller, D. E., and Kato, T., 1990, Field evidence for late Cenozoic kinematic transition in the Coyote Mountains, Imperial County, California [abs.]: Geol. Soc. Amer. Abs. Prog., v. 22, no. 3, p. 68.

————, 1991, Mid-Tertiary continental extension, SW Salton Trough, Calif. [abs.]: Geol. Soc. Amer. Abs. Prog., v. 23, no. 2, p. 79.

Mueller, K., J., and Rockwell, T. K., 1991, Late Quaternary structural evolution of the western margin of the Sierra Cucapa, northern Baja California, in Dauphin, J. P., and Simoneit, B. T., eds., The Gulf and Peninsular provinces of the Californias: Tulsa, OK, Amer. Assoc. Petrol. Geol. Memoir, v. 47, p. 249–260.

————, 1995, Late Quaternary activity of the Laguna Salada fault in northern Baja California, Mexico: Geol. Soc. Amer. Bull., v. 107, p. 8–18.

Nourse, J. A., Anderson, T. H., and Silver, L. T., 1994, Tertiary metamorphic core complexes in Sonora, northwestern Mexico: Tectonics, v. 13, no. 5, p. 1161–1182.

O'Brien, D. K., Wenk, H. R., Ratschbacher, L., and You, Z., 1987, Preferred orientation of phyllosilicates in phyllonites and ultramylonites: Jour. Struct. Geol., v. 9, p. 719–730.

Peterson, M. S., 1975, Geology of the Coachella Fanglomerate, in Crowell, J. C., ed., San Andreas fault in Southern California: Calif. Div. Mines Spec. Report 118, p. 119–126.

Pinault, C. T., 1984, Structure, tectonic geomorphology and neotectonics of the Elsinore fault zone between banner Canyon and the Coyote Mountains, southern California: Unpubl. M.S. thesis, San Diego State Univ., 231 p.

Powell, R. E., 1993, Balanced palinspastic reconstruction of pre-Late Cenozoic paleogeology, southern California: Geologic and kinematic constraints on evolution of the San Andreas fault system, in Powell, R. E., Weldon, R. J., II, and Matti, J. C., eds., The San Andreas fault system: Displacement, palinspastic reconstruction, and geologic evolution: Boulder, CO, Geol. Soc. Amer. Memoir, p. 1–106.

Powell, R. E., and Weldon, R. J., II, 1992, Evolution of the San Andreas fault: Ann. Rev. Earth Planet. Sci., v. 20, p. 431–468.

Pridmore, C. L., and Frost, E. G., 1992, Detachment faults: California's extended past: Calif. Geol., v. 45, p. 3–17.

Rockwell, T. K., and Lamar, D. L., 1986, Neotectonics of the Elsinore fault, southern California, in Ehlig, P. L., ed., Neotectonics and faulting in Southern California: Los Angeles, Cordill. Sect., Geol. Soc. Amer., p. 149–207.

Rogers, T. H., 1965, Geologic map of California, Santa Ana sheet: Calif. Div. Mines Geol., 1:250,000 scale.

Romero-Espejel, J. G. H., 1997, Estructura y petrología en el norte de Sierra Juárez, Baja California: Unpubl. M.S. thesis, Centro de Investigación Científica y de Educación Superior de Ensenada (CICESE), Baja California, Mexico, 155 p.

Rosendahl, B. R., Kilembe, E., and Kaczmarick, K., 1992, Comparison of the Tanganyika, Malawi, Rukwa and Turkana zones from analyses of seismic reflection data: Tectonophys., v. 213, p. 235–256.

Ruisaard, C. I., 1979, Stratigraphy of the Miocene Alverson Formation, Imperial County, California: Unpubl. M.S. thesis, San Diego State Univ., 125 p.

Rymer, M. J., Sarna-Wojcicki, A. M., Powell, C. L., II, and Barron, J. A., 1994, Stratigraphic evidence for late Miocene opening of the Salton Trough in southern California [abs.]: Geol. Soc. Amer. Abs. Prog., v. 26, no. 2, p. 87.

Savage, J. C., Lisowski, M., King, N. E., and Gross, W. K., 1994, Strain accumulation along the Laguna Salada fault, Baja California, Mexico: Jour. Geophys. Res., v. 99, p. 18,109–18,116.

Sawlan, M. G., 1991, Magmatic evolution of the Gulf of California rift, in Dauphin, J. P., and Simoneit, B. R. T., eds., The Gulf and Peninsular provinces of the Californias: Tulsa, OK, Amer. Assoc. Petrol. Geol. Memoir, v. 47, p. 301–370.

Schermer, E. R., Howell, D. G., and Jones, D. L., 1984, The origin of allochthonous terranes: Perspectives on the growth and shaping of continents: Ann. Rev. Earth Planet. Sci., v. 12, p. 107–131.

Schultejann, P. A., 1984, The Yaqui Ridge antiform and detachment fault: Mid-Cenozoic extensional terrane west of the San Andreas fault: Tectonics, v. 3, p. 677–691.

Sharp, R. V., 1967, San Jacinto fault zone in the Peninsular Ranges of southern California: Geol. Soc. Amer. Bull., v. 78, p. 705–730.

————, 1968, The San Andreas fault system and contrasting pre-San Andreas structures in the Peninsular Ranges of southern California, in Dickinson, W. R., and Grantz, A., eds., Proc. Conf. Geol. Prob. San Andreas Fault System: Stanford, CA, Stanford Univ., p. 292–293.

————, 1979, Some characteristics of the eastern Peninsular Ranges mylonite zone, in Proc. Conf. VIII: Analysis of actual fault zones in bedrock: U.S. Geol. Surv. Open File Report 79-1239, p. 258–267.

Siem, M. E., 1992, The structure and petrology of Sierra El Mayor, northeastern Baja California, Mexico: Unpubl. M.S. thesis, San Diego State Univ., 244 p.

Siem, M. E., and Gastil, R. G., 1994, Mid-Tertiary to Holocene extension associated with the development of the Sierra El Mayor metamorphic core complex, northeastern Baja California, Mexico, in McGill, S. F., and Ross, T. M., eds., Geological investigations of an active margin: GSA Cordilleran Section guidebook: Redlands, CA, San Bernardino County Museum Assoc., p. 107–119.

Simpson, C., 1984, Borrego Springs–Santa Rosa mylonite zone: A Late Cretaceous west-directed thrust in southern California: Geology, v. 12, p. 8–11.

————, 1985, Comment on "Late Mesozoic and Cenozoic tectonic history of south-central California" by A. E. J. Engel and P. A. Schultejann and on "The Yaqui Ridge antiform and detachment fault: Mid-Cenozoic extensional terrane west of the San Andreas fault" by Patricia A. Schultejann: Tectonics, v. 4, p. 595–596.

Smith, J. T., 1991, Cenozoic marine mollusks and paleogeography of the Gulf of California, in Dauphin, J. P., and Simoneit, B. R. T., eds., The Gulf and Peninsular provinces of the Californias: Tulsa, OK, Amer. Assoc. Petrol. Geol. Memoir, v. 47, p. 637–666.

Spencer, J. E., and Normark, W. R., 1979, Tosco-Abreojos fault zone: A Neogene transform plate boundary within the Pacific margin of southern Baja California, Mexico: Geology, v. 7, p. 554–557.

Spencer, J. E., and Patchett, P. J., 1997, Sr-isotope evidence for a lacustrine origin for the upper Miocene to Pliocene Bouse Formation, lower Colorado River trough, and implications for timing of Colorado Plateau uplift: Geol. Soc. Amer. Bull. v. 109, p. 767–778.

Spencer, J. E., and Reynolds, S. J., 1989, Middle Tertiary tectonics of Arizona and adjacent areas, in Jenney, J. P., and Reynolds, S. J., eds., Geologic evolution of Arizona: Arizona Geological Society digest: Tucson, AZ, Ariz. Geol. Soc.

Spencer, J. E., Richard, S. M., Reynolds, S. J., Miller, R. J., Shafiqullah, M., Gilbert, W. G., and Grubensky, M. J., 1995, Spatial and temporal relationships between mid-Tertiary magmatism and extension in southwestern Arizona: Jour. Geophys. Res., v. 100, p. 10,321–10,351.

Stinson, A. L., and Gastil, R. G., 1996, Mid- to Late-Tertiary detachment faulting in the Pinyon Mountains, San Diego County, California: A setting for long-runout landslides in the Split Mountain gorge area, in Abbott, P. L., and Seymour, D. C., eds., Sturzstroms and detachment faults, Anza-Borrego Desert State Park, California: Santa Ana, California, South Coast Geol. Soc., p. 221–244.

Stock, J. M., and Hodges, K. V., 1989, Pre-Pliocene extension around the Gulf of California and the transfer of Baja California to the Pacific plate: Tectonics, v. 8, p. 99–115.

Stock, J. M., and Lee, J., 1994, Do microplates in subduction zones leave a geological record?: Tectonics, v. 13, p. 1472–1488.

Stock, J. M., Martin-Barajas, A., and Tellez-Duarte, M., 1996, Early rift sedimentation and structure along the NE margin of Baja California, in Abbott, P. L., and Cooper, J. D., eds., Field conference guidebook and volume for the annual convention, San Diego, California, May, 1996: Bakersfield, CA, Pacific Sect., Amer. Assoc. Petrol. Geol., p. 337–380.

Strand, R. G., 1962, Geologic map of California, San Diego–El Centro sheet: Calif. Div. Mines Geol., 1:250,000.

Strangway, D. W., McMahon, B. E., Walker, T. R., and Larson, E. E., 1971, Anomalous Pliocene paleomagnetic pole positions from Baja California: Earth Planet Sci. Let., v. 13, p. 161–166.

Tamsett, D., 1984, Comments on the development of rifts and transform faults during continental breakup: Examples from the Gulf of Aden and northern Red Sea: Tectonophys., v. 104, p. 35–46.

Theodore, T. J., 1970, Petrogenesis of mylonites of high metamorphic grade in the Peninsular Ranges of southern California: Geol. Soc. Amer. Bull., v. 81, p. 435–450.

Tiercelin, J. J., Chorowicz, J., Bellon, H., Richert, J. P., Mwanbene, J. T., and Walgenwitz, F., 1988, East African Rift System: Offset, age, and tectonic significance of the Tanganyika-Rukwa-Malawi intracontinental transcurrent fault zone: Tectonophys., v. 148, p. 241–252.

Todd, V. R., 1977, Geologic map of Agua Caliente Springs Quadrangle, San Diego County, California: U. S. Geol. Surv. Open-File Report 77-742 (1:24,000 scale), p. 1–20.

Todd, V. R., Erskine, B. G., and Morton, D. M., 1988, Metamorphic and tectonic evolution of the northern Peninsular Ranges Batholith, southern California, in Ernst, W. G., ed., Metamorphism and crustal evolution of the Western United States: Rubey Volume VII: Englewood Cliffs, NJ, Prentice-Hall, p. 894–937.

Tron, V., and Brun, J., 1991, Experiments on oblique rifting in brittle-ductile systems: Tectonophys., v. 188, p. 71–84.

Umhoefer, P. J., and Dorsey, R. J., 1997, Translation of terranes: Lessons from central Baja California, Mexico: Geology, v. 25, p. 1007–1010.

Vásquez-Hernández, S., 1996, Estratigrafía y ambientes de depósito de la secuencia al oriente de Laguna Salada, Baja California: Unpubl. M.S. thesis, Centro de Investigación Científica y de Educación Superior de Ensenada, Baja California, Mexico, 148 p.

Wallace, R. D., 1982, Evaluation of possible detachment faulting west of the San Andreas fault, southern Santa Rosa Mountains, California: Unpubl. M.S. thesis, San Diego State Univ., San Diego, California, 77 p.

Wallace, R. D., and English, D. J., 1982, Evaluation of possible detachment faulting west of the San Andreas, southern Santa Rosa Mountains, California, in Frost, E. G., and Martin, D. L., eds., Mesozoic-Cenozoic tectonic evolution of the Colorado River region, California, Arizona, and Nevada: San Diego, CA, Cordilleran Publ., p. 502–510.

Weaver, C. S., and Hill, D. P., 1978, Earthquake swarms and local crustal spreading along major strike-slip faults in California: Pure Appl. Geophys., v. 117, p. 51–64.

Weber, F. H., Jr., 1963, Geology and mineral resources of San Diego County, California: Calif. Div. Mines Geol. County Report 3, 309 p.

Wernicke, B., Axen, G. J., and Snow, J. K., 1988, Basin and Range extensional tectonics at the latitude of Las Vegas, Nevada: Geol. Soc. Amer. Bull., v. 100, p. 1738–1757.

Winker, C. D., and Kidwell, S. M., 1986, Paleocurrent evidence for lateral displacement of the Colorado River delta by the San Andreas fault system, southeastern California: Geology, v. 14, p. 788–791.

———, 1996, Stratigraphy of a marine rift basin: Neogene of the western Salton Trough, California, in

Abbott, P. L., and Cooper, J. D., eds., Field conference guidebook and volume for the annual convention, San Diego, California, May, 1996: Bakersfield, CA, Pacific Sect., Amer. Assoc. Petrol. Geol., p. 295–336.

Withjack, M. O., and Jamison, W. R., 1986, Deformation produced by oblique rifting: Tectonophysics, v. 126, p. 99–124.

Wolf, R. A., Farley, K. A., and Silver, L. T., 1997, Assessment of (U-Th)/He thermochronometry: The low-temperature history of the San Jacinto mountains, California: Geology, v. 25, p. 65–68.

Zoback, M. L., Zoback, M. D., Adams, J., Bell, S., Suter, M., Suarez, G., Jacob, K., Estabrook, C., and Magee, M., 1991, Stress map of North America: Continent-scale map 005: Geol. Soc. Amer., 1:5,000,000 scale.

Pacific–North America Plate Tectonics of the Neogene Southwestern United States: An Update

Tanya Atwater

Department of Geological Sciences, University of California, Santa Barbara California 93106-9630

and Joann Stock

Division of Geological and Planetary Sciences, California Institute of Technology 252-21, Pasadena, California 91125

Abstract

We use updated rotations within the Pacific–Antarctica–Africa–North America plate circuit to calculate Pacific–North America plate reconstructions for times since chron 13 (33 Ma). The direction of motion of the Pacific plate relative to stable North America was fairly steady between chrons 13 and 4, and then changed and moved in a more northerly direction from chron 4 to the present (8 Ma to the present). No Pliocene changes in Pacific–North America plate motion are resolvable in these data, suggesting that Pliocene changes in deformation style along the boundary were not driven by changes in plate motion. However, the chron 4 change in Pacific–North America plate motion appears to correlate very closely to a change in direction of extension documented between the Sierra Nevada and the Colorado Plateau. Our best solution for the displacement with respect to stable North America of a point on the Pacific plate that is now near the Mendocino triple junction is that from 30 to 12 Ma the point was displaced along an azimuth of ~N60°W at rate of ~33 mm/yr; from 12 Ma to about 8 Ma the azimuth of displacement was about the same as previously, but the rate was faster (~52 mm/yr); and since 8 Ma the point was displaced along an azimuth of N37°W at a rate of ~52 mm/yr.

We compare plate-circuit reconstructions of the edge of the Pacific plate to continental deformation reconstructions of North American tectonic elements across the Basin and Range province and elsewhere in order to evaluate the relationship of this deformation to the plate motions. The oceanic displacements correspond remarkably well to the continental reconstructions where deformations of the latter have been quantified along a path across the Colorado Plateau and central California. They also supply strong constraints for the deformation budgets of regions to the north and south, in Cascadia and northern Mexico, respectively.

We examine slab-window formation and evolution in a detailed re-analysis of the spreading geometry of the post-Farallon microplates, from 28 to 19 Ma. Development of the slab window seems linked to early Miocene volcanism and deformation in the Mojave Desert, although detailed correlations await clarification of early Miocene reconstructions of the Tehachapi Mountains. We then trace the post–20 Ma motion of the Mendocino slab window edge beneath the Sierran–Great Valley block and find that it drifted steadily north, then stalled just north of Sutter Buttes at ~4 Ma.

Introduction

Interactions between the North America plate and the plates of the northeastern Pacific basin have exerted a fundamental control on the tectonic development of the western United States and Mexico in Neogene time. The San Andreas transform system and its evolution through Neogene time is a clear manifestation of these interactions (e.g., Atwater, 1970, 1989), but a number of more subtle effects also are apparent. In particular, the piecewise demise of the subduction zone with the creation and evolution of slab-free regions beneath North America can be related to patterns of volcanism and uplift in the continent (e.g., Crough and Thompson, 1977; Dickinson and Snyder, 1979; Page and Engebretson, 1984; Atwater, 1989; Severinghaus and Atwater, 1990; Dickinson, 1997). Furthermore, it appears that deformation of the continental interior, including both extension and shear, may be strictly modulated by geometric constraints of the plate interactions.

A crucial step in working out the plate inter-actions along the continental rim is the calcula-tion of the relative positions of the Pacific plate with respect to stable North America for various past time steps. These calculations have been done in two ways—using either a global-plate-circuit or a fixed-hotspot assumption (e.g., Engebretson et al., 1985; Stock and Molnar, 1988). The weak link in the former is the assumption of a non-deforming Antarctic plate, whereas that of the latter is the assump-tion of fixity between the Pacific and Atlantic hotspots. We believe that for the late Cenozoic reconstructions used here, the former (global plate circuit) clearly is the more dependable solution, and hence have followed that method exclusively. There have been recent improve-ments in our knowledge of the details of the plate circuit, particularly in the southern oceans, as a result of additional fracture-zone constraints from satellite gravity maps (e.g., Sandwell and Smith, 1997) and shipboard data acquisition in critical, but previously unstudied, parts of the world's ocean basins, especially in the regions around Antarctica (Royer and Chang, 1991; Cande et al., 1995). In this paper, we revise the global-plate-circuit reconstructions, incorporating this new infor-mation. Such revision is an ongoing process; future surveys will continue to yield improve-ments in the plate circuit, and the results pre-sented here may need to be further refined.

Another crucial step for plate reconstruc-tions involves the undoing of internal North American deformations. Although some of the observations needed for this job have long been known, breakthroughs of the past decade have greatly enhanced our ability to make credible reconstructions. The conceptual acceptance of >100% extension in the Basin and Range (e.g., Crittenden et al., 1980; Wernicke, 1992) and its spatial and temporal quantification (e.g., Wer-nicke et al., 1988; Snow and Wernicke, 1998; Wernicke and Snow, 1998) are vital advances for the reconstruction of the interior. Likewise, refinement of block-rotation observations and models allows a tighter reconstruction of sev-eral southern California regions (e.g., Kamer-ling and Luyendyk, 1985; Legg, 1991; Luyendyk, 1991; Crouch and Suppe, 1993).

Furthermore, in the last decade there have been major advances in our conceptual under-standing of plate interactions. Examples include the ideas that: (1) the Pacific-Farallon Ridge could still have been some distance west of the trench when Farallon plate fragmentation began (e.g., Fernandez and Hey, 1991; Lonsdale, 1991), and (2) "slab capture" may have driven much of the coastal tectonic deformation after Farallon plate fragmentation took place (e.g., Nicholson et al., 1994; Bohannon and Parsons, 1995). These concepts have led to some changes in how one would reconcile the continental geology with plate-tectonic history. We attempt to integrate these new ideas into the results presented in this paper.

Reconstructions of the Relative Positions of the Pacific and North America Plates

Method

In our plate-circuit calculations, we derive the relative positions of the Pacific and North America plates by adding finite rotations across a series of boundaries in sequence: Pacific to Antarctica across the Pacific-Antarctic Ridge, then Antarctica to Africa across the Southwest Indian Ridge, and finally Africa to North Amer-ica across the Mid-Atlantic Ridge. Each calcula-tion must be done for the same position on the magnetic-reversal time scale in each ocean basin in order to be valid for that time in the past. This is not necessarily a straightforward process, because reconstructions published by different authors for different ocean basins often use slightly different events on the mag-netic-reversal time scale, and this must be taken into account. Pacific-Antarctic reconstructions (Cande et al., 1995) are available for selected positions, or "chrons," on the magnetic-rever-sal time scale that correspond to ~1 m.y. time spacing (following Atwater and Severinghaus, 1989). However, for the other boundaries, reconstructions at this level of detail are not available; rather, the norm is a 5 or 10 m.y. interval between available reconstructions, using only the most prominent magnetic anom-alies—i.e., chrons 5, 6, and 13 (Klitgord and Schouten, 1986; Royer and Chang, 1991). We call these the "global chrons." For our studies, we chose to augment the list of global chrons with some additional, intervening chrons, in order to make use of the extra detail now avail-able in the South Pacific. We calculated circuit

TABLE 1. Positions on Magnetic-Reversal Time Scale for Which
Reconstructions Are Discussed in This Paper

Chron	Position on magnetic-polarity time scale	Age[1]
2ay	Young edge	2.581
3o	Center of oldest normal in anomaly 3	5.105
4	Center	7.752
5o	Old edge	10.949
5a	Center of second normal within 5A	12.293
5b	Center of second normal	15.095
6o	Old edge	20.131
6c	Center of third normal	24.059
8y	Young edge	25.823
10y	Young edge	28.283
12o	Old edge	30.939
13y	Young edge	33.058

[1]After Cande and Kent, 1995.

reconstructions for these intervening chrons by combining the actual reconstructions from the South Pacific with interpolations from the other oceans. This seems justifiable since spreading was quite slow in the other oceans; any errors arising from the interpolations should be small.

We do our work in reference to seafloor magnetic isochrons, and thus we prefer to report our results in terms of chron numbers rather than millions of years, so that the solutions will remain valid through the continuing refinement of ages in the geomagnetic-reversal time scale. In this paper, whenever we address millions of years or rates, we use the chron ages listed in Table 1, from the new geomagnetic polarity time scale of Cande and Kent (1992), as revised by Cande and Kent (1995).

Uncertainties in the reconstructions for the global chrons 5, 6, and 13 are represented as covariance matrices following the formulation of Chang (1988) and Chang et al. (1990). The covariance matrices for the reconstructions across the Southwest Indian Ridge are given by Royer and Chang (1991) and those for the Pacific-Antarctic Ridge are part of the calculations used by Cande et al. (1995) (J. M. Stock, unpubl. data). For the central Mid-Atlantic Ridge, covariance matrices were constructed from the partial uncertainty rotations given by

Stock and Molnar (1988) following the technique described in Chang et al. (1990). The covariance matrices then were used to determine 95% confidence limits for the reconstructions. Uncertainties were only computed for the times of chrons 5o, 6o, and 13y (i.e., the old edges of chrons 5 and 6 and the young edge of chron 13), because these correspond most closely to the times for which covariance matrices were available for the Indian and Pacific oceans. Uncertainties for the intervening chrons are greater than those calculated for the global chrons, because of the additional uncertainty involved with using interpolations in the Atlantic and Indian oceans.

Results: Trajectories of Pacific plate points relative to North America

In Figures 1 and 2, our new plate circuit solutions were used to calculate displacements of the Pacific plate through time with respect to North America. Stable North America was employed as a fixed reference frame and we selected several arbitrary reference points on the Pacific plate to illustrate its displacements. The present locations of the Pacific reference points are shown as stars and their various reconstructed positions are labeled with chron numbers. By connecting the various positions

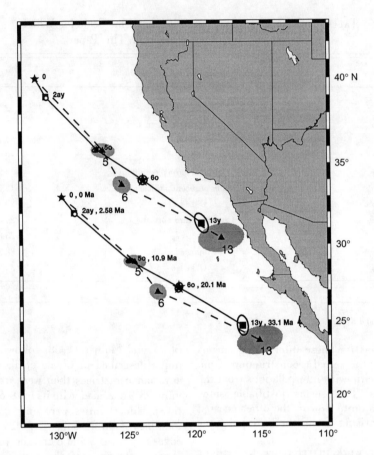

Fɪɢ. 1. Map showing tracks of two arbitrary reference points on the Pacific plate moving relative to a fixed North America plate. Present positions of the points are marked with small stars labeled "0." Past positions of these points are shown for the times of global chrons 5o, 6o, and 13y, reconstructed using the Pacific–Antarctica–Africa–North America global plate circuit. Ellipses represent the 95% confidence limits on the locations of these points. Locations of squares labeled "2ay" were calculated by extrapolating present-day velocities in the NUVEL-1A model (DeMets et al., 1994) to 2.58 Ma. Heavy open circles were located with a similar extrapolation, but using DeMets's (1995) modification of the Pacific–North America rate for NUVEL-1A. Dashed tracks with triangles labeled "5," "6," and "13" show past positions of the same reference points, as previously determined by Stock and Molnar (1988), with their 95% confidence ellipses shaded in grey for comparison. Note the differences between the new reconstructions and the older ones for chrons 6 and 13.

of a given reference point, we created a time trajectory for that part of the Pacific plate with respect to stable North America.

In Figure 1 we compared our new trajectories to those of the previous solutions by Stock and Molnar (1988) for the times of the global chrons 13y, 6o, and 5o and to solutions for present-day relative velocity extrapolated to chron 2ay. For the latter, we considered both the global NUVEL-1A plate-motion model by DeMets et al. (1994) (black squares labeled

2ay) and a variation of this model with an updated rate for Pacific–North America by DeMets (1995) (heavy open circles). In our new solutions, the reconstructions for chrons 13y and 6o are markedly different from the Stock and Molnar solutions, probably because of greatly improved mapping of small-offset fracture zones in the South Pacific and Indian Ocean. Small-offset fracture zones, while more difficult to map than large-offset fracture zones, are more reliable indicators of past

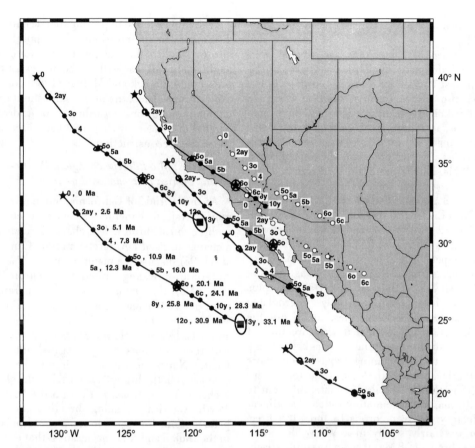

Fig. 2. Map showing tracks of arbitrary reference points assumed to move with the Pacific plate relative to a fixed North America plate. Present positions of the points are marked with symbols labeled "0." Past positions of these points are shown for chrons whose ages are listed in Table 1. Ellipses for chrons 5o, 6o, and 13y represent the 95% confidence limits on the locations of these points. Ellipses for other times are not shown but would be larger, because those reconstructions involve interpolations of rotations along the Southwest Indian Ridge and the Mid-Atlantic Ridge. Points now on the Pacific plate are shown only for the times that they have been present on the seafloor (e.g., a point located on seafloor of chron 10 age is not shown for times older than chron 10). Points now on North America (open symbols) are shown to illustrate the direction of motion that would be expected if the Pacific plate had been dragging North American crust with it. Note the major change in direction of Pacific–North America plate motion at chron 4 time (7.8 Ma). Heavy open circles are the locations predicted by extrapolating DeMets's (1995) modification of the Pacific–North America rate in the NUVEL-1A model to chron 2ay (2.58 Ma) as in Figure 1. Note the close correspondence of these circles to our chron 2ay circuit solutions.

instantaneous plate-motion directions, since they spend a much shorter time within the active transform fault and thus are less prone to overprinting by subsequent changes. For chron 5o, our new positions for the reference points are quite similar to positions resulting from the Stock and Molnar solution and are within the 95% confidence limits of those earlier calculations.

A change in the direction of Pacific–North America plate motion is clearly required by the global chron trajectories in Figure 1, since the average motion direction from chron 5o (11 Ma) to the present is distinctly more northward than the older directions. Furthermore, the circles and squares labeled 2ay on Figure 1 indicate a present-day velocity direction that is even more northerly than our 11 Ma average direction, suggesting that at least part of the change was younger than 11 Ma. In summary, the new solutions for the global chrons suggest a smooth trajectory between 33 and 11 Ma, and indicate one or more changes in direction since 11 Ma.

In order to take advantage of the very detailed kinematic model now available in the southwest Pacific, we interpolated steps in the other two (slow-spreading) oceans. When we included all the resulting 35 steps, the trajectory was, again, remarkably smooth, and a single change in direction was very clearly identified at or just preceding the time of chron 4, ~8 Ma. Furthermore, the direction and rate for the part of the track younger than chron 4 coincided almost exactly with that predicted by the NUVEL-1A extrapolation, described above.

Figure 2 shows our preferred new trajectories for various reference points on the Pacific plate with respect to stable North America. These trajectories include reconstructions for the global chrons with their uncertainties, plus selected intervening, partially interpolated chrons without uncertainties, to fill out the tracks. It is apparent that the direction of Pacific–North America motion has been changing with time, becoming progressively more northerly, although the exact trajectories vary with location on the Pacific plate. Adjacent to California, the plate motion followed a bilinear trajectory: between chrons 13 and 4 the direction was fairly steady in a WNW direction; since chron 4 (~8 Ma) it again was quite steady, but in a NNW direction. Farther south, the trajectory appears to have been more curved, with the chron 4 kink less noticeable than it is to the north.

The net displacements of the Pacific plate since the times of chron 8 and younger are important for calculations of the amount of net plate-boundary displacement that may need to be accommodated within the continental lithosphere of the western United States. For this purpose, we have calculated and listed in Table 2 the net displacements and their directions for a modern Pacific plate reference point near the Mendocino triple junction over a few select time intervals. In Figure 3, we have plotted the displacement and azimuth of this reference point through time. Again, the direction of motion is seen to be bilinear, changing at 8 Ma from ~N60°W to ~N37°W. The rate of motion also changed, from ~33 mm/yr to ~52 mm/yr, but the rate change seems to have occurred at ~12 Ma, which is earlier than the direction change.

It should be noted in passing that despite the differences in the positions of the points for chrons 6 and 13, the calculated values for coast-parallel slip all are within the uncertainties presented by Stock and Molnar (1988) for the same chrons. Thus, the new results should not change conclusions regarding San Andreas-parallel displacement that have been based on the earlier reconstructions.

Discussion: Mio-Pliocene change in Pacific–North America plate-motion direction

At the latitude of California, our new plate-motion trajectory includes a very clear change in direction at chron 4. This change is related to a change in Pacific-Antarctic motion. Cande et al. (1995) discussed a major change in Pacific-Antarctic spreading direction at chron 3ay (~5.9 Ma), the timing of which is constrained most precisely from a change in orientation of seafloor-spreading fabric that is visible on swath bathymetry. However, when the Pacific-Antarctic rotations are propagated into the Pacific–North America plate circuit, there are changes at both chrons 3ay and 4, but the chron 4 change has a stronger effect on the Pacific–North America spreading direction. Because plate motions for these chrons are interpolated in the Indian and Atlantic oceans—that is, they are assumed to be steady—any variation in spreading directions in these oceans would further change these results.

Several authors have inferred that there were one or more resolvable Pliocene changes in Pacific–North America plate motion. Harbert (1991) concluded that changes occurred at 2.48 Ma and between 3.4 and 3.9 Ma, resulting in a 12° clockwise change in the relative plate-motion vector along the Pacific–North America boundary in coastal California. Other estimates of the time of this change are ~5 Ma (Cox and Engebretson, 1985) and 3.2 to 5 Ma (Pollitz, 1986). These postulated changes are thought to have produced compression and uplift in the California Coast Ranges and offshore basins (Page and Engebretson, 1984; McCulloch, 1989; McIntosh et al., 1991) and development of strike-slip faults of more northerly trends within the San Andreas system (e.g., Harbert, 1991). Such changes also are thought to be linked to changes in the direction of absolute motion of the Pacific plate, manifested by an

TABLE 2. Total Displacement through Time, Relative to North America Plate, of Reference Point Now near Mendocino Triple Junction (38.5° N, 124° W)[1]

Chron interval and time span	Distance, degrees	Distance, km	Azimuth
0–3o (0 to 5.1 Ma)	2.53	280	N37°W
0–4 (0 to 7.8 Ma)	3.49	390	N37°W
0–5o (0 to 10.9 Ma)	5.13 ± 0.18	570 ± 25	N42°W ± 3°
0–5a (0 to 12.3 Ma)	5.71	635	N44°W
0–5b (0 to 15.1 Ma)	6.62	735	N45°W
0–6o (0 to 20.1 Ma)	8.22 ± 0.30	910 ± 35	N47° W ± 2°
0–6c (0 to 24.1 Ma)	9.20	1020	N48°W
0–8y (0 to 25.8 Ma)	9.70	1075	N48°W
0–10y (0 to 28.3 Ma)	10.48	1165	N48°W

[1]Uncertainties on reconstructions involving partial interpolations are not given, but they would be larger than the uncertainties calculated explicitly for chrons 5o and 6o.

inferred subtle change in direction of the Hawaiian-Emperor chain, which most recently has been assumed to be at 3 Ma (Wessel and Kroenke, 1997). None of these calculations included estimates of the uncertainties in the plate reconstructions.

In contrast to these earlier works, we cannot identify any resolvable changes during the Pliocene in our updated plate circuit. It is possible that there was a change and our interpolations for times younger than chron 5 missed some younger change of motion in either the Atlantic or Indian Ocean. Our results, however, suggest that this is not the case because of the very close match between our chron 4–0 direction and the direction given by the NUVEL-1A solution of DeMets et al. (1994) (heavy open circles in Fig. 2). If a change in Pacific–North America motion had occurred between chron 3 and chron 2a, we would expect that the NUVEL-1A direction, which is based upon the youngest magnetic anomalies (chrons 2a, 2, and 1) from all of the world's oceans, would differ from our vectors for chron 3 and older times. In fact, there is no resolvable difference between the NUVEL-1A direction and ours and no resolvable change in Pacific–North America motion direction younger than 8 Ma. Of course, some variations would be permitted within the uncertainties in the reconstructions, so we cannot rule out the possibility that small changes did take place in Pliocene time, but no such changes can actually be resolved.

The chron 4 change in motion of the Pacific plate relative to North America is clearly resolvable, but it is late Miocene in age (~8 Ma). Thus, it may be too old to have caused the uplift and compression that previously have been attributed to a Pliocene change in Pacific–North America plate motion. An alternative explanation would be that this compression was caused by some change in the component of extension in the Basin and Range province, so that it is related to internal deformation partitioning within the North America plate rather than to any external control from changing plate motions. For example, a modest counterclockwise rotation of the central Sierra Nevada–Great Valley block, postulated below for other reasons, could have caused the observed geological phenomena.

Reconstructed locations of the eastern edge of the oceanic Pacific plate and their constraints on continental deformations

Our new reconstructions of the Pacific plate locations place various constraints on the time-space budget of deformation within western North America. The strongest constraint arises from the simple fact that oceanic and continental lithosphere cannot occupy the same surface area at the same time. If North America is kept in its present shape, past reconstructions of the

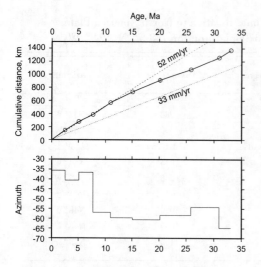

FIG. 3. Displacement of a point now on the Pacific plate at 38.5° N, 124.0° W, near the Mendocino triple junction, calculated from the global-plate-circuit solutions illustrated in Figure 2. A clear change in the rate of displacement is shown by a change in slope in the top plot at ~12 Ma. A clear change in the azimuth of displacement is seen in the bottom plot at ~8 Ma (chron 4). Note that the changes do not coincide in time.

edge of the Pacific plate result in significant, unacceptable overlaps of oceanic and continental lithosphere.

We illustrate this ocean-continent overlap problem in Figure 4. In this figure, the grey line shows the known edge of the oceanic Pacific plate lithosphere at the time of chron 6o (20.1 Ma), located using our new chron 6o around-the-world plate-circuit solution. Wherever the Pacific plate was in contact with the continent, this grey line traces the ocean-continent join along the base of the continental slope; wherever the Farallon or its derivative plates still lay between the Pacific and North America plates, the grey line traces transform faults and spreading centers along the active oceanic spreading system at the western edge of the Pacific plate. Assuming that the Pacific oceanic lithosphere has acted as a rigid plate, the overlap of the grey line over the edge of the continent shows the minimum total amount of retro-deformation within North America that is required in order to move its edge back out of the way.

In Figure 5, we present reconstructions of the edge of the oceanic Pacific plate lithosphere for selected Neogene time steps, including the edge just presented in Figure 4. It should be noted that the southern portions of the 6c, 6o, and 5b lines all trace lengthy segments of the still-active spreading system; remnants of the Farallon plate lay between the Pacific plate and Baja California until ~12 Ma. Any deformations within North America that are related to Pacific–North America plate boundary interactions may be expected to reflect the step-to-step displacements of the Pacific edge that are illustrated in Figure 5. Furthermore, although each overlap shown in Figure 5 literally constrains the deformation only within the overlap area itself, it is likely that the continental edge was a smooth curve (or at least it was not pre-indented in just the right location), so that the displacement of a much greater length of coast can be inferred. This possibility is explored below.

In order to quantify the plate-motion constraints for a North American deformation budget, we break down each motion/deformation estimate into coast-perpendicular and coast-parallel components of displacement, using N30°W as our approximate coast-parallel direction. The ocean-continent overlaps shown in Figure 4 are, therefore, a measure of the minimum coast-perpendicular deformation required within the continent to solve the overlap problem; i.e., the continental coast-perpendicular total must equal or exceed that calculated in the Pacific–North America plate-circuit solution. On the other hand, in the coast-parallel direction, the solutions supply the maximum internal deformation that might be expected. If we assume that the shear within the continent is driven by the plate interaction and that an unknown amount of slip may have occurred offshore, along the continent-ocean join, then the total coast-parallel component of deformation observed within the continent must be equal to or less than that calculated for Pacific–North America displacement. Furthermore, for reconstructions younger than 18 Ma, the plate-circuit solutions may place even tighter constraints on the internal continental deformation budget, since some evidence suggests that the central California continental rim was completely coupled to the Pacific plate starting at about that time (Nicholson et al., 1994). If this is true, the sum of continental deformations should be *equal* to the circuit displacements, within the uncertainties, for every time step.

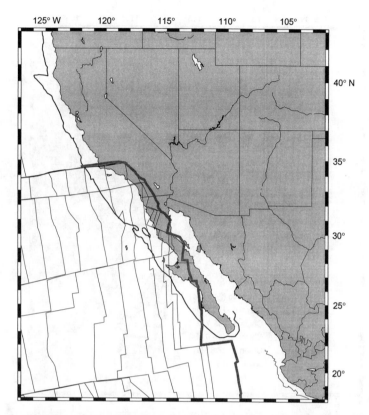

FIG. 4. Location of Pacific plate oceanic lithosphere at the time of chron 6o (20.1 Ma) relative to a fixed North America, plotted upon the present shape of North America. The heavy grey line is the eastern edge of known oceanic crust, drawn to trace either the spreading system that was active at chron 6o time or, where spreading and subduction had ceased, the edge of oceanic crust at the base of the continental slope. Light lines are older isochron patterns within the Pacific plate ocean floor, after Atwater and Severinghaus (1989). The solid line west of the North American coastline is the present-day base of the continental slope, inferred to be the present location of the western edge of North American continental crust. The overlap of the Pacific plate east of this line is an unacceptable overlap of oceanic and continental lithosphere. It demonstrates the minimum amount of internal deformation that is required to have occurred within the continent since 20.1 Ma if the plate reconstructions are correct.

For the reference point near Mendocino, the total displacement of the Pacific plate with respect to stable North America for each time step is given in Table 2. In Table 3 we break these down into their coast-perpendicular and coast-parallel components (right-hand columns labeled "Plate-circuit total") and compare them to an estimated continental strain budget for the path from stable North America to the Colorado Plateau to central California to the Pacific plate. Strain budgets have been attempted in the past (e.g., Hornafius et al., 1986; Dickinson, 1996; Dickinson and Wernicke, 1997) and we build upon and expand these works.

Continental Strain Budgets and the Reconstruction of Western North America for the Past

Observations of continental deformation

The 1980s and 1990s have seen a number of advances in our knowledge of the space and time patterns of continental deformation within western North America, so that we may soon be able to make quite precise reconstructions for many time steps at various latitudes. Figure 6 shows the major pieces of the continental puzzle, with letters, arrows, and rotation angles marking the various continental deformations for which there are quantitative esti-

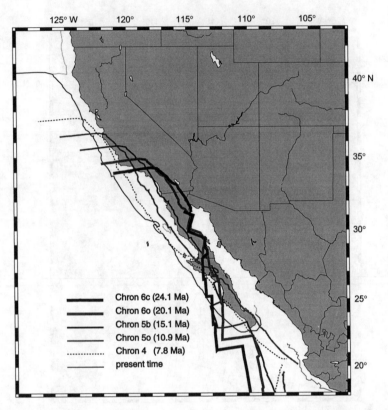

FIG. 5. Successive locations of the eastern edge of Pacific plate oceanic lithosphere, relative to a fixed North America, plotted upon the present shape of North America. The edge for each time step was drawn as described for Figure 4. The overlaps demonstrate the amount of internal deformation required within North America at each past time in order to avoid an unacceptable overlap of oceanic and continental lithosphere.

mates. These and other constraints and observations are summarized below.

1. For any time step, the *total continental strain* across western North America when compared to that calculated via the around-the-world plate circuit (Table 2) must equal or exceed the circuit solution in the coast-perpendicular direction (i.e., it should equal or exceed the amounts listed in the right-hand column of Table 3A). It must be equal to or less than the circuit solution in the coast-parallel direction (i.e., it should be equal to or less than the amounts listed in the right-hand column of Table 3B). Furthermore, we hypothesize that the continental and circuit strain totals should be about the same since 18 Ma. Essentially this amounts to assuming that, prior to 18 Ma, right-lateral strike-slip faulting and/or convergence may have taken place offshore, either within the continental margin or along the continent-

ocean contact zone, but since 18 Ma the continental margin has been attached to the Pacific plate.

2. The total Neogene opening across the *Rio Grande rift* was small—10 to 20 km. We assume, following Chapin and Cather (1994), that this deformation was accomplished by rotation of the Colorado Plateau 1.5° clockwise about a pole in northeastern Utah.

3. The *Colorado Plateau* acted as a rigid block without significant internal deformation.

4. The *Sierran–Great Valley block* acted rigidly, without significant internal deformation, except near its southern end. From paleomagnetic studies of the central portions of the Sierra Nevada, Frei (1986) reported a clockwise rotation of 6 ± 8° (i.e., indistinguishable from zero) since the early Late Cretaceous. In our reconstructions we violate this slightly, letting this block rotate counterclockwise approx-

TABLE 3. Approximate Coast-Perpendicular Displacement Budget for a Path across the Colorado Plateau and Central California[1]

Chron interval and time span[2]	Rio Grande rift[3]	Basin and Range,[4] A or B	Cent. San Andreas,[5] 1 or 2	Coastal slip[6]	Continental total[7]	Plate-circuit total[8]
A. Kilometers N60°E						
0–6c (0 to 24.1 Ma)	15	150 or 235	60	0	225 or 310	310
0–6o (0 to 20.1 Ma)	15	150 or 235	60	0	225 or 310	265
0–5b (0 to 15.1 Ma)	10	130 or 215	60	0	200 or 285	190
0–5o (0 to 10.9 Ma)	5	45 or 115	50 or 55	0	100–175	120
0–4 (0 to 7.8 Ma)	5	40 or 105	40 or 50	0	80–155	45
B. Kilometers N30°W						
0–6c (0 to 24.1 Ma)	5	220	310	250	785	972
0–6o (0 to 20.1 Ma)	5	220	310	250	785	870
0–5b (0 to 15.1 Ma)	0	205	290 or 310	230	725 or 745	710
0–5o (0 to 10.9 Ma)	0	150	260 or 290	110	520 or 550	560
0–4 (0 to 7.8 Ma)	0	130	200 or 255	80	410 or 465	385

[1]Compared to the plate-circuit solution for a Pacific plate reference point near Mendocino.
[2]Magnetic-reversal chron ages from Cande and Kent (1995).
[3]Rio Grande rift extension after "Miocene" rotation of Chapin and Cather (1994), as described in number 2 (under heading "Observations of continental deformation") in the text.
[4]Total of Basin and Range extension and dextral shear between the Sierran–Great Valley block and the Colorado Plateau, for point A near Bishop and for point B near Ridgecrest, California, as described in number 5 in the text. Components calculated from displacement estimates of Wernicke and Snow (1998).
[5]Displacements on the central San Andreas fault system, Pinnacles-Neenach offset. Partitioning of offset over time, as described in number 7 in the text: 1 = assuming significant early offset after Sims (1993), or 2 = assuming almost all offset was post-10 Ma, after Dickinson (1996). Coast-perpendicular displacements in Table 3A (for kilometers N60°E) arise from the fact that the San Andreas fault is not parallel to the coast.
[6]Displacements west of the central San Andreas fault, after Hornafius et al. (1986), as described in number 8 in the text.
[7]Sums of columns two through five. Up to 40 km of displacement might be added to each from the rotation of the Tehachapi Mountains, as described in number 6 in the text.
[8]Displacements of a reference point on the Pacific plate, from Table 2, broken into components (a) perpendicular and (b) parallel to N30°W.

imately 5° since 20.1 Ma. We do this in order to create smooth continental edges in the reconstructions, and we embrace it as a way to help create a triangular space for the Santa Maria Basin, described in number 8, below. We note that this postulated counterclockwise rotation of the Sierran–Great Valley block would not violate the paleomagnetic data if it were counteracting a rotation in the opposite sense during Laramide time, as suggested by Walcott (1993). Our rotation implies that Basin and Range opening was greater in northern Nevada than in the region described next.

5. The total opening since 16 Ma between the Colorado Plateau and the Sierra Nevada, across the *Basin and Range province* near the latitude of Las Vegas, Nevada, was very large (Wernicke et al., 1988; Snow and Wernicke, 1998). Wernicke and Snow (1998) reported the motions of two points—point A near Bishop, California and point B near Ridgecrest, California (A and B on Fig. 6) as follows: since ~10 Ma point A moved ~160 km N46°W; since ~10 Ma point B moved ~185 km N68°W; since 16 Ma point A moved ~265 km N65°W; and since 16 Ma point B moved ~325 km N77°W. It should be noted

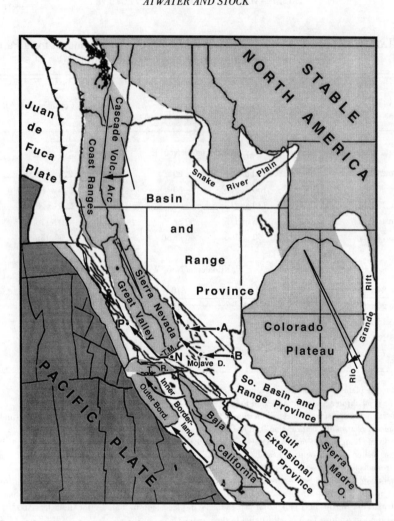

FIG. 6. Present locations of continental elements and known quantitative constraints (listed in the text) for their reconstructions to early Miocene locations. Dark grey = rigid Pacific plate; light grey = continental blocks that are believed to have suffered relatively little internal deformation during the Late Cenozoic; white = continental regions believed to have suffered significant Neogene deformation. A and B = reference points of Wernicke and Snow (1998) and arrows with dots show their trajectories 16 Ma–10 Ma–0 Ma, as described in number 5 in the text; P and N = Pinnacles and Neenach locations for reconstruction of the central San Andreas fault offset, as described in number 7 in the text; T. R. = western Transverse Ranges block; T. M. = Tehachapi Mountains.

that the displacements of these two points differ from one another. A literal use of both of these displacement paths implies that the Sierra Nevada block between the two points rotated 20° clockwise during the last 10 million years. This result could be accomplished by rotation of the entire Sierran–Great Valley block (as suggested by Wernicke and Snow [1998] in this issue), but this conflicts with loose geometric constraints described in numbers 4, 8, and 11. Alternatively, it could indicate significant internal deformation and flexure within the southern part of the block, an interpretation that is supported by observations of significant present seismicity and geodetic deformation on several known and implied fault zones within the southern Sierra Nevada (Bawden et al., 1997; G. W. Bawden and Michael, pers. commun., 1998). We adopt this flexural solution for now, even though it violates sparse paleomagnetic data suggesting minimal post–16 Ma rotation of the Tehachapi Mountains (described below).

Yet another alternative is to assume that the track for one or the other of the Wernicke and Snow points is in error and may be ignored, so that no young rotation is indicated. In that case, we would be required to use the larger (point B) displacement for the entire block in order to avoid an unacceptable oceanic overlap at the southernmost end, an assumption that seriously violates the displacement budget for the other track (point A) (B. P. Wernicke, pers. commun., 1998).

Geodetic measurements of displacements across the Great Basin yield a total present-day rate of ~12 mm/yr with a coast-parallel shear rate of ~11 mm/yr across the eastern California shear zone (Feigl et al., 1993; Dixon et al., 1995; Bennett et al., 1998). We note that these rates are somewhat slower than the long-term average implied by the point displacements described above.

6. The *Tehachapi Mountains,* at the southern edge of the Sierran–Great Valley block, are reported to have rotated 45° to 60° clockwise (Kanter and McWilliams, 1982; McWilliams and Li, 1985) between 23 and 16 Ma. Both the timing and deformation configuration here and in the northern Mojave are subjects of considerable controversy (e.g., Plescia et al., 1994; Dokka and Ross, 1995; Glazner et al., 1996). This deformation remains an unknown in our reconstructions. It may be responsible for displacements of 40 km each in the coast-parallel and coast-perpendicular directions (Dickinson, 1996).

7. Strike-slip displacement along the *central San Andreas fault* since 23 Ma was 315 ± 10 km, in a N40°W direction, to reconnect the Pinnacles to the Neenach volcanics (Matthews, 1976; Sims, 1993). Of special interest is the partitioning of this strain over time and, in particular, the amount of this slip that occurred after 8 Ma. Dickinson (1996) suggested that the bulk of the displacement was late and budgeted ~255 km since 8 Ma, whereas Sims (1993) implied that the post–8 Ma amount was ~200 km. We find that the latter estimate is more compatible with other post–8 Ma estimates, as discussed below, and so adopt it for now.

8. In *coastal California,* west of the San Andreas fault, two independent estimates of deformation have been made: (a) in central California, offsets on individual fault strands plus pervasive shear deformation of the ground

between them yields an estimate of ~250 km total, with ~80 km since 8 Ma (Hornafius et al., 1986) in an approximate coast-parallel direction; (b) a 110° clockwise rotation of the western Transverse Ranges block amounts to a coast-parallel displacement of ~270 km, with ~60 km since 8 Ma (Hornafius et al., 1986). In the coast-perpendicular direction, an extension about equal to the width of the inner borderland, ~100 km, is indicated for southern California, according to the assumption that it and the Santa Maria Basin were formed by "core-complex-like" openings (Kamerling and Luyendyk, 1985; Crouch and Suppe, 1993). However, north of the Santa Maria Basin, in central California, very little coast-perpendicular extension is evident. Indeed, the triangular shape of the Santa Maria Basin is difficult to understand in terms of purely translational offsets; simple transtension in the wake of the rotating western Transverse Ranges would have created a rhomb-shaped space. This odd configuration probably requires a rotation of the Sierran–Great Valley block, as described in number 4 above.

9. The *Oregon Coast Ranges* rotated 18° to 36° clockwise about a pivot point in Washington since 30–20 Ma and 10° to 15° since 15–12 Ma (summarized in Wells, 1990). We follow the model advanced by Magill and Cox (1981), Frei (1986), and Walcott (1993) that the southern end of the Oregon Coast Ranges moved with the northern end of the Sierran–Great Valley block.

10. The *Baja California Peninsula* moved ~300 km in a direction parallel to the Gulf of California transform faults since about 5 Ma. Since about 12 Ma, a coast-parallel dextral displacement of 250 to 300 km is postulated on the Pacific side of the Peninsula, along the offshore Tosco-Abreojos fault zone of Spencer and Normark (1979), in order to account for the offset of the Magdalena fan (Lyle and Ness, 1991). Also, a substantial but unknown amount of Miocene and/or younger extension with a major coast-perpendicular component occurred in northeastern Baja California, Sonora, and east of the Sierra Madre Occidental (e.g., Stock and Hodges, 1989; Gans, 1997; Henry, 1997).

11. We assume that the Early Cenozoic *continental edge* formed a smooth curve from Vancouver Island, British Columbia to Manzanillo,

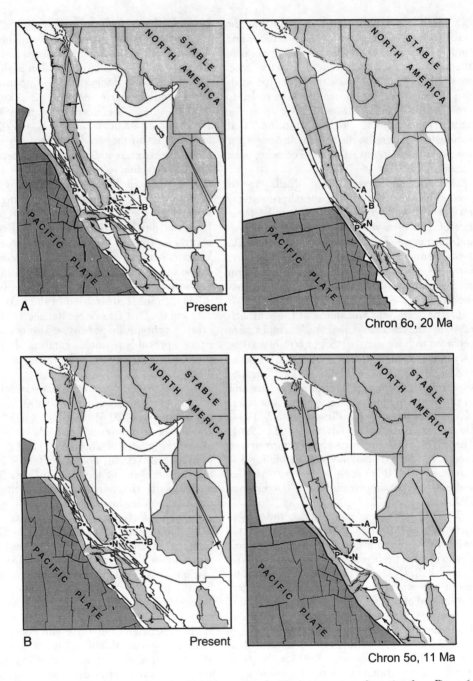

FIG. 7. A. Reconstruction for chron 6o, 20.1 Ma, compared with the present configuration from Figure 6. Individual continental elements (light grey) have been reconstructed using the relationships shown in Figure 6 and described in the text. Pacific seafloor with isochrons (dark grey) has been moved using the global-circuit solution for chron 6o, as illustrated in Figures 1, 2, 4, and 5. For reference, the dark line on left-hand image shows the location of isochron 6o within the present-day Pacific seafloor. B. Reconstruction for chron 5o, 10.9 Ma, compared with the present configuration from Figure 6. Individual continental elements (light grey) have been reconstructed using the relationships shown in Figure 6 and described in the text. Pacific seafloor with isochrons (dark grey) has been moved using the global-circuit solution for chron 5o, as illustrated in Figures 1, 2, and 5.

Mexico. Thus, reconstructions of some points along the continental edge can be used to estimate the placement of the rest of it.

Continental reconstructions and strain budgets

Figure 6 illustrates many of the constraints just described, and Figures 7A and 7B show our attempts to reconstruct North America and the Pacific plate using these constraints for chron 6o (20.1 Ma) and for chron 5o (10.9 Ma), respectively. There is only one complete path between stable North America and the Pacific plate along which we can attempt a quantitative reconstruction. This is the Colorado Plateau–central California path described in numbers 2–8, above. The approximate quantitative budgets for this path are listed in Table 3. We reconstruct the other parts of the Figure 7 maps using the other numbered observations and letting the unquantified regions take up the slack.

The coast-perpendicular budgets estimated in Table 3A constitute a very stringent constraint for mid-Cenozoic reconstructions. Indeed, the 24 Ma reconstruction can be made to fit along this path only if the largest allowed continental displacements are assumed (i.e., using point B in number 5). This very tight fit in the coast-perpendicular component is encouraging, suggesting that we are near to the actual solution. Furthermore, it implies that no significant additional area of the Pacific plate existed offshore at 24 Ma and has been subducted since that time.[1] This is a very important conclusion, as it allows us to use the present nearshore sea-floor patterns to describe the original Pacific–North America encounter, an assumption that is almost universally made. On the other hand, it does imply that layers imaged in coastal seismic refraction profiles that have been interpreted as underthrust Pacific plate (e.g., Page and Brocher, 1993) may need to be reinterpreted. They could, instead, be stalled pieces of the Farallon plate, or they could be mafic materials that were underplated onto the base of the continent during the opening of a slab window.

Ironically, by 8 Ma, the budget problem is reversed: significantly more coast-perpendicu-

lar deformation is implied by the post-8 Ma continental deformation than is needed to balance the plate motions. During this time interval, the Pacific plate reference point was outboard of the central Sierran–Great Valley block, so one way to resolve this difference would be to call on the block rotation advocated in number 4 and assume that that rotation occurred post-8 Ma.

For the coast-parallel budgets (Table 3B), the continental and oceanic totals are equivalent within the broad uncertainties of the continental data for ages younger than 18 Ma, as expected. In the fourth column ("Cent. San Andreas") we list the two alternative time-partitions of offset described in number 7 above. Note that the assumption that the offset on the San Andreas is mostly young (i.e., post-8 Ma) leads to a continental total (bottom row) that is too large.

Uncertainty concerning rotations of the Sierran–Great Valley block

An important uncertainty that arose several times in the above descriptions of continental deformations concerned the possible Cenozoic rotations of the Sierran–Great Valley block. Because of the important and pervasive implications of this problem, we reiterate and summarize it here. Paleomagnetic studies imply that since Cretaceous time, the main part of this block has not experienced a significant net rotation, but these results do not rule out any Cenozoic rotations that may have occurred but then were counteracted by other rotations in the opposite sense. Indeed, such a scenario might be expected, given the very different tectonic regimes of the Early and Late Cenozoic—Laramide subduction followed by San Andreas transtension (Walcott, 1993). Thus, at present we are quite free to postulate any convenient Neogene rotation for this block.

In our reconstructions, we assumed that the Paleogene continental edge (a subduction margin) formed a smooth curve; we accomplished this by assuming that the main Sierran–Great Valley block rotated ~5° counterclockwise during the Neogene (i.e., we rotate it back 5° clockwise to make our 20 Ma reconstruction). A rotation in the same sense may help explain to the triangular shape of the Santa Maria Basin, but we note here that the geometry of that basin actually suggests 15° to 30° of counterclock-

---

[1]The existence of such an area would require an even greater deformation within the continent in order to make room for it offshore.

wise Neogene rotation of its northeastern edge, depending on how the edges of the basin are chosen. Wernicke and Snow (1998) also mention a Neogene rotation of the Sierran–Great Valley block as a possible solution for the strain differences between their two reconstruction paths, but they call on a rotation in the opposite sense: 20° clockwise in the last 10 m.y. The situation is complicated by the likelihood that the southern end of the Sierran–Great Valley block has undergone major rotation—45° to 60° clockwise—apparently mostly in the early Miocene, and an internal deformation that is still ongoing.

Our present preference is to assume that the main Sierran–Great Valley block experienced a modest, late Neogene counterclockwise rotation, whereas the southern end experienced a major clockwise flexure, partly in early Miocene time in response to Mojave expansion and partly in the last 10 m.y. to satisfy the Wernicke and Snow reconstructions. We note, however, that this model is quite *ad hoc*. It mostly serves to emphasize the importance of obtaining more paleomagnetic information from Cenozoic rocks from all parts of the Sierran–Great Valley block.

Implications for northern and southern strain budgets

In Cascadia, north of the Sierran–Great Valley block, the coast-perpendicular deformation budget can be estimated by combining the central California solutions with the assumption of a smooth coastline described in number 11. This component of the deformation budget is fit very well by the Coast Range rotations, as has been noted by various authors, described in number 9. However, a substantial coast-parallel shortening, ~200 km since 16 Ma, also is mandated by the displacements of the Sierran–Great Valley block (as listed in the third column, labeled "Basin and Range," in Table 3B). To our knowledge, this aspect of the Sierran–Coast Range coupling has not previously been examined. Some of this shortening may have been accomplished by the thrust faults that surround the Olympic Peninsula and by a number of dextral shear zones that obliquely cross the Cascade arc (Snavely, 1987; Wells, 1990; Mann and Meyer, 1993). Furthermore, ongoing N-S compression is suggested by focal mechanisms and traces of active faults beneath the Puget Lowlands (Ludwin et al., 1991; Ma et al., 1996; Pratt et al., 1997). However, it remains to be seen whether NNW shortening on the order of 200 km can be documented.

In the Mexican portion of Figures 7A and 7B, we undo the oblique spreading that formed the Gulf of California, as described in number 10, and arbitrarily close up the Mexican Basin and Range province by the amount necessary to avoid overlap of Pacific oceanic plate with the continental crust of Baja California. We arbitrarily keep the Sierra Madre Occidental block in the middle of the Mexican Basin and Range province during these reconstructions. The correct placement for this block is unknown; it is clear that there has been major Neogene extension on both sides of the Sierra Madre Occidental, but present geologic data are insufficient to constrain the relative strain histories on the two sides (e.g., Gans, 1997; Henry, 1997). It should be noted that in our reconstructions (Figs. 7A and 7B), some of the expected coast-perpendicular extension occurs between chron 6o and chron 5o and some occurs after chron 5o time (i.e., after 10.9 Ma).

A quantitative discussion of the amount of coast-parallel slip offshore from the Mexican portion of the reconstructions is meaningful only for times since chron 5a (12.3 Ma), because prior to this time there was an active subduction zone immediately west of the southern half of the Baja California Peninsula (e.g., Stock and Hodges, 1989; Lonsdale, 1991). For times since 12 Ma, there is no obvious discrepancy between the coast-parallel slip determined from the plate circuit and that determined from summing the geological estimates (including closure of plate-boundary slip in the Gulf of California and postulated offset on the Pacific side of the Baja Peninsula, as described in number 10 above).

Creation and Evolution of Slab Windows beneath Western North America

An important and long-recognized consequence of the intersection of the East Pacific Rise with the North American subduction zone is the creation of slab-free regions, or "slab windows," beneath the continental plate. These windows, in turn, have been correlated to volcanic, uplift, and rifting events in the overriding plate (e.g., Dickinson and Snyder, 1979; Dickinson, 1997). However, there is no general agreement about the shapes of the windows, the relative robustness and importance of their various edges, their locations with respect to the overriding North America plate, or even what they actually represented in terms of the lateral variations in the region of the downgoing slab (e.g., Severinghaus and Atwater, 1990; Bohannon and Parsons, 1995). Thus, a careful analysis of the possible geometry of these windows seems warranted.

Breakup of the Farallon plate

During the Late Cretaceous, the Farallon-Pacific spreading system spanned 90 degrees of latitude and both plates were very large. During the Cenozoic, the Farallon plate has gradually broken up into various medium- and small-sized plates, as summarized in Atwater (1989). A break at about chron 24 (~52 Ma) spawned a semi-independent plate in the north, the Vancouver plate (the predecessor to the Juan de Fuca plate). This break occurred across a neck in the Farallon plate between the Pioneer and Murray fracture zones. The trace of this break—the Pacific-Farallon-Vancouver triple junction—is recorded in the isochron 23–13 pattern that presently stretches across the seafloor west of Monterey, California. It also can be seen as a subtle but distinct difference in trends of the Pioneer, Mendocino, and other northern fracture zones as compared to the trends of the Murray and all other fracture zones to the south. It appears that the new Vancouver plate remained somewhat coupled to the Farallon plate until chron 10y (28 Ma) because the directions and rates of the two plates continued to be quite similar (Rosa and Molnar, 1988). This first break probably did not create a significant slab window beneath the continent, but it did establish a weak zone for later, major breakage.

The isochron patterns in the seafloor just west of central California, shown in Figure 8, provide a detailed record of the approach, breakup, and demise of the East Pacific Rise in this area, as follows. By the mid-Cenozoic, the spreading center just south of the Pioneer fracture zone had come very near to the North American subduction zone. At the time of chron 10y (28 Ma), the last narrow section of

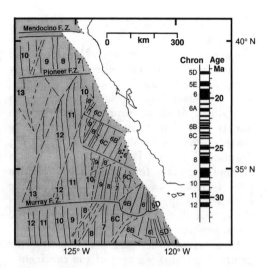

FIG. 8. Present-day seafloor isochron patterns and fracture zones mapped in the Pacific seafloor off central California, after Severinghaus and Atwater (1990). Heavy dotted line (at center) marks the location of the stalled Pacific-Monterey spreading center, after Lonsdale (1991). Labels are magnetic-reversal chron numbers. Magnetic-reversal time scale shows ages of the relevant chrons according to Cande and Kent (1995).

the intervening plate broke abruptly into two small plates—the Monterey and Arguello microplates (Atwater, 1970, 1989; Severinghaus and Atwater, 1990; Fernandez and Hey, 1991; Lonsdale 1991). We also, by somewhat arbitrary convention, change the name of the northern plate from the Vancouver plate to the Juan de Fuca plate at this time. Subduction became very slow in the adjacent subduction segment. The remaining larger oceanic plates to the north and south—the Juan de Fuca and Farallon plates—continued their fast subduction but became more erratic in their motions with respect to the Pacific plate and with respect to one another, suggesting that the contact between them had been lost (Wilson, 1988; Atwater, 1989).

The timing of this sudden breakup of the fast-subducting plates is quite important because of its on-land geologic implications. The changes in direction and rate are clearly recorded in the isochron patterns within the Pacific plate. They suggest that the breakup occurred between chrons 10 and 9, at ~28 Ma on the time scale of Cande and Kent (1995). This is 2 m.y. younger than generally reported previously, primarily because of revisions of the polarity-reversal time scale.

After the breakup, the Monterey and Arguello microplates continued to spread away from the Pacific, albeit slowly and obliquely, and to subduct beneath North America, also very slowly. At about chron 5E (~18 Ma) the last remnant of the Monterey-Pacific spreading center stalled and the Monterey microplate was "captured" by the Pacific plate. With this microplate capture, the Pacific–North America plate boundary was completed all along the coast from Cape Mendocino to Santa Lucia Bank, near Point Conception, a segment 700 km in length.

In our reconstructions, we assume that the central California segment of the continental rim has been rigidly attached to the Pacific plate and moving with it since the capture of the Monterey microplate at ~18 Ma. Although this is not the only possible assumption, we feel quite confident that it is valid. Significant strike-slip along the toe of the continent (i.e., between the Pacific plate and the continental edge) appears to be ruled out by the deep-seismic imaging of the Morro fracture zone beneath the continental shelf. If significant ocean-continent shear had occurred since its emplacement, this feature would no longer be aligned with its offshore counterpart (Nicholson et al., 1994).

Mid-Cenozoic slab window evolution

The fragmentation of the Farallon plate, as just described, is known from seafloor isochron patterns that have been mapped in the offshore Pacific plate. These patterns also have implications for the geometry of the breaks that must have occurred within the subducting plates that lay beneath North America. In Figure 9 we present images of the possible evolution of these subcontinental breaks and the resulting slab windows during their period of formation, 28 to 18 Ma. For these constructions, we assumed no slab dip. Various additional assumptions had to be made in order to construct each of the various portions of the windows (identified by the letters A through D on Figure 9B), with quite different resulting uncertainties, as follows.

Window region A. This window is the gap formed starting at 28 Ma, when the Monterey microplate broke off and moved southeast away

from the Juan de Fuca plate. An opening of this area in about this location is required by the isochron geometry. We feel most confident about the existence, location, and geometry of this part of the window.

Window region B. This is the slab-window region that would have formed starting at about chron 7 (26 Ma) if the Mendocino-Pioneer spreading-center segment entered the subduction zone directly, with no creation of microplates. Such a direct entry seems likely, since the Mendocino-Pioneer strip of the subducting plate was attached across the Mendocino fracture zone to the old, strong, easily subducted plate to the north. This geometry is similar to— and even more pronounced than—the present configuration of the South Chile Rise, where a segment of the spreading center is half subducted without any sign of slowing or breakage of the subducting plate (Herron et al., 1981; Tebbens et al., 1997). Alternatively, if a microplate did break off along the subducted Mendocino fracture zone (e.g., as postulated by Bohannon and Parsons, 1995), a slab-window region would still be formed with the area shown; its location would simply be shifted eastward. Furthermore, such a microplate, if it did form and attach itself to the Pacific plate, would have been surrounded by windows on the south and east and by a fast-subducting plate on the north, so it probably would not have stayed attached to the surface Pacific plate for long.

Window regions C and D. These two window regions are the least well located. They were drawn to illustrate the gaps that would have appeared somewhere in the downgoing slab after the Monterey and Arguello microplates broke away and slowed, assuming that the previously subducted parts of the Juan de Fuca and Farallon plates farther east remained intact and continued to subduct. We made the arbitrary assumption that the original break occurred along a line ~50 km inboard of the trench (grey serrated line containing "<" symbols in Fig. 9A). If the break had been closer to the trench, we assume that subduction would have stopped. Since the microplates continued to subduct, we suppose that the break occurred at or farther east than the position of this line. The assumption that the portions of the subducting slabs east of regions C and D remained intact is suspect, since they were quite young when they

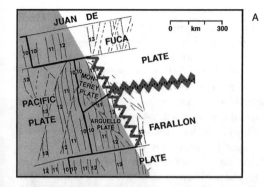

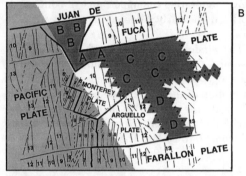

FIG. 9. Mid-Cenozoic slab-free window configurations, constructed using the seafloor isochron patterns shown in Figure 8 and assuming symmetrical spreading and no slab dip. A. Inferred plate configurations at chron 10y (28.3 Ma), the moment of formation of the Monterey and Arguello microplates. Light grey shows undersea regions. New plate breaks arbitrarily are assumed to have occurred along a transform fault between the microplates and along a line ~50 km beneath the lip of the continent (serrated grey line containing small "<" symbols), although the latter break line could have been located somewhat farther east. The break between the Juan de Fuca and Farallon plates is shown in its previously established position (wide, serrated grey line containing small "x" symbols). B. Inferred plate and window configurations at chron 6c (24.1 Ma). Light grey shows undersea regions, dark grey shows slab-window regions beneath the continent where no slab exists. Window edges: heavy lines = window edges located with some

confidence; serrated edges with "<" signs = window edges that were arbitrarily located in Figure 9A, then displaced with their respective plates; serrated grey edges containing "x" symbols = the inherited diffuse boundary between the Juan de Fuca and Farallon plates. Letters A through D refer to sections of the windows that are located with differing degrees of confidence, as discussed in the text. Only regions A and B are well located. C. Inferred plate and window configurations at chron 6y (19.0 Ma). Light grey shows undersea regions. Dark grey shows slab-window regions beneath the continent where no slab exists. Shading and window edges are the same as in Figure 9B.

subducted and thus had had little time beneath the ocean to cool and strengthen (Severinghaus and Atwater, 1990). Furthermore, in order to draw regions C and D, we assumed that the boundary between the two microplates was a transform fault in the direction of relative motion between the microplates and that the break between the rapidly subducting Juan de Fuca plate and the moderately rapidly subducting Farallon plate was in the middle of the Pioneer-Murray panel, utilizing the long-term Vancouver-Farallon break already established there (ragged grey region containing "x" symbols on Fig. 9B). These are the simplest geometric assumptions, but they are not necessarily correct. Given the arbitrary aspects of all these various assumptions, we conclude only that slab-free areas roughly equivalent to the spaces marked C and D should have appeared at about these latitudes at these times, at or to the east of the locations shown, but their actual locations and shapes are unknown.

Locations of slab windows with respect to North American features

The most interesting aspect of the slab windows is their possible causal relationship to tectonic features and events in the overriding North America plate. In Figure 10 we used our new circuit solutions to place the windows beneath our 20 Ma continental reconstruction, combining information from Figures 5, 7A, and 9. We do not know the dip of the mid-Cenozoic slab, but we supposed that it was similar to the 15° to 20° dip presently observed for the uppermost parts of the Cascadia slab (Crosson and Owens, 1987; Clowes et al., 1995) and of many other slabs (Jarrard, 1986). In fact, in Figure 10 we simulated an 18° slab dip by

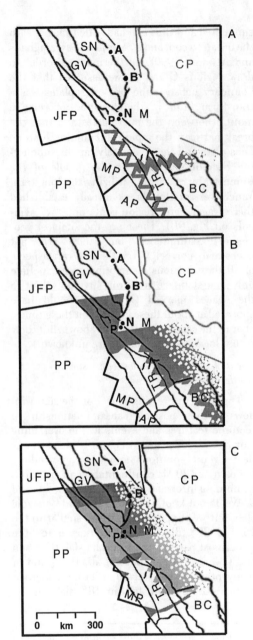

shortening the patterns from Figure 9 toward the coast by 5%. In general, the resulting windows lie beneath the Mojave Desert and southernmost Great Valley, as asserted by previous workers (e.g., Dokka and Ross, 1995; Dickinson, 1997, Dokka et al., 1998), although they extend farther north beneath the Sierran–Great Valley block than has been proposed previously. In detail, the placement depends upon the deformation, timing, and configuration of the Tehachapi Mountains, as described in number 6 above, reiterating the importance of continued work on the early Miocene tectonics in that area.

The windows in Figures 9 and 10 were drawn assuming that the coastline followed the Pacific plate westward—i.e., that the coast-perpendicular motion of the continental rim matched that of the Pacific plate. This motion amounted to ~65 km of continental expansion in the interval from 26 to 20 Ma. The earliest Miocene is a

FIG. 10. Mid-Cenozoic slab-window evolution with respect to the overriding North America plate. Slab-window shapes (grey shading) from Figure 9 are located beneath the 20 Ma reconstruction of continental elements from Figure 7A, using the circuit solutions of Figure 5 for coast-parallel placement and assuming that the continent expanded to keep pace with the coast-perpendicular motion of the oceanic plate. Oceanic plates: PP = Pacific plate; JFP = Juan de Fuca plate; MP = Monterey plate; AP = Arguello plate. Continental elements: SN and GV = Sierran–Great Valley block; CP = Colorado Plateau; BC = Baja California; TR = western Transverse Ranges in their pre-rotated position; A and B = Basin and Range reconstruction points; P and N = the Pinnacles and Neenach points for San Andreas fault reconstruction, all as illustrated in Figures 6 and 7 and described in numbers 5 and 7 in the text. Window shapes have been shortened 5% toward the coast to simulate an 18° slab dip and are shown fading out to the east to simulate loss of contact between the slab and overriding plate. Note that because pre-20 Ma continental deformation is not included in these figures, the positions of the slab elements relative to North American geological features are progressively more uncertain going back in time. A. Configuration at chron 10y (28.3 Ma), showing breaks in the slab inferred to have formed when the Monterey and Arguello microplates separated from the larger plates. B. Configuration at chron 6c (24.1 Ma). Dark grey tone shows the window regions that developed from 28 to 24 Ma beneath North America. C. Configuration at chron 6y (19.0 Ma). The Pacific-Monterey spreading center is about to stall. Dark grey tone shows the new window regions that developed from 24 to 19 Ma beneath North America; light grey tone shows slab-free regions formed earlier. From this time on, only the northern, Mendocino edge is believed to be a significant geologic factor. The underthrust Monterey microplate (white space beneath TR) has reached its maximum extent prior to its "capture" by the Pacific plate, although its eastern edge may have extended farther east if the chron 10y plate break occurred farther beneath the continental edge than assumed in Figure 9A.

time of large-magnitude detachment-style extension in the Mojave Desert (e.g., Dokka, 1986, 1989; Walker et al., 1990, 1995; Fletcher et al., 1995; Ingersoll et al., 1996; Fillmore and Walker, 1996) and abrupt deepening of the southernmost San Joaquin Valley (Davis and Legoe, 1988; Goodman et al., 1989; Graham et al., 1990; Goodman and Malin, 1992), so a continental expansion at this time seems likely. However, since the details of the early Miocene continental deformation have not been quantified, we used our 20 Ma reconstruction for all the reconstructions in Figure 10, recognizing that this is only a crude approximation. Also, we drew the continental edge as straight, but noted that a local bulge in the coastline, possibly formed during this early localized extension, would permit the granites that are now in the Salinian block to have been pulled west of the main Cretaceous batholithic belt, in a position where they could easily be sliced off and carried northwestward along the coast (e.g., Mattinson and James, 1985; Mattinson, 1990; James, 1992).

The configurations shown in Figure 10 were placed assuming an 18° slab dip. The subducting Farallon and Vancouver slabs are thought to have re-established a standard dipping configuration by this time (following a postulated Laramide flat-slab episode), but if the dip were steeper or shallower than 18°, all window patterns in Figure 10 must be shifted westward or eastward, respectively. Also, as the slabs descended into the mantle, they would have lost contact with the overriding plate at some point. This phenomenon is depicted as speckled fadeouts along the right-hand sides of Figure 10, but we do not know how far inland this actually occurred. Furthermore, we assume that as a slab window forms, asthenosphere rises to fill the gap and freezes onto the continental underside. Thus, the effective geologic life span of a given portion of a window should be short. To illustrate this, Figure 10C shows the older slab-window regions as light grey and only the youngest portions as dark grey. In any event, we conclude that after about chron 6o time (20 Ma) the only geologically relevant slab-window edge beneath the United States was the northern, Mendocino edge.

Coming forward in time, the Mendocino slab-window edge migrated northward with the Pacific plate. In Figure 11 we construct the time displacement of this edge with respect to the Sierran–Great Valley block. We drew these displacements by combining the motions of the Pacific plate implied by our circuits with the motions of the Sierran–Great Valley block described by Wernicke and Snow (1998), and since the rotation of the main Sierran–Great Valley block is uncertain, we assumed no rotation for this construction. After 6 Ma the motion of the Juan de Fuca–Gorda plate with respect to the Pacific plate shifted from eastward to ESE, changing the direction of subduction. We adopt the careful analysis of Wilson (1989) of these plate-motion changes and the resulting shapes of the 6, 4, 2, and 0 Ma edges of the downgoing slab.[2] The most noteworthy aspect of our successive reconstructions (Fig. 11) is that from 4 Ma to the present, the slab edge is stationary beneath the Sierran–Great Valley block at a (present) latitude of ~39.5° N, just north of Sutter Buttes.

One other interesting aspect of the constructions in Figure 10 is the configuration of the underthrust Monterey microplate (white region beneath the western Transverse Ranges [TR] in Figs. 10B and 10C). This microplate is interpreted to have stalled and attached itself to the Pacific plate at ~18 Ma. The subsequent displacement of this flap of Pacific plate beneath the western Transverse Ranges block is suggested by Nicholson et al. (1994) to have caused the unusual rotation of the overriding block. Furthermore, the underthrust plate area shown in Figure 10C is the minimum area of oceanic microplate underthrust. Some of this oceanic plate might still be present beneath southern California today, and it may be the piece of oceanic lithosphere postulated to be presently descending into the mantle beneath the western Transverse Ranges and northwestern Mojave Desert (Bird and Rosenstock, 1984; Humphreys, 1995).

Discussion

Our ultimate objective in determining the Pacific–North America plate reconstructions is to compare them to the geology within the

---

[2]The differences between our map view and that of Wilson arose because we added the motion of the Sierran–Great Valley block with respect to stable North America.

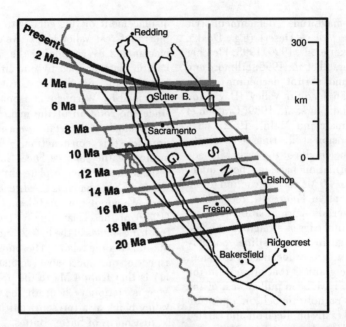

FIG. 11. Placement of the Mendocino edge of the subducting Juan de Fuca plate beneath the Sierran–Great Valley block, from 20 Ma to present. Drift of oceanic plates is interpolated from our circuit solutions; displacement of the Sierran–Great Valley block is drawn following Wernicke and Snow (1998); the shape of the Mendocino edges from 6 to 0 Ma is from Wilson (1989). Light grey coastline and state boundaries are given in their present-day locations for orientation purposes only.

North American continent. Particular emphasis is on two issues—(1) the relationship of the plate displacements to the magnitude and direction of continental extension and shear and (2) the relationship of the slab windows to the tectonics of the overlying plate.

Our results do suggest a close relationship between the relative Pacific–North America plate displacements and the magnitude and direction of continental extension in the Basin and Range province. The most recent update of the history of extension at the latitude of Las Vegas, Nevada is given by Wernicke and Snow (1998) in this issue from integrating the displacement direction and timing of various normal and strike-slip fault systems between the Sierra Nevada of California and the Colorado Plateau. These geological observations show that the direction of motion of the Sierran–Great Valley block, relative to the Colorado Plateau, was approximately E-W during the interval from 16 to 10 Ma, and then changed to become more northwesterly from 10 Ma to the present. The exact direction of northwest motion varied with latitude, but, nevertheless,

the northwestward change of the displacement direction at ~10 Ma is quite striking. We speculate that this 10 Ma change may correlate with the chron 4 northward change in direction of relative motion between the Pacific and North America plates (Fig. 2). The uncertainties in the geological data are such that this change in direction of slip within the Basin and Range province could have occurred at chron 4 (8 Ma, rather than 10 Ma). Note that we do not expect the direction of extension in the Basin and Range province to exactly match the plate-motion direction either before or after the clockwise change in plate motion, because some of the plate-boundary deformation was taken up on the San Andreas and related faults.

The slab windows shown in Figure 10 were drawn assuming that the slabs had an 18° dip and were rigid. In any interpretation of the relationship of the slab windows to the geology of the overlying North America plate, it must be remembered that: (1) the paleo-dip of the slabs is not known, so that the boundaries of the windows could be shifted somewhat to the east or to the west; and (2) the downgoing plate may not have been rigid; it may have undergone plastic deformation and stretching and contortion in the vicinity of the slab windows. Thus, despite the precision with which we can reconstruct the relevant plate motions and the expected slab-window shapes, the locations of the slab-window edges may never be very well known, especially in their E-W placements.

The interrelationship of the plate-boundary geometry with plate-margin volcanism is also an interesting issue. This relationship has been recently summarized by Dickinson (1997). Our updated Pacific–North America plate circuit does not fundamentally change any of his conclusions, since the positions of the triple junctions along the margin are similar to previous estimates (Stock and Molnar, 1988).

Conclusions

We present a new global-plate-circuit solution for the Late Cenozoic displacement of the Pacific plate with respect to North America. The new reconstruction for "global chron" 5 (10.9 Ma) matches the previous solution very closely, but those for "global chrons" 6 and 13 (20.1 and 33.1 Ma, respectively) are significantly changed. We also include reconstructions for some intervening semi-interpolated chrons to augment the solution. The resulting displacement path is much smoother, in both rate and azimuth, than previous solutions, and at the young end it agrees quite precisely with the semi-independent NUVEL-1A solution.

Our best solution for the displacement of a point on the Pacific plate, now near the Mendocino triple junction, relative to stable North America, is that from 30 to 12 Ma the point was displaced along an azimuth of ~N60°W, at a rate of ~33 mm/yr; from 12 Ma to ~8 Ma the azimuth of displacement still was about N60°W, but the rate was faster, ~52 mm/yr; and since 8 Ma the point was displaced along an azimuth of N37°W at a rate of ~52 mm/yr.

Our solutions for the latitude of central California include a distinct direction change at chron 4 time (~8 Ma), from more offshore to more coast-parallel. Previous models included a similar change and the onsets of various compressive events in coastal California have been attributed to that change. However, the change was generally believed to have occurred in Pliocene time, whereas we calculate the primary change to have taken place at ~8 Ma, which is distinctly older.

Our new circuit solutions yield coast-parallel displacements through time that are quite similar to those predicted by previous models. On the other hand, for times older than 10 Ma, we calculate significantly greater coast-perpendicular displacements than in previous models. We calculate more than 300 km of coast-perpendicular displacement since chron 6c (24 Ma), which, in turn, requires a Neogene coast-perpendicular expansion of the North American continental lithosphere of 300 km or more. Our reconstructions and space budgets thus rely quite heavily upon the very large magnitude extensions reported and quantified for the detachment-faulted terranes of the Basin and Range province by Wernicke and Snow (1998) in this issue. Indeed, our results require these large deformations in order to avoid the unacceptable overlaps of oceanic and continental lithosphere that otherwise result.

Our reconstructions place the early Pacific–North America plate contact region in southern California. The final reconstruction of mid-Cenozoic North America thus particularly depends upon the deformation budgets of the Mojave region and of the southernmost part of the Sierra Nevada block. The future quantification of the Neogene deformation of these regions, presently a subject replete with controversy, takes on even more urgency.

At present, a quantitative reconstruction of the mid-Cenozoic continent can be attempted only along one path—stepping from stable North America to the Colorado Plateau to the Sierran–Great Valley block to the central California margin. The fact that this reconstruction path gives a deformation budget quite similar to the one independently derived via the oceanic circuit gives us confidence that we are on the right track. A single additional assumption—that the margin of the continent had a smooth shape inherited from the preceding subduction era—allows us to make estimates for the deformation budgets in regions to the north and south. In the north, we predict a substantial (~200 km) coast-parallel shortening in addition to the long-recognized rotations of the Cascadia Coast Ranges. In Mexico, the budgets require percentages of coast-perpendicular expansion similar to those known from the Basin and Range province in the United States, both east and west of the Sierra Madre Occidental block.

We use isochron patterns in the Pacific plate to trace the evolution of the Farallon, Juan de Fuca, Monterey, and Arguello plates during their mid-Cenozoic interaction with the rim of North America. From these patterns, we construct potential shapes and sizes of the resulting "slab windows" beneath the continent. Our reconstructions place the most robust window beneath the Mojave region during the 26 to 19 Ma time step, reinforcing suggestions that the early Miocene volcanism and extension of this region may have resulted from asthenospheric upwelling into a sublithospheric slab window there.

Finally, we examined the 20 to 0 Ma drift of the Mendocino slab window edge beneath California by combining our circuit solutions for Pacific plate motions with a construction by Wilson of the shape of the southern edge of the subducted Juan de Fuca–Gorda plate and with the estimates of Wernicke and Snow for the motions of the Sierran–Great Valley block. This analysis suggests that the edge migrated north quite steadily until 4 Ma, at which time it stalled with respect to the Sierran–Great Valley block just north of Sutter Buttes.

Acknowledgments

We thank Brian Wernicke and J. Kent Snow for allowing us to use their results in advance of publication. We thank Gene Humphreys, John Crowell, Bruce Luyendyk, Craig Nicholson, Gary Axen, Michael Singer, and Marcy Davis for helpful reviews and Brian Wernicke, Doug Wilson, Gene Humphreys, Rob Twiss, Bob Butler, Wayne Thatcher, and Peter Weigand for helpful conversations, advice, and suggestions. We thank the Hall Symposium participants for lively feedback and Gary Ernst for his reviews, advice, and patient good humor. This work was supported by NSF Grant EAR-9614674 to J. Stock. California Institute of Technology, Division of Geological and Planetary Sciences, Contribution No. 8534.

REFERENCES

Atwater, T. M., 1970, Implications of plate tectonics for the Cenozoic tectonic evolution of western North America: Geol. Soc. Amer. Bull., v. 81, p. 3513–3536.

————, 1989, Plate tectonic history of the northeast Pacific and western North America, *in* Winterer, E. L., Hussong, D. M., and Decker, R. W., eds., The geology of North America, v. N: The northeastern Pacific Ocean and Hawaii: Boulder, CO, Geol. Soc. Amer., p. 21–72.

Atwater, T. M., and Severinghaus, J. P., 1989, Tectonic maps of the northeast Pacific, *in* Winterer, E. L., Hussong, D. M., and Decker, R. W., eds., The geology of North America, v. N: The northeastern Pacific Ocean and Hawaii: Boulder, CO, Geol. Soc. Amer., p. 15–20.

Bawden, G. W., Donnellan, A., Kellogg, L. H., Dong, D., and Rundle, J. B., 1997, Geodetic measurements of horizontal strain near the White Wolf fault, Kern County, California: Jour. Geophys. Res., v. 102, p. 4957–4968.

Bennett, R. A., Wernicke, B. P., and Davis, J. L., 1998, Continuous G. P. S. measurements of contemporary deformation across the northern Basin and Range province: Geophys. Res. Lett., v. 25, p. 563–566.

Bird, P., and Rosenstock, R. W., 1984, Kinematics of present crust and mantle flow in southern California: Geol. Soc. Amer. Bull., v. 95, p. 946–957.

Bohannon, R. G., and Parsons, T., 1995, Tectonic implications of post–30 Ma Pacific and North American relative plate motions: Geol. Soc. Amer. Bull., v. 107, p. 937–959.

Cande, S. C., and Kent, D. V., 1992, A new geomagnetic polarity time scale for the Late Cretaceous and Cenozoic: Jour. Geophys. Res., v. 97, p. 13,917–13,951.

————, 1995, Revised calibration of the geomagnetic polarity time scale for the Late Cretaceous and Cenozoic: Jour. Geophys. Res., v. 100, p. 6093–6096.

Cande, S. C., Raymond, C. A., Stock, J., and Haxby, W. F., 1995, Geophysics of the Pitman fracture zone and Pacific-Antarctic plate motions during the Cenozoic: Science, v. 270, p. 947–953.

Chang, T., 1988, Estimating the relative rotation of two tectonic plates from boundary crossings: Jour. Amer. Stat. Assoc., v. 83, p. 1178–1183.

Chang, T., Stock, J., and Molnar, P., 1990, The rotation group in plate tectonics and the representation of uncertainties of plate reconstructions: Geophys. Jour. Int., v. 101, p. 649–661.

Chapin, C. E., and Cather, S. M., 1994, Tectonic setting of the axial basins of the northern and central Rio Grande rift, *in* Keller, C. G., and Cather, S. M.., eds., Basins of the Rio Grande rift: Structure, stratigraphy, and tectonic setting: Geol. Soc. Amer. Spec. Pap. 291, p. 5–25.

Clowes, R. M., Zelt, C. A., Amor, J. R., and Ellis, R. M., 1995, Lithospheric structure in the southern Canadian Cordillera from a network of seismic refraction lines: Can. Jour. Earth Sci., v. 32, p. 1485–1513.

Cox, A., and Engebretson, D., 1985, Change in motion of the Pacific plate at 5 Myr BP: Nature, v. 313, p. 472–474.

Crittenden, M. D., Jr., Coney, P.J., and Davis, G. H., eds., 1980, Cordilleran metamorphic core complexes: Geol. Soc. Amer. Memoir 153, 490 p.

Crosson, R. S., and Owens, T. J., 1987, Slab geometry of the Cascadia subduction zone beneath Washington from earthquake hypocenters and teleseismic converted waves: Geophys. Res. Lett., v. 14, p. 824–827.

Crouch, J. K., and Suppe, J., 1993, Late Cenozoic tectonic evolution of the Los Angeles basin and California Borderland: A model for core complex-like crustal extension: Geol. Soc. Amer. Bull., v. 105, p. 1415–1434.

Crough, S. T., and Thompson, G. A., 1977, Upper mantle origin of the Sierra Nevada uplift: Geology, v. 5, p. 396–399.

Davis, T. L., and Legoe, M. B., 1988, A structural interpretation of major tectonic events affecting the western and southern margins of the San Joaquin Valley, California, in Graham, S. A., ed., Studies of the geology of the San Joaquin basin: Los Angeles, Pacific Sect. Soc. Econ. Paleontol. Mineral., p. 65–87.

DeMets, D. C., 1995, A reappraisal of seafloor spreading lineations in the Gulf of California—implications for the transfer of Baja California to the Pacific plate and estimates of Pacific–North America motion: Geophys. Res. Lett., v. 22, p. 3545–3548.

DeMets, D. C., Gordon, R. G., and Stein, S., 1994, Effects of recent revisions to the geomagnetic-reversal time scale on estimates of current plate motions: Geophys. Res. Lett., v. 21, p. 2191–2194.

Dickinson, W. R., 1996, Kinematics of transrotational tectonism in the California Transverse Ranges and its contribution to cumulative slip along the San Andreas transform fault system: Geol. Soc. Amer. Spec. Pap. 305.

————, 1997, Tectonic implications of Cenozoic volcanism in coastal California: Geol. Soc. Amer. Bull., v. 109, p. 936–954.

Dickinson, W. R., and Snyder, W. S., 1979, Geometry of triple junctions related to San Andreas transform: Jour. Geophys. Res., v. 84, p. 561–572.

Dickinson, W. R., and Wernicke, B. P., 1997, Reconciliation of San Andreas slip discrepancy by a combination of interior Basin and Range extension and transrotation near the coast: Geology, v. 25, p. 663–665.

Dixon, T. H., Robaudo, S., Lee, J., and Reheis, M. C., 1995, Constraints on present-day Basin and Range deformation from space geodesy: Tectonics, v. 14, p. 755–772.

Dokka, R. K., 1986, Patterns and modes of early Miocene crustal extension, central Mojave Desert, California, in Meyer, L., ed., Extensional tectonics of the Southwestern United States: A perspective on processes and kinematics: Geol. Soc. Amer. Spec. Pap. 208, p. 75–95.

————, 1989, The Mojave extensional belt of southern California: Tectonics, v. 8, p. 363–390.

Dokka, R. K., and Ross, T. M., 1995, Collapse of southwestern North America and the evolution of early Miocene detachment faults, metamorphic core complexes, the Sierra Nevada orocline, and the San Andreas fault system: Geology, v. 23, p. 1075–1078.

Dokka, R. K., Ross, T. M., and Lu, G., 1998, The trans-Mojave–Sierran shear zone and its role in Early Miocene collapse of southwestern North America, in Hodsworth, B., Dewye, J., and Strachan, R., eds., Continental transpressional and transtensional tectonics: Geol. Soc. Lond. Spec. Publ. (in press).

Engebretson, D. C., Cox, A., and Gordon, R. G., 1985, Relative motions between oceanic and continental plates in the Pacific basin: Geol. Soc. Amer. Spec. Pap. 206, 59 p.

Fernandez, L. S., and Hey, R. N., 1991, Late Tertiary tectonic evolution of the seafloor spreading system off the coast of California between the Mendocino and Murray fracture zones: Jour. Geophys. Res., v. 96, p. 17,955–17,979.

Feigl, K. L., Agnew, D. C., Bock, Y., Dong, D., Donnellan, A., Hager, B. H., Herring, T. A., Jackson, D. D., Jordan, T. H., King, R. W., Larsen, K. M., Murray, M. H., Shen, Z., and Webb, F. H., 1993, Space geodetic measurement of crustal deformation in central and southern California, 1984–1992: Jour. Geophys. Res., v. 98, p. 21,677–21,712.

Fillmore, R. P., and Walker, J. D., 1996, Evolution of a supradetachment extensional basin: The Lower Miocene Pickhandle basin, central Mojave Desert, California, in Beratan, K. K., ed., Reconstructing the history of Basin and Range extension using sedimentology and stratigraphy: Geol. Soc. Amer. Spec. Pap. 303, p. 107–126.

Fletcher, J. M., Bartley, J. M., Martin, M. W., Glazner, A. F., and Walker, J. D., 1995, Large-magnitude continental extension: An example from the central Mojave metamorphic core complex: Geol. Soc. Amer. Bull., v. 107, p. 1468–1483.

Frei, L. S., 1986, Additional paleomagnetic results from the Sierra Nevada: Further constraints on Basin and Range extension and northward displacement in the western United States: Geol. Soc. Amer. Bull., v. 97, p. 840–849.

Frei, L. S., Magill, J. R., and Cox, A., 1984, Paleomagnetic results from the central Sierra Nevada: Constraints on reconstructions of the western United States: Tectonics, v. 3, p. 157–177.

Gans, P. B., 1997, Large-magnitude Oligo-Miocene extension in southern Sonora: Implications for the tectonic evolution of northwest Mexico: Tectonics, v. 16, p. 388–408.

Glazner, A. F., Bartley, J. M., and Ingersoll, R. V., 1996, Collapse of southwestern North America and the evolution of early Miocene detachment faults, metamorphic core complexes, the Sierra Nevada orocline, and the San Andreas fault system: Comment and Reply: Geology, v. 24, p. 858–860.

Goodman, E. D., and Malin, P. E., 1992, Evolution of the southern San Joaquin basin and mid-Tertiary "transitional" tectonics, central California: Tectonics, v. 11, p. 478–498.

Goodman, E. D., Malin, P. E., Ambos, E. L., and Crowell, J. C., 1989, The southern San Joaquin Valley as an example of Cenozoic basin evolution in California, in Price, R. A., ed., Origin and evolution of sedimentary basins and their energy and mineral resources: Amer. Geophys. Union, Geophys. Monog. 48, IUGC series 4, p. 87–107.

Graham, S. A., Decelles, P. G., Carroll, A. R., and Goodman, E. D., 1990, Middle Tertiary contractile, uplift, extension, and rotation in the San Emigdio range, southern California: Amer. Assoc. Petrol. Geol. Bull., v. 74, p. 665.

Harbert, W., 1991, Late Neogene relative motion of the Pacific and North America plates: Tectonics, v. 10, p. 1–15.

Henry, C. D., 1997, Tie between proto-Gulf and Basin and Range extension in northwestern Mexico: Trans. Amer. Geophys. Union (EOS), v. 78, no. 46, fall meeting supplement, p. F843.

Herron, E. M., Cande, S. C., and Hall, B. R., 1981, An active spreading center collides with a subduction zone: A geophysical survey of the Chile margin triple junction, in Kulm, L. D., Dymond, J., Dasch, E. J., and Hussong, D. M., eds., Nazca plate: Crustal formation and Andean convergence: Geol. Soc. Amer. Memoir 154, p. 683–701.

Hornafius, J. S., Luyendyk, B. P., Terres, R. R., and Kamerling, M. J., 1986, Timing and extent of Neogene tectonic rotation in the western Transverse Ranges, California: Geol. Soc. Amer. Bull., v. 97, p. 1476–1487.

Humphreys, E. D., 1995, Post-Laramide removal of the Farallon slab, western United States: Geology, v. 23, p. 987–990.

Ingersoll, R. V., Devaney, K. A., Geslin, J. K., Cavazza, W., Diamond, D. S., Heins, W. A., Jagiello, K. J., Marsaglia, K. M., Paylor, E. D., II, and Short, P. F., 1996, The Mud Hills, Mojave Desert, California: Structure, stratigraphy, and sedimentology of a rapidly extended terrane, in Beratan, K. K., ed., Reconstructing the history of Basin and Range

extension using sedimentology and stratigraphy: Geol. Soc. Amer. Spec. Pap. 303, p. 61–84.

James, E. W., 1992, Cretaceous metamorphism and plutonism in the Santa Cruz Mountains, Salinian block, California, and correlation with the southernmost Sierra Nevada: Geol. Soc. Amer. Bull., v. 104, p. 1326–1339.

Jarrard, R. D., 1986, Relations among subduction parameters: Rev. Geophys., v. 24, p. 217–284.

Kamerling, M. J., and Luyendyk, B. P., 1985, Paleomagnetism and Neogene tectonics of the northern Channel Islands, California: Jour. Geophys. Res., v. 90, p. 12,485–12,502.

Kanter, L. R., and McWilliams, M. O., 1982, Rotation of the southernmost Sierra Nevada, California: Jour. Geophys. Res., v. 87, p. 3819–3830.

Klitgord, K. D., and Schouten, H., 1986, Plate kinematics of the Central Atlantic, in Vogt, P. R., and Tucholke, B. E., eds., The geology of North America, v. M: The western North Atlantic region: Boulder, CO, Geol. Soc. Amer.

Legg, M. R., 1991, Developments in understanding the tectonic evolution of the California Continental Borderland, in Osborne, R. H., ed., From shoreline to abyss: Soc. Econ. Paleontol. Mineral., Spec. Publ. 46, p. 291–312.

Lonsdale, P., 1991, Structural patterns of the Pacific floor offshore of Peninsular California, in Dauphin, J. P., and Simoneit, B. R. T., eds., Gulf and Peninsular provinces of the Californias: Amer. Assoc. Petrol. Geol. Memoir 47, p. 87–125.

Ludwin, R. S., Weaver, C. S., and Crosson, R. S., 1991, Seismicity of Washington and Oregon, in Slemmons, D. B., Engdahl, E. R., Zoback, M. D., and Blackwell, D. D., eds., The geology of North America: Neotectonics of North America: Boulder, CO: Geol. Soc. Amer., p. 77–98.

Luyendyk, B. P., 1991, A model for Neogene crustal rotations, transtension, and transpression in southern California: Geol. Soc. Amer. Bull., v. 103, p. 1528–1536.

Lyle, M., and Ness, G., 1991, The opening of the southern Gulf of California, in Dauphin, J. P., and Simoneit, B. R. T., eds., Gulf and Peninsular provinces of the Californias: Amer. Assoc. Petrol. Geol. Memoir 47, p. 403–423.

Ma, L., Crosson, R., and Ludwin, R., 1996, Western Washington earthquake focal mechanisms and their relationship to regional tectonic stress, in Rogers, A. M., Walsh, T. J., Kockelman, W. J., and Priest, G. R., eds., Assessing earthquake hazards and reducing risk in the Pacific Northwest: U. S. Geol. Surv. Prof. Pap. 1560, p. 257–283.

Magill, J., and Cox, A., 1981, Post-Oligocene tectonic rotation of the Oregon western Cascade Range and the Klamath mountains: Geology, v. 9, p. 127–131.

Mann, G. M., and Meyer, C. E., 1993, Late Cenozoic structure and correlations to seismicity along the Olympic-Wallowa lineament, northwest United States: Geol. Soc. Amer. Bull., v. 105, p. 853–871.

Matthews, V., III, 1976, Correlation of Pinnacles and Neenach volcanic formations and their bearing on the San Andreas problem: Amer. Assoc. Petrol. Geol. Bull., v. 60, p. 2128–2141.

Mattinson, J. M., 1990, Petrogenesis and evolution of the Salinian magmatic arc, in Anderson, J. L., ed., The nature and origin of cordilleran magmatism: Geol. Soc. Amer. Memoir 174, p. 237–250.

Mattinson, J. M., and James, E. W., 1985, Salinian block U/Pb age and isotopic variations: Implications for origin and emplacement of the Salinian terranes, in Howell, D. G., ed., Tectonostratigraphic terranes of the Circum-Pacific Region: Circum-Pacific Council for Energy and Mineral Resources, Earth Science Series, v. 1, p. 215–226.

McCulloch, D. S., 1989, Evolution of the offshore central California margin, in Winterer, E. L., Hussong, D. M., and Decker, R. W., eds., Geology of North America, v. N: The eastern Pacific Ocean and Hawaii: Boulder, CO, Geol. Soc. Amer., p. 439–470.

McIntosh, K. D., Reed, D. L., Silver, E. A., and Meltzer, A. S., 1991, Deep structure and structural inversion along the central California continental margin from EDGE seismic profile RU-3: Jour. Geophys. Res., v. 96, p. 6459–6473.

McWilliams, M. O., and Li, Y., 1985, Oroclinal bending of the southern Sierra Nevada batholith: Science, v. 230, p. 172–175.

Nicholson, C., Sorlien, C. C., Atwater, T., Crowell, J. C., and Luyendyk, B. P., 1994, Microplate capture, rotation of the western Transverse Ranges, and initiation of the San Andreas transform as a low-angle fault system: Geology, v. 22, p. 491–495.

Page, B. M., and Brocher, T. M., 1993, Thrusting of the central California margin over the edge of the Pacific plate during the transform regime: Geology, v. 21, p. 635–638.

Page, B. M., and Engebretson, D. C., 1984, Correlation between the geologic record and computed plate motions for central California: Tectonics, v. 3, p. 133–155.

Plescia, J. B., Calderone, G. J., and Snee, L. W., 1994, Paleomagnetic analysis of Miocene basalt flows in the Tehachapi Mountains, California: U.S. Geol. Surv. Bull. 2100, 11 p.

Pollitz, F. F., 1986, Pliocene change in Pacific plate motion: Trans. Amer. Geophys. Union (EOS), v. 66, p. 1062.

Pratt, T. L., Johnson, S., Potter, C., Stephenson, W., and Finn, C., 1997, Seismic reflection images beneath Puget Sound, western Washington State: The Puget

Lowland thrust sheet hypothesis: Jour. Geophys. Res., v. 102, p. 27,469–27,489.

Rosa, J. W. C., and Molnar, P., 1988, Uncertainties in reconstructions of the Pacific, Farallon, Vancouver, and Kula plates and constraints on the rigidity of the Pacific and Farallon (and Vancouver) plates between 72 and 34 Ma: Jour. Geophys. Res., v. 93, p. 2997–3008.

Royer, J.-Y., and Chang, T., 1991, Evidence for relative motions between the Indian and Australian plates during the last 20 m.y. from plate tectonic reconstructions: Implications for deformation of the Indo-Australian plate: Jour. Geophys. Res., v. 96, p. 11,779–11,802.

Sandwell, D. T., and Smith, W. F., 1997, Marine gravity anomaly from Geosat and ERS-1 satellite altimetry: Jour. Geophys. Res., v. 102, p. 10,039–10,054.

Sims, J. D., 1993, Chronology of displacement on the San Andreas fault in central California: Evidence from reversed positions of exotic rock bodies near Parkfield, California, in Powell, R. E., Weldon, R.J., II, and Matti J. C., eds., The San Andreas fault system: Displacement, palinspastic reconstruction, and geologic evolution: Geol. Soc. Amer. Memoir 178, p. 231–256.

Severinghaus, J., and Atwater, T. M., 1990, Cenozoic geometry and thermal state of the subducting slabs beneath North America, in Wernicke, B. P., ed., Basin and Range extensional tectonics near the latitude of Las Vegas: Geol. Soc. Amer. Memoir 176, p. 1–22.

Snavely, P. D., Jr., 1987, Tertiary geologic framework, neotectonics, and petroleum potential of the Oregon-Washington continental margin, in Scholl, D. W., Grantz, A., and Vedder, J. G., eds., Geology and resource potential of the continental margin of western North America and adjacent ocean basins— Beaufort Sea to Baja California: Circum-Pacific Council for Energy and Mineral Resources, Earth Sci. Series, v. 6, p. 305–335.

Snow, J. K., and Wernicke, B. P., 1998, Cenozoic tectonism in the central Basin and Range: Magnitude, rate, and distribution of upper crustal strain: Amer. Jour. Sci., in review.

Spencer, J. E., and Normark, W. R., 1979, Tosco-Abreojos fault zone: A Neogene transform plate boundary within the Pacific margin of southern Baja California, Mexico: Geology, v. 7, p. 554–557.

Stock, J. M., and Hodges, K. V., 1989, Pre-Pliocene extension around the Gulf of California and the transfer of Baja California to the Pacific plate: Tectonics, v. 8, p. 99–115.

Stock, J. M., and Molnar, P., 1988, Uncertainties and implications of the Late Cretaceous and Tertiary position of North America relative to the Farallon,

Kula, and Pacific plates: Tectonics, v. 7, p. 1339–1384.

Tebbens, S., Cande, S. C., Kovacs, L., Parra, J. C., LaBrecque, J. L., and Vergara, H., 1997, The Chile Ridge: A tectonic framework: Jour. Geophys. Res., v. 102, p. 12,035–12,059.

Walcott, D., 1993, Neogene tectonics and kinematics of western North America: Tectonics, v. 12, p. 326–333.

Walker, J. D., Bartley, J. M., and Glazner, A., 1990, Large-magnitude Miocene extension in the Central Mojave Desert: Implications for Paleozoic to Tertiary paleogeography and tectonics: Jour. Geophys. Res., v. 95, p. 557–569.

Walker, J. D., Fletcher, J. M., Fillmore, R. P., Martin, M. W., Taylor, W. J., Glazner, A., and Bartley, J. M., 1995, Connection between igneous activity and extension in the central Mojave metamorphic core complex, California: Jour. Geophys. Res., v. 100, p. 10,477–10,494.

Wells, R. E., 1990, Paleomagnetic rotations and the Cenozoic tectonics of the Cascade arc, Washington, Oregon, and California: Jour. Geophys. Res., v. 95, p. 19,409–19,417.

Wernicke, B. P., 1992, Cenozoic extensional tectonics of the U. S. Cordillera, in Burchfiel, B. C., Lipman, P. W., and Zoback, M. L., eds., The geology of North America, v. G-3: The Cordilleran orogen: Conterminous U.S.: Boulder, CO, Geol. Soc. Amer., p. 553–581.

Wernicke, B. P., Axen, G. J., and Snow, J. K., 1988, Basin and Range extensional tectonics at the latitude of Las Vegas, Nevada: Geol. Soc. Amer. Bull., v. 100, p. 1738–1757.

Wernicke, B. P., and Snow, J. K., 1998, Cenozoic tectonism in the central Basin and Range: Motion of the Sierran–Great Valley Block: INT. GEOL. REV., v. 40, p. 403–410.

Wessel, P., and Kroenke, L. W., 1997, A geometric technique for relocating hotspots and refining absolute plate motions: Nature, v. 387, p. 365–369.

Wilson, D. S., 1988, Tectonic history of the Juan de Fuca ridge over the last 40 million years: Jour. Geophys. Res., v. 93, p. 11,863–11,876.

————, 1989, Deformation of the so-called Gorda Plate: Jour. Geophys. Res., v. 94, p. 3065–3075.

Isotopic Constraints on the Petrogenesis of Jurassic Plutons, Southeastern California

David P. Mayo, J. Lawford Anderson,

Department of Earth Sciences, University of Southern California, Los Angeles, CA 90089-0704

and Joe L. Wooden

Branch of Isotope Geology, U.S. Geological Survey, Mail Stop 937, 345 Middlefield Road, Menlo Park, California 94025

Abstract

The 165 Ma Eagle Mountain intrusion is a heterogeneous, enclave-bearing, metaluminous remnant of the Cordilleran Jurassic arc that cuts regionally metamorphosed pre-Mesozoic rocks in the southeastern Mojave Desert of California. The main phase of the intrusion consists of granodiorite to tonalite host facies, diorite mixed facies, and homogeneous monzogranite facies. The host facies contains microdiorite enclaves interpreted as intermingled masses of mafic magma. Late-phase leucogranite stocks cut the main phase. Mineral equilibria indicate emplacement at ~6.5 km depth, with solidus temperatures ranging from 760°C for diorite to 700°C for felsic granodiorite.

Although uniform radiogenic-isotope compositions (Sr_i = 0.7085, ϵNd_i = –9.4) suggest derivation from a single source, no known source has the composition required. A hybrid source is proposed, consisting of various proportions of juvenile mantle and recycled lower crust. Calculations indicate that the source of the Eagle Mountain intrusion comprised >60% juvenile mantle and <40% recycled crust. On the basis of their isotopic compositions, other mafic Jurassic plutons in the region were derived from sources containing different proportions of mantle and crustal components.

Introduction

IN THE MOJAVE DESERT of southern California, Jurassic and Cretaceous plutons, remnants of two separate continental magmatic arcs, comprise over 75% of the exposed pre-Tertiary basement rock. The typical country rock for the plutons is high-grade Proterozoic gneiss overlain in some areas by variably metamorphosed Precambrian to Paleozoic sedimentary sequences transitional between cratonal and miogeoclinal facies (Tosdal et al., 1989). Petrologic studies of the Mojave plutons have revealed a variety of magma sources and emplacement conditions. Most of the plutons appear to contain both mantle and crustal components (Miller and Barton, 1990; Miller and Wooden, 1994; Barth et al., 1995; Miller and Glazner, 1995), but uncertainties remain as to the composition of the crustal component, the degree of enrichment of the mantle component, and the mechanism by which the components were blended. In general, pluton compositions require increasingly enriched and isotopically evolved mantle, or larger crustal components, or both, moving from west to east across the region.

This paper presents the results of a study in which radiogenic-isotope data were used to place limits on the proportions of juvenile mantle and recycled crust in the Jurassic Eagle Mountain intrusion. This intrusion, with an area of ~150 km², forms the southern end of a large, unnamed Jurassic batholith exposed in the Bullion, Pinto, and northern Eagle mountains (Fig. 1). The Eagle Mountain intrusion is more easily accessible than the northern part of the batholith, which lies within a restricted Marine Corps Air-Ground Combat Area.

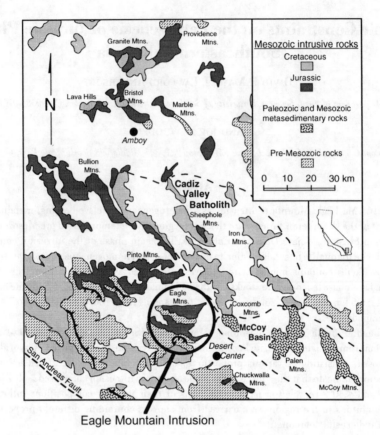

FIG. 1. Outcrop map of the southeastern Mojave Desert region, showing the location of the Eagle Mountain intrusion.

Geologic Setting and Field Relations

The Eagle Mountain intrusion was emplaced ~165 Ma (Wooden et al., 1991) into regionally metamorphosed Proterozoic gneiss overlain by upper Precambrian to Paleozoic quartzite, metapelite, and subordinate marble. Powell (1982) estimated peak metamorphic conditions between 3.5 to 4 kbar and 525° to 625°C for the metapelite. This metamorphism pre-dates emplacement of the Eagle Mountain intrusion, which cross-cuts regional isograds. A NW-trending septum of metasedimentary country rock divides the intrusion into northern and southern halves (Fig. 1). Relict bedding strikes WNW, parallel to the length of the septum, and dips northeast. The Eagle Mountain mine is located at the southeastern end of the septum where metacarbonate rocks were extensively replaced by magnetite-hematite ore during intrusion.

The Eagle Mountain intrusion and its country rocks are cut by NW-striking mafic and felsic dikes, some of which have been radiometrically dated (James, 1989) and are correlative with the 148 Ma Independence dike swarm (Chen and Moore, 1961; Moore and Hopson, 1961). A Cretaceous (?) pluton cuts the Late Jurassic dikes and older rocks in the southern Eagle Mountains. A second, Tertiary dike set, also NW-striking, cuts Mesozoic and older rocks in the eastern Eagle Mountains.

The Eagle Mountain intrusion consists of a compositionally heterogeneous, metaluminous main phase cut by late leucogranitic bodies. The main phase consists of three facies: a mixed facies with a predominantly dioritic composition, a host facies of tonalite to granodiorite containing microdiorite enclaves, and a homogeneous facies of monzogranitic composition. The host facies accounts for about half of the exposed main phase of the intrusion, the mixed

TABLE 1. Representative Modal Analyses[1]

	Enclaves		Mixed facies		Host facies		Homogeneous facies
	EM25e d	EM28e d	EM16 qd	EM28h gd	EM26 gd	EM25h qt	EM1 mg
Plagioclase	68.4	60.2	52.7	47.0	47.7	45.4	31.5
K-feldspar	0.6	0.2	5.2	14.7	15.1	2.2	34.7
Quartz	4.0		8.2	22.9	19.6	44.8	25.9
Augite	11.3	12.4	1.3	tr.	0.2	0.4	
Hornblende	0.6		15.3	3.8	5.3		1.8
Biotite	12.4	18.7	7.3	9.3	7.2	6.1	4.7
Magnetite	2.3	8.6	5.4	2.2	2.3	1.0	1.4
Sphene	0.3		0.6	0.2	0.6	tr.	tr.
Apatite	tr.	tr.	tr.	tr.	tr.	tr.	tr.
Zircon			tr.	tr.	tr.	tr.	tr.

[1]Approximately 1000 points counted per sample; "tr." indicates trace amount. Rock-type abbreviations: d = diorite; qd = quartz diorite; gd = granodiorite; qt = quartz-rich tonalite; mg = monzogranite.

facies about one quarter, and the homogeneous facies the remaining quarter. Contacts between the facies are highly gradational. No systematic compositional zonation is apparent. Foliation, where present, is defined by schlieren and mafic enclaves with long axes trending approximately E-W.

All of the main-phase rocks contain the same minerals—only the proportions are different. The assemblage is plagioclase, quartz, orthoclase, biotite, hornblende, magnetite, and augite, with accessory sphene, apatite, and zircon. The host facies consists primarily of quartz-poor, biotite-hornblende-sphene granodiorite (samples EM28h and EM26 in Table 1), but includes subordinate quartz-rich tonalite (sample EM25h in Table 1). Color indices range from 15 to 30 in quartz-poor granodiorite to less than 10 in quartz-rich tonalite. Granodiorite includes a porphyritic subfacies with blocky, pink to pale lavender orthoclase phenocrysts up to 4 cm long. Plagioclase grains commonly feature patchy, inclusion-rich cores (An_{37-33}) and slightly more calcic, normally zoned rims (An_{43-32}). Inclusion minerals are biotite, augite, magnetite, and apatite. Brown biotite in host-facies rocks is more abundant than hornblende and has euhedral faces against hornblende. Opaque oxide grains are essentially pure magnetite enclosing a few exsolved blebs of ilmenite ($Ilm_{93}Hem_7$). Subhedral augite grains, partially pseudomorphed by green amphibole, are fairly common. Mineral textures record early crystallization of plagioclase, biotite, augite, magnetite, and apatite. Hornblende commenced crystallizing after biotite and before interstitial quartz and orthoclase.

Microdiorite enclaves account for up to 50% of some host-facies outcrops, although 30% or less is more common. The enclaves are interpreted as masses of mafic magma intermingled with more felsic host magma (Mayo and Wooden, 1993). Enclave shapes are suggestive of flow-related distortion (Fernandez and Barbarin, 1991). Microtextures are igneous, with solid-state deformation limited to undulatory extinction of interstitial quartz, providing indications that the distortion occurred while the enclaves were still largely molten. Consistent with chemical equilibration prior to rim growth, rims of plagioclase grains in enclaves and host rocks have identical compositions (An_{40})—a condition that suggests the presence of interstitial liquid facilitating ion diffusion. Overall fine grain size (0.2 to 1 mm) and abundant acicular apatite inclusions in plagioclase rims are consistent with a period of rapid cooling of enclave magma as it thermally equilibrated with cooler host magma (Wyllie et al., 1962).

Enclaves, with color indices ranging from 25 to 45, have higher proportions of ferromagnesian silicates than do host rocks (see samples EM25e and EM28e in Table 1). As in the host facies, some plagioclase grains in enclaves (An_{46-40}) have patchy, inclusion-rich cores and clean, concentrically zoned rims. Biotite is particularly abundant, but amphibole is rare except in the smallest enclaves. Trace orthoclase (Or_{93}) fills interstices and poikilitically encloses euhedral plagioclase, biotite, and augite grains.

Next to microdiorite enclaves, the mixed facies (sample EM16 in Table 1) is the most mafic component of the intrusion. Field relations, textures, petrography, and mass-balance calculations all suggest that the mixed facies is a mixture of microdiorite enclave magma and host-facies magma. Mixed-facies rocks vary from fine to coarse grained and from diorite to quartz diorite to quartz monzodiorite. Patchy plagioclase cores contain an early-crystallizing assemblage of biotite, augite, opaque oxides, and apatite. Hornblende is generally more abundant than either biotite or augite, and is typically interstitial to all other major minerals except quartz and orthoclase.

Host-facies granodiorite grades into a relatively homogeneous facies comprising medium-grained, biotite-hornblende-sphene monzogranite (sample EM1 in Table 1). The monzogranite facies contains blocky plagioclase (An_{37-35}) that is concentrically zoned and inclusion free. Pale lavender orthoclase is particularly noticeable in hand sample. Hornblende occurs as euhedral to subhedral grains interlocked with plagioclase and as a pseudomorphic replacement of rare augite crystals. Plagioclase, augite, hornblende, and magnetite precipitated first, followed by biotite, orthoclase, and quartz.

Late-phase leucogranite is texturally and mineralogically diverse. Samples EM30 and EM17 are metaluminous, containing subequal amounts of quartz, plagioclase, and perthitic orthoclase; small amounts of greenish hornblende and brown biotite; and accessory sphene, zircon, and apatite. These rocks represent late differentiates of the main phase of the intrusion. Other examples are not clearly related to the main phase. Sample EM31A is a medium-grained plagioclase-quartz rock containing minor actinolitic hornblende and accessory sphene, apatite, zircon, and tourmaline. Sample EM31B contains microperthitic orthoclase and fluid inclusion–rich quartz that in places form a poorly developed graphic texture. Accessory minerals include chloritized biotite, granular sphene, and rare grains of metamict zircon and anhedral apatite.

Emplacement Conditions

A sharp intrusive contact and well-defined metasomatic aureole suggest upper-crustal emplacement of the Eagle Mountain intrusion. Virtually all of the main-phase rocks contain the requisite assemblage for Al-in-hornblende barometry. The Anderson and Smith (1995) calibration yields an estimated emplacement pressure of 1.7 ± 0.2 kbar, which converts to an emplacement depth of 6.3 ± 0.7 km. Hornblende-plagioclase thermometry, using the calibration of Blundy and Holland (1990), yields estimated solidus temperatures ranging from $\sim 760\,°C$ for mixed-facies diorite to $700\,°C$ for homogeneous-facies monzogranite. Other calibrations yield similar results for both pressure and temperature. Computations based on the biotite breakdown reaction (calibration of Wones, 1981) indicate essentially constant $f(O_2)$ of about 10^{-15} bars during crystallization of the main phase of the intrusion. Pegmatite dikes and segregations, which might be taken as indicators of water oversaturation during crystallization, are very rare in the main phase of the intrusion. In fact, the tendency for crystallization of biotite before hornblende in the mixed-facies diorite and host-facies granodiorite may be evidence of slight water undersaturation, based on the experimental observation that biotite crystallizes before hornblende in potassic, water-undersaturated granodiorite (Wones and Gilbert, 1982; Naney, 1983; Hewitt and Wones, 1984).

Whole-Rock Chemistry

Analytical procedures

Major- and trace-element concentrations were determined on an automated, wavelength-dispersive, Rigaku 3070 X-ray fluorescence spectrometer in the Earth Sciences Department at the University of Southern California. Radiogenic-isotope ratios were measured on a Finnigan-MAT 262 mass spectrometer at the Branch of Isotope Geology, U.S. Geological Survey, Menlo Park, California. Measured Pb-isotopic ratios for whole rocks and feldspar separates were corrected for thermal fractionation by 0.11% per mass unit on the basis of hundreds of analyses of NBS-981 and NBS-982. Analytical precision of measured ratios is 0.1% or less for multiple runs of standards and unknowns. Average fractionation-corrected values for 28 analyses of BCR-1 are $^{206}Pb/^{204}Pb$ = 18.812, $^{207}Pb/^{204}Pb$ = 15.625, and $^{208}Pb/^{204}Pb$ = 38.689. Elemental Pb concentrations were obtained by X-ray fluorescence.

Measured strontium-isotopic ratios were normalized to $^{86}Sr/^{88}Sr$ = 0.11940. Analytical precision of measured $^{87}Sr/^{86}Sr$ is $\pm$ 0.00002 or less. Periodic analyses of NBS-987 yielded an average $^{87}Sr/^{86}Sr$ = 0.71024 $\pm$ 2 (2σ). Rb and Sr concentrations were determined by X-ray fluorescence.

Elemental concentrations and isotopic ratios for Sm and Nd were determined from a bulk REE fraction separated during Sr column work using the standard isobutyric acid technique. Measured neodymium ratios were normalized to $^{146}Nd/^{144}Nd$ = 0.7219. Analytical precision for $^{147}Nd/^{144}Nd$ is $\pm$ 0.2%. BCR-1 has an average $^{143}Nd/^{144}Nd$ = 0.512633 $\pm$ 10 (2σ). Present-day chondritic values used were $^{143}Nd/^{144}Nd$ = 0.512635 and $^{147}Sm/^{144}Nd$ = 0.1967.

Oxygen-isotopic analyses of whole rocks and mineral separates were measured on a VG Isogas Prism Series II mass spectrometer in the Earth Sciences Department at the University of Southern California. Oxygen gas was liberated from powdered samples in nickel reaction vessels using BrF_5, and converted to CO_2 gas for the mass spectrometer by reaction with hot graphite. Results are reported as the per mil difference in $^{18}O/^{16}O$ from Standard Mean Ocean Water:

$$\delta^{18}O = 1000 \times \left[\frac{(^{18}O/^{16}O)_{SMOW}}{(^{18}O/^{16}O)_{Sample}} - 1 \right].$$

Instrumental precision based on repeated measurements of a standard gas (R7901) is $\pm$ 0.2‰ (1σ). Total analytical precision (including sample preparation errors + instrumental errors) was determined by repeatedly preparing and analyzing an aliquot of pure quartz standard NCSU-Quartz. The standard was analyzed 45 times during the course of this investigation. Measured $\delta^{18}O$ values ranged from 10.3 to 12.8‰, and averaged 11.3 $\pm$ 0.3‰ (1σ).

NCSU-Quartz has an accepted $\delta^{18}O$ value of 11.7‰.

Major and trace elements

Samples from the Eagle Mountain intrusion define a metaluminous, high-potassium, alkali-calcic suite with a Peacock Index of ~55 (Table 2; Figs. 2 and 3). The main phase of the intrusion (i.e., the mixed facies, host facies, and homogeneous facies) spans a range of SiO_2 from 52 to 68 wt% and exhibits approximately linear trends for most major elements versus SiO_2. Microdiorite enclaves lie on the same trend, extending SiO_2 down to 48 wt%. Late-phase leucogranite also lies on the same trend, extending SiO_2 up to 77 wt%. Strontium falls from an average 626 ppm in microdiorite enclaves to about 463 ppm in homogeneous-facies monzogranite. Microdiorite enclaves have high levels of K_2O, Rb, and Ba, comparable to the host facies.

Isotope compositions

Common Pb in the Eagle Mountain intrusion was determined by measuring the isotopic composition of fresh feldspar separates from five main-phase rocks ranging from diorite to monzogranite. Measured ratios are uniform, averaging $^{206}Pb/^{204}Pb$ = 18.79, $^{207}Pb/^{204}Pb$ = 15.66, and $^{208}Pb/^{204}Pb$ = 39.07 (Table 3). These values fall within the ranges of initial ratios calculated from ten main-phase whole rocks at 165 Ma ($^{206}Pb/^{204}Pb$ = 18.46 to 18.94, $^{207}Pb/^{204}Pb$ = 15.62 to 15.66, and $^{208}Pb/^{204}Pb$ = 38.88 to 39.27) (Table 4). A feldspar separate from late-phase leucogranite EM31B (Table 3) yielded slightly more radiogenic values ($^{206}Pb/^{204}Pb$ = 19.08, $^{207}Pb/^{204}Pb$ = 15.70, and $^{208}Pb/^{204}Pb$ = 39.45). Initial ratios calculated from EM31B whole-rock data ($^{206}Pb/^{204}Pb$ = 19.07, $^{207}Pb/^{204}Pb$ = 15.68, and $^{208}Pb/^{204}Pb$ = 40.33) also exceed the ratios calculated for main-phase whole rocks.

Wooden et al. (1988) divided the southwestern United States into Pb-isotopic provinces on the basis of different Early Proterozoic crustal histories. The delineation of isotopic provinces was facilitated by the fact that feldspars from Mesozoic plutons in the region have the same range of common Pb-isotopic compositions as the intruded Proterozoic crust. The Eagle Mountains lie in the Mojave province,

TABLE 2. Major- and Trace-Element Chemistry[1]

	Enclaves						Mixed facies				
	EM23e d	EM25e d	EM24e d	EM18e d	EM28e d	EM8e d	EM19 qd	EM9 d	EM7 qd	EM16 qmd	EM11 qmd
wt%											
SiO_2	48.22	49.83	50.57	51.14	52.99	53.13	52.28	53.48	54.05	55.92	57.55
TiO_2	1.26	1.05	1.25	1.13	1.04	1.06	1.12	1.00	1.07	0.91	0.78
Al_2O_3	18.64	19.35	18.99	18.40	17.72	17.60	18.17	19.04	18.72	17.85	17.78
FeO	10.90	8.95	9.38	9.42	8.95	9.11	8.68	7.90	8.03	7.36	6.90
MgO	4.22	3.97	3.93	4.04	3.85	3.91	3.90	3.11	3.32	2.98	2.83
MnO	0.24	0.21	0.20	0.21	0.19	0.19	0.17	0.16	0.16	0.15	0.15
CaO	8.19	8.42	7.30	7.63	7.90	7.93	7.26	7.01	6.69	6.41	6.12
Na_2O	4.10	4.15	3.87	3.86	3.86	3.86	3.67	4.12	3.85	3.80	3.82
K_2O	2.06	2.17	2.45	2.39	1.92	1.89	2.78	2.48	2.64	2.80	2.81
P_2O_5	0.37	0.34	0.37	0.37	0.25	0.25	0.36	0.36	0.38	0.34	0.29
LOI	0.51	0.81	0.78	0.69	0.82	0.79	0.69	0.12	1.06	0.89	1.16
Total	98.71	99.25	99.10	99.27	99.49	99.70	99.09	98.76	99.98	99.42	100.18
ppm											
Rb	78	101	108	129	76	75	131	103	121	109	99
Sr	682	638	552	637	628	617	644	675	627	616	597
Ba	1352	685	710	1067	1026	1014	1222	810	805	1130	1021
Ga	24.7	23.4	22.7	23.3	22.2	21.7	22.7	23.0	22.1	20.5	20.4
Y	31.2	34.8	31.2	31.7	27.6	28.0	25.1	32.1	24.9	28.6	18.0
La	59.1	50.7	51.0	52.6	30.5	44.9	51.2	46.2	71.5	63.4	44.3
Zr	192	212	217	143	220	223	159	262	245	223	226
Nb	10.6	10.2	8.0	15.5	7.4	7.4	9.7	12.1	13.5	12.5	11.7
Cr	17.8	23.4	16.7	18.9	46.3	23.7	14.7	10.7	7.3	9.0	12.8
Ni	13.0	21.2	15.3	12.6	31.1	25.0	14.6	13.5	10.6	12.8	13.2
Th	0.44	1.79	5.34	9.76	2.42	0.00	7.44	6.09	8.83	11.06	9.15
U	0.97	1.25	3.81	2.04	0.95	0.93	2.52	3.23	4.56	6.34	2.70
Pb	14.6	12.2	11.4	13.6	10.8	11.0	10.1	11.7	12.2	13.7	11.2
Zn	172.2	119.2	137.5	158.1	124.3	124.1	110.0	100.1	103.9	101.0	91.9
Cu	69.1	23.1	48.8	75.9	41.2	40.2	48.8	45.3	28.7	38.1	37.9

	Host facies											
	EM8h qd	EM20 qmd	EM18h gd	EM21 gd	EM12 gd	EM28h gd	EM32 gd	EM26 gd	EM29 gd	EM10 gd	EM33 gd	EM4 qt	EM25 qt
wt%												
SiO_2	56.61	57.37	58.66	59.05	59.41	59.98	60.36	60.51	61.36	62.70	63.90	65.02	68.04
TiO_2	0.87	0.69	0.81	0.69	0.83	0.82	0.78	0.86	0.79	0.66	0.66	0.58	0.51
Al_2O_3	18.57	18.54	17.72	17.75	17.58	16.86	17.46	16.60	16.70	16.85	16.41	17.10	15.44
FeO	6.63	5.76	6.53	5.71	5.66	5.95	5.28	5.94	5.36	4.91	5.33	3.99	3.40
MgO	2.69	2.20	2.42	2.19	2.29	2.39	1.93	2.37	2.00	2.00	2.05	1.53	1.38
MnO	0.13	0.11	0.13	0.13	0.11	0.13	0.11	0.12	0.12	0.09	0.10	0.10	0.07
CaO	6.25	5.05	5.68	5.27	5.24	5.41	4.79	5.34	5.11	5.02	4.75	4.83	4.24
Na_2O	4.19	4.21	3.82	3.75	4.04	4.14	3.82	3.89	4.05	3.77	3.66	3.91	3.71
K_2O	2.47	3.69	2.88	3.30	2.75	2.99	4.02	3.06	3.10	3.23	2.64	2.54	2.12
P_2O_5	0.33	0.28	0.31	0.28	0.29	0.33	0.32	0.33	0.30	0.26	0.24	0.19	0.16
LOI	1.07	1.16	0.80	1.18	1.22	0.86	0.88	0.81	1.02	0.67	0.95	0.92	1.34
Total	99.79	99.05	99.76	99.30	99.41	99.86	99.75	99.82	99.90	100.15	100.69	100.71	100.41

(continued)

TABLE 2. (*continued*)

	EM8h	EM20	EM18h	EM21	EM12	EM28h	EM32	EM26	EM29	EM10	EM33	EM4	EM25
	qd	qmd	gd	gd	gd	gd	gd	gd	gd	gd	gd	qt	qt

						ppm							
Rb	85	108	109	112	85	92	106	98	96	105	92	121	74
Sr	658	601	639	547	555	572	577	546	537	564	504	619	494
Ba	882	2218	1156	1283	1200	1182	2151	1282	1128	1208	726	318	431
Ga	21.8	21.0	20.4	18.9	20.7	19.3	19.8	19.4	19.4	18.5	19.8	20.5	16.0
Y	21.7	20.1	29.5	25.2	37.4	35.4	49.4	34.2	37.7	21.7	20.6	20.5	12.2
La	54.4	40.0	52.4	42.9	60.1	58.8	56.4	65.7	54.9	42.5	22.3	31.5	20.7
Zr	275	235	265	249	283	278	279	268	278	203	176	194	147
Nb	12.6	9.2	12.3	8.1	14.1	13.3	15.9	11.8	16.8	7.5	14.5	9.0	4.7
Cr	10.4	6.6	9.3	12.6	2.6	16.3	6.2	9.9	21.8	6.6	29.7	7.2	12.2
Ni	8.6	7.1	10.2	9.3	1.5	11.0	4.6	10.7	10.1	7.1	14.7	10.3	7.1
Th	5.80	8.25	13.36	14.97	16.72	11.10	10.87	12.06	13.84	10.72	6.18	10.30	6.60
U	1.53	3.41	2.40	3.49	3.03	1.97	1.76	3.97	4.26	3.37	1.78	2.19	2.23
Pb	12.3	10.0	13.1	14.2	13.4	11.0	14.9	14.6	12.7	11.5	15.0	12.3	10.0
Zn	81.6	50.2	88.2	74.2	70.2	72.2	72.5	84.0	81.4	53.1	74.0	53.3	47.3
Cu	19.4	24.7	28.5	28.8	28.5	25.1	21.8	19.4	17.5	20.5	9.0	7.4	7.7

	Homogeneous facies					Leucogranite					
	EM2	EM1	EM3	EM6	EM5	EM30	EM31A	EM13	EM7X	EM31B	EM17
	mg	mg	mg	mg	mg						

					wt%						
SiO$_2$	66.26	67.32	67.44	67.84	68.25	69.21	69.77	70.57	72.33	77.01	77.31
TiO$_2$	0.49	0.45	0.40	0.50	0.39	0.42	0.47	0.35	0.14	0.11	0.14
Al$_2$O$_3$	16.37	15.56	15.38	15.49	15.26	14.95	16.21	14.52	14.36	12.17	12.19
FeO	3.20	3.40	3.22	3.23	3.35	2.12	0.72	2.27	1.26	0.15	0.57
MgO	1.18	1.10	1.04	1.19	1.12	0.90	1.4	0.84	0.22	0.07	0.14
MnO	0.09	0.09	0.08	0.07	0.09	0.05	0.03	0.05	0.03	0.02	0.02
CaO	3.41	3.40	3.10	3.27	3.08	3.36	5.47	2.42	1.71	0.82	0.91
Na$_2$O	3.35	3.36	3.14	3.16	3.21	3.72	5.4	2.92	4.28	2.83	2.11
K$_2$O	4.53	4.23	4.65	4.49	4.61	4.33	0.37	5.16	5.15	5.55	6.15
P$_2$O$_5$	0.15	0.14	0.12	0.14	0.13	0.14	0.17	0.10	0.07	0.02	0.00
LOI	1.01	0.71	0.70	0.88	0.88	0.77	0.58	0.85	0.86	0.81	0.82
Total	100.03	99.76	99.26	100.26	100.36	99.96	100.6	100.05	100.39	99.55	100.36

					ppm						
Rb	147	115	122	112	121	109	10	147	121	175	118
Sr	578	448	444	412	435	387	465	201	252	98	293
Ba	2318	1529	1707	1420	1686	873	89	489	919	200	694
Ga	18.3	17.5	16.9	15.2	16.4	15.1	16.6	10.2	13.9	11.4	13.5
Y	25.6	23.8	20.7	25.5	16.7	28.0	26.8	11.4	37.0	10.3	18.5
La	40.8	49.8	46.0	47.3	53.0	43.2	32.4	44.3	142.5	11.7	50.5
Zr	191	194	170	176	170	184	195	63	97	78	152
Nb	13.3	7.9	18.1	8.1	9.5	17.3	24.0	4.1	10.6	17.4	9.9
Cr	6.9	6.9	6.7	0.0	6.7	9.4	5.6	5.1	5.7	4.9	5.6
Ni	8.4	8.8	7.6	0.0	7.6	5.9	1.3	0.0	1.9	0.0	1.3
Th	12.07	21.90	13.80	21.54	14.30	22.03	23.79	12.90	8.50	34.20	16.78
U	4.05	5.87	5.84	3.98	3.43	4.35	4.94	3.26	2.56	5.46	3.54
Pb	17.1	17.0	16.2	16.4	15.8	12.6	8.9	17.4	3.0	10.4	15.5
Zn	43.8	42.6	39.3	38.6	41.6	25.8	14.5	8.7	6.3	11.9	34.2
Cu	6.5	10.0	6.9	4.2	7.9	4.5	5.0	3.3	5.2	4.8	4.3

[1]Rock-type abbreviations: d = diorite; qmd = quartz monzodiorite; qt = quartz tonalite; gd = granodioriorite; mg = monzogranite.

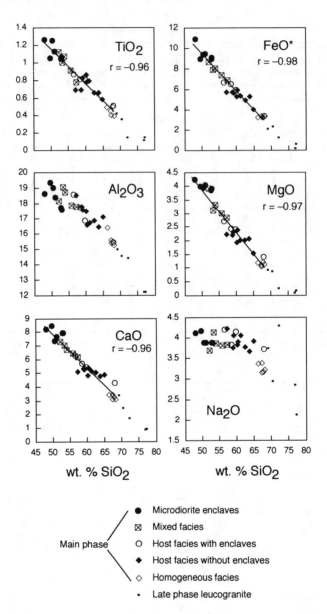

FIG. 2. Silica variation diagrams for major elements. Lines calculated by linear regression and correlation coefficients apply to main-phase data only.

which comprises southern Nevada and southeastern California. A boundary roughly coincident with the Colorado River separates the Mojave province from the Arizona province to the east. The Arizona province has a MORB-like mantle-Pb signature, whereas the Mojave province is more radiogenic. Feldspars from Jurassic and Cretaceous plutons in the Mojave Pb-isotopic province define a linear field in coordinates of $^{207}Pb/^{204}Pb$ vs. $^{206}Pb/^{204}Pb$ that Wooden et al. (1988) interpreted as a tertiary isochron with a slope of $\sim$1.6 Ga (Fig. 4). The Eagle Mountain feldspar data cluster together at the more radiogenic end of the Mojave Mesozoic feldspar field. Both uranogenic and thorogenic Pb ratios in the Eagle Mountain

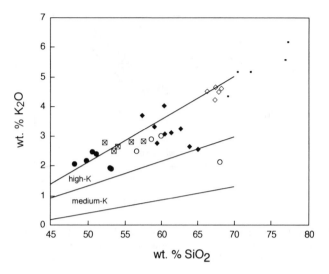

FIG. 3. K_2O-SiO_2 variation diagram. Boundaries between high-K and medium-K fields are from Gill (1981). Symbols are the same as in Figure 2.

TABLE 3. Feldspar Pb-Isotopic Compositions

Sample	Rock type	$^{206}Pb/^{204}Pb$	$^{207}Pb/^{204}Pb$	$^{208}Pb/^{204}Pb$
		Main phase		
EM16-FSP	quartz monzodiorite	18.780	15.651	39.030
EM8h-FSP	quartz diorite	18.870	15.639	39.047
EM25h-FSP	quartz-rich tonalite	18.773	15.664	39.180
EM12-FSP	granodiorite	18.757	15.663	39.064
EM6-FSP	monzogranite	18.758	15.666	39.050
Average		18.788	15.657	39.074
S. D. (1σ)		0.047	0.011	0.060
		Late phase		
EM31B-FSP	leucogranite	19.078	15.701	39.449

feldspars exceed the values for average crust of Jurassic age as modeled by Stacey and Kramers (1975).

Strontium-isotopic compositions were determined for 18 main-phase and 4 late-phase samples from the Eagle Mountain intrusion (Table 4). Sixteen of the main-phase samples have calculated values of Sr_i between 0.7083 and 0.7094 at the assumed crystallization age of 165 Ma. Two host-facies granodiorite samples (EM26 and EM28h) have slightly higher Sr_i = 0.7094. Four microdiorite enclaves have Sr_i between 0.7084 and 0.7086. Late-phase rocks have Sr_i between 0.7092 and 0.7102, also assuming a 165 Ma crystallization age.

Main-phase samples have a limited range of $^{87}Rb/^{86}Sr$ and exhibit scatter on a plot of $^{87}Sr/^{86}Sr$ vs. $^{87}Rb/^{86}Sr$ (Fig. 5). Despite the scatter, the slope of a line fitted to the main-phase data (not shown) yields a date of 160 Ma, close to the 165 Ma U-Pb zircon date for the intrusion. Reference 165 Ma isochrons in Figure 6 illustrate the range of calculated initial ratios. The four late-phase samples have a much wider range of $^{87}Rb/^{86}Sr$ and scatter slightly about a 173 Ma isochron (Fig. 6).

Values of Sr_i determined for the Eagle Mountain intrusion are sufficiently high to clearly indicate the involvement of a crustal component or an unusually radiogenic mantle compo-

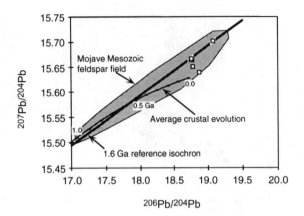

FIG. 4. $^{207}Pb/^{204}Pb$ vs. $^{206}Pb/^{204}Pb$ for Eagle Mountain feldspars (squares). Mojave Mesozoic feldspar field with 1.6 Ga reference isochron is from Wooden et al. (1988). Average crustal-evolution curve is from the two-stage model of Stacey and Kramers (1975) and has tick marks at 100 Ma intervals.

nent in magma evolution. Even the lowest calculated Sr_i value of 0.708 exceeds the maximum values of ~0.706 observed in young, mantle-derived oceanic basalts (DePaolo, 1988).

Nd-isotopic compositions were determined for four main-phase and two late-phase rocks (Table 4). Measured values of $^{143}Nd/^{144}Nd$ are plotted vs. $^{147}Sm/^{144}Nd$ in Figure 7, along with reference isochrons for 165 Ma. The range of $^{147}Sm/^{144}Nd$ (0.08 to 0.12) is small, and the poor correlation between $^{143}Nd/^{144}Nd$ and $^{147}Sm/^{144}Nd$ precludes fitting an isochron to the data. The four main-phase samples have calculated ϵNd_i ranging from –8.9 to –9.8, with the most mafic rock analyzed, quartz diorite EM19, having the lowest ratio. The two late-phase samples yielded values of –9.0 and –10.1. These ϵNd values are lower than the minimum values of ~–6 observed in young, mantle-derived oceanic basalts (DePaolo, 1988). Thus, the Nd data, like the Sr data, require the involvement of a crustal component or an unusually radiogenic mantle component in the evolution of the intrusion.

Oxygen-isotopic compositions for seven main-phase whole rocks (Table 4) are displayed in a series of histograms in Figure 8. The data generally exhibit a positive correlation between $\delta^{18}O$ and whole-rock SiO_2. Two microdiorite enclaves (<53 wt% SiO_2) have $\delta^{18}O$ values between 6 and 8‰. The more silicic rocks have $\delta^{18}O$ values between 7 and 9‰. Quartz separated from granodiorite EM8h and monzogranite EM6 have $\delta^{18}O$ values between 9 and 10‰.

Taylor (1968) demonstrated that fresh, mantle-derived gabbroic rocks generally have $\delta^{18}O$ values between 5.5 and 7.4‰, whereas fresh tonalite, granodiorite, and granite have slightly higher $\delta^{18}O$ values, in the range from 7.8 to 10.2‰. Plutonic igneous rocks with $\delta^{18}O$ values exceeding 10‰ are generally peraluminous granites that probably contain a substantial metasedimentary component. Comparison with these ranges reveals that the oxygen-isotopic compositions of the Eagle Mountain rocks (6 to 9‰) are typical for calc-alkaline plutonic rocks that contain some crust but little or no metasedimentary component. The most likely crustal component involved in the evolution of the intrusion is mid-Proterozoic orthogneiss, which forms a large fraction of the pre-Mesozoic wall rock in the Mojave Desert region. The mid-Proterozoic orthogneiss has calc-alkaline, igneous-type $\delta^{18}O$ values between 8 and 11.5‰. These values are only slightly greater than the range established for the Eagle Mountain intrusion, decreasing the sensitivity of oxygen-isotopic signatures to assimilation of Proterozoic crust.

Isotopic Constraints on Mantle/Crust Proportions

Combined Nd and Sr data

Combined Sr- and Nd-isotopic data provide a powerful tool for estimating the proportions of juvenile mantle versus recycled crust in a plu-

TABLE 4. Isotope Geochemistry

Sample[1]	Enclaves				Mixed facies			
	EM25e d	EM18e d	EM28e d	EM8e d	EM19 qd	EM7 qd	EM16 qmd	EM11 qmd
Rb (ppm)	101	129	76	75	131	121	109	99
Sr (ppm)	638	637	628	617	644	627	616	597
$^{87}Rb/^{86}Sr$	0.458	0.586	0.350	0.352	0.589	0.558	0.512	0.480
$^{87}Sr/^{86}Sr$	0.70966	0.70973	0.70946	0.70946	0.70978	0.70981	0.70974	0.70952
Sr_i^2	0.70859	0.70836	0.70864	0.70863	0.70840	0.70850	0.70854	0.70839
Sm (ppm)					5.69		6.5	
Nd (ppm)					32.06		37.08	
$^{147}Sm/^{144}Nd$					0.1074		0.1060	
$^{143}Nd/^{144}Nd$					0.51204		0.51206	
ϵNd_i^3					-9.8		-9.4	
U (ppm)		2.04		0.93			6.34	
Pb (ppm)		13.6		11.0			13.7	
$^{206}Pb/^{204}Pb$		19.030		18.849			19.303	
$^{207}Pb/^{204}Pb$		15.643		15.646			15.663	
$^{208}Pb/^{204}Pb$		39.278		39.132			39.390	
$^{206}Pb/^{204}Pb_i^2$		18.778		18.708			18.522	
$^{207}Pb/^{204}Pb_i^2$		15.631		15.639			15.624	
$^{208}Pb/^{204}Pb_i^2$		38.884		39.132			38.945	
$\delta^{18}O$	7.1			6.8			8.6	
$\delta^{18}O_{quartz}$								

Sample[1]	Host facies							
	EM8h qd	EM18h gd	EM28h gd	EM25h qt	EM20 qmd	EM12 gd	EM26 gd	EM10 gd
Rb (ppm)	85	109	92	74	108	85	98	105
Sr (ppm)	658	639	572	494	601	555	546	564
$^{87}Rb/^{86}Sr$	0.374	0.494	0.465	0.433	0.520	0.503	0.519	0.539
$^{87}Sr/^{86}Sr$	0.70933	0.70946	0.71053	0.70962	0.71003	0.70986	0.71064	0.70970
Sr_i^2	0.70845	0.70830	0.70944	0.70860	0.70881	0.70868	0.70942	0.70844
Sm (ppm)				2.47				4.44
Nd (ppm)				16.28				26.4
$^{147}Sm/^{144}Nd$				0.0916				0.1016
$^{143}Nd/^{144}Nd$				0.51205				0.51208
ϵNd_i^3				-9.3				-8.9
U (ppm)	1.53		1.97	2.23	3.41			
Pb (ppm)	12.3		11.0	10.0	10.0			
$^{206}Pb/^{204}Pb$	19.154		19.235	18.758	19.034			
$^{207}Pb/^{204}Pb$	15.667		15.676	15.664	15.647			
$^{208}Pb/^{204}Pb$	39.451		39.829	39.384	39.406			
$^{206}Pb/^{204}Pb_i^2$	18.944		18.931	18.717	18.460			
$^{207}Pb/^{204}Pb_i^2$	15.657		15.661	15.645	15.619			
$^{208}Pb/^{204}Pb_i^2$	39.191		39.270	39.021	38.953			
$\delta^{18}O$	7.7			7.7				7.8
$\delta^{18}O_{quartz}$	9.3							

(*continued*)

TABLE 4. (*continued*)

| Sample[1] | Host facies
EM4
qt | Homogeneous facies
EM1
mg | Leucogranite | | |
			EM30	EM31A	EM31B	EM17
Rb (ppm)	121	115	109	10	175	118
Sr (ppm)	619	448	387	465	98	293
$^{87}Rb/^{86}Sr$	0.566	0.743	0.815	0.0622	5.17	1.17
$^{87}Sr/^{86}Sr$	0.71014	0.71044	0.71108	0.71014	0.72233	0.71211
Sr_i[2]	0.70881	0.70870	0.70917	0.71000	0.71019	0.70938
Sm (ppm)				5.23		4.71
Nd (ppm)				26.18		35.99
$^{147}Sm/^{144}Nd$				0.1208		0.0791
$^{143}Nd/^{144}Nd$				0.51204		0.51205
ϵNd_i[3]				−10.1		− 9.0
U (ppm)	2.19	5.87			5.46	
Pb (ppm)	12.3	17.0			10.4	
$^{206}Pb/^{204}Pb$	19.167	19.202			19.979	
$^{207}Pb/^{204}Pb$	15.677	15.660			15.727	
$^{208}Pb/^{204}Pb$	39.427	39.764			40.626	
$^{206}Pb/^{204}Pb_i$[2]	18.867	18.617			19.069	
$^{207}Pb/^{204}Pb_i$[2]	15.662	15.631			15.682	
$^{208}Pb/^{204}Pb_i$[2]	38.966	39.051			40.329	
$\delta^{18}O$		7.7				
$\delta^{18}O_{quartz}$		9.4[4]				

[1]Rock abbreviations: d = diorite; qd = quartz diorite; qmd = quartz monzodiorite; gd = granodiorite; qt = quartz-rich tonalite; mg = monzogranite.
[2]Recalculated at crystallization age = 165 Ma.
[3]Calculated at crystallization age = 165 Ma, using $^{143}Nd/^{144}Nd_{CHUR, 0 \, Ma}$ = 0.512635, and $^{147}Sm/^{144}Nd_{CHUR, 0 \, Ma}$ = 0.1967.
[4]Quartz separate from monzogranite EM6.

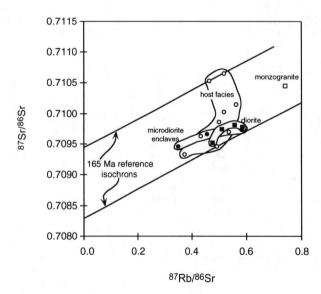

FIG. 5. $^{87}Sr/^{86}Sr$ vs. $^{87}Rb/^{86}Sr$ for main-phase rocks, with 165 Ma reference isochrons.

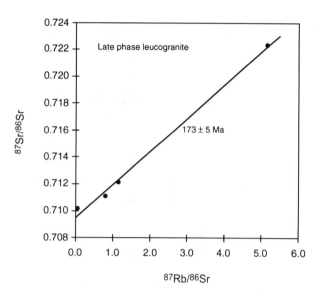

FIG. 6. ^{87}Sr/^{86}Sr vs. ^{87}Rb/^{86}Sr for late-phase leucogranite. Isochron slope yields a date of 173 ± 5 Ma and an apparent range of initial ^{87}Sr/^{86}Sr between 0.7090 and 0.70995.

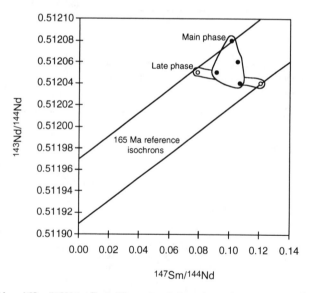

FIG. 7. ^{143}Nd/^{144}Nd vs. ^{147}Sm/^{144}Nd for Eagle Mountain whole rocks, with 165 Ma reference isochrons.

ton. Figure 9 is a plot of time-corrected Sr- and Nd-isotopic compositions of four different Jurassic intrusions in southeastern California. From isotopically most primitive to most evolved, these are the 155 Ma Granite Mountains diorite (Young et al., 1992), the 165 Ma Eagle Mountain intrusion, the 145 Ma Ship Mountains pluton and related dikes (Miller and Wooden, 1994), and the 160 Ma Clipper pluton (Miller and Wooden, 1994). Figure 10 shows the same data, along with the time-corrected compositions of end-member reservoirs that could have contributed to pluton genesis through mixing or assimilation.

Pre-Jurassic crustal components that represented significant isotopic reservoirs are largely

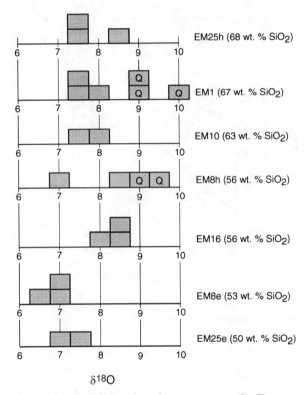

FIG. 8. Oxygen-isotope compositions of whole rocks and quartz separates (Q). The quartz analyses shown with monzogranite EM1 are actually from monzogranite EM6 (68 wt% SiO_2).

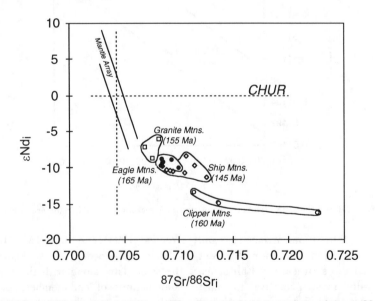

FIG. 9. Initial Sr- and Nd-isotopic compositions of four Jurassic intrusions in the southeastern Mojave Desert. Data are corrected to crystallization ages (in parentheses) determined by U-Pb in zircon. Data sources: Granite Mountains diorite (Young et al., 1992); Eagle Mountain intrusion (this study); Ship Mountains pluton and Clipper pluton (Miller and Wooden, 1994). Abbreviations: CHUR = chondritic uniform reservoir.

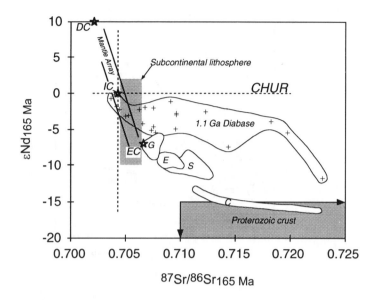

FIG. 10. Time-corrected isotopic compositions of reservoirs that may have contributed to Jurassic pluton genesis. Ratios are adjusted to 165 Ma. The derivation of the fields characterizing subcontinental lithosphere and Proterozoic crust are described in the text. Arrows mark the maximum εNd and minimum $^{87}Sr/^{86}Sr$ values on the Proterozoic crust field. Data for the 1.1 Ga diabase are from Hammond and Wooden (1990). Fields marked G, E, S, and C represent Jurassic plutons in the Granite, Eagle, Ship, and Clipper mountains, respectively (see Fig. 10 for data points). Stars mark the compositions of hypothetical mantle reservoirs used in model caclulations. Abbreviations: DC = MORB-like depleted component; IC = bulk earth–like intermediate component; EC = enriched component.

Proterozoic in age. The most widely exposed Proterozoic unit in the Eagle Mountains is 1.7 Ga granitic orthogneiss (Powell, 1981). Other Proterozoic units include 1.2 Ga syenite correlated with a large anorthosite-syenite complex in the San Gabriel Mountains north of Los Angeles (Powell, 1981; Carter and Silver, 1982) and mafic dikes that probably correlate with a widespread, 1.1 Ga diabase dike suite in southern California and Arizona (Hammond and Wooden, 1990). The field labeled "Proterozoic crust" in Figure 10 is bounded by the approximate minimum $^{87}Sr/^{86}Sr$ (0.71) and maximum εNd (–15) of the 1.7 Ga orthogneiss and the 1.2 Ga syenite at 165 Ma. Young et al. (1992) and Miller and Wooden (1994) employed similar fields to characterize pre-Mesozoic crust elsewhere in southeastern California. The 1.1 Ga diabase was significantly more enriched in ^{143}Nd at 165 Ma.

The field labeled "subcontinental lithosphere" in Figure 10 encompasses Tertiary alkali olivine basalts of the Sierra Nevada province that have been interpreted as partial melts of subcontinental lithosphere isolated since the Middle Proterozoic (Menzies et al., 1983; Musselwhite et al., 1989). The "mantle array," from DePaolo (1981b), is essentially a projection of the MORB Sr-Nd isotopic correlation line through more evolved "bulk-earth" ratios.

The isotopic compositions of the four Jurassic plutons overlap to form a concave-upward curve extending from the most evolved end of the mantle array into the Proterozoic crustal field. Individual Jurassic plutons have fairly restricted compositional ranges, compared to the entire range represented by the curve. With the exception of the most isotopically evolved sample from the Clipper pluton, the Jurassic data require the involvement of more than one isotopic reservoir in pluton genesis, and can be explained by two different hypotheses. One possibility is simple mixing of a partial melt of an isotopically primitive reservoir with a partial melt of isotopically evolved Proterozoic crust. The other hypothesis involves assimilation during fractional crystallization of a partial melt of an isotopically primitive reservoir while assim-

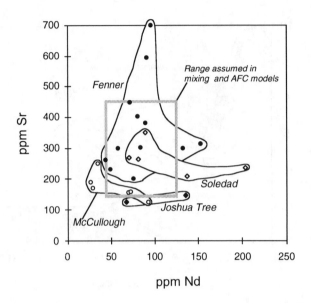

FIG. 11. Sr and Nd concentrations of "post-kinematic" 1.7 Ga gneisses exposed in the southeastern Mojave Desert region. The shaded square indicates the range of Sr (145 to 425 ppm) and Nd (45 to 125 ppm) concentrations assumed to represent Proterozoic crust in mixing and AFC models. Data from Bender (1995).

ilating Proterozoic crust. The primitive reservoir could be mantle, subcontinental lithosphere, or underplated lower crust with isotopic compositions similar to the most primitive diabase. The products of the mixing or AFC (assimilation and fractional crystallization) processes would be parental magmas for the Jurassic plutons or hybrid rocks from which parental magmas could be extracted by a second generation of partial melting. If either of these hypotheses is correct, then each Jurassic intrusion contains different proportions of primitive and crustal end members, and therefore each reflects a different degree of crustal recycling.

Model calculations and assumptions

Mass-balance calculations were made as a simple test of these hypotheses. The calculations were based on a conventional two-component mixing equation and the AFC equation of DePaolo (1981a). In their simplest forms, these models assume compositionally homogeneous end members, and only account for the generation of compositionally homogeneous plutons. The approach was to constrain both the isotopic composition of the primitive end member and the proportions of primitive and Proterozoic crustal end members that may have contributed

melt to the Eagle Mountain intrusion. Miller and Wooden (1994) applied a similar analysis to Mesozoic plutons in the Old Woman Mountains, located ~80 km northeast of the Eagle Mountains.

Specifically, both mixing and AFC curves were calculated that reproduce the elemental and isotopic composition of the least-fractionated sample from the Eagle Mountain intrusion, while passing approximately through the Jurassic plutonic Sr-Nd array. In this way, the curves are effectively "pinned" to a control sample from the Eagle Mountain intrusion, but qualitatively fit the data from the other Jurassic intrusions. Mixed-facies diorite sample EM19 was chosen for the control sample. This rock is a hornblende-biotite quartz diorite with 52 wt% SiO_2 and Mg# = 44. The sample contains 644 ppm Sr with Sr_i = 0.70840 and 32 ppm Nd with ϵNd_i = –9.8.

Proterozoic gneiss is the most likely crustal end member. Proterozoic gneiss (1.7 Ga) and granite (1.4 Ga) from localities throughout the southwestern United States have ϵNd (165 Ma) ranging from approximately –15 to –20 (Fig. 11; calculated from data in Bennett and DePaolo, 1987). An average value of –17.5 was assumed in the calculations. The Sr-isotopic composition of Proterozoic rocks in southeastern California is highly variable. Miller and Wooden (1994), for example, reported $^{87}Sr/^{86}Sr$ (100 Ma) ranging from 0.71 to 0.79 for Proterozoic rocks in the Old Woman Mountains. Therefore, the Sr-isotopic composition of Proterozoic crust was left unconstrained in the calculations and was adjusted to obtain solutions that precisely matched sample EM19 from the Eagle Mountain intrusion. The calculations assume limited ranges of Sr and Nd concentrations for Proterozoic crust. The assumed ranges were obtained from analyses of 1.7 Ga gneiss in the Eagle Mountains and correlative gneiss elsewhere in the region ("post-kinematic" gneiss of Bender, 1995). These rocks have Sr concentrations between 100 and 450 ppm, and Nd concentrations between 30 and 150 ppm (Fig. 11). Average Sr and Nd concentrations are 283 ± 140 ppm and 86 ± 41 ppm, respectively. With these data as a guide, crustal Sr was allowed to vary from 145 to 425 ppm, whereas crustal Nd was limited to values between 45 and 125 ppm. No restrictions were placed on the covariation of Sr and Nd in the models, because the observed concentrations are not strongly correlated (Fig. 11).

Following the approach taken by Miller and Wooden (1994), three different primitive end-member compositions were used in the calculations: a depleted component, an intermediate component, and an enriched component (DC, IC, and EC in Fig. 10). These components represent basaltic partial melts of isotopically variable magma sources in the mantle or lower crust at 165 Ma. The assumed isotopic composition of the DC ($^{87}Sr/^{86}Sr$ = 0.7025, ϵNd = +10) was patterned after MORB. A MORB-like source seems unlikely, considering the convergent tectonic setting of the Mojave region during the mid-Jurassic. Nevertheless, Leventhal et al. (1995) suggested the presence of a MORB-like source under the region as early as the Late Cretaceous, on the basis of the isotopic systematics of a gabbroic xenolith enclosed in Cenozoic basalt of the Cima volcanic field. The isotopic composition assumed for the IC ($^{87}Sr/^{86}Sr$ = 0.70431, ϵNd = 0) is close to bulk earth, and resembles ocean-island basalts at 165 Ma. The assumed isotopic composition for the EC ($^{87}Sr/^{86}Sr$ = 0.7065, ϵNd = −7) is the same as the least-evolved sample from the Granite Mountains diorite, which forms the most primitive end of the Jurassic Sr-Nd iso-

topic array. Young et al. (1992) concluded that this rock was derived by partial melting of enriched subcontinental lithosphere. Sr and Nd concentrations of the primitive end members were adjusted to obtain mixing and AFC curves that precisely reproduced the representative composition of sample EM19 from the Eagle Mountain intrusion.

For AFC calculations, a value of 0.4 was assumed for the mass ratio of assimilated to crystallizing material (r value). This value is sufficiently large to represent a reasonable estimate of assimilation rates in the lower crust. Bulk-distribution coefficients for Sr and Nd were calculated for dioritic samples from the Eagle Mountain intrusion, using modal mineralogy and partition coefficients for basaltic to intermediate rocks (Henderson, 1982). Calculated values of D_{Sr} range from 1.0 to 1.6, with the higher values for rocks containing orthoclase (K_{Sr} = 9.4) as well as plagioclase (K_{Sr} = 1.8) and the lower values for rocks lacking orthoclase. For the AFC calculations, a D_{Sr} value of 1.0 was used. This value is appropriate for a fractionating assemblage that contains ~50% plagioclase and no orthoclase. Bulk-distribution coefficients for Nd are strongly dependent on the fractionated amounts of apatite (K_{Nd} = 50) and, to a lesser extent, clinopyroxene (K_{Nd} = 0.6). Calculated values of D_{Nd} for the Eagle Mountain rocks range from 0.1 to 0.6 for an assumed range of 0% to 1% apatite in the fractionating assemblage. An intermediate value of D_{Nd} = 0.35 was used in the AFC calculations.

Results

The results of mixing and AFC calculations are summarized in Tables 5 and 6. The models are organized in groups of four, based on the primitive component involved in the calculations. The first model in each group represents the minimum allowable $^{87}Sr/^{86}Sr$ value for Proterozoic crust, given the assumed constraints on elemental concentrations. The second model in each group represents the maximum allowable $^{87}Sr/^{86}Sr$ value for Proterozoic crust, given the same constraints. For example, Mixing Model no. 1 (Table 5) is a mixture of 81% enriched mantle component and 19% Pro-

TABLE 5. Mixing Models Based on Combined Sr and Nd Data[1]

Model number	Component				Proterozoic crust				Pct. of component[2]
	Sr, ppm	87Sr/86Sr	Nd, ppm	εNd	Sr, ppm	87Sr/86Sr	Nd, ppm	εNd	
	Enriched component (EC)								
1	695	0.70650	29.0	−7.0	425	0.72170	45	−17.5	81
2	680	0.70650	25.3	−7.0	145	0.83050	125	−17.5	93
3	749	0.70650	29.0	−7.0	193	0.74000	45	−17.5	81
4	665	0.70650	25.8	−7.0	425	0.74000	99	−17.5	91
	Intermediate component (IC)								
5	789	0.70431	23.5	0.0	425	0.71988	45	−17.5	60
6	680	0.70431	16.5	0.0	425	0.74760	125	−17.5	86
7	947	0.70431	23.5	0.0	185	0.74000	45	−17.5	60
8	690	0.70431	17.1	0.0	425	0.74000	103	−17.5	83
	Depleted component (DC)								
9	874	0.70250	18.4	10.0	425	0.71993	45	−17.5	49
10	694	0.70250	11.0	10.0	425	0.75081	125	−17.5	82
11	1114	0.70250	18.5	10.0	197	0.74000	45	−17.5	49
12	713	0.70250	11.8	10.0	425	0.74000	96	−17.5	76

[1]Models represent mixtures of variably enriched primitive components with Proterozoic crust. The last column contains the percentage of primitive component that precisely yields the observed elemental and isotopic composition of the least-fractionated sample (EM19) from the Eagle Mountain intrusion. See text for further explanation.

[2]Percentage of enriched component (model nos. 1–4), of intermediate component (model nos. 5–8), and of depleted component (model nos. 9–12).

TABLE 6. AFC Models Based on Combined SR and Nd Data[1]

Model number	Component				Proterozoic crust				Pct. of component[2]
	Sr, ppm	87Sr/86Sr	Nd, ppm	εNd	Sr, ppm	87Sr/86Sr	Nd, ppm	εNd	
	Enriched component (EC)								
1	687	0.70650	21.1	−7.0	425	0.72410	45	−17.5	77
2	659	0.70650	22.6	−7.0	425	0.75110	125	−17.5	91
3	726	0.70650	21.1	−7.0	223	0.74000	45	−17.5	77
4	665	0.70650	22.3	−7.0	425	0.74000	92	−17.5	87
	Intermediate component (IC)								
5	738	0.70431	11.3	0.0	425	0.72500	45	−17.5	59
6	676	0.70431	13.0	0.0	425	0.75258	125	−17.5	81
7	814	0.70431	11.3	0.0	246	0.74000	45	−17.5	59
8	690	0.70431	12.5	0.0	425	0.74000	88	−17.5	75
	Depleted component (DC)								
9	766	0.70250	6.8	10.0	425	0.72736	45	−17.5	51
10	686	0.70250	8.1	10.0	425	0.75845	125	−17.5	77
11	847	0.70250	6.8	10.0	282	0.704000	45	−17.5	51
12	712	0.70250	7.6	10.0	425	0.74000	78	−17.5	67

[1]Models represent fractional crystallization of magma derived from variably enriched primitive components with simultaneous assimilation of Proterozoic crust. The last column contains the percentage of liquid remaining that precisely yields the observed elemental and isotopic composition of the least-fractionated sample (EM19) from the Eagle Mountain intrusion. All calculations assume r = 0.4, D_{Sr} = 1, and D_{Nd} = 0.35. See text for further explanation.

[2]Percentage of enriched component (model nos. 1–4), of intermediate component (model nos. 5–8), and of depleted component (model nos. 9–12).

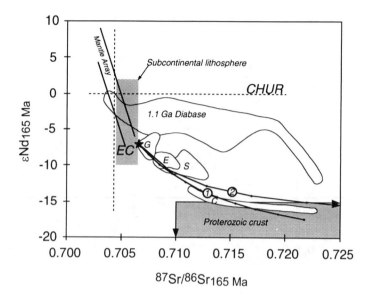

Fig. 12. Mixing between an enriched mantle component (EC) and compositionally variable Proterozoic crust. Models 1 and 2 from Table 5 are plotted. Model curves are marked at 10% increments. EC has Sr = 695 ppm, $^{87}Sr/^{86}Sr$ = 0.70650, Nd = 29 ppm, ϵNd = –7.0. Model no. 1 represents a mixture of 81% EC and 19% Proterozoic crust with Sr = 425 ppm, $^{87}Sr/^{86}Sr$ = 0.72170, Nd = 45, and ϵNd = –17.5. Model no. 2 depicts a mixture containing 93% EC and 7% Proterozoic crust with Sr = 145, $^{87}Sr/^{86}Sr$ = 0.83050, Nd = 125, and ϵNd = –17.5. Both models precisely reproduce the elemental concentrations and isotopic ratios of the least-fractionated sample from the Eagle Mountain intrusion, and generally mimic the curved Jurassic plutonic array. Models 1 and 2, respectively, represent the minimum and maximum crustal $^{87}Sr/^{86}Sr$ that is compatible with the observed range of crustal Sr and Nd elemental concentrations.

terozoic crust having $^{87}Sr/^{86}Sr$ = 0.72170. Mixing Model no. 2 is a mixture of 93% enriched mantle component and 7% Proterozoic crust having $^{87}Sr/^{86}Sr$ = 0.83050. The higher crustal $^{87}Sr/^{86}Sr$ in Mixing Model no. 2 compensates for a smaller proportion of crust in the mixture. Crustal concentrations of Sr and Nd differ between the two models, but remain within the ranges defined in Figure 11. Mixing Models 1 and 2 are plotted in Figure 12 to illustrate the approximate fit to the Jurassic plutonic array. AFC Model no. 1 is plotted in Figure 13.

The third and fourth models in each group illustrate the effect of variable crustal Sr and Nd concentrations for a constant intermediate crustal $^{87}Sr/^{86}Sr$ of 0.74000. For example, the decrease from 19% Proterozoic crust in Mixing Model no. 3 to 9% Proterozoic crust in Mixing Model no. 4 is strictly a function of different Sr and Nd elemental concentrations. Mixing Models 3 and 4 are both limiting cases in terms of crustal Sr and Nd concentrations. In Model no.

3, the crustal Nd concentration has bottomed out at 45 ppm, whereas in Model no. 4 the crustal Sr has topped out at 425 ppm.

The composition of sample EM19 can be reproduced by mixing 81% to 93% enriched mantle component (ϵNd = –7.0, Nd = 25 to 29 ppm, $^{87}Sr/^{86}Sr$ = 0.7065, Sr = 665 to 749 ppm) with 19% to 7% Proterozoic crust (ϵNd = –17.5, Nd = 45 to 125 ppm, $^{87}Sr/^{86}Sr$ = 0.72 to 0.83, Sr = 145 to 425 ppm), or by mixing 60% to 86% bulk earth–like mantle component (ϵNd = 0.0, Nd = 27 to 24 ppm, $^{87}Sr/^{86}Sr$ = 0.7043, Sr = 680 to 947 ppm) with 40% to 14% Proterozoic crust (ϵNd = –17.5, Nd = 45 to 125 ppm, $^{87}Sr/^{86}Sr$ = 0.72 to 0.75, Sr = 185 to 425 ppm). AFC calculations require 9% to 23% crystallization of an enriched component or 19% to 41% crystallization of a bulk earth–like component during assimilation of Proterozoic crust (r = 0.4) to reproduce the composition of sample EM19. The involvement of a MORB-like, depleted-mantle component can be ruled out

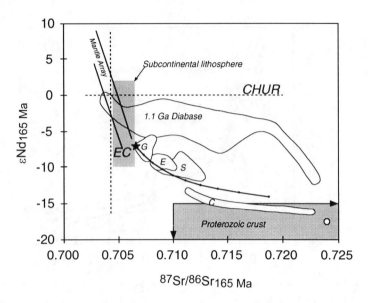

Fig. 13. AFC model based on fractional crystallization of magma derived from an enriched mantle component (EC) while assimilating Proterozoic crust. Model 1 from Table 5 is plotted. EC has Sr = 687 ppm, $^{87}Sr/^{86}Sr$ = 0.70650, Nd = 21 ppm, ϵNd = −7.0. Proterozoic crust has Sr = 425 ppm, $^{87}Sr/^{86}Sr$ = 0.72410, Nd = 45, and ϵNd = −17.5 (open circle). Model assumes r = 0.4, D_{Sr} = 1, and D_{Nd} = 0.35. Model curve has tick marks at 10% increments of liquid remaining. This particular model precisely reproduces the elemental concentrations and isotopic ratios of the least-fractionated sample from the Eagle Mountain intrusion (EM19) at 77% liquid remaining, and represents the minimum crustal $^{87}Sr/^{86}Sr$ that is compatible with the observed range of crustal Sr and Nd elemental concentrations. The model curve also generally mimics the curved Jurassic plutonic array.

because of the high Sr concentrations (>690 ppm) required by the data (see Tables 5 and 6).

Implications for other Jurassic plutons

The Eagle Mountain intrusion appears to contain, or to have been derived from, a source containing >60% juvenile material, with the remainder composed of a component similar to exposed Proterozoic crust. The Granite Mountains diorite lies closer to mantle compositions (Fig. 12) and should contain a larger juvenile component. Young et al. (1992) concluded that the Granite Mountains diorite contained approximately 90% juvenile, enriched mantle. The Ship and Clipper plutons have more crust-like compositions and should contain larger crustal fractions than the Eagle Mountain intrusion. Miller and Wooden (1994) estimated crustal contributions of 25% to 100% for these plutons.

The results of the modeling described in this study suggest derivation of the Mesozoic plutons in the Mojave region from hybridized sources containing variable proportions of

juvenile mantle and recycled crustal components. Formation of such hybridized sources would require a large flux of mantle-derived magma into the lower crust to induce crustal melting, followed by assimilation and mixing of mantle and crustal melts. This is essentially the MASH model of Hildreth and Moorbath (1988).

Conclusions

No single source could have yielded melts with the radiogenic isotopic composition of the Eagle Mountain intrusion. Nevertheless, the uniformity of isotopic compositions within the intrusion suggests derivation from a single source. A hybrid source is proposed that consists of various proportions of juvenile mantle–derived magma and recycled lower-crustal magma. The source-level hybridization proposed here is not to be confused with the mixing of enclave and host magmas that occurred during upper-crustal emplacement to form heterogeneous, mixed-facies diorite. Mixing and AFC calculations support a hybrid source for the

Eagle Mountain intrusion, containing >60% enriched mantle material and <40% crustal material with the isotopic composition of exposed Proterozoic crust.

Hybridization is envisioned to occur in lower-crustal zones of mixing and assimilation (MASH zones of Hildreth and Moorbath, 1988), where rising pulses of mantle-derived magma provide heat to partially melt hot lower-crustal rocks. The hybridized zones then serve as the source of mafic, partially differentiated magmas with isotope compositions intermediate between mantle and lower-crustal melts. Lateral variations in the proportions of mantle and crust in the hybridized source zone would lead to lateral variations in the isotopic signatures of derivative magmas. In this way, Jurassic plutons from different locations in the Mojave Desert region have isotopic affinities ranging from enriched mantle to exposed Proterozoic continental crust.

REFERENCES

Anderson, J. L., and Smith, D. R., 1995, The effects of temperature and fO_2 on the Al-in-hornblende barometer: Amer. Mineral., v. 80, p. 549–559.

Barth, A. P., Wooden, J. L., Tosdal, R. M., and Morrison, J., 1995, Crustal contamination in the petrogenesis of a calc-alkalic rock series: Josephine Mountain intrusion, California: Geol. Soc. Amer. Bull., v. 107, p. 202–212.

Bender, E. E., 1995, Petrology of early Proterozoic granitoids from the southwestern US: Implications for genesis and tectonics of the Mojave crustal province: Unpubl. Ph.D. thesis, Univ. of Southern California.

Bennett, V. C., and DePaolo, D. J., 1987, Proterozoic crustal history of the western United States as determined by neodymium isotopic mapping: Geol. Soc. Amer. Bull., v. 99, p. 674–685.

Blundy, J. D., and Holland, T. J. B., 1990, Calcic amphibole equilibria and a new amphibole-plagioclase geothermometer: Contrib. Mineral. Petrol., v. 104, p. 208–224.

Carter, B. C., and Silver, L. T., 1982, Geology of the San Gabriel anorthosite-syenite body, Los Angeles County, California, *in* Geology and Mineral Wealth of the California Transverse Ranges: Santa Ana, California, South Coast Geol. Soc., p. 294–296.

Chen, J. H., and Moore, J. G., 1961, Late Jurassic Independence dike swarm in eastern California: Geology, v. 7, p. 129–133.

DePaolo, D., 1981a, Trace element and isotopic effects of combined wallrock assimilation and fractional crystallization: Earth Planet. Sci. Lett., v. 53, p. 189–202.

————, 1981b, A neodymium and strontium isotopic study of the Mesozoic calc-alkaline granitic batholiths of the Sierra Nevada and Peninsular Ranges, California: Jour. Geophys. Res., v. 86, p. 10470–10488.

————, 1988, Neodymium isotope geochemistry: New York, Springer-Verlag, p. 187.

Fernandez, A. N., and Barbarin, B., 1991, Relative rheology of coeval mafic and felsic magmas: Nature of resulting interaction processes and shape and mineral fabrics of mafic microgranular enclaves, *in* Didier, J., and Barbarin, B., eds., Enclaves and granite petrology: Amsterdam, Elsevier, p. 263–275.

Gill, J. B., 1981, Orogenic andesites and plate tectonics: New York, Springer-Verlag, 390 p.

Hammond, J. G., and Wooden, J. L., 1990, Isotopic constraints on the petrogenesis of Proterozoic diabase in southwestern USA, *in* Parker, A. J., Rickwood, P. C., and Tucker, D. H., eds., Mafic dikes and emplacement mechanisms: Rotterdam, Balkema, p. 145–156.

Henderson, P., 1982, Inorganic geochemistry: Oxford, UK, Pergamon Press, 353 p.

Hewitt, D. A., and Wones, D. R., 1984, Experimental phase relations of the micas, *in* Bailey, S. W., ed., Micas: Mineral. Soc. Amer., Rev. Mineral. Vol. 13, p. 201–256.

Hildreth, W. and Moorbath, S., 1988, Crustal contributions to arc magmatism in the Andes of central Chile: Contrib. Mineral. Petrol., v. 98, p. 455–489.

James, E. W., 1989, Southern extension of the Independence dike swarm of eastern California: Geology, v. 17, p. 587–590.

Leventhal, J. A., Reid, M. R., Montana, A., and Holden, P., 1995, Mesozoic invasion of crust by MORB-source asthenospheric magmas, United States Cordilleran Interior: Geology, v. 23, p. 399–402.

Mayo, D. P., and Wooden, J. L., 1993, Mingled mafic and felsic magmas in the Jurassic Eagle Mountain pluton, southeastern California [abs.]: Geol. Soc. Amer. Abs. Prog., v. 25, p. 116.

Menzies, M. A., Leeman, W. P., and Hawkesworth, C. J., 1983, Isotope geochemistry of Cenozoic volcanic rocks reveals mantle heterogeneity below western USA: Nature, v. 303, p. 205–209.

Miller, C. F., and Barton, M. D., 1990, Phanerozoic plutonism in the Cordilleran Interior, U.S.A., *in* Kay, S. M., and Rapela, C.W., eds., Plutonism from Antarctica to Alaska: Geol. Soc. Amer. Spec. Pap. 241, p. 213–231.

Miller, C. F., and Wooden, J. L., 1994, Anatexis, hybridization, and the modification of ancient crust: Mesozoic plutonism in the Old Woman Mountains area, California: Lithos, v. 32, p. 111–133.

Miller, J. S., and Glazner, A. F., 1995, Jurassic plutonism and crustal evolution in the central Mojave Desert, California: Contrib. Mineral. Petrol., v. 118, p. 379–395.

Moore, J. G., and Hopson, C. A., 1961, The Independence dike swarm in eastern California: Amer. Jour. Sci., v. 259, p. 241–259.

Musselwhite, D. S., DePaolo, D. J., and McCurry, M., 1989, The evolution of a silicic magma system: Isotopic and chemical evidence from the Woods Mountains volcanic center, eastern California: Contrib. Mineral. Petrol., v. 101, p. 19–29.

Naney, N. T., 1983, Phase equilibria of rock-forming ferromagnesian silicates in granitic systems: Amer. Jour. Sci., v. 283, p. 993–1033.

Powell, R. E., 1981, Geology of the crystalline basement complex, eastern central Transverse Ranges, southern California: Constraints on regional tectonic interpretation: Unpubl. Ph.D. thesis, California Inst. Technol., 441 p.

——————, 1982, Crystalline basement terranes in the southern eastern Transverse Ranges, California, in Frost, E. G. and Martin, D. L., eds., Mesozoic-Cenozoic tectonic evolution of the Colorado River region, California, Arizona, and Nevada: Boulder, CO: Geol. Soc. Amer., p. 109–136.

Stacey, J. S., and Kramers, J. D., 1975, Approximation of terrestrial lead isotope evolution by a two-stage model: Earth Planet. Sci. Lett., v. 26, p. 207–221.

Taylor, H. P., Jr., 1968, The oxygen-isotope geochemistry of igneous rocks: Contrib. Mineral. Petrol., v. 19, p. 1–71.

Tosdal, R. M., Haxel, G. B., and Wright, J. E., 1989, Jurassic geology of the Sonoran Desert region, southern Arizona, southeastern California, and northernmost Sonora: Construction of a continental-margin magmatic arc, in Jenney, J. P., and Reynolds, S. J., eds., Geologic evolution of Arizona: Ariz. Geol. Soc. Digest, v. 17, p. 397–434.

Wones, D. R., 1981, Mafic silicates as indicators of intensive variables in granitic magmas: Mining Geol., v. 31, p. 191–212.

Wones, D. R., and Gilbert, M. C., 1982, Amphiboles in the igneous environment, in Veblen, D. R., and Ribbe, P. H., eds., Amphiboles: Petrology and experimental phase relations: Mineral. Soc. Amer., Rev. Mineral Vol. 9B, p. 355–390.

Wooden, J. L., Powell, R. E., Howard, K. A., and Tosdal, R. M., 1991, Eagle Mountains 30' × 60' quadrangle, southern California: II. Isotopic and chronologic studies [abs.]: Geol. Soc. Amer. Abs. Prog., v. 23, p. 478.

Wooden, J. L., Stacey, J. S., Howard, K. A., Doe, B. R., and Miller, D. M., 1988, Pb isotopic evidence for the formation of Proterozoic crust in the southwestern United States, in Ernst, W. G., ed., Metamorphism and crustal evolution of the western United States, Rubey Vol. VII: Englewood Cliffs, NJ, Prentice Hall, p. 68–83.

Wyllie, P. J., Cox, K. G., and Biggar, G. M., 1962, The habit of apatite in synthetic systems and igneous rocks: Jour. Petrol., v. 3, p. 238–243.

Young, E. D., Wooden, J. L., Shieh, Y.-N. and Farber, D., 1992, Geochemical evolution of Jurassic diorites from the Bristol Lake region, California, U.S.A. and the role of assimilation: Contrib. Mineral. Petrol., v. 110, p. 68–86.

Deformation and Metamorphism of the Marble Mountain and Pony Camp Areas, Western Triassic and Paleozoic Belt, Central Klamath Mountains, Northwestern California

DAVID E. MILLER AND W. G. ERNST

Department of Geological and Environmental Sciences, Stanford University, Stanford, California 94305-2115

Abstract

The Western Triassic and Paleozoic belt (WTrPz) is a regionally extensive, composite terrane correlative with Cache Creek–affinity rocks, a major crust-forming lithotectonic entity of the North American Cordillera. New structural, stratigraphic, and petrologic data suggest that a large tract of greenschist- to amphibolite-grade metavolcanic and metasedimentary rock, previously considered to consist of several separate oceanic terranes, is, instead, a single fault-bounded, volcanic island arc, the Sawyers Bar terrane. It represents a mid-Jurassic, relatively intact, recrystallized nappe complex 5 to 10 km thick, extending over 100 km along strike in the central Klamaths. Protoliths of the complex are interpreted to be Lower Triassic(?) to mid-Jurassic supracrustal, volcanic arc–related units deposited, deformed, and metamorphosed within a suprasubduction zone adjacent to the continental margin. Metamorphism increases monotonically with depth in the nappe, ranging from prehnite-pumpellyite to lower greenschist-grade in the Pony Camp area on the south, through greenschist–grade in the medial Sawyers Bar area, to low-pressure amphibolite–grade metamorphism in the Marble Mountains on the north. The Pony Camp area generally lacks penetrative deformation. In the Marble Mountains, peak metamorphism largely postdates intense deformation; nevertheless, folding of fabrics and brittle deformation are common.

The complex is bounded by low-angle, W-vergent, crustal-scale, mid-Jurassic thrusts. The Soap Creek Ridge fault juxtaposes Stuart Fork blueschists over the Sawyers Bar complex. The lower thrust is not definitely established, but must be situated beneath tectonic levels postulated by earlier workers. It may coincide with the previously unrecognized brittle-plastic Isinglass shear zone in the Marble Mountains, and a poorly exposed, unnamed low-angle fault in the Virgin Buttes region west of Pony Camp. In this area, mapping indicates that the Twin Sisters fault is a relatively minor high-angle break within the WTrPz, rather than being a crustal-scale terrane suture. Synmagmatic, brittle extensional faults are common, as are syn- and postmetamorphic, regionally extensive, high-angle faults that internally imbricate the WTrPz; the latter are marked by sheared serpentinite. Folds within the Sawyers Bar nappe complex are NE- to NW-trending and W-vergent. Structural evidence suggests that W-vergent thrusting, E-W contraction, regional Siskiyou metamorphism, penetrative deformation, and crustal thickening occurred at ~170 to 165 Ma, and preceded voluminous 167 to 162 Ma calc-alkaline plutonism. In the study areas, waning stages of Siskiyou deformation were characterized by thermal relaxation, uplift, extension, crustal thinning, and E-directed tectonic transport. Nevadan age contraction ($\approx$155 to 150 Ma), prevalent to the west at lower structural levels of the WTrPz, is not recognized in the Sawyers Bar nappe; however, regionally developed open folding of Siskiyou metamorphic fabrics and rare superposed folding and axial-plane cleavage development in the Marble Mountains may reflect a Nevadan event. Brittle deformation that clearly post-dates Siskiyou folding is younger than 150 Ma, but is older than ~130 Ma, the age of the oldest marine strata that overlie the Klamath province regionally. Kinematic evidence from the eastern Marble Mountains suggests sinistral transtension of possibly latest Jurassic–Early Cretaceous age. Late-stage brittle deformation is permissibly Cenozoic; the Sawyers Bar thrust sheet was tilted a maximum of 30° to the south along the flanks of the Condrey Mountain dome during Cenozoic uplift.

The Sawyers Bar nappe complex is similar to other composite terranes in Phanerozoic convergent suture zones throughout the world. Like the Klamath Mountains, these areas also may represent different exposure levels within a single fault-bounded entity rather than an amalgam of disparate terranes.

Introduction and Scope

CRUSTAL ACCRETION at convergent plate boundaries is an incompletely understood process.
Within accreted packages of rocks, internal
deformation and metamorphism at different
structural levels further complicate the record
of continental growth. The Klamath Mountains
provide a remarkably complete, well-exposed,
and accessible record of sialic crustal evolution
that spans most of the Paleozoic and Mesozoic
eras (Irwin, 1966; Irwin and Mankinen, 1998).
The terrane concept, in which continental
growth is accomplished by the accretion of
exotic, fault-bounded lithotectonic units, arose
from seminal studies by Irwin (1972) in this
mountain belt. The largest and perhaps least
well understood terrane within the Klamath
Mountains is the Western Triassic and Paleozoic Belt (WTrPz). It is generally considered to
be part of the Cache Creek assemblage, a regionally extensive, composite lithotectonic terrane
that constitutes a significant component of the
Cordilleran orogen in western North America
(Davis et al., 1978; Burchfiel and Davis, 1981;
Monger et al., 1982). The geographic distribution of assemblages with Cache Creek affinity is
illustrated in Figure 1. This lithotectonic belt
has been interpreted to represent far-traveled
paleo-Pacific crust accreted to North America
in the Mesozoic, and as such records the processes of continental growth at the western
sialic margin (Silberling et al., 1984). More
recent studies have suggested that much of the
Cache Creek assemblage actually formed in a
suprasubduction-zone setting in proximity to
North America (Ernst, 1990; Saleeby, 1990;
Ernst et al., 1991; Hacker et al., 1993).

The goals of this work are: (1) to examine the
local record of deformation and metamorphism
at an accretionary convergent margin; (2) to
illuminate the paleotectonic setting of well-
exposed portions of the Cache Creek assemblage that formed at contrasting crustal levels;
and (3) to relate these new data to more generalized models of Cordilleran orogenesis and
processes of continental growth. Two areas of
the WTrPz were chosen for detailed mapping
and structural, petrographic, and stratigraphic
analyses (Fig. 2A). Both areas are characterized
by glaciated mountains with significant topographic relief, and are well exposed. The Marble
Mountain study area is located in the

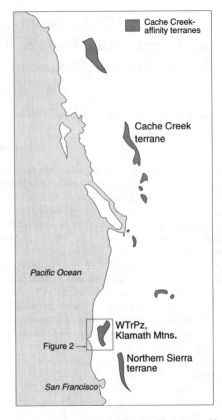

FIG. 1. Distribution of Cache Creek–affinity assemblages
in the North American Cordillera, after Miller (1987).

Marble Mountain Wilderness west of Yreka,
California; lithotectonic units cropping out
here are from low structural levels of the
WTrPz. The Pony Camp study area is located in
the western part of the Trinity Alps Wilderness;
exposures in this area are from high structural
levels of the WTrPz. Between these two areas
lies the Sawyers Bar area, investigated by Ernst
(1987, 1990, 1993, 1998), Ernst at al. (1991),
and Hacker et al. (1992, 1993, 1995). The
Sawyers Bar area provides a geologically
and geochemically well-characterized bridge
between the two study areas.

Regional Geologic Setting of the WTrPz

The Klamath Mountains consist of diverse
oceanic and arc-related rocks that preserve a
clear record of Phanerozoic continental accretion. Irwin (1966) divided the province into
four N-S–striking, arcuate lithologic belts.

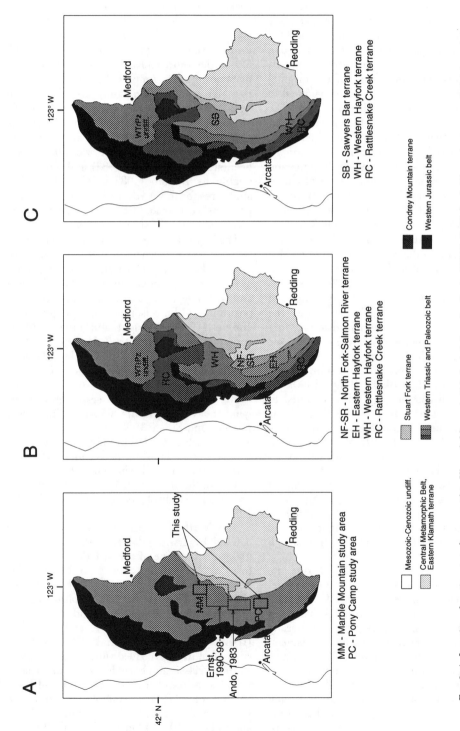

Fig. 2. A. Location of pertinent study areas within Klamath Mountain lithologic belts, after Irwin (1981). B. Klamath Mountain terrane subdivision, after Wright and Wyld (1994). C. Klamath Mountain terrane subdivision, this study.

From structurally lowest on the west to highest on the east, these are: (1) the Western Jurassic belt; (2) the Western Triassic and Paleozoic belt; (3) the Central Metamorphic belt; and (4) the Eastern Klamath belt. These units form a structural stack of predominantly W-vergent thrust sheets (Fig. 2A). Some of the original lithologic belts of Irwin now are considered to be amalgamated terranes (Irwin, 1972). The WTrPz is a composite lithotectonic unit that has been further divided into five subterranes, mainly on the basis of work in the southern Klamaths (e.g., Wright, 1982; Wright and Fahan, 1988). From structurally lowest to highest, these subterranes are: (a) the Rattlesnake Creek terrane (RC); (b) the Western Hayfork terrane (WH); (c) the Eastern Hayfork terrane (EH); (d) the North Fork–Salmon River terrane (NF-SR); and (e) the Stuart Fork terrane (SF). Figure 2B illustrates the terrane subdivision proposed by Wright and Wyld (1994).

These subdivisions are not clearly recognized in other parts of the WTrPz, including the localities reported on in this investigation. Only the transitional blueschist/greenschist–grade SF, the structurally highest subterrane, can be confidently traced from north to south across the orogen (Goodge, 1989a, 1989b, 1990). In subsequent discussions, the SF is elevated to the status of an individual terrane, on the basis of its unique metamorphic history relative to its neighbors (Hotz et al., 1977) and the well-defined crustal-scale faults that define its boundaries. The term WTrPz is used herein to refer to all other rock units of the original WTrPz belt as defined by Irwin (1966), exclusive of the SF (e.g., Ernst, 1983). Our alternative terrane subdivision, according to this and previous studies (Hacker et al., 1993), is shown in Figure 2C.

The Rattlesnake Creek terrane forms the tectonic base of the WTrPz. The most structurally disrupted subterrane, the RC is characterized by landslides and earthflows that cover surface exposures. This terrane is generally described as mélange consisting of dismembered ophiolitic rocks (Irwin, 1972; Wright, 1982). Chert within the mélange contains Triassic and Early Jurassic radiolarians (Irwin et al., 1983), and olistolithic limestone pods and lenses contain Devonian(?), Late Paleozoic, and Late Triassic fossils (Irwin and Galanis, 1976; Irwin et al., 1982). Gray (1986) and

Wright and Wyld (1994) described arc-related rocks that may depositionally overlie the mélange. Plutonic rocks, possible intrusive equivalents of the arc-related supracrustal units, have U/Pb ages ranging from 193 to 207 Ma. In the southern Klamaths, the RC is feebly metamorphosed. Amphibolite-grade rocks in the Marble Mountain study area have been considered higher-grade equivalents of the RC, although significant protolithic differences exist (Donato, 1987; Rawson and Petersen, 1982). Rocks in the Marble Mountains have been studied by Welsh (1982) and most thoroughly by Donato (1985, 1987, 1989). The study area for this investigation overlaps that of previous workers and lies directly north of the area studied by Ernst (1987, 1998).

The Hayfork terrane structurally overlies the RC; it was subdivided by Wright (1982) into the Western Hayfork and Eastern Hayfork terranes. WH rocks are predominantly crystal-lithic tuff and tuff breccias of andesitic to basaltic composition, and have isotopic ages ranging from 168 to 177 Ma (Wright and Fahan, 1988); superjacent units are intruded by the ~172 Ma Ironside Mountain batholith. The EH is a mélange consisting of argillite, chert, quartzose sandstone, mafic to silicic volcanic rocks, exotic limestone pods, and serpentinite overlying the WH along the Wilson Point thrust (Wright and Fahan, 1988). Chert contains Triassic to Early Jurassic(?) radiolarians (Irwin et al., 1982), and limestone pods contain Permian Tethyan fusilinids (Irwin and Galanis, 1976). In the southern Klamath Mountains, metamorphism is generally of greenschist grade (Wright, 1982).

The North Fork–Salmon River terrane, as defined by Irwin (1981), is the structurally highest subterrane of the WTrPz. These rocks form a N-S–striking zone 1 to 10 km wide bounded by high-angle faults in the southern Klamaths. They consist of gabbro, plagiogranite, diabase, serpentinite, and interlayered pillow basalt, chert, argillite, and limestone (Irwin, 1972; Ando et al., 1983). Chert and siliceous tuff interbedded with mafic volcanics contain Triassic and Early Jurassic radiolarians, whereas far-traveled lenses of chert and limestone contain Permian radiolarians and Late Paleozoic fusilinids and foraminifers (Irwin and Galanis, 1976; Blome and Irwin, 1983). A discordant, Late Paleozoic U/Pb age was reported by Ando et al. (1983) from a plagio-granite pod within a shear zone, whereas Hacker et al. (1993) obtained an Ar/Ar age of 200 Ma on hornblende from gabbro within this terrane. These rocks have been metamorphosed to greenschist grade. Rocks within the Pony Camp study area lie on strike to the south from areas studied by Ando et al. (1983) and Ernst (1987, 1998). The present investigation attempts to integrate this and previous studies in a regional tectonic synthesis of the central WTrPz.

Marble Mountain Study Area

General geology

The study area straddles the poorly under-stood transition between pairs of three pre-sumed subterranes of the WTrPz—the superjacent North Fork–Salmon River and sub-jacent Marble Mountain terranes, and interven-ing rocks of uncertain terrane designation, but generally correlated with the Western Hayfork terrane (Donato, 1987; Coleman et al., 1988). Amphibolite-grade rocks of the Marble Moun-tains have been correlated with the feebly meta-morphosed Rattlesnake Creek terrane of the southern Klamaths (Rawson and Petersen, 1982). Besides differences in metamorphic grade, differences in rock types and deforma-tion style are reported to exist among the three terranes (Donato, 1989; Miller and Hacker, 1993).

Map units of the Marble Mountain area

Rocks of the Marble Mountains can be divided into two regionally extensive units on the basis of structural position and metamor-phic texture. The tectonically lower unit is informally named the Boulder Creek amphibo-lite (BCa); the higher unit is termed the Wright Lakes assemblage (WLa). These rock units are juxtaposed along the previously unrecognized, gently dipping Isinglass shear zone, described in a later section. Both BCa and WLa have been invaded by calc-alkaline plutons ± ultramafic cold intrusions. The investigated region is located in Figure 3. Figures 4–6 present detailed geology of portions of the Marble Mountains area, mapped at a scale of 1:6,000; cross sec-tions also are presented in these figures.

Boulder Creek amphibolite. The Boulder Creek amphibolite, the tectonically lowest rock unit

in the study area, is exposed along creeks and cliffs south of the Scott River at elevations below 5000 to 6000 feet (~1500 to 1800 m) in the northern part of the study area (Figs. 5 and 6). The BCa has a structural thickness of at least 1.5 km. It has a well-defined L-S tectonite fabric parallel to compositional layering; foliation and compositional layering dip gently to moderately south. During mapping, this unit was further subdivided into three lithologies—predomi-nantly mafic amphibolite with subordinate quartzofeldspathic schist, subequal proportions of quartzofeldspathic schist and interlayered mafic amphibolite, and a disrupted mixture of various rock types found along the Isinglass shear zone. All rock types are interlayered at the meter scale, have well-developed tectonite fab-rics, and lack recognizable protolith textures. These lithologies are described in detail by Miller (1998).

Wright Lakes assemblage. The Wright Lakes assemblage is exposed along creeks and glaci-ated ridges in the southern part of the study area (Figs. 4–6). The WLa has a structural thickness of at least 2.5 km. It is juxtaposed against subjacent rocks of the Boulder Creek amphibolite by the Isinglass shear zone. Upper levels of the WLa are overlain and interlayered with mafic metavolcanic rocks of the Sawyers Bar area. The Wright Lakes assemblage consists of volcanic + sedimentary rocks and tec-tonically interleaved meta-ultramafic rocks + associated amphibolite tectonite. Amphibolite-grade metavolcanic rocks comprise most of this unit; metasedimentary rocks represent a lesser, although volumetrically significant, part. The Wright Lakes assemblage can be further sub-divided into mappable units based on lithology: metadacite, felsic-intermediate metavolcanic rocks, mafic metavolcanic rocks, metacarbo-nate, quartzite-metachert, pelitic schist + meta-tuff, polymict breccia + metaconglomerate, mixed metasedimentary rocks + gabbroic-dio-ritic dikes/sills, and a unique assemblage of felsic-mafic metavolcanic rocks termed the Boulder Peak unit (Figs. 4–6). Meta-ultramafic rocks and associated amphibolite tectonite are sheared into these supracrustal rocks. In con-trast to the BCa, the WLa displays multiple folds, possesses a variably developed tectonite fabric, and has well-preserved protolith tex-

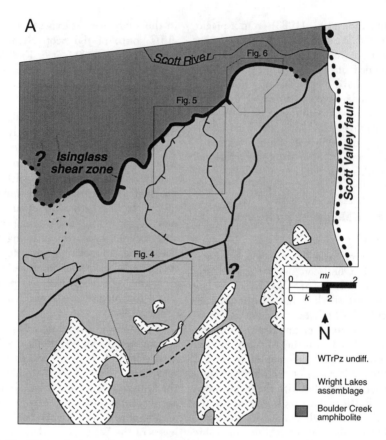

FIG. 3. A. Simplified geologic overview of the Marble Mountains and locations of detailed study areas (Fig. 4 = Shackleford Creek, Fig. 5 = Wright Lakes, Fig. 6 = Isinglass Lakes). B (facing page). Map units for the Marble Mountain study area.

tures. Most of the rock types listed above are interlayered at the outcrop scale and have demonstrable stratigraphic contacts. Facing indicators (pillow basalts and grain size or density stratification of clastic rocks) are rare. The WLa is presumed to have formed an originally intact stratigraphic sequence. Individual lithologies of this subunit are described in detail by Miller (1998).

Plutonic rocks. The WLa is intruded by the gabbroic to dioritic Heather Lake and Shelley Lake plutons and by numerous, small gabbroic to dioritic stocks, dikes, and sills. The proportion of exposed plutonic rock is much greater in the WLa than in the subjacent BCa. Also, in contrast to intrusions within the BCa, many of the larger plutons in the WLa have well-defined contact metamorphic aureoles extending outward tens to hundreds of meters; several of the

smaller intrusions show well-defined chilled margins. Hornblende diorite, hornblende quartz diorite, hornblende gabbro, and hornblende tonalite are the most abundant intrusive types. Some stocks have retained primary igneous fabrics, whereas others are moderately to weakly foliated, especially along their margins, similar to plutonic rocks in the Isinglass shear zone and elsewhere in the study area. Foliation in intrusives, where present, is usually concordant with country-rock layering.

Meta-ultramafic rocks. Metaperidotites and associated tectonite amphibolites are structurally interleaved with the WLa and, to a much lesser extent, with the BCa. Meta-ultramafics consist of roughly tabular sheets and lenses that are tens to hundreds of meters thick. Lenses and sheets are complexly folded and deformed. The contacts of meta-ultramafic rocks with

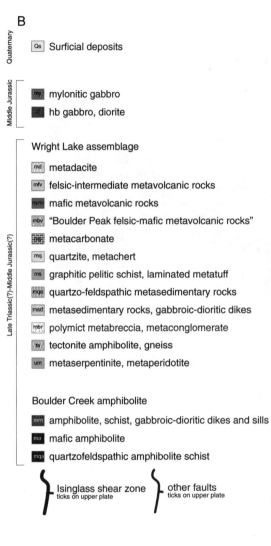

FIG. 3 (contd.).

amphibolites are generally concordant with foliation in the amphibolites, but locally crosscut the foliation in metasedimentary and metavolcanic rocks of the WLa, suggesting post-metamorphic faulting along rheologically weak metaserpentinite horizons. Metaperidotites are of two types: those that preserve relict mantle fabrics and those that exhibit superposed penetrative fabrics. The first type occurs within the interiors of larger lenses and sheets, whereas the second type is found along the margins of tectonic slivers and in fault zones.

Paleotectonic setting of the Marble Mountain protoliths

Previous studies and interpretations of rocks in the study area emphasized the presence of lithologies with oceanic petrologic and geochemical signatures and mélange-like natures (e.g., Donato, 1987). In contrast, this investigation reports the presence of quartz-rich metaclastic rocks, abundant felsic-intermediate metalavas, and metavolcaniclastic rocks. Such rock types are more characteristic of calc-alkaline volcanic arcs and Andean continental margins. Although complexly deformed, intact stratigraphic contacts between most rock types are demonstrable in the field, suggesting that units of the study area were once part of a coherent layered sequence.

Boulder Creek amphibolite. The protoliths of amphibolites in the Boulder Creek amphibolite probably were a mixture of mafic volcanic and quartzofeldspathic sedimentary rocks. Carbonate protoliths are scarce; limestone beds of the Marble Mountain area are considered to be part of the Wright Lakes assemblage. Quartz-rich layers such as chert or quartz arenites also are minor in the BCA at this level of exposure.

Rocks of the BCa are difficult to interpret, but may represent the more thoroughly recrystallized basement of the WLa sequence. However, such an interpretation is not supported by the general lack of meta-ultramafic rocks and paucity of quartzite, metachert, and metacarbonate BCa compared to metasedimentary rocks in the WLa. The BCa may represent a higher-grade equivalent of the Western Hayfork terrane, although it contains an apparently greater percentage of quartzofeldspathic metasediments compared to the Western Hayfork. The BCa may represent a higher-grade equivalent of the Rattlesnake Creek terrane. Support for this interpretation is provided by the presence of blocks of distinctive high-grade metamorphic rocks in both the BCa and Rattlesnake Creek terrane. Evidence against this correlation includes differences in rock types and their relative proportions between the terranes: for example, the Rattlesnake Creek terrane contains large amounts of argillite and serpentinite matrix mélange (Wright and Wyld, 1994), whereas meta-ultramafic rocks are rare at this structural level in the BCa. Similar to the WLa,

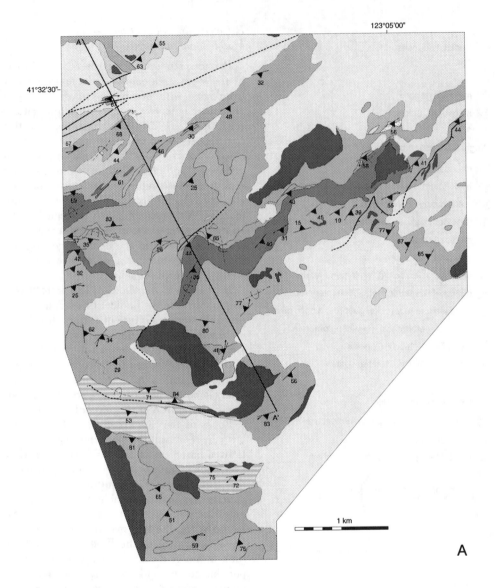

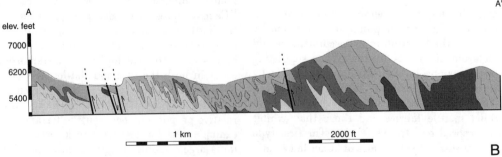

FIG. 4. Geologic map (A) and cross section (B) of the Shackleford Creek area, Marble Mountain study area. See Figure 3B for rock-unit patterns.

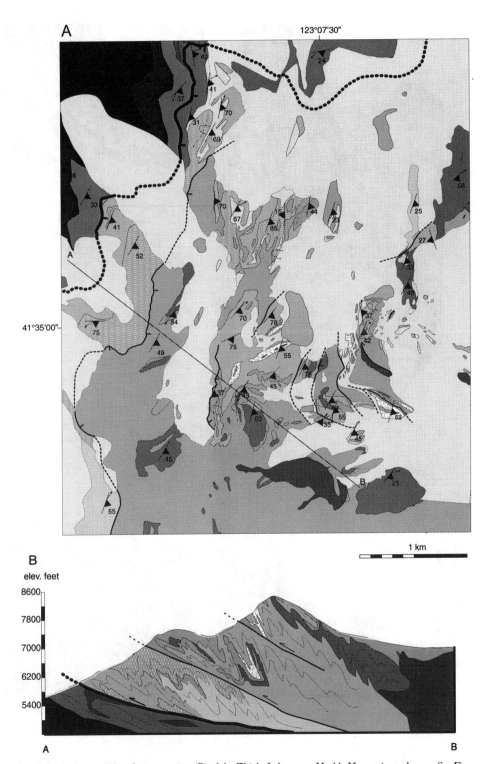

FIG. 5. Geologic map (A) and cross section (B) of the Wright Lakes area, Marble Mountain study area. See Figure 3B for rock-unit patterns.

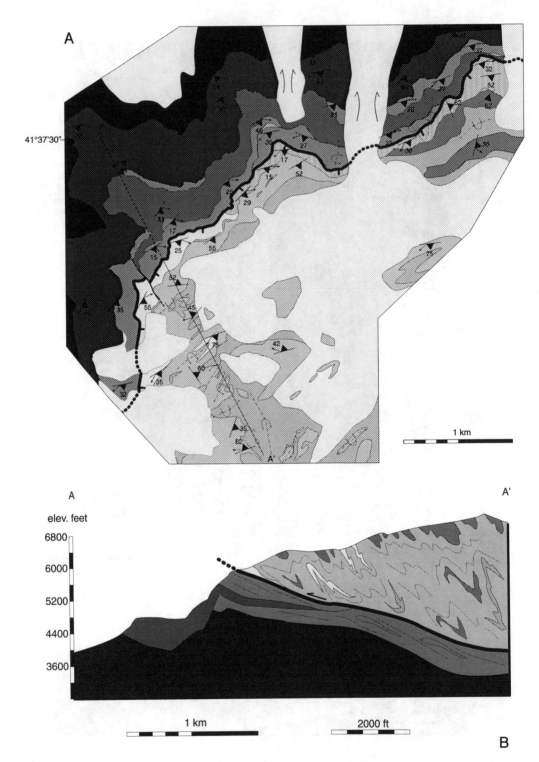

FIG. 6. Geologic map (A) and cross section (B) of the Isinglass Lakes area, Marble Mountain study area. See Figure 3B for rock unit patterns.

the BCa may represent a cryptic volcanic/sedimentary terrane.

Wright Lakes assemblage. Protoliths in the WLa consist of lava and volcaniclastic rocks in subequal amounts. They exhibit broad variations in compositions, but possess the same chemical ranges. Lavas and volcaniclastic rocks with felsic, intermediate, and mafic compositions are interlayered at the meter scale. Lavas preserve massive, pillowed, vesicular, and flow-banded textures. Volcaniclastic rocks consist predominantly of angular pebble- to cobble-sized clasts with basaltic, andesitic, and dacitic compositions in a crystal-rich matrix dominated by sand-sized angular fragments of plagioclase, pyroxene, hornblende, and quartz. Crystal-rich laminated tuffs, crystal lapilli tuffs, and presumed pumice fragments also are present within the volcaniclastics. On the basis of angularity of fragments, interbedded lavas, and abrupt lateral and vertical facies changes, volcaniclastic rocks are interpreted to contain juvenile first-cycle detritus deposited close to eruptive centers. These centers contemporaneously erupted a compositionally diverse range of lavas and pyroclastics. Subaqueous deposition is indicated by the presence of pillow lavas and by volcaniclastic rocks containing graded bedding and density stratification of crystal clasts. Shallow-marine deposition is suggested by: (1) pillow lavas with interpillow carbonate; (2) vesicular lavas with large, centimeter-scale flow-aligned vesicles; (3) well-rounded, well-sorted metaconglomerates; and (4) quartzites with planar, heavy-mineral laminations. Flow-banded metadacites suggest possible local subaerial deposition. Juvenile, felsic to intermediate, crystal-rich volcaniclastic deposits and lesser amounts of flow rock suggest deposition in proximity to a volcanic arc. Igneous units that possess arc-tholeiite, calc-alkaline volcanic arc, and within-plate geochemical signatures (Donato, 1987, 1989; Ernst, 1987; Ernst et al., 1991, Hacker et al., 1992) are interlayered on a meter scale. This diverse compositional range may record unique tectonic events, such as transtension within an arc/forearc/backarc tectonic setting, possibly related to ridge or hotspot subduction. Associated quartzose terrigenous sediments indicate deposition close to a continental margin.

Metasedimentary rocks are interlayered with metavolcanics at a meter scale. Fine-grained strata contain delicate laminations of quartz-rich silt and felsic tuff. Presumed soft-sediment deformation at the contacts of lavas and laminated, siliceous meta-argillite indicate that lavas were deposited on virtually unconsolidated sediment. Coarse-grained metasedimentary rocks contain angular pebble- to boulder-sized clasts consisting of varying mixtures of predominantly locally derived volcanic rocks and sedimentary rocks. Evidently the metasedimentary and metavolcanic rocks are part of the same stratigraphic sequence. Interbedded, laminated, graphitic pelitic schist, siliceous argillite, and chert reflect continuing sedimentation in a restricted basin during hiatuses in both volcanism and coarse clastic sedimentation.

Regional implications. Rocks of the Wright Lakes assemblage form a complexly deformed and disrupted but resolvable stratigraphic sequence. Lithostratigraphic units of the WLa were deposited in a suprasubduction, shallow-marine to marine restricted basin that was in proximity to both an active volcanic arc and a quartz-rich, continental-affinity source. We speculate that protoliths were deposited during syndepositional, extensional tectonism. This view contrasts with that of some previous workers who interpreted this assemblage to represent an oceanic, ophiolitic mélange (Silberling et al., 1984; Donato, 1987).

WLa rocks are detached from their basement and constitute a nappe or thrust plate. Provenance of coarse-grained clastics suggests that the original basement consisted of sedimentary rocks, chert, and plutonic + volcanic-arc rocks that may represent older forearc and intra-arc basin deposits. Ophiolites apparently were not exposed at the surface. Meta-ultramafic rocks were emplaced early in the deformational history, however. Lithologic assemblages in the study area resemble rocks deposited in modern suprasubduction-zone extensional basins in the western Pacific (e.g., Bloomer and Hawkins, 1983; Ishii, 1985; Ogawa et al., 1985). Although stratigraphic thicknesses and areal extents of these rocks are difficult to determine, original thicknesses probably did not exceed 1 km, which would be comparable to the volume of rocks erupted from a single relatively short-lived forearc or arc eruptive center. Even including Sawyers Bar metavolcanic and meta-

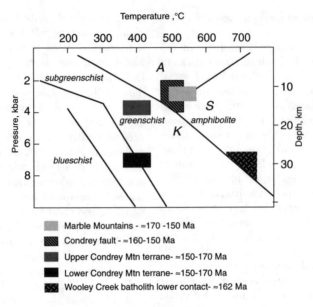

FIG. 7. P-T estimates of metamorphism, Marble Mountain region (Barnes et al., 1986; Helper, 1986; Coleman et al., 1988; Donato,1989).

sedimentary rocks to the south, total thicknesses probably were only a few kilometers.

These rocks also bear remarkable similarities to forearc and interarc extensional-basin deposits of Late Triassic to Early Jurassic age exposed throughout the Cordillera of the U.S. Southwest (Busby-Spera, 1990), even to the degree of containing quartz arenites whose possible source was the Mesozoic Navajo sand sea of the western United States. Sedimentary strata in the study area also resemble the Upper Triassic–Lower Jurassic cover sequence of the Rattlesnake Creek terrane in the southern Klamaths (Wright and Wyld, 1986). Differences between the clastic strata in the two terranes include a lack of ophiolitic debris in Marble Mountain metasedimentary rocks compared to those of the Rattlesnake Creek terrane and the presence of quartz arenites in the former. Moreover, Marble Mountain cover units are detached from their basement, which may have consisted of older forearc and arc-related volcanic, plutonic, and sedimentary rocks, whereas in contrast, Rattlesnake Creek superjacent strata maintain their original depositional relationships with a basement of ophiolitic mélange.

Metamorphism of the Marble Mountain tectonic stack

Metamorphic parageneses. Prograde metamorphic mineral assemablages in the study area have been reported by Welsh (1982), Burton (1982), Ernst (1987, 1990, 1998), Donato (1989), and Hacker et al. (1992). Statically recrystallized fabrics in many deformed rocks and the unstrained, granoblastic textures of most peak-metamorphic minerals indicate that thermal equilibration was attained after the main phase of ductile deformation. Figure 7 summarizes P-T conditions estimated for different areas in the central Klamaths.

In the subjacent BCa, amphibolites contain neoblastic clinopyroxene, and ultramafic rocks contain the assemblage olivine + enstatite + anthophyllite (Welsh, 1982; Donato, 1989; this investigation). Immediately to the north of the study area at structurally lower levels, Burton (1982) determined temperatures and pressures of ~650°C and 4.5 to 9 kbar, based on poorly constrained calc-silicate assemblages. Although possibly due to bulk-rock compositional variations and proximity to intrusions, these assemblages suggest higher peak temperatures in rocks below the Isinglass shear zone. Coleman et al. (1988) and Donato (1989) described localized high-grade amphibolite- and granulite-facies metamorphic assemblages that are clearly out of equilibrium with regional assemblages. These anomalous assemblages also are sited structurally below the Isinglass shear zone within the BCa.

In the superjacent WLa, conditions estimated from prograde equilibrium mineral assemblages and garnet-biotite geothermometry are 480° to 560°C and <3.7 kbar (Donato, 1989). At slightly higher structural levels, actinolite + plagioclase (≥An21) and actinolite or hornblende + plagioclase (≥An21) + sodic plagioclase (≤An20) ± epidote in metabasites indicate transitional greenschist-amphibolite conditions (Liou et al., 1985; Donato, 1989). At still higher structural levels, in rocks that are interlayered with and immediately overlie the WLa, estimated temperatures and pressures are 350° to 550°C and ~3 kbar, with the characteristic assemblage in metabasites consisting of actinolitic hornblende ± phengite + epidote + sodic plagioclase ± microcline + chlorite + titanite + hematite + quartz (Ernst, 1990, 1998; Hacker et al., 1992).

Retrograde greenschist assemblages are locally present in both subjacent and superjacent rocks, especially along late-stage shear zones in the vicinity of the Isinglass thrust, the Shackleford fault, and the Sniktaw shear zone, and around some stocks and small intrusions. In the vicinity of these structures, quartz + carbonate veins + fracture fillings as well as oxidative alteration suggest high fluid flow. In the Kidder Lake area, retrograde assemblages consisting of biotite + muscovite ± chlorite ± quartz overprint pre-existing amphibolite assemblages, define a second foliation, and are spatially associated with an unnamed pluton. Well-defined, prograde contact metamorphic effects are present around several of the intrusions and stocks. The Heather Lake pluton shows contact effects extending hundreds of meters outward that overprint earlier metamorphic fabrics and assemblages. In the Mill Creek and Shelley Lake areas, small plutons exhibit contact effects extending outward 20 to 100 m. Contact metamorphic mineral parageneses include actinolite replaced by hornblende and chlorite by biotite. The anorthite content of plagioclase also increases toward the granitoid plutons (Hacker et al., 1992). The Wooley Creek batholith is exposed approximately 10

km west of the study area. Contact metamorphic assemblages along the northeast contact of the batholith, at about the same structural level as the lower WLa and upper BCa, indicate P-T conditions of 6.5 to 8.5 kbar and 650° to 750°C (Barnes et al., 1986).

Hence, at least three distinct stages of subsolidus recrystallization are recognized in the Marble Mountains: (1) prograde greenschist- to amphibolite-facies metamorphism attending and outlasting regional penetrative deformation; (2) thermal upgrading accompanying granitoid pluton emplacement; and (3) superposed retrogression and greenschist-facies metamorphism associated with possible late-stage or subsequent tectonism or terrane exhumation. In addition, a cryptic, earlier recrystallization is suggested by high-grade metamorphosed blocks exposed below the Isinglass shear zone.

Age of metamorphism. The times of metamorphism are poorly constrained. Several Ar/Ar ages directly to the south, reported by Hacker et al. (1995), indicate cooling through the closing temperature of hornblende (~500° to 525°C) at about 150 Ma. Contact metamorphism by the Heather Lake pluton overprints the regional fabric at the contact, and dikes interpreted to be associated with the pluton are folded and deformed. The igneous crystallization age of the Heather Lake pluton is 167 ± 0.6 Ma (Ar/Ar, hornblende) (Hacker et al., 1993). Igneous crystallization ages for metadikes that intrude the WTrPz to the north and south of the study area are 172 ± 2 Ma (U/Pb, zircon) (Saleeby, in Hill, 1985) and 173.2 ± 3.7 Ma, 174.6 ± 1.3 Ma (Ar/Ar, hornblende) (Hacker et al., 1993). Wooley Creek batholith contact metamorphism overprints the regional fabric and is dated at ~162 Ma (Barnes et al., 1986; Wright and Fahan, 1988). To the south of the study area, in the Sawyers Bar region, regional greenschist-facies metamorphic fabrics are overprinted by contact metamorphism of the English Peak batholith, which crystallized at about 165 Ma (Ernst, 1990; Hacker and Ernst, 1993). Caution should be exercised when interpreting relationships between contact and regional metamorphism, inasmuch as the regional fabric may only represent a local maximum (Barton et al., 1988) within an area undergoing multiple intrusions of large-scale plutons over a 10 to 15 m.y. interval.

Thus, ages of regional and contact metamorphism are constrained to be conservatively 170 to 150 Ma, and quite possibly restricted to the interval 170 to 165 Ma. From mapped geologic relationships, we interpret the regional recrystallization as accompanying the suturing of the Sawyers Bar terrane against and beneath the Stuart Fork and more easterly lithostratigraphic belts. In contrast, Irwin and Mankinen (1998) have postulated a sequential docking of progressively farther Pacificward units; they estimated that the North Fork terrane accreted at ~198 to 193 Ma, and the outboard Eastern Hayfork at ~180 Ma. However that may be, retrograde greenschist-facies overprinting may postdate 155 to 150 Ma in the Sawyers Bar area. A minimum age for greenschist metamorphism is ~130 Ma because Valinginian marine sedimentary rocks overlie the Klamath Province along a regional erosion surface. Fission-track dating of zircon in the Slinkard and Wooley Creek batholiths yielded ages of ~91 ± 10 Ma (Lewison, 1984). Exhumation to shallow-crustal levels evidently was completed by mid-Cretaceous time.

Implications for crustal evolution and regional tectonics. The Marble Mountains represent a regional low-pressure, moderate-temperature metamorphic terrane. Barton et al. (1988) discussed models for creation of such complexes, emphasizing the importance of magmatic heat flux. Monotonically decreasing grade upsection and away from the Condrey Mountain dome indicates vertical and lateral temperature gradients. No discontinuities in metamorphic conditions were observed across the study area. Mineralogic and geologic evidence supports regional models of a Middle Jurassic thermal maximum associated with magmatic heat transport.

Anomalous, high-grade amphibolite- and granulite-grade blocks reported by Coleman et al. (1988) and Donato (1989) may reflect an earlier, cryptic, higher-grade metamorphic event. Alternatively, they may represent vestiges of high-grade blocks incorporated in a mélange that never re-equilibrated during regional low-P, moderate-T metamorphism. All are confined to the footwall of the Isinglass shear zone. Coleman et al. (1988) tentatively correlated these exotics with similar high-grade blocks incorporated in subgreenschist-grade tectonic mélange of the Rattlesnake Creek terrane in the southern Klamaths. The correlation of Marble Mountain high-grade blocks with the Rattlesnake Creek terrane supports the interpretation of the Isinglass shear zone as a terrane-bounding fault that occupies the same structural position as the Wilson Point thrust in the southern Klamaths.

Even with conservative thermodynamic estimates, the ~162 Ma Wooley Creek contact metamorphism apparently occurred at much higher pressures (6.5 to 8.5 kbar) (Barnes et al., 1986) than those recorded by regionally metamorphosed rocks at equivalent structural positions (<3.7 kbar) in the Marble Mountains. Possible magmatic epidote (Barnes et al., 1986) in the structurally lower, coeval Slinkard pluton suggests similar high pressures. Implications of these data generally have been downplayed in regional syntheses (e.g., Coleman et al., 1988; Hacker et al., 1995). If the regional low-P, low-T metamorphism recorded in host rocks in the study area is indeed older than Wooley Creek crystallization, Wooley Creek contact metamorphism may record substantial crustal thickening during terminal stages of the Siskiyou orogeny, involving thrust emplacement of Stuart Fork ± Eastern Klamath terranes(?), and following the regional low-P amphibolite-facies metamorphism. Crustal thickening also is implied by Barnes et al. (1986), who described unique isotopic characteristics of Wooley Creek and related plutonics that suggest anatexis of lower-crustal rocks of graywacke composition. Crustal thickening and anatexis probably were immediately followed by crustal collapse and attenuation, inasmuch as regionally metamorphosed rocks do not record these high pressures, although aureole temperatures were apparently above 500° to 525°C until ~150 Ma.

Crustal collapse and attenuation also is supported by the presence of Lower Cretaceous marine strata (Sliter et al., 1984) that overlie the Klamath province along a regional erosion surface, indicating exhumation and exposure. The time-averaged (162 to 130 Ma), post–Wooley Creek uplift rate is 0.8 mm/year, but could have been much greater following Wooley Creek intrusion. It must have been sufficiently rapid to prevent re-equilibration of regionally metamorphosed rocks to higher-pressure assemblages, but is ill constrained. The cryptic formation of high-grade blocks reported by

Coleman et al. (1988) and discussed previously records P-T conditions similar to those of the Wooley Creek contact aureole. These exotic metamorphics have not been dated directly in the study area, but comparable blocks in the southern Klamaths have recrystallization ages much older than the Siskiyou orogeny (Coleman et al., 1988).

Geochemical data

Previous work. Donato (1987) investigated the bulk-rock chemistry of mafic volcanic rocks in the Marble Mountains and reported predominantly volcanic-arc geochemical signatures with a few MORB, within-plate (OIB), or ambiguous geochemical signatures from structurally lower levels. Ernst et al. (1991) and Hacker et al. (1992) analyzed many additional metabasalt samples and reported within-plate and volcanic-arc (IAT) geochemical signatures from the same area. They interpreted the data to suggest the presence of two terranes with distinct mafic volcanic bulk-rock compositions: (1) the structurally lower Marble Mountains (Rattlesnake Creek?) terrane displaying mid-ocean-ridge-basalt geochemistry; (2) and a structurally higher Sawyers Bar terrane possessing volcanic-arc and within-plate signatures. The distinction between these two terranes as conceived by previous workers may be more apparent than real. Reinterpretation of geochemical data based on detailed mapping indicates that metabasaltic rocks with an arc signature are present throughout the Marble Mountains; mafic volcanics with MORB and within-plate signatures are interbedded with volcanic-arc rocks at the meter scale. The presence of these geochemically diverse protoliths suggests unique tectonic circumstances, such as formation of an oceanic island arc, intra-arc extension, or hot-spot/ridge subduction (Ernst, 1987).

Electron-microprobe data. Electron-microprobe analyses were performed on six amphiboles from BCa mafic amphibolites, BCa quartzofeldspathic amphibolites, WLa metabasites, and an amphibole sample from a WLa metabasite interpreted on textural evidence to be a relict igneous phase. Analytical data are presented by Miller (1998).

Metamorphic amphiboles from quartzofeldspathic Boulder Creek amphibolites have total Na+K and Al contents an order of magnitude higher and $Mg/Mg+Fe^{2+}$ ratios lower than analogues in associated mafic amphibolites. The former plot in the edenitic hornblende field of discriminant diagrams, whereas the latter plot in the tremolite field (Leake, 1978). Neoblastic amphiboles from metabasites of the WLa have intermediate Na+K contents and intermediate to high Al contents, compared to amphibolites from the BCa. They lie in the magnesio-hornblende, actinolitic hornblende, and ferroan pargasitic hornblende fields on discriminant plots. The single analyzed igneous amphibole in a WLa metabasite is aluminous tschermakitic hornblende.

Oxygen-isotope data. To provide constraints on fluid flow and metasomatism during metamorphism, bulk-rock $^{18}O/^{16}O$ compositions were obtained for eight specimens from the Marble Mountains. Figure 8 shows sample localities. Analyses were performed in the laboratory of Yehoshua Kolodny at the Hebrew University, Jerusalem. Table 1 lists results. Samples were run in duplicate and are reported with an error $\pm$ 0.3 per mil.

Mafic amphibolites from the subjacent Boulder Creek amphibolite have $\delta^{18}O$ ave$_2$ = +11.2 $\pm$ 0.14 per mil. Because fresh basalts typically possess $\delta^{18}O$ values of approximately +6, mafic amphibolites could have exchanged oxygen with seawater (Ernst, 1987; Hacker et al., 1992) if they were erupted in a submarine arc. Mafic amphibolites from the superjacent Wright Lakes assemblage have $\delta^{18}O$ ave$_4$ = +9.4 $\pm$ 0.24, insignificantly less than the typical value found for greenschist-grade rocks of similar lithology at structurally higher levels of this unit directly to the south (Ernst et al., 1991). The WLa is intruded by granitic plutons and numerous small bodies. Sample localities lie 2 to 6 km from major plutonic contacts. Analyzed rocks are sufficiently distant from the plutons that their isotopic composition probably reflects submarine alteration within an arc. Alternatively, the large percentage of plutonic rocks and presence of highly fractured, meta-ultramafic breccias in the WLa compared to the BCa may have contributed to large-scale regional fluid flow during intrusion, high-T metamorphism, and deformation.

Two quartz-bearing veins with variable lithology were sampled, one from each unit. Vein material has enriched $\delta^{18}O$ values of +13.8 (BCa) and +15.2 (WLa). These compositions,

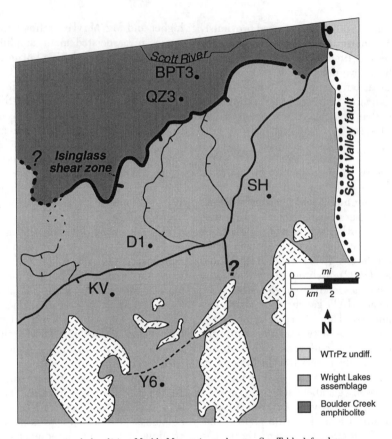

FIG. 8. Oxygen-isotope sample localities, Marble Mountain study area. See Table 1 for data.

especially that of the Wright Lakes assemblage quartz vein, may reflect the fact that aqueous fluids were derived from ^{18}O-rich metasedimentary units that were heated, devolatilized, and recrystallized during granitoid emplacement.

Geochemical summary. Geochemical data reported here support more extensive results reported in previous studies of Marble Mountain and contiguous lithologies (Welch, 1982; Donato, 1989; Hacker et al., 1992; Ernst and Kolodny, 1997). Both mineral chemistry and oxygen-isotope analyses show differences between rocks above and below the low-angle Isinglass shear zone, supporting the interpretation that this structure is a major regional discontinuity. Retrogression of mineral phases near the Isinglass shear zone also is suggested by the mineral chemistry. The oxygen-isotope signature of the WLa may reflect the large percentage of calk-alkaline plutons and pres-

ence of highly fractured, meta-ultramafic breccias in the WLa compared to other regions. Alternatively, contrasts in the oxygen-isotope signatures may have been inherited from different degrees of submarine alteration of the protoliths in an oceanic-arc environment.

Structural geology

General relationships. The Marble Mountain study area straddles a presumed suture zone. The location and kinematics of this terrane-bounding fault are poorly known (Welsh, 1982; Blake et al., 1982; Donato, 1987; Ernst, 1987, 1998; Hacker et al., 1995). Also, the geologic entities that the terrane boundary is presumed to separate are not well established. The discontinuity generally has been interpreted to be a thrust fault that figures prominently on regional maps (Irwin, 1981, 1994). It is thought to represent a major fault contact between the

TABLE 1. Oxygen-Isotope Analyses from the Marble Mountain Terrane

Sample no.	Map unit	Rock type	$\delta^{18}O \pm 0.3$
D1	Wright Lakes assemblage	metavolcanic	9.5
KV	Wright Lakes assemblage	metavolcanic	9.2
Y6	Wright Lakes assemblage	metavolcanic	9.7
SH1	Wright Lakes assemblage	trans. amphibolite	9.2
Average $\pm$ 1σ			9.4 $\pm$ 0.24
SH1q	Wright Lakes assemblage	quartz vein	15.2
QZ3	Boulder Creek amphibolite	amphibolite	11.1
BPT3	Boulder Creek amphibolite	amphibolite	11.3
Average $\pm$ 1σ			11.2 $\pm$ 0.14
BPT3f	Boulder Creek amphibolite	qtz-plag-garn vein	13.8

Marble Mountain terrane and (a) the Western Hayfork terrane (Wright and Wyld, 1994); (b) the Salmon River terrane (Silberling et al., 1984); or (c) the Sawyers Bar terrane (Hacker et al., 1993). It also has been interpreted as a faulted depositional contact between the Marble Mountain and Western Hayfork terranes (Donato, 1987) and as a major normal fault between the Marble Mountain and Sawyers Bar terranes (Hacker et al., 1992). A contribution of this study involves detailed mapping across the site of the putative terrane boundary. The present interpretation of new map and structural data is that the terrane-bounding structures as previously described do not exist. However, the following sections describe three previously unrecognized regional faults. All of these breaks can be interpreted as intraterrane features, although one—the Isinglass shear zone—may represent a terrane-bounding, crustal-scale structure. These regional faults also divide the study area into domains that have distinctly different fold and fabric orientations.

Tilting and rotation. Mortimer and Coleman (1985) presented abundant evidence for Late Cenozoic tilting and doming in the Klamath Mountains. The study area lies on the south flank of the Condrey Mountain dome, but the absence of Late Mesozoic to Cenozoic rocks in the immediate area makes determination of the precise direction, timing, and amount of tilting difficult to quantify. Barnes et al. (1986) presented evidence from the mineralogic architec-

ture of the pluton and contact metamorphic phase assemblages that indicates that the 162 Ma Wooley Creek batholith, exposed ~20 km west of the study area, was tilted a minimum of 20° to 30° toward the SSW sometime after intrusion.

In addition, maps by Coleman et al. (1988) and other workers (e.g., Welsh, 1982; Donato, 1989) show km-scale antiforms and synforms that control the regional outcrop pattern. These antiforms and synforms presumably rotated structural elements from 10° to 30°. Broad open folds with different orientations also are observed at outcrop scale and add dispersion to orientation data. Tilting of structural elements previously attributed to major regional faults (e.g., Hacker et al., 1995) may actually reflect rotation along regional antiforms and synforms. Mankinen et al. (1989) and Mankinen and Irwin (1990) reviewed paleomagnetic data from the WTrPz, including four Jurassic plutons that intrude the WTrPz in the northern Klamaths. Three plutons show postcrystallization clockwise rotations about vertical axes from 53° to 113°, whereas the slightly younger Ashland pluton shows minor counterclockwise rotation. Thus, the current N-S to NNE trend of Jurassic structural elements may have been more westerly during Jurassic regional penetrative deformation (Irwin and Mankinen, 1998).

Emplacement of ultramafic rocks. Ultramafic rocks evidently were emplaced along faults that now are complexly folded and deformed. Serpentinized peridotites consist of thin, folded, moderately SE-dipping tabular lenses bounded by ultramafic fault breccias. Rock types above and below the tabular zones are the same. Paleomagnetic data (USGS OFR 79-1228, 1979) support modeling of the serpentinized peridotites as thin, tabular, rootless slabs that do not extend deeply into the subsurface. These data indicate that ultramafic rocks do not mark a major suture zone, remnants of a closed ocean basin, or an intra-oceanic fault zone. Instead, they may have been emplaced along relatively minor, early-formed intraterrane faults similar to the those described from the Pony Camp area in the second part of this report. Tabular zones of uncompetent ultramafic rock localized subsequent faulting, including post-metamorphic readjustments.

Faulting. Three major, regional-scale faults cut the Marble Mountains study area: (1) the Isinglass shear zone, the contact between the superjacent WLa and subjacent BCa; (2) the Shackleford fault, an ENE-striking, S-dipping, high-angle fault within the WLa; and (3) the Sniktaw shear zone, a complex NNE-striking, steeply E-dipping deformation zone along the easternmost Marble Mountains range front. The regional significance and kinematic history of these faults were generally unrecognized by previous workers. Structures were identified in the field by abrupt discontinuities in lithology and fabric, and from the presence of mylonitic, protomylonitic, and cataclastic rocks within the fault zones. In addition, numerous minor, steeply and gently dipping faults cut rocks in the study area. Of note are a series of moderately E-dipping faults, spaced ~2 km apart, that imbricate the WLa between the Isinglass shear zone and the Shackleford fault. Details of the structural investigation were documented by Miller (1998), and only the main conclusions are presented here.

The Isinglass shear zone is a major, low-angle fault between the subjacent BCa and the superjacent WLa; it separates a lower plate of gently dipping, amphibolite-grade L-S tectonites that lack relict protolith textures from an upper plate of multiply folded amphibolite and transitional greenschist- to amphibolite-grade metamorphic rocks with well-preserved relict textures. The Isinglass shear zone strikes NE to ENE and dips gently to moderately south, although post-kinematic open folding has

changed the orientation locally; it is 10 to hundreds of meters wide and consists of anastomosing, 1 to 10 m thick mylonitic, phyllonitic, and brittle fault zones. These narrow, deformed zones bound outcrop- to map-scale lenses and sheets of less deformed quartzite, quartzofeldspathic schist, amphibolite, metacarbonate, rare meta-ultramafic, and numerous small gabbroic-to-intermediate intrusive rocks. Kinematic evidence indicates that W-directed transport of upper-plate relative to lower-plate rocks occurred initially on this shear zone. W-directed transport also is indicated by fold asymmetry and by rotation of fold axes into the mineral elongation direction. Less abundant kinematic evidence also suggests that W-directed transport was coeval with, or followed by, E-directed movement on mylonitic zones within the Isinglass shear zone. E-directed transport could represent local space accommodation around deformed gabbroic sills, minor antithetic shears, backfolding during progressive W-directed thrusting, extensional backsliding of a thickened orogenic welt, or a separate tectonic episode. E-directed kinematic indicators previously were unknown from this section of the Klamath Mountains. Alternatively, the Isinglass shear zone may be one of several internal faults within the nappe complex. These faults include those breaks that form a regional duplex structure in the Marble Mountains and faults that separate domains of rocks that have discordant structural orientations. If the Isinglass shear zone is internal to the nappe complex, the structurally lower Condrey fault may represent the lower terrane-bounding fault (Fig. 9).

The Shackleford fault follows the prominent ENE-trending topographic lineament of Shackleford and Wooley creeks. It is exposed along the Pacific Crest Trail and discontinuously within the streambed of Shackleford Creek. The fault strikes ENE and dips steeply to moderately south. It separates similar rock types that have discordant structural orientations. Tectonically lower rocks north of the Shackleford fault are multiply folded, whereas structurally higher rocks south of the fault show less complex fold patterns. Meta-ultramafic rocks and distinctive porphyritic volcanic- arc rocks are present on both sides of the fault, but south of the fault, exposures of meta-ultramafic rocks are less common, and outcrops

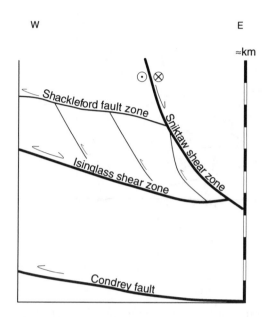

FIG. 9. Schematic cross section of regional-scale faults, Marble Mountain study area.

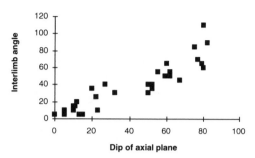

FIG. 10. Measured interlimb angles versus axial-plane dip, unrotated, Marble Mountain study area.

of porphyritic arc volcanics are much more extensive compared to the area north of the fault.

The Sniktaw shear zone is a complex zone of anastamosing, steeply E-dipping, brittle and less commonly ductile faults along the eastern side of the study area. It strikes NNE and is up to 2 km wide. It cuts the Shackleford fault and probably also the Isinglass shear zone, although the junction of these two faults is poorly exposed. Extension of the Sniktaw shear zone to the south, east of the Shelley Lake pluton, is likely but as yet unproven. Rocks within the shear zone consist of a wide range of amphibolite-, transitional amphibolite-, and greenschist-grade supracrustal and hypabyssal intrusive rocks. The Quaternary Scott Valley fault, which forms the eastern range front of the Marble Mountains, may have been localized within this basement shear zone.

Structural conclusions. On the basis of previous discussions, rocks of the Marble Mountains are interpreted to represent a metamorphosed nappe complex consisting of supracrustal island-arc rocks. Figure 9 illustrates an interpretive down-plunge view of the allochthon. Internal structural and lithologic breaks are present, but on a regional scale the terrane exhibits a fairly consistent pattern. Metamorphic grade increases monotonically with depth. Structural and fabric data also indicate gradual changes downward within the nappe complex: deeper levels deformed more plastically and are charactized by well-developed fabrics and recumbent isoclinal folds; middle levels are characterized by tight to isoclinal, recumbent to upright folds, multiply folded domains, and variably developed deformational fabric; upper levels are characterized by a single fold generation with a relatively uniform orientation. Supporting these conclusions, measured axial plane dip and interlimb fold angles systematically decrease with increasing depth, as illustrated in Figure 10.

Multiply folded domains may reflect rheological differences between constituent rock types, refolding of originally non-planar layers, progressive deformation of a metamorphosed nappe complex, and/or discrete deformation events. Rheological differences between constituent rock types and refolding of originally non-planar layers probably contributed to complex deformation patterns in the Marble Mountains. The regional extent of multiply folded domains across contrasting rock types and the consistent location within discrete structural levels of the complex suggest that regional factors, such as progressive deformation and/or discrete regional deformation episodes, also were important. We interpret the observed structures to represent progressive penetrative deformation within an intensely metamorphosed thrust sheet. In this model (e.g., Ramsay and Huber, 1983), superposed folding and deformation results from the evolution of deeper, higher-strain rocks into areas of lower

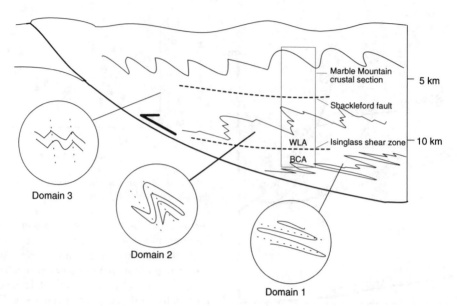

FIG. 11. Simplified progressive deformation in a metamorphosed thrust sheet, after Ramsay and Huber (1983).

strain as thrusting and deformation progressed. Figure 11 schematically illustrates locations of the various structural domains. According to this interpretation, the Isinglass shear zone and Shackleford fault would represent intra-nappe faults that formed at discrete horizons within the evolving complex, across which deformation style, P-T conditions, and/or rheologic conditions changed significantly.

Evidence for discrete deformational episodes includes: divergent orientations of superposed fabrics, differing kinematics of superposed fabrics, and strongly contrasting contact and regional metamorphism, implying changing heat flow, crustal thickness, and tectonic regimes. Previously presented data and regional considerations suggest a multistage deformational history. It involves detachment of supracrustal rocks of the WLa and BCa from basement in a suprasubduction-zone setting, and evolution within a W-vergent, contractional nappe system during the Siskiyou orogeny. W-vergent folds and W-directed mylonitic rocks formed at this time. Tectonism was closely followed by E-vergent extension and/or extensional backsliding during waning phases of the Siskiyou orogeny (or perhaps early stages of Josephine ophiolite–related extension), which formed E-directed mylonites and minor extensional faults. Less intense reactivation

and tightening of Siskiyou structures occurred during Nevadan E-W contraction, possibly promoting the scattered development of minor, local superposed fabrics and/or N-S extension. Sinistral transtension occurred during the Early Cretaceous along the Sniktaw shear zone and minor ductile-to-brittle extensional faults within the study area.

Geologic history of the Marble Mountains area

Rocks of the Marble Mountains are interpreted to have formed in a suprasubduction-zone setting that was kinematically coupled to the North American plate. Thus, the study area is viewed as having developed relatively *in situ* and is not an exotic, far-traveled complex. Whether the Marble Mountains study area was in a forearc, intra-arc, or backarc tectonic environment is difficult to determine and subject to the shifting patterns of subduction-related magmatism, but the general trend was one of westward migration of arc magmatism and outward growth of the continent, with the study area progressively evolving from a forearc, to intra-arc, to backarc tectonic regime during the Mesozoic. The following geologic history emphasizes the evolution of the WLa, for which paleotectonic, structural, and geochronologic data are most complete (this study;

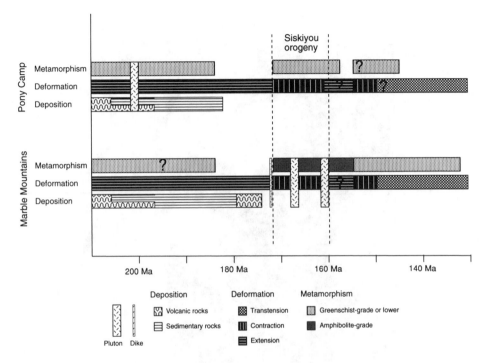

FIG. 12. Summary of Mesozoic geologic and tectonic history of the Marble Mountain and Pony Camp study areas, central WTrPz.

Hacker et al., 1993). Development is summarized in Figure 12 as series of time slices within the ranges of age data for a particular group of events.

220 to 170 Ma. Deposition of arc volcanics and continental-affinity clastics occurred against a background of Late Triassic(?)–early Middle Jurassic hemipelagic sedimentation in a restricted, intra-arc extensional basin. Arc rocks consisted mainly of fragmental andesitic/basaltic rocks but also included dacite domes and alkalic flows. Sedimentary strata included fault-scarp breccias and compositionally mature, continentally derived quartz arenites. Basement consisted of older, accreted forearc deposits and pre-existing island-arc basement, uplifted along extensional faults. Rapid retreat of the subduction zone relative to the North American continental margin may have contributed to arc extension. The rock record is discontinuous, and older cryptic deformation + recrystallization, hinted at by high-grade metamorphic blocks, may have been produced at this time.

170 to 165 Ma. Supracrustal rocks were detached from their basement during this time

interval, and the study area underwent E-W contraction, W-directed thrusting, regional penetrative deformation, probable crustal thickening, and low-pressure greenschist-to amphibolite-grade metamorphism. The Marble Mountains were buried under 10 to 15+ km thick thrust plates of the Stuart Fork terrane, the Central Metamorphic belt, and yet more easterly terranes. Ultramafic rocks were tectonically inserted early in the deformational history; continuing orogeny involved movement on both the Isinglass and Shackleford faults. Low heat flow promoted formation of the Condrey Mountain blueschists. This time corresponds to the Siskiyou orogeny and to slip on the Soap Creek Ridge thrust, the major crustal-scale, terrane-bounding fault that forms the upper tectonic contact of the WTrPz. Rapid westward advance of North America relative to the continental-margin subduction zone may have occurred, possibly reflecting extension in the backarc region.

165 to 160 Ma. Lower-crustal melting of tectonically thickened crust and extensive subduction-related plutonism (Wooley Creek and related plutonic bodies) occurred during this

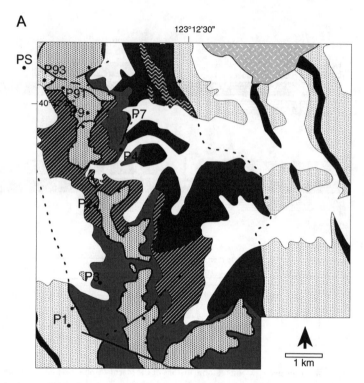

Fig. 13. Geologic map (A) and rock units (B, facing page) for the Pony Camp study area.

stage. At the end of this time, extension probably occurred at structurally higher levels of the WLa. The main locus of detachment and thrusting stepped outboard and deeper within the middle crust (e.g., the Condrey Mountain fault), which was thermally weakened by crust-derived melts. Movement continued along the Isinglass and Shackleford faults, however, which localized the intrusion of small plutonic bodies. Metamorphism continued, attending conditions of moderate heat flow.

160 to 155 Ma. Uplift of the study area to moderately shallow crustal levels and formation of minor E-directed and extensional structures occurred during this time. Attenuation evidently characterized upper levels of the tectonically thickened WLa, whereas contraction dominated lower levels (the Condrey Mountain fault).

155 to 145 Ma. Minor E-W contraction, W-directed thrusting related to Nevadan deformation farther west, and cooling of the WLa through ~500°C occurred during this time frame.

145 to 125 Ma. In the Early Cretaceous, uplift and sinistral transtension along the Sniktaw shear zone and minor retrograde metamorphism and formation of extensional structures in the study area occurred during oblique northward movement of North America relative to the fringing continental margin. Rocks of the Klamath province were exposed at the surface by Valinginian time (~130 Ma).

Pony Camp Study Area

General geology

The Pony Camp igneous complex (PCIC) is exposed along creeks and glaciated ridges in the western part of the Trinity Alps Wilderness (Fig. 2A). It has a structural thickness of at least 1 km. Its current orientation is subhorizontal, but the eastern part of the study area is tilted gently to the east. The geology of the complex was first studied by Cox (1956). The PCIC is separated from subjacent rocks of the Eastern Hayfork terrane on the west by the Twin Sisters fault, an inferred terrane boundary (Wright,

B

Qs	Quaternary surficial deposits
Ji	Middle to Late Jurassic hornblende diorite
sp	massive serpentinite

Pony Camp igneous complex

mv	metavolcanic rocks
mvd	dikes, metavolcanic rocks
mid	mafic-intermediate dike complex
gbs	gabbroic sill complex
gb	pyroxene hornblende gabbro
um	ultramafic rocks

high-angle fault
ball on downthrown side

low-angle fault
square on upper plate

Fɪɢ. 13 (contd.).

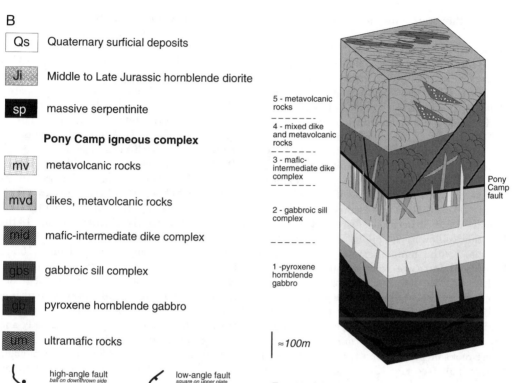

5 - metavolcanic rocks
- - - - - - - -
4 - mixed dike and metavolcanic rocks
- - - - - - - -
3 - mafic-intermediate dike complex
- - - - - - -
2 - gabbroic sill complex

- - - - - - -

1 - pyroxene hornblende gabbro

≈100m

Pony Camp fault

Fɪɢ. 14. Schematic stratigraphic column, Pony Camp study area.

1982). It is thrust beneath superjacent rocks of the more easterly Stuart Fork terrane along the Soap Creek Ridge fault (Hotz, 1977). The PCIC is roughly correlative with the North Fork terrane of Ando et al. (1983) and the Salmon River terrane of Irwin (1981; see also Silberling et al., 1984). The study area lies ~20 km along strike to the south of rocks mapped by Ando et al. (1983) and Ernst (1987, 1998).

Map units of the Pony Camp area

Rocks of the Pony Camp igneous complex. The PCIC consists of a sequence of subgreenschist- to lower greenschist–grade, mafic plutonic rocks and overlying metavolcanics. Units lack penetrative deformation; igneous textures are generally well preserved, but hydrothermal alteration is common and locally intense. Geologic relationships are illustrated in Figure 13. The following descriptions are given in terms of original igneous lithologies. The Pony Camp

igneous complex consists of a sequence of five mappable units described from structurally lowest to highest (Fig. 14) and labeled 1 through 5, respectively. Contacts between units 1, 2, and 3 are intrusive. Most contacts juxtaposing units 3, 4, and 5 are faults. The contact between units 3 and 4 is a low-angle fault that is interpreted to be synmagmatic and informally termed the Pony Camp fault. Weak recrystallization of protoliths produced the assemblage chl + qtz + ab + ep + sph + seri ± preh ± act.

Unit 1 is 100 to 500+ m thick and is exposed at the base of the PCIC. It consists of massive, coarse-grained, pyroxene hornblende gabbro, hornblende gabbro, and pyroxene gabbro with minor pegmatitic hornblendite, clinopyroxenite, and cumulate peridotite. Textures are predominantly subhedral granular with minor cumulate and hypersolidus, protoclastic textures. Unit 2 is 100 to 500 m thick and represents structurally coherent, massive, fine- to medium-grained, equant, subhedral-granular hornblende gabbro and pyroxene gabbro. This plutonic member consists of multiple, tabular horizontal sheets, tens of meters thick. Contacts within this unit are intrusive. Dikes increase in abundance upsection. Unit 3 is a structurally coherent, hornblende-phyric mafic-intermediate dike complex, 0 to 200 m thick. Chilled, multiple intrusive contacts are common. Dikes dip steeply and consistently strike northeast. Unit 4 consists of mafic-intermediate dikes and metavolcanic rocks, and is 0 to 200 m thick. It is a structurally disrupted, strongly altered diabasic and hornblende-phyric mafic-intermediate dike complex containing screens of metavolcanic rocks. Dikes exhibit diverse orientations. A series of metavolcanic rocks, 600 to 1000+ m thick, constitutes Unit 5. It consists of structurally disrupted, massive flow rock, pillow basalt, pillow breccia, and tuff breccia, with minor crystal lithic tuff, hypabyssal intrusive rock, radiolarian chert, and oölitic carbonate. Lenses of breccia contain cobble-sized clasts of hornblende gabbro.

Metasedimentary rocks. The area west of the study area is underlain by a large area of chert, chert-argillite breccia, and minor limestone. These rocks lie predominantly west of the Twin Sisters fault (see Fig. 13) and have been previously correlated with the Eastern Hayfork terrane. Although this area was not investigated in detail, reconnaissance mapping provided important structural, paleoenvironmental, and regional tectonic data. Chert and limestone are in depositional contact with underlying pillow basalt and volcanic breccia interpreted to be part of the PCIC on the western side of the study area. Thick layers of chert- argillite breccia are interbedded with chert and are regarded as olistostromes (Cox, 1956).

Age of the rock units. No age data are available from within the study area. Paleontologic ages and radiometric dates from rocks adjacent to the Pony Camp study area are chiefly Middle and Late Triassic. Radiolarian biostratigraphy provides protolith ages of chert to the north and south. Radiolaria of Late Triassic and permissibly Early Jurassic age are common within relatively coherent chert sequences exposed along strike in supracrustal rocks of the PCIC. Unequivocal Early Jurassic (Pleinsbachian) radiolaria have been found farther to the north and to the south (Irwin et al., 1982). Conodont data support these radiolarian age determinations (Irwin et al., 1983). Also along strike of the PCIC, Late Permian radiolaria and Permian Tethyan fusilinids have been found within

blocks that have uncertain structural and stratigraphic relationships to surrounding rocks (Irwin et al., 1982). Ando et al. (1983) reported a discordant U/Pb zircon date of 265 to 310 Ma from a plagiogranite phacoid within a fault zone. Because of discordant isotope sytematics and uncertain structural and stratigraphic relationships to surrounding rocks, this date is suspect for the North Fork terrane and thus also for the PCIC crystallization age. Hacker et al. (1993) reported an Ar/Ar hornblende date of 200.4 ± 1.4 Ma from hornblende gabbro intruding diabase 20 km north of the study area. This gabbro is correlated with Unit 2 of the PCIC and represents an igneous crystallization age. In the WTrPz at this latitude, Middle to Late Jurassic granitoid plutons ranging in age from ~165 to 145 Ma crosscut major structures and are coeval with or postdate regional subgreenschist/greenschist–grade metamorphism (Davis et al., 1965; Goodge, 1989a). Although not dated directly, plutons mineralogically and petrologically identical to dated plutons intrude the study area and provide a minimum geologic age for PCIC crystallization, deformation, and metamorphism.

On the basis of available evidence, the main body of PCIC and related metasedimentary rocks are interpreted to be Late Triassic–Early Jurassic in age. Older rocks are confined to fault-bounded blocks within shear zones or are blocks with uncertain field relationships with the surroundings. Some may represent fragments of basement on which the PCIC was constructed. These fragments are interpreted to have been entrained in fault zones or deposited as blocks within olistostromes in the study area.

Paleotectonic setting of the Pony Camp protoliths

Previous investigations interpreted the PCIC as a segment of ophiolite or an oceanic seamount. Although the PCIC superficially resembles a sliver of the upper levels of oceanic crust, mineralogy and geochemical data (discussed in a subsequent section) indicate that it was erupted within an extensional suprasubduction-zone setting, possibly a forearc or intra-arc setting. Evidence for submarine deposition of volcanic rocks includes the presence of pillow basalts and interpillow carbonate and chert. Oölitic limestone suggests local shallow-water conditions. Chert and chert-argillite olistostromes stratigraphically overlying the mafic igneous complex indicate volcanic quiescence, local high relief, and possible continued tectonism in a marine environment. Abundant, coarse-grained intraformational breccias also testify to rugged topography. Premetamorphic brittle faults suggest the possibility of synmagmatic tectonism; this is also reflected by abundant dikes, rare kinematic indicators on synmagmatic faults, and the gross aspect and crosscutting relationships of an intraformational, low-angle extensional break, the Pony Camp fault (Fig. 13). Suprasubduction-zone extension led to the formation of new, thin lithosphere of ophiolitic affinity. Attenuation occurred in a N-S linear belt that currently extends throughout the central WTrPz. The PCIC is similar in lithology, structure, metamorphism, and volume to extensional suprasubduction-zone volcanoplutonic complexes described from the western Pacific (e.g., Bloomer and Hawkins, 1983; Ishii, 1985; Ogawa et al., 1985). Detailed mapping by Ando et al. (1983), Ernst (1998), and this study indicate that rock units of the PCIC can be traced continuously for ~100 km northward into the Marble Mountains. Thus, lithologies of the Marble Mountains, Sawyers Bar, and the PCIC are broadly correlative and probably evolved within the same island-arc system.

Attenuation recorded in the PCIC may be related to the extension described from the Marble Mountain study area, and to a broad region of suprasubduction-zone extension recorded throughout the North American Cordillera in the Late Triassic–Early Jurassic (Busby-Spera et al., 1990). Rock types in the PCIC and Marble Mountains are similar, including the presence of a distinctive sequence of alkalic metavolcanic flows/breccias, metacarbonates, and metacherts, although the PCIC consists of a greater volume of tholeiitic, mafic volcanic rocks and coeval shallow intrusives, a lesser amount of intermediate-felsic volcanic rocks, and still lesser volumes of interbedded sedimentary breccias and medium- to fine-grained clastics compared with the Marble Mountains. Similar to the Marble Mountains, the PCIC is apparently detached from its original basement. Slivers of older ophiolitic rocks, cherts, and ultramafics within intraterrane shear zones are interpreted to be samples of

original basement that may represent a tectonic mélange of older accreted material.

Possible paleotectonic settings for PCIC magmatism include the following: (1) arc-axis basaltic activity related to an immature oceanic-island arc; (2) intra-arc extension or transtension; (3) near-trench magmatism related to the initiation of an island arc; (4) forearc magmatism related to unique subduction conditions such as underflow of a leaky transform, spreading ridge, or hotspot; (5) near-trench eruption related to extension or transtension within the forearc; or (6) backarc spreading. Unlike the Marble Mountains, an intra-arc environment for the Pony Camp igneous complex is not favored because of the paucity of arc-derived pyroclastics and the presence instead of a thick chert-argillite sequence that lacks juvenile volcanic rocks. The PCIC may have occupied a forearc or backarc position relative to the Marble Mountains area. A regime based on regional correlations and structural relationships is favored. The presence of blocks of both exotic accreted material (Permian Tethyan fusilinid-bearing limestone and chert) and inboard, native-derived debris (McCloud limestone) within overlying sedimentary rocks suggests that the PCIC extensional basin was within depositional range of both paleo-Pacific off-scrapings in an accretionary subduction mélange and inboard Klamath terranes. A forearc basin is arguably a more likely place for mixing of accreted and *in situ* clastic components. The amount of extension in the PCIC was sufficient to allow creation of new oceanic crust. This event probably was short lived and/or extrusion took place slowly because, as currently exposed, the crust is thin and areally limited.

Metamorphism of the Pony Camp Igneous Complex

Metamorphic parageneses. The PCIC is not penetratively deformed and only weakly and incompletely recrystallized. Primary igneous features such as chilled margins, pillows, and diabasic textures are generally well preserved. In mafic metavolcanic rocks, the subgreenschist- to lower greenschist–facies assemblage chl + qtz + ab + ep + sph + sericite is ubiquitous. Pyroxene and hornblende are recrystallized to chlorite, and epidote is common on fractures and along grain boundaries. Calcite accompanies chlorite and epidote in replacing pyroxene. Plagioclase is recrystallized to albite, sericite, and epidote. Prehnite is present in albitized plagioclase, in vesicles, and in veinlets throughout the study area. North of the Pony Camp area, near the Salmon-Trinity Divide, mafic volcaniclastic rocks contain the assemblage prehnite + pumpellyite + chlorite. Actinolite is present in recrystallized fault breccia and gouge and less commonly as fringes and patches on pyroxene and hornblende. In three samples, fibrous actinolite rims on pyroxene and hornblende are fringed, in turn, by ragged chlorite and epidote.

In dike rocks, prehnite is less common and actinolite is more common compared to overlying metavolcanics. The igneous hornblende in dike rocks is generally recrystallized to green chlorite, epidote, actinolite, and opaque minerals along fractures and grain boundaries. Most pyroxenes are completely recrystallized to chlorite + epidote ± actinolite. Biotite is present in one sample as small ragged flakes rimming pyroxene. The biotite, in turn, is rimmed by green chlorite. Recrystallization of mafic plutonic rocks is incomplete and variable. In many samples, recrystallization of mafic minerals is restricted to fringes along grain boundaries and cracks. In other samples, mafic minerals, especially pyroxene, are replaced by fine-grained aggregates of pale green actinolite, chlorite, epidote, and opaque minerals.

Chert and argillaceous metasedimentary rocks west of the study area contain white mica + chlorite + quartz ± albite. Sporadic fine-grained, neoblastic biotite is present within argillaceous partings in chert and within argillaceous rocks in structurally lower areas several kilometers west of the study area (Cox, 1956). Biotite defines a weak foliation that becomes better developed as the low-angle fault exposed on Virgin Buttes is approached.

Conditions of metamorphism. Assuming a close approach to local domain equilibrium, the assemblage prehnite + pumpellyite + chlorite suggests temperatures of ~275°C and pressures of ~2.5 kbar (Liou et al., 1985) within mafic volcaniclastic rocks at high structural/stratigraphic levels of the PCIC. At somewhat lower structural levels, the assemblage prehnite + chlorite ± actinolite suggests temperatures of ~275 to 325°C and pressures <3.0 kbar (Liou et al., 1985). The assemblage actinolite + chlo-

rite ± epidote, predominantly in hypabyssal rocks, formed at somewhat higher temperatures, on the order of 350°C. Rare biotite in gabbro indicates unambiguous greenschist-facies conditions. In general, equilibrium metamorphic assemblages indicate prehnite-pumpellyite to transitional, lower greenschist–grade metamorphic conditions.

Age of metamorphism. Critical for the discussion of the timing of recrystallization is the ability to differentiate between igneous and deuteric mineral assemblages acquired in the environment in which the PCIC formed, and later assemblages produced during subsequent localized heating and regional deformation. Metamorphic mineral assemblages may represent Late Triassic to mid-Jurassic events, including: (1) autometamorphic assemblages of hypabyssal rocks that reflect somewhat higher temperature conditions than the regionally metamorphosed country rock; (2) contact metamorphism spatially associated with shallow calc-alkaline intrusions; (3) hydrothermal and cataclastic fault-related recrystallization and vein formation; (4) burial metamorphism in a hot volcanoplutonic complex; and (5) sea-floor alteration. Except where spatially localized by intrusions and faults, many of the metamorphic assemblages produced during these episodes are difficult to distinguish from those formed during regional subgreenschist to greenschist-grade metamorphism reported by various authors for this area (Ando et al., 1983; Goodge, 1989a; Hacker at al., 1992; Ernst, 1998). Regional metamorphism of the southern part of the WTrPz is generally subgreenschist to greenschist grade and is considered to be coeval with deformation along several regional W-vergent thrust faults dated at ~169 to 165 Ma (Wright and Fahan, 1988; Goodge, 1989b). Coleman et al. (1988) correlated this dynamothermal event with the Siskiyou orogeny of the central Klamaths. Somewhat earlier suturing events, however, have been postulated by Irwin and Mankinen (1998).

Discussion. Progressive dynamothermal recrystallization has not been studied in detail in the southern Klamaths. Compilation of existing studies suggests that its intensity may increase from subgreenschist in the west to greenschist in the eastern parts of the WTrPz at this latitude, but this may be a sampling artifact. In the PCIC, it is especially difficult to distinguish between neoblastic assemblages formed regionally within an evolving volcano-plutonic complex and those formed during subsequent contact metamorphism. In mafic metavolcanic rocks, act + chl ± ep assemblages are spatially associated with shear zones and deformational fabrics. A feeble axial-plane cleavage defined by aligned white mica, chlorite, and rarely biotite is incompletely developed in folded metasedimentary rocks adjacent to these shear zones; such structures are interpreted to have formed during Siskiyou-age W-vergent thrusting.

Contact metamorphism by Middle to Late Jurassic, post-Siskiyou calc-alkaline plutons is faint and was not studied in detail. Cox (1956) described hornfels-textured metapelitic rocks in zones a few meters wide around apparently Middle to Late Jurassic plutons adjacent to the study area; these narrow aureoles contain muscovite, biotite, and cordierite. Goodge (1989a) described post-Siskiyou contact metamorphic parageneses in metasedimentary rocks from the Stuart Fork terrane; the degree of recrystallization of this overprint is spatially related to granitic plutons. Estimated P-T conditions are <3 kbar and approximately 400°C. These assemblages contain muscovite + biotite ± garnet ± cordierite. Goodge also described a pre-existing, regionally developed greenschist-grade overprint of Triassic blueschist metamorphic assemblages that is generally correlated with the Siskiyou orogeny. Higher temperatures of late contact metamorphism may be related to the higher density of Middle to Late Jurassic granitic plutons in the Stuart Fork terrane compared to the PCIC at this level of exposure. It is unclear if temperatures recorded by metamorphic mineral assemblages increase smoothly across the Soap Creek Ridge fault or if this thrust places a higher-temperature Stuart Fork terrane over a slightly lower temperature PCIC.

With increasing structural depth to the west of the study area, neoblastic biotite occurs sporadically in cherts and in pelitic metasedimentary rocks, where it defines a weak foliation. In the Virgin Buttes area, metacherts and metapelites are in low-angle fault contact with underlying, well-foliated lineated quartzite, quartz-muscovite schist, and actinolite schist. Metamorphic and structural relationships are similar to those described by Wright and Fahan (1988) for the Wilson Point thrust, 60 km to the south.

Geochemical data

Bulk-rock geochemistry. Samples of mafic metavolcanic rock were collected for analysis. Data were determined employing optical-emission spectroscopy at the U. S. Geological Survey, Office of Mineral Resources, Denver, Colorado, and are reported in Miller (1998). Optical-emission spectroscopy is less precise and less accurate than X-ray fluorescence (XRF) techniques in determining bulk-rock compositions. However, in other mafic metavolcanic rocks from the Klamaths for which both optical spectroscopic and XRF results from the same laboratory are available, these techniques produced similar results for the same specimen. Optical-emission data were used to discriminate among mafic volcanic rocks of basaltic composition, on the basis of the ratios of Zr/Ti to Nb/Y. This subpopulation was further investigated employing geochemical plots in order to identify specific tectonic environments. Subpopulations consistently plotted in the island-arc tholeiite (IAT) field of discriminant diagrams that utilize the relatively immobile elements Cr, T, and Y (Fig. 15). These rocks are correlated with the Salmon River greenstones of Ando et al. (1983) and analogous metavolcanics of the Sawyers Bar area (Ernst et al., 1991). New geochemical data presented here further confirm that island-arc volcanic rocks constitute a large portion of the central WTrPz.

Electron-microprobe data. Electron-microprobe anayses were performed on PCIC magmatic amphiboles, PCIC neoblastic amphiboles, and amphiboles from a post-tectonic mid-Jurassic calc-alkaline pluton. Data are reported in Miller (1998). Metamorphic hornblendes have lower total Na+K and Al contents and lower Mg/Mg+Fe^{2+} ratios compared to magmatic hornblendes of the PCIC. Metamorphic amphiboles plot consistently in the actinolite and actinolitic hornblende field of discriminant plots. Gabbroic igneous amphiboles plot in the pargasitic hornblende field. Amphiboles from mid-Jurassic granitoids plot in the edenitic hornblende field. Mg-rich igneous amphibole also is characteristic of Marble Mountain and Sawyers Bar metavolcanics (Ernst et al., 1991; Hacker et al., 1992) and may be typical of immature island-arc volcanic rocks.

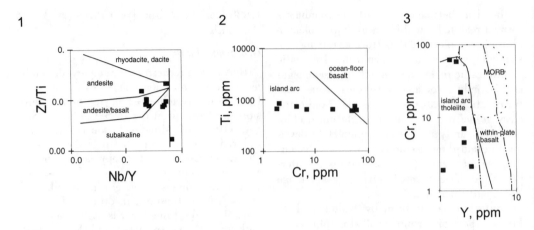

Fig. 15. Bulk-rock geochemical discriminant plots for basaltic rocks, Pony Camp study area.

Oxygen-isotope data. To provide constraints on fluid flow and metasomatism accompanying recrystallization, bulk-rock $^{18}O/^{16}O$ compositions were obtained for 13 samples from the Pony Camp study area. Sample localities are shown in Figure 16. Analyses were performed in the laboratory of Yehoshua Kolodny, Hebrew University, Jerusalem. Table 2 lists analytical results. Samples were run in duplicate and are reported to ± 0.3 per mil.

Subgreenschist-grade mafic metavolcanic rocks have $\delta^{18}O$ ave$_6$ = +11.5 ± 0.81 per mil. This value is typical of intense isotopic exchange reulting from submarine hydrothermal alteration (Taylor, 1978). Lower greenschist–grade metaplutonic rocks have $\delta^{18}O$ ave$_6$ = +8.7 ± 1.32. Because original igneous values probably closely approximated MORB compositions of $\delta^{18}O$ = +6.0, this value may reflect alteration in deeper, hotter hydrothermal systems or a less thorough low-T exchange with seawater in massive, less-fractured plutonic rocks. Analyzed samples of metabasaltic rocks are from the upper plate of the presumed regional-scale, low-angle, Pony Camp normal fault, whereas analyzed samples of metagabbroic rocks are from the lower plate. The data also are compatible with the hypothesis that prior to tectonic juxtaposition, the upper and lower plates were subjected to different degrees of oxygen-isotopic exchange and/or were reequilibrated with hydrothermal fluids of contrasting isotopic composition or temperature.

A single quartz-bearing vein from an upper-plate metavolcanic rock was sampled. This vein material has an enriched $\delta^{18}O$ value of +15.5, indicating a lower temperature of equilibration than the submarine-altered metavolcanic rocks or, more likely, exchange with an aqueous fluid enriched in ^{18}O relative to ocean water (Ernst and Kolodny, 1997).

Structural geology

General relationships. Shallow intrusive rocks of the PCIC are coherent and massive. Except for a few discontinuous zones within gabbroic units, they are not intensely faulted. In contrast, overlying supracrustal and hypabyssal rocks are extremely disrupted and cut by multiple generations of brittle faults. The contact between structurally coherent, shallow intrusive rocks and overlying, disrupted extrusive and hypabyssal rocks is a zone of intense brecciation and hydrothermal alteration. No discernible contact-metamorphic effects were observed. Dikes in the structurally lower complex are truncated at the contact, but several undeformed dikes intrude it. This contact is sinuous in map view (Fig. 13) and is interpreted to be a gently dipping extensional break, the Pony Camp fault. Crosscutting and mutually intrusive relationships suggest that movement on this fault was syn- to postmagmatic. Orientations of nearly vertical dikes within the structurally coherent dike complex strike consistently northeast, indicating NW-SE extension.

Brittle faults are common in the overlying metavolcanic and hypabyssal units. Cataclastic faults are characterized by zones of breccia and

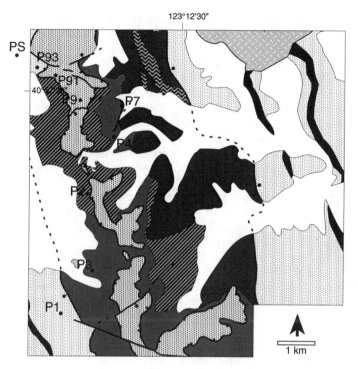

FIG. 16. Oxygen-isotope sample localities, Pony Camp igneous complex. See Table 2 for data.

TABLE 2. Oxygen-Isotope Analyses from the Pony Camp Igneous Complex

Sample no.	Map unit	Rock type	$\delta^{18}O \pm 0.3$
P1a	PCIC metavolcanic	basalt	11.4
P91	PCIC metavolcanic	pillow basalt	11.2
P92a	PCIC metavolcanic	pillow basalt	10.7
P93	PCIC metavolcanic	pillow breccia	12.2
PS	PCIC metavolcanic	pillow basalt	10.7
P2c	PCIC metavolcanic	diabase dike	12.7
Average $\pm 1\sigma$			11.5
P3b	PCIC metaplutonic	gabbro dike	9.8
P2	PCIC metaplutonic	gabbro dike	9.3
P3a	PCIC metaplutonic	px hb gabbro	9.4
P4	PCIC metaplutonic	px hb gabbro	8.4
P7a	PCIC metaplutonic	hb gabbro	9.4
P7c	PCIC metaplutonic	px hb gabbro	6.5
Average $\pm 1\sigma$			8.7 $\pm$ 1.32
P92av	PCIC vein	qtz-epidote vein	15.5

gouge up to one meter wide, with matrix recrystallized to randomly oriented intergrowths of chlorite, epidote, actinolite, quartz, calcite, and prehnite. Both brecciated and relatively undeformed veins and veinlets are common within fault zones. Rare striations indicate that the most recent movement on these faults was dip slip. Bent crystal-fiber lineations on one fault suggest normal displacement. Orientations of faults, although variable, are generally consistent with the NW-SE extension direction recorded in the structurally coherent dike complex. Paleohorizontal constraints regarding eruption, intrusion, and extensional faulting were not found. A possible geopetal indicator is present as crude density stratification of mafic and felsic minerals within gabbroic sills. The average strike and dip of seven measurements of these layers is N-S, $10°E$, with a 95% confidence cone of $8.8°$.

Cherty metasedimentary rocks to the west of both the study area and the Twin Sisters fault contain outcrop-scale concentric folds. Axial planes strike NNE and chiefly dip steeply eastward; fold axes trend NNE and plunge gently north and south. Structural asymmetry is dominantly W-verging (Ando et al., 1983; Goodge, 1989b). A feeble axial plane cleavage, defined by aligned white mica, chlorite, and rare biotite, is indistinctly developed in structurally lower levels of the metasedimentary unit along with a rare crenulation cleavage coplanar with axial planes. Folds are interpreted to have developed during regional W-vergent thrusting that occurred between ~169 and 165 Ma (Wright and Fahan, 1988).

The gross aspect of the PCIC and overlying rocks suggests an open to tight, W-vergent regional antiform, similar to that suggested by Ando et al. (1983) for PCIC-correlative rocks to the north. Figure 17 illustrates an interpretative regional cross-section across the WTrPz at the latitude of the PCIC. Conservative palinspastic restorations suggest approximately 17% regional shortening across the belt, with an indeterminate amount of additional compression taken up by internally folded rocks.

Regional fault zones and terrane boundaries. The PCIC is bounded on the east and west by N-S-striking, vertical to steeply E-dipping shear zones that are marked by foliated, sheared serpentinite. Shear zones vary in thickness from meters to hundreds of meters along strike, are anastomosing in map view, and contain lenses and slices of adjacent units. Several subparallel, NNW-striking, serpentinite-filled shear zones are present on the east side of the PCIC (Fig. 13). The easternmost and struc-

turally highest shear zone separates subjacent, lower greenschist–grade metavolcanic and metasedimentary rocks of PCIC Unit 5 from a thin slab of superjacent greenschist-transitional blueschist rocks of the Stuart Fork terrane. Rocks below this thrust possess a weak, penetrative foliation and are more thoroughly recrystallized. Where measured, layering in rock units is rotated into parallelism with the fault. This discontinuity is clearly a major terrane-bounding structure, the Soap Creek Ridge thrust of Hotz (1977). It places Triassic blueschists over rocks feebly metamorphosed at shallow crustal levels. Slip probably occurred during the Early Jurassic to early Middle Jurassic.

To the west, NNW-striking, steeply E-dipping serpentinite shear zones beneath the Soap Creek Ridge fault juxtapose rocks of similar lithology and metamorphic grade (prehnite-pumpellyite to lower greenschist–grade metavolcanic rocks + hornblende-phyric hypabyssals + metasedimentary strata correlated with Unit 5 of the PCIC). Near these shear zones, rocks are more intensely brecciated and contain abundant fractures + veinlets compared to sections farther away, but are not penetratively deformed. Lithologic layering is crosscut at a high angle by these faults and locally rotated into parallelism with them. In the study area, minor shear zones are intruded and truncated by an undeformed, relatively unrecrystallized hornblende diorite body; hence faulting is probably older than late Middle to Late Jurassic.

On the western side of the PCIC, the Twin Sisters fault (Fig. 13) is a presumed terrane boundary that separates largely meta-igneous rocks of the PCIC from predominantly metasedimentary rocks of the Eastern Hayfork terrane. This fault strikes NNW, dips steeply to the east, and contains thin selvages of serpentinite. Rocks interpreted to be Unit 5 of the PCIC and its stratigraphically overlying metasedimentary cover sequence are exposed in both hanging wall and footwall. Original stratigraphic contacts between meta-igneous and metasedimentary rocks are locally preserved on both sides of the fault. Although fracturing and oxidative alteration increase near this break, there is no evidence of penetrative deformation, as is common for other presumed terrane-bounding

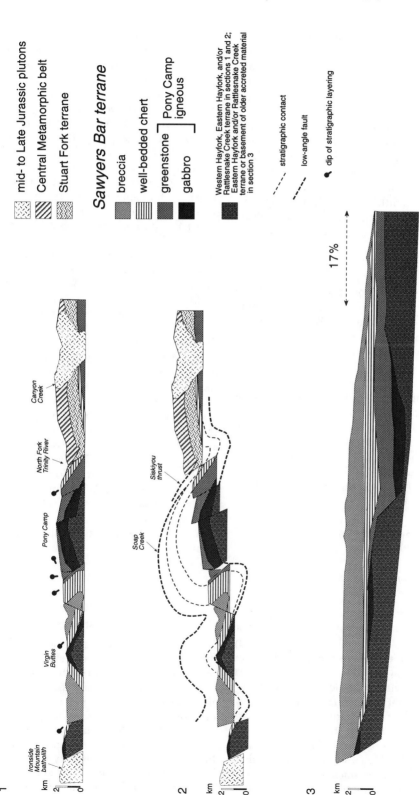

Fig. 17. Interpretative regional cross section, Pony Camp study area.

faults in the WTrPz. Rock layering is transected at a high-angle by the Twin Sisters fault and is locally rotated into parallelism with it. The Twin Sisters fault is interpreted here to represent a minor discontinuity that internally imbricates supracrustal rocks of the PCIC.

In the Virgin Buttes area to the west of the study area, a previously unrecognized, gently dipping shear zone, exposed in creek beds and canyons, separates superjacent, greenschist-grade chert and chert-argillite breccia with well-preserved protolith textures from subjacent, amphibolite-grade, thoroughly recrystallized quartzose tectonite and mafic amphibolite. Superjacent rocks become penetratively deformed near the contact. This poorly exposed shear zone is probably the best candidate for a crustal-scale terrane-bounding structure on the western side of the PCIC. Subjacent rocks could be correlated with either the Western Hayfork or Rattlesnake Creek terrane. This fault zone may be the southern equivalent of the Isinglass shear zone of the Marble Mountains.

Evidence for post-Siskiyou extension, E-directed transport, and/or sinistral transtension is generally lacking in the PCIC, compared to the Marble Mountains. Offset of regional rock units across some intraterrane shear zones and faults indicates syn- to post-Siskiyou normal and reverse slip on these high-angle faults (Fig. 17). Vertical displacements are limited to 1 to 2 km, but horizontal offsets could be 10 to 100+ km on faults that parallel the regional trend of units, as shown by the strike length of high-angle faults.

Geological history of the Pony Camp Igneous Complex

Evidence presented above suggests the following geologic history for the PCIC, summarized in Figure 12. In the Late Triassic to Early Jurassic, basaltic volcanism and shallow-level intrusion within an attenuating submarine arc reconstituted the shallow-level crust in a narrow belt over 100 km long. The basement probably consisted of older arc and accretionary complexes. Extensional tectonism included movement on the low-angle Pony Camp fault. Short-lived, local mafic magmatism subsequently died out. Subsidence and extensional tectonism continued, leading to the deposition

of chert, limestone, and chert-argillite olisto-stromes in a tectonically active, rifted basin that formed along the former magmatic axis. Beginning at ~170 Ma, supracrustal rocks and shallow intrusives were detached from the basement and were thrust westward along a poorly exposed fault in the Virgin Buttes area during the Siskiyou orogeny (Fig. 17). This fault may be correlative with the Wilson Point thrust and/or the Isinglass shear zone. Thrusting and contraction occurred at upper-crustal levels under prehnite-pumpellyite to lower green-schist–grade metamorphic conditions. The Stuart Fork terrane and Central Metamorphic belt were thrust over the PCIC at this time, and the various components of the WTrPz were amalgamated and accreted to the Eastern Klamaths by ~165 Ma (Wright and Fahan, 1988).

In the PCIC, shallow-level intrusives behaved as rigid bodies and formed the core of a regional W-vergent antiform, whereas overlying meta-sedimentary rocks were folded, but not penetratively deformed. Formation of NNW-striking, steeply E-dipping, intraterrane, serpentinite-invaded shear zones was coeval with and followed thrusting. Vertical movement along these shear zones was probably less than 2 km, but strike-slip movement is permissibly 10 to 100+ km. Beginning at ~165 Ma and continuing into the Late Jurassic to Early Cretaceous (~135 Ma), calc-alkaline plutons and dikes were emplaced at shallow crustal levels throughout the region. Minor, Late Jurassic and younger, normal and reverse motion and/or strike-slip displacement apparently occurred on high-angle faults.

Petrotectonic History of the Sawyers Bar Terrane

This study, through geologic mapping and detailed description of the structures, metamorphism, and content/distribution of rock units, sheds light on several issues: the regional three-dimensional structural and metamorphic evolution of the Sawyers Bar nappe complex, a metamorphosed thrust sheet within a continental-margin volcanic-arc setting; origin and evolution of Cache Creek–affinity terranes of the Klamath Mountains; and Mesozoic accretion of the westernmost North American Cordillera.

Contrasts in metamorphism and deformation within the Sawyers Bar nappe complex

The WTrPz represents a regional low-pressure, low- to moderate-temperature metamorphic terrane. The observed monotonically upward-decreasing grade from low-pressure amphibolite to transitional greenschist-amphibolite grade in the Marble Mountains area, and from lower greenschist–grade to prehnite-pumpellyite assemblages in the Pony Camp area, is consistent with heat flow in arcs and intra-arc rifts. Discontinuities in metamorphic conditions were not detected across the study areas. Metamorphic parageneses support regional models of a Middle Jurassic thermal maximum associated with arc-related magmatic heat flow. The intensity of recrystallization and deformation increase northward from Pony Camp → Sawyers Bar → Marble Mountains.

Oxygen-isotope data document contrasting $\delta^{18}O$ bulk-rock values with structural depth, and between shallow-intrusive and supracrustal rocks. Changes may reflect depth-dependent variations in the presence of isotopically heavy metasedimentary rocks, or control of fluid flow by regional low-angle faults, variations in hydrothermal systems, or increased permeability of pervasively faulted supracrustal rocks. In the feebly recrystallized PCIC, it is difficult to distinguish burial metamorphism within a hot volcanic pile from superimposed low-grade regional metamorphic assemblages.

Lower structural levels of the Sawyers Bar nappe complex in the Marble Mountains area are characterized by penetrative L-S tectonite fabrics, isoclinal folds with gently dipping axial planes parallel to foliation, and intrusive rocks that show only modest contact effects. Middle levels are characterized by the development of multiple superposed folds with gently to steeply dipping axial planes, minor crenulation foliations, and intrusive rocks with well-defined contact effects. Upper levels are characterized by tight to isoclinal folds with steeply dipping axial planes. Structures are most simply interpreted to have formed during progressive deformation within an evolving, recrystallized thrust sheet (Fig. 11). Within the nappe, internal faults commonly bound domains with distinct deformational style, structural orientation, and depth of recrystallization. Distinctive associations of rock types can be traced across internal

faults, indicating that these structures accommodated only limited displacement. Without detailed mapping of structures and rock types, it would have been tempting to interpret these domains as separate lithotectonic terranes.

Deformation in the PCIC occurred at lower temperatures and slightly shallower depths than that in the Marble Mountains. The PCIC lacks a penetrative fabric. Synmagmatic brittle faults are well preserved. High-angle faults marked by brecciation and/or sheared serpentinite internally imbricate supracrustal rocks of the PCIC, whereas the shallow-intrusive complex behaved as a rigid, coherent mass. Probable crustal-scale terrane-bounding faults generated a weak, penetrative fabric parallel to the zones of dislocation, as well as a slight apparent metamorphic upgrading. In contrast, intraterrane faults are characterized by increased brecciation, but did not produce penetrative fabrics, and typically cut layering at high angles.

Metamorphic rocks in the Marble Mountains are low-pressure amphibolites to transitional greenschists. To the south, PCIC-phase assemblages reflect prehnite-pumpellyite and lower-greenschist facies and were produced at lower T and P. These data indicate a lateral temperature gradient over a distance of ~100 km and suggest that the thermal maxima for Siskiyou metamorphism were located in the central Klamaths near the Condrey Mountain dome, where crustal thickening probably reached a maximum. This area also coincides with the locus of maximum Cenozoic uplift. Coupled with structural information, mineral parageneses suggest that the Sawyers Bar nappe complex may be an exhumed lens-shaped allochthon, thickening and deepening to the north. The lithologic section in the Marble Mountains was buried under a pile of thrust sheets ≥15 km thick during Siskiyou deformation. In contrast, the Pony Camp igneous complex evidently was overridden by allochthons aggregating <10 km in thickness.

Implications for the WTrPZ and the Klamath Mountains

Rocks of the study area have been considered to be representatives of diverse lithotectonic entities, including the Western Hayfork, Eastern Hayfork, North Fork–Salmon River, and Marble Mountain terranes (Fig. 2). Detailed mapping across putative terrane boundaries in this study demonstrates that such faults either do not exist or are minor intraformational breaks. Our terrane interpretation generally follows that of Hacker et al. (1993) and Ernst (1998), but differs in detail. The name Sawyers Bar terrane is applied to a regionally extensive belt of arc-related rocks that form the eastern part of the WTrPz. The Sawyers Bar terrane is bounded above by the crustal-scale Soap Creek Ridge fault and below by the crustal-scale Wilson Point thrust in the southern Klamaths and possibly the Isinglass shear zone in the central Klamaths.

The Sawyers Bar terrane is interpreted to represent a relatively intact metamorphic nappe complex. It is detached from its basement of older accretionary + volcanic-arc complexes and consists of intensely deformed upper levels of a volcanic arc. We postulate that magmatism and sedimentation within the Sawyers Bar terrane is Late Triassic to Early or Middle Jurassic in age, correlative with volcanoplutonic sequences of this age exposed throughout the Cordillera. Most faunal and radiometric ages from the Sawyers Bar terrane are Triassic to Middle Jurassic; all fossil ages from coherent, bedded sequences are Late Triassic to Early Jurassic. Small blocks with Permian faunal ages are probably samples of older, exotic oceanic basement incorporated in the Sawyers Bar terrane along intraterrane shear zones or as blocks within olistostromes, as is a discordant radiometric date from a plagiogranite pod within a shear zone (Ando et al., 1983). We suspect that these older rocks are not genetically related to the Sawyers Bar terrane and do not date deposition and magmatism within the terrane. More age data and a detailed structural analysis of Permian blocks from the region are clearly needed. High-angle faults within the Sawyers Bar nappe complex that are marked by sheared serpentinite selvages are interpreted to have formed from internal imbrication of a single lithotectonic assemblage rather than as crustal-scale sutures or closed ocean basins, as interpreted by some previous workers (Irwin, 1981; Mortimer, 1984).

Integrating data from this study with those of Hacker et al. (1993, 1995) and Ernst (1998) indicates that arc-related rocks are more abundant than MORB within the WTrPz. These arc-related lithologies record synmagmatic extension. Such attenuated arc complexes probably have a high preservation potential along convergent margins compared to offscrapings of oceanic plates. The arc evidently lay within depositional range of quartz-rich continent-derived sediments and rocks of the Eastern Klamath terrane. Regional deformation and metamorphism were variable in space and time, with layer-parallel extension and contraction occurring more or less simultaneously (at the resolution of geochronologic methods) at different crustal levels, or alternating on time scales <5 Ma, as summarized in Figure 12. Metamorphism and deformation were spatially controlled by local magmatism and enhanced by thermally weakened crust.

Tectonic models

Previous studies (e.g., Ernst, 1983; Donato, 1987; Wright and Fahan, 1988; Hacker et al., 1993; Irwin and Mankinen, 1998) have emphasized the evolution of WTrPz rocks above an E-dipping subduction zone and general oceanward growth and younging of accreted material. This model is generally accepted, but new structural and stratigraphic data presented here require the modification of details.

Eastern Hayfork metasedimentary rocks are interpreted to be interbedded with rocks of the Sawyers Bar terrane. Although these units contain older accreted material, the depositional age of the Eastern Hayfork metasedimentary rocks is interpreted to be Late Triassic to Early Jurassic and perhaps as young as Middle Jurassic. The source for these rocks was older accreted material, possibly the Rattlesnake Creek terrane, the Eastern Klamath terrane, and the underthrust basement of the Sawyers Bar arc.

The Rattlesnake Creek terrane contains Late Triassic–Early Jurassic arc volcanoplutonic complexes built on a mélange of older accreted materials. Although it contains lithotectonic units coeval with those of Sawyers Bar, the Rattlesnake Creek terrane occurs in an outboard, out-of-place position relative to the latter. Unlike the Sawyers Bar terrane, the Rattlesnake Creek arc apparently is still attached to its ophiolitic basement. The Rattlesnake Creek arc may have occupied a more oceanic, outward, fringing-arc position relative to the Sawyers Bar terrane, but the former contains Eastern Klamath–derived detritus along with materials probably scraped off a subducting plate (Gray, 1986; Wright and Wyld, 1994). It is difficult to imagine Eastern Klamath debris being transported across two arc-trench systems to be deposited within the Rattlesnake Creek terrane. Thus, the latter may have been continuous with presumed Sawyers Bar basement and was rifted away to form a fringing arc in the Late Triassic. The rift basin has since disappeared, presumably subducted, but may be represented by protoliths of the Condrey Mountain terrane. A third model postulates that the Late Triassic–Early Jurassic complex has been doubled up by arc-parallel, strike-slip faulting. Although available paleomagnetic evidence suggests minimal Mesozoic latitudinal displacement of WTrPz terranes (May and Butler, 1986; Mankinen and Irwin, 1990) relative to each other, substantial displacements of 600 to 700 km are within the error range of the data. Some exotic deep-sea cherts and ophiolite scraps appear to be truly far traveled, however (Mankinen et al., 1996).

Sawyers Bar rocks and volcanoplutonic complexes of the WTrPz also lie outboard of coeval Eastern Klamath arc rocks, thus introducing yet a third possible arc-trench system into Late Triassic–Early Jurassic tectonic models. Eastern Klamath–derived material in Upper Triassic(?)–Lower Jurassic deposits of the WTrPz suggests proximity to the Eastern Klamaths at this time. The Siskiyou + Nevadan orogenies may represent a minimum 100 to 200 km shortening between WTrPz and Eastern Klamaths in the Middle Jurassic. Stratigraphic resolution within the Eastern Klamath arc rocks permits depositional hiatuses of >1 m.y., and thus the axis of arc magmatism may have shifted temporarily outboard, into the Sawyers Bar–WTrPz area, consistent with the relatively small volume and episodicity of magmatism in the outer-arc region. Alternately, Sawyers Bar magmatism may represent unique circumstances in a fore-arc, such as ridge subduction. Another possibility is that the Sawyers Bar–WTrPz–Eastern Klamath arc-trench system formed oblique to the continental margin, similar to the Kamchatka-Aleutian island-arc system in the North Pacific. Increase in the westward motion vector of North America in the Middle Jurassic may have caused an accordian-like collapse of this arc-trench system before and during the Siskiyou orogeny.

Another model discussed above is that the Late Triassic–Early Jurassic complexes of the Klamaths formed in a single arc-trench system that has been tripled by strike-slip faulting similar to that proposed for the Philippines (Karig et al., 1986). Both accordian-like collapse of an oblique arc-trench system and slivering of a single arc along arc-parallel strike-slip faults would explain structural repetition of Late Triassic–Early Jurassic arc volcanoplutonic complexes in the Klamaths and would support the model postulating generation of complexes within a single arc-trench system. Both models have analogues in modern arc-trench systems. Multiple fringing arcs on separate plates would require basins and trenches between fringing arcs, for which evidence is generally lacking in the Klamaths. Figure 18 illustrates a possible, speculative tectonic model in which structurally repeated arc terranes of the Klamaths and Sierran Foothills evolved within a single continental-margin arc.

Differences between Sierra and Klamath arcs

Volcanoplutonic complexes in the WTrPz are found in Middle Jurassic W-vergent thrust sheets or nappe complexes detached from basement. Available age data favor a Late Triassic through early Middle Jurassic age for arc magmatism in the central Klamath Mountains. Correlations often are made between the WTrPz and Sierran Foothill terranes, and the lithologic similarities are striking (Davis, 1969; Saleeby, 1990; Hacker et al., 1993), supporting the concept of a broad region of suprasubduction-zone extension and magmatism during Late Triassic–Early Jurassic time. Such a process apparently produced the Cache Creek–affinity rocks. However, significant structural differences exist between Klamath and Sierran Cache Creek assemblages. The Eastern Hayfork terrane is often correlated with Upper Paleozoic–Lower Mesozoic Calaveras-type rocks, but evidence summarized here suggests that the protolith of the Eastern Hayfork terrane was an Upper Triassic–Lower Jurassic(?) sedimentary deposit within the Sawyers Bar terrane. Although these rocks contain older accreted material, the depositional age of the metasedimentary rocks is probably Triassic–Early(?) Jurassic.

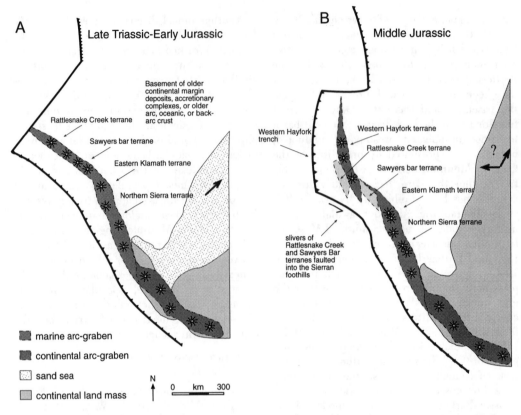

Fig. 18. Speculative tectonic model for the WTrPz belt in the Klamath Mountains. (A) Late Triassic–Early Jurassic time. (B) Middle Jurassic time.

The Rattlesnake Creek terrane compares favorably to ophiolitic-rich Calaveras/Cache Creek–type mélange terranes in the Sierra Foothills. If this correlation is accepted, then the Sierra Foothills terranes lack the inboard, crustal-scale, regionally extensive, arc-nappe complexes such as Sawyers Bar or Western Hayfork terrane that are present in the Klamaths. In the Sierra, rocks possibly correlative with Sawyers Bar rocks (Peñon Blanco, Sullivan Creek, Slate Creek, and Tuolumne River complexes) occur as smaller, discontinuous, fault-bounded slivers, in some cases still attached to basement and in other cases within the upper plate of E-vergent thrusts. Thus, the Sierra equivalents to Sawyers Bar rocks are not as regionally extensive and underwent a different and probably more complex post-magmatic deformational history compared with those of the WTrPz.

Implications for Cordillera and Cache Creek–affinity terranes

The origin and tectonic setting of Cache Creek–affinity terranes of the North American Cordillera is controversial and has been the subject of numerous studies. Cache Creek assemblages were originally considered to consist of allochthonous paleo-Pacific lithosphere accreted to North America in conjunction with Mesozoic convergence. This and other studies (e.g., Miller, 1987) indicate that much of the accreted material was generated in the hanging wall of a subduction zone, rather than representing exotic paleo-Pacific lithosphere. Most workers (e.g., Gray, 1986; Ernst, 1990, 1998; Hacker et al., 1993; Wright and Wyld, 1994; this study) regarded WTrPz magmatism to have occurred within an island arc. Saleeby (1990) and Busby-Spera et al. (1990) interpreted Late

Triassic–Early Jurassic Cordilleran magmatism within Cache Creek–affinity terranes to represent near-trench activity in a forearc setting. The broad regional extent, total volume, and locally evolved compositions of magmatic rocks of Late Triassic–Early Jurassic age within the WTrPz and related terranes argue for construction of a continental-margin arc on Cache Creek–affinity basement rather than near-trench magmatism. What, then, is the relationship of Cache Creek magmatism to inboard, roughly coeval continental-arc rocks of the Sierra and Klamaths?

A short-lived westward jump of the main axis of arc magmatism may have marked retreat of the North American plate relative to the continental-margin subduction zone and/or steeply dipping subduction of old Panthalassa lithosphere (Busby-Spera, 1990). The Lower Jurassic deposits of the inboard continental-margin arc are characterized by local volcanic quiescence and deposition of continent-derived quartz arenite, which may record the arc-axis jump. Alternatively, the areal extent of arc magmatism may have been exceptionally broad and variable in space or time in the Late Triassic–Early Jurassic (Fig. 18).

Implications for crustal growth, accretion, and terrane interpretations

Data collected in this study indicate that the eastern WTrPz in the Klamath Mountains, once regarded as the type locality of a terrane amalgam formed from disparate, far-traveled, unrelated lithotectonic fragments, actually consists of a single metamorphosed thrust sheet. Detailed description and mapping of structures, metamorphism, and content + distribution of rock units indicates that differences among WTrPz areas do not represent separate terranes, but instead reflect different depths of exposure within the nappe or along-strike variations within a single volcanic-arc terrane. Composite terranes and areas of multiple terranes in convergent zones throughout the world may similarly represent different exposure (exhumation) levels within single fault-bounded entities. Detailed field work is required to resolve terrane boundaries and to determine whether faulted contacts represent crustal-scale suture zones or rather the internal imbrication of a single lithostratigraphic assemblage.

Detailed mapping of fault-bounded ultramafic rocks in the Marble Mountain and Pony Camp areas, previously thought to represent ocean-continent suture zones or closed ocean basins, indicates that serpentinites were emplaced along internal faults with relatively minor displacement. Another assumption of geologists working in convergent margins is that tectonic mélange commonly represents a subduction-zone accretionary complex. As shown through detailed mapping in the Marble Mountains, a mélange mapped at 1:24,000 scale is a multiply folded and faulted pseudo-stratigraphic sequence when mapped at 1:6000 scale, and it probably formed inboard of a subduction zone within a volcanic arc.

As documented by geologic mapping (e.g., Ernst, 1998) a majority of the WTrPz consists of *in situ* volcanic-arc-related rocks. Unequivocal foreign material offscraped from a subducting plate is a less important constituent of the WTrPz. Extrapolated to other convergent-plate junctions, these data suggest that the contribution of material decoupled from downgoing oceanic plates and underplated along continental margins may be less voluminous than previously thought. Certain accretionary terranes may form within the hanging wall of subduction zones and are tectonically coupled to continental plates. Rapidly alternating contraction and attenuation as well as diverse magmatic products in the WTrPz also suggest that continental-margin complexes, such as Cache Creek–affinity terranes of the North American Cordillera, may be particularily sensitive to changes in plate motions. As shown in this study, intra-arc extension played an important role in the formation and preservation of rocks within the WTrPz. Extensional arcs may have high preservation potential along continental margins, creating basins in which volcanosedimentary material accumulates, locally leading to the generation of new juvenile crust. If this is the case, sedimentary, magmatic, and structural signatures of regional extension should be preferentially preserved in continental-margin accretionary assemblages. Where rift basins are not identified, it would be easy to misinterpret these lithic sections as individual terranes. In the study area, provenance of sedimentary rocks indicates local, intrabasin derivation as well as supply from inboard terranes, from a quartz-rich continental source, and from outboard, far-traveled oceanic materials. Variable provenance may be characteristic of continental-margin accretionary assemblages.

In the WTrPz, intra-arc extension was punctuated by episodic thrusting and crustal thickening, which led to local generation of crustal melts. In the Klamath Mountains, repeated deformation created a strongly layered forearc/arc crustal column consisting of thin, recrystallized thrust sheets with marked rheologic contrasts. In addition, margin-parallel strike-slip faults with displacements of a few hundred kilometers, although difficult to identify with certainty, may have structurally repeated a single volcanic arc in the Klamath Mountains, leading to the erroneous conclusion of multiple separate arc terranes.

Acknowledgments

Field and laboratory research summarized in this report was supported by the U. S. Department of Energy through grant DE FG03-90ER14154 and by Stanford University. Elizabeth Miller and R. G. Coleman provided critical reviews of a first-draft manuscript that guided revisions and led to a much-improved final version. Discussions on the outcrop and in the laboratory with these reviewers and with M. O. McWilliams, Porter Irwin, C. G. Barnes, B. R. Hacker, Don Elder, and Mary Donato have been very helpful. None are to be held accountable for the interpretations expressed here, of course. The authors are grateful to the above-named institutions and researchers for support.

REFERENCES

Ando, C. J., Irwin, W. P., Jones, D. L., and Saleeby, J. B., 1983, The ophiolitic North Fork terrane in the Salmon River region, central Klamath Mountains, California: Geol. Soc. Amer. Bull., v. 94, p. 236–252.

Barnes, C. G., Rice, J. M., and Gribble, R. F., 1986, Tilted plutons in the Klamath Mountains of California and Oregon: Jour. Geophys. Res., v. 91, p. 6059–6071.

Barton, M. D., Battles, D. A., Bebout, G. E., Capo, R. C., Christensen, J. N., Davis, S. R., Hansen, R. B., Michelsen, G. J., and Trim, H. E., 1988, Mesozoic contact metamorphism in the western United States, in Ernst, W. G., ed., Metamorphism and crustal evolution of the western United States. Rubey Vol. VII: Englewood Cliffs, NJ, Prentice-Hall, p. 110–178.

Blake, M. C., Howell, D. G., and Jones, D. L., 1982, Preliminary tectonostratigraphic terrane map of California: U.S. Geol. Surv. Open File Rep. 82-593.

Blome, C. D., and Irwin, W. P., 1983, Tectonic significance of late Paleozoic to Jurassic radiolarians from the North Fork terrane, Klamath Mountains, California, in Stevens, C. H., ed., Pre-Jurassic rocks in western North America suspect terranes: Soc. Econ. Paleontol. Mineral., Rocky Mountain Sect., p. 77–89.

Bloomer, S. H. and Hawkins, J. W., 1983, Gabbroic and ultramafic rocks from the Mariana trench: An island arc ophiolite, in Hayes, D. E., ed., Tectonic and geologic evolution of southeast Asia seas and islands: Amer. Geophys. Union Monog. 27, p. 294–317.

Burchfiel, B. C., and Davis, G. A., 1981, Triassic and Jurassic tectonic evolution of the Klamath Mountains–Sierra Nevada geologic terrane, in Ernst, W. G., ed., The geotectonic development of California: Englewood Cliffs, NJ, Prentice-Hall, p. 50–70.

Burton, W. C., 1982, Geology of the Scott Bar Mountains, northern California: Unpubl. M.S. thesis, Univ. of Oregon, 120 p.

Busby-Spera, C. J., Mattinson, J. M., Riggs, N. R., and Schermer, E. R., 1990, The Triassic-Jurassic magmatic arc in the Mojave-Sonoran Deserts and the Sierran-Klamath region, in Harwood, D. S., and Miller, M. M., eds., Paleozoic and Early Mesozoic paleogeographic relations: Sierra Nevada, Klamath Mountains, and related terranes: Geol. Soc. Amer., Spec. Pap. 255, p. 93–114.

Coleman, R. G., Manning, C. E., Donato, M. M., Mortimer, N., and Hill, L. B., 1988, Tectonic and regional metamorphic framework of the Klamath Mountains and adjacent Coast Ranges, California and Oregon, in Ernst, W. G., ed., Metamorphism and crustal evolution of the western United States. Rubey Vol. VII: Englewood Cliffs, NJ, Prentice-Hall, p. 1061–1097.

Cox, D. P., 1956, Geology of the Helena Quadrangle, Trinity County, California: Unpubl. Ph.D. dissertation, Stanford Univ., 123 p.

Davis, G. A., 1969, Tectonic correlations, Klamath Mountains and western Sierra Nevada, California: Geol. Soc. Amer. Bull., v. 80, p. 1095–1108.

Davis, G. A., Holdaway, M. J., Lipman, P. W., and Romey, W. D., 1965, Structure, metamorphism, and plutonism in the south-central Klamath Mountains, California: Geol. Soc. Amer. Bull., v. 76, p. 933–966.

Davis, G. A., Monger, J. W. H., and Burchfiel, B. C., 1978, Mesozoic construction of the Cordilleran "collage," central British Columbia to central California, in Howell, D. G., and McDougall, K. A., eds., Mesozoic paleogeography of the western United States: Los Angeles, Soc. Econ. Paleontol. Mineral., Pacific Sect., p. 1–3.

Donato, M. M., 1985, Metamorphic and structural evolution of an ophiolitic tectonic mélange, Marble Mountains, northern California: Unpubl. Ph.D. dissertation, Stanford Univ., 258 p.

—————, 1987, Evolution of an ophiolitic tectonic mélange, Marble Mountains, northern California Klamath Mountains: Geol. Soc Amer. Bull., v. 98, p. 448–464.

—————, 1989, Metamorphism of an ophiolitic tectonic mélange, northern California Klamath Mountains, USA: Jour. Metamor. Geol., v. 7, p. 515–528.

—————, 1983, Phanerozoic continental accretion and metamorphic evolution of northern and central California: Tectonophys., v. 100, p. 287–320.

—————, 1987, Mafic meta-igneous arc rocks of apparent komatiitic affinities, Sawyers Bar area, central Klamath Mountains, California: Geochem. Soc., Spec. Publ. No. 1, p. 191–208.

—————, 1990, Accretionary terrane in the Sawyers Bar area of the Western Triassic and Paleozoic belt, central Klamath Mountains, northern California, in Harwood, D. S., and Miller, M. M., eds., Paleozoic and Early Mesozoic paleogeographic relations: Sierra Nevada, Klamath Mountains, and related terranes: Geol. Soc. Amer., Spec. Pap. 255, p. 297–305.

—————, 1993, Chemically distinct mafic dike/sill sequences of contrasting age ranges, Sawyers Bar area, central Klamath Mountains, northern California: Jour. Petrol., v. 34, p. 63–75.

—————, 1998, Geologic map of the Sawyers Bar area, scale 1:48,000—geochemical/petrotectonic evolution of an oceanic island arc, central Klamath Mountains, California: Calif. Div. Mines and Geol., Map Sheet 47, scale 1:48,000, accompanying text 32 p.

Ernst, W. G., Hacker, B. R., Barton, M. D., and Sen, G., 1991, Occurrence, geochemistry and igneous petrogenesis of magnesian metavolcanic rocks from the WTrPz belt, central Klamath Mountains, northern California: Geol. Soc. Amer. Bull., v. 103, p. 56–72.

Ernst, W. G., and Kolodny, Y., 1997, Submarine and superimposed contact metamorphic oxygen isotopic exchange in an oceanic arc, Sawyers Bar area, central Klamath Mountains, California, USA: Geochim. et Cosmochim. Acta, v. 61, p. 821–834.

Goodge, J. W., 1989a, Polyphase metamorphism of the Stuart Fork terrane, a Late Triassic subduction complex, Klamath Mountains, northern California: Amer. Jour. Sci., v. 289, p. 874–943.

—————, 1989b, Early to middle Mesozoic deformation of a convergent margin complex, Klamath Mountains, northern California: Tectonics, v. 8, p. 845–864.

—————, 1990, Tectonic evolution of a coherent Late Triassic subduction complex, Stuart Fork terrane, Klamath Mountains, northern California: Geol. Soc. Amer. Bull., v. 102, p. 86–101.

Gray, G. G., 1986, Native terranes of the central Klamath Mountains: Tectonics, v. 5, p. 1043–1053.

Hacker, B. R., and Ernst, W. G., 1993, Jurassic orogeny in the Klamath Mountains: A geochronological approach, in Howell, D. G., and McDougall, K. A., eds., Mesozoic paleogeography of the western United States: Los Angeles, Soc. Econ. Paleontol. Mineral., Pacific Sect., p. 37–60.

Hacker, B. R., Ernst, W. G., and Barton, M. D., 1992, Metamorphism, geochemistry, and origin of magnesian volcanic rocks, Klamath Mountains, California: Jour. Metamor. Geol., v. 10, p. 55–69.

Hacker, B. R., Ernst, W. G., and McWilliams, M. O., 1993, Genesis and evolution of a Permian-Jurassic magmatic arc accretionary wedge, and evaluation of terranes in the central Klamath Mountains: Tectonics, v. 12, p. 387–409.

Hacker, B. R., Donato, M. M., Barnes, C. G., McWilliams, M. O., and Ernst, W. G., 1995, Timescales of orogeny: Jurassic construction of the Klamath Mountains: Tectonics, v. 14, p. 677–703.

Helper, M. A., 1986, Deformation and high P/T metamorphism in the central part of the Condrey Mountain window, north-central Klamath Mountains, California and Oregon: Geol. Soc. Amer. Memoir 164, p. 125–141.

Hill, L. B., 1985, Metamorphic, deformational, and temporal constraints on terrane assembly, northern Klamath Mountains, California, in Howell, D. G., ed., Tectonostratigraphic terranes of the Circum-Pacific Region: Houston, Earth Sci. Ser., Circum-Pacific Council for Energy Min. Resources, p. 173–186.

Hotz, P. E., 1977, Geology of the Yreka quadrangle, Siskiyou County, California: U. S. Geol. Surv. Bull. 1436, 72 p.

Hotz, P. E., Lanphere, M. A., and Swanson, D. A., 1977, Triassic blueschist from northern California and north-central Oregon: Geology, v. 5, p. 659–663.

Irwin, W. P., 1966, Geology of the Klamath Mountains province: Calif. Div. Mines Geol. Bull. 190, p. 17–36.

—————, 1972, Terranes of the western Paleozoic and Triassic belt in the southern Klamath Mountains, California: U. S. Geol. Surv. Prof. Paper 800C, p. 103–111.

—————, 1981, Tectonic accretion of the Klamath Mountains, in Ernst, W. G., ed., The geotectonic development of California: Englewood Cliffs, NJ, Prentice-Hall, p. 29–49.

—————, 1994, Geologic map of the Klamath Mountains, California and Oregon: U. S. Geol. Surv. Misc. Investig. Ser., Map I-2148.

Irwin, W. P., and Galanis, J. R., Jr., 1976, Map showing limestone and selected fossil localities in the Klamath Mountains, California and Oregon: U. S.

Geol. Surv. Misc. Field Studies, Map MF-749, scale 1:500,000.

Irwin, W. P., and Mankinen, E. A., 1998, Rotational and accretionary evolution of the Klamath Mountains, California and Oregon, from Devonian to present time: U. S. Geol. Surv. Open-File Report 98-114.

Irwin, W. P., Jones, D. L., and Blome, C. D., 1982, Map showing radiolarian localities in the Western Paleozoic and Triassic belt, Klamath Mountains, California: U. S. Geol. Surv. Misc. Field Studies, Map MF-1399, scale 1:250,000.

Irwin, W. P., Wardlaw, B. R., and Kaplan, T. A., 1983, Conodonts of the western Paleozoic and Triassic belt, Klamath Mountains, California and Oregon: Jour. Paleontol., v. 57, p. 1030-1039.

Ishii, T., 1985, Dredged samples from the Ogasawara forearc seamount or Ogasawara paleoland forearc ophiolite, in Nasu, N., Kobayashi, K., Uyeda, S., Kushiro, I., and Kagami, H., eds., Formation of active ocean margins: Tokyo, Terra Sci. Publ., p. 307-342.

Karig, D. E., Sarewitz, S. R., and Haeck, G. D., 1986, Role of strike-slip faulting in the evolution of allochthonous terranes in the Philippines: Geology, v. 14, p. 852-855.

Leake, B. E., 1978, Nomenclature of amphiboles: Can. Mineral., v. 16., p. 501-520.

Lewison, M. A., 1984, Fission-track ages from two plutons in the central Klamath Mountains, California: Unpubl. M.S. thesis, Univ. of Oregon, 66 p.

Liou, J. G., Maruyama, S., and Cho, M., 1985, Phase equilibria and mineral parageneses of metabasites in low grade metamorphism: Mineral. Mag., v. 49, p. 321-334.

Mankinen, E. A., and Irwin, W. P., 1990, Review of paleomagnetic data from the Klamath Mountains, Blue Mountains, and Sierra Nevada, in Harwood, D. S., and Miller, M. M. eds., Paleozoic and Early Mesozoic paleogeographic relations: Sierra Nevada, Klamath Mountains, and related terranes: Geol. Soc. Amer., Spec. Pap. 255, p. 93-114.

Mankinen, E. A., Irwin, W. P., and Gromme, C. S., 1989, Paleomagnetic study of the Eastern Klamath terrane, California, and implications for the tectonic history of the Klamath Mountains province: Jour. Geophys. Res., v. 94, p. 10,444-10,472.

Mankinen, E. A., Irwin, W. P., and Blome, C. D., 1996, Far-travelled Permian chert of the North Fork terrane, Klamath Mountains, California: Tectonics, v. 15, p. 314-328.

May, S. R., and Butler, R. F., 1986, North American Jurassic apparent polar wander: Implications for plate motion, paleogeography and Cordilleran tectonics: Jour. Geophys. Res., v. 91, p. 11519-11544.

Miller, D. E., 1998, Deformation and metamorphism in the Western Triassic and Paleozoic belt, Klamath Mountains, California: Unpubl. Ph.D. dissertation, Stanford Univ., 189 p.

Miller, D. E., and Hacker, B. R., 1993, Detailed structure and stratigraphy of the eastern Marble Mountain terrane, Klamath Mountains, CA [abs.]: Geol. Soc. Amer., Abs. Prog., v. 25, no. 5, p. 121.

Miller, M. M., 1987, Dispersed remnants of a northeast Pacific fringing arc: Upper Paleozoic island arc terranes of Permian McCloud faunal affinity, western U.S.: Tectonics, v. 6, p. 807-830.

Monger, J. W. H., Price, R. A., and Tempelman-Kluit, D. J., 1982, Tectonic accretion and origin of the two major metamorphic and plutonic belts in the Canadian Cordillera: Geology, v. 10, p. 70-75.

Mortimer, N., 1984, Petrology and structure of Permian to Jurassic rocks near Yreka, Klamath Mountains, California: Unpubl. Ph.D. dissertation, Stanford Univ., 83 p.

Mortimer, N., and Coleman, R. G., 1985, A Neogene structural dome in the Klamath Mountains, California and Oregon: Geology, v. 13, p. 253-256.

Ogawa, Y., Naka, J., and Taniguchi, H., 1985, Ophiolite based forearcs, in Nasu, N., Kobayashi, K., Uyeda, S., Kushiro, I., and Kagami, H., eds., Formation of active ocean margins: Tokyo, Terra Sci. Publ., p. 719-746.

Ramsay, J. G., and Huber, M. I., 1983, The techniques of modern structural geology: New York, Academic Press, 307 p.

Rawson, S. A., and Petersen, S. W., 1982, Structural and lithologic equivalence of the Rattlesnake Creek terrane and high-grade rocks of the Western Triassic and Paleozoic belt, north central Klamath Mountains, California [abs.]: Geol. Soc. Amer. Abs. Prog., v. 14, no. 4, p. 226.

Saleeby, J. B., 1990, Geochronological and tectonostratigraphic framework of Sierran-Klamath ophiolitic assemblages, in Harwood, D. S., and Miller, M. M., eds., Paleozoic and Early Mesozoic paleogeographic relations, Sierra Nevada, Klamath Mountains, and related terranes: Geol. Soc. Amer., Spec. Pap. 255, p. 93-114.

Silberling, N. J., Jones, D. L., Blake, M. C., Jr., and Howell, D. G., 1984, Lithotectonic terrane map of the North American Cordillera, Part C: U. S. Geol. Surv. Open-File Report 84-523, scale 1:2,500,000.

Sliter, W. V., Jones, D. L., and Throckmorton, C. K., 1984, Age and correlation of the Cretaceous Hornbrook Formation, in Nilsen, T. H., ed., Geology of the Upper Cretaceous Hornbrook Formation, Oregon and California: Los Angeles, Soc. Econ. Paleontol. Mineral., Pacific Sect., p. 89-98.

Taylor, H. P., 1978, Oxygen and hydrogen isotope studies of plutonic granitic rocks: Earth Planet. Sci. Lett., v. 38, p. 177-210.

Welsh, J. L., 1982, Structure, petrology, and metamorphism of the Marble Mountains area, Siskiyou County, California: Unpubl. Ph.D. dissertation, Univ. of Wisconsin, Madison, 250 p.

Wright, J. E., 1982, Permian-Triassic accretionary subduction complex, southwestern Klamath Mountains, northern California: Jour. Geophys. Res., v. 87, p. 3805-3818.

Wright, J. E., and Fahan, M. R., 1988, An expanded view of Jurassic orogenesis in the western U.S. Cordillera: Middle Jurassic (pre-Nevadan) regional metamorphism and thrust faulting within an active arc environment: Geol. Soc. Amer. Bull., v. 100, p. 859-876.

Wright, J. E., and Wyld, S. J., 1986, Significance of xenocrystic Precambrian zircon contained within the southern continuation of the Josephine ophiolite: Devils Elbow ophiolite remnant, Klamath Mountains, northern California: Geology, v. 14, p. 671-674.

————, 1994, The Rattlesnake Creek terrane, Klamath Mountains, California: An early Mesozoic volcanic arc and its basement of tectonically disrupted oceanic crust: Geol. Soc. Amer. Bull., v. 106, p. 1033-1056.

Miocene Paleogeography of Southwestern California and Its Implications Regarding Basin Terminology

A. Eugene Fritsche

Department of Geological Sciences, California State University, Northridge, California 91330-8266

Abstract

A new palinspastic reconstruction for the latest Oligocene of southwestern California is created by: (1) backsliding the eastern part of the western Transverse Ranges west of the curved San Gabriel–Sierra Madre fault in a counterclockwise, rotational, left-slip direction in order to close the gap created by medial Miocene transrotational extension of the easternmost Los Angeles basin; and (2) bending the rocks in the westernmost Transverse Ranges, west of the Santa Monica Mountains, through an additional counterclockwise backrotation until they are in contact with the present southern California coast. This reconstruction restores Eocene forearc basin deposits of the southern California coast and the western Transverse Ranges regions into straight alignment with Eocene forearc-basin deposits to the north in the San Rafael Mountains. During the Oligocene, this forearc basin was divided into two depositional basins that received mostly nonmarine deposits. The northern of the two basins is named the DiSoCuMa depositional basin and the southern one the AnaVent depositional basin. Subsidence occurred during the early Miocene and flooded the two basins with marine deposits. During the medial Miocene, subsidence continued as the western side of the AnaVent basin (today's western Transverse Ranges) began to pull away from the southern California coast and rotate clockwise around its northern end. This transrotational process served to enlarge both basins by crustal extension and produced extensive areas of volcanism. Throughout the late Miocene, transrotation and subsidence continued, the basins grew in size and depth to their present configuration, and internal isostatic adjustments produced several new marine depositional basins within the previous two-basin framework.

Introduction

PRELIMINARY PALEOGEOGRAPHIC reconstructions of a regional nature for the Miocene of southwestern California include those by Reed (1933), Corey (1954), and Fritsche (1977, 1981). These reconstructions utilized a present-day geographic map of California for a base map because, except for estimates of slip on the San Andreas fault documented by Crowell (1962), knowledge of the Tertiary tectonic history of southern California was not sufficient to create a reasonably accurate Tertiary palinspastic map. The suggestion by Jones et al. (1976), Hamilton (1978), and Kamerling and Luyendyk (1979), that the western Transverse Ranges (Fig. 1) had rotated ~90° since the medial Miocene, was a concept that further complicated the tectonic picture of southwestern California. During the next decade, several palinspastic reconstruction models were proposed for the region (Luyendyk et al., 1980; Hornafius, 1985; Hornafius et al., 1986; Luyen-

dyk and Hornafius, 1987; Luyendyk, 1991). These models used right-shearing shutter panels in the inner and outer Continental Borderland regions and in the Santa Maria basin (Fig. 1) to account for rotation of the western Transverse Ranges. None of these models, however, achieved wide acceptance because they did not adequately account for a missing section of lower and middle Tertiary rocks in the Los Angeles and Santa Maria basins.

Prior to paleomagnetic studies of the rotation of the western Transverse Ranges, Yeats (1968, 1976) proposed that the California Continental Borderland originated by an extension process similar to the type taking place today in the Gulf of California. Such an extension process, if completed during the medial Miocene, would account for the absence of lower and middle Tertiary rocks in the Los Angeles basin. Crouch (1979), Kamerling and Luyendyk (1985), and Crouch and Suppe (1993) combined the concepts of rotation and extension to produce a

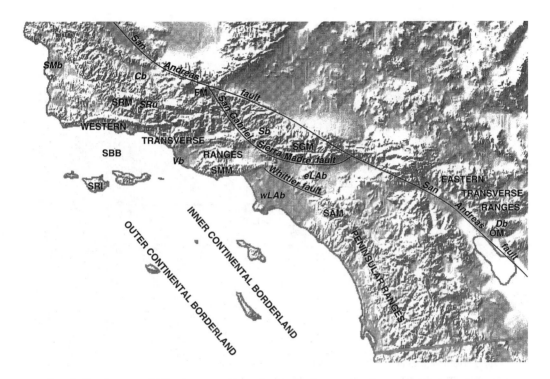

Fig. 1. Southwestern California geographic and geologic place names that are referred to in the text. Abbreviations (roman letters): FM = Frazier Mountain; OM = Orocopia Mountains; SAM = Santa Ana Mountains; SBB = Santa Barbara Basin; SGM = San Gabriel Mountains; SMM = Santa Monica Mountains; SRI = Santa Rosa Island; SRM = San Rafael Mountains. Abbreviations for geologic features (italics): *Cb* = Cuyama basin; *Db* = Diligencia basin; *eLAb* = eastern Los Angeles basin; *Sb* = Soledad basin; *SMb* = Santa Maria basin; *SRu* = San Rafael uplift; *Vb* = Ventura basin; *wLAb* = western Los Angeles basin. The base map in this figure and Figures 2–10 and 18 is modified from a digitized map of southern California (copyright © 1995) found in the Johns Hopkins University Applied Physics Laboratory Color Landform Atlas of the United States (http://fermi.jhuapl.edu/states/maps1/ca _south.gif) and is used with permission.

palinspastic model that eliminated the right-shearing shutter panels and restored the western Transverse Ranges to a position parallel with and immediately adjacent to the Peninsular Ranges before rotation and extension. This model received support from Nicholson et al. (1994), who suggested that capture of the partially subducted Monterey microplate by the Pacific plate provides a mechanism for the operation of the rotation-extension model.

This rotation-extension model, however (Crouch, 1979; Kamerling and Luyendyk, 1985; Crouch and Suppe, 1993), does not address three geologic factors that must be resolved in any palinspastic reconstruction model: (1) the amount of rotation, as demonstrated by the paleomagnetic data (Hornafius, 1985; Dickinson, 1996), must increase from

east to west along the length of the western Transverse Ranges; (2) rocks on the adjacent eastern and western sides of the San Gabriel–Sierra Madre fault (Fig. 1) must remain in contact while rotation and extension occur; and (3) Mesozoic plutonic and sedimentary trends in the Santa Ana Mountains and the Santa Monica Mountains must be restored to alignment prior to extension and rotation.

Palinspastically Restored Base Maps

Figure 2 is a map of southwestern California that shows the lines along which the map must be cut and the two areas that Crouch and Suppe (1993) suggested must be removed in order to provide an accurate palinspastic restoration.

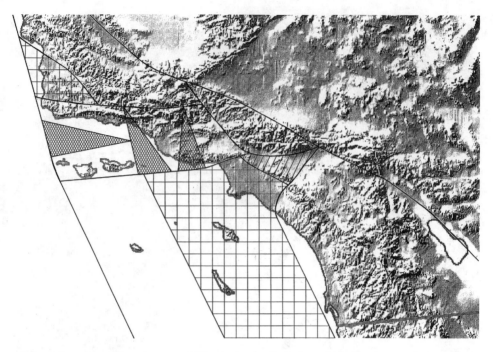

FIG. 2. Digitized map of southwestern California showing lines along which the map must be cut and areas (patterned) that must be removed in order to allow palinspastic restoration of southwestern California back to the latest Oligocene (~25 Ma). The Los Angeles basin–inner Continental Borderland and the Santa Maria basin regions (square cross-hatching) are areas created by post-Oligocene extension, according to Crouch and Suppe (1993). The easternmost Los Angeles basin (diagonal lines) is proposed herein as an additional area of post-Oligocene extension. Triangular areas in the western Transverse Ranges (diamond cross-hatching) were removed in order to accomplish realignment of the westward-increasing paleomagnetic vectors as described in the text.

These two areas—south and north of the western Transverse Ranges block (the Los Angeles basin–inner Continental Borderland region and the Santa Maria basin region)—are areas that were created by extension during rotation of the western Transverse Ranges block, and they did not exist before that time. Within the western Transverse Ranges block (Fig. 2) are additional triangular areas that have been removed in order to accomplish realignment of the westward-increasing paleomagnetic vectors described by Hornafius (1985) and Dickinson (1996). In reality, the realignment of these vectors could be accomplished by a uniform bending process from one end of the block to the other, but this is not possible with the non-plastic medium of paper, so the triangular areas were removed for the convenience of reconstruction.

Figure 3 shows the remaining non-extended areas of Figure 2 in their prerotation position at ~25 Ma. Dickinson's (1996) analysis of southern California paleomagnetic data indicates that rocks within the San Gabriel Mountains block rotated 37° clockwise during rotation, whereas rocks to the west of the San Gabriel–Sierra Madre fault, outside the San Gabriel Mountains block, rotated 56° clockwise. The difference of 19° of rotation across the fault can be accounted for merely by right slip along the curved surface of the fault. I propose, therefore, that the San Gabriel–Sierra Madre fault did not originate as a major strand of the San Andreas fault system, as suggested by Crowell (1975), but that it was created in its curved form by rotational shearing in the hinge region of the rotation, and thereafter served as a curved fault surface along which 19° of rotation occurred. Why this happened in this manner may be the result of the thickness, density, and relative strength of the Precambrian gabbroic and anorthositic basement rocks in the

FIG. 3. Palinspastic restoration of southwestern California during the latest Oligocene (~25 Ma), modified from proposals of Hornafius (1985) and Nicholson et al. (1994) and from the compilation of Dickinson (1996).

San Gabriel Mountains at this location. Further comments on the importance of these Precambrian rocks to the sedimentary and tectonic history of the region are made below.

In the palinspastic reconstruction shown in Figure 3, areas farther to the west of the San Gabriel–Sierra Madre fault, in the western Transverse Ranges block, are backrotated sufficiently to bring them into agreement with the paleomagnetic data of Hornafius (1985) and the analysis of Dickinson (1996). The result of this backrotation is that the western Transverse Ranges block, as shown in Figure 3, begins its history as a bent block that slowly straightens as differential rotation proceeds.

Rotation of the San Gabriel Mountains block (Fig. 3) is not constrained by movement along the San Andreas fault because the San Andreas fault did not exist at the time of rotation of the San Gabriel Mountains block. This rotation occurred in conjunction with the simultaneous rotation of the eastern Transverse Ranges block (Figs. 1 and 3) (Terres, 1984; Luyendyk et al., 1985), which was adjacent to the San Gabriel Mountains block at the time.

In the Crouch and Suppe (1993) model, the triangular area from the Whittier fault (Fig. 1) eastward to the San Gabriel–Sierra Madre fault was not considered as part of the extensional

Los Angeles basin. Wright (1991), however, showed that basement rocks—or in many places the lack of information on the distribution of basement rocks—for this area is the same as that for the Los Angeles basin to the west of the Whittier fault. In Figures 2 and 3, therefore, this triangular segment is considered to be part of the extensional Los Angeles basin. This allows the western Transverse Ranges block in Figure 3 to be backrotated along the San Gabriel–Sierra Madre fault until the extensional gap is closed, thus realigning the Mesozoic plutonic and sedimentary trends in the Santa Ana Mountains and the Santa Monica Mountains, a process that cannot be accommodated in the Crouch and Suppe (1993) model. Figures 4, 5, and 6 show the relative positions of blocks at ~20 Ma, ~15 Ma, and ~10 Ma, respectively, as suggested by Nicholson et al. (1994).

Paleogeographic Maps

Latest Oligocene

Figures 7 through 10 are simplified, small-scale paleogeographic maps of the area, each one drawn on top of its time-corresponding, palinspastically restored base map (Figs. 3–6). Prior to 25 Ma, during the Cretaceous and the Paleogene, deposition in the southern Califor-

FIG. 4. Palinspastic restoration of southwestern California during the early Miocene (~20 Ma), modified from proposals of Hornafius (1985) and Nicholson et al. (1994) and from the compilation of Dickinson (1996).

nia region was determined by subduction tectonics and occurred in a forearc basin between a volcanic arc to the east and a low, sometimes-emergent, forearc ridge to the west (Hamilton, 1978; Crouch, 1979; Kamerling and Luyendyk, 1985; Nilsen, 1987).

At the end of the Paleogene (~25 Ma; Fig. 7), the paleogeography reflects this forearc origin, but the area was relatively uplifted and deposition in the forearc basin was almost totally fluvial. The western boundary of the forearc basin, the forearc ridge, is represented in the rock record by an unconformity between Eocene and Miocene rocks that has long been known in the easternmost part of the western Transverse Ranges as the E-W-trending San Rafael uplift (Fig. 1) (Reed, 1933; Corey, 1954; Fischer, 1976). This highland on the reconstructed map is oriented generally NW-SE and to the west of the forearc basin on the south half of the map. Its continuance to the north is in the present-day San Rafael Mountains, where it also is recognized by an Eocene/Miocene unconformity. A topographic high point in the forearc basin occurred at the site of the soon-to-be-elevated or proto-San Gabriel-Frazier Mountains, a Miocene mountain range that combined the present-day San Gabriel Moun-

tains and Frazier Mountain into a single range before the two ranges were separated by movement on the San Gabriel-Sierra Madre fault.

I suggest that what caused the uplift of the proto-San Gabriel-Frazier Mountains is related to the Precambrian gabbroic and anorthositic rocks in those mountains. Perhaps this terrane had a dense root whose basal lithospheric boundary extended deeper into the asthenosphere than in adjacent areas. As subduction of the Monterey microplate below this root slowed and ceased, and post-subduction isostatic adjustments to the new tectonic regime took place, the proto-San Gabriel-Frazier Mountains area was uplifted more than the surrounding regions, thus dividing the former forearc basin into two basins—a N-sloping "northern basin" to the north of the uplift and a S-sloping "southern basin" to the south.

North of the proto-San Gabriel-Frazier Mountains high point, a river entered the "northern basin" and flowed northward in the basin, depositing the Vasquez Formation and the Simmler Formation (Bohannon, 1975, 1976; Blake, 1981, 1982; Hendrix and Ingersoll, 1987). Volcanism in this northern area at that time is recorded by the Morro Rock-Islay

FIG. 5. Palinspastic restoration of southwestern California during the medial Miocene (~15 Ma), modified from proposals of Hornafius (1985) and Nicholson et al. (1994) and from the compilation of Dickinson (1996).

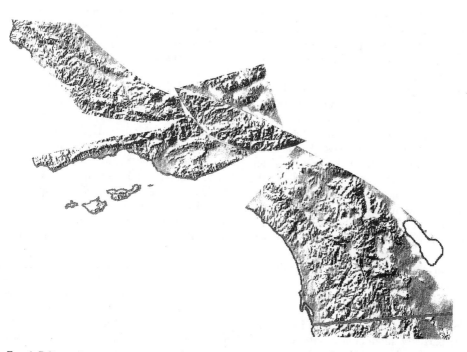

FIG. 6. Palinspastic restoration of southwestern California during the late Miocene (~10 Ma), modified from proposals of Hornafius (1985) and Nicholson et al. (1994) and from the compilation of Dickinson (1996).

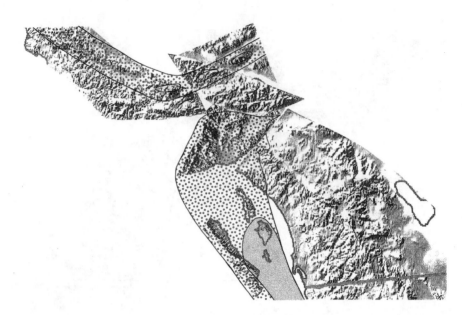

FIG. 7. Paleogeographic map of southwestern California during the latest Oligocene (~25 Ma), drawn on the palinspastic restoration shown in Figure 3. Highland areas are unmarked, areas of nonmarine deposition are marked with open circles, areas of marine deposition are finely stippled, and areas of volcanism are marked with a V-shaped pattern. Paleogeography is interpreted on the basis of references cited in the text.

Hill Complex, the Rocky Butte Dacite, and the Cambria Felsite (Hall, 1981) as well as by volcanic rocks within the Plush Ranch Formation, the Vasquez Formation, and the Orocopia Formation (Frizzell and Weigand, 1993).

South of the proto–San Gabriel–Frazier Mountains high point, a second river entered the "southern basin" and flowed southward, depositing the Sespe Formation (McCracken, 1969, 1972; Taylor, 1983, 1984; Howard and Lowry, 1995; Howard, 1996). A marine environment at the extreme southern end of the "southern basin" is represented by the marine Alegria Formation, which presently interfingers with the nonmarine Sespe Formation at the western end of the western Transverse Ranges. This is the setting that marks the end of subduction tectonics and the beginning of transform tectonics.

Early Miocene

By ~20 Ma (Fig. 8), subduction had ceased and the partially subducted Monterey microplate was captured by the Pacific plate (Nicholson et al., 1994), thus causing the initiation of extension, but not yet rotation. As extension began, the area subsided, leading to transgres-

sion of lower Miocene marine sedimentary units into the depositional basin, a basin that had formed tectonically as a forearc basin and was still geographically the same basin, but by this time was an extensional basin.

From the north, transgression proceeded southward up the basin slope of the "northern basin" toward the newly emergent San Gabriel–Frazier Mountains, depositing first the shallow-marine Vaqueros Formation and then the deeper-marine Saltos Shale (Lagoe, 1984, 1985; Freitag and Fritsche, 1988; Oldershaw, 1988, 1990; Freitag, 1989). The Vaqueros Formation interfingered northward with a part of the nonmarine, deltaic Caliente Formation to the north of the San Gabriel–Frazier Mountain area.

From the south, transgression proceeded northward up the basin slope of the "southern basin," depositing the shallow-marine Vaqueros Formation (Blundell, 1981, 1983; Oborne, 1987, 1993; Daniel, 1989; Daniel-Lyle, 1995; Anderson, 1996), which interfingered with a coeval part of the nonmarine, deltaic Sespe Formation (Belyea, 1984; Belyea and Minch, 1989) south of the newly emergent San Gabriel–Frazier Mountain area. The two basins

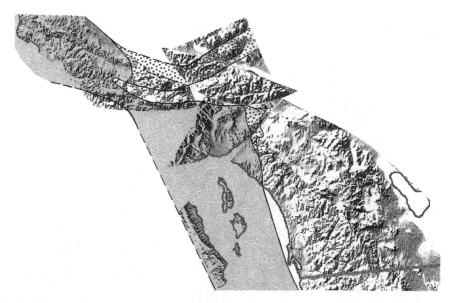

FIG. 8. Paleogeographic map of southwestern California during the early Miocene (~20 Ma), drawn on the palinspastic restoration shown in Figure 4. Highland areas are unmarked, areas of nonmarine deposition are marked with open circles, and areas of marine deposition are finely stippled. Paleogeography is interpreted on the basis of references cited in the text.

eventually were connected by a marine strait to the west of the San Gabriel–Frazier Mountain area, through which flowed a S-directed marine current (Reid, 1978, 1979).

Medial Miocene

Rotation of the western Transverse Ranges block had begun by ~15 Ma (Fig. 9; Nicholson et al., 1994) and the two depositional basins mentioned above began to change significantly in size and shape. The initiation of rotation was marked by the eruption of volcanic rocks along two generally NW-SE–oriented linear zones on the western and eastern sides of the western Transverse Ranges block. Volcanism started on the western side of the western Transverse Ranges block near the south end of the block at ~18 to 17 Ma. This volcanic event is recorded by the Tranquillon Volcanics and volcanic rocks in the Temblor Formation and the Lospe Formation (Hall, 1981; Fritsche and Thomas, 1990; Stanley et al., 1996). Volcanism continued northwestward up the western side of the western Transverse Ranges block to produce the volcanic rocks in the Obispo Formation at ~15 Ma (Hall, 1981). At present, the E-W–oriented belt of Tranquillon Volcanics and the NE-

SW–oriented belt of Temblor and Obispo volcanic rocks meet at an acute angle in the San Rafael Mountains (Fig. 1). Hall (1981) attempted to decipher the origin of these volcanic rocks by a leaky transform fault and their distribution by counterclockwise rotation of the volcanic rocks. Paleomagnetic data do not support his model. In the palinspastic reconstruction of Crouch and Suppe (1993) and Nicholson et al. (1994), the two belts of volcanic rocks are opened out into a nearly straight line, a model that is supported by the paleomagnetic data.

Initiation of volcanism on the eastern side of the western Transverse Ranges block is marked by hypabyssal intrusions on Santa Rosa Island, dated at ~19 Ma (Luyendyk et al., 1998). As on the western side of the western Transverse Ranges block, volcanism proceeded northwestward, culminating in the Conejo Volcanics (~13 Ma) and the El Modeno Volcanics (~11 Ma) (Weigand, 1994; Luyendyk et al., 1998). The apparent age progression of volcanism from southeast to northwest on the two sides of the western Transverse Ranges block suggests dual propagating rifts (Luyendyk et al., 1998). These volcanic rocks formed as decompression melt-

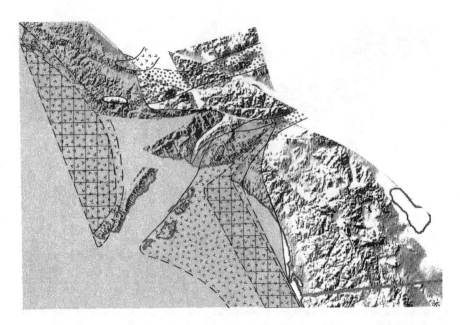

FIG. 9. Paleogeographic map of southwestern California during the medial Miocene (~15 Ma), drawn on the palinspastic restoration shown in Figure 5. Highland areas are unmarked, areas of nonmarine deposition are marked with open circles, areas of marine deposition are finely stippled, areas of volcanism are marked with a V-shaped pattern, one known subaerial volcano is indicated with diagonal cross-hatching, and new crustal surface areas are marked with square cross-hatching. Paleogeography is interpreted on the basis of references cited in the text.

ing of rising asthenosphere produced magmas that made their way to the surface while extension stretched and thinned the crust (Savage, 1996; Savage and Weigand, 1997). The most extensive volcanism is recorded by the Conejo Volcanics, which began as submarine extrusions and grew into subaerial island volcanoes (Dibblee and Ehrenspeck, 1993; Stadum and Weigand, 1998). The eruptive site of the Conejo Volcanics is located along the eastern, inside bend of the prerotation western Transverse Ranges block at the place where straightening of the block during rotation would have caused the greatest extension.

As rotational extension in the Los Angeles–inner Continental Borderland rift area (the "southern basin") continued, basement rock, the Catalina Schist, was uplifted, exposed, eroded, and incorporated as clasts into the San Onofre Breccia and the Topanga Formation (Vedder and Howell, 1976; Vedder, 1979; Stuart, 1979a, 1979b; Wright, 1991). Environments during deposition of the Topanga Forma-

tion in the "southern basin" varied from fluvial and deltaic in the northeast to shallow-marine and eventually deep-marine toward the south and southwest (Flack, 1990, 1993).

To the north, in the "northern basin," the delta represented by the Caliente Formation continued to grow (Fritsche, 1988; Menzie et al., 1989), but by this time it was interfingering westward and northwestward with the middle Miocene, shallow-marine Branch Canyon Formation (Perri and Fritsche, 1988; Perri, 1990). The Branch Canyon Formation, in turn, interfingered farther westward with the middle Miocene, deep-water Hurricane Deck Formation, which spread into the ever-expanding and deepening Santa Maria rift (Van Wagoner, 1981; Yaldezian, 1984; Popelar, 1988; Thomas et al., 1988; Condon, 1989; Thomas, 1989). The San Gabriel Mountain block and the western Transverse Ranges block were rotating as a unit at this time, and shear stress between the two had not yet initiated movement on the San Gabriel–Sierra Madre fault.

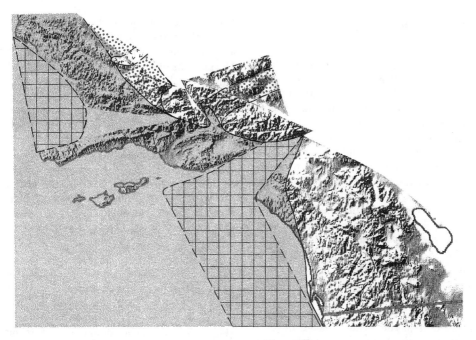

FIG. 10. Paleogeographic map of southwestern California during the late Miocene (~10 Ma) drawn on the palinspastic restoration shown in Figure 6. Highland areas are unmarked, areas of nonmarine deposition are marked with open circles, areas of marine deposition are finely stippled, areas of volcanism are marked with a V-shaped pattern, and new crustal surface areas are marked with square cross-hatching. Paleogeography is interpreted on the basis of references cited in the text.

Late Miocene

Major changes were occurring in the area by ~10 Ma (Fig. 10). Rotation of the western Transverse Ranges block continued during the late Miocene, thus causing the Santa Maria rift to widen in an E-W direction and narrow in a N-S direction. The Los Angeles–inner Continental Borderland rift area was much larger, and differential uplift and subsidence in various portions of the newly exposed schistose crust produced an irregular topography of islands or shoals and small intervening basins. The late Miocene was a time of widespread subsidence and ocean expansion (Mayer, 1987; Wright, 1991). Previous highlands were flooded and most of the region, both to the north and to the south, was occupied by deep-ocean water where the Monterey Shale was deposited. Several turbidite fans formed in the areas that were nearest to the coastline (Wright, 1991). The San Gabriel–Sierra Madre fault had been mov-

ing right-laterally for ~2 to 3 m.y. through the proto–San Gabriel–Frazier Mountains, thus separating present-day Frazier Mountain from the present-day San Gabriel Mountains. On the block west of the San Gabriel–Sierra Madre fault, the Frazier Mountain area moved relatively northward until it blocked the course of the river that previously had flowed northwestward through the Cuyama region into the ocean. This lateral movement forced the river to flow southward through the gap between the San Gabriel Mountains and the Frazier Mountain areas and into the ocean at the southwest corner of the San Gabriel Mountains. In the area to the east of Frazier Mountain, lacustrine deposits of the Mint Canyon Formation formed in a local basin during the late Miocene, but as subsidence continued, the late Miocene sea transgressed into this basin from the south and deposited the shallow-marine Castaic Formation (Stanton, 1967).

Basin Terminology

Introduction

As the study of geology developed in California in the early 1900s, petroleum exploration became one of the leading contributors to our knowledge of the geology of the state. Petroleum reservoirs at that time were most easily discovered in Neogene rocks that existed in structural basins throughout the state, these structural basins being surrounded by structural highs of Paleogene or older rocks of sedimentary, igneous, or metamorphic origin that did not contain easily obtainable petroleum. In order to expedite communication, these structural basins were given names such as Ventura basin, Los Angeles basin, Santa Maria basin, Cuyama basin, Soledad basin, etc. These basins are structurally low areas, and it has been common to consider them as topographically low areas. Questions and statements such as "when did deposition in the Cuyama basin begin?," "deposition in the Soledad basin was mostly nonmarine," and "deposition in the Ventura basin was continuous from the Eocene through to the Pliocene" have arisen because of this perception. Unfortunately, the depositional history of California has nothing to do with the well-known and named structural basins, and to describe the depositional history in this manner is misleading. The differences between topographic, depositional, and structural basins are reviewed below in order to understand the discussion and conclusions regarding the Miocene paleogeography of southwestern California.

Topographic, depositional, and structural basins

Three kinds of basins are recognized and described by paleogeographers. A *topographic basin* is defined by a topographic or drainage low point surrounded by drainage divides (Fig. 11). The low point is recognized geologically by: (1) the convergence point of all downslope paleocurrent directions and (2) the paleobathymetry of associated fossils. Topographic basins should be shown on paleogeographic maps.

A *depositional basin* is defined by the area of sediment accumulation in a topographic basin (Fig. 12). This area of sediment accumulation is recognized stratigraphically as a basin sequence, which is defined as a package of sedimentary units that is bounded below, above, and on all sides by unconformities (Fig. 13).

The extent, variation in thickness, and depocenter (location of maximum thickness) of the basin sequence are illustrated by isopach maps. The margins of the basin sequence may contain numerous short-lived rock sequences marked by unconformities related to eustatic or local tectonic changes, but the depocenter consists of a continuous, uninterrupted sedimentary record. Depositional basins also should be shown on paleogeographic maps.

A *structural basin* is defined by the dip of the rocks, which are inclined toward the center or trough of the basin (Fig. 14). Structural basins are formed after deposition of the rocks and generally are unrelated to any associated topographic or depositional basins. Structural basins are not shown on paleogeographic maps and should not be considered as potential sites of former depositional basins.

In addition, depositional basins are divided into three types. In a *marine depositional basin* (Fig. 15), the basin sequence that forms is entirely marine in origin. The basin sequence is thinner on the divides than at the depocenter, but commonly covers the entire basin. In a *nonmarine depositional basin* (Fig. 16), the basin sequence is totally nonmarine in origin. Deposition is concentrated in the center of the basin and unconformities occur where the divides or topographic barriers are located. The *marginal-marine depositional basin* (Fig. 17) is the least understood of the three types. The basin sequence consists of interfingering marine and nonmarine rocks. Deposition is thickest along one side of the basin; unconformities occur at the location of the divides on the nonmarine side of the basin and marine deposits cover the divides on the marine side of the basin.

Examination of the modern-day Santa Barbara Basin, a marginal-marine topographic and depositional basin, will serve to elucidate the above definitions. Figure 18 shows that the Santa Barbara topographic basin is bounded on the west by an ocean sill or shoal; on the southwest by the E-W crestal trends of four islands and the intervening sills between the islands; and on the southeast, east, and north by the crest lines (drainage divides) of several mountain ranges. The Santa Barbara topographic basin, therefore, includes an oceanic part in the southwest, the drainage basins of three major rivers in the east, and the drainage

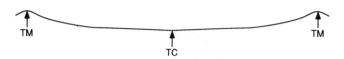

FIG. 11. Cross section of a topographic basin. Abbreviations: TM = topographic margin or drainage divide on the edge of the topographic basin; TC = topographic center or low point in the basin.

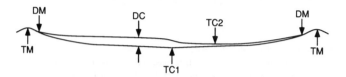

FIG. 12. Cross section of a depositional basin that is infilling a topographic basin mainly from one side. Abbreviations: TM = topographic margin or drainage divide on the edge of the topographic basin; TC1 = topographic center of the basin when filling began; TC2 = topographic center of the basin when deposition ceased; DM = depositional margin or location of the zero isopach around the edge of the depositional basin; DC = depocenter, location of the thickest deposits in the depositional basin.

FIG. 13. Diagram of a basin sequence (see text for discussion).

basins of many smaller and shorter creeks along the northwest. The Santa Barbara depositional basin, within the topographic basin, contains all the marine sediment that is accumulating today in the oceanic part of the topographic basin, all the nonmarine alluvial sediment that is accumulating along the rivers and creeks in the topographic basin and that has a continuous physical connection with the marine sediment, and all the older, underlying sediment that shows continuous deposition from the origin of the basin to the present.

Implications and Recommendations for Basin Terminology

In the northern portion of Figures 7, 8, and 9 is depicted a marginal-marine depositional basin in which deposition began in the Oligocene after a brief period of erosion during late Eocene–early Oligocene time. Sedimentation in this depositional basin ended for the most part in the Pliocene, but may still be occurring in the ocean at the extreme western end of the

basin. This marginal-marine depositional basin, referred to above as the "northern basin," bears a close resemblance to the present-day Santa Barbara depositional basin outlined above. Since cessation of deposition, the "northern basin" has been deformed by folding and faulting into four structural basins—(1) the Diligencia basin east of the San Andreas fault (Fig. 1), (2) the Soledad basin within the San Gabriel Mountains block, and (3) the Cuyama and (4) Santa Maria basins to the west. These structural basins did not exist until latest Miocene or Pliocene time, when structural deformation of the area created them. If post-depositional structural terms and names are used to describe pre-deformational geographic features, confusion can occur. I propose that the "northern basin" described above be referred to as the "DiSoCuMa depositional basin," an acronym consisting of the first two letters of the four structural basins (**Di**ligencia, **So**ledad, **Cu**yama, and Santa **Ma**ria) that ultimately resulted from deformation of the depositional basin. The rocks in these four structural

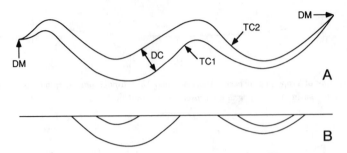

Fig. 14. Cross section of the folded sedimentary deposits of a depositional basin. "A" shows the entire folded sequence before any erosion; "B" shows the two structural basins that remain after erosion. Symbols are the same as in Figure 12. Note that after deformation and erosion, DM, DC, TC1, and TC2 are no longer directly observable and their location must be interpreted.

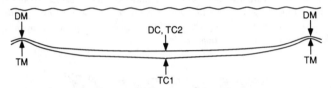

Fig. 15. Cross section of an entirely marine depositional basin. Symbols are the same as those used in Figure 12. TM and DM commonly are synonymous. TC1, TC2, and DC may or may not be synonymous, depending on variations in subsidence rates throughout the basin.

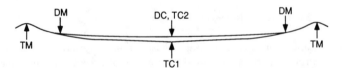

Fig. 16. Cross section of an entirely nonmarine depositional basin. Symbols are the same as those used in Figure 12. TC1, TC2, and DC may or may not be synonymous, depending on variations in subsidence rates throughout the basin.

basins provide evidence for the original depositional basin history, and this relationship is preserved in the basin's name.

In the southern part of Figures 7, 8, and 9 is another marginal-marine depositional basin within which deposition began in early Eocene time after a period of erosion during Paleocene time. Deposition in some parts of this "southern basin" continues today. Rocks deposited on the western side of this "southern basin" are commonly referred to as having been deposited in the Ventura basin. The Ventura basin is an oil-producing structural basin that did not originate until the Pliocene, after cessation of deposition of the lower Neogene rocks. Rocks on the eastern side of the "southern basin" have not as yet been connected with any named basin, but these rocks are present in the region around the

city of Santa Ana. It is inappropriate and misleading to refer to this "southern basin" as the Ventura depositional basin when deposition was taking place off coastal southernmost California and far from Ventura. I propose that this "southern basin" be named the "AnaVent depositional basin," an acronym that combines parts of the names of the two now widely separated structural basins (Santa **Ana** and **Vent**ura) in which are preserved the remnants of the former depositional basin.

Between 13 and 12 Ma, the headwaters part of the DiSoCuMa depositional basin was captured by the AnaVent depositional basin as a result of movement along the San Gabriel–Sierra Madre fault. The lower part of the Mint Canyon Formation was deposited in a fluvial depositional system north of the San Gabriel Mountains in

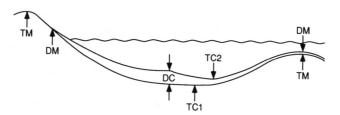

FIG. 17. Cross section of a marginal-marine basin. Symbols are the same as those used in Figure 12. TM and DM commonly are synonymous along the offshore edge of the basin. The majority of the fill comes from the onshore side of the basin.

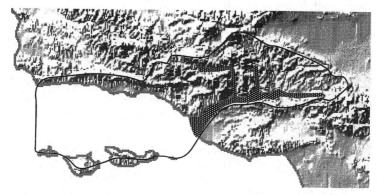

FIG. 18. Area outlined on the map encloses the Santa Barbara topographic basin. The outline follows the topographic margin or rim of the basin. The Santa Barbara depositional basin consists of marine rocks on the west end, which are being deposited in the ocean between the islands and the northern coastline, and coeval nonmarine rocks (patterned) on the eastern end, which are being deposited in the rivers that empty into the ocean. The marine and nonmarine rocks of the depositional basin interfinger at the site of a wave-dominated delta along the coastline.

the DiSoCuMa basin. Once the block west of the San Gabriel–Sierra Madre fault moved far enough northward to isolate the upper part of the DiSoCuMa basin, a local lacustrine basin was formed into which the upper, lacustrine part of the Mint Canyon Formation was deposited. During the short existence of this lacustrine basin, three depositional basins existed in the southwestern California region—(1) a marginal-marine basin that consisted of only the western or "CuMa" (**Cu**yama–Santa **Ma**ria) part of the previous DiSoCuMa basin, (2) a completely nonmarine basin that occupied the eastern, beheaded or "DiSo" (**Di**ligencia-**So**ledad) part of the previous DiSoCuMa basin, and (3) the still-intact AnaVent basin. As deformation along the San Gabriel–Sierra Madre fault system and subsidence within the area continued, the late Miocene ocean transgressed northward from the AnaVent basin and breached the sill between itself and the DiSo

nonmarine depositional basin to the north, and the Castaic Formation was deposited unconformably on top of the upper Miocene Mint Canyon Formation, in what by that time was the DiSo arm of the AnaVent basin (Fig. 10). In a relatively short period of time, a geographic area within what is known as the Soledad structural basin passed through an evolutionary history involving three different depositional basins.

Finally, Figures 10 and 11 show that as the AnaVent basin evolved through time, it was extended and its western border rotated clockwise and northward. The processes of stretching and isostatic adjustment created several new depositional basins within the confines of the old AnaVent basin—a northern, Ventura (or Santa Barbara) marginal-marine depositional basin, an eastern, Santa Ana marginal-marine depositional basin (the two being the split halves of the original AnaVent basin), and— between the two—several new depositional basins, including the Los Angeles basin, whose boundaries in the past have not yet been documented, but which are clearly demonstrable in the Continental Borderland of the modern ocean.

Conclusions

1. In the new model for medial Tertiary palinspastic reconstruction of southwestern California presented herein (Fig. 3), the western Transverse Ranges block began originally as a curved block that straightened during medial Miocene rotation. This proposed reconstruction best fits the paleomagnetic data that show increasing rotation vectors toward the western end of the block.

2. A triangular portion of the easternmost Los Angeles basin, east of the Whittier fault, is added to that part of the Los Angeles basin that was created by medial Miocene extension, thus allowing room for the eastern end of the western Transverse Ranges block to be backrotated into that triangular gap in order to realign the Mesozoic plutonic and sedimentary trends of the Santa Ana Mountains and the Santa Monica Mountains.

3. The San Gabriel–Sierra Madre fault system did not originate as a major strand of the San Andreas fault system, but instead was created as a curved fault surface by rotational shearing between 13 and 12 Ma. Right-lateral movement along the curved fault line of the San Gabriel–Sierra Madre fault system promoted differential rotation between the San Gabriel Mountains and western Transverse Ranges blocks.

4. The Mesozoic-Paleogene forearc basin of California continued as a topographic feature into the Oligocene, but it was divided in the latest Oligocene (~25 Ma) into two mostly nonmarine depositional basins that were aligned end-to-end in a NW-SE direction and were separated by a highland that existed in the proto–San Gabriel–Frazier Mountains region. The northern of the two basins is named the DiSoCuMa depositional basin and the southern the AnaVent depositional basin.

5. Subsidence occurred during the early Miocene and flooded the two basins with marine deposits. During the medial Miocene, subsidence continued as the western side of the AnaVent basin (today's western Transverse Ranges) began to pull away from the southern California coast and rotate clockwise around its northern end. This transrotational process served to enlarge both of the basins by crustal extension, which in turn produced extensive areas of volcanism. Throughout the late Miocene, transrotation and subsidence continued, the basins grew in size and depth to their present configuration, and internal isostatic adjustments produced several new marine depositional basins within the confines of the previous two-basin framework.

6. Structural basins are not synonymous with depositional basins. Describing depositional and paleogeographic history through the use of post-depositional structural terms is confusing and inaccurate. The terminology for depositional basins is completely different from the terminology used to describe structural basins.

Acknowledgments

I would like to thank Clarence A. Hall, Jr., Peter W. Weigand, and W. Gary Ernst for their critical reading and thoughtful comments on the manuscript. Bruce P. Luyendyk also provided helpful insights. Additional thanks go to my many students over the years at California State University, Northridge, who through their research have helped to make these palinspastic maps and this paleogeographic compilation possible.

REFERENCES

Anderson, D. W., 1996, Depositional environments and paleogeography of the Vaqueros and Rincon Formations, lower Sespe Creek area, Ventura County, California: Unpubl. M.S. thesis, California State Univ., Northridge, 136 p.

Belyea, R. R., 1984, Stratigraphy and depositional environments of the Sespe Formation, northern Peninsular Ranges, California: Unpubl. M.S. thesis, San Diego State Univ., 206 p.

Belyea, R. R., and Minch, J. A., 1989, Stratigraphy and depositional environments of the Sespe Formation, northern Santa Ana Mountains, California, in Colburn, I. P., Abbott, P. L., and Minch, J. A., eds., Conglomerates in basin analysis: A symposium dedicated to A. O. Woodford: Los Angeles, Soc. Econ. Paleontol. and Mineral. (SEPM), Pacific Sect., no. 62, p. 281–300.

Blake, T. F., 1981, Depositional environments of the Simmler Formation in southern Cuyama Valley, Santa Barbara and Ventura counties, California: Unpubl. M.S. thesis, California State Univ., Northridge, 151 p.

————, 1982, Depositional environments of the Simmler Formation in southern Cuyama Valley, Santa Barbara and Ventura counties, California, in Ingersoll, R. V., and Woodburne, M. O., eds., Cenozoic nonmarine deposits of California and Arizona: Soc. Econ. Paleontol. Mineral., Pacific Sect., p. 35–50.

Blundell, M. C., 1981, Depositional environments of the Vaqueros Formation in the Big Mountain area, Ventura County, California: Unpubl. M.S. thesis, California State Univ., Northridge, 102 p., 2 pls.

————, 1983, Depositional environments of the Vaqueros Formation, Big Mountain area, Ventura County, California, in Squires, R. L., and Filewicz, M. V., eds., Cenozoic geology of the Simi Valley area, southern California: Los Angeles, Soc. Econ. Paleontol. Mineral., Pacific Sect., p. 161–171.

Bohannon, R. G., 1975, Mid-Tertiary conglomerates and their bearing on Transverse Range tectonics, southern California: California Div. Mines Geol. Bull. 118, p. 75–82.

————, 1976, Mid-Tertiary nonmarine rocks along the San Andreas fault in southern California: Unpubl. Ph.D. dissertation, Univ. of California, Santa Barbara, 311 p.

Condon, M. W., 1989, Stratigraphic analysis of the Hurricane Deck Formation, Sierra Madre, Santa Barbara County, California: Unpubl. M.S. thesis, California State Univ., Northridge, 87 p.

Corey, W. H., 1954, Tertiary basins of southern California, in Jahns, R. H., ed., Geology of southern California: California Div. Mines Bull. 170, chap. 3, p. 73–83.

Crouch, J. K., 1979, Neogene tectonic evolution of the California Continental borderland and western Transverse Ranges: Geol. Soc. Amer. Bull., v. 90, p. 338–345.

Crouch, J. K., and Suppe, J., 1993, Late Cenozoic tectonic evolution of the Los Angeles basin and inner California borderland: A model for core complex-like crustal extension: Geol. Soc. Amer. Bull., v. 105, p. 1415–1434.

Crowell, J. C., 1962, Displacement along the San Andreas fault, California: Geol. Soc. Amer. Spec. Pap. 71, 61 p.

————, 1975, The San Gabriel fault and Ridge basin, southern California: California Div. Mines Geol. Bull. 118, p. 208–219.

Daniel, L. L., 1989, Stratigraphy and depositional environments of the lower Miocene Vaqueros Formation, Santa Ana Mountains, California: Unpubl. M.S. thesis, California State Univ., Northridge, 100 p.

Daniel-Lyle, L., 1995, Depositional environments and paleogeography of the lower Miocene Vaqueros Formation, Santa Ana Mountains, California, in Fritsche, A. E., ed., Cenozoic paleogeography of the western United States—II: SEPM (Soc. Sediment. Geol.), Pacific Sect., book 75, p. 9–21.

Dibblee, T. W., Jr., and Ehrenspeck, H. E., 1993, Field relations of Miocene volcanic and sedimentary rocks of the western Santa Monica Mountains, California, in Weigand, P. W., Fritsche, A. E., and Davis, G. E., eds., Depositional and volcanic environments of middle Tertiary rocks in the Santa Monica Mountains, southern California: SEPM (Soc. Sediment. Geol.), Pacific Sect., book 72, p. 75–92.

Dickinson, W. R., 1996, Kinematics of transrotational tectonism in the California Transverse Ranges: Geol. Soc. Amer. Spec. Pap. 305, 46 p.

Fischer, P. J., 1976, Late Neogene–Quaternary tectonics and depositional environments of the Santa Barbara Basin, California, in Fritsche, A. E., TerBest, H., Jr., and Wornardt, W. W., The Neogene symposium: Soc. Econ. Paleontol. Mineral., Pacific Sect., p. 33–52.

Flack, M. E., 1990, Depositional environments of the Topanga Canyon Formation, central Santa Monica Mountains, Los Angeles County, California: Unpubl. M.S. thesis, California State Univ., Northridge, 122 p.

————, 1993, Depositional environments of the "Topanga Canyon" Formation, the Encinal Tongue of the Rincon Shale, and the Fernwood Tongue of the Sespe Formation, central Santa Monica Mountains, California, in Weigand, P. W., Fritsche, A. E., and Davis, G. E., eds., Depositional and volcanic environments of middle Tertiary rocks in the Santa Monica Mountains, southern California: SEPM (Soc. Sediment. Geol.), Pacific Sect., book 72, p. 45–74.

Freitag, G. A., 1989, Depositional environments of the Vaqueros Formation, southeastern Cuyama basin, California: Unpubl. M.S. thesis, California State Univ., Northridge, 138 p.

Freitag, G. A., and Fritsche, A. E., 1988, Facies and preliminary depositional environments of the Vaqueros Formation, southeastern Cuyama Valley, California, in Bazeley, W. J. M., ed., Tertiary tectonics and sedimentation in the Cuyama basin, San Luis Obispo, Santa Barbara, and Ventura counties, California: Soc. Econ. Paleontol. Mineral., Pacific Sect., book 59, p. 61–69.

Fritsche, A. E., 1977, Miocene paleogeography of California, in Nilsen, T. H., ed., Late Mesozoic and

Cenozoic sedimentation and tectonics in California: San Joaquin Geol. Soc. Short Course, p. 109–119.

————, 1981, Preliminary middle Tertiary paleogeographic maps of area represented by two-degree Los Angeles map sheet, California: Amer. Assoc. Petrol. Geol. Bull., v. 65, p. 927–928.

————, 1988, Origin and paleogeographic development of the Tertiary Cuyama depositional basin, southern California, in Bazeley, W. J. M., ed., Tertiary tectonics and sedimentation in the Cuyama basin, San Luis Obispo, Santa Barbara, and Ventura counties, California: Soc. Econ. Paleontol. Mineral., Pacific Sect., book 59, p. 159–162.

Fritsche, A. E., and Thomas, G. D., 1990, New early Miocene K-Ar date for basalt in the Hurricane Deck Formation, central Santa Barbara County, California [abs.]: Geol. Soc. Amer. Abs. Prog., v. 22, no. 3, p. 23–24.

Frizzell, V. A., Jr., and Weigand, P. W., 1993, Whole-rock ages and geochemical data from middle Cenozoic volcanic rocks, southern California: A test of correlations across the San Andreas fault, in Powell, R. E., Weldon, R. J., II, and Matti, J. C., eds., The San Andreas fault system: Displacement, palinspastic reconstruction, and geologic evolution: Boulder, CO, Geol. Soc. Amer. Mem. 178, p. 273–287.

Hall, C. A., Jr., 1981, San Luis Obispo transform fault and middle Miocene rotation of the western Transverse Ranges, California: Jour. Geophys. Res., v. 86, p. 1015–1031.

Hamilton, W., 1978, Mesozoic tectonics of the western United States, in Howell, D. G., and McDougall, K. A., eds., Mesozoic paleogeography of the western United States: Los Angeles, Soc. Econ. Paleontol. Mineral., Pacific Coast Paleogeog. Symp. 2, p. 33–70.

Hendrix, E. D., and Ingersoll, R. V., 1987, Tectonics and alluvial sedimentation of the upper Oligocene/lower Miocene Vasquez Formation, Soledad basin, southern California: Geol. Soc. Amer. Bull., v. 98, p. 647–663.

Hornafius, J. S., 1985, Neogene tectonic rotation of the Santa Ynez Range, western Transverse Ranges, California, suggested by paleomagnetic investigation of the Monterey Formation: Jour. Geophys. Res., v. 90, p. 12,503–12,522.

Hornafius, J. S., Luyendyk, B. P., Terres, R. R., and Kamerling, M. J., 1986, Timing and extent of Neogene tectonic rotation in the western Transverse Ranges, California: Geol. Soc. Amer. Bull., v. 97, p. 1476–1487.

Howard, J. L., 1996, Paleocene to Holocene paleodeltas of ancestral Colorado River offset by the San Andreas fault system, southern California: Geology, v. 24, p. 783–786.

Howard, J. L., and Lowry, W. D., 1995, Medial Cenozoic paleogeography of the Los Angeles area, south-western California, and adjacent parts of the United States, in Fritsche, A. E., ed., Cenozoic paleogeography of the western United States—II: SEPM (Soc. Sediment. Geol.), Pacific Sect., book 75, p. 22–41.

Jones, D. L., Blake, M. C., Jr., and Rangin, C., 1976, The four Jurassic belts of northern California and their significance to the geology of the southern California borderland, in Howell, D. G., ed., Aspects of the geologic history of the California Continental Borderland: Amer. Assoc. Petrol. Geol., Pacific Sect., Misc. Publ. 24, p. 343–362.

Kamerling, M. J., and Luyendyk, B. P., 1979, Tectonic rotations of the Santa Monica Mountains region, western Transverse Ranges, California, suggested by paleomagnetic vectors: Geol. Soc. Amer. Bull., v. 90, p. 331–337.

————, 1985, Paleomagnetism and Neogene tectonics of the northern Channel Islands, California: Jour. Geophys. Res., v. 90, p. 12,485–12,502.

Lagoe, M. B., 1984, Paleogeography of Monterey Formation, Cuyama basin, California: Amer. Assoc. Petrol. Geol. Bull., v. 68, p. 610–627.

————, 1985, Depositional environments in the Monterey Formation, Cuyama basin, California: Geol. Soc. Amer. Bull., v. 96, p. 1296–1312.

Luyendyk, B. P., 1991, A model for Neogene crustal rotations, transtension, and transpression in southern California: Geol. Soc. Amer. Bull., v. 103, p. 1528–1536.

Luyendyk, B. P., Gans, P. B., and Kamerling, M. J., 1998, $^{40}Ar/^{39}Ar$ geochronology of southern California Neogene volcanism, in Weigand, P. W., Contributions to the geology of the northern Channel Islands, southern California: Amer. Assoc. Petrol. Geol., Pacific Sect., Misc. Publ. 45, in press.

Luyendyk, B. P., and Hornafius, J. S., 1987, Neogene crustal rotations, fault slip, and basin development in southern California, in Ingersoll, R. V., and Ernst, W. G., eds., Cenozoic basin development of coastal California. Rubey Volume VI: Englewood Cliffs, NJ, Prentice-Hall, p. 259–283.

Luyendyk, B. P., Kamerling, M. J., and Terres, R. R., 1980, Geometric model for Neogene crustal rotations in southern California: Geol. Soc. Amer. Bull., v. 91, p. 211–217.

Luyendyk, B. P., Kamerling, M. J., Terres, R. R., and Hornafius, J. S., 1985, Simple shear of southern California during Neogene time suggested by paleomagnetic declinations: Jour. Geophys. Res., v. 90, p. 12,454–12,466.

Mayer, L. 1987, Subsidence analysis of the Los Angeles basin, in Ingersoll, R. V., and Ernst, W. G., eds., Cenozoic basin development of coastal California. Rubey Volume VI: Englewood Cliffs, NJ, Prentice-Hall, p. 299–320.

McCracken, W. A., 1969, Sespe Formation on upper Sespe Creek, in Dickinson, W. R., ed., Geologic setting of upper Miocene gypsum and phosphorite deposits, upper Sespe Creek and Pine Mountain, Ventura County, California: Soc. Econ. Paleontol. Mineral., Pacific Sect., field trip guidebook, p. 41–48.

————, 1972, Paleocurrents and petrology of Sespe sandstones and conglomerates, Ventura basin, California: Unpubl. Ph.D. dissertation, Stanford Univ., 192 p.

Menzie, R. J., Jr., Horton, R. A., Jr., and Fritsche, A. E., 1989, Marine rocks in nonmarine Miocene Caliente Formation, northern Cuyama Badlands, Ventura County, California: Amer. Assoc. Petrol. Geol. Bull., v. 73, p. 545–546.

Nicholson, C., Sorlien, C. C., Atwater, T., Crowell, J. C., and Luyendyk, B. P., 1994, Microplate capture, rotation of the western Transverse Ranges, and initiation of the San Andreas transform as a low-angle fault system: Geology, v. 22, p. 491–495.

Nilsen, T. H., 1987, Paleogene tectonics and sedimentation of coastal California, in Ingersoll, R. V., and Ernst, W. G., eds., Cenozoic basin development of coastal California. Rubey Volume VI: Englewood Cliffs, NJ, Prentice-Hall, p. 81–123.

Oborne, J. G., 1987, Stratigraphy and depositional environments of the Vaqueros Formation, central Santa Monica Mountains, California: Unpubl. M.S. thesis, California State Univ., Northridge, 95 p., 2 pls.

————, 1993, Stratigraphy and depositional environments of the Vaqueros Formation, central Santa Monica Mountains, California, in Weigand, P. W., Fritsche, A. E., and Davis, G. E., eds., Depositional and volcanic environments of middle Tertiary rocks in the Santa Monica Mountains, southern California: SEPM (Soc. Sediment. Geol.), Pacific Sect., book 72, p. 25–44.

Oldershaw, M. W., 1988, Preliminary study of the depositional environments of the Painted Rock Sandstone Member of the Miocene Vaqueros Formation in the eastern Caliente Range, San Luis Obispo County, California, in Bazeley, W. J. M., ed., Tertiary tectonics and sedimentation in the Cuyama basin, San Luis Obispo, Santa Barbara, and Ventura counties, California: Soc. Econ. Paleontol. Mineral., Pacific Sect., book 59, p. 49–60.

————, Depositional environments and paleogeography of the Painted Rock Sandstone Member of the Vaqueros Formation, Caliente Range: Unpubl. M.S. thesis, California State Univ., Northridge, 125 p.

Perri, M. L., 1990, Stratigraphic analysis of the Branch Canyon Formation in the Sierra Madre, Santa Barbara County, California: Unpubl. M.S. thesis, California State Univ., Northridge, 114 p.

Perri, M. L., and Fritsche, A. E., 1988, Stratigraphy and depositional environments of the Miocene Branch Canyon Formation in the Sierra Madre, Caliente Range, and Sespe Creek areas, California, in Bazeley, W. J. M., ed., Tertiary tectonics and sedimentation in the Cuyama basin, San Luis Obispo, Santa Barbara, and Ventura counties, California: Soc. Econ. Paleontol. Mineral., Pacific Sect., book 59, p. 87–98.

Popelar, S. J., 1988, Miocene geology of the southwestern portion of the San Rafael Wilderness, Santa Barbara County, California: Unpubl. M.S. thesis, California State Univ., Northridge, 109 p.

Reed, R. D., 1933, Geology of California: Tulsa, OK, Amer. Assoc. Petrol. Geol., 355 p.

Reid, S. A., 1978, Mid-Tertiary depositional environments and paleogeography along upper Sespe Creek, Ventura County, California: Soc. Econ. Paleontol. Mineral., Pacific Sect., Pacific Coast paleogeog. field guide 3, p. 27–41.

————, 1979, Depositional environments of the Vaqueros Formation along Sespe Creek, Ventura County, California: Unpubl. M.S. thesis, California State Univ., Northridge, 129 p.

Savage, K. L., 1996, The geochemistry and petrogenesis of the Conejo Volcanics, Santa Monica Mountains, California: Unpubl. M.S. thesis, California State Univ., Northridge, 126 p.

Savage, K. L., and Weigand, P. W., 1997, Petrogenesis of the mid-Miocene Conejo Volcanics, western Santa Monica Mountains, California—calc-alkaline magmatism in an extensional environment [abs.]: Geol. Soc. Amer. Abs. Prog., v. 29, no. 5, p. 62–63.

Stadum, C. J., and Weigand, P. W., 1998, Fossil wood from the middle Miocene Conejo Volcanics, Santa Monica Mountains, California: Southern California Acad. Sci. Bull., submitted.

Stanley, R. G., Johnson, S. Y., Swisher, C. C., III, Mason, M. A., Obradovich, J. D., Cotton, M. L., Filewicz, M. V., and Vork, D. R., 1996, Age of the Lospe Formation (early Miocene) and origin of the Santa Maria basin, California: U.S. Geol. Surv. Bull. 1995-M, p. M1–M37.

Stanton, R. J., 1967, The effects of provenance and basin-edge topography on sedimentation in the basal Castaic Formation (upper Miocene, marine), Los Angeles County, California: California Div. Mines Spec. Report 92, p. 21–31.

Stuart, C. J., 1979a, Middle Miocene paleogeography of coastal southern California and the California borderland—evidence from schist-bearing sedimentary rocks, in Armentrout, J. M., Cole, M. R., and Ter-Best, H., eds., Cenozoic paleogeography of the western United States: Soc. Econ. Paleontol. Mineral., Pacific Sect., Pacific Coast Paleogeog. Symp. 3, p. 29–44.

————, 1979b, Lithofacies and origin of the San Onofre Breccia, coastal southern California, *in* Stuart, C. J., ed., A guidebook to Miocene lithofacies and depositional environments, coastal southern California and northwestern Baja California: Soc. Econ. Paleontol. Mineral., Pacific Sect., p. 25–42.

Taylor, G. E., 1983, Braided-river and flood-related deposits of the Sespe Formation, northern Simi Valley, California, *in* Squires, R. L., and Filewicz, M. V., eds., Cenozoic geology of the Simi Valley area, southern California: Soc. Econ. Paleontol. Mineral., Pacific Sect., p. 129–140.

————, 1984, Depositional environments of the Eocene through Oligocene Sespe Formation in the northern Simi Valley area, Ventura County, southern California: Unpubl. M.S. thesis, California State Univ., Northridge, 74 p.

Terres, R. R., 1984, Paleomagnetism and tectonics of the central and eastern Transverse Ranges, southern California: Unpubl. Ph.D. dissertation, Univ. of California, Santa Barbara, 364 p.

Thomas, G., 1989, Stratigraphic analysis and paleogeography of the Hurricane Deck Formation, San Rafael Mountains, Santa Barbara County, California: Unpubl. M.S. thesis, California State Univ., Northridge, 144 p.

Thomas, G. D., Fritsche, A. E., and Condon, M. W., 1988, Stratigraphy and depositional environments of the Hurricane Deck Formation, a new lower and middle Miocene submarine fan sandstone unit in the Sierra Madre and San Rafael Mountains, northeastern Santa Barbara County, California, *in* Bazeley, W. J. M., ed., Tertiary tectonics and sedimentation in the Cuyama basin, San Luis Obispo, Santa Barbara, and Ventura counties, California: Soc. Econ. Paleontol. Mineral., Pacific Sect., book 59, p. 71–86.

Van Wagoner, S. L., 1981, Geology of a part of the Zaca Lake Quadrangle, Santa Barbara County, California: Unpubl. M.S. thesis, California State Univ., Northridge, 143 p.

Vedder, J. G., 1979, The Topanga Formation in the San Joaquin Hills, Orange County, California, *in* Stuart, C. J., ed., A guidebook to Miocene lithofacies and depositional environments, coastal southern California and northwestern Baja California: Soc. Econ. Paleontol. Mineral., Pacific Sect., p. 19–24.

Vedder, J. G., and Howell, D. G., 1976, Review of the distribution and tectonic implications of Miocene debris from the Catalina Schist, California Continental Borderland and adjacent coastal areas, *in* Howell, D. G., ed., Aspects of the geologic history of the California Continental Borderland: Amer. Assoc. Petrol. Geol., Pacific Sect., Misc. Publ. 24, p. 326–340.

Weigand, P. W., 1994, Middle Miocene igneous rocks in the El Modeno, San Joaquin Hills, and Laguna Beach areas, *in* Hughes, P., Lozinsky, R. P., and Roquemore, G. R., eds., Field geology in Orange County, southern California—1994 Field Conference Guidebook: Nat. Assoc. Geol. Teachers, Far Western Section, p. 55–84.

Wright, T. L., 1991, Structural geology and tectonic evolution of the Los Angeles basin, California, *in* Biddle, K. T., ed., Active margin basins: Amer. Assoc. Petrol. Geol. Memoir 52, p. 35–134.

Yaldezian, J. G., II, 1984, Miocene geology of the east-central portion of the San Rafael Wilderness, Santa Barbara County, California: Unpubl. M.S. thesis, California State Univ., Northridge, 145 p.

Yeats, R. S., 1968, Rifting and rafting in the southern California borderland, in Dickinson, W. R., and Grantz, A., eds., Proceedings of conference on geologic problems of the San Andreas fault system: Stanford Univ. Publ., Geol. Sci., v. 11, p. 307–322.

————, 1976, Extension versus strike-slip origin of the southern California borderland, *in* Howell, D. G., ed., Aspects of the geologic history of the California Continental Borderland: Amer. Assoc. Petrol. Geol., Pacific Sect., Misc. Publ. 24, p. 455–485.